D1302614

TORTS:
CASES AND PROBLEMS

TORTS:
CASES AND PROBLEMS

Third Edition

Frank J. Vandall
Professor of Law
Emory University School of Law

Ellen Wertheimer
Professor of Law
Villanova University School of Law

Mark C. Rahdert
Professor of Law
Temple University Beasley School of Law

ISBN: 978–0–7698–4690–3

Library of Congress Cataloging-in-Publication Data
Vandall, Frank J.
Torts : cases and problems / Frank J. Vandall, Ellen Wertheimer, Mark C. Rahdert. -- 3rd ed.
p. cm.
Includes index.
ISBN 978-0-7698-4690-3
1. Torts--United States--Cases. I. Wertheimer, Ellen. II. Rahdert, Mark C., 1952- III. Title.
KF1249.V36 2012
346.7303--dc23
2011052279

> ## NOTE TO USERS
> To ensure that you are using the latest materials available in this area, please be sure to periodically check the LexisNexis Law School web site for downloadable updates and supplements at www.lexisnexis.com/lawschool.

Editorial Offices
121 Chanlon Rd., New Providence, NJ 07974 (908) 464-6800
201 Mission St., San Francisco, CA 94105-1831 (415) 908-3200
www.lexisnexis.com

MATTHEW◆BENDER

Dedications

I dedicate this book to my wife Sheila, my children Megan and Josh, and my grandchildren, Madison, Keegan and Emma. — *Frank Vandall*

We dedicate this book to our children, Chris and Lise. — *Ellen Wertheimer & Mark C. Rahdert*

Acknowledgments

For the Third Edition, I am indebted to my research assistant, Ruth Dawson. Mistakes are mine, however. The book relies on the organizational and computer expertise of Marianne D'Souza. I am especially indebted to her. I also appreciate the support and encouragement of Dean David Partlett and Dean Robert Schapiro. — *Frank Vandall*

For the Third Edition, I am deeply in the debt of my research assistants, Vincent Cannizarro, Amy Dudash, Erin Hehn, and Andrew Hubley. My assistant, Mira Baric, was invaluable. Without her calm good sense and superb skills, this project would have proven much more difficult and anxiety-producing.

I want also to thank Dean John Gotanda and Associate Dean Steve Chanenson for their unfailing support for this project. — *Ellen Wertheimer*

For the Third Edition, I wish to acknowledge the extremely helpful research assistance that I received from Joshua Brand, the technical assistance I received from Shannon Markley, the library support I received from Noa Kaumeheiwa, and the encouragement I received from Dean JoAnne Epps and my faculty colleagues at Temple University Beasley School of Law. I also received financial support from the Clifford Scott Green research fund at Temple, for which I am most grateful. I would like to thank Frank Vandall and Ellen Wertheimer for involving me in this project, and I would like to thank my family — Ellen, Chris, and Lise — for their continued support in all my professional endeavors. — *Mark C. Rahdert*

Preface

For the Third Edition, our goal was to "polish the apple" by replacing cases that were not effective in class and adding new and important ones. One of our goals was also to include cases with human interest in the book.

New cases include:

- *Walmart*: what is the impact of locking Mexican employees in the store during the night shift?

- *Wrinkle*: can a landowner be liable for negligent clothesline placement when the plaintiff is injured while pursuing cattle on the defendant's property?

- *John B. v. Superior Court of Los Angeles County*: when must an HIV carrier warn of the disease?

- *Yates*: is a law school liable for intentional emotional distress to an impoverished applicant?

- *Langan v. St. Vincent's Hospital*: does the New York wrongful death statute include actions by the surviving partner in a same-sex civil union?

For this edition, we also tried to incorporate comments we have received from those who have adopted the casebook. We hope we have been responsive.

Enjoy.

Frank J. Vandall
Professor of Law
Emory University School of Law

Ellen Wertheimer
Professor of Law
Villanova University School of Law

Mark C. Rahdert
Charles Klein Professor of Law and Government
Temple University Beasley School of Law
August 8, 2011

Table of Contents

Table of Contents

Table of Contents

Table of Contents

Table of Contents

Table of Contents

Table of Contents

Table of Contents

Table of Contents

Table of Contents

Table of Contents

Table of Contents

Table of Contents

Chapter 1

INTRODUCTION

Torts is a deceptively simple subject because there is only one question in each case: Who will pay the damages, plaintiff or defendant? This is a matter of justice and involves a weighing of numerous factors. Answering the question of whether the defendant will be liable or the loss left with the plaintiff, in each case, involves an evaluation of history, tort doctrine, and social policy. An examination of these subjects is the text of the course.

A tort is any civil action other than contract. The usual remedy is damages awarded after a jury trial. In fact, ninety-two percent are settled before trial. Another six percent are "settled on the court house steps." Therefore ninety-eight percent are settled. Injunctions are rare. There are several fundamental purposes for tort law: compensate the injured party, prevent self-help (violence), and deter the conduct in the future. Very simply, in today's world, the law of torts exists to give people an alternative to violence.

The foundation of tort law is absolute liability. Before 1300, the plaintiff merely had to prove that the defendant was a cause of his injury in order to prevail. Fault was not required:

> At your request I accompany you when you are about your own affairs; my enemies fall upon and kill me, you must pay for my death. You take me to see a wild beast show or that interesting spectacle, a mad man; beast or mad man kills me; you must pay. You hang up your sword; someone else knocks it down so that it cuts me; you must pay. In none of these cases can you honestly swear that you did nothing that helped to bring about death or wound.

W. Malone, *Ruminations on the Role of Fault in the History of the Common Law of Torts*, 31 La. L. Rev. 1, 3 (1970).

In torts as in most law school courses, you will learn the law by studying actual cases.

Before an attorney can take a case, she must first have an injured person as a client. The attorney must decide that the injury is worth the expense of a lawsuit.

Because the civil procedure course usually begins with appellate issues, rather than the complaint and answer, a few procedural points on bringing a torts suit are in order.

Basically, jurisdiction refers to the state the suit will be filed in and the appropriate court for filing the complaint, within the jurisdiction. These points are important in writing the complaint and statement of the facts. The complaint is filed with the appropriate court.

In the torts cases we read, usually the case has been tried and a verdict rendered. We will be reading appeals from trial courts to intermediate appellate courts, or the state supreme court. Occasionally, we will read a federal case, rarely one decided by the U.S. Supreme Court. All of the above is covered in the last part of your civil procedure course.

"Tort reform" is a hot topic and functions to leave the loss on the victim.

---

1. What if, in Malone's examples, the defendant had exercised care or the plaintiff was careless?

2. In the above example, should not the attacker be liable rather than the invitor? Why not hold the circus liable for the attack of the wild beast?

3. Does absolute liability have any relevance today? Most would say no, but see F.J. Vandall, *Reallocating the Costs of Smoking: The Application of Absolute Liability to Cigarette Manufacturers*, 52 Ohio State L.J. 406 (1991).

4. In *Weaver v. Ward*, Hobart 134, 80 Eng. Rep. 284 (1616), the court stated:

Weaver brought an action of trespass of assault and battery against Ward. The defendant pleaded, that he was amongst others by the commandment of the Lords of the Council a trained soldier in London, of the band of one Andrews captain; and so was the plaintiff, and that they were skirmishing with their muskets charged with powder for their exercise in re militari, against another captain and his band; and as they were so skirmishing, the defendant casualiter & per infor-tunium & contra voluntatem suam, in discharging of his piece did hurt and wound the plaintiff, which is the same, &c. absque hoc, that he was guilty aliter sive alio modo. And upon demurrer by the plaintiff, judgment was given for him; for though it were agreed, that if men tilt or turney in the presence of the King, or if two masters of defence playing their prizes kill one another, that this shall be no felony; or if a lunatick kill a man, or the like, because felony must be done animo felonico: yet in trespass, which tends only to give damages according to hurt or loss, it is not so; and therefore if a lunatick hurt a man, he shall be answerable in trespass: and therefore no man shall be excused of a trespass (for this is the nature of an excuse, and not of a justification, prout ei bene licuit) except it may be judged utterly without his fault.

As if a man by force take my hand and strike you, or if here the defendant had said, that the plaintiff ran cross his piece when it was discharging, or had set forth the case with the circumstances, so as it had appeared to the court that it had been inevitable, and that the defendant had committed no negligence to give occasion to the hurt.

What is a demurrer? What did the plaintiff plead? How did the defendant answer? What was the legal basis for the plaintiffs demurrer? How does the court respond to the demurrer? Why does the defendant lose? What message does the court provide for future cases? How does the court define fault?

5. Personal injury cases are often presented on the newspaper's front page. Torts is a "hot" topic and commonly the subject of legislative reform because of a perceived crisis (dramatic expansion in the number of cases and the size of the awards). A recent study suggests a need for facts and caution, however. Professors Thomas A. Eaton and Susette M. Talarico conclude that "[T]ort fights are fewer and simpler and end in victories for defendants more often than the public thinks." They conclude that "tort filings are level, not rising, and represent a much smaller proportion [5%] of total civil litigation than is widely believed." Eaton stated that "there is [not an explosion of personal injury cases]. The general trend is really one of relative stability. We are not seeing an increase in the number of cases filed. And this holds true on a national level. Year-by-year, the tort filing levels [in Georgia] did not rise or fall dramatically. Federal and other available state court data indicate that tort filings have remained flat for 10 years." Eaton also made clear that "only 7 percent of tort claims filed ever get to trial." *Tort Crisis a Myth*, Fulton County Daily Report 1 (May 30, 1996), reporting of a speech based on Thomas A. Eaton & Susette M. Talarico, *A Profile of Tort Litigation in Georgia and Reflections on Tort Reform*, 30 Ga. L. Rev. 627 (1996).

6. Every lawyer, it is said, gets a dog case. Therefore, we present the following "simple" dog case for your elucidation and enjoyment.

BROWN v. KENDALL
Supreme Judicial Court of Massachusetts, 1850
6 Cush. (60 Mass.) 292

This was an action of trespass for assault and battery, originally commenced against George K. Kendall, the defendant. . . .

It appeared in evidence, on the trial, . . . that two dogs, belonging to the plaintiff and the defendant, respectively, were fighting in the presence of their masters; that the defendant took a stick about four feet long, and commenced beating the dogs in order to separate them; that the plaintiff was looking on, at the distance of about a rod, and that he advanced a step or two towards the dogs. In their struggle, the dogs approached the place where the plaintiff was standing. The defendant retreated backwards from before the dogs, striking them as he retreated; and as he approached the plaintiff, with his back towards him, in raising his stick over his shoulder, in order to strike the dogs, he . . . hit the plaintiff in the eye, inflicting upon him a severe injury.

Whether it was necessary or proper for the defendant to interfere in the fight between the dogs; whether the interference, if called for, was in a proper manner, and what degree of care was exercised by each party on the occasion; were the subject of controversy between the parties, upon all the evidence in the case, of which the foregoing is an outline.

The judge . . . left the case to the jury under the following instructions: "If the defendant, in beating the dogs, was doing a necessary act, or one which it was his duty under the circumstances of the case to do, and was doing it in a proper way;

then he was not responsible in this action, provided he was using ordinary care at the time of the blow. If it was not a necessary act; if he was not in duty bound to attempt to part the dogs, but might with propriety interfere or not as he chose; the defendant was responsible for the consequences of the blow, unless it appeared that he was in the exercise of extraordinary care, so that the accident was inevitable, using the word inevitable not in a strict but a popular sense."

"If, however, the plaintiff, when he met with the injury, was not in the exercise of ordinary care, he cannot recover, and this rule applies, whether the interference of the defendant in the fight of the dogs was necessary or not. If the jury believe, that it was the duty of the defendant to interfere, then the burden of proving negligence on the part of the defendant, and ordinary care on the part of the plaintiff, is on the plaintiff. If the jury believes that the act of interference in the fight was unnecessary, then the burden of proving extraordinary care on the part of the defendant, or want of ordinary care on the part of the plaintiff, is on defendant."

The jury under these instructions returned a verdict for the plaintiff; whereupon the defendant alleged exceptions.

SHAW, C. J. . . .

The facts set forth in the bill of exceptions preclude the supposition, that the blow, inflicted by the hand of the defendant upon the person of the plaintiff, was intentional. The whole case proceeds on the assumption, that the damages sustained by the plaintiff, from the stick held by the defendant, was inadvertent and unintentional; and the case involves the question how far, and under what qualifications, the party by whose unconscious act the damage was done is responsible for it. We use the term "unintentional" rather than involuntary, because in some of the cases, it is stated, that the act of holding and using a weapon or instrument, the movement of which is the immediate cause of hurt to another, is a voluntary act, although its particular effect in hitting and hurting another is not within the purpose or intention of the party doing the act.

It appears to us, that some of the confusion in the cases on this subject has grown out of the long-vexed question, under the rule of the common law, whether a party's remedy, where he has one, should be sought in an action of the case, or of trespass. This is very distinguishable from the question, whether in a given case, any action will lie. The result of these cases is, that if the damage complained of is the immediate effect of the act of the defendant, trespass *vi et armis* lies; if consequential only, and not immediate, case is the proper remedy. . . .

In these discussions, it is frequently stated by judges, that when one receives injury from the direct act of another, trespass will lie. But we think this is said in reference to the question, whether trespass and not case will lie, assuming that the facts are such, that some action will lie. These *dicta* are no authority, we think, for holding, that damage received by a direct act of force from another will be sufficient to maintain an action of trespass, whether the act was lawful or unlawful, and neither wilful, intentional, or careless. . . .

We think, as the result of all the authorities, the rule is correctly stated by Mr. Greenleaf, that the plaintiff must come prepared with evidence to show either that the *intention* was unlawful, or that the defendant was *in fault;* for if the injury was unavoidable, and the conduct of the defendant was free from blame, he will not be liable. . . . If, in the prosecution of a lawful act, a casualty purely accidental arises, no action can be supported for an injury arising therefrom. . . . In applying these rules to the present case, we can perceive no reason why the instructions asked for by the defendant ought not to have been given; to this effect, that if both plaintiff and defendant at the time of the blow were using ordinary care, or if at that time the defendant was using ordinary care, and the plaintiff was not, or if at that time, both the plaintiff and defendant were not using ordinary care, then the plaintiff could not recover.

In using this term, ordinary care, it may be proper to state that what constitutes ordinary care will vary with the circumstances of cases. In general, it means that kind and degree of care which prudent and cautious men would use, such as is required by the exigency of the case, and such as is necessary to guard against probable danger. A man, who should have occasion to discharge a gun, on an open and extensive marsh, or in a forest, would be required to use less circumspection and care, than if he were to do the same thing in an inhabited town, village, or city. To make an accident, or casualty, or as the law sometimes states it, inevitable accident, it must be such an accident as the defendant could not have avoided by the use of the kind and degree of care necessary to the exigency, and in the circumstances in which he was placed.

We are not aware of any circumstances in this case, requiring a distinction between acts which it was lawful and proper to do, and acts of legal duty. There are cases, undoubtedly, in which officers are bound to act under process, for the legality of which they are not responsible, and perhaps some others in which this distinction would be important. We can have no doubt that the act of the defendant in attempting to part the fighting dogs, one of which was his own, and for the injurious acts of which he might be responsible, was a lawful and proper act, which he might do by proper and safe means. If, then, in doing this act, using due care and all proper precautions necessary to the exigency of the case, to avoid hurt to others, in raising his stick for that purpose, he accidentally hit the plaintiff in his eye, and wounded him, this was the result of pure accident, or was involuntary and unavoidable, and therefore the action would not lie. . . .

The court instructed the jury, that if it was not a necessary act, and the defendant was not duty bound to part the dogs, but might with propriety interfere or not as he chose, the defendant was responsible for the consequences of the blow, unless it appeared that he was in the exercise of extraordinary care, so that the accident was inevitable, using the word not in a strict but a popular sense. This is to be taken in connection with the charge afterwards given, that if the jury believed, that the act of interference in the fight was unnecessary (that is, as before explained, not a duty incumbent on the defendant), then the burden of proving extraordinary care on the part of the defendant, or want of ordinary care on the part of plaintiff, was on the defendant.

The court are of opinion that these directions were not conformable to law. If the act of hitting the plaintiff was unintentional, on the part of the defendant, and done in the doing of a lawful act, then the defendant was not liable, unless it was done in the want of exercise of due care, adapted to the exigency of the case, and therefore such want of due care became part of the plaintiffs case, and the burden of proof was on the plaintiff to establish it. . . .

Perhaps the learned judge, by the use of the term extraordinary care, in the above charge, explained as it is by the context, may have intended nothing more than that increased degree of care and diligence, which the exigency of particular circumstances might require, and which men of ordinary care and prudence would use under like circumstances, to guard against danger. If such was the meaning of this part of the charge, then it does not differ from our views, as above explained. But we are of opinion, that the other part of the charge, that the burden of proof was on the defendant, was incorrect. Those facts which are essential to enable the plaintiff to recover, he takes the burden of proving. The evidence may be offered by the plaintiff or by the defendant; the question of due care, or want of care, may be essentially connected with the main facts, and arise from the same proof; but the effect of the rule as to the burden of proof is this, that when the proof is all in, and before the jury, from whatever side it comes, and whether directly proved, or inferred from circumstances, if it appears that the defendant was doing a lawful act, and unintentionally hit and hurt the plaintiff, then unless it also appears to the satisfaction of the jury, that the defendant is chargeable with some fault, negligence, carelessness, or want of prudence, the plaintiff fails to sustain the burden of proof, and is not entitled to recover.

New trial ordered.

---

1. What did the plaintiff and the defendant apparently argue in the trial court?

2. Until *Brown*, what had been the rule for direct injuries? What did Judge Shaw say of this rule?

3. After *Brown*, what must a person show in order to recover for a physical injury?

4. What policy supports the decision in *Brown*? What would corporate America think of this case at the time it was decided?

5. Who has the burden of proving fault after *Brown*?

6. *See* Gregory, *Trespass to Negligence to Absolute Liability*, 37 Va. L. Rev. 359 (1951).

HAMMONTREE v. JENNER
Court of Appeal of California, 1971
20 Cal. App. 3d 528, 97 Cal. Rptr. 739

LILLIE, J.

Plaintiffs Maxine Hammontree and her husband sued defendant for personal injuries and property damage arising out of an automobile accident. The cause was tried to a jury. Plaintiffs appeal from judgment entered on a jury verdict returned against them and in favor of defendant.

The evidence shows that on the afternoon of April 25, 1967, defendant was driving his 1959 Chevrolet home from work; at the same time plaintiff Maxine Hammontree was working in a bicycle shop owned and operated by her and her husband; without warning defendant's car crashed through the wall of the shop, struck Maxine and caused personal injuries and damage to the shop.

Defendant claimed he became unconscious during an epileptic seizure losing control of his car. He did not recall the accident but his last recollection before it, was leaving a stop light after his last stop, and his first recollection after the accident was being taken out of his car in plaintiffs' shop. Defendant testified he has a medical history of epilepsy and knows of no other reason for his loss of consciousness except an epileptic seizure; prior to 1952 he had been examined by several neurologists whose conclusion was that the condition could be controlled and who placed him on medication; in 1952 he suffered a seizure while fishing; several days later he went to Dr. Benson Hyatt who diagnosed his condition as petit mal seizure and kept him on the same medication; thereafter he saw Dr. Hyatt every six months and then on a yearly basis several years prior to 1967; in 1953 he had another seizure, was told he was an epileptic and continued his medication; in 1954 Dr. Kershner prescribed dilantin and in 1955 Dr. Hyatt prescribed phelantin; from 1955 until the accident occurred (1967) defendant had used phelantin on a regular basis which controlled his condition; defendant has continued to take medication as prescribed by his physician and has done everything his doctors told him to do to avoid a seizure; he had no inkling or warning that he was about to have a seizure prior to the occurrence of the accident.

In 1955 or 1956 the Department of Motor Vehicles was advised that defendant was an epileptic and placed him on probation under which every six months he had to report to the doctor who was required to advise it in writing of defendant's condition. In 1960 his probation was changed to a once-a-year report.

Dr. Hyatt testified that during the times he saw defendant, and according to his history, defendant "was doing normally" and that he continued to take phelantin; that "[the] purpose of the [phelantin] would be to react on the nervous system in such a way that where, without the medication, I would say to raise the threshold so that he would not be as subject to these episodes without the medication, so as not to have the seizures. He would not be having the seizures with the medication as he would without the medication compared to taking medication"; in a seizure it would be impossible for a person to drive and control an automobile; he believed it was safe for defendant to drive.

Appellants' contentions that the trial court erred in refusing to grant their motion for summary judgment on the issue of liability and their motion for directed verdict on the pleadings and counsel's opening argument are answered by the disposition of their third claim that the trial court committed prejudicial error in refusing to give their jury instruction on absolute liability.[1]

---

[1] "When the evidence shows that a driver of a motor vehicle on a public street or highway loses his

Under the present state of the law found in appellate authorities beginning with *Waters v. Pacific Coast Dairy, Inc.*, 55 Cal. App. 2d 789, 791-793 [131 P.2d 588] (driver rendered unconscious from sharp pain in left arm and shoulder) through *Ford v. Carew & English*, 89 Cal. App. 2d 199, 203-204 [200 P.2d 828] (fainting spells from strained heart muscles), *Zabunoff v. Walker*, 192 Cal. App. 2d 8, 11 [13 Cal. Rptr. 463] (sudden sneeze), and *Tanny-hill v. Pacific Motor Trans. Co.*, 227 Cal. App. 2d 512, 520 [38 Cal. Rptr. 774] (heart attack), the trial judge properly refused the instruction. The foregoing cases generally hold that liability of a driver, suddenly stricken by an illness rendering him unconscious, for injury resulting from an accident occcurring during that time rests on principles of negligence. However, herein during the trial plaintiffs withdrew their claim of negligence and, after both parties rested and before jury argument, objected to the giving of any instructions on negligence electing to stand solely on the theory of absolute liability. The objection was overruled and the court refused plaintiffs' requested instruction after which plaintiffs waived both opening and closing jury arguments. Defendant argued the cause to the jury after which the judge read a series of negligence instructions and, on his own motion, BAJI 4.02 (res ipsa loquitur).

Appellants seek to have this court override the established law of this state which is dispositive of the issue before us as outmoded in today's social and economic structure, particularly in the light of the now recognized principles imposing liability upon the manufacturer, retailer and all distributive and vending elements and activities which bring a product to the consumer to his injury, on the basis of strict liability in tort expressed first in Justice Traynor's concurring opinion in *Escola v. Coca Cola Bottling Co.*, 24 Cal. 2d 453, 461-468 [150 P.2d 436]; and then in *Greenman v. Yuba Power Products, Inc.*, 59 Cal. 2d 57 [27 Cal. Rptr. 697, 377 P.2d 897; . . . These authorities hold that "A manufacturer [or retailer] is strictly liable in tort when an article he places on the market, knowing that it is to be used without inspection for defects, proves to have a defect that causes injury to a human being." (*Greenman v. Yuba Power Products, Inc.*, supra, 59 Cal. 2d 57, 62; . . .) Drawing a parallel with these products liability cases, appellants argue, with some degree of logic, that only the driver affected by a physical condition which could suddenly render him unconscious and who is aware of that condition can anticipate the hazards and foresee the dangers involved in his operation of a motor vehicle, and that the liability of those who by reason of seizure or heart failure or some other physical condition lose the ability to safely operate and control a motor vehicle resulting in injury to an innocent person should be predicated on strict liability.

We decline to superimpose the absolute liability of products liability cases upon drivers under the circumstances here. The theory on which those cases are predicated is that manufacturers, retailers and distributors of products are engaged in the business of distributing goods to the public and are an integral part of the over-all producing and marketing enterprise that should bear the cost of injuries from defective parts. (*Vandermark v. Ford Motor Co.*, 61 Cal. 2d 256, 262 [37 Cal.

---

ability to safely operate and control such vehicle because of some seizure or health failure, that driver is nevertheless legally liable for all injuries and property damage which an innocent person may suffer as a proximate result of the defendant's inability to so control or operate his motor vehicle.

"This is true even if you find the defendant driver had no warning of any such impending seizure or health failure."

Rptr. 896, 391 P.2d 168];. . . .) This policy hardly applies here and it is not enough to simply say, as do appellants, that the insurance carriers should be the ones to bear the cost of injuries to innocent victims on a strict liability basis. In *Maloney v. Rath*, 69 Cal. 2d 442 [71 Cal. Rptr. 897, 445 P.2d 513], . . . appellant urged that defendant's violation of a safety provision (defective brakes) of the Vehicle Code makes the violator strictly liable for damages caused by the violation. While reversing the judgment for defendant upon another ground, the California Supreme Court refused to apply the doctrine of strict liability to automobile drivers. The situation involved two users of the highway but the problems of fixing responsibility under a system of strict liability are as complicated in the instant case as those in *Maloney v. Rath* (p. 447), and could only create uncertainty in the area of its concern. As stated in *Maloney*, at page 446: "To invoke a rule of strict liability on users of the streets and highways, however, without also establishing in substantial detail how the new rule should operate would only contribute confusion to the automobile accident problem. Settlement and claims adjustment procedures would become chaotic until the new rules were worked out on a case-by-case basis, and the hardships of delayed compensation would be seriously intensified. Only the Legislature, if it deems it wise to do so, can avoid such difficulties by enacting a comprehensive plan for the compensation of automobile accident victims in place of or in addition to the law of negligence."

The instruction tendered by appellants was properly refused for still another reason. Even assuming the merit of appellants' position under the facts of this case in which defendant knew he had a history of epilepsy, previously had suffered seizures and at the time of the accident was attempting to control the condition by medication, the instruction does not except from its ambit the driver who suddenly is stricken by an illness or physical condition which he had no reason whatever to anticipate and of which he had no prior knowledge.

The judgment is affirmed.

WOOD, P.J., and THOMPSON, J., concur.

---

1. Who bears the loss in *Hammontree*? Why do you think the jury did not find the defendant negligent?

2. What is the reasoning underlying the court of appeals decision?

3. What is the policy underlying strict liability for defective products? Why does this court reject that policy?

4. What result if the defendant had been operating a taxi?

5. Argue that the plaintiff should or should not recover because the defendant has insurance. Note that few cases discuss insurance. Why?

6. Does not the plaintiff have a strong case for strict liability, because she is innocent and on her own property? For an affirmative answer, see *Louisville Ry. Co. v. Sweeney*, 157 Ky. 620, 163 S.W. 739 (1914).

7. What result if the defendant had fallen asleep at the wheel of the car? For an article arguing for strict liability in sleeping and seizure cases, see Kaufman & Kantrowitz, *The Case of the Sleeping Motorist*, 25 N.Y.U. L.Q. Rev. 362 (1950).

8. The cases often use absolute liability and strict liability without drawing a distinction. To recover in absolute liability, the plaintiff need only prove causation. To recover under strict liability for a product, however, the plaintiff must prove causation and that the product is defective. He or she does not have to prove intent or negligence, but may be subject to defenses, such as assumption of risk or contributory negligence. This will be further considered in the Products Liability chapter.

LANGAN v. VALICOPTERS, INC.
Supreme Court of Washington, 1977
88 Wash. 2d 855, 567 P.2d 218

DOLLIVER, J.

This is an appeal from a judgment against appellants for damages resulting from their crop spraying activities. Patrick and Dorothy Langan, respondents, own a small (2 1/2 to 3 acre) farm in the Yakima Valley. The Langans are organic farmers: that is, they use no nonorganic fertilizers, insecticides or herbicides to aid them in their farming but rely on natural fertilizers and natural pest control agents. They had planned to can and sell their produce to organic food buyers.

Valicopters, Inc., is a Washington corporation which engages in the aerial application of agricultural pesticides. Gene Bepple, one of the owners of Valicopters, Inc., was the helicopter pilot at the time of the incident giving rise to this lawsuit. The Thalheimers, doing business as Thalheimer Farms, owned and farmed the land adjoining that of the respondents. It was their land that was being sprayed by Valicopters. Simplot Soilbuilders sold the agricultural chemical to Thalheimers for aerial application.

On June 3, 1973, Bepple sprayed for Colorado beetle infestation on the Thalheimer farm with a chemical pesticide known as Thiodan. A small patch of the farm was sprayed with the chemical Guthion. While applying the pesticides to Thalheimers' property, Bepple traveled approximately 45 miles per hour while 6 to 8 feet off the ground with a 42-foot application boom extending from the sides of the helicopter. Patrick Langan testified that, during one spraying pass, the helicopter began spraying while it was over his property. This testimony was disputed. He further testified that the spray settled on the entire length of their tomato, bean, garlic, cucumber and Jerusalem artichoke rows.

The Langans and other organic farmers founded and are members of the Northwest Organic Food Producers' Association (NOFPA). The bylaws of NOFPA contain the following pertinent provisions:

> 7. No poisonous insecticides, repellents, herbicides, artificial fertilizers, stimulants or hormones may be used on food or in soil in which products are grown or animals are grazed. If any such item is applied by the grower to

any committed acreage that has been previously committed and certified, the acreage will be withdrawn from certification and this farmer cannot be recertified without approval of the Executive Committee.

9. No member shall be allowed to market foods or advertise food as certified organically grown by NOFPA if laboratory tests on the finished crop indicates [sic] the presence of more than ten percent (10%) of the maximum pesticide residue tolerances allowable by the Food and Drug Administration. In the event the finished crop reflects a residue higher than the allowable tolerances set forth in this section, the member's seal for any such crop shall immediately be suspended and public notice made thereof.

NOFPA Bylaws, art. 4, §§ 7, 9.

A laboratory test conducted after the spraying indicated the presence of 1.4 parts per million by weight of Thiodan on the Langans' crop tissue. The United States Department of Health Education and Welfare, Food and Drug Administration's tolerance for Thiodan on tomatoes and beans is 2.0 parts per million. Following the test results, the board of directors of NOFPA revoked the Langans' certification as organic food growers in conformance with bylaw No. 7. The Langans' entire property was decertified in conformance with the NOFPA rule which requires decertification when a portion of the land is contaminated.

Due to the decertification, the Langans did not grow their tomatoes and beans to fruition. Instead, they pulled them from the ground to prevent further contamination of the soil. The Langans had no contract to sell the contaminated tomatoes and beans commercially.

After a jury trial, a judgment in the amount of $5,500 was entered against appellants. They appealed to the Court of Appeals, Division Three. That court certified the case to this court and we accepted certification.

At the outset, it must be determined whether there was substantial evidence to support the jury's finding that respondents' damage occurred as a result of the spraying. Appellants contend that NOFPA erroneously interpreted its own bylaws. They argue that neither rule No. 7 nor rule No. 9 required immediate decertification of appellants' property and that the tomatoes and beans should have been tested for chemicals when those crops had fully matured. The bylaws of that organization are essentially a contract between NOFPA and its members. . . .

A director of NOFPA testified that their interpretation of rule No. 7, coupled with the basic purpose of NOFPA (to insure consumers that the products are organically grown if they are sold under the organization's seal) required decertification of respondents' farm. The Langans apparently agreed with this interpretation and did not question the legitimacy of the decertification. This decertification, which prompted the Langans to pull the crops, provided substantial evidence for the jury to conclude that they suffered damage as a result of crop spraying.

The next issue is whether the trial court erred by instructing the jury that appellants would be strictly liable for damage that was proximately caused by their aerial spraying. The trial judge gave the following instruction:

If you find that defendants' chemicals fell upon plaintiffs' crops, you are instructed that as a matter of law the defendants are liable for such damage to plaintiffs' crops, if any, as you find was proximately caused by defendants' spray application.

Liability for damage caused by crop dusting or spraying generally is imposed on the basis of either negligence or strict liability. . . . The courts in most jurisdictions that have held crop dusters liable have used the theory of negligence. . . . However, other opinions which have ostensibly relied upon the principles of negligence have been criticized by legal writers because the reasoning is not clear or more nearly resembles strict liability. Comment, Crop Dusting: Two Theories of Liability? 19 Hastings L.J. 476, 482-89 (1968); Note, "Crop Dusting: Legal Problems in a New Industry," 6 Stan. L. Rev. 69, 75-80 (1953).

Three jurisdictions have held crop dusting to be an activity to which the principles of strict liability apply. . . . In *Loe v. Lenhardt*, [227 Or. 242, 362 P.2d 312 (1961)] *supra*, Justice Goodwin, writing for the majority, noted that the dangers of spraying agricultural chemicals by aircraft has been the subject of considerable legislative attention nationwide, citing the laws of 29 states. These laws, he concluded, were evidence of the dangerous character of aerial spraying. The court recognized the activity was one capable of inflicting damage notwithstanding the exercise of utmost care by the applicator, and that the damage was within the scope of the risk created by spraying an adjoining field. The court cited *Bedell v. Goulter*, 199 Ore. 344, 362-63, 261 P.2d 842 (1953), a case involving strict liability for blasting, in which it stated:

"... Basic to the problem is 'an adjustment of conflicting interests,'... of the right of the blaster, on the one hand, to pursue a lawful occupation and the right of an owner of land, on the other, to its peaceful enjoyment and possession. Where damage is sustained by the latter through the nonculpable activities of the former, who should bear the loss — the man who caused it or a 'third person,' as Judge Hand says, 'who has no relation to the explosion, other than that of injury'?"

Loe v. Lenhardt, supra at 253-54.

In Washington, this court has adopted the Restatement (Second) of Torts §§ 519, 520 (Tent. Draft No. 10, 1964). *Pacific Northwest Bell Tel. Co. v. Port of Seattle*, 80 Wn. 2d 59, 491 P.2d 1037 (1971); *Siegler v. Kuhlman*, 81 Wn. 2d 448, 502 P.2d 1181 (1972). Section 519 of the Restatement provides:

(1) One who carries on an abnormally dangerous activity is subject to liability for harm to the person, land or chattels of another resulting from the activity, although he has exercised the utmost care to prevent such harm.

(2) Such strict liability is limited to the kind of harm, the risk of which makes the activity abnormally dangerous.

Section 520 lists the factors to be used when determining what constitutes an abnormally dangerous activity:

In determining whether an activity is abnormally dangerous, the following factors are to be considered:

(a) Whether the activity involves a high degree of risk of some harm to the person, land or chattels of others;

(b) Whether the gravity of the harm which may result from it is likely to be great;

(c) Whether the risk cannot be eliminated by the exercise of reasonable care;

(d) Whether the activity is not a matter of common usage;

(e) Whether the activity is inappropriate to the place where it is carried on; and

(f) The value of the activity to the community.

Whether an activity is abnormally dangerous is a question of law for the court to decide. *Siegler v. Kuhlman, supra;* Restatement (Second) of Torts § 520, comment (1) (Tent. Draft No. 10, 1964). In making this determination, we have considered each of the factors listed in the Restatement, section 520.

The essential question is whether the risk created is so unusual, either because of its magnitude or because of the circumstances surrounding it, as to justify the imposition of strict liability for the harm which results from it, even though it is carried on with all reasonable care.

Restatement (Second) of Torts § 520, comment (f) (Tent. Draft No. 10, 1964). *See generally* Peck, "Negligence and Liability Without Fault in Tort Law," 46 Wash. L. Rev. 225 (1971). However, in this case, each test of the Restatement is met. [The court then applied the six Restatement factors to crop dusting.]

. . . .

There is no doubt that pesticides are socially valuable in the control of insects, weeds and other pests. They may benefit society by increasing production. Whether strict liability or negligence principles should be applied amounts to a balancing of conflicting social interest — the risk of harm versus the utility of the activity. In balancing these interests, we must ask who should bear the loss caused by the pesticides. . . .

In the present case, the Langans were eliminated from the organic food market for 1973 through no fault of their own. If crop dusting continues on the adjoining property, the Langens [sic] may never be able to sell their crops to organic food buyers. Appellants, on the other hand, will all profit from the continued application of pesticides. Under these circumstances, there can be an equitable balancing of social interests only if appellants are made to pay for the consequences of their acts.

We realize that farmers are statutorily bound to prevent the spread of insects, pests, noxious weeds and diseases. RCW 15.08.030 and RCW 17.10.140,. 150. But the fulfillment of that duty does not mean the ability of an organic farmer to produce organic crops must be destroyed without compensation.

Thus, for the reasons mentioned above, we find that the trial court did not err by instructing the jury on strict liability.

. . . .

There is no reversible error; the judgment of the trial court is affirmed.

––––––––––––

1. What is the policy behind strict liability in *Langan*?

2. Would it be fair to say that strict liability impedes progress? What do you think of the statement in *Spano v. Perini Corp.*, 25 N.Y.2d 11, 302 N.Y.S.2d 527, 250 N.E.2d 31 (1969): "The plaintiff . . . was not seeking, as the court implied, to 'exclude the defendant from blasting' . . . he was merely seeking compensation for the damage which was inflicted upon his own property as a result of that blasting. The question . . . was not *whether* it was lawful or proper to engage in blasting but *who* should bear the cost of any resulting damage — the person who engaged in the dangerous activity or the innocent neighbor injured thereby."

3. What could plaintiff or defendant have done to prevent the injury in *Langan*?

4. Note that this is strict liability for an abnormally dangerous activity (like blasting), but in *Hammontree* the plaintiff was arguing for strict liability derived from defective products theory. What is the difference?

5. Note that the law has come full circle since the early middle ages. Wex Malone told us that, as of 1300, tort law was founded on absolute liability. In 1616, we saw a wisp of negligence in *Weaver v. Ward*. Negligence emerged as a fully feathered cause of action in 1850. Indeed, it appeared that absolute and strict liability were perhaps dead. Then strict liability emerged for abnormally dangerous activities, such as blasting and crop dusting, as presented in *Langan*. Strict liability for defective products, suggested in *Escola* (presented in *Hammontree*), became the dominant cause of action for cases involving defective products following the *Greenman* decision (also presented in *Hammontree*) in 1963. Strict liability and products liability will be discussed in later chapters. Much of our effort will now be devoted to the various aspects of intentional torts and negligence.

6. For an economic analysis of negligence and strict liability, see A. M. Polinsky, An Introduction to Law and Economics (1983); R. A. Posner, Economic Analysis of Law 137–42 (2d ed. 1977); S. Shavell, *Strict Liability Versus Negligence*, 9 J. Legal Stud. 1 (1980); F.J. Vandall, Strict Liability, Legal and Economic Analysis (1989).

Chapter 2

INTENTIONAL TORTS

The element of intent distinguishes the intentional torts from torts based on negligence or strict liability. Whether a tort is intentional or the product of negligence (accidental) has a major impact upon what the plaintiff must prove and upon what the defendant must pay should he or she be found liable.

The concept of intent has led to differences in treatment between intentional torts, on the one hand, and negligence and strict liability based torts, on the other. One difference of particular significance to plaintiffs seeking a substantial recovery is that the doctrine of respondeat superior is inapplicable in intentional tort cases. Under respondeat superior, an employer is liable for the negligent torts committed by an employee when the employee is acting within the scope of his or her employment. Except in certain situations involving occupations like security guards and bouncers, intentional torts are, virtually by definition, not within the scope of employment because of their intentional nature, and thus an employer who is liable when his or her employee commits a negligent tort is not liable when the tort is intentional. Another difference appears in the context of causation. There is no concept of proximate cause in the world of intentional torts: the defendant is simply liable for all of the consequences of his or her intentional act. Another difference appears in the realm of damages. If the tort was intentional, the courts do not generally require evidence of actual injury in order for the plaintiff to recover. Of course, if there was injury, the plaintiff will recover for that injury, but even if there was none, the plaintiff may recover nominal or other damages for the dignitary harm inflicted by the very fact that the intentional tort took place. Moreover, punitive damages, rarely available in negligence or strict liability contexts, may be awarded if the tort involved was intentional.

Perhaps because of the moral content inherent in the idea that the tort was committed at least to some extent on purpose, with the corollary availability of punitive damages, courts are adamant that the elements of each intentional tort be precisely proven in order for the plaintiff to prevail. In this respect, the intentional torts are easier to learn than the inherently more nebulous negligence or strict liability based torts. The court has its checklist of elements, and systematically marks off each one as the plaintiff makes his or her way through the case.

A.   INTENT IN GENERAL

The element of intent divides the intentional torts from those which are the products of negligence. Thus, defining intent becomes central to the question of whether any intentional tort took place at all. Many courts use cases involving children as a vehicle for defining intent.

15

GARRATT v. DAILEY
Supreme Court of Washington, 1955
279 P.2d 1091

HILL, JUSTICE.

The liability of an infant for an alleged battery is presented to this court for the first time. Brian Dailey (age five years, nine months) was visiting with Naomi Garratt, an adult and a sister of the plaintiff, Ruth Garratt, likewise an adult, in the back yard of the plaintiffs home, on July 16, 1951. It is plaintiffs contention that she came out into the back yard to talk with Naomi and that, as she started to sit down in a wood and canvas lawn chair, Brian deliberately pulled it out from under her. The only one of the three persons present so testifying was Naomi Garratt. (Ruth Garratt, the plaintiff, did not testify as to how or why she fell.) The trial court, unwilling to accept this testimony, adopted instead Brian Dailey's version of what happened, and made the following findings:

> "III. . . . that while Naomi Garratt and Brian Dailey were in the back yard the plaintiff, Ruth Garratt, came out of her house into the back yard. Some time subsequent thereto defendant, Brian Dailey, picked up a lightly built wood and canvas lawn chair which was then and there located in the back yard of the above described premises, moved it sideways a few feet and seated himself therein, at which time he discovered the plaintiff, Ruth Garratt, about to sit down at the place where the lawn chair had formerly been, at which time he hurriedly got up from the chair and attempted to move it toward Ruth Garratt to aid her in sitting down in the chair; that due to the defendant's small size and lack of dexterity he was unable to get the lawn chair under the plaintiff in time to prevent her from falling to the ground. That plaintiff fell to the ground and sustained a fracture of her hip, and other injuries and damages as hereinafter set forth.

> "IV. That the preponderance of the evidence in this case establishes that when the defendant, Brian Dailey, moved the chair in question *he did not have any willful or unlawful purpose* in doing so; that *he did not have any intent to injure the plaintiff or any intent to bring about any unauthorized or offensive contact with her person* or any objects appurtenant thereto; that the circumstances which immediately preceded the fall of the plaintiff established that the defendant, *Brian Dailey, did not have purpose, intent or design to perform a prank or to effect an assault and battery upon the person of the plaintiff*" (Italics ours, for a purpose hereinafter indicated.)

It is conceded that Ruth Garratt's fall resulted in a fractured hip and other painful and serious injuries. To obviate the necessity of a retrial in the event this court determines that she was entitled to a judgment against Brian Dailey, the amount of her damage was found to be $11,000. Plaintiff appeals from a judgment dismissing the action and asks for the entry of a judgment in that amount or a new trial.

The authorities generally, but with certain notable exceptions, state that when a minor has committed a tort with force he is liable to be proceeded against as any other person would be.

In our analysis of the applicable law, we start with the basic premise that Brian, whether five or fifty-five, must have committed some wrongful act before he could be liable for appellant's injuries.

. . . .

It is urged that Brian's action in moving the chair constituted a battery. A definition (not all-inclusive but sufficient for our purpose) of a battery is the intentional infliction of a harmful bodily contact upon another. The rule that determines liability for battery is given in 1 Restatement, Torts, 29, § 13, as:

> "An act which, directly or indirectly, is the legal cause of a harmful contact with another's person makes the actor liable to the other, if
>
> "(a) the act is done with the intention of bringing about a harmful or offensive contact or an apprehension thereof to the other or a third person, and
>
> "(b) the contact is not consented to by the other or the other's consent thereto is procured by fraud or duress, and
>
> "(c) the contact is not otherwise privileged."

We have in this case no question of consent or privilege. We therefore proceed to an immediate consideration of intent and its place in the law of battery. In the comment on clause (a), the Restatement says:

> "*Character of actor's intention.* In order that an act may be done with the intention of bringing about a harmful or offensive contact or an apprehension thereof to a particular person, either the other or a third person, the act must be done for the purpose of causing the contact or apprehension or with knowledge on the part of the actor that such contact or apprehension is substantially certain to be produced." *See, also,* Prosser on Torts 41, § 8.

We have here the conceded volitional act of Brian, *i.e.*, the moving of a chair. Had the plaintiff proved to the satisfaction of the trial court that Brian moved the chair while she was in the act of sitting down, Brian's action would patently have been for the purpose or with the intent of causing the plaintiffs bodily contact with the ground, and she would be entitled to a judgment against him for the resulting damages.

The plaintiff based her case on that theory, and the trial court held that she failed in her proof and accepted Brian's version of the facts rather than that given by the eyewitness who testified for the plaintiff. After the trial court determined that the plaintiff had not established her theory of a battery (*i.e.*, that Brian had pulled the chair out from under the plaintiff while she was in the act of sitting down), it then became concerned with whether a battery was established under the facts as it found them to be.

In this connection, we quote another portion of the comment on the "Character of actor's intention," relating to clause (a) of the rule from the Restatement heretofore set forth:

> "It is not enough that the act itself is intentionally done and this, even though the actor realizes or should realize that it contains a very grave risk of bringing about the contact or apprehension. Such realization may make the actor's conduct negligent or even reckless but unless he realizes that to a substantial certainty, the contact or apprehension will result, the actor has not that intention which is necessary to make him liable under the rule stated in this section."

A battery would be established if, in addition to plaintiffs fall, it was proved that, when Brian moved the chair, he knew with substantial certainty that the plaintiff would attempt to sit down where the chair had been. If Brian had any of the intents which the trial court found, in the italicized portions of the findings of fact quoted above, that he did not have, he would of course have had the knowledge to which we have referred. The mere absence of any intent to injure the plaintiff or to play a prank on her or to embarrass her, or to commit an assault and battery on her would not absolve him from liability if in fact he had such knowledge. Without such knowledge, there would be nothing wrongful about Brian's act in moving the chair and, there being no wrongful act, there would be no liability.

While a finding that Brian had no such knowledge can be inferred from the findings made, we believe that before the plaintiffs action in such a case should be dismissed there should be no question but that the trial court had passed upon that issue; hence, the case should be remanded for clarification of the findings to specifically cover the question of Brian's knowledge, because intent could be inferred therefrom. If the court finds that he had such knowledge the necessary intent will be established and the plaintiff will be entitled to recover, even though there was no purpose to injure or embarrass the plaintiff. If Brian did not have such knowledge, there was no wrongful act by him and the basic premise of liability on the theory of a battery was not established.

It will be noted that the law of battery as we have discussed it is the law applicable to adults, and no significance has been attached to the fact that Brian was a child less than six years of age when the alleged battery occurred. The only circumstance where Brian's age is of any consequence is in determining what he knew, and there his experience, capacity, and understanding are of course material.

From what has been said, it is clear that we find no merit in plaintiffs contention that we can direct the entry of a judgment for $11,000 in her favor on the record now before us.

Nor do we find any error in the record that warrants a new trial.

. . . .

The cause is remanded for clarification, with instructions to make definite findings on the issue of whether Brian Dailey knew with substantial certainty that the plaintiff would attempt to sit down where the chair which he moved had been, and to change the judgment if the findings warrant it.

. . . .

Remanded for clarification.

SCHWELLENBACH, DONWORTH, and WEAVER, JJ., concur.

---

1. Why didn't Ruth Garratt, the plaintiff, testify as to why she fell?

2. How does the court define intent? Did the court require that Brian know that the plaintiff might fall, or did the court require that Brian know that the plaintiff might be injured? If the plaintiff had not been injured, would Brian win?

3. If Brian had been an adult, what might this opinion have looked like?

4. In *Garratt*, the court focused on the fact question of whether, in fact, Brian had the intent necessary to treat the tort as an intentional one. Brian's age, as such, was irrelevant; what was important was whether he possessed the requisite intent. While his age may be significant in answering this question, it is only significant insofar as it contributes to the jury's ability to decide whether he, in fact, intended the results of his action.

Some courts treat children under seven as incapable of possessing the intent required for liability for an intentional tort as a matter of law, drawing the analogy to the rule in their jurisdictions that children under seven are, as a matter of law, incapable of contributory negligence. *DeLuca v. Bowden*, 329 N.E.2d 109 (Ohio 1975).

Garratt v. Dailey and *DeLuca v. Bowden* illustrate the alternative approaches to children taken in negligence cases as well as intentional tort cases. Some courts apply "bright line" rules, with the standard of care and potential liability of the child depending on that child's age. Other courts look at the individual child, irrespective of age, to determine whether *that* child has the capacity to act negligently or intentionally.

WALLACE v. ROSEN
Indiana Court of Appeals, Second District, 2002
765 N.E.2d 192

KIRSCH, JUDGE.

Mable Wallace appeals the jury verdict in favor of Indianapolis Public Schools (IPS) and Harriet Rosen, a teacher for IPS. On appeal, Wallace raises the following issues:

> I. Whether the trial court erred in refusing to give her tendered jury instruction regarding battery.

> II. Whether the trial court erred in instructing the jury regarding the defense of incurred risk.

We affirm.

FACTS AND PROCEDURAL HISTORY

In 1994, Rosen was a teacher at Northwest High School in Indianapolis. On April 22, 1994, the high school had a fire drill while classes were in session. The drill was not previously announced to the teachers and occurred just one week after a fire was extinguished in a bathroom near Rosen's classroom.

On the day the alarm sounded, Wallace was at the high school delivering homework to her daughter Lalaya. Because Wallace was recovering from foot surgery and Lalaya's class was on the second floor, Lalaya's boyfriend Eric Fuqua accompanied Wallace up the stairs. Wallace and Fuqua were near the top of the staircase when they saw Lalaya and began to speak with her. Jamie Arnold, a student who knew Lalaya and her mother, joined the conversation. The alarm then sounded and students began filing down the stairs while Wallace took a step or two up the stairs to the second floor landing.

In response to the alarm, Rosen escorted her class to the designated stairway and noticed three or four people talking together at the top of the stairway and blocking the students' exit. Rosen did not recognize any of the individuals but approached "telling everybody to move it." *Transcript* at 35. Wallace, with her back to Rosen, was unable to hear Rosen over the noise of the alarm and Rosen had to touch her on the back to get her attention. *Id.* at 259. Rosen then told Wallace, "you've got to get moving because this is a fire drill." *Id.* 259.

At trial, Wallace testified that Rosen pushed her down the stairs. *Id.* at 128. Rosen denied pushing Wallace and testified that Wallace had not fallen, but rather had made her way down the stairs unassisted and without losing her balance. *Id.* at 265–66.

At the close of the trial, Wallace tendered an instruction concerning civil battery. Over Wallace's objection, the court refused to read the instruction to the jury. IPS and Rosen tendered an instruction concerning the defense of incurred risk on the basis that Wallace had continued up the stairs after hearing the alarm, had stopped at the landing to talk, and had blocked the students' exit. Over Wallace's objection, the court gave the incurred risk instruction. The jury found in favor of IPS and Rosen, and Wallace now appeals.

I. Battery Instruction

Wallace first argues that it was error for the trial court to refuse to give the jury the following tendered instruction pertaining to battery:

> A battery is the knowing or intentional touching of one person by another in a rude, insolent, or angry manner.

> Any touching, however slight, may constitute an assault and battery.

> Also, a battery may be recklessly committed where one acts in reckless disregard of the consequences, and the fact the person does not intend that the act shall result in an injury is immaterial.

Wallace argues that the omission of the instruction was error because the instruction was an accurate statement of the law, was supported by the evidence, and was not covered by any other instruction read to the jury. Appellees respond that the instruction was properly omitted because there was no evidence presented that supported a battery instruction.

. . . .

[I]t is correct to tell the jury that, relying on circumstantial evidence, they may infer that the actor's state of mind was the same as a reasonable person's state of mind would have been. Thus, . . . the defendant on a bicycle who rides down a person in full view on a sidewalk where there is ample room to pass may learn that the factfinder (judge or jury) is unwilling to credit the statement, "I didn't mean to do it."

On the other hand, the mere knowledge and appreciation of a risk — something short of substantial certainty — is not intent. The defendant who acts in the belief or consciousness that the act is causing an appreciable risk of harm to another may be negligent, and if the risk is great the conduct may be characterized as reckless or wanton, but it is not an intentional wrong. In such cases the distinction between intent and negligence obviously is a matter of degree. The line has to be drawn by the courts at the point where the known danger ceases to be only a foreseeable risk which a reasonable person would avoid, and becomes in the mind of the actor a substantial certainty.

The intent with which tort liability is concerned is not necessarily a hostile intent, or a desire to do any harm. Rather it is an intent to bring about a result which will invade the interests of another in a way that the law forbids. The defendant may be liable although intending nothing more than a good-natured practical joke, or honestly believing that the act would not injure the plaintiff, or even though seeking the plaintiff's own good.

W. Page Keeton et al., Prosser and Keeton on the Law of Torts, § 8, at 33, 36-37 (5th ed. 1984) (footnotes omitted).

Wallace, Lalaya, and Fuqua testified that Rosen touched Wallace on the back causing her to fall down the stairs and injure herself. For battery to be an appropriate instruction, the evidence had to support an inference not only that Rosen intentionally touched Wallace, but that she did so in a rude, insolent, or angry manner, i.e., that she intended to invade Wallace's interests in a way that the law forbids.

Professors Prosser and Keeton also made the following observations about the intentional tort of battery and the character of the defendant's action:

In a crowded world, a certain amount of personal contact is inevitable and must be accepted. *Absent expression to the contrary, consent is assumed to all those ordinary contacts which are customary and reasonably necessary to the common intercourse of life, such as a tap on the shoulder to attract attention,* a friendly grasp of the arm, or a casual jostling to make a passage. . . . .

The time and place, and the circumstances under which the act is done, will necessarily affect its unpermitted character, and so will the relations between the parties. A stranger is not to be expected to tolerate liberties which would be allowed by an intimate friend. But unless the defendant has special reason to believe that more or less will be permitted by the individual plaintiff, the test is what would be offensive to an ordinary person not unduly sensitive as to personal dignity.

Keeton et al., § 9, at 42 (emphasis added).

. . . .

Viewed most favorably to the trial court's decision refusing the tendered instruction, the evidence . . . indicates that Rosen placed her fingertips on Wallace's shoulder and turned her 90 degrees toward the exit in the midst of a fire drill. The conditions on the stairway of Northwest High School during the fire drill were an example of Professors Prosser and Keeton's "crowded world." Individuals standing in the middle of a stairway during the fire drill could expect that a certain amount of personal contact would be inevitable. Rosen had a responsibility to her students to keep them moving in an orderly fashion down the stairs and out the door. Under these circumstances, Rosen's touching of Wallace's shoulder or back with her fingertips to get her attention over the noise of the alarm cannot be said to be a rude, insolent, or angry touching. Wallace has failed to show that the trial court abused its discretion in refusing the battery instruction.

Furthermore, even if an instruction on battery was appropriate, Wallace's inclusion of language that "a battery may be recklessly committed" created an instruction that was likely to mislead or confuse the jury under the facts of this case. . . . *Mercer v. Corbin*, 117 Ind. 450, 20 N.E. 132 (1889) (the supreme court, ignoring the defendant's statement that he didn't mean to hit the plaintiff, found that the defendant committed assault and battery when he rode his bicycle over the plaintiff who was standing on one side of a fourteen-foot-wide sidewalk in broad daylight); *Reynolds v. Pierson*, 29 Ind. App. 273, 64 N.E. 484 (1902) ("horse play" in which the defendant jerked and pulled with sufficient force to throw the plaintiff off another's arm and injure him revealed a reckless disregard of the consequences and thus supplied grounds for inferring defendant's constructive intent and the willful act of battery).

The facts in this case can be distinguished from those cited by the Committee. Rosen's actions were clearly not intentional like the facts in *Kline*, nor can it be said that Rosen's touching arose from a recklessness or wanton disregard of human life and safety found in *Mercer*. Quite the contrary, the actions that Rosen took were intended to keep the student traffic flowing out of the building and away from any potential danger. . . . The inclusion of the reckless instruction with the intentional tort of battery under the facts of this case would have allowed the jury to use a lesser standard to convict Rosen and IPS of battery. We find that the inclusion of the "reckless" language in the battery instruction would have been misleading and made the instructions as a whole confusing to the jury.

A fire had been actually set in the bathroom on Rosen's floor less than a week before the fire alarm sounded. On April 22, 1994, with no prior knowledge whether the alarm signaled a drill or a fire, Rosen exercised ordinary and reasonable care when she tried to get the students to exit as quickly as possible. Finding Wallace and three others creating a bottleneck at the top of the staircase required Rosen to take quick action. It was necessary for Rosen to both raise her voice and touch Wallace's back to get her attention. When Wallace objected to being touched and did not move, it was also reasonable for Rosen to turn Wallace toward the stairs and tell her to get moving. Failing to give the battery instruction was not error because, even if given, the facts of this case would not have supported a claim for intentional battery.

. . . .

Affirmed.

SULLIVAN, J., concurs with separate opinion.

ROBB, J., concurs in part and concurs in result in part with separate opinion.

VOSBURG v. PUTNEY
Supreme Court of Wisconsin, 1891
80 Wis. 523, 50 N.W. 403

APPEAL from the Circuit Court for Waukesha County.

The action was brought to recover damages for an assault and battery, alleged to have been committed by the defendant upon the plaintiff on February 20, 1889. The answer is a general denial.

The injury complained of was caused by a kick inflicted by defendant upon the leg of the plaintiff, a little below the knee. The transaction occurred in a school-room in Waukesha, during school hours, both parties being pupils in the school. A former trial of the cause resulted in a verdict and judgment for the plaintiff for $2,800. The defendant appealed from such judgment to this court, and the same was reversed for error, and a new trial awarded.

The case has been again tried in the circuit court, and the trial resulted in a verdict for plaintiff for $2,500. The facts of the case, as they appeared on both trials, are sufficiently stated in the opinion by MR. JUSTICE ORTON on the former appeal, and require no repetition.

. . . .

LYON, J.

[The facts of this case are included in the opinion of ORTON, J. in an earlier appeal of this case at 47 N.W. 99 (Wisc. 1890). They are briefly as follows: The plaintiff was about fourteen years of age, and the defendant about eleven years of age. On the 20th day of February, 1889, they were sitting opposite to each other across an aisle in the high school of the village of Waukesha. The defendant reached across the aisle with his foot, and hit with his toe the shin of the right leg of the plaintiff. The touch was slight. The plaintiff did not feel it, either on account of its being so slight or of loss of sensation produced by the shock. In a few moments he felt a violent pain in that place, which caused him to cry out loudly. The next day he was sick, and had to be helped to school. On the fourth day he was vomiting, and Dr. Bacon was sent for, but could not come, and he sent medicine to stop the vomiting, and came to see him the next day, on the 25th. There was a slight discoloration of the skin entirely over the inner surface of the tibia an inch below the bend of the knee. The doctor applied fomentations, and gave him anodynes to quiet the pain. This treatment was continued, and the swelling so increased by the 5th day of March that counsel was called, and on the 8th of March an operation was performed on the limb by making an incision, and a moderate amount of pus escaped. A drainage tube was inserted, and an iodoform dressing put on. On the sixth day after this, another incision was made to the bone, and it was found that destruction was going on in the bone, and so it has continued exfoliating pieces of bone. He will never recover the use of his limb. There were black and blue spots on the shin bone, indicating that there had been a blow. On the 1st day of January before, the plaintiff received an injury just above the knee of the same leg by coasting, which appeared to be healing up and drying down at the time of the last injury. The theory of at least one of the medical witnesses was that the limb was in a diseased condition when this touch or kick was given, caused by microbes entering in through the wound above the knee, and which were revivified by the touch, and that the touch was the exciting or remote cause of the destruction of the bone, or of the plaintiffs injury. It does not appear that there was any visible mark made or left by this touch or kick of the defendant's foot, or any appearance of injury until the black and blue spots were discovered by the physician several days afterwards, and then there were more spots than one. There was no proof of any other hurt, and the medical testimony seems to have been agreed that this touch or kick was the exciting cause of the injury to the plaintiff. The jury rendered a verdict for the plaintiff of $2,800.

The rule of damages in actions for torts was held in *Brown v. C, M. & St. P. R. Co. 54 Wis. 342*, to be that the wrongdoer is liable for all injuries resulting directly from the wrongful act, whether they could or could not have been foreseen by him.

. . .

---

1. What is the nature of the intent required as an element in intentional tort cases? Is it subjective or objective? What is recklessness?

2. The intent of a defendant is measured by his or her acts, and not by what the defendant happened to be thinking at the time of the acts. Why did the court in *Garratt v. Bailey* focus on what the defendant actually knew or might actually have been thinking? Does the idea of the "crowded world" require some examination of intent? By what standard should the crowded world be measured?

3. A defendant may be liable for battery where no harm was intended. The intent required is the intent to make unconsented-to contact; the defendant is liable for the contact and any harm that results from the contact. *Vosburg v. Putney* is perhaps the best-known case standing for this proposition. Incidentally, there was

a truly startling number of appeals and remands in this case before the litigation ended.

Vosburg also illustrates the rule that the defendant is liable for all of the consequences of his or her intentional tort, whether foreseeable or not negligence cases, the defendant is liable for all injury proximately caused by his or her negligent actions. The concept of proximate cause enables courts to sever the chain of causation in cases where the consequences were not foreseeable to the defendant. One acts negligently only in failing to avoid foreseeable dangers; one cannot be held liable for unreasonably failing to avoid a danger which no one could have predicted. In intentional tort cases, on the other hand, reasonable avoidance is not an issue because the act was intentional. Thus, the defendant is liable for all consequences of his or her intentional tort, no matter how farfetched those consequences may be. In negligence, the defendant's conduct is evaluated by its potential for harm. In intentional torts, the defendant's conduct is evaluated by its character, and its consequences are important only insofar as they cast light upon the intentional nature of the initial act itself and serve as the basis for an award of damages.

Another case illustrating the principle that the defendant is liable for all of the consequences of his or her actions, whether foreseeable or not, is *Caudle v. Betts*, 512 So. 2d 389 (La. 1987). In *Caudle*, the defendant, as a practical joke, caused a minor electrical shock to be administered to the plaintiff. This minor electrical shock caused severe and unforeseeable nerve damage to the plaintiff, for which the defendant had to pay.

The defendant may be liable for consequences that extend beyond the intended plaintiff. In *Keel v. Hainline*, 331 P.2d 397 (Okla. 1958), the court ruled that the defendants, who contrary to school rules were engaged in throwing erasers and other projectiles at each other, were liable for battery when the projectiles struck a classmate who was not participating in the activity. The intent of the defendants to strike each other was transferred to the person who was in fact struck, and the fact that the defendants had not intended to strike the plaintiff was irrelevant.

4. It is clear that not all contact should serve as the basis for a lawsuit. Where should courts draw the line between the kinds of contact individuals should be required to tolerate and the kinds of contact for which individuals should be able to file suit?

PROBLEM

H, a ten-year-old child, decides to see what will happen if he throws a glass soda bottle against a telephone pole. He fails to look up before throwing the bottle. He throws the bottle, and it shatters. A piece of the bottle strikes a telephone company worker who is working at the top of the pole.

The telephone company worker files suit for battery. Assuming that the worker may sue H, what arguments will the parties make on the question of intent?

B. BATTERY

Battery is the classic intentional tort. What is particularly interesting about the following cases is the way in which an apparently archaic tort can fit modern contexts and needs.

MINK v. UNIVERSITY OF CHICAGO
United States District Court for the Northern District of Illinois, 1978
460 F. Supp. 713

Memorandum Opinion

GRADY, DISTRICT JUDGE.

Plaintiffs have brought this [diversity] action on behalf of themselves and some 1,000 women who were given diethylstilbestrol ("DES") as part of a medical experiment conducted by the defendants, University of Chicago and Eli Lilly & Company, between September 29, 1950, and November 20, 1952. The drug was administered to the plaintiffs during their prenatal care at the University's Lying-in Hospital as part of a double blind study to determine the value of DES in preventing miscarriages. The women were not told they were part of an experiment, nor were they told that the pills administered to them were DES. Plaintiffs claim that as a result of their taking DES, their daughters have developed abnormal cervical cellular formations and are exposed to an increased risk of vaginal or cervical cancer. Plaintiffs also allege that they and their sons have suffered reproductive tract and other abnormalities and have incurred an increased risk of cancer.

. . . .

The complaint seeks recovery on three causes of action. The first alleges that the defendants committed a series of batteries on the plaintiffs by conducting a medical experiment on them without their knowledge or consent. The administration of DES to the plaintiffs without their consent is alleged to be an "offensive invasion of their persons" which has caused them "severe mental anxiety and emotional distress due to the increased risk to their children of contracting cancer and other abnormalities.' . . . Throughout the complaint plaintiffs claim the defendants intentionally concealed the fact of the experiment and information concerning the relationship between DES and cancer from the plaintiffs.

Both defendants have moved to dismiss the complaint for failure to state a claim. We will deny the motions as to the first cause of action [.] . . .

Battery

We must determine whether the administration of a drug, DES, to the plaintiffs without their knowledge or consent constitutes a battery under Illinois law. The defendants argue that the plaintiffs' first count is really a "lack of informed consent" case premised on negligence. Because the named plaintiffs have not alleged specific physical injury to themselves, the defendants contend they have failed to state a claim for negligence and the count should be dismissed. However, if we find the action to be based on a battery theory, it may stand notwithstanding the lack of an allegation of personal physical injury.

True "informed consent" cases concern the duty of the physician to inform his patient of risks inherent in the surgery or treatment to which he has consented. While early cases treated lack of informed consent as vitiating the consent to treatment so there was liability for battery, the modern view "is that the action . . . is in reality one for negligence in failing to conform to the proper standard, to be determined on the basis of expert testimony as to what disclosure should be made." W. Prosser, Law of Torts § 32, at 165 (4th ed. 1971). Nonetheless, a battery action may still be appropriate in certain circumstances. Where the patient has not consented to the treatment, it is meaningless to ask whether the doctor should have revealed certain risks necessary to make the consent an "informed" one. The distinction between battery and negligence is elucidated in *Trogun v. Fruchtman*, 58 Wis. 2d 569, 596, 207 N.W.2d 297, 311-12 (1973):

> The courts of this country have recognized essentially two theories of liability for allegedly unauthorized medical treatment or therapy rendered by physicians to their patients. The first of these theories is the traditional intentional tort of battery or assault and battery which is simply defined as the unauthorized touching of the person of another. Underlying this theory of liability is, of course, the general feeling that a person of sound mind has a right to determine, even as against his physician, what is to be done to his body. Under this theory, liability is imposed upon a physician who has performed non-emergency treatment upon a patient without his consent.
>
> . . . .
>
The second theory of liability, permitted by a majority of courts, is grounded upon negligence principles rather than on intentional tort. . . . "[This] doctrine of 'informed consent'. . . concerns the duty of the physician or surgeon to inform the patient of the risk which may be involved in treatment or surgery."

As for the application of the distinction, we find the analysis of the court in *Cobbs v. Grant*, 8 Cal. 3d 229, 104 Cal. Rptr. 505, 512, 502 P.2d 1, 8 (1972), persuasive:

> The battery theory should be reserved for those circumstances when a doctor performs an operation to which the patient has not consented. When the patient gives permission to perform one type of treatment and the doctor performs another, the requisite element of deliberate intent to deviate from the consent given is present. However, when the patient consents to certain treatment and the doctor performs that treatment but an undisclosed inherent complication with a low probability occurs, no intentional deviation from the consent given appears; rather, the doctor in obtaining consent may have failed to meet his due care duty to disclose pertinent information. In that situation the action should be pleaded in negligence.

Illinois courts have adopted the modern approach to true informed consent cases, and have treated them as negligence actions. However, they have not overruled earlier cases which recognize a cause of action in battery for surgery performed without a patient's consent. Thus, it appears the two separate theories continue to exist in Illinois, and battery may be the proper cause of action in certain situations, for example, where there is a total lack of consent by the patient.[4]

The question thus becomes whether the instant case is more akin to the performance of an unauthorized operation than to the failure to disclose the potential ramifications of an agreed to treatment. We think the situation is closer to the former. The plaintiffs did not consent to DES treatment; they were not even aware that the drug was being administered to them. They were the subjects of an experiment whereby non-emergency treatment was performed upon them without their consent or knowledge.

. . . .

Battery is defined as the unauthorized touching of the person of another. To be liable for battery, the defendant must have done some affirmative act, intended to cause an unpermitted contact. "[I]t is enough that the defendant sets a force in motion which ultimately produces the result. . . . Proof of the technical invasion of the integrity of the plaintiffs person by even an entirely harmless, but offensive, contact entitles him to vindication of his legal right by an award of nominal damages, and the establishment of the tort cause of action entitles him also to compensation for the mental disturbance inflicted upon him." W. Prosser, Law of Torts § 9, at 35 (4th ed. 1971).

"The gist of the action for battery is not the hostile intent of the defendant, but rather the absence of consent to the contact on the part of the plaintiff." *Id.* at 36. "The essence . . . [of the] question in a battery case involving a physician is what did the patient agree with the physician to have done, and was the ultimate contact by the physician within the scope of the patient's consent." *Cathemer v. Hunter*, 27 Ariz. App. 780, 558 P.2d 975, 978 (1976). In sum, to state a cause of action for battery, the plaintiffs must allege intentional acts by the defendants resulting in offensive contact with the plaintiffs' persons, and the lack of consent to the Defendants' conduct.

The administration of DES to the plaintiffs was clearly intentional. It was part of a planned experiment conducted by the defendants. The requisite element of intent is therefore met, since the plaintiffs need show only an intent to bring about the contact; an intent to do harm is not essential to the action. Prosser at 36.

The act of administering the drug supplies the contact with the plaintiffs' persons. "It is not necessary that the contact with the other's person be directly caused by some act of the actor. All that is necessary is that the actor intend to cause the other, directly or indirectly, to come in contact with a foreign substance in a manner which the other will reasonably regard as offensive." Restatement (Second) of Torts § 18, Comment c at 31 (1965). We find the administration of a drug without the patient's knowledge comports with the meaning of offensive contact. Had the drug been administered by means of a hypodermic needle, the element of physical contact would clearly be sufficient. We believe that causing the patient to physically

---

[4] We disagree with defendants that the battery theory is applicable only in cases of uncon-sented operations. The gravamen of a battery action is the plaintiffs lack of consent, not the form of the touching.

ingest a pill is indistinguishable in principle.

Finally, there is the question of consent. As previously stated, this is the real crux of the issue in cases involving a physician's treatment of his patient. If the patient has assented to the doctor's treatment, he may not later maintain an action in battery. The defendants argue that the plaintiffs consented to treatment when they admitted themselves to the University's Lying-in Hospital for prenatal care. The scope of the plaintiffs' consent is crucial to their ultimate recovery in a battery action. The Defendants' privilege is limited at least to acts substantially similar to those to which the plaintiffs consented. If the defendants went beyond the consent given, to perform substantially different acts, they may be liable. The time, place and circumstances will affect the nature of the consent given. "It is . . . possible that the consent given will be sufficiently general in its terms to cover the particular operation [or treatment], or that the surgeon may be authorized with complete freedom to do whatever he thinks best to remedy whatever he finds, particularly where the patient has signed one of the written forms in common use in hospitals." Prosser at 104. These questions, however, are questions of fact which are to be determined by the jury, not by this court on a motion to dismiss. The plaintiffs have alleged sufficient lack of consent to the treatment involved to state a claim for battery against both defendants.

. . . .

Conclusion

The motions to dismiss of defendants University of Chicago and Eli Lilly & Co. are denied as to the plaintiffs' first cause of action. The first count states a claim for relief for battery and is not barred by the statute of limitations or the doctrine of charitable immunity.

. . . .

———

1. What is the nature of the contact here? Why did the plaintiffs bring this suit as a battery case?

2. The concept of consent appears both here and in the Privileges chapter. This is because there is an inherent ambiguity in battery law: Is consent a defense or is its absence something the plaintiff must prove? As will appear further in the Privileges and Negligence chapters, there is also a wide gulf between those cases in which the plaintiff alleges that there was no consent whatever (which are adjudicated as battery cases) and those cases in which the plaintiff alleges that there was incomplete consent (which tend to be treated as negligence cases).

FISHER v. CARROUSEL MOTOR HOTEL, INC.
Supreme Court of Texas, 1967
424 S.W.2d 627

GREENHILL, JUSTICE.

This is a suit for actual and exemplary damages growing out of an alleged assault and battery. The plaintiff Fisher was a mathematician with the Data Processing Division of the Manned Spacecraft Center, an agency of the National Aeronautics and Space Agency, commonly called NASA, near Houston. The defendants were the Carrousel Motor Hotel, Inc., located in Houston, the Brass Ring Club, which is located in the Carrousel, and Robert W. Flynn, who as an employee of the Carrousel was the manager of the Brass Ring Club. Flynn died before the trial, and the suit proceeded as to the Carrousel and the Brass Ring. Trial was to a jury which found for the plaintiff Fisher. The trial court rendered judgment for the defendants notwithstanding the verdict. The Court of Civil Appeals affirmed. 414 S.W.2d 774. The questions before this Court are whether there was evidence that an actionable battery was committed, and, if so, whether the two corporate defendants must respond in exemplary [punitive] as well as actual damages for the malicious conduct of Flynn.

The plaintiff Fisher had been invited by Ampex Corporation and Defense Electronics to a one day's meeting regarding telemetry equipment at the Carrousel. The invitation included a luncheon. . . . After the morning session, the group of 25 or 30 guests adjourned to the Brass Ring Club for lunch. The luncheon was buffet style. . . . As Fisher was about to be served, he was approached by Flynn, who snatched the plate from Fisher's hand and shouted that he, a Negro, could not be served in the club. Fisher testified that he was not actually touched, and did not testify that he suffered fear or apprehension of physical injury; but he did testify that he was highly embarrassed and hurt by Flynn's conduct in the presence of his associates.

The jury found that Flynn "forceably dispossessed plaintiff of his dinner plate" and "shouted in a loud and offensive manner" that Fisher could not be served there, thus subjecting Fisher to humiliation and indignity. . . .

The Court of Civil Appeals held that there was no assault because there was no physical contact and no evidence of fear or apprehension of physical contact. However, it has long been settled that there can be a battery without an assault, and that actual physical contact is not necessary to constitute a battery, so long as there is contact with clothing or an object closely identified with the body. 1 Harper & James, The Law of Torts 216 (1956); Restatement of Torts 2d, §§ 18 and 19. In Prosser, Law of Torts 32 (3d Ed. 1964), it is said:

> "The interest in freedom from intentional and unpermitted contacts with the plaintiffs person is protected by an action for the tort commonly called battery. The protection extends to any part of the body, or to anything which is attached to it and practically identified with it. Thus contact with the plaintiffs clothing, or with a cane, a paper, or any other object held in his hand will be sufficient; . . . The plaintiffs interest in the integrity of his

person includes all those things which are in contact or connected with it."

Under the facts of this case, we have no difficulty in holding that the intentional grabbing of plaintiffs plate constituted a battery. The intentional snatching of an object from one's hand is as clearly an offensive invasion of his person as would be an actual contact with the body. "To constitute an assault and battery, it is not necessary to touch the plaintiffs body or even his clothing; knocking or snatching anything from plaintiffs hand or touching anything connected with his person, when, done in an offensive manner, is sufficient." *Morgan v. Loyacomo*, 190 Miss. 656, 1 So. 2d 510 (1941).

. . . .

The rationale for holding an offensive contact with such an object to be a battery is explained in 1 Restatement of Torts 2d § 18 (Comment p. 31) as follows:

"Since the essence of the plaintiffs grievance consists in the offense to the dignity involved in the unpermitted and intentional invasion of the inviolability of his person and not in any physical harm done to his body, it is not necessary that the plaintiffs actual body be disturbed. Unpermitted and intentional contacts with anything so connected with the body as to be customarily regarded as part of the other's person and therefore as partaking of its inviolability is actionable as an offensive contact with his person. There are some things such as clothing or a cane or, indeed, anything directly grasped by the hand which are so intimately connected with one's body as to be universally regarded as part of the person."

We hold, therefore, that the forceful dispossession of plaintiff Fisher's plate in an offensive manner was sufficient to constitute a battery, and the trial court erred in granting judgment notwithstanding the verdict on the issue of actual damages.

. . . .

---

1.   Under the Federal Civil Rights Act, 42 U.S.C. § 2000a *et seq.* (1964), all businesses accommodating the public and affecting interstate commerce must serve their customers "without discrimination or segregation on the ground of race, color, religion, or national origin."

2.   In Texas, the employer can be held liable for the intentional torts of the employee if the actor was a manager, the act was "authorized," or if the employer "ratifies" the tortious acts, *Fisher* at 631.

PROBLEM

Mrs. Clayton went roller skating at defendant's rink. While skating, she fell over some chewing gum on the rink surface and broke her arm. Defendant told Mrs. Clayton that he was not a doctor but that he had experience in dealing with injuries. In an effort to be helpful, he then tried to set the broken bone despite objections from Mrs. Clayton, causing her additional pain.

You are Mrs. Clayton's attorney. What will you allege in your suit against defendant?

LAMBERTSON v. UNITED STATES
United States Court of Appeals for the Second Circuit, 1976
528 F.2d 441

Before MOORE, OAKES and VAN GRAAFEILAND, CIRCUIT JUDGES.

VAN GRAAFEILAND, CIRCUIT JUDGE:

This is an appeal from an order of Judge Edmund Port of the United States District Court for the Northern District of New York dismissing plaintiffs action against the United States as barred by 28 U.S.C. § 2680(h). We affirm.

Appellant, an employee of Armour & Co., sustained serious injuries to his mouth as a result of the actions of one William Boslet, a meat inspector for the United States Department of Agriculture [who was on duty at the time]. For the most part, the circumstances of the incident are not in dispute. . . .

On August 30, 1972, a truck shipment of beef arrived at the receiving dock of Armour's Syracuse plant. Plaintiff was one of the employees assigned to unload this truck. While he was so engaged, he was suddenly and without warning jumped by Boslet who, screaming "boo," pulled plaintiffs wool stocking hat over his eyes and, climbing on his back, began to ride him piggyback. As a result of this action, plaintiff fell forward and struck his face on some meat hooks located on the receiving dock [no more than six inches away] suffering severe injuries to his mouth and teeth.

It is apparently agreed by all witnesses that the mishap was the result of one-sided horseplay with no intention on Boslet's part to injure plaintiff. Indeed, immediately after the incident Boslet apologized to plaintiff, telling him that he was only playing around and meant no harm.

Seeking redress for his injuries, plaintiff commenced the instant action against the United States pursuant to the Federal Tort Claims Act, 28 U.S.C. § 1346(b).

Traditionally, the sovereign has always been immune from suit. To alleviate the harshness of this rule, Congress enacted the Federal Tort Claims Act which permits civil actions against the United States for personal injury and property damage caused by the "negligent or wrongful act or omission of any employee of the Government while acting within the scope of his office or employment." 28 U.S.C. § 1346(b). 28 U.S.C. § 2680, however, lists several claims expressly excepted from the purview of the Act, among which are any claims arising out of an assault or battery.[3] Since the United States has not consented to be sued for these torts, federal courts are without jurisdiction to entertain a suit based on them.

Although his order contains no express statement to that effect, the parties agree

---

[3] Section 2680 reads in pertinent part as follows:

The provisions of this chapter and section 1346(b) of this title shall not apply to — (h) Any claim arising out of assault, battery, false imprisonment, false arrest, malicious prosecution, abuse of process, libel, slander, misrepresentation, deceit, or interference with contract rights.

that the sole basis for Judge Port's dismissal was his conclusion that Boslet's actions constituted a battery.

Appellant contests this conclusion and steadfastly maintains that his complaint sounds in negligence.

. . . .

It is hornbook law in New York, as in most other jurisdictions, that the intent which is an essential element of the action for battery is the intent to make contact, not to do injury.

> A plaintiff in an action to recover damages for an assault founded on bodily contact must prove only that there was bodily contact; that such contact was offensive; and that the defendant intended to make the contact. The plaintiff is not required to prove that defendant intended physically to injure him. Certainly he is not required to prove an intention to cause the specific injuries resulting from the contact.

Harper and James put it that "it is a battery for a man . . . to play a joke upon another which involves a harmful or offensive contact." Prosser says that a "defendant may be liable where he has intended only a joke." *Accord* Restatement (Second) of Torts § 13, comment c (1965). Since there is not the remotest suggestion that Boslet's leap onto plaintiffs back, his piggy back ride and his use of plaintiffs hat as a blindfold might have been accidental, there was no error in the District Court's determination that it was a battery.

. . . .

Affirmed.

Oakes, Circuit Judge (concurring):

Were we writing on a clean slate, a good argument could be made for the proposition that the 'battery" exclusion in 28 U.S.C. § 2680(h) was intended to apply only to cases where bodily harm was intended and not to cases involving a "technical battery."

---

1. What is a technical battery? What damages should be available for such a battery?

2. Under what circumstances do you think that an employer should be liable for the intentional torts of an employee?

3. A corollary of the rule that the defendant is liable for all consequences of his or her intentional tort, no matter their foreseeability, is the principle that no actual damage is necessary in order for liability to attach. Even in the absence of actual damage, the plaintiff has been injured by the fact of the contact or other intentional tort. The defendant remains liable for the intentional tort, even if there is evidence that the intentional tort caused no actual damage to the plaintiff (or, indeed, evidence that the intentional tort benefited the plaintiff). *Harmony Ditch v.*

Sweeney, 222 P. 577 (Wyo. 1924) (trespass to land).

PROBLEM

Sally, sitting on her bike, flicks the ash off the end of her cigarette. It hits Jim's hand. He calls her a jackwood, and hits her bike tire with a stick. Jim catches his thumb under the stick and breaks his thumb. Five weeks later, Jim's infected thumb must be amputated.

Consider both sides.

C. ASSAULT

CONLEY v. DOE
Superior Court of Massachusetts, 2001
2001 Mass. Super. LEXIS 490

RALPH D. GANTS, JUSTICE OF THE SUPERIOR COURT.

The plaintiff, Mary Conley ("Ms. Conley"), is a sixth grade teacher at a suburban middle school in the Boston metropolitan area. The defendant John Doe ("John") was a sixth grade student in her English class and homeroom last school year. According to her Complaint, on Friday, January 12, 2001, in study hall, she saw John writing on a piece of paper with a black marker and observed that he had written the words, "People I Want to Kill," across the top of the paper. No names had been written on the paper. Ms. Conley confiscated the paper and brought John to the school office, informing school authorities of what she had found.

On Wednesday, January 17, Ms. Conley learned that school authorities had discovered on January 12 a second piece of paper that had been written by John and that also was entitled, "People I Want to Kill," but this paper included the names of nine people, including Ms. Conley. This second piece of paper was written less neatly than the piece of paper that Ms. Conley had found. Therefore, she inferred that John was either re-writing this first piece of paper onto a new page when she discovered him in study hall, or was seeking to add more names to the list, since he had run out of room on the second piece of paper. When Ms. Conley learned of the piece of paper that included her name on January 17, she left the school building and is "deathly afraid" of returning.

At roughly 1:30 p.m. on January 19, 2001, school officials met with John's parents, James Doe and Jane Moe ("John's parents" or "the parents"), telling them that John could not return to school until, among other things, he had completed a psychological evaluation. Early that same evening, one of John's parents accompanied John to school before a school dance and delivered to a school official what the parent contended was a full and complete psychological evaluation of John, as had been required by the school. Having received that evaluation, the school allowed John to attend the school dance that evening. Ms. Conley contends that this purported psychological evaluation could not have been a genuine full and complete psychological evaluation of John, because it was produced in too short a time. She alleges that the psychological evaluation submitted to the school was a misleading and fraudulent document, having been prepared by one or both of John's parents, or by another person who was under their control and supervision.

Ms. Conley alleges in her Complaint that the school failed to take any meaningful disciplinary action against John and allowed him to return to school, even though he may pose a serious risk of harm. She further alleges that the school's failure to take meaningful disciplinary action against John resulted from threats and intimidation by John's parents, including the threat by John's mother of a lawsuit if the school took strong disciplinary action or publicized what he had done.

Ms. Conley alleges eight counts in her complaint. . . .

The defendants now move to dismiss all eight counts of the Complaint, contending that each fails to state a claim under Mass.R.Civ.P. 12(b)(6). After hearing, for the reasons stated below, the motion to dismiss the Complaint is *ALLOWED*.

DISCUSSION

When evaluating the sufficiency of a complaint pursuant to Mass. R. Civ. P. 12(b)(6), the court must accept as true the factual allegations of the complaint and all reasonable inferences favorable to the plaintiff which can be drawn from those allegations. . . .

Count 2 — Assault

For John to have committed the tort of assault, he must have engaged in conduct that put Ms. Conley in reasonable apprehension of an imminent harmful or offensive contact with her person. *Commonwealth v. Delgado*, 367 Mass. 432, 437 n.3 (1975), quoting Restatement 2d: Torts, § 31(1965). Words alone cannot constitute the tort of assault "unless together with other acts or circumstances they put the other in reasonable apprehension of an imminent harmful or offensive contact with his person." *Id.*

Here, the Complaint alleges nothing more than words written on two sheets of paper. These words cannot constitute even a criminal *threat* unless they were communicated by John to Ms. Conley. The Complaint does not allege that John communicated any words, orally or in writing, to Ms. Conley; she observed John writing the first piece of paper (which did not contain her name) in study hall and was informed by school authorities that the second piece of paper (which did contain her name) had been found. Nor is there any other conduct alleged, apart from the mere writing of these words, that put Ms. Conley in reasonable apprehension of an imminent harmful or offensive contact with John. Mere uncommunicated words, no matter how frightening, are not sufficient to constitute a tortious assault.

This Court is mindful that Ms. Conley alleges that she feared that John would carry out these words, and the Court respects that she is sincere in her fear. But the fact remains that a sixth grader does not assault a teacher by privately writing that he wants to kill her. Otherwise, a student writing such thoughts at home in his private journal would be assaulting a teacher once she somehow obtains a copy of the journal entry. At the very least, the student must in some fashion act to communicate that intention to the teacher before the expression of these private thoughts becomes a tortious assault. Here, since the Complaint makes clear that John did not act to communicate those thoughts to Ms. Conley, she has failed to state a claim for assault. . . .

Dean Prosser argues that a "gesture" is needed for an assault. Why? W. Page Keeton et al., Prosser and Keeton on Torts 45 (5th ed. 1984).

BOUTON v. ALLSTATE INSURANCE CO.
Court of Appeal of Louisiana, First Circuit, 1986
491 So. 2d 56

SHORTESS, JUDGE.

This suit arose from the unfortunate events of Halloween night in 1981. Jeffrey Scott Trammel, aged 15, Robert Martin Landry, Jr., aged 13, and Daniel Breaux, aged 13, went trick-or-treating that evening. About 6:30 p.m., Trammel and Breaux rang Robert Bouton's (plaintiff) front door bell while Landry waited at the sidewalk. Plaintiff opened the door and saw Breaux standing before him. Breaux was dressed in military fatigues and was holding a plastic model submachine gun. Plaintiff shut the door immediately and locked it, then armed himself with a .357 magnum pistol. He returned to the door, opened it, and saw a flash of light, caused, he alleges, by Trammel's triggering a photographic flash. Plaintiffs pistol then discharged, the bullet striking and killing Breaux.

Plaintiff brought this suit against Allstate Insurance Company (Allstate), insurer of Landry and Breaux, and Independent Fire Insurance Company (Independent), insurer of Trammel. He alleged that the three boys' actions were tortious and caused him to be indicted and tried for second-degree murder,[1] incur substantial attorney fees, lose his job, and suffer unfavorable publicity. Allstate filed motions for summary judgment, and Independent raised the peremptory exception of no cause of action. LSA-C.C.P. arts. 966 and 927. The trial court granted the summary judgment motions and sustained the exception of no cause of action. From that action plaintiff brings this appeal.

If what these boys did on that Halloween night is to be deemed tortious, it must be either an intentional tort or one arising from their negligence.

Intentional Tort

Plaintiff claims that the boys committed an assault, causing him to become frightened and triggering the tragic series of events which ensued. Plaintiff must prove an intentional act by the defendants which would have put a person in reasonable apprehension of receiving a battery. We find that the pleadings and

---

[1] Plaintiff's trial ended with an acquittal.

evidence fail to establish any right to relief because, under the facts as set out by the plaintiff, he could not have had a *reasonable* apprehension of an impending battery or physical harm. Although it is *possible* for one who opens his door to trick-or-treaters on Halloween to become so frightened that he believes a battery is imminent, under the circumstances here, such an apprehension is not reasonable. Any reasonable person expects to see an endless array of ghouls, beasts, and characters on this evening, especially when he is, as was plaintiff, passing out candy at his doorstep.

Plaintiff contends that "the sole determining issue in this case" is whether we judge the boys' actions from their point of view or from his. We do neither. Instead, "we place the average reasonable [person] . . . in the very situation which confronted the plaintiff and ask of him oracularly" if an apprehension of a battery could be reasonably expected to follow from such a situation. We do not believe that a reasonable person acting reasonably would have been apprehensive of a battery when confronted with this situation on Halloween.[2] Therefore, we hold that plaintiff was not the victim of an assault.

. . . .

For the foregoing reasons, the judgment of the trial court is affirmed at plaintiff's cost.

Affirmed.

How much of a threat should be required before a defendant can be held liable for assault? Should mere words ever be enough?

D.   FALSE IMPRISONMENT

False imprisonment, in addition to requiring study of the defendant's intent, also necessitates examination of the plaintiff's perceptions. An unconscious plaintiff cannot seek recovery for false imprisonment, because the plaintiff was not aware that he or she was imprisoned. Because the test applied to the plaintiff is in this sense subjective, the analysis in the cases can begin to sound highly psychological. Courts in this area can easily become bogged down in the facts of who perceived what and how they felt about it.

---

[2] Because of this ruling, we need not address the question of the boys' intent, plaintiff being required to establish both the intentional act and the apprehension.

ZAVALA v. WAL-MART STORES, INC.
United States District Court for the District of New Jersey, 2005
393 F. Supp. 2d 295

GREENAWAY, J., U.S. DISTRICT JUDGE.

Defendant Wal-Mart, by its own account, is the nation's largest private employer. The named plaintiffs are undocumented immigrants who worked as janitors in various Wal-Mart retail store locations across the country.

. . . .

The Alleged Criminal Enterprise

Plaintiffs claim that the Wal-Mart Enterprise systematically employed, harbored, and trafficked in the labor of immigrants, aided and abetted violation of the immigration laws, failed to pay their wages and overtime and benefits as required, and concealed their profits and practices from detection.

More specifically, the Wal-Mart Enterprise operated as follows: participants in the Wal-Mart Enterprise violated the immigration laws to secure workers who could be exploited easily based on their undocumented status. It targeted, encouraged, harbored, trafficked, and employed undocumented aliens, specifically because they were a vulnerable population. The Wal-Mart Enterprise exploited them in any number of ways — by obligating them to work in excess of the statutory maximum number of hours, every day of the week, denying them of lawful pay and benefits under the [Fair Labor Standards Act], as well as time for sick leave, meals or breaks, and paying them in cash without withholding payroll taxes. The Wal-Mart Enterprise also easily could, and did, hide them from law enforcement authorities, by threatening them with deportation or locking them into the stores for the duration of their shifts.

DISCUSSION

Defendant Wal-Mart has moved to dismiss the compliant in its entirety. There are five counts to the complaint, [the fifth being] common law false imprisonment. For the reasons set forth below, this Court . . . denies the motion with respect to Count . . . 5.

Count 5 — False Imprisonment Claim

Wal-Mart asserts that, despite the inflammatory allegations at Count 5, Plaintiffs have not alleged sufficient facts to state a claim for false imprisonment.

This Court disagrees. Assuming the truth of Plaintiff's allegations and granting all favorable inferences to the non-moving party, . . . this Court concludes that Plaintiffs have stated a claim for false imprisonment. . . .

Plaintiffs allege that Wal-Mart intentionally engaged in a widespread, systematic practice of locking janitors into their stores during their shifts, against their will, causing them physical and emotional harm. The complaint further asserts that Wal-Mart:

> Compelled the labor of the janitors through its widespread and systematic practice of intentionally locking these vulnerable workers into its stores during its shifts. The [plaintiffs] knew they were so confined to the stores by Wal-Mart. Such confinement was against their will and resulted in physical and emotional injury of plaintiffs and coerced plaintiffs to work for Wal-Mart whether they wanted to or not.

For purposes of deciding this motion, this Court shall apply New Jersey law. . . . In New Jersey, a person "is falsely imprisoned when that person's freedom of movement is constrained . . . by force or by threats of force communicated through conduct or words. But for threats to be held to be a constraint, they must be such as would 'induce a reasonable apprehension of force and the means of coercion [must be] at hand.' "

> The essential thing is the constraint of the person. This constraint may be caused by threats as well as by actionable force, and the threats may be by conduct or by words. If the words or conduct are such as to induce a reasonable apprehension of force and the means of coercion is at hand, a person may be as effectually restrained and deprived of liberty as by prision bars. (*101 A.2d at 539*).

Physical force does not amount to an actionable restraint if there is a safe avenue of escape through an exit, but in the absence of a "reasonable means of escape," there may be an actionable restraint.

In order for allegations of threats of force to support a claim for false imprisonment, the threat of force must be sufficient for a person to be placed in reasonable apprehension of force, in order to state a claim. For example, the fact that an alarm might sound if a plaintiff exits through an employee exit, or that there is moral pressure, or that one's job is being threatened, is not sufficiently adequate to constitute an actionable constraint by threat of force. Id.

Plaintiffs' claim of false imprisonment appears to be rooted in their allegation that some of them were locked into their stores during their shifts, as part of a widespread practice and policy – against their will. . . . [B]ased on the allegations and granting all reasonable inferences therefrom in favor of Plaintiffs, Defendant's motion to dismiss Count 5 is denied.

As stated earlier, Plaintiffs allege that some of them were threatened with deportation. [T]he parties briefed the issue of whether or not the alleged threats of deportation are sufficient to state a claim for false imprisonment.

. . . .

In this Court's view, the authority is not decisive, one way or the other, in this matter. The Supreme Court has stated that "it is impossible that threatening . . . an immigrant with deportation could constitute the threat of legal coercion that induces involuntary servitude, . . .

1. These workers are potentially a vulnerable population, due to their immigration status and potential language or educational barrier. Should the law accord them any different treatment because of this vulnerability?

Vulnerable means "1) Can be wounded or physically injured; 2) Open to attack, [or] easily hurt." Websters New World Dictionary (3d ed. 1988).

2. In situations where there is an inherent imbalance of power and difference in privilege (employer vs. employee, legal status vs. undocumented status, business savvy vs. uninformed), do the courts have a role to play in leveling the playing field?

3. What policies does the court consider in deciding the case?

4. What if, instead of physically locking the plaintiffs in the stores, the defendant had threatened them with deportation or other legal action if they left the store during their shift? Would this constitute false imprisonment?

5. Did the workers consent to the confinement by accepting employment?

WHITTAKER v. SANFORD

Supreme Judicial Court of Maine, 1912

85 A. 399

Savage, J.

Action for false imprisonment. The plaintiff recovered a verdict for $1,100. The case comes up on defendant's exceptions and motion for a new trial.

The case shows that for several years prior to 1910, at a locality called "Shiloh," in Durham, in this state, there had been gathered together a religious sect, of which the defendant was at least the religious leader. They dwelt in a so-called colony. There was a similar colony under the same religious leadership at Jaffa, in Syria. The plaintiff was a member of this sect, and her husband was one of its ministers. For the promotion of the work of the "movement," as it is called, a Yacht Club was incorporated, of which the defendant was president. The Yacht Club owned two sailing yachts, the *"Kingdom"* and the *"Coronet"*. So far as this case is concerned, these yachts were employed in transporting members of the movement, back and forth, between the coast of Maine and Jaffa.

The plaintiff, with her four children, sailed on the *Coronet* to Jaffa in 1905. Her husband was in Jerusalem, but came to Jaffa, and there remained until he sailed, a year later, apparently to America. The plaintiff lived in Jerusalem and Jaffa, as a member of the colony, until March, 1909. At that time she decided to abandon the movement, and from that time on ceased to take part in its exercise or to be recognized as a member. She made her preparations to return to America by steamer, but did not obtain the necessary funds therefore until December 24, 1909. At that time the *Kingdom* was in the harbor at Jaffa, and the defendant was on board. . . . The plaintiff fearing, as she says, that if she came on board the defendant's yacht she would not be let off until she was "won to the movement" again, discussed that subject with the defendant, and he assured her repeatedly that under no circumstances would she be detained on board the vessel after they got into port, and that she should be free to do what she wanted to the moment they reached shore. Relying upon this promise, she boarded the *Kingdom* on December 28th and sailed for America. She had her four children with her. The defendant was also on board.

The *Kingdom* arrived in Portland Harbor on the afternoon of Sunday, May 8, 1910. The plaintiffs husband, who was at Shiloh, was telephoned to by someone, and went at once to Portland Harbor, reaching the yacht about midnight of the same day. The *Coronet* was also in Portland Harbor at that time. Later both yachts sailed to South Freeport, reaching there Tuesday morning, May 10th. From this time until June 6th following the plaintiff claims that she was prevented from leaving the *Kingdom*, by the defendant, in such manner as to constitute false imprisonment.

The Exceptions

. . . .

2. The plaintiff claimed and testified that on two or three occasions the defendant personally refused to furnish her with a boat so that she could leave the *Kingdom* — that when she wanted to go ashore "they," evidently referring to the defendant and her husband, "had talked against it"; that the defendant "had spoken plainly that it was out of the question"; that when she spoke to him about it he said he would leave it to her husband to do what he wanted to, that he would not take the responsibility of separating families, but that, when she asked her husband to take her ashore, he replied, "We will see Mr. Sandford about it and see what he says." The plaintiff contended that in this way the defendant and her husband in effect played into each other's hands, and shifted the responsibility from one to the other, while she was the victim of this play of battledore and shuttlecock. It was contended that by virtue of the peculiar religious character attributed to the defendant by those who were in the movement, of whom the plaintiffs husband was one, being a minister of that faith, he possessed and exercised supreme control over the members, both on sea and on land, and that his wish was law both to their wills and consciences, and that the plaintiffs husband, whatever part he took in the matter, was either merely the defendant's instrument, or else was colleagued with him. . . .

The court instructed the jury that the plaintiff to recover must show that the restraint was physical, and not merely a moral influence; that it must have been actual physical restraint, in the sense that one intentionally locked into a room would be physically restrained but not necessarily involving physical force upon the person; that it was not necessary that the defendant, or any person by his direction, should lay his hand upon the plaintiff; that if the plaintiff was restrained so that she could not leave the yacht *Kingdom* by the intentional refusal to furnish transportation as agreed, she not having it in her power to escape otherwise, it would be a physical restraint and unlawful imprisonment. We think the instructions were apt and sufficient. If one should, without right, turn the key in a door, and thereby prevent a person in the room from leaving, it would be the simplest form of unlawful imprisonment. The restraint is physical. The four walls and the locked door are physical impediments to escape. . . . The boat is the key. By refusing the boat he turns the key. The guest is as effectually locked up as if there were walls along the sides of the vessel. The restraint is physical. The impassible sea is the physical barrier.

There are other exceptions, but the points involved are all covered by the foregoing discussion. The exceptions must all be overruled.

. . . .

---

1. This case is perhaps one of the earliest religious cult cases on record. In modern times, the tort of false imprisonment has been revived in religious cult cases, both as a tool to combat those who would separate the individual from the cult and as a tool for those seeking to leave the cult.

2. Frank Weston Sanford, the founder of the cult in this case, died in 1948 at age 85. Life for those who followed him was far from easy; many died of disease and starvation. At the peak of his popularity, Sanford ran communities in Maine, England, Egypt, and Jerusalem. The cult went into decline after Sanford's arrest, trial, and three-year jail sentence for the deaths by starvation and disease of six of the crew on one of his ships. *See* Pamela Rohland, Book Review of *Fair, Clear, and Terrible: The Story of Shiloh* by Shirley Nelson (British American Publishing, 1996), Philadelphia Inquirer, July 9, 1996, at D9.

DUPLER v. SEUBERT
Supreme Court of Wisconsin, 1975
230 N.W.2d 626

WILKIE, CHIEF JUSTICE.

This is a false imprisonment action. On April 23, 1971, plaintiff-appellant Ethel M. Dupler was fired from her job with the defendant-respondent Wisconsin Telephone Company. She was informed of her discharge during an hour-and-a-half session with her two superiors, defendants-respondents Keith Peterson and Helen Seubert, who Dupler claims, falsely imprisoned her during a portion of this time period. A jury found that Peterson and Seubert did falsely imprison Dupler and fixed damages at $7,500. The trial court gave Dupler the option of accepting a lower amount — $500 — or a new trial on the issue of damages. The option was not exercised, judgment for $500 was entered, and Mrs. Dupler appeals. We reverse and remand for a new trial on the issue of damages, but give plaintiff-appellant an option to accept $1,000 damages in lieu of a new trial.

Dupler had worked for the Telephone Company as a customer service representative since 1960. At approximately 4:30 on April 23rd, Seubert asked Dupler to come to Peterson's office. When all three were inside, sitting down, with the door closed, Seubert told Dupler the Telephone Company would no longer employ her and that she could choose either to resign or be fired. Dupler testified that she refused to resign and that in the conversation that followed, Peterson discussed several alternatives short of dismissal, all of which had been considered but rejected.

At approximately five o'clock, Dupler testified, she began to feel sick to her stomach and said "You have already fired me. Why don't you just let me go." She made a motion to get up but Peterson told her to sit down in "a very loud harsh voice." Then, Dupler testified, she began to feel violently ill and stated "I got to go. I can't take this anymore. I'm sick to my stomach. I know I'm going to throw up." She got up and started for the door but Seubert also arose and stood in front of the door. After Dupler repeated that she was sick, Seubert allowed her to exit, but followed her to the men" washroom, where Dupler did throw up. Following this, at approximately 5:25, Seubert asked Dupler to return to Peterson's office where she had left her purse to discuss the situation further. Dupler testified that she went back to the office and reached for her purse; Seubert again closed the door and Peterson said "[i]n a loud voice 'Sit down. I'm still your boss. I'm not through with you.' " At approximately 5:40 Dupler told Peterson her husband was waiting for her outside in a car and Peterson told her to go outside and ask her husband to come inside. Dupler then went outside and explained the situation to her husband who said, "You get back in there and get your coat and if you aren't right out I'll call the police." Dupler returned to Peterson's office and was again told in a loud tone of voice to sit down. She said Seubert and Peterson were trying to convince her to resign rather than be fired and again reviewed the alternatives that had been considered. Dupler then said: "What's the sense of all this. Why keep torturing me. Let me go. Let me go." She stated that

Peterson replied: "No, we still aren't finished. We have a lot of things to discuss, your retirement pay, your vacation, other things." Finally, at approximately 6:00 Peterson told Dupler they could talk further on the phone or at her house, and Dupler left. When asked why she had stayed in Peterson's office for such a long time, Dupler replied:

"Well, for one thing, Helen, Mrs. Seubert, had blocked the door, and tempers had been raised with all the shouting and screaming, I was just plain scared to make an effort. There were two against one."

The issue raised by a motion for review filed by defendants-respondents is: *Is the jury's verdict, finding that Dupler was falsely imprisoned, supported by the evidence?*

The essence of false imprisonment is the intentional, unlawful, and uncon-sented restraint by one person of the physical liberty of another. In *Maniaci v. Marquette University*, the court adopted the definition of false imprisonment contained in sec. 35 of the Restatement of Torts 2d, which provides in part:

"False Imprisonment

"(1) An actor is subject to liability to another for false imprisonment if

"(a) he acts intending to confine the other or a third person within boundaries fixed by the actor, and

"(b) his act directly or indirectly results in such a confinement of the other, and

"(c) the other is conscious of the confinement or is harmed by it."

Secs. 39[9] and 401[10] provide that the confinement may be caused by physical force or the threat of physical force, and the comment to sec. 40 indicates the threat may either be express, or inferred from the person's conduct. As Prosser comments:

"Character of Defendant's Act

"The restraint may be by means of physical barriers, or by threats of force which intimidate the plaintiff into compliance with orders. It is sufficient that he submits to an apprehension of force reasonably to be understood from the conduct of the defendant, although no force is used or even expressly threatened. . . . This gives rise, in borderline cases, to questions of fact, turning upon the details of the testimony, as to what was reasonably to be understood and implied from the defendant's conduct, tone of voice and the like, which seldom can be reflected accurately in an appellate record, and normally are for the jury."[11]

This is precisely such a case and we conclude that the record contains sufficient evidence from which the jury could have concluded that Mrs. Dupler was intentionally confined, against her will, by an implied threat of actual physical restraint. . . .

. . . .

We conclude . . . that the jury could properly find that defendants falsely imprisoned Dupler by compelling her to remain in Peterson's office against her will after 5 p.m. We conclude the imprisonment ceased when Dupler left the building to visit her husband, but resumed when she reentered Peterson's office to get her coat in order to leave, but was commanded to stay.

. . . .

Order affirmed; judgment modified with new trial ordered on the issue of damages unless, within twenty days of remittitur, plaintiff-appellant Ethel Dupler elects to accept judgment for $1,000, and, as modified affirmed.

———————

How is the imprisonment aspect of the tort established? In other words, what kind of escape attempts should be required of a plaintiff before that plaintiff can claim imprisonment? What about climbing out of the window of a school bus? Testing threats by ignoring them? What if you are pathologically frightened of cats, and there is a cat between you and the door?

———————

[9] (1971), 50 Wis. 2d 287, 184 N.W.2d 168.

[10] *Id.* at page 59:

"39. Confinement by Physical Force

"The confinement may be by overpowering physical force, or by submission to physical force."

"40. Confinement by Threats of Physical Force."

"The confinement may be by submission to a threat to apply physical force to the other's person immediately upon the other's going or attempting to *go* beyond the area in which the actor intends to confine him."

[11] Prosser, Torts (4th ed. 1971), sec. 11, p. 44.

PROBLEM

Two police officers are called to the scene of a noisy party. At the scene, they find one Parvi, who is intoxicated. Parvi claims that he has nowhere to go. The police officers load the semiconscious Parvi into their car, drive him to a golf course outside the city limits, and leave him there. In an effort to return home, Parvi, who has no idea where he is or what has happened, wanders out onto the highway which is near the golf course, is struck by an automobile, and is severely injured.

Does Parvi have a cause of action for false imprisonment?

E. INTENTIONAL INFLICTION OF EMOTIONAL DISTRESS

The tort of intentional infliction of emotional distress has become an important tool in the modern world. It is perhaps the only intentional tort to be added to the list of intentional torts in modern times, and it fills the gap left when the elements of the other torts cannot be met, but when the message needs to be sent that certain conduct will not be tolerated in a civilized society.

Intentional infliction of emotional distress, like false imprisonment, requires an examination of the psychological facts of the case from the points of view of both parties. The defendant's acts must be reprehensible; the plaintiffs perceptions must be traumatic. Unlike false imprisonment, however, intentional infliction of emotional distress merges into negligence-based torts through the tort of negligent infliction of emotional distress. Intentional infliction of emotional distress lies on a continuum with the most grotesquely intentional acts on one end, and purely negligent acts on the other. Drawing the line between the intentional and the negligent can be difficult, as there is no easily perceived division between the two. The dividing line can be important in a particular case, however, because the plaintiff in the intentional tort context may recover damages for all injuries resulting from the commission of the tort, whether proximately caused by the defendant or not, and may also recover punitive damages which would be unavailable if the tort were based in negligence.

Intentional infliction of emotional distress applies where the defendant's conduct has been so appalling that to deny any recovery to the plaintiff would be unacceptable. The operative concept is that of intent: the defendant has intentionally caused suffering to the plaintiff, and should be made to pay for the consequences of his or her behavior. The tort allows the courts to deter conduct that is simply not acceptable in a civilized society.

HARRIS v. JONES
Court of Appeals of Maryland, 1977
380 A.2d 611

MURPHY, CHIEF JUDGE.

In *Jones u. Harris*, 35 Md. App. 556, 371 A.2d 1104 (1977), a case of first impression in Maryland, the Court of Special Appeals, in a scholarly opinion by Judge W. Albert Menchine, recognized intentional infliction of emotional distress as a new and independent tort in this jurisdiction. It found that a majority of the states now recognize intentional infliction of emotional distress as a separate and distinct basis of tort liability, apart from any other tort, thus repudiating earlier holdings that claims for emotional distress could not be sustained except as a parasitic element of damage accompanying a recognized tort. We granted certiorari to review the decision of the Court of Special Appeals and to decide whether, if intentional infliction of emotional distress is a viable tort in Maryland, the court erred in reversing judgments entered on jury verdicts for the plaintiff on that cause of action.

The plaintiff, William R. Harris, a 26-year-old, 8-year employee of General Motors Corporation (GM), sued GM and one of its supervisory employees, H. Robert Jones, in the Superior Court of Baltimore City. The declaration alleged that Jones, aware that Harris suffered from a speech impediment which caused him to stutter, and also aware of Harris' sensitivity to his disability, and his insecurity because of it, nevertheless "maliciously and cruelly ridiculed . . . [him] thus causing tremendous nervousness, increasing the physical defect itself and further injuring the mental attitude fostered by the Plaintiff toward his problem and otherwise intentionally inflicting emotional distress." It was also alleged in the declaration that Jones' actions occurred within the course of his employment with GM and that GM ratified Jones' conduct.

The evidence at trial showed that Harris stuttered throughout his entire life. While he had little trouble with one syllable words, he had great difficulty with longer words or sentences, causing him at times to shake his head up and down when attempting to speak.

During part of 1975, Harris worked under Jones' supervision at a GM automobile assembly plant. Over a five-month period, between March and August of 1975, Jones approached Harris over 30 times at work and verbally and physically mimicked his stuttering disability. In addition, two or three times a week during this period, Jones approached Harris and told him, in a "smart manner," not to get nervous. As a result of Jones' conduct, Harris was "shaken up" and felt "like going into a hole and hide."

. . . .

Harris had been under the care of a physician for a nervous condition for six years prior to the commencement of Jones' harassment. He admitted that many things made him nervous, including "bosses." Harris testified that Jones' conduct heightened his nervousness and his speech impediment worsened. He saw his physician on one occasion during the five-month period that Jones was mistreating him; the physician prescribed pills for his nerves.

Harris admitted that other employees at work mimicked his stuttering. Approximately 3,000 persons were employed on each of two shifts, and Harris acknowledged the presence at the plant of a lot of "tough guys," as well as profanity, name-calling and roughhousing among the employees. He said that a bad day at work caused him to become more nervous than usual. He admitted that he had problems with supervisors other than Jones, that he had been suspended or relieved from work 10 or 12 times, and that after one such dispute, he followed a supervisor home on his motorcycle, for which he was later disciplined.

. . . .

On this evidence, the case was submitted to the jury after the trial court denied the Defendants' motions for directed verdicts; the jury awarded Harris $3,500 compensatory damages and $15,000 punitive damages against both Jones and GM.

In concluding that the intentional infliction of emotional distress, standing alone, may constitute a valid tort action, the Court of Special Appeals relied upon Restatement (Second) of Torts, ch. 2, Emotional Distress, § 46 (1965), which provides, in pertinent part:

"§ 46. Outrageous Conduct Causing Severe Emotional Distress

(1) One who by extreme and outrageous conduct intentionally or recklessly causes severe emotional distress to another is subject to liability for such emotional distress, and if bodily harm to the other results from it, for such bodily harm."

The court noted that the tort was recognized, and its boundaries defined, in W. Prosser, Law of Torts § 12, at 56 (4th ed. 1971), as follows:

"So far as it is possible to generalize from the cases, the rule which seems to have emerged is that there is liability for conduct exceeding all bounds usually tolerated by decent society, of a nature which is especially calculated to cause, and does cause, mental distress of a very serious kind."

. . ..

Illustrative of the cases which hold that a cause of action will lie for intentional infliction of emotional distress, unaccompanied by physical injury, is *Womack v. Eldridge*, 215 Va. 338, 210 S.E.2d 145 (1974). There, the defendant was engaged in the business of investigating cases for attorneys. She deceitfully obtained the plaintiffs photograph for the purpose of permitting a criminal defense lawyer to show it to the victims in several child molesting cases in an effort to have them identify the plaintiff as the perpetrator of the offenses, even though he was in no way involved in the crimes. While the victims did not identify the plaintiff, he was nevertheless questioned by the police, called repeatedly as a witness and required to explain the circumstances under which the defendant had obtained his photograph. As a result, plaintiff suffered shock, mental depression, nervousness and great anxiety as to what people would think of him and he feared that he would be accused of molesting the boys. The court, in concluding that a cause of action had been made out, said:

. . . .

> "In *Samms [v. Eccles*, 11 Utah 2d 289, 358 P.2d 344 (1961)], the Supreme
> Court of Utah aptly stated:
>
>> ' . . . [T]he best considered view recognizes an action for severe
>> emotional distress, though not accompanied by bodily impact or physical
>> injury, where the defendant intentionally engaged in some conduct
>> toward the plaintiff, (a) with the purpose of inflicting emotional distress,
>> *or*, (b) where any reasonable person would have known that such would
>> result; and his actions are of such a nature as to be considered
>> outrageous and intolerable in that they offend against the generally
>> accepted standards of decency and morality' " 210 S.E.2d at 147-148.

The court in *Womack* identified four elements which must coalesce to impose
liability for intentional infliction of emotional distress:

> (1) The conduct must be intentional or reckless;
>
> (2) The conduct must be extreme and outrageous;
>
> (3) There must be a causal connection between the wrongful conduct and
> the emotional distress;
>
> (4) The emotional distress must be severe.

Essentially, these are the elements of the tort set forth in § 46 of the
Restatement, *supra*. We agree that the independent tort of intentional infliction of
emotional distress should be sanctioned in Maryland. . . .

As to the first element of the tort, § 46 of the Restatement, *supra*, comment i,
states, and the cases generally recognize, that the defendant's conduct is intentional
or reckless where he desires to inflict severe emotional distress, and also where he
knows that such distress is certain, or substantially certain, to result from his
conduct; or where the defendant acts recklessly in deliberate disregard of a high
degree of probability that the emotional distress will follow.

Whether the conduct of a defendant has been "extreme and outrageous," so as to
satisfy that element of the tort, has been a particularly troublesome question.
Section 46 of the Restatement, comment d, states that "Liability has been found
only where the conduct has been so outrageous in character, and so extreme in
degree, as to go beyond all possible bounds of decency, and to be regarded as
atrocious, and utterly intolerable in a civilized community." The comment goes on to
state that liability does not extend, however:

> "to mere insults, indignities, threats, annoyances, petty oppressions, or
> other trivialities. The rough edges of our society are still in need of a good
> deal of filing down, and in the meantime plaintiffs must necessarily be
> expected and required to be hardened to a certain amount of rough
> language, and to occasional acts that are definitely inconsiderate and
> unkind."

. . . .

Comment f states that the extreme and outrageous character of the conduct "may arise from the actor's knowledge that the other is peculiarly susceptible to emotional distress, by reason of some physical or mental condition or peculiarity."

[Professor Calvert Magruder] observed at 1035 that "Against a large part of the frictions and irritations and clashing of temperaments incident to participation in a community life, a certain toughening of the mental hide is a better protection than the law could ever be."

. . . .

In determining whether conduct is extreme and outrageous, it should not be considered in a sterile setting, detached from the surroundings in which it occurred. The personality of the individual to whom the misconduct is directed is also a factor. "There is a difference between violent and vile profanity addressed to a lady, and the same language to a Butte miner and a United States marine." Prosser, *Intentional Infliction of Mental Suffering: A New Tort*, 37 Mich. L. Rev. 874, 887 (1939).

. . . .

It is for the court to determine, in the first instance, whether the defendant's conduct may reasonably be regarded as extreme and outrageous; where reasonable men may differ, it is for the jury to determine whether, in the particular case, the conduct has been sufficiently extreme and outrageous to result in liability.

The Court of Special Appeals found that Jones' conduct was intended to inflict emotional distress and was extreme and outrageous. As to the other elements of the tort, it concluded that the evidence was legally insufficient to establish either that a causal connection existed between Jones' conduct and Harris' emotional distress, or that Harris' emotional distress was severe.

While it is crystal clear that Jones' conduct was intentional, we need not decide whether it was extreme or outrageous, or causally related to the emotional distress which Harris allegedly suffered.[2] The fourth element of the tort — that the emotional distress must be severe — was not established by legally sufficient evidence justifying submission of the case to the jury. That element of the tort requires the plaintiff to show that he suffered a *severely* disabling emotional response to the defendant's conduct. The severity of the emotional distress is not only relevant to the amount of recovery, but is a necessary element to any recovery. Comment j of § 46 of the Restatement, *supra*, elaborates on this requirement:

> "Emotional distress passes under various names, such as mental suffering, mental anguish, mental or nervous shock, or the like. It includes all highly unpleasant mental reactions, such as fright, horror, grief, shame, humiliation, embarrassment, anger, chagrin, disappointment, worry, and nausea. It is only where it is extreme that the liability arises."

---

[2] The fact that Harris may have had some pre-existing susceptibility to emotional distress does not necessarily preclude liability if it can be shown that the conduct intensified the pre-existing condition of psychological stress.

" . . . Severe distress must be proved; but in many cases the extreme and outrageous character of the defendant's conduct is in itself important evidence that the distress has existed. . . ."

"The distress must be reasonable and justified under the circumstances, and there is no liability where the plaintiff has suffered exaggerated and unreasonable emotional distress, unless it results from a peculiar susceptibility to such distress of which the actor has knowledge. . . ."

"It is for the court to determine whether on the evidence severe emotional distress can be found; it is for the jury to determine whether, on the evidence, it has in fact existed."

Assuming that a causal relationship was shown between Jones' wrongful conduct and Harris' emotional distress, we find no evidence, legally sufficient for submission to the jury, that the distress was "severe" within the contemplation of the rule requiring establishment of that element of the tort. The evidence that Jones' reprehensible conduct humiliated Harris and caused him emotional distress, which was manifested by an aggravation of Harris' preexisting nervous condition and a worsening of his speech impediment, was vague and weak at best. It was unaccompanied by any evidentiary particulars other than that Harris, during the period of Jones' harassment, saw his physician on one occasion for his nerves, for which pills were prescribed — the same treatment which Harris had been receiving from his physician for six years prior to Jones' mistreatment. The intensity and duration of Harris' emotional distress is nowhere reflected in the evidence. All that was shown was that Harris was "shaken up" by Jones' misconduct and was so humiliated that he felt "like going into a hole and hide." While Harris' nervous condition may have been exacerbated somewhat by Jones' conduct, his family problems antedated his encounter with Jones and were not shown to be attributable to Jones' actions. Just how, or to what degree, Harris' speech impediment worsened is not revealed by the evidence. Granting the cruel and insensitive nature of Jones' conduct toward Harris, and considering the position of authority which Jones held over Harris, we conclude that the humiliation suffered was not, as a matter of law, so intense as to constitute the "severe" emotional distress required to recover for the tort of intentional infliction of emotional distress.

Judgment affirmed; costs to be paid by appellant.

———————

1. To what extent does the tort of intentional infliction of emotional distress protect individual sensitivity? Can you think of a standard which would protect the rights of plaintiffs and defendants?

2. The Americans with Disabilities Act, 42 U.S.C. § 12101 *et seq.* (1990), now provides some protection to disabled persons. Does this reflect an enhanced societal perception that conduct such as that in *Harris v. Jones* is inappropriate?

3. In *Taylor v. Vallelunga*, 339 P.2d 910 (Cal. Ct. App. 1959), the court dismissed the second count of a complaint for intentional infliction of emotional distress. In the dismissed count, the daughter of a man who had been beaten by the defendants sought damages against the defendants for the emotional distress she suffered as a result of watching the beating. The court dismissed her claim on the ground that she had failed to allege that the defendants had been aware of her presence as a witness to the beating. Thus, the defendants did not know that their conduct was likely to cause her to suffer severe emotional distress. Is this result consistent with the rule that a person who commits an intentional tort (in this case, battery) is liable for all the consequences of the tort, whether foreseeable or not?

4.   If the defendant takes advantage of the victim's special sensitivity, he may be liable for intentional infliction of emotional distress, although a normal person would not experience distress.

In *Nickerson v. Hodges*, 84 So. 37 (La. 1920), several people buried a "pot of gold" and enabled the victim to find it. She was old and known to suffer from mental illness. They intended the victim to find the pot as a practical joke. She found it and passed out, withered and died when she discovered it was filled with manure. Her representatives recovered from the insensitive abusers.

YATES v. JOHN MARSHALL LAW SCHOOL
United States District Court for the Northern District of Illinois, 2009
2009 U.S. Dist. LEXIS 39819

Aspen, Marvin E., District Judge.

On November 5, 2008, Plaintiff Francine Yates filed a multi-count Amended Complaint against the John Marshall Law School ("JMLS"), the Chicago Transit Authority ("CTA"), the City of Chicago ("the City"), and the State of Illinois ("the State"). Yates alleges that JMLS violated various civil rights statutes and Illinois law by denying her admission into law school. Presently before us is JMLS's motion to dismiss, which we grant for the reasons discussed below.

BACKGROUND

According to the Amended Complaint, Yates applied for admission to JMLS for the January 2008 and August 2008 semesters. She indicated on both applications that she was homeless. JMLS ignored her first application because she failed to pay the application fee. On May 5, 2008, JMLS informed Yates by letter that her second application had been rejected. Thereafter, on or about May 12, 2008, Yates went to speak with William Powers, Dean of JMLS. At that time, she complained to Powers about "the continued harassment, retaliation and coercion that she was being subjected to by . . . Mayor Richard Daley to fraudulently embezzle money from CTA's claim fund." Among other things, she also informed Powers of her Christian faith and homelessness, as well as her mental disabilities. Indeed, in 2003, Yates was diagnosed with "major depression, anxiety and high blood pressure." After hearing Yates's complaints and disclosures, Powers agreed to review her file and "let her know of the board's decision by Friday, May 23, 2008." He emailed Yates on May 30, 2008, again reporting that she had been denied admission. At some point, Powers informed Yates that her application was rejected because her LSAT score was too low.

Yates met again with Powers in June 2008 and told him that she was falsely arrested on May 26, 2008 for battery. On one occasion, on June 5, 2008, Yates attempted to meet with Powers but was told that he was unavailable to meet with her, although he appeared to be "surfing the web." Although she scheduled an appointment with Powers on June 10, 2008, that appointment was cancelled by email dated June 6, 2008, wherein Powers informed Yates that "he had attempted to answer all of her questions via email and did not feel that he had anything more to impart." On June 9, 2008, JMLS informed Yates that it would not refund her application fee, which she had borrowed from a church, or return her admissions paperwork.

. . . .

Based on the above, Yates asserts the following claims: (1) intentional infliction of emotional distress ("IIED") and negligent infliction of emotional and mental distress ("NIED"); . . . Yates requests various remedies, including compensatory and punitive damages. She asks, *inter alia*, that we discipline and disbar her harassers. She also requests that JMLS admit her, provide her with J.D. and LL.M. degrees, and pay the full cost of her tuition, living expenses, law books and all bar fees.

. . . .

ANALYSIS

. . . .

C. Intentional Infliction of Emotional Distress

In Count II, Yates asserts that JMLS committed the tort of IIED by wrongfully denying her access into the law school. She alleges that JMLS showed a "reckless disregard for the likelihood of causing [her] distress" by rejecting her application after "she opposed unlawful discrimination, complained about it and disclosed her disabilities to William Powers" on or around May 12, 2008. She states JMLS was aware of her mental illness and homelessness and nonetheless took advantage of her, because Powers refused to meet with her and she was harassed by a JMLS employee when she retrieved her admissions paperwork. She alleges that these events exacerbated her emotional distress and lead to physical injuries, such as hair loss and incontinence.

To state an IIED claim, Yates must allege that: (1) JMLS's conduct was extreme and outrageous; (2) JMLS intended that its conduct would "cause severe emotional distress or [was] aware of a high probability of causing severe emotional distress;" and (3) JMLS's conduct actually caused severe emotional distress. Liability for IIED "does not extend to mere insult, indignities, threats, annoyances, petty oppressions or trivialities" and can attach "only in circumstances where the defendant's conduct is so outrageous in character, and so extreme in degree, as to go beyond all possible bounds of decency." Indeed, the "distress inflicted must be so severe that no reasonable person could be expected to endure it." "Whether the conduct is extreme and outrageous is judged on an objective standard, based on the facts of the particular case."

Here, Yates has not clearly alleged that JMLS intended to cause her severe emotional distress or was aware of a high probability of doing so. She alleges that JMLS exhibited a "reckless disregard for the likelihood of causing [her] distress" by denying her admission and access to the school, but this allegation is not equivalent to a claim that JMLS knowingly engaged in conduct with knowledge of a "high probability" of inflicting severe emotional harm.

Even assuming that Yates sufficiently pled the second element required to an IIED claim, JMLS persuasively argues that its alleged conduct cannot be considered "extreme and outrageous." Yates does not address this issue in her response brief and we conclude that, as a matter of law, the conduct alleged is not sufficiently "extreme and outrageous" to state a claim for IIED. Reviewing Yates's allegations on the whole, and drawing all inferences in her favor, JMLS's May 30, 2008 denial of her application to law school and all subsequent behavior — including its initial refusal to provide admissions paperwork, later acquiescence to that request, and alleged forcing her off of JMLS property — is not so outrageous "as to go beyond all possible bounds of decency." Yates describes quite trivial slights, such as Powers's refusal to meet with her repeatedly in June 2008, after having met with her on May 12, or JMLS's apparently insulting offer of a one-day bus pass to defray her transportation expenses. Her more substantive complaints, such as harassment off of JMLS property, fare no better, as they objectively are not "so severe that no reasonable person could be expected to endure it." Yates does not allege, for example, that she was physically attacked, threatened or verbally abused, or that JMLS's offensive conduct continued for any length of time. Indeed, even JMLS's May 30 rejection of her law school application with knowledge of her alleged vulnerability cannot rise to the level of extreme and outrageous conduct under these circumstances. Law schools deny applications routinely, and these necessary decisions cannot be deemed objectively outrageous for purposes of an IIED claim, barring some truly extreme factual scenario not alleged here. For the above reasons, we grant JMLS's motion. . ..

HUSTLER MAGAZINE, INC. v. JERRY FALWELL
Supreme Court of the United States, 1988
485 U.S. 46

REHNQUIST, C.J., delivered the opinion of the Court, in which BRENNAN, MARSHALL, BLACKMUN, STEVENS, O'CONNOR, and SCALIA, JJ., joined. WHITE, J., filed an opinion concurring in the judgment. KENNEDY, J., took no part in the consideration or decision of the case.

CHIEF JUSTICE REHNQUIST delivered the opinion of the Court.

Petitioner Hustler Magazine, Inc., is a magazine of nationwide circulation. Respondent Jerry Falwell, a nationally known minister who has been active as a commentator on politics and public affairs, sued petitioner and its publisher, petitioner Larry Flynt, to recover damages for invasion of privacy, libel, and intentional infliction of emotional distress. The District Court directed a verdict against respondent on the privacy claim, and submitted the other two claims to a jury. The jury found for petitioners on the defamation claim, but found for respondent on the claim for intentional infliction of emotional distress and awarded damages. We now consider whether this award is consistent with the First and Fourteenth Amendments of the United States Constitution.

The inside front cover of the November 1983 issue of Hustler Magazine featured a "parody" of an advertisement for Campari Liqueur that contained the name and picture of respondent and was entitled "Jerry Falwell talks about his first time." This parody was modeled after actual Campari ads that included interviews with various celebrities about their "first times." Although it was apparent by the end of each interview that this meant the first time they sampled Campari, the ads clearly played on the sexual double entendre of the general subject of "first times." Copying the form and layout of these Campari ads, Hustler's editors chose respondent as the featured celebrity and drafted an alleged "interview" with him in which he states that his "first time" was during a drunken incestuous rendezvous with his mother in an outhouse. The Hustler parody portrays respondent and his mother as drunk and immoral, and suggests that respondent is a hypocrite who preaches only when he is drunk. In small print at the bottom of the page, the ad contains the disclaimer, "ad parody — not to be taken seriously." The magazine's table of contents also lists the ad as "Fiction; Ad and Personality Parody."

Soon after the November issue of Hustler became available to the public, respondent brought this diversity action . . . against Hustler Magazine, Inc., Larry C. Flynt, and Flynt Distributing Co. Respondent stated in his complaint that publication of the ad parody in Hustler entitled him to recover damages for libel, invasion of privacy, and intentional infliction of emotional distress. The case proceeded to trial. . . . The jury ruled for respondent on the intentional infliction of emotional distress claim. . . . Petitioners' motion for judgment notwithstanding the verdict was denied.

On appeal, the United States Court of Appeals for the Fourth Circuit affirmed the judgment against petitioners. . . . Given the importance of the constitutional issues involved, we granted certiorari. 480 U.S. 945 (1987).

This case presents us with a novel question involving First Amendment limitations upon a State's authority to protect its citizens from the intentional infliction of emotional distress. We must decide whether a public figure may recover damages for emotional harm caused by the publication of an ad parody offensive to him, and doubtless gross and repugnant in the eyes of most. Respondent would have us find that a State's interest in protecting public figures from emotional distress is sufficient to deny First Amendment protection to speech that is patently offensive and is intended to inflict emotional injury, even when that speech could not reasonably have been interpreted as stating actual facts about the public figure involved. This we decline to do.

At the heart of the First Amendment is the recognition of the fundamental importance of the free flow of ideas and opinions on matters of public interest and concern. "[T]he freedom to speak one's mind is not only an aspect of individual liberty — and thus a good unto itself — but also is essential to the common quest for truth and the vitality of society as a whole." *Bose Corp. v. Consumers Union of United States, Inc.*, 466 U.S. 485, 503-504 (1984). We have therefore been particularly vigilant to ensure that individual expressions of ideas remain free from governmentally imposed sanctions. The First Amendment recognizes no such thing as a "false" idea. *Gertz v. Robert Welch, Inc.*, 418 U.S. 323, 339 (1974). As Justice Holmes wrote, "when men have realized that time has upset many fighting faiths, they may come to believe even more than they believe the very foundations of their own conduct that the ultimate good desired is better reached by free trade in ideas — that the best test of truth is the power of the thought to get itself accepted in the competition of the market. . . ." *Abrams v. United States*, 250 U.S. 616, 630 (1919) (dissenting opinion).

The sort of robust political debate encouraged by the First Amendment is bound to produce speech that is critical of those who hold public office or those public figures who are "intimately involved in the resolution of important public questions or, by reason of their fame, shape events in areas of concern to society at large." *Associated Press v. Walker* decided with *Curtis Publishing Co. v. Butts*, 388 U.S. 130, 164 (1967) (Warren, C.J., concurring in result). Justice Frankfurter put it succinctly in *Baumgartner v. United States*, 322 U.S. 665, 673-674 (1944), when he said that "[o]ne of the prerogatives of American citizenship is the right to criticize public men and measures." Such criticism, inevitably, will not always be reasoned or moderate; public figures as well as public officials will be subject to "vehement, caustic, and sometimes unpleasantly sharp attacks," *New York Times, supra*, at 270.
. . .

Of course, this does not mean that *any* speech about a public figure is immune from sanction in the form of damages. Since *New York Times Co. v. Sullivan*, 376 U.S. 254 (1964), we have consistently ruled that a public figure may hold a speaker liable for the damage to reputation caused by publication of a defamatory falsehood, but only if the statement was made "with knowledge that it was false or with reckless disregard of whether it was false or not." *Id.*, at 279-280. . . . "Freedoms of expression require 'breathing space.'" *Philadelphia Newspapers, Inc. v. Hepps*, 475 U.S. 767, 772 (1986) (quoting *New York Times, supra*, 376 U.S., at 272). This breathing space is provided by a constitutional rule that allows public figures to recover for libel or defamation only when they can prove *both* that the statement was false and that the statement was made with the requisite level of culpability.

. . . In respondent's view, and in the view of the Court of Appeals, so long as the utterance was intended to inflict emotional distress, was outrageous, and did in fact inflict serious emotional distress, it is of no constitutional import whether the statement was a fact or an opinion, or whether it was true or false. . . .

Thus while such a bad motive may be deemed controlling for purposes of tort liability in other areas of the law, we think the First Amendment prohibits such a result in the area of public debate about public figures.

Were we to hold otherwise, there can be little doubt that political cartoonists and satirists would be subjected to damages awards without any showing that their work falsely defamed its subject. Webster's defines a caricature as "the deliberately distorted picturing or imitating of a person, literary style, etc. by exaggerating features or mannerisms for satirical effect." . . .

— an exploration often calculated to injure the feelings of the subject of the portrayal. The art of the cartoonist is often not reasoned or evenhanded, but slashing and one-sided. One cartoonist expressed the nature of the art in these words:

> "The political cartoon is a weapon of attack, of scorn and ridicule and satire; it is least effective when it tries to pat some politician on the back. It is usually as welcome as a bee sting and is always controversial in some quarters." Long, *The Political Cartoon: Journalism's Strongest Weapon*, The Quill, 56, 57 (Nov. 1962).

. . . .

Respondent contends, however, that the caricature in question here was so "outrageous" as to distinguish it from more traditional political cartoons. . . . "Outrageousness" in the area of political and social discourse has an inherent subjectiveness about it which would allow a jury to impose liability on the basis of the jurors' tastes or views, or perhaps on the basis of their dislike of a particular expression. An "outrageousness" standard thus runs afoul of our longstanding refusal to allow damages to be awarded because the speech in question may have an adverse emotional impact on the audience. . . .

> "[T]he fact that society may find speech offensive is not a sufficient reason for suppressing it. Indeed, if it is the speaker's opinion that gives offense, that consequence is a reason for according it constitutional protection. For it is a central tenet of the First Amendment that the government must remain neutral in the marketplace of ideas." *Id.*, at 745-746. . . .

. . . .

We conclude that public figures and public officials may not recover for the tort of intentional infliction of emotional distress by reason of publications such as the one here at issue without showing in addition that the publication contains a false statement of fact which was made with "actual malice," i.e., with knowledge that the statement was false or with reckless disregard as to whether or not it was true. This is not merely a "blind application" of the *New York Times* standard, see *Time, Inc. v. Hill*, 385 U.S. 374, 390 (1967); it reflects our considered judgment that such a standard is necessary to give adequate "breathing space" to the freedoms protected by the First Amendment.

Here it is clear that respondent Falwell is a "public figure" for purposes of First Amendment law. The jury found against respondent on his libel claim when it decided that the Hustler ad parody could not "reasonably be understood as describing actual facts about [respondent] or actual events in which [he] participated." App. to Pet. for Cert. Cl. The Court of Appeals interpreted the jury's finding to be that the ad parody "was not reasonably believable," 797 F.2d, at 1278, and in accordance with our custom we accept this finding. Respondent is thus relegated to his claim for damages awarded by the jury for the intentional infliction of emotional distress by "outrageous" conduct. But for reasons heretofore stated this claim cannot, consistently with the First Amendment, form a basis for the award of damages when the conduct in question is the publication of a caricature such as the ad parody involved here. The judgment of the Court of Appeals is accordingly

Reversed.

How thick-skinned should we require public figures to be? Should there be a difference between public figures who seek the limelight and those who are dragged into the public eye?

PROBLEM

A national newpaper publishes a cartoon depicting X, a media star, as intoxicated. X sues the newspaper for intentional infliction of emotional distress. In the lawsuit, X points out that X's father died of alcoholism, and that X was therefore extremely distressed by the cartoon. What result?

F. TRESPASS

1. In General

The entire social system of Western Europe in the middle ages revolved around land ownership. Thus, the tort of trespass to land attained early significance in the development of the common law. Much blood was spilled in resolving questions of land ownership, and many lives were saved when boundary conflicts moved into the courts. A lawsuit based on defendant putting a toe across the line where plaintiff thinks his or her property begins may seem silly. The issue is not really one of the damage caused to the plaintiff by the toe, however; the issue may well be the far more fundamental one of where the boundary line in fact should be drawn.

DOUGHERTY v. STEPP
Supreme Court of North Carolina, 1835
18 N.C. 371

Every unauthorized intrusion into the land of another is a sufficient trespass to support an action for *breaking the close*, whether the land be actually enclosed or not. And from every such entry the law infers some damage; if nothing more, the treading down the grass or shrubbery.

Trespass quare clausum fregit, tried at Buncombe, on the last circuit, before his Honor, Judge Martin. The only proof introduced by the plaintiff to establish an act of trespass was, that the defendant had entered on the unenclosed land of the plaintiff, with a surveyor and chain-carriers, and actually surveyed a part of it, claiming it as his own, but without marking trees or cutting bushes. This, his Honor held not be a trespass, and the jury, under his instructions, found a verdict for the defendant, and the plaintiff appealed.

RUFFIN, C.J. In the opinion of the Court, there is error in the instructions given to the jury. The amount of damages may depend on the acts done on the land, and the extent of injury to it therefrom. But it is an elementary principle that every unauthorized, and therefore unlawful, entry into the close of another, is a trespass. From every such entry against the will of the possessor the law infers some damage; if nothing more, the treading down the grass or the herbage, or as here, the shrubbery. . . . It is the entry that constitutes the trespass. . . . Let the judgment be reversed and a new trial granted.

Per curiam.

Judgment reversed.

———

1. What amount of damages should a property owner receive in a case like *Dougherty v. Stepp.*

2. *Mistake.* Dean Prosser argues that mistake is not a defense to an intentional tort. This is because the result was intended and defendant "acted under an erroneous belief that circumstances existed which would justify his conduct." W. Page Keeton et al., Prosser and Keeton on Torts 110 (1984).

3. Under the common law, the owner of real estate owned from his or her parcel down to the center of the earth and up to the heavens. This rule has not remained intact. "The common law doctrine that ownership of land extends to the periphery of the universe has no place in the modern world." *United States v. Causby*, 328 U.S. 256, 260 (1946).

2. Trespass to Land and Nuisance

J.H. BORLAND, SR. v. SANDERS LEAD CO.
Supreme Court of Alabama, 1979
369 So. 2d 523

JONES, JUSTICE.

This appeal involves the right of a property owner, in an action for trespass, to recover damages for pollution of his property. The case was tried *ore tenus* to the trial Judge without a jury, and judgment was rendered for the Defendant. We reverse and remand for a new trial.

J.H. Borland, Sr., and Sarah M. Borland, Appellants, own approximately 159 acres of land, located just south of Troy, Alabama, on Henderson Road. On this property, Appellants raise cattle, grow several different crops, and have a large pecan orchard.

In 1968, the Appellee, Sanders Lead Company, started an operation for the recovery of lead from used automobile batteries. This operation is conducted on property just east of the Borlands' property across Henderson Road. The Appellee's smelter was placed on the west edge of their property, that part nearest to the Appellants' property. The smelter is used to reduce the plates from used automobile batteries. It is alleged by Appellants that the smelting process results in the emission of lead particulates and sulfoxide gases.

It is undisputed that Appellee installed a filter system, commonly known as a "bag house," to intercept these lead particulates which otherwise would be emitted into the atmosphere. The "bag house" is a building containing fiber bags. The smoke emitting from the furnace is passed through two cooling systems before passing through the "bag house" so that the fiber bags will not catch fire. If properly installed and used, an efficient "bag house" will recover over 99% of the lead emitted. On two occasions, the cooling system at Appellee's smeltering plant has failed to function properly, resulting in the "bag house's" catching fire on both occasions. There is a dispute as to the efficiency of Appellee's "bag house" throughout its operation.

Appellants allege that, because of the problems with the "bag house," their property has been damaged by a dangerous accumulation of lead particulates and sulfoxide deposits on their property. . . .

It is apparent . . . that the trial Court was under the mistaken impression that compliance with the Alabama Air Pollution Control Act shielded the Defendant from liability for damages caused by pollutants emitting from its smelter. This is not the law in this State. Furthermore, the trial Court incorrectly applied the law of this State in concluding that, because there was evidence showing that the Plaintiffs' farm had increased in value as industrial property, due to its proximity to the lead plant, Plaintiffs could not recover of the Defendant. Such a rule, in effect, would permit private condemnation, which, unquestionably, is impermissible. A discussion of the applicable rule of damages appears later in this opinion.

The Alabama Air Pollution Control Act is codified at § 22-28-1, *et seq.*, Alabama Code 1975. § 22-28-23, Alabama Code 1975, specifically provides:

> *[N]othing in this section shall be construed to limit or abrogate any private remedies now available to any person* for the alleviation, abatement, control, correction or prevention of air pollution *or restitution for damage resulting therefrom.* (Emphasis added.)

Alabama law clearly provides an appropriate remedy for Plaintiffs who have been directly injured by the deleterious effects of pollutants created by another party's acts.

In *Rushing v. Hooper-McDonald, Inc.*, . . . a trespass need not be inflicted directly on another's realty, but may be committed by discharging foreign polluting matter at a point beyond the boundary of such realty. *Rushing* specifically held that a trespass is committed by one who knowingly discharges asphalt in such a manner that it will in due course invade a neighbor's realty and cause harm. . . .

Rushing further cited with approval the case of *Martin v. Reynolds Metals Co.*, 221 Or. 86, 342 P.2d 790, *cert. denied*, 362 U.S. 918, 80 S. Ct. 672, 4 L. Ed. 2d 739 (1959). In *Martin*, a case remarkably similar to the present case, the Plaintiffs sought recovery from the Defendant, aluminum company, for trespass. The Plaintiffs in *Martin* alleged that the operation by Defendants of an aluminum reduction plant caused certain fluoride compounds in the form of gases and particulates, invisible to the naked eye, to become airborne and settle on Plaintiffs' property, rendering it unfit for raising livestock. Plaintiffs in the present case allege that the operation of Defendant's lead reduction plant causes an emission of lead particulates, and S02, invisible to the naked eye, which emissions have settled on their property, making it unsuitable for raising cattle or growing crops.

The Defendants in *Martin* contended that there had not been a sufficient invasion of Plaintiffs' property to constitute trespass, but, at most, Defendant's acts constituted a nuisance. This would have allowed the Defendants to set up Oregon's two-year statute of limitations applicable to non-possessory injuries to land rather than Oregon's six-year statute for trespass to land.

The *Martin* Court pointed out that . . . trespass protecting the possessor's interest in exclusive possession of property and nuisance protecting the interest in use and enjoyment.

The confusion surrounding trespass and nuisance is due in a large part to the influence of common law forms of action. The modern action for trespass to land stemmed inexorably from the common law action for trespass which lay when the injury was both direct and substantial. Nuisance, on the other hand, would lie when injuries were indirect and less substantial. . . .

The *Martin* Court rejected the dimensional test and substituted in its place a force and energy test, stating:

> . . . "[W]e prefer to emphasize the object's energy or force rather than its size. Viewed in this way we may define trespass as an intrusion which invades the possessor's protected interest in exclusive possession, whether that intrusion is by visible or invisible pieces of matter or by energy which can be measured only by the mathematical language of the physicist."

> "We are of the opinion, therefore, that the intrusion of the fluoride particulates in the present case constituted a trespass."

In deciding what acts constitute a trespass, the Oregon Supreme Court cited earlier cases recognizing that a trespass is committed by a defendant's blasting operation when the vibrations and concussions to earth and air cause damage to the plaintiffs property. . . .

. . . Suffice it to say that here we are not dealing with a vibration/concussion case. Moreover, it is clear from a thorough reading of *Martin* that the reliance by the Oregon Supreme Court on the trespass theory of the earlier blasting case was not essential to the *Martin* holding deposits of fluoride particulates constituted a trespass upon the plaintiffs' land.

Having shown trespass and nuisance are not always mutually exclusive remedies, we do not wish to intimate that there is no longer a distinction in the two remedies. Indeed, this distinction is evident in the case of *Wilson v. Parent*, 228 Or. 354, 365 P.2d 72 (1961). There, Plaintiff alleged that her son-in-law, who resided on adjoining property, made vile and obscene gestures toward her and directed vile, obscene and profane language at her. The Plaintiff framed her complaint in nuisance, but a significant portion of the opinion was devoted to the question of whether the intrusions were trespasses. . . .

. . . But we hasten to point out that there is a point where the entry is so lacking in substance that the law will refuse to recognize it, applying the maxim *de minimis non curat lex* — the law does not concern itself with trifles. In the present case, however, we are not faced with a trifling complaint.

The Plaintiffs in this case have suffered, if the evidence is believed, a real and substantial invasion of a protected interest.

. . . Whether an invasion of a property interest is a trespass or a nuisance does not depend upon whether the intruding agent is "tangible" or "intangible." Instead, an analysis must be made to determine the interest interfered with. If the intrusion interferes with the right to exclusive possession of property, the law of trespass applies. If the intrusion is to the interest in use and enjoyment of property, the law of nuisance applies. As previously observed, however, the remedies of trespass and nuisance are not necessarily mutually exclusive.

. . . Under the modern theory of trespass, the law presently allows an action to be maintained in trespass for invasions that, at one time, were considered indirect and, hence, only a nuisance. In order to recover in trespass for this type of invasion [i.e., the asphalt piled in such way as to run onto plaintiffs property, or the pollution emitting from a defendant's smoke stack, such as in the present case], a plaintiff must show 1) an invasion affecting an interest in the exclusive possession of his property; 2) an intentional doing of the act which results in the invasion; 3) reasonable foreseeability that the act done could result in an invasion of plaintiff s possessory interest; and 4) substantial damages to the *res*.

A further clarification of our nuisance/indirect trespass dichotomy is appropriate at this point. In the traditional sense, the law of nuisance applies where the invasion results in no substantial damage to the *res*, but where there is interference with the use and enjoyment of one's property. The classic cases of the barking dog, the neighboring bawdy house, noise, smoke, fumes, or obnoxious odors generally invoke the doctrine of the law of nuisance. These intrusions do not typically result in any actionable damage to the *res;* the injury caused by such acts usually results in a diminution of the use value of the property causally related to the harmful conduct made the basis of the claim.

We emphasize that these intrusions are not relegated to the nuisance remedy simply because of their indirect nature; rather, they do not constitute a trespass because all of the requisite elements of trespass to land are not present. For an indirect invasion to amount to an actionable trespass, there must be an interference with plaintiffs exclusive possessory interest; that is, through the defendant's intentional conduct, and with reasonable foreseeability, some substance has entered upon the land itself, affecting its nature and character, and causing substantial actual damage to the *res*. For example, if the smoke or polluting substance emitting from a defendant's operation causes discomfort and annoyance to the plaintiff in his use and enjoyment of the property, then the plaintiffs remedy is for nuisance; but if, as a result of the defendant's operation, the polluting substance is deposited upon the plaintiffs property, thus interfering with his exclusive possessory interest by causing substantial damage to the *res*, then the plaintiff may seek his remedy in trespass, though his alternative remedy in nuisance may co-exist.

Reversed and remanded.

All the Justices concur.

---

1. To what extent should nuisance law be available as an antipollution tool? Clearly, a property owner may file suit for trespass if some noxious substance crosses the boundary lines of his or her property, but what about odors? What about pollution of a stream with invisible chemicals upstream from the plaintiffs property?

2. In *Public Service Company of Colorado v. Van Wyk*, 27 P.3d 377 (Colo. 2001), the court held that: for a trespass, the plaintiff must prove actual physical damages, and "noise, radiations, and electromagnetic fields" from high tension electric lines were not "physical intrusions" and not physical damages. Therefore, plaintiffs lost in trespass.

PROBLEM

Y, a homeowner, decides to install solar power on the roof of her house. Her neighbor, Z, dislikes the appearance of the solar panels, and plants trees on her (Z's) land so that the panels will not be visible to Z. The trees planted by Z block the sunlight which Y's panels need in order to generate power. Y sues Z to compel Z to trim the trees so that the sunlight may reach Y's panels. What arguments will the parties raise? What result?

3. Trespass to Chattels

Impairing the condition, quality, or value of a chattel upon brief interference can constitute a trespass to the chattel. Restatement (Second) of Torts § 226.

HUFFMAN & WRIGHT LOGGING CO. v. WADE
Supreme Court of Oregon, 1993
857 P.2d 101

GRABER, JUSTICE.

In an action for trespass to chattels, the jury awarded compensatory and punitive damages to plaintiff. Defendants concede their liability for trespass and for compensatory damages, but argue that Article I, sections 8 and 26, of the Oregon Constitution, and the First and Fourteenth Amendments to the Constitution of the United States[2] prohibit an award of punitive damages against them, because their trespassory conduct was "expressive" political speech designed to change government policies. The Court of Appeals affirmed the judgment for punitive damages.

---

[2] The First Amendment provides in part:

"Congress shall make no law . . . abridging the freedom of speech, or of the press; or the right of the people peaceably to assemble, and to petition the Government for a redress of grievances."

The First Amendment is made applicable to the states by the Due Process Clause of the Fourteenth Amendment. New York Times Co. v. Sullivan, 376 U.S. 254, 264 n. 4, 84 S. Ct. 710, 11 L. Ed. 2d 686 (1964).

Huffman and Wright Logging Co. v. Wade, 109 Or. App. 37, 817 P.2d 1334 (1991). We also affirm.

The material facts are not disputed. Plaintiff is a private corporation that operates a logging business. Defendants are six members of "Earth First!" In July 1987, defendants participated in a demonstration on a United States Forest Service logging road in the North Kalmiopsis area of the Siskiyou National Forest. The demonstration was organized to protest Forest Service policies regarding the area. During the demonstration, five of the six defendants climbed on, and chained themselves to, plaintiffs logging equipment. The sixth defendant climbed to the top of a yarder belonging to plaintiff and hung a large banner that read: "FROM HERITAGE TO SAWDUST — EARTH FIRST!" The banner also depicted two trees being turned into sawdust. While defendants were attached to the equipment, they made statements, sang songs, and chanted slogans relating to their beliefs about the need for greater environmental protection of the North Kalmiopsis area. The demonstration was widely publicized.

Defendants did not have permission to be on, or otherwise to interfere with the use of, plaintiffs personal property, and they knew that they did not. Defendants' actions caused part of plaintiff s logging operation to be suspended for most of a day. Defendants were arrested and charged with criminal mischief in the third degree, ORS 164.345. After a trial to the court on stipulated facts, defendants were convicted. Each defendant served two weeks in jail, and each was ordered to pay a $250 fine and to make full restitution to plaintiff for its lost revenues resulting from Defendants' actions.

Plaintiff then filed this civil action against defendants. As material here, the complaint alleged that defendants committed a trespass by "intentionally and wrongfully interfering with and depriving Plaintiff of the use and possession of [its] logging equipment." Plaintiff sought compensatory damages for lost revenues in the amount of $7,818.26, plus punitive damages of $50,000.

Defendants conceded liability for compensatory damages (although they disputed the amount). As an affirmative defense to the claim for punitive damages, they asserted that Article I, sections 8 and 26, of the Oregon Constitution, and the First and Fourteenth Amendments to the Constitution of the United States precluded the imposition of punitive damages for their actions. . . . The jury returned a verdict in plaintiffs favor, awarding $5,717.34 in compensatory damages and $25,000 in punitive damages. Defendants moved for judgment notwithstanding the verdict on the claim for punitive damages, continuing to assert the same constitutional theories. The trial court denied that motion and entered judgment for plaintiff.

Defendants sought review only with respect to the constitutionality of the award of punitive damages, and we allowed their petition.

Defendants contend that, as a matter of law, no punitive damages are recoverable, because *all* their activity was "expressive conduct" protected from an award of punitive damages by the state and federal constitutions.

. . ..

Article I, Section 8

The jury awarded compensatory and punitive damages for trespass to chattels. From the evidence presented, the jury could have found that the acts of trespass were Defendants' climbing on plaintiffs logging equipment, chaining themselves to it, affixing an object to it, and rendering the equipment inoperable during that time. Although those acts undoubtedly had a communicative effect, in the sense that most purposive human activity communicates something about the frame of mind of the actor, the acts were conduct, not speech. The question becomes, then, whether defendants are nonetheless constitutionally immune from potential responsibility for punitive damages because of the message that their conduct assertedly was trying to convey, the reason for their conduct, or the fact that speech accompanied their conduct.

Two lines of cases from this court demonstrate that the answer under Article I, section 8, is "no." . . .

We conclude that there are, indeed, some intentional torts that are concerned only with forbidden effects and that the tort that we consider in this case, trespass to chattels, is such a tort.

"In actions for trespass to personal property the gist of the action is the disturbance of the plaintiffs possession." *Swank v. Elwert*, 55 Or. 487, 496, 105 P. 901 (1910). That is, the tort of trespass to chattels focuses on the *effect* — the disturbance of the owner's possession. . . . [R]esponsibility for punitive damages may accompany an intentional tort — like the tort of trespass — that permits liability for harm not caused by speech. With respect to such a tort, liability for both compensatory and punitive damages rests on conduct. A defendant still may assert, however, that punitive damages cannot constitutionally be applied to the particular conduct involved. Where a defendant . . . makes such an assertion, the defendant — like a defendant in a second-category tort case — may be entitled to a limiting instruction.

If a tort permits liability for the content of speech, punitive damages are not recoverable. If a tort permits liability for speech-caused harm, then a defendant who requests it is entitled to an instruction limiting the tortious predicate for punitive damages to conduct not protected by the free speech provision of Article I, section 8.

. . . .

Defendants' conduct consisted of several acts: climbing on plaintiffs logging equipment, chaining themselves to the equipment, affixing an object to one piece of logging equipment, and thereby disrupting plaintiffs use of its property. We conclude that the jury was entitled to find that Defendants' acts caused the disturbance of plaintiff s possession of its personal property, wholly apart from any motivating opinion, underlying message, or accompanying speech. The trespassory acts were, therefore, "non-expressive conduct" within the meaning of Article I, section 8. The message that defendants sought to convey by their conduct, the reason for their conduct, and the spoken and written words accompanying their conduct did not transform Defendants' conduct into speech.

. . . Liability for Defendants' conduct in this case could have been assessed independently of any accompanying expression of views. A properly instructed jury could have awarded punitive damages based on the predicate of Defendants' trespassory conduct alone. Defendants did not choose to request a limiting instruction. Having failed to request such an instruction, defendants cannot prevail in their Article I, section 8, challenge to the award of punitive damages against them. . . .

First Amendment

Having rejected Defendants' state constitutional arguments, we turn to their arguments under the federal constitution. Defendants assert that the First Amendment to the Constitution of the United States protects them from an award of punitive damages in a case of this kind.

The Supreme Court of the United States recently reaffirmed the principle that "violence or other types of potentially expressive activities that produce special harms distinct from their communicative impact are entitled to no constitutional protection. . . .

We already have held that the tort of trespass to chattels is aimed at conduct not protected by the free expression provision of the Oregon Constitution. The same conclusion obtains with respect to the First Amendment. In this case, Defendants' conduct, although accompanied by expressive activity, produced a special cognizable harm (an interference with plaintiffs possessory interest in its property), distinct from any communicative impact. "[T]he State, no less than a private owner of property, has power to preserve the property under its control for the use to which it is lawfully dedicated").

In addition, the First Amendment does not apply to private property that is not devoted to public use. For an owner of private property to be subject to the proscriptions of the First Amendment, the property must "assume to some significant degree the functional attributes of public property devoted to public use." *Central Hardware Co. v. NLRB*, 407 U.S. 539, 547, 92 S. Ct. 2238, 33 L. Ed. 2d 122 (1972). Devotion of private property to public use requires, at a minimum, the owner's invitation to the general public to enter the premises. *See Marsh v. Alabama*, 326 U.S. 501, 506, 66 S. Ct. 276, 90 L. Ed. 265 (1946) ("The more an owner . . . opens up his property for use by the public in general, the more do his rights become circumscribed by the statutory and constitutional rights of those who use it."). *See also Lloyd Corporation v. Whiffen, supra*, 315 Or. at 510-11, 849 P.2d 446 (citing and agreeing with the above-quoted passage from *Marsh v. Alabama*). Nothing in the First Amendment cases of the Supreme Court suggests that a different rule applies to private personal property than to private real property; the former, like the latter, is not subject to the proscriptions of the First Amendment unless it is devoted to public use. Here, plaintiff did not invite members of the general public to climb on or chain themselves to its equipment or otherwise subject itself to the proscriptions of the First Amendment.

Finally, defendants rely on the assembly and petition clauses of the First Amendment. They argue that the imposition of punitive damages violates their federally protected rights to assemble and to petition the government.

. . ..

The First and Fourteenth Amendments do not preclude an award of punitive damages against defendants in this case.

The jury's verdict awarding plaintiff $25,000 in punitive damages was permissible. The decision of the Court of Appeals and the judgment of the circuit court are affirmed.

––––––––––

Why were punitive damages allowed in this case? When do you think that the First Amendment should serve as a defense in a case alleging trespass to chattels? Trespass to land? What about picketing in shopping malls? Are there kinds of private property which are so open to the public that they should lose their private character, at least for some purposes?

G. CONVERSION

The line between trespass to chattels and conversion can be difficult to perceive. One court defined the difference as follows:

> . . . the difference between the two torts is fundamentally one of degree, trespass constituting a lesser interference with another's chattel, conversion a more serious exercise of dominion or control over it. *See* Restatement (Second) of Torts, § 222A, Comment (1965).

> Thus, a trespass has been defined as an intentional use or intermeddling with the chattel in possession of another, Restatement (Second) of Torts, § 217(b), such intermeddling occurring, *inter alia*, when "the chattel is impaired as to its condition, quality, or value." Restatement (Second) of Torts, § 218(b). *See also Walser v. Resthaven Memorial Gardens, Inc.*, 98 Md. App. 371, 395, 633 A.2d 466 (1993).

A "conversion," on the other hand, has been defined as:

> [A]n intentional exercise of dominion or control over a chattel which so seriously interferes with the right of another to control it that the actor may justly be required to pay the other the full value of the chattel. Restatement (Second) of Torts, § 222A(1). Whereas impairing the condition, quality or value of a chattel upon brief interference can constitute a trespass, intentional destruction or material alteration of a chattel will subject the actor to liability for conversion. Restatement (Second) of Torts, § 226.

A number of factors are considered in determining whether interference with a chattel is serious enough to constitute a conversion as opposed to a trespass. These include:

a) the extent and duration of the actor's exercise of dominion or control;

b) the actor's intent to assert a right in fact inconsistent with the other's right of control;

c) the actor's good faith;

d) the extent and duration of the resulting interference with the other's right of control;

e) the harm done to the chattel;

f) the inconvenience and expense caused to the other.[9]

United States v. Arora, 860 F. Supp. 1091 (D. Md. 1994).

DICKENS v. DEBOLT
Supreme Court of Oregon, 1979 (en banc)
602 P.2d 246

Tongue, Justice.

This is an action for conversion by a fisherman against a state police officer who seized a sturgeon which he mistakenly believed to have been caught illegally and may have then eaten most of the "evidence." The case was tried before a jury, which returned a verdict of $250 in general damages and $750 punitive damages. The Attorney General appealed from the resulting judgment on behalf of the state police officer. The Court of Appeals reversed the judgment upon the ground that Oregon statutes confer complete and absolute immunity upon a state police officer in such a case. 39 Or. App. 575, 592 P.2d 1082 (1979).[1] We allowed plaintiffs petition for review.

The facts are bizarre. On September 12, 1977, plaintiff with his wife, an uncle and an aunt, drove over 150 miles from their home to fish for sturgeon in the Columbia River below the John Day Dam.

At about sundown plaintiff hooked a fish. After a good fight lasting about 30 minutes he landed his prize, a sturgeon — a "royal fish" — 43 inches in length and weighing between 40 and 45 pounds.[2] Being concerned over the fish spoiling and it being too late to drive home, plaintiff put the end of a rope through the gills of the

---

[9] It is inconsequential that the actor may have received no benefit from the act. Maryland Casualty Co. v. Wolff, 180 Md. 513, 25 A.2d 665 (1942).

[Citation], quoting Restatement (Second) of Torts, § 222A(2).

[1] ORS 496.620, relied upon by the Court of Appeals, provides:

"No person authorized to enforce the wildlife laws shall suffer any civil liability for the enforcement or attempted enforcement of any provisions of the wildlife laws . . ." ORS 30.265(3)(c), also referred to by the Court of Appeals, provides:

"(3) Every public body and its officers, employees and agents acting within the scope of their employment or duties are immune from liability for:

"(c) Any claim based upon the performance of or the failure to exercise or perform a discretionary function or duty, whether or not the discretion is abused."

[2] Under English common law, a sturgeon was a "royal fish" which belonged to the king and no subject could take such a fish without a royal grant. Arnold v. Mundy, 6 N.J.L. 1, 76 (1821).

sturgeon and tied the other end of the rope to a cable under the platform, leaving the fish alive and in the river.

Because Golden and Elliot were still fishing and had a mobile home parked nearby, plaintiff asked them to "keep an eye" on his sturgeon. Plaintiff and his party then went to a motel about one mile away in Rufus, where they had dinner and spent the night.

On returning to the river the next morning to get his sturgeon, plaintiff found the rope cut and the fish gone. He was then told by Rans Golden that a state police officer had taken the fish and had said that if plaintiff wanted it he "would have to call." Plaintiff testified that he then called the desk sergeant of the state police at Arlington, told him what had happened and asked for his fish, but was told that he would not get it back. Plaintiff also testified that he told the desk sergeant that he had witnesses who had seen him catch the fish, and was told that "if we went to court all seven of us could go to jail for perjury."

Plaintiff never saw his sturgeon again. He testified that the "going price" for the 40 to 45 pounds of meat, which he had planned to eat, was $5.65 per pound and that the rope was a ski rope worth from $10 to $15. He was never interviewed by the state police, much less arrested or charged with catching the sturgeon illegally.

Defendant was the state police officer who took plaintiff's sturgeon. He testified that on the evening of that day he observed two persons fishing on the platform below the dam and saw one of them catch a sturgeon at about 10:00 p.m., it then being illegal to fish for sturgeon. He also saw them tie a rope through its gills and tie the rope to a cable under the platform. Defendant arrested the two fishermen, Rans Golden and Gregory Elliot, for angling after hours. He then looked over the platform and saw one sturgeon tied to a cable. He testified that he took the fish "as evidence" in the case against Golden and Elliot. He admitted, however, that they told him that the sturgeon "belonged to some people that were in a motel in Rufus," but that he did not "check (that) out," apparently because he did not believe Golden and Elliot, who had not told him that there were two sturgeon tied to cables under the platform, including the one that he had seen them catch and which he believed to be the fish that he took "as evidence."

Defendant then took plaintiff's sturgeon to Arlington, where he lived. He testified that because the state police "didn't have any deep freeze facilities there," it "seemed like a reasonable thing to do" for him to put the sturgeon in the freezer at his home.

Before doing so, however, defendant skinned and fileted the sturgeon, and "packaged it up." He testified that he also put a state police evidence tag "on the package," with his name and number and also the names of Elliot and Golden and the charge against them. At the trial defendant produced a package of frozen fish with such a tag on it.

Defendant testified that after the fish was fileted, the meat weighed 8 pounds. He also testified that he had not eaten any of the sturgeon. A professional fish buyer called as a witness by the defense to testify to a market value of $.85 per pound for the sturgeon, if dressed, also testified that a 40 pound sturgeon, after dressing by removal of head and entrails, would "lose at least 15 percent," depending on the size of the head (or at least 6 pounds, with up to 34 pounds of the 40 pound fish remaining).

The answer filed by the Attorney General on behalf of defendant, in addition to denying most of the facts alleged in plaintiffs complaint for conversion, alleged the following affirmative defenses:

> "At all times material herein, defendant was acting in his official capacity as a trooper of the Oregon State Police, and seized said sturgeon and water ski rope as the fruits of a crime and at the time of and pursuant to a valid arrest." (ORS 496.620)

and,

> "At all times material herein, defendant, a trooper of the Oregon State Police, was performing a discretionary function." (ORS 30.265(3)(c)).

At the conclusion of the testimony defendant moved for a directed verdict upon the ground, among others, that ORS 496.620 conferred complete and absolute immunity upon defendant. Later, after the jury verdict in favor of plaintiff, defendant moved for a judgment notwithstanding the verdict on the same grounds. In the order denying that motion the trial judge held as follows:

> The storage of the fish in the private freezer might have been within the defendant's scope of employment, but there is no way a State Policeman's duties include the eating of filet of sturgeon."

We agree with the trial judge.

In holding that the trial judge erred in denying defendant's motion for directed verdict, the Court of Appeals recognized that the jury could have properly inferred from the facts that "there was an unexplained shrinkage in the amount of sturgeon still available at the time of trial," not only that "the officer had eaten a portion of the fish," but also that "the officer intended to do so when he seized the fish." (39 Or. App. at 580, 592 P.2d at 1085).

. . . .

As we analyze the problem presented by this case, however, the issue to be decided in determining whether ORS 496.620 provides immunity to the defendant is not whether he acted in good faith or in bad faith, but whether he was engaged in "the enforcement or attempted enforcement of . . . the wild life laws" or in "the exercise or attempted exercise of any of the duties or privileges granted to or imposed by law upon" the defendant when he "ate most of the evidence," as the jury was entitled to find.

We may agree that when a state police officer seizes a fish that he believes to have been caught illegally he is entitled to immunity under ORS 496.620. We do not believe, however, that this statute can properly be construed to mean when a state police officer "eats the evidence" he is then engaged in either the "enforcement or attempted enforcement" of the game laws or the "exercise or attempted exercise" of any of his "duties or privileges" as an officer. It follows, in our opinion, that the reasoning on which the Court of Appeals based its decision of this case is faulty and that it was in error in holding that ORS 496.620 granted an immunity to the defendant as a complete defense to this case.

For similar reasons, we hold that ORS 30.265(3)(c) of the Oregon Tort Claims Act does not confer immunity upon defendant as for the performance of a discretionary function or duty. Thus, we hold that when defendant ate most of the sturgeon, as the jury could properly find, he was not then acting "within the scope of (his) employment or duties," within the meaning of that statute.

. . . .

Both in instructions requested at the time of trial on behalf of the defendant and in the brief filed on his behalf in the Court of Appeals, it is contended by the Attorney General that a conversion in such a case is to be defined as held by this court in *Mustola v. Toddy*, 253 Or. 658, 456 P.2d 1004 (1969) (also an action for conversion against a state police officer), in which this court (at 663-64, 456 P.2d 1004) adopted Restatement (Second) of Torts § 222A (1965) as a definition of conversion for application in such a case and which reads as follows:

§ 222A. What Constitutes Conversion

"(1) Conversion is an intentional exercise of dominion or control over a chattel which so seriously interferes with the right of another to control it that the actor may justly be required to pay the other the full value of the chattel.

(2) In determining the seriousness of the interference and the justice of requiring the actor to pay the full value, the following factors are important: [The list of factors is presented earlier with the definition of conversion.]

. . . .

ORS 496.620 would protect the officer from the legal consequences of that conversion only as long as he held the fish for the purpose which the statute protects; i.e., attempted enforcement of the wild life laws. The same is also true of ORS 30.265(3)(c). For reasons previously stated, we hold that those statutes do not confer such an immunity. It follows, in our opinion, that the trial court properly denied defendant's motion for a directed verdict and that the Court of Appeals erred in holding to the contrary.

. . . .

If, however, this defendant ate most of the sturgeon and at that time was *not* acting within the course and scope of his employment, as the jury was entitled to find from the evidence of this case, he would then be subject to punitive damages on the same basis as any other person who commits an act of conversion. This court has held that punitive damages may properly be awarded by a jury in actions for conversion when the circumstances are sufficiently aggravated.

Because the trial court erred in failing to give two of defendant's requested instructions, this case must be remanded to it for a new trial.

[Reversed] and remanded.

The reasons for the reversal of the trial court had nothing to do with the substance of the opinion.

How did the court know that the defendant had eaten the fish? What should the defendant have done with the fish instead? What relationship did the fact that the defendant ate the fish bear to the conclusion that his employer would not be held liable for his conduct?

PEARSON v. DODD
United States Court of Appeals for the District of Columbia Circuit, 1969
410 F.2d 701

J. Skelly Wright, Circuit Judge:

This case arises out of the exposure of the alleged misdeeds of Senator Thomas Dodd of Connecticut by newspaper columnists Drew Pearson and Jack Anderson. The District Court has granted partial summary judgment to Senator Dodd, appellee here, finding liability on a theory of conversion. At the same time, the court denied partial summary judgment on the theory of invasion of privacy. Both branches of the court's judgment are before us on interlocutory appeal. We affirm the District Court's denial of summary judgment for invasion of privacy and reverse its grant of summary judgment for conversion.

The undisputed facts in the case were stated by the District Court as follows:

" . . . [O]n several occasions in June and July, 1965, two former employees of the plaintiff, at times with the assistance of two members of the plaintiffs staff, entered the plaintiffs office without authority and unbeknownst to him, removed numerous documents from his files, made copies of them, replaced the originals, and turned over the copies to the defendant Anderson, who was aware of the manner in which the copies had been obtained. The defendants Pearson and Anderson thereafter published articles containing information gleaned from these documents."[2]

        . . . .

II

The District Court ruled that appellants' receipt and subsequent use of photo-copies of documents which appellants knew had been removed from Appellee's files without authorization established appellants' liability for conversion. We conclude that appellants are not guilty of conversion on the facts shown.

Dean Prosser has remarked that "[conversion is the forgotten tort."[21] That it is not entirely forgotten is attested by the case before us. History has largely defined its contours, contours which we should now follow except where they derive from clearly obsolete practices or abandoned theories.[22]

---

[2] Dodd v. Pearson, D.D.C., 279 F. Supp. 101, 102 (1968).

[21] Prosser, *The Nature of Conversion*, 42 Corn. L.Q. 168 (1957).

[22] *Cf.* id. at 169: "The hand of history lies heavy upon the tort of conversion."

Conversion is the substantive tort theory which underlay the ancient common law form of action for trover. A plaintiff in trover alleged that he had lost a chattel which he rightfully possessed,[23] and that the defendant had found it and converted it to his own use. With time, the allegations of losing and finding became fictional, leaving the question of whether the defendant had "converted" the property the only operative one.

The most distinctive feature of conversion is its measure of damages, which is the value of the goods converted. The theory is that the "converting" defendant has in some way treated the goods as if they were his own, so that the plaintiff can properly ask the court to decree a forced sale of the property from the rightful possessor to the converter.

Because of this stringent measure of damages, it has long been recognized that not every wrongful interference with the personal property of another is a conversion. Where the intermeddling falls short of the complete or very substantial deprivation of possessory rights in the property, the tort committed is not conversion, but the lesser wrong of trespass to chattels.

The Second Restatement of Torts has marked the distinction by defining conversion as:

> " . . . [A]n intentional exercise of dominion or control over a chattel which so seriously interferes with the right of another to control it that the actor may justly be required to pay the other the full value of the chattel."[29]

Less serious interferences fall under the Restatements definition of trespass.[30]

The difference is more than a semantic one. The measure of damages in trespass is not the whole value of the property interfered with, but rather the actual diminution in its value caused by the interference. More important for this case, a judgment for conversion can be obtained with only nominal damages, whereas liability for trespass to chattels exists only on a showing of actual damage to the property interfered with.[32]

---

[23] A threshold question, not briefed by either party and hence not decided by us, is the nature of the property right held by appellee in the contents of the files in his Senate office. Those files, themselves paid for by the United States, are maintained in an office owned by the United States, by employees of the United States. They are meant to contribute to the work of appellee as an officer of the United States. The question thus is not entirely free from doubt whether appellee has title to the contents of the files or has a right of exclusive possession of those contents, or is a bailee, or even a mere custodian of those contents.

[29] Restatement (Second) of Torts § 222A(1) (1965).

[30] Id., § 217: "A trespass to a chattel may be committed by intentionally (a) dispossessing another of the chattel, or (b) using or intermeddling with a chattel in the possession of another."

[32] "To support an action of trespass to a chattel where the invasion of interests does not result in its destruction or in a dispossession thereof, it was early held there must be some physical harm to the chattel or to its possessor. Unlike the action of trespass quare clausum fregit in the case of land, no action could be maintained for a mere harmless intermeddling with goods. The possessor's proprietary interest in the inviolability of his personal property did not receive that protection which the similar interest in the possession of land or the dignitary interest in the inviolability of the person receives. . . ." 1 F. Harper & F. James, *supra* Note 25, § 2.3. (Footnotes omitted.)

It is clear that on the agreed facts appellants committed no conversion of the physical documents taken from Appellee's files. Those documents were removed from the files at night, photocopied, and returned to the files undamaged before office operations resumed in the morning. Insofar as the documents' value to appellee resided in their usefulness as records of the business of his office, appellee was clearly not substantially deprived of his use of them.

This of course is not an end of the matter. It has long been recognized that documents often have value above and beyond that springing from their physical possession. They may embody information or ideas whose economic value depends in part or in whole upon being kept secret. The question then arises whether the information taken by means of copying Appellee's office files is of the type which the law of conversion protects. The general rule has been that ideas or information are not subject to legal protection,[34] but the law has developed exceptions to this rule.

Where information is gathered and arranged at some cost and sold as a commodity on the market, it is properly protected as property. Where ideas are formulated with labor and inventive genius, as in the case of literary works or scientific researches, they are protected. Where they constitute instruments of fair and effective commercial competition, those who develop them may gather their fruits under the protection of the law.

The question here is not whether appellee had a right to keep his files from prying eyes, but whether the information taken from those files falls under the protection of the law of property, enforceable by a suit for conversion. In our view, it does not. The information included the contents of letters to appellee from supplicants, and office records of other kinds, the nature of which is not fully revealed by the record. Insofar as we can tell, none of it amounts to literary property, to scientific invention, or to secret plans formulated by appellee for the conduct of commerce. Nor does it appear to be information held in any way for sale by appellee, analogous to the fresh news copy produced by a wire service.

Appellee complains, not of the misappropriation of property bought or created by him, but of the exposure of information either (1) injurious to his reputation or (2) revelatory of matters which he believes he has a right to keep to himself. Injuries of this type are redressed at law by suit for libel and invasion of privacy respectively, where Defendants' liability for those torts can be established under the limitations created by common law and by the Constitution.

Because no conversion of the physical contents of Appellee's files took place, and because the information copied from the documents in those files has not been shown to be property subject to protection by suit for conversion, the District Court's ruling that appellants are guilty of conversion must be reversed.

So ordered.

---

[34] The traditional rule has been that conversion will lie only for the taking of tangible property, or rights embodied in a tangible token necessary for the enforcement of those rights. [Citations.] This overly restrictive rule has recently been relaxed in favor of the reasonable proposition that any intangible generally protected as personal property may be the subject matter of a suit for conversion.

Tamm, Circuit Judge (concurring):

Some legal scholars will see in the majority opinion — as distinguished from its actual holding — an ironic aspect.

Conduct for which a law enforcement officer would be soundly castigated is, by the phraseology of the majority opinion, found tolerable; conduct which, if engaged in by government agents would lead to the suppression of evidence obtained by these means, is approved when used for the profit of the press. . . .

---

1.   Must property be tangible in order to be converted? In *National Surety Corp. v. Applied Sys.*, 418 So. 2d 847 (Ala. 1982), the court decided that computer programs could be the subject of a suit for conversion. In an era when the most valuable property may well be intangible, the conclusion that conversion does not require tangibility is an important one.

2.   What analytic difficulties does the application of conversion law to intangible property create?

3.   For further reading on modern approaches to conversion, see Jeff C. Dodd, *Rights in Information: Conversion and Misappropriation Causes of Action in Intellectual Property Cases*, 32 Hous. L. Rev. 459 (1995); Val D. Ricks, *The Conversion of Intangible Property: Bursting the Ancient Trover Bottle with New Wine*, 1991 B.Y.U. L. Rev. 1681.

Chapter 3

PRIVILEGES

This chapter deals with the privileges which, if applicable, justify or exempt from liability the intentional act that is the basis of the underlying intentional tort suit. When arguing that an action was privileged, the defendant basically concedes that the facts as alleged are correct, but contends that he or she should not be liable for the reason covered by the privilege. The defendant in these cases is not arguing that any element of the intentional tort is missing. Rather, the argument is that the defendant's acts, which would subject the defendant to liability in the absence of a privilege, should not subject the defendant to liability because of the operation of the privilege. Under the privileges discussed in this chapter, the defendant basically agrees that the act that is the basis for the tort suit occurred, but contends that he or she should not be liable because the act was privileged.

A.   CONSENT AS A DEFENSE TO BATTERY

In the Intentional Torts chapter, we saw that the courts reject good intentions as a defense. Similarly, the fact that the act at issue benefitted the plaintiff does not constitute a defense in an intentional tort suit. The injury in a battery case is the unconsented-to touching itself, irrespective of whether this touching benefitted the plaintiff. This contrasts sharply with torts based on negligence; in negligence-based jurisprudence, if there are no damages, there is no liability.

1.   The Medical Arena

MOHR v. WILLIAMS
Supreme Court of Minnesota, 1905
104 N.W. 12

BROWN, J.

Defendant is a physician and surgeon of standing and character, making disorders of the ear a specialty, and having an extensive practice in the city of St. Paul. . . . He informed plaintiff of the result of his examination, and advised an operation for the purpose of removing the polyp and diseased ossicles. After consultation with her family physician, and one or two further consultations with defendant, plaintiff decided to submit to the proposed operation. She was not informed that her left ear was in any way diseased, and understood that the necessity for an operation applied to her right ear only. She repaired to the hospital, and was placed under the influence of anesthetics; and, after being made unconscious, defendant made a thorough examination of her left ear, and found it in a more serious condition than her right one. A small perforation was discovered high up in the drum membrane, hooded, and with granulated edges, and the bone of the inner wall of the middle ear was diseased and dead. He called this discovery to the attention of Dr. Davis — plaintiff's family physician, who attended the operation at her request — who also examined the ear, and confirmed defendant in his diagnosis. Defendant also further examined the right ear, and found its condition less serious than expected, and finally concluded that the left, instead of the right, should be operated upon; devoting to the right ear other treatment. He then performed the operation of ossiculectomy on plaintiff's left ear; removing a portion of the drum membrane, and scraping away the diseased portion of the inner wall of the ear. The operation was in every way successful and skillfully performed. It is claimed by plaintiff that the operation greatly impaired her hearing, seriously injured her person, and, not having been consented to by her, was wrongful and unlawful, constituting an assault and battery; and she brought this action to recover damages therefor. The trial in the court below resulted in a verdict for plaintiff for $14,322.50. Defendant thereafter moved the court for judgment notwithstanding the verdict [or for a new trial], on the ground that, on the evidence presented, plaintiff was not entitled to recover. . . . The trial court denied the motion for judgment, but granted a new trial on the ground, as stated in the order, that the damages were excessive. Defendant appealed from the order denying the motion for judgment, and plaintiff appealed from the order granting a new trial.

2. We come then to a consideration of the questions presented by defendant's appeal from the order denying his motion for judgment notwithstanding the verdict. It is contended that final judgment should be ordered in his favor for the following reasons: (a) That it appears from the evidence received on the trial that plaintiff consented to the operation on her left ear. (b) If the court shall find that no such consent was given, that, under the circumstances disclosed by the record, no consent was necessary, (c) That, under the facts disclosed, an action for assault and battery will not lie; it appearing conclusively, as counsel urge, that there is a total lack of evidence showing or tending to show malice or an evil intent on the part of defendant, or that the operation was negligently performed.

We shall consider first the question whether, under the circumstances shown in the record, the consent of plaintiff to the operation was necessary. If, under the particular facts of this case, such consent was unnecessary, no recovery can be had, for the evidence fairly shows that the operation complained of was skillfully performed and of a generally beneficial nature. But if the consent of plaintiff was necessary, then the further questions presented become important. This particular question is new in this state. . . . [W]e are unable to concur with counsel for defendant in their contention that the consent of plaintiff was unnecessary. . . . It cannot be doubted that ordinarily the patient must be consulted, and his consent given, before a physician may operate upon him. It was said in the case *of Pratt v. Davis*, 37 Chicago Leg. News, 213, referred to and commented on in Cent. Law J. 452: "Under a free government, at least, the free citizen's first and greatest right, which underlies all others — the right to the inviolability of his person; in other words, the right to himself — is the subject of universal acquiescence, and this right necessarily forbids a physician or surgeon, however skillful or eminent, who has been asked to examine, diagnose, advise, and prescribe (which are at least necessary first steps in treatment and care), to violate, without permission, the bodily integrity of his patient by a major or capital operation, placing him under an anaesthetic for that purpose, and operating upon him without his consent or knowledge." 1 Kinkead on Torts, § 375, states the general rule on this subject as follows: "The patient must be the final arbiter as to whether he will take his chances with the operation, or take his chances of living without it. Such is the natural right of the individual, which the law recognizes as a legal one. Consent, therefore, of an individual, must be either expressly or impliedly given before a surgeon may have the right to operate." . . . It is not, however, contended by defendant that under ordinary circumstances consent is unnecessary, but that, under the particular circumstances of this case, consent was implied; that it was an emergency case, such as to authorize the operation without express consent or permission. [Emergency] If a person should be injured to the extent of rendering him unconscious, and his injuries were of such a nature as to require prompt surgical attention, a physician called to attend him would be justified in applying such medical or surgical treatment as might reasonably be necessary for the preservation of his life or limb, and consent on the part of the injured person would be implied. And again, if, in the course of an operation to which the patient consented, the physician should discover conditions not anticipated before the operation was commenced, and which, if not removed, would endanger the life or health of the patient, he would, though no express consent was obtained or given, be justified in extending the operation to remove and overcome them. But such is not the case at bar. The diseased condition of plaintiff's left ear was not discovered in the course of an operation on the right, which was authorized, but upon an independent examination of that organ, made after the authorized operation was found unnecessary. Nor is the evidence such as to justify the court in holding, as a matter of law, that it was such an affection as would result immediately in the serious injury of plaintiff, or such an emergency as to justify proceeding without her consent. She had experienced no particular difficulty with that ear, and the questions as to when its diseased condition would become alarming or fatal, and whether there was an immediate necessity for an operation, were, under the evidence, questions of fact for the jury.

3. The contention of defendant that the operation was consented to by plaintiff is not sustained by the evidence. . . .

4. The last contention of defendant is . . . an entire absence of any evidence tending to show an evil intent, the court should say, as a matter of law, that no assault and battery was committed, even though she did not consent to the operation. In other words, that the absence of a showing that defendant was actuated by a wrongful intent, or guilty of negligence, relieves the act of defendant from the charge of an unlawful assault and battery. We are unable to reach that conclusion, though the contention is not without merit. It would seem to follow from what has been said on the other features of the case that the act of defendant amounted at least to a technical assault and battery. If the operation was performed without plaintiff's consent, and the circumstances were not such as to justify its performance without, it was wrongful; and, if it was wrongful, it was unlawful. As remarked in 1 Jaggard on Torts, 437, every person has a right to complete immunity of his person from physical interference of others, except in so far as contact may be necessary under the general doctrine of privilege; and any unlawful or

unauthorized touching of the person of another, except it be in the spirit of pleasantry, constitutes an assault and battery. In the case at bar, as we have already seen, the question whether defendant's act in performing the operation upon plaintiff was authorized was a question for the jury to determine. If it was unauthorized, then it was, within what we have said, unlawful. It was a violent assault, not a mere pleasantry; and, even though no negligence is shown, it was wrongful and unlawful. The case is unlike a criminal prosecution for assault and battery, for there an unlawful intent must be shown. But that rule does not apply to a civil action, to maintain which it is sufficient to show that the assault complained of was wrongful and unlawful or the result of negligence.

The amount of plaintiff's recovery, if she is entitled to recover at all, must depend upon the character and extent of the injury inflicted upon her, in determining which the nature of the malady intended to be healed and the beneficial nature of the operation should be taken into consideration, as well as the good faith of the defendant.

Order affirmed.

JAGGARD, J., took no part.

----

1. The court states that the beneficial nature of the procedure should be taken into account in assessing damages, and implies that a battery might occur but no damages be awarded. Is this consistent with the nature of the injury? What is the nature of the injury in *Mohr*?

2. What if the unconsented-to touching were entirely beneficial, such that there was no injury other than the unconsented-to touching itself? What might an award of damages look like in such a case?

3. A doctor may be liable for battery if he or she exceeds the scope of the consent given, even in the absence of negligence and the presence of good faith. *Rogers v. Lumbermens Mut. Cas. Co.*, 119 So. 2d 649 (La. Ct. App. 1960) (patient consented to appendectomy, doctor performed hysterectomy, no emergency).

What can a doctor do prior to an operation to foreclose such liability?

PAUSCHER v. IOWA METHODIST MEDICAL CENTER
Supreme Court of Iowa, 1987
408 N.W.2d 355

[The doctrine of informed consent has its roots in the tort of battery. Originally, the failure to inform the plaintiff about the proposed treatment vitiated the consent (if any), and the defendant would thus be liable for battery. Informed consent has, however, metamorphosed into a negligence doctrine. Thus, *Pauscher v. Iowa Methodist Medical Center* appears in Chapter 5, Negligence, and not in this chapter.]

In battery cases, the injury includes the unconsented-to contact itself. Because informed consent is now part of negligence doctrine, the concept of the injury has changed. Many informed consent cases are lost by plaintiffs because the plaintiffs cannot show that the lack of information caused them any harm: in order to recover for a failure of informed consent, the plaintiff must prove that he or she would have chosen differently had he or she possessed the information that the doctor neglected to provide.

ASHCRAFT v. KING
California Court of Appeal, Second District, 1991
278 Cal. Rptr. 900

JOHNSON, ASSOCIATE JUSTICE.

Plaintiff appeals from a judgment for defendant in this medical malpractice case. Because plaintiff was erroneously nonsuited on her battery cause of action we reverse the judgment as to that cause of action. In all other respects the judgment is affirmed.

Facts and Proceedings Below

In 1983, plaintiff Daisy Ashcraft, age 16, was diagnosed as having scoliosis, a curvature of the spine, destined to become debilitating if not corrected. Ms. Ashcraft was referred to defendant John King, M.D., an orthopedic surgeon.

Ms. Ashcraft went to Dr. King's office for a consultation. She was accompanied by her mother, Lulu Ashcraft. At that meeting Dr. King recommended surgery and described the procedure generally. During the course of the consultation Dr. King and the Ashcrafts discussed the subject of blood transfusions, including the use of family donated blood in the operation.

. . . [P]laintiffs mother testified she insisted the operation be performed using only family donated blood. Dr. King conceded the subject of family donated blood was discussed but only in terms of whether it was "possible" for the family to donate blood to be used in Ms. Ashcraft's operation. Both parties agree Dr. King informed Ms. Ashcraft and her mother they should contact officials at Children's Hospital, where the operation would be performed, to arrange for family donated blood.

Ms. Ashcraft's mother and father and several other relatives went to Children's Hospital and gave blood before and during the operation. None of this blood ever went to Daisy Ashcraft. Instead, all of the blood Ms. Ashcraft received during the operation came from the general supplies on hand at Children's Hospital.

At the time of this surgery, in 1983, no test was available to determine whether blood was contaminated with the Human Immuno-deficiency Virus (HIV), the cause of AIDS. It was not until 1987 the hospital discovered Daisy Ashcraft had been transfused during surgery with blood from an HIV positive donor. Ms. Ashcraft went to the hospital for a blood test the day she received this information. The test was positive.

In her medical malpractice suit against Dr. King, Ms. Ashcraft sought damages on the theories of negligence and battery. The battery theory rested on Ms. Ashcraft" contention she had specifically conditioned her consent to surgery on the understanding only family donated blood would be used in her transfusions but Dr. King willfully ignored that condition.

After all the evidence was received, the trial court granted Dr. King's motion for nonsuit on the battery cause of action. The case was submitted to the jury only on the negligence theory. After five days of deliberation, the jury returned a verdict in favor of defendant by a vote of nine to three.

I. A Patient Has the Right to Impose Express Limitations or Conditions on a Doctor's Authority to Perform an Operation.

A. Doctor Is Subject to Liability for Battery for Exceeding the Conditions Imposed by the Patient.

As a general rule, one who consents to a touching cannot recover in an action for battery. (Rest. 2d Torts, § 892A.) Thus, one who gives informed consent to a surgery cannot recover for resulting harm under a theory of battery. However, it is well-recognized a person may place conditions on the consent. If the actor exceeds the terms or conditions of the consent, the consent does not protect the actor from liability for the excessive act. (Rest. 2d Torts, § 89A(3), (4), comment h, p. 369.)

. . . .

In the present case, Ms. Ashcraft's claim of battery rested on the theory that although the operation was consented to, the consent was subject to a specific condition: only family donated blood would be used. If Ms. Ashcraft could establish the existence of this condition and its breach by Dr. King, she would establish a battery.

II. Plaintiff Introduced Sufficient Evidence of Battery to Have the Claim Determined by the Jury.

At the close of evidence from both parties the trial court granted defendant's motion for nonsuit as to the cause of action for battery. For the reasons discussed below, granting the motion was prejudicial error.

. . . .

It is equally well settled what elements Ms. Ashcraft had to introduce evidence of in order to survive a motion for nonsuit. A battery is any intentional, unlawful and harmful contact by one person with the person of another. A harmful contact, intentionally done is the essence of a battery. A contact is "unlawful" if it is unconsented to. In order to recover on a theory of battery, Ms. Ashcraft had to establish: (1) her consent to the operation was conditioned on the use of only family donated blood; (2) defendant intentionally violated this condition while performing the operation; (3) Ms. Ashcraft suffered harm as a result of defendant's violation of the condition.

At trial it was undisputed no family donated blood was used in the operation on Ms. Ashcraft. It was also undisputed some of the blood given Ms. Ashcraft in the operation was contaminated with the Human Immuno-deficiency Virus (HIV), the cause of AIDS, and that as a result Ms. Ashcraft is HIV positive. Therefore, the questions on appeal are whether, accepting all evidence favorable to the plaintiff as true, . . . there was sufficient evidence from which the jury could have determined Ms. Ashcraft's consent to the operation was conditioned on the use of family donated blood only and that defendant intentionally exceeded this condition in performing the operation.

We have concluded Ms. Ashcraft's evidence was sufficient to meet this test and, thereby, overcome the motion for nonsuit.

A. Consent Conditional On Family Donated Blood

Based on the testimony of Ms. Ashcraft and her mother that they wanted only "family blood" used in the operation and defendant's acknowledgement: "that's fine," and his instruction to the Ashcrafts to contact the hospital to make arrangements, the jury could have found Ms. Ashcraft's consent to the operation was conditioned on the use of "family blood."

B. Intent to Act in Excess of the Conditional Consent

In an action for civil battery the element of intent is satisfied if the evidence shows defendant acted with a "willful disregard" of the plaintiff's rights. In the context of battery in a medical procedure, "[w]hen the patient gives permission to perform one type of treatment and the doctor performs another, the requisite element of deliberate intent to deviate from the consent given is present."

Evidence in this case showed defendant had permission to operate on condition he used family donated blood but that he operated using blood from the hospital's general supply. . . . [T]his evidence was sufficient to allow the jury to infer an intent to willfully disregard plaintiff's conditional consent.

Disposition

The judgment is reversed only as to plaintiff's cause of action for battery and, as to that cause of action, the matter is remanded to the trial court for further proceedings consistent with this opinion. In all other respects, the judgment is affirmed. Each party to bear its own costs on appeal.

LILLIE, P.J., and FRED WOODS, J., concur.

The court's list of the elements that the plaintiff had to prove included the requirement that she "suffered harm as a result of defendant's violation of the condition." What does the court mean by this? Would there have been an injury to the plaintiff if the blood had not been tainted?

2. The Sports Arena

MARCHETTI v. KALISH
Supreme Court of Ohio, 1990
559 N.E.2d 699

In June 1982, thirteen-year-old plaintiff-appellee, Angela Marchetti, had several neighborhood friends over to her house, including Richard Kalish, age fifteen, to play a game called "kick the can." . . .

On the day in question, the children were playing a modified version of the game. Their variations included the use of a ball instead of a can, and the first player captured immediately became the new "it." While appellee was the person designated "it," she spotted appellant and ran to home base. Appellee placed her left foot on the ball and shouted appellant's name. Under the rules of the game, appellant was supposed to stop and in turn become "it." Appellant, however, continued to run towards appellee, colliding with her and kicking the ball out from under her foot. Appellee fell to the ground, and her right leg was broken in two places.

Appellee filed a complaint on October 19, 1987, alleging appellant had "negligently and/or willfully, wantonly and maliciously" caused the above injury. The trial court granted appellant's motion for summary judgment, relying on *Hanson v. Kynast* (1987), 38 Ohio App. 3d 58, 526 N.E.2d 327, for the proposition that a participant in a recreational or athletic sporting event can recover only for an intentional tort. The trial court found that in the appellee's deposition she admitted that she did not believe that the defendant had intended to injure her during the game. The trial court also held that as a voluntary participant in the game, appellee had assumed the risk of her injury.

The court of appeals reversed the trial court and remanded the cause, holding that an issue of fact existed as to whether appellee consented to appellant's action through her participation in the game. The court adopted 1 Restatement of the Law 2d, Torts (1965), Section 50, and 4 Restatement of the Law 2d, Torts (1979), Section 892A, and rejected the holding in *Hanson, supra*. Finding its decision to be in conflict with the decision of the Fifth District Court of Appeals in *Hanson*, the court certified the record of this case to this court for review and final determination.

ALICE ROBIE RESNICK, JUSTICE.

The issue for this court's determination is whether a participant in a recreational or sporting activity can recover for personal injuries received during the course of the activity absent evidence of reckless or intentional conduct.[2] Stated differently,

---

[2] We will employ the term "intentional" as it is defined in 1 Restatement of the Law 2d, Torts (1965) 15, Section 8A. Likewise, we shall employ the term "reckless" as it is defined in 2 Restatement of the Law 2d, Torts (1965) 587, Section 500. Respectively, these definitions are as follows:

"The word 'intent' is used throughout the Restatement of this Subject to denote that the actor desires to cause consequences of his act, or that he believes that the consequences are substantially certain to result from it." Restatement of Torts 2d, Section 8A.

the question is whether a showing of negligence will suffice to allow recovery under these circumstances. The court of appeals adopted Sections 50 and 892A of the Restatement of Torts 2d, and essentially applied a negligence standard. Since these issues have not been previously addressed by this court, we must determine the proper standard as to the liability of persons engaging in a recreational or sporting activity.

I

Legal commentators have identified three distinct standards which are used by some jurisdictions to permit recovery for injuries received during sports and recreational activities: (1) intentional tort, i.e., assault and battery; (2) willful or reckless misconduct; and (3) negligence. However, courts traditionally have not been inclined to allow a cause of action for injuries received during participation in such activities. In *Kuehner v. Green* (Fla. 1983), 436 So. 2d 78, 81, Justice Boyd, concurring specially, noted that "[h]istorically, the courts have been reluctant to allow persons to recover money damages for injuries received while participating in a sport, especially a contact sport, unless there was a deliberate attempt to injure. In denying recovery, the courts have often explained that a person who participates in a sport assumes the risk that he or she may be injured. Only recently have some courts allowed a sport participant to recover damages for injuries resulting from unintentional but reckless misconduct. These courts reasoned that a sport participant does not assume the risk of injuries resulting from bodily contact uncustomary to or prohibited by the rules of the particular sport."

Likewise, while allowing a recovery for a sports injury based on intentional tort, a Michigan court has stated that "[participation in a game involves a manifestation of consent to those bodily contacts which are permitted by the rules of the game. Restatement of Torts, 2d, § 50, comment b. However, there is a general agreement that an intentional act causing injury, which goes beyond what is ordinarily permissible, is an assault and battery for which recovery may be had." *Overall v. Kadella* (1984), 138 Mich. App. 351, 361 N.W.2d 352, 355. Thus, courts generally allow a cause of action for injuries sustained in recreational or sports activities only under reckless or intentional tort theories.

In *Hanson, supra,* the court of appeals held that there is no liability for participants in an athletic competition for conduct which falls short of an intentional tort. The court in *Hanson* was confronted with a plaintiff injured while competing in a collegiate lacrosse match. The court stated that " . . . the only cause of action in the instant situation that can exist (and thus survive a summary judgment motion) is an intentional tort. . . ." *Id.*, 38 Ohio App. 3d at 60, 526 N.E.2d at 329. . . .

"The actor's conduct is in reckless disregard of the safety of another if he does an act or intentionally fails *to* do an act which it is his duty to the other *to* do, knowing or having reason to know of facts which would lead a reasonable man to realize, not only that his conduct creates an unreasonable risk of physical harm to another, but also that such risk is substantially greater than that which is necessary to make his conduct negligent." Restatement of Torts 2d, Section 500.

II

Appellee argues that [the] cases from other jurisdictions are distinguishable from the present case because here we are dealing with children involved in a simple neighborhood game rather than an organized contact sport. However, courts in other jurisdictions have not made this distinction as to whether the injury arises in an organized activity, neighborhood game, or whether it involves children or adults.

The common thread in [the cited] cases and the instant case is that the children involved were engaging in some type of recreational or sports activity. Whether the activity is organized, unorganized, supervised or unsupervised is immaterial to the standard of liability. To hold otherwise would open the floodgates to a myriad of lawsuits involving the backyard games of children. Furthermore, the courts in [the cited cases] did not differentiate between adults' and children's recreational and sports activities. Rather, the courts applied the same standard of liability to children's sports activities as to those of adults.

Additionally, appellee urges this court to follow the court of appeals in adopting the view taken in the Restatement of Torts 2d, Sections 50 and 892A. These sections provide as follows:

"892A. Effect of Consent

"(1) One who effectively consents to conduct of another intended to invade his interests cannot recover in an action of tort for the conduct or for harm resulting from it.

"(2) To be effective, consent must be

"(a) by one who has the capacity to consent or by a person empowered to consent for him, and

"(b) to the particular conduct, or to substantially the same conduct.

"(3) Conditional consent or consent restricted as to time, area or in other respects is effective only within the limits of the condition or restriction.

"(4) If the actor exceeds the consent, it is not effective for the excess.

"(5) Upon termination of consent its effectiveness is terminated, except as it may have become irrevocable by contract or otherwise, or except as its terms may include, expressly or by implication, a privilege to continue to act."

"50. Apparent Consent.

"The rule stated in § 892(2) as to apparent consent to the invasion of an interest applies to the intentional invasion of interests of personality."

Comment b to Section 50 of the Restatement provides as follows:

"*Taking part in a game.* Taking part in a game manifests a willingness to submit to such bodily contacts or restrictions of liberty as are permitted by its rules or usages. Participating in such a game does not manifest consent to contacts which are prohibited by rules or usages of the game if such rules or usages are designed to protect the participants and not merely to secure the better playing of the game as a test of skill. This is true although the player knows that those with or against whom he is playing are habitual violators of such rules."

The position taken by the Restatement involves an examination of the injured person's scope of consent in the context of the particular rules of the recreational or sports activity involved. Hence, the emphasis under the Restatement would be initially on the consent of the plaintiff rather than on the conduct of the other player. The next step would entail an analysis by the trial court of the applicable rules of the game or sport, and then superimposing these rules on the plaintiff's state of mind to determine the scope of his or her consent. The present case, or indeed any case involving children's recreational or sport activities, demonstrates the difficulty associated with this standard. We believe that requiring courts to delve into the minds of children to determine whether they understand the rules of the recreational or sports activity they are engaging in could lead to anomalous results. In this context, we perceive no reason to distinguish between children and adults. The policy which we and other courts seek to advance was set forth in *Nabozny [v. Barnhill*, 31 Ill. App. 3d 212, 215, 334 N.E.2d 258, 260 (1975)]: "[T]he law should not place unreasonable burdens on the free and vigorous participation in sports by our youth. However, we also believe that organized, athletic competition does not exist in a vacuum. Rather, some of the restraints of civilization must accompany every athlete onto the playing field. One of the educational benefits of organized athletic competition to our youth is the development of discipline and self-control." . . . [O]ur goal is to strike a balance between encouraging vigorous and free participation in recreational or sports activities, while ensuring the safety of the players. The standard announced today does not curtail, but indeed enhances this objective, regardless of whether the participants are children or adults.

We therefore decline to adopt the analysis under the Restatement of Torts 2d, Sections 50 and 892A. Traditional tort concepts place the emphasis on the conduct or actions of the tort-feasor. Thus, we join the weight of authority set forth above and require that before a party may proceed with a cause of action involving injury resulting from a recreational or sports activity, reckless or intentional conduct must exist.[3] We hold that where individuals engage in recreational or sports activities,

---

[3] Comments *f* and *g* to Section 500 of the Restatement of Torts 2d, *supra*, at 590, provide a concise analysis which differentiates between the three mental states of tortious conduct with which we are confronted. Without further discourse, we cite to these comments with approval. They provide as follows:

"*f. Intentional misconduct and recklessness contrasted.* Reckless misconduct differs from intentional wrongdoing in a very important particular. While an act to be reckless must be intended by the actor, the actor does not intend to cause the harm which results from it. It is enough that he realizes or, from facts which he knows, should realize that there is a strong probability that harm may result, even though he hopes or even expects that his conduct will prove harmless. However, a strong probability is a different thing from the substantial certainty without which he cannot be said to intend the harm in which his act results."

"*g. Negligence and recklessness contrasted.* Reckless misconduct differs from negligence in several important particulars. It differs from that form of negligence which consists in mere inadvertence, incompetence, unskillfulness, or a failure to take precautions to enable the actor adequately to cope with a possible or probable future emergency, in that reckless misconduct requires a conscious choice of a course of action, either with knowledge of the serious danger to others involved in it or with knowledge of facts which would disclose this danger to any reasonable man. It differs not only from the above-mentioned form of negligence, but also

they assume the ordinary risks of the activity and cannot recover for any injury unless it can be shown that the other participant's actions were either "reckless" or "intentional" as defined in Sections 500 and 8A of the Restatement of Torts 2d.

In the present case, plaintiff-appellee's own testimony demonstrates that appellant did not act either recklessly or intentionally. Thus, there is no question of fact that needs to be resolved regarding this material issue. Additionally, appellee is deemed to have assumed the risk by voluntarily participating in the game. Since there has been no showing of reckless or intentional conduct on the part of appellant, the trial court was correct in granting summary judgment in appellant's favor. We reverse the judgment of the court of appeals and reinstate the trial court's judgment.

Judgment reversed.

MOYER, C.J., concurs separately.

KOFFMAN v. GARNETT
Supreme Court of Virginia, 2003
574 S.E.2d 258

LACY, J.

In the fall of 2000, Andrew W. Koffman, a 13-year old middle school student at a public school in Botetourt County, began participating on the school's football team. It was Andy's first season playing organized football, and he was positioned as a third-string defensive player. James Garnett was employed by the Botetourt County School Board as an assistant coach for the football team and was responsible for the supervision, training, and instruction of the team's defensive players.

The team lost its first game of the season. Garnett was upset by the defensive players' inadequate tackling in that game and became further displeased by what he perceived as inadequate tackling during the first practice following the loss.

Garnett ordered Andy to hold a football and "stand upright and motionless" so that Garnett could explain the proper tackling technique to the defensive players. Then Garnett, without further warning, thrust his arms around Andy's body, lifted him "off his feet by two feet or more," and "slammed" him to the ground. Andy weighed 144 pounds, while Garnett weighed approximately 260 pounds. The force of the tackle broke the humerus bone in Andy's left arm. During prior practices, no coach had used physical force to instruct players on rules or techniques of playing football.

---

from that negligence which consists in intentionally doing an act with knowledge that it contains a risk of harm to others, in that the actor to be reckless must recognize that his conduct involves a risk substantially greater in amount than that which is necessary to make his conduct negligent. The difference between reckless misconduct and conduct involving only such a quantum of risk as is necessary to make it negligent is a difference in the degree of the risk, but this difference of degree is so marked as to amount substantially to a difference in kind."

In his second amended motion for judgment, Andy, by his father and next friend, Richard Koffman, and Andy's parents, Richard and Rebecca Koffman, individually, (collectively "the Koffmans") alleged that Andy was injured as a result of Garnett's . . . intentional acts of assault and battery. Garnett filed a demurrer and plea of sovereign immunity, asserting that the second amended motion for judgment did not allege sufficient facts to support a lack of consent to the tackling demonstration and, therefore, did not plead causes of action for either, . . . assault, or battery. The trial court dismissed the action, finding that . . . the facts alleged were insufficient to state causes of action for gross negligence, assault, or battery because the instruction and playing of football are "inherently dangerous and always potentially violent."

In this appeal, the Koffmans . . . assert that they pled sufficient facts in their second amended motion for judgment to sustain their claims of . . . assault and battery. . . .

The second amended motion for judgment is sufficient, however, to establish a cause of action for the tort of battery. The Koffmans pled that Andy consented to physical contact with players "of like age and experience" and that neither Andy nor his parents expected or consented to his "participation in aggressive contact tackling by the adult coaches." Further, the Koffmans pled that, in the past, coaches had not tackled players as a method of instruction. Garnett asserts that, by consenting to play football, Andy consented to be tackled, by either other football players or by the coaches.

Whether Andy consented to be tackled by Garnett in the manner alleged was a matter of fact. Based on the allegations in the Koffmans' second amended motion for judgment, reasonable persons could disagree on whether Andy gave such consent. Thus, we find that the trial court erred in holding that the Koffmans' second amended motion for judgment was insufficient as a matter of law to establish a claim for battery.

For the above reasons, we will reverse the trial court's judgment that the Koffmans' second amended motion for judgment was insufficient as a matter of law to establish the cause of action for . . . battery and remand the case for further proceedings consistent with this opinion.

Reversed and remanded.

DISSENT

JUSTICE KINSER, concurring in part and dissenting in part.

I agree with the majority opinion except with regard to the issue of consent as it pertains to the intentional tort of battery. In my view, the second amended motion for judgment filed by the plaintiff was insufficient as a matter of law to state a claim for battery.

Absent fraud, consent is generally a defense to an alleged battery. In the context of this case, "taking part in a game manifests a willingness to submit to such bodily

contacts or restrictions of liberty as are permitted by its rules or usages."
*Restatement (Second) of Torts β 50, cmt. b (1965), quoted in Thompson v. McNeill,
53 Ohio St. 3d 102, 559 N.E.2d 705, 708 (Ohio 1990).* However, participating in a
particular sport "does not manifest consent to contacts which are prohibited by
rules or usages of the game if such rules or usages are designed to protect the
participants and not merely to secure the better playing of the game as a test of
skill." *Restatement (Second) of Torts β 50, cmt. b (1965) quoted in Thompson, 559
N.E.2d at 708.*

. . . .

---

1. How is this situation different from that in *Marchetti*? In other words, why
can battery be alleged here and not in *Marchetti*?

2. Is this case more similar, in facts and reasoning, to *Marchetti* or *Hackbart,
infra*?

3. Should the court consider Koffman's age (13 years) to show inability to
consent? How does this case differ from *C.C.H v. Philadelphia Phillies, Inc., infra*,
where the nature of the tort in question was sexual?

HACKBART v. CINCINNATI BENGALS, INC.
United States Court of Appeals, Tenth Circuit, 1979
601 F.2d 516

Before DOYLE, MCKAY and LOGAN, CIRCUIT JUDGES.

DOYLE, CIRCUIT JUDGE,

The question in this case is whether in a regular season professional football
game an injury which is inflicted by one professional football player on an opposing
player can give rise to liability in tort where the injury was inflicted by the
intentional striking of a blow during the game.

The injury occurred in the course of a game between the Denver Broncos and the
Cincinnati Bengals, which game was being played in Denver in 1973. The Broncos'
defensive back, Dale Hackbart, was the recipient of the injury and the Bengals'
offensive back, Charles "Booby" Clark, inflicted the blow which produced it.

By agreement the liability question was determined by the United States
District Court for the District of Colorado without a jury. The judge resolved the
liability issue in favor of the Cincinnati team and Charles Clark. Consistent with this
result, final judgment was entered for Cincinnati and the appeal challenges this
judgment. In essence the trial court's reasons for rejecting plaintiff's claim were
that professional football is a species of warfare and that so much physical force is
tolerated and the magnitude of the force exerted is so great that it renders injuries
not actionable in court; that even intentional batteries are beyond the scope of the
judicial process.

Clark was an offensive back and just before the injury he had run a pass pattern to the right side of the Denver Broncos' end zone. The injury flowed indirectly from this play. The pass was intercepted by Billy Thompson, a Denver free safety, who returned it to mid-field. The subject injury occurred as an aftermath of the pass play.

As a consequence of the interception, the roles of Hackbart and Clark suddenly changed. Hackbart, who had been defending, instantaneously became an offensive player. Clark, on the other hand, became a defensive player. Acting as an offensive player, Hackbart attempted to block Clark by throwing his body in front of him. He thereafter remained on the ground. He turned, and with one knee on the ground, watched the play following the interception.

The trial court's finding was that Charles Clark, "acting out of anger and frustration, but without a specific intent to injure . . . stepped forward and struck a blow with his right forearm to the back of the kneeling plaintiff's head and neck with sufficient force to cause both players to fall forward to the ground." Both players, without complaining to the officials or to one another, returned to their respective sidelines since the ball had changed hands and the offensive and defensive teams of each had been substituted. Clark testified at trial that his frustration was brought about by the fact that his team was losing the game.

Due to the failure of the officials to view the incident, a foul was not called. However, the game film showed very clearly what had occurred. Plaintiff did not at the time report the happening to his coaches or to anyone else during the game. However, because of the pain which he experienced he was unable to play golf the next day. He did not seek medical attention, but the continued pain caused him to report this fact and the incident to the Bronco trainer who gave him treatment. Apparently he played on the specialty teams for two successive Sundays, but after that the Broncos released him on waivers. (He was in his thirteenth year as a player.) He sought medical help and it was then that it was discovered by the physician that he had a serious neck fracture injury.

Despite the fact that the defendant Charles Clark admitted that the blow which had been struck was not accidental, that it was intentionally administered, the trial court ruled as a matter of law that the game of professional football is basically a business which is violent in nature, and that the available sanctions are imposition of penalties and expulsion from the game. Notice was taken of the fact that many fouls are overlooked; that the game is played in an emotional and noisy environment; and that incidents such as that here complained of are not unusual.

The trial court spoke as well of the unreasonableness of applying the laws and rules which are a part of injury law to the game of professional football, noting the unreasonableness of holding that one player has a duty of care for the safety of others. He also talked about the concept of assumption of risk and contributory fault as applying and concluded that Hackbart had to recognize that he accepted the risk that he would be injured by such an act.

I.

THE ISSUES AND CONTENTIONS

1. Whether the trial court erred in ruling that as a matter of policy the principles of law governing the infliction of injuries should be entirely refused where the injury took place in the course of the game.

. . . .

II.

WHETHER THE EVIDENCE SUPPORTED THE JUDGMENT

The evidence at the trial uniformly supported the proposition that the intentional striking of a player in the head from the rear is not an accepted part of either the playing rules or the general customs of the game of professional football. The trial court, however, believed that the unusual nature of the case called for the consideration of underlying policy which it defined as common law principles which have evolved as a result of the case to case process and which necessarily affect behavior in various contexts. From these considerations the belief was expressed that even *intentional* injuries incurred in football games should be outside the framework of the law. The court recognized that the potential threat of legal liability has a significant deterrent effect, and further said that private civil actions constitute an important mechanism for societal control of human conduct. Due to the increase in severity of human conflicts, a need existed to expand the body of governing law more rapidly and with more certainty, but that this had to be accomplished by legislation and administrative regulation. The judge compared football to coal mining and railroading insofar as all are inherently hazardous. Judge Matsch said that in the case of football it was questionable whether social values would be improved by limiting the violence.

Thus the district court's assumption was that Clark had inflicted an intentional blow which would ordinarily generate civil liability and which might bring about a criminal sanction as well, but that since it had occurred in the course of a football game, it should not be subject to the restraints of the law; that if it were it would place unreasonable impediments and restraints on the activity. The judge also pointed out that courts are ill-suited to decide the different social questions and to administer conflicts on what is much like a battlefield where the restraints of civilization have been left on the sidelines.

We are forced to conclude that the result reached is not supported by evidence.

III.

WHETHER INTENTIONAL INJURY IS ALLOWED BY EITHER WRITTEN RULE OR CUSTOM

Plaintiff, of course, maintains that tort law applicable to the injury in this case applies on the football field as well as in other places. On the other hand, plaintiff does not rely on the theory of negligence being applicable. This is in recognition of the fact that subjecting another to unreasonable risk of harm, the essence of negligence, is inherent in the game of football, for admittedly it is violent. Plaintiff maintains that in the area of contributory fault, a vacuum exists in relationship to intentional infliction of injury. Since negligence does not apply, contributory negligence is inapplicable. Intentional or reckless contributory fault could theoretically at least apply to infliction of injuries in reckless disregard of the rights of others. This has some similarity to contributory negligence and undoubtedly it would apply if the evidence would justify it. But it is highly questionable whether a professional football player consents or submits to injuries caused by conduct not within the rules, and there is no evidence which we have seen which shows this. However, the trial court did not consider this question and we are not deciding it.

Contrary to the position of the court then, there are no principles of law which allow a court to rule out certain tortious conduct by reason of general roughness of the game or difficulty of administering it.

Indeed, the evidence shows that there are rules of the game which prohibit the intentional striking of blows. Thus, Article 1, Item 1, Subsection C, provides that:

> All players are prohibited from striking on the head, face or neck with the heel, back or side of the hand, wrist, forearm, elbow or clasped hands.

Thus the very conduct which was present here is expressly prohibited by the rule which is quoted above.

The general customs of football do not approve the intentional punching or striking of others. That this is prohibited was supported by the testimony of all of the witnesses. They testified that the intentional striking of a player in the face or from the rear is prohibited by the playing rules as well as the general customs of the game. Punching or hitting with the arms is prohibited. Undoubtedly these restraints are intended to establish reasonable boundaries so that one football player cannot intentionally inflict a serious injury on another. Therefore, the notion is not correct that all reason has been abandoned whereby the only possible remedy for the person who has been the victim of an unlawful blow is retaliation.

. . . .

The cause is reversed and remanded for a new trial in accordance with the foregoing views.

----

1. Is it possible to formulate a general rule for courts to apply where the injuries are incurred during a sporting event? If so, what would such a rule look like?

2. Should a rule for sporting events differentiate among professional, amateur, and informal contexts? If so, what is the basis for treating such contexts differently? If not, why not?

3. When a sporting event involves children, what standard should the court use? What if a child has no idea what the risks are?

4. What role should the rules and regulations of a game play in a court's decision? If the player has been penalized by an official such as a referee, should the imposition of the penalty have an impact upon the court's decision? If so, what should that impact be? The court in *Hackbart* rejected the idea that the game should be governed solely by referees, with the corollary that judges should stay out of it.

PROBLEMS

1. P, who is nine, plays softball with a league that uses a pitching machine instead of a person, so that each pitch will be perfect. One day, the pitching machine is out of order. The league officials agree that the teams which are scheduled to play that day will use their coaches as pitchers instead of the machine.

P, while up at bat, is struck in the chest by a pitch and severely injured. P sues the coach for battery. What result?

2. C and D play for different professional football teams. They have hated each other for years, and their rivalry, which is highly promoted by the television network which carries football games, is a source of higher television ratings for their teams, as the viewers enjoy the enhanced competition and roughness of the games when C and D's teams play against each other.

C and D, who often end up brawling but who rarely hurt each other seriously, engage in a fight during a playoff game. This time, C is seriously injured. When an intrepid referee tries to stop the fight, he is trampled by both players, neither of whom sees him before stepping on him.

C sues D for battery. The referee sues C, D, their teams, and the network for battery. What arguments will the parties make? How will the court rule?

3. Consent in Other Arenas

TEOLIS v. MOSCATELLI
Supreme Court of Rhode Island, 1923
119 A. 161

RATHBURN, J.

This is an action of trespass for assault and battery. The trial in the superior court resulted in a verdict for plaintiff for $750. [The trial court denied defendants' motion for a new trial, and defendants appealed.] . . .

The assault resulted from a dispute between the plaintiff and defendants relative to a division fence. The plaintiff accepted the challenge of defendant Moscatelli to go into the highway and fight. After proceeding to the highway plaintiff removed his coat, and was immediately stabbed with a knife by defendant Moscatelli. Plaintiff testified that defendant Neri held him and told Moscatelli to "give it to him."

The defendants contend that the plaintiff, having agreed to fight, consented to the assault, and that such consent is a bar to recovery. The plaintiff agreed to engage in a fist fight. He never consented to being assaulted with a knife or held by Neri while Moscatelli wielded the knife.

The defendants' contention that an agreement to fight is a bar to recovery for injuries received in the course of combat by one of the participants and inflicted by the other is also untenable. As an agreement to break the peace is void, the maxim, "Volenti non fit injuria," does not apply. See authorities cited in 5 Corpus Juris, page 630, where the rule is stated as follows:

"By the weight of authority consent will not avail as a defense in a case of mutual combat, as such fighting is unlawful; and hence the acceptance of a challenge to fight, and voluntarily engaging in a fight by one party with another, because of the challenge, cannot be set up as a defense in a civil suit for damages for an assault and battery, although it seems that such consent may be shown in mitigation of damages."

. . . .

All of the defendants' exceptions are overruled, and the case is remitted to the superior court, with direction to enter Judgement on the verdict.

One of the most important reasons for the development of battery law (and, indeed, intentional tort law generally) was to keep the peace by preventing parties from taking the law into their own hands. Requiring that parties go to court to settle their differences accomplished this goal, because parties could obtain a remedy without the need to resort to violence. In order to make the availability of a remedy a complete cure for the problem of individual violence, however, the courts needed to penalize those who bypass the legal remedy and continue to take the law into their own hands.

In this case, the court states the rule applicable when one participant in an illegal fight sues the other. Under this rule, consent cannot operate as a defense in a battery action for injuries received in the fight, because one has no power to consent to an illegal act. On the hypothesis that the plaintiff will usually be the loser of the fight, does this rule deter illegal fighting? How should the situation be handled in order to accomplish the goal of deterring breaches of the peace?

C.C.H. v. PHILADELPHIA PHILLIES, INC.
Supreme Court of Pennsylvania, 2008
596 Pa. 23, 940 A.2d 336

Appellant T.G., a minor girl, was 11 years of age at the time she was allegedly sexually assaulted by Appellees Joseph Fabrizzio, John Scaruzzi, and Michael Ibbetson. She subsequently brought a civil action seeking damages against the individual defendants . . . The individual defendants defended, in part, by asserting that T.G. consented to sexual activities with them and, therefore, there was no sexual assault. There is no dispute that, given T.G.'s age, 11, consent would not be available as a defense if the individual defendants were charged criminally. The question before us regarding the individual defendants is whether the defense of consent may be asserted in this civil action. The trial court and the Superior Court concluded that, in the context of a civil trial, defendants are permitted to raise a minor victim's consent. For the following reasons, we conclude that, where the victim is less than 13 years of age, evidence of the victim's consent to sexual contact, like in criminal proceedings, is not an available defense in determining a defendant's civil liability. Accordingly, we reverse the Order of the Superior Court affirming the trial court with respect to the individual defendants, and remand the matter to the Superior Court with instructions to remand to the trial court for a new trial.

The Pennsylvania Criminal Code defines various crimes so as to make the defense of consent invalid where the victim is a minor under 13 years of age. For example, where a person commits rape of a child less than 13.

The relevant facts of this case are as follows. On August 9, 2000, T.G. was attending a Phillies baseball game at Veteran's Stadium in Philadelphia with an adult family friend. At some point during the game, T.G. was separated from her guardian and became lost inside the stadium. T.G. asserts that she then sought help from the Phillies' security personnel, who T.G. alleges failed to assist her in finding her guardian, in contravention to the team's "Lost People Policy." It is undisputed, however, that she eventually encountered the individual defendants, who were then 15 and 16 years old and employed at a concession stand at the stadium. According to T.G., these defendants offered to help her locate a telephone, but instead led her to a secluded area outside the stadium where they forcibly removed her clothes and sexually assaulted her. [W]hile the parties disagree on whether intercourse occurred, they all agree that some type of sexual contact took place.

Reversed and remanded.

---

1. Should it matter that T.G. flirted with the boys or went outside with them voluntarily, as one of the defense attorneys stated? Do these actions have a strong enough relation with consent to sexual activity to matter in the court's analysis?

2. This is an intentional tort. Will the Philadelphia Phillies, Inc. be held liable for the acts of their employees?

THOMAS v. BEDFORD
Court of Appeal of Louisiana, Second Circuit, 1980
389 So. 2d 405

Before PRICE, JASPER E. JONES and FRED W. JONES, JR., JJ.

FRED W. JONES, JR., JUDGE.

Anna Spear Goff Thomas, as the natural tutrix of her minor son, Joseph A. Goff, filed this suit against Carter Bedford, a Caddo Parish school teacher, the Caddo Parish School Board, and the latter's liability insurance carrier, Reliance Insurance Company, for injuries allegedly sustained by the minor because of a battery committed by Bedford at a Caddo Parish School.

Plaintiff appeals from a district court judgment rejecting her demands. We reverse and render judgment for plaintiff.

The incident in question occurred in February 1979 at the Northwood High School in Caddo Parish. Goff, a student at the school, was 14 years of age, weighed between 95 and 100 pounds, and was 4 feet 9 inches in height. Bedford, a teacher at the school, was 26 years of age, weighed between 135 and 140 pounds, and was 5 feet 9 inches in height. The two had become acquainted the previous year when Goff was in one of Bedford's classes. The record indicated that, although not a serious disciplinary problem, Goff tended to engage in mischievous behavior, some of which had been occasionally directed at Bedford.

On the afternoon of February 15, 1979, while Bedford was standing outside a classroom at the high school conversing with two other teachers, Goff came up and struck Bedford a light blow in the back with his hand. Instead of going to his class as instructed by Bedford, Goff picked up a rubber band and from a distance of about two feet propelled it into Bedford's face. Goff then turned and ran into his classroom, chased by Bedford who threw a two foot long 1 by 2 board at the youngster, but missed him.

Bedford left and went to his classroom where he remained for ten or fifteen minutes. He then returned to Goff's classroom and pulled the youngster into an adjoining vacant "project" room where the altercation in question took place. Bedford testified that he gave Goff a "severe shaking." On the other hand, Goff stated that Bedford struck him three or four times on the body with his fist. The statement of the physician who examined Goff, finding that the youngster had contusions of the chest, arms and back, tended to corroborate Goff's version of the incident.

It is now recognized that "corporal punishment, reasonable in degree, administered by a teacher to a pupil for disciplinary reasons, is permitted in Louisiana." *Roy v. Continental Insurance Co.*, 313 So. 2d 349 (La. App. 3rd Cir. 1975). Further elaborating, the court in *Roy* commented:

"It is also a well established rule in general tort law that a teacher is immune from civil liability for physical corporal punishment, reasonable in degree, administered to a student. But it is likewise clear under tort law that this discretionary right of a teacher to use physical punishment is a limited one and immunity or privilege from liability requires a showing that said punishment was administered neither unreasonably nor excessively, measured in part by such factors as the nature of the punishment itself, the misconduct of the child, the teacher's motive in the discipline, and the age and physical condition of the pupil. The question of 'reasonableness' or 'excessiveness' is determined on a case by case basis. . . ."

The rationale of these cases, which we adopt, is that a minor's school teacher, while the youngster is attending school, stands in the place of the parent for the purpose of enforcing discipline and, in connection therewith, may use a reasonable degree of corporal punishment. The factual question presented by each individual case is whether the punishment was unreasonable or excessive under the circumstances.

In his written reasons for judgment in this case the trial judge concluded that "although the teacher's action *greatly exceeded reasonable force* (emphasis added), nevertheless, there is sufficient provocation by plaintiff for Mr. Bedford to have lost his temper in rendering corporal punishment on Joseph Goff." In a previous portion of that opinion the minor had been characterized as the "aggressor."

The "aggressor doctrine" contemplates an altercation provoked by the aggressor against a party who defends himself. Even if, under the facts of this case, Goff's striking Bedford in the back and hitting him with a rubber band rendered him an aggressor, it is obvious that the subsequent altercation in the "project" room, some 10 or 15 minutes later after Bedford had admittedly calmed down, was in fact a separate incident and not a spontaneous reaction to the original provocation. Therefore, the "aggressor doctrine" is inapplicable. The pivotal issue here is whether the corporal punishment meted out by Bedford was unreasonable. The trial judge explicitly answered that question in the affirmative. Since this is a factual question and our review of the record does not show that the trial judge was clearly wrong in his conclusion, we must accept that ruling. Consequently, under our jurisprudence Bedford, his employer and the latter's insurance carrier are liable for Goff's injuries.

Legitimate concern for disciplinary problems in our schools ably articulated by the conscientious trial judge, does not permit us to disregard our responsibility to accord due deference to the rights of *all* those participants in the educational process, students as well as teachers and administrators. Needless to say, our law does not by any means render the latter impotent in the face of rule infractions. Where appropriate, corporal punishment may be administered in a reasonable manner as a measured, rational response to serious acts of misconduct.

. . . .

For the reasons set forth, we reverse the judgment of the trial court. . . .

———————

Assume that B (with a gun) is coming at A. A therefore shoots at B, but misses and hits C.

Reasonable Force. A, the person threatened, is privileged to use reasonable force to defend himself. The force used must parallel the force threatened. If B is unarmed, A cannot shoot him.

Injury to a Bystander. C, the bystander, does not recover, if the force used by A was reasonable and parallel. W. Page Keeton et al., Prosser and Keeton on Torts 124–25 (5th ed. 1984)

———

1.   Would the result in this case have been different if Bedford had immediately "punished" Goff instead of waiting the ten or fifteen minutes in question?

2.   Should a school be able to administer corporal punishment over parental objections? *See Suits v. Glover*, 71 So. 2d 49 (Ala. 1954).

3.   The Eighth Amendment to the United States Constitution forbids cruel and unusual punishment. Is it constitutional for teachers and administrators to administer corporal punishment for disciplinary purposes? *See Baker v. Owen*, 395 F. Supp. 294 (M.D.N.C.), *aff'd*, 423 U.S. 907 (1975).

4.   *Retreating to the Wall.* Before deadly force is used the "northern" rule is that the person using deadly force must "retreat to the wall." The "southern" rule does not require that the person using deadly force must first "retreat to the wall." *See* W. Page Keeton et al., Prosser and Keeton on Torts 124–25 (5th ed. 1984).

B.   DEFENSES TO FALSE IMPRISONMENT

NOGUCHI v. NAKAMURA
Intermediate Court of Appeals of Hawaii, 1982
638 P.2d 1383

Before Hayashi, C.J., and Padgett and Burns, JJ.

Per Curiam.

This is an appeal from an order granting a directed verdict on a claim of false imprisonment. We reverse.

The complaint herein asserted two claims for relief: one based on negligence and one on false imprisonment. The court below directed a verdict on the false imprisonment claim and the jury found for the appellee on the negligence claim.

Basically, appellant testified that she and appellee had been girlfriend and boyfriend. She had come to the conclusion that she did not wish to go out with him anymore. On the day in question, he came to see her and asked her to go with him on a date that evening. She refused. After some conversation, he asked her to at least go to the store with him and she consented on the condition, which he agreed to, that he would bring her right back. She then entered his car and they proceeded to the store and returned, stopping in front of her house. She was seated in the car with the car door open when he suddenly drove off. At some point thereafter, she fell, was pushed or jumped from the car, sustaining the injuries complained of.

The tort of false imprisonment is defined in 2 Restatement of Torts 2d, § 35 (1965) as follows:

False Imprisonment

(1) An actor is subject to liability to another for false imprisonment if

(a) he acts intending to confine the other or a third person within boundaries fixed by the actor, and

(b) his act directly or indirectly results in such a confinement of the other, and

(c) the other is conscious of the confinement or is harmed by it.

Of course, it goes without saying that one who consents to being placed within a limited and enclosed space by the other is not legally confined.

Obviously, a moving automobile, because of the danger of any egress therefrom, can constitute a place of confinement. 2 Restatement of Torts 2d, § 36 (1965), ex. 9 at 56.

Appellee contends, however, that since appellant originally entered the car voluntarily, some threat against her to prevent her leaving must have been made or she was at least under an obligation when the car was stopped in front of her parents' home to express a refusal to go further. We do not regard such to be the law. She had refused to go anywhere on the day in question with the appellee but to the store and back. She was back; she was in front of her parents' house, and she had the car door open when appellee suddenly started off. A jury could well have found from her testimony that her consent to go anywhere with the appellee on the day in question was limited to going to the store and back; that she had previously expressly told him she would not go out with him that evening, so that the limited consent had expired; and that her having the door open in the stopped car in front of her parents' home reindicated her lack of consent to any further movement.

. . . .

[T]here was sufficient evidence to go to the jury on the claim of false imprisonment.

Because of our disposition of the question of the sufficiency of the evidence, we do not reach the other errors alleged.

Reversed and remanded for a new trial.

---

1. How subjective should determinations of consent be? From whose perspective, the plaintiff's or defendant's, should the issue of consent be approached? Should a reasonable person standard simply be used for everyone involved?

2. What amount of damages should the plaintiff recover? Should the amount of recovery depend upon why the plaintiff fell from the car? If she jumped from the car, should her injuries be compensable? Does the answer to this depend upon why

she jumped (if she did)?

PETERSON v. SORLIEN
Supreme Court of Minnesota, 1980
299 N.W.2d 123

SHERAN, CHIEF JUSTICE.

This action by plaintiff Susan Jungclaus Peterson for false imprisonment and intentional infliction of emotional distress arises from an effort by her parents, in conjunction with other individuals named as defendants, to prompt her disaffiliation from an organization known as The Way Ministry.

At trial, the Hennepin County District Court directed a verdict in favor of defendant Paul Sorlien, plaintiff's former minister, finding the evidence proffered against him insufficient as a matter of law. The jury returned a verdict exonerating Mr. and Mrs. Jungclaus and the other remaining defendants of the charge of false imprisonment; however, the jury found defendants Veronica Morgel and Kathy Mills liable for intentional infliction of emotional distress, assessing against each of them $1 compensatory damages and $4,000 and $6,000 respectively as punitive damages.

Plaintiff asserts that the trial court erred by 1) failing to grant a judgment notwithstanding the verdict on the claim of false imprisonment; 2) permitting the admission of evidence concerning her involvement in The Way and its activities. . . .

[W]e affirm the determination of the district court.

Viewing the evidence in the light most favorable to the prevailing defendants, this case marks the emergence of a new cultural phenomenon: youth-oriented religious or pseudo-religious groups which utilize the techniques of what has been termed "coercive persuasion" or "mind control" to cultivate an uncritical and devoted following. Commentators have used the term "coercive persuasion," originally coined to identify the experience of American prisoners of war during the Korean conflict to describe the cult-induction process. The word "cult" is not used pejoratively but in its dictionary sense to describe an unorthodox system of belief characterized by "[g]reat or excessive devotion or dedication to some person, idea, or thing." Webster's New International Dictionary of the English Language Unabridged 552 (1976). Coercive persuasion is fostered through the creation of a controlled environment that heightens the susceptibility of a subject to suggestion and manipulation through sensory deprivation, physiological depletion, cognitive dissonance, peer pressure, and a clear assertion of authority and dominion. The aftermath of indoctrination is a severe impairment of autonomy and the ability to think independently, which induces a subject's unyielding compliance and the rupture of past connections, affiliations and associations. *See generally* Delgado, *Religious Totalism: Gentle and Ungentle Persuasion under the First Amendment,* 51 S. Cal. L. Rev. 1 (1977). One psychologist characterized the process of cult indoctrination as "psychological kidnapping." *Id.* at 23.

At the time of the events in question, Susan Jungclaus Peterson was 21 years old.

For most of her life, she lived with her family on a farm near Bird Island, Minnesota. In 1973, she graduated with honors from high school, ranking second in her class. She matriculated that fall at Moorhead State College. A dean's list student during her first year, her academic performance declined and her interests narrowed after she joined the local chapter of a group organized internationally and identified locally as The Way of Minnesota, Inc.

. . . .

The operation of The Way is predicated on the fund-raising activities of its members. The Way's fund-raising strategy centers upon the sale of prerecorded learning programs. Members are instructed to elicit the interest of a group of ten or twelve people and then play for them, at a charge of $85 per participant, a taped introductory course produced by The Way International. Advanced tape courses are then offered to the participants at additional cost, and training sessions are conducted to more fully acquaint recruits with the orientation of the group and the obligations of membership. Recruits must contribute a minimum of 10 percent of their earnings to the organization; to meet the tithe, student members are expected to obtain part-time employment. Members are also required to purchase books and other materials published by the ministry, and are encouraged to make larger financial contributions and to engage in more sustained efforts at solicitation.

By the end of her freshman year, Susan was devoting many hours to The Way, listening to instructional tapes, soliciting new members and assisting in training sessions. As her sophomore year began, Susan committed herself significantly, selling the car her father had given her and working part-time as a waitress to finance her contributions to The Way. Susan spent the following summer in South Dakota, living in conditions described as appalling and overcrowded, while recruiting, raising money and conducting training sessions for The Way.

As her junior year in college drew to a close, the Jungclauses grew increasingly alarmed by the personality changes they witnessed in their daughter; overly tired, unusually pale, distraught and irritable, she exhibited an increasing alienation from family, diminished interest in education and decline in academic performance. The Jungclauses, versed in the literature of youth cults and based on conversations with former members of The Way, concluded that through a calculated process of manipulation and exploitation Susan had been reduced to a condition of psychological bondage.

On May 24, 1976, defendant Norman Jungclaus, father of plaintiff, arrived at Moorhead to pick up Susan following the end of the third college quarter. Instead of returning to their family home, defendant drove with Susan to Minneapolis to the home of Veronica Morgel. Entering the home of Mrs. Mor-gel, Susan was greeted by Kathy Mills and several young people who wished to discuss Susan's involvement in the ministry. Each of those present had been in some way touched by the cult phenomenon. Kathy Mills, the leader of the group, had treated a number of former cult members, including Veronica Morgel's son. It was Kathy Mills [,] a self-styled professional deprogrammer, to whom the Jungclauses turned, and intermittently for the next sixteen days, it was in the home of Veronica Morgel that Susan stayed.

The avowed purpose of deprogramming is to break the hold of the cult over the individual through reason and confrontation. Initially, Susan was unwilling to discuss her involvement; she lay curled in a fetal position, in the downstairs bedroom where she first stayed, plugging her ears and crying while her father pleaded with her to listen to what was being said. This behavior persisted for two days during which she intermittently engaged in conversation, at one point screaming hysterically and flailing at her father. But by Wednesday Susan's demeanor had changed completely; she was friendly and vivacious and that night slept in an upstairs bedroom. Susan spent all day Thursday reading and conversing with her father and on Saturday night went roller-skating. On Sunday she played Softball at a nearby park, afterwards enjoying a picnic lunch. The next week Susan spent in Columbus, Ohio, flying there with a former cult member who had shared with her the experiences of the previous week. While in Columbus, she spoke every day by telephone to her fiance who, playing tapes and songs from the ministry's headquarters in Minneapolis, begged that she return to the fold. Susan expressed the desire to extricate her fiance from the dominion of the cult.

Susan returned to Minneapolis on June 9. Unable to arrange a controlled meeting so that Susan could see her fiance outside the presence of other members of the ministry, her parents asked that she sign an agreement releasing them from liability for their past weeks' actions. Refusing to do so, Susan stepped outside the Morgel residence with the puppy she had purchased in Ohio, motioned to a passing police car and shortly thereafter was reunited with her fiance in the Minneapolis headquarters of The Way. Following her return to the ministry, she was directed to counsel and initiated the present action.

1. Plaintiff seeks a judgment notwithstanding the verdict on the issue of false imprisonment, alleging that defendants unlawfully interfered with her personal liberty by words or acts which induced a reasonable apprehension that force would be used against her if she did not otherwise comply. The jury, instructed that an informed and reasoned consent is a defense to an allegation of false imprisonment and that a nonconsensual detention could be deemed consensual if one's behavior so indicated, exonerated defendants with respect to the false imprisonment claim.

The period in question began on Monday, May 24, 1976, and ceased on Wednesday, June 9, 1976, a period of 16 days. The record clearly demonstrates that Susan willingly remained in the company of defendants for at least 13 of those days. During that time she took many excursions into the public sphere, playing softball and picnicking in a city park, roller-skating at a public rink, flying aboard public aircraft and shopping and swimming while relaxing in Ohio. Had Susan desired, manifold opportunities existed for her to alert the authorities of her allegedly unlawful detention; in Minneapolis, two police officers observed at close range the softball game in which she engaged; en route to Ohio, she passed through the security areas of the Twin Cities and Columbus airports in the presence of security guards and uniformed police; in Columbus she transacted business at a bank, went for walks in solitude and was interviewed by an F.B.I, agent who sought assurances of her safety. At no time during the 13-day period did she complain of her treatment or suggest that defendants were holding her against her will. If one is aware of a reasonable means of escape that does not present a danger of bodily or material harm, a restriction is not total and complete and does not constitute unlawful imprisonment. Damages may not be assessed for any period of detention to which one freely consents.

In his summation to the jury, the trial judge instructed that to deem consent a defense to the charge of false imprisonment for the entire period or for any part therein, a preponderance of the evidence must demonstrate that such plaintiff voluntarily consented. The central issue for the jury, then, was whether Susan voluntarily participated in the activities of the first three days. The jury concluded that her behavior constituted a waiver.

We believe the determination to have been consistent with the evidence. Were the relationship other than that of parent and child, the consent would have less significance.

To determine whether the findings of the jury can be supported upon review, the behavior Susan manifested during the initial three days at issue must be considered in light of her actions in the remainder of the period. Because, it is argued, the cult conditioning process induces dramatic and non-consensual change giving rise to a new temporary identity on the part of the individuals whose consent is under examination, Susan's volitional capacity prior to treatment may well have been impaired. Following her readjustment, the evidence suggests that Susan was a different person, "like her old self." As such, the question of Susan's consent becomes a function of time. We therefore deem Susan's subsequent affirmation of defendants' actions dispositive.

. . . .

In light of our examination of the record and rules of construction providing that upon review the evidence must be viewed in a manner most favorable to the prevailing party, we find that a reasonable basis existed for the verdict exonerating defendants of the charge of false imprisonment. Although carried out under color ably religious auspices, the method of cult indoctrination, viewed in a light most favorable to the prevailing party, is predicated on a strategy of coercive persuasion that undermines the capacity for informed consent. While we acknowledge that other social institutions may utilize a degree of coercion in promoting their objectives, none do so to the same extent or intend the same consequences. Society, therefore, has a compelling interest favoring intervention. The facts in this case support the conclusion that plaintiff only regained her volitional capacity to consent after engaging in the first three days of the deprogramming process. As such, we hold that when parents, or their agents, acting under the conviction that the judgmental capacity of their adult child is impaired, seek to extricate that child from what they reasonably believe to be a religious or pseudo-religious cult, and the child at some juncture assents to the actions in question, limitations upon the child's mobility do not constitute meaningful deprivations of personal liberty sufficient to support a judgment for false imprisonment. But owing to the threat that deprogramming poses to public order, we do not endorse self-help as a preferred alternative. In fashioning a remedy, the First Amendment requires resort to the least restrictive alternative so as to not impinge upon religious belief. *Cantwell v. Connecticut*, 310 U.S. 296, 60 S. Ct. 900, 84 L. Ed. 1213 (1940).

. . . .

Affirmed.

PETERSON, JUSTICE (concurring specially).

I concur in the result.

AMDAHL and SIMONETT, JJ., not having been members of this court at the time of the argument and submission, took no part in the consideration or decision of this case.

WAHL, JUSTICE (dissenting in part, concurring in part).

I must respectfully dissent. In every generation, parents have viewed their children's religious and political beliefs with alarm and dismay if those beliefs were different from their own. Under the First Amendment, however, adults in our society enjoy freedoms of association and belief. In my view, it is unwise to tamper with those freedoms and with longstanding principles of tort law out of sympathy for parents seeking to help their "misguided" offspring, however well-intentioned and loving their acts may be.

. . . .

OTIS, JUSTICE (dissenting in part).

I join in the views expressed by Justice Wahl, and particularly take issue with a rule which authorizes what is euphemistically described as "limitations upon the adult child's mobility" whenever a parent, or indeed a stranger acting for a parent, subjectively decides, without the benefit of a professional opinion or judicial intervention, that the adult child's "judgmental capacity" is impaired and that she should be "extricated" from what is deemed to be a religious or pseudo-religious cult.

At age 21, a daughter is no longer a child. She is an adult. Susan Peterson was not only an adult in 1976 but she was a bright, well-educated adult. For whatever reason, she was experiencing a period of restlessness and insecurity which is by no means uncommon in students of that age. But to hold that for seeking companionship and identity in a group whose proselyting tactics may well be suspect, she must endure without a remedy the degrading and humiliating treatment she received at the hands of her parents, is, in my opinion, totally at odds with the basic rights of young people to think unorthodox thoughts, join unorthodox groups, and proclaim unorthodox views. I would reverse the denial of recovery as to that cause of action.

―――――――

How should courts balance the rights to freedom of belief against concerns that the individual no longer has the capacity to consent, whether to cult membership or to deprogramming? How can one tell whether the will of the individual has in fact been overborne? Who should make such a decision?

BONKOWSKI v. ARLAN'S DEPARTMENT STORE
Court of Appeals of Michigan, Division No. 3, 1968
162 N.W.2d 347

NEAL E. FITZGERALD, JUDGE.

This appeal from a jury verdict for false arrest and slander, rendered against the defendant store whose agent stopped and questioned the plaintiff whom he suspected of larceny, surprisingly presents questions that are novel to the appellate courts of this jurisdiction.

The plaintiff, Mrs. Marion Bonkowski, accompanied by her husband, had left the defendant's Saginaw, Michigan store about 10:00 p.m. on the night of December 18, 1962 after making several purchases, when Earl Reinhardt, a private [uniformed] policeman on duty that night in the defendant's store, called to her to stop as she was walking to her car about 30 feet away in the adjacent parking lot. Reinhardt motioned to the plaintiff to return toward the store, and when she had done so, Reinhardt said that someone in the store had told him the plaintiff had put three pieces of costume jewelry into her purse without having paid for them. Mrs. Bonkowski denied she had taken anything unlawfully, but Reinhardt told her he wanted to see the contents of her purse. On a cement step in front of the store, plaintiff emptied the contents of her purse into her husband's hands. The plaintiff produced sales slips for the items she had purchased, and Reinhardt, satisfied that she had not committed larceny, returned to the store.

Plaintiff brought this action against Earl Reinhardt and Arlan's Department Store, seeking damages on several counts. She complains that as a result of defendant's tortious acts she has suffered numerous psychosomatic symptoms, including headaches, nervousness, and depression. Arlan's Department Store filed a third-party complaint against Earl Reinhardt's employer, Gerald Kaweck, doing business as Michigan Security Police Service, who defaulted. On the counts of false arrest and slander the case went to the jury, who returned a verdict of $43,750. The defendant's motions for judgment notwithstanding the verdict, remittitur, and new trial were denied by the trial court.

Numerous errors are alleged on appeal; we consider those necessary to the disposition of the case.

We conclude the plaintiff established a case entitling her to go to the jury on a charge of false arrest.[1]

But we conclude on the record before us that the cause of action on the ground of slander was not established. . . . Therefore, there must be a new trial.

We first consider briefly the issue whether defendant, Arlan's Department Store, can be held responsible for the acts of Earl Reinhardt, the private respect to the incident giving rise to this action, was acting within the scope of his authority as the agent of Arlan's Department Store, which must respond for his acts.

---

[1] Although the distinctions are not always clearly set out in the authorities, false arrest, or unlawful arrest, is a species of the common-law action for false imprisonment.

To the common-law tort of false arrest, privilege is a common-law defense, and we recognize as applicable here a privilege similar to that recognized by the American Law Institute in the Restatement of Torts, 2d. In section 120A, the Institute recognizes a privilege in favor of a merchant to detain for reasonable investigation a person whom he reasonably believes to have taken a chattel unlawfully. We adopt the concept embodied in section 120A, and we state the rule for this action as follows: if defendant Arlan's agent, Earl Reinhardt, reasonably believed the plaintiff had unlawfully taken goods held for sale in the defendant's store, then he enjoyed a privilege to detain her for a reasonable investigation of the facts.

The Commissioners' comment states the strong reason behind recognizing such a privilege:

> "The privilege stated in this section is necessary for the protection of a shopkeeper against the dilemma in which he would otherwise find himself when he reasonably believes that a shoplifter has taken goods from his counter. If there were no such privilege, he must either permit the suspected person to walk out of the premises and disappear, or must arrest him, at the risk of liability for false arrest if the theft could not be proved."
> 1 Restatement of Torts, 2d, page 202.

That the problem of shoplifting, faced by merchants, has reached serious dimensions is common knowledge, and we find compelling reason to recognize such a privilege, similar to that recognized in other jurisdictions.

. . . .

The privilege we recognize here goes beyond that set forth in the Restatement, for the Commissioners there stated a caveat that "the Institute expresses no opinion as to whether there may be circumstances under which this privilege may extend to the detention of one who has left the premises but is in their immediate vicinity." 1 Restatement of Torts, 2d, page 202.

In their comment, the Commissioners state that, by their caveat, in the absence of express authority, they intended to leave the question open. 1 Restatement of Torts, 2d, page 204. We think the privilege should be so extended here because we think it entirely reasonable to apply it to the circumstances of the case at bar, for the reason that a merchant may not be able to form the reasonable belief justifying a detention for a reasonable investigation before a suspected person has left the premises.

. . . .

On remand on the cause for false arrest, therefore, it will be the duty of the jury to determine in accordance with the rule we have set down, whether or not the defendant's agent, Earl Reinhardt, reasonably believed the plaintiff had unlawfully taken any goods held for sale at the defendant's store. If the jury finds the defendant's agent did so reasonably believe, then it must further determine whether the investigation that followed was reasonable under all the circumstances. If the jury finds the defendant does not come within this privilege, then from the facts as discussed above, it could find a false arrest.

. . . .

Reversed and remanded for new trial in accordance with this opinion. The award of costs to await final determination of the cause.

If a plaintiff has the chance of escape, must he or she take it? How much danger should an imprisoned plaintiff be required to confront? What about jumping from a school bus window? Risking being fired from employment? Should the standard used by the courts be subjective (*this* plaintiff) or objective (a reasonable person)?

C. PRIVILEGES IN SUITS ALLEGING TRESPASS TO LAND AND CHATTELS

PROBLEM

Several vigilantes from Texas, including Smith, kicked, punched and detained several Mexican aliens shortly after they crossed the border into Texas. The Mexicans had entered the United States illegally, stole water, two chickens and defecated on Smith's Texas property.

Discuss.

KATKO v. BRINEY
Supreme Court of Iowa, 1971
183 N.W.2d 657

MOORE, CHIEF JUSTICE.

The primary issue presented here is whether an owner may protect personal property in an unoccupied boarded-up farm house against trespassers and thieves by a spring gun capable of inflicting death or serious injury.

We are not here concerned with a man's right to protect his home and members of his family. Defendants' home was several miles from the scene of the incident to which we refer infra.

Plaintiff's action is for damages resulting from serious injury caused by a shot from a 20-gauge spring shotgun set by defendants in a bedroom of an old farm house which had been uninhabited for several years. Plaintiff and his companion, Marvin McDonough, had broken and entered the house to find and steal old bottles and dated fruit jars which they considered antiques.

At defendants' request plaintiff's action was tried to a jury consisting of residents of the community where defendants' property was located. The jury returned a verdict for plaintiff and against defendants for $20,000 actual and $10,000 punitive damages.

After careful consideration of defendants' motions for judgment notwithstanding the verdict and for new trial, the experienced and capable trial judge overruled them and entered judgment on the verdict. Thus we have this appeal by defendants.

. . . .

II. Most of the facts are not disputed. In 1957 defendant Bertha L. Briney inherited her parents' farm land in Mahaska and Monroe Counties. Included was an 80-acre tract in southwest Mahaska County where her grandparents and parents had lived. No one occupied the house thereafter. Her husband, Edward, attempted to care for the land. He kept no farm machinery thereon. The outbuildings became dilapidated.

For about 10 years, 1957 to 1967, there occurred a series of trespassing and housebreaking events with loss of some household items, the breaking of windows and "messing up of the property in general." The latest occurred June 8, 1967, prior to the event on July 16, 1967 herein involved.

Defendants through the years boarded up the windows and doors in an attempt to stop the intrusions. They had posted "no trespass" signs on the land several years before 1967. The nearest one was 35 feet from the house. On June 11, 1967 defendants set "a shotgun trap" in the north bedroom. After Mr. Briney cleaned and oiled his 20-gauge shotgun, the power of which he was well aware, defendants took it to the old house where they secured it to an iron bed with the barrel pointed at the bedroom door. It was rigged with wire from the doorknob to the gun's trigger so it would fire when the door was opened. Briney first pointed the gun so an intruder would be hit in the stomach but at Mrs. Briney's suggestion it was lowered to hit the legs. He admitted he did so "because I was mad and tired of being tormented" but "he did not intend to injure anyone." He gave no explanation of why he used a loaded shell and set it to hit a person already in the house. Tin was nailed over the bedroom window. The spring gun could not be seen from the outside. No warning of its presence was posted.

Plaintiff lived with his wife and worked regularly as a gasoline station attendant in Eddyville, seven miles from the old house. He had observed it for several years while hunting in the area and considered it as being abandoned. He knew it had long been uninhabited. In 1967 the area around the house was covered with high weeds. Prior to July 16, 1967 plaintiff and McDonough had been to the premises and found several old bottles and fruit jars which they took and added to their collection of antiques. On the latter date about 9:30 p.m. they made a second trip to the Briney property. They entered the old house by removing a board from a porch window which was without glass. While McDonough was looking around the kitchen area plaintiff went to another part of the house. As he started to open the north bedroom door the shotgun went off striking him in the right leg above the ankle bone. Much of his leg, including part of the tibia, was blown away. Only by McDonough's assistance was plaintiff able to get out of the house and after crawling some distance was put in his vehicle and rushed to a doctor and then to a hospital. He remained in the hospital 40 days.

. . . .

IV. The main thrust of defendants' defense in the trial court and on this appeal is that, "the law permits use of a spring gun in a dwelling or warehouse for the purpose of preventing the unlawful entry of a burglar or thief." They repeated this contention in their exceptions to the trial court's instructions 2, 5 and 6. They took no exception to the trial court's statement of the issues or to other instructions.

In the statement of issues the trial court stated plaintiff and his companion committed a felony when they broke and entered defendants' house. In instruction 2 the court referred to the early case history of the use of spring guns and stated under the law their use was prohibited except to prevent the commission of felonies of violence and where human life is in danger. The instruction included a statement breaking and entering is not a felony of violence.

Instruction 5 stated: "You are hereby instructed that one may use reasonable force in the protection of his property, but such right is subject to the qualification that one may not use such means of force as will take human life or inflict great bodily injury. Such is the rule even though the injured party is a trespasser and is in violation of the law himself."

Instruction 6 stated: "An owner of premises is prohibited from willfully or intentionally injuring a trespasser by means of force that either takes life or inflicts great bodily injury; and therefore a person owning a premise is prohibited from setting out 'spring guns' and like dangerous devices which will likely take life or inflict great bodily injury, for the purpose of harming trespassers. The fact that the trespasser may be acting in violation of the law does not change the rule. The only time when such conduct of setting a 'spring gun' or a like dangerous device is justified would be when the trespasser was committing a felony of violence or a felony punishable by death, or where the trespasser was endangering human life by his act."

Instruction 7, to which defendants made no objection or exception, stated: "To entitle the plaintiff to recover for compensatory damages, the burden of proof is upon him to establish by a preponderance of the evidence each and all of the following propositions:

1. That defendants erected a shotgun trap in a vacant house on land owned by defendant, Bertha L. Briney, on or about June 11, 1967, which fact was known only by them, to protect household goods from trespassers and thieves.

2. That the force used by defendants was in excess of that force reasonably necessary and which persons are entitled to use in the protection of their property.

3. That plaintiff was injured and damaged and the amount thereof.

4. That plaintiff's injuries and damages resulted directly from the discharge of the shotgun trap which was set and used by defendants.

The overwhelming weight of authority, both textbook and case law, supports the trial court's statement of the applicable principles of law.

Prosser on Torts, Third Edition, pages 116-118, states:

" . . . [T]he law has always placed a higher value upon human safety than upon mere rights in property, it is the accepted rule that there is no privilege to use any force calculated to cause death or serious bodily injury to repel the threat to land or chattels, unless there is also such a threat to the defendant's personal safety as to justify a self-defense. . . . [S]pring guns and other mankilling devices are not justifiable against a mere trespasser, or even a petty thief. They are privileged only against those upon whom the landowner, if he were present in person would be free to inflict injury of the same kind."

Restatement of Torts, section 85, page 180, states: "The value of human life and limb, not only to the individual concerned but also to society, so outweighs the interest of a possessor of land in excluding from it those whom he is not willing to admit thereto that a possessor of land has, as is stated in § 79, no privilege to use force intended or likely to cause death or serious harm against another whom the possessor sees about to enter his premises or meddle with his chattel, unless the intrusion threatens death or serious bodily harm to the occupiers or users of the premises. . . . A possessor of land cannot do indirectly and by a mechanical device that which, were he present, he could not do immediately and in person. Therefore, he cannot gain a privilege to install, for the purpose of protecting his land from intrusions harmless to the lives and limbs of the occupiers or users of it, a mechanical device whose only purpose is to inflict death or serious harm upon such as may intrude, by giving notice of his intention to inflict, by mechanical means and indirectly, harm which he could not, even after request, inflict directly were he present."

In Volume 2, Harper and James, The Law of Torts, section 27.3, pages 1440, 1441, this is found: "The possessor of land may not arrange his premises intentionally so as to cause death or serious bodily harm to a trespasser. The possessor may of course take some steps to repel a trespass. If he is present he may use force to do so, but only that amount which is reasonably necessary to effect the repulse. Moreover if the trespass threatens harm to property only — even a theft of property — the possessor would not be privileged to use deadly force, he may not arrange his premises so that such force will be inflicted by mechanical means. If he does, he will be liable even to a thief who is injured by such device."

Affirmed.

All Justices concur except LARSON, J., who dissents.

———————

1.   How far should one be allowed to go to protect one's property? Should what constitutes reasonable force vary depending upon where the property one seeks to protect is located? Upon what is acceptable in the community?

2.   What if Briney had posted a sign outside the property proclaiming the presence of a spring gun inside? Would he still be liable?

3.   What should the contours of the privilege of self-defense be? Defense of property? What does *Katko* tell us about these privileges? Should the use of deadly force ever be privileged when it has been used to protect property and not human life? If the putative victim can run away rather than use deadly force to protect him or herself, should the privilege be applicable at all?

4. The law of Texas:

§ 9.41. Protection of One's Own Property

A person in lawful possession of land . . . is justified in using force against another when and to the degree the actor reasonably believes the force is immediately necessary to prevent or terminate the other's trespass.

. . .

§ 9.42. Deadly Force to Protect Property

A person is justified in using deadly force against anther to protect land

. . .

(1) . . . to the degree he reasonably believes the deadly force is immediately necessary:

(A) to prevent the other's imminent commission of arson, burglary, robbery, . . . or theft during the nighttime; or

(B) to prevent the other who is fleeing immediately after committing burglary, robbery, . . . or theft during the nighttime from escaping with the property; and

(2) he reasonably believes that:

(A) the land . . . cannot be protected . . . by any other means; or

(B) the use of force other than deadly force to protect or recover the land or . . . would expose the actor . . . to a substantial risk of death or serious bodily injury.

§ 9.44. Use of Device to Protect Property

The justification afforded by Sections 9.41 and 9.43 applies to the use of a device to protect land . . . if:

(1) the device is not designed to cause . . . substantial risk of causing, death or serious bodily injury; and

(2) use of the device is reasonable under all the circumstances . . . Vernon's Texas Statutes (2008).

5. How much protection is afforded the "shooter" by the phrase "the land cannot be protected by any other means."

6. How is the "device" statute different from *Katko*?

D.   NECESSITY

1.   Private Necessity

PLOOF v. PUTNAM
Supreme Court of Vermont, 1907
71 A. 188

MUNSON, J.

It is alleged as the ground of recovery that on the 13th day of November, 1904, the defendant was the owner of a certain island in Lake Champlain, and of a certain dock attached thereto, which island and dock were then in charge of the defendant's servant; that the plaintiff was then possessed of and sailing upon said lake a certain loaded sloop, on which were the plaintiff and his wife and two minor children; that there then arose a sudden and violent tempest, whereby the sloop and the property and persons therein were placed in great danger of destruction; that, to save these from destruction or injury, the plaintiff was compelled to, and did, moor the sloop to defendant's dock; that the defendant, by his servant, unmoored the sloop, whereupon it was drive [n] upon the shore by the tempest, without the plaintiff's fault; and that the sloop and its contents were thereby destroyed, and the plaintiff and his wife, and children cast into the lake and upon the shore, receiving injuries. This claim is set forth in two counts — one in trespass, charging that the defendant by his servant with force and arms willfully and designedly unmoored the sloop; the other in case, alleging that it was the duty of the defendant by his servant to permit the plaintiff to moor his sloop to the dock, and to permit it to remain so moored during the continuance of the tempest, but that the defendant by his servant, in disregard of this duty, negligently, carelessly, and wrongfully unmoored the sloop. Both counts are demurred to generally.

There are many cases in the books which hold that necessity, and an inability to control movements inaugurated in the proper exercise of a strict right, will justify entries upon land and interferences with personal property that would otherwise have been trespasses. A reference to a few of these will be sufficient to illustrate the doctrine. In *Miller v. Fandrye*, Poph. 161, trespass was brought for chasing sheep, and the defendant pleaded that the sheep were trespassing upon his land, and that he with a little dog chased them out, and that, as soon as the sheep were off his land, he called in the dog. It was argued that, although the defendant might lawfully drive the sheep from his own ground with a dog, he had no right to pursue them into the next ground; but the court considered that the defendant might drive the sheep from his land with a dog, and that the nature of a dog is such that he cannot be withdrawn in an instant, and that, as the defendant had done his best to recall the dog, trespass would not lie. In trespass of cattle taken in A., defendant pleaded that he was seised of C. and found the cattle there damage feasant, and chased them towards the pound, and they escaped from him and went into A., and he presently retook them; and this was held a good plea. If one have a way over the land of another for his beasts to pass, and the beasts, being properly driven feed the grass by morsels in passing, or run out of the way and are promptly pursued and brought back, trespass will not lie. A traveler on a highway who finds it obstructed from a sudden and temporary cause may pass upon the adjoining land without becoming a trespasser because of the necessity. An entry upon land to save goods which are in danger of being lost or destroyed by water or fire is not a trespass. In *Proctor v. Adams*, 113 Mass. 376, 18 Am. Rep. 500, the defendant went upon the plaintiff's beach for the purpose of saving and restoring to the lawful owner a boat which had been driven ashore, and was in danger of being carried off by the sea; and it was held no trespass.

This doctrine of necessity applies with special force to the preservation of human life. One assaulted and in peril of his life may run through the [land] of another to escape from his assailant. One may sacrifice the personal property of another to save his life or the lives of his fellows. In *Mouse's Case*, 12 Co. 63, the defendant was sued for taking and carrying away the plaintiff's casket and it[s] contents. It appeared that the ferryman of Gravesend took 47 passengers into his barge to pass to London, among whom were the plaintiff and defendant; and the barge being upon the water a great tempest happened, and a strong wind, so that the barge and all the passengers were in danger of being lost if certain ponderous things were not cast out, and the defendant thereupon cast out the plaintiff's casket. It was resolved that in case of necessity, to save the lives of the passengers, it was lawful for the defendant, being a passenger, to cast the plaintiff's casket out of the barge; that, if the ferryman surcharge the barge, the owner shall have his remedy upon the surcharge against the ferryman, but that if there be no surcharge, and the danger accrue only by the act of God, as by tempest, without fault of the ferryman, every one ought to bear his loss to safeguard the life of a man.

It is clear that an entry upon the land of another may be justified by necessity, and that the declaration before us discloses a necessity for mooring the sloop. But the defendant questions the sufficiency of the counts because they do not negative the existence of natural objects to which the plaintiff could have moored with equal safety. The allegations are, in substance, that the stress of a sudden and violent tempest compelled the plaintiff to moor to defendant's dock to save his sloop and the people in it. The averment of necessity is complete, for it covers not only the necessity of mooring, but the necessity of mooring to the dock; and the details of the situation which created this necessity, whatever the legal requirements regarding them are matters of proof, and need not be alleged. It is certain that the rule suggested cannot be held applicable irrespective of circumstance, and the question must be left for adjudication upon proceedings had with reference to the evidence or the charge.

. . . .

Judgment affirmed and cause remanded.

VINCENT v. LAKE ERIE TRANSP. CO.
Supreme Court of Minnesota, 1910
124 N.W. 221

O'BRIEN, J.

The steamship *Reynolds*, owned by the defendant, was for the purpose of discharging her cargo on November 27, 1905, moored to plaintiffs' dock in Duluth. While the unloading of the boat was taking place a storm from the northeast developed, which at about 10 o'clock p.m., when the unloading was completed, had so grown in violence that the wind was then moving at 50 miles per hour and continued to increase during the night. There is some evidence that one, and perhaps two, boats were able to enter the harbor that night, but it is plain that navigation was practically suspended from the hour mentioned until the morning of the 29th, when the storm abated, and during that time no master would have been justified in attempting to navigate his vessel, if he could avoid doing so. After the discharge of the cargo the *Reynolds* signaled for a tug to tow her from the dock, but none could be obtained because of the severity of the storm. If the lines holding the ship to the dock had been cast off, she would doubtless have drifted away; but, instead, the lines were kept fast, and as soon as one parted or chafed it was replaced, sometimes with a larger one. The vessel lay upon the outside of the dock, her bow to the east, the wind and waves striking her starboard quarter with such force that she was constantly being lifted and thrown against the dock, resulting in its damage, as found by the jury, to the amount of $500.

We are satisfied that the character of the storm was such that it would have been highly imprudent for the master of the *Reynolds* to have attempted to leave the dock or to have permitted his vessel to drift away from it. . . . Nothing more was demanded of [the master] than ordinary prudence and care, and the record in this case fully sustains the contention of the appellant that, in holding the vessel fast to the dock, those in charge of her exercised good judgment and prudent seamanship.

. . . .

The appellant contends by ample assignments of error that, because its conduct during the storm was rendered necessary by prudence and good seamanship under conditions over which it had no control, it cannot be held liable for any injury resulting to the property of others, and claims that the jury should have been so instructed. An analysis of the charge given by the trial court is not necessary, as in our opinion the only question for the jury was the amount of damages which the plaintiffs were entitled to recover, and no complaint is made upon that score.

The situation was one in which the ordinary rules regulating properly [sic] rights were suspended by forces beyond human control, and if, without the direct intervention of some act by the one sought to be held liable, the property of another was injured, such injury must be attributed to the act of God, and not to the wrongful act of the person sought to be charged. If during the storm the *Reynolds* had entered the harbor, and while there had become disabled and been thrown against the plaintiffs' dock, the plaintiffs could not have recovered. Again, if which attempting to hold fast to the dock the lines had parted, without any negligence, and the vessel carried against some other boat or dock in the harbor, there would be no liability upon her owner. But here those in charge of the vessel deliberately and by their direct efforts held her in such a position that the damage to the dock resulted, and, having thus preserved the ship at the expense of the dock, it seems to us that her owners are responsible to the dock owners to the extent of the injury inflicted.

In *Depue v. Flatau*, 100 Minn. 299, 111 N.W. 1, 8 L.R.A. (N.S.) 485, this court held that where the plaintiff, while lawfully in the defendants' house, became so ill that he was incapable of traveling with safety, the defendants were responsible to him in damages for compelling him to leave the premises. If, however, the owner of the premises had furnished the traveler with proper accommodations and medical attendance, would he have been able to defeat an action brought against him for their reasonable worth?

In *Ploof v. Putnam*, 71 Atl. 188, 20 L.R.A. (N.S.) 152, the Supreme Court of Vermont held that where, under stress of weather, a vessel was without permission moored to a private dock at an island in Lake Champlain owned by the defendant, the plaintiff was not guilty of trespass, and that the defendant was responsible in damages because his representative upon the island unmoored the vessel, permitting it to drift upon the shore, with resultant injuries to it. If, in that case, the vessel had been permitted to remain, and the dock had suffered an injury, we believe the shipowner would have been held liable for the injury done.

Theologians hold that a starving man may, without moral guilt, take what is necessary to sustain life; but it could hardly be said that the obligation would not be upon such person to pay the value of the property so taken when he became able to do so. And so public necessity, in times of war or peace, may require the taking of private property for public purposes; but under our system of jurisprudence compensation must be made.

Let us imagine in this case that for the better mooring of the vessel those in charge of her had appropriated a valuable cable lying upon the dock. No matter how justifiable such appropriation might have been, it would not be claimed that, because of the overwhelming necessity of the situation, the owner of the cable could not recover its value.

This is not a case where life or property was menaced by any object or thing belonging to the plaintiff, the destruction of which became necessary to prevent the threatened disaster. Nor is it a case where, because of the act of God, or unavoidable accident, the infliction of the injury was beyond the control of the defendant, but is one where the defendant prudently and advisedly availed itself of the plaintiffs' property for the purpose of preserving its own more valuable property, and the plaintiffs are entitled to compensation for the injury done.

Order affirmed.

Lewis, J.

I dissent.

. . . .

I am of the opinion that one who constructs a dock to the navigable line of waters, and enters into contractual relations with the owner of a vessel to moor at the same, takes the risk of damage to his dock by a boat caught there by a storm, which event could not have been avoided in the exercise of due care. . . .

JAGGARD, J., concurs herein.

Shouldn't the defendant compensate the plaintiff for damage done by the defendant in the course of preserving his or her property? What if the defendant causes more damage to the plaintiff's property than the defendant would have suffered if the defendant had not made use of the plaintiff's property? In other words, suppose that the damage done by the defendant to the plaintiff's property is more extensive than the damage that would have been done to the defendant's property if the defendant had not used the plaintiff's property to save his or her own. Would this defeat a necessity defense?

PROBLEM

A, while boating on a lake, decides that a severe storm is about to arise and, without B's consent, moors her boat to B's dock. In the mooring process, A causes severe damage to B's dock. The storm fails to materialize.

B sues A for damages to B's dock. What will A argue in defense of her actions?

2.   Public Necessity

SUROCCO v. GEARY
Supreme Court of California, 1853
3 Cal. 69

MURRAY, CHIEF JUSTICE, delivered the opinion of the Court. HEYDENFELDT, JUSTICE, concurred.

This was an action, commenced in the court below, to recover damages for blowing up and destroying the plaintiffs' house and property, during the fire of the 24th of December, 1849.

Geary, at that time Alcalde of San Francisco, justified, on the ground that he had the authority, by virtue of his office, to destroy said building and also that it had been blown up by him to stop the progress of the conflagration then raging.

It was in proof, that the fire passed over and burned beyond the building of the plaintiffs', and that at the time said building was destroyed, they were engaged in removing their property, and could, had they not been prevented, have succeeded in removing more, if not all of their goods.

The cause was tried by the court sitting as a jury, and a verdict rendered for the plaintiffs, from which the defendant prosecutes this appeal under the Practice Act of 1850.

The only question for our consideration is, whether the person who tears down or destroys the house of another, in good faith, and under apparent necessity, during the time of a conflagration, for the purpose of saving the buildings adjacent, and stopping its progress, can be held personally liable in an action by the owner of the property destroyed.

This point has been so well settled in the courts of New York and New Jersey, that a reference to those authorities is all that is necessary to determine the present case.

The right to destroy property, to prevent the spread of a conflagration, has been traced to the highest law of necessity, and the natural rights of man, independent of society or civil government. "It is referred by moralists and jurists to the same great principle which justifies the exclusive appropriation of a plank in a shipwreck, though the life of another be sacrificed; with the throwing overboard goods in a tempest, for the safety of a vessel; with the trespassing upon the lands of another, to escape death by an enemy. It rests upon the maxim, *Necessitas inducit privilegium quod jura private.*"

The common law adopts the principles of the natural law, and places the justification of an act otherwise tortious precisely on the same ground on necessity. (*See American Print Works v. Lawrence*, 1 Zab. 258, 264, and the cases there cited.)

This principle has been familiarly recognized by the books from the time of the saltpetre case, and the instances of tearing down houses to prevent a conflagration, or to raise bulwarks for the defence of a city, are made use of as illustrations, rather than as abstract cases, in which its exercise is permitted. At such times, the individual rights of property give way to the higher laws of impending necessity.

A house on fire, or those in its immediate vicinity, which serve to communicate the flames, becomes a nuisance, which it is lawful to abate, and the private rights of the individual yield to the consideration of general convenience, and the interests of society. Were it otherwise, one stubborn person might involve a whole city in ruin, by refusing to allow the destruction of a building which would cut off the flames and check the progress of the fire, and that, too, when it was perfectly evident that his building must be consumed.

The respondent has invoked the aid of the constitutional provision which prohibits the taking of private property for public use, without just compensation being made therefor. This is not "a taking of private property for public use," within the meaning of the Constitution.

The right of taking individual property for public purposes belongs to the State, by virtue of eminent domain, and is said to be justified on the ground of state necessity; but this is not a taking or a destruction for a public purpose, but a destruction for the benefit of the individual or the city, but not properly of the State.

The counsel for the respondent has asked, who is to judge of the necessity of the destruction of property?

This must, in some instances, be a difficult matter to determine. The necessity of blowing up a house may not exist, or be as apparent to the owner, whose judgment is clouded by interest, and the hope of saving his property, as to others. In all such cases the conduct of the individual must be regarded by his own judgment as to the exigencies of the case. If a building should be torn down without apparent or actual necessity, the parties concerned would undoubtedly be liable in an action of trespass. But in every case the necessity must be clearly shown. It is true, many cases of hardship may grow out of this rule, and property may often in such cases be destroyed, without necessity, by irresponsible persons, but this difficulty would not be obviated by making the parties responsible in every case, whether the necessity existed or not.

The legislature of the State possess the power to regulate this subject by providing the manner in which buildings may be destroyed, and the mode in which compensation shall be made; and it is to be hoped that something will be done to obviate the difficulty, and prevent the happening of such events as those supposed by the respondent's counsel.

In the absence of any legislation on the subject, we are compelled to fall back upon the rules of the common law.

The evidence in this case clearly establishes the fact, that the blowing up of the house was necessary, as it would have been consumed had it been left standing. The plaintiffs cannot recover for the value of the goods which they might have saved; they were as much subject to the necessities of the occasion as the house in which they were situate; and if in such cases a party was held liable, it would too frequently happen, that the delay caused by the removal of the goods would render the destruction of the house useless.

The court below clearly erred as to the law applicable to the facts of this case. The testimony will not warrant a verdict against the defendant.

Judgment reversed.

What if the defendant had blown up the plaintiff's house and it turned out that the fire would not have reached it?

WEGNER v. MILWAUKEE MUTUAL INSURANCE CO.
Supreme Court of Minnesota, 1991
479 N.W.2d 38

The salient facts are not in dispute. Around 6:30 p.m. on August 27, 1986, Minneapolis police were staking out an address in Northeast Minneapolis in the hope of apprehending two suspected felons who were believed to be coming to that address to sell stolen narcotics. The suspects arrived at the address with the stolen narcotics. Before arrests could be made, however, the suspects spotted the police and fled in their car at a high rate of speed with the police in pursuit. Eventually, the suspects abandoned their vehicle, separated and fled on foot. The police exchanged gunfire with one suspect as he fled. This suspect later entered the house of Harriet G. Wegner (Wegner) and hid in the front closet. Wegner's granddaughter, who was living at the house, and her fiance then fled the premises and notified the police.

The police immediately surrounded the house and shortly thereafter called an "Operation 100" around 7:00 p.m. The term "Operation 100" refers to the calling of the Minneapolis Police Department's Emergency Response Unit (ERU) to the scene. The ERU, commonly thought of as a "SWAT" team, consists of personnel specially trained to deal with barricaded suspects, hostage-taking, or similar high-risk situations. Throughout the standoff, the police used a bullhorn and telephone in an attempt to communicate with the suspect. The police, receiving no response, continued efforts to establish contact with the suspect until around 10:00 p.m. At that time the police decided, according to ERU procedure, to take the next step in a barricaded suspect situation, which was to deliver chemical munitions. The police fired at least 25 rounds of chemical munitions or "tear gas" into the house in an attempt to expel the suspect. The police delivered the tear gas to every level of the house, breaking virtually every window in the process. In addition to the tear gas, the police cast three concussion or "flash-bang" grenades into the house to confuse the suspect. The police then entered the home and apprehended the suspect crawling out of a basement window.

The tear gas and flash-bang grenades caused extensive damage to the Wegner house. . . . Wegner alleges damages of $71,000. The City denied Wegner's request for reimbursement, so she turned to her insurance carrier, Milwaukee Mutual Insurance Company (Milwaukee Mutual) for coverage. Milwaukee Mutual paid Wegner $26,595.88 for structural damage, $1,410.06 for emergency board and glass repair and denied coverage for the rest of the claim. Milwaukee Mutual is subrogated to the claims of Wegner against the City to the extent of its payments under the policy.

Wegner commenced an action against both the City of Minneapolis and Milwaukee Mutual to recover the remaining damages. In conjunction with a trespass claim against the City, Wegner asserted that the police department's actions constituted a compensable taking under Minn. Const, art. I, § 13. Milwaukee Mutual cross-claimed against the City for its subrogation interest and any additional amounts the insurer may be found liable for in the future.

Milwaukee Mutual and the City both brought motions for summary judgment on all claims. The district court granted partial summary judgment in favor of the City on the "taking" issue, holding that "Eminent domain is not intended as a limitation on [the] police power." Both Wegner and Milwaukee Mutual appealed the trial court's determination.

The court of appeals affirmed the trial court, reasoning that although there was a "taking" within the meaning of Minn. Const, art. I, § 13, the "taking" was noncompensable under the doctrine of public necessity. *Wegner v. Milwaukee Mut. Ins. Co.*, 464 N.W.2d 543 (Minn. App. 1990).

I.

Article I, section 13, of the Minnesota Constitution provides: "Private property shall not be taken, destroyed or damaged for public use without just compensation, first paid or secured." This provision "imposes a condition on the exercise of the state's inherent supremacy over private property rights." *Johnson v. City of Plymouth*, 263 N.W.2d 603, 605 (Minn. 1978). This type of constitutional inhibition "was designed to bar Government from forcing -some people alone to bear public burdens which, in all fairness and justice, should be borne by the public as a whole." *Armstrong v. United States*, 364 U.S. 40, 49, 80 S. Ct. 1563, 1569, 4 L. Ed. 2d 1554 (1960).

The purpose of the damage clause is to ensure that private landowners are compensated, not only for physical invasion of their property, but also damages caused by the state where no physical invasion has occurred. A more significant restriction on recovery under this provision is the requirement that the taking or damaging must be for a public use. What constitutes a public use under this provision is a judicial question which this court historically construes broadly.

The City contends there was no taking for a public use because the actions of the police constituted a legitimate exercise of the police power. The police power in its nature is indefinable.[2]

However, simply labeling the actions of the police as an exercise of the police power "cannot justify the disregard of the constitutional inhibitions." *Petition of Dreosch*, 233 Minn. 274, 282, 47 N.W.2d 106, 111 (1951).

The City argues that Wegner and Milwaukee Mutual are confusing the concept of police power and eminent domain. We agree that this is not an eminent domain action and should not be analyzed as such. This action is based on the plain meaning of the language of Minn. Const, art I, § 13, which requires compensation when property is damaged for a public use. Consequently, the issue in this case is not the reasonableness of the use of chemical munitions to extricate the barricaded suspect but rather whether the exercise of the city's admittedly legitimate police power resulted in a "taking."

In resolving this case of first impression, the well-reasoned decision of *Steele v. City of Houston*, 603 S.W.2d 786 (Tex. 1980) provides guidance. In *Steele*, the Texas Supreme Court addressed a constitutional taking claim involving facts strikingly similar to the present case. There, a group of escaped prisoners had taken refuge in a house apparently selected at random. After discovering the prisoners in the house, the Houston police discharged incendiary material into the house for the purpose of causing the house to catch fire. The police allegedly let the house burn, even after the fire department arrived, in order to ensure all the prisoners had been forced out. The court, interpreting the taking provision of the Texas Constitution, which is virtually identical to the Minnesota taking provision, stated, "this court has moved beyond the earlier notion that the government's duty to pay for taking property rights is excused by labeling the taking as an exercise of police powers."

---

[2] One commentator explained:

> [The police power] is used by the court to identify those state and local governmental restrictions and prohibitions which are valid and which may be invoked without payment of compensation. . . .

Sax, *Takings and the Police Power*, 74 Yale L.J. 36, n.6 (1966).

Id. at 789. In discussing the city's governmental immunity argument, the court stated:

> The Constitution itself is the authorization for compensation for the destruction of property and is a waiver of governmental immunity for the taking, damaging or destruction of property for public use.

The court further stated:

> The City argues that the destruction of the property as a means to apprehend escapees is a classic instance of police power exercised for the safety of the public. We do not hold that the police officers wrongfully ordered the destruction of the dwelling; we hold that the innocent third parties are entitled by the Constitution to compensation for their property.

Id. at 791, 793. The court reversed the grant of summary judgment and remanded the case to the trial court so the plaintiffs could prove that the house was intentionally set on fire and that the destruction of the house and its contents was for a public use.

It is unnecessary to remand this case for a determination of whether the police intentionally damaged the Wegner house for a public use. It is undisputed the police intentionally fired tear gas and concussion grenades into the Wegner house. Similarly, it is clear that the damage inflicted by the police in the course of capturing a dangerous suspect was for a public use within the meaning of the constitution.

. . . .

We hold that where an innocent third party's property is damaged by the police in the course of apprehending a suspect, that property is damaged within the meaning of the constitution.

II.

We briefly address the application of the doctrine of public necessity to these facts. The Restatement (Second) of Torts § 196 describes the doctrine as follows:

> One is privileged to enter land in the possession of another if it is, or if the actor reasonably believes it to be, necessary for the purpose of averting an imminent public disaster.

See McDonald v. City of Red Wing, 13 Minn. 38 (Gil. 25) (1868) (city excused from paying compensation under the doctrine of "public safety" where city officers destroyed building to prevent the spread of fire). Prosser, apparently somewhat troubled by the potential harsh outcomes of this doctrine, states:

> It would seem that the moral obligation upon the group affected to make compensation in such a case should be recognized by the law, but recovery usually has been denied.

Prosser and Keeton, The Law of Torts, § 24 (5th ed. 1984); *see also* Restatement (Second) of Torts § 196 comment h. Here, the police were attempting to apprehend a dangerous felon who had fired shots at pursuing officers. The capture of this individual most certainly was beneficial to the whole community. In such circumstances, an individual in Wegner's position should not be forced to bear the entire cost of a benefit conferred on the community as a whole.

Although the court of appeals found there to be a "taking" under Minn. Const, art. I, § 13, the court ruled the "taking" was noncompensable based on the doctrine of public necessity. We do not agree. Once a "taking" is found, compensation is required by operation of law. Thus, if the doctrine of public necessity were to apply to a given fact situation, no taking could be found under Minn. Const, art. I, § 13.

We are not inclined to allow the city to defend its actions on the grounds of public necessity under the facts of this case. We believe the better rule, in situations where an innocent third party's property is taken, damaged or destroyed by the police in the course of apprehending a suspect, is for the municipality to compensate the innocent party for the resulting damages. The policy considerations in this case center around the basic notions of fairness and justice. At its most basic level, the issue is whether it is fair to allocate the entire risk of loss to an innocent homeowner for the good of the public. We do not believe the imposition of such a burden on the innocent citizens of this state would square with the underlying principles of our system of justice. Therefore, the City must reimburse Wegner for the losses sustained.

As a final note, we hold that the individual police officers, who were acting in the public interest, cannot be held personally liable. Instead, the citizens of the City should all bear the cost of the benefit conferred.

The judgments of the courts below are reversed and the cause remanded for trial on the issue of damages.

Affirmed in part, reversed in part and remanded.

---

1. Why is the result in *Wegner* different from the result in *Surocco*?

2. Can a police officer "borrow" a car in order to pursue a fleeing bank robber? A person who has run a red light? A fleeing murderer? If the police officer has an accident during the pursuit, who should pay for the damage to the borrowed car? For the injuries to the bystanders caused by the accident?

Chapter 4

DUTY

The negligence formula provides that five elements must be proven in order to win in a suit: duty, breach of duty, cause-in-fact, proximate cause, and damages. Many students have difficulty dealing with duty when it is presented at some other place (after proximate cause) in the book. They ask, "How can you limit or cut off duty by proximate cause before it has been established?" Therefore, duty is presented here. In truth, duty is a term of art, and the courts use it to find liability or to limit liability. Thus understood, duty is merely a branch of the social policy analysis considered in the proximate cause chapter. There is no rule for duty, and the courts consider many factors in deciding whether a duty exists.

The general duty theory presented in *Heaven v. Fender* has not been accepted, except perhaps in automobile collision cases:

> The proposition which these recognised cases suggest, and which is, therefore, to be deduced from them, is that whenever one person is by circumstances placed in such a position with regard to another that every one of ordinary sense who did think would at once recognise that if he did not use ordinary care and skill in his own conduct with regard to those circumstances he would cause danger of injury to the person or property of the other, a duty arises to use ordinary care and skill to avoid such danger.

11 Q.B.D. 503 (C.A. 1883).

This chapter will consider specific situations where the defendant has argued that the law does not extend a duty to this plaintiff for these injuries.

A. THE OBLIGATION TO ASSIST OTHERS

PROBLEM

Anna and Bob were both second-year law students. For their first date, they decided to go to a movie and then to a motel. At the motel, they took a shower together. Bob left the shower first. When Anna stepped from the shower, she slipped and fell, breaking her leg. She was bleeding and unable to move. Bob refused her requests to call for help. Two hours after the fall, Anna was able to crawl to the phone and call 911. Consider whether Bob had a duty to Anna to call for assistance.

YANIA v. BIGAN
Pennsylvania Supreme Court, 1959
397 Pa. 316, 155 A.2d 343

BENJAMIN R. JONES, JUSTICE.

A bizarre and most unusual circumstance provides the background of this appeal.

On September 25, 1957 John E. Bigan was engaged in a coal strip-mining operation in Shade Township, Somerset County. On the property being stripped were large cuts or trenches created by Bigan when he removed the earthen overburden for the purpose of removing the coal underneath. One cut contained water 8 to 10 feet in depth with side walls or embankments 16 to 18 feet in height; at this cut Bigan had installed a pump to remove the water.

At approximately 4 p.m. on that date, Joseph F. Yania, the operator of another coal strip-mining operation, and one Boyd M. Ross went upon Bigan's property for the purpose of discussing a business matter with Bigan, and, while there, were asked by Bigan to aid him in starting the pump. Ross and Bigan entered the cut and stood at the point where the pump was located. Yania stood at the top of one of the cut's side walls and then jumped from the side wall — a height of 16 to 18 feet — into the water and was drowned.

Yania's widow, in her own right and on behalf of her three children, instituted wrongful death and survival actions against Bigan contending Bigan was responsible for Yania's death. Preliminary objections, in the nature of demurrers, to the complaint were filed on behalf of Bigan. The court below sustained the preliminary objections; from the entry of that order this appeal was taken.

. . . .

Lastly, it is urged that Bigan failed to take the necessary steps to rescue Yania from the water. The mere fact that Bigan saw Yania in a position of peril in the water imposed upon him no legal, although a moral, obligation or duty to go to his rescue.
. . .

Order affirmed.

---

1. How do you respond to the argument that the law does not deal with purely moral obligations? What is the difference between causing and preventing an injury?

2. Was it costless for Bigan to render aid? Apply the cost-benefit analysis of *Carroll Towing, infra* to *Yania.*

3. What if a person on a bridge refused to throw a rope to a stranger drowning in the river below? What if a doctor in Atlanta is the only doctor capable of saving a person in Chicago?

4. Vermont requires a rescue in some situations: "A person who knows that another is exposed to grave physical harm shall, to the extent that the same can be rendered without danger or peril to himself . . . give reasonable assistance to the exposed person unless that assistance or care is being provided by others." Vt. Stat. Ann. tit. 12, § 519 (1973). What problems do you see with the Vermont statute?

5. The duty to rescue issue has been discussed in: Epstein, *A Theory of Strict Liability*, 2 J. Legal Stud. 151, 197–201 (1973); Epstein, *Causation and Corrective Justice: A Reply to Two Critics*, 8 J. Legal Stud. 477 (1979); Franklin, *Vermont Requires Rescue: A Comment*, 25 Stan. L. Rev. 51 (1972).

6. A duty to exercise care for another person usually rests on a special relation. The following are common special relations:

> Carriers have a duty to aid passengers who are known to be in peril [*Yu v. New York, N. H. & H. R. Co.*, 145 Conn. 451, 144 A.2d 56 (1958)]; employers similarly are required to render aid to employees [*Anderson v. Atchison, T. & S.F.R. Co.*, 333 U.S. 821, 68 S. Ct. 854, 92 L. Ed. 1108 (1948); *Bessemer Land & Improvement Co. v. Campbell*, 121 Ala. 50, 25 So. 793 (1898); *Carey v. Davis*, 190 Iowa 720, 180 N.W. 889 (1921)]; innkeepers to their guests [*West v. Spratling*, 204 Ala. 478, 86 So. 32 (1920)]; a jailer to his prisoner [*Farmer v. State*, 224 Miss. 96, 79 So. 2d 528 (1955)].

> Maritime law has imposed a duty upon masters to rescue crewmen who fall overboard. *Harris v. Pennsylvania R. Co.*, 50 F.2d 866 (4th Cir. 1931). *See* Prosser, Torts, *supra*; 2 Harper & James, *supra*, at 1048–49.

7. In *Farwell*, two boys followed two girls for several blocks. Friends of the girls severely beat one of the boys, Farwell. The other boy, Siegrist, applied ice and drove *Farwell* around for several hours and then parked the car containing him at *Farwell's* grandparents' house. *Farwell* died three days later. The court held:

> "Where performance clearly has begun, there . . . is a duty of care."

> "Farwell and Siegrist were companions on a social venture. Implicit in such a common undertaking is that one will render assistance to the other . . ."

> *Farwell v. Keaton*, 240 N.W.2d 217 (Mich. 1976).

The case has not been followed. Why not?

8. How is Hutchinson (the yacht captain) different from the person on the bridge who refused to throw a rope to a drowning person?

9. Some courts have refused to find a duty where there was inaction, looking instead for some act. What does *Farwell* say of the nonfeasance-misfeasance distinction?

10. Because the doctor, nurse, or good Samaritan who rescues negligently may be liable, states have adopted statutes such as the following:

51-1-29 Liability of persons rendering emergency care.

Any person, including any person licensed to practice medicine and surgery pursuant to Article 2 of Chapter 34 of Title 43 and including any person licensed to render services ancillary thereto, who in good faith renders emergency care at the scene of an accident or emergency to the victim or victims thereof without making any charge therefor shall not be liable for any civil damages as a result of any act or omission by such person in rendering emergency care or as a result of any act or failure to act to provide or arrange for further medical treatment or care for the injured person.

Ga. Code Ann. § 51-1-29 (1962).

11. In *L.S. Ayres & Co. v. Hicks*, 220 Ind. 86, 40 N.E.2d 334, 41 N.E.2d 195 (1942), a duty was found to a six-year-old boy, who got his finger caught in defendant's escalator, when defendant delayed stopping the escalator. The court reasoned: "[T]here may be a legal obligation . . . to effect the rescue . . . when the one proceeded against is [an] . . . invitor, or when the injury resulted from the use of an instrumentality under the control of the defendant." Are both required?

12. Old cases state that one who innocently injures another does not have a duty to help. In *Union Pac. R. Co. v. Cappier*, 66 Kan. 649, 72 P. 281 (1903), no duty to rescue was found where a train operated by the railroad ran over a trespasser and he bled to death.

This approach was rejected in *Maldonado v. Southern Pac. Transp. Co.*, 129 Ariz. 165, 629 P.2d 1001 (Ct. App. 1981), where the plaintiff fell off the train and had his arm severed. The railroad knew of his situation and did not render aid. The railroad was held liable.

13. A person involved in a highway collision is required to provide assistance by statute. A failure to do so will likely be interpreted as negligence per se. *See Brumfield v. Wofford*, 143 W. Va. 332, 102 S.E.2d 103 (1958).

SOLDANO v. O'DANIELS
Court of Appeals of California, 1983
141 Cal. App. 3d 443, 190 Cal. Rptr. 310

ANDREEN, ASSOCIATE JUSTICE.

Does a business establishment incur liability for wrongful death if it denies use of its telephone to a good Samaritan who explains an emergency situation occurring without and wishes to call the police?

. . . Both briefs on appeal adopt the defense averments:

"This action arises out of a shooting death occurring on August 9, 1977. Plaintiff's father [Darrell Soldano] was shot and killed by one Rudolph Villanueva on that date at defendant's Happy Jack's Saloon. This defendant owns and operates the Circle Inn which is an eating establishment located across the street from Happy Jack's. Plaintiff's . . . cause of action against this defendant is one for negligence."

"Plaintiff alleges that on the date of the shooting, a patron of Happy Jack's Saloon came into the Circle Inn and informed a Circle Inn employee that a man had been threatened at Happy Jack's. He requested the employee either call the police or allow him to use the Circle Inn phone to call the police. That employee allegedly refused to call the police and allegedly refused to allow the patron to use the phone to make his own call. Plaintiff alleges that the actions of the Circle Inn employee were a breach of the legal duty that the Circle Inn owed to the decedent."

. . . .

Comment c of section 314 [Restatement (Second) of Torts] is instructive on the basis and limits of the rule and is set forth in the footnote. The distinction between malfeasance and nonfeasance, between active misconduct working positive injury and failure to act to prevent mischief not brought on by the defendant, is founded on "that attitude of extreme individualism so typical of anglo-saxon legal thought."

Defendant argues that the request that its employee call the police is a request that it do something. He points to the established rule that one who has not created a peril ordinarily does not have a duty to take affirmative action to assist an imperiled person.

. . . .

We turn now to the concept of duty in a tort case. The Supreme Court has identified certain factors to be considered in determining whether a duty is owed to third persons. These factors include: "the foreseeability of harm to the plaintiff, the degree of certainty that the plaintiff suffered injury, the closeness of the connection between the defendant's conduct and the injury suffered, the moral blame attached to the defendant's conduct, the policy of preventing future harm, the extent of the burden to the defendant and consequences to the community of imposing a duty to exercise care with resulting liability for breach, and the availability, cost, and prevalence of insurance for the risk involved."

. . . .

We examine those factors in reference to this case. (1) The harm to the decedent was abundantly foreseeable; it was imminent. The employee was expressly told that a man had been threatened. The employee was a bartender. As such he knew it is foreseeable that some people who drink alcohol in the milieu of a bar setting are prone to violence. (2) The certainty of decedent's injury is undisputed. (3) There is arguably a close connection between the employee's conduct and the injury: the patron wanted to use the phone to summon the police to intervene. . . .

The consequences to the community of imposing a duty, the remaining factor is termed "the administrative factor" by Professor Green in his analysis of determining whether a duty exists in a given case. (Green, *The Duty Problem in Negligence Cases*, I (1929) 28 Colum. L. Rev. 1014, 1035-1045; *reprinted in* Green, The Litigation Process in Tort Law; No Place to Stop in the Development of Tort Law (2d ed. 1977) pp. 174-184.) The administrative factor is simply the pragmatic concern of fashioning a workable rule and the impact of such a rule on the judicial machinery. It is the policy of major concern in this case.

. . . .

The facts of this case come very nearly within section 327 of the Restatement . . . which provides that if one knows that a third person is ready to give aid to another and negligently prevents the third person from doing so, he is subject to liability for harm caused by the absence of the aid. . . .

We conclude that the bartender owed a duty to the plaintiff's decedent to permit the patron from Happy Jack's to place a call to the police or to place the call himself.

It bears emphasizing that the duty in this case does not require that one must go to the aid of another. That is not the issue here. The employee was not the good Samaritan intent on aiding another. The patron was.

. . . .

We conclude there are sufficient justifiable issues to permit the case to go to trial and therefore reverse.

———

1.   After *Soldano*, what remains of the action-nonaction distinction? What is the difference between the bartender permitting the patron to make a phone call and the bartender making it?

2.   The *Soldano* court cited several special relationships:

. . . California courts have found special relationships in *Ellis v. D'Angelo* (1953) 116 Cal. App. 2d 310, 253 P.2d 675 (upholding a cause of action against parents who failed to warn a babysitter of the violent proclivities of their child), *Johnson v. State of California* (1968) 69 Cal. 2d 782, 73 Cal. Rptr. 240, 447 P.2d 352 (upholding suit against the state for failure to warn foster parents of the dangerous tendencies of their ward), *Morgan u. County of Yuba* (1964) 230 Cal. App. 2d 938, 41 Cal. Rptr. 508. . . .

3.   Might a doctor have a duty to warn a previous patient of new information that a medical device is defective? An affirmative answer was given in *Tresemer v. Barke*, 86 Cal. App. 3d 656, 150 Cal. Rptr. 384 (1978), where several years earlier, the defendant physician had inserted a Dalkon Shield.

4.   Will a duty rest on a bare promise? A negative answer was given in *Thorne v. Deas*, 4 Johns. 84 (N.Y. Sup. Ct. 1809), where a co-owner in a ship promised to obtain insurance on the cargo, but failed. The boat and cargo sank. Why not extend tort liability to all broken promises?

If there is a promise by the defendant and physical injury plus reliance by the plaintiff, the answer may be yes. In *Marsalis v. La Salle*, 94 So. 2d 120 (La. Ct. App. 1957), the plaintiff was bitten by the defendant's cat. The defendant promised to keep the cat in the house in order to determine if it had rabies, but the cat escaped. The plaintiff underwent painful treatment, and the court found a duty.

5.   For an authoritative discussion, see Seavey, *Reliance upon Gratuitous Promises or Other Conduct*, 64 Harv. L. Rev. 913 (1951).

B. PRIVITY: SUITS BY THIRD PARTIES

H.R. MOCH CO. v. RENSSELAER WATER CO.
Court of Appeals of New York, 1928
247 N.Y. 160, 159 N.E. 896

CARDOZO, C.J.

The defendant, a water works company under the laws of this State, made a contract with the city of Rensselaer for the supply of water during a term of years. Water was to be furnished to the city for sewer flushing and street sprinkling; for service to schools and public buildings; and for service at fire hydrants, the latter service at the rate of $42.50 a year for each hydrant. Water was to be furnished to private takers within the city at their homes and factories and other industries at reasonable rates, not exceeding a stated schedule. While this contract was in force, a building caught fire. The flames, spreading to the plaintiff's warehouse nearby, destroyed it and its contents. The defendant according to the complaint was promptly notified of the fire, "but omitted and neglected after such notice, to supply or furnish sufficient or adequate quantity of water, with adequate pressure to stay, suppress or extinguish the fire before it reached the warehouse of the plaintiff, although the pressure and supply which the defendant was equipped to supply and furnish, and had agreed by said contract to supply and furnish, was adequate and sufficient to prevent the spread of the fire to and the destruction of the plaintiff's warehouse and its contents." By reason of the failure of the defendant to "fulfill the provisions of the contract between it and the city of Rensselaer," the plaintiff is said to have suffered damage, for which judgment is demanded. A motion, in the nature of a demurrer, to dismiss the complaint, was denied at Special Term. The Appellate Division reversed by a divided court.

We think the action is not maintainable as one for breach of contract.

No legal duty rests upon a city to supply its inhabitants with protection against fire. That being so, a member of the public may not maintain an action under *Lawrence v. Fox* against one contracting with the city to furnish water at the hydrants, unless an intention appears that the promisor is to be answerable to individual members of the public as well as to the city for any loss ensuing from the failure to fulfill the promise. No such intention is discernible here. . . .

We think the action is not maintainable as one for a common-law tort.

"It is ancient learning that one who assumes to act, even though gratuitously, may thereby become subject to the duty of acting carefully, if he acts at all." . . . A time-honored formula often phrases the distinction as one between misfeasance and non-feasance. . . . If conduct has gone forward to such a stage that inaction would commonly result, not negatively merely in withholding a benefit, but positively or actively in working an injury, there exists a relation out of which arises a duty to go forward. . . . So the surgeon who operates without pay, is liable though his negligence is in the omission to sterilize his instruments; . . . the maker of automobiles, at the suit of someone other than the buyer, though his negligence is merely in inadequate inspection. . . . The query always is whether the putative wrongdoer has advanced to such a point as to have launched a force or instrument of harm, or has stopped where inaction is at most a refusal to become an instrument for good. . . .

The plaintiff would have us hold that the defendant, when once it entered upon the performance of its contract with the city, was brought into such a relation with everyone who might potentially be benefited through the supply of water at the hydrants as to give to negligent performance, without reasonable notice of a refusal to continue, the quality of a tort. . . . We are satisfied that liability would be unduly and indeed indefinitely extended by this enlargement of the zone of duty. . . . Every one making a promise having the quality of a contract will be under a duty to the promisee by virtue of the promise, but under another duty, apart from contract, to an indefinite number of potential beneficiaries when performance has begun. The assumption of one relation will mean the involuntary assumption of a series of new relations, inescapably hooked together. Again we may say in the words of the Supreme Court of the United States, "The law does not spread its protection so far."

. . . .

We think the action is not maintainable as one for the breach of a statutory duty.

. . . .

The judgment should be affirmed with costs.

---

1. What is the holding in *Moch*? What is Cardozo's reasoning? Do you believe that the defendant's conduct had gone forward to such an extent as to work an injury? If so, what are the real reasons for the decision? Why didn't Cardozo state them?

2. If the true basis of *Moch* is lack of privity, in that the plaintiffs were not in contract with the defendants, the city (in privity) should be able to recover when its property is burned. A negative answer was provided in *Town of Ukiah v. Ukiah Water & Improvement Co.*, 142 Cal. 173, 75 P. 773 (1904).

If there is action, e.g., water containing typhoid is supplied, the plaintiff (not in privity) may be able to recover. *Hayes v. Torrington Water Co.*, 88 Conn. 609, 92 A. 406 (1914). Can *Moch*, *Ukiah*, and *Hayes* be synthesized?

3. Water companies have been held liable on facts similar to *Moch*, on the basis that the defendant began to perform, *Doyle v. South Pittsburgh Water Co.*, 414 Pa. 199, 199 A.2d 875 (1964), and the plaintiff was a third-party beneficiary of the water company's contract with the city. *See Harlan Water Co. v. Carter*, 220 Ky. 493, 295 S.W. 426 (1927).

4. For a scholarly discussion of privity and the water company cases, see Seavey, *The Water Works Cases and Stare Decisis*, 66 Harv. L. Rev. 84 (1952).

STRAUSS v. BELLE REALTY CO.
Court of Appeals of New York, 1985
65 N.Y.2d 399, 492 N.Y.S.2d 555, 482 N.E.2d 34

Kaye, Justice.

On July 13, 1977, a failure of defendant Consolidated Edison's power system left most of New York City in darkness. In this action for damages allegedly resulting from the power failure, we are asked to determine whether Con Edison owed a duty of care to a tenant who suffered personal injuries in a common area of an apartment building, where his landlord — but not he — had a contractual relationship with the utility. We conclude that in the case of a blackout of a metropolis of several million residents and visitors, each in some manner necessarily affected by a 25-hour power failure, liability for injuries in a building's common areas should, as a matter of public policy, be limited by the contractual relationship.

. . . .

Plaintiff, Julius Strauss, then 77 years old, resided in an apartment building in Queens. Con Edison provided electricity to his apartment pursuant to agreement with him, and to the common areas of the building under a separate agreement with his landlord, defendant Belle Realty Company. As water to the apartment was supplied by electric pump, plaintiff had no running water for the duration of the blackout. Consequently, on the second day of the power failure, he set out for the basement to obtain water, but fell on the darkened, defective basement stairs, sustaining injuries. In this action against Belle Realty and Con Edison, plaintiff alleged negligence against the landlord, in failing to maintain the stairs or warn of their dangerous condition, and negligence against the utility in the performance of its duty to provide electricity.

. . . Con Edison cross-moved for summary judgment dismissing the complaint, maintaining it had no duty to a noncustomer.

. . . .

A defendant may be held liable for negligence only when it breaches a duty owed to the plaintiff. . . . The essential question here is whether Con Edison owed a duty to plaintiff, whose injuries from a fall on a darkened staircase may have conceivably been foreseeable, but with whom there was no contractual relationship for lighting in the building's common areas.

Duty in negligence cases is defined neither by foreseeability of injury nor by privity of contract. . . .

But while the absence of privity does not foreclose recognition of a duty, it is still the responsibility of courts, in fixing the orbit of duty, "to limit the legal consequences of wrongs to a controllable degree." . . . "In fixing the bounds of that duty, not only logic and science, but policy play an important role." . . . The courts' definition of an orbit of duty based on public policy may at times result in the exclusion of some who might otherwise have recovered for losses or injuries if traditional tort principles had been applied.

Considerations of privity are not entirely irrelevant in implementing policy. Indeed, in determining the liability of utilities for consequential damages for failure to provide service — a liability which could obviously be "enormous," and has been described as "sui generis," rather than strictly governed by tort or contract law principles — courts have declined to extend the duty of care to noncustomers. . . . The court denied recovery [in *Moch*], concluding that the proposed enlargement of the zone of duty would unduly extend liability. . . . In the view of the Appellate Division dissenter, *Moch* does not control because the injuries here were foreseeable and plaintiff was a member of a specific, limited, circumscribed class with a close relationship with Con Edison.

. . . .

Central to these decisions was an ability to extend the defendant's duty to cover specifically foreseeable parties but at the same time to contain liability to manageable levels. . . .

Additionally, we deal here with a system-wide power failure occasioned by what has already been determined to be the utility's gross negligence. If liability could be found here, then in logic and fairness the same result must follow in many similar situations. For example, a tenant's guests and invitees, as well as persons making deliveries or repairing equipment in the building, are equally persons who must use the common areas, and for whom they are maintained.

In sum, Con Edison is not answerable to the tenant of an apartment building injured in a common area as a result of Con Edison's negligent failure to provide electric service as required by its agreement with the building owner. Accordingly, the order of the Appellate Division should be affirmed, with costs.

———————

1. What is the court's reasoning in *Strauss*? What role, if any, does privity play? What is the most important factor in the decision?

2. Why doesn't foreseeability or the fact that the plaintiff is a member of a "specific, limited, circumscribed class" control?

3. What result if Strauss had fallen in his own home because of the blackout? Have we returned to privity as the guiding concept?

C. PROFESSIONALS

LUCAS v. HAMM
Supreme Court of California, 1961
56 Cal. 2d 583, 15 Cal. Rptr. 821, 364 P.2d 685, *cert. denied*,
368 U.S. 987 (1962)

GIBSON, CHIEF JUSTICE.

The allegations of the first and second causes of action are summarized as follows: Defendant agreed with the testator, for a consideration, to prepare a will and codicils thereto for him by which plaintiffs were to be designated as beneficiaries of a trust. . . . Defendant, . . . negligently prepared testamentary instruments containing phraseology that was invalid by virtue of . . . the rule against perpetuities.

The reasoning underlying the denial of tort liability in the *Buckley* case, i.e., the stringent privity test, was rejected in *Biakanja v. Irving*, 49 Cal. 2d 647, 648-650 [320 P.2d 16, 65 A.L.R.2d 1358], where we held that a notary public who, although not authorized to practice law, prepared a will but negligently failed to direct proper attestation was liable in tort to an intended beneficiary who was damaged because of the invalidity of the instrument. It was pointed out that since 1895, when *Buckley* was decided, the rule that in the absence of privity there was no liability for negligence committed in the performance of a contract had been greatly liberalized. . . . In restating the rule it was said that the determination whether in a specific case the defendant will be held liable to a third person not in privity is a matter of policy and involves the balancing of various factors, among which are the extent to which the transaction was intended to affect the plaintiff, the foreseeability of harm to him, the degree of certainty that the plaintiff suffered injury, the closeness of the connection between the defendant's conduct and the injury, and the policy of preventing future harm. . . . The same general principle must be applied in determining whether a beneficiary is entitled to bring an action for negligence in the drafting of a will when the instrument is drafted by an attorney rather than by a person not authorized to practice law.

. . . .

We are of the view that the extension of his liability to beneficiaries injured by a negligently drawn will does not place an undue burden on the profession, particularly when we take into consideration that a contrary conclusion would cause the innocent beneficiary to bear the loss.

It follows that the lack of privity between plaintiffs and defendant does not preclude plaintiffs from maintaining an action in tort against defendant. . . .

We conclude that intended beneficiaries of a will who lose their testamentary rights because of failure of the attorney who drew the will to properly fulfill his obligations under his contract with the testator may recover as third-party beneficiaries.

However, an attorney is not liable either to his client or to a beneficiary under a will for errors of the kind alleged in the first and second causes of action.

. . . The attorney is not liable for every mistake he may make in his practice; he is not, in the absence of an express agreement, an insurer of the soundness of his opinions or of the validity of an instrument that he is engaged to draft; and he is not liable for being in error as to a question of law on which reasonable doubt may be entertained by well-informed lawyers. . . .

The complaint, as we have seen, alleges that defendant drafted the will in such a manner that the trust was invalid because it violated the rules relating to perpetuities. . . . Of the California law on perpetuities and restraints it has been said that few, if any, areas of the law have been fraught with more confusion or concealed more traps for the unwary draftsman; that members of the bar, probate courts, and title insurance companies make errors in these matters. . . .

The judgment is affirmed.

---

1. What happened to the privity defense? What happened to the "crushing burden" defense?

2. As a law student, what do you think of the attorney's defense that the rule against perpetuities is very difficult to understand and to apply?

3. In *Clagett v. Dacy*, 47 Md. App. 23, 420 A.2d 1285 (1980), the attorney, who was auctioning his employer's property, was held not liable because of no duty to a person who bid on the property.

4. In *Heyer v. Flaig*, 74 Cal. Rptr. 225, 449 P.2d 161 (1969), where the attorney who had negligently drafted a will defended on the basis of the statute of limitations, the court held that the statute did not begin to run against the plaintiff beneficiaries until the client's death.

D. DUTY TO CONTROL OTHERS

PROBLEM

Carl, a State University student, becomes a patient of Dr. Block, a psychiatrist, in the University health system. Carl says, "I will kill a female student." Dr. Block informs the campus police of Carl's statement, but does nothing more. Two weeks after the statement, Carl kills Helen, a University student. Discuss a suit by Helen's representatives against Dr. Block and the University.

TARASOFF v. THE REGENTS OF THE UNIVERSITY OF CALIFORNIA

Supreme Court of California, 1976
17 Cal. 3d 425, 131 Cal. Rptr. 14, 551 P.2d 334

TOBRINER, JUSTICE.

On October 27, 1969, Prosenjit Poddar killed Tatiana Tarasoff. Plaintiffs, Tatiana's parents, allege that two months earlier Poddar confided his intention to kill Tatiana to Dr. Lawrence Moore, a psychologist employed by the Cowell Memorial Hospital at the University of California at Berkeley. They allege that on Moore's request, the campus police briefly detained Poddar, but released him when he appeared rational. They further claim that Dr. Harvey Powelson, Moore's superior, then directed that no further action be taken to detain Poddar. No one warned plaintiffs of Tatiana's peril.

Concluding that these facts set forth causes of action against neither therapists and policemen involved, nor against the Regents of the University of California as their employer, the superior court sustained defendants' demurrers to plaintiffs' second amended complaints without leave to amend. This appeal ensued.

Plaintiffs' complaints predicate liability on . . . defendants' failure to warn plaintiffs of the impending danger. . . . Defendants, in turn, assert that they owed no duty of reasonable care to Tatiana. . . .

The second cause of action can be amended to allege that Tatiana's death proximately resulted from defendants' negligent failure to warn Tatiana or others likely to apprise her of her danger. Plaintiffs contend that as amended, such allegations of negligence and proximate causation, with resulting damages, establish a cause of action. Defendants, however, contend that in the circumstances of the present case they owed no duty of care to Tatiana or her parents. . . .

[Liability should be imposed "for injury occasioned to another by his want of ordinary care or skill" . . . "whenever one person is by circumstances placed in such a position with regard to another . . . that if he did not use ordinary care and skill in his own conduct . . . he would cause danger of injury to the person or property of the other, a duty arises to use ordinary care and skill to avoid such danger." [Heaven v. Pender]

We depart from "this fundamental principle" only upon the "balancing of a number of considerations"; major ones "are the foreseeability of harm to the plaintiff, the degree of certainty that the plaintiff suffered injury, the closeness of the connection between the defendant's conduct and the injury suffered, the moral blame attached to the defendant's conduct, the policy of preventing future harm, the extent of the burden to the defendant and consequences to the community of imposing a duty to exercise care with resulting liability for breach, and the availability, cost and prevalence of insurance for the risk involved."

Although, as we have stated above, under the common law, as a general rule, one person owed no duty to control the conduct of another . . . nor to warn those endangered by such conduct the courts have carved out an exception to this rule in cases in which the defendant stands in some special relationship to either the person whose conduct needs to be controlled or in a relationship to the foreseeable victim of that conduct. . . .

Although plaintiffs' pleadings assert no special relation between Tatiana and defendant therapists, they establish as between Poddar and defendant therapists the special relation that arises between a patient and his doctor or psychotherapist. Such a relationship may support affirmative duties for the benefit of third persons. Thus, for example, a hospital must exercise reasonable care to control the behavior of a patient which may endanger other persons. A doctor must also warn a patient if the patient's condition or medication renders certain conduct, such as driving a car, dangerous to others.

Although the California decisions that recognize this duty have involved cases in which the defendant stood in a special relationship both to the victim and to the person whose conduct created the danger, we do not think that the duty should logically be constricted to such situations. Decisions of other jurisdictions hold that the single relationship of a doctor to his patient is sufficient to support the duty to exercise reasonable care to protect others against dangers emanating from the patient's illness. The courts hold that a doctor is liable to persons infected by his patient if he negligently fails to diagnose a contagious disease {*Hofmann v. Blackmon* (Fla. App. 1970) 241 So. 2d 752), or, having diagnosed the illness, fails to warn members of the patient's family. . . .

Defendants contend, however, that imposition of a duty to exercise reasonable care to protect third persons is unworkable because therapists cannot accurately predict whether or not a patient will resort to violence. In support of this argument amicus representing the American Psychiatric Association and other professional societies cites numerous articles which indicate that therapists, in the present state of the art, are unable reliably to predict violent acts; their forecasts, amicus claims, tend consistently to overpredict violence, and indeed are more often wrong than right. Since predictions of violence are often erroneous, amicus concludes, the courts should not render rulings that predicate the liability of therapists upon the validity of such predictions.

. . . .

We recognize the difficulty that a therapist encounters in attempting to forecast whether a patient presents a serious danger of violence. Obviously, we do not require that the therapist, in making that determination, render a perfect performance; the therapist need only exercise "that reasonable degree of skill, knowledge, and care ordinarily possessed and exercised by members of [that professional specialty] under similar circumstances." . . .

In the instant case, however, the pleadings do not raise any question as to failure of defendant therapists to predict that Poddar presented a serious danger of violence. On the contrary, the present complaints allege that defendant therapists did in fact predict that Poddar would kill, but were negligent in failing to warn.

Amicus contends, however, that even when a therapist does in fact predict that a patient poses a serious danger of violence to others, the therapist should be absolved of any responsibility for failing to act to protect the potential victim. In our view, however, once a therapist does in fact determine, or under applicable professional standards reasonably should have determined, that a patient poses a serious danger of violence to others, he bears a duty to exercise reasonable care to protect the foreseeable victim of that danger. While the discharge of this duty of due care will necessarily vary with the facts of each case, in each instance the adequacy of the therapist's conduct must be measured against the traditional negligence standard of the rendition of reasonable care under the circumstances. . . .

The risk that unnecessary warnings may be given is a reasonable price to pay for the lives of possible victims that may be saved. . . .

Defendants further argue that free and open communication is essential to psychotherapy . . . ; that "Unless a patient . . . is assured that . . . information [revealed by him] can and will be held in utmost confidence, he will be reluctant to make the full disclosure upon which diagnosis and treatment . . . depends." . . . The giving of a warning, defendants contend, constitutes a breach of trust which entails the revelation of confidential communications. We recognize the public interest in supporting effective treatment of mental illness and in protecting the rights of patients to privacy . . . and the consequent public importance of safeguarding the confidential character of psychotherapeutic communication.

Against this interest, however, we must weigh the public interest in safety from violent assault. The Legislature has undertaken the difficult task of balancing the countervailing concerns. In Evidence Code section 1014, it established a broad rule of privilege to protect confidential communications between patient and psychotherapist. In Evidence Code section 1024, the Legislature created a specific and limited exception to the psychotherapist-patient privilege: "There is no privilege . . . if the psychotherapist has reasonable cause to believe that the patient is in such mental or emotional condition as to be dangerous to himself or to the person or property of another and that disclosure of the communication is necessary to prevent the threatened danger."

Our current crowded and computerized society compels the interdependence of its members. In this risk-infested society we can hardly tolerate the further exposure to danger that would result from a concealed knowledge of the therapist that his patient was lethal. If the exercise of reasonable care to protect the threatened victim requires the therapist to warn the endangered party or those who can reasonably be expected to notify him, we see no sufficient societal interest that would protect and justify concealment. The containment of such risks lies in the public interest. For the foregoing reasons, we find that plaintiffs' complaints can be amended to state a cause of action against defendants Moore, Powelson, Gold, and Yandell and against the Regents as their employer, for breach of a duty to exercise reasonable care to protect Tatiana.

. . . .

---

1. How is *Tarasoff* an extension of previous duty cases? What defenses did the psychotherapists raise?

2. How would you respond to a doctor who said that the courts have no understanding of the doctor's duty of confidentiality?

3. In California, therapists are immune from liability for failure to warn, "except when the patient has communicated to the psychotherapist a serious threat of physical violence against a reasonably identifiable victim or victims." Cal. Civ. Code § 43.92.

In *Thompson v. County of Alameda*, 27 Cal. 3d 741, 167 Cal. Rptr. 70, 614 P.2d 728 (1980), a juvenile was released from confinement although the county knew that he had said he would take the life of a child living in the neighborhood. He did, and the decedent's mother sued. The court distinguished *Tarasoff* on the basis that here no specific person was identified by the killer.

4. If the doctor discloses, he or she runs the risk of being sued by the patient. *See* Fleming & Maximov, *The Patient or His Victim: The Therapist's Dilemma*, 62 Cal. L. Rev. 1025 (1974).

5. Is there a duty to warn the parents of the child's threat to commit suicide? Yes, *Eisel v. Board of Educ., Montgomery County*, 324 Md. 376, 597 A.2d 447 (1991). No, *Bellah v. Greenson*, 81 Cal. App. 3d 614, 146 Cal. Rptr. 535 (1978).

6. What if you hear a classmate say, "I am going to kill Jim," also a classmate? Do you have a duty to inform Jim?

7. What is the duty of a hospital that learns that one of its surgeons has tested HIV positive? Must the hospital warn the patient of the risk? The court answered in the affirmative:

> It is the court's view that the risk of transmission is not the sole risk involved. The risk of a surgical accident, i.e., a needlestick or scalpel cut, during surgery performed by an HIV-positive surgeon, may subject a previously uninfected patient to months or even years of continual HIV testing. Both of these risks are sufficient to meet the *Jansen* standard of "probability of harm" and the *Largey* standard requiring disclosure.

Estate of Behringer, M.D. v. Medical Center at Princeton, 249 N.J. Super. 597, 592 A.2d 1251 (1991).

VINCE v. WILSON
Supreme Court of Vermont, 1989
151 Vt. 425, 561 A.2d 103

MAHADY, JUSTICE.

This personal injury action requires us to further refine our definition of the tort of negligent entrustment. Plaintiff, seriously injured in an automobile accident, brought suit against defendant Wilson, who had provided funding for her grand-nephew, the driver of the car in which plaintiff was a passenger at the time of the accident, to purchase the vehicle. Subsequently Ace Auto Sales, Inc. and its president Gary Gardner were added as defendants. Ace sold the vehicle to the driver; Gardner was the salesman of the vehicle.

At the close of plaintiff's case, the trial court directed verdicts in favor of defendants Ace and Gardner. Plaintiff appeals from this ruling. The claim against Wilson, on the other hand, was submitted to the jury, which returned a substantial verdict in favor of plaintiff. Wilson appeals from the judgment entered against her on the jury verdict. For the reasons stated below, we hold that the trial court erred in directing verdicts in favor of Ace and Gardner. As to the judgment against Wilson, we affirm the court's decision to submit the question to the jury, and remand for proceedings consistent with this opinion.

The tort of negligent entrustment has long been recognized in Vermont. *See Giguere v. Rosselot*, 110 Vt. 173, 179, 3 A.2d 538, 540 (1939). In *Dicranian v. Foster*, 114 Vt. 372, 45 A.2d 650 (1946), we noted that such "liability . . . arises out of the combined negligence of both, the negligence of one in entrusting the automobile to an incompetent driver and of the other in its operation." . . .

Plaintiff argues that the rule should be applied to a person who knowingly provides funding to an incompetent driver to purchase a vehicle and to a person who knowingly sells a vehicle to an incompetent driver. We have not previously had an opportunity to address this issue. In *Giguere*, the defendant negligently entrusted a firearm and ammunition to his child, who negligently discharged the firearm resulting in the death of the plaintiff's intestate. In *Dicranian*, the defendant negligently entrusted his motor vehicle to an incompetent operator whose negligent operation of the vehicle caused injury to the plaintiff.

Defendants urge us to follow those courts which have limited recovery under a claim of negligent entrustment to situations where the defendant "is the owner or has the right to control" the instrumentality entrusted. . . . These courts have denied liability where a father sold a car to his son who was known to have a drinking problem . . . ; where a vehicle was given to an incompetent operator; or where a bailee automobile dealer returned an automobile after repair to its obviously intoxicated owner. . . .

Other courts have applied the rule more broadly. For example, courts have allowed recovery against an automobile dealer who sold a vehicle to an inexperienced and incompetent driver whose driving injured several people when the seller knew or should have known of the incompetency. . . . These courts hold that the fact that a defendant had ownership and control over the instrumentality at the time it was turned over to an incompetent individual is sufficient. . . . Thus, a father was held liable for funding the purchase of an automobile by a son whom the father knew to be an irresponsible driver, . . . and a complaint against a father who purchased a vehicle for his epileptic son was held to state a cause of action. . . .

Both lines of cases derive their rule from the Restatement of Torts, which provides:

> One who supplies directly or through a third person a chattel for the use of another whom the supplier knows or has reason to know to be likely because of his youth, inexperience, or otherwise, to use it in a manner involving unreasonable risk of physical harm to himself and others whom the supplier should expect to share in or be endangered by its use, is subject to liability for physical harm resulting to them.

Restatement (Second) of Torts § 390 (1965). The comments to the Restatement support those decisions which extend the rule to individuals such as sellers:

> The rule stated applies to anyone who supplies a chattel for the use of another. It applies to sellers, lessors, donors or lenders, and to all kinds of bailors, irrespective of whether the bailment is gratuitous or for a consideration.

Id., comment a.

The cases noted above which restrict the rule to situations where the defendant is the owner or has the right to control the instrumentality have been severely criticized. *See, e.g.*, Notes, 32 Chi. Kent L. Rev. 237, 239 (1954) ("liability in these cases arises not from ownership or agency but from the combined negligence of the owner in entrusting the vehicle to the incompetent driver and of the driver in carelessly operating the same"); 43 Ky. L.J. 178, 183 (1954) ("mere passing of title does not change the character of the negligence of the defendant, and . . . the law should not operate to relieve him of his responsibility for the natural and probable consequences of his own negligent act"); 29 N.Y.U. L. Rev. 530 (1954); 33 B.U.L. Rev. 538 (1953).

[T]he leading commentators on the law of torts have said that such decisions "look definitely wrong," explaining: It is the negligent entrusting which creates the unreasonable risk; and this is none the less when the goods are conveyed. Prosser and Keeton on Torts § 104, at 718 (5th ed. 1984). Seen in this light, the issue is clearly one of negligence to be determined by the jury under proper instruction; the relationship of the defendant to the particular instrumentality is but one factor to be considered. The key factor is that "[t]he negligent entrustment theory requires a showing that the entrustor knew or should have known some reason why entrusting the item to another was foolish or negligent." . . .

With regard to plaintiff's claim against defendant Wilson, we must view the evidence in the light most favorable to plaintiff because of the jury's verdict in plaintiff's favor. . . . With regard to plaintiff's claims against defendants Ace and Gardner, the trial court directed a verdict in favor of the defendants; as such, we must view the evidence in the light most favorable to plaintiff, excluding the effect of any modifying evidence.

So viewed, the evidence indicates that Wilson knew that the operator for whom she provided funding to purchase the vehicle had no driver's license and had failed the driver's test several times. Indeed, she communicated this fact to defendant Gardner, an agent of defendant Ace, prior to the sale of the vehicle. Defendant Wilson was also aware of the fact that her grandnephew abused alcohol and other drugs. The evidence also tended to show that the operator's inexperience and lack of training contributed to the accident which caused plaintiff's injuries. The evidence was sufficient to make out a prima facie case of negligent entrustment, and the trial court properly submitted the question to the jury.

Verdicts should not have been directed in favor of defendants Ace and Gardner, however. There was evidence which, if believed by the jury, would establish that they knew the operator had no operator's license and that he had failed the driver's test several times. Viewed in the light most favorable to plaintiff, the evidence tends to demonstrate negligence on the part of Ace and Gardner, and the issue should have been determined by the jury. . . .

Cause remanded for further proceedings not inconsistent with this opinion.

---

1. What was Wilson's defense? What was the basis of the car dealer's liability? How would this decision be viewed by the general public?

2. Should liability be different, for one who sells, lends, or gives, from one who provides the money for the purchase? Explain.

3. Does *Vince* place a duty on a car dealer to inquire about the use of alcohol by the purchaser and the nature of the purchaser's driver's license?

4. Which is more helpful in deciding cases, the Restatement or the cases? Why?

5. In *Olivia N. v. National Broadcasting Co.*, 126 Cal. App. 3d 488, 178 Cal. Rptr. 888 (1981), *cert. denied*, 458 U.S. 1108 (1982), a young girl was raped on a beach by means of a soda bottle. She sued NBC, claiming that the rapist had imitated a rape scene on a recent television program where the actor had used a plumber's helper. The court rejected the plaintiff's tort duty argument and relied on the First Amendment:

> Appellant . . . asserts civil liability premised on traditional negligence concepts. But the chilling effect of permitting negligence actions for a television broadcast is obvious. "The fear of damage awards . . . may be markedly more inhibiting than the fear of prosecution under a criminal statute." . . . Realistically, television networks would become significantly more inhibited in the selection of controversial materials if liability were to be imposed on a simple negligence theory. "[T]he pall of fear and timidity imposed upon those who would give voice to public criticism is an atmosphere in which the First Amendment freedoms cannot survive." . . . the deterrent effect of subjecting the television networks to negligence liability because of their programming choices would lead to self-censorship which would dampen the vigor and limit the variety of public debate. . . .

Can you argue against this?

6. A duty may rest on a voluntary undertaking. In *Crowley v. Spivey*, 285 S.C. 397, 329 S.E.2d 774, 780 (1985), the defendant grandparents agreed to watch the grandchildren while the mother visited them. The defendants knew of the mother's mental instability and that she might have a gun. Indeed, they searched for it. The mother murdered her children, and the father (Timothy) sued the grandparents for negligence. The court found a duty:

> The duty of care in this case is grounded in the legal proposition that one who assumes to act, even though under no obligation to do so, may become subject to the duty to act with due care. . . .Timothy's testimony is unequivocal that he allowed visitation to resume because the Spiveys undertook to provide supervision over the children's visits with Lynette in Beaufort. The evidence also warrants the conclusion that Timothy was swayed to permit visitation because the Spiveys undertook a search for the pistol and were satisfied that Lynette no longer had it. Although the Spiveys were not obligated to so act, once their performance began, a common law duty to exercise reasonable care arose. . . .

E.   NEGLIGENT INFLICTION OF EMOTIONAL DISTRESS

PROBLEM

Latisha entered the Big Peach Circus (a small, one ring circus) and sat in the front row beside the ring. About a third of the way through the performance, the elephants were led in by Carla. Jumbo, a huge gray elephant backed up and evacuated his bowels into Latisha's lap. Most everyone at the circus laughed, but Latisha was extremely humiliated and embarrassed.

Discuss.

QUILL v. TRANS WORLD AIRLINES
Court of Appeals of Minnesota, 1985
361 N.W.2d 438

LESLIE, JUDGE.

. . . .

On April 4, 1979, TWA flight 841 from New York to Minneapolis was cruising at an altitude of 39,000 feet when it suddenly rolled over and plunged downward. Its tailspin continued for the next 40 seconds at speeds just below the speed of sound, causing the plane to violently shake. At approximately 5,000 feet the pilots regained control of the plane, about 5 seconds before it would have struck ground. The force exerted on the plane and the passengers equalled approximately 6 G's. Testimony indicated that force wrinkled the fuselage skin of the aircraft and bent its wings.

Plaintiff is a medical doctor who does not practice; he teaches and consults on nuclear energy and environmental policy issues. He is 48 years old and married. His work requires him to make approximately 20 business trips per year, involving about 60 flights. On this flight he was returning to Minneapolis from Europe via New York. When the plane rolled over and started its accelerating dive, he believed that his death was certain. He testified that the G force was so strong that he could not lift his arm to reach the oxygen masks which had shaken loose. Plaintiff believed even if the child in the seat next to him had been screaming he could not have heard over the incredible noise generated.

. . . .

The pilot informed the passengers over the intercom that they had experienced some problems and that they would make an emergency landing in Detroit, Michigan. The flight crew, however, did not explain the problem, indicate the condition of the plane, or assure the passengers that they would land safely.

During the next forty minutes the plane continued to shake and make considerable noise. . . .

Since the incident, plaintiff has continued to fly for business purposes. On about 50 percent of the flights he experiences anxiety and recalls his feelings that night. His anxiety is often triggered by sudden changes in an aircraft's direction. Plaintiffs fear manifests itself physically in adrenaline surges, sweaty hands, elevated pulse and blood pressure. In a few instances plaintiff has not been able to take his scheduled flight, because of his concerns, and has taken a later plane instead. His wife says it sometimes takes him two days to relax after a flight. Plaintiff has not consulted any medical professionals about his problem because, as a doctor, he believes they could do nothing for him.

ISSUES

1. Did plaintiff present a prima facie case for negligent infliction of emotional

distress?

. . . .

The seminal Minnesota case on negligent infliction of emotional distress is *Purcell v. St Paul City Railway*, 48 Minn. 134, 50 N.W. 1034 (1892). In *Purcell* a pregnant woman was severely frightened when the cable car she was riding in nearly collided with another cable car. Her fear caused her to convulse violently, leading her to miscarry her child. She sued for damages for her miscarriage, alleging the railway company negligently caused the near collision. The supreme court said:

> The mind and body operate reciprocally on each other. Physical injury or illness sometimes causes mental disease. A mental shock or disturbance sometimes causes injury or illness of body, especially of the nervous system. Now, if the fright was the natural consequence of — was brought about, caused by — the circumstances of peril and alarm in which defendant's negligence placed plaintiff, and the fright caused the nervous shock and convulsions and consequent illness, the negligence was the proximate cause of those injuries. . . .

Later cases have modified the rules for recovery of damages for emotional distress. In cases like the present one where the plaintiff did not suffer a contemporaneous physical injury, the "zone of danger" rule applies. . . . In *Langeland v. Farmers State Bank*, 319 N.W.2d 26 (Minn. 1982) the supreme court wrote:

> [T]he general rule regarding the negligent infliction of emotional distress has been that there can be no recovery absent some accompanying physical injury. See W. Prosser, Handbook of the Law of Torts § 54, at 328-29 (4th ed. 1971). In cases in which physical symptoms occur subsequent to and because of the plaintiff's emotional disturbance, many jurisdictions, including this one, require the plaintiff to have been in some personal physical danger caused by the defendant's negligence before awarding damages for emotional distress.

Id. at 31.

The Minnesota cases establish that damages for emotional distress are compensable under the zone of danger rule, but leave unanswered the narrower question raised here: How severely must the emotional distress physically manifest itself before the law will provide a remedy under the zone of danger theory?

Two Minnesota cases allowing recovery for emotional distress fit squarely under the zone of danger rule: *Purcell* and *Okrina v. Midwestern Corp.*, 282 Minn. 400, 165 N.W.2d 259 (1969). In *Okrina* a wall of the store in which plaintiff was shopping collapsed making a thunderous noise. Plaintiff was afraid the whole building would collapse but she escaped without being struck by any debris. Following the incident she felt numb and sought hospital care. She spent five days receiving treatment for severe pain in her head, back and leg. Her doctor testified that her condition resulted from her fright, that her personality had been altered, and that it was unlikely she would improve. The court said:

Here, there was a physical injury sustained as a result of Mrs. Okrina's fear and not merely mental anguish unaccompanied by symptoms of physical suffering. . . .

. . . .

TWA argues a recent decision should guide our analysis. In *Hubbard v. United Press International, Inc.*, 330 N.W.2d 428 (Minn. 1983) the Minnesota Supreme Court recognized for the first time the independent tort of intentional infliction of emotional distress. *Hubbard* ended a long period in Minnesota law where damages for emotional distress could only be recovered under the negligence theory outlined above, or under a "parasitic tort" theory. *See* Note, "Minnesota's 'New Tort': Intentional Infliction of Emotional Distress," 10 Wm. Mitchell L. Rev. 349 (1984) (recovery was parasitic because the emotional suffering must have arisen out of an [sic] "host" tort such as assault or mistreatment of a corpse).

. . . .

[W]e decide that the *Hubbard* standard does not apply to negligent infliction of emotional distress cases. . . .

Our issue remains whether plaintiff has satisfied the physical injury or symptom requirement. This requirement is a judicial obstacle designed to insure a plaintiff's claim is real. *See* Restatement (Second) of Torts, § 436A, com. b. (1965). Our task is problematic for no clear line can be drawn between mental and physical injury. Comment, *Negligently Inflicted Mental Distress: The Case for an Independent Tort*, 59 Geo. L. J. 1237, 1241 (1971). Cases taking varying positions on what meets the physical injury requirement illustrate the difficulty. *See Bowman v. Williams*, 164 Md. 397, 404, 165 A. 182, 184 (1933) (weakness and nervousness sufficient physical symptoms); *Cosgrove v. Beymer*, 244 F. Supp. 824, 826 (D. Del. 1965) (dizziness, mild headaches and nervousness insufficient symptoms of bodily harm). *See also Daley v. LaCroix*, 384 Mich. 4, 179 N.W.2d 390 (1970) (majority and dissenting views on what constitutes physical injury). The problem has led some jurisdictions to abandon altogether the physical injury or symptom requirement which Minnesota continues to employ. . . .

Although plaintiff's symptoms are less severe than those in *Okrina* and *Purcell*, we hold under the circumstances of this case that he has stated a prima facie case. The trial court upheld the jury's verdict finding that the "unique nature of the accident in this case [resolves] all doubts of the genuineness of the claim." This reasoning accords with Prosser's discussion of two types of cases allowing recovery for emotional distress without physical injury:

> What all of these cases appear to have in common is an especial likelihood of genuine and serious mental distress, arising from the special circumstances, which serves as a guarantee that the claim is not spurious. There may perhaps be other such cases. Where the guarantee can be found, and the mental distress is undoubtedly real and serious, there is no essential reason to deny recovery. But cases will obviously be rare in which "mental anguish," not so severe as to cause physical harm, will be so clearly a serious wrong worthy of redress, or sufficiently attested by the circumstances of the case.

Prosser, § 54, at 328.

This case does not fit in one of Prosser's recognized categories, but we believe the unusually disturbing experience plaintiff endured combined with his physical symptoms assure that his claim is real. There can be few experiences as terrifying as being pinned to a seat by gravity forces as an airplane twists and screams toward earth at just under the speed of sound. The nature of that experience guarantees plaintiff suffered severe emotional distress during the descent and the emergency detour to Detroit. This conclusion is supported by the suffering of many others who shared his experience. Plaintiff's recurring distress is no doubt genuine as well. His sweaty hands, elevated blood pressure and other signs of distress provide, in this case, sufficient physical symptoms to warrant the law's recognition of his claim. Therefore we hold that the law permits recovery of damages for plaintiff's emotional distress.

. . . .

---

1. Why are the courts concerned about permitting recovery for the negligent infliction of emotional distress?

2. Why do some courts require a resulting physical illness? How does *Quill* define the required physical injury? Examples?

3. Was Quill's spouse within the "zone of danger"? Was her mental distress foreseeable? *See* Leebron, *Final Moments: Damages for Pain and Suffering Prior to Death*, 64 N.Y.U. L. Rev. 256 (1989).

4. Does *Quill* require both resulting physical injury and "zone of danger"?

5. What was the key factor that led Quill's attorney to conclude that he had a good case?

6. In *Daley v. La Croix*, 384 Mich. 4, 179 N.W.2d 390 (1970), the court found a resulting physical injury even though: "There was no expert or medical testimony offered on behalf of the minor, Timothy. Extremely vague lay testimony was offered to the effect he was nervous. It was so vague and uncertain it did not, in the court's opinion, reach the dignity of possessing any evidentiary value whatever. It afforded the jury nothing into which the jury could put its damage-assessment teeth." In *Daley*, a "great electrical explosion" in plaintiff's house resulted because the defendant's vehicle crashed into a utility pole.

POTTER v. FIRESTONE TIRE & RUBBER CO.
Supreme Court of California, 1993
6 Cal. 4th 965, 25 Cal. Rptr. 2d 550, 863 P.2d 795

BAXTER, JUSTICE.

We granted review in this case to consider:

> (1) whether emotional distress engendered by a fear of cancer or other serious physical illness or injury following exposure to a carcinogen or

other toxic substance is an injury for which damages may be recovered in a negligence action in the absence of physical injury;

. . . .

(3) whether the cost of future medical monitoring to detect the onset of cancer is a recoverable item of damage when, as a result of a defendant's negligence, a plaintiff has an increased risk of future illness but suffers no present physical injury or illness; and

. . . .

Our analysis of existing case law and policy considerations relevant to the availability of damages for emotional distress leads us to conclude that, generally, in the absence of a present physical injury or illness, recovery of damages for fear of cancer in a negligence action should be allowed only if the plaintiff pleads and proves that the fear stems from a knowledge, corroborated by reliable medical and scientific opinion, that it is more likely than not that the feared cancer will develop in the future due to the toxic exposure.

. . . .

On the issue of medical monitoring costs, we hold that such costs are a compensable item of damages in a negligence action where the proofs demonstrate, through reliable medical expert testimony, that the need for future monitoring is a reasonably certain consequence of the plaintiffs' toxic exposure and that the recommended monitoring is reasonable.

. . . .

This is a toxic exposure case brought by four landowners living adjacent to a landfill. As a result of defendant Firestone's practice of disposing of its toxic wastes at the landfill, the landowners were subjected to prolonged exposure to certain carcinogens. While none of the landowners currently suffers from any cancerous or precancerous condition, each faces an enhanced but unquantified risk of developing cancer in the future due to the exposure.

. . . .

Crazy Horse, a class II sanitary landfill owned by the City of Salinas, covers approximately 125 acres suitable for the disposal of household and commercial solid waste. Unlike dump sites that are classified class I, class II landfills such as Crazy Horse prohibit toxic substances and liquids because of the danger that they will leach into the groundwater and cause contamination.

. . . .

Frank and Shirley Potter owned property and lived adjacent to Crazy Horse. . . .

The court further concluded that since plaintiffs now live with an increased vulnerability to serious disease, it was axiomatic that they should receive periodic medical monitoring to detect the onset of disease at the earliest possible time and that early diagnosis was unquestionably important to increase the chances of effective treatment. Accordingly, the court awarded damages totaling $142,975 as the present value of the costs of such monitoring, based on plaintiffs' life expectancies.

. . . .

[T]he only damages at issue here are the fear of cancer component of the emotional distress award, [and] the award for medical monitoring costs. . . .

"Fear of cancer" is a term generally used to describe a present anxiety over developing cancer in the future.

The availability of damages for fear of cancer as a result of exposure to carcinogens or other toxins in negligence actions is a relatively novel issue for California courts. Other jurisdictions, however, have considered such claims and the appropriate limits on recovery.

We must now consider whether, pursuant to California precedent, emotional distress engendered by the fear of developing cancer in the future as a result of a toxic exposure is a recoverable item of damages in a negligence action.

1. *Parasitic Recovery: Immune System Impairment and I or Cellular Damage as Physical Injury*

Because it initially appeared plaintiffs might have suffered damage to their immune systems, we solicited the views of the parties on whether such damage constitutes physical injury. We did so because it is settled in California that in ordinary negligence actions for physical injury, recovery for emotional distress caused by that injury is available as an item of parasitic damages. (*Crisci v. Security Insurance Co.* (1967) 66 Cal. 2d 425, 433 [58 Cal. Rptr. 13, 426 P.2d 173]; *Merenda v. Superior Court* (1992) 3 Cal. App. 4th 1, 8-9 [4 Cal. Rptr. 2d 87].) Where a plaintiff can demonstrate a physical injury caused by the defendant's negligence, anxiety specifically due to a reasonable fear of a future harm attributable to the injury may also constitute a proper element of damages. . . .

Although the availability of parasitic damages for emotional distress engendered by a fear of developing cancer in the future appears to be an issue of first impression in California, other jurisdictions have concluded that such damages are recoverable when they are derivative of a claim for serious physical injuries. For example, the court in *Ferrara v. Galluchio* (1958) 5 N.Y.2d 16, 21-22 [176 N.Y.S.2d 996, 1000, 152 N.E.2d 249, 253] upheld an award of emotional distress damages based on the plaintiff's fear of cancer where she had been negligently burned in X-ray treatments and later advised by a dermatologist to have her tissue examined every six months as cancer might develop. (*Accord, Dempsey v. Hartley* (E.D. Pa. 1951) 94 F. Supp. 918, 920-921 [fear of breast cancer due to traumatic breast injury]; *Alley v. Charlotte Pipe & Foundry Co.* (1912) 159 N.C. 327 [74 S.E. 885, 886] [fear stemming from sarcoma liable to ensue from burn wound].) In these cases, the existence of a present physical injury, rather than the degree of probability that the disease may actually develop, is determinative.

Plaintiffs, citing several such cases, contend that immune system impairment and cellular damage is a physical injury for which parasitic damages for emotional distress are available. . . .

Conversely, Firestone contends that mere subcellular changes that are unaccompanied by clinically verifiable symptoms of illness or disease do not constitute a physical injury sufficient to support a claim for parasitic emotional distress damages. . . .

It is not clear from the record in this case, however, that these plaintiffs' emotional distress is parasitic to this type of supposed injury. . . .

2. *Nonparasitic Fear of Cancer Recovery*

. . . .

That is already the law in California. . . . The tort is negligence, a cause of action in which a duty to the plaintiff is an essential element. . . . Firestone did violate a duty imposed on it by law and regulation to dispose of toxic waste only in a class I landfill and to avoid contamination of underground water. The violation led directly to plaintiffs' ingestion of various known and suspected carcinogens, and thus to their fear of suffering the very harm which the Legislature sought by statute to avoid. Their fear of cancer was proximately caused by Firestone's unlawful conduct which threatened serious physical injury. . . .

B. *Absence of Physical Injury*

Amici curiae argue that no recovery for emotional distress arising from fear of cancer should be allowed in any case unless the plaintiff can establish a present physical injury such as a clinically verifiable cancerous or precancerous condition. . . . Amici curiae next contend that substantial policy reasons nevertheless support a physical injury requirement for recovery of fear of cancer damages where no preexisting relationship exists. They suggest that allowing recovery in the absence of a physical injury would create limitless liability and would result in a flood of litigation which thereby would impose onerous burdens on courts, corporations, insurers and society in general. Allowing such recovery would promote fraud and artful pleading, and would also encourage plaintiffs to seek damages based on a subjective fear of cancer. In amici curiae's view, a physical injury requirement is thus essential to provide meaningful limits on the class of potential plaintiffs and clear guidelines for resolving disputes over liability without the necessity for trial.

This argument overlooks the reasons for our decision to discard the requirement of physical injury. As we observed more than a decade ago, "[t]he primary justification for the requirement of physical injury appears to be that it serves as a screening device to minimize a presumed risk of feigned injuries and false claims. . . ."

In *Molien, supra,* 27 Cal. 3d 916, we perceived two significant difficulties with the physical injury requirement. First, "the classification is both overinclusive and underinclusive when viewed in the light of its purported purpose of screening false claims." (27 Cal. 3d at p. 928.) It is overinclusive in that it permits recovery whenever the suffering accompanies or results in physical injury, no matter how trivial (ibid.), yet underinclusive in that it mechanically denies court access to potentially valid claims that could be proved if the plaintiffs were permitted to go to trial (at p. 929).

Second, we observed that the physical injury requirement "encourages extravagant pleading and distorted testimony." . . .

Our reasons for discarding the physical injury requirement in *Molien, supra,* 27 Cal. 3d 916, remain valid today and are equally applicable in a toxic exposure case. That is, the physical injury requirement is a hopelessly imprecise screening device — it would allow recovery for fear of cancer whenever such distress accompanies or results in any physical injury, no matter how trivial, yet would disallow recovery in all cases where the fear is both serious and genuine but no physical injury has yet manifested itself.

Unless an express exception to this general rule is recognized, in the absence of a present physical injury or illness, damages for fear of cancer may be recovered only if the plaintiff pleads and proves that (1) as a result of the defendant's negligent breach of a duty owed to the plaintiff, the plaintiff is exposed to a toxic substance which threatens cancer; and (2) the plaintiff's fear stems from a knowledge, corroborated by reliable medical or scientific opinion, that it is more likely than not that the plaintiff will develop the cancer in the future due to the toxic exposure. Under this rule, a plaintiff must do more than simply establish knowledge of a toxic ingestion or exposure and a significant increased risk of cancer. The plaintiff must further show that based upon reliable medical or scientific opinion, the plaintiff harbors a serious fear that the toxic ingestion or exposure was of such magnitude and proportion as to likely result in the feared cancer.

. . . .

C. Medical Monitoring Costs

In the context of a toxic exposure action, a claim for medical monitoring seeks to recover the cost of future periodic medical examinations intended to facilitate early detection and treatment of disease caused by a plaintiff's exposure to toxic substances. . . .

In light of the foregoing, we believe the *Miranda* court's analysis appropriately recognizes that medical science may necessarily and properly intervene in the absence of physical injury where there is a significant but not necessarily likely risk of serious disease. Accordingly, consistent with *Miranda, supra,* 17 Cal. App. 4th 1651, and the cases cited above, we hold that the cost of medical monitoring is a compensable item of damages where the proofs demonstrate, through reliable medical expert testimony, that the need for future monitoring is a reasonably certain consequence of a plaintiff's toxic exposure and that the recommended monitoring is reasonable. In determining the reasonableness and necessity of monitoring, the following factors are relevant: (1) the significance and extent of the plaintiff's exposure to chemicals; (2) the toxicity of the chemicals; (3) the relative increase in the chance of onset of disease in the exposed plaintiff as a result of the exposure, when compared to (a) the plaintiff's chances of developing the disease had he or she not been exposed, and (b) the chances of the members of the public at large of developing the disease; (4) the seriousness of the disease for which the plaintiff is at risk; and (5) the clinical value of early detection and diagnosis. Under this holding, it is for the trier of fact to decide, on the basis of competent medical testimony, whether and to what extent the particular plaintiff's exposure to toxic chemicals in a given situation justifies future periodic medical monitoring.

We are confident that our holding will not, as Firestone and amici curiae warn, open the floodgates of litigation. . . .

D. Smoking and Comparative Fault

In this case, all four plaintiffs were long-time cigarette smokers. . . .

In other cases, however, when a defendant demonstrates that a plaintiff's smoking is negligent and that a portion of the plaintiff's fear of developing cancer is attributable to the smoking, comparative fault principles may be applied in determining the extent to which the plaintiff's emotional distress damages for such fear should be reduced to reflect the proportion of such damages for which the plaintiff should properly bear the responsibility. . . .

Finally, we also observe that evidence of smoking by a plaintiff is relevant to whether the plaintiffs fear is reasonable and genuine. Thus, if a plaintiff had smoked heavily for 20 years without fearing cancer, the trier of fact may consider that evidence in assessing the legitimacy of the plaintiffs fear of cancer claim.

. . . .

---

1. What is the concern of the courts with cancerphobia? Has *Potter* kept the lid on the box, or will there be a flood of such suits?

2. What interests were the *amici* trying to protect?

3. What is the rule in regard to parasitic recovery? Absent physical injury, when is recovery for emotional distress permitted?

4. What policy reasons support a physical injury requirement? Why is it dropped? Is it out for all future cases?

5. When is smoking negligent or non-negligent? If smoking is as addictive as heroin, how can it be negligent? If the plaintiff was negligent for smoking, what might happen to the jury's view of his or her damages (fear of cancer)?

6. *See* Lumpkin, Note, *Recovery of Emotional Distress Damages in AIDS-Phobia Cases: A Suggested Approach for Virginia*, 51 Wash. & Lee L. Rev. 717 (1994).

PROBLEMS

1. An observant Jewish couple gave express instructions to the hospital that their newborn son was to be ritualistically circumcised, on his eighth day, by a *mohel*, in accordance with the tenets of their religion. Instead, due to the negligence of the hospital, the baby was circumcised on his fourth day by a physician. Discuss.

2. Carol sees and hears Nurse Smith negligently drop Carol's baby to the floor in the hospital. Carol suffers emotional distress and is not able to work for six months. Discuss whether Nurse Smith has a duty to Carol.

THING v. LA CHUSA
Supreme Court of California, 1989 (en banc)
48 Cal. 3d 644, 257 Cal. Rptr. 865, 771 P.2d 814

EAGLESON, JUSTICE.

The narrow issue presented by the parties in this case is whether the Court of Appeal correctly held that a mother who did not witness an accident in which an automobile struck and injured her child may recover damages from the negligent driver for the emotional distress she suffered when she arrived at the accident scene. The more important question this issue poses for the court, however, is whether the "guidelines" enunciated by this court in *Dillon v. Legg* (1968) 68 Cal. 2d 728 [69 Cal. Rptr. 72, 441 P.2d 912, 29 A.L.R.3d 1316] are adequate, or if they should be refined to create greater certainty in this area of the law.

. . . It is in that context that we consider the appropriate application of the concept of "duty". . . .

On December 8, 1980, John Thing, a minor, was injured when struck by an automobile operated by defendant James V. La Chusa. His mother, plaintiff Maria Thing, was nearby, but neither saw nor heard the accident. She became aware of the injury to her son when told by a daughter that John had been struck by a car. She rushed to the scene where she saw her bloody and unconscious child, who she believed was dead, lying in the roadway. Maria sued defendants, alleging that she suffered great emotional disturbance, shock, and injury to her nervous system as a result of these events, and that the injury to John and emotional distress she suffered were proximately caused by defendants' negligence.

The trial court granted defendants' motion for summary judgment, ruling that, as a matter of law, Maria could not establish a claim for negligent infliction of emotional distress because she did not contemporaneously and sensorily perceive the accident. . . .

[I]n negligence cases the right to recover for emotional distress had been limited to circumstances in which the victim was himself injured and emotional distress was a "parasitic" item of damages, or if a plaintiff who had been in the "zone of danger" did not suffer injury from impact, but did suffer physical injury as a result of the emotional trauma.

But shortly before *Dillon*, in *Amaya v. Home Ice, Fuel & Supply Co., supra*, 59 Cal. 2d 295, the court had declined the opportunity to broaden the right to recover for emotional distress. *Amaya*, after confirming that the "impact rule" making a contemporaneous physical impact a prerequisite to recovery for negligently induced fright or shock was not applicable in California, held damages could not be recovered by persons outside the zone of danger created by the defendant's negligence even when that shock was reflected in physiological symptoms.

The *Amaya* view was short lived, however. Only five years later, the decision was overruled in *Dillon v. Legg.* . . .

In *Dillon* itself, the issue was limited. The mother and sister of a deceased infant each sought damages for "great emotional disturbance and shock and injury to her nervous system" which had caused them great mental pain and suffering. Allegedly these injuries were caused by witnessing the defendant's negligently operated vehicle collide with and roll over the infant as she lawfully crossed a street. The mother was not herself endangered by the defendant's conduct. The sister may have been. The trial court had therefore granted the defendant's motion for judgment on the pleadings as to the mother, but had denied it with respect to the sister of the decedent. Faced with the incongruous result demanded by the "zone of danger" rule which denied recovery for emotional distress and consequent physical injury unless the plaintiff himself had been threatened with injury, the court overruled *Amaya.*

. . . .

The difficulty in defining the limits on recovery anticipated by the *Amaya* court was rejected as a basis for denying recovery, but the court did recognize that "to limit the otherwise potentially infinite liability which would follow every negligent act, the law of torts holds defendant amenable only for injuries to others which to defendant at the time were reasonably foreseeable." (*Dillon, supra*, 68 Cal. 2d at p. 739.) Thus, while the court indicated that foreseeabihty of the injury was to be the primary consideration in finding duty, it simultaneously recognized that policy considerations mandated that infinite liability be avoided by restrictions that would somehow narrow the class of potential plaintiffs. But the test limiting liability was itself amorphous.

The expectation of the *Dillon* majority that the parameters of the tort would be further defined in future cases has not been fulfilled. Instead, subsequent decisions of the Courts of Appeal and this court, have created more uncertainty. And, just as the "zone of danger" limitation was abandoned in *Dillon* as an arbitrary restriction on recovery, the *Dillon* guidelines have been relaxed on grounds that they, too, created arbitrary limitations on recovery.

. . . .

Both the physical harm and accident or sudden occurrence elements were eliminated, however, in *Molien v. Kaiser Foundation Hospitals, supra*, 27 Cal. 3d 916, at least as to those plaintiffs who could claim to be "direct victims" of the defendant's negligence. The court held in *Molien* that a defendant hospital and doctor owed a duty directly to the husband of a patient who had been diagnosed erroneously as having syphilis, and had been told to so advise the husband in order that he could receive testing and, if necessary, treatment.

In finding the existence of a duty to the husband of the patient, the court reasoned that the risk of harm to the husband was reasonably foreseeable, and that the tortious conduct was directed to him as well as the patient. . . . The status of the plaintiff mother in *Dillon* was distinguished as she suffered her injury solely as a "percipient witness" to the infliction of injury on another. She was therefore a "bystander" rather than a "direct victim."

. . . .

The subtleties in the distinction between the right to recover as a "bystander" and as a "direct victim" created what one Court of Appeal has described as an "amorphous nether realm". . . . "The problem which arises from this cryptic explanation is: how are we to distinguish between 'direct victim' cases and 'bystander' cases? An impression is given that the foreseeability of the particular injury to the husband alone explains the result. The inference suggested is that a 'direct victim' is a person whose emotional distress is a reasonably foreseeable consequence of the conduct of the defendant. This does not provide criteria which delimit what counts as reasonable foreseeability. It leads into the quagmire of novel claims which the Supreme Court foresaw as an unacceptable consequence of a 'pure' foreseeability analysis. . . ."

. . . If the consequences of a negligent act are not limited an intolerable burden is placed on society. A "bright line in this area of the law is essential."

. . . .

The impact of personally observing the injury-producing event in most, although concededly not all, cases distinguishes the plaintiff's resultant emotional distress from the emotion felt when one learns of the injury or death of a loved one from another, or observes pain and suffering but not the traumatic cause of the injury. Greater certainty and a more reasonable limit on the exposure to liability for negligent conduct is possible by limiting the right to recover for negligently caused emotional distress to plaintiffs who personally and contemporaneously perceive the injury-producing event and its traumatic consequences.

Similar reasoning justifies limiting recovery to persons closely related by blood or marriage since, in common experience, it is more likely that they will suffer a greater degree of emotional distress than a disinterested witness to negligently caused pain and suffering or death. Such limitations are indisputably arbitrary since it is foreseeable that in some cases unrelated persons have a relationship to the victim or they are so affected by the traumatic event that they suffer equivalent emotional distress. As we have observed, however, drawing arbitrary lines is unavoidable if we are to limit liability and establish meaningful rules for application by litigants and lower courts.

No policy supports extension of the right to recover for [the negligent infliction of emotional distress] to a larger class of plaintiffs. Emotional distress is an intangible condition experienced by most persons, even absent negligence, at some time during their lives. Close relatives suffer serious, even debilitating, emotional reactions to the injury, death, serious illness, and evident suffering of loved ones. . . . The overwhelming majority of "emotional distress" which we endure, therefore is not compensable.

. . . In identifying those persons and the circumstances in which the defendant will be held to redress the injury, it is appropriate to restrict recovery to those persons who will suffer emotional impact beyond the impact that can be anticipated whenever one learns that a relative is injured, or dies, or the emotion felt by a "disinterested" witness. The class of potential plaintiffs should be limited to those who because of their relationship suffer the greatest emotional distress. When the right to recover is limited in this manner, the liability bears a reasonable relationship to the culpability of the negligent defendant.

We conclude, therefore, that a plaintiff may recover damages for emotional distress caused by observing the negligently inflicted injury of a third person if, but only if, said plaintiff: (1) is closely related to the injury victim; (2) is present at the scene of the injury producing event at the time it occurs and is then aware that it is causing injury to the victim; and (3) as a result suffers serious emotional distress — a reaction beyond that which would be anticipated in a disinterested witness and which is not an abnormal response to the circumstances.

. . . .

The undisputed facts establish that plaintiff was not present at the scene of the accident in which her son was injured. She did not observe defendant's conduct and was not aware that her son was being injured. She could not, therefore, establish a right to recover for the emotional distress she suffered when she subsequently learned of the accident and observed its consequences. The order granting summary judgment was proper.

The judgment of the Court of Appeal is reversed.

---

1. What are the policies for and against a recovery by a third party for the negligent infliction of emotional distress?

2. What was the function of the impact rule, and what problems did it create?

3. As plaintiff's attorney, apply the *Dillon* test to the *Thing* plaintiff prior to the *Thing* decision.

4. Was it foreseeable that the mother in the *Thing* case would suffer emotional distress? Why not permit a recovery? Why is "foreseeability alone" not a useful guideline?

5. Draw the line between a "bystander" (*Dillon*, mother) and a "direct victim" (*Molien*, husband)?

6. Does a person who cohabits with another have a close enough relation to recover under the *Dillon* test? No. *Elden v. Sheldon*, 46 Cal. 3d 267, 250 Cal. Rptr. 254, 758 P.2d 582 (1988).

7. In *St. Elizabeth Hosp. v. Garrard*, 730 S.W.2d 649 (Tex. 1987), the Texas Supreme Court appeared to give up after struggling with the physical injury requirement. The patient and her husband brought an action seeking damages for mental anguish after their stillborn daughter's body had been disposed of in an unmarked, common grave, without their knowledge or consent. The court stated:

> The question presented in this personal injury case is whether the physical manifestation requirement remains an element of claims for negligent infliction of mental anguish. . . . We hold that proof of physical injury is no longer required in order to recover for negligent infliction of mental anguish and therefore affirm the judgment of the court of appeals.

. . . .

By eliminating the physical manifestation requirement Texas joins an established trend in American jurisprudence which recognizes the tort of negligent infliction of mental anguish without imposing arbitrary restrictions on recovery in such actions. The distinction between physical injury and emotional distress is no longer defensible. The problem is one of proof, and to deny a remedy in all cases because some claims may be false leads to arbitrary results which do not serve the best interests of the public. Jurors are best suited to determine whether and to what extent the defendant's conduct caused compensa-ble mental anguish by referring to their own experience.

Thus, we hold that the Garrards' petition states a cause of action despite the absence of allegations that the mental anguish suffered resulted in physical injury.

Then came the following decision.

BOYLES v. KERR
Supreme Court of Texas, 1993
855 S.W.2d 593

PHILLIPS, CHIEF JUSTICE.

Respondent's motion for rehearing is overruled. Our opinion of December 2, 1992, is withdrawn and the following is substituted in its place.

This is a suit for the negligent infliction of emotional distress. We hold that there is no general duty in Texas not to negligently inflict emotional distress. A claimant may recover mental anguish damages only in connection with defendant's breach of some other legal duty. Because Respondent proceeded below only on the theory of negligent infliction of emotional distress, we reverse the judgment of the court of appeals in her favor. 806 S.W.2d 255. However, in the interest of justice, we remand for a new trial.

On August 10, 1985, Petitioner Dan Boyles, Jr., then seventeen, covertly videotaped nineteen-year-old Respondent Susan Leigh Kerr engaging in sexual intercourse with him. Although not dating steadily, they had known each other a few months and had shared several previous sexual encounters. Kerr testified that she had not had sexual intercourse prior to her relationship with Boyles.

. . . .

Boyles took possession of the tape shortly after it was made, and subsequently showed it on three occasions, each time at a private residence. Although he showed the tape to only ten friends, gossip about the incident soon spread among many of Kerr and Boyles' friends in Houston. Soon many students at Kerr's school, Southwest Texas State University, and Boyles' school, the University of Texas at Austin, also became aware of the story. . . .

The tape stigmatized Kerr with the reputation of "porno queen" among some of her friends, and she claimed that the embarrassment and notoriety affected her academic performance. Kerr also claimed that the incident made it difficult for her to relate to men, although she testified to having had subsequent sexually-active relationships. Eventually, she sought psychological counselling.

. . . Before the case was submitted to the jury, however, Kerr dropped all causes of action except for negligent infliction of emotional distress. The jury returned a verdict for Kerr on that claim, assessing $500,000 in actual damages. . . .

While the holding of *Garrard* was correct, we conclude that its reasoning was based on an erroneous interpretation *of Hill v. Kimball*, and is out of step with most American jurisdictions. Therefore, we overrule the language of *Garrard* to the extent that it recognizes an independent right to recover for negligently inflicted emotional distress. Instead, mental anguish damages should be compensated only in connection with defendant's breach of some other duty imposed by law. . . .

By overruling the language *of Garrard*, we hold only that there is no general duty not to negligently inflict emotional distress. Our decision does not affect a claimant's right to recover mental anguish damages caused by defendant's breach of some other legal duty. *See, e.g., Fisher v. Coastal Transp. Co.* (negligent infliction of direct physical injury); *Moore v. Lillebo* (wrongful death); *Fisher v. Carrousel Motor Hotel, Inc.* (battery); *Stuart v. Western Union Tel. Co.* (failure of telegraph company to timely deliver death message); *Billings v. Atkinson*, (invasion of privacy); *Leyendecker & Assocs., Inc., v. Wechter*, (defamation); *Pat H. Foley & Co. u. Wyatt* (negligent handling of corpse).

Also, our holding does not affect the right of bystanders to recover emotional distress damages suffered as a result of witnessing a serious or fatal accident. Texas has adopted the bystander rules originally promulgated by the California Supreme Court in *Dillon v. Legg.* . . .

We also are not imposing a requirement that emotional distress manifest itself physically to be compensable. . . .

Most other jurisdictions do not recognize a general duty not to negligently inflict emotional distress. Many limit recovery by requiring proof of a physical manifestation. Others allow recovery where the claimant establishes the breach of some independent duty. A few jurisdictions recognize a general right to recover for negligently inflicted emotional distress, but these jurisdictions are squarely in the minority.

We find the experience in California to be instructive. . . . *Thing v. La Chusa.* . . .

We therefore reverse the judgment of the court of appeals in favor of Kerr on the ground of negligent infliction of emotional distress.

. . . .

We denied recovery not because Boyles breached no duty toward Kerr, but because the only theory which she chose . . . negligent infliction of emotional distress — was overly broad and would encompass other cases involving merely rude or insensitive behavior. We reaffirm that conclusion today.

Kerr cannot recover based on the cause of action under which she proceeded. It may well be, however, that she failed to assert and preserve alternative causes of action because of her reliance on our holding in *Garrard.* . . . We therefore reverse the judgment of the court of appeals and remand this cause to the trial court for a new trial.

. . . .

Concurring Opinion on Motion for Rehearing

GONZALEZ, JUSTICE.

What happened to Ms. Kerr in this case is grossly offensive conduct which no one should tolerate. As such the law should, and does, provide a remedy. However, as a result of the posturing by the dissenting justices, what has been lost in the shuffle is the pivotal role that insurance played in this case.

The young men who videotaped Ms. Kerr's sexual encounter intentionally positioned the camera to capture the event on film. They intentionally showed the videotape to their friends. There was nothing accidental or careless about their outrageous conduct. However, Ms. Kerr intentionally gave up her right to receive redress under two other theories of recovery which she had pleaded: willful invasion of privacy, a cause of action which was recognized by this Court sixteen years before the jury verdict in this case in *Billings v. Atkinson*, 489 S.W.2d 858, 860-61 (Tex. 1973), and intentional infliction of emotional distress. . . . Her lawyers gambled when they made a strategic decision to proceed only with the questionable legal theory of negligent infliction of emotional distress.

. . . .

It does not take a rocket scientist to determine why Ms. Kerr's lawyers elected to proceed solely on the tort of negligent infliction of emotional distress. In fact, her lawyers explained their strategy to the trial court. At the close of the evidence, the defense attorneys made a motion for directed verdict on the negligence theories of recovery:

THE COURT: Under what basis?

MR. DRABECK [defendant's attorney]:

Under the basis that intentional tort cannot be the result of negligent conduct. That the case has been tried from start to finish as an intentional tort by the lawyers over here. We'd ask that the Court recognize that. There has never been one question asked of anybody as to whether or not they failed to exercise ordinary care on the occasion in question, whether they negligently inflicted some sort of mental distress on her. It would appear by virtue of the record as placed by the plaintiffs themselves that every single question was directed toward intentional conduct.

MR. KRIST: [plaintiff's attorney]:

Your Honor, the — to begin with, let the record reveal, for whatever purposes, it might be at a later date, that should the Court adopt counsel's suggestion, counsel would have dropped his client in the grease in that he would have gotten totally out of coverage.

THE COURT:

It's your case . . . and I am going to give you your requested charge. If you don't ask for an intentional tort, I ain't asking it, . . . I'm not going to make you prosecute a lawsuit that you didn't want to prosecute. So don't worry about that. Nobody is going to get intentional tort unless they ask for it.

In Texas, a home owners policy covers only accidents or careless conduct and excludes intentional acts. . . .

---

1. Why did plaintiff's attorneys limit the suit to negligent infliction of mental distress? What remains of the holding in *Garrard*? Is it limited to its facts, interference with dead bodies?

2. In Texas, after *Boyles v. Kerr*, when can a plaintiff recover for the negligent infliction of mental distress?

3. Some jurisdictions do not require a physical injury in two cases: (1) the negligent interference with dead bodies and (2) mistakes in sending telegrams reporting death. *Lott v. State*, 32 Misc. 2d 296, 225 N.Y.S.2d 434 (Ct. Cl. 1962) (dead bodies); *Johnson v. State*, 37 N.Y.2d 378, 372 N.Y.S.2d 638, 334 N.E.2d 590 (1975) (death telegram).

4. Does *Boyles v. Kerr* turn "back the clock to a time when the sexual exploitation of unwilling women was socially acceptable" and send "a message to the women of Texas that sexual harassment and abuse is O.K."? (*Boyles* at 605).

5. What are the chances for settlement prior to retrial? Argue for the defendant.

6. Can the parents recover for emotional distress when their infant is abducted from the defendant hospital because of negligence? The court rejected the claim holding that the parents were not within the "zone of danger" and the hospital owed "no direct duty" to them. A direct duty was owed only to the child. *Johnson v. Jamaica Hosp.*, 62 N.Y.2d 523, 467 N.E.2d 502, 478 N.Y.2d 838 (1984).

The "no direct duty" rationale was extended to the misdiagnosis of disease in *Jacobs v. Horton Mem. Hosp.*, 130 A.D.2d 546, 515 N.Y.S.2d 281 (1987), where a wife had sued for the emotional distress resulting from the negligent diagnosis of pancreatic cancer in her husband. Have we returned to the privity of contract concept?

7. In general, today either spouse can recover for the loss of consortium. *See Diaz v. Eli Lilly & Co.*, 364 Mass. 153, 302 N.E.2d 555 (1973). Can children recover for the loss of parental society? No, *Borer v. American Airlines, Inc.*, 19 Cal. 3d 441, 138 Cal. Rptr. 302, 563 P.2d 858 (1977). Yes, *Ferriter v. Daniel O'Connell's Sons, Inc.*, 381 Mass. 507, 413 N.E.2d 690 (1980).

CHAPA v. TRACIERS & ASSOCIATES, INC.
Court of Appeals of Texas, 2008
267 S.W.3d 386

GUZMAN, J.

FACTUAL AND PROCEDURAL BACKGROUND

Ford Motor Credit Corp. ("FMCC") hired Traciers & Associates ("Traciers") to repossess a white 2002 Ford Expedition owned by Marissa Chapa, who was in default on the associated promissory note. Traciers assigned the job to its field manager, Paul Chambers, and gave him an address where the vehicle could be found. FMCC, Traciers, and Chambers were unaware that the address was that of Marissa's brother, Carlos Chapa. Coincidentally, Carlos and his wife Maria Chapa also had purchased a white Ford Expedition financed by FMCC. Their vehicle, however, was a 2003 model, and the Chapas were not in default.

On the night of February 6, 2003, Chambers went to the address and observed a white Ford Expedition. The license number of the vehicle did not match that of the vehicle he was told to repossess, and he did not see the vehicle's vehicle identification number ("VIN"), which was obscured. Chambers returned early the next morning and still could not see the Expedition's VIN. He returned to his own vehicle, which was parked two houses away.

Unseen by Chambers, Maria Chapa left the house and helped her two sons, ages ten and six, into the Expedition for the trip to school. Her mother-in-law's vehicle was parked behind her, so Maria backed her mother-in-law's vehicle into the street, then backed her Expedition out of the driveway and parked on the street. She left the keys to her truck in the ignition with the motor running while she parked her mother-in-law's car back in the driveway and reentered the house to return her mother-in-law's keys.

After Chambers saw Maria park the Expedition on the street and return to the house, it took him only thirty seconds to back his tow truck to the Expedition, hook it to his truck, and drive away. Chambers did not leave his own vehicle to perform this operation, and it is undisputed that he did not know the Chapa children were inside. When Maria emerged from the house, the Expedition, with her children, was gone. Maria began screaming, telephoned 911, and called her husband at work to tell him the children were gone.

Chambers did not see the children in the back seat through the tinted windows of the Expedition.

Meanwhile, on an adjacent street, Chambers noticed that the Expedition's wheels were turning, indicating to him that the vehicle's engine was running. He stopped the tow truck and heard a sound from the Expedition. Looking inside, he discovered the two Chapa children. After he persuaded one of the boys to unlock the vehicle, Chambers drove the Expedition back to the Chapas's house. He returned the keys to Maria, who was outside her house, crying. By the time emergency personnel and Carlos Chapa arrived, the children were back home and Chambers had left the scene.

Maria testified that the incident caused her to have an anxiety attack, including chest pain and numbness in her arm. She states she has continued to experience panic attacks and has been diagnosed with an anxiety disorder. In addition, both Carlos and Maria have been diagnosed with post-traumatic stress disorder.

Acting individually and on behalf of their children, Carlos and Maria Chapa sued Traciers, Chambers, and FMCC. Appellees settled the children's claims but contested the individual claims of Carlos and Maria. The trial court granted summary judgment on the parents' claims in favor of Traciers, Chambers, and FMCC, and this appeal ensued.

ANALYSIS

The claims of Carlos and Maria Chapa . . . more closely resemble a common-law claim of negligent infliction of emotional distress. This tort consists of "mental or emotional harm (such as fright or anxiety) that is caused by the negligence of another and that is not directly brought about by a physical injury, but that may manifest itself in physical symptoms." With limited exceptions, claims of negligent infliction of emotional distress are not recognized under Texas law. *Boyles v. Kerr, 855 S.W.2d 593, 594 (Tex. 1993)* (op. on mot. for reh'g) ("[T]here is no general duty in Texas not to negligently inflict emotional distress. A claimant may recover mental anguish damages only in connection with defendant's breach of some other legal duty."). And although the Chapas argue that their physical manifestations of emotional distress are distinct physical injuries, the cases on which they rely do not support recovery for such physical manifestations . . . and are otherwise distinguishable on the facts.

Because the Chapas' claims consist of negligently inflicted mental anguish and its physical manifestations, we conclude that general negligence law [does not support] the Chapas' claims. We therefore overrule the Chapas' first issue.

Bystander Claim

A bystander claim falls within an exception to the general rule barring recovery for negligent infliction of emotional distress. . . . Under this legal theory, mental-anguish damages are recoverable for the contemporaneous sensory perception of a serious or fatal injury to a close relative. . . . When the material facts are undisputed, the question of whether a plaintiff is entitled to recover as a bystander is a question of law. . . .

To determine whether a plaintiff has a valid bystander claim, courts consider:

(1) Whether the plaintiff was located near the scene of the accident as contrasted with one who was a distance away from it.

(2) Whether the shock resulted from a direct emotional impact upon the plaintiff from the sensory and contemporaneous observance of the accident, as contrasted with learning of the accident from others after its occurrence.

(3) Whether the plaintiff and the victim were closely related, as contrasted with an absence of any relationship or the presence of only a distant relationship.

Freeman v. City of Pasadena, 744 S.W.2d 923, 923-24 *(Tex. 1988)* (adopting the "bystander" elements set forth in *Dillon v. Legg,* 68 Cal. 2d 728, 69 Cal. Rptr. 72, 441 P.2d 912, 920 (Cal. 1968)). Here, the material facts are undisputed, but the parties disagree about whether these facts satisfy the second element of the test.

The Chapas argue that Maria, who was out of sight of the Expedition for only about 30 seconds, was a contemporaneous observer of the "accident." They further contend that Chambers's act of removing the vehicle and the children constituted a continuing tort; thus, Maria's observation of their absence renders her a bystander. . . . ("[A]ctual observance of the accident is not required if there is otherwise an experiential perception of it, as distinguished from a learning of it from others after its occurrence."). (phrase "contemporaneous perception of the accident" contemplates a sudden and brief event causing injury). But on this record and under existing law, we cannot say that the requirements for bystander recovery have been satisfied.

. . . .

Such cases illustrate the distinction between the perception of circumstances that would cause a parent intense fear and uncertainty regarding a child's well-being and actually witnessing the realization of such fears first-hand.

Maria Chapa unquestionably experienced fear and shock when she observed an empty street where her vehicle should have been. Although the elements of a bystander claim are applied flexibly and on a case-by-case basis, this case presents an important disjunction between the alleged cause of injury to the primary victim — *i.e.,* the "accident" — and the circumstances observed by the relative. Texas courts have reserved recognition of bystander claims for those cases in which the emotional impact results from a sensory and contemporaneous observance of the accident that caused the close relative's harm. (holding family members are not bystanders where they discovered, but did not witness, the removal of decedent's eyes). Here, however, the evidence is undisputed that Maria did not "sense" her children's serious injury or death; to the contrary, she admittedly had *no* knowledge of what had happened to her vehicle or her children until they were returned. (holding that parents who "did not contemporaneously perceive the injury to their daughter" are not bystanders). The requirement that a parent bystander's mental anguish "result[] from a direct emotional impact upon plaintiff from the sensory and contemporaneous observance of the accident" necessarily excludes circumstances in which the parent saw nothing, heard nothing, does not know what happened to the child, and does not know if the child is injured. Here, Maria seeks to recover not for a terrible injury to her children that she witnessed, but for her fear of not knowing where they were or whether they were seriously injured.

After Chambers returned the vehicle, Maria learned of the "accident" and the condition of her children, but she acquired this knowledge from others. She did not witness the accident or the injuries, but learned of them from her children after the occurrence.

. . . .

On this record, we conclude that the second requirement of the bystander test has not been satisfied. . . .

CONCLUSION

We therefore affirm the judgment of the trial court.

––––––––––

1. Was the court's negative holding driven by the fact that the children were not physically injured?

2. Does the holding suggest that Texas is unsympathetic to a victim's mental distress? If so, why?

3. What result if Maria had seen the tow-truck drive off with her car attached, knowing her children were inside?

––––––––––

BINNS v. WESTMINSTER MEMORIAL PARK
Court of Appeal of California, 2009
171 Cal. App. 4th 700, 89 Cal. Rptr. 3d 890

ARONSON, J.

In 1977, plaintiff's mother purchased a burial plot for plaintiff's deceased father in defendant's cemetery. A few months later, plaintiff's mother purchased three additional plots adjacent to the plot in which plaintiff's father was interred, intended for herself, plaintiff, and plaintiff's wife or, if plaintiff did not marry, plaintiff's brother. As part of the transaction, plaintiff's mother executed a purchase agreement with defendant. Plaintiff's mother died in 1986 and was interred in the plot next to plaintiff's father.

On Easter 2005, plaintiff visited his parents' graves and discovered a stranger, Maria Vallejo, buried in the plot immediately adjacent to his mother, which had been reserved for plaintiff. Plaintiff immediately brought the situation to the attention of Lydia Navas, defendant's family services counselor, who reviewed some records and promised to obtain further information. The following day, Navas contacted plaintiff, confirmed Vallejo had been buried in plaintiff's plot, and promised to rectify the problem. A few days later, Navas again contacted plaintiff to inform him the cemetery had removed Vallejo from plaintiff's plot and reinterred the corpse in another location. Defendant had not notified plaintiff it would disturb Vallejo's remains to rectify the situation.

. . . .

In awarding plaintiff emotional distress damages, the trial court relied exclusively on plaintiff's cause of action for negligent infliction of emotional distress. Damages for severe emotional distress are recoverable in a negligence action "when they result from the breach of a duty owed the plaintiff that is assumed by the defendant or imposed on the defendant as a matter of law, or that arises out of a relationship between the two." Defendant contends plaintiff's claim fails because it did not owe plaintiff a duty to prevent the temporary burial of Vallejo in his burial plot. We disagree.

Civil Code section 1714, subdivision (a), presents the general rule concerning a person's legal responsibility to others: "Everyone is responsible, not only for the result of his or her willful acts, but also for an injury occasioned to another by his or her want of ordinary care or skill in the management of his or her property or person, except so far as the latter has, willfully or by want of ordinary care, brought the injury upon himself or herself." The Supreme Court has observed that ' "[i]n the absence of a statutory provision limiting this rule, exceptions to the general principle imposing liability for negligence are recognized only when clearly supported by public policy." '

Generally, nonstatutory limitations on legal duty turn on (1) the reasonable foreseeability of the risk of injury, and (2) a weighing of policy considerations for and against imposition of liability. In elaborating upon the relationship between these two elements, the court in *Quesada v. Oak Hill Improvement Co. (1989) 213 Cal.App.3d 596, 608 [261 Cal. Rptr. 769]* (*Quesada*) explained that "although the court . . . utilize[s] foreseeability to begin a determination of duty, the final determination . . . is tempered by policy considerations."

The seminal case of *Rowland v. Christian (1968) 69 Cal.2d 108 [70 Cal. Rptr. 97, 443 P.2d 561]* set forth the major factors in determining the scope of a person's legal duty: "the foreseeability of harm to the plaintiff, the degree of certainty that the plaintiff suffered injury, the closeness of the connection between the defendant's conduct and the injury suffered, the moral blame attached to the defendant's conduct, the policy of preventing future harm, the extent of the burden to the defendant and consequences to the community of imposing a duty to exercise care with resulting liability for breach, and the availability, cost, and prevalence of insurance for the risk involved."

. . . . In *Christensen v. Superior Court (1991) 54 Cal.3d 868 [2 Cal. Rptr. 2d 79, 820 P.2d 181]* (*Christensen*), decided two years after *Quesada*, the mortuary defendants contracted with the cemetery defendants to perform cremations. The cemetery defendants mishandled the decedents' remains. The defendant mortuaries knew or should have known of the cemetery's malfeasance. (*Christensen, at pp. 878-879.*) The Supreme Court held family members could recover emotional distress damages because the mortuaries and crematories owed them an independent tort duty arising from a special relationship. (*Id. at p. 891.*) The court recognized that " '[o]nce a mortuary . . . undertakes to accept the care, custody and control of the remains, a duty of care must be found running to the members of decedent's bereaved family.' "

The *Christensen* court determined it was foreseeable that mishandling human remains likely would cause serious emotional distress to members of the decedent's immediate family.

. . . .

Although the issue is close, we conclude it is foreseeable a person could suffer severe emotional distress upon discovery a stranger had been buried in their family gravesite.

. . . Though unintentional, defendant's negligent interment of a stranger in plaintiff's family burial plot compromised the purpose underlying the agreement between the family and the cemetery, i.e., the emotional tranquility arising from the cemetery's promise that plaintiff will be buried next to his loved ones. While other relatives may be upset to discover a stranger buried in a family plot, it is the intended user of the plot who is most likely to suffer emotional distress from the incident.

. . . Finally, we note that recognizing a duty here supports the principle that "[a]s a society we want those who are entrusted with the bodies of our dead to exercise the greatest of care."

. . . "Emotional distress includes suffering, anguish, fright, horror, nervousness, grief, anxiety, worry, shock, humiliation, and shame." (*CACI No. 1604*; see also Black's Law Dict. (8th ed. 2004) p. 563 [defining emotional distress].) At trial, plaintiff presented evidence that when he discovered Vallejo's body buried in his own plot, he began trembling and felt as if he had been "struck by lightning." He was "horrified," believing he had been "spiritually violated." Plaintiff viewed the plot as having been desecrated because Vallejo" soul had been disturbed when she was moved from what was to have been her final resting place. As a result of defendant's error, plaintiff testified he suffered from nightmares, loss of appetite, and cold sweats. Plaintiff testified he did not seek medical care because he could not afford it

. . . .

The judgment and order are affirmed. In the interests of justice, each side is to bear its own costs on appeal.

DISSENT

BEDSWORTH, Acting P. J., Concurring and Dissenting

. . . .

It seems to me we started out with a perfectly intelligible and easily applicable rule . . . that conduct amounting to a breach of contract becomes tortious only when it also violates an independent duty arising from principles of tort law. In applying this rule to funerary/mortuary services, it held that such an independent duty arises when one party agrees with another *to handle the remains* of a deceased loved one. It did not hold that such a duty arises when someone agrees to provide a plot for burial, and I see no reason to create such a rule.

---

1. What is it about improperly handling the remains of dead bodies that makes it one of the only actions that consistently supports a claim for negligent infliction of emotional distress?

2.   Aren't there other actions that can be seen as just as consistently disturbing? Couldn't the same be said for improperly handling the birth of a child, for example?

3.   Make an argument in favor of the cemetery in this case. Do cases such as this one place too heavy a burden on those who are in the business of handling the deceased?

4.   Should it be sufficient that the cemetery quickly moved Maria Vallejo's remains out of plaintiff's plot?

F.   INJURY TO UNBORN CHILDREN

PROBLEM

Dale negligently crashes into Karen's car, causing Karen to give birth to Rick three months early. Because of the early birth, Rick suffers brain damage. Would you take Rick's suit against Dale? What if Rick had been stillborn?

RENSLOW v. MENNONITE HOSPITAL
Supreme Court of Illinois, 1977
67 Ill. 2d 348, 367 N.E.2d 1250

MORAN, JUSTICE.

. . . .

There is but one issue: Does a child, not conceived at the time negligent acts were committed against its mother, have a cause of action against the tortfeasors for its injuries resulting from their conduct?

Plaintiff's six-count complaint for negligence . . . alleges that in October of 1965, when her mother was 13 years of age, the defendants, on two occasions, negligently transfused her mother with 500 cubic centimeters of Rh-positive blood. The mother's Rh-negative blood was incompatible with, and was sensitized by, the Rh-positive blood. Her mother had no knowledge of an adverse reaction from the transfusions and did not know she had been improperly transfused or that her blood had been sensitized. In December 1973 she first discovered her condition when a routine blood screening was ordered by her physician in the course of prenatal care. Plaintiff further asserts that the defendants discovered they had administered the incompatible blood, but at no time notified her mother or the mother's family.

The resulting sensitization of the mother's blood allegedly caused prenatal damage to plaintiff's hemolitic processes, which put her life in jeopardy and necessitated her induced premature birth. . . . It is further alleged that, as a result of the defendants' acts, plaintiff suffers from permanent damage to various organs, her brain, and her nervous system.

The trial court dismissed plaintiff's cause of action because she was not "at the time of the alleged infliction of the injury conceived." . . . [T]he appellate court found no reason to deny a cause of action to a person simply because he had not yet been conceived at the time of the wrongful conduct.

. . . [I]n *Allaire v. St. Luke's Hospital* (1900), 184 Ill. 359, 56 N.E. 638, 641, . . . Mr. Justice Boggs [dissent] pointed out that it was clearly demonstrable that "at a period of gestation in advance of . . . parturition the foetus is capable of independent and separate life, and that though within the [mother's body] it is not merely a part of her body, for her body may die in all of its parts and the child remain alive and capable of maintaining life when separated from the dead body of the mother." . . . [T]he impact of Mr. Justice Boggs' dissent eventually turned the tide toward prenatal recovery. *Bonbrest v. Kotz* (D.D.C. 1946), 65 F. Supp. 138, was the first decision to recognize a common law right of action for prenatal injuries. It relied heavily on Mr. Justice Boggs' reasoning — that an infant should be recognized as having a legal existence separate from its mother's at such time as it was capable of sustaining life separate from her. . . . This court in *Amann v. Faidy* . . . held that there is a right of action for the wrongful death of a viable child, injured in utero, who is born alive but thereafter dies. *Rodriguez v. Patti* . . . extended a common law right of action for personal injuries to an infant viable when wrongfully injured in utero. In *Chrisafogeorgis v. Brandenberg* . . . this rationale was further extended to permit a wrongful death action for a viable child wrongfully injured in utero and thereafter born dead. . . .

Although we have not decided whether a surviving infant has a right of action for injuries sustained in utero during a previable state of its development, our appellate courts have answered that question in the affirmative. *Sana v. Brown* (1962), 35 Ill. App. 2d 425; *Daley v. Meier* (1961), 33 Ill. App. 2d 218. *See also Rapp v. Hiemenz* (1969), 107 Ill. App. 2d 382, where an action for wrongful death as the result of prenatal injuries to a previable fetus, born dead, was denied.

The complaint in the case sub judice contains no allegation that the plaintiff was viable when her injuries were sustained. We, therefore, must consider whether the plaintiff must allege that she was viable at the time her injuries were sustained.

The rule permitting a cause of action only where the child is viable at the time of the injury has been criticized as a "most unsatisfactory criterion, since [viability] is a relative matter, depending on the health of mother and child and many other matters in addition to the stage of development." (Prosser, Torts sec. 55, at 337 (4th ed. 1971). . . .

Because the appellate court found the risk of harm reasonably foreseeable, it assumed duty was established, and concluded that the delay between the act and the injury was not a bar to the action.

The implication in the appellate court's opinion that duty and foreseeability are identical in scope is not altogether correct. In *Cunis v. Brennan* (1974), 56 Ill. 2d 372, 375, it was pointed out that "the existence of a legal duty is not to be bottomed on the factor of foreseeability alone." There, quoted with approval, was Dean Leon Green's observation:

"[H]owever valuable the foreseeability formula may be in aiding a jury or judge to reach a decision on the negligence issue, it is altogether inadequate for use by the judge as a basis of determining the duty issue and its scope. The duty issue, being one of law, is broad in its implication; the negligence issue is confined to the particular case and has no implications for other cases. There are many factors other than foreseeability that may condition a judge's imposing or not imposing a duty in the particular case. . . ." Green, *Foreseeability in Negligence Law*, 61 Colum. L. Rev. 1401, 1417-18. . . .

The cases allowing relief to an infant for injuries incurred in its previable state make it clear that a defendant may be held liable to a person whose existence was not apparent at the time of his act. We therefore find it illogical to bar relief for an act done prior to conception where the defendant would be liable for this same conduct had the child, unbeknownst to him, been conceived prior to his act. We believe that there is a right to be born free from prenatal injuries foreseeably caused by a breach of duty to the child's mother.

The extension of duty in such a case is further supported by sound policy considerations. Medical science has developed various techniques which can mitigate or, in some cases, totally alleviate a child's prenatal harm. In light of these substantial medical advances it seems to us that sound social policy requires the extension of duty in this case.

. . . .

Since the liability announced herein represents an extension of duty to a new class of plaintiffs, we hold that it be given prospective application. Therefore, except as to the plaintiff herein, the rule shall apply only to cases arising out of future conduct. . . .

The decision of the appellate court, reversing the trial court's dismissal of this claim for failure to state a cause of action, is therefore affirmed and the cause remanded to the trial court for further proceedings.

---

1. What factors influenced the court to find a duty in *Renslow*? What is the problem with foreseeability as a test?

2. Argue for the hospital that *Renslow* goes too far in permitting a nonexisting (at time of injury) infant to recover.

3. Some courts permit an infant, injured while viable, to recover. If the child is stillborn, no recovery is permitted, however. Also, if the child is killed before birth, no recovery is available. Others drop the viability requirement and permit a child injured *in utero* to recover if born alive. *See Endresz v. Friedberg*, 24 N.Y.2d 478, 301 N.Y.S.2d 65, 248 N.E.2d 901 (1969), where the representative of stillborn twins was not permitted to recover. They were delivered stillborn two days after a car crash that injured the mother.

The majority of states permit a suit by an unborn child for wrongful death, however. *See Volk v. Baldazo*, 103 Idaho 570, 651 P.2d 11 (1982); Gordon, *The Unborn Plaintiff*, 63 Mich. L. Rev. 579 (1965).

PROBLEM

Cheyanne, age fourteen, became pregnant following seduction by her biofeedback therapist. What damages can the child, Tom, recover from the therapist, Art? Tom is a healthy child.

VICCARO v. MILUNSKY

Supreme Judicial Court of Massachusetts, 1990
406 Mass. 777, 551 N.E.2d 8

WILKINS, JUSTICE.

A judge of the United States District Court for the District of Massachusetts has certified novel questions of Massachusetts law to this court. The judge asks whether a child who was born with a genetic defect and his parents have bases under Massachusetts law for recovery against a physician whose negligent preconception counseling led the parents to decide to conceive children.

The facts presented to us in association with the certified questions are brief. In November, 1976, not then married, the Viccaros consulted the defendant physician, a specialist in genetics, genetic disorders, and genetic counseling, concerning the possibility that Amy might have, or be a carrier of, a genetic disorder known as ectodermal dysplasia.[2] The defendant concluded that Amy did not have the disease and that there should be no likelihood of her developing the disorder or of having affected children. In October, 1977, the Viccaros were married. Relying on the defendant's assurances, they bore children. Their first child, a daughter, was born in July, 1980, apparently healthy, without manifestations of the disorder. On March 27, 1984, Adam was born severely afflicted with anhidrotic ectodermal dysplasia. He will require special medical care throughout his life and will suffer substantial physical pain and mental anguish. The Viccaros have suffered and will continue to suffer severe emotional distress and substantial physical injuries (whose nature and cause are not disclosed on the record). Their complaint seeks, in addition to emotional distress damages, recovery of the extraordinary expenses for Adam's care, support, and education; their loss of companionship of a normal son; and their loss of the services and earnings of a normal son.[3]

---

[2] For the purposes of certifying the questions to us, the judge accepted as correct the allegations of the complaint that several members of Amy's family were afflicted with ectodermal dysplasia, a severely disfiguring disorder that affects the skin, hair, nails, teeth, nerve cells, sweat glands, parts of the eyes and ears, and other organs of the body.

[3] In other jurisdictions, the claim that Adam asserts has generally been characterized as a "wrongful life" claim, one made by a child with a genetic defect who was born as a result of the defendant's negligence. The claim the Viccaros assert has generally been termed a "wrongful birth" claim, a claim by parents that, because of the defendant's negligence, they gave birth to a child with a genetic or other congenital defect. The claim asserted in *Burke v. Rivo*, ante 764 (1990), which we decide today, has often been placed in the category of "wrongful conception" or "wrongful pregnancy." That claim is that the birth of a normal, healthy child was a consequence of a negligently performed sterilization procedure or some other negligence without which the unwanted child would not have been born. These labels are not instructive. Any "wrongfulness" lies not in the life, the birth, the conception, or the pregnancy, but in the negligence of the physician. The harm, if any, is not the birth itself but the effect of the defendant's

The Parents' Claim

We think it preferable to consider and decide questions concerning the parents' claim first. . . .

If a child is born with a congenital or genetic disorder, almost all courts have allowed the parents to recover against a negligent physician the extraordinary medical, educational, and other expenses that are associated with and are consequences of the disorder.

We agree with the general rule that the Viccaros are entitled to recover the extraordinary medical and educational expenses and other extraordinary costs associated with caring for Adam. If the Viccaros prove that, when Adam attains his majority, they will remain liable for Adam's support, they will be entitled to recover for the extraordinary expenses they will incur during Adam's majority. In Massachusetts, a parent is liable for the support of an adult child if the child is physically or mentally impaired and incapable of supporting himself. The emotional distress the Viccaros sustain as a result of the defendant's negligence and any physical harm caused by that emotional distress are also recoverable. *See Burke v. Rivo, supra* at 768.

The Viccaros' claim for the loss of Adam's society and companionship as a normal child lacks merit. The defendant is not responsible for the fact that Adam is afflicted with a substantial genetic disease. Although the defendant may be liable for certain damages because, had he not been negligent, according to the complaint, the Viccaros would not have conceived a child, the defendant cannot be liable for the Viccaros' loss of the companionship of a normal child.

We summarize our conclusions as to the parents' claims. Question 3, concerning the existence of a cause of action in the parents, we answer in the affirmative. There is one. We need not answer question 4 (a) because the Viccaros do not press a claim for all financial burdens associated with raising Adam. In response to the two parts of question 4 (b), we answer affirmatively that the Viccaros may recover for Adam's extraordinary medical needs and, as to the second question in question 4 (b), in certain circumstances the Viccaros could recover for extraordinary expenses they may incur after Adam's majority. Because the Viccaros may recover damages for the cost of the extraordinary care that Adam needs, we answer the first question in question 4 (c) in the affirmative. We do not have sufficient information, however, to answer the second part of question 4 (c), concerning the parents' right to recover for wages they lost or will lose in providing extraordinary care to Adam. In general, damages should be measured by the fair market value of the necessary extraordinary services. Perhaps the parents' lost wages will be an appropriate measure of recovery in some special circumstance. As to question 4 (d), the parents may recover for emotional distress and for physical harm caused by that emotional distress, offset by whatever emotional benefits they may derive from the existence of their

---

negligence on the parents' physical, emotional, and financial well-being resulting from the denial to the parents of their right, as the case may be, to decide whether to bear a child or whether to bear a child with a genetic or other defect. We abstained from using any label in the *Burke* opinion, such as wrongful pregnancy, and shall similarly abstain in this case from using the labels "wrongful life" or "wrongful birth."

first child and offset (as the Viccaros concede) by any benefits that may be derived from the existence of Adam. We do not know what other physical injuries this question may refer to. For completeness, although we are not asked to comment on the point, whatever emotional benefits the parents may derive from the children may also be offset against the extraordinary expenses the parents may incur.

We see no basis for the Viccaros to recover for the loss of Adam's society and companionship as a normal child, and thus we answer question 4 (e) in the negative. Question 4 (f) we answer in the negative because the Viccaros make no serious argument that they are entitled to recover for the loss of Adam's services as a normal child.

The Child's Claim

The judge has also asked us: "Does Massachusetts recognize a cause of action for wrongful life, where a minor child, afflicted with a genetic defect, alleges that the negligent preconception genetic counseling of his parents by a geneticist induced his parents to conceive and give birth to the child?" We answer the question in the negative. Because, as alleged by his parents, Adam would not have been born if the defendant had not been negligent, there is a fundamental problem of logic if Adam were allowed to recover against the defendant in a negligence-based tort action.

The almost universal rule in this country is that a physician is not liable to a child who was born because of the physician's negligence. . . .

A few courts, however, have allowed a child who was born with a defect to recover against a negligent physician the extraordinary expenses that he or she will incur during his or her lifetime because of the hereditary defect. . . .

We faced a somewhat similar, but not identical, question in *Payton v. Abbott Labs*, 386 Mass. 540, 557-560 (1982), where we concluded that a woman, who would not have been born but for her mother's use of a drug manufactured by the defendants, was barred from recovery for physical or emotional damage she suffered as a result of her mother's ingestion of the drug. We said that "[t]he provider of the probable means of a plaintiff's very existence should not be liable for unavoidable, collateral consequences of the use of that means." *Id.* at 560. By the same token, the defendant whose negligence (it is asserted) is a reason for Adam's very existence should not be liable for the unfortunate consequences of Adam's birth with a genetic disease, such as his pain and suffering, emotional distress, and loss of his parents' consortium.

On a theoretical basis, it is difficult to conclude that the defendant physician was in breach of any duty owed to Adam. It is alleged, however, that Adam does exist as a result of the defendant's negligence and that he may incur substantial and extraordinary expenses for medical care, educational, and other needs. It is this pragmatic consideration that has moved a few jurisdictions, as noted above, to allow a child like Adam to recover those extraordinary expenses that he will incur during his lifetime because of his genetic defect. As long, however, as Adam's parents are entitled to recover against the defendant for the extraordinary costs they will incur because of Adam's genetic disease, Adam need not have his own cause of action for those expenses. We do not know Adam's life expectancy nor whether he has a reasonable prospect of supporting himself in adulthood. We do not totally discount the possibility that we might impose liability for the extraordinary expenses of caring for a person like Adam after his parents' deaths, perhaps in order to keep such a person from being a public charge. That is not this case, as far as we are told, and certainly no question has been asked of us in these specific terms.

. . . .

---

1. What did the court mean in *Payton* when it said, "the provider of the probable means of a plaintiff's very existence should not be liable. . . ."?

2. Do Adam's extraordinary costs mirror those of his parents?

3. Should the emotional benefits that a parent receives from having a child be set off against the actual expenses of raising the child?

4. Should the parent's claim be denied because:

[A]n assumption that a judge or jury can measure the net loss to parents of the birth of a normal child is so inconsistent with the reverence we should have for human life that the harm to society from such an inquiry, augmented by the harm to the family and child, outweighs the value of compensating parents for the wrong they allege. My position in this case is the same. Although I recognize that the burden of raising an impaired child may be considerably heavier than the burden associated with raising a normal child, the controlling values and principles are the same.

(*Viccaro* dissent, 406 Mass. at 785–86.) What if the family is very poor?

5. The calculation of damages in wrongful life cases has been viewed as impossible:

"The *Gleitman v. Cosgrove* Court found it impossible to compare the infant's condition if the doctor had not been negligent with the infant's impaired condition as a result of the negligence. Measurement of the Value of life with impairments against the nonexistence of life itself was, the court declared, a logical impossibility. Consequently the Court rejected the infant's [entire] claim." . . .

"The *Berman v. Allan* Court also declined to recognize a cause of action in an infant born with birth defects. [E]ven a life with serious defects is more valuable than non-existence, the alternative for the infant plaintiff if his mother chose to have an abortion."

Procanik by Procanik v. Cillo, 97 N.J. 339, 478 A.2d 755 (1984). Does *Gleitman* or *Berman* have anything to recommend it?

6. What damages might Adam face in fact? *See* Kelly, *The Rightful Position in "Wrongful Life" Actions*, 42 Hastings L.J. 505 (1991).

7. There may be substantial cause in fact issues, and a need for expert testimony in these cases, when the parents argue that the death or impairment of the child was caused by prescription drugs. The Supreme Court recently held:

Faced with a proffer of expert scientific testimony, . . . the trial judge must determine . . . whether the expert is proposing to testify to (1) scientific knowledge that (2) will assist the trier of fact to understand or determine a fact in issue. This entails a preliminary assessment of whether the reasoning or methodology underlying the testimony is scientifically valid and of whether that reasoning or methodology properly can be applied to the facts in issue. . . . Many factors will bear on the inquiry. . . .

Daubert v. Merrell Dow Pharmaceuticals, Inc., 509 U.S. 579, 113 S. Ct. 2786 (1993).

BURKE v. RIVO
Supreme Judicial Court of Massachusetts, 1990
406 Mass. 764, 551 N.E.2d 1

WILKINS, JUSTICE.

. . . .

In December, 1983, the plaintiff Carole Burke met with the defendant physician to discuss her desire not to have more children. The Burke family was experiencing financial difficulties. She wanted to return to work to support her family and to fulfil her career goals. The Burkes assert that the defendant recommended that Carole undergo a bipolar cauterization procedure and that he guaranteed that she would not again become pregnant if she did so. In February, 1984, the defendant performed a laparoscopic bilateral tubal ligation by bipolar cauterization.

On June 25, 1985, a pregnancy test confirmed that Carole was pregnant. On February 12, 1986, she give [sic] birth to a fourth child, and the next day she underwent a second sterilization procedure, known as bilateral salpingectomy. A pathology report showed that there had been a recanalization of the left fallopian tube. The Burkes assert that, if the defendant had told Carole of the risk of recanalization, however small, she would initially have selected a different sterilization procedure.

The judge has only reported questions concerning damages. . . . The matters of liability are, however, not before us, and remain to be proved.

. . . We reject his arguments that in Massachusetts there should be no liability for negligently performing a sterilization procedure when the result is the conception of a child; no liability for negligently failing to advise a patient of the risks of conceiving a child following a particular sterilization operation (where the patient, properly informed, would have selected a different and more certain sterilization operation); and no liability for breach of a guarantee that following a sterilization procedure there would be no further pregnancy.

The great weight of authority permits the parents of a normal child born as a result of a physician's negligence to recover damages directly associated with the birth (sometimes including damage for the parents' emotional distress), but courts are divided on whether the parents may recover the economic expense of rearing the child. . . .

The judge below recognized that damages properly would include the cost of the unsuccessful sterilization procedure and costs directly flowing from the pregnancy: the wife's lost earning capacity; medical expenses of the delivery and care following the birth; the cost of care for the other children while the wife was incapacitated; the cost of the second sterilization procedure and any expenses flowing from that operation; and the husband's loss of consortium. We would add the wife's pain and suffering in connection with the pregnancy and birth and with the second sterilization procedure. We also see no reason why the plaintiffs should not recover for emotional distress they sustained as a result of the unwanted pregnancy. Emotional distress could be the probable consequence of a breach of the duty the defendant owed directly to the plaintiffs. . . .

The principal issue is whether the plaintiffs are entitled, if they establish liability, to the cost of raising their child. Under normal tort and contract principles, that cost is both a reasonably foreseeable and a natural and probable consequence of the wrongs that the plaintiffs allege. The question is whether there is any public policy consideration to which we should give effect to limit traditional tort and contract damages. We conclude that there is none as to parents who have elected sterilization for economic reasons.

Many justifications often relied on for declining to allow recovery of the cost of rearing a healthy child born as a result of a physician's negligence are outstandingly unimpressive. . . . The judicial declaration that the joy and pride in raising a child always outweigh any economic loss the parents may suffer, thus precluding recovery for the cost of raising the child . . . simply lacks verisimilitude. The very fact that a person has sought medical intervention to prevent him or her from having a child demonstrates that, for that person, the benefits of parenthood did not outweigh the burdens, economic and otherwise, of having a child. The extensive use of contraception and sterilization and the performance of numerous abortions each year show that, in some instances, large numbers of people do not accept parenthood as a net positive circumstance. We agree with those courts that have rejected the theory that the birth of a child is for all parents at all times a net benefit. . . . While we firmly reject a universal rule that the birth of an unexpected healthy child is always a net benefit, we also firmly reject any suggestion that the availability of abortion or of adoption furnishes a basis for limiting damages payable by a physician but for whose negligence the child would not have been conceived. . . .

We are also unimpressed with the reasoning that child-rearing expenses should not be allowed because some day the child could be adversely affected by learning that he or she was unwanted and that someone else had paid for the expense of rearing the child. . . . Courts expressing concern about the effect on the child nevertheless allow the parents to recover certain direct expenses from the negligent physician without expressing concern about harm to the child when the child learns that he or she was unwanted. . . . The once unwanted child's knowledge that someone other than the parents had been obliged to pay for the cost of rearing him or her may in fact alleviate the child's distress at the knowledge of having been once unwanted. . . . In any event, it is for the parents, not the courts, to decide whether a lawsuit would adversely affect the child and should not be maintained.

We see no validity to the arguments, sometimes made, that the costs of child-rearing are too speculative or are unreasonably disproportionate to the doctor's negligence. . . . The determination of the anticipated costs of child-rearing is no more complicated or fanciful than many calculations of future losses made every day in tort cases. If a physician is negligent in caring for a newborn child, damage calculations would be made concerning the new-born's earning capacity and expected medical expenses over an entire lifetime. The expenses of rearing a child are far more easily determined. If there is any justification for denying recovery of normal tort damages in a case of this character, it is not that the cost of rearing a child is incapable of reasonable calculation or is too great to impose on a negligent physician.

A substantial number of jurisdictions have allowed recovery of the cost of rearing a normal child to adulthood, offset, however, by the benefits that the parents receive in having a normal, healthy child . . . ("allowing the plaintiff to prove that raising a child constitutes damage is the course of greater justice"). Such a balancing by the trier of fact requires a comparison of the economic loss of child-rearing with the emotional gains of having a normal, healthy child (converted into a dollar value). These courts have thought the comparison appropriate under the general principle expressed in Restatement (Second) of Torts § 920 (1979). A few courts have thought that, because the benefit conferred did not affect the economic interest that was harmed, no mitigation of the cost of child-rearing should be recognized. . . .

If the parents' desire to avoid the birth of a child was founded on eugenic reasons (avoidance of a feared genetic defect) or was founded on therapeutic reasons (concern for the mother's health) and if a healthy, normal baby is born, the justification for allowing recovery of the cost of rearing a normal child to maturity is far less than when, to conserve family resources, the parents sought unsuccessfully to avoid conceiving another child. *See University of Ariz. Health Sciences Center v. Superior Court*, 136 Ariz. 579, 585 (1983) ("For example, where the parent sought sterilization in order to avoid the danger of genetic defect, the jury could easily find that the uneventful birth of a healthy, non-defective child was a blessing rather than a 'damage' "). . . .

We conclude that, in addition to the recoverable damages described earlier in this opinion, parents may recover the cost of rearing a normal, healthy but (at least initially) unwanted child if their reason for seeking sterilization was founded on economic or financial considerations. In such a situation, the trier of fact should offset against the cost of rearing the child the benefit, if any, the parents receive and will receive from having their child. We discern no reason founded on sound public policy to immunize a physician from having to pay for a reasonably foreseeable consequence of his negligence or from a natural and probable consequence of a breach of his guarantee, namely, the parents' expenses in rearing the child to adulthood.

. . . .

1. Should a suit for loss of consortium be denied because the child might someday discover defendant paid for its upbringing? Justice O'Connor, in dissent, argued:

> The court states that it is "unimpressed with the reasoning [of several courts] that child-rearing expenses should not be allowed because some day the child could be adversely affected by learning that he or she was unwanted and that someone else had paid for the expense of rearing the child." The court concludes that "it is for the parents, not the courts, to decide whether a lawsuit would adversely affect the child and should not be maintained." I disagree. The State's interest in strengthening and encouraging family life for the protection and care of children is legitimate and strong. Indeed, it is for the State to determine whether to adopt a rule of damages that would encourage litigation harmful to families — litigation designed to produce the result, ultimately to be discovered by the child, that he or she was supported not by the parents, because they did not want him or her, but by an unwilling stranger.

Burke, 551 N.E.2d at 7, 8. Might the child say, "Cool"?

2. Is the jury capable of the "economic" balancing that the court requires? Argue that the birth of a child is always a net benefit. Argue that the availability of an abortion is relevant.

3. How is the argument in *Burke* different from other emotional harm actions in this chapter?

Chapter 5

NEGLIGENCE

A. INTRODUCTION

Negligence has been the core concept in personal injury law since at least 1850. Substantial debate exists as to the nature of personal injury law before 1850, however. There are four different theories concerning the nature of tort law before 1850. First, Professor Wex Malone argues that the law rested on absolute liability. If the plaintiff was able to show cause in fact, the defendant was absolutely liable, and fault was not an issue:

> At your request I accompany you when you are about your own affairs; my enemies fall upon and kill me, you must pay for my death. You take me to see a wild beast show or that interesting spectacle, a mad man; beast or mad man kills me; you must pay. You hang up your sword; someone else knocks it down so that it cuts me; you must pay. In none of these cases can you honestly swear that you did nothing that helped to bring about death or wound.

W. Malone, *Ruminations on the Role of Fault in the History of the Common Law of Torts*, 31 La. L. Rev. 1, 3 (1970).

Second, Professor Robert Rabin argues that there was no tort law, merely a broad sea of immunities before 1850:

> Throughout the "heyday of negligence," the common law courts wrestled with issues that forced a choice between powerful no-liability principles and a fledgling doctrine of fault liability. Gradually the no-liability principles — immunities, privileges, and no-duty considerations imported from other conceptual systems (property, contract and such) — retreated, like a melting glacier in a hostile environment, before the successive onslaughts of fault and, later, strict liability rules.

Rabin, Perspectives on Tort Law 44 (2d ed. 1983).

Third, Professor Schwartz suggests a vacuum of knowledge; we just don't have enough information to evaluate the nature of the law:

> The meager quality of the English and American evidence counsels caution in making any dramatic assertions about pre-nineteenth century tort doctrine.

Schwartz, *Tort Law and the Economy in Nineteenth-Century America: A Reinterpretation*, 90 Yale L.J. 1722 (1981).

Fourth, Professor William Prosser suggests that prior to 1850, personal injury law rested on the distinction between two writs, trespass and case. Whenever someone wanted to bring a personal injury action, he or she obtained a writ of trespass to proceed before the king's common-law court. If the facts were outside the writ of trespass, he or she had to claim under the writ of trespass on the case. Trespass was available for direct and immediate injuries, while case was used for indirect injuries. Trespass did not require a showing of actual damages, but they were a requirement for case. W. Page Keeton et al., Prosser and Keeton on Torts 29–30 (5th ed. 1984).

The distinction between the writ of trespass and the writ of trespass on the case is shown in the following example:

> [I]f a man throws a log into the highway, and in that act it hits me; I may maintain trespass, because it is an immediate wrong; but if as it lies there I tumble over it, and receive an injury, I must bring an action upon the case; because it is only prejudicial in consequence, for which originally I could have no action at all.

Reynolds v. Clarke, 1 Strange 634, 92 Eng. Rep. 410 (1726).

Over the years the intentional torts grew out of trespass and therefore do not require a showing of damages. Negligence grew out of trespass on the case, and therefore damages must be shown to recover for negligence. *See Brown v. Kendall*, 6 Cush. (60 Mass.) 292 (1850).

B.   THE CORE CONCEPT

In order for a plaintiff to recover in negligence, he or she must show five elements:

1. *Duty.* The plaintiff must show that a legal obligation extends from the defendant to this plaintiff for this injury.

2. *Breach of Duty.* The plaintiff must show that the defendant breached his duty to the plaintiff. This is referred to as negligence and will be considered in this chapter.

3. *Cause-in-Fact.* The plaintiff must show that the defendant's conduct was a cause-in-fact of the plaintiff's injury. Cause-in-fact is often a matter of science. Did the defendant's conduct have something to do with the plaintiff's injury as a matter of science?

4. *Proximate Cause.* This is a matter of social policy, of practical politics. Liability cannot run-on or extend forever. A line must be drawn at some point, and proximate cause is the concept and the process for drawing that line. The question is whether the defendant's negligent conduct, although a cause-in-fact of the injury, is also the proximate cause. Proximate cause is often used to protect a negligent corporation from liability, especially when the damages caused were large.

5. *Damages.* In order to recover in negligence, the plaintiff must show that the defendant's conduct caused damages to the plaintiff.

Note that the term negligence is used in two ways: one, the five elements that must be shown to win in court, and two, the second requirement of the five-part negligence formula (2. Breach of Duty).

PROBLEM

John (age nine), a little league baseball player, was shifted from second base to right field during a regular baseball game. (Second base is his usual position.) A fly ball was hit, and in John's attempt to catch the ball, he was hit in the eye by the ball and seriously injured. (John said the sun was in his eyes.)

John, by means of his parents, wants to sue the coach on the basis that the coach failed to instruct the boy how to shield his eyes from the sun when he caught a fly ball. Assume that the coach is a father of one of the players, a volunteer. John's parents have consulted you for advice. Discuss.

C.   THE STANDARD OF CARE

BLYTH v. BIRMINGHAM WATERWORKS CO.
Court of Exchequer, 1856
11 Exch. 781, 156 Eng. Rep. 1047

[The defendant had installed water mains with fireplugs in the street. A large quantity of water escaped from a leak, where the fireplug joins the main, and forced its way through the ground into the plaintiff's house. One of the defendant's engineers stated that the leak might have been caused by the recent frost, one of the most severe frosts on record. The water main and fireplugs had been installed 25 years earlier and had functioned without problems. The judge left it to the jury to decide whether the defendant had used proper care. The jury found a verdict for the plaintiff. Defendant appealed.]

ALDERSON, B. I am of opinion that there was no evidence to be left to the jury. The case turns upon the question, whether the facts proved show that the defendants were guilty of negligence. Negligence is the omission to do something which a reasonable man, guided upon those considerations which ordinarily regulate the conduct of human affairs, would do, or doing something which a prudent and reasonable man would not do. The defendants might have been liable for negligence, if, unintentionally, they omitted to do, or doing something which a prudent and reasonable man would not do. The defendants might have been liable for negligence, if, unintentionally, they omitted to do that which a reasonable person would have done, or did that which a person taking reasonable precautions would not have done. A reasonable man would act with reference to the average circumstances of the temperature in ordinary years. The defendants had provided against such frosts as experience would have led men, acting prudently, to provide against; and they are not guilty of negligence, because their precautions proved insufficient against the effects of the extreme severity of the frost of 1855, which penetrated to a greater depth than any which ordinarily occurs south of the polar regions. Such a state of circumstances constitutes a contingency against which no reasonable man can provide. The result was an accident, for which the defendant cannot be held liable.

[The concurring opinions are omitted.] Verdict to be entered for the defendants.

———————

1.   Where did the court obtain the negligence concept?

2.   What would it cost to rebury the water mains? How important is providing water to the community? How often would this injury occur?

3.   Would it be helpful, in deciding whether the defendant was negligent, to know the exact damage to the plaintiff?

4.   Should a drug manufacturer be liable for risks that premarket testing did not reveal?

UNITED STATES v. CARROLL TOWING CO.
United States Court of Appeals, Second Circuit, 1947
159 F.2d 169

[During strong winds, a barge named the *Anna C.* broke loose, drifted down river, collided with a tanker and sank. Several acts contributed to the sinking. Because of the negligence of the harbormaster and a tug (the *Carroll)* deckhand, in adjusting the lines holding the *Anna C*, she broke free while they were moving (drilling) another barge. This is a suit in admiralty to recover for the value of the *Anna C.* and her cargo (flour) owned by the United States. The issue discussed here is whether the recovery by the owners of the *Anna C.* should be reduced because the plaintiff's bargee was absent from his post (contributory negligence). If present, he could have reattached the lines and called for help to pump out the sinking *Anna C.*]

LEARNED HAND, CIRCUIT JUDGE.

. . . It appears from the foregoing review that there is no general rule to determine when the absence of a bargee or other attendant will make the owner of the barge liable for injuries to other vessels if she breaks away from her moorings. However, in any case where he would be so liable for injuries to others, obviously he must reduce his damages proportionately, if the injury is to his own barge. It becomes apparent why there can be no such general rule, when we consider the grounds for such a liability. Since there are occasions when every vessel will break from her moorings, and since, if she does, she becomes a menace to those about her; the owner's duty, as in other similar situations, to provide against resulting injuries is a function of three variables: (1) The probability that she will break away; (2) the gravity of the resulting injury, if she does; (3) the burden of adequate precautions. Possibly it serves to bring this notion into relief to state it in algebraic terms: if the probability be called P; the injury, L; and the burden, B; liability depends upon whether B is less than L multiplied by P: i.e., whether $B < PL$. Applied to the situation at bar, the likelihood that a barge will break from her fasts and the damage she will do, vary with the place and time; for example, if a storm threatens, the danger is greater; so it is, if she is in a crowded harbor where moored barges are constantly being shifted about. On the other hand, the barge must not be the bargee's prison, even though he lives aboard; he must go ashore at times. We need not say whether, even in such crowded waters as New York Harbor a bargee must be aboard at night at all; it may be that the custom is otherwise . . . and that, if so, the situation is one where custom should control. We leave that question open; but we hold that it is not in all cases a sufficient answer to a bargee's absence without excuse, during working hours, that he has properly made fast his barge to a pier, when he leaves her. In the case at bar the bargee left at five o'clock in the afternoon of January 3rd and the flotilla broke away at about two o'clock in the afternoon of the following day, twenty-one hours afterwards. The bargee had been away all the time, and we hold that his fabricated story was affirmative evidence that he had no excuse for his absence. At the locus in quo — especially during the short January days and in the full tide of war activity — barges were being constantly "drilled" in and out. Certainly it was not beyond reasonable expectation that, with the inevitable haste and bustle, the work might not be done with adequate care. In such circumstances we hold — and it is all that we do hold — that it was a fair requirement that the Conners Company should have a bargee aboard (unless he had some excuse for his absence), during the working hours of the daylight.

[The reduction of the recovery was affirmed.]

———————

1.   Is this a negligence case, a proximate cause case, or a duty case? The court says that it is a duty case. Should it be placed in the duty chapter? Why is it here?

2.   In applying Hand's formula, how do you obtain numbers for probability, gravity, burden, and injury (before the collision and sinking)?

3.   Apply the Hand formula to *Blyth v. Birmingham Waterworks Co.* Is the formula helpful?

4.   If you plan to marry, will you use such an equation to compare one choice with another? What factors will you weigh, and where will you get the numbers?

5.   The cost-benefit nature of Judge Hand's formula has made it the keystone of the law and economics movement. *See* Richard Posner, *A Theory of Negligence*, 1 J. Legal Stud. 29, 32–33 (1972). For an evaluation of Posner's theory, see Frank Vandall, *Judge Posner's Negligence-Efficiency Theory: A Critique*, 35 Emory L.J. 383 (1986).

6.   Seven years before *Carroll Towing*, Judge Learned Hand stated: "The degree of care demanded of a person by an occasion is the resultant of three factors: the likelihood that his conduct will injure others, taken with the seriousness of the injury if it happens, and balanced against the interest which he must sacrifice to avoid the risk. All these are practically not susceptible of any quantitative estimate — even theoretically. For this reason a solution always involves some preference or choice among incommensurables, and is consigned to a jury. . . ." *Conway v. O'Brien*, 111 F.2d 611, 612 (2d Cir. 1940).

What does this mean?

7.   Judge Posner has recently concluded that developing numerical values for tort policies may not be possible:

Ordinarily, and here, the parties do not give the jury the information required to quantify the variables that the Hand Formula picks out as relevant. That is why the formula has greater analytic than operational significance. Conceptual as well as practical difficulties in monetizing personal injuries may continue to frustrate efforts to measure expected accident costs with the precision that is possible, in principle at least, in measuring the other side of the equation — the cost or burden of precaution.

. . . For many years to come juries may be forced to make rough judgments of reasonableness, intuiting rather than measuring the factors in the Hand Formula; and so long as their judgment is reasonable, the trial judge has no right to set it aside, let alone substitute his own judgment.

McCarty v. Pheasant Run, Inc., 826 F.2d 1554 (7th Cir. 1987). What does Judge Posner mean by saying the Hand formula has "greater analytic than operational significance?" What has more predictive value, the Hand formula or a Torts hornbook?

ADAMS v. BULLOCK
Court of Appeals of New York, 1919
227 N.Y. 208, 125 N.E. 93

CARDOZO, J. The defendant runs a trolley line in the city of Dunkirk, employing the overhead wire system. At one point, the road is crossed by a bridge or culvert which carries the tracks of the Nickle Plate and Pennsylvania railroads. Pedestrians often use the bridge as a short cut between streets, and children play on it. On April 21, 1916, the plaintiff, a boy of twelve years, came across the bridge, swinging a wire about eight feet long. In swinging it, he brought it in contact with the defendant's trolley wire, which ran beneath the structure. The side of the bridge was protected by a parapet eighteen inches wide. Four feet seven and three-fourths inches below the top of the parapet, the trolley wire was strung. The plaintiff was shocked and burned when the wires came together. He had a verdict at Trial Term, which has been affirmed at the Appellate Division by a divided court.

We think the verdict cannot stand. The defendant in using an overhead trolley was in the lawful exercise of its franchise. Negligence, therefore, cannot be imputed to it because it used that system and not another. . . . There was, of course, a duty to adopt all reasonable precautions to minimize the resulting perils. We think there is no evidence that this duty was ignored. The trolley wire was so placed that no one standing on the bridge or even bending over the parapet could reach it. Only some extraordinary casualty, not fairly within the area of ordinary provision, could make it a thing of danger. Reasonable care in the use of a destructive agency imports a high degree of vigilance. . . . But no vigilance, however alert, unless fortified by the gift of prophecy, could have predicted the point upon the route where such an accident would occur. It might with equal reason have been expected anywhere else. At any point upon the route, a mischievous or thoughtless boy might touch the wire with a metal pole, or fling another wire across it. . . . If unable to reach it from the walk, he might stand upon a wagon or climb upon a tree. No special danger at this bridge warned the defendant that there was need of special measures of precaution.

No like accident had occurred before. No custom had been disregarded. We think that ordinary caution did not involve forethought of this extraordinary peril. . . . There is, we may add, a distinction, not to be ignored, between electric light and trolley wires. The distinction is that the former may be insulated. Chance of harm, though remote, may betoken negligence, if needless. Facility of protection may impose a duty to protect. With trolley wires, the case is different. Insulation is impossible. Guards here and there are of little value. To avert the possibility of this accident and others like it at one point or another on the route, the defendant must have abandoned the overhead system, and put the wires underground. Neither its power nor its duty to make the change is shown. To hold it liable upon the facts exhibited in this record would be to charge it as an insurer.

The judgment should be reversed and a new trial granted.

---

1. What factors did the court weigh in deciding whether there was evidence of negligence to give to the jury?

2. Would the "lawful franchise" argument be effective today? Why not?

3. In *Gulf Refining Co. v. Williams*, 183 Miss. 723, 185 So. 234 (1938), the plaintiff was injured while removing the bung hole cap from a drum of gasoline. The drum exploded from a spark. The defense was that "no such happening had ever before been heard of." The "spark was produced by the condition of unrepair in the threads of the bung cap."

The court found for the plaintiff, because a reasonable person should have known of "the condition [of the bung threads] and should reasonably have anticipated . . . that a sudden fire or explosion would be caused by the stated condition of unrepair." Why did the Court in *Gulf Refining* decide for the plaintiff? What does this add to the negligence equation? Why did the court reach a verdict contrary to *Adams*?

4. Does a golfer, preparing to drive a ball, have a duty to warn persons not in the intended line of flight who are on another tee or fairway? No. *Rinaldo v. McGovern*, 587 N.E.2d 264 (N.Y. 1991). *See also Bolton v. Stone*, [1951] A.C. 850.

RIVERA v. NEW YORK CITY TRANSIT AUTHORITY
Court of Appeals of New York, 1991
77 N.Y.2d 322, 567 N.Y.S.2d 629, 569 N.E.2d 432

BELLACOSA, JUDGE.

In 1980, Milton Rivera fell from the platform of the 42nd Street and 6th Avenue Manhattan subway station onto the tracks and was struck by an arriving train. He died several hours later. His widow sued the New York City Transit Authority (TA) for damages. After a trial, the jury returned a verdict in plaintiff's favor. . . .

The theory of plaintiff's case was that the subway operator was negligent in speeding into the station and in not taking measures to stop the train as soon as he first observed the decedent on the platform. The defendant TA contends principally on this appeal that the trial court erred in refusing its requested instructions on the emergency doctrine. . . . This argument has merit and a new trial is required.

Viewing the evidence, as we must, in the light most favorably towards giving the requested emergency doctrine instruction to the jury, we conclude that it was reversible error for the trial court to deny the TA's request. . . . This doctrine recognizes that when an actor is faced with a sudden and unexpected circumstance which leaves little or no time for thought, deliberation or consideration, or causes the actor to be reasonably so disturbed that the actor must make a speedy decision without weighing alternative courses of conduct, the actor may not be negligent if the actions taken are reasonable and prudent in the emergency context. . . . A person in such an emergency situation "cannot reasonably be held to the same accuracy of judgment or conduct as one who has had full opportunity to reflect, even though it later appears that the actor made the wrong decision." . . . A party requesting the emergency instruction is entitled to have the jury so charged if some evidence of a qualifying emergency is presented. If, under some reasonable view of the evidence, an actor was confronted by a sudden and unforeseen occurrence not of the actor's own making, then the reasonableness of the conduct in the face of the emergency is for the jury, which should be appropriately instructed. . . .

The evidence in this case presents a person, awaiting the arrival of the train, suddenly and unexpectedly falling off the platform and onto the tracks. In light of defendant's expert's testimony that the operator was driving the train at a reasonable and prudent speed upon entering the station, the jury — if it believed that witness — could reasonably have concluded that the train was not traveling at an excessive speed and that the accident was unavoidable. Evidence was also adduced indicating that an operator entering the station can observe passengers within only 3 1/2 feet of the edge of the platform. Thus, a reasonable view of the evidence could support the conclusion that the accident was sudden and unexpected in that when the operator first saw Rivera he was standing normally near the edge of the platform but then staggered and fell onto the tracks without warning. A disinterested eyewitness confirmed these key details. Despite some conflicting testimony from other witnesses, the jury could reasonably have concluded that the operator released the brake handle as soon as he observed decedent's sudden, inseparable act of staggering and falling. The entire incident unfolded within seconds, during which flash of time the operator had to assess, deliberate, consider alternatives, and react to attempt to make the safest and speediest choice. The operator, in addition to everything else, also had to be mindful of the consequences to passengers on his train if the train were subjected to a sudden emergency stop. . . .

HANCOCK, JUDGE (dissenting).

I would affirm. The Appellate Division properly held that an emergency charge was not warranted. The emergency doctrine is predicated on the notion that an actor confronted with a sudden and unexpected event which leaves little or no time for thought, deliberation or consideration, or which reasonably causes the actor to make a quick decision without weighing alternative courses of action, cannot be judged in the same way as someone who has had a full opportunity to reflect before acting. . . .

That the actor is confronted with a sudden and unexpected event does not, without more, implicate the emergency doctrine. If that were the law, an emergency charge would be required in almost every accident case because an accident by its very nature is sudden and unexpected. What justifies the charge is the effect that the sudden and unexpected event has on the actor in the particular circumstances — i.e., whether it puts the actor in a position of having to make a split second choice or decision concerning the preferred course of conduct necessary to avoid harm to the endangered party. . . . In such a situation, there is no negligence if the choice or decision is reasonable under the circumstances, even though the actor did not use the best judgment. . . . In this case, neither plaintiff's nor defendant's version of the facts requires an assessment of the reasonableness of the motorman's choice of action in the face of an emergency.

According to plaintiff, the motorman saw or should have seen plaintiff's decedent staggering near the edge of the platform for several seconds prior to decedent's fall onto the tracks. The train then was still 200 to 344 feet away. Had the motorman taken steps then to stop or slow down, the accident could have been avoided. The claim of negligence is that he did not do so. This claim has nothing to do with the motorman's choice of action when confronted with an emergency. On the contrary, it involves the motorman's failure to act some seconds before any emergency arose. That this failure undoubtedly contributed to the emergency situation which later developed does not, of course, call for an emergency charge, but actually militates against it. . . . Thus, the emergency doctrine cannot apply if plaintiff's evidence is accepted.

---

1. Why did the trial court fail to charge on the emergency doctrine? Define the doctrine.

2. What are the limits of the emergency doctrine? Why not raise it in every case? What if the defendant created the emergency?

WIDMYER v. SOUTHEAST SKYWAYS, INC.
Supreme Court of Alaska, 1978
584 P.2d 1

BOOCHEVER, CHIEF JUSTICE.

On November 15, 1974, a DeHavilland Beaver airplane, owned by Southeast Skyways, Inc, and piloted by Richard Norvell, crashed in the waters of False Bay, Chichagof Island, Alaska. The pilot and three passengers, Peggy Rae Welch, Joshua John Welch and Dermott R. O'Toole, were killed in the crash. Appellants, Carmelita Widmyer and A. Dermott OToole, personal representatives of the estates of the deceased passengers, brought this action for wrongful death against appellees, Southeast Skyways, Inc., and James Norvell, personal representative of the estate of Richard Norvell.

A jury returned a verdict for Skyways. . . .

It is not disputed that Skyways owed plaintiffs' deceased a duty of care. The controversy on appeal concerns the nature of that duty.

Plaintiffs submitted the following proposed instruction to the court:

> Common carriers owe a duty of utmost care and the vigilance of a very cautious person toward their passengers. They are responsible for any, even the slightest, negligence, and are required to do all that human care, vigilance and foresight reasonably can do under all the circumstances.

The instruction was not given. . . .

Although there is no Alaska statute to the contrary, we believe that a general duty of due care instruction is inadequate with respect to common carriers transporting passengers for hire. Singular treatment of common carriers is deeply rooted in common law and retains continuing validity in public policy.[10] Airline passengers are completely at the mercy of the carrier and are entitled to assume that the highest degree of care is being taken for their safety. . . .

Skyways cites no case in which the higher degree of care imposed on common carriers has been abandoned. Indeed, the rule has been repeatedly reaffirmed. We hold that the superior court erred in denying plaintiffs' proposed instruction.

. . . .

Reversed and remanded.

---

1. Draw the line between negligence and "utmost care." How is utmost care different from strict liability? How does the "utmost care" standard affect settlement negotiations?

2. Is a commercial bus or a cab a common carrier? Suppose your client's four-year-old child was being transported to the zoo in a nine-passenger van owned by the day-care center, does the carrier rule apply to the day-care center?

3. The standard of care in Georgia is: "Ordinary care and diligence is that care and diligence which every prudent man takes under the same and similar circumstances." *Sanders v. Central of Ga. Ry. Co.*, 123 Ga. 763, 51 S.E. 728 (1905).

4. Degrees of Negligence, Automobile Guest Passenger Statutes, and Good Samaritan Acts.

---

[10] Congress has recognized this policy. 49 U.S.C. § 1421 provides in part:

(a) the Administrator [of the Federal Aviation Administration] is empowered and it shall be his duty to promote safety of flight of civil aircraft in air commerce by prescribing and revising from time to time [various standards, rules and regulations]. . . .

(b) in prescribing standards, rules, and regulations, and in issuing certificates under this subchapter, the Administrator shall give full consideration to perform their services with the highest possible degree of safety in the public interest. . . .

Degrees of Negligence

In order to make negligence analysis more precise, several jurisdictions divided negligence cases into categories. The three categories, based on degrees of negligence, were (1) slight negligence, (2) ordinary negligence, and (3) gross negligence. The courts applied the doctrine of degrees of negligence to automobile guest statutes and good Samaritan laws. Illinois and Kansas extended the doctrine to all negligence cases, however. *See Wabash R.R. Co. v. Henks*, 91 Ill. 406 (1879); *Wichita & Western Rwy. Co. v. Davis*, 37 Kan. 743, 16 P. 78 (1887). The distinctions are as follows:

1. *Slight negligence* involves a failure to exercise great care.

2. *Ordinary negligence* is the failure to exercise ordinary or reasonable care.

3. *Gross negligence* is the absence of the exercise of slight care or is the omission or commission of an act with a conscious indifference to consequences.

Some jurisdictions equate gross negligence with "recklessness," "willfulness," and "wantonness." *See* Edwin H. Byrd, *Reflections on Willful, Wanton, Reckless, and Gross Negligence*, 48 La. L. Rev. 1383 (1988).

Over the years of trying to apply degrees of negligence, courts were flooded with appeals as they attempted to differentiate among the categories. The degrees of negligence doctrine proved to be too burdensome for the courts, but some continue to refer to gross negligence when instructing the jury on punitive damages. *See* Nanette A. O'Donnell, *Punitive Damages in Florida Negligence Cases: How Much Negligence Is Enough?*, 42 U. Miami L. Rev. 803 (1988).

Automobile Guest Passenger Statutes

A guest passenger statute allows a guest passenger to recover for personal injury against his host driver *only* when the host's conduct amounts to more than ordinary negligence. This required higher degree of negligence must be willful, wanton, reckless, or gross negligence.

The policy behind these statutes, which originated in the early twentieth century, was (1) to prevent collusion and fraud between the host driver and the guest against insurance companies and (2) to preserve the hospitality of a host driver. The theory was that the insurance companies would be flooded with collusive claims, where the driver and the passenger would conceal the truth from the court.

However, definitional problems such as "who is a guest," "are family members guests," "what if the guest bought the gasoline," "what if the host had some social or business desire in providing the guest with a ride," plagued the statutes. *See* W. Page Keeton et al., Prosser and Keeton on Torts § 34 (5th ed. 1984); Peter A. R. Lardy, *Guest Statutes: Have Recent Cases Brought Them to the End of the Road?*, 49 Notre Dame Law. 446, 446–47 (1973).

The most important guest passenger statute case is *Brown v. Merlo*, 8 Cal. 3d 855, 106 Cal. Rptr. 388, 506 P.2d 212 (1973). *Brown* found the California guest statute unconstitutional for violating the equal protection clauses of the California and U.S. Constitutions. The vast majority of states have repealed their guest statutes.

See Stanley W. Widger, *The Present Status of Automobile Guest Statutes*, 59 Cornell L. Rev. 659 (1974); William J. Brooks, *Guest Statutes and the Common Law Categories: An Inseparable Duality?*, 51 Notre Dame Law. 467 (1976).

Good Samaritan Acts

A physician who sees an injured motorist in need of urgent medical attention can refuse to help without fear of liability. In response, courts created exceptions to the no duty to rescue rule. To encourage physicians to render assistance, all fifty states and the District of Columbia have enacted Good Samaritan Acts. These acts protect the physician from liability if he or she stops and provides aid. *See Colby v. Schwartz*, 78 Cal. App. 3d 885, 892, 144 Cal. Rptr. 624, 628 (1978). To complement these statutes, immunity statutes were also enacted to protect virtually every type of health care professional who offers his or her services in emergencies. Some states do not extend immunity to acts constituting gross negligence or willful and wanton misconduct. *See Dahl v. Turner*, 80 N.M. 564, 458 P.2d 816 (1969); *Ballou v. Sigma Nu General Fraternity*, 291 S.C. 140, 352 S.E.2d 488 (Ct. App. 1986); Henry R. Stiepel, *Good Samaritans and Hospital Emergencies*, 54 S. Cal. L. Rev. 417 (1981); Martin A. Kotler, *Motivation and Tort Law: Acting for Economic Gain as a Suspect Motive*, 41 Vand. L. Rev. 63 (1988) (comparing automobile guest statutes with good Samaritan laws); Note, *Good Samaritans and Liability for Medical Malpractice*, 64 Colum. L. Rev. 1301 (1964).

PROBLEM

Tiwana was robbed and shot at 10:00 p.m. while obtaining money from an automated teller machine (ATM). Is there evidence of the bank's negligence to give to the jury? What other facts do you need?

1.   The Reasonable Person

VAUGHAN v. MENLOVE
Court of Common Pleas, 1837
3 Bing. (N.C.) 467, 132 Eng. Rep. 490

[A fire ignited on the defendant's land and spread causing damage to the plaintiff's buildings. The defendant had built a hay rick near the border of his property and had been told that the rick was likely to ignite, spread, and damage the plaintiff's cottages. The defendant denied that he was negligent.]

At the trial it appeared that the rick in question had been made by the defendant near the boundary of his own premises; that the hay was in such a state when put together, as to give rise to discussion on the probability of fire; that though there were conflicting opinions on the subject, yet during a period of five weeks, the Defendant was repeatedly warned of his peril; that his stock was insured; and that upon one occasion, being advised to take the rick down to avoid all danger, he said "he would chance it." He made an aperture or chimney through the rick; but in spite, or perhaps in consequence of this precaution, the rick at length burst into flames from the spontaneous heating of its materials; the flames communicated to the Defendant's barn and stables, and thence to the Plaintiff's cottages, which were entirely destroyed.

Patteson, J. before whom the cause was tried, told the jury that the question for them to consider was whether the fire had been occasioned by gross negligence on the part of the Defendant; adding, that he was bound to proceed with such reasonable caution as a prudent man would have exercised under such circumstances.

A verdict having been found for the Plaintiff, a rule nisi for a new trial was obtained, on the ground that the jury should have been directed to consider, not whether the Defendant had been guilty of gross negligence with reference to the standard of ordinary prudence, a standard too uncertain to afford any criterion; but whether he had acted bona fide to the best of his judgment; if he had, he ought not to be responsible for the misfortune of not possessing the highest order of intelligence. The action under such circumstances was of the first impression.

. . . .

TINDAL, C.J. I agree that this is a case primae impressionis. . . . [T]here is a rule of law which says you must so enjoy your own property as not to injure that of another; and according to that rule the Defendant is liable for

> the consequence of his own neglect; and though the Defendant did not himself light the fire, yet mediately, he is as much the cause of it as if he had himself put a candle to the rick; for it is well known that hay will ferment and take fire if it be not carefully stacked. . . .

It is contended, however, that the learned Judge was wrong in leaving this to the jury as a case of gross negligence, and that the question of negligence was so mixed up with reference to what would be the conduct of a man of ordinary prudence that the jury might have thought the latter the rule by which they were to decide; that such a rule would be too uncertain to act upon; and that the question ought to have been whether the Defendant had acted honestly and bona fide to the best of his own judgment. . . . The care taken by a prudent man has always been the rule laid down; and as to the supposed difficulty of applying it, a jury has always been able to say, whether taking that rule as their guide, there has been negligence on the occasion in question.

Instead, therefore, of saying that the liability for negligence should be coextensive with the judgment of each individual, which would be as variable as the length of the foot of each individual, we ought rather to adhere to the rule which requires in all cases a regard to caution such as a man of ordinary prudence would observe. That was in substance the criterion presented to the jury in this case, and therefore the present rule must be discharged. . . .

----

1. How can a person hold himself or herself to a standard other than what he or she thinks is best?

2. The "reasonable man" was the standard, but the "reasonable person" is now the accepted term.

3. What policy is the law trying to promote with the reasonable person standard?

4. For a further discussion, see Leon Green, *The Negligence Issue*, 37 Yale L.J. 1029 (1928).

5. Should a person who has driven trucks for 20 years be held to the standard of a "professional"? Pennsylvania answered in the negative.

> The standard of ordinary care is "already difficult to grasp and apply justly." To begin to vary the standard according to the driver's experience would render the application of any reasonably uniform standard impossible. There is only one degree of care in the law, and that is the standard of care which may reasonably be required or expected under all the circumstances. . . .

Fredericks v. Castora, 360 A.2d 696 (Pa. Super. Ct. 1976).

6. Is a layperson able to understand the nature of a truck driver's work? A medical doctor's?

7. In *Delair v. McAdoo*, 324 Pa. 392, 188 A. 181 (1936), the court stated:

> The accident occurred when defendant, proceeding in the same direction as plaintiff, sought to pass him. As defendant drew alongside of plaintiff, the left rear tire of his car blew out, causing it to swerve and come into contact with the plaintiff's car. The latter's theory at trial was that defendant was negligent in driving with defective tires.
>
>   . . . .
>
> There is always a duty of reasonable inspection.
>
> "Generally speaking, it is the duty of one operating a motor vehicle on the public highways to see that it is in reasonably good condition and properly equipped, so that it may be at all times controlled, and not become a source of danger to its occupants or to other travellers. To this end, the owner or operator of a motor vehicle must exercise reasonable care in the inspection of the machine and is chargeable with notice of everything that such inspection would disclose."
>
> It has been held in other states that the question whether a particular person is negligent in failing to know that his tires are in too poor a condition for ordinary operation on the highways is a question of fact for the jury. . . . In the instant case the testimony relative to the defect was as follows: A witness for the plaintiff stated that the tire "was worn pretty well through. You could see the tread in the tire — the inside lining." The witness later described this inside lining as the "fabric." The fact that the tire was worn through to and into the fabric over its entire area was corroborated by another witness. The repairman who replaced the tire which had blown out stated that he could see "the breaker strip" which is

just under the fabric of a tire. This testimony was contradicted by the defendant.

> . . . It is apparent that a tire so worn that the fabric is exposed is not in a condition for safe driving, and that such a defect will support a finding by a jury of negligence.

Is an expert required to testify in regard to the nature of the bald tires? What other things will a reasonable person be held to know?

BERBERIAN v. LYNN
Supreme Court of New Jersey, 2004
179 N.J. 290, 845 A.2d 122

WALLACE, J.

Plaintiffs, Mary Berberian, the head nurse in a long-term care facility, and her husband, Emmanuel Berberian, sued defendant Edmund Gernannt, an institutionalized patient with Alzheimer's dementia, his estate (defendant), Diane Lynn, in her capacity as Gernannt's guardian, and M.H. Rainey, M.D., to recover damages for personal injuries she sustained when Gernannt pushed her. After closing arguments, the trial court instructed the jury that the applicable standard of negligence was that of "a reasonably prudent person who has Alzheimer's dementia." The jury found in favor of defendant. On appeal, plaintiffs argued that the trial court should have applied an objective "reasonable person" standard without taking into account Gernannt's mental disability. The Appellate Division disagreed with plaintiffs and affirmed the trial court. . . .

I.

On October 3, 1997, Gernannt, now deceased, was involuntarily committed to Bergen Pines County Hospital (Bergen Pines) with a diagnosis of senile dementia, Alzheimer's type. On October 13, 1997, he was transferred from the long-term care unit to the acute geriatric psychiatric unit because he became increasingly agitated and assaultive towards the staff. On November 5, 1997, Gernannt was transferred to the eighth floor, where a number of other Alzheimer's and dementia patients were housed.

Plaintiff first met Gernannt on November 8, 1997. At that time, she was a nurse supervisor in the long-term care unit and had over twenty years of experience working with Alzheimer's patients. She knew that Gernannt had dementia and a history of agitation, including prior acts of violence towards staff. With respect to that behavior, plaintiff reported in her notes that Gernannt "refused to go to bed[,] . . . was combative, agitated," and "[t]ried to hit staff." Plaintiff was also aware of the Bergen Pines standard patient aggression policy. That policy stated that if a patient with dementia is violent, aggressive, resistant or unredirectable, the nurse should retreat from the patient and call security for assistance.

On November 11, 1997, Gernannt attempted to leave the unit by way of the fire exit and set off the alarm. Nurse Christine Schell tried to redirect him, but he began hitting her. Schell backed away and walked down the hall to call security. Plaintiff then approached him and extended her hand to help him to his room. Gernannt grabbed plaintiff's hand, pulled her toward him and then pushed her back, causing her to fall and fracture her right leg.

On January 26, 1998, plaintiffs filed a complaint against Lynn, Gernannt, . . . While not disputing that Gernannt was an adjudicated incompetent, plaintiffs alleged that he, "without provocation negligently, recklessly and carelessly" struck plaintiff, causing her injuries. . . .

. . . .

After the close of the evidence portion of the trial, plaintiffs requested a "reasonable man" standard instruction. The trial court denied the request and charged as follows:

Now in determining the standard of care that defendant, Edmund Gernannt should have used on November 11th, 1997, you must measure his actions as you would *a reasonably prudent person who has Alzheimer's dementia*

. . . .

The jury returned a verdict in favor of defendant.

Plaintiffs appealed. The Appellate Division affirmed, holding that "the appropriate capacity-based standard of care for mentally incompetent defendants, such as Gernannt, is that of a reasonable prudent person who has Alzheimer's disease in light of the defendant's capacity." . . . In a concurring opinion, Judge Lintner concluded that Gernannt had no duty of care because his "dementia and corresponding inability to act reasonably . . . is the very reason for his being institutionalized and under the care of plaintiff." Based on that reasoning, Judge Lintner concluded that the trial court should have granted defendant's motion for involuntary dismissal. *Ibid.*

II.

Plaintiffs contend that it was error to use a capacity-based standard of care for the mentally incompetent Gernannt. Plaintiffs urge that this Court's ruling in *Cowan v. Doering, 111 N.J. 451, 545 A.2d 159 (1988)*, which held that capacity-based standards should be used in comparative negligence cases against mentally disturbed persons, does not apply here.

. . . .

A.

Generally, the reasonable person standard applies to a mentally deficient person. *Restatement (Second) of Torts Section 283B (1965)* provides that:

> Unless the actor is a child, his insanity or other mental deficiency does not relieve the actor from liability for conduct which does not conform to the standard of a reasonable man under like circumstances.

"The rule that a mentally deficient adult is liable for his torts is an old one, dating back at least to 1616, at a time when the action for trespass rested upon the older basis of strict liability, without regard to any fault of the individual." *Id. at Section 283B comment b.*

The rule's persistence in modern law has been justified on the following grounds:

1. The difficulty of drawing any satisfactory line between mental deficiency and those variations of temperament, intellect, and emotional balance which cannot, as a practical matter, be taken into account in imposing liability for damage done.

2. The unsatisfactory character of the evidence of mental deficiency in many cases, together with the ease with which it can be feigned. . . .

. . .

3. The feeling that if mental defectives are to live in the world they should pay for the damage they do, and that it is better that their wealth, if any, should be used to compensate innocent victims than that it should remain in their hands.

4. The belief that their liability will mean that those who have charge of them or their estates will be stimulated to look after them, keep them in order, and see that they do not do harm.

. . . .

However, the Restatement limits the distinction with respect to the standards of care governing the tort liability of children and *physically* disabled persons, but *not mentally* disabled persons. *See Id. At Section 283A* (providing that a child must conform his or her conduct to that of "a reasonable person of like age, intelligence, and experience under like circumstances"); *see also Id. at Section 283C* (providing that a physically disabled individual must conform his or her conduct to "that of a reasonable man under like disability").

III.

. . . . We hold that a mentally disabled patient, who does not have the capacity to control his or her conduct, does not owe his or her caregiver a duty of care.

. . .

Most important, Gernannt was involuntarily admitted to Bergen Pines to prevent the very type of injury that is at the center of this lawsuit.

Conversely, plaintiff had knowledge of Gernannt's potential for violence and was trained to enlist the assistance of security when necessary. Plaintiff could readily control her behavior to deal with the foreseeable harm. In these circumstances, it would not be fair to impose a duty of care on Gernannt to his professional caregiver when the caregiver's job duties included preventing Gernannt from injuring himself and others. Moreover, plaintiff has the benefit of worker's compensation for her work-related injuries.

. . . .

---

1. Did the third point under the given Restatement section sound punitive to you? "The feeling that if mental defectives are to live in the world they should pay for the damage they do, and that it is better that their wealth, if any, should be used to compensate innocent victims than that it should remain in their hands." Restatement (Second) of Torts § 283B, Comment B (1965).

2. Do you think it was intentional for the Restatement to allow for subjectivity in determining negligence of children (age) and physically disabled persons (blind), without mentioning the standard for mentally disabled persons? Why?

ROBERTS v. STATE OF LOUISIANA
Court of Appeals of Louisiana, 1981
396 So. 2d 566

LABORDE, JUDGE.

In this tort suit, William C. Roberts sued to recover damages for injuries he sustained in an accident in the lobby of the U.S. Post Office Building in Alexandria, Louisiana. Roberts fell after being bumped into by Mike Burson, the blind operator of the concession stand located in the building.

Plaintiff sued the State of Louisiana, through the Louisiana Health and Human Resources Administration, advancing two theories of liability:

respondeat superior and negligent failure by the State to properly supervise and oversee the safe operation of the concession stand. The stand's blind operator, Mike Burson, is not a party to this suit although he is charged with negligence. The trial court ordered plaintiff's suit dismissed. . . .

We affirm the trial court's decision for the reasons which follow.

On September 1, 1977, at about 12:45 in the afternoon, operator Mike Bur-son left his concession stand to go to the men's bathroom located in the building. As he was walking down the hall, he bumped into plaintiff who fell to the floor and injured his hip. Plaintiff was 75 years old, stood 5'6" and weighed approximately 100 pounds. Burson, on the other hand, was 25 to 26 years old, stood approximately 6' and weighed 165 pounds.

At the time of the incident, Burson was not using a cane nor was he utilizing the technique of walking with his arm or hand in front of him.

Even though Burson was not joined as a defendant, his negligence or lack thereof is crucial to a determination of the State's liability. Because of its importance, we begin with it.

Plaintiff contends that operator Mike Burson traversed the area from his concession stand to the men's bathroom in a negligent manner. To be more specific, he focuses on the operator's failure to use his cane even though he had it with him in his concession stand.

In determining an actor's negligence, various courts have imposed differing standards of care to which handicapped persons are expected to perform. Professor William L. Prosser expresses one generally recognized modern standard of care as follows:

"As to his physical characteristics, the reasonable man may be said to be identical with the actor. The man who is blind . . . is entitled to live in the world and to have allowance made by others for his disability, and he cannot be required to do the impossible by conforming to physical standards which he cannot meet . . . At the same time, the conduct of the handicapped individual must be reasonable in the light of his knowledge of his infirmity, which is treated merely as one of the circumstances under which he acts . . . It is sometimes said that a blind man must use a greater degree of care than one who can see; but it is now generally agreed that as a fixed rule this is inaccurate, and that the correct statement is merely that he must take the precautions, be they more or less, which the ordinary reasonable man would take if he were blind." . . .

A careful review of the record in this instance reveals that Burson was acting as a reasonably prudent blind person would under these particular circumstances.

Mike Burson is totally blind. Since 1974, he has operated the concession stand located in the lobby of the post office building. It is one of twenty-three vending stands operated by blind persons under a program funded by the federal government and implemented by the State through the Blind Services Division of the Department of Health and Human Resources. Burson hired no employees, choosing instead to operate his stand on his own.

Prior to running the vending stand in Alexandria, Burson attended Arkansas Enterprises for the blind where he received mobility training. In 1972, he took a refresher course in mobility followed by a course on vending stand training. In that same year, he operated a concession stand in Shreveport, his first under the vending stand program. He later operated a stand at Centenary before going to Alexandria in 1974 to take up operations there.

On the date of the incident in question, Mike Burson testified that he left his concession stand and was on his way to the men's bathroom when he bumped into plaintiff. He, without hesitancy, admitted that at the time he was not using his cane, explaining that he relies on his facial sense which he feels is an adequate technique for short trips inside the familiar building. Burson testified that he does use a cane to get to and from work.

Plaintiff makes much of Burson's failure to use a cane when traversing the halls of the post office building. Yet, our review of the testimony received at trial indicates that it is not uncommon for blind people to rely on other techniques when moving around in a familiar setting. For example George Marzloff, the director of the Division of Blind Services, testified that he can recommend to the blind operators that they should use a cane but he knows that when they are in a setting in which they are comfortable, he would say that nine out of ten will not use a cane and in his personal opinion, if the operator is in a relatively busy area, the cane can be more of a hazard than an asset. Mr. Marzloff further testified that he felt a reasonably functioning blind person would learn his way around his work setting as he does around his home so that he could get around without a cane. Mr. Marzloff added that he has several blind people working in his office, none of whom use a cane inside that facility.

The only testimony in the record that suggests that Burson traversed the halls in a negligent manner was that elicited from plaintiff's expert witness, William Henry Jacobson. Jacobson is an instructor in peripathology, which he explained as the science of movement within the surroundings by visually impaired individuals. Jacobson, admitting that he conducted no study or examination of Mike Burson's mobility skills and that he was unfamiliar with the State's vending program, nonetheless testified that he would require a blind person to use a cane in traversing the areas outside the concession stand. He added that a totally blind individual probably should use a cane under any situation where there in an unfamiliar environment or where a familiar environment involves a change, whether it be people moving through that environment or strangers moving through that environment or just a heavy traffic within that environment.

Upon our review of the record, we feel that plaintiff has failed to show that Burson was negligent. Burson testified that he was very familiar with his surroundings, having worked there for three and a half years. He had special mobility training and his reports introduced into evidence indicate good mobility skills. He explained his decision to rely on his facial sense instead of his cane for these short trips in a manner which convinces us that it was a reasoned decision. Not only was Burson's explanation adequate, there was additional testimony from other persons indicating that such a decision is not an unreasonable one. Also important is the total lack of any evidence in the record showing that at the time of the incident, Burson engaged in any acts which may be characterized as negligence on his part. For example, there is nothing showing that Burson was walking too fast, not paying attention, et cetera. Under all of these circumstances, we conclude that Mike Burson was not negligent.

Our determination that Mike Burson was not negligent disposes of our need to discuss liability on the part of the State.

For the above and foregoing reasons, the judgment of the trial court dismissing plaintiff's claims against defendant is affirmed and all costs of this appeal are assessed against the plaintiff-appellant.

Affirmed.

----

1. What other disabilities might qualify for this treatment? What about a short or weak man or woman? What policy is being applied here? *See* Restatement (Second) of Torts § 283C.

2. What result where the blind plaintiff suffers injury because he or she cannot see? *See Hill v. Glenwood*, 124 Iowa 479, 100 N.W. 522 (1904).

3. *See* Jacobus tenBroek, *The Right to Live in the World: The Disabled in the Law of Torts*, 54 Cal. L. Rev. 841 (1966).

4. What if the defendant is drunk, or high on pot?

5. Does the result change if the plaintiff is intoxicated? In *Robinson v. Pioche, Bayerque & Co.*, 5 Cal. 460 (1855), the court stated: "A drunken man is as much entitled to a safe street as a sober one, and much more in need of it." What is required for this theory to apply?

6. A paraplegic, who is licensed to drive, runs a stoplight in a van because he or she is not paying attention. What standard applies?

PROBLEM

A sixteen-year-old was shot while hunting deer by his seventeen-year-old companion, the defendant. Does an adult standard or the child standard for negligence apply? Assume that the case arose in Arkansas. What policies are applicable?

ROBINSON v. LINDSAY
Supreme Court of Washington, 1979 (en banc)
92 Wash. 2d 410, 598 P.2d 392

UTTER, CHIEF JUSTICE.

An action seeking damages for personal injuries was brought on behalf of Kelly Robinson who lost full use of a thumb in a snowmobile accident when she was 11 years of age. The petitioner, Billy Anderson, 13 years of age at the time of the accident, was the driver of the snowmobile. After a jury verdict in favor of Anderson, the trial court ordered a new trial.

The single issue on appeal is whether a minor operating a snowmobile is to be held to an adult standard of care. The trial court failed to instruct the jury as to that standard and ordered a new trial because it believed the jury should have been so instructed. We agree and affirm the order granting a new trial.

The trial court instructed the jury under WPI 10.05 that:

> In considering the claimed negligence of a child, you are instructed that it is the duty of a child to exercise the same care that a reasonably careful child of the same age, intelligence, maturity, training and experience would exercise under the same or similar circumstances.

Respondent properly excepted to the giving of this instruction and to the court's failure to give an adult standard of care.

. . . Children are traditionally encouraged to pursue childhood activities without the same burdens and responsibilities with which adults must contend. *See* Bahr, *Tort Law and the Games Kids Play*, 23 S.D.L. Rev. 275 (1978). As a result, courts evolved a special standard of care to measure a child's negligence in a particular situation.

In *Roth v. Union Depot Co.*, 13 Wash. 525, 43 P. 641 (1896), Washington joined "the overwhelming weight of authority" in distinguishing between the capacity of a child and that of an adult. As the court then stated, at page 544:

> [I]t would be a monstrous doctrine to hold that a child of inexperience —
> and experience can come only with years — should be held to the same
> degree of care in avoiding danger as a person of mature years and
> accumulated experience.

The court went on to hold, at page 545:

> The care or caution required is according to the capacity of the child, and
> this is to be determined ordinarily by the age of the child.
>
> " . . . a child is held . . . only to the exercise of such degree of care and
> discretion as is reasonably to be expected from children of his age."

The current law in this state is fairly reflected in WPI 10.05, given in this case.
In the past we have always compared a child's conduct to that expected of a
reasonably careful child of the same age, intelligence, maturity, training and
experience. This case is the first to consider the question of a child's liability for
injuries sustained as a result of his or her operation of a motorized vehicle or
participation in an inherently dangerous activity.

Courts in other jurisdictions have created an exception to the special child
standard because of the apparent injustice that would occur if a child who caused
injury while engaged in certain dangerous activities were permitted to defend
himself by saying that other children similarly situated would not have exercised a
degree of care higher than his, and he is, therefore, not liable for his tort. Some
courts have couched the exception in terms of children engaging in an activity which
is normally one for adults only. *See, e.g., Dellwo v. Pearson*, 259 Minn. 452, 107
N.W.2d 859, 97 A.L.R.2d 866 (1961) (operation of a motorboat). We believe a better
rationale is that when the activity a child engages in is inherently dangerous, as is
the operation of powerful mechanized vehicles, the child should be held to an adult
standard of care.

Other courts adopting the adult standard of care for children engaged in adult
activities have emphasized the hazards to the public if the rule is otherwise. We
agree with the Minnesota Supreme Court's language in its decision in *Dellwo v.
Pearson, supra* at 457-58:

> Certainly in the circumstances of modern life, where vehicles moved by
> powerful motors are readily available and frequently operated by immature
> individuals, we should be skeptical of a rule that would allow motor vehicles
> to be operated to the hazard of the public with less than the normal
> minimum degree of care and competence.

Dellwo applied the adult standard to a 12-year-old defendant operating a motorboat. Other jurisdictions have applied the adult standard to minors engaged in
analogous activities. *Goodfellow v. Coggburn*, 98 Idaho 202, 203-04, 560 P.2d 873
(1977) (minor operating tractor); *Williams v. Esaw*, 214 Kan. 658, 668, 522 P.2d 950
(1974) (minor operating motorcycle); *Perricone v. DiBartolo*, 14 Ill. App. 3d 514, 520,
302 N.E.2d 637 (1973) (minor operating gasoline-powered minibike); *Krahn v.
LaMeres*, 483 P.2d 522, 525-26 (Wyo. 1971) (minor operating automobile). The
holding of minors to an adult standard of care when they operate motorized vehicles

is gaining approval from an increasing number of courts and commentators. . . .

The operation of a snowmobile likewise requires adult care and competence. . . .

At the time of the accident, the 13-year-old petitioner had operated snowmobiles for about 2 years. When the injury occurred, petitioner was operating a 30-horsepower snowmobile at speeds of 10 to 20 miles per hour. The record indicates that the machine itself was capable of 65 miles per hour. Because petitioner was operating a powerful motorized vehicle, he should be held to the standard of care and conduct expected of an adult.

The order granting a new trial is affirmed.

---

1. What would happen if there were no special standard for children? What incentive would be created?

2. When you see a six-year-old on a bicycle coming at you, what thoughts go through your mind? What are your thoughts when you see a snowmobile coming at you at fifty miles per hour?

3. In a Pennsylvania case a five-year-old hit a six-year-old with a stick. The court held that the five-year-old was conclusively presumed incapable of negligence:

> The application of this standard is clarified by the use of several presumptions delineating convenient points to aid in drawing the uncertain line between capacity to appreciate and guard against danger and incapacity: (1) minors under the age of seven years are conclusively presumed incapable of negligence; (2) minors between the ages of seven and fourteen years are presumed incapable of negligence, but the presumption is a rebuttable one that weakens as the fourteenth year is approached; (3) minors over the age of fourteen years are presumptively capable of negligence, with the burden placed on the minor to prove incapacity.

Dunn v. Teti, 280 Pa. Super. 399, 421 A.2d 782 (1980). What is the policy behind *Dunn*? Argue for the plaintiff.

2. The Professional

BOYCE v. BROWN
Supreme Court of Arizona, 1938
51 Ariz. 416, 77 P.2d 455

LOCKWOOD, JUDGE. Berlie B. Boyce and Nannie E. Boyce, his wife, hereinafter called plaintiffs, brought suit against Edgar H. Brown, hereinafter called defendant, to recover damages for alleged malpractice by the defendant upon the person of Nannie E. Boyce. The case was tried to a jury and, at the close of the evidence for plaintiffs, the court granted a motion for an instructed verdict in favor of the defendant, . . . Judgment was rendered on the verdict, and, after the usual motion for new trial was overruled, this appeal was taken.

About September 1, 1927, plaintiffs engaged the services of defendant, who for many years had been a practicing physician and surgeon in Phoenix, to reduce a fracture of Mrs. Boyce's ankle. This was done by means of an operation which consisted, in substance, of making an incision at the point of fracture, bringing the broken fragments of bone into apposition, and permanently fixing them in place by means of a metal screw placed in the bone. Defendant continued to attend Mrs. Boyce for three or four weeks following such operation until a complete union of the bone had been established, when his services terminated. There is no serious contention in the record that defendant did not follow the approved medical standard in the treatment of the fractured bone up to this time. No further professional relations existed between the parties until years later, in November, 1934, when Mrs. Boyce again consulted him, complaining that her ankle was giving her considerable pain. He examined the ankle, wrapped it with adhesive tape, and then filed the edge of an arch support, which he had made for her seven years before, and which, from use, had grown so thin that the edge was sharp. About a week later he removed the bandage. Her ankle, however, did not improve after this treatment, but continued to grow more painful until January, 1936, some two years later. At this last-mentioned time she returned to defendant, who again examined the ankle. A few days later she went to visit Dr. Kent of Mesa, who, on hearing the history of the case, and noticing some discoloration and swelling, caused an X-ray of the ankle to be made. This X-ray showed that there had been some necrosis of the bone around the screw. Dr. Kent operated upon Mrs. Boyce, removing the screw, and she made an uneventful recovery, the ankle becoming practically normal.

There are certain general rules of law governing actions of malpractice, which are almost universally accepted by the courts, and which are applicable to the present situation. We state them as follows: (1) One licensed to practice medicine is presumed to possess the degree of skill and learning which is possessed by the average member of the medical profession in good standing in the community in which he practices, and to apply that skill and learning, with ordinary and reasonable care, to cases which come to him for treatment. . . . (3) In order to sustain a verdict for the plaintiffs in an action for malpractice, the standard of medical practice in the community must be shown by affirmative evidence, and, unless there is evidence of such a standard, a jury may not be permitted to speculate as to what the required standard is, or whether the defendant has departed therefrom. *Butler v. Rule, supra; Rising v. Veatch, 117 Cal. App. 404, 3 Pac. (2d) 1023; Connelly v. Cone, 205 Mo. App. 395, 224 S.W. 1011.* (4) Negligence on the part of a physician or surgeon in the treatment of a case is never presumed, but must be affirmatively proven, and no presumption of negligence nor want of skill arises from the mere fact that a treatment was unsuccessful, failed to bring the best results, or that the patient died. 48 C.J. 1142, 1143, and cases cited. (5) The accepted rule is that negligence on the part of a physician or surgeon, by reason of his departure from the proper standard of practice, must be established by expert medical testimony, unless the negligence is so grossly apparent that a layman would have no difficulty in recognizing it. . . .

The . . . question is whether the examination and treatment given by defendant departed from the established standard for cases like that of Mrs. Boyce. The only testimony we have which, in any manner, bears upon medical standards or the proper treatment of Mrs. Boyce in November, 1934, is that of Dr. Kent, who performed the operation on the ankle in January, 1936, and of defendant. The latter testified that he did what was required by Mrs. Boyce's condition as it existed then. Dr. Kent's testimony as to the condition he found in 1936, and what he did, is clear and distinct. He was asked as to how long prior to that time the screw should have been removed, and stated that he could not answer; that, if the ankle was in the same condition as it was when he operated, he would say that the screw should have been removed, but that it was impossible for him to testify as to when the condition justifying removal arose. . . . On cross-examination he testified that the method of uniting bone used by defendant was a standard one, and that the screw was not removed, as a rule, unless it made trouble. Nowhere, however, did Dr. Kent testify as to what was the proper standard of medical care required at the time defendant treated Mrs. Boyce in 1934, or as to whether, in his opinion, the treatment given deviated from that standard. The nearest he came to such testimony was the statement that he personally would have had an X-ray taken, but he did not say the failure to do so was a deviation from the proper standard of treatment.

Counsel for plaintiffs . . . urge that this comes within the exception to the general rule, in that a failure to [take an X-ray] is such obvious negligence that even a layman knows it to be a departure from the proper standard. We think this contention cannot be sustained. It is true that most laymen know that the X-ray usually offers the best method of diagnosing physical changes of the interior organs of the body, and particularly of the skeleton, short of an actual opening of the body for ocular examination, but laymen cannot say that in all cases where there is some trouble with the internal organs that it is a departure from standard medical practice to fail to take and X-ray. Such things are costly and do not always give a satisfactory diagnosis, or even as good a one as other types of examination may give. . . . [W]e think it is going too far to say that the failure to take an X-ray of Mrs. Boyce's ankle at that time was so far a departure from ordinary medical standards that even laymen would know it to be gross negligence. Since, therefore, there was insufficient evidence in the record to show that defendant was guilty of malpractice, . . . the court properly instructed a verdict in favor of the defendant.

The judgment of the superior court is affirmed.

---

1.   The requirement of an expert witness in a medical malpractice case means that the plaintiff may lose if he cannot obtain one. Often doctors (and lawyers) do not wish to testify against their colleagues. *See Bernstein v. Alameda-Contra Costa Medical Assoc.*, 139 Cal. App. 2d 241, 293 P.2d 862 (1956). What are some solutions?

2.   Formerly, the rule was that the medical expert must be from the same "community" as the defendant doctor. This was expanded to the same "locality" and is now often rejected. In *Smith v. Hospital Authority of Terrell County*, 161 Ga. App. 657, 288 S.E.2d 715 (1982), the court said:

> The rationale [s] for applying general standards to physicians [are] "Reasons for the more narrow rule [community] which might have obtained in times past, where transportation was difficult, medical schools and hospitals often inaccessible, and doctors licensed to practice with little or no

formal training, no longer have any validity. Medical practitioners frequently receive a part or all of their education in States other than the one in which they settle to practice . . ."

For a critique of the "same community standard," see Dan Dobbs, The Law of Torts 635–36 (2000).

3.   A professional is one whose work calls for special skills. They include doctors, dentists, psychiatrists, attorneys, architects, engineers and accountants. *See* W. Page Keeton et al., Prosser and Keeton on Torts (5th ed. 1984).

What about college teachers?

JONES v. O'YOUNG
Supreme Court of Illinois, 1992
154 Ill. 2d 39, 607 N.E.2d 224

Johnny Jones and Loretta Jones, plaintiffs, brought a medical malpractice action in the circuit court of Cook County against Roseland Community Hospital and Doctors Richard O'Young, Armanda Pacis, Ramasamy Kali-muthu and James So. . . . Dr. Kalimuthu is board certified in plastic surgery and general surgery. Dr. O'Young is an orthopedic surgeon and Dr. Pacis is a general surgeon. [The plaintiff, following a car crash, developed an infection that allegedly led to the amputation of his leg.]

. . . The court certified the following question of law:

"In order to testify concerning the standard of care required of and deviations from the standard of care by a defendant physician specializing in an area of medicine, must the plaintiff's expert also specialize in the same area of medicine as the defendant, so that, in this case, the plaintiff's infectious disease specialist would not be qualified to testify against the defendant plastic surgeon, orthopedic surgeon, or general surgeon with regard to each defendant's care and treatment of the infectious disease, Pseudomonas osteomyelitis?"

We answer the question in the negative. We are not reviewing the trial court's decision as to the competency of Dr. Deam to testify and are considering only the question certified by the trial court. See *Purtill v. Hess*, 111 Ill. 2d 229, 251, 95 Ill. Dec. 305, 489 N.E.2d 867 (1986).

In *Purtill v. Hess*, 111 Ill. 2d 229, 95 Ill. Dec. 305, 489 N.E.2d 867 (1986), this court articulated the requirements necessary to demonstrate an expert physician's qualifications and competency to testify. First, the physician must be a licensed member of the school of medicine about which he proposes to testify. (*Purtill*, 111 Ill. 2d at 242–43, citing *Dolan v. Galluzzo*, 77 Ill. 2d 279, 32 Ill. Dec. 900, 396 N.E.2d 13 (1979).) Second, "the expert witness must show that he is familiar with the methods, procedures, and treatments ordinarily observed by other physicians, in either the defendant physician's community or a similar community." (*Purtill*, 111 Ill. 2d at 243.) Once the foundational requirements have been met, the trial court has the discretion to determine whether a physician is qualified and competent to state his opinion as an expert regarding the standard of care. *Purtill*, 111 Ill. 2d at 243.

By hearing evidence on the expert's qualifications and comparing the medical problem and the type of treatment in the case to the experience and background of the expert, the trial court can evaluate whether the witness has demonstrated a sufficient familiarity with the standard of care practiced in the case. The foundational requirements provide the trial court with the information necessary to determine whether an expert has expertise in dealing with the plaintiff's medical problem and treatment. Whether the expert is qualified to testify is not dependent on whether he is a member of the same specialty or subspecialty as the defendant but, rather, whether the allegations of negligence concern matters within his knowledge and observation.

> If the plaintiff fails to satisfy either of the foundational requirements of *Purtill*, the trial court must disallow the expert's testimony. (*Purtill*, 111 Ill. 2d at 244.) The requirements are a threshold beneath which the plaintiff cannot fall without failing to sustain the allegations of his complaint. They monitor the course the plaintiff's action will take, and are sufficiently comprehensive in alerting the trial court to the concerns relevant in determining the admissibility of the expert's testimony.

If the trial court determines that the expert is qualified, the defendant is then in the position to direct the jury's attention to any infirmities in his testimony or his competency to testify. Cross-examination, argument and jury instructions provide defense counsel with the opportunity and means to challenge the expert's qualifications as well as the opinion he offers. Restricting the qualification of experts to those physicians who are members of the same specialty or subspecialty as the defendant would only upset the balance necessary to an adversarial system without any compensating benefit. Accordingly, we reaffirm this court's position in *Purtill* without qualification.

In its order, the trial court stated that "there is substantial ground for difference of opinion on this issue based upon the conflict" in the appellate court among the opinions in *Petkus, Northern Trust* and *Thomas*. We disagree.

. . . We believe the trial courts in these matters correctly applied the law as contained in *Purtill v. Hess*. We answer the question certified by the trial court in this matter in the negative and in so doing, reaffirm this court's decisions in *Purtill v. Hess*.

The cause is remanded to the circuit court for further proceedings.

---

1. *Avret v. McCormick*, 246 Ga. 401, 271 S.E.2d 832 (1980), held that a nurse who had drawn blood over 2,000 times was qualified as an expert to testify against a doctor on the question of "standards of care in keeping sterile a needle used to draw blood from a patient."

HEATH v. SWIFT WINGS, INC.

Court of Appeals of North Carolina, 1979
40 N.C. App. 158, 252 S.E.2d 526

On 3 August 1975 a Piper 180 Arrow airplane crashed immediately after takeoff from the Boone-Blowing Rock Airport. Killed in the crash was the pilot, Fred Heath; his wife, Jonna; their son, Karl; and a family friend, Vance Smathers. Valerie Heath, a daughter of Fred and Jonna Heath, and sister of Karl, became the sole survivor of the Heath family. This action was instituted by Richard E. Heath as ancillary administrator of the estates of Jonna and Karl Heath against (1) Swift Wings, Inc., the corporate owner of the aircraft, on the grounds of agency; (2) the four shareholders of Swift Wings, Inc. — Fred Heath, Frank Kish, Richard Kish, and Kermit Rockett — alleging they actually constituted a de facto partnership, and (3) The Bank of Virginia Trust Company, Executor of the Estate of Frederick B. Heath, Jr.

Plaintiff's evidence, except to the extent it is quoted from the record, is briefly summarized as follows: Mary Payne Smathers Curry, widow of Vance Smathers, observed the takeoff of the Piper aircraft shortly after 5:00 o'clock on 3 August 1975. She observed Fred Heath load and reload the passengers and luggage, apparently in an effort to improve the balance of the aircraft. He also "walked around [the airplane] and looked at everything . . . She remembers seeing him and thinking that he's doublechecking it to be sure no one has slashed the tires." The airplane engine started promptly and the plane was taxied to the end of the runway where it paused for approximately five minutes before takeoff. The airplane came very close to the end of the runway before takeoff. However, "[t]he engine sounded good the entire time, and she did not recall hearing the engine miss or pop or backfire." After takeoff, the airplane "gained altitude but it didn't go up very high" and then "leveled off pretty low."

William B. Gough, Jr., a free-lance mechanical engineering consultant and pilot, testified concerning the operation and flight performance of the Piper 180 Arrow. He testified concerning the many factors affecting the takeoff capabilities of the Piper and the calculations to be made by the pilot before takeoff, utilizing flight performance charts. He testified that in his opinion, according to his calculations, the pilot should have used flaps to aid in the takeoff. Furthermore, he stated that in his opinion the reasonably prudent pilot should have made a controlled landing in the cornfield shortly after takeoff if he were experiencing difficulty attaining flight speed, and that if he had done so Jonna Heath and Karl Heath would have survived.

. . . .

After the customary motions at the conclusion of all the evidence, the case was submitted to the jury upon voluminous instructions by the trial court. The jury returned a verdict answering the following issue as indicated: "1. Was Fred Heath, Jr., negligent in the operation of PA — 28R 'Arrow' airplane on August 3, 1975 as alleged in the complaint?" Answer: "No." Plaintiff appeals assigning error to the exclusion of certain evidence and to the charge to the jury. Defendants cross-appeal assigning error to the denial of the motions for a directed verdict by Swift Wings, Inc.

MORRIS, CHIEF JUDGE. . . .

Assignment of error No. 4 is directed to the trial court's charge concerning the definition of negligence and the applicable standard of care:

> "Negligence, ladies and gentlemen of the jury, is the failure of someone to act as a reasonably and careful and prudent person would under the same or similar circumstances. Obviously, this could be the doing of something or the failure to do something, depending on the circumstances. With respect to aviation negligence could be more specifically defined as the failure to exercise that degree of ordinary care and caution, which an ordinary prudent pilot having the same training and experience as Fred Heath, would have used in the same or similar circumstances."

It is a familiar rule of law that the standard of care required of an individual, unless altered by statute, is the conduct of the reasonably prudent man under the same or similar circumstances. . . . While the standard of care of the reasonably prudent man remains constant, the quantity or degree of care required varies significantly with the attendant circumstances. . . .

The trial court improperly introduced a subjective standard of care into the definition of negligence by referring to the "ordinary care and caution, which an ordinary prudent pilot having the same training and experience as Fred Heath, would have used in the same or similar circumstances." (Emphasis added.) We are aware of the authorities which support the application of a greater standard of care than that of the ordinary prudent man for persons shown to possess special skill in a particular endeavor. . . . Indeed, our courts have long recognized that one who engages in a business, occupation, or profession must exercise the requisite degree of learning, skill, and ability of that calling with reasonable and ordinary care. . . . Furthermore, the specialist within a profession may be held to a standard of care greater than that required of the general practitioner. . . . Nevertheless, the professional standard remains an objective standard. For example, the recognized standard for a physician is established as "the standard of professional competence and care customary in similar communities among physicians engaged in his field of practice." . . .

Such objective standards avoid the evil of imposing a different standard of care upon each individual. The instructions in this case concerning the pilot's standard of care are misleading at best, and a misapplication of the law. They permit the jury to consider Fred Heath's own particular experience and training, whether outstanding or inferior, in determining the requisite standard of conduct, rather than applying a minimum standard generally applicable to all pilots. The plaintiff is entitled to an instruction holding Fred Heath to the objective minimum standard of care applicable to all pilots.

[F]or prejudicial errors in the charge, there must be a *New trial.*

---

1.   What is the error in the charge to the jury? What is the appellate court's concern?

2.   What is the standard of care for a pilot? Why?

3. What is the standard for the medical doctor? Without such a standard, what might the jury infer? With such a standard, what expense must the plaintiff bear?

4. What standard will be applied to a "shade tree" mechanic who works on his friend's automobile?

5. The test for whether an expert must be provided to testify is whether a lay person can understand the nature of the defendant's work. If a lay person cannot understand, because the work is technical, an expert will be required. *See Aetna Ins. Co. v. Hellmuth, Obata & Kassabaum, Inc.*, 392 F.2d 472 (8th Cir. 1968):

> Most of the cases stating the general rule on expert testimony to establish the standard of professional care required deal with physicians and surgeons, but the same principle is applicable to attorneys, architects and engineers and other professional men. . . .

> Prosser notes that expert testimony is necessary to establish the standard of care required of those engaged in practicing medicine, as laymen are normally incompetent to pass judgment on questions of medical science or technique, but that

> "Where the matter is regarded as within the common knowledge of laymen, as where the surgeon saws off the wrong leg, or there is injury to a part of the body not within the operative field, it has been held that the jury may infer negligence without the aid of any expert." Prosser, Law of Torts 164 (3rd ed.)

> It is a matter of common knowledge that it is often difficult to secure the services of a professional man to testify in a case involving a claim of dereliction of duty by a fellow member in the profession. This undoubtedly holds true in architectural circles as well as others. . . . It does appear that there are certain duties patently required of the architect that are within the common knowledge and experience of laymen serving as jurors. It requires no particular technical knowledge on the part of the jury to pass upon the failure to supervise the back-filling of the sewer ditch when specifically required under the contract, the failure to correct misaligned forms utilized in retaining and supporting a poured concrete wall, or the significance of a sewer pipe that is misaligned and crooked. The jury is competent to pass on these issues without knowledge of the professional skills and competency required of architects in the ordinary performance of their skilled duties. Questions relating to stress and strain and weight-bearing capacities of structural elements are beyond the ordinary comprehension of most laymen and the court and jury require expert enlightenment on issues of this type. It, therefore, appears that the general rule requiring expert testimony to establish a reasonable standard of professional care is necessary when issues are presented that are beyond the ordinary competency of laymen jurors, but is not necessary in passing on commonplace factual situations that the ordinary jury layman can readily grasp and understand.

6. In medical malpractice cases, the general rule is that the plaintiff's case will be dismissed, if the plaintiff does not provide an expert who will testify that the defendant doctor failed to exercise reasonable care. The Georgia Code provides:

Sec. 9-11-9.1. Affidavit to accompany charge of professional malpractice

(a) In any action for damages alleging professional malpractice, the plaintiff shall be required to file with the complaint an affidavit of an expert competent to testify, which affidavit shall set forth specifically at least one negligent act or omission claimed to exist and the factual basis for each such claim. . . .

. . . .

(e) . . . if a plaintiff fails to file an affidavit as required by this Code section contemporaneously with a complaint alleging professional malpractice and the defendant raises the failure to file such an affidavit in its initial responsive pleading, such complaint is subject to dismissal for failure to state a claim. . . .

O.C.G.A. § 9-11-9.1 (1995). What is the policy behind this? Why not obtain the standard from the defendant at trial? What policy is at work here? What does this requirement mean for the plaintiff? For the defendant? *See* Danzon, Medical Malpractice: Theory, Evidence, and Public Policy (1985).

7. *Furey v. Thomas Jefferson Univ. Hosp.*, 325 Pa. Super. 212, 472 A.2d 1083 (1984), presents the "two schools of thought" doctrine:

This doctrine is called into play in medical malpractice cases where there is more than one method of accepted treatment for the patient's disease or injury. The rule is that, where competent medical authority is divided, a physician will not be liable if in the exercise of his judgment he followed a course of treatment supported by reputable, respectable, and reasonable medical experts.

. . . .

Here, the medical authority on the treatment of a severe bacterial infection was diametrically opposed. Dr. Bass testified that treatment should absolutely be limited to antibiotic therapy. The defense experts stated that surgical intervention was imperative, and that it would have constituted malpractice to have failed to operate at once.

. . . .

The testimony clearly showed a difference of medical opinion, expressed by physicians and surgeons of unquestioned standing and reputation, and the defendants were not negligent for having adopted the view held by the majority of their brethren who testified.

How does this differ from the case where two experts disagree over the standard in the specific case?

PROBLEM

Will broke his nose in a football game. He went to Dr. Callier to have it set. Will showed the doctor a picture of his face and said, "That is what my nose should look like."

Dr. Callier straightened the nose and took a little off the tip. He also removed an unsightly mole from Will's chin. There are dark marks where the skin was cut and stitched.

Will is furious because of the marks and because the nose on his face does not resemble his nose. To most observers, however, it looks very good. Discuss.

PAUSCHER v. IOWA METHODIST MEDICAL CENTER
Supreme Court of Iowa, 1987
408 N.W.2d 355

Reynoldson, Chief Judge.

August 1, 1982, Becky, age twenty-six, entered Iowa Methodist Medical Center (IMMC) to deliver her first child. The child, Brad, was born the next day and Becky was scheduled to be released August 6.

On the day she was to leave the hospital, Becky developed a fever and pain in her right side. She also began to discharge large amounts of blood in her urine. As a result, Becky's obstetrician, Dr. Mark, delayed her release and prescribed Macrodantin, a bacteriostatic drug.

Becky's symptoms continued on August 7, 1982. Dr. Mark telephoned defendant Dr. John Bardole, a urology specialist. The latter feared a potentially life-threatening obstruction might be present in Becky's urinary tract.

Bardole ordered intravenous administration of a more aggressive bacterial drug, Mandol. Blood tests were instituted. Bardole also ordered an intravenous pyelogram (IVP) to be run the next morning, August 8, to determine whether Becky's urinary tract was obstructed.

An IVP is a diagnostic procedure in which an iodine-containing contrast material, in this case Reno-M-60, is injected into the patient's veins. X-rays then taken of the urinary tract, highlighted by the dye material, often enable the physician to determine whether it is obstructed.

Administration of an IVP is not without risk. A relatively small percent of individuals will suffer some discomfort, including flushing, hives, and nausea. More serious reactions include significant trouble breathing and a severe drop in blood pressure. The record made in this trial also indicates 1 person in 100,000 to 1 person in 150,000 will die as a result of an IVP, less often than fatal reactions to penicillin.

Before the IVP was administered neither Dr. Bardole nor defendant Dr. Jeff Watters, the only radiologist present in IMMC's radiology department on the Sunday morning Becky died, ever saw or talked to her. Two of the shift nurses who had attended Becky testified they separately told Becky she was to have an IVP and briefly described its purpose. One told Becky she could get a mild reaction, like hives, or a severe reaction, like difficult breathing. The other nurse described only the possibility of a mild reaction, "just the warmth of the dye, that sort of thing."

These discussions were noted in Becky's charts four days after her death, as "a late entry," at the request of a supervisor. Neither nurse was acting at the direction of a doctor in visiting with Becky about the IVP, neither nurse told her a severe reaction could include anaphylactic shock and death, and neither asked Becky if she consented to the procedure.

. . . .

In this action the plaintiff, Becky's husband, the administrator of her estate, alleges Bardole and Watters failed to inform Becky about the possibility she could die from an IVP, and thus they failed to obtain her informed consent to the procedure. He also claims IMMC failed to adopt or carry out procedures sufficient to insure that Becky's informed consent was obtained before the IVP was administered.

At trial, plaintiff presented no expert testimony on the issue whether Bardole and Watters deviated from professional standards when they failed to inform Becky the administration of an IVP entailed a very remote risk of death. In the absence of such evidence the trial court, following our 1966 decision in *Grosjean v. Spencer*, 258 Iowa 685, 140 N.W.2d 139 (1966), granted the defendant doctors' motions for directed verdict. The court also granted IMMC's motion for directed verdict on the same ground, and apparently because the obligation to inform a patient of such risks is upon the doctor, not the hospital.

I. In this appeal we first address the issue whether the "patient rule" or the "professional rule" should apply in circumstances such as these. The two standards were identified and extensively discussed in *Cowman v. Hornaday*, . . . in which we applied the "patient rule" in a case of elective surgery. . . . We since have applied the same rule in *Moser v. Stallings*, . . . an elective cosmetic surgery situation, and, apparently without it becoming an issue, in *Van Iperen v. Van Bramer*, . . . a case that involved medication for a serious illness, not elective surgery.

As we noted in *Cowman*, the doctrine of informed consent arises out of the unquestioned principle that absent extenuating circumstances a patient has the right to exercise control over his or her body by making an informed decision concerning whether to submit to a particular medical procedure. . . . Thus, a doctor recommending a particular procedure generally has, among other obligations, the duty to disclose to the patient all material risks involved in the procedure. . . .

The "professional rule" we followed in *Grosjean* recognized the treating doctor's duty to "disclose danger of which he has knowledge and the patient does not — but should have — in order to determine whether to consent to the risk." . . . At the same time, however, we left the question whether that duty had been satisfied to the medical profession when we held this was "primarily a question of medical judgment." Because there was no expert testimony that the treating doctor "failed to do that which should have been done in . . . advising . . . plaintiff . . . [a] jury question on negligence was not created." We thus affirmed a judgment based on a directed verdict for the defendant doctor.

Recognizing the inherently paternalistic and authoritarian nature of the professional rule of disclosure, an expanding number of jurisdictions have rejected it for a judicially-fashioned standard [16 states]. . . .

Similarly, the professional rule has come under a barrage of criticism from current commentators. . . .

The authoritarian rationale that undergirds the professional rule is apparent in the record before us. Both defendant doctors testified the practice in the profession would be to avoid mentioning a risk of death to a patient scheduled for an IVP. Although both doctors took into consideration the remote chance of such a fatality — a factor we discuss later — both justified withholding this information on the ground it would produce an anxiety in the patient that might adversely affect the patient's condition during the procedure.

In this connection plaintiff's evidence disclosed the manufacturer's package insert accompanying the dye material contained no warning relating to a patient with anxiety, but did contain the following information:

> Adverse reactions accompanying the use of iodine-containing intravascular contrast agents are usually mild and transient although severe and life-threatening reactions, including fatalities, have occurred. . . .
>
> . . . The histamine-liberating effect of these compounds may induce an allergic-like reaction which may range in severity from rhinitis or angioneurotic edema to laryngeal or bronchial spasm or anaphylactoid shock.

Each doctor, however, testified that if the patient asked what might happen, he would reply that the patient could die from the IVP. The professional rule thus provides this information for the patient already apprehensive enough to ask, but denies it to one so lacking in anxiety that he or she is not motivated to inquire. A rule resulting in such anomalous treatment of patients has little to commend it.

On the other hand, under the patient rule we adopted for elective surgery in *Cowman*, the physician's duty to disclose is measured by the patient's need to have access to all information material to making a truly informed and intelligent decision concerning the proposed medical procedure. . . . In *Cowman* we concluded that in the elective surgery situation no valid reasons existed for allowing the medical community the exclusive determination of what information would be material to a patient's decision to consent to a particular medical procedure. . . . Today we confirm, as we implied in *Van Iperen*, . . . that the patient rule is applicable in all informed consent cases, in both elective and nonelective medical procedures.

Compelling grounds justify this conclusion. The patient's right to make an intelligent and informed decision cannot be exercised when information material to that decision is withheld. Although most aspects of the physician-patient relationship necessarily must be dominated by the superior skill and knowledge of the physician, the decision to consent to a particular medical procedure is not a medical decision. Instead, it ordinarily is a personal and often difficult decision to be made by the patient with the physician's advice and consultation. In order to make his or her informed decision, the patient has the right to expect the information reasonably necessary to that process will be made available by the physician. To force a layperson patient to prove the professional community's standard and its violation allows the exceptions to swallow the rule — the hallmark of the professional rule as demonstrated by this case — and forces the patient to prove the withholding of material information was not medically justified. In contrast, the patient rule makes full disclosure the rule but allows for numerous exceptions which the physician, who has access to the medical knowledge involved, can assert.

Adoption of the patient rule in all circumstances does not provide an easy burden for the patient, who generally must establish the following:

(1) The existence of a material risk unknown to the patient;

(2) A failure to disclose that risk on the part of the physician;

(3) Disclosure of the risk would have led a reasonable patient in plaintiff's position to reject the medical procedure or choose a different course of treatment;

(4) Injury.

. . . Further, the patient ordinarily will be required to present expert testimony relating to the nature of the risk and the likelihood of its occurrence, in order for the jury to determine, from the standpoint of the reasonable patient, whether the risk is in fact a material one. . . .

As we noted in *Cowman*, a number of situations may be established by the defendant physician as a defense to an informed consent action, constituting exceptions to the duty to disclosure. These include:

(1) Situations in which complete and candid disclosure might have a detrimental effect on the physical or psychological well-being of the patient;

(2) Situations in which a patient is incapable of giving consent by reason of mental disability or infancy;

(3) Situations in which an emergency makes it impractical to obtain consent;

(4) Situations in which the risk is either known to the patient or is so obvious as to justify a presumption on the part of the physician that the patient has knowledge of the risk;

(5) Situations in which the procedure itself is simple and the danger remote and commonly appreciated to be remote;

(6) Situations in which the physician does not know of an otherwise material risk and should not have been aware of it in the exercise of ordinary care. . . .

Dr. Bardole's brief contends for the professional rule "as a matter of public policy," on the ground the decision to withhold information from the patient, for the patient's best interests, is a uniquely medical judgment call to be measured by what physicians under similar circumstances do. . . .

Our holding that the patient rule is applicable in both elective and nonelective medical procedures and thus applicable here, means that trial court's basis for directed verdict in favor of the defendant doctors, although understandable in light of our former case law, was erroneous.

II. The above determination does not end our inquiry, however, for defendants' motions also asserted there was insufficient competent evidence from which a jury could find they were guilty of negligence.

As the evidence developed from plaintiff's use of defendant doctors as witnesses, Becky's symptoms indicated a strong possibility of a serious and life-threatening infection, gram-negative sepsis. On the other hand, the risk of death posed by the IVP was 1 in 100,000 to 1 in 150,000.

We here confront not an action for battery, which may lie when a patient consents to one type of treatment and the physician intentionally deviates from the consent and performs a substantially different treatment. . . . Rather, we view these situations as sounding in negligence and imposing upon the doctor a duty reasonably to disclose information material to the patient's decision.

. . . .

In this case there was little dispute about the operative facts. A patient with a potentially life-threatening illness was not told there was a 1 in 100,000 chance she could die from a diagnostic procedure. We must answer the question whether a jury reasonably could conclude this withheld information was material to Becky's decision. In *Cowman v. Hornaday*, . . . we discussed the "subjective test" and the "objective test."

The subjective test focuses on whether the particular patient would have considered the nondisclosed information sufficiently significant to affect his or her decision. Although embraced occasionally by commentators, . . . most courts have rejected the subjective test in favor of the objective test. . . .

In *Cowman*, 329 N.W.2d at 425, we quoted the definition of materiality, in this context, that was adopted by the court in *Wilkinson v. Vesey*, 110 R.I. 606, 295 A.2d 676 (1972): Materiality may be said to be the significance a reasonable person, in what the physician knows or should know is his [or her] patient's position, would attach to the disclosed risk or risks in deciding whether to submit . . . to surgery or treatment.

After careful consideration, we are unable to conclude, applying the above objective test for materiality, that a jury could reasonably find the withheld information relating to the extremely remote risk of death, shown by this record, would have been significant to a reasonable person in Becky's circumstances, or would have affected such a person's willingness to undergo the IVP. Plainly, the risk involved in every informed consent action is not so significant as to generate a jury question. It is generally acknowledged that not all risks need be disclosed, only the material risks. . . . Cases involving the remoteness of the risk, falling on both sides of a necessarily obscure line, are collected in *Canterbury*, 464 F.2d at 788. . . . Plaintiff's proof in this case, although reflecting a most tragic situation, does not generate a jury question under the principles above noted. Trial court thus properly granted the defendant doctors' motions for directed verdict. . . . ("No prudent juror could reasonably have considered the [1 in 100,000] risk of permanent paresthesia material to a decision on whether to consent to the procedure. . . . ").

III. There remains the question whether the trial court properly granted IMMC's motion for directed verdict. Without the citation of any authority directly supporting the proposition, plaintiff argues IMMC "had a duty either to disseminate the necessary information and secure the patient's response or to adopt policies and procedures which allow physicians practicing in the hospital to perform medical procedures only with the patient's informed consent." In the circumstances of this case, we hold no jury issue relating to IMMC's liability was generated.

In Iowa as elsewhere a hospital does not practice medicine. . . . This court has not imposed on a hospital a duty to inform a patient of matters that lie at the heart of the doctor-patient relationship. . . . In similar situations other jurisdictions have held the responsibility of obtaining informed consent is the duty of the doctor and the hospital should not intervene. . . .

To the extent any of our prior decisions are inconsistent with our holding in division I of this opinion, the same are overruled. We affirm the judgment of the district court.

---

1. Define informed consent. What is a "material risk"? What is the problem with the "professional rule"? What is the problem with a "patient rule"?

2. What is the policy underlying the informed consent doctrine?

3. Why might a doctor want to avoid informing a patient of all the material risks? Should the rule be different for nonelective surgery?

4. What is the "objective" test? What would be an example of an emergency?

5. Note that the informed consent rule may allow a case to reach the jury without expert testimony.

6. If the doctor performs surgery without consent, or removes something without consent, the patient may sue in battery, *Mohr v. Williams*, 95 Minn. 261, 104 N.W. 12 (1905). What is the procedural difference between a battery suit and an informed consent (negligence) suit?

7. The doctor may be liable for failing to inform the patient of what might happen if the patient rejects the procedure. In *Truman v. Thomas*, 27 Cal. 3d 285, 165 Cal. Rptr. 308, 611 P.2d 902 (1980), the doctor was held liable for failing to inform the patient of the risk of death if the Pap smear test was rejected. The patient rejected the procedure, contracted cervical cancer, and died.

8. The doctor may have a duty to find the patient and warn her of risk that developed after he or she last saw her. Two years after inserting a Dalkon Shield (interuterine device) into the plaintiff, the doctor learned of the risks of migration, serious infection, and death. He was held liable for failing to notify his patient and to provide her with the opportunity to have it removed. *Tresemer v. Barke*, 86 Cal. App. 3d 656, 150 Cal. Rptr. 384 (1978).

9. In informed consent, the doctor is liable although he was not negligent in diagnosis or treatment. Is this fair to the doctor?

10. Some states have codified informed consent. The Georgia Code provides:

(a) [A]ny person who undergoes any surgical procedure under general anesthesia, spinal anesthesia, or major regional anesthesia or any person who undergoes an amniocentesis diagnostic procedure or a diagnostic procedure which involves the intravenous injection of a contrast material must consent to such procedure and shall be informed in general terms of the following:

(1) A diagnosis of the patient's condition requiring such proposed surgical or diagnostic procedure;

(2) The nature and purpose of such proposed surgical or diagnostic procedure;

(3) The material risks generally recognized and accepted by reasonably prudent physicians of infection, allergic reaction, severe loss of blood, loss or loss of function of any limb or organ, paralysis or partial paralysis, paraplegia or quadriplegia, disfiguring scar, brain damage, cardiac arrest, or death involved in such proposed surgical or diagnostic procedure which, if disclosed to a reasonably prudent person in the patient's position, could reasonably be expected to cause such prudent person to decline such proposed surgical or diagnostic procedure on the basis of the material risk of injury that could result from such proposed surgical or diagnostic procedure;

(4) The likelihood of success of such proposed surgical or diagnostic procedure;

(5) The practical alternatives to such proposed surgical or diagnostic procedure which are generally recognized and accepted by reasonably prudent physicians; and

(6) The prognosis of the patient's condition if such proposed surgical or diagnostic procedure is rejected.

. . . .

O.C.G.A. § 31-9-6.1 (1989). How is this different from the informed consent doctrine developed in *Pauscher v. Iowa Methodist Medical Center*?

11. In *Doreika*, the defendant was a chiropractor. He argued that informed consent did not apply, because it was not required by the Georgia statute (no anesthetic). The court held that there was a common law and a constitutional right to informed consent and therefore he should have informed his patient of the risks of a neck adjustment. *Doreika v. Blotner* 666 S.E.2d 21 (Ga. Ct. App. 2008). What has this done to informed consent in Georgia?

JOHN B. v. SUPERIOR COURT OF LOS ANGELES COUNTY
Supreme Court of California, 2006
137 P.3d 153

BAXTER, J.

This is a sad case. Bridget B., the plaintiff in the underlying action and real party in interest herein, is infected with the human immunodeficiency virus (HIV), the probable causative agent of acquired immune deficiency syndrome (AIDS). So is her husband, petitioner herein and defendant in the underlying action, John B.

Bridget alleges that John became infected with HIV first, as a result of engaging in unprotected sex with multiple men before and during their marriage, and that he then knowingly or negligently transmitted the virus to her. John, who now has full-blown AIDS, alleges in his answer that Bridget infected *him* and offers as proof a negative HIV test conducted in connection with his application for life insurance on August 17, 2000, six weeks before Bridget discovered she was infected with HIV.

This factual scenario raises a number of interesting questions: What duty does an HIV-positive individual have to avoid transmitting the virus? What level of awareness should be required before a court imposes a duty of care on an HIV-positive individual to avoid transmission of the virus? What responsibility does the victim have to protect himself or herself against possible infection with the virus? . . .

Bridget's complaint for damages alleges the following:

Plaintiff Bridget B. and defendant John B. met in September 1998 and began dating shortly thereafter. The couple became engaged in late 1999 and were married in July 2000. During this period, John represented to Bridget that he was healthy, disease-free, and monogamous. Indeed, it was John who insisted that the couple stop using condoms during intercourse. Based on John's representations, Bridget complied with his demand to engage in unprotected sex. In September 2000, however, Bridget began to suffer from exhaustion and high fevers.

On October 1, 2000, Bridget learned that she had tested positive for HIV. She was advised to undergo a second test and to have her husband tested as well. The second test confirmed that Bridget was HIV positive. John, too, was determined to be HIV positive. John's doctor told Bridget that she had "brought the HIV into the marriage." The doctor prescribed medications for John that made his viral load virtually undetectable. Bridget, on the other hand, was not offered treatment; she was informed that she had "had the illness for a long time." Bridget became depressed that she had infected her husband with this deadly disease.

In September 2001, John began telling others that Bridget had infected him with HIV. The next month, after defendant refused to continue his treatment, he became much sicker and developed sores on his face and scalp. Although he was diagnosed with AIDS, he refused all treatments and medications except those that treated the visible signs of the disease.

. . . .

The fourth cause of action (negligence) incorporates the foregoing allegations and alleges that John owed Bridget a duty of care to disclose the fact that he was HIV positive, that he breached this duty, and that he thereby infected her with HIV.

. . . .

This court has not yet had occasion to consider the tort of negligent transmission of a sexually transmitted disease, but the tort is far from novel. Our sister jurisdictions have long imposed liability on individuals who have harmed others by transmitting communicable diseases. . . . In particular, courts throughout the United States have recognized a cause of action for the negligent transmission of sexually transmitted diseases. . . . We agree with these courts that "[t]o be *stricken with disease* through another's negligence is in legal contemplation as it often is in the seriousness of consequences, no different from *being struck with an automobile* through another's negligence."

. . . .

John concedes that a person who actually knows he or she is infected with a sexually transmitted disease based on a test from an accredited laboratory or a medical diagnosis has a duty to use ordinary care to see that the disease is not transmitted to others. The foreseeability of harm in such a circumstance is manifest. John also concedes the viability of the tort of negligent transmission of HIV. In his view, though, a duty under this tort exists only when the actor has actual knowledge of being HIV positive; constructive knowledge of the infection is insufficient.

. . . Extending liability to those who have constructive knowledge of the disease, as [other] jurisdictions have done, comports with general principles of negligence. Indeed, the "very concept of negligence presupposes that the actor either does foresee an unreasonable risk of injury, or could foresee it if he conducted himself as a reasonably prudent person." (3 Harper et al., The Law of Torts (2d ed. 1986) Section 16.5, p. 397. . . .

It must be noted, though, that "constructive knowledge," which means knowledge "that one using reasonable care or diligence should have, and therefore is attributed by law to a given person" (Black's Law Dict. (7th ed. 1999) p. 876), encompasses a variety of mental states, ranging from one who is deliberately indifferent in the face of an unjustifiably high risk of harm (to one who merely should know of a dangerous condition. . . .

In this case, we conclude that the tort of negligent transmission of HIV does not depend solely on actual knowledge of HIV infection and would extend at least to those situations where the actor, under the totality of the circumstances, has *reason to know* of the infection. Under the reason-to-know standard, "the actor has information from which a person of reasonable intelligence or of the superior intelligence of the actor would infer that the fact in question exists, or that such person would govern his conduct upon the assumption that such fact exists."

Imposing liability for the transmission of HIV where the actor knows or has reason to know he or she is HIV positive is consistent with the general principle of California law that " '[a]ll persons are required to use ordinary care to prevent others being injured as the result of their conduct.' " The factor that " 'plays a very significant role in this calculus' " is the foreseeability of the particular harm, which (like the reason-to-know standard) is assessed by an objective test.

. . . .

. . . . We need not consider the existence or scope of a duty for persons whose relationship does not extend beyond the sexual encounter itself, whose relationship does not contemplate sexual exclusivity, who have not represented themselves as disease-free, or who have not insisted on having sex without condoms.

. . . .

---

1. Weigh the policy considerations in this case. Did the court get them right?

2. Do you agree with the assertion that, "[t]o be stricken with disease through another's negligence is in legal contemplation as it often is in the seriousness of consequences, no different from being struck with an automobile through another's negligence"? *Billo v. Allegheny Steel Co.*, 328 Pa. 97, 195 A. 110, 114 (1937). Does it depend on the severity of the specific disease?

3. Do you think the same rule should extend to casual sex?

Why does the court dodge this issue? Is contracting HIV through casual dating still "getting hit with a car"?

4. Would the analysis be different if the transmission were of a more common sexually transmitted disease, such as syphilis or genital herpes? The majority stated that diseases such as syphilis and HPV "are also life-threatening," and that HIV is not " 'unique' in the approbrium with which those infected are viewed." (*John B.*, 38 Cal. 4th at 1195–96.)

MOORE v. THE REGENTS OF THE UNIVERSITY OF CALIFORNIA
Supreme Court of California, 1990
51 Cal. 3d 120, 271 Cal. Rptr. 146, 793 P.2d 479

[John Moore was diagnosed by his doctor, defendant Golde, at the U.C.L.A. Medical Center as having hairy-cell leukemia. He had his spleen removed and blood removed during his many visits to the medical center. From Moore's cells, Dr. Golde and others patented a cell line and "leased" it to Genetics Institute and Sandoz Pharmaceuticals.

Moore brought 13 causes of action, including informed consent, conversion and breach of fiduciary duty, against Golde, the university Regents, Genetics Institute and Sandoz.]

PENELLI, JUSTICE. . . .

A. *Breach of Fiduciary Duty and Lack of Informed Consent*

Moore repeatedly alleges that Golde failed to disclose the extent of his research and economic interests in Moore's cells before obtaining consent to the medical procedures by which the cells were extracted. These allegations, in our view, state a cause of action against Golde for invading a legally protected interest of his patient. This cause of action can properly be characterized either as the breach of a fiduciary duty to disclose facts material to the patient's consent or, alternatively, as the performance of medical procedures without first having obtained the patient's informed consent.

Our analysis begins with three well-established principles. First, "a person of adult years and in sound mind has the right, in the exercise of control over his own body, to determine whether or not to submit to lawful medical treatment." . . . Second, "the patient's consent to treatment, to be effective, must be an informed consent." . . . Third, in soliciting the patient's consent, a physician has a fiduciary duty to disclose all information material to the patient's decision. . . .

These principles lead to the following conclusions: (1) a physician must disclose personal interests unrelated to the patient's health, whether research or economic, that may affect the physician's professional judgment; and (2) a physician's failure to disclose such interests may give rise to a cause of action for performing medical procedures without informed consent or breach of fiduciary duty.

. . . "The scope of the physician's communication to the patient . . . must be measured by the patient's need, and that need is whatever information is material to the decision." . . .

Indeed, the law already recognizes that a reasonable patient would want to know whether a physician has an economic interest that might affect the physician's professional judgment. As the Court of Appeal has said, "[c]ertainly a sick patient deserves to be free of any reasonable suspicion that his doctor's judgment is influenced by a profit motive." . . . A physician who adds his own research interests to this balance may be tempted to order a scientifically useful procedure or test that offers marginal, or no, benefits to the patient.[8]

The possibility that an interest extraneous to the patient's health has affected the physician's judgment is something that a reasonable patient would want to know in deciding whether to consent to a proposed course of treatment. It is material to the patient's decision and, thus, a prerequisite to informed consent. . . .

Golde argues that the scientific use of cells that have already been removed cannot possibly affect the patient's medical interests. The argument is correct in one instance but not in another. If a physician has no plans to conduct research on a patient's cells at the time he recommends the medical procedure by which they are taken, then the patient's medical interests have not been impaired. In that instance

---

[8] This is, in fact, precisely what Moore has alleged with respect to the postoperative withdrawals of blood and other substances.

the argument is correct. On the other hand, a physician who does have a preexisting research interest might, consciously or unconsciously, take that into consideration in recommending the procedure. In that instance the argument is incorrect: the physician's extraneous motivation may affect his judgment and is, thus, material to the patient's consent.

Accordingly, we hold that a physician who is seeking a patient's consent for a medical procedure must, in order to satisfy his fiduciary duty and to obtain the patient's informed consent, disclose personal interests unrelated to the patient's health, whether research or economic, that may affect his medical judgment.

. . . .

The decision of the Court of Appeal is affirmed in part and reversed in part. The case is remanded to the Court of Appeal, which shall direct the superior court to: (1) overrule Golde's demurrers to the causes of action for breach of fiduciary duty and lack of informed consent; (2) sustain, with leave to amend, the demurrers of the Regents, Quan, Sandoz, and Genetics Institute to the purported causes of action for breach of fiduciary duty and lack of informed consent; (3) sustain, without leave to amend, all defendants' demurrers to the purported cause of action for conversion; and (4) hear and determine all defendants' remaining demurrers.

[The concurring and dissenting opinions have been omitted.]

---

1. Upon being informed of the physician's personal interest, as required by the opinion, is there a risk that the patient will be distracted from health considerations?

2. In some cases, might "a physician's research interest . . . play such an insignificant role in the decision . . . that disclosure should not be required because the interest is not material?" The court answered yes. What are examples of such trivial research interests?

3. The court held that the cause of action in conversion did not cover Moore's cells in part because there was no precedent. *Moore*, 793 P.2d at 487–97. Argue that the taking of his cells falls within conversion.

4. What will be the impact of the *Moore* decision on medical research? What damages, if any, should Moore recover? *See* Anne T. Corrigan, *A Paper Tiger: Lawsuits Against Doctors for Non-Disclosure of Economic Interests in Patients' Cells, Tissues and Organs*, 42 Case W. Res. L. Rev. 565 (1992); Jennifer Lavoie, Note, *Ownership of Human Tissue: Life After* Moore v. Regents of the University of California, 75 Va. L. Rev. 1363 (1989).

5. Assume that the physician sends the patient to a diagnostic lab for tests. Must the physician inform the patient of his or her part ownership in the lab?

3. Custom

PROBLEM

Barbara took her car to Anita's Garage to have the transmission repaired. Anita removed the transmission, but parked the car in the adjacent parking lot overnight. During the night, the engine from the car was stolen. Anita has several local garage owners who will testify that they generally leave customers' cars parked outside overnight.

Will you take Barbara's suit against Anita's Garage?

THE T.J. HOOPER I
District Court, S.D. New York, 1931
53 F.2d 107

Coxe, District Judge.

These cases grow out of the foundering of the coal barges Northern 17 and Northern 30 in a storm off the New Jersey coast in March, 1928. Libels have been filed by the owners of the coal on the two barges for cargo loss against the barge owner. The owner of the tugs T. J. Hooper and Montrose has also instituted limitation proceedings, in which it seeks to be relieved from liability, and, at the same time, denies fault. In these limitation proceedings, the barge owner has answered, asserting negligent towage by the tugs, and claiming for the value of the barges. The cargo owners have also answered, alleging negligent towage, and contesting the right to limit. The cases have all been tried together as one action.

. . . .

This raises the question whether the Hooper and Montrose were required to have effective radio sets to pick up weather reports broadcast along the coast. Concededly, there is no statutory law on the subject applicable to tugs of that type, the radio statute applying only to steamers "licensed to carry, or carrying, fifty or more persons;" and excepting by its terms "steamers plying between ports, or places, less than two hundred miles apart." U.S. Code Annotated, title 46, § 484. The standard of seaworthiness is not, however, dependent on statutory enactment, or condemned to inertia or rigidity, but changes "with advancing knowledge, experience, and the changed appliances of navigation." *The Titania* (D.C.) 19 F. 101, 106; *The Southwark*, 191 U.S. 1, 24 S. Ct. 1, 48 L. Ed. 65. It is particularly affected by new devices of demonstrated worth, which have become recognized as regular equipment by common usage.

Radio broadcasting was no new or untried thing in March, 1928. Everywhere, and in almost every field of activity, it was being utilized as an aid to communication, and for the dissemination of information. And that radio sets were in widespread use on vessels of all kinds is clearly indicated by the testimony in this case. Twice a day the government broadcast from Arlington weather reports forecasting weather conditions. Clearly this was important information which navigators could not afford to ignore.

Captain Powell, master of the Menominee, who was a witness for the tugs, testified that prior to March, 1928, his tug, and all other seagoing tugs of his company, were equipped by the owner with efficient radio sets, and that he regarded a radio as part "of the necessary equipment" of every reasonably well-equipped tug in the coastwise service. He further testified that 90 per cent of the coastwise tugs operating along the coast were so equipped. It is, of course, true that many of these radio sets were the personal property of the tug master, and not supplied by the owner. This was so with the Mars, Wal-tham, and Menominee; but, notwithstanding that fact, the use of the radio was shown to be so extensive as to amount almost to a universal practice in the navigation of coastwise tugs along the coast. I think therefore there was a duty on the part of the tug owner to supply effective receiving sets.

How have the tugs met this requirement? The Hooper had a radio set which belonged to her master, but was practically useless even before the tug left Hampton Roads, and was generally out of order. Similarly, the radio on the Montrose was the personal property of Captain Walton, and was "a home made set," which was not in very good working order, and was admittedly ineffective. Neither tug received any of the radio reports broadcast on March 8th. And Captain Savage of the Hooper admitted that if he had received such reports he would "quite likely" have turned into the breakwater. . . . Likewise, Captain Walton of the Montrose admitted that if he had received the weather reports on the 8th, which were received by the other tug captains, he "certainly would have gone into Breakwater." . . .

I hold therefore . . . (2) that the tugs T. J. Hooper and Montrose were unsea-worthy in failing to have effective radio sets, capable of receiving weather reports on March 8th . . . (3) that the claims of the cargo owners against the tugs should be allowed. . . .

What was the custom of the tug owners? What was the custom of the tug captains?

THE T.J. HOOPER II
United States Court of Appeals, Second Circuit, 1932
60 F.2d 737

[This is the previous case now in the court of appeals. The court first held that the tugs would have sailed to the protection of the Delaware Breakwater if they had received the radio broadcasts.]

L. Hand, Circuit Judge. . . .

They did not, because their private radio receiving sets, which were on board, were not in working order. These belonged to them personally, and were partly a toy, partly a part of the equipment, but neither furnished by the owner, nor supervised by it. It is not fair to say that there was a general custom among coastwise carriers to so equip their tugs. One line alone did it; as for the rest, they relied upon their crews, so far as they can be said to have relied at all. An adequate receiving set suitable for a coastwise tug can now be got at small cost and is reasonably reliable if kept up; obviously it is a source of great protection to their tows. Twice every day they can receive these predictions, based upon the widest possible information, available to every vessel within two or three hundred miles and more. Such a set is the ears of the tug to catch the spoken word, just as the master's binoculars are her eyes to see a storm signal ashore. Whatever may be said as to other vessels, tugs towing heavy coal laden barges, strung out for half a mile, have little power to maneuver, and do not, as this case proves, expose themselves to weather which would not turn back stauncher craft. They can have at hand protection against dangers of which they can learn in no other way.

Is it then a final answer that the business had not yet generally adopted receiving sets? There are, no doubt, cases where courts seem to make the general practice of the calling the standard of proper diligence; we have indeed given some currency to the notion ourselves. . . . Indeed in most cases reasonable prudence is in fact common prudence; but strictly it is never its measure; a whole calling may have unduly lagged in the adoption of new and available devices. It never may set its own tests, however persuasive be its usages. Courts must in the end say what is required; there are precautions so imperative that even their universal disregard will not excuse their omission. . . . But here there was no custom at all as to receiving sets; some had them, some did not; the most that can be urged is that they had not yet become general. Certainly in such a case we need not pause; when some have thought a device necessary, at least we may say that they were right, and the others too slack. The statute (section 484, title 46, U.S. Code [46 USCA § 484]) does not bear on this situation at all. It prescribes not a receiving, but a transmitting set, and for a very different purpose; to call for help, not to get news. We hold the tugs therefore [sic] because had they been properly equipped, they would have got the Arlington reports. The injury was a direct consequence of this unseaworthiness.

Decree affirmed. [The claims against the tugs were allowed.]

---

1.   Why would the owners decide not to supply radios? Is it the function of the courts to uphold the business decisions of the owners, the captains, or neither?

2.   Argue that since this was a commercial case, the market decision by the owners should control.

3.   Could it be that barges tend to sink, but tugs do not? In prior suits, perhaps the barges lost and tug owners won because storms were viewed as acts of God. Might the tug owners have reacted to the law (storms are acts of God), not the market (cheaper not to have radios)?

4.   The plaintiff fell through a hole in the floor of a coal mine. Reflecting custom, the hole was unlit and unfenced. The court held that the custom was so careless that it was inadmissible as evidence. *Mayhew v. Sullivan Mining Co.*, 76 Me. 100 (1884).

5.   In *Trimarco v. Klein*, 56 N.Y.2d 98, 451 N.Y.S.2d 52, 436 N.E.2d 502 (1982), the plaintiff was injured when the shower door shattered, and the court held that

the custom was to replace the glass doors with safety glass. The landlord was negligent in replacing the non-safety glass with the same type.

6. For an evaluation, see R.A. Epstein, *The Path to* The T.J. Hooper: *The Theory and History of Custom in the Law of Tort*, 21 J. Legal Stud. 1 (1992).

D.   THE RELATIONSHIP BETWEEN JUDGE AND JURY

The judge has the opportunity and the responsibility to control the jury. In this section the judge does this by stating a rule of law. The judge may also look to a statute or the regulation for the standard (Section E. Violation of Statute), follow the standard of the reasonable person (Section C, Subsection 1), or apply the relevant custom (Section C, Subsection 3).

BALTIMORE & OHIO RAILROAD CO. v. GOODMAN
Supreme Court of the United States, 1927
275 U.S. 66, 48 S. Ct. 24, 72 L. Ed. 167

MR. JUSTICE HOLMES delivered the opinion of the Court.

This is a suit brought by the widow and administratrix of Nathan Goodman against the petitioner for causing his death by running him down at a grade crossing. The defence is that Goodman's own negligence caused the death. At the trial, the defendant asked the Court to direct a verdict for it, but the request, and others looking to the same direction, were refused, and the plaintiff got a verdict and a judgment which was affirmed by the Circuit Court of Appeals. . . .

Goodman was driving an automobile truck in an easterly direction and was killed by a train running southwesterly across the road at a rate of not less than sixty miles an hour. The line was straight, but it is said by the respondent that Goodman 'had no practical view' beyond a section house two hundred and forty-three feet north of the crossing until he was about twenty feet from the first rail, or, as the respondent argues, twelve feet from danger, and that then the engine was still obscured by the section house. He had been driving at the rate of ten or twelve miles an hour, but had cut down his rate to five or six miles at about forty feet from the crossing. It is thought that there was an emergency in which, so far as appears, Goodman did all that he could.

We do not go into further details as to Goodman's precise situation, beyond mentioning that it was daylight and that he was familiar with the crossing, for it appears to us plain that nothing is suggested by the evidence to relieve Goodman from responsibility for his own death. When a man goes upon a railroad track he knows that he goes to a place where he will be killed if a train comes upon him before he is clear of the track. He knows that he must stop for the train, not the train stop for him. In such circumstances it seems to us that if a driver cannot be sure otherwise whether a train is dangerously near he must stop and get out of his vehicle, although obviously he will not often be required to do more than to stop and look. It seems to us that if he relies upon not hearing the train or any signal and takes no further precaution he does so at his own risk. If at the last moment

Goodman found himself in an emergency it was his own fault that he did not reduce his speed earlier or come to a stop. It is true . . . that the question of due care very generally is left to the jury. But we are dealing with a standard of conduct, and when the standard is clear it should be laid down once for all by the courts. . . .

Judgment reversed.

---

1. Why did Justice Holmes state the standard? What is it? Was the standard reasonable?

2. Why does the Supreme Court rarely take a torts case? Was it appropriate here? Read on.

POKORA v. WABASH RAILWAY CO.
Supreme Court of the United States, 1934
292 U.S. 98, 54 S. Ct. 580, 78 L. Ed. 1149

MR. JUSTICE CARDOZO delivered the opinion of the Court.

John Pokora, driving his truck across a railway grade crossing in the city of Springfield, Illinois, was struck by a train and injured. Upon the trial of his suit for damages, the District Court held that he had been guilty of contributory negligence, and directed a verdict for the defendant. The Circuit Court of Appeals (one judge dissenting) affirmed, 66 F.2d 166, resting its judgment on the opinion of this court in *B. & O. R. Co. v. Goodman*, 275 U.S. 66. A writ of certiorari brings the case here.

Pokora was an ice dealer, and had come to the crossing to load his truck with ice. The tracks of the Wabash Railway are laid along Tenth Street, which runs north and south. There is a crossing at Edwards Street running east and west. Two ice depots are on opposite corners of Tenth and Edward Streets, one at the northeast corner, the other at the southwest. Pokora, driving west along Edwards Street, stopped at the first of these corners to get his load of ice, but found so many trucks ahead of him that he decided to try the depot on the other side of the way. In this crossing of the railway, the accident occurred.

The defendant has four tracks on Tenth Street, a switch track on the east, then the main track, and then two switches. Pokora, as he left the northeast corner where his truck had been stopped, looked to the north for approaching trains. He did this at a point about ten or fifteen feet east of the switch ahead of him. A string of box cars standing on the switch, about five to ten feet from the north line of Edwards Street, cut off his view of the tracks beyond him to the north. At the same time he listened. There was neither bell nor whistle. Still listening, he crossed the switch, and reaching the main track was struck by a passenger train coming from the north at a speed of twenty-five to thirty miles an hour.

. . . .

The argument is made, however, that our decision in *B. & O. R. Co. v. Goodman, supra,* is a barrier in the plaintiff's path, irrespective of the conclusion that might

commend itself if the question were at large. There is no doubt that the opinion in
that case is correct in its result. Goodman, the driver, traveling only five or six miles
an hour, had, before reaching the track, a clear space of eighteen feet within which
the train was plainly visible. With that opportunity, he fell short of the legal
standard of duty established for a traveler when he failed to look and see. This was
decisive of the case. But the court did not stop there. It added a remark,
unnecessary upon the facts before it, which has been a fertile source of controversy.
"In such circumstances it seems to us that if a driver cannot be sure otherwise
whether a train is dangerously near he must stop and get out of his vehicle,
although obviously he will not often be required to do more than to stop and look."

There is need at this stage to clear the ground of brushwood that may obscure
the point at issue. We do not now inquire into the existence of a duty to stop,
disconnected from a duty to get out and reconnoitre. The inquiry, if pursued, would
lead us into the thickets of conflicting judgments. Some courts apply what is often
spoken of as the Pennsylvania rule, and impose an unyielding duty to stop, as well
as to look and listen, no matter how clear the crossing or the tracks on either side.
. . . Other courts, the majority, adopt the rule that the traveler must look and listen,
but that the existence of a duty to stop depends upon the circumstances, and hence
generally, even if not invariably, upon the judgment of the jury. . . . The subject has
been less considered in this court, but in none of its opinions is there a suggestion
that at any and every crossing the duty to stop is absolute, irrespective of the
danger. Not even in *B. & O. R. Co. v. Goodman, supra*, which goes farther than the
earlier cases, is there support for such a rule. To the contrary, the opinion makes it
clear that the duty is conditioned upon the presence of impediments whereby sight
and hearing become inadequate for the traveler's protection. . . .

Choice between these diversities of doctrine is unnecessary for the decision of
the case at hand. Here the fact is not disputed that the plaintiff did stop before he
started to cross the tracks. If we assume that by reason of the box cars, there was
a duty to stop again when the obstructions had been cleared, that duty did not arise
unless a stop could be made safely after the point of clearance had been reached.
. . . For reasons already stated, the testimony permits the inference that the truck
was in the zone of danger by the time the field of vision was enlarged. No stop would
then have helped the plaintiff if he remained seated on his truck, or so the triers of
the facts might find. His case was for the jury unless as a matter of law he was
subject to a duty to get out of the vehicle before it crossed the switch, walk forward
to the front, and then, afoot, survey the scene. We must say whether his failure to
do this was negligence so obvious and certain that one conclusion and one only is
permissible for rational and candid minds.

Standards of prudent conduct are declared at times by courts, but they are taken
over from the facts of life. To get out of a vehicle and reconnoitre is an uncommon
precaution, as everyday experience informs us. Besides being uncommon, it is very
likely to be futile, and sometimes even dangerous. If the driver leaves his vehicle
when he nears a cut or curve, he will learn nothing by getting out about the perils
that lurk beyond. By the time he regains his seat and sets his car in motion, the
hidden train may be upon him. . . . Often the added safeguard will be dubious
though the track happens to be straight, as it seems that this one was, at all events
as far as the station, about five blocks to the north. A train traveling at a speed of

thirty miles an hour will cover a quarter of a mile in the space of thirty seconds. It may thus emerge out of obscurity as the driver turns his back to regain the waiting car, and may then descend upon him suddenly when his car is on the track. Instead of helping himself by getting out, he might do better to press forward with all his faculties alert. So a train at a neighboring station, apparently at rest and harmless, may be transformed in a few seconds into an instrument of destruction. At times the course of safety may be different. One can figure to oneself a roadbed so level and unbroken that getting out will be a gain. Even then the balance of advantage depends on many circumstances and can be easily disturbed. Where was Pokora to leave his truck after getting out to reconnoitre? If he was to leave it on the switch, there was the possibility that the box cars would be shunted down upon him before he could regain his seat. The defendant did not show whether there was a locomotive at the forward end, or whether the cars were so few that a locomotive could be seen. If he was to leave his vehicle near the curb, there was even stronger reason to believe that the space to be covered in going back and forth would make his observations worthless. One must remember that while the traveler turns his eyes in one direction, a train or a loose engine may be approaching from the other.

Illustrations such as these bear witness to the need for caution in framing standards of behavior that amount to rules of law. The need is the more urgent when there is no background of experience out of which the standards have emerged. They are then, not the natural flowerings of behavior in its customary forms, but rules artificially developed, and imposed from without. Extraordinary situations may not wisely or fairly be subjected to tests or regulations that are fitting for the common-place or normal. In default of the guide of customary conduct, what is suitable for the traveler caught in a mesh where the ordinary safeguards fail him is for the judgment of a jury. . . . The opinion in Goodman's case has been a source of confusion in the federal courts to the extent that it imposes a standard for application by the judge, and has had only wavering support in the courts of the states. We limit it accordingly.

The judgment should be reversed and the cause remanded for further proceedings in accordance with this opinion.

Reversed.

---

1. Why does Justice Cardozo object to the *Goodman* standard? What rule does he present in its place? Does he say that the courts should never state a firm rule?

2. If it was economically sound to subsidize the railroads in 1927, by placing the loss on the victim, had the strength of the railroads improved by 1933? Is Cardozo merely reflecting such strength? *See* Green, *The Duty Problem in Negligence Cases*, 29 Colum. L. Rev. 255 (1929). Does the court have a legitimate role in social engineering?

3. One case has rejected the professional standard of care as established by the customary practice of doctors. In spite of numerous office visits over several years, the defendant ophthalmologist did not test the patient for glaucoma. The accepted practice was to not give glaucoma tests to persons under age forty. The court

rejected the medical standard and found for the plaintiff, stating:

> The incidence of glaucoma in one out of 25,000 persons under the age of 40 may appear quite minimal. However, that one person, the plaintiff in this instance, is entitled to the same protection, as afforded persons over 40, essential for timely detection of the evidence of glaucoma where it can be arrested to avoid the grave and devastating result of this disease. The test is a simple pressure test, relatively inexpensive. There is no judgment factor involved, and there is no doubt that by giving the test the evidence of glaucoma can be detected. The giving of the test is harmless if the physical condition of the eye permits.
>
> Under the facts of this case reasonable prudence required the timely giving of the pressure test to this plaintiff. The precaution of giving this test to detect the incidence of glaucoma to patients under 40 years of age is so imperative that irrespective of its disregard by the standards of the ophthalmology profession, it is the duty of the courts to say what is required to protect patients under 40 from the damaging results of glaucoma.

Helling v. Carey, 83 Wash. 2d 514, 519 P.2d 981 (1974). What factors did the court balance in rejecting the professional standard?

Does the hard rule established in *Helling* fly in the face of *Pokora*? Would any other rule be unjust to those under age forty? What other policies are important?

E. VIOLATION OF STATUTE

PROBLEM

A father of a child whose brain is permanently damaged has come to you for advice. The child was severely beaten by the mother's boyfriend. The child has bruises, a broken arm, and strangulation marks on his neck, and will never weigh over forty pounds. The boyfriend is in prison serving a ten-year sentence, and the mother is a waitress.

What questions do you ask of the father and others?

HETHERTON v. SEARS, ROEBUCK & CO.
United States Court of Appeals, Third Circuit, 1979
593 F.2d 526

A. LEON HIGGINBOTHAM, JR., CIRCUIT JUDGE.

In this appeal we are asked to decide whether a retail store can be held liable under Delaware law when the ammunition it sold was used to injure an innocent person in an attempted murder and robbery.

We conclude that the district court was in error in granting a summary judgment for the defendant and therefore we will reverse the judgment.

I.

On February 25, 1976, Lloyd Fullman, Jr. purchased from Sears, Roebuck and Co. (Sears) a.22 caliber rifle and rifle cartridges. Six weeks later, in an attempted robbery of a Wilmington restaurant, Fullman, using the rifle and ammunition purchased at Sears, shot the plaintiff, James Hetherton, in the head. At the time, Hetherton, an off-duty police officer, was employed as a guard in the restaurant. Hetherton was injured seriously and, as of the time of the suit, still had "13 fragments of the projectile in his head." In the related criminal proceeding in state court, Fullman was convicted of attempted second degree murder, attempted robbery, possession of a deadly weapon during the commission of a felony, possession of a deadly weapon by a person prohibited and conspiracy of the second degree. These convictions, however, were not Fullman's first "brush with the law." He had been convicted previously of the felonies of attempted robbery, conspiracy of the second degree, and falsely reporting an incident. As a result of these prior felony convictions Fullman was prohibited under Delaware law from purchasing the rifle and cartridges obtained from Sears. Additionally, Delaware law required Sears, prior to sale, to receive from two freeholders the positive identification of a purchaser of any "deadly weapon." No freeholders identified Fullman when he made his purchase. He merely produced a Delaware driver's license and completed a Federal Firearms Transaction Record, Form 4473. Although Fullman had a criminal record, he indicated on Form 4473 that he had never been convicted of a felony.

Hetherton and his wife brought this suit alleging that Sears was negligent when it sold the gun and ammunition to Fullman and Sears was therefore liable for Hetherton's injuries. They asserted that Sears was negligent because it had failed to require at least two freeholders to identify Fullman before making the sale as required by 24 Del. C. § 904. . . .

A.

At least since 1911, Delaware has had a number of statutes regulating the sale and possession of guns and ammunition including 24 Del. C. § 904, on which the Hethertons rely for a theory of liability.

Section 904 provides that:

> Any person desiring to engage in the business described in this chapter shall keep and maintain in his place of business at all times a book which shall be furnished him by the State Tax Department. In such book he shall enter the date of the sale, the name and address of the person purchasing *any deadly weapon*, the number and kind of *deadly weapon* so purchased, the color of the person so purchasing the same, the apparent age of the purchaser, and the names and addresses of at least 2 freeholders resident in the county wherein the sale is made who shall positively identify the purchaser before the sale can be made, (emphasis added)[6]

---

[6] We note that § 904 was amended after the Fullman purchase to strike the words "freeholders resident in the county wherein the sale is made" from the second sentence and to substitute the words

The starting point in this case has to be what is a "deadly weapon," or more specifically, was the ammunition Fullman purchased from Sears a "deadly weapon" under section 904. Sears argues that neither the rifle nor the ammunition it sold Fullman were "deadly weapons" within the meaning of the statute and therefore Sears was not required to comply with section 904 when it made the sale. While the plaintiffs agree that the rifle was not a "deadly weapon" as defined by the statute, they urge that the rifle cartridges were "deadly weapons" for the purpose of section 904.

Section 904 is a provision of chapter nine, title 24 of the Delaware Code. This chapter regulates "deadly weapons dealers." The chapter includes a definition of "deadly weapons" which is controlling for each of the chapter sections. "Deadly weapons" is defined in section 901 to mean "any pistol or revolver, or Revolver or pistol cartridges, stiletto, steel or brass knuckles, or other deadly weapon made especially for the defense of one's person." 24 Del. C. § 901 (emphasis added). The ammunition which Fullman purchased was sold as "Sears.22 Long Rifle Extra-Range Hollow Point Cartridges." These ".22 caliber rifle cartridges . . . can be used in many types of pistols and revolvers. Thus, although the ammunition which Fullman purchased was labeled as rifle cartridges, it can also be described as 'revolver or pistol cartridges.'" *Hetherton*, 445 F. Supp. at 297-98 (footnote omitted). Sears asserts that the sale of the ammunition did not fall within the statute because the ammunition was sold and labeled as rifle ammunition and not as pistol or revolver cartridges. As the district court noted:

It is unlikely that the legislature intended to permit dealers to evade either the licensing requirements of § 901 or the recording requirements of § 904 merely by selling a product under one label rather than another. *Id.* at 298.

We agree and hold that cartridges which can be used, without alteration, as pistol cartridges are covered by section 904 regardless of the fortuity of labeling by the retailer.

B.

Having found that the ammunition was a "deadly weapon" covered by section 904, we must also decide whether Sears' violation of the statute results in liability to the Hethertons. First, it must be determined whether section 904 was enacted for the safety of others. If the statute was enacted for the safety of others, its violation is negligence per se. *See, e.g., Schwartzman v. Weiner*, 319 A.2d 48 (Del. Super. Ct. 1974) (landlord negligent when he failed to provide a handrail on a staircase in violation of housing code); *Farrow v. Hoffecker*, 23 Del. 223, 79 A. 920 (Del. Super. Ct. 1906) (defendant negligent when he violated ordinance prohibiting shooting within the city limits). Second, it must be determined whether Hetherton was among the group of individuals the legislature intended to protect. *Wealth v. Renai*, 49 Del. 289, 114 A.2d 809 (Del. Super. Ct. 1955) (pedestrians among the class of

---

"residents of the State of Delaware." House Bill No. 876, 66 Del. Laws 406 (June 30, 1978). This amendment does not change our disposition of this case. Moreover, it reinforces our belief that section 904 is not an obscure provision providing for an antiquated means of identification but one that reflects Delaware's current concerns with an important and sensitive problem.

persons to be protected by statute prohibiting automobile passing at intersections.)

Recognizing the deadliness of firearms and their related components ammunition, it seems incomprehensible that the primary concern of the legislature in enacting provisions regulating "deadly weapons dealers" could have been anything other than the safety of citizens and the prevention of injuries caused by "deadly weapons." Yet, as so often occurs, our conclusions must be based on the logic of experience rather than any other indication of legislative intent. For in this case, we have found neither relevant legislative history nor pertinent Delaware cases construing the statute in issue.

However, our construction is consistent with cases reviewing gun control legislation from other jurisdictions. For example, in *State v. Sima*, 142 N.J. Super. 187, 192, 361 A.2d 58, 61 (1976), the New Jersey court noted that New Jersey's gun control legislation was designed "to prevent criminals and other unfit elements from acquiring firearms." The United States Supreme Court in construing federal gun control legislation in *Huddleston v. United States*, 415 U.S. 814, 94 S. Ct. 1262, 39 L. Ed. 2d 782 (1974) noted that:

> Information drawn from records kept by dealers was a prime guarantee of the Act's effectiveness in keeping "these lethal weapons out of the hands of criminals, drug addicts, mentally disordered persons, juveniles, and other persons whose possession of them is too high a price to pay in danger to us all to allow."

Id. at 825, 94 S. Ct. at 1269, Quoting 114 Cong. Rec. 13219 (1968) (remarks of Sen. Tydings). *See also Franco v. Bunyard*, 261 Ark. 144, 547 S.W.2d 91 (Ark. 1977) (The purpose of federal gun control laws and regulations is to keep weapons out of the hands of criminals).

We therefore conclude that section 904 was enacted for the safety of others and that the legislature intended to protect innocent persons who might otherwise be injured during the commission of a crime. Thus, Sears' failure to require two freeholders to identify Fullman constituted negligence per se.

C.

The final question under section 904 liability is whether Sears' negligence was the proximate cause of the Hetherton's injuries. If not, the violation does not result in liability. . . .

Sears asserts and the district court agreed that Sears' failure to comply with the statute did not proximately cause Hetherton's injuries as a matter of law. It asserts that the requirement that a deadly weapons purchaser produce two freeholders serves *only* to verify the identity of the purchaser. It asserts that because Fullman properly identified himself, compliance with the statute would not have affected the sale.

We disagree. We note that the requirement that a purchaser produce two freeholders is a burdensome procedure which reduces the ease and simplicity of obtaining a "deadly weapon." It seems reasonable to conclude that the Delaware legislature was aware of the inconvenience of the requirement and that the legislature intended the inconvenience. It might have been difficult, if not impossible, for someone like Fullman, who could not legally purchase "deadly weapons," to meet the additional identification requirement. Compliance with the statute would have prevented consummation of the sale at least at that time because Fullman was not accompanied by two freeholders.

In *Franco v. Bunyard, supra,* the Arkansas court discussed issues somewhat similar to those presented by this case. In *Franco* the plaintiffs requested damages for the wrongful deaths and personal injuries which resulted from the defendant's sale of a weapon to an escaped convict. The defendant had sold the weapon without requiring the purchaser to complete Form 4473 as required by federal law. On the issue of proximate cause the court stated:

> (It) is enough to point out that the tragedies could not have occurred as they did if the federal rules had been obeyed. That is, Graham had no means of identification, an essential prerequisite to the purchase of a gun. This is not, as the appellees argue, a mere matter of record keeping. Form 4473 required the seller to obtain and record Graham's identification *before* handing over the gun. Graham had no identification. Thus, had the law been obeyed, he could not have obtained possession of the gun and could not have used it to shoot innocent men the next day. On the issue of foreseeability, we need say only that the very purpose of the law is to keep pistols out of the hands of such persons as Graham, who was both a convicted criminal and a fugitive from justice. It certainly cannot be said that his use of the gun in such a way as to injure others was not foreseeable. Of course it is not required that the precise sequence of events leading to the injury be foreseeable. 547 S.W.2d at 93.

We do not conclude that as a matter of law a jury must find that Sears' failure to comply with the statute was the proximate cause of Hetherton's injuries. Proximate cause is usually a question for the jury and not an issue for the judge to decide. . . .

We will therefore reverse the judgment of the district court and will remand for further proceedings consistent with this opinion. In such proceedings, there will remain for the consideration of a jury the issues of proximate cause and damages.

---

1. *Hetherton* was reversed in the second appeal on the ground that the statute's "two freeholders" requirement was unconstitutional. 652 F.2d 1152 (3d Cir. 1981).

2. The plaintiff must be within the class intended to be protected by the statute. The plaintiff owned a hotel that was damaged when a car crashed into it. The defendant, heading north, turned left in front of a car heading south. The two cars collided, and the defendant's car hit the plaintiff's building. The statute prohibited left turns. The court refused to apply the negligence per se doctrine because the plaintiff was outside the class intended to be protected by the right-of-way statute. *Erickson v. Kongsli,* 40 Wash. 2d 79, 240 P.2d 1209 (1952).

3. The hazard must be the one intended to be protected by the statute. The plaintiff's sheep were washed off the defendant's ship during a storm, and the plaintiff sued for failure to fence the sheep as required by statute. The court refused to apply negligence per se because the statute was intended to prevent the spread of disease, not protect against the perils of the sea. *Gorris v. Scott*, L.R. 9 Ex. 125 (1874). What hazard was the statute in *Hetherton* intended to prevent?

4. The Restatement (Second) of Torts § 288 provides that the court will not adopt, as the standard of the reasonable person, a statute intended to apply to a different class, interest, harm, or hazard than the one before the court.

5. Once the court decides that the statute applies to this plaintiff (class) for this injury (hazard), there is no issue of proximate cause. *See* W. Page Keeton et al., Prosser and Keeton on Torts 223–24 (5th ed. 1984).

In *Hetherton*, was Judge Higginbotham considering proximate cause, as he stated, or merely whether the statute applied to this class of persons? Was he considering whether violation of the statute was a cause in fact of the injury?

TEDLA v. ELLMAN
Court of Appeals of New York, 1939
280 N.Y. 124, 19 N.E.2d 987

LEHMAN, JUDGE.

While walking along a highway, Anna Tedla and her brother, John Bachek, were struck by a passing automobile, operated by the defendant Ellman. She was injured and Bachek was killed. Bachek was a deaf-mute. His occupation was collecting and selling junk. His sister, Mrs. Tedla, was engaged in the same occupation. They often picked up junk at the incinerator of the village of Islip. At the time of the accident they were walking along "Sunrise Highway" and wheeling baby carriages containing junk and wood which they had picked up at the incinerator. It was about six o'clock, or a little earlier, on a Sunday evening in December. Darkness had already set in. Bachek was carrying a lighted lantern, or, at least, there is testimony to that effect. The jury found that the accident was due solely to the negligence of the operator of the automobile. The defendants do not, upon this appeal, challenge the finding of negligence on the part of the operator. They maintain, however, that Mrs. Tedla and her brother were guilty of contributory negligence as a matter of law.

The Legislature in the first five subdivisions of section 85 of the Vehicle and Traffic Law has provided regulations to govern the conduct of pedestrians and of drivers of vehicles when a pedestrian is crossing a road. Until, by chapter 114 of the Laws of 1933, it adopted subdivision 6 of section 85, quoted above, there was no special statutory rule for pedestrians walking along a highway. Then for the first time it reversed, for pedestrians, the rule established for vehicles by immemorial custom, and provided that pedestrians shall keep to the left of the center line of a highway.

The plaintiffs showed by the testimony of a State policeman that "there were very few cars going east" at the time of the accident, but that going west there was "very heavy Sunday night traffic." [The plaintiffs were hit from behind while walking on the east side (right).] . . .

The analogy [to *Martin v. Herzog*] is, however, incomplete. The "established rule" should not be weakened either by subtle distinctions or by extension beyond its letter or spirit into a field where "by the very terms of the hypothesis" it can have no proper application. At times the indefinite and flexible standard of care of the traditional reasonably prudent man may be, in the opinion of the Legislature, an insufficient measure of the care which should be exercised to guard against a recognized danger; . . . . Then the Legislature may by statute prescribe additional safeguards and may define duty and standard of care in rigid terms; and when the Legislature has spoken, the standard of the care required is no longer what the reasonably prudent man would do under the circumstances but what the Legislature has commanded. That is the rule established by the courts and "by the very terms of the hypothesis" the rule applies where the Legislature has prescribed safeguards "for the benefit of another that he may be preserved in life or limb." In that field debate as to whether the safeguards so prescribed are reasonably necessary is ended by the legislative fiat. . . .

The statute upon which the defendants rely is of different character. It does not prescribe additional safeguards which pedestrians must provide for the preservation of the life or limb or property of others, or even of themselves, nor does it impose upon pedestrians a higher standard of care. What the statute does provide is rules of the road to be observed by pedestrians and by vehicles, so that all those who use the road may know how they and others should proceed, at least under usual circumstances. . . .

Negligence is failure to exercise the care required by law. Where a statute defines the standard of care and the safeguards required to meet a recognized danger, then, as we have said, no other measure may be applied in determining whether a person has carried out the duty of care imposed by law. Failure to observe the standard imposed by statute is negligence, as matter of law. On the other hand, where a statutory general rule of conduct fixes no definite standard of care which would under all circumstances tend to protect life, limb or property but merely codifies or supplements a common-law rule, which has always been subject to limitations and exceptions; or where the statutory rule of conduct regulates conflicting rights and obligations in manner calculated to promote public convenience and safety, then the statute, in the absence of clear language to the contrary, should not be construed as intended to wipe out the limitations and exceptions which judicial decisions have attached to the common-law duty; nor should it be construed as an inflexible command that the general rule of conduct intended to prevent accidents must be followed even under conditions when observance might cause accidents. We may assume reasonably that the Legislature directed pedestrians to keep to the left of the center of the road because that would cause them to face traffic approaching in that lane and would enable them to care for their own safety better than if the traffic approached them from the rear. We cannot assume reasonably that the Legislature intended that a statute enacted for the preservation of the life and limb of pedestrians must be observed when observance would subject them to more imminent danger.

[A] pedestrian is, of course, at fault if he fails without good reason to observe the statutory rule of conduct. The general duty is established by the statute, and deviation from it without good cause is a wrong and the wrongdoer is responsible for the damages resulting from his wrong. . . .

In each action, the judgment [in favor of the plaintiffs] should be affirmed, with costs.

---

1. *Martin v. Herzog*, 228 N.Y. 164, 126 N.E. 814 (1920), referred to in *Tedla*, was a contributory negligence case. The defendant's car negligently ran into the front of the plaintiff's wagon, but the plaintiff was charged with contributory negligence for not having lights on the front of his wagon as required by statute. Judge Cardozo wrote:

> We think the unexcused omission of the statutory signals is more than some evidence of negligence. It is negligence in itself. Lights are intended for the guidance and protection of other travelers on the highway. Highway Law, § 329a. By the very terms of the hypothesis, to omit, willfully or heedlessly, the safeguards prescribed by law for the benefit of another that he may be preserved in life or limb, is to fall short of the standard of diligence to which those who live in organized society are under a duty to conform. That, we think, is now the established rule in this state. . . .
>
> In the case at hand, we have an instance of the admitted violation of a statute intended for the protection of travelers on the highway, of whom the defendant at the time was one. Yet the jurors were instructed in effect that they were at liberty in their discretion to treat the omission of lights either as innocent or as culpable. They were allowed to "consider the default as lightly or gravely" as they would (Thomas, J., in the court below). . . . Jurors have no dispensing power, by which they may relax the duty that one traveler on the highways owes under the statute to another. It is error to tell them that they have. The omission of these lights was a wrong, and, being wholly unexcused, was also a negligent wrong. No license should have been conceded to the triers of the facts to find it anything else.

2. In *Martin* and *Tedla*, what do the judges think is the relationship between the legislature and the court?

3. Can the judge refuse to apply a statute or ordinance to which he or she has an objection? What is Cardozo's view in *Martin*? Lehman's view in *Tedla*?

4. Judge Traynor stated:

> A statute, that provides for a criminal proceeding only, does not create a civil liability; if there is no provision for a remedy by civil action to persons injured by a breach of the statute it is because the Legislature did not contemplate one. A suit for damages is based on the theory that the conduct inflicting the injuries is a common-law tort. . . . The decision as to what the civil standard should be still rests with the court, and the standard formulated by a legislative body in a police regulation or criminal statute becomes the standard to determine civil liability only because the court accepts it. In the absence of such a standard the case goes to the jury, which must determine whether the defendant has acted as a reasonably prudent man would act in similar circumstances. The jury then has the burden of deciding not only what the facts are but what the unformulated standard is

of reasonable conduct. When a legislative body has generalized a standard from the experience of the community and prohibits conduct that is likely to cause harm, the court accepts the formulated standards and applies them. . . .

Clinkscales v. Carver, 22 Cal. 2d 72, 136 P.2d 777 (1943). How is Traynor's view different from Lehman's and Cardozo's? Are they fundamentally different, or will they vary with the statute and the facts of the case?

5. In these discussions we are assuming that the legislature provided no express civil standard. Why didn't the legislature provide a civil remedy?

6. Students often overlook the question of what weight should be given to the violation of the statute once the judge decides that the statutory standard applies to the case. There are three approaches: rebuttable presumption, negligence per se, and evidence of negligence.

A. *Violation of Statute as Rebuttable Presumption.* In a growing number of states, the rule concerning the proper role of a penal statute in a civil action for damages is that violation of the statute which has been found to apply to a particular set of facts establishes only a prima facie case of negligence, a presumption which may be rebutted by a showing on the part of the party violating the statute of an adequate excuse under the facts and circumstances of the case.

[An] attraction of this approach is that it is fair. "If there is sufficient excuse or justification there is ordinarily no violation of a statute and the statutory standard is inapplicable."

B. *Violation of Statute as Negligence Per Se.* While some Michigan cases seem to speak of negligence per se as a kind of strict liability . . . an examination indicates that there are a number of conditions that attempt to create a more reasonable approach than would result from an automatic application of a per se rule.

Despite such limitations, the judge-made rule of negligence per se has still proved to be too inflexible and mechanical to satisfy thoughtful commentators and judges. It is forcefully argued that no matter how a court may attempt to confine the negligence per se doctrine, if defendant is liable despite the exercise of due care and the availability of a reasonable excuse, this is really strict liability, and not negligence. Prosser, The Law of Torts (4th ed.), § 36, p. 197. . . .

C. *Violation of Statute as Evidence of Negligence.* Just as the rebuttable presumption approach to statutory violations in a negligence context arose, at least in part, from dissatisfaction with the result of a mechanical application of the per se rule, a parallel of administrative development in our state with respect to infractions of ordinances and regulations, has been that violations of these amount to only evidence of negligence. . . .

We have not chosen to join that small minority which has decreed that violation of a statute is only evidence of negligence. . . .

An accurate statement of our law is that when a court adopts a penal statute as the standard of care in an action for negligence, violation of that statute establishes a prima facie case of negligence, with the determination to be made by the finder of fact whether the party accused of violating the statute has established a legally sufficient excuse. If the finder of fact determines such an excuse exists, the appropriate standard of care then becomes that established by the common law.

Zeni v. Anderson, 397 Mich. 117, 243 N.W.2d 270 (1976). Which approach makes more sense?

7. Why is the weight to be given a statutory violation "a tempest in a teapot" from the plaintiff's perspective?

8. The defendant may argue that his or her compliance with a statute or ordinance creates a presumption of due care. This is a common argument in products liability litigation. In *Alvarado v. J.C. Penney Co.*, 735 F. Supp. 371 (D. Kan. 1990), the court rejected a presumption of due care in the following statute:

When the injury-causing aspect of the product was, at the time of manufacture, in compliance with legislative regulatory standards or administrative regulatory safety standards relating to design or performance, the product shall be deemed not defective by reason of design or performance.
. . .

[W]e are now of the belief that we incorrectly interpreted [the statute] in our previous opinion. . . . This means that a plaintiff can attempt to demonstrate by a preponderance of the evidence that a regulatory or administrative standard does not meet the necessary level of safety.

9. The Restatement (Third) of Products Liability Tentative Draft No. 2 (1995) Sec. 7(b) takes a middle of the road position:

[A] product's compliance with an applicable product safety statute or regulation is properly considered in determining whether a product is defective . . . but does not necessarily preclude . . . a finding of product defect.

What role does a regulated industry have in the drafting of a statute? Why is it often said that an agency should be disbanded after five years?

PROBLEM

While carefully driving to work, Matt is hit by Niles' car. Niles was negligent but claims that Matt was also negligent because he had no license. Matt's driver's license expired three days before the crash.

What result and why?

BROWN v. SHYNE
Court of Appeals of New York, 1926
242 N.Y. 176, 151 N.E. 197

LEHMAN, J.

The plaintiff employed the defendant to give chiropractic treatment to her for a disease or physical condition. The defendant had no license to practice medicine, yet he held himself out as being able to diagnose and treat disease, and under the provisions of the Public Health Law (Cons. Laws, ch. 45) he was guilty of a misdemeanor. The plaintiff became paralyzed after she had received nine treatments by the defendant. She claims, and upon this appeal we must assume, that the paralysis was caused by the treatment she received. She has recovered judgment in the sum of $10,000 for the damages caused by said injury.

The plaintiff in her complaint alleges that the injuries were caused by the defendant's negligence. If negligence on the part of the defendant caused the injury, the plaintiff may recover the consequent damages. Though the defendant held himself out, and the plaintiff consulted him, as a chiropractor and not as a regular physician, he claimed to possess the skill requisite for diagnosis and treatment of disease, and in the performance of what he undertook to do he may be held to the degree of skill and care which he claimed to possess. At the trial the plaintiff gave testimony in regard to the manner in which she was treated. . . .

At the close of the plaintiff's case the plaintiff was permitted to amend the complaint to allege "that in so treating the plaintiff the defendant was engaged in the practice of medicine contrary to and in violation of the provisions of the Public Health Law of the State of New York in such case made and provided, he at the time of so treating plaintiff not being a duly licensed physician or surgeon of the State of New York." Thereafter the trial judge charged the jury that they might bring in a verdict in favor of the plaintiff if they found that the evidence established that the treatment given to the plaintiff was not in accordance with the standards of skill and care which prevail among those treating disease. He then continued: "This is a little different from the ordinary malpractice case, and I am going to allow you, if you think proper under the evidence in the case, to predicate negligence upon another theory. The public health laws of this State prescribe that no person shall practice medicine unless he is licensed so to do by the Board of Regents of this State and registered pursuant to statute. . . . This statute to which I have referred is a general police regulation. Its violation, and it has been violated by the defendant, is some evidence, more or less cogent, of negligence which you may consider for what it is worth, along with all the other evidence in the case. . . ."

In so charging the jury that from the violation of the statute the jury might infer negligence which produced injury to the plaintiff, the trial justice in my opinion erred.

The provisions of the Public Health Law prohibiting the practice of medicine without a license granted upon proof of preliminary training and after examination intended to show adequate knowledge, are of course intended for the protection of the general public against injury which unskilled and unlearned practitioners might cause. If violation of the statute by the defendant was the proximate cause of the plaintiff's injury, then the plaintiff may recover upon proof of violation; if violation of the statute has no direct bearing on the injury, proof of the violation becomes irrelevant. For injury caused by neglect of duty imposed by the penal law there is civil remedy; but of course the injury must follow from the neglect.

Proper formulation of general standards of preliminary education and proper examination of the particular applicant should serve to raise the standards of skill and care generally possessed by members of the profession in this State; but the license to practice medicine confers no additional skill upon the practitioner; nor does it confer immunity from physical injury upon a patient if the practitioner fails to exercise care. Here, injury may have been caused by lack of skill or care; it would not have been obviated if the defendant had possessed a license yet failed to exercise the skill and care required of one practicing medicine. True, if the defendant had not practiced medicine in this State, he could not have injured the plaintiff, but the protection which the statute was intended to provide was against risk of injury by the unskilled or careless practitioner, and unless the plaintiff's injury was caused by carelessness or lack of skill, the defendant's failure to obtain a license was not connected with the injury. The plaintiff's cause of action is for negligence or malpractice. The defendant undertook to treat the plaintiff for a physical condition which seemed to require remedy. Under our law such treatment may be given only by a duly qualified practitioner who has obtained a license.

The defendant in offering to treat the plaintiff held himself out as qualified to give treatment. He must meet the professional standards of skill and care prevailing among those who do offer treatment lawfully. If injury follows through failure to meet those standards, the plaintiff may recover. The provisions of the Public Health Law may result in the exclusion from practice of some who are unqualified. Even a skilled and learned practitioner who is not licensed commits an offense against the State; but against such practitioners the statute was not intended to protect, for no protection was needed, and neglect to obtain a license results in no injury to the patient and, therefore, no private wrong. The purpose of the statute is to protect the public against unfounded assumption of skill by one who undertakes to prescribe or treat for disease. In order to show that the plaintiff has been injured by defendant's breach of the statutory duty, proof must be given that defendant in such treatment did not exercise the care and skill which would have been exercised by qualified practitioners within the State, and that such lack of skill and care caused the injury. Failure to obtain a license as required by law gives rise to no remedy if it has caused no injury. . . .

For these reasons the judgments should be reversed and a new trial granted, with costs to abide the event.

---

1. What did the court mean when it said: "We must assume that 'paralysis was caused by the treatment' "?

2. What evidence was there to show that the treatment was negligent? What is the narrow issue here?

3. If the "failure to obtain a license was not connected with the injury," what was the purpose of the statute?

4. Formerly, the rule in New Hampshire was that anyone driving on the road without a license was an outlaw and liable for injuries without a need to show negligence. This has been reversed. *See Fuller v. Sirois*, 97 N.H. 100, 82 A.2d 82 (1951). *Compare* Mass. Laws ch. 250 (1959). For negligence, should failure to have an automobile driver's license be treated differently from failure to have a medical license?

RUSHINK v. GERSTHEIMER
Supreme Court of New York, 1981
82 A.D.2d 944, 440 N.Y.S.2d 738

Before MAHONEY, P.J., and SWEENEY, KANE, CASEY and WEISS, JJ.

Memorandum Decision.

Cross appeals from an order of the Supreme Court at Special Term (Miner, J.), entered October 21, 1980 in Sullivan County, which denied both plaintiff's and defendant's motions for summary judgment. On August 9, 1978, defendant Mary Jane Gerstheimer, a stenographer employed by the Letchworth Village Developmental Center, drove an automobile owned by her husband, defendant George F. Gerstheimer, to a pharmacy located on the grounds of the Middletown Psychiatric Center. After parking the automobile in front of the pharmacy, she left it unattended with the keys in the ignition. Moments later, Stephen E. Rushink, a resident patient at the facility, drove away in the vehicle and met his death soon thereafter when it left the road and struck a tree. After issue was joined, plaintiff moved at Special Term for summary judgment contending that there were no triable issues of fact since defendant Mary Jane Gerstheimer violated subdivision (a) of section 1210 of the Vehicle and Traffic Law and that the violation of the statute was the proximate cause of the occurrence. Defendants opposed the motion arguing that subdivision (a) of section 1210 of the Vehicle and Traffic Law is not applicable to the instant case and, assuming it was, that the alleged violation was not the proximate cause of plaintiff's decedent's accident. Defendants also moved for summary judgment to dismiss the complaint. Special Term denied both motions and these appeals ensued. Subdivision (a) of section 1210, which prohibits a person in charge of a vehicle from leaving it unattended without removing or hiding the key, was enacted to deter theft and injury from the operation of motor vehicles by unauthorized persons. . . . In our view, however, its provisions were plainly not designed to protect such unauthorized users from the consequences of their own actions. . . . That plaintiff's decedent may not have been capable of forming a larcenous intent is irrelevant to our conclusion that he could not have been within the class of persons the enactment was meant to protect. Of course, redress for wrongs suffered by one under a legal disability may be pursued in a common-law negligence action wholly apart from statutory considerations. The instant complaint is sufficient to support such a cause of action and, since there are obvious factual issues to be resolved in determining defendants' liability, if any, the motions for summary judgment were properly denied. Order affirmed, without costs.

SWEENEY, KANE and CASEY, JJ., concur.

MAHONEY, P.J., and WEISS, J., concur in the following memorandum by MAHONEY, P.J.

MAHONEY, PRESIDING JUDGE (concurring).

While we concur in the majority's holding that the order denying both plaintiff's and defendants' motions for summary judgment must be affirmed, we cannot accept the view that subdivision (a) of section 1210 of the Vehicle and Traffic Law does not create a class of persons entitled to be protected by the statute, and, further, that plaintiff's decedent is not among its membership. In recommending the enactment of section 1210, the Joint Legislative Committee on Motor Vehicle Problems stated that the proposed law was "designed to obviate the risk of a vehicle moving from the place where it was left parked and possibly injuring the person or property of others as well as itself being damaged. It serves to lessen the likelihood of theft" (NY Legis Doc, 1954, No. 36, pp. 106-107). Since at common law the owner was not liable, as a matter of law, for the negligence of a thief, on the basis that the use of the car by the thief intervened between the occurrence of the negligence of the owner and the unskillful operation of the car by the thief . . . , the statute changed the common law and made it clear that the intervention of an unauthorized person no longer operates to break the chain of causation. Where, as here, the legislative intent to protect the public generally from the consequences that foreseeably flow from unauthorized use of motor vehicles is clear, and, again as here, the violation of subdivision (a) of section 1210 is undisputed, it is patently unfair to deny to plaintiff the evidentiary weight of such violation and leave him to the more vigorous burden of establishing common-law negligence.

---

1. Was the plaintiff within the hazard and class protected by the statute?

2. Why was Rushink not permitted to argue to the jury that the statute set the standard?

3. What is Rushink's course of action now? What problems lie ahead?

4. What would have been the result if Rushink had run into another car and injured the driver? *See Ney v. Yellow Cab Co.*, 2 Ill. 2d 74, 117 N.E.2d 74 (1954).

5. The plaintiff obtained drinks at the defendant's bar and was injured when her car later hit a tree. She alleged that she received the drinks after she was intoxicated. Although the statute provided that the sale of alcoholic beverages to a noticeably intoxicated person was a crime, the court found in favor of the bar: "[F]or at least 94 years it has been the law of this State that the statute . . . does not create any civil liability on the part of the sellers of alcoholic beverages." *Riverside Enters. v. Rahn*, 171 Ga. App. 674, 320 S.E.2d 595 (1984).

6. Some statutes are interpreted as providing strict liability without any excuses. *See*, for example, the Pure Food Act discussed in *Doherty v. S.S. Kresge Co.*, 227 Wis. 661, 278 N.W. 437 (1938). Child labor acts are another example. *See*

Blanton v. Kellioka Coal Co., 192 Ky. 220, 232 S.W. 614 (1921).

7.   Statutory violations can be excused as follows: the actor is incapacitated, he or she does not know of the need for compliance, he or she exercises reasonable diligence, an emergency, and compliance with the act involves a greater risk of harm than violation. Restatement (Second) of Torts § 288A.

8.   A mentally ill plaintiff is only held to be contributorily negligent if he or she can appreciate the nature of the conduct. *See Emory Univ. v. Lee*, 97 Ga. App. 680, 104 S.E.2d 234 (1958).

9.   Some states enact legislation holding the commercial providers of alcohol liable when an intoxicated customer injures someone. Such laws are called Dram Shop Acts. *See Ling v. Jan's Liquors*, 237 Kan. 629, 703 P.2d 731 (1985).

F.   PROVING THE NEGLIGENCE CASE BEFORE THE JUDGE AND THE JURY

There are three types of evidence: direct, real, and circumstantial. Direct evidence is the statement of a witness about a fact in issue that he or she saw. The witness, for example, said that the defendant's car was traveling at 110 miles per hour when it hit the plaintiff's car. Real evidence is the knife used in the stabbing or a rug with a hole in it. Circumstantial evidence is evidence of fact A (not in issue) from which fact B (in issue) can be inferred. For example, five people ate at the defendant's restaurant on Tuesday and developed ptomaine poisoning. P ate at the restaurant on Tuesday and developed ptomaine poisoning. The jury may infer that P also contracted ptomaine poisoning from the defendant's restaurant. *See* L. R. Patterson, *The Types of Evidence: An Analysis*, 19 Vand. L. Rev. 1 (1965).

Most evidence in torts cases is circumstantial. There are few smoking guns.

1.   Circumstantial Evidence

PROBLEM

Duane has an open-air market located beside a two-lane highway in Texas. About half the produce is displayed outside in boxes or on the ground. While "Bootsie" was picking up a pumpkin located outside, she was bitten by a rattlesnake. Discuss.

NEGRI v. STOP & SHOP, INC.
Court of Appeals of New York, 1985
65 N.Y.2d 625, 491 N.Y.S.2d 151, 480 N.E.2d 740

Memorandum.

. . . .

The record contains some evidence tending to show that defendant had constructive notice of a dangerous condition which allegedly caused injuries to its customer.

There was testimony that the injured plaintiff, while shopping in defendant's store, fell backward, did not come into contact with the shelves, but hit her head directly on the floor where "a lot of broken jars" of baby food lay; that the baby food was "dirty and messy"; that a witness in the immediate vicinity of the accident did not hear any jars falling from the shelves or otherwise breaking during the 15 or 20 minutes prior to the accident; and that the aisle had not been cleaned or inspected for at least 50 minutes prior to the accident — indeed, some evidence was adduced that it was at least two hours.

Viewing the evidence in a light most favorable to the plaintiffs and according plaintiff the benefit of every reasonable inference . . . , it cannot be said, as a matter of law, that the circumstantial evidence was insufficient to permit the jury to draw the necessary inference that a slippery condition was created by jars of baby food which had fallen and broken a sufficient length of time prior to the accident to permit defendant's employees to discover and remedy the condition. . . . Plaintiff having made out a prima facie case, it was error to dismiss the complaint.

----

1.   What kind of evidence did the plaintiff introduce? How convincing is it?

2.   Compare *Negri* with *Goddard:*

   Action by Wilfred H. Goddard against the Boston & Maine Railroad Company for personal injuries received by falling upon a banana skin lying upon the platform at defendant's station at Boston. The evidence showed that plaintiff was a passenger who had just arrived, and was about the length of the car from where he alighted when he slipped and fell. There was evidence that there were many passengers on the platform. Verdict directed for defendant, and plaintiff excepts. Exceptions overruled.

   HOLMES, C. J. The banana skin upon which the plaintiff stepped and which caused him to slip may have been dropped within a minute by one of the persons who was leaving the train. It is unnecessary to go further to decide the case.

   Exceptions overruled.

Goddard v. Boston & Maine R.R. Co., 179 Mass. 52, 60 N.E. 486 (1901). Why did the plaintiff lose?

3.   What inference in the following slip-and-fall case? Should the case be submitted to the jury?

   The plaintiff arrived on one of defendant's cars on the upper level of the Dudley Street terminal; other passengers arrived on the same car, but it does not appear how many. She waited until the crowd had left the platform, when she inquired of one of defendant's uniformed employees the direction to another car. He walked along a narrow platform, and she, following a few feet behind him toward the stairway he had indicated, was injured by slipping upon a banana peel. It was described by several who examined it in these terms: It "felt dry, gritty, as if there were dirt upon it," as if "trampled over a good deal," as "flattened down, and black in color," "every bit of it was black, there wasn't a particle of yellow," and as "black, flattened out and gritty." It was one of the duties of employees of the defendant, of whom there was one at this station all the time, to observe and remove whatever was upon the platform to interfere with the safety of travelers. These might have been found to be the facts.

Anjou v. Boston Elevated R.R. Co., 208 Mass. 273, 94 N.E. 386 (1911). How is *Anjou* different from *Goddard* in regard to the weight of the evidence?

4. The constructive notice principle was clearly presented in *Gordon v. American Museum of Nat. History*, 67 N.Y.2d 836, 492 N.E.2d 774, 501 N.Y.S.2d 646 (1986):

Plaintiff was injured when he fell on defendant's front entrance steps. He testified that as he descended the upper level of steps he slipped on the third step and that while he was in midair he observed a piece of white, waxy paper next to his left foot. He alleges that this paper came from the concession stand that defendant had contracted to have present and which was located on the plaza separating the two tiers of steps and that defendant was negligent insofar as its employees failed to discover and remove the paper before he fell on it. The case was submitted to the jury on the theory that defendant had either actual or constructive notice of the dangerous condition presented by the paper on the steps. The jury found against defendant on the issue of liability. A divided Appellate Division affirmed and granted defendant leave to appeal on a certified question.

There is no evidence in the record that defendant had actual notice of the paper and the case should not have gone to the jury on that theory. To constitute constructive notice, a defect must be visible and apparent and it must exist for a sufficient length of time prior to the accident to permit defendant's employees to discover and remedy it (*Negri v. Stop & Shop* . . .). The record contains no evidence that anyone including plaintiff, observed the piece of white paper prior to the accident. Nor did he describe the paper as being dirty or worn, which would have provided some indication that it had been present for some period of time (*cf. Negri v. Stop & Shop* . . .). Thus on the evidence presented, the piece of paper that caused plaintiff's fall could have been deposited there only minutes or seconds before the accident and any other conclusion would be pure speculation.

. . . The defect in plaintiff's case here, however, is not an inability to prove the causation element of his fall but the lack of evidence establishing constructive notice of the particular condition that caused his fall.

5. Suppose the plaintiff slips on a piece of freshly cooked pizza;

In her attempt to meet the requirement of notice, plaintiff did not claim or show that the alleged pizza was placed or dropped on the floor directly by the defendant or its employees, or that defendant knew of its presence. . . . Rather, it was her contention that defendant's method of selling pizza was one which leads inescapably to such mishaps as her own, and that in such a situation conventional notice requirements need not be met. We agree.

The dangerous condition was created by the store's method of sale. The steps taken to constantly clean the floor show that the store owner recognized the danger.

The practice of extensive selling of slices of pizza on waxed paper to customers who consume it while standing creates the reasonable probability that food will drop to the floor. Food on a terrazzo floor will create a dangerous condition. In such a situation, notice to the proprietor of the specific item on the floor need not be shown.

[Directed verdict in favor of defendant, reversed.] *Jasko v. F.W. Woolworth Co.*, 177 Colo. 418, 494 P.2d 839 (1972).

PIETRONE v. AMERICAN HONDA MOTOR CO.
Court of Appeals of California, 1987
189 Cal. App. 3d 1057, 235 Cal. Rptr. 137

Opinion by: GATES, J.

Defendant American Honda Motor Company, Inc., appeals from the judgment entered pursuant to a jury verdict in favor of plaintiff Alison Pietrone. . . .

Plaintiff presented evidence that she was a passenger on her husband's 1974 Honda CB 450 motorcycle on the afternoon of April 26, 1979. As they entered the intersection of Towne Avenue and Arrow Highway in the City of Pomona the driver of an oncoming automobile began a U-turn. Her husband moved to the right in an unsuccessful attempt to avoid the vehicle. The auto's bumper struck the lower portion of plaintiff's left leg, breaking it.

This impact was so slight it merely created a "wobbling sensation" in the motorcycle rather than causing it to overturn. Nonetheless, plaintiff's now unstable leg came into contact with the exposed spokes of its rear wheel behind the shock absorber, but "[not] very long, because it came out, and while it was coming out it was rotating." As it rotated two full revolutions, it "was also moving out and forward." As it did so her foot "caught the shock absorber, which brought it back in again," lodging it tightly into the equally open area located in front of the shock absorber and above the chain guard.

So powerful were the forces that had been exerted upon plaintiff's foot, she was required to sit, helplessly trapped, for many agonizing minutes. In fact, she was freed only after firemen arrived armed with an instrument known as the "jaws of life" with which they were able to cut away the shock absorber. As a result of her experience, it was necessary for this 21-year-old plaintiff to undergo a below-the-knee amputation of her leg.

After presenting the foregoing evidence, but before formally resting, counsel for plaintiff advised the court it was his "understanding of the law, as it exists now in product liability cases, that it is the responsibility of a plaintiff to meet her burden of proof that she present a prima facie case. That . . . a design feature, and in this case that would be the open, exposed, rotating wheel of this motorcycle, was a proximate cause of her injury. Having established a prima facie case to that extent, . . . the burden of proof then shifts to the defendant" who "must now prove and produce evidence that the benefit of this design feature outweighs the risk of injury, as has been presented by the plaintiff." Counsel expressed his belief that plaintiff had met this burden and sought the court's concurrence. He also informed the court that he had additional witnesses, specifically engineers, who could be called to defend "against whatever evidence the defendants present on their burden of proof."

The court declined to make an "anticipatory" ruling, but did indicate that in considering motions the defense might make, it "would see no prejudice to the defense to reopen in the event that [plaintiff] left something out which [the court] [deemed] critical." Plaintiff responded, "And I will rest, based upon that."

When proceedings commenced following a four-day recess, Honda's counsel opined that in his view plaintiff had failed to prove her case. He announced that . . . the defendant will rest at this point of time without producing any additional evidence, other than that which has been produced on cross-examination of the witnesses called by plaintiff and will move this court for a directed verdict." He additionally advised the court, "one of the reasons that we have decided to rest, rather than move for non-suit, was the fact that there has been no expert testimony that would indicate any way, any method, that this motorcycle could have been designed, in order to prevent the unusual type of injury that occurred in this particular case."

In the instant case the evidence conclusively established that a design feature of Honda's product — the open, exposed, rotating rear wheel in close proximity to the passenger's foot pegs — was a proximate cause of plaintiff's injury. Without more, the burden then shifted to Honda to justify its adoption and utilization of that particular design. . . . Further, even were it to be assumed that plaintiff's burden under *Barker v. Lull* . . . exceeded such a showing and required that she demonstrate the existence of some alternative design which would have prevented or lessened her injury, this burden was met by the jury's mere inspection of the photographs introduced into evidence. That is to say, no more than a cursory examination of this machine's configuration makes apparent both the danger of its design and potential solutions thereto.

Given that such alternative designs were so self-evident as to obviate the need to present express testimony, expert or otherwise, on the subject, it is equally clear counsel for plaintiff did not commit misconduct by mentioning during argument that items which "would avoid contact" such as saddlebags, luggage racks, fairings, shields, etc., could be so placed as to partially enclose the motorcycle's rotating rear wheel. The existence of such devices on other models is a matter of general knowledge and their potential effectiveness in preventing the sort of accident which occurred here is patent.

. . . .

The judgment is affirmed.

---

1. Why did Honda rest without challenging plaintiff's evidence? Why did the court reject Honda's appellate argument?

2. Is this evidence real or circumstantial?

3. *Pietrone* rests on a strict liability cause of action. Would the result be different if it rested on negligence?

4. The Tentative Draft of the Restatement (Third) of Products Liability, § 2(b) (1995), provides: A "product is defective in design when the foreseeable risks of harm posed by the product could have been reduced . . . by the adoption of a reasonable alternative design by the seller . . . and the omission . . . renders the product not reasonably safe."

Because of § 2(b), would Honda win a case brought today? If every plaintiff must bring evidence of a "reasonable alternative design," what has happened to the costs of such suits? For evaluations of the Restatement (Third) of Products Liability, see M.S. Shapo, *In Search of the Law of Products Liability: The ALI Restatement Project*, 48 Vand. L. Rev. 631 (1995); F.J. Vandall, *The Restatement (Third) of Torts, Products Liability, Section 2(b): Design Defect*, 68 Temp. L. Rev. 167 (1995).

2. Res Ipsa Loquitur

The plaintiff was bound to give affirmative proof of negligence. But there was not a scintilla of evidence, unless the occurrence is of itself evidence of negligence. . . . [Pollock, C.B. interrupted the defense's argument to say: "There are certain cases of which it may be said res ipsa loquitur, and this seems one of them. In some cases the Courts have held that the mere fact of the accident having occurred is evidence of negligence, . . ."]

The present case upon the evidence comes to this, a man is passing in front of the premises of a dealer in flour, and there falls down upon him a barrel of flour. I think it apparent that the barrel was in the custody of the defendant who occupied the premises, and who is responsible for the acts of his servants who had the control of it; and in my opinion the fact of its falling is prima facie evidence of negligence, and the plaintiff who was injured by it is not bound to show that it could not fall without negligence, but if there are any facts inconsistent with negligence it is for the defendant to prove them.

Byrne v. Boadle, 2 H & C 722, 159 Eng. Rep. 299 (Ct. Ex. 1863).

PROBLEM

When Calla picked up her two-and-a-half-year-old daughter at the nursery room in her church, she discovered a serious eye injury. The two adults who supervised the children could not explain what happened, and an inspection of the toys in the nursery revealed no sharp objects. Is there an inference of negligence on the part of the supervisors and the church to give to the jury?

ESCOLA v. COCA-COLA BOTTLING CO.
Supreme Court of California, 1944
24 Cal. 2d 453, 150 P.2d 436

Opinion by: GIBSON, J.

Plaintiff, a waitress in a restaurant, was injured when a bottle of Coca Cola broke in her hand. She alleged that defendant company, which had bottled and delivered the alleged defective bottle to her employer, was negligent in selling "bottles containing said beverage which on account of excessive pressure of gas or by reason of some defect in the bottle was dangerous . . . and likely to explode." This appeal is from a judgment upon a jury verdict in favor of plaintiff.

Defendant's driver delivered several cases of Coca-Cola to the restaurant, placing them on the floor, one on top of the other, under and behind the counter, where they remained at least thirty-six hours. Immediately before the accident, plaintiff picked up the top case and set it upon a near-by ice cream cabinet in front of and about three feet from the refrigerator. She then proceeded to take the bottles from the case with her right hand, one at a time, and put them into the refrigerator. Plaintiff testified that after she had placed three bottles in the refrigerator and had moved the fourth bottle about eighteen inches from the case "it exploded in my hand." The bottle broke into two jagged pieces and inflicted a deep five-inch cut, severing blood vessels, nerves and muscles of the thumb and palm of the hand. Plaintiff further testified that when the bottle exploded, "It made a sound similar to an electric light bulb that would have dropped. It made a loud pop." Plaintiff's employer testified, "I was about twenty feet from where it actually happened and I heard the explosion." A fellow employee, on the opposite side of the counter, testified that plaintiff "had the bottle, I should judge, waist high, and I know that it didn't bang either the case or the door or another bottle . . . when it popped. It sounded just like a fruit jar would blow up. . . ." The witness further testified that the contents of the bottle "flew all over herself and myself and the walls and one thing and another."

The top portion of the bottle, with the cap, remained in plaintiff's hand, and the lower portion fell to the floor but did not break. The broken bottle was not produced at the trial, the pieces having been thrown away by an employee of the restaurant shortly after the accident. Plaintiff, however, described the broken pieces, and a diagram of the bottle was made showing the location of the "fracture line" where the bottle broke in two.

. . . .

Plaintiff then rested her case, having announced to the court that being unable to show any specific acts of negligence she relied completely on the doctrine of res ipsa loquitur.

Defendant contends that the doctrine of res ipsa loquitur does not apply in this case, and that the evidence is insufficient to support the judgment.

Many jurisdictions have applied the doctrine in cases involving exploding bottles of carbonated beverages. . . . It would serve no useful purpose to discuss the reasoning of the foregoing cases in detail, since the problem is whether under the facts shown in the instant case the conditions warranting application of the doctrine have been satisfied.

Res ipsa loquitur does not apply unless (1) defendant had exclusive control of the thing causing the injury and (2) the accident is of such a nature that it ordinarily would not occur in the absence of negligence by the defendant. . . .

Many authorities state that the happening of the accident does not speak for itself where it took place sometime after defendant had relinquished control of the instrumentality causing the injury. Under the more logical view, however, the doctrine may be applied upon the theory that defendant had control at the time of the alleged negligent act, although not at the time of the accident, provided plaintiff first proves that the condition of the instrumentality had not been changed after it left the defendant's possession. . . . As said in *Dunn v. Hoffman Beverage Co.*, 126 N.J.L. 556 [20 A.2d 352, 354], "defendant is not charged with the duty of showing affirmatively that something happened to the bottle after it left its control or management; . . . to get to the jury the plaintiff must show that there was due care during that period." Plaintiff must also prove that she handled the bottle carefully. The reason for this prerequisite is set forth in Prosser on Torts, *supra*, at page 300, where the author states: "Allied to the condition of exclusive control in the defendant is that of absence of any action on the part of the plaintiff contributing to the accident. Its purpose, of course, is to eliminate the possibility that it was the plaintiff who was responsible." . . .

Upon an examination of the record, the evidence appears sufficient to support a reasonable inference that the bottle here involved was not damaged by any extraneous force after delivery to the restaurant by defendant. It follows, therefore, that the bottle was in some manner defective at the time defendant relinquished control, because sound and properly prepared bottles of carbonated liquids do not ordinarily explode when carefully handled.

. . . .

The judgment is affirmed. Concur by: TRAYNOR, J.

---

1. Before the decision in *Byrne v. Boadle*, the plaintiff had to present affirmative evidence of negligence by means of witnesses who saw the occurrence. What is the import of res ipsa loquitur (the thing speaks for itself)?

2. If the defendant presents no evidence, after the court permits an inference of negligence, what may happen? Is this unfair to the defendant?

3. *Escola* is best known for the concurring opinion [omitted] by Judge Traynor, where he presents the policy foundation for strict liability in products cases.

4. Isn't there a possibility that someone bumped the Coca-Cola bottle after it left the seller? Who should have the burden of proving that the bump occurred? What if such proof is not available?

5. Is it also possible that the plaintiff bumped the bottle? How does Judge Gibson deal with that possibility?

COX v. NORTHWEST AIRLINES
United States Court of Appeals, Seventh Circuit, 1967
379 F.2d 893

Castle, Circuit Judge.

The appellant, Northwest Airlines, Inc., prosecutes this appeal from a judgment entered against it in an admiralty action instituted in the District Court by the libellant-appellee, Irene Cox, administratrix. Libellant sought recovery of damages under the Death on the High Seas Act (46 U.S.C.A. § 761 et seq.) for the death of her husband. The action was tried to the court without a jury. The court made and entered findings of fact and conclusions of law, and awarded judgment against the appellant for $329,956.59.

The record discloses that the libellant's decedent, her husband, Randall S. Cox, a Captain in the United States Army, 29 years of age, was a passenger on appellant's Douglas DC-7C airplane . . . which crashed in the Pacific Ocean on June 3, 1963 during a flight from McChord Air Force Base, near Seattle, Washington, to Elmendorf, Alaska, at approximately 11:12 A.M. at a point about one hundred sixteen miles west-southwest of Annette Island off the west coast of Canada. The flight had taken off from McChord at about 8:32 A.M. after having been briefed on the weather by both its dispatch office at the Seattle Airport and by a U.S. Air Force weather specialist at McChord, and having followed the usual procedures in preparation for flight. The crew reported by radio at 11:07 A.M. that it had been over Domestic Annette at an altitude of 14,000 feet and requested clearance to climb to 18,000 feet. No reason for the requested change in altitude was given. Domestic Annette is a fix-point at which directional radio bearings are obtained along the air route from McChord to Elmendorf. This was the last known transmission made by the crew of the aircraft. On the following day, June 4, 1963, floating debris was sighted in the Pacific Ocean about 35 nautical miles west of Domestic Annette. Approximately 1,500 pounds of wreckage identified as being from the aircraft, including life vests still encased in their plastic containers and extremely deformed seat frames, was recovered. The bodies of none of the crew or passengers were ever recovered.

. . . The court's conclusion that the negligence of appellant was the proximate cause of decedent's death is predicated upon the court's finding that:

As a result of the occurrence Randall S. Cox met his death. The instrumentality which produced the death of Randall S. Cox was under the exclusive control and management of the [appellant] and that the occurrence in question was such as does not ordinarily occur in the absence of negligence, and, further, that there is no possibility of contributing conduct which would make Randall S. Cox responsible; that the facts herein justify a finding of negligence.

The appellant recognizes that the doctrine of res ipsa loquitur may properly have application in actions involving airline accidents. But the appellant contends that in the instant case it was error to apply that doctrine in resolving the issue of liability because there is substantial proof of the exercise of due care by the appellant and no countervailing evidence of specific negligence or even of unusual circumstances.

Appellant urges that evidence of due care on its part precludes any inference of negligence arising from the occurrence in the absence of at least minimal supporting evidence. . . .

The evidence of due care to which appellant alludes concerns its maintenance records and procedures with respect to the aircraft involved; the qualified and certified status, and the competence, of the operating personnel of the aircraft and of the dispatcher; the safety training received by the crew; and the evidence that the flight was properly dispatched and the weather normal.

There is no evidence as to the cause of the aircraft's crash into the ocean or concerning what happened to affect the operation of the aircraft during the period following 11:07 A.M. and prior to the crash. In the absence of such evidence, the probative value of appellant's general evidence of due care is not of substantial import. Whether due care was exercised by the operating personnel of the aircraft in the face of whatever occurred to affect the operation of the aircraft can be appraised only in the light of knowledge of what that occurrence was, whether human or mechanical failure or some other incident, and of what if anything was or could have been done about it.

We perceive nothing in appellant's due care evidence which precludes an application of the res ipsa loquitur doctrine or conditions such application upon the libellant's responding with evidence to support some specific negligent act or omission on the part of appellant. Here the cause of the crash which resulted in the death of Randall S. Cox is wholly unexplained. And, as was cogently observed in *Johnson v. United States* . . . :

No act need be explicable only in terms of negligence in order for the rule of res ipsa loquitur to be invoked. The rule deals only with permissible inferences from unexplained events.

We are of the opinion that the court properly applied the doctrine of res ipsa loquitur and that its finding of negligence was a permissible one — warranted though not compelled . . . and that the court's conclusion on the issue of appellant's liability is thus supported by the evidence and the application of correct legal criteria. . . .

Affirmed in part and remanded with directions to modify damages awarded.

-----

1. What inferences may be drawn from the plaintiff's evidence? Why does the court refuse to draw inferences from the defendant's evidence of care? Why aren't the jury and the court merely guessing on the issue of negligence in *Cox*?

2. In another plane crash case brought by a passenger, the court refused to apply res ipsa loquitur against the pilot:

The record is barren of any demonstrable proof of what occurred after the aircraft disappeared from view. Except for the time and location of the crash, everything else relating to the fatal accident is a matter of conjecture and speculation. The scant evidence gathered at the crash site, at which fire followed impact, revealed nothing concerning the course and position of the plane or the actions of the pilot immediately before the crash.

Campbell v. First Nat'l Bank in Albuquerque, NM., 370 F. Supp. 1096 (D.N.M. 1973). The pilot had just rented the small plane in the morning, and there were difficult mountains around the airfield. Why a different result from *Cox*?

3.   In contrast, res ipsa loquitur was applied to direct a verdict against the pilot in *Newing v. Cheatham*, 15 Cal. 3d 351, 124 Cal. Rptr. 193, 540 P.2d 33 (1975).

YBARRA v. SPANGARD
Supreme Court of California, 1944
25 Cal. 2d 486, 154 P.2d 687

GIBSON, CHIEF JUSTICE.

This is an action for damages for personal injuries alleged to have been inflicted on plaintiff [Ybarra] by defendants during the course of a surgical operation. The trial court entered judgments of nonsuit as to all defendants and plaintiff appealed.

On October 28, 1939, plaintiff consulted defendant Dr. Tilley, who diagnosed his ailment as appendicitis, and made arrangements for an appendectomy to be performed by defendant Dr. Spangard at a hospital owned and managed by defendant Dr. Swift. Plaintiff entered the hospital, was given a hypodermic injection, slept, and later was awakened by Doctors Tilley and Spangard and wheeled into the operating room by a nurse whom he believed to be defendant Gisler, an employee of Dr. Swift. Defendant Dr. Reser, the anesthetist, also an employee of Dr. Swift, adjusted plaintiff for the operation, pulling his body to the head of the operating table and, according to plaintiff's testimony, laying him back against two hard objects at the top of his shoulders, about an inch below his neck. Dr. Reser then administered the anesthetic and plaintiff lost consciousness. When he awoke early the following morning he was in his hospital room attended by defendant Thompson, the special nurse, and another nurse who was not made a defendant.

Plaintiff testified that prior to the operation he had never had any pain in, or injury to, his right arm or shoulder, but that when he awakened he felt a sharp pain about half way between the neck and the point of the right shoulder. He complained to the nurse, and then to Dr. Tilley, who gave him diathermy treatments while he remained in the hospital. The pain did not cease, but spread down to the lower part of his arm, and after his release from the hospital the condition grew worse. He was unable to rotate or lift his arm, and developed paralysis and atrophy of the muscles around the shoulder. He received further treatments from Dr. Tilley until March, 1940, and then returned to work, wearing his arm in a splint on the advice of Dr. Spangard. . . .

Plaintiff's theory is that the foregoing evidence presents a proper case for the application of the doctrine of res ipsa loquitur. . . . Defendants take the position that, assuming that plaintiff's condition was in fact the result of an injury, there is no showing that the act of any particular defendant, nor any particular instrumentality, was the cause thereof. They attack plaintiff's action as an attempt to fix liability "en masse" on various defendants, some of whom were not responsible for the acts of others; and they further point to the failure to show which defendants had control of the instrumentalities that may have been involved. Their main defense may be briefly stated in two propositions: (1) that where there are several defendants, and there is a division of responsibility in the use of an instrumentality causing the injury, and the injury might have resulted from the separate act of either one of two or more persons, the rule of res ipsa loquitur cannot be invoked against any one of them; and (2) that where there are several instrumentalities, and no showing is made as to which caused the injury or as to the particular defendant in control of it, the doctrine cannot apply. We are satisfied, however, that these objections are not well taken in the circumstances of this case.

The doctrine of res ipsa loquitur has three conditions: "(1) the accident must be of a kind which ordinarily does not occur in the absence of someone's negligence; (2) it must be caused by an agency or instrumentality within the exclusive control of the defendant; (3) it must not have been due to any voluntary action or contribution on the part of the plaintiff." . . .

. . . If the doctrine is to continue to serve a useful purpose, we should not forget that "the particular force and justice of the rule, regarded as a presumption throwing upon the party charged the duty of producing evidence, consists in the circumstance that the chief evidence of the true cause, whether culpable or innocent, is practically accessible to him but inaccessible to the injured person." . . .

The present case is of a type which comes within the reason and spirit of the doctrine more fully perhaps than any other. The passenger sitting awake in a railroad car at the time of a collision, the pedestrian walking along the street and struck by a falling object or the debris of an explosion, are surely not more entitled to an explanation than the unconscious patient on the operating table. Viewed from this aspect, it is difficult to see how the doctrine can, with any justification, be so restricted in its statement as to become inapplicable to a patient who submits himself to the care and custody of doctors and nurses, is rendered unconscious, and receives some injury from instrumentalities used in his treatment. Without the aid of the doctrine a patient who received permanent injuries of a serious character, obviously the result of someone's negligence, would be entirely unable to recover unless the doctors and nurses in attendance voluntarily chose to disclose the identity of the negligent person and the facts establishing liability. . . . If this were the state of the law of negligence, the courts, to avoid gross injustice, would be forced to invoke the principles of absolute liability, irrespective of negligence, in actions by persons suffering injuries during the course of treatment under anesthesia. But we think this juncture has not yet been reached, and that the doctrine of res ipsa loquitur is properly applicable to the case before us.

The condition that the injury must not have been due to the plaintiff's voluntary action is of course fully satisfied under the evidence produced herein; and the same is true of the condition that the accident must be one which ordinarily does not occur unless someone was negligent. We have here no problem of negligence in treatment, but of distinct injury to a healthy part of the body not the subject of treatment, nor within the area covered by the operation. The decisions in this state make it clear that such circumstances raise the inference of negligence, and call upon the defendant to explain the unusual result. . . .

The argument of defendants is simply that plaintiff has not shown an injury caused by an instrumentality under a defendant's control, because he has not shown which of the several instrumentalities that he came in contact with while in the hospital caused the injury; and he has not shown that any one defendant or his servants had exclusive control over any particular instrumentality. Defendants assert that some of them were not the employees of other defendants, that some did not stand in any permanent relationship from which liability in tort would follow, and that in view of the nature of the injury, the number of defendants and the different functions performed by each, they could not all be liable for the wrong, if any.

We have no doubt that in a modern hospital a patient is quite likely to come under the care of a number of persons in different types of contractual and other relationships with each other. For example, in the present case it appears that Doctors Smith, Spangard and Tilley were physicians or surgeons commonly placed in the legal category of independent contractors; and Dr. Reser, the anesthetist, and defendant Thompson, the special nurse, were employees of Dr. Swift and not of the other doctors. But we do not believe that either the number or relationship of the defendants alone determines whether the doctrine of res ipsa loquitur applies. Every defendant in whose custody the plaintiff was placed for any period was bound to exercise ordinary care to see that no unnecessary harm came to him and each would be liable for failure in this regard. Any defendant who negligently injured him, and any defendant charged with his care who so neglected him as to allow injury to occur, would be liable. The defendant employers would be liable for the neglect of their employees; and the doctor in charge of the operation would be liable for the negligence of those who became his temporary servants for the purpose of assisting in the operation.

. . . .

It may appear at the trial that, consistent with the principles outlined above, one or more defendants will be found liable and others absolved, but this should not preclude the application of the rule of res ipsa loquitur. The control, at one time or another, of one or more of the various agencies or instrumentalities which might have harmed the plaintiff was in the hands of every defendant or of his employees or temporary servants. This, we think, places upon them the burden of initial explanation. Plaintiff was rendered unconscious for the purpose of undergoing surgical treatment by the defendants; it is manifestly unreasonable for them to insist that he identify any one of them as the person who did the alleged negligent act.

The other aspect of the case which defendants so strongly emphasize is that plaintiff has not identified the instrumentality any more than he has the particular guilty defendant. Here, again, there is a misconception which, if carried to the extreme for which defendants contend, would unreasonably limit the application of the res ipsa loquitur rule. It should be enough that the plaintiff can show an injury resulting from an external force applied while he lay unconscious in the hospital; this is as clear a case of identification of the instrumentality as the plaintiff may ever be able to make.

. . . .

In the face of these examples of liberalization of the tests for res ipsa loquitur, there can be no justification for the rejection of the doctrine in the instant case. As pointed out above, if we accept the contention of defendants herein, there will rarely be any compensation for patients injured while unconscious. A hospital today conducts a highly integrated system of activities, with many persons contributing their efforts. There may be, e.g., preparation for surgery by nurses and interns who are employees of the hospital; administering of an anesthetic by a doctor who may be an employee of the hospital, an employee of the operating surgeon, or an independent contractor; performance of an operation by a surgeon and assistants who may be his employees, employees of the hospital, or independent contractors; and post surgical care by the surgeon, a hospital physician, and nurses. The number of those in whose care the patient is placed is not a good reason for denying him all reasonable opportunity to recover for negligent harm. It is rather a good reason for re-examination of the statement of legal theories which supposedly compel such a shocking result.

. . . .

We . . . hold that where a plaintiff receives unusual injuries while unconscious and in the course of medical treatment, all those defendants who had any control over his body or the instrumentalities which might have caused the injuries may properly be called upon to meet the inference of negligence by giving an explanation of their conduct.

The judgment is reversed.

---

1. What is the plaintiff's argument? What is the defendant's response to the plaintiff's contentions? Why does the court agree with the plaintiff?

2. If res ipsa had not applied in *Ybarra*, what would have been the result?

3. The remand was held before a judge sitting without a jury. The defendants all testified that they saw nothing, and the judge found for the plaintiff:

> All of the defendants except the owner of the hospital, who was not personally in attendance upon the respondent, gave evidence and each testified that while he was present he saw nothing occur which could have produced the injury to respondent's arm and shoulder. Upon this evidence appellants insist that the prima facie case made under the res ipsa doctrine was overcome. But it was for the trial judge to weigh the circumstantial evidence which made the prima facie case under the res ipsa rule against the positive testimony of the appellants and to determine whether the prima facie case had been met. . . . There is nothing inherent in direct testimony which compels a trial court to accept it over the contrary inferences which may reasonably be drawn from circumstantial evidence. The view taken of the evidence by the trial judge is illustrated by the following remark made at the hearing of the motion for new trial:

I believe it arose from a traumatic condition. Now, where did it happen? That puts the court right back. Even though their explanations were honest, that there was something they did not appreciate happened in the course of the operation, in the course of handling the patient. That is the way I figured the case and that was my decision.

Ybarra v. Spangard, 93 Cal. App. 2d 43, 208 P.2d 445 (1949).

4.   *Ybarra* has not been widely applied. Why? *See* Thode, *The Unconscious Patient: Who Should Bear the Risk of Unexplained Injuries to a Healthy Part of His Body?*, 1969 Utah L. Rev. 1.

5.   In medical malpractice cases, res ipsa loquitur has been applied to a sponge left in the body, *Truhitte v. French Hosp.*, 128 Cal. App. 3d 332, 180 Cal. Rptr. 152 (1982), and to severe burns the plaintiff received while unconscious following a Caesarean operation, *Timbrell v. Suburban Hosp.*, 4 Cal. 2d 68, 47 P.2d 737 (1935).

6.   Does res ipsa loquitur apply when a patient undergoes abdominal surgery and receives a spinal anesthesia, but awakens with a paralyzed leg? No. Here the negligence must be grounded upon expert testimony. *Ayers v. Parry*, 192 F.2d 181 (3d Cir. 1951).

7.   The plaintiff had a tumor removed from his spinal cord. In the recovery room it was discovered that he was hemorrhaging. He was returned to the operating room, and Gelfoam was applied to stop the bleeding. It failed. The defendant doctor therefore packed Surgicel into the area of the spine with the hemorrhage. Surgicel swells 10% to 20% when exposed to blood. It stopped the bleeding. In the recovery room, the plaintiff discovered that the lower portion of his body was paralyzed. Does res ipsa loquitur apply against the doctor? The court found for the defendant:

This brings us to a consideration of whether the accident in this case is of a kind which ordinarily does not occur in the absence of someone's negligence. The plaintiff in his brief argues that the proper question is: "Is paralysis of the lower body as a result of surgery to remove a tumor from the chest the kind of an accident which ordinarily does not occur in the absence of negligence?" We cannot agree. [T]he question is: "Is paralysis of the lower body resulting from packing Surgicel against the spinal cord in an attempt to halt extensive hemorrhaging an accident of the kind which ordinarily does not occur in the absence of someone's negligence?"

The test is not whether a particular injury rarely occurs, but rather, when it occurs, is it ordinarily the result of negligence. . . .

The fact that a particular injury suffered by a patient as the result of an operation is something that rarely occurs does not in itself prove that the injury was probably caused by the negligence of those in charge of the operation.

"To permit an inference of negligence under the doctrine of res ipsa loquitur solely because an uncommon complication develops would place too great a burden upon the medical profession and might result in an undesirable limitation on the use of operations or new procedures involving an inherent risk of injury even when due care is used. Where risks are inherent in an operation and an injury of a type which is rare does occur, the doctrine should not be applicable unless it can be said that, in light of past experience, such an occurrence is more likely the result of negligence than some cause for which the defendant is not responsible."

We hold that it is not common knowledge that the result in this case does not ordinarily occur in the absence of negligence.

There are risks inherent in the use of Surgicel against the spinal cord and, even though injury from this cause is rare, res ipsa loquitur is not applicable unless it can be shown through expert witnesses that the injury is more likely the result of negligence than some other cause. No doctor testified that under the facts of this case there was bad medical practice, and no doctor testified that where, under the present facts, injury does occur it is more likely than not the result of negligence.

Brannon v. Wood, 251 Or. 349, 444 P.2d 558 (1968).

8. There are two situations where res ipsa loquitur does not apply. First, the "calculated risk." In *Brannon*, the doctor knew that paralysis was a risk of using Surgicel. Second, the "bad result." There is a risk of death whenever a general anesthetic is used, for example. The "calculated risk" and the "bad result" may occur in the absence of negligence. W. Page Keeton et al., Prosser and Keeton on Torts (5th ed. 1984).

What is the doctor's informational obligation when a "calculated risk" or "bad result" may occur during treatment?

ANDERSON v. SOMBERG
Supreme Court of New Jersey, 1975
67 N.J. 291, 338 A.2d 1

PASHMAN, JUSTICE.

These negligence-products liability actions had their inception in a surgery performed in 1967 on the premises of defendant St. James Hospital (Hospital). Plaintiff was undergoing a laminectomy, a back operation, performed by defendant Dr. Somberg. During the course of the procedure, the tip or cup of an angulated pituitary rongeur, a forceps-like instrument, broke off while the tool was being manipulated in plaintiff's spinal canal. The surgeon attempted to retrieve the metal but was unable to do so. After repeated failure in that attempt, he terminated the operation. The imbedded fragment caused medical complications and further surgical interventions were required. Plaintiff has suffered significant and permanent physical injury proximately caused by the rongeur fragment which lodged in his spine.

Plaintiff sued: (1) Dr. Somberg for medical malpractice, alleging that the doctor's negligent action caused the rongeur to break: (2) St. James Hospital, alleging that it negligently furnished Dr. Somberg with a defective surgical instrument; (3) Reinhold-Schumann, Inc. (Reinhold), the medical supply distributor which furnished the defective rongeur to the hospital, on a warranty theory, and (4) Lawton

Instrument Company (Lawton), the manufacturer of the rongeur, on a strict liability in tort claim, alleging that the rongeur was a defective product. In short, plaintiff sued all who might have been liable for his injury, absent some alternative explanation such as contributory negligence.

. . . .

The position adopted by the Appellate Division majority seems to us substantially correct: that is, at the close of all the evidence, it was apparent that at least one of the defendants was liable for plaintiff's injury, because no alternative theory of liability was within reasonable contemplation. Since defendants had engaged in conduct which activated legal obligations by each of them to plaintiff, the jury should have been instructed that the failure of any defendant to prove his nonculpability would trigger liability; and further, that since at least one of the defendants could not sustain his burden of proof, at least one would be liable. A no cause of action verdict against all primary and third-party defendants will be unacceptable and would work a miscarriage of justice sufficient to require a new trial. . . .

In the ordinary case, the law will not assist an innocent plaintiff at the expense of an innocent defendant. However, in the type of case we consider here, where an unconscious or helpless patient suffers an admitted mishap not reasonably foreseeable and unrelated to the scope of the surgery (such as cases where foreign objects are left in the body of the patient), those who had custody of the patient, and who owed him a duty of care as to medical treatment, or not to furnish a defective instrument for use in such treatment can be called to account for their default. They must prove their nonculpa-bility, or else risk liability for the injuries suffered.

This case resembles the ordinary medical malpractice foreign-objects case, where the patient is sewn up with a surgical tool or sponge inside him. In those cases, res ipsa loquitur is used to make out a prima facie case. . . .

The rule of evidence we set forth does not represent the doctrine of res ipsa loquitur as it has been traditionally understood. Res ipsa loquitur is ordinarily impressed only where the injury more probably than not has resulted from negligence of the defendant. . . . The doctrine has been expanded to include, as in the instant matter, multiple defendants . . . , although even this expansion has been criticized. . . . It has also been expanded to embrace cases where the negligence cause was not the only or most probable theory in the case, but where the alternate theories of liability accounted for the only possible causes of injury. . . . That is the situation in this case, where we find negligence, strict liability in tort and breach of warranty all advanced as possible theories of liability. In such cases, defendants are required to come forward and give their evidence. The latter development represents a substantial deviation from earlier conceptions of res ipsa loquitur and has more accurately been called "akin to res ipsa loquitur". . . .

We hold that in a situation like this, the burden of proof in fact does shift to defendants. All those in custody of that patient or who owed him a duty, as here, the manufacturer and the distributor, should be called forward and should be made to prove their freedom from liability. The rule would have no application except in those instances where the injury lay outside the ambit of the surgical procedure in question; for example, an injury to an organ, when that organ was itself the object of medical attention, would not by itself make out a prima facie case for malpractice or shift the burden of proof to defendants. . . .

The judgment of the Appellate Division is hereby affirmed, and the cause remanded for trial upon instructions consonant with this opinion.

MOUNTAIN, J., dissenting.

This Court has reached an extraordinary result in a very remarkable way. As I shall hope to make clear, the structure of argument as presented in the Court's opinion is rested upon an assumed factual premise which does not exist. In part because of this, the concluding and most significant part of the argument suffers from the defect of visiting liability, in a wholly irrational way, upon parties who are more probably than not totally free of blame. I respectfully dissent.

During the course of the Court's opinion there appear statements to the effect that all those who might have been in any way responsible for plaintiff's injury are before the court. Hence, the argument continues, a process of selection properly undertaken by the finder of fact cannot fail to implicate the true culprit or culprits. Indeed, as I read the opinion, the entire argument is made to rest upon this premise: each and every person who may have brought about the imperfection in the surgical instrument or who may have caused the injury by its misuse is before the court; it remains only to identify him.

And yet we know — and everyone who has been associated with this case has always known — that this assumption is not in fact true. The only four defendants in the case are: the surgeon, Dr. Harold Somberg, who performed the operation; St. James Hospital, the medical facility in which the operation took place; Lawton Instrument Co., which manufactured the rongeur; and Rheinhold-Schumann, Inc., the distributor which sold it to the hospital. There is no other defendant in the case. And yet the record is replete with testimony that other surgeons — perhaps as many as twenty — have used the rongeur during the four years that it has formed part of the surgical equipment of the hospital, and that any one or more of them may perfectly well have been responsible for so injuring the instrument that it came apart while being manipulated in plaintiff's incision; or that it may have been weakened to near breaking point by cumulative misuse, entirely by persons not now before the court. . . .

I would vote to reverse the judgment of the Appellate Division and to reinstate the judgment of the trial court.

---

1.   Who did the plaintiff sue? Why cast such a broad net? What were the causes of action?

2.   As clerk for the trial court judge, formulate the charge to the jury on the remand of *Anderson*.

3.   Is this a radical case? If so, why? If judges are generally conservative, why did these draft such an extreme decision?

4. What point does the dissent overlook?

5. *Car crashes.* Res ipsa loquitur applies against the driver, in a suit brought by a passenger, when the car leaves the road and crashes into a tree. *Badela v. Karpowich*, 152 Conn. 360, 206 A.2d 838 (1965).

It does not apply against the other driver, when two cars crash into each other, because the jury would be required to guess as to negligence.

However, in a collision between a bus and a car, the bus passenger can go to the jury by arguing res ipsa loquitur. This is because the driver of a common carrier is held to the highest standard of care, and it is likely he or she violated this very high standard. *See* W. Page Keeton et al., Prosser and Keeton on Torts 252 (5th ed. 1984).

PROBLEM

Over 100 high school juniors and seniors rent rooms in the Gobstopper Hotel, a huge hotel in a large city, for New Year's Eve. The hotel has an atrium 20 stories tall. In some cases, parents rented the rooms; in others, the students used fake identification. Tom, a junior, who is a guest of a senior who rented the room, gets drunk and jumps or falls from the 18th floor in the atrium. He dies.

Discuss a possible suit against the Gobstopper Hotel. What assumptions have you made?

CONNOLLY v. NICOLLET HOTEL
Supreme Court of Minnesota, 1959
254 Minn. 373, 95 N.W.2d 657

Murphy, Justice.

Action by Marcella A. Connolly against The Nicollet Hotel, a copartnership, . . . for the loss of the sight of her left eye alleged to have been caused by defendants' negligence.

The accident occurred about midnight June 12, 1953, during the course of the 1953 National Junior Chamber of Commerce Convention which had its headquarters at The Nicollet Hotel in Minneapolis. It was occasioned when plaintiff was struck in her left eye by a substance falling from above her as she walked on a public sidewalk on Nicollet Avenue adjacent to the hotel.

The 1953 National Junior Chamber of Commerce Convention, Inc., was joined as a defendant in the action, but at the close of the testimony a verdict was directed in its favor. The jury returned a verdict against The Nicollet Hotel copartnership, which will hereinafter be designated defendants, in the sum of $30,000. This is an appeal from an order of the trial court granting judgment for such defendants notwithstanding the verdict. On appeal plaintiff contends that defendants were negligent in failing to maintain order and control the conduct of their guests . . . and that hence the court erred in granting judgment notwithstanding the verdict.

. . . .

Plaintiff, in company with one Margaret Hansen, had just left the hotel via its Nicollet Avenue entrance and was walking southerly toward Third Street on the west side of Nicollet Avenue. When she had traveled approximately six to ten steps from the canopy extending over such entrance, she observed two people walking toward her. She then heard a noise which sounded like a small explosion and saw something strike the walk in front of her. She observed that one of the persons approaching her was struck on the left shoulder by some substance. She then exclaimed, "We better get off this sidewalk, . . . or somebody is going to get hit." Immediately thereafter she glanced upward and was struck in the left eye by a substance she described as a mud-like substance or a "handful of dirt." Margaret Hansen testified that she also saw the substance falling from eye level to the sidewalk a step or two in front of her. She described the sound made by the striking object as explosive and accompanied by a splattering. The only place from which the article might have fallen from above was the hotel building.

The blow which struck plaintiff caused her to lose her balance but not to fall. Her knees buckled and she was caught by Margaret Hansen and held on her feet. Following the blow, she stated that she could not open her left eye and the left side of her face and head became numb, and her shoulders, hair, and the left side of her face were covered with dirt. A dark substance which looked like mud was found imbedded in her left eye. After the accident the assistant manager of the hotel attempted to remove a "mud like substance" from plaintiff's eye by using a cotton applicator. As a result of the foregoing accident, plaintiff lost the sight of the injured eye.

As stated above, the 1953 National Junior Chamber of Commerce Convention occupied a substantial portion of the hotel at the time of the accident. In connection therewith various delegates and firms maintained hospitality centers there where intoxicants, beer, and milk were served to guests and visitors. Two of such centers were located on the Nicollet Avenue side of the building.

The assistant manager of the hotel on duty at the time of the accident and in charge of maintaining order had received notice that water bags had been thrown from the hotel during the previous days of the convention. The night engineer testified that on the Hennepin Avenue side of the hotel he had observed liquor and beer bottles and cans on the sidewalk and described the accumulation in this area as greater than he had ever witnessed during the 18-month period he had been employed at the hotel. He also testified that he had found cans and beer bottles upon the fire escape at the third-floor level during the convention.

. . . .

It is generally agreed that a hotel owner or innkeeper owes a duty to the public to protect it against foreseeable risk of danger attendant upon the maintenance and operation of his property . . . ; and to keep it in such condition that it will not be of danger to pedestrians using streets adjacent thereto. . . .

The failure of a hotel owner and operator to take reasonable precautions to eliminate or prevent conditions of which he is or should be aware and which might reasonably be expected to be dangerous to the public may constitute negligence. . . .

There are certain controlling principles of law which must be kept in mind in considering the merits of the plaintiff's claims as they are established by the record. It is recognized that one who assembles a large number of people upon his premises for the purpose of financial gain to himself assumes the responsibility for using all reasonable care to protect others from injury from causes reasonably to be anticipated. In the exercise of this duty it is necessary for him to furnish a sufficient number of guards or attendants and to take other precautions to control the actions of the crowd. Whether the guards furnished or the precautions taken are sufficient is ordinarily a question for the jury to determine under all of the circumstances.

. . . .

The defendants contend that the proof is circumstantial and that there is no evidence that the object which struck the plaintiff came from the hotel. The plaintiff was struck in the eye by a mass of moist dirt or earth. The jury could find that this object was not an accumulation of dirt which fell from the structure. . . . We think that under the facts in this case the evidence presents inferences which make the question of where the mass of mud came from one for the jury.

. . . .

Reversed.

---

1. At what point did the hotel's duty of care arise? For the hotel, what was reasonable care under these circumstances?

Notice the hotel's duty extends outside the boundary of the property.

2. Is there any evidence that the plaintiff was contributorily negligent?

3. Res ipsa loquitur was not applied against the hotel when an overstuffed chair was thrown out of a hotel window and hit the plaintiff, a pedestrian. The guests in the hotel were celebrating V-J Day, and the court held that the hotel lacked exclusive control. *Larson v. St. Francis Hotel*, 83 Cal. App. 2d 210, 188 P.2d 513 (1948). Compare *Larson* with *Connolly*. Why the different result?

4. The plaintiff ate turkey salad at a luncheon put on by eleven high school band mothers. She contracted food poisoning from the salad. The court refused to apply res ipsa loquitur against the eleven mothers:

> Some of the elements of res ipsa have been proved. The evidence leads to the conclusion that salmonella would not exist in the turkey salad without someone's negligence, but exclusive control in any one of the defendants or in the defendants collectively, on a theory of vicarious liability, has not been shown either by proof or by inference.

Samson v. Riesing, 62 Wis. 2d 698, 215 N.W.2d 662 (1974). What are the other reasons for the decision? Why is the result different from *Ybarra*?

5. In some jurisdictions there may be a debate as to the weight to be given to circumstantial evidence in a case where res ipsa loquitur applies:

While we agree that these facts made a case of res ipsa loquitur, we do not agree that they, though unexplained, required an inference or finding of negligence, or that the jury could not reasonably refuse to find negligence and return a verdict for defendant, or that there was no evidence to support their verdict for him.

It is true there has been confusion in the case as to the procedural effect of res ipsa loquitur, some cases giving it one and some another of these three different effects:

(1) It warrants an *inference* of negligence which the jury may draw or not, as their judgment dictates. . . .

(2) It raises a *presumption* of negligence which requires the jury to find negligence if defendant does not produce evidence sufficient to rebut the presumption. . . .

(3) It not only raises such a presumption but also *shifts the ultimate burden of proof to* defendant and requires him to prove by a preponderance of all the evidence that the injury was not caused by his negligence.

The effect of a case of res ipsa loquitur, like that of any other case of circumstantial evidence varies from case to case, depending on the particular facts of each case; and therefore such effect can no more be fitted into a fixed formula or reduced to a rigid rule than can the effect of other cases of circumstantial evidence. The only generalization that can be safely made is that, in the words of the definition of res ipsa loquitur, it affords "reasonable evidence," in the absence of an explanation by defendant, that the accident arose from this negligence.

The weight or strength of such "reasonable evidence" will necessarily depend on the particular facts of each case, and the cogency of the inference of negligence from such facts may of course vary in degree all the way from practical certainty in one case to reasonable probability in another.

In exceptional cases the inference may be so strong as to require a directed verdict for plaintiff, as in cases of objects falling from defendant's premises on persons in the highway, such as *Byrne u. Boadle.* . . .

In the ordinary case, however, res ipsa loquitur merely makes a case for the jury — merely permits the jury to choose the inference of defendant's negligence in preference to other permissible or reasonable inferences. . . .

Sullivan v. Crabtree, 36 Tenn. App. 469, 258 S.W.2d 782 (1953).

6. While chewing tobacco, the plaintiff's mouth began to burn. He found a human toe in the plug of tobacco. Does res ipsa loquitur apply? As judge would you direct a verdict for the plaintiff? The court said: "We can imagine no reason why, with ordinary care, human toes could not be left out of chewing tobacco, and if toes are found in chewing tobacco, it seems to us that somebody has been very careless." *Pillars v. R.J. Reynolds Tobacco Co.*, 117 Miss. 490, 78 So. 365 (1918).

7.   Does res ipsa loquitur apply when two trains run into each other head-on? As the judge would you direct a verdict for the plaintiff? *See Moore v. Atchison, T. & S.F.R. Co.*, 28 Ill. App. 2d 340, 171 N.E.2d 393 (1960); *Rouse v. Hornsby*, 67 F. 219 (8th Cir. 1895).

8.   What about a dental patient who has a tooth removed and emerges from the procedure with a broken finger? *See Wolfe v. Feldman*, 158 Misc. 656, 286 N.Y.S. 118 (1936).

Chapter 6

CAUSE IN FACT

A. INTRODUCTION

Some authors include cause in fact and proximate cause in the same causation chapter. That leads to analytical confusion because cause in fact and proximate cause are not closely related. The only thing they have in common is the term "causation." Proximate cause is a matter of policy and answers the question of whether this particular defendant should be liable for this specific injury. Proximate cause should not be considered until cause in fact has been shown.

In contrast, cause in fact is a matter of science: did the defendant's act have something to do with the plaintiffs injury as a matter of science? There are two tests for cause in fact: the "but for" test and the "substantial factor" test. Cause in fact is necessary for liability, but it is not sufficient by itself to prove liability. For all injuries, there is more than one cause in fact. *See* Malone, *Ruminations on Cause-in-Fact*, 9 Stan. L. Rev. 60 (1958).

PROBLEM

Marilyn was a guest at the Old Tyme Hotel when she received a cut on her forehead from a piece of glass that fell from the transom (a window above the door). The injury occurred when Marilyn opened the door to her room. Assume that the Old Tyme Hotel was negligent in regard to the maintenance of the transom. The wound would not heal, and a specialist found that at the point of injury, skin cancer had developed.

For what damages will Marilyn be able to recover?

NEW YORK CENTRAL RAILROAD CO. v. GRIMSTAD
United States Court of Appeals, Second Circuit, 1920
264 F. 334

Before WARD, ROGERS, and HOUGH, CIRCUIT JUDGES.

WARD, CIRCUIT JUDGE. This is an action under the Federal Employers' Liability Act (Comp. St. §§ 8657-8665) to recover damages for the death of Angell Grimstad, captain of the covered barge, Gray ton, owned by the defendant railroad company. The charge of negligence is failure to equip the barge with proper life-preservers . . . , for want of which the decedent having fallen into the water, was drowned.

The barge was lying on the port side of the steamer Santa Clara, on the north side of Pier 2, Erie Basin, Brooklyn, loaded with sugar in transit from Havana to St. John, N.B. The tug *Mary M*, entering the slip between Piers 1 and 2, bumped against the barge. The decedent's wife, feeling the shock, came out from the cabin, looked on one side of the barge, and saw nothing, and then went across the deck to the other side, and discovered her husband in the water about ten feet from the barge holding up his hands out of the water. He did not know how to swim. She immediately ran back into the cabin for a small line, and when she returned with it he had disappeared.

. . . The court left it to the jury to say whether the defendant was negligent in not equipping the barge with life-preservers and whether, if there had been a life-preserver on board, Grimstad would have been saved from drowning.

The jury found as a fact that the defendant was negligent in not equipping the barge with life-preservers. Life-preservers and life belts are intended to be put on the body of a person before getting into the water, and would have been of no use at all to the decedent. On the other hand, life buoys are intended to be thrown to a person when in the water, and we will treat the charge in the complaint as covering life buoys.

Obviously the proximate cause of the decedent's death was his falling into the water, and in the absence of any testimony whatever on the point, we will assume that this happened without negligence on his part or on the part of the defendant. On the second question, whether a life buoy would have saved the decedent from drowning, we think the jury were left to pure conjecture and speculation. A jury might well conclude that a light near an open hatch or a rail on the side of a vessel's deck would have prevented a person's falling into the hatch or into the water, in the dark. But there is nothing whatever to show that the decedent was not drowned because he did not know how to swim, nor anything to show that, if there had been a life buoy on board, the decedent's wife would have got it in time, that is, sooner than she got the small line, or, if she had, that she would have thrown it so that her husband could have seized it, or, if she did, that he would have seized it, or that, if he did, it would have prevented him from drowning.

The court erred in denying the defendant's motion to dismiss the complaint at the end of the case.

Judgment reversed.

---

1.   What does the court mean when it says, "Obviously the proximate cause of the decedent's death was his falling into the water . . . ?"

Does the court mean that a cause in fact of his death was falling into the water?

2.   Does the court apply the "but for" test or the "substantial factor" test?

3.   For about sixty dollars it is possible to obtain a gas-inflatable personal flotation device (PFD) that is about the size of a "fanny" pack. Today, would the case go to the jury if the defendant barge owner failed to provide such PFD's in a case with the same facts as *Grimstad?*

4. The defendant was cutting ice on a lake and was negligent in failing to fence a large hole. The plaintiffs horses ran across the ice and into the hole and drowned. The court found that the horses were uncontrollable, and therefore would not have been stopped by the fence. The absence of a fence was not a cause in fact of the drownings. Is there anyone in the class who knows anything about horses? Is the court correct? *Stacy v. Knickerbocker Ice Co.*, 84 Wis. 614, 54 N.W. 1091 (1893).

5. A widow of a seaman who drowned while swimming in the ocean after jumping overboard brought a Jones Act action against the shipowner. The district court denied relief, and the widow appealed. The court of appeals held that (1) it was appropriate to conclude that the seaman was legally drunk at the time of his death; (2) the lack of the required line-throwing device, coupled with the shipowner's duty to rescue, established that the shipowner was negligent as a matter of law; (3) the existence of causation was presumed, and the burden was on the shipowner to show that the ship's inaction and regulatory violations could not have been even a contributory cause of the seaman's death.

The Court of Appeals stated:

> From the foregoing discussion, it is apparent that the element of causation in this situation turns on a number of either ambiguous or hypothetical issues of fact. Determining the causation element in this case is made most difficult by the facts that (i) the ship lacked required equipment which could conceivably have been used for rescue and by (ii) the actual failure of the ship to even attempt a rescue. These omissions are solely the fault of the ship.

> We refuse to place such a difficult burden of proving causation on the widow of the deceased seaman. Instead, the District Court on remand is to presume the existence of causation and defendant-appellee shall have the burden of overcoming that presumption. A number of considerations support this allocation of the burden of proving causation.

> The "search and rescue" branch of the rescue doctrine already recognizes such a rebuttable presumption of causation in favor of a seaman's representative.

Reyes v. Vantage Steamship Co., 609 F.2d 140, 144 (5th Cir. 1980).

6. A father and his son drowned in the defendant's motel pool. The motel violated a statute that required a lifeguard and failed to warn of the absence of a lifeguard. The court held:

> [W]e have concluded that under the facts presented at trial, plaintiffs, in demonstrating defendants' failure to provide a lifeguard at the pool as required by statute, sustained their initial burden of proof and that defendants then bore the burden of showing that this statutory violation was not a cause of the deaths. Although defendants failed to meet this burden at the initial trial, we have determined that inasmuch as the parties' respective burdens were not clearly defined at that time, the judgment should be reversed and the cause be remanded for a new trial.

Haft v. Lone Palm Hotel, 3 Cal. 3d 756, 761, 91 Cal. Rptr. 745, 747, 478 P.2d 465, 467 (1970). On retrial, how will the motel prove that the failure to have a lifeguard and the failure to warn of the absence of a guard did not cause in fact the drownings?

7. A 250-pound woman fell down the steps at a railroad station and sued the railroad for failing to provide a handrail and failing to light the steps. The railroad argued that the cause in fact of her falling was her weight. The court held for the plaintiff, stating: "[W]here the negligence of the defendant greatly multiplies the chance of the accident . . . and is of a character naturally leading to its occurrence, the mere possibility that it might have happened without the negligence is not sufficient to break the chain of cause and effect. . . ." *Reynolds v. Texas & Pac. Ry. Co.*, 37 La. Ann. 694 (1885). *But see McInturff v. Chicago Title & Trust*, 243 N.E.2d 657 (Ill. App. Ct. 1968).

B. CONCURRENT CAUSES

ANDERSON v. MINNEAPOLIS, ST. PAUL & SAULT STE. MARIE RAILWAY CO.
Supreme Court of Minnesota, 1920
146 Minn. 430, 179 N.W. 45

LEES, C. This is a fire case brought against the defendant railway company. . . . Plaintiff had a verdict. The appeal is from an order denying a motion in the alternative for judgment notwithstanding the verdict or for a new trial. . . .

Plaintiffs case in chief was directed to proving that in August, 1918, one of defendant's engines started a fire in a bog near the west side of plaintiffs land; that it smoldered there until October 12, 1918, when it flared up and burned his property shortly before it was reached by one of the great fires which swept through northeastern Minnesota at the close of that day.

Defendant introduced evidence to show that on and prior to October 12 fires were burning west and northwest of and were swept by the wind towards plaintiffs premises. . . .

In instructing the jury, the court said in part:

> If you find that other fire or fires not set by one of the defendant's engines mingled with one that was set by one of the defendant's engines, there may be difficulty in determining whether you should find that the fire set by the engine was a material or substantial element in causing plaintiffs damage. If it was, the defendant is liable, otherwise it is not. . . .

> If you find that bog fire was set by the defendant's engine and that some greater fire swept over it before it reached the plaintiffs land, then it will be for you to determine whether that bog fire . . . was a material or substantial factor in causing plaintiffs damage. If it was . . . defendant is liable. If it was not, defendant is not liable. . . .

The following proposition is stated in defendant's brief and relied on for a reversal:

If plaintiff's property was damaged by a number of fires combining, one . . . being the fire pleaded . . . the others being of no responsible origin, but of such sufficient or such superior force that they would have produced the damage to plaintiff's property regardless of the fire pleaded, then defendant was not liable.

This proposition is based upon *Cook v. Minneapolis, St. P. & S.S.M. Ry. Co.* 98 Wis. 624, 74 N.W. 561. . . . If the *Cook* case merely decides that one who negligently sets a fire is not liable if another's property is damaged, unless it is made to appear that the fire was a material element in the destruction of the property, there can be no question about the soundness of the decision. But if it decides that if such fire combines with another of no responsible origin, and after the union of the two fires they destroy the property, and either fire independently of the other would have destroyed it, then, irrespective of whether the first fire was or was not a material factor in the destruction of the property, there is no liability, we are not prepared to adopt the doctrine as the law of this state. If a fire set by the engine of one railroad company unites with a fire set by the engine of another company, there is joint and several liability, even though either fire would have destroyed plaintiff's property. But if the doctrine of the *Cook* case is applied and one of the fires is of unknown origin, there is no liability. . . . We, therefore, hold that the trial court did not err in refusing to instruct the jury in accordance with the rule laid down in the *Cook* case.

We find no error requiring a reversal, and hence the order appealed from is affirmed.

---

1. The *Cook* case (cited in the principal case), decided in 1898, was also a suit against a railroad for damage from merged fires, one unknown and one caused by the railroad. The court found for the railroad. What happened to the railroads between 1898 (*Cook*) and 1920 (Anderson)? What was the reason for the decision in *Cook*?

2. Suppose that Sally negligently drives into Tom, who is walking across the street, and severely injures his right leg. Carl negligently runs over Tom's same leg, as he is lying in the street awaiting an ambulance. Either contact would have been sufficient to necessitate amputation of the leg. The leg is amputated. Who is liable? *See People v. Lewis*, 124 Cal. 551, 57 P. 470 (1899) (criminal case).

3. California has adopted the "substantial factor" test by way of jury instructions as the test for cause in fact. *See Mitchell v. Gonzales*, 54 Cal. 3d 1041, 1 Cal. Rptr. 2d 913, 819 P.2d 872 (1991).

4. In contemporary products liability cases, only the substantial factor test is generally used by the courts. Why?

5. The Restatement (Third) of Torts provides:

§ 26: *Factual Cause*

Tortious conduct must be a factual cause of physical harm for liability to be imposed. Conduct is a factual cause of harm when the harm would not have occurred absent the conduct.

In 1993 the American Law institute (A.L.I), publishers of the Restatement, began a campaign to make it more difficult for victims to sue corporations who manufactured toxic substance such as, tobacco, asbestos, and defective pharmaceuticals. The attack on victims took the form of removing strict liability from the attorney's arsenal. *See* Frank J. Vandall, *Constructing a Roof Before the Foundation Is Prepared: The Restatement (Third) Products Liability: Section 2(b) Design Defect*, 30 Mich. J.L.R. 261 (1997).

The second offensive by the A.L.I. was to argue that joint and several liability was unfair to corporate defendants. They advocated for several liability. This means the victims will lose a percentage or all of her damages. *See* Frank J. Vandall, *A Critique of the Restatement (Third), Apportionment as It Affects Joint and Several Liability*, 49 Emory L.J. 565 (2000).

A recent challenge by the A.L.I. to victims of toxic substance is to require proof of cause in fact solely by use of the "but for" test and to deep six the "substantial factor" test: The black letter of § 27 [Restatement (Third) of Torts] states: "If multiple acts occur, each of which under § 26 alone would have been a factual cause of the physical harm at the same time in the absence of the other act(s), each act is regarded as a factual cause of harm." *June v. Union Carbide Corp.*, 577 F.3d 1234 (10th Cir. 2009).

The problem is that when a smoker dies from cancer of the lungs, she very often also has other diseases. The same can be said of prescription drug victims, they are often sick from other illnesses. Therefore, use of the "but for" test makes it extremely difficult or impossible for the victim to win. The result is that the victims go uncompensated and corporate balance sheets are enhanced with a windfall. *See* Frank J. Vandall, A History of Civil Litigation: Political and Economic Perspectives (Oxford University Press 2011).

PROBLEM

A developer would like to purchase Jane's property because it is located between two streams (A and B) that join to form a third stream. Strong odors emanate from stream A, because of the material that Alvin discharges into stream A upstream of Jane. Likewise, unpleasant odors waft up from stream B because of Ben's discharges into stream B upstream from Jane. The developer refuses to buy until the odors are abated. If Jane sues under the "but for" test, what result? (Assume the case occurred prior to 1972. What happened to the law in 1972?)

C. FAILURE TO IDENTIFY THE SPECIFIC ACTOR

SUMMERS v. TICE
Supreme Court of California, 1948
33 Cal. 2d 80, 199 P.2d 1

Actions by Charles A. Summers against Harold W. Tice and against Ernest Simonson for negligently shooting plaintiff while hunting. From judgments for plaintiff, defendants appeal, and the appeals were consolidated pursuant to stipulation.

CARTER, JUSTICE.

. . . .

Plaintiffs action was against both defendants for an injury to his right eye . . . as the result of being struck by bird shot discharged from a shotgun. . . . Defendant Tice flushed a quail which rose in flight to a 10-foot elevation and flew between plaintiff and defendants. Both defendants shot at the quail, shooting in plaintiff s direction. . . . One shot struck plaintiff in his eye. . . . [I]t was found by the court that as the direct result of the shooting by defendants the shots struck plaintiff . . . and that defendants were negligent in so shooting and plaintiff was not contributorily negligent.

. . . .

The problem presented in this case is whether the judgment against both defendants may stand. It is argued by defendants that they are not joint tort feasors, and thus jointly and severally liable, as they were not acting in concert, and that there is not sufficient evidence to show which defendant was guilty of the negligence which caused the injuries. . . . The one shot that entered plaintiffs eye was the major factor in assessing damages and that shot could not have come from the gun of both defendants. It was from one or the other only.

It has been held that where a group of persons are on a hunting party, or otherwise engaged in the use of firearms, and two of them are negligent in firing in the direction of a third person who is injured thereby, both of those so firing are liable for the injury suffered by the third person, although the negligence of only one of them could have caused the injury. . . . These cases speak of the action of defendants as being in concert as the ground of decision, yet it would seem they are straining that concept and the more reasonable basis appears in *Oliver v. Miles*, 110 So. 666. There two persons were hunting together. Both shot at some partridges and in so doing shot across the highway injuring plaintiff who was travelling on it. The court stated they were acting in concert and thus both were liable. The court then stated: "We think that . . . each is liable for the resulting injury to the boy, although no one can say definitely who actually shot him. *To hold otherwise would be to exonerate both from liability, although each was negligent, and the injury resulted from such negligence*" [Emphasis added.] . . . "The real reason for the rule that each joint tortfeasor is responsible for the whole damage is the practical unfairness of denying the injured person redress simply because he cannot prove how much damage each did, when it is certain that between them they did all; let them be the ones to apportion it among themselves." . . . (Wigmore, Select Cases on the Law of Torts, sec. 153.) . . .

When we consider the relative position of the parties and the results that would flow if plaintiff was required to pin the injury on one of the defendants only, a requirement that the burden of proof on that subject be shifted to defendants becomes manifest. They are both wrongdoers — both negligent toward plaintiff. They brought about a situation where the negligence of one of them injured the plaintiff, hence it should rest with them each to absolve himself if he can. The injured party has been placed by defendants in the unfair position of pointing to which defendant caused the harm. If one can escape the other may also and plaintiff is remediless. Ordinarily defendants are in a far better position to offer evidence to determine which one caused the injury. . . .

[I]t should be pointed out that the same reasons of policy and justice shift the burden to each of defendants to absolve himself if he can — relieving the wronged person of the duty of apportioning the injury to a particular defendant, apply here where we are concerned with whether plaintiff is required to supply evidence for the apportionment of damages. If defendants are independent tort feasors and thus each liable for the damage caused by him alone, and, at least, where the matter of apportionment is incapable of proof, the innocent wronged party should not be deprived of his right to redress. The wrongdoers should be left to work out between themselves any apportionment. . . .

We have seen that for the reasons of policy discussed herein, the case is based upon the legal proposition that, under the circumstances here presented, each defendant is liable for the whole damage whether they are deemed to be acting in concert or independently.

The judgment is affirmed.

———————

1.   Determining cause in fact in multiple-car crashes may be challenging. Suppose three cars negligently collide with each other and Barbara, a passenger in one of the cars, is injured. Does the rule in Summers apply? *See Murphy v. Taxicabs of Louisville, Inc.*, 330 S.W.2d 395 (Ky. 1959).

How is this different from the res ipsa loquitur car crashes we looked at in the Negligence chapter? There we said that res ipsa loquitur does not apply when the only evidence is that one car crashed into another and a passenger was injured.

2.   Don negligently drove his car onto the railroad tracks after the crossing light began blinking. The gate operator negligently lowered both gates, trapping Don's car on the tracks. Wanda, a passenger in Don's car, jumped out and broke her leg trying to escape from the oncoming train. How is this case different from *Summers?* What result? *Washington & Georgetown R.R. Co. v. Hickey*, 166 U.S. 521 (1897).

3.   In *Hill v. Edmonds*, 26 A.D.2d 554, 270 N.Y.S.2d 1020 (1966), the court held: "Where separate acts of negligence combine to produce directly a single injury each

tortfeasor is responsible for the entire result, even though his act alone might not have caused it."

4. Thirty-seven Canadian families sued three corporations, located across the Detroit River in the United States, for emitting noxious pollutants. Does the *Summers* rule apply? Yes. The defendants were treated as joint tort-feasors because "the independent acts of several actors concur to produce indivisible harmful consequences." *Michie v. Great Lakes Steel Div., Nat'l Steel Corp.*, 495 F.2d 213 (1974).

5. The introductory paragraph to this chapter states that cause in fact is a question of fact, but proximate cause is a question of policy. What policies are involved in *Summers v. Tice?*

HYMOWITZ v. ELI LILLY & CO.
Court of Appeals of New York, 1989
73 N.Y.2d 487, 541 N.Y.S.2d 941, 539 N.E.2d 1069, *cert. denied*, 493 U.S. 944, 110 S. Ct. 350

WACHTLER, CHIEF JUDGE.

Plaintiffs in these appeals allege that they were injured by the drug diethylstilbestrol (DES) ingested by their mothers during pregnancy. They seek relief against defendant DES manufacturers. While not class actions, these cases are representative of nearly 500 similar actions pending in the courts in this State. . . . With this in mind, we now resolve the issue twice expressly left open by this court, and adopt a market share theory, using a national market, for determining liability and apportioning damages in DES cases in which identification of the manufacturer of the drug that injured the plaintiff is impossible. . . .

In 1947, the FDA began approving the NDAs (New Drug Application) of manufacturers to market DES for the purpose of preventing human miscarriages. . . . In 1971, however, the FDA banned the use of DES as a miscarriage preventative, when studies established the harmful latent effects of DES upon the offspring of mothers who took the drug. Specifically, tests indicated that DES caused vaginal adenocarcinoma, a form of cancer, and adenosis, a precancerous vaginal or cervical growth.

. . . [N]ot only is identification of the manufacturer of the DES ingested in a particular case generally impossible, but, due to the latent nature of DES injuries, many claims were barred by the Statute of Limitations before the injury was discovered.

The identification problem has many causes. All DES was of identical chemical composition. Druggists usually filled prescriptions from whatever was on hand. Approximately 300 manufacturers produced the drug, with companies entering and leaving the market continuously during the 24 years that DES was sold for pregnancy use. The long latency period of a DES injury compounds the identification problem; memories fade, records are lost or destroyed, and witnesses die. Thus the pregnant women who took DES generally never knew who produced the drug they took, and there was no reason to attempt to discover this fact until many years after ingestion, at which time the information is not available.

[I]n DES cases it is a "practical impossibility for most victims [to] pinpoint . . . the manufacturer directly responsible for their particular injury". . . .

The present appeals are before the court in the context of summary judgment motions. In all of the appeals defendants moved for summary judgment dismissing the complaints because plaintiffs could not identify the manufacturer of the drug that allegedly injured them. . . . The trial court denied all of these motions. . . .

In a products liability action, identification of the exact defendant whose product injured the plaintiff is, of course, generally required. . . . The record now before us, however, presents the question of whether a DES plaintiff may recover against a DES manufacturer when identification of the producer of the specific drug that caused the injury is impossible.

. . . [T]he accepted tort doctrines of alternative liability and concerted action are available in some personal injury cases to permit recovery where the precise identification of a wrongdoer is impossible. However, we agree with the near unanimous views of the high State courts that have considered the matter that these doctrines in their unaltered common-law forms do not permit recovery in DES cases. . . .

The paradigm of alternative liability is found in the case of *Summers v. Tice.* . . .

In DES cases, however, there is a great number of possible wrongdoers, who entered and left the market at different times, and some of whom no longer exist. Additionally, in DES cases many years elapse between the ingestion of the drug and injury. Consequently, DES defendants are not in any better position than are plaintiffs to identify the manufacturer of the DES ingested in any given case, nor is there any real prospect of having all the possible producers before the court. Finally, while it may be fair to employ alternative liability in cases involving only a small number of potential wrongdoers, that fairness disappears with the decreasing probability that any one of the defendants actually caused the injury. This is particularly true when applied to DES where the chance that a particular producer caused the injury is often very remote. . . . Alternative liability, therefore, provides DES plaintiffs no relief.

Nor does the theory of concerted action, in its pure form, supply a basis for recovery. This doctrine, seen in drag racing cases, provides for joint and several liability on the part of all defendants having an understanding, express or tacit, to participate in "a common plan or design to commit a tortious act". . . . There is nothing in the record, however, beyond this similar conduct to show any agreement, tacit or otherwise, to market DES for pregnancy use without taking proper steps to ensure the drug's safety. . . .

In short, extant common-law doctrines, unmodified, provide no relief for the DES plaintiff unable to identify the manufacturer of the drug that injured her. . . .

We conclude that the present circumstances call for recognition of a realistic avenue of relief for plaintiffs injured by DES. . . . [W]e perceive that here judicial action is again required to overcome the "'inordinately difficult problems of proof'" . . .

Indeed, it would be inconsistent with the reasonable expectations of a modern society to say to these plaintiffs that because of the insidious nature of an injury that long remains dormant, and because so many manufacturers, each behind a curtain, contributed to the devastation, the cost of injury should be borne by the innocent and not the wrongdoers. This is particularly so where the Legislature consciously created these expectations by reviving hundreds of DES cases. Consequently, the ever-evolving dictates of justice and fairness, which are the heart of our common-law system, require formation of a remedy for injuries caused by DES. . . .

We stress, however, that the DES situation is a singular case, with manufacturers acting in a parallel manner to produce an identical, generically marketed product, which causes injury many years later, and which has evoked a legislative response reviving previously barred actions. Given this unusual scenario, it is more appropriate that the loss be borne by those that produced the drug for use during pregnancy, rather than by those who were injured by the use, even where the precise manufacturer of the drug cannot be identified in a particular action. We turn then to the question of how to fairly and equitably apportion the loss occasioned by DES, in a case where the exact manufacturer of the drug that caused the injury is unknown. . . .

A narrower basis for liability, tailored more closely to the varying culpable-ness of individual DES producers, is the market share concept. . . . It first loosened the requirement that all possible wrongdoers be before the court, and instead made a "substantial share" sufficient. The court then held that each defendant who could not prove that it did not actually injure plaintiff would be liable according to that manufacturer's market share. The court's central justification for adopting this approach was its belief that limiting a defendant's liability to its market share will result, over the run of cases, in liability on the part of a defendant roughly equal to the injuries the defendant actually caused. . . .

In the recent case of *Brown v. Superior Ct.* (44 Cal. 3d 1049, 751 P.2d 470), the California Supreme Court resolved some apparent ambiguity in *Sindell v. Abbott Labs.* [26 Cal. 3d 588, 163 Cal. Rptr. 132, 607 P.2d 924], and held that a manufacturer's liability is several only, and, in cases in which all manufacturers in the market are not joined for any reason, liability will still be limited to market share, resulting in a less than 100% recovery for a plaintiff. Finally, it is noteworthy that determining market shares under *Sindell v. Abbott Labs*, proved difficult and engendered years of litigation. After attempts at using smaller geographical units, it was eventually determined that the national market provided the most feasible and fair solution. . . .

Turning to the structure to be adopted in New York, we heed both the lessons learned through experience in other jurisdictions and the realities of the mass litigation of DES claims in this State. Balancing these considerations, we are led to the conclusion that a market share theory, based upon a national market, provides the best solution. . . .

Consequently, for essentially practical reasons, we adopt a market share theory using a national market. We are aware that the adoption of a national market will likely result in a disproportion between the liability of individual manufacturers and the actual injuries each manufacturer caused in this State. Thus our market share theory cannot be founded upon the belief that, over the run of cases, liability will approximate causation in this State. . . . Nor does the use of a national market provide a reasonable link between liability and the risk created by a defendant to a particular plaintiff. . . . Instead, we choose to apportion liability so as to correspond to the over-all culpability of each defendant, measured by the amount of risk of injury each defendant created to the public-at-large. Use of a national market is a fair method, we believe, of apportioning defendants' liabilities according to their total culpability in marketing DES for use during pregnancy. Under the circumstances, this is an equitable way to provide plaintiffs with the relief they deserve, while also rationally distributing the responsibility for plaintiffs' injuries among defendants.

To be sure, a defendant cannot be held liable if it did not participate in the marketing of DES for pregnancy use; if a DES producer satisfies its burden of proof of showing that it was not a member of the market of DES sold for pregnancy use, disallowing exculpation would be unfair and unjust. Nevertheless, because liability here is based on the over-all risk produced, and not causation in a single case, there should be no exculpation of a defendant who, although a member of the market producing DES for pregnancy use, appears not to have caused a particular plaintiffs injury. It is merely a windfall for a producer to escape liability solely because it manufactured a more identifiable pill, or sold only to certain drugstores. These fortuities in no way diminish the culpability of a defendant for marketing the product, which is the basis of liability here.

Finally, we hold that the liability of DES producers is several only, and should not be inflated when all participants in the market are not before the court in a particular case. We understand that, as a practical matter, this will prevent some plaintiffs from recovering 100% of their damages. However, we eschewed exculpation to prevent the fortuitous avoidance of liability, and thus, equitably, we decline to unleash the same forces to increase a defendant's liability beyond its fair share of responsibility.[3]

---

[3] The dissenter misapprehends the basis for liability here. We have not by the backdoor adopted a theory of concerted action. We avoided extending this theory, because its concomitant requirement of joint and several liability expands the burden on small manufacturers beyond a rational or fair limit. This result is reached by the dissent, not by the majority, so that criticism on this front is misplaced.

We are confronted here with an unprecedented identification problem, and have provided a solution that rationally apportions liability. We have heeded the practical lessons learned by other jurisdictions, resulting in our adoption of a national market theory with full knowledge that it concedes the lack of a logical link between liability and causation in a single case. The dissent ignores these lessons, and, endeavoring to articulate a theory it perceives to be closer to traditional law, sets out a construct in which liability is based upon chance, not upon the fair assessment of the acts of defendants. Under the dissent's theory, a manufacturer with a large market share may avoid liability in many cases just because it manufactured a memorably shaped pill. Conversely, a small manufacturer can be held jointly liable for the full amount of every DES injury in this State simply because the shape of its product was not remarkable, even though the odds, realistically, are exceedingly long that the small manufacturer caused the injury in any one particular case.

Therefore, although the dissent's theory based upon a "shifting the burden of proof and joint and

The constitutionality of the revival statute remains to be considered (see L. 1986, ch. 682, § 4). This section revives, for the period of one year, actions for damages caused by the latent effects of DES, tungsten-carbide, asbestos, chlordane, and polyvinylchloride. . . .

As it pertains to DES, surely the revival statute has a rational basis, and the Legislature acted within its broad range of discretion in enacting the law. . . . Accordingly, in each case the order of the Appellate Division should be affirmed, with costs, and the certified question answered in the affirmative.

MOLLEN, JUDGE (concurring in *Hymowitz and Hanfling*; and dissenting in part in *Tigue* and *Dolan*).

. . . .

The principle of market share liability in DES litigation was first espoused by the California Supreme Court in *Sindell v. Abbott Labs, (supra)*, as a valid theory of manufacturer's liability based upon each manufacturer's share of the market. This approach provides DES plaintiffs with a means by which to recover damages for their injuries without the plaintiffs being held to the traditional tort requirement of identifying the actual wrongdoer. The public policy underpinnings of the *Sindell* rationale is that, from a perspective of fairness and equity, the DES manufacturers are in a better position than the innocent plaintiffs who have sustained grievous injuries to bear the cost of such injuries. Thus, the *Sindell* court held that once a plaintiff has joined a "substantial share" of the DES manufacturers of the relevant market in the action and has established that the sustained injuries were caused by the ingestion of DES by the plaintiffs mother during pregnancy, the burden of proof shifts to each defendant to demonstrate, by a preponderance of the evidence, that it did not produce or market the pill ingested by the plaintiffs mother. Those DES defendants who could not exculpate themselves, would then be liable for the proportion of the judgment which represented its share of the market. The intended result of the *Sindell* approach is that, "each manufacturer's liability for [a particular DES] injury would be approximately equivalent to the damage caused by the DES it manufactured". . . .

I cannot agree that the imposition of liability on drug companies, in this case DES manufacturers, solely upon their contribution, in some measure, to the risk of injury by producing and marketing a defective drug, without any consideration given to whether the defendant drug companies actually caused the plaintiffs injuries, is appropriate or warranted. Rather, I would adopt a market share theory of liability, based upon a national market, which would provide for the shifting of the burden of proof on the issue of causation to the defendants and would impose liability upon all of the defendants who produced and marketed DES for pregnancy purposes, except those who were able to prove that their product could not have caused the injury. Under this approach, DES plaintiffs, who are unable to identify

---

several liability is facially reminiscent of prior law, in the case of DES it is nothing more than advocating that bare fortuity be the test for liability. When faced with the novel identification problem posed by DES cases, it is preferable to adopt a new theory that apportions fault rationally, rather than to contort extant doctrines beyond the point at which they provide a sound premise for determining liability.

the actual manufacturer of the pill ingested by their mother, would only be required to establish, (1) that the plaintiffs mother ingested DES during pregnancy; (2) that the plaintiffs injuries were caused by DES; and (3) that the defendant or defendants produced and marketed DES for pregnancy purposes. Thereafter, the burden of proof would shift to the defendants to exculpate themselves by establishing, by a preponderance of the evidence, that the plaintiffs mother could not have ingested their particular pill. Of those defendants who are unable to exculpate themselves from liability, their respective share of the plaintiffs damages would be measured by their share of the national market of DES produced and marketed for pregnancy purposes during the period in question.

---

1.   There have been numerous permutations of the Sindell decision. Wisconsin, for example, held that if the defendant manufactured the same color of DES pill as consumed by plaintiffs mother, the plaintiff could recover 100% of her damages from that single manufacturer. *Collins v. Eli Lilly Co.*, 116 Wis. 2d 166, 342 N.W.2d 37 (1984).

In Washington, the plaintiff was required to sue only one manufacturer of DES, and the burden was then shifted to the defendant to implead other manufacturers. *Martin v. Abbott Labs*, 102 Wash. 2d 581, 689 P.2d 368 (1984). *See also Conley v. Boyle Drug Co.*, 570 So. 2d 275 (Fla. 1990).

2.   In terms of whether DES caused the cancer, the case is somewhat simple because the DES cancer is a "signature disease." Only DES causes that particular type of cancer.

3.   What is the difference between joint liability and several liability? What makes more sense in DES cases? *See Brown v. Superior Ct.*, 44 Cal. 3d 1049, 245 Cal. Rptr. 412, 751 P.2d 470 (1988).

4.   What percentage of damages does the plaintiff recover in *Hymowitz?* Under *Hymowitz*, does the plaintiff have to join a "substantial share" of the market?

5.   Is it fair to not permit defendants to be dismissed from the suit if they can prove that they did not manufacture the DES pill that the plaintiffs mother took? (Different color, sold to other pharmacy.)

6.   Courts have adopted market share theory outside the DES context. Most notable are Factor VIII (HIV-tainted blood clotting agents for hemophiliacs) in *Smith v. Cutter Biological, Inc.*, Div. of Miles, Inc., 823 P.2d 717 (Haw. 1991), *Ray v. Cutter Labs., Div. of Miles, Inc.*, 754 F. Supp. 193 (M.D. Fla. 1991), and *Doe v. Cutter Biological, Inc., A Division of Miles, Inc.*, 971 F.2d 375 (9th Cir. 1992) (applying Hawaii law); asbestos-lined brake pads in California in *Wheeler v. Raybestos-Manhattan*, 8 Cal. App. 4th 1152, 11 Cal. Rptr. 2d 109 (1992), and *Richie v. Bridgestone/Firestone, Inc.*, 22 Cal. App. 4th 335, 27 Cal. Rptr. 2d 418 (1994); lead paint in *Jackson v. Glidden Co.*, 98 Ohio App. 3d 100, 647 N.E.2d 879 (1995); and the vaccine for DPT in *Morris v. Parke, Davis & Co.*, 667 F. Supp. 1332 (C.D. Cal. 1987).

Many courts have been reluctant to extend market share liability outside the DES context, however. *See Skipworth v. Lead Indus. Assoc.*, 665 A.2d 1288 (Pa. Super. Ct. 1995) (lead paint); *White v. Celotex Corp.*, 907 F.2d 104 (9th Cir. 1990) (applying Arizona law) (asbestos); *In re New York State Silicone Breast Implant Litig.*, 166 Misc. 2d 85, 631 N.Y.S.2d 491 (Sup. Ct. 1995) (breast implants); *Doe v. Cutter Biological, A Div. of Miles, Inc.*, 852 F. Supp. 909 (D. Idaho 1994) (Factor VIII); *Miller v. Wyeth Labs.*, 43 F.3d 1483 (10th Cir. 1994) (applying Oklahoma law) (DPT vaccine); *Bixler v. Avondale Mills*, 405 N.W.2d 428 (Minn. Ct. App. 1987) (cotton flannel nightshirt).

The highest courts of the following states have rejected market share liability in the DES context and require the plaintiff to prove the identity of the tort-feasor: *Gorman v. Abbott Labs.*, 599 A.2d 1364 (R.I. 1991); *Smith v. Eli Lilly & Co.*, 137 Ill. 2d 222, 560 N.E.2d 324 (1990); *Mulcahy v. Eli Lilly & Co.*, 386 N.W.2d 67 (Iowa 1986); *Zafft v. Eli Lilly & Co.*, 676 S.W.2d 241 (Mo. 1984).

7. The first case to hold several defendants liable, including those who could not have caused the injury, was *Hall v. E.I. DuPont de Nemours & Co.*, 345 F. Supp. 353 (E.D.N.Y. 1972). Thirteen children were injured by the explosion of blasting caps in twelve separate incidents. The court held that the six manufacturers of blasting caps had acted in concert because they agreed on one formula and worked through a common trade association to produce an interchangeable and faulty product. *Sindell* and *Hymowitz* rejected *Hall* because there was no "concert of action" by the DES manufacturers.

8. The "market share" theory has its origin in a student note, Comment, *DES and a Proposed Theory of Enterprise Liability*, 46 Fordham L. Rev. 963 (1978). *See also* Fischer, *Products Liability — An Analysis of Market Share Liability*, 34 Vand. L. Rev. 1623 (1981); Schwartz & Mahshigian, *Failure to Identify the Defendant in Tort Law: Towards a Legislative Solution*, 73 Cal. L. Rev. 941 (1985).

D. DIFFICULTIES IN PROOF OF CAUSATION

FALCON v. MEMORIAL HOSPITAL
Supreme Court of Michigan, 1990
436 Mich. 443, 462 N.W.2d 44

LEVIN, JUSTICE.

The deposition testimony of plaintiff Ruby Falcon's[1] expert witness tended to show that had the defendant physician, S.N. Kelso, Jr., followed the procedures the expert witness claims should have been followed, the patient, Nena J. Falcon, would have had a 37.5 percent opportunity[2] of surviving the medical accident that was a cause of her death.

The trial court dismissed the complaint because Falcon's evidence did not show

---

[1] The plaintiff is Ruby Falcon, administratrix of the estate of her granddaughter, Nena Falcon.

[2] While "chance" and "opportunity" can be used interchangeably, "chance" includes "the absence of any cause of events that can be predicted, understood, or controlled," Random House Dictionary of the English Language, 2d ed, unabridged, p. 344, and "opportunity" includes "a situation or condition favorable for attainment of a goal." *Id.*, 1359.

that Nena Falcon probably — defined as more than fifty percent — would have survived if the procedure had not been omitted. The Court of Appeals reversed, stating that Falcon need only "establish that the omitted treatment or procedure had the potential for improving the patient's recovery or preventing the patient's death." . . . The Court added that "while a plaintiff must show some probability that the treatment would be successful, that probability need not be greater than fifty percent." We affirm.

I

The defendants contend that because the proofs at a trial of Falcon's claim would not show that it was probable, measured as more than fifty percent, that Nena Falcon would have avoided physical harm had the procedure not been omitted, Falcon cannot show that the asserted negligence of defendants caused her physical harm. . . .

II

Under the more probable, measured as more than fifty percent, approach to causation, a plaintiff who establishes that the patient would have had more than a fifty percent opportunity of not suffering physical harm had the defendant not acted negligently, recovers one hundred percent of the damages.

The better than even opportunity is compensated as if it were a certainty, although the patient's chances of a better result are significantly less than one hundred percent.

III

Other courts have permitted recovery for physical harm on a showing that the lost opportunity was a substantial, albeit fifty percent or less, factor in producing the harm. . . .

Some courts have held that the plaintiff need only show that the defendant's conduct was a substantial factor in producing the physical harm. Other courts allow recovery for loss of a fifty percent or less opportunity of achieving a better result without clearly articulating a standard of causation. A number of courts have so held on the basis of language in the Restatement Torts, 2d.

IV

Nena Falcon, a nineteen-year-old woman, gave birth to a healthy baby, Justice Eugene Falcon, in the early morning hours of March 21, 1973. Moments after delivery, Nena Falcon coughed, gagged, convulsed, became cyanotic, and suffered a complete respiratory and cardiac collapse. Attempts to revive her were unsuccessful. She was pronounced dead soon thereafter.

The autopsy report indicated that amniotic fluid embolism,[15] an unprevent-able complication that occurs in approximately one out of ten or twenty thousand births, was the cause of death. The survival rate of amniotic fluid embolism is, according to Falcon's expert witness, 37.5 percent if an intravenous line is connected to the patient before the onset of the embolism. In this case, an intravenous line had not been established.

Falcon's theory . . . is the intravenous line could have been used to infuse life-saving fluids into Nena Falcon's circulatory system, providing her a 37.5 percent opportunity of surviving. By not inserting the intravenous line, the physician deprived her of a 37.5 percent opportunity of surviving the embolism.

V

The defendant's failure to act is largely responsible for the uncertainty regarding causation.

Had the defendants in the instant case inserted an intravenous line, one of two things would have happened, Nena Falcon would have lived, or she would have died. . . . The United States Court of Appeals for the Fourth Circuit, observed:

> When a defendant's negligent action or inaction has effectively terminated a person's chance of survival, it does not lie in the defendant's mouth to raise conjectures as to the measure of the chances that he has put beyond the possibility of realization. If there was any substantial possibility of survival and the defendant has destroyed it, he is answerable. . . . The law does not in the existing circumstances require the plaintiff to show to a certainty that the patient would have lived had she been hospitalized and operated on promptly. . . ." [Emphasis in original.]

VI

. . . .

The physician expects the patient to pay or provide payment for the services, whether the likelihood of there in fact being any benefit to the patient is only one through fifty percent or is greater than fifty percent.

. . . [The defendants] contend that they should be subject to liability only for acts or omissions likely, to the extent of more than fifty percent, to have caused physical harm to the patient:

> The reasoning of the district court herein . . . in essence, declares open season on critically ill or injured persons as care providers would be free of

---

[15] An amniotic fluid embolism occurs when the amniotic fluid infuses into the mother's circulatory system, most often through a rent in the uterus or through the mother's pelvic veins. The amniotic fluid is not clear. It may contain undissolved matter such as fetal skin cells, lanugo, mucus, or meconium (excrement from the fetus' intestinal tract). The debris-filled fluid is taken up into the mother's circulatory system, pumped through her heart and into her lungs where the embolus lodges, causing injury, and often, death. Amniotic fluid embolism may be diagnosed in an autopsy by the presence of amniotic debris in the body's lungs.

liability for even the grossest malpractice if the patient had only a fifty-fifty chance of surviving the disease or injury even with proper treatment." . . .

. . . In reducing Nena Falcon's opportunity of living by failing to insert an intravenous line, her physician caused her harm, although it cannot be said, more probably than not, that he caused her death. A 37.5 percent opportunity of living is hardly the kind of opportunity that any of us would willingly allow our health care providers to ignore.

. . . .

VII

A number of courts have recognized, as we would, loss of an opportunity for a more favorable result, as distinguished from the unfavorable result, as compensable in medical malpractice actions. Under this approach, damages are recoverable for the loss of opportunity although the opportunity lost was less than even, and thus it is not more probable than not that the unfavorable result would or could have been avoided.

Under this approach, the plaintiff must establish more-probable-than-not causation. He must prove, more probably than not, that the defendant reduced the opportunity of avoiding harm.

VIII

We are persuaded that loss of a 37.5 percent opportunity of living constitutes a loss of a substantial opportunity of avoiding physical harm. We need not now decide what lesser percentage would constitute a substantial loss of opportunity.

IX

. . . In this case, 37.5 percent times the damages recoverable for wrongful death would be an appropriate measure of damages.

. . . .

We would affirm the Court of Appeals reversal of the entry of summary judgment for the defendants, and remand the case for trial.

---

1. What damages does the plaintiff recover in Falcon? The dissenting opinion in Falcon states:

> The lost chance theory is most fully explained in King, *Causation, Valuation, and Chance in Personal Injury Torts Involving Preexisting Conditions and Future Consequences*, 90 Yale L.J. 1353 (1981). The theory is premised on the reasoning that chance itself is an injury entitled to redress, and that chance should be measured by a mathematical percentage probability test:

> > A plaintiff ordinarily should be required to prove by the applicable

standard of proof that the defendant caused the loss in question. *What* caused a loss, however, should be a separate question from what the *nature and extent* of the loss are. This distinction seems to have eluded the courts, with the result that lost chances in many respects are compensated either as certainties or not at all.

To illustrate, consider the case in which a doctor negligently fails to diagnose a patient's cancerous condition until it has become inoperable. Assume further that even with a timely diagnosis the patient would have had only a 30% chance of recovering from the disease and surviving over the long term. There are two ways of handling such a case. Under the traditional approach, this loss of a not-better-than-even chance of recovering from the cancer would not be compensable because it did not appear more likely [than] not that the patient would have survived with proper care. Recoverable damages, if any, would depend on the extent to which it appeared that cancer killed the patient sooner than it would have with timely diagnosis and treatment, and on the extent to which the delay in diagnosis aggravated the patient's condition, such as by causing additional pain. A more rational approach, however, would allow recovery for the loss of the chance of cure even though the chance was not better than even. The probability of long-term survival would be reflected in the amount of damages awarded for the loss of the chance. While the plaintiff here could not prove by a preponderance of the evidence that he was denied a cure by the defendant's negligence, he could show by a preponderance that he was deprived of a 30% chance of a cure. *Id.*, pp. 1363-1364.

A number of cases adopting the lost chance of survival theory also adopt Professor King's statistical approach, holding that if a decedent had, for example, a thirty percent chance of survival, then compensation should be awarded for thirty percent of the value of the decedent's life.

Falcon, 462 N.W.2d at 63, 64.

2. Justice Boyle's concurring opinion in *Falcon* raises the issue of injuries other than death:

I concur in the recognition of "lost opportunity to survive" as injury for which tort law should allow recovery in proportion to the extent of the lost chance of survival, . . . provided that the negligence of the defendant more probably than not caused the loss of opportunity. However, I would emphasize that the Court today is called upon to decide the viability of a claim for "lost opportunity" only where the ultimate harm to the victim is death. Thus, any language in the lead opinion suggesting that a similar cause of action might lie for a lost opportunity of avoiding lesser physical harm is dicta. Whether the social and policy factors which justify compensation for a lost chance of survival would justify recovery for the loss of a chance to avoid some lesser harm is a question for another day.

Falcon, 462 N.W.2d at 57, 58.

If Nena Falcon had suffered partial paralysis of her legs because of the embolism and the failure to connect an intravenous line, should she be able to recover? Why might the courts draw the line of recovery at death?

3. Does the lost chance of survival theory fundamentally alter the meaning of causation? Justice Riley (dissenting) argued:

> The recognition of a lost chance as a cognizable injury is necessarily based on the reasoning that but for the defendant's negligence, the plaintiff *might possibly* have avoided an adverse result. Thus, recognition of lost chance as a recoverable interest contradicts the very notion of cause in fact. Professor King aptly characterizes a lost chance as a "raffle ticket" destroyed by the defendant's negligence. King, *supra*, p. 1378. King advocates compensation for "statistically demonstrable losses," *id.*, p. 1377, so that a person deprived of a forty percent chance of survival should be compensated for forty percent of the compensable value of his life. *Id.*, p. 1382. Thus, tort law is transformed from a compensatory system to a payout scheme on the basis of a statistical chance that the defendant caused the plaintiff's death.

Falcon, 462 N.W.2d at 65. Critique Riley's reasoning.

4. In *Herskovits v. Group Health Coop, of Puget Sound*, 99 Wash. 2d 609, 664 P.2d 474 (1983), the court permitted recovery for a 14% reduction in the opportunity for survival. The case involved a failure to diagnose cancer in a patient who was certain to die of the disease. The *Falcon* majority stated:

> The Supreme Court of Washington permitted the personal representative of the patient to maintain an action where there was expert testimony of a fourteen percentage point reduction — from thirty-nine percent to twenty-five percent — in the patient's opportunity for survival, which was claimed to have resulted from a delay in diagnosis of lung cancer. *Herskovits v. Group Health Cooperative of Puget Sound*, 99 Wash. 2d 609; 664 P.2d 474 (1983). The majority, . . . agreed, that recovery for "[causing reduction of the opportunity to recover (loss of chance) by one's negligence, however, does not necessitate a total recovery against the negligent party for all damages caused by the victim's death."

Falcon, 462 N.W.2d at 54.

5. The loss of chance theory was rejected in *Fennell v. Southern Md. Hosp. Center, Inc.*, 320 Md. 776, 580 A.2d 206 (1990). The plaintiff sued for loss of a 40% chance of surviving meningitis. The majority reasoned:

> Since loss of chance damages are only permitted when the patient dies, it is also arguable that, when we strip away the rhetoric, damages are really being awarded for the *possibility* that the negligence was a cause of the death. Maryland law clearly does not allow damages based on mere possibilities.
>
> Another factor weighing against adoption of a loss of chance damages approach is its practical application in civil jury trials. Probabilities and statistical evidence comprise a substantial portion of the evidence submit-

ted to the trier of fact in loss of chance actions. This evidence will generally be in the form of opinions based on statistics that show chance of survival of other individuals similarly situated to the victim. The use of statistics in trials is subject to criticism as being unreliable, misleading, easily manipulated, and confusing to a jury. When large damage awards will be based on the statistical chance of survival before the negligent treatment, minus the statistical chance of survival after the negligent treatment, times the value of the lost life, we can imagine the bewildering sets of numbers with which the jury will be confronted, as well as the difficulties juries will have in assessing the comparative reliability of the divergent statistical evidence offered by each side.

Id. at 213. Argue against the Maryland court's reasoning, or for it.

6. Informed consent, discussed in the Negligence chapter, may be important in these cases.

7. Suppose a singer, who is very popular with teenagers, records a song that says: "When your girlfriend leaves you, parents throw you out and you are failing math and gym, take a gun or pills and check out." Chucky, age 17, is found dead with the teenage angst CD in the player. Argue for cause in fact against the record company and the singer. *See McCollum v. CBS, Inc.*, 202 Cal. App. 3d 989, 249 Cal. Rptr. 187 (1988), where liability was rejected.

What about a rape that is presented on television and later imitated on the street? *See Olivia N. v. National Broadcasting Co.*, 126 Cal. App. 3d 488, 178 Cal. Rptr. 888 (1981), rejecting liability on constitutional principles. *See* Krattenmaker & Powe, *Televised Violence: First Amendment Principles and Social Science Theory*, 64 Va. L. Rev. 1123 (1978).

PROBLEM

Several states sued tobacco manufacturers to recover the medical costs of treating patients for sickness and disease allegedly caused by smoking. The manufacturers will likely argue that each patient must prove that smoking caused his or her specific illness. Argue for or against the proposition that the costs of treating numerous patients can be grouped together in one suit and that statistical proof (smoking caused 30% of these illnesses) is sufficient to send the case to the jury.

GEORGIA-PACIFIC CORP. v. BOSTIC
Court of Appeals of Texas, 2010
2010 Tex. App. LEXIS 7072

FILLMORE, J.

. . . . In February 2003, Timothy Bostic's wife, son, father, and mother brought wrongful death claims and a survival action against Georgia-Pacific and numerous other entities alleging Timothy's death was caused by exposure to asbestos. At the time of trial, Georgia-Pacific was the sole remaining defendant, the other named defendants having settled or been dismissed. . . . The jury returned a verdict in favor of appellees, finding Georgia-Pacific seventy-five percent liable and Knox Glass, Inc., a non-party former employer of Timothy, twenty-five percent liable for Timothy's death. The jury awarded $7,554,907 in compensatory damages and $6,038,910 in punitive damages.

Georgia-Pacific appealed.

LEGAL SUFFICIENCY OF THE EVIDENCE

In its first issue, Georgia-Pacific asserts there is legally insufficient evidence that Georgia-Pacific asbestos-containing joint compound caused Timothy's mesothelioma, a form of cancer usually linked to asbestos exposure. Georgia-Pacific asserts there is no evidence Timothy was exposed to Georgia-Pacific asbestos-containing joint compound, and even if there was evidence of exposure, there is no evidence of dose. Further, Georgia-Pacific asserts that even if there was evidence of exposure and dose, the record contains no epidemiological studies showing that persons similar to Timothy with exposure to asbestos-containing joint compound had an increased risk of developing mesothelioma. . . . Georgia-Pacific asserts that for each of these reasons, appellees' negligence and defective marketing claims against Georgia-Pacific fail as a matter of law.

Joint compound, sometimes called "drywall mud," is used to connect and smooth the seams of adjoining pieces of drywall, also called sheetrock, and to cover nail heads on sheets of drywall. Joint compound is spread in a thin coat and then smoothed. After it dries, uneven areas are further smoothed by sanding. This process is sometimes carried out multiple times in further refining the surface.

. . . .

In 2002, Timothy was diagnosed with mesothelioma at the age of forty. He died in 2003. Appellees claim Timothy's mesothelioma was caused by his exposure to asbestos-containing joint compound manufactured by Georgia-Pacific. Georgia-Pacific acknowledged there is some evidence that Timothy used or was present during the use of joint compound between 1967 and 1977, but contends there is no evidence of exposure to Georgia-Pacific asbestos-containing joint compound. (fundamental principle of products liability law is plaintiff must prove defendant supplied product which caused injury).

. . . .

Timothy testified he had been around drywall work his entire life, and he recalled that before the age of ten, he observed his father performing drywall work. He stated he mixed and sanded joint compound from the age of five. He testified he recalled at a young age helping his father "mud the holes" with joint compound. While he did not provide any more specifics of drywall work he performed with his father before 1977, he believed he used and was exposed to Georgia-Pacific joint compound before he graduated from high school in 1980. Timothy's work history sheets also indicate he worked with and around other brands of asbestos-containing joint compounds.

. . . .

Harold [Tim's father] testified he used Georgia-Pacific joint compound ninety-eight percent of the time that he did drywall work. He testified he tried one or two other brands of joint compound, but he always returned to Georgia-Pacific's product. With one exception listed below, Harold said he could not positively associate Georgia-Pacific's product with any specific drywall job. On this record, we disagree with Georgia-Pacific's argument that there is no evidence Timothy was exposed to Georgia-Pacific asbestos-containing joint compound.

Substantial-Factor Causation

. . . .

Georgia-Pacific contends that appellees failed to introduce evidence sufficient to satisfy the "substantial factor" standard of causation set forth in Flores, because appellees produced no evidence of cause-in-fact. In the context of an asbestos case, the Texas Supreme Court explained that "asbestos in the defendant's product [must be] a substantial factor in bringing about the plaintiff's injuries." *Flores, 232 S.W.3d at 770.* The court agreed that the "frequency, regularity, and proximity" test for exposure to asbestos set out in *Lohrmann v. Pittsburgh Corning Corp., 782 F.2d 1156 (4th Cir. 1986),* is appropriate. *Flores, 232 S.W.3d at 769; see also Lohrmann, 782 F.2d at 1162-63* (to support reasonable inference of substantial causation from circumstantial evidence, there must be evidence of exposure to specific product on regular basis over extended period of time in proximity to where plaintiff actually worked). The supreme court stated, however, that the terms "frequency," "regularity," and "proximity" do not "capture the emphasis [Texas] jurisprudence has placed on causation as an essential predicate to liability," and agreed with *Lohrmann's* analysis that the asbestos exposure must be a substantial factor in causing the asbestos-related disease. *Fleers, 232 S.W.3d at 769; see also Lohrmann, 782 F.2d at 1162.*

. . . .

Appellees assert that *Flores* does not require "but-for" causation in proving specific causation and that Flores requires only that appellees prove Timothy's exposure to Georgia-Pacific asbestos-containing joint compound was a "substantial factor" in contributing to his risk of mesothelioma. We disagree. The Texas Supreme Court [has] recognized that '[c]ommon to both proximate and producing cause is causation in fact, including the requirement that the defendant's conduct or product be a substantial factor in bringing about the plaintiff's injuries. Thus, to establish substantial-factor causation, a plaintiff must prove that the defendant's conduct was a cause-in-fact of the harm. *See Flores, 232 S.W.3d at 770.* "In asbestos cases, then, we must determine whether the asbestos in the defendant's product was a substantial factor in bringing about the plaintiff's injuries" and without which the injuries would not have occurred. *Id.; see also Stephens, 239 S.W.3d at 308-09.*

Appellees acknowledged in their brief and at oral submission that their only expert who opined on specific causation of Timothy's mesothelioma was pathologist Samuel Hammar, M.D. However, Dr. Hammar testified he could not opine that Timothy would not have developed mesothelioma absent exposure to Georgia-Pacific asbestos-containing joint compound. Because a plaintiff must prove that the defendant's conduct was a cause-in-fact of the harm, appellees' evidence is insufficient to satisfy the required substantial-factor causation element for maintaining this negligence and product liability suit. *See Flores, 232 S.W.3d at 770.*

. . . .

On this record, appellees' evidence is insufficient to provide quantitative evidence of Timothy's exposure to asbestos fibers from Georgia-Pacific's asbestos-containing joint compound or to establish Timothy's exposure was in amounts sufficient to increase his risk of developing mesothelioma. Therefore, appellees' evidence is legally insufficient to establish substantial-factor causation mandated by *Flores.*

. . . .

CONCLUSION

There is legally insufficient evidence of causation to support the verdict against Georgia-Pacific. We reverse the trial court's judgment and render judgment that appellees take nothing on their claims against Georgia-Pacific.

----

1. How does the reasoning in this case contrast with that in *Falcon*? Is one case's reasoning more logical than the other, or are they both logical, but applicable to different circumstances?

2. What seems like the more reasonable test for mesothelioma: the "but for" test or the "substantial factor" test?

3. In the real world, will a plaintiff ever be able to prove the standard required by the court in Georgia-Pacific Corp.? Explain.

4. Would you apply "market share liability" here?

DAUBERT v. MERRELL DOW PHARMACEUTICALS, INC.
United States Supreme Court, 1993
509 U.S. 579

JUSTICE BLACKMUN delivered the opinion of the Court.

. . . Petitioners Jason Daubert and Eric Schuller are minor children born with serious birth defects. They and their parents sued respondent in California state court, alleging that the birth defects had been caused by the mothers' ingestion of Bendectin, a prescription anti-nausea drug marketed by respondent. Respondent removed the suits to federal court on diversity grounds.

After extensive discovery, respondent moved for summary judgment, contending that Bendectin does not cause birth defects in humans and that petitioners would be unable to come forward with any admissible evidence that it does. In support of its motion, respondent submitted an affidavit of Steven H. Lamm, physician and epidemiologist, who is a well-credentialed expert on the risks from exposure to various chemical substances. Doctor Lamm stated that he had reviewed all the literature on Bendectin and human birth defects – more than 30 published studies involving over 130,000 patients. No study had found Bendectin to be a human teratogen (i.e., a substance capable of causing malformations in fetuses). On the basis of this review, Doctor Lamm concluded that maternal use of Bendectin during the first trimester of pregnancy has not been shown to be a risk factor for human birth defects.

Petitioners did not (and do not) contest this characterization of the published record regarding Bendectin. Instead, they responded to respondent's motion with the testimony of eight experts of their own, each of whom also possessed impressive credentials. These experts had concluded that Bendectin can cause birth defects. Their conclusions were based upon "in vitro" (test tube) and "in vivo" (live) animal studies that found a link between Bendectin and malformations; pharmacological studies of the chemical structure of Bendectin that purported to show similarities between the structure of the drug and that of other substances known to cause birth defects; and the "reanalysis" of previously published epidemiological (human statistical) studies.

The District Court granted respondent's motion for summary judgment. The court stated that scientific evidence is admissible only if the principle upon which it is based is "sufficiently established to have general acceptance in the field to which it belongs." *Daubert v. Merrell Dow Pharmaceuticals, Inc.*, 727 F. Supp. 570, 572 (S.D. Cal. 1989), quoting *United States v. Kilgus*, 571 F.2d 508, 510 (9th Cir. 1978). The court concluded that petitioners' evidence did not meet this standard. Given the vast body of epidemiological data concerning Bendectin, the court held, expert opinion which is not based on epidemiological evidence is not admissible to establish causation. 727 F. Supp., at 575. Thus, the animal-cell studies, live-animal studies, and chemical-structure analyses on which petitioners had relied could not raise by themselves a reasonably disputable jury issue regarding causation. Petitioners' epidemiological analyses, based as they were on recalculations of data in previously published studies that had found no causal link between the drug and birth defects, were ruled to be inadmissible because they had not been published or subjected to peer review.

The United States Court of Appeals for the Ninth Circuit affirmed. 951 F.2d 1128 (1991). Citing *Frye v. United States*, 293 F. 1013, 1014, 54 App. D.C. 46, 47 (1923), the court stated that expert opinion based on a scientific technique is inadmissible unless the technique is "generally accepted" as reliable in the relevant scientific community. 951 F.2d, at 1129-1130.

. . . We granted certiorari in light of sharp divisions among the courts regarding the proper standard for the admission of expert testimony. . . .

In the 70 years since its formulation in the *Frye* case, the "general acceptance" test has been the dominant standard for determining the admissibility of novel scientific evidence at trial. Although under increasing attack of late, the rule continues to be followed by a majority of courts, including the Ninth Circuit.

. . . They contend that the *Frye* test was superseded by the adoption of the Federal Rules of Evidence. We agree.

. . . [T]here is a specific Rule that speaks to the contested issue. Rule 702, governing expert testimony, provides:

> If scientific, technical, or other specialized knowledge will assist the trier of fact to understand the evidence or to determine a fact in issue, a witness qualified as an expert by knowledge, skill, experience, training, or education, may testify thereto in the form of an opinion or otherwise.

That the *Frye* test was displaced by the Rules of Evidence does not mean, however, that the Rules themselves place no limits on the admissibility of purportedly scientific evidence. Nor is the trial judge disable from screening such evidence. To the contrary, under the Rules the trial judge must ensure that any and all scientific testimony or evidence admitted is not only relevant, but reliable.

The primary locus of this obligation is Rule 702, which clearly contemplates some degree of regulation of the subjects and theories about which an expert may testify. "If scientific, technical, or other specialized knowledge will assist the trier of fact to understand the evidence or to determine a fact in issue" an expert "may testify thereto." The subject of an expert's testimony must be "scientific . . . knowledge." The adjective "scientific" implies a grounding in the methods and procedures of science. Similarly, the word "knowledge" connotes more than subjective belief or unsupported speculation. The term "applies to any body of known facts or to any body of ideas inferred from such facts or accepted as truths on good grounds." Webster's Third New International Dictionary 1252 (1986). Of course, it would be unreasonable to conclude that the subject of scientific testimony must be "known" to a certainty; arguably, there are no certainties in science. But, in order to qualify as "scientific knowledge," an inference or assertion must be derived by the scientific method. Proposed testimony must be supported by appropriate validation, i.e., "good grounds," based on what is known. In short, the requirement that an expert's testimony pertain to "scientific knowledge" establishes a standard of evidentiary reliability.

Rule 702 further requires that the evidence or testimony "assist the trier of fact to understand the evidence or to determine a fact in issue." This condition goes primarily to relevance. . . .

Faced with a proffer of expert scientific testimony, then, the trial judge must determine at the outset, pursuant to Rule 104(a), whether the expert is proposing to testify to (1) scientific knowledge that (2) will assist the trier of fact to understand or determine a fact in issue. This entails a preliminary assessment of whether the reasoning or methodology underlying the testimony is scientifically valid and of whether that reasoning or methodology properly can be applied to the facts in issue. . . .

Ordinarily, a key question to be answered in determining whether a theory or technique is scientific knowledge that will assist the trier of fact will be whether it can be (and has been) tested. "Scientific methodology today is based on generating hypotheses and testing them to see if they can be falsified; indeed, this methodology is what distinguishes science from other fields of human inquiry." E. Green & C. Nesson, Problems, Cases, and Materials on Evidence 649, 645 (1983). See also C. Hempel, Philosophy of Natural Science 49 (1966) ([T]he statements constituting a scientific explanation must be capable of empirical test"). . . .

Another pertinent consideration is whether the theory or technique has been subjected to peer review and publication. Publication (which is but one element of peer review) is not a sine qua of admissibility; it does not necessarily correlate with reliability, and in some instances well-grounded but innovative theories will not have been published. Some propositions, moreover are too particular, too new, or of too limited interest to be published.

Finally, "general acceptance" can yet have a bearing on the inquiry. . . . Widespread acceptance can be an important factor in ruling particular evidence admissible, and "a known technique that has been able to attract only minimal support within the community," Downing, supra, at 1238, may be properly be viewed with skepticism.

To summarize: "general acceptance" is not a necessary precondition to the admissibility of scientific evidence under the Federal Rules of Evidence. . . .

The inquiries of the District Court and the Court of Appeals focused almost exclusively on "general acceptance," as gauged by publication and the decisions of other courts. Accordingly, the judgment of the Court of Appeals is vacated and the case is remanded for further proceedings consistent with this opinion.

It is so ordered.

---

1. *The Scientific vs. The Technical Expert. In Kumho Tire Co., Ltd. v. Carmichael*, 526 U.S. 137 (1999), the Court held that the Daubert standard applied to expert testimony based on technical or other specialized knowledge, as well as testimony based on scientific knowledge.

Daubert and *Kumho* are binding on federal, but not state, courts. How does a trial court judge come to grips with questions of science that she may not understand?

2. In *Daubert v. Merrell Dow Pharmaceuticals, Inc.*, 43 F.3d 1311 (9th Cir. 1995), Judge Kozinski said:

> On remand from the United States Supreme Court, we undertake "the task of ensuring that an expert's testimony both rests on a reliable foundation and is relevant to the task at hand." . . .

> Two minors brought suit against Merrell Dow Pharmaceuticals, claiming they suffered limb reduction birth defects because their mothers had taken Benedectin, a drug prescribed for morning sickness to about 17.5 million pregnant women in the United States between 1957 and 1982. This appeal deals with an evidentiary question: whether certain expert scientific testimony is admissible to prove that Bendectin caused the plaintiffs' birth defects.

> For the most part, we don't know how birth defects come about. We do know they occur in 2-3% of births, whether or not the expectant mother has taken Benedectin. . . .

Not knowing the mechanism whereby a particular agent causes a particular effect is not always fatal to a plaintiff's claim, . . . One method of proving causation in these circumstances is to use statistical evidence. . . .

The opinions proffered by plaintiffs' expert do not, to understate the point, reflect the consensus within the scientific community. . . . Every published study here and abroad — and there have been many — concludes that Bendectin is not a teratogen. . . .

It is largely because the opinions proffered by plaintiffs' experts run counter to the substantial consensus in the scientific community that we affirmed the district court's grant of summary judgment the last time the case appeared before us. . . .

Federal judges ruling on the admissibility of expert scientific testimony face a far more complex and daunting task in a post-*Daubert* world than before. The judge's task under *Frye* was relatively simple: to determine whether the method employed by the experts is generally accepted in the scientific community. Under *Daubert*, we must engage in a difficult, two-part analysis. First, we must determine nothing less than whether the experts' testimony reflects "scientific knowledge," whether their findings are "derived by the scientific method," and whether their work product amounts to "good science." Second, we must ensure that the proposed expert testimony is "relevant to the task at hand," i.e., that it logically advances a material aspect of the proposing party's case. The Supreme Court referred to this second prong of the analysis as the "fit" requirement. . . .

Our responsibility, then, unless we badly misread the Supreme Court's opinion, is to resolve disputes among respected, well-credentialed scientists about matters squarely within their expertise, in areas where there is no scientific consensus as to what is and is not "good science," and occasionally to reject such expert testimony because it was not "derived by the scientific method." . . .

Establishing that an expert's proffered testimony grows out of prelitigation research or that the expert's research has been subjected to peer review are the two principal ways the proponent of expert testimony can show that the evidence satisfies the first prong of Rule 702. Where such evidence is unavailable, the proponent of expert scientific testimony may attempt to satisfy its burden through the testimony of its own experts. For such a showing to be sufficient, the experts must explain precisely how they went about reaching their conclusions and point to some objective source — a learned treatise, the policy statement of a professional association, a published article in a reputed scientific method, as it is practiced by (at least) a recognized minority of scientists in their field. . . .

. . . We've been presented with only the experts' qualifications, their conclusions and their assurances of reliability. Under *Daubert*, that's not enough. . . .

[W]hat plaintiffs must prove it not that Bendectin causes some birth defects, but that it caused their birth defects. To show this, plaintiffs' experts would have had to testify either that Bendectin actually cause plaintiffs' injuries (which they could not say) or that Bendectin more than doubled the likelihood of limb reduction birth defects (which they did not say).

The district court's grant of summary judgment is AFFIRMED.

3. What are the cause in fact issues in a suit brought by a woman with silicone breast implants who sues to recover for connective tissue injury? *See Hopkins v. Dow Corning Corp.*, 33 F.3d 1116 (9th Cir. 1994). What are the cause in fact issues in a suit brought by the survivors of people shot by a person taking Prozac (a medication for depression)? *See Forsyth v. Eli Lilly & Co.*, 904 F. Supp. 1153 (D. Haw. 1995) (dismissing the Food and Drug Administration as a party).

4. Parents of children with severe limb deformities brought suit against Dow Chemical Company alleging that the fathers' exposures to Agent Orange (a defoliant) in Viet Nam caused the problems. Although the plaintiffs had substantial problems proving cause in fact, the judge urged both sides to settle:

> There are serious factual problems with plaintiffs' case, the chief one being doubt that present scientific knowledge would support a finding of causality. . . .

> Many plaintiffs suffer from diseases that can be caused by dioxin. . . . The logical and practical difficulty with their argument is that the diseases referred to may result from causes other than dioxin poisoning. . . .

> In conclusion, all that can be said is that persuasive evidence of causality has not been produced. . . .

> Defendants contend that even if anyone was injured by Agent Orange, plaintiffs cannot establish that the harm to any one of them was caused by any individual defendant. . . .

> Plaintiffs have several difficult legal hurdles to overcome. The first results from the conceded inability of any veteran to identify the manufacturer of the herbicide to which he was exposed. Second, all of the ailments and conditions class members allegedly suffer from, with the possible exception of chloracne, are not unique to Agent Orange or dioxin exposure and occur in the population at large. . . . Given the desirability of resolving the indeterminate plaintiff problem using a form of proportional liability or some other acceptable method, a dismissal of the class action would be unwarranted. The statistical theory, available data, and public policy are far from settled. Particularly during this period of rapidly changing scientific approaches and increased threats to the environment, we should not unduly restrict development of legal theory and practice — both substantive and procedural — by dismissing a class action such as the one now before us although the hazards of an ultimate dismissal must be considered in assessing the fairness of the settlement.

In re "Agent Orange" Prod. Liab. Litig., 597 F. Supp. 740, 775–843 (E.D.N.Y. 1984).

5.   For a discussion of the cause in fact problems in suits brought by public hospitals and states to recover the costs of treating patients for tobacco-caused illnesses, see R.E. Gangarosa, F.J. Vandall & B.M. *Willis, Suits by Public Hospitals to Recover Expenditures for the Treatment of Disease, Injury and Disability Caused by Tobacco and Alcohol,* 22 Fordham Urb. L.J. 81 (1994).

6.   Cause in fact may be a problem in fear of cancer cases and emotional distress cases that are discussed in the Duty chapter.

Chapter 7

PROXIMATE CAUSE

The terms cause-in-fact and proximate cause are often confused by judges, attorneys and law students. Cause-in-fact is a matter of science: did the defendant's conduct have something to do with the plaintiff's injury as a matter of science? In contrast, proximate cause is a matter of social policy, and asks does the defendant's liability extend to this specific plaintiff for this particular injury. Proximate cause is based on or assumes that the defendant's conduct was the cause-in-fact of the plaintiff's injury. Proximate cause is a matter of line drawing and was developed by the courts to control the jury. The court considers many factors in deciding the question of proximate cause. There is no rule for proximate cause, and the facts of each case are critical.

You will see that often, when proximate cause is a determinative issue, the party protected by it is a large corporation.

A. THE BASIC THEORIES

PROBLEM

While adjusting his CD player, A crashes into B's car. B's car trunk explodes into flames, injuring B and destroying the car. C, standing beside the car, is injured by flying debris, and D, two blocks away, is hit on the head by a shingle that was dislodged by the blast.

E, an attorney located four blocks from the explosion, is frightened by the sound of the blast and therefore drops his infant, F. The child suffers brain damage, and E becomes depressed, can no longer work, loses his law practice, and then is divorced by his wife. Where would the proximate cause line be drawn, and why?

IN RE ARBITRATION BETWEEN POLEMIS & FURNESS, WITHY & CO.
Court of Appeal, 1921
3 K.B. 560

BANKES L.J.

[T]he respondents chartered their vessel to the appellants. . . . The vessel was employed by the charterers to carry a cargo to Casablanca in Morocco. The cargo included a quantity of benzine or petrol in cases. While discharging at Casablanca a heavy plank fell into the hold in which the petrol was stowed, and caused an explosion, which set fire to the vessel and completely destroyed her. The owners claimed the value of the vessel from the charterers alleging that the loss of the vessel was due to the negligence of the charterers' servants. The charterers contended that . . . the damages claimed were too remote. The claim was referred to arbitration, and the arbitrators stated a special case for the opinion of the court. The arbitrators found that the ship was lost by fire; that the fire arose from a spark igniting the petrol vapour in the hold; that the spark was caused by the falling board coming into contact with some substance in the hold; and that the causing of the spark could not reasonably have been anticipated from the falling of the board, though some damage to the ship might reasonably have been anticipated. . . .

In the present case the arbitrators have found as a fact that the falling of the plank was due to the negligence of the defendants' servants. The fire appears to me to have been directly caused by the falling of the plank. Under these circumstances I consider that it is immaterial that the causing of the spark by the falling of the plank could not have been reasonably anticipated. The appellants' junior counsel sought to draw a distinction between the anticipation of the extent of damage resulting from a negligent act, and the anticipation of the type of damage resulting from such an act. He admitted that it could not lie in the mouth of a person whose negligent act had caused damage to say that he could not reasonably have foreseen the extent of the damage, but he contended that the negligent person was entitled to rely upon the fact that he could not reasonably have anticipated the type of damage which resulted from his negligent act. I do not think that the distinction can be admitted. Given the breach of duty which constitutes the negligence, and given the damage as a direct result of that negligence, the anticipations of the person whose negligent act has produced the damage appear to me to be irrelevant. I consider that the damages claimed are not too remote.

. . . .

Scrutton L.J. The steamship *Thrasyvoulos* was lost by fire while being discharged by workmen employed by the charterers. Experienced arbitrators, by whose findings of fact we are bound, have decided that the fire was caused by a spark igniting petrol vapour in the hold, the vapour coming from leaks from cargo shipped by the charterers, and that the spark was caused by the . . . workmen employed by the charterers negligently knocking a plank out of a temporary staging erected in the hold, so that the plank fell into the hold, and in its fall by striking something made the spark which ignited the petrol vapour.

. . . .

The . . . defence is that the damage is too remote from the negligence, as it could not be reasonably foreseen as a consequence. . . . To determine whether an act is negligent, it is relevant to determine whether any reasonable person would foresee that the act would cause damage; if he would not, the act is not negligent. But if the act would or might probably cause damage, the fact that the damage it in fact causes is not the exact kind of damage one would expect is immaterial, so long as the damage is in fact directly traceable to the negligent act, and not due to the operation of independent causes having no connection with the negligent act, except that they could not avoid its results. Once the act is negligent, the fact that its exact operation was not foreseen is immaterial. In the present case it was negligent in discharging cargo to knock down the planks of the temporary staging, for they might easily cause some damage either to workmen, or cargo, or the ship. The fact that they did directly produce an unexpected result, a spark in an atmosphere of petrol vapour which caused a fire, does not relieve the person who was negligent from the damage which his negligent act directly causes.

For these reasons the experienced arbitrators and the judge appealed from came, in my opinion, to a correct decision, and the appeal must be dismissed with costs.

Appeal dismissed.

[The concurring opinion of WARRINGTON L.J. is omitted.]

----

1.   What is the function of the term "foreseeable"? What does the court mean by "direct"?

2.   In *Ryan v. New York Central R.R. Co.*, 35 N.Y. 210, 91 Am. Dec. 49 (1866), the railroad, through careless management of one of its engines, set fire to its woodshed. The plaintiff's house, located 130 feet from the railroad's shed, soon caught fire from the sparks and was consumed. In finding for the railroad, the court stated:

> Thus far the law is settled, and the principle is apparent. If, however, the fire communicates from the house of A. to that of B., and that is destroyed, is the negligent party liable for his loss? And if it spreads thence to the house of C, and thence to the house of D., and thence consecutively through the other houses, until it reaches and consumes the house of Z., is the party liable to pay the damages sustained by these twenty-four sufferers? The counsel for the plaintiff does not distinctly claim this, and I think it would not be seriously insisted, that the sufferers could recover in such case. Where, then, is the principle upon which A. recovers and Z. fails?
>
>   . . . .
>
> Without deciding upon the importance of this distinction, I prefer to place my opinion upon the ground that, in the one case, to wit, the destruction of the building upon which the sparks were thrown by the negligent act of the party sought to be charged, the result was to have been anticipated, the moment the fire was communicated to the building; that its destruction was the ordinary and natural result of its being fired. In the second, third or twenty-fourth case, as supposed, the destruction of the building was not a natural and expected result of the first firing. That a building upon which sparks and cinders fall should be destroyed or seriously injured, must be expected, but that the fire should spread and other buildings be consumed, is not a necessary or an usual result. That it is possible, and that it is not unfrequent, cannot be denied. The result, however, depends, not upon any necessity of a further communication of the fire, but upon a concurrence of accidental circumstances, such as the degree of the heat, the state of the atmosphere, the condition and materials of the adjoining structures and the direction of the wind. These are accidental and

varying circumstances; the party has no control over them, and is not responsible for their effects.

My opinion, therefore, is, that this action cannot be sustained, for the reason that the damages incurred are not the immediate but the remote result of the negligence of the defendants. The immediate result was the destruction of their own wood and sheds; beyond that, it was remote.

. . . .

In a country where wood, coal, gas and oils are universally used, where men are crowded into cities and villages, where servants are employed, and where children find their home in all houses, it is impossible, that the most vigilant prudence should guard against the occurrence of accidental or negligent fires. A man may insure his own house, or his own furniture, but he cannot insure his neighbor's building or furniture for the reason that he has no interest in them. To hold that the owner must not only meet his own loss by fire, but that he must guaranty the security of his neighbors on both sides, and to an unlimited extent, would be to create a liability which would be the destruction of all civilized society. No community could long exist, under the operation of such a principle. In a commercial country, each man, to some extent, runs the hazard of his neighbor's conduct, and each, by insurance against such hazards, is enabled to obtain a reasonable security against loss.

Does this decision make sense in a community where insurance is available? What decision would you expect in a state where insurance was not available for crops such as grain? *See Atchison, T. & S.F. R.R. Co. v. Stanford*, 12 Kan. 354, 15 Am. Rep. 362 (1874).

3. *Ryan* is one of the earliest cases to mention insurance. What should be the role of insurance in proximate cause decisions? Today, it is rare to see insurance discussed as a decisional factor. Does that mean it is not a factor?

4. In *Ryan*, was the spread of fire natural, expected, usual, immediate, or remote?

5. "For an intended injury the law is astute to discover even very remote causation. For one which the defendant merely ought to have anticipated it has often stopped at an earlier stage of the investigation of causal connection." *Derosier v. New England Tel. & Tel. Co.*, 81 N.H. 451, 130 A. 145 (1925).

BARTOLONE v. JECKOVICH
Supreme Court of New York, 1984
103 A.D.2d 632, 481 N.Y.S.2d 545

DENMAN, JUSTICE.

On October 4, 1976, plaintiff was involved in a four-car chain reaction collision in Niagara Falls for which defendants were found liable. Plaintiff sustained relatively minor injuries consisting of whiplash and cervical and lower back strain for which he was treated with muscle relaxants and physical therapy but was not hospitalized. Subsequently, however, he suffered an acute psychotic breakdown from which he has not recovered. The theory on which plaintiff's case was tried was that the accident aggravated a preexisting paranoid schizophrenic condition which has totally and permanently disabled him. The jury returned a verdict of $500,000 in plaintiff's favor. The court granted defendants' motion to set aside the verdict and ordered a new trial unless plaintiff would stipulate to a reduced verdict of $30,000. Plaintiff refused and took this appeal. The order should be reversed and the verdict reinstated.

At the time of the accident, plaintiff was a 48-year-old man who lived alone in one room and worked out of a union hall as a carpenter. He was very proud of his physique and his strength, spending on the average of four hours daily at the local YMCA engaged in body building. On weekends, in order to conserve his strength, he pursued nonphysical interests such as painting and sculpture, singing and playing the guitar and trombone. Since the accident, plaintiff has been in a degenerative psychotic condition in which he is withdrawn, hostile, delusional, hears voices and sees shadows, refuses to cut his hair, shave or bathe and no longer participates in any of his former interests. In the words of his treating psychiatrist, he is "a life lost."

Three psychiatrists and one neurosurgeon testified on behalf of plaintiff. From their testimony a strange and sad profile emerged: Plaintiff's mother had died of cancer when he was a very young boy. His sister had also died of cancer. Probably as a consequence, plaintiff had developed a fear and dislike of doctors and engaged in body building in order to avoid doctors and ward off illness. His bodily fitness was extremely important to him because it provided him with a sense of control over his life so that he was able to function in a relatively normal way. He had adopted a life-style in which he was something of a "loner," but he was self-supporting, had no complaints and lived a rather placid existence. After the accident, although his physical injuries were minor, he perceived that his bodily integrity was impaired and that he was physically deteriorating. Because he had such an intense emotional investment in his body, his perception of this impairment made him incapable of his former physical feats and he was thus deprived of the mechanism by which he coped with his emotional problems. As a consequence, he deteriorated psychologically and socially as well. He increasingly isolated himself and felt himself to be a victim of powerful forces over which he had no control. It was the consensus of plaintiff's medical experts that he had suffered from a preexisting schizophrenic illness which had been exacerbated by the accident and that he was now in a chronic paranoid schizophrenic state which is irreversible.

Defendants' expert, who had never seen the plaintiff, even at trial, agreed that plaintiff suffered from schizophrenia but stated that, in his opinion, it had not been exacerbated by the accident and that defendant was merely attempting to make money. The jury, who had an opportunity to see the plaintiff and hear his testimony, returned a verdict of $500,000. The court set that verdict aside stating that there was no basis on which the jury could conclude that plaintiff's total mental breakdown could be attributed to a minor accident.

We find, to the contrary, that there was ample proof in the record to support the jury's verdict. There is precedent for such determination. In *Bonner v. United States* (339 F. Supp. 640), plaintiff was a passenger in a car which was rear-ended. She received a whiplash injury resulting in cervical spasms and lumbar-sacral strain for which she was treated with muscle relaxants and physiotherapy. She later developed numbness, headaches, hearing difficulties, inability to keep her eyes open, deteriorated personal hygiene, degeneration in appearance, facial tics and jerking and twitching of her head, all of which were determined to be of a psychological rather than neurological origin. The psychiatric testimony established that she had a preexisting underlying psychotic illness with which she was able to cope until the accident but that the accident had precipitated a chronic psychosis which was totally disabling.

The circumstances of those cases as well as those of the case before us illustrate the truth of the old axiom that a defendant must take a plaintiff as he finds him and hence may be held liable in damages for aggravation of a preexisting illness.

The record presents ample evidence that plaintiff, although apparently suffering from a quiescent psychotic illness, was able to function in a relatively normal manner but that this minor accident aggravated his schizophrenic condition leaving him totally and permanently disabled.

Accordingly, the order should be reversed and the jury's verdict reinstated.

Order unanimously reversed with costs, motion denied and verdict reinstated.

———

1. What would a nonlawyer say of the plaintiff's recovery in *Bartolone*? How would you answer the nonlawyer?

2. The theory that you take the plaintiff as you find him or her (the thin skull rule) is supported by *Dulieu v. White*, [1901] 2 K.B. 669, where a pregnant woman recovered for a shock-induced premature birth of a child with mental illness. Plaintiff was behind the bar in a public house when the defendant's servant negligently drove his horse-drawn wagon into the house. There was no impact with the plaintiff. How would *Dulieu* be decided today in terms of cause-in-fact?

OVERSEAS TANKSHIP (U.K.) LTD. v. MORTS DOCK & ENGINEERING CO. (THE WAGON MOUND NO. 1)
Privy Council, 1961
[1961] A.C. 388

Viscount Simonds:

Appeal from an order of the Full Court of the Supreme Court of New South Wales dismissing an appeal by the appellants, Overseas Tankship (U.K.) Ltd., from a judgment . . . in an action in which the appellants were defendants and the respondents, Morts Dock & Engineering Co. Ltd., were plaintiffs.

The plaintiffs at the relevant time carried on the business of ship-building, ship-repairing and general engineering at Morts Bay, Balmain, in the Port of Sydney. They owned and used for their business the Sheerlegs Wharf, a timber wharf about 400 feet in length and 40 feet wide, where there was a quantity of tools and equipment. In October and November, 1951, a vessel known as the *Corrimel* was moored alongside the wharf and was being refitted by the respondents. Her mast was lying on the wharf and a number of the respondents' employees were working both upon it and upon the vessel itself, using for that purpose electric and oxy-acetylene welding equipment.

At the same time the defendants were charterers . . . of the *s.s. Wagon Mound*, an oil-burning vessel, which was moored at the Caltex Wharf on the northern shore of the harbour at a distance of about 600 feet from the Sheerlegs Wharf. She was there . . . for the purpose of discharging gasolene products and taking in bunkering oil.

During the early hours of October 30, 1951, a large quantity of bunkering oil was, through the carelessness of the defendants' servants, allowed to spill into the bay, and by 10:30 on the morning of that day it had spread over a considerable part of the bay, being thickly concentrated in some places and particularly along the foreshore near the respondents' property. The defendants made no attempt to disperse the oil. The *Wagon Mound* unberthed and set sail very shortly after.

. . . .

For the remainder of October 30 and until about 2 p.m. on November 1 work was carried on as usual, the condition and congestion of the oil remaining substantially unaltered. But at about that time the oil under or near the wharf was ignited and a fire, fed initially by the oil, spread rapidly and burned with great intensity. The wharf and the *Corrimal* caught fire and considerable damage was done to the wharf and the equipment upon it.

The outbreak of fire was due, as the judge found, to the fact that there was floating in the oil underneath the wharf a piece of debris on which lay some smoldering cotton waste or rag which had been set on fire by molten metal falling from the wharf: that the cotton waste or rag burst into flames: that the flames from the cotton waste set the floating oil afire either directly or by first setting fire to a wooden pile coated with oil, and that after the floating oil became ignited the flames spread rapidly over the surface of the oil and . . . severely damaged the wharf.

. . . .

[The trial court found that the defendants did not know that the oil could be ignited while floating on top of the water. The plaintiff won in the trial court and this was affirmed by the Supreme Court of New South Wales. Defendants appealed to the Privy Council. They reversed the decision and stated:]

[T]he authority of *Polemis* has been severely shaken though lip-service has from time to time been paid to it. In their Lordships' opinion it should no longer be regarded as good law. It is not probable that many cases will for that reason have a different result, though it is hoped that the law will be thereby simplified, and that in some cases, at least, palpable injustice will be avoided. For it does not seem consonant with current ideas of justice or morality that for an act of negligence, however slight or venial, which results in some trivial foreseeable damage the actor should be liable for all consequences however unforeseeable and however grave, so

long as they can be said to be "direct." It is a principle of civil liability, subject only
to qualifications which have no present relevance, that a man must be considered to
be responsible for the probable consequences of his act. To demand more of him is
too harsh a rule, to demand less is to ignore that civilized order requires the
observance of a minimum standard of behaviour.

This concept applied to the slowly developing law of negligence has led to a great
variety of expressions which can, as it appears to their Lordships, be harmonised
with little difficulty with the single exception of the so-called rule in *Polemis*. For,
if it is asked why a man should be responsible for the natural or necessary or
probable consequences of his act (or any other similar description of them) the
answer is that it is not because, since they are natural or necessary or probable, but
because, since they have this quality, it is judged by the standard of the reasonable
man that he ought to have foreseen them. Thus it is that over and over again it has
happened that in different judgments in the same case, and sometimes in a single
judgment, liability for a consequence has been imposed on the ground that it was
natural or necessary or probable. The two grounds have been treated as cotermi-
nous, and so they largely are. But, where they are not, the question arises to which
the wrong answer was given in *Polemis*. For, if some limitation must be imposed
upon the consequences for which the negligent actor is to be held responsible — and
all are agreed that some limitation there must be — why should that test
(reasonable foreseeability) be rejected which, since he is judged by what the
reasonable man ought to foresee, corresponds with the common conscience of
mankind, and a test (the "direct" consequence) be substituted which leads to
no-where by the never-ending and insoluble problems of causation. . . .

It is, no doubt, proper when considering tortious liability for negligence to
analyze its elements and to say that the plaintiff must prove a duty owed to him by
the defendant, a breach of that duty by the defendant, and consequent damage. But
there can be no liability until the damage has been done. It is not the act but the
consequences on which tortious liability is founded. Just as (as it has been said)
there is no such thing as negligence in the air, so there is no such thing as liability
in the air. Suppose an action brought by A for damage caused by the carelessness
(a neutral word) of B, for example, a fire caused by the careless spillage of oil. It
may, of course, become relevant to know what duty B owed to A, but the only
liability that is in question is the liability for damage by fire. It is vain to isolate the
liability from its context and to say that B is or is not liable, and then to ask for what
damage he is liable. For his liability is in respect of that damage and no other. If,
as admittedly it is, B's liability (culpability) depends on the reasonable foreseeability of the consequent damage, how is that to be determined except by the
foreseeability of the damage which in fact happened — the damage in suit?

But, it is said, a different position arises if B's careless act has been shown to be
negligent and has caused some foreseeable damage to A. Their Lordships have
already observed that to hold B liable for consequences however unforeseeable of a
careless act, if, but only if, he is at the same time liable for some other damage
however trivial, appears to be neither logical nor just. This becomes more clear if it
is supposed that similar unforeseeable damage is suffered by A and — but other
foreseeable damage, for which B is liable, by A only. A system of law which would
hold B liable to A but not to — for the similar damage suffered by each of them

could not easily be defended. Fortunately, the attempt is not necessary. For the same fallacy is at the root of the proposition. It is irrelevant to the question whether B is liable for unforeseeable damage that he is liable for foreseeable damage, as irrelevant as would the fact that he had trespassed on Whiteacre be to the question whether he has trespassed on Blackacre. Again, suppose a claim by A for damage by fire by the careless act of B. Of what relevance is it to that claim that he has another claim arising out of the same careless act? It would surely not prejudice his claim if that other claim failed: it cannot assist it if it succeeds. Each of them rests on its own bottom, and will fail if it can be established that the damage could not reasonably be foreseen. . . .

Their Lordships will humbly advise Her Majesty that this appeal should be allowed, and the respondents' action so far as it related to damage caused by the negligence of the appellants be dismissed with costs. . . . The respondents must pay the costs of the appellants of this appeal and in the courts below.

---

1. Why did the court dislike the rule in *Polemis*?

2. Does the court in *Wagon Mound* feel it is developing a rule or merely deciding the case before it?

3. What is the policy behind the new rule? What is left of *Polemis*?

4. When the defendant served "foul smelling" shrimp, could it be held to foresee that the plaintiff would slip on a customer's vomit? *Crankshaw v. Piedmont Driving Club*, 115 Ga. App. 820, 156 S.E.2d 208 (1967).

5. Will a doctor who negligently fails to identify a battered child be held to foresee the damage later inflicted by his parents? Should the criminal acts of the parents (beatings) cut off the doctor's liability? *See Landeros v. Flood*, 17 Cal. 3d 399, 131 Cal. Rptr. 69, 551 P.2d 389 (1976).

6. If a telephone company negligently places a phone booth too close to the road, will it be held to foresee that a drunk driver might run into the phone booth and cause the plaintiff (using the booth) serious injury? Should the drunk driver sever the phone company's liability? *See Bigbee v. Pacific Tel. & Tel. Co.*, 34 Cal. 3d 49, 192 Cal. Rptr. 857, 665 P.2d 947 (1983).

7. For articles discussing the *Wagon Mound* case, see Fleming, *The Passing of* Polemis, 39 Can. B. Rev. 489 (1961); Green, *Foreseeability in Negligence Law*, 61 Colum. L. Rev. 1401 (1961).

8. In a second suit, *Wagon Mound No. 2*, the owners of the *Corrimal* sued the charterers of the *Wagon Mound* on the same facts as found in *Wagon Mound No. 1*. The Privy Council reversed the trial court and held in favor of plaintiffs:

> In the present case the evidence led was substantially different from the evidence led in *The Wagon Mound (No. 1)* and the findings of Walsh J. are significantly different. That is not due to there having been any failure by the plaintiffs in *The Wagon Mound (No. 1)* in preparing and presenting their case. The plaintiffs there were no doubt embarrassed by a difficulty which does not affect the present plaintiffs. The outbreak of the fire was

consequent on the act of the manager of the plaintiffs in *The Wagon Mound (No. 1)* in resuming oxy-acetylene welding and cutting while the wharf was surrounded by this oil. So if the plaintiffs in the former case had set out to prove that it was foreseeable by the engineers of the *Wagon Mound* that this oil could be set alight, they might have had difficulty in parrying the reply that this must also have been foreseeable by their manager. Then there would have been contributory negligence and at that time contributory negligence was a complete defence in New South Wales.

. . . .

In *The Wagon Mound (No. 1)* the Board were not concerned with degrees of foreseeability because the finding was that the fire was not foreseeable at all. So Lord Simonds had no cause to amplify the statement that the "essential factor in determining liability is whether the damage is of such a kind as the reasonable man should have foreseen." But here the findings show that some risk of fire would have been present to the mind of a reasonable man in the shoes of the ship's chief engineer. So the first question must be what is the precise meaning to be attached in this context to the words "foreseeable" and "reasonably foreseeable."

. . . .

[I]t does not follow that, no matter what the circumstances may be, it is justifiable to neglect a risk of such a small magnitude. A reasonable man would only neglect such a risk if he had a valid reason for doing so, e.g., that it would involve considerable expense to eliminate the risk. He would weigh the risk against the difficulty of eliminating it.

. . . .

In the present case there was no justification whatever for discharging the oil into Sydney Harbour. Not only was it an offence to do so, but it involved considerable loss financially. If the ship's engineer had thought about the matter, there could have been no question of balancing the advantages and disadvantages. From every point of view it was both his duty and his interest to stop the discharge immediately.

It follows that in their Lordships' view the only question is whether a reasonable man having the knowledge and experience to be expected of the chief engineer of the *Wagon Mound* would have known that there was a real risk of the oil on the water catching fire in some way: if it did, serious damage to ships or other property was not only foreseeable but very likely.

. . . .

In the present case the evidence shows that the discharge of so much oil onto the water must have taken a considerable time, and a vigilant ship's engineer would have noticed the discharge at an early stage. The findings show that he ought to have known that it is possible to ignite this kind of oil on water, and that the ship's engineer probably ought to have known that this had in fact happened before. The most that can be said to justify inaction is that he would have known that this could only happen in very exceptional circumstances. But that does not mean that a reasonable man would dismiss such a risk from his mind and do nothing when it was so easy to prevent it. If it is clear that the reasonable man would have realised or foreseen and prevented the risk, then it must follow that the *[Wagon Mound]* is liable in damages.

Overseas Tankships [U.K.], Ltd. v. Miller Steamship Co. (Wagon Mound No. 2), [1967] 1 A.C. 617.

9. What rule was decided in *Wagon Mound No. 2*? What has happened to the *Polemis* rule?

10. For an article discussing the *Wagon Mound No. 2*, see Green, The Wagon Mound No. 2 — *Foreseeability Revisited*, 1967 Utah L. Rev. 197.

PROBLEM

Alex was walking along Main Street when he suddenly felt the call of nature. He saw a Porta-Potty looking device and stepped inside. As soon as he closed the door, the potty exploded. Alex was severely injured, as was his son who was standing outside the "Potty" door.

The device is not a true "Porta-Potty." Instead of a liquid chemical in the base of the potty, it drains into an underground sewer below. The sewer and the potty are owned by Salient Green, a private corporation.

Two weeks ago, Salient Green began to permit Hogs We Are (a large pig farm) to dump hog manure into the sewer.

Assume that Hogs We Are is judgment-proof. Assume also that Alex lit his cigarette as he stepped inside the "Potty".

Discuss.

PALSGRAF v. THE LONG ISLAND RAILROAD CO.
Court of Appeals of New York, 1928
248 N.Y. 339, 162 N.E. 99

Appeal from a judgment of the Appellate Division of the Supreme Court in the second judicial department, entered December 16, 1927, affirming a judgment in favor of plaintiff entered upon a verdict.

CARDOZO, CH. J.

Plaintiff was standing on a platform of defendant's railroad after buying a ticket to go to Rockaway Beach. A train stopped at the station, bound for another place. Two men ran forward to catch it. One of the men reached the platform of the car without mishap, though the train was already moving. The other man, carrying a package, jumped aboard the car, but seemed unsteady as if about to fall. A guard on the car, who had held the door open, reached forward to help him in, and another guard on the platform pushed him from behind. In this act, the package was dislodged, and fell upon the rails. It was a package of small size, about fifteen inches long, and was covered by a newspaper. In fact it contained fireworks, but there was nothing in its appearance to give notice of its contents. The fireworks when they fell exploded. The shock of the explosion threw down some scales at the other end of the platform, many feet away. The scales struck the plaintiff, causing injuries for which she sues.

The conduct of the defendant's guard, if a wrong in its relation to the holder of the package, was not a wrong in its relation to the plaintiff, standing far away. Relatively to her it was not negligence at all. Nothing in the situation gave notice that the falling package had in it the potency of peril to persons thus removed. Negligence is not actionable unless it involves the invasion of a legally protected interest, the violation of a right. "Proof of negligence in the air, so to speak, will not do." . . .

If no hazard was apparent to the eye of ordinary vigilance, an act innocent and harmless, at least to outward seeming, with reference to her, did not take to itself the quality of a tort because it happened to be a wrong, though apparently not one involving the risk of bodily insecurity, with reference to someone else. "In every instance, before negligence can be predicated of a given act, back of the act must be sought and found a duty to the individual complaining, the observance of which would have averted or avoided the injury." . . . "The ideas of negligence and duty are strictly correlative." . . . The plaintiff sues in her own right for a wrong personal to her, and not as the vicarious beneficiary of a breach of duty to another.

A different conclusion will involve us, and swiftly too, in a maze of contradictions. A guard stumbles over a package which has been left upon a platform. It seems to be a bundle of newspapers. It turns out to be a can of dynamite. To the eye of ordinary vigilance, the bundle is abandoned waste, which may be kicked or trod on with impunity. Is a passenger at the other end of the platform protected by the law against the unsuspected hazard concealed beneath the waste? If not, is the result to be any different, so far as the distant passenger is concerned, when the guard stumbles over a valise which a truckman or a porter has left upon the walk? The passenger far away, if the victim of a wrong at all, has a cause of action, not derivative, but original and primary. His claim to be protected against invasion of his bodily security is neither greater nor less because the act resulting in the invasion is a wrong to another far removed. In this case, the rights that are said to have been violated, the interests said to have been invaded, are not even of the same order. The man was not injured in his person nor even put in danger. The purpose of the act, as well as its effect, was to make his person safe. If there was a wrong to him at all, which may very well be doubted, it was a wrong to a property interest only, the safety of his package. Out of this wrong to property, which threatened injury to nothing else, there has passed, we are told, to the plaintiff by derivation or succession a right of action for the invasion of an interest of another order, the right to bodily security. The diversity of interests emphasizes the futility of the effort to build the plaintiffs right upon the basis of a wrong to someone else. The gain is one of emphasis, for a like result would follow if the interests were the same. Even then, the orbit of the danger as disclosed to the eye of reasonable vigilance would be the orbit of the duty. One who jostles one's neighbor in a crowd does not invade the rights of others standing at the outer fringe when the unintended contact casts a bomb upon the ground. The wrongdoer as to them is the man who carries the bomb, not the one who explodes it without suspicion of the danger. . . .

The argument for the plaintiff is built upon the shifting meanings of such words as "wrong" and "wrongful," and shares their instability. What the plaintiff must show is "a wrong" to herself, i.e., a violation of her own right, and not merely a wrong to someone else, nor conduct "wrongful" because unsocial, but not "a wrong" to anyone. We are told that one who drives at reckless speed through a crowded city street is guilty of a negligent act and, therefore, of a wrongful one irrespective of the consequences. Negligent the act is, and wrongful in the sense that it is unsocial, but wrongful and unsocial in relation to other travelers, only because the eye of vigilance perceives the risk of damage. If the same act were to be committed on a speedway or a race course, it would lose its wrongful quality. The risk reasonably to be perceived defines the duty to be obeyed, and risk imports relation; it is risk to another or to others within the range of apprehension. . . . The range of reasonable apprehension is at times a question for the court, and at times, if varying inferences are possible, a question for the jury. Here, by concession, there was nothing in the situation to suggest to the most cautious mind that the parcel wrapped in newspaper would spread wreckage through the station. If the guard had thrown it down knowingly and willfully, he would not have threatened the plaintiff's safety, so far as appearances could warn him. His conduct would not have involved, even then, an unreasonable probability of invasion of her bodily security. Liability can be no greater where the act is inadvertent.

Negligence, like risk, is thus a term of relation. Negligence in the abstract, apart from things related, is surely not a tort, if indeed it is understandable at all. . . .

The law of causation, remote or proximate, is thus foreign to the case before us. The question of liability is always anterior to the question of the measure of the consequences that go with liability. If there is no tort to be redressed, there is no occasion to consider what damage might be recovered if there were a finding of a tort. We may assume, without deciding, that negligence, not at large or in the abstract, but in relation to the plaintiff, would entail liability for any and all consequences, however novel or extraordinary. . . . There is room for argument that a distinction is to be drawn according to the diversity of interests invaded by the act, as where conduct negligent in that it threatens an insignificant invasion of an interest in property results in an unforeseeable invasion of an interest of another order, as, e.g., one of bodily security. Perhaps other distinctions may be necessary. We do not go into the question now. The consequences to be followed must first be rooted in a wrong.

The judgment of the Appellate Division and that of the Trial Term should be reversed, and the complaint dismissed, with costs in all courts.

ANDREWS, J. (dissenting). Assisting a passenger to board a train, the defendant's servant negligently knocked a package from his arms. It fell between the platform and the cars. Of its contents the servant knew and could know nothing. A violent explosion followed. The concussion broke some scales standing a considerable distance away. In falling they injured the plaintiff, an intending passenger.

Upon these facts may she recover the damages she has suffered in an action brought against the master? The result we shall reach depends upon our theory as to the nature of negligence. Is it a relative concept — the breach of some duty owing to a particular person or to particular persons? Or where there is an act which unreasonably threatens the safety of others, is the doer liable for all its proximate consequences, even where they result in injury to one who would generally be thought to be outside the radius of danger? This is not a mere dispute as to words. We might not believe that to the average mind the dropping of the bundle would seem to involve the probability of harm to the plaintiff standing many feet away whatever might be the case as to the owner or to one so near as to be likely to be struck by its fall. If, however, we adopt the second hypothesis we have to inquire only as to the relation between cause and effect. We deal in terms of proximate cause, not of negligence. . . .

But we are told that "there is no negligence unless there is in the particular case a legal duty to take care, and this duty must be one which is owed to the plaintiff himself and not merely to others." . . . This, I think too narrow a conception. Where there is the unreasonable act, and some right that may be affected there is negligence whether damage does or does not result. That is immaterial. Should we drive down Broadway at a reckless speed, we are negligent whether we strike an approaching car or miss it by an inch. The act itself is wrongful. It is a wrong not only to those who happen to be within the radius of danger but to all who might have been there — a wrong to the public at large. Such is the language of the street. Such the language of the courts when speaking of contributory negligence. Such again and again their language in speaking of the duty of some defendant and discussing proximate cause in cases where such a discussion is wholly irrelevant on any other theory. . . .

It may well be that there is no such thing as negligence in the abstract. "Proof of negligence in the air, so to speak, will not do." In an empty world negligence would not exist. It does involve a relationship between man and his fellows. But not merely a relationship between man and those whom he might reasonably expect his act would injure. Rather, a relationship between him and those whom he does in fact injure. If his act has a tendency to harm someone, it harms him a mile away as surely as it does those on the scene. . . .

In the well-known *Polemis* Case (1921, 3 K. B. 560), Scrutton, L. J., said that the dropping of a plank was negligent for it might injure "workman or cargo or ship." Because of either possibility the owner of the vessel was to be made good for his loss. The act being wrongful the doer was liable for its proximate results. Criticized and explained as this statement may have been, I think it states the law as it should be and as it is. . . .

The proposition is this. Every one owes to the world at large the duty of refraining from those acts that may unreasonably threaten the safety of others. Such an act occurs. Not only is he wronged to whom harm might reasonably be expected to result, but he also who is in fact injured, even if he be outside what would generally be thought the danger zone. There needs be duty due the one complaining but this is not a duty to a particular individual because as to him harm might be expected. Harm to someone being the natural result of the act, not only that one alone, but all those in fact injured may complain. We have never, I think, held otherwise. . . .

If this be so, we do not have a plaintiff suing by "derivation or succession." Her action is original and primary. Her claim is for a breach of duty to herself — not that she is subrogated to any right of action of the owner of the parcel or of a passenger standing at the scene of the explosion.

. . . But there is one limitation. The damages must be so connected with the negligence that the latter may be said to be the proximate cause of the former.

These two words have never been given an inclusive definition. What is a cause in a legal sense, still more what is a proximate cause, depend in each case upon many considerations, as does the existence of negligence itself. . . .

As we have said, we cannot trace the effect of an act to the end, if end there is. Again, however, we may trace it part of the way. A murder at Serajevo may be the necessary antecedent to an assassination in London twenty years hence. An overturned lantern may burn all Chicago. We may follow the fire from the shed to the last building. We rightly say the fire started by the lantern caused its destruction.

A cause, but not the proximate cause. What we do mean by the word "proximate" is, that because of convenience, of public policy, of a rough sense of justice, the law arbitrarily declines to trace a series of events beyond a certain point. This is not logic. It is practical politics. Take our rule as to fires. Sparks from my burning haystack set on fire my house and my neighbor's. I may recover from a negligent railroad. He may not. Yet the wrongful act as directly harmed the one as the other. We may regret that the line was drawn just where it was, but drawn somewhere it had to be. We said the act of the railroad was not the proximate cause of our neighbor's fire. Cause it surely was. The words we used were simply indicative of our notions of public policy. Other courts think differently. But somewhere they reach the point where they cannot say the stream comes from any one source.

. . . .

It is all a question of expediency. There are no fixed rules to govern our judgment. . . .

There are some hints that may help us. The proximate cause, involved as it may be with many other causes, must be, at the least, something without which the event would not happen. The court must ask itself whether there was a natural and continuous sequence between cause and effect. Was the one a substantial factor in producing the other? Was there a direct connection between them, without too many intervening causes? Is the effect of cause on result not too attenuated? Is the cause likely, in the usual judgment of mankind, to produce the result? Or by the exercise of prudent foresight could the result be foreseen? Is the result too remote from the cause, and here we consider remoteness in time and space. . . . We draw an uncertain and wavering line, but draw it we must as best we can.

Once again, it is all a question of fair judgment, always keeping in mind the fact that we endeavor to make a rule in each case that will be practical and in keeping with the general understanding of mankind.

. . . .

This last suggestion is the factor which must determine the case before us. The act upon which defendant's liability rests is knocking an apparently harmless package onto the platform. The act was negligent. For its proximate consequences the defendant is liable. If its contents were broken, to the owner; if it fell upon and crushed a passenger's foot, then to him. If it exploded and injured one in the immediate vicinity, to him also as to A in the illustration. Mrs. Palsgraf was standing some distance away. How far cannot be told from the record — apparently twenty-five or thirty feet. Perhaps less. Except for the explosion, she would not have been injured. We are told by the appellant in his brief "it cannot be denied that the explosion was the direct cause of the plaintiff's injuries." So it was a substantial factor in producing the result — there was here a natural and continuous sequence — direct connection. The only intervening cause was that instead of blowing her to the ground the concussion smashed the weighing machine which in turn fell upon her. There was no remoteness in time, little in space. And surely, given such an explosion as here it needed no great foresight to predict that the natural result would be to injure one on the platform at no greater distance from its scene than was the plaintiff. Just how no one might be able to predict. Whether by flying fragments, by broken glass, by wreckage of machines or structures no one could say. But injury in some form was most probable.

Under these circumstances I cannot say as a matter of law that the plaintiff's injuries were not the proximate result of the negligence. That is all we have before us. The court refused to so charge. No request was made to submit the matter to the jury as a question of fact, even would that have been proper upon the record before us.

The judgment appealed from should be affirmed, with costs.

POUND, LEHMAN and KELLOGG, JJ., concur with CARDOZO, CH. J.; ANDREWS, J., dissents in opinion in which CRANE and O'BRIEN, JJ., concur.

Judgment reversed, etc.

---

1. What are Judge Cardozo's and Judge Andrew's theories in regard to duty, negligence, cause-in-fact, proximate cause, and damages?

2. What does Judge Cardozo mean when he says: "Negligence . . . is a term of relation"?

3. *Palsgraf* is probably the best known case in torts. Why?

4. Judge Cardozo may have obtained portions of his theory at a meeting of the American Law Institute. *See* Robert Keeton, *A Palsgraf Anecdote*, 56 Tex. L. Rev. 513 (1978).

5. For articles discussing *Palsgraf*, see William Prosser, Palsgraf *Revisited*, 52 Mich. L. Rev. 1 (1953); and Leon Green, *The* Palsgraf *Case*, 30 Colum. L. Rev. 789 (1930).

PETITIONS OF THE KINSMAN TRANSIT CO.
United States Court of Appeals, Second Circuit, 1964
338 F.2d 708, *cert. denied*, 380 U.S. 944 (1965)

FRIENDLY, CIRCUIT JUDGE:

We have here six appeals, from an interlocutory decree in admiralty adjudicating liability. The litigation, in the District Court for the Western District of New York, arose out of a series of misadventures on a navigable portion of the Buffalo River during the night of January 21, 1959. The owners of two vessels petitioned for exoneration from or limitation of liability. . . . The proceedings were consolidated for trial before Judge Burke. We shall summarize the facts as found by him:

The Buffalo River flows through Buffalo from east to west, with many turns and bends, until it empties into Lake Erie. Its navigable western portion is lined with docks, grain elevators, and industrial installations; during the winter, lake vessels tie up there pending resumption of navigation on the Great Lakes, without power and with only a shipkeeper aboard. About a mile from the mouth, the City of Buffalo maintains a lift bridge at Michigan Avenue. Thaws and rain frequently cause freshets to develop in the upper part of the river and its tributary, Cazenovia Creek; currents then range up to fifteen miles an hour and propel broken ice down the river, which sometimes overflows its banks.

 . . . .

The *MacGilvray Shiras*, owned by The Kinsman Transit Company, was moored at the dock of the Concrete Elevator, operated by Continental Grain Company, on the south side of the river about three miles upstream of the Michigan Avenue Bridge. She was loaded with grain owned by Continental. The berth, east of the main portion of the dock, was exposed in the sense that about 150' of the *Shiras'* forward end, pointing upstream, and 70' of her stern — a total of over half her length — projected beyond the dock. This left between her stem and the bank a space of water seventy-five feet wide where the ice and other debris could float in and accumulate. . . . From about 10 P.M. large chunks of ice and debris began to pile up between the *Shims'* starboard bow and the bank; the pressure exerted by this mass on her starboard bow was augmented by the force of the current and of floating ice against her port quarter. The mooring lines began to part, and a 'deadman,' to which the No. 1 mooring cable had been attached, pulled out of the ground, the judge finding that it had not been properly constructed or inspected. About 10:40 P.M. the stern lines parted, and the *Shiras* drifted into the current.

Careening stern first down the S-shaped river, the *Shiras*, at about 11 P.M., struck the bow of the *Michael K. Tewksbury*. . . . Her shipkeeper had left around 5 P.M. and spent the evening watching television with a girl friend and her family. The collision caused the *Tewksbury's* mooring lines to part; she too drifted stern first down the river, followed by the *Shiras*. The collision caused damage to the Steamer *Druckenmiller* which was moored opposite the *Tewksbury*.

 . . . [T]he Coast Guard, . . . called the city fire station on the river, which in turn warned the crew on the Michigan Avenue Bridge, this last call being made about

10:48 P.M. . . . [T]he bridge was just being raised when, at 11:17 P.M., the *Tewksbury* crashed into its center. . . .

The *Shiras* ended her journey with her stern against the *Tewksbury* and her bow against the north side of the river. So wedged, the two vessels substantially dammed the flow, causing water and ice to back up and flood installations on the banks with consequent damage as far as the Concrete Elevator, nearly three miles upstream. . . .

We see little similarity between the *Palsgraf* case and the situation before us. The point of *Palsgraf* was that the appearance of the newspaper-wrapped package gave no notice that its dislodgement could do any harm save to itself and those nearby, and this by impact, perhaps with consequent breakage, and not by explosion. In contrast, a ship insecurely moored in a fast flowing river is a known danger not only to herself but to the owners of all other ships and structures down-river, and to persons upon them. No one would dream of saying that a shipowner who "knowingly and willfully" failed to secure his ship at a pier on such a river "would not have threatened" persons and owners of property downstream in some manner. The shipowner and the wharfinger in this case having thus owed a duty of care to all within the reach of the ship's known destructive power, the impossibility of advance identification of the particular person who would be hurt is without legal consequence. . . . Similarly the foreseeable consequences of the City's failure to raise the bridge were not limited to the *Shiras* and the *Tewksbury*. Collision plainly created a danger that the bridge towers might fall onto adjoining property, and the crash of two uncontrolled lake vessels, one 425 feet and the other 525 feet long, into a bridge over a swift ice-ridden stream, with a channel only 177 feet wide, could well result in a partial damming that would flood property upstream. As to the City also, it is useful to consider, by way of contrast, Chief Judge Cardozo's statement that the Long Island would not have been liable to Mrs. Palsgraf had the guard wilfully thrown the package down. If the City had deliberately kept the bridge closed in the face of the onrushing vessels, taking the risk that they might not come so far, no one would give house-room to a claim that it "owed no duty" to those who later suffered from the flooding. Unlike Mrs. Palsgraf, they were within the area of hazard.

. . . .

Since all the claimants here met the *Palsgraf* requirement of being persons to whom the actors owed a "duty of care," we are not obliged to reconsider whether that case furnishes as useful a standard for determining the boundaries of liability in admiralty for negligent conduct. . . . But this does not dispose of the alternative argument that the manner in which several of the claimants were harmed, particularly by flood damage, was unforeseeable and that recovery for this may not be had. . . .

Although the obvious risks from not raising the bridge were damage to itself and to the vessels, the danger of a fall of the bridge and of flooding would not have been unforeseeable under the circumstances to anyone who gave them thought. And the same can be said as to the failure of Kinsman's shipkeeper to ready the anchors after the danger had become apparent. The exhibits indicate that the width of the channel between the Concrete Elevator and the bridge is at most points less than two hundred fifty feet. If the *Shiras* caught up on a dock or vessel moored along the shore, the current might well swing her bow across the channel so as to block the ice floes, as indeed could easily have occurred at the Standard Elevator dock where the stern of the *Shiras* struck the *Tewksbury's* bow. . . . Nor was it unforeseeable that the drawbridge would not be raised since, apart from any other reason, there was no assurance of timely warning. What may have been less foreseeable was that the *Shiras* would get that far down the twisting river, but this is somewhat negated both by the known speed of the current when freshets developed and by the evidence that, on learning of the *Shiras'* departure, Continental's employees and those they informed foresaw precisely that.

. . . Foreseeability of danger is necessary to render conduct negligent; whereas here the damage was caused by just those forces whose existence required the exercise of greater care than was taken — the current, the ice, and the physical mass of the *Shiras*, the incurring of consequences other and greater than foreseen does not make the conduct less culpable or provide a reasoned basis for insulation. . . . The oft encountered argument that failure to limit liability to foreseeable consequences may subject the defendant to a loss wholly out of proportion to his fault seems scarcely consistent with the universally accepted rule that the defendant takes the plaintiff as he finds him and will be responsible for the full extent of the injury. . . .

The weight of authority in this country rejects the limitation of damages to consequences foreseeable at the time of the negligent conduct when the consequences are "direct," and the damage, although other and greater than expectable, is of the same general sort that was risked. . . .

We see no reason why an actor engaging in conduct which entails a large risk of small damage and a small risk of other and greater damage, of the same general sort, from the same forces, and to the same class of persons, should be relieved of responsibility for the latter simply because the chance of its occurrence, if viewed alone, may not have been large enough to require the exercise of care. By hypothesis, the risk of the lesser harm was sufficient to render his disregard of it actionable; the existence of a less likely additional risk that the very forces against whose action he was required to guard would produce other and greater damage than could have been reasonably anticipated should inculpate him further rather than limit his liability. This does not mean that the careless actor will always be held for all damages for which the forces that he risked were a cause in fact. Somewhere a point will be reached when courts will agree that the link has become too tenuous — that what is claimed to be consequence is only fortuity. . . . [W]hat courts do in such cases makes better sense than what they, or others, say. Where the line will be drawn will vary from age to age; as society has come to rely increasingly on insurance and other methods of loss-sharing, the point may lie further off than a century ago. Here it is surely more equitable that the losses from the operators' negligent failure to raise the Michigan Avenue Bridge should be ratably borne by Buffalo's taxpayers than left with the innocent victims of the flooding; yet the mind is also repelled by a solution that would impose liability solely on the City and exonerate the persons whose negligent acts of commission and omission were the precipitating force of the collision with the bridge and its sequelae. We go only so far as to hold that where, as here, the damages resulted from the same physical forces whose existence required the exercise of greater care than was displayed and were of the same general sort that was expectable, unforeseeability of the exact developments and of the extent of the loss will not limit liability.

. . . .

———————

1. How is the proximate cause issue facing the court in *Kinsman* different from *Palsgraf*? To what extent does the decision in *Kinsman* extend *Palsgraf*?

2. Compare the decision in *Kinsman* with *Polemis, Wagon Mound No. 1*, and *Wagon Mound No. 2*.

3. What factors does the court weigh in *Kinsman*?

PROBLEM

Several years ago, Hemi Car Co. went into bankruptcy. This usually takes several years. Hemi emerged from bankruptcy in a few weeks after discontinuing many "small" dealers. This lightning-fast turnaround was assisted by the United States Government. Assume the small dealers lost millions of dollars each and were not compensated by Hemi.

Several small dealers, who were dropped, have asked you for assistance. Consider:

A. Under the Federal Torts Claims Act, should this be negligence on the part of government, or viewed as a "discretionary function" of high ranking government officials and therefore protected from suit?

B. In a tort suit (assume that you cannot sue Hemi), would proximate cause protect the government officials who designed and implemented the bankruptcy program for Hemi to discontinue the small dealers?

HAMBLIN v. STATE; MARICOPA COUNTY ADULT PROBATION DEPARTMENT
Court of Appeals of Arizona, 2006
143 P.3d 388

THOMPSON, J.

Appellants, the survivors of Russell Hamblin (the Hamblins), brought suit for his wrongful death against the State of Arizona and the Maricopa County Adult Probation Department (collectively MCAPD). The Hamblins appeal the summary judgment entered against them. Because we find that MCAPD was not the proximate cause of Russell Hamblin's death, we affirm.

FACTS AND RELEVANT PROCEEDINGS

Russell Hamblin was shot and killed by Roy Salinas (Salinas) during an armed robbery committed by Salinas and two others. At the time of the murder, fifteen-year-old Salinas was on adult probation with MCAPD for having assaulted a corrections officer while detained by the Arizona Department of Juvenile Corrections. Salinas pled guilty to attempted aggravated assault on a corrections officer, a class 6 offense, and was awaiting the start of his deferred jail term when he shot Russell Hamblin during a robbery.

The Hamblins alleged that MCAPD had a duty to supervise Salinas to ensure that he followed the terms of his probation, that MCAPD was grossly negligent when they failed to arrest Salinas or to seek a warrant for his arrest when Salinas violated his probationary terms, and that MCAPD's willful ignorance of Salinas's conduct allowed Salinas to murder Russell Hamblin.

We noted that there was an outstanding issue of causation urged below by MCAPD that the trial court had not ruled on. MCAPD argued that causation was lacking and that the Hamblins' claim required speculation that different supervision would have resulted in revocation of Salinas's probation, causing him to be incarcerated on the date that Russell Hamblin was killed. Our reversal of the dismissal order left the Hamblins with the task of developing evidence to support all of the allegations of their complaint and to establish the elements of their claim, including the element of causation.

Proximate Cause

. . . .

Causation is a two-part inquiry. Both elements, cause in fact and proximate cause, must be present for legal liability to attach. . . .

The second part of the causation inquiry is proximate cause. Our supreme court defines proximate cause as "that which, in a natural and continuous sequence, unbroken by any efficient intervening cause, produces an injury, and without which the injury would not have occurred." . . . That definition highlights the importance of the cause in fact element to proximate cause. Without cause in fact, proximate cause will never be shown. Whether a defendant's conduct that in-fact caused harm is too attenuated from the consequential harm is a question of proximate cause for the court.

In general, proximate cause embodies "ideas of what justice demands, or of what is administratively possible and convenient." Any examination of causation should recognize that "public policy undergirds concepts such as 'proximate cause'." "[P]roximate causation is a matter of public policy and therefore subject to the changing attitudes and needs of society." *See* Keeton, et al., *supra* P 11, Section 39, at p. 244.

. . . .

That there are policy limits inherent in proximate cause is neither a new nor a particularly revolutionary notion. The *Blue Shield* Court cited the seminal 1928 tort case *Palsgraf v. Long Island Railroad Company* for the proposition that:

> What we mean by the word 'proximate' is, that because of convenience, of public policy, of a rough sense of justice, the law arbitrarily declines to trace a series of events beyond a certain point.

. . . .

"Proximate cause" is not a logical proposition but a legal conclusion about when a party is to be held responsible for a loss; . . . proximate cause is a question of legal policy related directed at determining how far the protection of the law should extend; Leon Green, The Causal Relation Issue in Negligence Law, 60 Mich. L. Rev. 543, 548-49 (1960).

. . . .

As a policy matter, it is untenable to hold probation officers liable for all crimes committed by a person on probation. This is true even if the officer knows that the defendant has committed technical violations of his probation. To hold otherwise would give hindsight too much play and derogate the social utility of a probation officer's judgment and discretion. Our legislature outlined the powers and duties of probation officers in *A.R.S. Section 12-253* (2005). *Section 12-253(7)* states that a probation officer has the power and duty to

> [b]ring defaulting probationers into court when in his judgment the conduct
> of the probationer justifies the court to revoke suspension of the sentence.

The plain language of *A.R.S. Section 12-253(7)* recognizes that not all probation violations warrant a change in status. The probation officer has a duty to bring probationers into court when "in his judgment" the violation would be likely to cause the court to alter the probationer's status.

. . . .

―――――――

1. In general, courts tend to not hold governments liable for negligent acts such as this one. This seems appropriate in a practical sense. But in terms of checks on government, should there be the possibility of bringing such a tort against the government?

2. The trial court initially dismissed the Hamblins' claims against MCAPD for failure to state a claim on grounds of governmental immunity. On appeal from that decision this court reversed, holding that the alleged failure to supervise was not covered by immunity from civil liability, citing *Acevedo v. Pima County Adult Probation Department*, 142 Ariz. 319, 322, 690 P.2d 38, 41 (1984). Note that the Court's finding of "no proximate cause" accomplishes the same thing as immunity under the Federal Torts Claims Act.

B. INTERVENING CAUSES

PROBLEM

Al was cleaning a coin-operated vending machine with a solvent in an eight-foot by ten-foot room when a rat ran out of the machine and sought refuge under a gas heater with an open flame, located in the room. The now-flaming rodent returned to the machine, which exploded into flames, and as a result Al was severely burned. Al is nineteen-years-old and sues the manufacturer of the vending machine whose instructions said that it could be cleaned with a solvent. What defense?

WEIRUM v. RKO GENERAL, INC.
Supreme Court of California, 1975
15 Cal. 3d 40, 123 Cal. Rptr. 468, 539 P.2d 36

Mosk, Justice.

A rock radio station with an extensive teenage audience conducted a contest which rewarded the first contestant to locate a peripatetic disc jockey. Two minors driving in separate automobiles attempted to follow the disc jockey's automobile to its next stop. In the course of their pursuit, one of the minors negligently forced a car off the highway, killing its sole occupant. In a suit filed by the surviving wife and children of the decedent, the jury rendered a verdict against the radio station.

. . . .

On that day, Donald Steele Revert, known professionally as "The Real Don Steele," a KHJ disc jockey and television personality, traveled in a conspicuous red automobile to a number of locations in the Los Angeles metropolitan area. Periodically, he apprised KHJ of his whereabouts and his intended destination, and the station broadcast the information to its listeners. The first person to physically locate Steele and fulfill a specified condition received a cash prize. . . . The following excerpts from the July 16 broadcast illustrate the tenor of the contest announcements:

"9:30 and The Real Don Steele is back on his feet again with some money and he is headed for the Valley. Thought I would give you a warning so that you can get your kids out of the street."

. . . .

The primary question for our determination is whether defendant owed a duty to decedent arising out of its broadcast of the giveaway contest. The determination of duty is primarily a question of law. . . . It is the court's "expression of the sum total of those considerations of policy which lead the law to say that the particular plaintiff is entitled to protection." . . . Any number of considerations may justify the imposition of duty in particular circumstances, including the guidance of history, our continually refined concepts of morals and justice, the convenience of the rule, and social judgment as to where the loss should fall. . . . While the question whether one owes a duty to another must be decided on a case-by-case basis, every case is governed by the rule of general application that all persons are required to use ordinary care to prevent others from being injured as the result of their conduct. . . . [F]oreseeability of the risk is a primary consideration in establishing the element of duty. . . . Defendant asserts that the record here does not support a conclusion that a risk of harm to decedent was foreseeable.

While duty is a question of law, foreseeability is a question of fact for the jury. . . . The verdict in plaintiffs' favor here necessarily embraced a finding that decedent was exposed to a foreseeable risk of harm. . . .

We conclude that the record amply supports the finding of foreseeability. These tragic events unfolded in the middle of a Los Angeles summer, a time when young people were free from the constraints of school and responsive to relief from vacation tedium. Seeking to attract new listeners, KHJ devised an "exciting" promotion. Money and a small measure of momentary notoriety awaited the swiftest response. It was foreseeable that defendant's youthful listeners, finding the prize had eluded them at one location, would race to arrive first at the next site and in their haste would disregard the demands of highway safety.

. . . ."The mere fact that a particular kind of an accident has not happened before does not . . . show that such accident is one which might not reasonably have been anticipated." . . . Thus, the fortuitous absence of prior injury does not justify relieving defendant from responsibility for the foreseeable consequences of its acts.

It is of no consequence that the harm to decedent was inflicted by third parties acting negligently. Defendant invokes the maxim that an actor is entitled to assume that others will not act negligently. . . . This concept is valid, however, only to the extent the intervening conduct was not to be anticipated. . . . If the likelihood that a third person may react in a particular manner is a hazard which makes the actor negligent, such reaction whether innocent or negligent does not prevent the actor from being liable for the harm caused thereby. . . . Here, reckless conduct by youthful contestants, stimulated by defendant's broadcast, constituted the hazard to which decedent was exposed.

. . . .

Defendant's contention that the giveaway contest must be afforded the deference due society's interest in the First Amendment is clearly without merit. The issue here is civil accountability for the foreseeable results of a broadcast which created an undue risk of harm to decedent. The First Amendment does not sanction the infliction of physical injury merely because achieved by word, rather than act.

Defendant, relying upon the rule stated in section 315 of the Restatement Second of Torts, urges that it owed no duty of care to decedent. The section provides that, absent a special relationship, an actor is under no duty to control the conduct of third parties. As explained hereinafter, this rule has no application if the plaintiff's complaint, as here, is grounded upon an affirmative act of defendant which created an undue risk of harm.

The rule stated in section 315 is merely a refinement of the general principle embodied in section 314 that one is not obligated to act as a "good Samaritan." . . . This doctrine is rooted in the common law distinction between action and inaction, or misfeasance and nonfeasance. Misfeasance exists when the defendant is responsible for making the plaintiff's position worse, i.e., defendant has created a risk. Conversely, nonfeasance is found when the defendant has failed to aid plaintiff through beneficial intervention. As section 315 illustrates, liability for nonfeasance is largely limited to those circumstances in which some special relationship can be established. If, on the other hand, the act complained of is one of misfeasance, the question of duty is governed by the standards of ordinary care discussed above.

Here, there can be little doubt that we review an act of misfeasance to which section 315 is inapplicable. Liability is not predicated upon defendant's failure to intervene for the benefit of decedent but rather upon its creation of an unreasonable risk of harm to him. . . .

The judgment and the orders appealed from are affirmed. Plaintiffs shall recover their costs on appeal. The parties shall bear their own costs on the cross-appeal.

---

1.   In *Weirum*, who was the intervening cause? What arguments could you make for cutting off the radio station's liability?

2.   How would you flesh out the court's First Amendment discussion?

3.   How would you answer the following argument in *Weirum*: "Defendant is fearful that entrepreneurs will henceforth be burdened with an avalanche of obligations: an athletic department will owe a duty to an ardent sports fan injured while hastening to purchase one of a limited number of tickets . . ." (539 P.2d 36)? In *Riley v. Triplex Commun., Inc.*, 874 S.W.2d 333 (Tex. App. 1994), the radio station was found liable for negligently promoting a weekly Ladies' Night with ninety-four cent drinks at a local bar after a drunk customer injured two police officers.

4.   In *Derdiarian v. Felix Contracting Corp.*, 51 N.Y.2d 308, 434 N.Y.S.2d 166, 414 N.E.2d 666 (1980), defendant Felix Contracting Corp. was excavating a worksite in a street when defendant Dickens suffered an epileptic seizure, allowing his vehicle to crash into the worksite and hit plaintiff, throwing him into the air. When plaintiff landed, he was splattered with boiling enamel from a kettle that had been struck by the automobile. Plaintiff Derdiarian was an employee of a subcontractor at the worksite. Defendant Felix argued that there was no causal link between Felix' breach of duty and plaintiff's injuries. Dickens' seizure and crash was held not to be a superseding cause of Felix' liability:

> Where the acts of a third person intervene between the defendant's conduct and the plaintiff's injury, the causal connection is not automatically severed. In such a case, liability turns upon whether the intervening act is a normal or foreseeable consequence of the situation created by the defendant's negligence. If the intervening act is extraordinary under the circumstances, not foreseeable in the normal course of events, or independent of or far removed from the defendant's conduct, it may well be a superseding act which breaks the causal nexus. Because questions concerning what is foreseeable and what is normal may be the subject of varying inferences, as is the question of negligence itself, these issues generally are for the fact finder to resolve.
>
> [I]n the present case, we cannot say as a matter of law that defendant Dickens' negligence was a superseding cause which interrupted the link between Felix's negligence and plaintiff's injuries. From the evidence in the record, the jury could have found that Felix negligently failed to safeguard the excavation site. A prime hazard associated with such dereliction is the possibility that a driver will negligently enter the work site and cause injury to a worker. That the driver was negligent, or even reckless, does not insulate Felix from liability. Nor is it decisive that the driver lost control of

the vehicle through a negligent failure to take medication, rather than a driving mistake. The precise manner of the event need not be anticipated. The finder of fact could have concluded that the foreseeable, normal and natural result of the risk created by Felix was the injury of a worker by a car entering the improperly protected work area. An intervening act may not serve as a superseding cause, and relieve an actor of responsibility, where the risk of the intervening act occurring is the very same risk which renders the actor negligent.

In a similar vein, plaintiff's act of placing the kettle on the west side of the excavation does not, as a matter of law, absolve defendant Felix of responsibility. Serious injury, or even death, was a foreseeable consequence of a vehicle crashing through the work area. The injury could have occurred in numerous ways, ranging from a worker being directly struck by the car to the car hitting an object that injures the worker. Placement of the kettle, or any object in the work area, could affect how the accident occurs and the extent of injuries. That defendant could not anticipate the precise manner of the accident or the exact extent of injuries, however, does not preclude liability as a matter of law where the general risk and character of injuries are foreseeable.

PROBLEM

Casey rents an apartment in an urban area from GHI, which has advertised night security. However, one night, an employee caretaker of the apartment complex walks into Casey's apartment with a key and murders one of Casey's guests, Jim. Casey and Jim's heirs sue the management of GHI and the security agency, claiming the negligent hiring of the employee and negligent security were the proximate cause of Jim's murder. What result?

WATSON v. KENTUCKY & INDIANA BRIDGE & RAILROAD CO.

Court of Appeals Kentucky, 1910
137 Ky. 619, 126 S.W. 146

[A gasoline tank car owned by defendant railroad was derailed because of a faulty roadbed thereby causing gasoline to flow into the streets of Louisville. The gasoline was ignited and damage done when Duerr lit a match. He said he was lighting a cigar. Others testified:

> Duerr, who had been a telegraph operator in the employ of the appellee Bridge & Railroad Company, was on the morning of the day of the explosion discharged from its service, and that 20 minutes before the explosion Duerr remarked to his companion, in the hearing of Giacometti and Darnall, "Let us go and set the damn thing on fire."

Plaintiff appeals a directed verdict in favor of the defendant.]

SETTLE, J. . . . .

The lighting of the match of Duerr having resulted in the explosion, the question is, was that act merely a contributing cause, or the efficient and, therefore, proximate cause of appellant's injuries? The question of proximate cause is a question for the jury. In holding that Duerr in lighting or throwing the match acted maliciously or with intent to cause the explosion, the trial court invaded the province of the jury. There was, it is true, evidence tending to prove that it was inadvertently or negligently done by Duerr. It was therefore for the jury and not the court to determine from all the evidence whether the lighting of the match was done by Duerr inadvertently or negligently, or whether it was a wanton and malicious act.

. . . .

If the presence on Madison street in the city of Louisville of the great volume of loose gas that arose from the escaping gasoline was caused by the negligence of the appellee Bridge & Railroad Company, it seems to us that the probable consequences of its coming in contact with fire and causing an explosion was too plain a proposition to admit of doubt. Indeed, it was most probable that someone would strike a match to light a cigar or for other purposes in the midst of the gas. In our opinion, therefore, the act of one lighting and throwing a match under such circumstances cannot be said to be the efficient cause of the explosion. It did not of itself produce the explosion, nor could it have done so without the assistance and contribution resulting from the primary negligence, if there was such negligence, on the part of the appellee Bridge & Railroad company in furnishing the presence of the gas in the street. This conclusion, however, rests upon the theory that Duerr inadvertently or negligently lighted and threw the match in the gas.

If, however, the act of Duerr in lighting the match and throwing it into the vapor or gas arising from the gasoline was malicious, and done for the purpose of causing the explosion, we do not think appellees would be responsible, for while the appellee Bridge & Railroad Company's negligence may have been the efficient cause of the presence of the gas in the street, and it should have understood enough of the consequences thereof to have foreseen that an explosion was likely to result from the inadvertent or negligent lighting of a match by some person who was ignorant of the presence of the gas or of the effect of lighting or throwing a match in it, it could not have foreseen or deemed it probable that one would maliciously or wantonly do such an act for the evil purpose of producing the explosion. Therefore, if the act of Duerr was malicious, we quite agree with the trial court that it was one which the appellees could not reasonably have anticipated or guarded against, and in such case the act of Duerr, and not the primary negligence of the appellee Bridge & Railroad Company, in any of the particulars charged, was the efficient or proximate cause of appellant's injuries. The mere fact that the concurrent cause or intervening act was unforeseen will not relieve the defendant guilty of the primary negligence from liability, but if the intervening agency is something so unexpected or extraordinary as that he could not or ought not to have anticipated it, he will not be liable, and certainly he is not bound to anticipate the criminal acts of others by which damage is inflicted and hence is not liable therefor.

. . . .

[T]he judgment is . . . reversed as to the Bridge & Railroad Company, and cause remanded for a new trial consistent with the opinion.

———

1. In *Brower v. New York Central & H. R.R.*, 91 N.J.L. 190, 103 A. 166 (1918), the train, because of negligence, crashed into plaintiff's wagon. As a result, the barrels that were in the wagon were stolen. The court found that "the act of the thieves did not intervene between defendant's negligence and the plaintiff's loss."

2. Is the line between negligence and maliciousness drawn by the court in *Watson* clear?

3. Argue that the railroad should not escape liability even if Duerr's act was malicious.

4. Criminal behavior does not always break the chain of causation. *See* Restatement (Second) of Torts §§ 448–49. Examples:

a. Two minor students steal chemical explosives from defendant school's unlocked storage room. The plaintiff child is injured when the chemicals explode. Is the school liable? *Kush by Marszalek v. City of Buffalo*, 59 N.Y.2d 26, 462 N.Y.S.2d 831, 449 N.E.2d 725 (1983).

b. Defendant train misses plaintiff's stop and drops her one mile away from her stop in a dangerous area. The plaintiff, on her way home, is raped by two individuals. Is the railroad company liable? *Hines v. Garrett*, 108 S.E. 690 (Va. 1921).

c. The defendant pharmacist sold poison to the wife's husband, who then used it to kill her. The wife's survivors sue for wrongful death. Is the pharmacist liable? *January v. Peace*, 738 S.W.2d 355 (Tex. App. 1987).

d. The plaintiff freelance photographer is attacked and beaten while photographing a hotel in Mexico. The defendant newspaper had not informed the plaintiff that the newspaper had previously printed an article alleging that the owner of the hotel was a drug kingpin. Is the newspaper liable for plaintiff's injuries? *Gutierrez v. Scripps-Howard*, 823 S.W.2d 696 (Tex. App. 1992).

e. The defendant tenant violates a fire code by stacking trash next to a building. A fire destroys the building. Arson may have been the cause of fire, yet the plaintiff landlord sues the tenant for the loss of the building. Is the tenant liable? *Britton v. Wooten*, 817 S.W.2d 443 (Ky. 1991).

BRAUN v. SOLDIER OF FORTUNE MAGAZINE, INC.
United States Court of Appeals, Eleventh Circuit, 1992
968 F.2d 1110, *cert. denied*, 506 U.S. 1071, 113 S. Ct. 1028 (1993)

[The sons of a murder victim brought this wrongful death action against *Soldier of Fortune* (S.O.F.) magazine and its parent company, alleging that the defendants negligently published an advertisement that created an unreasonable risk of solicitation of violent criminal activity. The jury awarded compensatory damages of

$4.3 million.]

ANDERSON, CIRCUIT JUDGE:

. . . .

In January 1985, Michael Savage submitted a personal service advertisement to SOF. After several conversations between Savage and SOF's advertising manager, Joan Steel, the following advertisement ran in the June 1985 through March 1986 issues of SOF:

> GUN FOR HIRE: 37 year old professional mercenary desires jobs. Vietnam Veteran. Discrete [sic] and very private. Body guard, courier, and other special skills. All jobs considered. Phone (615) 436-9785 (days) or (615) 436-4335 (nights), or write: Rt. 2, Box 682 Village Loop Road, Gatlinburg, TN 37738.

Savage testified that, when he placed the ad, he had no intention of obtaining anything but legitimate jobs. Nonetheless, Savage stated that the overwhelming majority of the 30 to 40 phone calls a week he received in response to his ad sought his participation in criminal activity such as murder, assault, and kidnapping. The ad also generated at least one legitimate job as a bodyguard, which Savage accepted.

In late 1984 or early 1985, Bruce Gastwirth began seeking to murder his business partner, Richard Braun. Gastwirth enlisted the aid of another business associate, John Horton Moore, and together they arranged for at least three attempts on Braun's life, all of which were unsuccessful. Responding to Savage's SOF ad, Gastwirth and Moore contacted him in August 1985 to discuss plans to murder Braun.

On August 26, 1985, Savage, Moore, and another individual, Sean Trevor Doutre, went to Braun's suburban Atlanta home. As Braun and his sixteen year-old son Michael were driving down the driveway, Doutre stepped in front of Braun's car and fired several shots into the car with a MAC 11 automatic pistol. The shots hit Michael in the thigh and wounded Braun as well. Braun managed to roll out of the car, but Doutre walked over to Braun and killed him by firing two more shots into the back of his head as Braun lay on the ground.

. . . .

The district court, sitting in Alabama, properly looked to Georgia law in resolving appellees' negligence claims. . . .

. . . .

The district court found that publishers like SOF have a duty to the public when they publish an advertisement if "the ad in question contains a clearly identifiable unreasonable risk, that the offer in the ad is one to commit a serious violent crime, including murder." SOF argues that the district court erred in finding that a publisher has a duty "to reject ambiguous advertisements that pose a threat of harm," Brief for Appellants at 24, and contends that a publisher should be held liable for publishing an ad only if the ad explicitly solicits a crime. . . .

Georgia courts recognize a "general duty one owes to all the world not to subject them to an unreasonable risk of harm." . . . Accordingly, the district court properly found that SOF had a legal duty to refrain from publishing advertisements that subjected the public, including appellees, to a clearly identifiable unreasonable risk of harm from violent criminal activity. To the extent that SOF denies that a publisher owes any duty to the public when it publishes personal service ads, its position is clearly inconsistent with Georgia law. We believe, however, that the crux of SOF's argument is not that it had no duty to the public, but that, as a matter of law, the risk to the public presented when a publisher prints an advertisement is "unreasonable" only if the ad openly solicits criminal activity. . . .

. . . .

[W]e find that the district court properly . . . instructed that the jury could hold SOF liable for printing Savage's advertisement only if the advertisement on its face would have alerted a reasonably prudent publisher to the clearly identifiable unreasonable risk of harm to the public that the advertisement posed. . . . [T]he duty of care the district court imposed on publishers was an appropriate reconciliation of Georgia's interest in providing compensation to victims of tortious conduct with the First Amendment concern that state law not chill protected speech. Accordingly, we reject SOF's argument that the district court's instructions "placed an intolerable burden upon the press." . . . SOF's sole remaining claim is that the jury erred in finding that SOF's publication of Savage's ad was the proximate cause of appellees' injuries. SOF argues that the events that intervened between its publication of Savage" ad and the carrying out of the murder plot were entirely unforeseeable and, therefore, that SOF's publication of Savage's ad was too remote in the chain of events leading to appellees' injuries for the jury to hold SOF liable. Since the proximate cause issue does not implicate any constitutional values, we review the jury's factual finding under the traditional standard of deference to the fact finder. . . .

We find that the jury had ample grounds for finding that SOFs publication of Savage's ad was the proximate cause of appellees' injuries. Georgia law recognizes that, "generally, the intervening criminal act of a third party, without which the injury would not have occurred, will be treated as the proximate cause of the injury, superseding any negligence of the defendant . . ." . . . If, however, "the criminal act was a reasonably foreseeable consequence of the defendant's conduct, the casual connection between that conduct and the injury is not broken." . . . We have already held that the language of Savage's ad should have alerted a reasonably prudent publisher to the clearly identifiable unreasonable risk that Savage was soliciting violent and illegal jobs. It follows that a reasonable jury could conclude that the criminal act that harmed appellees was reasonably foreseeable and, accordingly, that the chain of causation was not broken.

For the foregoing reasons, we AFFIRM the district court's judgment.

Affirmed.

1.   As compared with *Watson*, what makes *Braun* more challenging in dealing with proximate cause?

2.   Liability of S.O.F. was denied in *Eimann v. Soldier of Fortune Magazine*, 880 F.2d 830 (5th Cir. 1989), *cert. denied*, 493 U.S. 1024 (1990), based on the following advertisement:

> EX-MARINES — 67-69 'Nam Vets, Ex-DI, weapons specialist-jungle warfare, pilot, M.E., high risk assignments, U.S. or overseas. (404) 991-2684.

Compare this to the ad in *Braun*. What are the differences?

3.   In *Way v. Boy Scouts of Am., Nat'l Shooting Sports Found., Inc.*, 856 S.W.2d 230 (Tex. App. 1993), for example, a mother sued a youth magazine publisher for advertising shooting sports, claiming the advertisement caused the death of her son. The mother claimed that her son, after having read the advertisement, was motivated to experiment with a rifle that discharged and killed him. The court found there was no breach of duty and that Texas does not recognize a cause of action for negligent publication.

4.   In *Braun*, the court rejected S.O.F.'s First Amendment arguments and concluded:

> Supreme Court cases discussing the limitations the First Amendment places on state defamation law indicate that there is no constitutional infirmity in Georgia Law holding publishers liable under a negligence standard with respect to the commercial advertisements they print.
>
> . . . .
>
> Based upon the foregoing authorities, we conclude that the First Amendment permits a state to impose upon a publisher liability forcompensatory damages for negligently publishing a commercial advertisement where the ad on its face, and without the need for investigation, makes it apparent that there is a substantial danger of harm to the public. The absence of a duty requiring publishers to investigate the advertisements they print and the requirement that the substance of the ad itself must warn the publisher of a substantial danger of harm to the public guarantee that the burden placed on publishers will not impermissibly chill protected commercial speech. 968 F.2d 1110, 1119.

5.   In "Hit Man" the author wrote a manual for those who wished to kill someone. A reader committed a triple murder. In the civil suit, the publisher defended on the basis of free speech, but the U.S. Court of Appeals rejected that argument: "The mail-order book had no legitimate purpose beyond the promotion and teaching of murder." The court said, "In at least these circumstances, we are confident that the First Amendment does not erect an absolute bar to the imposition of civil liability . . ." Atlanta Journal Constitution A-10, Nov. 11, 1997.

6.   If the owner of a car leaves the keys in the ignition, is he or she the proximate cause of the damage to the plaintiff where a thief steals the defendant's car and negligently runs into the plaintiff's car?

The answer may be yes where there is a statute on point. In *Ney v. Yellow Cab Co.*, 2 Ill. 2d 74, 117 N.E.2d 74 (1954), the statute provided: "No person driving . . . a motor vehicle shall permit it to stand unattended without first . . . removing the car key."

The answer may also be yes where the theft is especially foreseeable because of the neighborhood or the goods in the back of the truck, *Hergenrether v. East*, 61 Cal. 2d 440, 39 Cal. Rptr. 4, 393 P.2d 164 (1964).

The car thief is likely to be a superseding cause of the owner's negligence in cases without a statute and without strong facts suggesting foreseeability. *See Ross v. Nutt*, 177 Ohio St. 113, 203 N.E.2d 118 (1964).

PROBLEM

Ann is the fourteen-year-old daughter of Jack. Jack went out of town for the weekend and left Ann with neighbors. Ann went home, allegedly to feed her cat. While there, she had a party for ten friends, which soon exploded to 100 teenagers. Everyone brought alcohol and consumed it. While driving home from the party, Bob (age seventeen) crashed into the plaintiff's car and seriously injured him. Bob was drunk. You represent the plaintiff. Discuss.

What if Jack had left a large amount of alcohol in the house and Ann had appropriated it for the party?

KELLY v. GWINNELL
Supreme Court of New Jersey, 1984
96 N.J. 538, 476 A.2d 1219

WILENTZ, C.J.

This case raises the issue of whether a social host who enables an adult guest at his home to become drunk is liable to the victim of an automobile accident caused by the drunken driving of the guest. Here the host served liquor to the guest beyond the point at which the guest was visibly intoxicated. We hold the host may be liable under the circumstances of this case. At the trial level, the case was disposed of, insofar as the issue before us is concerned, by summary judgment in favor of the social host. The record on which the summary judgment was based (pleadings, depositions, and certifications) discloses that defendant Donald Gwinnell, after driving defendant Joseph Zak home, spent an hour or two at Zak's home before leaving to return to his own home. During that time, according to Gwinnell, Zak, and Zak's wife, Gwinnell consumed two or three drinks of scotch on the rocks. Zak accompanied Gwinnell outside to his car, chatted with him, and watched as Gwinnell then drove off to go home. About twenty-five minutes later Zak telephoned Gwin-nell's home to make sure Gwinnell had arrived there safely. The phone was answered by Mrs. Gwinnell, who advised Zak that Gwinnell had been involved in a head-on collision. The collision was with an automobile operated by plaintiff, Marie Kelly, who was seriously injured as a result.

After the accident Gwinnell was subjected to a blood test, which indicated a blood alcohol concentration of 0.286 percent. Kelly's expert concluded from that reading that Gwinnell had consumed not two or three scotches but the equivalent of thirteen drinks; that while at Zak's home Gwinnell must have been showing unmistakable signs of intoxication; and that in fact he was severely intoxicated while at Zak's residence and at the time of the accident.

Kelly sued Gwinnell and his employer; those defendants sued the Zaks in a third party action; and thereafter plaintiff amended her complaint to include Mr. and Mrs. Zak as direct defendants. The Zaks moved for summary judgment, contending that as a matter of law a host is not liable for the negligence of an adult social guest who has become intoxicated while at the host's home. The trial court granted the motion on that basis. . . .

Under the facts here defendant provided his guest with liquor, knowing that thereafter the guest would have to drive in order to get home. Viewing the facts most favorably to plaintiff (as we must, since the complaint was dismissed on a motion for summary judgment), one could reasonably conclude that the Zaks must have known that their provision of liquor was causing Gwinnell to become drunk, yet they continued to serve him even after he was visibly intoxicated. By the time he left, Gwinnell was in fact severely intoxicated. A reasonable person in Zak's position could foresee quite clearly that this continued provision of alcohol to Gwinnell was making it more and more likely that Gwinnell would not be able to operate his car carefully. Zak could foresee that unless he stopped providing drinks to Gwinnell, Gwinnell was likely to injure someone as a result of the negligent operation of his car. The usual elements of a cause of action for negligence are clearly present: an action by defendant creating an unreasonable risk of harm to plaintiff, a risk that was clearly foreseeable, and a risk that resulted in an injury equally foreseeable. Under those circumstances the only question remaining is whether a duty exists to prevent such risk or, realistically, whether this Court should impose such a duty.

In most cases the justice of imposing such a duty is so clear that the cause of action in negligence is assumed to exist simply on the basis of the actor's creation of an unreasonable risk of foreseeable harm resulting in injury. In fact, however, more is needed, "more" being the value judgment, based on an analysis of public policy, that the actor owed the injured party a duty of reasonable care. . . .

When the court determines that a duty exists and liability will be extended, it draws judicial lines based on fairness and policy. In a society where thousands of deaths are caused each year by drunken drivers, where the damage caused by such deaths is regarded increasingly as intolerable, where liquor licensees are prohibited from serving intoxicated adults, and where long-standing criminal sanctions against drunken driving have recently been significantly strengthened to the point where the Governor notes that they are regarded as the toughest in the nation, see Governor's Annual Message to the N. J. State Legislature, Jan. 10, 1984, the imposition of such a duty by the judiciary seems both fair and fully in accord with the State's policy. Unlike those cases in which the definition of desirable policy is the subject of intense controversy, here the imposition of a duty is both consistent with and supportive of a social goal — the reduction of drunken driving — that is practically unanimously accepted by society.

. . . .

The argument is made that the rule imposing liability on licensees is justified because licensees, unlike social hosts, derive a profit from serving liquor. We reject this analysis of the liability's foundation and emphasize that the liability proceeds from the duty of care that accompanies control of the liquor supply. Whatever the motive behind making alcohol available to those who will subsequently drive, the provider has a duty to the public not to create foreseeable, unreasonable risks by this activity.

We therefore hold that a host who serves liquor to an adult social guest, knowing both that the guest is intoxicated and will thereafter be operating a motor vehicle, is liable for injuries inflicted on a third party as a result of the negligent operation of a motor vehicle by the adult guest when such negligence is caused by the intoxication. We impose this duty on the host to the third party because we believe that the policy considerations served by its imposition far outweigh those asserted in opposition. While we recognize the concern that our ruling will interfere with accepted standards of social behavior; will intrude on and somewhat diminish the enjoyment, relaxation, and camaraderie that accompany social gatherings at which alcohol is served; and that such gatherings and social relationships are not simply tangential benefits of a civilized society but are regarded by many as important, we believe that the added assurance of just compensation to the victims of drunken driving as well as the added deterrent effect of the rule on such driving outweigh the importance of those other values. . . .

The liability we impose here is analogous to that traditionally imposed on owners of vehicles who lend their cars to persons they know to be intoxicated. . . . If, by lending a car to a drunk, a host becomes liable to third parties injured by the drunken driver's negligence, the same liability should extend to a host who furnishes liquor to a visibly drunken guest who he knows will thereafter drive away.

Some fear has been expressed that the extent of the potential liability may be disproportionate to the fault of the host. A social judgment is therein implied to the effect that society does not regard as particularly serious the host's actions in causing his guests to become drunk, even though he knows they will thereafter be driving their cars. We seriously question that value judgment; indeed, we do not believe that the liability is disproportionate when the host's actions, so relatively easily corrected, may result in serious injury or death. The other aspect of this argument is that the host's insurance protection will be insufficient. While acknowledging that homeowners' insurance will cover such liability, this argument notes the risk that both the host and spouse will be jointly liable. The point made is not that the level of insurance will be lower in relation to the injuries than in the case of other torts, but rather that the joint liability of the spouses may result in the loss of their home and other property to the extent that the policy limits are inadequate. If only one spouse were liable, then even though the policy limits did not cover the liability, the couple need not lose their home because the creditor might not reach the interest of the spouse who was not liable. . . . We observe, however, that it is common for both spouses to be liable in automobile accident cases. It may be that some special form of insurance could be designed to protect the spouses' equity in their homes in cases such as this one. In any event, it is not clear that the loss of a home by spouses who, by definition, have negligently caused the injury, is disproportionate to the loss of life of one who is totally innocent of any wrongdoing.

Given the lack of precedent anywhere else in the country, however, we believe it would be unfair to impose this liability retroactively. . . . Homeowners who are social hosts may desire to increase their policy limits; apartment dwellers may want to obtain liability insurance of this kind where perhaps they now have none. The imposition of retroactive liability could be considered unexpected and its imposition unfair. We therefore have determined that the liability imposed by this case on social hosts shall be prospective, applicable only to events that occur after the date of this decision. We will, however, apply the doctrine to the parties before us on the usual theory that to do otherwise would not only deprive the plaintiff of any benefit resulting from her own efforts but would also make it less likely that, in the future, individuals will be willing to claim rights, not yet established, that they believe are just.

. . . .

We are satisfied that our decision today is well within the competence of the judiciary. Defining the scope of tort liability has traditionally been accepted as the responsibility of the courts. Indeed, given the courts' prior involvement in these matters, our decision today is hardly the radical change implied by the dissent but, while significant, is rather a fairly predictable expansion of liability in this area.

It should be noted that the difficulties posited by the dissent as to the likely consequence of this decision are purely hypothetical. Given the facts before us, we decide only that where the social host directly serves the guest and continues to do so even after the guest is visibly intoxicated, knowing that the guest will soon be driving home, the social host may be liable for the consequences of the resulting drunken driving. We are not faced with a party where many guests congregate, nor with guests serving each other, nor with a host busily occupied with other responsibilities and therefore unable to attend to the matter of serving liquor, nor with a drunken host. We will face those situations when and if they come before us, we hope with sufficient reason and perception so as to balance, if necessary and if legitimate, the societal interests alleged to be inconsistent with the public policy considerations that are at the heart of today's decision. The fears expressed by the dissent concerning the vast impact of the decision on the "average citizen's" life are reminiscent of those asserted in opposition to our decisions abolishing husband-wife, parent-child, and generally family immunity. . . .

We recognize, however, that the point of view expressed by the dissent conforms, at least insofar as the result is concerned, with the view, whether legislatively or judicially expressed, of practically every other jurisdiction that has been faced with this question. It seems to us that by now it ought to be clear to all that the concerns on which that point of view is based are minor compared to the devastating consequences of drunken driving. This is a problem that society is just beginning to face squarely, and perhaps we in New Jersey are doing so sooner than others.

For instance, the dissent's emphasis on the financial impact of an insurance premium increase on the homeowner or the tenant should be measured against the monumental financial losses suffered by society as a result of drunken driving. By our decision we not only spread some of that loss so that it need not be borne completely by the victims of this widespread affliction, but, to some extent, reduce the likelihood that the loss will occur in the first place. Even if the dissent's view of the scope of our decision were correct, the adjustments in social behavior at parties, the burden put on the host to reasonably oversee the serving of liquor, the burden on the guests to make sure if one is drinking that another is driving, and the burden on all to take those reasonable steps even if, on some occasion, some guest may become belligerent: those social dislocations, their importance, must be measured against the misery, death, and destruction caused by the drunken driver. Does our society morally approve of the decision to continue to allow the charm of unrestrained social drinking when the cost is the lives of others, sometimes of the guests themselves?

If we but step back and observe ourselves objectively, we will see a phenomenon not of merriment but of cruelty, causing misery to innocent people, tolerated for years despite our knowledge that without fail, out of our extraordinarily high number of deaths caused by automobiles, nearly half have regularly been attributable to drunken driving.

. . . .

We therefore reverse the judgment in favor of the defendants Zak and remand the case to the Law Division for proceedings consistent with this opinion.

GARIBALDI, J., dissenting.

[T]he almost limitless implications of the majority's decision lead me to conclude that the Legislature is better equipped to effectuate the goals of reducing injuries from drunken driving and protecting the interests of the injured party, without placing such a grave burden on the average citizen of this state.

---

1. Arguably, *Kelly* has had a substantial impact on how individuals, groups, and private clubs serve alcohol. Argue that the question is for the legislature or the courts.

2. What factors did the court consider in reaching its decision? Is the amount and availability of insurance an appropriate factor for consideration under proximate cause?

3. If you believe that the court would have reached a different decision twenty years ago, what has changed in the interim?

4. After the decision in *Kelly*, the New Jersey legislature passed a statute limiting the impact of the case. The statute provides social host liability for "willfully and knowingly" providing alcoholic beverages to "a person who was visibly intoxicated in the host's presence. . . ." An irrebutable presumption that the driver was not visibly intoxicated is provided if the blood alcohol concentration was less than.10%, and a rebuttable presumption of nonintoxi-cation between.10% and.15%. The social host's liability is not joint and several. *See* N.J. Stat. Ann. §§ 2A:15-5.6 to 2A:15-5.8.

5. Dramshop Acts. Statutes often provide that commercial vendors of liquor are civilly and criminally liable for damages caused by intoxicated customers. For a summary of these acts, see *Ling v. Jan's Liquors*, 237 Kan. 629, 703 P.2d 731 (1985).

6. A majority of the courts, faced with the question, have refused to hold the social host liable for damages brought about by the guest. *See Overbaugh v. McCutcheon*, 396 S.E.2d 153 (W. Va. 1990). Why?

7. A mother purchased beer and supervised its consumption by teenagers, including her child. Although concerned, she permitted an intoxicated teen to drive home. He crashed into a car and killed the driver. The mother was held liable. *Sutter v. Hutchings*, 254 Ga. 194, 327 S.E.2d 716 (1985). When a drunken wedding guest injures someone, will the bride's parents be liable because they paid for the reception?

8. A bar owner who provided jumper cables to a visibly intoxicated person was held liable to third persons who suffered injuries in a collision. *Leppke v. Segura*, 632 P.2d 1057 (Colo. App. 1981). An extreme result?

WAGNER v. INTERNATIONAL RAILWAY CO.
Court of Appeals of New York, 1921
232 N.Y. 176, 133 N.E. 437

CARDOZO, J.

The action is for personal injuries. The defendant operates an electric railway between Buffalo and Niagara Falls. There is a point on its line where an overhead crossing carries its tracks . . . upwards over a trestle. . . . A turn is then made to the left at an angle of from sixty-four to eighty-four degrees. After making this turn, the line passes over a bridge, which is about one hundred and fifty-eight feet long from one abutment to the other. Then comes a turn to the right at about the same angle down the same kind of an incline to grade. Above the trestles, the tracks are laid on ties, unguarded at the ends. There is thus an overhang of the cars, which is accentuated at curves. . . .

Plaintiff and his cousin Herbert boarded a car at a station near the bottom of one of the trestles. Other passengers, entering at the same time, filled the platform, and blocked admission to the aisle. The platform was provided with doors, but the conductor did not close them. Moving at from six to eight miles an hour, the car, without slackening, turned the curve. There was a violent lurch, and Herbert Wagner was thrown out, near the point where the trestle changes to a bridge. The cry was raised, "Man overboard." The car went on across the bridge, and stopped near the foot of the incline. Night and darkness had come on. Plaintiff walked along the trestle, a distance of four hundred and forty-five feet, until he arrived at the bridge, where he thought to find his cousin's body. He says that he was asked to go there by the conductor. He says, too, that the conductor followed with a lantern. Both these statements the conductor denies. Several other persons, instead of ascending the trestle, went beneath it, and discovered under the bridge the body they were seeking. As they stood there, the plaintiff's body struck the ground beside them. Reaching the bridge, he had found upon a beam his cousin's hat, but nothing else. About him, there was darkness. He missed his footing, and fell.

. . . .

Danger invites rescue. The cry of distress is the summons to relief. The law does not ignore these reactions of the mind in tracing conduct to its consequences. It recognizes them as normal. It places their effects within the range of the natural and probable. The wrong that imperils life is a wrong to the imperilled victim; it is a wrong also to his rescuer. The state that leaves an opening in a bridge is liable to the child that falls into the stream, but liable also to the parent who plunges to its aid. . . . The railroad company whose train approaches without signal is a wrongdoer toward the traveler surprised between the rails, but a wrongdoer also to the bystander who drags him from the path. . . . The risk of rescue, if only it be not wanton, is born of the occasion. The emergency begets the man. The wrongdoer may not have foreseen the coming of a deliverer. He is accountable as if he had. . . .

The defendant says that we must stop, in following the chain of causes, when action ceases to be "instinctive." By this, is meant, it seems, that rescue is at the peril of the rescuer, unless spontaneous and immediate. If there has been time to deliberate, if impulse has given way to judgment, one cause, it is said, has spent its force, and another has intervened. In this case, the plaintiff walked more than four hundred feet in going to Herbert's aid. He had time to reflect and weigh; impulse had been followed by choice; and choice, in the defendant's view, intercepts and breaks the sequence. We find no warrant for thus shortening the chain of jural causes. We may assume, though we are not required to decide, that peril and rescue must be in substance one transaction; that the sight of the one must have aroused the impulse to the other; in short, that there must be unbroken continuity between the commission of the wrong and the effort to avert its consequences. If all this be assumed, the defendant is not aided. Continuity in such circumstances is not broken by the exercise of volition. . . . The law does not discriminate between the rescuer oblivious of peril and the one who counts the cost. It is enough that the act, whether impulsive or deliberate, is the child of the occasion.

. . . The reason that was exacted of him was not the reason of the morrow. It was reason fitted and proportioned to the time and the event.

Whether Herbert Wagner's fall was due to the defendant's negligence, and whether plaintiff in going to the rescue, as he did, was foolhardy or reasonable in the light of the emergency confronting him, were questions for the jury.

The judgment of the Appellate Division and that of the Trial Term should be reversed, and a new trial granted, with costs to abide the event.

---

1. Note that *Wagner* was decided seven years before *Palsgraf* (1928). Does *Palsgraf* follow *Wagner*? Must it?

2. Suppose a cruise ship sinks because of negligence on the part of the captain. Would a private rescuer who is drowned in a hurricane be able to recover from the cruise line? What about a rescuing sailor who is a doctor and suffers a heart attack from overwork while treating the passengers? What if the doctor is employed by the cruise line for such emergencies and suffers a heart attack from strain after having been flown to the site of the sinking? See *Carter v. Taylor Diving & Salvage Co.*, 341 F. Supp. 628 (E.D. La. 1972), *aff'd mem.*, 470 F.2d 995 (5th Cir. 1973).

3. What limit does the court place on the rescuer's recovery?

4. The plaintiff fell and injured her leg while running from the defendant's railroad car that had jumped the track. The court rejected the argument that the plaintiff's fear was a superseding cause and upheld the plaintiff's verdict. *Tuttle v. Atlantic City R.R. Co.*, 66 N.J.L. 327, 49 A. 450 (1901).

5. Should a professional, i.e., firefighter, police officer, or doctor, who is injured in the line of duty be able to recover when defendant is negligent? The "fireman's rule," now more commonly referred to as the "professional rescuer" doctrine, bars recovery for a professional. However, some states have abolished or limited this rule. *See Christensen v. Murphy*, 296 Or. 610, 678 P.2d 1210 (1984) (holding the rule is no longer a bar to recovery for personal injury); *Bates v. McKeon*, 650 F. Supp. 476 (D. Conn. 1986) (holding that police officer could recover compensatory and punitive damages for intentional tort of assault and battery).

6. Suppose the plaintiff passenger is injured in a bus collision, resulting from the bus driver's negligence. The doctor treating the plaintiff performs unnecessary surgery on the plaintiff, whose injuries are therefore further aggravated. The plaintiff sues the bus driver and bus owner for all injuries. What result? *Ponder v. Cartmell*, 301 Ark. 409, 784 S.W.2d 758 (1990).

7. A recurring problem is where the first defendant injures the plaintiff in a car crash and on the way to the hospital, the plaintiff is injured by a second defendant, who crashes into the ambulance, or at the hospital, a doctor (defendant three) prescribes the wrong medicine or removes the wrong leg. The proximate cause issue becomes whether the first defendant is liable for the negligent acts of the later defendants.

In *Weber v. Charity Hospital*, 475 So. 2d 1047 (La. 1985), following a car crash, the plaintiff received a blood transfusion containing hepatitis. The negligent car driver was held liable for the damages from the hepatitis.

In *Pridham v. Cash & Carry*, 359 A.2d 193 (N.H. 1976), the plaintiff died when the ambulance driver had a heart attack and the ambulance crashed into a tree. The court said:

> "[I]f a [defendant's] negligence causes harm to another which requires the other to receive medical . . . services, and bodily harm results from a normal effort of persons rendering such services, whether done in a proper or negligent manner, the [first defendant] is a legal cause of the injuries received. . . ." The court held for the plaintiff on the intervening cause issue.

In *Anaya v. Superior Court*, 93 Cal. Rptr. 2d 228 (Ct. App. 2000), because of injuries caused by defendant one, the plaintiff was being rushed to the hospital in a helicopter when it crashed and killed her. In finding against the first defendant, the Court said:

> An actor may be liable if the actor's negligence is a substantial factor in causing an injury, and the actor is not relieved of liability because of the intervening act of a third party if such act was reasonably foreseeable at the time of the original negligent conduct. . . . The allegations that the

helicopter malfunctioned and the manufacturer is strictly liable . . . do not establish the manufacturer as a superseding actor.

Sometimes a line is drawn, however. *In Purchase v. Seelye*, 121 N.E. 413 (Mass. 1918), the first defendant's liability was severed when the hospital operated on the wrong patient. The Court said:

> It is well settled in this commonwealth . . . that in an action for personal injuries arising out of the alleged negligence of the defendant, the plaintiff is entitled to recover for the injuries resulting from the defendant's negligence although such injuries are aggravated by the negligence of an attending physician if, in his selection and employment the plaintiff was in the exercise of reasonable care.

> . . . We are of opinion that the general rule as above stated is not applicable to the case at bar. There was sufficient evidence to show that the defendant made a mistake in the identity of the plaintiff at the time the operation was performed. . . . The reason why a wrongdoer is held liable for the negligence of a physician whose unskillful treatment aggravates an injury, is that such unskilled treatment is a result which reasonably ought to have been anticipated by him.

FULLER v. PREIS
New York Court of Appeals, 1974
35 N.Y.2d 425, 363 N.Y.S.2d 568, 322 N.E.2d 263

BREITEL, CHIEF JUDGE.

. . . .

Decedent, Dr. Lewis, committed suicide some seven months after an automobile accident from which he had walked away believing he was uninjured. In fact he had suffered head injuries with consequences to be detailed later. The theory of the case was that defendants, owner and operator of the vehicle which struck decedent's automobile, were responsible in tort for the suicide as a matter of proximate cause. . . . The issue is whether plaintiff's evidence of cause of the suicide was sufficient.
. . .

On December 2, 1966, decedent Dr. Lewis, a 43-year-old surgeon, was involved in an intersection collision. Upon impact, the left side of his head struck the frame and window of his automobile. Suffering no evident injuries, he declined aid and drove himself home. . . .

Two days after the accident, Dr. Lewis had a seizure followed by others. . . .

Then ensued a period of deterioration and gradual contraction of his professional and private activities. . . .

On July 9, after experiencing three seizures that day, he went to the bathroom of his home, closed the door and shot himself in the head. He died the following day.
. . .

[T]he act of suicide, as a matter of law, is not a superseding cause in negligence law precluding liability. . . .

That suicide may be encouraged by allowing recovery for suicide, a highly doubtful proposition in occidental society, is unpersuasive to preclude recovery for the suicide of a mentally deranged person. The remote possibility of fraudulent claims connecting a suicide with mental derangement affords no basis for barring recovery.

The obvious difficulty in proving or disproving causal relation should not bar recovery. . . .

Thus, there is neither public policy nor precedent barring recovery for suicide of a tortiously injured person driven "insane" by the consequence of the tortious act.
. . .

[T]he jury was instructed, primarily, upon the theory of liability for a suicide by an accident victim suffering from ensuing mental disease, who was unable to control the "irresistible impulse" to destroy himself. . . .

Dr. Lewis was physically and mentally healthy immediately prior to the automobile accident in which he struck his head against the interior of his own vehicle. After the accident he suffered several epileptic seizures, often with unconsciousness. Before the accident he had never suffered a seizure. For seven months between the accident and his death, Dr. Lewis experienced no fewer than 38 separate seizures. . . .

The only authentic issue is whether the suicide was an "irresistible impulse" caused by traumatic organic brain damage. . . .

On the day of the suicide, only seven months after the accident, when Dr. Lewis had had three seizures, his daughter tried to speak with him but he did not respond. After the third seizure he seemed unable to recognize his wife, had a strange look, and locked himself in the bathroom. Twenty minutes later, his wife heard him mutter, "I must do it, I must do it," and then a gunshot rang out. Dr. Lewis had shot himself in the head and died the following day. . . .

In tort law, as contrasted with criminal law, there is recognition that one may retain the power to intend, to know, and yet to have an irresistible impulse to act and therefore be incapable of voluntary conduct. . . . The issue in this case was, precisely, whether Dr. Lewis, who obviously knew what he was doing and intended to do what he did, nevertheless, was because of mental derangement, incapable of resisting the impulse to destroy himself. Precedents and modern knowledge say that that could have been. The jury found that it was so.

When the suicide is preceded by a history of trauma, brain damage, epileptic seizures, aberrational conduct, depression and despair, it is at the very least a fair issue of fact whether the suicide was the rational act of a sound mind or the irrational act or irresistible impulse of a deranged mind evidenced by a physically damaged brain. . . .

Since the Appellate Division, in reversing, stated that in any event it would have set the verdict aside as contrary to the weight of the evidence, the verdict in favor of plaintiff may not be reinstated and a new trial is required.

Accordingly, the order of the Appellate Division should be reversed, with costs, and a new trial directed.

---

1. How does the court resolve the cause-in-fact issue?

2. What is the proximate cause issue? Would your thinking be affected by the fact that Dr. Lewis' mother-in-law was suffering from cancer and his wife was extremely sick?

3. Are you able to suggest a better test than "irresistible impulse" for suicides?

4. In older cases, courts found that suicide breaks the chain of causation. *See Scheffer v. Railroad Co.*, 105 U.S. 249 (1882). However, in more recent cases, the question is often left to the jury. *See Stafford v. Neurological Med., Inc.*, 811 F.2d 470 (8th Cir. 1987).

ENRIGHT v. ELI LILLY & CO.
Court of Appeals of New York, 1991
77 N.Y.2d 377, 568 N.Y.S.2d 550, 570 N.E.2d 198

WACHTLER, CHIEF JUDGE.

The question in this case is whether the liability of manufacturers of the drug diethylstilbestrol (DES) should extend to a so-called "third generation" plaintiff, the granddaughter of a woman who ingested the drug. According to the allegations of the complaint, the infant plaintiff's injuries were caused by her premature birth, which in turn resulted from damage to her mother's reproductive system caused by the mother's in utero exposure to DES. We hold, in accord with our decision in *Albala v. City of New York* (54 N.Y.2d 269), that in these circumstances no cause of action accrues in favor of the infant plaintiff against the drug manufacturers.

The plaintiffs in this case are Karen Enright, born August 9, 1981, and her parents, Patricia and Earl Enright. According to their complaint, the events underlying this action began more than 30 years ago, when Karen Enright's maternal grandmother ingested DES during a pregnancy which resulted in the birth of plaintiff Patricia Enright on January 29, 1960. Plaintiffs allege that because of her in utero exposure to DES, Patricia Enright developed a variety of abnormalities and deformities in her reproductive system. As a result, several of her pregnancies terminated in spontaneous abortions and another resulted in the premature birth of Karen Enright. Karen suffers from cerebral palsy and other disabilities that plaintiffs attribute to her premature birth and, ultimately, to her grandmother's ingestion of DES.

. . . .

We note that no issues are raised on this appeal regarding the still pending claims of Patricia and Earl Enright based on the injuries allegedly sustained by Patricia Enright due to her own in utero exposure to DES.

. . . .

The tragic DES tale is well documented in this Court's decisions and need not be recounted here. . . . It is sufficient to note that between 1947 and 1971, the drug, a synthetic estrogen-like substance produced by approximately 300 manufacturers, was prescribed for use and ingested by millions of pregnant women to prevent miscarriages. In 1971, the Food and Drug Administration banned the drug's use for the treatment of problems of pregnancy after studies established a link between in utero exposure to DES and the occurrence in teen-age women of a rare form of vaginal and cervical cancer. Plaintiffs allege that in utero exposure to DES has since been linked to other genital tract aberrations in DES daughters, including malformations or immaturity of the uterus, cervical abnormalities, misshapen Fallopian tubes and abnormal cell and tissue growth, all of which has caused in this population a marked increase in the incidence of infertility, miscarriages, premature births and ectopic pregnancies.

The Legislature and this Court have both expressed concern for the victims of this tragedy by removing legal barriers to their tort recovery — barriers which may have had their place in other contexts, but which in DES litigation worked a peculiar injustice because of the ways in which DES was developed, marketed and sold and because of the insidious nature of its harm.

For example, prior to 1986, the long-standing rule in this State was that a cause of action for personal injuries caused by a toxic substance accrued and the limitations period began to run upon exposure to the substance. . . . The Legislature, recognizing that under this rule claims for injuries caused by exposure to DES and other toxic substances were often time barred before the harmful effects of the exposure could be discovered, changed the law to provide that the limitations period in exposure cases begins to run upon discovery of the injury. . . . At the same time, the Legislature revived for one year previously time-barred causes of action based on exposure to DES and four other toxic substances. . . .

More recently, this Court responded to the fact that — for a variety of reasons unique to the DES litigation context — a DES plaintiff generally finds it impossible to identify the manufacturer of the drug that caused her injuries. We held that liability could be imposed upon DES manufacturers in accordance with their share of the national DES market, notwithstanding the plaintiff's inability to identify the manufacturer particularly at fault for her injuries. . . .

In the present case, we are asked to do something significantly different. We are asked, not to remove some barrier to recovery that presents unique problems in DES cases, but to recognize a cause of action not available in other contexts simply (or at least largely) because this is a DES case.

In *Albala v. City of New York* . . . , we were presented with the question "whether a cause of action lies in favor of a child for injuries suffered as a result of a preconception tort committed against the mother." There, the mother suffered a perforated uterus during the course of an abortion. Four years later, she gave birth to a brain-damaged child, whose injuries were allegedly attributable to the defendants' negligence in perforating the mother's uterus. We declined, as a matter of policy, to recognize a cause of action on behalf of the child, believing that to do so would "require the extension of traditional tort concepts beyond manageable bounds." . . . Among other things, we were concerned with "the staggering implications of any proposition which would honor claims assuming the breach of an identifiable duty for less than a perfect birth" and the difficulty, if such a cause of action were recognized, of confining liability by other than artificial and arbitrary boundaries. . . .

The case now before us differs from *Albala* only in that the mother's injuries in this case were caused by exposure to DES instead of by medical malpractice. A different rule is justified, therefore, only if that distinction alters the policy balance we struck in *Albala*.

The primary thrust of plaintiffs' argument and the Appellate Division's decision is that DES itself alters that balance. From the Legislature's actions in modifying the applicable Statute of Limitations and reviving time-barred DES cases and from our adoption of a market-share liability theory in *Hymowitz*, plaintiffs perceive a public policy favoring a remedy for DES-caused injuries sufficient to overcome the countervailing policy considerations we identified in *Albala*. The implication, of course, is that the public interest in providing a remedy for those injured by DES is stronger than the public interest in providing a remedy for those injured by other means — medical malpractice, for example. We do not believe that such a preference has been established.

To be sure, recent developments demonstrate legislative and judicial solicitude for the victims of DES, but they do not establish DES plaintiffs as a favored class for whose benefit all traditional limitations on tort liability must give way. To the extent that special rules have been fashioned, they are a response to unique procedural barriers and problems of proof peculiar to DES litigation.

. . . .

As in *Albala*, the cause of action plaintiffs ask us to recognize here could not be confined without the drawing of artificial and arbitrary boundaries. For all we know, the rippling effects of DES exposure may extend for generations. It is our duty to confine liability within manageable limits. . . . Limiting liability to those who ingested the drug or were exposed to it in utero serves this purpose. . . .

But in light of the FDA's responsibility in this area, the need for the tort system to promote prescription drug safety is at least diminished. . . .

More important, however, is recognition that public policy favors the availability of prescription drugs even though most carry some risks. . . . That is not to say that drug manufacturers should enjoy immunity from liability stemming from their failure to conduct adequate research and testing prior to the marketing of their products. They do not enjoy such immunity, as evidenced by our recognition of liability in favor of those who have been injured by ingestion or in utero exposure to DES. But we are aware of the dangers of overdeterrence — the possibility that research will be discouraged or beneficial drugs withheld from the market. These dangers are magnified in this context, where we are asked to recognize a legal duty toward generations not yet conceived.

In sum, the distinctions between this case and *Albala* provide no basis for a departure from the rule that an injury to a mother which results in injuries to a later-conceived child does not establish a cause of action in favor of the child against the original tort-feasor. For this reason, we decline to recognize a cause of action on behalf of plaintiff Karen Enright. Accordingly, the order of the Appellate Division should be modified, with costs to defendants, by granting defendants' motions for summary judgment dismissing the third cause of action and, as so modified, affirmed. The certified question should be answered in the affirmative.

---

1.   This is a New York case with an issue as to whether the plaintiff is foreseeable. Why is there no discussion of *Palsgraf*, zone of danger, foreseeability, or directness?

2.   What policies does the court present for not finding a duty, a "new" cause of action?

3.   How would Judge Wachtler have decided *Polemis, Wagon Mound No. 1*, and *Palsgraf*? What is the difference in analytical approach between those three cases and *Enright*? Which approach do you prefer and why?

4.   Why might a court be more accurate and clear in deciding proximate cause in products cases than other cases?

5.   Is this a proximate cause or a products liability case? What is the distinction?

C.   ECONOMIC LOSS

PROBLEM

Dr. Jones told Chuck that, because of cancer, Chuck had only six months to live. Chuck therefore retired early and suffered substantial financial loss because Dr. Jones was wrong and negligent. Will Chuck be able to recover his financial losses from Dr. Jones?

PEOPLE EXPRESS AIRLINES v. CONSOLIDATED RAIL CORP.

Supreme Court of New Jersey, 1985
100 N.J. 246, 495 A.2d 107

[The airline sued the various defendants including the railroad for damages it suffered due to evacuation of its offices following a tank car accident at a nearby railroad yard, although the airline suffered no physical damages. The Superior Court, Law Division, Essex County, entered summary judgment for the defendants, and the airline appealed. The Superior Court reversed and remanded, and defendants appealed.]

HANDLER, J.

. . . .

On July 22, 1981, a fire began in the Port Newark freight yard of defendant Consolidated Rail Corporation (Conrail) when ethylene oxide manufactured by defendant BASF Wyandotte Company (BASF) escaped from a tank car, punctured during a "coupling" operation with another rail car, and ignited. The tank car was owned by defendant Union Tank Car Company (Union Car) and was leased to defendant BASF.

The plaintiff asserted at oral argument that at least some of the defendants were aware from prior experiences that ethylene oxide is a highly volatile substance; further, that emergency response plans in case of an accident had been prepared. When the fire occurred that gave rise to this lawsuit, some of the defendants' consultants helped determine how much of the surrounding area to evacuate. The municipal authorities then evacuated the area within a one-mile radius surrounding the fire to lessen the risk to persons within the area should the burning tank car explode. The evacuation area included the adjacent North Terminal building of Newark International Airport, where plaintiff People Express Airlines' (People Express) business operations are based. Although the feared explosion never occurred, People Express employees were prohibited from using the North Terminal for twelve hours.

The plaintiff contends that it suffered business-interruption losses as a result of the evacuation. These losses consist of canceled scheduled flights and lost reservations because employees were unable to answer the telephones to accept bookings; also, certain fixed operating expenses allocable to the evacuation time period were incurred and paid despite the fact that plaintiff's offices were closed. No physical damage to airline property and no personal injury occurred as a result of the fire.

. . .

The single characteristic that distinguishes parties in negligence suits whose claims for economic losses have been regularly denied by American and English courts from those who have recovered economic losses is, with respect to the successful claimants, the fortuitous occurrence of physical harm or property damage, however slight. It is well-accepted that a defendant who negligently injures a plaintiff or his property may be liable for all proximately caused harm, including economic losses. *See Palsgraf.* . . . Nevertheless, a virtually *per se* rule barring recovery for economic loss unless the negligent conduct also caused physical harm has evolved throughout this century, based, in part, on *Robins Dry Dock & Repair Co. v. Flint*, 275 U.S. 303, 48 S. Ct. 134, 72 L. Ed. 2d 290 (1927). . . .

The reasons that have been advanced to explain the divergent results for litigants seeking economic losses are varied. Some courts have viewed the general rule against recovery as necessary to limit damages to reasonably foreseeable consequences of negligent conduct. This concern in a given case is often manifested as an issue of causation and has led to the requirement of physical harm as an element of proximate cause. In this context, the physical harm requirement functions as part of the definition of the causal relationship between the defendant's negligent act and the plaintiff's economic damages; it acts as a convenient clamp on otherwise boundless liability. . . . The physical harm rule also reflects certain deep-seated concerns that underlie courts' denial of recovery for purely economic losses occasioned by a defendant's negligence. These concerns include the fear of fraudulent claims, mass litigation, and limitless liability, or liability out of proportion to the defendant's fault. . . .

The troublesome concern reflected in cases denying recovery for negligently-caused economic loss is the alleged potential for infinite liability, or liability out of all proportion to the defendant's fault. . . .

Judicial discomfiture with the rule of nonrecovery for purely economic loss throughout the last several decades has led to numerous exceptions in the general rule. Although the rationalizations for these exceptions differ among courts and cases, two common threads run throughout the exceptions. The first is that the element of foreseeability emerges as a more appropriate analytical standard to determine the question of liability than a per se prohibitory rule. The second is that the extent to which the defendant knew or should have known the particular consequences of his negligence, including the economic loss of a particularly foreseeable plaintiff, is dispositive of the issues of duty and fault.

. . . .

Courts have found it fair and just in all of these exceptional cases to impose liability on defendants who, by virtue of their special activities, professional training or other unique preparation for their work, had particular knowledge or reason to know that others, such as the intended beneficiaries of wills . . . or the purchasers of stock who were expected to rely on the company's financial statement in the prospectus . . . would be economically harmed by negligent conduct. In this group of cases, even though the particular plaintiff was not always foreseeable, the particular class of plaintiffs was foreseeable as was the particular type of injury.

A very solid exception allowing recovery for economic losses has also been created in cases akin to private actions for public nuisance. Where a plaintiff's business is based in part upon the exercise of a public right, the plaintiff has been able to recover purely economic losses caused by a defendant's negligence. *See, e.g., Louisiana ex rel. Guste v. M/V Testbank*, 752 F.2d 1019 (5th Cir. 1985) (en banc) (defendants responsible for ship collision held liable to all commercial fishermen, shrimpers, crabbers and oystermen for resulting pollution of Mississippi River). . . . The theory running throughout these cases, in which the plaintiffs depend on the exercise of the public or riparian right to clean water as a natural resource, is that the pecuniary losses suffered by those who make direct use of the resource are particularly foreseeable because they are so closely linked, through the resource, to the defendants' behavior.

Particular knowledge of the economic consequences has sufficed to establish duty and proximate cause in contexts other than those already considered. . . .

These exceptions expose the hopeless artificiality of the *per se* rule against recovery for purely economic losses. When the plaintiffs are reasonably foreseeable, the injury is directly and proximately caused by defendant's negligence, and liability can be limited fairly, courts have endeavored to create exceptions to allow recovery. . . .

One thematic motif that may be extrapolated from these decisions to differentiate between those cases in which recovery for economic losses was allowed and denied is that of foreseeability as it relates to both the duty owed and proximate cause. . . .

We hold therefore that a defendant owes a duty of care to take reasonable measures to avoid the risk of causing economic damages, aside from physical injury, to particular plaintiffs or plaintiffs comprising an identifiable class with respect to whom defendant knows or has reason to know are likely to suffer such damages from its conduct. A defendant failing to adhere to this duty of care may be found liable for such economic damages proximately caused by its breach of duty.

We stress that an identifiable class of plaintiffs is not simply a foreseeable class of plaintiffs. For example, members of the general public, or invitees such as sales and service persons at a particular plaintiff's business premises, or persons travelling on a highway near the scene of a negligently-caused accident, such as the one at bar, who are delayed in the conduct of their affairs and suffer varied economic losses, are certainly a foreseeable class of plaintiffs. Yet their presence within the area would be fortuitous, and the particular type of economic injury that could be suffered by such persons would be hopelessly unpredictable and not realistically foreseeable. Thus, the class itself would not be sufficiently ascertainable. An identifiable class of plaintiffs must be particularly foreseeable in terms of the type of persons or entities comprising the class, the certainty or predictability of their presence, the approximate numbers of those in the class, as well as the type of economic expectations disrupted. . . .

In these cases, the courts will be required to draw upon notions of fairness, common sense and morality to fix the line limiting liability as a matter of public policy, rather than an uncritical application of the principle of particular foreseeability. . . .

. . . .

Among the facts that persuade us that a cause of action has been established is the close proximity of the North Terminal and People Express Airlines to the Conrail freight yard; the obvious nature of the plaintiff's operations and particular foreseeability of economic losses resulting from an accident and evacuation; the defendants' actual or constructive knowledge of the volatile properties of ethylene oxide; and the existence of an emergency response plan prepared by some of the defendants (alluded to in the course of oral argument), which apparently called for the nearby area to be evacuated to avoid the risk of harm in case of an explosion. We do not mean to suggest by our recitation of these facts that actual knowledge of the eventual economic losses is necessary to the cause of action; rather, particular foreseeability will suffice. The plaintiff still faces a difficult task in proving damages, particularly lost profits, to the degree of certainty required in other negligence cases. The trial court's examination of these proofs must be exacting to ensure that damages recovered are those reasonably to have been anticipated in view of the defendants' capacity to have foreseen that this particular plaintiff was within the risk created by their negligence. . . .

Accordingly, the judgment of the Appellate Division is modified, and, as modified, affirmed. The case is remanded for proceedings consistent with this opinion.

———

1. Define economic loss.

2. In *State of Louisiana ex rel. Guste v. M/V Testbank*, 752 F.2d 1019 (5th Cir. 1985), two ships collided, releasing an acidic white haze and forcing the closing of the Mississippi River. Owners of restaurants, vessels delayed upriver, and bait stores were not able to recover damages, such as lost business, because there was no physical damage to their property.

How would New Jersey decide *Testbank*? What is the built-in limit in *People Express*?

3. In *Kinsman II*, when the Buffalo River was closed due to the collision of two ships, the plaintiff had to purchase more grain and use trucks, rather than ships, to transport the grain. His suit for economic loss was rejected:

> On the previous appeal we stated aptly: "somewhere a point will be reached when courts will agree that the link has become too tenuous — that what is claimed to be consequence is only fortuity." . . . We believe that this point has been reached. . . . The instant claims occurred only because the downed bridge made it impossible to move traffic along the river. Under all the circumstances of this case, we hold that the connection between the defendants' negligence and the claimants' damages is too tenuous and remote to permit recovery. "The law does not spread its protection so far." Holmes, J., in *Robins Dry Dock, supra*, 275 U.S. at 309, 48 S. Ct. at 135.
>
> . . . As we have previously noted, . . . we return to Judge Andrews' frequently quoted statement in *Palsgraf* . . . (dissenting opinion): "It is all a question of expediency . . . of fair judgment, always keeping in mind the fact that we endeavor to make a rule in each case that will be practical and in keeping with the general understanding of mankind."

Kinsman Transit Co. v. Buffalo, 388 F.2d 821 (2d Cir. 1968). Were the plaintiffs foreseeable under the *Palsgraf* test? Does *People Express* alter the guideline presented in Andrews' dissent in *Palsgraf*?

4. For articles on economic loss, see Bishop, *Economic Loss in Tort*, 2 Oxford J. Legal Stud. 1 (1982); Rizzo, *The Economic Loss Problem: A Comment on Bishop*, 2 Oxford J. Legal Stud. 197 (1982).

D. DUTY VERSUS PROXIMATE CAUSE: GREEN'S THEORY

1. Eliminate Proximate Cause

Over sixty years ago, Dean Leon Green suggested that proximate cause should be deleted from tort analysis. He reasoned that it created problems because proximate cause was often confused with cause-in-fact. He also wanted to make clear the limited but foundational role of cause-in-fact and to clarify the role of the judge in controlling the jury. He therefore advocated the elimination of proximate cause and the adoption of the duty concept.

2. Green's Duty Analysis

At the center of Green's duty theory is the question: Does the defendant's duty extend to this particular plaintiff for this particular injury? Green makes clear that negligence analysis cannot be done with a broad brush, but rather each plaintiff and each injury must be evaluated separately.

Dean Green also made clear that the concept of foreseeability has only a vestigial role in duty theory. He argued that foreseeability under proximate cause analysis carries too much baggage and that any careful reader should wonder whether foreseeability can carry the weight that is placed upon it by the courts. Its cure-all function is too broad. When the jury is given the negligence charge, under Green's theory, they are asked whether the defendant, as a reasonable person, could have foreseen this injury. That is all that remains of the foreseeability concept.

3. Three Questions

In applying the duty theory, Dean Green argued that before the duty question is considered, two other questions should be asked. First, is there evidence of cause-in-fact? In some cases where causation is discussed, what is at issue is cause-in-fact, not proximate cause or duty. If there is no evidence of cause-in-fact, the case is over. The second question that should be asked is: Is there evidence of negligence? In some of the proximate cause cases, the real question is was there any evidence of negligence. That is, the court is not actually talking about scope of liability but rather whether the defendant was at fault. If there is no such evidence, the case is over. If the cause-in-fact and the negligence question are both answered in the plaintiff's favor, the third question may be reached: Does the defendant's duty extend to this particular plaintiff for this particular injury?

4. Relevant Factors

In answering the question whether the defendant's duty extends to this particular plaintiff for this particular injury, the court must consider several factors such as the following: economics, the administrative role of the courts, loss shifting, who can best obtain insurance, the impact upon society of placing a duty on the defendant, precedent, justice, and prevention.

The administrative factor refers to the task of a court in deciding to take a case and the ability of the court to deal with the problems presented by the case. We see administrative problems most clearly in negligent infliction of mental distress cases. The court is there concerned about a flood of suits and where to draw the line in the next case. Faked claims are also a problem.

Loss shifting asks whether this loss should be placed on the actor rather than the victim. With the insurance factor, Dean Green asks the court to consider who among the parties is best able to insure. With the impact factor, he asks what might be the effect on society of making this defendant bear this loss.

With precedent, Dean Green asks the court to consider whether the question has been decided in a previous case. If it has, it should, by all means, be followed in this case, but if it has not, it is the responsibility of the court to weigh the various factors.

It must be noted, however, that Dean Green was loath to list the factors to be considered by the court and felt strongly that each case should be decided on its own merits. Indeed, he believed it was better for the court to decide the case and say nothing, rather than to mislead by using vague terms such as causation and foreseeability.

5.   Conclusion

Why should we go through the duty analysis? The answer Dean Green gives is that it fosters clear analysis. It makes more sense to talk about social policy under duty, rather than cloud analysis with the term causation. Proximate cause (foreseeability) misleads attorneys, judges, and juries. Duty makes clear the role of the judge in guiding the jury and the demarcation between cause-in-fact and social policy.

While Dean Green's theory has struggled and not been widely accepted in ordinary negligence cases, it has leapfrogged to the forefront in products liability cases. The dominant issue in products liability cases is whether the product is defective. The most popular approach for answering this question is risk-utility analysis. Risk-utility analysis rests on a weighing of all relevant factors. To that extent, Dean Green's theory points us in the right direction for answering challenging products liability defect questions: weigh the relevant factors. On the other hand, foreseeability analysis is almost useless in products liability cases, because the injury that resulted is often foreseeable. For example, when an automobile manufacturer builds a car, he or she knows what will happen when the car rolls over at twenty, thirty or forty miles per hour. He or she knows precisely what forces will cause the roof to collapse. It is not helpful to ask if it was foreseeable that the roof would collapse. It is helpful, however, to ask what factors the manufacturer considered in designing the roof and if these were the appropriate factors.

For a further discussion of Dean Green's duty theory, see the following articles: Leon Green, *Proximate Cause in Texas Negligence Law*, 28 Tex. L. Rev. (I) 471, (II) 621, (III) 755 (1950); Leon Green, *The Duty Problem in Negligence Cases*, 29 Colum. L. Rev. 255 (1929); Leon Green, *The Duty Problem in Negligence Cases*, 28 Colum. L. Rev. 1014, 1034 (1928); Frank Vandall, *Duty: The Continuing Vitality of Dean Green's Theory*, 15 Quinnipiac L. Rev. 343 (1995).

Chapter 8

MULTIPLE DEFENDANTS: JOINT AND SEVERAL LIABILITY

Many cases involve multiple defendants. This reality creates numerous problems that can overlap into other aspects of tort law such as causation and comparative negligence. They can also involve other areas of law such as contracts (for example, the law of settlements and releases).

PROBLEM

Paul and Kathy negligently drive into each other's cars. Kathy's car then bounces into Tom's car. In the crash, Tom's leg is broken, and he suffers $100,000 in damages. Assume that Tom was also negligent, and Paul is 30% at fault, Kathy is 60% at fault, and Tom is 10% at fault.

1. What result if Tom wants to sue both Paul and Kathy, but Kathy lacks insurance and is bankrupt?

2. Kathy pays $60,000 and obtains a release from Tom. Tom suffered $100,000 in damages. What might Kathy be able to recover from Paul? Problems?

3. What result if the place of the tort has a statute providing: "Each party is liable only to the extent of his or her fault?"

Under the common law, where two or more persons plotted to injure or kill someone, they could be liable as joint tort-feasors because of the conspiracy even if only one actually did the deed. The injury or death was viewed as a single act. More recently, joint liability has been extended to cases where multiple defendants have caused a single indivisible result. Each defendant may be liable for the whole amount when there is no practical basis for apportioning the damages.

BIERCZYNSKI v. ROGERS
Supreme Court of Delaware, 1968
239 A.2d 218

HERRMANN, JUSTICE.

This appeal involves an automobile accident in which the plaintiffs claim that the defendant motorists were racing on the public highway, as the result of which the accident occurred.

The plaintiffs Cecil B. Rogers and Susan D. Rogers brought this action against Robert C. Race and Ronald Bierczynski, ages 18 and 17 respectively, alleging concurrent negligences in that they violated various speed statutes and various other statutory rules of the road, and in that they failed to keep a proper lookout and failed to keep their vehicles under proper control. The jury, by answer to interrogatories in its special verdict, expressly found that Race and Bierczynski were each negligent and that the negligence of each was a proximate cause of the accident. Substantial verdicts were entered in favor of the plaintiffs against both defendants jointly. The defendant Bierczynski appeals therefrom. The defendant Race does not appeal; rather, he joins with the plaintiffs in upholding the judgment below.

. . . .

Cecil Rogers testified as follows: He was returning from a Girl Scout trip with his daughter, headed for their home located about three blocks from the scene of the accident. He entered Lore Avenue from Governor Printz Boulevard, thus driving in a westerly direction on Lore Avenue. At a point about 300 feet east of River Road, Rogers' car was struck by Race's car which approached him sideways, moving in an easterly direction on the westbound lane. Rogers saw Race's car coming at him; he stopped in the westbound lane; but he was unable to move out of the way because there was a guard rail along that part of the road and no shoulder. Rogers first saw the Race vehicle when it was about 550 feet up Lore Avenue — or about 250 feet west of River Road. At that point, the Race car was being driven easterly on Lore Avenue in the westbound lane, almost along-side the Bierczynski car which was moving easterly in the eastbound lane. The front bumper of the Race car was opposite the back bumper of the Bierczynski car. Both cars were moving at about 55 or 60 m.p.h. down the hill. Before reaching River Road, Race swerved back into the eastbound lane behind Bierczynski, who was about a car length in front. As it crossed River Road, the Race automobile "bottomed on the road"; and it "careened down against the pavement and gave an impression of an explosion"; dust "flew everywhere" sufficiently to obscure the Race car momentarily from Rogers' view. At that point, the Race and Bierczynski automobiles were only "inches apart." The Race car then emerged from behind the Bierczynski car and careened sideways, at about 70 m.p.h., a distance of about 300 feet to the Rogers car standing in the westbound lane. The left side of the Race car struck the front of the Rogers car. Meanwhile, the Bierczynski car was brought to a stop in the eastbound lane, about 35 feet from the area of impact. The Bierczynski car did not come into contact with the Rogers vehicle.

Bierczynski's contention as to lack of proximate cause is based mainly upon the facts that his automobile remained in the proper lane at all times and was stopped about 35 feet before reaching the area of impact, without coming into contact with the Rogers car. These facts notwithstanding, the foregoing testimony of the plaintiff constituted sufficient evidence of proximate cause, in our opinion, to warrant the submission of that issue to the jury as to both drivers.

A reasonable inference capable of being drawn from the above testimony of Rogers, in the light of the surrounding circumstances, is that Race and Bierczynski were engaged in a speed contest as they came down the hill of Lore Avenue approaching its intersection with River Road. It is unimportant whether it was technically a "race," in the terminology of the defendants who deny that they were "racing." Clearly, the inference of a deliberate and intentional speed competition, as they came down the hill practically side-by-side at twice the legal speed, was permissible from Rogers' testimony; clearly, the inference that Bierczynski maintained his greatly excessive speed deliberately to prevent Race from passing him, was also permissible from Rogers' testimony. We classify both of these courses of conduct as improper racing on the highway. In either of the latter situations, the issue of whether Bierczynski's conduct was a proximate cause of Race's loss of control and collision with Rogers, was a proper issue for the jury.

In many States, automobile racing on a public highway is prohibited by statute, the violation of which is negligence per se. . . . Delaware has no such statute. Nevertheless, speed competition in automobiles on the public highway is negligence in this State, for the reason that a reasonably prudent person would not engage in such conduct. This conclusion is in accord with the general rule, prevailing in other jurisdictions which lack statutes on the subject, that racing motor vehicles on a public highway is negligence. . . .

It is also generally held that all who engage in a race on the highway do so at their peril, and are liable for injury or damage sustained by a third person as a result thereof, regardless of which of the racing cars directly inflicted the injury or damage. The authorities reflect generally accepted rules of causation that all parties engaged in a motor vehicle race on the highway are wrongdoers acting in concert, and that each participant is liable for harm to a third person arising from the tortious conduct of the other, because he has induced and encouraged the tort. . . .

We subscribe to those rules; and hold that, as a general rule, participation in a motor vehicle race on a public highway is an act of concurrent negligence imposing liability on each participant for any injury to a non-participant resulting from the race. If, therefore, Race and Bierczynski were engaged in a speed competition, each was liable for the damages and injuries to the plaintiffs herein, even though Bierczynski was not directly involved in the collision itself. Bierczynski apparently concedes liability if a race had, in fact, been in progress. Clearly there was ample evidence to carry to the jury the issue of a race — and with it, implicit therein, the issue of proximate cause as to Bierczynski.

The foregoing disposes of the appellant's contention that there was no evidence upon which it was proper for plaintiffs' counsel to argue to the jury that the defendants were racing.

. . . .

We find no error as asserted by the appellant. The judgments below are affirmed.

———————

1. In *Biercynski*, the activity of drag racing is a joint one, which essentially means that the parties jointly created the risk. They are thus defined as acting in concert, and both are equally liable for the whole amount of damages, although the plaintiff only recovers once. What if they had just happened to crash simultaneously into the plaintiff while driving negligently on a highway? Does the fact that the

defendants were acting intentionally or even illegally play a role? What if two defendants cause a single injury, but only one of them was acting intentionally?

2. What result if during the race, but before the crash, Bierczynski's hubcap had come off and hit a bystander?

3. Why did Race not appeal?

4. The first classification of joint tort is acting in concert, which was discussed above. The second classification involves two or more parties who fail in a common duty and cause injury to the plaintiff. An example would be where two defendants have the duty to maintain a party-wall. The wall collapses because they neglected their duty, and it injures the plaintiff. *See Johnson v. Chapman*, 43 W. Va. 639, 28 S.E. 744 (1897); *Schaffer v. Pennsylvania R.R. Co.*, 101 F.2d 369 (7th Cir. 1939) (jointly owned railway tracks).

5. Joint liability is often confused with permissive joinder, in which additional parties are brought into the case in order to resolve the dispute. The common-law rule was that only persons acting in concert could be joined. This proved to be wasteful because it led to failed cases and numerous trials. Therefore, the New York Code of Procedure (1848) (First Report of New York Commissioners on Pleading and Practice, 1848) provided that a party that might be helpful in settling the dispute could be brought before the court. This is referred to as joinder. Section 20(a) of the Federal Rules of Civil Procedure now broadly provides that joinder is permitted when the claims arise from "the same transaction, occurrence, or series of transactions or occurrences and if any question of law or fact common to all defendants will arise in the action." Permissive joinder is usually discussed in the Civil Procedure course.

6. The third classification of joint liability involves multiple defendants and a single indivisible result.

RAVO v. ROGATNICK
Court of Appeals of New York, 1987
514 N.E.2d 1104

ALEXANDER, JUDGE.

In this medical malpractice action, defendant, Dr. Irwin L. Harris, appeals from an order of the Appellate Division unanimously affirming an amended judgment of Supreme Court, entered on a jury verdict, finding him jointly and severally liable with Dr. Sol Rogatnick for injuries negligently inflicted upon plaintiff, Josephine Ravo, and resulting in brain damage that has rendered her severely and permanently retarded. The issue presented is whether joint and several liability was properly imposed upon defendant under the circumstances of this case where, notwithstanding that the defendants neither acted in concert nor concurrently, a single indivisible injury — brain damage — was negligently inflicted. For the reasons that follow, we affirm.

I.

Uncontroverted expert medical evidence established that plaintiff, Josephine Ravo, who at the time of trial was 14 years of age, was severely and permanently retarded as a result of brain damage she suffered at birth. The evidence demonstrated that the child was born an unusually large baby whose mother suffered from gestational diabetes which contributed to difficulties during delivery. The evidence further established that Dr. Rogatnick, the obstetrician who had charge of the ante partum care of Josephine's mother and who delivered Josephine, failed to ascertain pertinent medical information about the mother, incorrectly estimated the size of the infant, and employed improper surgical procedures during the delivery. It was shown that Dr. Harris, the pediatrician under whose care Josephine came following birth, misdiagnosed and improperly treated the infant's condition after birth. Based upon this evidence, the jury concluded that Dr. Rogatnick committed eight separate acts of medical malpractice, and Dr. Harris committed three separate acts of medical malpractice.

Although Dr. Rogatnick's negligence contributed to Josephine's brain damage, the medical testimony demonstrated that Dr. Harris' negligence was also a substantial contributing cause of the injury. No testimony was adduced, however, from which the jury could delineate which aspects of the injury were caused by the respective negligence of the individual doctors. Indeed, plaintiff's expert, Dr. Charash, testified that while the hypoxia and trauma directly attributable to Dr. Rogatnick's negligence were two major villains — being the most common causes of perinatal difficulty — the hyperbilirubinemia and excessively high hematocrit level inadequately addressed by Dr. Harris could not be excluded as having a contributing effect. The expert concluded that neither he nor anybody else could say with certainty which of the factors caused the brain damage. Similarly, Dr. Perrotta, testifying on behalf of plaintiff, opined that she could not tell whether the excessively high hematocrit level contributed "10 percent, 20 percent, or anything like that" to the injury. Nor, as the Appellate Division found, did Dr. Harris adduce any evidence that could support a jury finding that he caused an identifiable percentage of the infant plaintiff's brain damage. Indeed, Dr. Harris' entire defense appears to have been that he was not responsible for the plaintiff's injury to any degree.

The trial court instructed the jury that if they found that both defendants were negligent, and that their separate and independent acts of negligence were direct causes of a single injury to the plaintiff, but that it was not possible to determine what proportion each contributed to the injury, they could find each responsible for the entire injury even though the act of one may not have caused the entire injury, and even though the acts of negligence were not equal in degree. The court further instructed the jury that if they found that both defendants were negligent, they would have "to compare their negligence on the basis of 100 percent." The court also instructed the jury that if they found both defendants responsible for the plaintiff's injury "then you will evaluate their respective faults in contributing to the infant's condition."

These instructions were explanatory of an interrogatory, previously accepted without objection by Dr. Harris, and submitted to the jury, that requested the standard *Dole v. Dow* apportionment of fault. . . . Notwithstanding his failure to object to this interrogatory, Dr. Harris raised for the first time, after the jury was charged, an objection to the instructions, contending that he was only "liable for what injury he puts [sic] on top of the injury that exists," and therefore responsible only as a successive and independent tort-feasor. The trial court rejected defendant's contention, and the jury returned a verdict for plaintiff in the total amount of $2,750,000 attributing 80% of the "fault" to Dr. Rogatnick and 20% of the "fault" to Dr. Harris.

In a postverdict motion, Dr. Harris sought an order directing entry of judgment limiting the plaintiff's recovery against him to $450,000 (20% of the $2,250,000 base recovery — the court having set off $500,000 received by plaintiff in settlement of claims against other defendants) based upon his contention that his liability was not joint and several, but rather was independent and successive. This motion was denied. The Appellate Division dismissed Harris' appeal from the order denying the postverdict motion and affirmed the amended judgment entered on the jury's verdict.

II.

When two or more tort-feasors act concurrently or in concert to produce a single injury, they may be held jointly and severally liable. . . . This is so because such concerted wrongdoers are considered "joint tort-feasors" and in legal contemplation, there is a joint enterprise and a mutual agency, such that the act of one is the act of all and liability for all that is done is visited upon each. . . . On the other hand, where multiple tort-feasors "neither act in concert nor contribute concurrently to the same wrong, they are not joint tort-feasors; rather, their wrongs are independent and successive". . . . Under successive and independent liability, of course, the initial tort-feasor may well be liable to the plaintiff for the entire damage proximately resulting from his own wrongful acts, including aggravation of injuries by a successive tort-feasor. . . . The successive tort-feasor, however, is liable only for the separate injury or the aggravation his conduct has caused. . . .

It is sometimes the case that tort-feasors who neither act in concert nor concurrently may nevertheless be considered jointly and severally liable. This may occur in the instance of certain injuries which, because of their nature, are incapable of any reasonable or practicable division or allocation among multiple tort-feasors. . . .

We had occasion to consider such a circumstance in *Slater v. Mersereau* (64 N.Y. 138, *supra*), where premises belonging to the plaintiff were damaged by rainwater as a result of the negligent workmanship by a general contractor and a subcontractor. We held that where two parties by their separate and independent acts of negligence, cause a single, inseparable injury, each party is responsible for the entire injury: "Although they acted independently of each other, they did act at the same time in causing the damages . . . each contributing towards it, and although the act of each, alone and of itself, might not have caused the entire injury, under the circumstances presented, there is no good reason why each should not be liable for the damages caused by the different acts of all. . . . The water with which each of the parties were instrumental in injuring the plaintiffs was one mass and inseparable, and no distinction can be made between the different sources from whence it flowed, so that it can be claimed that each caused a separate and distinct injury for which each one is separately responsible . . . [the] contractor and subcontractors were separately negligent, and although such negligence was not concurrent, yet the negligence of both these parties contributed to produce the damages caused at one and the same time". . . .

Our affirmance in *Hawkes v. Goll* (281 N.Y. 808, *affg* 256 App. Div. 940, *supra)* demonstrates that simultaneous conduct is not necessary to a finding of joint and several liability when there is an indivisible injury. In that case, the decedent was struck by the vehicle driven by the defendant Farrell and was thrown across the roadway, where very shortly thereafter he was again struck, this time by the vehicle driven by the defendant Goll, and dragged some 40 to 50 feet along the highway. He was taken to the hospital where he expired within the hour. The Appellate Division stated (256 App. Div. 940): "As the result of his injuries the plaintiff's intestate died within an hour. There could be no evidence upon which the jury could base a finding of the nature of the injuries inflicted by the first car as distinguished from those inflicted by the second car. The case was submitted to the jury upon the theory that if both defendants were negligent they were jointly and severally liable. While the wrongful acts of the two defendants were not precisely concurrent in point of time, the defendants may nevertheless be joint tort feasors where, as here, their several acts of neglect concurred in producing the injury."

. . . .

Similarly, here the jury was unable to determine from the evidence adduced at trial the degree to which the defendants' separate acts of negligence contributed to the brain damage sustained by Josephine at birth. Certainly, a subsequent tort-feasor is not to be held jointly and severally liable for the acts of the initial tort-feasor with whom he is not acting in concert in every case where it is difficult, because of the nature of the injury, to separate the harm done by each tort-feasor from the others (. . . *see generally*, Prosser, *Joint Torts and Several Liability*, 25 Calif. L. Rev. 413). Here, however, the evidence established that plaintiff's brain damage was a single indivisible injury, and defendant failed to submit any evidence upon which the jury could base an apportionment of damage.

Harris argues, however, that since the jury ascribed only 20% of the fault to him, this was in reality an apportionment of damage, demonstrating that the injury was divisible. This argument must fail. Clearly, the court's instruction, and the interrogatory submitted in amplification thereof, called upon the jury to determine the respective responsibility in negligence of the defendants so as to establish a basis for an apportionment between them, by way of contribution, for the total damages awarded to plaintiff. . . .

As we said in *Schauer v. Joyce* (54 N.Y.2d 1, 5): " CPLR 1401, which codified this court's decision in *Dole v. Dow Chem. Co.* (30 N.Y.2d 143), provides that 'two or more persons who are subject to liability for damages for the same personal injury, injury to property or wrongful death, may claim contribution among them whether or not an action has been brought or a judgment has been rendered against the person from whom contribution is sought.' The section 'applies not only to joint tortfeasors, but also to concurrent successive, independent, alternative, and even intentional tortfeasors (Siegel, New York Practice, § 172, p 213)." The focus and purpose of the *Dole v. Dow* inquiry, therefore, is not whether, or to what degree, a defendant can be cast in damages to a plaintiff for a third party's negligence, . . . rather, it seeks to determine "whether each defendant owed a duty to plaintiff and whether, by breaching their respective duties, they contributed to plaintiff's ultimate injury" claimed to have been caused by each defendant. . . .

Here, the jury determined that the defendants breached duties owed to Josephine Ravo, and that these breaches contributed to her brain injury. The jury's apportionment of fault, however, does not alter the joint and several liability of defendants for the single indivisible injury. Rather, that aspect of the jury's determination of culpability merely defines the amount of contribution defendants may claim from each other, and does not impinge upon plaintiff's right to collect the entire judgment award from either defendant (CPLR 1402). As we stated in *Graphic Arts Mut. Ins. Co. v. Bakers Mut. Ins. Co.* (45 N.Y.2d 551, 557): "The right under the Dole-Dow doctrine to seek equitable apportionment based on relative culpability is not one intended for the benefit of the injured claimant. It is a right affecting the distributive responsibilities of tort-feasors inter sese. . . . It is elementary that injured claimants may still choose which joint tort-feasors to include as defendants in an action and, regardless of the concurrent negligence of others, recover the whole of their damages from any of the particular tort-feasors sued. . . ." This being so, in light of the evidence establishing the indivisibility of the brain injury and the contributing negligence of Dr. Harris, and of the manner in which the case was tried and submitted to the jury, we conclude that joint and several liability was properly imposed.

Accordingly, the order of the Appellate Division should be affirmed.

BANKS v. ELKS CLUB PRIDE OF TENNEESEE
Supreme Court of Tennessee, Nashville, 2010
301 S.W.3d 214

WILLIAM C. KOCH, JR., J., delivered the opinion of the court, in which JANICE M. HOLDER, C.J., CORNELIA A. CLARK, GARY R. WADE, and SHARON G. LEE, JJ., joined.

WILLIAM C. KOCH, JR., J.

This appeal involves the continuing viability in Tennessee of the common-law principle that imputes liability to an original tortfeasor for enhanced physical harm caused by the normal efforts of third persons to render aid which an injured party reasonably requires. A guest at a private club was injured on the club's premises. The injuries to the guest's back were compounded first by the conduct of her surgeon and second by the actions or inactions of a nursing home where the guest was a patient following her surgery. The guest filed separate lawsuits against the private club and her surgeon in the Circuit Court for Davidson County. After the cases were consolidated, the club and the surgeon moved to amend their answers to assert comparative fault claims against the nursing home. The trial court denied their motions but granted them permission to pursue an interlocutory appeal. After the Court of Appeals declined to consider the interlocutory appeal, the club and the surgeon sought this Court's permission for an interlocutory appeal. We granted their application. We now hold that an original tortfeasor is not jointly and severally liable for the further aggravation of an original injury caused by a subsequent tortfeasor's medically negligent treatment of the injury caused by the original tortfeasor's negligence. Therefore, we have determined that the trial court erred by denying the motions of the club and the surgeon to amend their complaints to assert comparative fault claims against the nursing home.

I.

Alice J. Banks attended a social event at an Elks Lodge in Nashville on March 24, 2006. While she was there, the chair on which she was seated collapsed, causing serious injuries to Ms. Banks's back. Ms. Banks consulted with Dr. Robert H. Boyce, a physician affiliated with Premier Orthopaedics and Sports Medicine, P.C. ("Premier Orthopaedics"), who recommended lumbar surgery at the L3–L4 and L4–L5 levels. The procedure consisted of a decompression laminectomy and fusion. Ms. Banks agreed to have the procedure performed.

On May 16, 2006, Ms. Banks underwent surgery at Centennial Medical Center. While Dr. Boyce's operative report indicates that he performed a lumbar laminectomy and fusion at the L3–L4 and L4–L5 vertebrae as intended, he actually performed the surgery upon the L2–L3 and L3–L4 vertebrae. It was only after the surgery was completed that Dr. Boyce realized he mistakenly performed the surgery at the L2–L3, rather than the L4–L5 vertebrae. As a result, Ms. Banks was required to undergo a second surgery on May 17, 2006.

Following Ms. Banks's surgeries, she was transferred to Cumberland Manor Nursing Home ("Cumberland Manor") for further recuperation and rehabilitation. While a patient at Cumberland Manor, Ms. Banks developed a serious staphylococcus infection that required additional surgeries and extensive care and treatment.

On March 23, 2007, Ms. Banks filed suit in the Circuit Court for Davidson County against the Elks Club Pride of Tennessee 1102, Pride of Tennessee Lodge of Elks No. 1102 Improved Benevolent, and Elks Lodge 1102 Pride of Tennessee ("Elks Lodge defendants"). She alleged that the negligence of the Elks Lodge defendants had caused her back injuries. The case was assigned to the Sixth Circuit Court.

On May 10, 2007, Ms. Banks filed a separate lawsuit against Dr. Boyce and Premier Orthopaedics ("Dr. Boyce") in the Circuit Court for Davidson County. She asserted claims of medical negligence and medical battery based on Dr. Boyce's performance of an unauthorized procedure. This case was assigned to the Fifth Circuit Court.

Dr. Boyce later requested the Fifth Circuit Court to transfer Ms. Banks's lawsuit against him to the Sixth Circuit Court where her lawsuit against the Elks Lodge defendants was pending. Ms. Banks agreed to the transfer. . . .

On May 30, 2008, the Elks Lodge defendants filed a Tenn. R. Civ. P. 15.01 motion to amend their answer to assert a comparative fault defense against Cumberland Manor. They alleged that they had learned during the discovery process that

Cumberland Manor's improper care and treatment had contributed to Ms. Banks's staphylococcus infection. They also asserted that this infection had aggravated Ms. Banks's injuries and damages and that Ms. Banks was seeking to hold them responsible for these additional injuries and damages. The Elks Lodge defendants also reserved the right "to amend their comparative fault defense to allege fault of others throughout the course of discovery and trial." On June 2, 2008, Dr. Boyce also sought to amend his answer to assert a comparative fault defense against Cumberland Manor, adopting the same language set forth in the Elks Lodge defendants' motion.

Ms. Banks opposed the defendants' motions to amend their answers to assert a comparative fault defense against Cumberland Manor. She argued that the defendants' efforts to assert a comparative fault defense "against a subsequent healthcare provider for alleged negligent medical treatment that was brought on by the injuries negligently caused by the named defendants is inappropriate." In their trial court briefs, the parties argued vigorously over whether what they referred to as the "original tortfeasor rule" or the "original tortfeasor doctrine"[3] survived this Court's decision in *McIntyre v. Balentine*, 833 S.W.2d 52 (Tenn. 1992) and its progeny.

On August 15, 2008, the trial court entered an order denying the Elks Lodge defendants' and Dr. Boyce's motion to amend their complaints to assert comparative fault claims against Cumberland Manor. The court reasoned that "the holdings in the cases of *Transports, Inc. v. Perry*, 220 Tenn. 57, 414 S.W.2d 1 (1967) and *Atkinson v. Hemphill*, 1994 Tenn. App. LEXIS 480 (Tenn.Ct.App.1994), [are] still good law and the proposed amendments would be futile and therefore must be denied under Rule 15, Tennessee Rules of Civil Procedure." On its own motion, the court also suggested that pursuing a Tenn. R.App. P. 9 interlocutory appeal from its decision would be appropriate. The Elks Lodge defendants and Dr. Boyce pursued an interlocutory appeal; however, on September 10, 2008, the Court of Appeals denied their application for an interlocutory appeal without comment.

On October 9, 2008, the Elks Lodge defendants and Dr. Boyce filed a Tenn. R.App. P. 9 application for permission to appeal. We granted the application on December 15, 2008. Following our decision to grant permission to appeal, Ms. Banks, seeking to avoid potentially adverse statute of limitations impact should this Court determine that the trial court erred in not permitting the Elks Lodge defendants or Dr. Boyce to amend their answers to assert an affirmative defense against Cumberland Manor, amended her complaint to name Cumberland Manor as a tortfeasor.

---

[3] The terms "original tortfeasor rule" and "original tortfeasor doctrine" are actually shorthand references to a concatenation of two common-law principles. The first principle is that "if one is injured by the negligence of another, and these injuries are aggravated by medical treatment (either prudent or negligent), the negligence of the wrongdoer causing the original injury is regarded as the proximate cause of the damage subsequently flowing from the medical treatment." *Transports, Inc. v. Perry*, 220 Tenn. 57, 64-65, 414 S.W.2d 1, 4-5 (1967). The second principle is that the original tortfeasor is jointly and severally liable for the full extent of the injuries caused by the original tortfeasor and the successive tortfeasor. J.D. Lee & Barry A. Lindahl, *Modern Tort Law: Liability and Litigation* § 6:3 (2d ed. 2009) (hereinafter "Lee & Lindahl").

II.

Eighteen years ago, this Court produced a sea-change in Tennessee's tort law by replacing the common-law concept of contributory negligence with the concept of contributory fault. *McIntyre v. Balentine*, 833 S.W.2d at 56. We expressly recognized at that time that many of the issues arising from the transition to a comparative fault regime would be addressed in later cases. *McIntyre v. Balentine*, 833 S.W.2d at 57. Accordingly, it has come to pass that this Court has been presented with many opportunities since 1992 to revisit, refine, and clarify many of the central tenets of *McIntyre v. Balentine* and to address their impact on Tennessee tort law.

One of the central tenets of *McIntyre v. Balentine* is that the doctrine of joint and several liability was "obsolete" because it was inconsistent with the doctrine of comparative fault. *McIntyre v. Balentine*, 833 S.W.2d at 58. We explained that the doctrine of comparative fault, which would more closely link liability and fault, could not be reconciled with joint and several liability which could "fortuitously impose a degree of liability that is out of all proportion to fault." *McIntyre v. Balentine*, 833 S.W.2d at 58.

The announcement that the doctrine of joint and several liability was obsolete, while later characterized as dictum, was not met with universal acceptance. Mr. McIntyre and one of the parties who filed an amicus curiae brief requested a rehearing to address "the advisability of retaining joint and several liability in certain limited circumstances." This Court declined to grant the petition for rehearing, stating that "such further guidance should await an appropriate controversy." *McIntyre v. Balentine*, 833 S.W.2d at 60.

Thus, the *McIntyre v. Balentine* decision left behind some ambiguity regarding the continuing viability of any application of the doctrine of joint and several liability. On one hand, the Court had declared the doctrine "obsolete." On the other hand, the Court had left open the possibility that it might retain the doctrine "in certain limited circumstances" in future cases. As a result, the practicing bar set out to create opportunities for the Court to decide in what circumstances, if any, the doctrine of joint and several liability could rise from the ashes of obsolescence.

In the first comparative fault cases considered by the Court, we reaffirmed that our decision in *McIntyre v. Balentine* "did abolish the doctrine of joint and several liability to the extent that it allows a plaintiff to sue and obtain a full recovery against any one or more of several parties against whom liability could be established." *Bervoets v. Harde Ralls Pontiac–Olds, Inc.*, 891 S.W.2d 905, 907 (Tenn. 1994). The following year, we repeated that "one of the corollaries to the adoption of comparative fault . . . was the abolition of the doctrine of joint and several liability," and we "confirm[ed] that the doctrine of joint and several liability was rendered obsolete by our decision in *McIntyre v. Balentine*." *Volz v. Ledes*, 895 S.W.2d at 680. We made the same point in 1995. *Whitehead v. Toyota Motor Corp.*, 897 S.W.2d 684, 686 (Tenn. 1995).

Thus, during the three years immediately following *McIntyre v. Balentine*, the Court exhibited little inclination to return the doctrine of joint and several liability, in any of its common-law applications, to useful service. The tide, however, began to turn in 1996. In the face of the broad obsolescence language in *McIntyre v. Balentine, Bervoets v. Harde Ralls Pontiac – Olds, Inc., Volz v. Ledes*, and *Whitehead v. Toyota Motor Corp.*, the Court announced that it had "not . . . disapproved of the doctrine of joint and several liability *in a general sense* . . . it [had] disapproved joint and several liability *in a particular sense*, that is, where the defendants were charged with separate, independent acts of negligence." *Owens v. Truckstops of Am.*, 915 S.W.2d 420, 431 n. 13 (Tenn. 1996).

This change in direction prompted the author of *McIntyre v. Balentine* to point out in dissent that the Court was "resurrecting joint and several liability." *Owens v. Truckstops of Am., Inc.*, 915 S.W.2d at 437 (Drowota, J., dissenting in part). In response, the Court declared that "[j]oint and several liability need not be 'resurrected' . . . because it has continued to be an integral part of the law, except where specifically abrogated." *Owens v. Truckstops of Am.*, 915 S.W.2d at 431 n. 13. The Court then recalibrated the extent of the obsolescence of the doctrine of joint and several liability to circumstances "where the separate, independent negligent acts of more than one tortfeasor combine to cause a single, indivisible injury." *Owens v. Truckstops of Am.*, 915 S.W.2d at 430. In this circumstance, "each tortfeasor will be liable only for that proportion of the damages attributable to its fault. As to those tortfeasors, liability is not joint and several but several only, even though two or more tortfeasors are joined in the same action." *Owens v. Truckstops of Am.*, 915 S.W.2d at 430.

During the past fourteen years, this Court has reaffirmed its holding that the doctrine of joint and several liability, as it existed prior to 1992, is obsolete. *Ali v. Fisher*, 145 S.W.3d 557, 561 (Tenn. 2004); *Carroll v. Whitney*, 29 S.W.3d 14, 16 (Tenn. 2000); *Sherer v. Linginfelter*, 29 S.W.3d 451, 455 (Tenn. 2000). At the same time, however, we have determined that the doctrine remains viable in several well-defined circumstances. We approved joint and several liability for defendants in the chain of distribution of a product in a products liability action. *Owens v. Truckstops of Am.*, 915 S.W.2d at 433. We determined that the doctrine of joint and several liability was not obsolete in cases involving injury caused by multiple defendants who have breached a common duty. *Resolution Trust Corp. v. Block*, 924 S.W.2d 354, 355, 357 (Tenn. 1996). We have likewise approved the application of the doctrine in cases wherein the plaintiff's injury was caused by the concerted actions of the defendants. *Gen. Elec. Co. v. Process Control Co.*, 969 S.W.2d 914, 916 (Tenn. 1998).

To the extent that the doctrine of vicarious liability can be considered a species of joint and several liability, we have held that the adoption of comparative fault in *McIntyre v. Balentine* did not undermine the continuing viability of various vicarious liability doctrines, including the family purpose doctrine, *Camper v. Minor*, 915 S.W.2d 437, 447–48 (Tenn. 1996), "respondeat superior, or similar circumstance where liability is vicarious due to an agency-type relationship between the active, or actual wrongdoer and the one who is vicariously responsible." *Browder v. Morris*, 975 S.W.2d 308, 311–12 (Tenn. 1998). Finally, we determined that tortfeasors who have a duty to protect others from the foreseeable intentional acts of third persons are jointly and severally liable with the third person for the injuries caused by the third person's intentional acts. *Limbaugh v. Coffee Med. Ctr.*, 59 S.W.3d 73, 87 (Tenn. 2001); *White v. Lawrence*, 975 S.W.2d 525, 531 (Tenn. 1998); *Turner v. Jordan*, 957 S.W.2d 815, 823 (Tenn. 1997).

Ever since we handed down our decision in *McIntyre v. Balentine*, this Court's goal has been to assure that Tennessee's comparative fault regime strikes the proper balance between the plaintiff's interest in being made whole with the defendant's interest in paying only those damages for which the defendant is responsible. *Brown v. Wal – Mart Discount Cities*, 12 S.W.3d 785, 787 (Tenn. 2000). We have found this balance in proceedings that link liability to fault. *Biscan v. Brown*, 160 S.W.3d 462, 474 (Tenn. 2005); *Ali v. Fisher*, 145 S.W.3d at 563–64; *Carroll v. Whitney*, 29 S.W.3d at 16–17, 21. Thus, we have embraced an approach in which a tortfeasor may seek to reduce its proportional share of the damages by successfully asserting as an affirmative defense that a portion of the fault for the plaintiff's damages should be allocated to another tortfeasor.

Throughout this period, we have repeatedly emphasized four core principles of the comparative fault regime that we ushered in when we decided *McIntyre v. Balentine*. These principles are: (1) that when "the separate, independent negligent acts of more than one tortfeasor combine to cause a single, indivisible injury, all tortfeasors must be joined in the same action, unless joinder is specifically prohibited by law"; (2) that when "the separate, independent negligent acts of more than one tortfeasor combine to cause a single, indivisible injury, each tortfeasor will be liable only for that proportion of the damages attributed to its fault"; (3) that the goal of linking liability with fault is not furthered by a rule that allows a defendant's liability to be determined by the happenstance of the financial wherewithal of the other defendants; and (4) that the purpose of the comparative fault regime is to prevent fortuitously imposing a degree of liability that is out of all proportion to fault.

III.

This Court has not addressed the continuing viability of the original tortfeasor rule since deciding *McIntyre v. Balentine* in 1992. Despite the Court of Appeals's belief to the contrary, we do not view *McIntyre v. Balentine* as being incompatible with the common-law rule permitting a tortfeasor to be found liable for subsequent negligent conduct of third parties that is a foreseeable result of the original tortfeasor's negligence. Even though our decision in *McIntyre v. Balentine* altered the common-law rules for determining the apportionment of the liability among multiple tortfeasors, it did not alter the common-law rules for determining when tortfeasors are liable for the harm they cause.

A.

McIntyre v. Balentine did not require this Court to determine the role that the original tortfeasor rule would play following the advent of comparative fault. During the intervening years, the Court of Appeals has decided on three occasions that the original tortfeasor rule — embracing both the liability of the original tortfeasor for subsequent negligent acts and the concept of joint and several liability — was not affected by our decision in *McIntyre v. Balentine*.

In the first case presented to the Court of Appeals, the court observed that "to allow a tortfeasor to reduce his damages by alleging the subsequent negligence of a medical provider would for all practical purposes abolish the common law rule." *Atkinson v. Hemphill*, No. 01A01–9311–CV–00509, 1994 Tenn. App. LEXIS 480, at *2 (Tenn.Ct.App. Aug.24, 1994) (No Tenn. R.App. P. 11 application filed). Believing that the abolition of the common-law original tortfeasor rule would "penalize injured parties in several inequitable ways," the court concluded, "[w]e do not believe that the Supreme Court intended this result." *Atkinson v. Hemphill*, 1994 Tenn. App. LEXIS 480, at *2.

The Court of Appeals followed the *Atkinson v. Hemphill* decision four years later. *Troy v. Herndon*, No. 03A01–9707–CV–00271, 1998 Tenn. App. LEXIS 793, at *1–2 (Tenn.Ct.App. Nov.24, 1998) (No Tenn. R.App. P. 11 application filed). When the issue was next presented in 2003, the Court of Appeals again followed *Atkinson v. Hemphill*, but for the first time, the defendant requested this Court to review the decision. While we did not review the case, we designated the Court of Appeals' decision "Not for Citation." *Jackson v. Hamilton*, No. W2000–01992–COA–R3–CV, 2003 Tenn. App. LEXIS 787, at *5–6 (Tenn.Ct.App. Nov.4, 2003), *perm. app. denied, designated not for citation* (Tenn. May 10, 2004). This designation signified that the opinion could not be considered persuasive authority. Tenn. Sup.Ct. R. 4(G)(1).

We have concluded that the Court of Appeals analyses in the three cases it considered failed to differentiate between the two principles embodied in the original tortfeasor rule — the original tortfeasor's liability for subsequent negligent acts of third parties and the original tortfeasor's joint and several liability with the subsequent negligent actors. Accordingly, we now take this occasion to disapprove the holdings in *Atkinson v. Hemphill*, *Troy v. Herndon*, and *Jackson v. Hamilton* with regard to the original tortfeasor rule.

B.

The principles governing liability for successive injuries are settled. They recognize that there are circumstances in which an earlier tortfeasor may be held liable not only for the injury caused by its own negligent conduct but also for later injury caused by the negligent conduct of another tortfeasor. Restatement (Second) of Torts § 433A, cmt. c (1965); *Prosser and Keeton* § 52, at 352. Liability in these circumstances arises when the subsequent negligent conduct is a foreseeable or natural consequence of the original tortfeasor's negligence. 2 Jacob A. Stein, *Stein on Personal Injury Damages* § 11:7 (3d ed.2009) (hereinafter "Stein"); *see also McClenahan v. Cooley*, 806 S.W.2d 767, 775 (Tenn. 1991) (noting that "[a]n intervening act, which is a normal response created by negligence, is not a superseding, intervening cause so as to relieve the original wrongdoer of liability, provided the intervening act could have reasonably been foreseen and the conduct was a substantial factor in bringing about the harm").

Negligence in subsequent medical treatment of a tortiously caused injury is the most common invocation of this rule. Lee & Lindahl, at § 6:3; *Prosser and Keeton* § 52, at 352; 2 Stein, at § 11:7. The first two Restatements of Torts recognized this principle. Restatement (Second) of Torts § 457, at 496; Restatement of Torts § 457, at 1214 (1934). It has also been carried forward in the Proposed Final Draft of the Restatement (Third) of Torts: Liability for Personal Injury in the following form:

An actor whose tortious conduct is a factual cause of physical harm to another is subject to liability for any enhanced harm the other suffers due to the efforts of third persons to render aid reasonably required by the other's injury, so long as the harm arises from a risk that inheres in the effort to render aid.

Restatement (Third) of Torts: Liability for Physical Harm § 35, at 693 (Proposed Final Draft No. 12005) ("Restatement (Third) of Torts: Liability for Physical Harm").

Tennessee's courts have recognized and applied this principle for over one hundred years. This Court first alluded to it in *Arkansas River Packet Co. v. Hobbs*, 105 Tenn. 29, 44–46, 58 S.W. 278, 282 (1900). In 1931, we invoked it as an alternate basis for preventing an injured employee from filing a medical malpractice suit against an employer-provided physician after the employee obtained a judgment against the employer. *Revell v. McCaughan*, 162 Tenn. 532, 538, 39 S.W.2d 269, 271 (1931). In 1967, characterizing the principle as a "well settled principle of law," we employed it for the first time to decide a dispute that did not arise out of a workplace injury. *Transports, Inc. v. Perry*, 220 Tenn. at 64–65, 414 S.W.2d at 4–5. Ten years later in another case involving a workplace injury, we noted that this now well settled principle "applies to the general field of tort law." *McAlister v. Methodist Hosp.*, 550 S.W.2d 240, 242 (Tenn. 1977).

C.

McIntyre v. Balentine involved a straightforward intersection crash involving two intoxicated drivers. It did not raise an issue of liability for successive injuries, and thus, this Court had no occasion to determine how the new comparative fault regime would mesh with the principle that, in proper circumstances, an earlier tortfeasor could be liable for the later negligent acts of another tortfeasor. To understand the effect of *McIntyre v. Balentine* on the original tortfeasor rule, the two principles in that rule — the original tortfeasor's liability for subsequent negligent acts of third parties and the original tortfeasor's joint and several liability with the subsequent negligent actors — must be unraveled and considered separately.

Today, we state unequivocally that our decision regarding joint and several liability in *McIntyre v. Balentine* did not alter Tennessee's common-law rules with regard to liability of tortfeasors for injuries caused by subsequent medical treatment for the injuries they cause. That rule is a rule that determines "when defendants are liable for the harm they caused." Restatement (Third) of Torts: Liability for Physical Injury § 35, cmt. d, at 696–97. Thus, the rule in Tennessee is now, as it was before *McIntyre v. Balentine* was decided, that an actor whose tortious conduct causes physical harm to another is liable for any enhanced harm the other suffers due to the efforts of third persons to render aid reasonably required by the other's injury, as long as the enhanced harm arises from a risk that inheres in the effort to render aid. *See* Restatement (Third) of Torts: Liability for Physical Injury § 35, at 693.

However, at the same time, we again reaffirm our earlier decisions holding that following *McIntyre v. Balentine*, the doctrine of joint and several liability no longer applies to circumstances in which separate, independent negligent acts of more than one tortfeasor combine to cause a single, indivisible injury. *Sherer v. Linginfelter*, 29 S.W.3d at 455; *Samuelson v. McMurtry*, 962 S.W.2d at 476; *Owens v. Truckstops of Am., Inc.*, 915 S.W.2d at 430. This decision is not inconsistent with our decision to retain the rule imposing liability on tortfeasors for subsequent negligent medical care for the injuries caused by the original tortfeasor. As the drafters of the proposed Restatement (Third) of Torts: Liability for Physical Injury have explained:

> Nor does modification of joint and several liability require or imply any change in the rule contained in . . . Section [35]. Modern adoption of pure several liability limits the liability of each defendant liable for the same harm to that defendant's comparative share of the harm. See Restatement Third, Torts: Apportionment of Liability § 11.[12] Several liability, however, does not provide rules about when defendants are liable for harm that they caused. When two or more defendants are liable for the enhanced harm suffered by a plaintiff, as may occur under this Section, and the governing law imposes several liability, each of the defendants is held liable for the amount of damages reflecting the enhanced harm discounted by the comparative share responsibility assigned by the factfinder to that defendant.

Restatement (Third) of Torts: Liability for Physical Harm § 35, cmt. d., at 697.

The Court of Appeals in *Atkinson v. Hemphill* overstated the effect of *McIntyre v. Balentine* when it observed that applying the decision in circumstances such as this one would "penalize injured parties in several inequitable ways." *Atkinson v. Hemphill*, 1994 Tenn. App. LEXIS 480, at *3. To the contrary, as observed by the American Law Institute, "[c]omparative responsibility provides a different and easier method for apportioning liability among severally liable parties." Restatement (Third) of Torts: Apportionment of Liability § 11, at cmt. b., at 109. It spares injured plaintiffs, as well as the courts and other parties, the time and expense of multiple trials. As we noted over ten years ago, Tennessee's comparative fault regime "retains the efficiency of joint liability and the fairness of comparative fault." *Samuelson v. McMurtry*, 962 S.W.2d at 476.

Most of the states that have adopted the principles of comparative fault or comparative responsibility have done so by statute rather than by judicial decision. The substance of these statutes differs because states have balanced the rights and interests of the parties in different ways. Accordingly, decisions from other state courts construing their own comparative fault statute provide only limited guidance to us. However, we note that a significant number of state courts that have addressed the same question we address in this case have, like this Court, concluded that comparative fault does not prevent the continuing imposition of liability on an

---

[12] Restatement (Third) of Torts: Apportionment of Liability § 11 (2000) provides: "When, under applicable law, a person is severally liable to an injured person for an indivisible injury, the injured person may recover only the severally liable person's comparative-responsibility share of the injured person's damages."

original tortfeasor for subsequent negligent medical care for the injuries caused by the original tortfeasor.

D.

Finally, Ms. Banks and the Tennessee Association for Justice assert that public policy dictates retaining joint and several liability in circumstances where an injured person suffers enhanced physical harm due to the efforts of third persons to render aid to the injured person for injuries caused by the defendant's negligence. They assert that joint and several liability is appropriate because (1) the original defendant is the proximate cause of the entire injury and (2) doing away with joint and several liability will require injured persons to make difficult choices with regard to filing suit against their treating physicians.

The proximate cause argument overlooks the fact that in cases of this sort, the original tortfeasor's conduct is not the sole proximate cause of the plaintiff's indivisible injury. To the contrary, the independent tortious conduct of the original tortfeasor and one or more other parties are both proximate causes of the injury. The tortfeasors are not acting in concert, have not breached common duty, and do not have a relationship triggering the application of vicarious liability. Therefore, this circumstance is governed by our consistent holding that joint and several liability is no longer applicable in circumstances "where the separate, independent negligent acts of more than one tortfeasor combine to cause a single, indivisible injury." *Sherer v. Linginfelter*, 29 S.W.3d at 455. As we noted more than one century ago, where "there is no intent that the combined acts of all shall culminate in the injury resulting therefrom, . . . it is just that each should only be held liable so far as his acts contribute to the injury." *Swain v. Tenn. Copper Co.*, 111 Tenn. 430, 439, 78 S.W. 93, 94 (1903).

Ms. Banks and the Tennessee Association for Justice also insist that not applying joint and several liability in circumstances like the one involved in this case will place plaintiffs in the difficult position of being forced to sue their treating physicians and, thereby, adding the complexity of a medical negligence claim to an otherwise straightforward ordinary negligence case. The force of this argument is somewhat undermined by the fact that Ms. Banks is not being drawn into reluctantly suing her treating physician because she has already sued Dr. Boyce. In any event, we have concluded that these concerns are overstated.

When a defendant tortfeasor files an answer asserting the affirmative defense[13] that a nonparty healthcare provider is at fault for the plaintiff's injuries, the plaintiff has two options. First, it can decide not to name the healthcare provider as a defendant under Tenn.Code Ann. § 20-1-119(a) (2009) and run the risk of a diminished recovery if the defendant succeeds in convincing the trier of fact that the nonparty healthcare provider is partially or completely at fault. Second, the plaintiff can amend its complaint in accordance with Tenn.Code Ann. § 20-1-119(a) and thereby preserve its opportunity for an undiminished recovery.

---

[13] One of the affirmative defenses included in Tenn. R. Civ. P. 8.03 is "comparative fault (including the identity or description of the other alleged tortfeasors)."

When a plaintiff elects to amend its complaint to name as a defendant a healthcare provider whom the original defendant identified as liable for the plaintiff's injury, the burden of proof regarding the healthcare provider's negligence does not shift entirely to the plaintiff. It remains with the original defendant who asserted the affirmative defense of comparative fault. Thus, the plaintiff is not required to shoulder the difficulty and expense of proving medical negligence unless, for some reason, it chooses to do so, just as Ms. Banks has already done in this case. That burden remains with the defendant who asserted the affirmative defense of comparative fault in the first place.[14]

Leaving the burden of proof with the defendant asserting the comparative fault defense does not prejudice plaintiffs who elect to amend their complaint to name a healthcare provider as a defendant after the original defendant has asserted that the healthcare provider is comparatively at fault. If the original defendant is unable to prove that the healthcare provider is liable, the plaintiff may still obtain a complete recovery from the original defendant, just as it originally set out to do. If, however, the original defendant is successful in proving that the healthcare provider is liable, then the plaintiff may obtain a complete recovery apportioned between the original defendant and the healthcare provider based on their fault.

Plaintiffs are not required to amend their complaints to add as defendants third parties whom a defendant identifies as a contributing tortfeasor. That decision remains entirely in their control. Amending a complaint to add as a defendant a third-party tortfeasor identified by the original defendant also does not force the plaintiff to try a case it was not prepared to try. Therefore, amending a complaint pursuant to Tenn.Code Ann. § 20-1-119(a) to name as a defendant a third party named by a defendant as a contributing tortfeasor is neither burdensome nor costly.

IV.

In addition to their argument that they should have been permitted to assert a comparative fault defense against Cumberland Manor, the Elks Lodge defendants assert that the original tortfeasor principle is inconsistent with this Court's opinion in *Mercer v. Vanderbilt University, Inc.*, 134 S.W.3d 121 (Tenn. 2004). They argue that *Mercer v. Vanderbilt University, Inc.* stands for the proposition that a "negligent actor should not be held responsible for the subsequent negligence of a healthcare provider under Tennessee's law of comparative fault." The Elks Lodge defendants have placed more weight on the Mercer opinion than it can bear.

The principles that dictated the result in *Mercer v. Vanderbilt University, Inc.* do not apply to cases like this one for two reasons. First, unlike *Mercer* where we declined to extend comparative fault to patients who sue their physicians for

---

[14] Accordingly, if a plaintiff amends its complaint to add a new defendant identified by the original defendant as contributing to the plaintiff's indivisible injuries, trial courts would not act on the new defendant's motion for a directed verdict until the close of all the proof in order to permit the original defendant to present its evidence regarding the new defendant's fault. A directed verdict at the close of the plaintiff's proof would be appropriate only when the original defendant states that it lacks sufficient evidence to send the issue of the new defendant's fault to the jury. If the new defendant's motion for directed verdict is granted, the jury cannot be requested to allocate any portion of the fault to the now-dismissed defendant.

negligence because doing so would prevent any recovery for injured patients who were found to be more than fifty percent at fault, applying comparative fault in this case will not prevent an injured plaintiff from recovering. *See Mercer v. Vanderbilt Univ., Inc.*, 134 S.W.3d at 129–30. It will simply enable the trier of fact to apportion the fault between the defendants whose conduct caused or contributed to the plaintiff's injuries.

Second, holding that original tortfeasors will not be liable for the enhanced injuries caused from the efforts of physicians or other healthcare providers to render aid to an injured plaintiff would be contrary to the basic tenets of Tennessee tort law, more than one century of Tennessee common-law precedents, and the general principles of liability reflected in the Restatement of Torts. Negligence is conduct that violates a person's obligation to exercise reasonable care to avoid engaging in behavior that creates an unreasonable danger to others. *Satterfield v. Breeding Insulation Co.*, 266 S.W.3d 347, 363 (Tenn. 2008). Persons who are negligent are liable for the natural and probable consequences of their conduct, *Doe v. Linder Constr. Co.*, 845 S.W.2d 173, 181 (Tenn. 1992), as long as their conduct was a substantial factor in bringing about the plaintiff's injury, the injury was reasonably foreseeable, and there is no statute or policy relieving them of liability. *Naifeh v. Valley Forge Life Ins. Co.*, 204 S.W.3d 758, 771 (Tenn. 2006).

Ever since the advent of comparative fault in 1992, we have emphasized that the doctrine of joint and several liability no longer applies to circumstances in which separate, independent negligent acts of more than one tortfeasor combine to cause a single, indivisible injury. Today, we have explicitly held that the doctrine of joint and several liability does not apply in cases where the injuries caused by the negligence of the original tortfeasor are enhanced by the subsequent negligence of physicians and other healthcare providers. Nothing in *Mercer v. Vanderbilt University, Inc.* dictates a contrary result. Accordingly, we decline the Elks Lodge defendants' invitation to extend our ruling in *Mercer v. Vanderbilt University, Inc.* to entirely eliminate the original tortfeasor rule.

V.

Dr. Boyce has raised four other issues, only one of which merits discussion. He argues that the original tortfeasor principle cannot be applied to him because he "cannot be simultaneously branded the original tortfeasor and a successive tortfeasor." We respectfully disagree. Dr. Boyce can, in fact, be both an original tortfeasor and a successive tortfeasor.

In cases involving successive acts of malpractice, many courts have recognized that the original treating physician may be liable for the injuries caused by the negligence of subsequent physicians for medical treatment undertaken to mitigate the harm caused by the original physician's malpractice.

The specific circumstance in which a physician qualifies both as an "original tortfeasor" and a "successive tortfeasor" was well addressed in *State ex rel. Blond v. Stubbs*, 485 S.W.2d 152 (Mo.Ct.App.1972). The plaintiff was injured as a result of a dangerous condition at a building operated by the Tenth and Main Corporation and was treated by three different physicians. He alleged that each of the physicians had treated him negligently and that their treatment enhanced the injuries for which the Tenth and Main Corporation and the earlier treating physicians were responsible. Applying the original tortfeasor rule, the Missouri Court of Appeals concluded:

> By reason of the operation of the foregoing rule, defendant Tenth and Main Corporation is liable not only for its own alleged negligence, but also for the alleged negligence of all [three] doctors; likewise, [the first in time physician] is liable, not only for his own alleged negligence, but also for that of the two succeeding doctors; likewise, [the second in time physician] is liable for his own alleged negligence and also that of [the third in time physician]. The net result of all this is that the alleged negligence of [the third in time physician] is a common occurrence for which all four defendants have potential liability.

State ex rel. Blond v. Stubbs, 485 S.W.2d at 154.

The continuing liability under the original tortfeasor rule is not tied to anything magical about being the "original" tortfeasor. It stems instead from being a proximate cause of an aggravated injury resulting from subsequent medical treatment of the negligent injury that one has caused or aggravated. *See Transports, Inc. v. Perry*, 220 Tenn. at 64–65, 414 S.W.2d at 4; Restatement (Third) of Torts: Liability for Physical Harm § 35, at 693. We agree with the approach employed by the Missouri Court of Appeals in *State ex rel. Blond v. Stubbs*. Accordingly, we find that Dr. Boyce can, in fact, simultaneously be an original tortfeasor, for purposes of the aggravation that he allegedly caused and a subsequent aggravation resulting from the alleged medical negligence of Cumberland Manor, and a successive tortfeasor, for purposes of the injury allegedly negligently caused by the Elks Lodge and allegedly negligently aggravated by Dr. Boyce.

VI.

We reiterate that the doctrine of joint and several liability no longer applies to circumstances in which separate, independent negligent acts of more than one tortfeasor combine to cause a single, indivisible injury. We hold that an actor whose tortious conduct causes physical harm to another is liable for any enhanced harm the other suffers due to the efforts of third persons to render aid reasonably required by the other's injury, as long as the enhanced harm arises from a risk that inheres in the effort to render aid. In light of our consistent holding that the doctrine of joint and several liability no longer applies to circumstances in which separate, independent negligent acts of more than one tortfeasor combine to cause a single, indivisible injury, it is improper to maintain joint and several liability in cases involving subsequent medical negligence where there is even less cause. We find that the trial court erred by refusing to permit the Elks Lodge defendants and Dr. Boyce to amend their answers to assert a comparative fault defense against Cumberland Manor. [Remanded.]

1. What is the court's rationale in *Ravo* for permitting the plaintiff to recover the whole amount from Dr. Harris? Is this fair? How would the *Banks* court handle this?

2. What is a successive tort-feasor? Why, in a successive tort, might the first tort-feasor be liable for later injuries? When might the second tort-feasor be liable for all the injuries?

3. What is the reason for holding two or more defendants liable when they produce a single indivisible injury? Should there be a difference between simultaneous and sequential acts?

4. If a joint defendant is required to pay the whole amount, how much should he recover from any codefendant? Should this affect his or her liability to the plaintiff?

WALT DISNEY WORLD v. WOOD
Supreme Court of Florida, 1987
515 So. 2d 198

GRIMES, JUSTICE.

Aloysia Wood was injured in November 1971 at the grand prix attraction at Walt Disney World (Disney), when her fiancé,[1] Daniel Wood, rammed from the rear the vehicle which she was driving. Aloysia Wood filed suit against Disney, and Disney sought contribution from Daniel Wood. After trial, the jury returned a verdict finding Aloysia Wood 14% at fault, Daniel Wood 85% at fault, and Disney 1% at fault. The jury assessed Wood's damages at $75,000. The court entered judgment against Disney for 86% of the damages. Disney subsequently moved to alter the judgment to reflect the jury's finding that Disney was only 1% at fault. The court denied the motion. On appeal, the fourth district affirmed the judgment on the basis of this Court's decision in *Lincenberg v. Issen*, 318 So. 2d 386 (Fla. 1975).

In *Hoffman v. Jones*, 280 So. 2d 431 (Fla. 1973), this Court discarded the rule of contributory negligence, which Florida had followed since at least 1886, and adopted the pure comparative negligence standard. . . .

Thereafter, in *Lincenberg v. Issen*, a faultless plaintiff obtained a verdict in which the jury determined that one defendant was 85% percent negligent and the other defendant was 15% negligent. The district court of appeal held that the jury should not have been asked to apportion fault between the defendants. *Issen v. Lincenberg*, 293 So. 2d 777 (Fla. 3d DCA 1974). On review, this Court concluded that the rationale of *Hoffman v. Jones* dictated the elimination of the rule against contribution among joint tortfeasors. The Court then said that since " 'no contribution' is no longer a viable principle in Florida, we were confronted with the problem of determining what procedure will most fully effectuate the principle that each party should pay the proportion of the total damages he has caused to the other party, and we considered several alternatives." *Lincenberg*, 318 So. 2d at 392 (footnote

---

[1] Wood married her fiancé prior to this action.

omitted). At this point, the Court stated in footnote 2 that among the alternatives considered was pure apportionment whereby the plaintiff may recover judgment against codefen-dants only for the percentage of damages caused by the negligence of each individual defendant. However, the Court noted that the legislature had just passed section 738.31, Florida Statutes (1975), which provided for contribution among joint tortfeasors and interpreted the statute as retaining the "full, joint, and several liability of joint tortfeasors to the plaintiff." Thus, the Court held:

> The plaintiff is entitled to a measurement of his full damages and the liability for these damages should be apportioned in accordance with the percentage of negligence as it relates to the total of all the defendants. The negligence attributed to the defendants will then be apportioned on a pro rata basis without considering relative degrees of fault although the multiparty defendants will remain jointly and severally liable for the entire amount.

Lincenberg, 318 So. 2d at 393-94.

While arising in the context of a faultless plaintiff, it cannot reasonably be said that the Court in *Lincenberg* did not pass on the question now before us. Understandably, courts addressing the issue in subsequent decisions, including this Court, have interpreted *Lincenberg* as upholding the doctrine of joint and several liability. . . .

The real issue before us is whether we should now replace the doctrine of joint and several liability with one in which the liability of codefendants to the plaintiff is apportioned according to each defendant's respective fault. According to Disney, this Court in *Hoffman* set for itself the goal of creating a tort system that fairly and equitably allocated damages according to the degrees of fault. Therefore, a defendant should only be held responsible to the extent of his fault in the same way as a plaintiff under comparative negligence.

Joint and several liability is a judicially created doctrine. *Louisville & N.R.R. v. Allen*, 67 Fla. 257, 65 So. 8 (1914). This Court may alter a rule of law where great social upheaval dictates its necessity. *Hoffman*, 280 So. 2d 431. The "social upheaval" which is said to have occurred here is the fundamental alteration of Florida tort law encompassed by the adoption of comparative negligence. Following the adoption of comparative negligence, some states have passed laws eliminating joint and several liability,[4] and the courts of several others have judicially abolished the doctrine. . . . The Kansas Supreme Court in *Brown v. Keill* reasoned:

> There is nothing inherently fair about a defendant who is 10% at fault paying 100% of the loss, and there is no social policy that should compel defendants to pay more than their fair share of the loss. Plaintiffs now take the parties as they find them. If one of the parties at fault happens to be a spouse or a governmental agency and if by reason of some competing social

---

[4] Some statutes limit the judgment entered against each defendant to that defendant's percentage of the plaintiff's damages. *E.g.*, Ohio Rev. Code Ann. § 2315.19(A) (Baldwin 1984); N.H. Rev. Stat. Ann. § 507.7?d (1986 Supp.). Others only limit the defendant's liability to the percentage of his negligence when his negligence is less than that of the plaintiffs. *E.g.*, Or. Rev. Stat. § 18.485 (1985); Tex. Civ. Prac. & Rem. Code Ann. § 33.001(b) (Vernon 1986).

policy the plaintiff cannot receive payment for his injuries from the spouse or agency, there is no compelling social policy which requires the codefendant to pay more than his fair share of the loss. The same is true if one of the defendants is wealthy and the other is not.

Brown, 224 Kan. at 203, 580 P.2d at 874.

On the other hand, the majority of courts which have faced the issue in jurisdictions with comparative negligence have ruled that joint and several liability should be retained. . . . The Illinois Supreme Court in *Coney v. J.L.G. Industries, Inc.* gave four reasons justifying the retention of joint and several liability:

(1) The feasibility of apportioning fault on a comparative basis does not render an indivisible injury "divisible" for purposes of the joint and several liability rule. A concurrent tortfeasor is liable for the whole of an indivisible injury when his negligence is a proximate cause of that damage. In many instances, the negligence of a concurrent tortfeasor may be sufficient by itself to cause the entire loss. The mere fact that it may be possible to assign some percentage figure to the relative culpability of one negligent defendant as compared to another does not in any way suggest that each defendant's negligence is not a proximate cause of the entire indivisible injury.

(2) In those instances where the plaintiff is not guilty of negligence, he would be forced to bear a portion of the loss should one of the tortfeasors prove financially unable to satisfy his share of the damages.

(3) Even in cases where a plaintiff is partially at fault, his culpability is not equivalent to that of a defendant. The plaintiff's negligence relates only to a lack of due care for his own safety while the defendant's negligence relates to a lack of due care for the safety of others; the latter is tortious, but the former is not.

(4) Elimination of joint and several liability would work a serious and unwarranted deleterious effect on the ability of an injured plaintiff to obtain adequate compensation for his injuries.

Coney, 97 Ill. 2d at 121-22, 454 N.E.2d at 205 (citations omitted).

. . . .

While recognizing the logic in Disney's position, we cannot say with certainty that joint and several liability is an unjust doctrine or that it should necessarily be eliminated upon the adoption of comparative negligence. In view of the public policy considerations bearing on the issue, this Court believes that the viability of the doctrine is a matter which should best be decided by the legislature. Consequently, we approve the decision of the district court of appeal.

It is so ordered.

———————

1. Chief Justice McDonald dissented in *Walt Disney World* as follows:

The majority opinion may make social sense, but it defies legal logic. The doctrines of joint and several liability and contributory negligence are consistent with each other. Each tortfeasor, as a part of the whole, is liable for the whole. Comparative negligence, which does not bar, but reduces a recovery to the extent of individual fault, requires a separation of fault between the injured party and the other tortfeasors. It would be a mismatch of legal concepts to have a separation theory for the plaintiffs and a joint liability responsibility for defendants. Comparative negligence recognized the ability of a court to determine and apportion damages in relation to the harm caused. Joint and several, in contrast, presumes the inability of the judiciary to divide fault among parties. We have now said that we can. Accordingly, when the comparative negligence doctrine comes into play, as it did in this case, the law of joint and several liability should be repudiated and each defendant held accountable for only the percentage of damages found by the trier of fact to have been caused by his conduct.

515 So. 2d 198, at 202 (McDonald, C.J., dissenting).

Has the adoption of comparative fault by the states eliminated the basis for joint liability, as Chief Justice McDonald and tort-reformers nationally suggest? What if one of the liable parties is bankrupt or otherwise unavailable? Who should bear the risk if part of the judgment is uncollectible? Is it appropriate for one or more of the defendants to benefit if a fellow-defendant cannot pay his or her share? What if one of the defendants in *Summers v. Tice* had been judgment-proof? Should the plaintiff only collect half of the judgment?

2.   Subsequent to *Walt Disney World*, the Florida legislature adopted section 768.81(3) Florida Statutes, which states:

(3) Apportionment of Damages. In cases to which this section applies, the court shall enter judgment against each party liable on the basis of such party's percentage of fault and not on the basis of the doctrine of joint and several liability; provided that with respect to any party whose percentage of fault equals or exceeds that of a particular claimant, the court shall enter judgment with respect to economic damages against that party on the basis of the doctrine of joint and several liability.

3.   In 2003, the National Conference of Commissioners on Uniform State Laws adopted the Uniform Apportionment of Tort Responsibility Act. This Act deals with many of the issues raised in this chapter. While it seems not to have been adopted whole in any state, the comments in the Act discuss many of the approaches taken by the states to the problems raised in this chapter.

In the Preface, the Act notes that, with the exception of multiple defendants who engage in concerted action who cause damage to the environment, "many jurisdictions today . . . have abolished joint and several liability and, thereby, any necessity to recognize rights of contribution among joint tortfeasors." Some highlights of the Act of particular relevance to this chapter include adoption of the following approaches:

1. Comparative negligence on the part of the plaintiff reduces the plaintiff's recovery by a percentage equal to that of the plaintiff's negli-

gence, and bars any recovery if the plaintiff's negligence is greater than the sum of the combined negligence of the other parties (Section 3(a) and (b));

2. The jury or factfinder must make findings apportioning responsibility to all parties, including ones who have been released (Section 4 (a)(2));

3. Liability of each defendant is based on its percentage of responsibility (several liability), with the exception that uncollectible portions of the damages are reallocated to solvent defendants in proportion to their responsibility for the injuries (Section 5 (b)).

4.   The Restatement of the Law Third: Torts: Apportionment of Liability (2000) discusses many of the issues raised in this chapter. In the Introduction, the authors note that "there is no majority rule" on how to handle joint and several liability. Instead of restating the law, the authors present various alternative approaches, anticipating that legislatures will act on the matter. Many have done so, as joint and several liability has proven to be a popular target for those who wish to curtail tort liability.

5.   *Release and Satisfaction.* Most personal injury actions are settled, either before trial or at some point in the proceedings. Releases, which are of course contracts, can bring with them major complications if the litigation proceeds against other parties. Under the Uniform Apportionment of Tort Responsibility Act, a release of one party in a multiple-defendant case reduces the potential liability of the other parties by the "percentage of responsibility attributed to the released person" (Section 8(b)).

A party that has settled with the plaintiff is very unlikely to continue to participate in the case after that point (indeed, avoiding litigation costs is a major incentive to settle). What difficulties may arise in terms of apportioning responsibility to that party? Within the bounds of the required honesty, might the other defendants be tempted to heap responsibility on the absent defendant, on the theory that the judgments against them are likely to be reduced under a several approach? Conversely, and also within the bounds of the required honesty, might the plaintiff be tempted to heap responsibility on the present parties, on the theory that minimizing the liability attributable to the absent party will maximize the judgment? Do these two incentives cancel each other out?

What if a plaintiff settles with one party in exchange for that party's testimony at trial? For example, in a medical malpractice case involving several physicians, the plaintiff might settle with one doctor with the testimony of that doctor against the other doctor(s) being part of the agreement. How, if at all, should this affect the allocation of responsibility and damages?

6.   In a case involving admiralty law, the Supreme Court adopted a similar approach to the approach that would later be taken in the Uniform Apportionment of Tort Responsibility Act. *See McDermott, Inc. v. AmClyde*, 511 U.S. 202 (1994). Recognizing that judges and scholars vary in their approaches to how much credit a nonsettling defendant is entitled to after a plaintiff releases other defendants, the Supreme Court reviewed the three major approaches, as identified by the Restatement (Second) of Torts § 886A:

(1) The money paid extinguishes any claim that the injured party has against the party released and the amount of his remaining claim against the other tortfeasor is reached by crediting the amount received; but the transaction does not affect a claim for contribution by another tortfeasor who has paid more than his equitable share of the obligation. . . .

(2) The money paid extinguishes both any claims on the part of the injured party and any claim for contribution by another tortfeasor who has paid more than his equitable share of the obligation and seeks contribution. [Pro Tanto Approach]. . . .

(3) The money paid extinguishes any claim that the injured party has against the released tortfeasor and also diminishes the claim that the injured party has against the other tortfeasors by the amount of the equitable share of the obligation of the released tortfeasor. [Proportionate Share Rule].

511 U.S. at 208–09.

Basing its decision on the precedent of comparative fault, promotion of settlement, and judicial economy, the Supreme Court explained that under the proportionate share method:

no suits for contribution from the settling defendants were permitted, nor are they necessary, because the nonsettling defendants pay no more than their share of the judgment. . . .

[The first Restatement approach] is clearly inferior to the other two, because it discourages settlement and leads to unnecessary ancillary litigation. It discourages settlement, because settlement can only disadvantage the settling defendant. . . .

The choice between [the pro tanto approach and the proportionate share method] is less clear. . . . Under the pro tanto approach, however, a litigating defendant's liability will frequently differ from its equitable share, because a settlement with one defendant for less than its equitable share requires the nonsettling defendant to pay more than its share. Such deviations from the equitable apportionment of damages will be common, because settlements seldom reflect an entirely accurate prediction of the outcome of the trial. . . .

The rule encourages settlements by giving the defendant that settles first an opportunity to pay less than its fair share of the damages, thereby threatening the non-settling defendant with the prospect of paying more than its fair share of the loss. By disadvantaging the party that spurns settlement offers, the pro tanto rule puts pressure on all defendants to settle. While public policy wisely encourages settlements, such additional pressure to settle is unnecessary. The parties' desire to avoid litigation costs, to reduce uncertainty, and to maintain ongoing commercial relationships is sufficient to ensure nontrial dispositions in the vast majority of cases. Under the proportionate share approach, such factors should ensure a similarly high settlement rate. The additional incentive to settlement provided by the pro tanto rule comes at too high a price in unfairness.

AmClyde, 511 U.S. at 209 (footnotes omitted).

7. *Mary Carter Agreements.* Mary Carter agreements are partial and often secret settlements in multiparty litigation where the plaintiff settles with one or more of the defendants, but not all of them. "A Mary Carter-type agreement is generally a secret agreement between adverse parties by which the contracting defendant remains in the lawsuit, guarantees plaintiff a certain monetary recovery, and the contracting defendant's liability is decreased in direct proportion to the increase in the non-agreeing defendants' liability." *American Nat'l Bank & Trust Co. v. Bic Corp.*, 880 P.2d 420, 422–23 (Okla. Ct. App. 1994). Each agreement will vary, but as long as it has the essential elements (secrecy and the settling defendant remaining a party against the plaintiff at trial), it will be deemed a Mary Carter agreement. Because nonsettling defendants are often disadvantaged by these agreements, much controversy arises as to whether certain settlements are Mary Carter agreements and, if so, whether the agreements should be disclosed or void as against public policy.

The name of these agreements originated from *Booth v. Mary Carter Paint Co.*, 202 So. 2d 8 (Fla. Dist. Ct. App. 1967), *overruled by Ward v. Ochoa*, 284 So. 2d 385 (Fla. 1973). The majority of courts, although recognizing that the agreements could skew the trial process, find them to be enforceable as long as certain procedural safeguards are met. Finding the agreement's secrecy to be the main disadvantage to the nonsettling defendant, many courts require the agreements to be fully disclosed to juries and judges. Disclosure will most likely compel the trier of fact to weigh the testimony and conduct of the settling defendant differently, possibly resulting in lesser liability for the non-settling defendant. However, the minority view finds these collusive settlements to be void for various public policy reasons. *See Trampe v. Wisconsin Tel. Co.*, 252 N.W. 675 (Wis. 1934); *Lum v. Stinnett*, 488 P.2d 347 (Nev. 1971); *Cox v. Kelsey-Hayes Co.*, 594 P.2d 354, 360 (Okla. 1978) (Mary Carter agreements are void as against public policy where the "agreeing defendant remains in the lawsuit."); *Elbaor v. Smith*, 845 S.W.2d 240 (Tex. 1992); *Dosdourian v. Carsten*, 624 So. 2d 241 (Fla. 1993). The Texas Supreme Court held that:

> We do not favor settlement arrangements that skew the trial process, mislead the jury, promote unethical collusion among nominal adversaries, and create the likelihood that a less culpable defendant will be hit with this full judgment. The bottom line is that our public policy favoring fair trials outweighs our public policy favoring partial settlements.

Elbaor, 845 S.W.2d at 248–50.

8. What if one of the participants in creating the injury is immune from suit for whatever reason? There are various approaches to this problem. The Uniform Apportionment of Tort Responsibility Act in section 9 treats these situations as though the immune party had signed a release with the plaintiff. The *Restatement Third, Torts: Apportionment of Responsibility* presents alternative approaches without adopting one.

RICHARDS v. BADGER MUTUAL INSURANCE CO.
Supreme Court of Wisconsin, 2008
749 N.W.2d 581

PATIENCE DRAKE ROGGENSACK, J.[*]

We are asked to review a decision of the court of appeals that reversed the circuit court's decision, which concluded that the stipulated facts of this case present a "common scheme or plan" that invokes joint and several liability under Wis. Stat. § 895.045(2) (2005-06). [WE AFFIRM.]

We conclude as follows: (1) Wis. Stat. § 895.045(2) is the legislative codification of the concerted action theory of liability; (2) the damages in this case resulted from the consumption of beer to the point of intoxication and the subsequent decision to drive while intoxicated; and (3) although Robert Zimmerlee, David Schrimpf, and Tomakia Pratchet acted "in accordance with a common scheme or plan" to procure beer, they did not so act in consuming beer to the point of intoxication and in the subsequent act of driving while intoxicated, and, therefore, David Schrimpf is not jointly and severally liable under § 895.045(2) for the death of Chris Richards. Accordingly, Badger Mutual Insurance Company is relieved from making any further payment to Michelle Richards.

I. BACKGROUND

An ill-conceived idea between teenagers to "get some beer" one evening culminated in tragedy the next morning when an intoxicated Robert Zimmerlee, 19, failed to stop for a stop sign and smashed into the driver's side of Christopher Richards' vehicle, killing him instantly. Chris' wife, Michelle Richards (Richards), sought to recover damages. She initially pursued a negligence claim against Zimmerlee and his insurer. The parties settled on for $1,312,500,[4] and Zimmerlee is therefore not a party to this appeal. After Richards received the settlement, she then brought a wrongful death action against David Schrimpf, 19, who was the passenger in Zimmerlee's car, and Schrimpf's insurer, Badger Mutual Insurance Company, pursuant to Wis. Stat. § 895.04. Richards alleged that Schrimpf illegally procured beer and that Zimmerlee's consumption of the beer resulted in Christopher Richards' wrongful death. Schrimpf joined Tomakia Pratchet, who purchased the beer for Zimmerlee and Schrimpf, in the litigation.

The parties have stipulated to the facts in this case. Events leading to the accident unfolded the prior evening, when Schrimpf and Zimmerlee decided to "go get some beer." Schrimpf was employed at a West Allis restaurant, and he said that one of his co-workers, Pratchet, would be able to purchase the beer for them because she was of-age.

Zimmerlee and Schrimpf drove together to Schrimpf's employer, where Pratchet was working that evening. Schrimpf entered and spoke with Pratchet about her purchasing beer for him and Zimmerlee. Pratchet agreed. Schrimpf also spoke with

---

[*] Paragraph numbers in original have been omitted — Eds.

[4] The parties stipulated that Richards' total damages equal $1,785,714.29.

another co-worker, Jennifer Spencer, who invited Schrimpf to a party at her home that evening.

From the restaurant, Zimmerlee, Schrimpf, and Pratchet traveled together to a nearby grocer, where Pratchet purchased an 18-pack of beer for Zimmerlee and Schrimpf with money Zimmerlee provided. The two dropped Pratchet off at a bus stop and Zimmerlee and Schrimpf went their separate ways for several hours, with the beer remaining in Zimmerlee's car.

Later that evening, Schrimpf and Zimmerlee reconnected, and with 18-pack in tow, arrived at Spencer's party between 12 midnight and 1:00 a.m. While Schrimpf drank "some" of the beer, Zimmerlee consumed "maybe half" of the 18 beers.

At approximately 7:30 a.m., the duo left Spencer's party. Schrimpf sat in the passenger seat, and Zimmerlee took the wheel of his car. They proceeded only half a block before colliding with Chris Richards' vehicle.

Two days before trial was set to commence, the parties entered into a settlement agreement. By the terms of that settlement agreement, the jury trial was waived and the parties agreed to allow the circuit judge to decide the question of whether Zimmerlee, Schrimpf, and Pratchet acted in accordance with a common scheme or plan that caused damage to Chris and Michelle Richards. The circuit court answered that question in the affirmative and held the parties jointly and severally liable for Richards' damages.

There is no dispute that Zimmerlee was negligent in the operation of his vehicle and that his negligence was a cause of the accident and death of Chris Richards. There is also no dispute that the beer was a substantial factor in causing the accident and the death. Both Schrimpf and Pratchet were "providers" of alcoholic beverages to Zimmerlee, as defined by Wis. Stat. § 125.035(2) and were therefore negligent under Wis. Stat. § 125.07(1)(a).

The parties also agreed to the apportionment of causal negligence among them: Zimmerlee at 72 percent; Schrimpf at 14 percent; and Pratchet at 14 percent. The parties stipulated to Richards' damages and that Schrimpf's and Pratchet's combined causal negligence resulted in $500,000 of the total damages, or $250,000 each. Accordingly, the parties agreed that Richards was to be paid $250,000, as Schrimpf's share of the total damages, regardless of the outcome of this lawsuit. If the final court decision in this case concluded that the parties did not act in accordance with a common scheme or plan that resulted in Richards' damages, Richards would not receive the 14 percent of the damages that remained unpaid. If, however, it was concluded that the parties did act in accordance with such common scheme or plan that caused Richards' damages, then Schrimpf and Pratchet would be jointly and severally liable to Richards and, therefore, Schrimpf, and thereby Badger Mutual, would be required to pay Richards an additional $250,000 to cover the remainder of the damages.

What the parties dispute is whether the foregoing stipulated facts give rise to joint and several liability under Wis. Stat. § 895.045(2). The parties contest whether Zimmerlee, Schrimpf, and Pratchet acted in accordance with a common scheme or plan that resulted in Richards' damages, as those terms are used in § 895.045(2).

The court of appeals concluded that the parties were not jointly and severally liable under Wis. Stat. § 895.045(2) for Richards' damages. It held that, although the parties "had an agreement to purchase alcohol," that agreement did not include Zimmerlee's driving while intoxicated, which resulted in the damages. *Richards v. Badger Mut. Ins. Co.*, 297 Wis.2d 699, 727 N.W.2d 69, 2006 WI App 255, ¶ 27. Richards petitioned for review, which we granted.

II. DISCUSSION

A. Standard of Review

The outcome of this case hinges on the interpretation and application of Wis. Stat. § 895.045(2). . . .

B. The Parties' Positions

Both parties posit that Wis. Stat. § 895.045(2) is unambiguous; however, they offer differing interpretations and applications of it under the facts before us. Before turning to a discussion of the language of the statute, it is instructive to recount briefly the parties' respective arguments.

1. Richards' position

Richards argues that the parties agree that Zimmerlee, Schrimpf, and Pratchet acted in accordance with a common scheme or plan to purchase beer. She also asserts that the parties agree that "as a result of drinking the beer bought for [Zimmerlee] pursuant to his and Schrimpf's joint scheme and plan, Zimmerlee killed Mr. Richards by the intoxicated use of his vehicle." Further, Richards asserts that the parties have stipulated that the beer was a substantial factor in the cause of Chris Richards' death. Richards refers to Judge Fine's dissent as a succinct presentation of her argument: The stipulated facts require the conclusion that Chris Richards "would not have been killed by Zimmerlee if Zimmerlee had not been drunk as a result of drinking alcohol [bought] for him by Pratchet." *Richards*, 297 Wis.2d 699, ¶ 34, 727 N.W.2d 69 (Fine, J., dissenting). Richards contends that those facts evidence a common scheme or plan that falls within Wis. Stat. § 895.045(2), resulting in joint and several liability for all three defendants.

Furthermore, Richards argues that cannons (*sic)* of statutory interpretation preclude this court's consideration of the title of Wis. Stat. § 895.045(2), "Concerted action," when interpreting the statute. Richards argues that, because the statute is plain on its face, it is improper for the court to consider extrinsic sources to facilitate its interpretation, and because Wisconsin law provides that titles of statutes are not part of the statute, the title to § 895.045(2) is an extrinsic source. The import of Richards' argument in this regard is twofold: (1) we have not adopted the concerted action theory of liability, as embodied in Restatement (Second) of Torts § 876, even though it is incorporated into Wisconsin Jury Instruction 1740 that attends § 895.045(2). Therefore, the so-called, but misnamed, "concerted action cases" that predate § 895.045(2) provide no guidance in interpreting the statute; and (2) the enactment of § 895.045(2) did not alter the law in Wisconsin that causal negligence is predicated on whether an act or omission is a substantial factor in causing harm. Here, it was stipulated that the beer was a substantial factor in causing the accident that killed Chris Richards.

2. Badger Mutual's position

In response, Badger Mutual argues that, while Richards correctly asserts that the statute is unambiguous, Richards nevertheless misapprehends the statute's meaning. First, Badger Mutual contends that "Concerted action" is the title for the theory of liability described in Wis. Stat. § 895.045(2), as shown by the discussions in Wisconsin cases. Badger argues that because the concerted action theory of liability embodied in § 895.045(2) is the concerted action referred to in Wisconsin case law, subsection (2) requires that all parties have equal causal negligence. Consequently, because the parties stipulated to apportionment of causal negligence among Zimmerlee, Schrimpf, and Pratchet, their liability to Richards falls within subsection (1), not within subsection (2) of § 895.045.

Second, Badger Mutual acknowledges that while Schrimpf's conduct was a substantial factor in causing the accident, it did not also constitute concerted action, as is required before it falls within Wis. Stat. § 895.045(2). Badger Mutual contends that the Restatement (Second) of Torts § 876 and the common law in regard to concerted action support its position. Badger Mutual contends that the common scheme or plan to purchase beer did not damage Chris Richards. It was the reckless driving while intoxicated that resulted in damage to Chris Richards. However, the reckless driving was not part of a common scheme or plan in which Zimmerlee, Schrimpf, and Pratchet participated. Accordingly, it concludes that Schrimpf's liability to Richards falls within the parameters of § 895.045(1), not those of subsection (2).

C. Interpretation of Wis. Stat. § 895.045(2)

1. General principles

Statutory interpretation "begins with the language of the statute." We assume that the meaning of a statute is expressed in the words the legislature chose. The context in which the operative language appears is important too because a statute's meaning may be affected by the context in which the words chosen by the legislature are used. If our focus on the statute's language yields a plain, clear meaning, then there is no ambiguity, and the statute is applied according to its plain terms. If the statutory language is unambiguous, it is unnecessary to consult extrinsic sources to facilitate interpretation.

However, if a statute is "capable of being understood by reasonably well-informed persons in two or more senses[,]" then the statute is ambiguous. When a statute is ambiguous, we may resort to extrinsic sources, such as legislative history, to assist our understanding of the statute's meaning.

2. Statutory history

A review of statutory history is part of a plain meaning analysis. Statutory history encompasses the previously enacted and repealed provisions of a statute. By analyzing the changes the legislature has made over the course of several years, we may be assisted in arriving at the meaning of a statute. Therefore, statutory history is part of the context in which we interpret the words used in a statute. Accordingly, we examine the statutory history that underlies the current version of Wis. Stat. § 895.045.

The early common law rule of contributory negligence that existed prior to 1931, when the predecessor to Wis. Stat. § 895.045(1) was enacted, required that any contributory negligence of a plaintiff was a complete bar to recovery. *Brewster v. Ludtke*, 211 Wis. 344, 346, 247 N.W. 449 (1933). Also at common law, joint and several liability was the rule, such that when multiple tortfeasors caused injury to a plaintiff who was not contributorily negligent, the plaintiff could recover his or her entire damages from any tortfeasor. *Group Health Coop. of Eau Claire v. Hartland Cicero Mut. Ins. Co.*, 164 Wis.2d 632, 634-35, 476 N.W.2d 302 (Ct.App.1991).

24 In 1931, the legislature established statutory comparative negligence. This change in the law permitted a plaintiff who was contributorily negligent to recover damages if his or her negligence was less than the negligence of the person from whom recovery was sought. *Lupie v. Hartzheim*, 54 Wis.2d 415, 416, 195 N.W.2d 461 (1972). However, the adoption of comparative negligence did not change the common law rule of joint and several liability for the tortfeasors. *Walker v. Kroger Grocery & Baking Co.*, 214 Wis. 519, 535, 252 N.W. 721 (1934).

In 1971, the legislature renumbered the comparative negligence statute to Wis. Stat. § 895.045. It continued to permit a plaintiff who was not more negligent than the defendant from whom recovery was sought to recover damages, reduced by the amount of the plaintiff's negligence. Once again, this change did not affect the common law rule of joint and several liability. *Group Health*, 164 Wis.2d at 637, 476 N.W.2d 302. Therefore, in suits involving multiple tortfeasors, a comparison of the negligence of the plaintiff with that of any tortfeasor continued to be made and the full amount of damages[7] could be recovered from any tortfeasor who was more negligent than the plaintiff, even though a second tortfeasor may have been more negligent than the tortfeasor from whom recovery was sought. *Matthies v. Positive Safety Mfg. Co.*, 2001 WI 82, ¶ 10, 244 Wis.2d 720, 628 N.W.2d 842.

The current version of Wis. Stat. § 895.045 was created by 1995 Wis. Act 17. That Act amended comparative negligence in subsection (1) and created subsection (2). In subsection (1), the legislature chose to significantly change the law of joint and several liability by limiting the circumstances under which joint and several liability could be applied. *Id.* The relevant portion of § 895.045(1) provides:

> Comparative negligence. . . . The negligence of the plaintiff shall be measured separately against the negligence of each person found to be causally negligent. The liability of each person found to be causally

---

[7] The amount due the plaintiff was always first reduced by the percentage of plaintiff's negligence. *See Matthies v. Positive Safety Mfg. Co.*, 2001 WI 82, ¶ 10, 244 Wis.2d 720, 628 N.W.2d 842.

negligent whose percentage of causal negligence is less than 51% is limited to the percentage of the total causal negligence attributed to that person. A person found to be causally negligent whose percentage of causal negligence is 51% or more shall be jointly and severally liable for the damages allowed.

Under revised subsection (1), a contributorily negligent plaintiff is precluded from recovering more of his or her damages from a tortfeasor than the tortfeasor's causal negligence bears to the total causal negligence. For those tortfeasors, the common law rule of joint and several liability is abrogated. Only when a tortfeasor is at least 51 percent causally negligent will the tortfeasor be jointly and severally liable for all damages attributed to all tortfeasors in the comparisons made under subsection (1). Therefore, in many cases involving joint tortfeasors and a contributorily negligent plaintiff, there no longer is joint and several liability.

In amending Wis. Stat. § 895.045 in 1995, the legislature also created subsection (2). This subsection retains the common law rule of joint and several liability in the circumstances described in the statute. Subsection (2) provides:

> Concerted action. Notwithstanding sub. (1), if 2 or more parties act in accordance with a common scheme or plan, those parties are jointly and severally liable for all damages resulting from that action, except as provided in § 895.043(5).[8]

Subsection (2), which the legislature chose to title "Concerted action," retains the common law rule of joint and several liability, if "that action" is taken in accordance with a common scheme or plan resulting in damages. However, while demonstrating a legislative choice to significantly reduce the occasions where joint and several liability may be awarded, the statutory history underlying § 895.045 does not resolve the meaning of the terms, "common scheme or plan" and "that action" "resulting" in damages that are before us in this review. Nor does it shed light on the title of subsection (2), "Concerted action." However, it does inform us that the legislature meant to proscribe the occasions for imposition of joint and several liability.[9]

3. Ambiguity

Richards urges us to interpret Wis. Stat. § 895.045(2) such that it applies to persons engaged in a common scheme or plan to accomplish a result that in combination with other acts ultimately causes harm. Richards asserts that common law concerted action is not what the legislature meant to describe in subsection (2). Badger Mutual contends that the action that causes the harm must be undertaken

---

[8] Wisconsin Stat. § 895.043(5) provides: "The rule of joint and several liability does not apply to punitive damages."

[9] The amicus brief of Wisconsin Academy of Trial Lawyers cites *Fuchsgruber v. Custom Accessories, Inc.*, 2001 WI 81, 244 Wis.2d 758, 628 N.W.2d 833, as support for its assertion that the 1995 amendments to Wis. Stat. § 895.045 did not intend to change the common law rule of joint and several liability. Reliance on *Fuchsgruber* for that proposition is misplaced. *Fuchsgruber* explained that a claim for strict products liability is not a negligence action under the common law; and therefore, because § 895.045(1) involves negligence, it has no application to claims of strict products liability. *Id.*, ¶¶ 1-3.

to facilitate the common scheme or plan and that subsection (2) does embody common law concerted action. These competing interpretations of the terms and the title of § 895.045(2) are both reasonable interpretations. They indicate that the statute is "capable of being understood by reasonably well-informed persons in two or more senses" and is therefore ambiguous.

When confronted with an ambiguous statute, we may resort to extrinsic sources to help uncover the statute's meaning. The legislative history now available that relates to the creation of subsection (2) of Wis. Stat. § 895.045 is sparse. However, the Legislative Reference Bureau Analysis of an earlier version of the 1995 changes in § 895.045 that were eventually enacted states:

> This bill modifies the comparative negligence system in several ways. The bill requires that the negligence of the plaintiff be measured separately against each of the joint tort-feasors. Under this bill, a joint tort-feasor's liability is limited to the percentage of the total causal negligence attributed to that party.
>
> The bill specifies that the changes in the rule of joint and several liability do not apply to parties whose concerted action results in damages . . .

Drafting File for 1995 Wis. Act 17, *Analysis by the Legislative Reference Bureau* of 1995 S.B. 11, Legislative Reference Bureau, Madison, Wis. The LRB's analysis supports our conclusion that the 1995 changes to § 895.045 were meant to significantly change the common law rule of joint and several liability that had applied to negligence actions in the past. However, the legislative history provides limited guidance with respect to the statutory terms in subsection (2) that we must interpret.

The title is not part of a statute according to Wis. Stat. § 990.001(6); however, it may be used to assist in understanding a statute's meaning. We note that the title to Wis. Stat. § 895.045(2) is "Concerted action." Concerted action is a theory of liability that comes from the common law, as do key words the legislature chose to use in subsection (2), such as "common scheme or plan." Accordingly, we review Wisconsin's common law and the learned treatises cited therein for guidance in interpreting the title and terms of subsection (2).

4. Wisconsin appellate decisions

Four published appellate opinions offer potential guidance on the meaning of Wis. Stat. § 895.045(2). *Danks v. Stock Bldg. Supply, Inc.*, 298 Wis.2d 348, 727 N.W.2d 846, 2007 WI App 8; *Bruttig v. Olsen*, 154 Wis.2d 270, 453 N.W.2d 153 (Ct.App.1989); *Collins v. Eli Lilly Co.*, 116 Wis.2d 166, 342 N.W.2d 37 (1984); and *Ogle v. Avina*, 33 Wis.2d 125, 146 N.W.2d 422 (1966).

Danks provides only the briefest interpretation of Wis. Stat. § 895.045(2). There, liability for a personal injury was at issue. Danks was injured while assisting his supervisor load a truss onto a truck belonging to the manufacturer of the truss, Stock Building Supply. *Danks*, 298 Wis.2d 348, ¶ 1, 727 N.W.2d 846. Stock Building Supply had given specific written instructions that the truss was not to be lifted in the manner used at the time of the accident. *Id.*, ¶ 6. When the truss failed due to the improper lift, it fell and Danks was injured. *Id.*, ¶ 13.

Danks had several theories under which he attempted to impose liability on Stock Building Supply. One of those theories was concerted action liability, in which Danks contended that the lifting of the truss was undertaken in accordance with a common scheme or plan pursuant to Wis. Stat. § 895.045(2). *Id.*, ¶ 38. The court of appeals decision concluding that Stock Building Supply was not liable turned on the lack of an affirmative act of negligence by Stock Building Supply. *Id.*, ¶ 22.

However, *Danks* does interpret Wis. Stat. § 895.045(2) as pertaining only to tortfeasors who take concerted action. *Id.*, ¶ 39. *Danks* does not discuss the meanings of "Concerted action" or "common scheme or plan," but it does note that those who act "in concert" will come within the parameters of subsection (2):

> Subsection (2) simply modifies subsection (1) of the statute to provide that all defendants who are legally responsible for causing a plaintiff's damages, and who acted in concert in so doing, are jointly and severally liable for the plaintiff's damages, irrespective of whether a given defendant's apportioned causal negligence is less than 51%.

Id. Danks continues to conclude that "§ 895.045(2) plays no role to determine *whether* a given defendant may be held liable." *Id.*, ¶ 40 (emphasis in original). Rather, a defendant must be liable before subsection (2) may be applied. *Id.* Stated otherwise, *Danks* determined that subsection (2) does not create a claim for relief, but instead applies only when a defendant is already liable for damages under the substantive law. That is, he or she is causally negligent to a greater extent than the plaintiff; and in addition, he or she participated in concerted action that resulted in the plaintiff's damages. *Id.*, ¶¶ 39-40.

Collins precedes *Danks* and the 1995 revisions of Wis. Stat. § 895.045. There we discussed concerted action as a theory of liability and relied on the explanation of that theory by Professor Prosser. *Collins*, 116 Wis.2d at 184, 342 N.W.2d 37. In it we explained that:

> The concerted action theory of liability rests upon the principle that "those who, in pursuance of a common plan or design to commit a tortious act, actively take part in it, or further it by cooperation or request, or who lend aid or encouragement to the wrongdoer, or ratify and adopt his acts done for their benefit, are equally liable with him. Express agreement is not necessary, and all that is required is that there be a tacit understanding."

Id. (quoting W. Prosser, *Handbook of The Law of Torts* § 46, at 292 (4th ed.1971)). However, we declined to apply the concerted action theory when the plaintiff, who sought damages from former manufacturers of the drug diethylstilbestrol (DES) that caused an aggressive form of cervical cancer, could not identify the specific manufacturer of the DES that was taken by her mother. *Id.* at 186, 342 N.W.2d 37.

Collins explained that the concerted action theory required an agreement among the parties. *Id.* at 185, 342 N.W.2d 37. The allegation of Collins was that the "defendants failed to adequately test [DES] or to give sufficient warning[s] of its dangers." *Id.* We noted that there had been "a substantial amount of parallel action by the defendants in producing and marketing DES" but that activity did not "rise to the level of 'acting in concert.' " *Id.* We so concluded because there was no agreement that the testing and warnings would be inadequate, and it was that type of "agreement" that would have been required to show concerted action caused the plaintiff's harm. *Id.*

Collins is helpful to our analysis. For example, the specificity of the subject matter of the common plan in *Collins* that we concluded was necessary to support the concerted action theory of liability is important to our consideration of the specificity of the subject matter of the common plan at issue in the case before us. That is, the action that harmed Collins must have been that which was undertaken to further the drug companies' agreement. *Id.* In addition, *Collins* equated "concerted action," the title of Wis. Stat. § 895.045(2) with "pursuance of a common plan," terms employed in the text of subsection (2). *Id.* at 184, 342 N.W.2d 37.

Bruttig also tackled the topic of concerted action. There the plaintiff, Brian Bruttig who was a minor, and two friends, also minors, engaged in a game of "snowmobile tag." Brian was injured and recovery was denied because his liability was greater than that of either of the other two tortfeasors. *Bruttig*, 154 Wis.2d at 273, 453 N.W.2d 153. On appeal, Brian argued that he and the two defendants were equally negligent "because the tag game created a situation of mutual stimulation where the negligence of each participant [was] entirely interrelated with that of the others and therefore each should be charged with the causal negligence of the other." *Id.* at 280, 453 N.W.2d 153. The court of appeals recognized the argument as the theory of concerted action liability in which "the jury would not be permitted to apportion damages." *Id.* (citing W. Prosser, *Handbook of The Law of Torts* § 46, at 291 (4th ed.1971)).

The court of appeals noted that the concerted action theory of liability has never been "explicitly adopted" in Wisconsin. *Id.* at 280, 453 N.W.2d 153. It also noted that Brian had not raised this theory of liability in the circuit court. Therefore, it rejected his argument to apply it on appeal. *Id.* at 281, 453 N.W.2d 153.

Bruttig' s discussion is helpful, as it reviews Brian's claim that the three boys "acted in concert," which terms are similar to the title of subsection (2): "Concerted action." *Bruttig* acknowledges that the theory that Brian is proffering is "a separate theory of liability, that of 'concerted action.' " *Id.* at 280, 453 N.W.2d 153. This is significant because Wis. Stat. § 895.045(2) requires proof of a separate theory of liability for one who may already be a tortfeasor under subsection (1), in order to accord joint and several liability. *Danks*, 298 Wis.2d 348, ¶ 39, 727 N.W.2d 846. That is, subsection (2) requires a plaintiff to prove that the tortfeasor acted "in accordance with a common scheme or plan" and also that the common scheme or plan the tortfeasor acted in accordance with resulted in damages. *Id.* Subsection (2) is not applicable in every case where joint tortfeasors are present.

Our review of Wisconsin case law that touches on the concerted action theory of liability concludes with *Ogle*. In *Ogle*, we held that both negligent participants in a "drag race" were equally liable for a fatal collision resulting from their negligence, even though only one of the tortfeasors struck a third automobile causing injury. *Ogle*, 33 Wis.2d at 135, 146 N.W.2d 422.

In *Ogle*, two cars were racing at a high rate of speed in the same direction down a highway, when the lead car collided with the plaintiff's car. *Id.* at 128- 30, 146 N.W.2d 422. In holding both defendants equally liable for the collision without specifically referencing "concerted action," we applied the principles of concerted action:

> We think when there is an understanding to reach a common destination and in doing so illegal speed is used and the cars are driven so closely together as to be practically in tandem, or to constitute a unit, that we have a situation of mutual stimulation where the negligence of each participant is so related to the negligence of the other participants that the participants should each be chargeable with the causal negligence of the other as to speed and their percentage of causal negligence should be equal.

Id. at 135, 146 N.W.2d 422. The mutual agreement to use excessive speed to reach an agreed upon destination formed the basis for the tortfeasors' concerted action. *Id.*

This court went on to explain in *Ogle* that the usual rule of apportioning causal negligence between tortfeasors whose negligence combined or concurred in causing injury does not apply with "mutual fault" for the injury that occurred. *Id.* Rather, the tortfeasors in *Ogle* each assumed the fault of the other and causal negligence was apportioned equally between them. *Id.* Badger Mutual argues that the concept of equal fault for tortfeasors in concerted actions is significant to the case before us because the parties have agreed to apportioned causal negligence. Richards maintains it has no relevancy.

5. Learned treatises

Because discussions of the concerted action theory of liability in Professor Prosser's *The Law of Torts*, as well as those provided by The Restatement (Second) of Torts, are so prominent in the cases that discuss the concerted action theory of liability, we review those learned treatises as well, before interpreting and applying Wis. Stat. § 895.045(2). Prosser's explanation of the historic context of the concerted action theory of liability is helpful. It provides:

> The original meaning . . . was that of vicarious liability for concerted action. All persons who acted in concert to commit a trespass, in pursuance of a common design, were held liable for the entire result. In such a case there was a common purpose, with mutual aid in carrying it out; in short, there was a joint enterprise, so that "all coming to do an unlawful act, and of one party, the act of one is the act of all of the same party being present." Each was therefore liable for the entire damage done. . . . [S]ince each was liable for all, the jury would not be permitted to apportion the damages.

W. Page Keeton, *Prosser and Keeton on The Law of Torts* § 46, at 322-23 (5th ed.1984) (quoted citations omitted). This historic framework for concerted action is helpful to our understanding of the mutuality of agreement that is necessary in order to have a common scheme or plan under the concerted action theory of liability, as well as to understanding the statutory terms used to express the concerted action theory of liability.

Section 876 of the Restatement (Second) of Torts is also helpful. It provides:

Persons Acting in Concert

For harm resulting to a third person from the tortious conduct of another, one is subject to liability if he

(a) does a tortious act in concert with the other or pursuant to a common design with him, or

(b) knows that the other's conduct constitutes a breach of duty and gives substantial assistance or encouragement to the other so to conduct himself, or

(c) gives substantial assistance to the other in accomplishing a tortious result and his own conduct, separately considered, constitutes a breach of duty to the third person.

Comment on Clause (a): Parties are acting in concert when they act in accordance with an agreement to cooperate in a particular line of conduct or to accomplish a particular result. The agreement need not be expressed in words and may be implied and understood to exist from the conduct itself. Whenever two or more persons commit tortious acts in concert, each becomes subject to liability for the acts of the others, as well as for his own acts. The theory of the early common law was that there was a mutual agency of each to act for the others, which made all liable for the tortious acts of any one.

Restatement (Second) of Torts § 876, at 315-16 (1979). The Comment to Clause (a) is particularly helpful in its description of mutual agency and that it was mutual agency that made all the actors liable for one another's tortious acts.

From our review of Wisconsin cases and learned treatises, wherein principles of concerted action are discussed, terms similar to those in Wis. Stat. § 895.045(2) are employed and the concerted action theory of liability is explained, we conclude that § 895.045(2) is the codification of the concerted action theory of liability. The statute is consistent with the concerted action theory as explained by Wisconsin courts and in learned treatises such as Prosser's *The Law of Torts* and the Restatement (Second) of Torts § 876. Our decision in this regard is supported by those who considered this question when drafting the Wisconsin Civil Jury Instruction 1740.

Our conclusion that Wis. Stat. § 895.045(2) is the codification of the concerted action theory of liability does not change Wisconsin law in regard to whether the actions of a tortfeasor were a substantial factor in causing harm sustained by another. This is so because in order to fit within the parameters of § 895.045(2), a tortfeasor must already be causally negligent under substantive law. *Danks*, 298 Wis.2d 348, ¶ 39, 727 N.W.2d 846. One is causally negligent when his or her conduct is a substantial factor in causing injury to another. *Johnson v. Misericordia Cmty. Hosp.*, 97 Wis.2d 521, 561, 294 N.W.2d 501 (Ct.App.1980). Accordingly, under our interpretation of § 895.045(2), a person who is causally negligent with regard to a recovering plaintiff will have proportionate liability under § 895.045(1), unless something more is proved about that tortfeasor's conduct that will bring it within the purview of subsection (2). *Danks*, 298 Wis.2d 348, ¶ 39, 727 N.W.2d 846.

6. Application of Wis. Stat. § 895.045(2)

There are two possible scenarios under the stipulated facts and the arguments made by Richards wherein she seeks to hold Schrimpf jointly and severally liable under Wis. Stat. § 895.045(2) for her damages: (1) Zimmerlee, Schrimpf, and Pratchet acted in accordance with a common scheme or plan to procure beer and that action resulted in her damages; or (2) Zimmerlee and Schrimpf acted in accordance with a common scheme or plan to drink to intoxication and then drive and that action resulted in her damages. Although Richards interweaves these two scenarios, we will examine them independently.

Concerted action liability is a separate theory of liability that does not apply to all who are proved to be causally negligent. *Danks*, 298 Wis.2d 348, ¶ 40, 727 N.W.2d 846; *see Bruttig*, 154 Wis.2d at 280, 453 N.W.2d 153; W. Page Keeton, *Prosser and Keeton on the Law of Torts* § 46, at 322-23 (5th ed.1984). Something more than causal negligence is required before the actions of a tortfeasor will come within the parameters of Wis. Stat. § 895.045(2). *Danks*, 298 Wis.2d 348, ¶ 40, 727 N.W.2d 846. Concerted action must be proved.

There are three factual predicates necessary to proving concerted action: First, there must be an explicit or tacit agreement among the parties to act in accordance with a mutually agreed upon scheme or plan. *See Collins*, 116 Wis.2d at 185, 342 N.W.2d 37. Parallel action, without more, is insufficient to show a common scheme or plan. *Id.* Second, there must be mutual acts committed in furtherance of that common scheme or plan that are tortious acts. *See Ogle*, 33 Wis.2d at 135, 146 N.W.2d 422. Third, the tortious acts that are undertaken to accomplish the common scheme or plan must be the acts that result in damages. *See Collins*, 116 Wis.2d at 184-85, 342 N.W.2d 37.

In regard to the actions of Zimmerlee, Schrimpf, and Pratchet, it is undisputed that they agreed to purchase beer. When Schrimpf asked Pratchet to purchase beer and Zimmerlee drove her to the grocery and gave her the money that she used to purchase the beer, they acted "in accordance with a common scheme or plan." Their procurement of beer was tortious. Wis. Stat. §§ 125.035(4)(b); 125.07(1). However, after that purchase, Pratchet had nothing further to do with the beer. She took a bus to an unnamed location. Zimmerlee and Schrimpf became parallel actors. Zimmerlee and Schrimpf separated, with Zimmerlee keeping the beer in his car. The scheme or plan that was common to these three defendants had been completed. Richards had suffered no damages because of actions taken to further that common plan. Something more was required. Therefore, the purchase of beer is insufficient to show concerted action, and to cause Schrimpf's conduct to fall within Wis. Stat. § 895.045(2).

In regard to concluding that there was concerted action between Zimmerlee and Schrimpf resulting in Zimmerlee's drinking until intoxicated and then driving, certainly, the consumption of the beer to the point of intoxication and Zimmerlee's driving while intoxicated resulted in Richards' damages. Moreover, the drinking by Zimmerlee and Schrimpf was tortious because they were both under age. Wis. Stat. § 125.07(4)(b). However, there is nothing in the record to show that their drinking was not merely parallel conduct and that Zimmerlee and Schrimpf did not have a common scheme or plan to drink until intoxicated and then to drive. Accordingly,

Schrimpf's conduct does not bring him within the parameters of Wis. Stat. § 895.045(2).[13]

In addition, pursuant to the parties' stipulation, Zimmerlee was 72 percent causally negligent in the death of Chris Richards; Schrimpf was 14 percent causally negligent, and Pratchet was 14 percent causally negligent. The apportioned negligence here reflects Schrimpf's and Pratchet's respective several liability. However, with a concerted action theory of liability, each party assumes the causal negligence of the other so that all are equally liable. *See Ogle*, 33 Wis.2d at 135, 146 N.W.2d 422. Therefore, the parties' stipulation to differing percentages of causal negligence further supports our conclusion that Richards' injury was not the result of concerted action.

In sum, we reach the following conclusions: (1) Zimmerlee, Schrimpf, and Pratchet acted in accordance with a common scheme or plan to procure alcohol, but since the action undertaken to accomplish that common scheme or plan was not the act that resulted in Richards' damages, Wis. Stat. § 895.045(2) is inapplicable and therefore Schrimpf is not jointly and severally liable; and (2) the action that did result in Richards' damages was Zimmerlee's drinking until he was intoxicated and his subsequent decision to drive while intoxicated, but since this action was not taken in accordance with a common scheme or plan, § 895.045(2) is again inapplicable and therefore Schrimpf is not jointly and severally liable in that context as well.

III. CONCLUSION

We conclude as follows: (1) Wis. Stat. § 895.045(2) is the legislative codification of the concerted action theory of liability; (2) the damages in this case resulted from the consumption of beer to the point of intoxication and the subsequent decision to drive while intoxicated; and (3) although Robert Zimmerlee, David Schrimpf, and Tomakia Pratchet acted "in accordance with a common scheme or plan" to procure beer, they did not so act in consuming beer to the point of intoxication and in the subsequent act of driving while intoxicated, and, therefore, David Schrimpf is not jointly and severally liable under § 895.045(2) for the death of Chris Richards. Accordingly, Badger Mutual Insurance Company is relieved from making any further payment to Michelle Richards.

The decision of the court of appeals is affirmed.

SHIRLEY S. ABRAHAMSON, C.J. (dissenting).

The issue presented is whether the defendants Schrimpf and Pratchet are jointly and severally liable under Wis. Stat. § 895.045(2) for their combined 28 percent

---

[13] Schrimpf's involvement with Zimmerlee after the parties purchased the beer resembles the involvement of the defendants in *Blakeslee*. There, the drivers of two vehicles alternately changed lanes on a highway, and the rear driver crashed after dipping his tires onto the right-hand shoulder of the highway. *Blakeslee*, 37 A.D.3d at 1022, 831 N.Y.S.2d 556. The court held that there was insufficient proof to hold the drivers jointly and severally liable under a concerted action theory of liability because the record did not demonstrate that the drivers had an express or implied agreement to engage in a "passing contest." *Id.* at 1022-23, 831 N.Y.S.2d 556.

causal negligence for the plaintiff's injury. These two engaged in a common scheme or plan to procure alcohol for an underage drinker (Zimmerlee, the driver-defendant with 72 percent causal negligence) who became intoxicated and caused damage to an innocent third party (the plaintiff) by the intoxicated use of a motor vehicle. In other words, the issue is whether Schrimpf is liable to the plaintiff not only for the damages attributed to his causal negligence but also for the damages attributed to Pratchet's causal negligence. . . .

The plain language of Wis. Stat. § 895.045(2) is that parties acting in accordance with a common scheme or plan are jointly and severally liable to the plaintiff for all the damages resulting to the plaintiff from that common scheme or plan. Wisconsin Stat. § 895.045(2) provides in full as follows:

> **(2) Concerted action.** Notwithstanding sub. (1), if 2 or more parties act in accordance with a common scheme or plan, those parties are jointly and severally liable for all damages resulting from that action, except as provided in § 895.043(5).

The parties, the circuit court, and the majority opinion agree that Schrimpf and Pratchet acted in accordance with a common scheme or plan to procure alcohol beverages for the underage driver in the present case. Furthermore, the parties, the circuit court, and the majority opinion agree that Schrimpf and Pratchet's procurement of the alcohol was tortious. Schrimpf and Pratchet stipulated that each was a "provider" of alcohol beverages to the underage driver for purposes of Wis. Stat. § 125.035(4), that is, that they each "procure[d] alcohol beverages for . . . an underage person in violation of § 125.07(1)(a)."

The parties, the circuit court, and the majority opinion also agree that Schrimpf and Pratchet's procurement of the alcohol caused damages to the plaintiff. Schrimpf and Pratchet stipulated that each was "causally negligent" with respect to the plaintiff's damages. Schrimpf and Pratchet stipulated that their combined negligence caused 28 percent of the total damages suffered by the plaintiff.[6]

Under these circumstances, the plain language of Wis. Stat. § 895.045(2) permits only one result: It provides that Schrimpf and Pratchet shall be jointly and severally liable for "all" damages resulting from their common scheme or plan to procure alcohol for the underage driver. No one disputes that 28 percent of the plaintiff's damages resulted from Schrimpf and Pratchet's procurement of alcohol for the underage driver. Wisconsin Stat. § 895.045(2) thus requires, about as clearly as any statute could, that Schrimpf and Pratchet be jointly and severally liable for 28 percent of the plaintiff's total damages.

The majority opinion errs. . . . in concluding that the question whether a common scheme or plan has resulted in damages for purposes of joint and several liability under Wis. Stat. § 895.045(2) is different from the question whether a common scheme or plan has resulted in damages for purposes of tort liability to the plaintiff. In other words, the majority opinion has concluded that Wis. Stat.

---

[6] The parties stipulated that the plaintiff's total damages were $1,785,714.29. The parties further stipulated that the underage driver-defendant's share of the causal negligence was 72 percent, Schrimpf's share was 14 percent, and Pratchet's share was 14 percent.

§ 895.045(2) changes the Wisconsin law on causation. Nothing in the text of Wis. Stat. § 895.045(2) states that the legislature is altering or modifying the substantial factor test of causation, as the majority opinions opine.

The end! No more need be said.

I write more, however, because in addition to ignoring the text of the statute, the majority opinion rests. . . . on "concepts that are not on point." The majority opinion errs by listening to the siren song of concerted action. The majority opinion errs by applying the common law doctrine of "concerted action" in a context in which it does not apply. The concept of concerted action in the Restatement (Second) of Torts § 876 and in the cases (upon which the majority opinion relies) is not on point in interpreting and applying Wis. Stat. § 895.045.

Concerted action in the Restatement and in the cases is a substantive rule of tort liability to determine which of multiple actors are causally negligent and liable to an injured plaintiff. Concerted action under the Restatement and in these cases relates to a theory of liability.[8]

The majority opinion lifts the doctrine of concerted action and applies it in a different legal context, namely in the allocation of damages among those tortfeasors already found at fault. Wisconsin Stat. § 895.045(2) does not determine fault; it apportions damages after liability has been determined.

The majority opinion compounds its mistake of applying the substantive doctrine of concerted action by treating the doctrine as one departing from Wisconsin's law of causation. According to the majority opinion, joint and several liability under Wis. Stat. § 895.045(2) applies only to tortfeasors who act in accordance with a common scheme or plan that is *the* direct and particular cause of the plaintiff's damages, rather than merely *a* cause of the plaintiff's damages. The majority opinion requires that damages be *the* direct and particular result of the common scheme or plan for purposes of § 895.045, rather than merely *a* result of the common scheme or plan.[9]

----

[8] Section 876 of the Restatement (Second) of Torts (1979) is a specific application of the rule stated in § 875 of the Restatement, which provides as follows:

> Each of two or more persons whose tortious conduct is a legal cause of a single and indivisible harm to the injured party is subject to liability to the injured party for the entire harm.

Comment c explains that § 875 is consistent with the rules of causation in negligence; any one of a number of persons whose tortious conduct is a substantial factor in causing harm is liable for the harm in the absence of a superseding cause.

Section 876 of the Restatement provides in relevant part as follows:

> For harm resulting to a third person from the tortious conduct of another, one is subject to liability if he . . . does a tortious act in concert with the other or pursuant to a common design with him. . . .

The Wisconsin cases upon which the majority relies similarly treat the common law doctrine of "concerted action" as a rule to determine causal negligence. *See Bruttig v. Olsen*, 154 Wis.2d 270, 280, 453 N.W.2d 153 (Ct.App. 1989) (stating that concerted action is "a separate theory of liability"); *Collins v. Eli Lilly Co.*, 116 Wis.2d 166, 185, 342 N.W.2d 37 (1984) ("The concerted action theory typically is applied to situations in which . . . a particular defendant is already identified as causing the plaintiff's harm, and the plaintiff desires to extend liability to those acting in league with that defendant.") (citation omitted); *Ogle v. Avina*, 33 Wis.2d 125, 133-35, 146 N.W.2d 422 (1966) (participant in a drag race causally negligent even though plaintiff's injuries were caused most directly by another participant in the race).

[9] "The test of cause in Wisconsin is whether the defendant's negligence was a substantial factor in

The majority opinion declares that for purposes of joint and several liability under § 895.045(2) the common scheme to procure the alcohol beverage in the instant case did not result in the plaintiff's damages, notwithstanding the parties' stipulation that the procurement of alcohol was a cause of damages to the plaintiff and that the providers were liable for their causal negligence. The majority opinion concludes that for purposes of joint and several liability under § 895.045(2), the only cause of the plaintiff's damages was the underage drinker's consumption of alcohol to the point of intoxication and subsequent decision to drive while intoxicated.

The majority opinion's reasoning is explained in a simple way in the third-party brief of the Wisconsin Insurance Alliance and Property Casualty Insurers Association of America. The brief urges that the words "that action" in Wis. Stat. § 895.045(2) mean that joint and several liability is applicable only in those cases where the damages result *solely* from the tortfeasors who act in accordance with a common scheme or plan. Applying this interpretation to the present case, the Alliance's brief concludes that "[i]n this case, the concerted action, or 'that action,' was buying beer, but the harm resulted from drunk driving-conduct different from 'that action.' "

I do not know on what basis the majority opinion determines that the common-law doctrine of concerted action (or Wis. Stat. § 895.045(2), which the majority opinion concludes is a codification of the common-law doctrine) applies only when damages result *solely* from acts that the tortfeasors undertake in accordance with a common scheme or plan. The majority opinion fails to cite any authority in support of its determination that for purposes of § 895.045(2), the plaintiff suffered no damages because of the defendants' common scheme or plan to procure alcohol. Even assuming that the majority opinion is correct to apply the substantive doctrine of concerted action to the present case, it does not appear that this doctrine distinguishes between "a" cause and "the" cause in the manner that the majority opinion does. The majority opinion cites no case or treatise dealing with a situation similar to the present case, in which the defendants' common scheme or plan caused some but not all of the plaintiff's damages.

In contrast to the majority opinion, I conclude that Wis. Stat. § 895.045 uses the concept of defendant tortfeasors acting in accordance with a common scheme or plan to allocate damages among the multiple tortfeasors already found to be at fault, not to determine (as § 876 of the Restatement does) whether each actor is liable to the plaintiff under a theory of liability. The multiple tortfeasors in the present case have been identified as contributing to a single injury and the responsibility of each is based upon the causal fault. In other words, tort liability has already been decided when § 895.045 is applied. I conclude that under § 895.045, Schrimpf is liable for damages attributed to Pratchet's causal negligence.

Several factors support the position I espouse.

---

producing the injury. It need not be the sole factor or the primary factor, only a 'substantial factor.' The phrase 'substantial factor' denotes that the defendant's conduct has such an effect in producing the harm as to lead the trier of fact, as a reasonable person, to regard it as a cause, using that word in the popular sense. There may be several substantial factors contributing to the same result." *Clark v. Leisure Vehicles, Inc.*, 96 Wis.2d 607, 617-18, 292 N.W.2d 630 (1980) (internal citations omitted).

First, the text of Wis. Stat. § 895.045 supports my view of "concerted action." Wisconsin Stat. § 895.045(1) modifies the common-law rule of joint and several liability. The common-law rule regarding joint and several liability allowed a plaintiff (who was not negligent) to recover the total judgment against any defendant who was liable-regardless of how much fault was attributable to that tortfeasor. Section 895.045(1) limits the plaintiff's recovery from a tortfeasor whose causal negligence is less than 51 percent to the percentage of the total causal negligence attributed to that person. Ordinarily, Wis. Stat. § 895.045(1) would preclude the plaintiff from recovering Pratchet's 14 percent share of liability from Schrimpf.

Wisconsin Stat. § 895.045(2), however, provides an exception to the statutory modification of joint and several liability. Subsection (2) provides that if 2 or more parties act in accordance with a common scheme or plan, those parties are jointly and severally liable for all damages resulting from that action.

The phrase "concerted action" does not appear in the text of Wis. Stat. § 895.045. The phrase is in the title to § 895.045(2). The phrase "concerted action" in the title to § 895.045(2) is obviously a shorthand for the lengthier statutory language "act in accordance with a common scheme or plan."[12] The concept of concerted action can play a role in § 895.045. The substantive law of concerted action may be used to interpret whether the defendant tortfeasors acted in accordance with a common scheme or plan under § 895.045(2).

Section 895.045(1) and (2) provide as follows:

> **(1) Comparative negligence.** Contributory negligence does not bar recovery in an action by any person or the person's legal representative to recover damages for negligence resulting in death or in injury to person or property, if that negligence was not greater than the negligence of the person against whom recovery is sought, but any damages allowed shall be diminished in the proportion to the amount of negligence attributed to the person recovering. The negligence of the plaintiff shall be measured separately against the negligence of each person found to be causally negligent. The liability of each person found to be causally negligent whose percentage of causal negligence is less than 51% is limited to the percentage of the total causal negligence attributed to that person. A person found to be causally negligent whose percentage of causal negligence is 51% or more shall be jointly and severally liable for the damages allowed.

> **(2) Concerted action.** Notwithstanding sub. (1), if 2 or more parties act in accordance with a common scheme or plan, those parties are jointly and severally liable for all damages resulting from that action, except as provided in s. 895.043(5).

As I see it, Wis. Stat. § 895.045 directs that each of the multiple actors who has acted in accordance with a common scheme or plan and whose causal negligence has been apportioned at less than 51 percent is liable to the plaintiff not only for his or

---

[12] Several states apparently have adopted the concept of "concerted action" as an exception to the modification of joint and several liability.

her own share of causal negligence but also for the share of causal negligence of another defendant with whom he acted in concert. Rather than decide the substantive tort liability of multiple actors, § 895.045 *apportions* damages after the liability of the multiple tortfeasors has already been determined. Section 895.045 does not change causal negligence.

Second, the court of appeals in *Danks v. Stock Building Supply, Inc.*, 298 Wis.2d 348, 727 N.W.2d 846, 2007 WI App 8, ¶ 39, is in accord with my interpretation, correctly describing Wis. Stat. § 895.045(2) as follows:

> Wisconsin Stat. § 895.045(1) sets forth Wisconsin's law of comparative negligence, specifying when a negligent plaintiff may recover from a negligent defendant. It also spells out Wisconsin law regarding joint and several liability among defendants, specifying when a given defendant may become liable for all damages assessed against multiple tortfeasors. Thus § 895.045(2) applies only *after* a judge or jury has determined, under applicable substantive law, that more than one tortfeasor is liable in some measure to the plaintiff. Subsection (2) simply modifies subsection (1) of the statute to provide that all defendants who are legally responsible for causing a plaintiff's damages, and who acted in concert in so doing, are jointly and severally liable for the plaintiff's damages, irrespective of whether a given defendant's apportioned causal negligence is less than 51%.

Third, other states have similarly interpreted "concerted action" in joint and several liability statutes. The North Dakota Supreme Court, for example, held that its joint and several liability statute with a special provision for "concerted action" "does not create an independent basis of liability, rather it deals with the allocation of damages among those already at fault."[14]

Fourth, my interpretation of Wis. Stat. § 895.045(2) comports with Restatement (Third) of the Law of Torts: Apportionment of Liability § 15 (2000), which does not replace Restatement (Second) § 876, but is an addition thereto. Section 15 provides for apportionment of liability when persons act in concert as follows:

> When persons are liable because they acted in concert, all persons are jointly and severally liable for the share of comparative responsibility assigned to each person engaged in concerted activity.

Comment *a* explains that § 15 applies when the "governing law determines that concerted activity took place and that the tortious acts of one or more of the

---

[14] North Dakota has a statute similar to Wis. Stat. § 895.045(2). The North Dakota statute provides in part (and provided at the time of the *Hurt* decision):

> When two or more parties are found to have contributed to the injury, the liability of each party is several only, and is not joint, and each party is liable only for the amount of damages attributable to the percentage of fault of that party, *except that any persons who act in concert in committing a tortious act or aid or encourage the act, or ratifies or adopts the act for their benefit, are jointly liable for all damages attributable to their combined percentage of fault.* Under this section, fault includes negligence, malpractice, absolute liability, dram shop liability, failure to warn, reckless or willful conduct, assumption of risk, misuse of product, failure to avoid injury, and product liability, including product liability involving negligence or strict liability or breach of warranty for product defect.

N.D. Cent.Code § 32-03.2-02 (2006) (emphasis added).

participants in the concerted activity was a legal cause of the plaintiff's indivisible injury." The comment further explains that "[t]he joint and several liability of those engaged in concerted activity is for the total comparative responsibility assigned to all who engage in the concerted activity." The Reporters' Note to § 15 of the Restatement (Third) of Torts: Apportionment of Liability interprets Wis. Stat. § 895.045 as retaining "full joint and several liability for concerted actors." According to the comment, the American Law Institute does not take a position on "whether a concerted-action tortfeasor is also jointly and severally liable for the share of comparative responsibility assigned to an independent tortfeasor who is also liable for the same indivisible injury."

Fifth, my interpretation of Wis. Stat. § 895.045(2) also comports with *Reilly v. Anderson*, 727 N.W.2d 102 (Iowa 2006), in which the Iowa Supreme Court had to decide whether the theory of concerted action is compatible with statutory comparative fault principles. The Iowa court explained, 727 N.W.2d at 109, that where an independent party (such as the underage drunken driver in the present case) had been assigned 55 percent fault and concerted actors # 1 and # 2 (here Schrimpf and Pratchet) had been assigned fault of 35 percent and 10 percent respectively, the concerted actors would at least be jointly and severally liable for 45 percent of plaintiff's damages. The Iowa court did not decide whether the concerted actors would be jointly and severally liable for the entire fault assigned to all defendants in the fact situation described.

For the reasons set forth, I dissent.

I am authorized to state that Justices Ann Walsh Bradley and Louis B. Butler, Jr. join this opinion.

Chapter 9

THE LIABILITY OF LANDOWNERS

The ownership of property (by which is meant real estate, a definition of some significance), at one time a highly protected activity, has come to bring with it obligations as well as rights in the modern world. The courts have safeguarded the interests of owners and other lawful occupiers of real estate for centuries; much property law goes back hundreds of years to the English courts. At the dawning of property law, the property owner had close to absolute dominion over the land, and the person entering upon the property had few rights. As society changed, persons other than the property owner gained status, and the owner of the property no longer ruled that property absolutely. This chapter deals with the difficulties courts must face in balancing the rights of the owner, the lessee, etc. to use his or her property in any manner that he or she deems appropriate against the rights of others not to be injured by whatever the owner does.

Because the courts are always engaging in an implicit balancing of the rights of property owners and those affected by them, and because so much property law is ancient, the law in this arena can become tangled in complex definitions. Some courts in the modern era have elected to eliminate the accretion of centuries and apply the same negligence and reasonableness doctrines to land cases as are applied in many tort cases, but other courts, perceiving a value in the traditional rules, have been unwilling to eliminate them.

A.   LIABILITY TO THOSE WHO ENTER ON THE LAND

1.   The Taxonomy of Plaintiffs

ROWLAND v. CHRISTIAN
Supreme Court of California, 1968 (en banc)
443 P.2d 561

PETERS, JUSTICE.

Plaintiff appeals from a summary judgment for defendant Nancy Christian in this personal injury action.

In his complaint plaintiff alleged that about November 1, 1963, Miss Christian told the lessors of her apartment that the knob of the cold water faucet on the bathroom basin was cracked and should be replaced; that on November 30, 1963, plaintiff entered the apartment at the invitation of Miss Christian; that he was injured while using the bathroom fixtures, suffering severed tendons and nerves of his right hand; and that he has incurred medical and hospital expenses. He further alleged that the bathroom fixtures were dangerous, that Miss Christian was aware of the dangerous condition, and that his injuries were proximately caused by the negligence of Miss Christian. Plaintiff sought recovery of his medical and hospital expenses, loss of wages, damage to his clothing, and $100,000 general damages. It does not appear from the complaint whether the crack in the faucet handle was obvious to an ordinary inspection or was concealed.

Miss Christian filed an answer containing a general denial except that she alleged that plaintiff was a social guest and admitted the allegations that she had told the lessors that the faucet was defective and that it should be replaced. Miss Christian also alleged contributory negligence and assumption of the risk. In connection with the defenses, she alleged that plaintiff had failed to use his "eyesight" and knew of the condition of the premises. Apart from these allegations, Miss Christian did not allege whether the crack in the faucet handle was obvious or concealed.

Miss Christian's affidavit in support of the motion for summary judgment alleged facts showing that plaintiff was a social guest in her apartment when, as he was using the bathroom, the porcelain handle of one of the water faucets broke in his hand causing injuries to his hand and that plaintiff had used the bathroom on a prior occasion. In opposition to the motion for summary judgment, plaintiff filed an affidavit stating that immediately prior to the accident he told Miss Christian that he was going to use the bathroom facilities, that she had known for two weeks prior to the accident that the faucet handle that caused injury was cracked, that she warned the manager of the building of the condition, that nothing was done to repair the condition of the handle, that she did not say anything to plaintiff as to the condition of the handle, and that when plaintiff turned off the faucet the handle broke in his hands severing the tendons and medial nerve in his right hand.

The summary judgment procedure is drastic and should be used with caution so that it does not become a substitute for an open trial. . . .

In the instant case, Miss Christian's affidavit and admissions made by plaintiff show that plaintiff was a social guest and that he suffered injury when the faucet handle broke; they do not show that the faucet handle crack was obvious or even nonconcealed. Without in any way contradicting her affidavit or his own admissions, plaintiff at trial could establish that she was aware of the condition and realized or should have realized that it involved an unreasonable risk of harm to him, that defendant should have expected that he would not discover the danger, that she did not exercise reasonable care to eliminate the danger or warn him of it, and that he did not know or have reason to know of the danger. Plaintiff also could establish, without contradicting Miss Christian's affidavit or his admissions, that the crack was not obvious and was concealed. Under the circumstances, a summary judgment is proper in this case only if, after proof of such facts, a judgment would be required as a matter of law for Miss Christian. The record supports no such conclusion.

. . . .

One of the areas where this court and other courts have departed from the fundamental concept that a man is liable for injuries caused by his carelessness is with regard to the liability of a possessor of land for injuries to persons who have entered upon that land. It has been suggested that the special rules regarding liability of the possessor of land are due to historical considerations stemming from the high place which land has traditionally held in English and American thought, the dominance and prestige of the landowning class in England during the formative period of the rules governing the possessor's liability, and the heritage of feudalism.

The departure from the fundamental rule of liability for negligence has been accomplished by classifying the plaintiff either as a trespasser, licensee, or invitee and then adopting special rules as to the duty owed by the possessor to each of the classifications. Generally speaking a trespasser is a person who enters or remains upon land of another without a privilege to do so; a licensee is a person like a social guest who is not an invitee and who is privileged to enter or remain upon land by virtue of the possessor's consent, and an invitee is a business visitor who is invited or permitted to enter or remain on the land for a purpose directly or indirectly connected with business dealings between them.

Although the invitor owes the invitee a duty to exercise ordinary care to avoid injuring him, the general rule is that a trespasser and licensee or social guest are obliged to take the premises as they find them insofar as any alleged defective condition thereon may exist, and that the possessor of the land owes them only the duty of refraining from wanton or willful injury. The ordinary justification for the general rule severely restricting the occupier's liability to social guests is based on the theory that the guest should not expect special precautions to be made on his account and that if the host does not inspect and maintain his property the guest should not expect this to be done on his account.

An increasing regard for human safety has led to a retreat from this position.

. . . .

The cases dealing with the active negligence and the trap exceptions are indicative of the subtleties and confusion which have resulted from application of the common law principles governing the liability of the possessor of land. Similar confusion and complexity exist as to the definitions of trespasser, licensee, and invitee.

In refusing to adopt the rules relating to the liability of a possessor of land for the law of admiralty, the United States Supreme Court stated: ["] . . . [T]he common law has moved, unevenly and with hesitation, towards 'imposing on owners and occupiers a single duty of reasonable care in all circumstances.' " (Footnotes omitted.)

The courts of this state have also recognized the failings of the common law rules relating to the liability of the owner and occupier of land. . . .

There is another fundamental objection to the approach to the question of the possessor's liability on the basis of the common law distinctions based upon the status of the injured party as a trespasser, licensee, or invitee. Complexity can be borne and confusion remedied where the underlying principles governing liability are based upon proper considerations. Whatever may have been the historical justifications for the common law distinctions, it is clear that those distinctions are not justified in the light of our modern society and that the complexity and confusion which has arisen is not due to difficulty in applying the original common law rules — they are all too easy to apply in their original formulation — but is due to the attempts to apply just rules in our modern society within the ancient terminology.

Without attempting to labor all of the rules relating to the possessor's liability, it is apparent that the classifications of trespasser, licensee, and invitee, the immunities from liability predicated upon those classifications, and the exceptions to those immunities, often do not reflect the major factors which should determine whether immunity should be conferred upon the possessor of land. Some of those factors, including the closeness of the connection between the injury and the defendant's conduct, the moral blame attached to the defendant's conduct, the policy of preventing future harm, and the prevalence and availability of insurance, bear little, if any, relationship to the classifications of trespasser, licensee and invitee and the existing rules conferring immunity.

Although in general there may be a relationship between the remaining factors and the classifications of trespasser, licensee, and invitee, there are many cases in which no such relationship may exist. Thus, although the foreseeability of harm to an invitee would ordinarily seem greater than the foreseeability of harm to a trespasser, in a particular case the opposite may be true. The same may be said of the issue of certainty of injury. The burden to the defendant and consequences to the community of imposing a duty to exercise care with resulting liability for breach may often be greater with respect to trespassers than with respect to invitees, but it by no means follows that this is true in every case. In many situations, the burden will be the same, i.e., the conduct necessary upon the defendant's part to meet the burden of exercising due care as to invitees will also meet his burden with respect to licensees and trespassers. The last of the major factors, the cost of insurance, will, of course, vary depending upon the rules of liability adopted, but there is no persuasive evidence that applying ordinary principles of negligence law to the land occupier's liability will materially reduce the prevalence of insurance due to increased cost or even substantially increase the cost.

Considerations such as these have led some courts in particular situations to reject the rigid common law classifications and to approach the issue of the duty of the occupier on the basis of ordinary principles of negligence. And the common law distinctions after thorough study have been repudiated by the jurisdiction of their birth.

A man's life or limb does not become less worthy of protection by the law nor a loss less worthy of compensation under the law because he has come upon the land of another without permission or with permission but without a business purpose. Reasonable people do not ordinarily vary their conduct depending upon such matters, and to focus upon the status of the injured party as a trespasser, licensee, or invitee in order to determine the question whether the landowner has a duty of care, is contrary to our modern social mores and humanitarian values. The common law rules obscure rather than illuminate the proper considerations which should govern determination of the question of duty.

It bears repetition that the basic policy of this state set forth by the Legislature in section 1714 of the Civil Code is that everyone is responsible for an injury caused to another by his want of ordinary care or skill in the management of his property. The factors which may in particular cases warrant departure from this fundamental principle do not warrant the wholesale immunities resulting from the common law classifications, and we are satisfied that continued adherence to the common law distinctions can only lead to injustice or, if we are to avoid injustice, further fictions with the resulting complexity and confusion. We decline to follow and perpetuate such rigid classifications. The proper test to be applied to the liability of the possessor of land in accordance with section 1714 of the Civil Code is whether in the management of his property he has acted as a reasonable man in view of the probability of injury to others, and, although the plaintiff's status as a trespasser, licensee, or invitee may in the light of the facts giving rise to such status have some bearing on the question of liability, the status is not determinative.

Once the ancient concepts as to the liability of the occupier of land are stripped away, the status of the plaintiff relegated to its proper place in determining such liability, and ordinary principles of negligence applied, the result in the instant case presents no substantial difficulties. . . . Where the occupier of land is aware of a concealed condition involving in the absence of precautions an unreasonable risk of harm to those coming in contact with it and is aware that a person on the premises is about to come in contact with it, the trier of fact can reasonably conclude that a failure to warn or to repair the condition constitutes negligence. Whether or not a guest has a right to expect that his host will remedy dangerous conditions on his account, he should reasonably be entitled to rely upon a warning of the dangerous condition so that he, like the host, will be in a position to take special precautions when he comes in contact with it.

. . . .

The judgment is reversed.

TRAYNOR, C.J., and TOBRINER, MOSK and SULLIVAN, JJ., concur.

BURKE, JUSTICE (dissenting).

I dissent. In determining the liability of the occupier or owner of land for injuries, the distinctions between trespassers, licensees and invitees have been developed and applied by the courts over a period of many years. They supply a reasonable and workable approach to the problems involved, and one which provides the degree of stability and predictability so highly prized in the law.

. . . .

In my view, it is not a proper function of this court to overturn the learning, wisdom and experience of the past in this field. Sweeping modifications of tort liability law fall more suitably within the domain of the Legislature, before which all affected interests can be heard and which can enact statutes providing uniform standards and guidelines for the future.

I would affirm the judgment for defendant.

McComb, J., concurs.

Does *Rowland* change the range of appropriate landowner conduct? For what sorts of conduct might a landowner be liable under *Rowland* that would not subject him or her to liability under the system *Rowland* abolished? Is the impact of *Rowland* solely in favor of plaintiffs, or are there some forms of conduct for which a defendant might be not liable under *Rowland* but might have been under the earlier system? Does *Rowland* have an impact upon the law applicable to trespassers?

GERCHBERG v. LONEY
Supreme Court of Kansas, 1978
576 P.2d 593

Fromme, Justice:

Rolf Gerchberg, a five year old boy, received burn injuries while playing on the premises of the neighbors, Mr. and Mrs. Roy Loney. At the close of plaintiff's evidence the district court directed a verdict in favor of defendants. The Court of Appeals reversed the judgment and remanded the case for trial on the theory of attractive nuisance. *See Gerchberg v. Loney*, 1 Kan. App. 2d 84, 562 P.2d 464.

The plaintiff-appellant urged the Court of Appeals to discard the traditional classification of trespassers, licensees and invitees, and to abolish the distinctions in our law as to the duty of care owed to each class. In place thereof he urged the court to adopt one duty of care owed to all who are on the premises of another, i.e., a duty of reasonable care under all facts and circumstances of the case. The Court of Appeals declined to do so and plaintiff-appellant sought review in this court.

. . . .

[In this case] the plaintiff Rolf Gerchberg, a five-year-old boy, received serious burns when he returned to an unattended smoldering fire in a barrel used by the defendants as an incinerator. Rodney Loney, the ten-year-old neighbor boy, had previously been directed to burn papers and had started the fire. Rolf was with him and saw Rodney place a stack of papers near the incinerator and start the fire. After a short while both boys left the premises. The fire had not been extinguished and was still smoldering on the Loney premises when Rolf returned to the barrel. He began putting the papers into the barrel. The fire blazed and his clothing caught on fire. Serious injuries resulted.

. . . .

Now let us turn our attention to plaintiff's argument that the traditional classification of trespassers, licensees and invitees should be discarded, and that the distinctions in our law covering the duty of care owed to each class be abandoned in favor of a single standard of reasonable care under the circumstances. Plaintiff contends there is no logical reason for protecting the possessor of premises by requiring his negligence to be wilful, wanton, or in reckless disregard for the safety of the trespasser or licensee before it is actionable.

Under the present law of Kansas a trespasser is one who enters on the premises of another without any right, lawful authority, or an express or implied invitation or license. The possessor of premises on which a trespasser intrudes owes a trespasser the duty to refrain from wilfully, wantonly, or recklessly injuring him.

A licensee is one who enters or remains on the premises of another by virtue of either the express or implied consent of the possessor of the premises, or by operation of law, so that he is not a trespasser thereon. The possessor of premises on which a licensee intrudes owes a licensee the duty to refrain from wilfully or wantonly injuring him. The parties agree that Rolf Gerchberg was a licensee under the facts of this case.

Under the law in this jurisdiction a social guest has the status of a licensee and his host owes him only the duty to refrain from wilfully, intentionally, or recklessly injuring him.

An invitee is one who enters or remains on the premises of another at the express or implied invitation of the possessor of the premises for the benefit of the inviter, or for the mutual benefit and advantage of both inviter and invitee. The possessor of premises on which an invitee enters owes a higher degree of care, that of reasonable or ordinary care for the invitee's safety. This duty is active and positive. It includes a duty to protect and warn an invitee against any danger that may be reasonably anticipated.

Under the law in this and other jurisdictions a child may be presumed conclusively incapable of contributory negligence. Children are not held to the same strict accountability to appreciate a danger and to care for themselves as persons of full age. Therefore the attractive nuisance exception has been recognized to accommodate for a child's incapacity to understand and appreciate the possible dangers to which he may be attracted.

. . . .

If the traditional classifications are discarded the legal distinctions which have heretofore governed the courts in imposing a particular standard of care are also discarded. In such case the standard, reasonable care under all the circumstances, would have to be applied by the jury to the specific facts of each case. Can a lay jury reasonably be expected to consider the proper relative effect of natural and artificial conditions on the premises which are or may be dangerous, the degree of danger inherent in such conditions, the extent of the burden which should be placed on the possessor of premises to alleviate the danger, the nature, use and location of the condition or force involved, the foreseeability of the presence of the plaintiff on the premises, the obviousness of such dangerous condition or the plaintiff's actual knowledge of the condition or force which resulted in injury? It would appear these considerations should be imparted to the jury if it is to be placed in a position to decide whether reasonable care was exercised by the possessor of the premises. Otherwise the jury will have a free hand to impose or withhold liability.

A majority of the members of this court do not feel that the traditional classifications of trespassers, licensees and invitees should be jettisoned. The traditional classifications were worked out and the exceptions were spelled out with much thought, sweat and even tears by generations of Kansas legal scholars who have gone before us. Should this body of law be discarded completely in favor of a free hand by a lay jury? We feel at this time there is too much of value in our premises law with respect to rights of possessors of premises to warrant its abandonment.

. . . .

It should be noted that the adoption of one standard of care not only will have the effect of lowering the standard of care owed to trespassers and licensees but also would lower the standard of care presently owed to invitees. Under our present law the duty owed to an invitee is active and positive. It includes a duty to protect and warn an invitee against any danger that may be reasonably anticipated. Not only does it extend to dangerous conditions known to the possessor but also to dangerous conditions discoverable in the exercise of a duty to inspect and keep the premises free of unreasonable risk of harm.

It has been suggested that the jury need not be left without guidance even though the traditional classifications are discarded. It is further suggested that after a jury is advised of the single standard of care the court can further instruct the jury by setting out the applicable rules found in the Restatement of the Law, Second, Torts, §§ 333 through 343B. The Restatement classifies these rules as follows: Title B. Liability of Possessors of Land to Trespassers; Title C. General Liability of Possessors of Land to Licensees and Invitees; Title D. Special Liability of Possessors of Land to Licensees; and Title E. Special Liability of Possessors of Land to Invitees. If such a suggestion is followed in advising the jury what if anything is gained by discarding the traditional rules? The traditional classifications (trespassers, licensees and invitees) are still to be considered by the court. If, as the appellant suggests, the traditional classifications are confusing, unreasonable and arbitrary any change which embraces the Restatement rules will be subject to similar charges. In such case we would be merely changing the extent of the duty owed by a possessor of premises. The extent of that duty would still be dictated by the circumstances surrounding entry on the premises, the danger involved and the burden to be placed on the possessor to make the premises reasonably safe. The traditional classifications would remain but the traditional rules worked out over so many years would be discarded and new rules governing a possessor's liability would have to be relearned.

A majority of this court feel if the mores and values of present society dictate changes such changes should be worked out individually as the circumstances of a particular case may warrant. Such changes will result in less general confusion and better understanding of each particular change.

. . . .

In conclusion we wish to acknowledge what has been referred to as a trend in this country toward abolition of the traditional classifications. Apparently the bellwether case in the United States was handed down in 1968, *Rowland v. Christian*, 69 Cal. 2d 108, 70 Cal. Rptr. 97, 443 P.2d 561. Our research indicates that in the ten years which have elapsed since *Rowland* only nine states have followed the lead. During this same period of time several states have elevated licensees to a common class with invitees, and five states have placed social guests in the category of invitees. During this same period of time a large majority of states have continued to follow the traditional common law classifications. At least six states have considered the advisability of following *Rowland v. Christian, supra,* and have declined to do so. The jurisdictions which have abolished all classifications are not sufficient in number to constitute a clear trend.

In the present case the plaintiff's evidence was sufficient to require submitting the case to a jury on the theory of attractive nuisance. . . .

Accordingly we approve the majority opinion of the Court of Appeals. The judgment of the District Court of Douglas County is reversed and the case is remanded for further proceedings.

PRAGER, JUSTICE, dissenting:

I respectfully dissent. Under the undisputed facts as shown in the record, the plaintiff has failed as a matter of law to establish that the defendants were negligent.

. . . .

I am also in disagreement with the position of the majority that the traditional classifications of trespassers, licensees, and invitees should be maintained and that the degree of care owed to each classification by a land occupier should be controlled solely by the status of the injured person. A cardinal principle of tort law today is that *all persons* should be required to use ordinary care under the circumstances to prevent others from being injured as the result of their conduct.

. . . .

MILLER, JUSTICE, dissenting:

I join in the dissent of Justice Prager. I would eliminate the distinction between licensees and invitees, and adopt reasonable care as the standard governing the duty of an occupier of land towards persons entering upon the land with consent. I would not abolish the trespasser classification, however, and would retain the present standard as to the duty owed to trespassers, i.e., the duty to refrain from the infliction of willful, wanton, or reckless injury.

OWSLEY, JUSTICE, concurring[.]

The following case highlights the fact that wandering cattle cases remain a phenomenon of the present. *Wrinkle* involves issues that refer back to the intentional tort chapters and to privileges for people who might otherwise be considered to be trespassers, and forward to the strict liability and defenses chapters.

WRINKLE v. NORMAN

Court of Appeals of Kansas, 2010
242 P.3d 1216

MARQUARDT J.

Rodney P. Wrinkle filed a negligence action against his neighbors, Gene and Charlene Norman (the Normans), after he sustained injuries on their property. The district court granted summary judgment in favor of the Normans, finding that they did not breach a duty to Wrinkle. Wrinkle appeals. We affirm.

At the time of Wrinkle's accident, Wrinkle lived across U.S. highway 59 from the Normans in Oskaloosa, Kansas. The Normans had 20 acres of pasture land along the west side of the highway on which they raised cattle. The pasture is fenced and has a 16–foot panel gate.

On March 10, 2006, while riding his lawn tractor, Wrinkle observed four or five cattle running loose in the ditch near the Normans' property, approximately 10 to 12 feet from the highway. Wrinkle herded the cattle onto the Normans' property toward a pen with an open gate. According to Wrinkle, the cattle were "returning from where they came from" and "knew where they was going." Wrinkle was able to get all of the cattle into the pen except for one that became entangled in a clothesline wire. Wrinkle removed the wire from around the animal's neck. As the animal ran toward the gate, the wire with a T–shaped clothesline pole attached to it flipped and hit the back of Wrinkle's legs. Wrinkle fell and fractured his back on a concrete path.

Wrinkle filed suit against the Normans, alleging they had negligently and carelessly allowed the clothesline wire to run across the ground, thereby creating a dangerous condition that presented an unreasonable risk of harm. Wrinkle claimed that he was lawfully on the Normans' property when he was injured.

The Normans moved for summary judgment, contending that Wrinkle entered their property without an invitation or permission and, as such, he was trespassing at the time of his injury. The Normans denied liability and argued that the only duty they owed Wrinkle was to refrain from willfully, wantonly, or recklessly causing him injury. The Normans further claimed that they had no notice or knowledge of cattle escaping from their fence on March 10, 2006, or of any defective condition relating to their fence or clothesline wire.

In response, Wrinkle asserted that summary judgment was not appropriate because he was a licensee on the Normans' property, not a trespasser. He claimed the Normans "owed a duty of reasonable care, under all of the circumstances, to maintain their property and keep it safe." Wrinkle relied upon the doctrine of private necessity in the Restatement of Torts (Second) § 197 (1965), alleging that he was privileged to enter the Normans' property in order to prevent serious harm to highway, individuals, or the cattle. Wrinkle also argued that summary judgment was inappropriate because the Normans were subject to liability under K.S.A. 47–123 for negligently confining their cattle.

After hearing arguments from counsel, the district court granted the Normans' summary judgment motion, holding that Wrinkle was a trespasser on the Normans' property; the Normans only owed Wrinkle a duty to refrain from willfully, wantonly, or recklessly causing him injury. The court found as a matter of law that the Normans did not breach a duty owed to Wrinkle. Wrinkle filed a motion to alter or amend the judgment, which the district court denied. Wrinkle timely appeals. . . .

TRESPASSER OR LICENSEE

To establish a claim for negligence, Wrinkle had to prove the existence of a duty, a breach of the duty, an injury, and a causal connection between the duty breached and the injury. The existence of a duty is a question of law. Whether the duty has been breached is a question of fact. *Reynolds v. Kansas Dept. of Transportation*, 273 Kan. 261, Syl. ¶ 1, 43 P.3d 799 (2002). The duty owed by defendants to Wrinkle is determined by Wrinkle's status while he was on the Normans' property. The question is whether he was an invitee, a licensee, or a trespasser.

Wrinkle contends that he was a licensee on the Normans' property and the district court erred in determining that he was a trespasser.

An invitee is " 'one who enters or remains on the premises of another at the express or implied invitation of the possessor of the premises for the benefit of the inviter, or for the mutual benefit and advantage of both inviter and invitee.' " *Jones v. Hansen*, 254 Kan. 499, 503, 867 P.2d 303 (1994). A licensee is " 'one who enters or remains on the premises of another by virtue of either the express or implied consent of the possessor of the premises, or by operation of law, so that he [or she] is not a trespasser thereon.' " 254 Kan. at 503, 867 P.2d 303. A trespasser is " 'one who enters on the premises of another without any right, lawful authority, or an express or implied invitation or license.' " 254 Kan. at 503, 867 P.2d 303.

Our Supreme Court has held that "[t]he duty owed by an occupier of land to invitees and licensees alike is one of reasonable care under all the circumstances." 254 Kan. at 509, 867 P.2d 303. In contrast, the duty owed by an occupier of land to trespassers is "to refrain from willfully, wantonly, or recklessly injuring" the trespasser. 254 Kan. at 510, 867 P.2d 303.

Wrinkle admits that he did not have express permission or consent to enter the Normans' property. Wrinkle was not an invitee. The question remains whether Wrinkle was a licensee or a trespasser. Wrinkle argues that he was a licensee, relying primarily on the Restatement (Second) of Torts § 197.

Section 197 provides, in relevant part: "One is privileged to enter or remain on land in the possession of another if it is or reasonably appears to be necessary to prevent serious harm to . . . the other or a third person, or the land or chattels of either. . . ." Comment a to § 197 provides:

> "The privilege [of private necessity] exists only where in an emergency the actor enters land for the purpose of protecting himself or the possessor of the land or a third person or the land or chattels of any such persons. Furthermore, the privilege must be exercised at a reasonable time and in a reasonable manner.". . . .

Wrinkle contends that he was privileged to enter the Normans' property because it was, or reasonably appeared to be, necessary to prevent serious harm to individuals or the Normans' cattle. Wrinkle acknowledges that Kansas courts have not expressly adopted or applied § 197 but urges this court to do so.

Wrinkle's argument is incomplete. Even if Wrinkle were privileged to enter the Normans' property, § 197 only relieves Wrinkle of liability for doing so and has nothing to do with the scope of the Normans' duty to Wrinkle. In order for Wrinkle's status to change pursuant to this section, this court would also have to adopt Restatement (Second) of Torts § 345 (1965), which states, in relevant part, that "the liability of a possessor of land to one who enters the land only in the exercise of a privilege, for either a public or a private purpose, and irrespective of the possessor's consent, is the same as the liability to a licensee." Wrinkle's brief focuses on § 197 and only gives passing mention to § 345; however, both sections are essential to establish an exception to the usual trespasser rule which would provide that a would-be trespasser who enters onto the land of another based on private necessity is classified as a licensee.

Like § 197, § 345 has never been adopted by Kansas courts. An Illinois Appellate Court implicitly adopted § 345 in *West v. Faurbo*, 66 Ill.App.3d 815, 817–18, 23 Ill.Dec. 663, 384 N.E.2d 457 (1978), and more recently held that a landowner does not automatically owe a higher duty to every trespasser who enters land pursuant to a private necessity. *Lange v. Fisher Real Estate Develop.*, 358 Ill.App.3d 962, 969, 295 Ill.Dec. 123, 832 N.E.2d 274 (2005). In so holding, the *Lange* court relied upon the reasoning in *Benamon v. Soo Line R.R. Co.*, 294 Ill.App.3d 85, 91–92, 228 Ill.Dec. 494, 689 N.E.2d 366 (1997):

> " 'One could argue, as the plaintiff does, that a trespasser who enters the property of another under private necessity, considered to be a licensee, is now entitled to the greater protection of reasonable care since there is no longer a distinction between licensees and invitees. We would disagree with such an argument. We believe that the abolishment of the licensee/invitee distinction in Illinois would not heighten the duties owed by a possessor of land to a person who enters his land under private necessity. There can be no logical reason to afford a greater protection of reasonable care to such a person, who, in actuality, is a trespasser and who enters the property without the possessor's permission and without benefit to the possessor.' "
> 358 Ill.App.3d at 970, 295 Ill.Dec. 123, 832 N.E.2d 274.

Kansas, like Illinois, has abolished the licensee/invitee distinction. *Jones*, 254 Kan. at 509, 867 P.2d 303. In the instant case, there was no evidence that the cattle were owned by the Normans. Wrinkle apparently assumed that the cattle belonged to the Normans because they were wandering near the Normans' property and ran toward a gate on the Normans' property. However, Gene Norman denied that his cattle were on his property on March 10, 2006. Gene testified that prior to March 5, 2006, he had about 30 head of cattle on his property. Gene also testified that he moves his cattle off of his property the first week of March every year and brings some of them back around the first of May. Gene provided names of other individuals who pasture cattle on either side of his property. Thus, Wrinkle not only entered the Normans' property without permission, but also arguably without benefit to the Normans. Accordingly, Wrinkle is not entitled to protection as a licensee under § 345.

The duty owed by the Normans to Wrinkle, a trespasser, was to refrain from willfully, wantonly, or recklessly causing him injury. See *Jones*, 254 Kan. at 510, 867 P.2d 303. There is nothing in the record to suggest, nor does Wrinkle contend, that a genuine issue of material fact exists regarding whether the Normans breached this duty.

The district court properly determined that Wrinkle was a trespasser.

K.S.A. 47–123 CLAIM

Wrinkle also contends that summary judgment was improper because there are material fact issues regarding whether the Normans are liable for their cattle running at large under K.S.A. 47–123.

Wrinkle did not plead a claim under K.S.A. 47–123 as a separate and distinct theory of liability in his original petition for damages but did reference the statutory provision in his response to the Normans' motion for summary judgment. Thereafter, Wrinkle requested leave to file a second amended petition which included a separate cause of action under K.S.A. 47–123. The district court denied the request, finding that the allegations in Wrinkle's proposed second amended petition were included in his response to the Normans' summary judgment motion and had been considered by the court. Although the district court did not explicitly rule on Wrinkle's K.S.A. 47–123 argument, by granting the Normans' summary judgment motion, the court implicitly rejected it.

K.S.A. 47–122 makes it "unlawful for any domestic animal, other than dogs and cats, to run at large." Further, K.S.A. 47–123 provides that any livestock owner in violation of K.S.A. 47–122 shall be "liable to the person injured for all damages resulting therefrom, and the person so damaged shall have a lien on said livestock for the amount of such damages."

The doctrines of strict liability and res ipsa loquitur do not apply in livestock escape cases. In order to recover for damages, the injured party must prove negligence, *i.e.*, that the livestock owner failed to exercise ordinary care to keep the livestock fenced. *Harmon v. Koch*, 24 Kan.App.2d 149, 153, 942 P.2d 669 (1997); *Walborn v. Stockman*, 10 Kan.App.2d 597, 598–599, 706 P.2d 465 (1985). An owner of animals is required to use reasonable care to confine his or her animals, but absolute security is not required. *Clark v. Carson*, 188 Kan. 261, 264–65, 362 P.2d 71 (1961). Accordingly, Wrinkle, as the party opposing summary judgment, must come forward with evidence to establish a dispute as to a material fact regarding the Normans' failure to exercise due care in keeping their cattle enclosed.

Wrinkle cannot meet this burden. First, ownership of the cattle involved in Wrinkle's accident was never established. Although Wrinkle assumed that the cattle belonged to the Normans, Gene Norman denied that they were his and provided the names of other individuals who pasture cattle on either side of his property.

Further, there was no evidence to show that the Normans failed to exercise due care in containing their cattle.

Wrinkle argues that the present case is similar to *Cooper v. Eberly*, 211 Kan. 657, 508 P.2d 943 (1973). In *Cooper*, evidence of a horse owner's negligence in failing to take reasonable precautions to confine his horses included a failure to padlock a gate which was found open after an accident and knowledge that horses had escaped on prior occasions. 211 Kan. at 660, 665–66, 669, 508 P.2d 943. Wrinkle contends that, as in *Cooper*, the Normans' pasture gate was found unsecured and partially open prior to the accident and there were reports that the Normans' cattle had been out of their pasture on at least three occasions prior to March 10, 2006. Wrinkle claims that these facts provide a sufficient basis to find that the Normans are liable under K.S.A. 47–123.

Although Wrinkle alleges that the gate he herded the cattle towards did not have a secure lock, there is no evidence in the record on appeal that the cattle actually escaped from this gate. As for Wrinkle's contentions that the Normans' cattle had been seen running loose on several occasions prior to March 10, 2006, there is no indication that the Normans ever had notice of these alleged prior escapes. Both Gene and Charlene testified that they could only recall one time, when a single calf got out of a fence on their property. Moreover, Wrinkle testified that he never notified the Normans on the occasions when he allegedly observed their cattle outside of their pen and did not know if anyone else had ever notified them.

It is well established that "[a] party opposing summary judgment may not rest merely on allegations, but must set forth specific facts to support its position." *Lloyd v. Quorum Health Resources, LLC*, 31 Kan.App.2d 943, 954, 77 P.3d 993 (2003); see K.S.A. 2009 Supp. 60–256(e). Furthermore, "[t]he law is clear that 'an inference cannot be based upon evidence which is too uncertain or speculative or which raises merely a conjecture or possibility.' " 31 Kan.App.2d at 954, 77 P.3d 993. The evidence in Wrinkle's response to the Normans' summary judgment motion merely created a conjecture or possibility that the Normans owned the cattle that he herded onto their property on March 10, 2006. Assuming that ownership of the cattle was established, the evidence brought forward by Wrinkle merely raised the possibility that the Normans had failed to exercise due care in containing their cattle. Therefore, Wrinkle's claim under K.S.A. 47–123 presents no genuine issues of material fact. [Affirmed.]

If you were a plaintiff, which would you prefer, the categories or a uniform reasonableness standard? If you were a defendant, which would you prefer? An insurance company selling homeowners' liability insurance? The question of the duty owed in a particular case is one for the judge; whether the defendant was negligent in light of that duty is for the jury. Does this allocation of responsibility at trial affect your answer?

ILLINOIS COMPILED STATUTES ANNOTATED
CHAPTER 740. CIVIL LIABILITIES — PREMISES LIABILITY ACT
740 ILCS 130/2 (1996)

§ 740 ICLS 130/2. [Common law distinction abolished]

Sec.2. The distinction under the common law between invitees and licensees as to the duty owed by an owner or occupier of any premises to such entrants is abolished.

The duty owed to such entrants is that of reasonable care under the circumstances regarding the state of the premises or acts done or omitted on them. The duty of reasonable care under the circumstances which an owner or occupier of land owes to such entrants does not include any of the following: a duty to warn of or otherwise take reasonable steps to protect such entrants from conditions on the premises that are known to the entrant, are open and obvious, or can reasonably be expected to be discovered by the entrant; a duty to warn of latent defects or dangers or defects or dangers unknown to the owner or occupier of the premises; a duty to warn such entrants of any dangers resulting from misuse by the entrants of the premises or anything affixed to or located on the premises; or a duty to protect such entrants from their own misuse of the premises or anything affixed to or located on the premises . . .

§ 740 ILCS 13013. [Trespasser]

Sec. 3. Nothing herein affects the law as regards the trespassing child entrant. An owner or occupier of land owes no duty of care to an adult trespasser other than to refrain from willful and wanton conduct that would endanger the safety of a known trespasser on the property from a condition of the property or an activity conducted by the owner or occupier on the property.

———————

1.   Why did the Illinois legislature retain the trespasser classification?

2.   The Second Restatement of Torts in Section 333 retains the trespasser classification and provides that "a possessor of land is not liable to trespassers for physical harm caused by his failure to exercise reasonable care." The landowner is under no obligation either to make the land safe for trespassers or to take their presence into account when using his or her land. Section 333 states that this rule "applies although from past experience or otherwise the possessor has every reason to realize that there is a strong probability that trespassers will intrude upon his land." There are, of course, exceptions to this rule of nonliability. Sections 334–39 of the Second Restatement describe six types of trespasser to whom the owner of the land will be liable — in other words, six types of trespasser who are excepted from the general rule of nonliability to trespassers. Three of these are: (1) trespassers of whose constant presence the landowner is or should be aware, where the landowner's activity involves a risk of death or serious injury to the trespasser (Section 334), (2) trespassers of whose constant presence the landowner is or should be aware,

where there is a highly dangerous artificial condition created or maintained by the landowner, where the trespassers are not likely to discover the condition, and where the landowner has failed to use reasonable care to warn the trespassers of the condition and the risk (Section 335), (3) trespassers of whose presence the landowner is or should be aware, where the landowner "fail[s] to carry on his activities upon the land with reasonable care for the trespasser's safety" (Section 336). How much of the nonliability principle remains after all these exceptions are applied? A court that has abandoned such classifications does not need to deal with the Restatement definitions; rather, that court will need to ask whether the landowner was negligent with respect to the plaintiffs involved.

3.   The California and Kansas courts reach opposite conclusions about whether the classifications of plaintiff should remain in place. How often do you think that the classifications make a difference in the result of a case? Aren't the classifications really a rule-oriented effort to embody foreseeability concepts? If the classification of trespasser were unavailable, wouldn't the defendant argue that the presence of the plaintiff on his or her land was unforeseeable, or if foreseeable, that the defendant did not act unreasonably with respect to the plaintiff by failing to make his or her land safe for that plaintiff?

2.   Natural and Unnatural Conditions On and Off the Land

SPRECHER v. ADAMSON COS.
Supreme Court of California, 1981 (en banc)
636 P.2d 1121

BIRD, CHIEF JUSTICE.

This case concerns the present validity of the old common law rule which immunized a possessor of land from liability for injury caused by a natural condition of his land to persons or property not on his land.

I.

The following facts are not in dispute. Respondent, South Winter Mesa Associates, a joint venture between respondents The Adamson Companies and Century-Malibu Ventures, Inc., owns a 90-acre parcel of land in Malibu, California. The parcel is bounded on the north by the Pacific Coast Highway and on the south by Malibu Road. Across Malibu Road and opposite the parcel are a number of beach front homes, including the home of appellant, Peter Sprecher.

Respondents' parcel of land contains part of an active landslide which extends seaward from the parcel for some 1,700 feet along Malibu Road and beyond the boundaries of respondents' property. The Sprecher property is situated within the toe of this slide. The landslide, which has been evident since the area was first developed in the early 1900's, is classified as active because it exhibits periodic cycles of activity and dormancy. The parties agree that the slide is a natural condition of the land which has not been affected by any of respondents' activities on the 90-acre parcel.

In March 1978, heavy spring rains triggered a major movement of the slide which caused appellant's home to rotate and to press against the home of his neighbor, Gwendolyn Sexton. As a result, Sexton filed an action against appellant, seeking to enjoin the encroachment of his home upon hers. Appellant cross-complained against Sexton, the County of Los Angeles and respondents. Specifically, appellant sought damages for the harm done to his home by the landslide. He alleged that such damage proximately resulted from respondents' negligent failure to correct or to control the landslide condition.

Respondents moved for summary judgment, arguing primarily that a possessor of land has no duty to remedy a natural condition of the land in order to prevent harm to property outside his premises. Since the landslide was a natural condition, they argued that they were not liable for the damage to appellant's home.

In opposition, appellant challenged the present validity of the common law rule of nonliability for a natural condition, arguing that the rule is neither premised upon sound public policy nor in accord with modern principles of tort liability.

The trial court ruled in favor of respondents and this appeal followed.

II.

Summary judgment is properly granted where the evidence in support of the moving party, here the respondents, is sufficient to establish a complete defense to appellant's claims and there is no triable issue of fact. Obviously, a rule of law, such as the traditional rule regarding natural conditions, which provides that a defendant has no duty to protect plaintiff is a complete defense to a claim of negligence. Its effect is to immunize or exempt the defendant from liability for negligence. Therefore, the first question this court must decide is whether a possessor of land should be immunized from liability for harm caused by a natural condition of his land to persons outside his premises. That is, should a possessor's exposure to liability be determined by reference to the origin of the condition causing harm or in accord with the ordinary principles of negligence.

Under the common law, the major important limitation upon the responsibility of a possessor of land to those outside his premises concerned the natural condition of the land.[3] While the possessor's liability for harm caused by artificial conditions[4] was determined in accord with ordinary principles of negligence, the common law gave him an absolute immunity from liability for harm caused by conditions considered natural in origin. No matter how great the harm threatened to his neighbor, or to one passing by, and no matter how small the effort needed to eliminate it, a possessor of land had no duty to remedy conditions that were natural in origin.

---

[3] The term " '[n]atural condition of the land' is used to indicate that the condition of land has not been changed by any act of a human being. . . . It is also used to include the natural growth of trees, weeds, and other vegetation upon land not artificially made receptive to them." (Rest. 2d Torts, § 363, com. b.

[4] "[A] structure erected upon land is a non-natural or artificial condition, as are trees or plants planted or preserved, and changes in the surface by excavation or filling, irrespective of whether they are harmful in themselves or become so only because of the subsequent operation of natural forces." (Rest. 2d Torts, § 363, com. b.)

This court has held that it will not depart from the fundamental concept that a person is liable for injuries caused "by his want of ordinary care . . . in the management of his property or person . . ." (Civ. Code, § 1714) except when such a departure is "clearly supported by public policy." *(Rowland v. Christian* (1968) 69 Cal. 2d 108, 112, 70 Cal. Rptr. 97, 443 P.2d 561.) Accordingly, common law distinctions resulting in wholesale immunities have been struck down when such distinctions could not withstand critical scrutiny.

In *Rowland,* this court stated that "[a] departure from [the] fundamental principle [of Civil Code section 1714] involves the balancing of a number of considerations[.] [T]he major ones are the foreseeability of harm to the plaintiff, the degree of certainty that the plaintiff suffered injury, the closeness of the connection between the defendant's conduct and the injury suffered, the moral blame attached to the defendant's conduct, the policy of preventing future harm, the extent of the burden to the defendant and [the] consequences to the community of imposing a duty to exercise care with resulting liability for breach and the availability, cost, and prevalence of insurance for the risk involved." *(Rowland v. Christian, supra,* 69 Cal. 2d at pp. 112-113, 70 Cal. Rptr. 97, 443 P.2d 561.)

Th[e] progression of the law in California mirrors what appears to be a general trend toward rejecting the common law distinction between natural and artificial conditions. Instead, the courts are increasingly using ordinary negligence principles to determine a possessor's liability for harm caused by a condition of the land. The early case of *Gibson v. Denton* (1896) 4 A.D. 198, 38 N.Y.S. 554 was a precursor of this trend. In *Gibson,* the court held a possessor of land liable for damage caused when a decayed tree on her premises fell on the home of her neighbor during a storm. After noting that the defendant clearly would be liable for the fall of a dilapidated building, or artificial structure, the court observed that it could "see no good reason why she should not be responsible for the fall of a decayed tree, which she allowed to remain on her premises." *(Id.,* at p. 555.) "[T]he tree was on her lot, and was her property. It was as much under her control as a pole or building in the same position would have been." *(Ibid.)* Thus, "[t]he defendant had no more right to keep, maintain, or suffer to remain on her premises an unsound tree . . . than she would have had to keep a dilapidated and unsafe building in the same position." *(Id.,* at pp. 555-556.)

In more recent years, at least 13 other states and the District of Columbia have begun applying ordinary negligence principles in determining a possessor's liability for harm caused by a natural condition.

. . . .

The courts are not simply creating an exception to the common law rule of nonliability for damage caused by trees and retaining the rule for other natural conditions of the land. Instead, the courts are moving toward jettisoning the common law rule in its entirety and replacing it with a single duty of reasonable care in the maintenance of property. This development is reflected in the Restatement Second of Torts, which now recognizes that a possessor of land may be subject to liability for harm caused not just by trees but by any natural condition of the land.

. . . .

The latest formulation of the duty owed by a possessor of land to persons outside his premises with regard to natural conditions which is set forth in the Restatement Second of Torts still limits the reach of the duty to persons traveling on the public streets and highways. (Rest. 2d Torts, § 840, subd. (2).) The American Law Institute, however, noted that at the time this formulation was promulgated, the authority was insufficient to support a position regarding whether the duty was owed adjoining landowners as well. (See Rest. 2d Torts, § 840, com. c.) Nevertheless, a number of jurisdictions have held a possessor of land liable for harm caused an adjoining landowner by a natural condition of the land. It is difficult to discern any reason to restrict the possessor's duty to individuals using the highways. To do so would create an unsatisfying anomaly: a possessor of land would have a duty of care toward strangers but not toward his neighbor.

In rejecting the common law rule of nonliability for natural conditions, the courts have recognized the inherent injustice involved in a rule which states that "a landowner may escape all liability for serious damage to his neighbors [or those using a public highway], merely by allowing nature to take its course." (Prosser, [Law of Torts (4th ed. 1971) § 57], at p. 355.) As one commentator has observed: "[w]here a planted tree has become dangerous to persons on the highway or on adjoining land, and causes harm, the fault lies not in the planting of the tree but in permitting it to remain after it has become unsafe." (Noel, *Nuisances from Land in its Natural Condition* 56 Harv. L. Rev. 772, 796-797 (1943).)

Historically, the consideration most frequently invoked to support the rule of nonliability for natural conditions was that it was merely an embodiment of the principle that one should not be obligated to undertake affirmative conduct to aid or protect others. This doctrine rested on the common law distinction between the infliction of harm and the failure to prevent it, or misfeasance and nonfeasance. (Rest. 2d Torts, § 314, com. c.) Misfeasance was determined to exist when a defendant played some part in the creation of a risk, even if his participation was innocent. Nonfeasance occurred when a defendant had merely failed to intervene in a plaintiff's behalf. Liability for nonfeasance, or the failure to take affirmative action, was ordinarily imposed only where some special relationship between the plaintiff and defendant could be established.

Proponents of the rule of nonliability for natural conditions argued that a defendant's failure to prevent a natural condition from causing harm was mere nonfeasance. A natural condition of the land was by definition, they argued, one which no human being had played a part in creating. Therefore, no basis for liability existed because a duty to exercise reasonable care could not arise out of possession alone. Since there was no special relationship between the possessor of land and persons outside the premises, there could be no liability. Conversely, a defendant's failure to prevent an artificial condition from causing harm constituted actionable misfeasance.

Whatever the rule may once have been, it is now clear that a duty to exercise due care can arise out of possession alone. One example is provided by modern cases dealing with the duty of a possessor of land to act affirmatively for the protection of individuals who come upon the premises. In days gone by, a possessor of land was deemed to owe such a duty of care only to invitees. That is, the duty to act affirmatively was grounded in the special relation between the possessor-invitor and the invitee. *Rowland* held that whether the individual coming upon the land was a trespasser, a licensee or an invitee made no difference as to the duty of reasonable care owed but was to be considered only as to the issue of whether the possessor had exercised reasonable care under all the circumstances. (*Rowland v. Christian, supra*, at pp. 118-119, 70 Cal. Rptr. 97, 443 P.2d 561.)

Modern cases recognize that after *Rowland*, the duty to take affirmative action for the protection of individuals coming upon the land is grounded in the possession of the premises and the attendant right to control and manage the premises.

. . . .

Thus, it becomes clear that the traditional characterization of a defendant's failure to take affirmative steps to prevent a natural condition from causing harm as nonactionable nonfeasance conflicts sharply with modern perceptions of the obligations which flow from the possession of land. Possession ordinarily brings with it the right of supervision and control. . . .

Another deficiency of the historical justification of the rule of nonliability is simply that it proves too much. Under the traditional analysis, a possessor of land should be excused from any duty to prevent harm to persons outside his land whenever he has played no part in the creation of the condition which threatens the harm, be it artificial or natural. However, most courts recognize that the possessor is under an affirmative duty to act with regard to a dangerous artificial condition even though the condition was created solely by some predecessor in title or possession (Rest. 2d Torts, § 366;[6] or by the unauthorized conduct of some other third person (Rest. 2d Torts, § 364, subd.(c)).[7]

. . . .

In addition, adherence to the rule in California would produce an anomalous result. A possessor of land would owe a duty of care to protect trespassers, invitees and licensees, but not his neighbor, from harms threatened by a natural condition of the land. It has long been established in California that a possessor of land is subject to liability for harm caused a person upon the land by a natural condition. It is difficult to see why this court should support a rule which would allow a

---

[6] Section 366 provides:

"One who takes possession of land upon which there is an existing structure or other artificial condition unreasonably dangerous to persons or property outside of the land is subject to liability for physical harm caused to them by the condition after, but only after,

"(a) the possessor knows or should know of the condition, and

"(b) he knows or should know that it exists without the consent of those affected by it, and

"(c) he has failed, after a reasonable opportunity, to make it safe or otherwise to protect such persons against it."

[7] Section 364, subdivision (c), provides:

"A possessor of land is subject to liability to others outside of the land for physical harm caused by a structure or other artificial condition on the land, which the possessor realizes or should realize will involve an unreasonable risk of harm, if . . .

"(c) the condition is created by a third person without the possessor's consent or acquiescence, but reasonable care is not taken to make the condition safe after the possessor knows or should know of it."

trespasser to bring an action in negligence that would be denied a neighbor, where both were standing on either side of the possessor's boundary line and were both struck by a dead limb from his tree.

Finally, it is apparent that the distinction between artificial and natural conditions, and the immunity from liability predicated on that distinction, bears little relationship to the major factors which should determine whether immunity should be given the possessor of land for harm done by a natural condition of the land. The foreseeability of harm to the plaintiff, the degree of certainty that the plaintiff suffered injury, the closeness of the connection between the defendant's conduct and the injury suffered, the moral blame attached to the defendant's conduct, the policy of preventing future harm, and the extent of the burden to the defendant and the consequence to the community of imposing a duty to exercise care have little, if any, relationship to the natural, as opposed to artificial, origin of the condition causing harm.

The remaining factors, the availability, cost, and prevalence of insurance may in some cases bear a relationship to the natural origin of the condition. Insurance may not be readily available for the risks posed by some natural conditions. On balance, however, it is clear that a departure from the fundamental concept that a person is liable for the harm caused "by his want of ordinary care . . . in the management of his property . . ." (Civ. Code, § 1714) is unwarranted as regards natural conditions of land.

The trend in the law is in the direction of imposing a duty of reasonable care upon the possessor of land with regard to natural conditions of land. The erosion of the doctrinal underpinning of the rule of nonliability is evident from even a cursory review of the case law. Also evident is the lack of congruence between the old common law rule of nonliability and the relevant factors which should determine whether a duty exists. All this leads to but one conclusion. The distinction between artificial and natural conditions should be rejected.

IV.

The judgment of the trial court is reversed and the cause remanded to the trial court for further proceedings consistent with the views expressed in this opinion.

TOBRINER, MOSK, NEWMAN, WORK and MCCLOSKY, JJ., concur.

RICHARDSON, JUSTICE, concurring.

I concur in the judgment of the court which reverses the trial court's entry of summary judgment in favor of respondents. It seems proper to require that landowners act reasonably with reference to their property, thus preventing damage to their neighbors. This is so regardless of whether the condition threatening the injury or damage is artificial or natural.

. . . .

1. What effect does extending liability to natural conditions have on insurance? What if you live on a mountaintop, and after a rainstorm, a mudslide runs from your property down onto your neighbor's house? How would you classify cattle?

2. As with many other areas of tort law, the concept of reasonable conduct in the circumstances may replace the proliferation of specific rules that the common law generated in the past. The issue becomes whether the defendant (and, for that matter, the plaintiff) acted reasonably; categorizing either party becomes unnecessary. This trend simplifies legal decisions enormously, not least because it creates a body of law that applies in all cases, no matter how bizarre or outside prior precedent the facts may be. Instead of having to figure out into which pigeonhole the facts fit, or having to invent a new pigeonhole if they don't fit anywhere, the court simply asks whether the parties acted reasonably.

One of the sets of pigeonholes that created problems involved natural and unnatural uses of or conditions of land. For example, the rules on trees could be unexpectedly complex. In some courts, any tree would be a natural condition; in others, a tree would be a natural condition only if it had grown by itself (as opposed to having been planted by the landowner). In still others, a tree would be a natural condition if it was of a native species, whether planted by the landowner or not. Any nonnative tree would then be an unnatural condition, however it appeared on the property. Such a welter of definitional problems can be eliminated when a reasonableness standard is used.

3. T, the owner of real estate, builds a garage for his car on his land. Because he likes to be in the shade when working on his car, he builds his garage in such a way that a large healthy tree on the property of his next-door neighbor, R, will cast shade onto that garage.

During a storm, the tree on R's land, which is several hundred years old, falls onto T's garage. Will R be liable for damage to the garage? Would your answer change depending upon whether the tree had been planted by an ancestor of R or had grown at its location by itself?

B.   ADDITIONAL CATEGORIES OF PLAINTIFFS

1.   Attractive Nuisances, Artificial Conditions, and Children

CRAWFORD v. PACIFIC WESTERN MOBILE ESTATES, INC.
Missouri Court of Appeals, Kansas City District, 1977
548 S.W.2d 216

Before WASSERSTROM, P.J. and SOMMERVILLE and TURNAGE, JJ.

WASSERSTROM, PRESIDING JUDGE.

Plaintiffs seek damages for wrongful death of their six year old son, Mark, who drowned in a settlement tank maintained by defendant Pacific Western Mobile

Estates, Inc., as part of its sewage treatment plant at Liberty Village Trailer Park in Clay County, Missouri. The jury returned a verdict of $30,000 against both Pacific Western and its resident manager Wilma Gilbert. However, the trial court, pursuant to after trial motions, set aside the verdict and entered judgment for defendants. Plaintiffs appeal. Reversed.

The sole issue presented is whether the evidence established a submissible case of negligence. . . .

The tragic accident in question occurred on November 22, 1973. Plaintiffs, together with their son Mark, were residents of Pacific Western's trailer park which accommodated 143 residential trailers. The southwest part of the park was reserved for non-family residents, while the southeast part was reserved for families with children. At the extreme northern part of the trailer park, and closer to the family portion than to the non-family section, Pacific Western maintained a sewage treatment plant of which the settlement tank was a part. The nearest trailer was approximately 200 yards from this sewage treatment facility.

The settlement tank itself resembled a swimming pool; it was approximately 25 feet long and 11 feet wide, with vertical concrete reinforced walls 7½ feet deep. The water level was maintained at a depth of 6 feet, which means that the surface of the effluent was 1½ feet below the top ledge of the tank (which is at ground level). There was no ladder or other device which would aid anyone who fell into the tank to climb out. The architect designed the tank with a cypress deck to completely cover the top of the tank. The deck was to rest upon a lip or indentation at either end of the tank and fit flush with the top. Although the tank does have the described lip or indentation, the tank has never been covered since the trailer park was acquired by Pacific Western in August, 1973, and manager Gilbert had never observed nor was she ever told about any covering of any kind.

The architect also designed a fence to be built around the tank, and a six foot tall solid wooden flat fence had been erected and was in place. Adjacent to this wooden fence and borrowing one side thereof, a rectangular area was fenced off with a chain link fence for use as a storage area. The chain link fence had a gate and there was also a gate between the storage area and the tank area. Gilbert testified that these gates were kept locked at all times.

After Pacific Western acquired the trailer park, the previous owner removed approximately 60 trailers from the trailer park, leaving behind on the ground concrete blocks which had been used to support those trailers. Pacific Western's maintenance employees gathered up these blocks and piled them against the wooden fence which enclosed the sewage settlement tank. These blocks were stacked in such a way so that "they were sort of like stairs going up" and reached to within 6 inches of the top of the fence. Although a child could not have gotten over the 6 foot wooden fence otherwise, the "stairway" of concrete blocks could be easily ascended by a child and there remained only a short jump to the ground inside of the sewage tank area.

A number of children lived in the trailer park with their parents, and they customarily played throughout the trailer park. There were no warning signs posted anywhere on the grounds to alert parents of any dangerous condition inside the wooden fence, nor were the tenants notified of the existence of the treatment facility. Mark's father testified that he did not know what was inside the fence until after the fatal accident. A neighbor who had lived in the court testified that she also was unaware of the sewage facility inside the fence until after the accident.

On the afternoon of the accident a number of children, aged six to ten, among whom Mark was one, were playing in the trailer park in the vicinity of the wooden fence described and they were seen playing on the concrete blocks piled next to the wooden fence. At about 3:30 an older boy walking by was hailed by the children and was told that someone was in the sewage tank. He climbed the blocks, but could see nothing but a ball floating on the surface of the murky effluent. Other children went to notify Mark's father, who was working beside his trailer, that someone was in the sewer. Mr. Crawford, unaware of the existence of a sewage treatment facility on the grounds, headed toward a storm sewer next to the street, but was corrected by the children. Mr. Crawford and a neighbor who had been summoned probed the pool with a rake and a two by twelve board and succeeded in locating and removing Mark's submerged body. Attempts at resuscitation were unsuccessful. In the course of these rescue attempts, Mr. Crawford saw a wooden ladder-like contraption lying across the width of the tank and which served as a bridge. Also lying across the width of the tank was a metal latticework which Mr. Crawford testified would probably not have borne the weight of a grown man but which might have borne the weight of a small child. Mr. Crawford also noticed small hand prints on one side of the concrete tank on the 1 1/2 foot vertical concrete wall above the surface of the effluent.

Defendants argue vigorously that defendants owed the deceased boy no duty which can be the foundation of recovery, because he was a trespasser when he entered the fenced area. Plaintiffs do not deny the classification of their son as a trespasser, but contend that the landowner nevertheless owed their son a duty of reasonable care under the standards of Section 339, 2 Restatement of the Law, Torts. Defendants deny that the facts here meet those requirements. The issue in this case accordingly narrows to the question of whether plaintiffs have brought this situation within the scope of the § 339 doctrine.

Section 339 of the Restatement (1965 Revision) provides as follows:

"§ 339. Artificial Conditions Highly Dangerous to Trespassing Children

"A possessor of land is subject to liability for physical harm to children trespassing thereon caused by an artificial condition upon the land if

(a) the place where the condition exists is one upon which the possessor knows or has reason to know that children are likely to trespass, and

(b) the condition is one of which the possessor knows or has reason to know and which he realizes or should realize will involve an unreasonable risk of death or serious bodily harm to such children, and

(c) the children because of their youth do not discover the condition or realize the risk involved in intermeddling with it or in coming within the area made dangerous by it, and

(d) the utility to the possessor of maintaining the condition and the burden of eliminating the danger are slight as compared with the risk to children involved, and

(e) the possessor fails to exercise reasonable care to eliminate the danger or otherwise to protect the children."

(a) *Reason to anticipate presence of children.* Treating these five requirements in order, the first question is whether defendants knew or had reason to know that children were likely to enter the fenced area. Defendants lay great stress upon the fact that the record contains no evidence that any children had ever before been in the sewage-treatment facility. That, however, misses the point. Merely because children had not trespassed in the past does not relieve the landowner from liability if there is some reasonable expectation that they might trespass. . . .

The evidence here shows that many of the families in the trailer court had young children who played all over the trailer court. . . . There was further evidence that children played on the concrete blocks which themselves allowed easy access to the sewage tank area itself. Defendant Gilbert, the resident manager of the trailer court, admitted that the kids "were like a bunch of damn monkeys and were down there all the time" and there was nothing she could do to keep them out.

Furthermore, the manager Gilbert had full knowledge of the piled up blocks which permitted of such easy access for children to get over the fence. . . .

The evidence in this case abundantly shows that defendants had good reason to know that children played in the immediate area of the settlement tank and that the conditions were such that the block stairway would provide easy access — if not an open invitation — for children to enter the sewage tank area. Defendants had ample reason to know that sooner or later some child was likely to enter the picket enclosure.

(b) *Reason to realize unreasonable risk.* The second requirement of § 339 is that defendants knew or had reason to know and which they realized or should have realized would involve an unreasonable risk of death *(sic)*. This requirement causes little difficulty under the facts of this case. The prospect of danger was so apparent from the beginning that the architect designed the settlement tank to be protected by both a wooden deck cover and also a six foot high fence. Although the deck cover was apparently never utilized, still the original owner of the trailer park showed a realization of the necessity of some protection by erecting the six foot fence and providing a locked gate to prevent inadvertent entrance into the area. After acquisition of the trailer park by Pacific Western, the necessity of such protection continued to be acknowledged by the defendants as shown by their custom, to which Mrs. Gilbert testified, of keeping the gate carefully locked at all times. Thus the general presence of danger requiring some protection has been established by the actions of defendants themselves. . . .

Yet, despite this awareness of danger against which the fence constituted the only protection, defendants permitted the piling up of concrete blocks against the fence in such a way as to completely negate the protection which the fence was designed to afford. No question is here presented about whether defendants knew of the location of those blocks — Pacific Western's own employees created that condition. Moreover, the resident manager was reminded by her own eyesight of the dangerous condition daily. The evidence amply shows that defendants had reason to know and to realize the unreasonable risk of death or injury.

(c) *Lack of realization of risk by trespassing child.* The third requirement for inquiry is whether Mark Crawford, because of his youth, failed to realize the risk involved. This element of plaintiffs' case represents by far the most difficult point of decision and it is the one which bears the heavy weight of defendant's attack. Defendants argue the Missouri courts have consistently denied recovery for the death of children who have drowned in ponds, pools or similar bodies of water and defendants contend that those cases decided under the attractive nuisance doctrine control here. As part of their reliance upon those cases, defendants insist in their brief that Restatement § 339 "is simply a rule setting forth the 'attractive nuisance doctrine.' "

Defendants' latter statement errs. The attractive nuisance doctrine originated as an effort by the courts to ameliorate the harsh rules relating to the extremely limited duty of a landowner to trespassers. The courts, however, confined that new doctrine to a very [narrow] scope, and legal thought grew in favor of further relief. Out of this current of thought grew § 339 of the Restatement. . . . Not until the decision in *Arbogast v. Terminal Railroad Assn. of St. Louis*, [452 S.W.2d 81 (Mo.)] in 1970, more than 35 years after the first publication of § 339, did the Missouri courts yield to the new rules of child trespasser liability. That this adoption would significantly extend the liability of the landowner was the very reason that the Missouri Supreme Court had for so long resisted the change. Now that the change has been accomplished, the old Missouri decisions applying the former attractive nuisance doctrine must be read with discrimination and applied only with the greatest of caution.

The pond and pool cases decided under the attractive nuisance doctrine, and upon which the defendants so heavily relied, went in part on the ground that these bodies of water constituted open and obvious danger which should be within the comprehension of any child old enough to be permitted to roam at large. To this extent, the pool and pond cases still state the law, and a landowner is not now (just as he was not previously) required to "child-proof" his premises against an obvious danger. The underlying concept mentioned has been expressly stated in Comment j under § 339 as follows:

> "There are many dangers, such a [sic] those of fire and water, or of falling from a height, which under ordinary conditions may reasonably be expected to be fully understood and appreciated by any child of an age to be allowed at large. To such conditions the rule stated in this Section ordinarily has no application, in the absence of some other factor creating a special risk that the child will not avoid the danger, such as the fact that the condition is so hidden as not to be readily visible, or a distracting influence which makes it likely that the child will not discover or appreciate it." . . .

Analysis of the present situation must therefore take the next step of examining whether the facts here show distracting elements which kept Mark Crawford from realizing the danger inherent in the settlement tank. Such distracting factors did exist. First of all, the effluent in the tank was dark and murky so as to be opaque. No one could tell from looking whether the depth was a few inches or several yards. Next a ball was floating on top of the effluent. Whether Mark Crawford climbed over the wall to recover the ball which he may have been playing with outside the wall or whether he saw the ball floating in the tank only after he got inside the enclosure, in either event the ball represented a plaything which naturally became the focus of distracting attention to this six-year-old boy.

Added to that situation, there stretched across the tank a wooden bridge and a metal bridge which invited the child out over the pool to bring himself into a position better able to reach toward the ball. The combination of these factors readily support the inference that Mark Crawford was in fact distracted from and did not realize the danger. Under these circumstances, it is easy to understand why this young boy who knew how to swim would not notice that the concrete wall of the tank stood a sheer 1 1/2 feet above the surface of the effluent and that there was no ladder or similar device by which he could get out of the pool in the event he fell in.

. . . .

[The facts in this case meet the requirements of § 339.]

(d) *Comparison of the burden of eliminating the danger with the character of the risk.* The fourth element to be proved under § 339 requires that the burden to the landowner of eliminating the danger be slight as compared to the risk to the trespassing children. Satisfaction of this requirement presents no problem here. All that was necessary to protect against the danger created by the open tank was to eliminate the stacked pile of concrete blocks immediately alongside the wooden fence enclosing the sewage treatment area. Nothing at all appears which would require those blocks to be stored in this particular location. They could have been piled up anywhere else, thereby eliminating the danger which led to Mark Crawford's death. Even pulling down the height of the stack of blocks would probably have been enough. The cost of so doing would have been negligible.

(e) The final requirement of § 339 is a showing that the landowner failed to exercise reasonable care to protect the children. Comment *o* under this section says that the purpose of this requirement is to create liability "only if the possessor fails to take the steps which a reasonable man would take under such circumstances. If the possessor has exercised all reasonable care to make the condition safe, or otherwise to protect the children, and has still not succeeded, there is no liability." The Comment goes on to say that in some circumstances a warning would be all that could be expected of a reasonable man, and if so the giving of a warning may satisfy the landowner's duty.

No such problem complicates the instant case. Defendants had a safe condition if they themselves had not eliminated the safety feature of the fence by piling the concrete blocks against it. That danger was created by the affirmative acts of their own workmen, and defendants did nothing at all to offset the consequent danger. Even if a warning would have been sufficient, no warning, either written or oral, was ever given by defendants to anyone. No question can exist but what plaintiffs made a submissible case as to defendants' negligence.

. . . .

It follows from the foregoing that the trial court erred in setting aside the jury verdict. The judgment is therefore reversed with instructions to the trial court to reinstate the jury verdict.

All concur.

---

1. How can landowners with ineradicable hazards on their property avoid liability to children? What is the standard of care to which a landowner should be held? A child? Would warning signs have been any use to the landowner in the above case? Why, or why not?

2. Children have for years presented special problems and issues in connection with so-called attractive nuisances. Certainly the structures which lure children into getting themselves injured on the property of others are attractive; the problem stems from the fact that the structures are often useful — like railroad trestles — and not true nuisances at all. The need to protect children (who are often highly creative at avoiding the protection), the cost of eliminating the dangers, and the general usefulness of the structure, in addition to the other factors involved, can lead to extremely involved calculations.

2. Public Employees: Firefighters and Police Officers

ROSA v. DUNKIN' DONUTS OF PASSAIC
Supreme Court of New Jersey, 1991
583 A.2d 1129

GARIBALDI, J.

[In a 1960 case] we adopted the fireman's rule that "the owner or occupier is not liable to a paid fireman for negligence with respect to the creation of a fire." In [1960], we extended the rule to police officers.

This appeal concerns the scope of the immunity granted by the fireman's rule. The issue [here] is: does the fireman's rule bar liability only where the injuries arise from an ordinary act of negligence that is the reason for the firefighter or police officer being on the premises, or does it likewise bar liability where the injuries arise from an ordinary act of negligence that firefighters and police in the normal course of their duties should expect to meet?

I

The facts are essentially undisputed. While on duty, plaintiff, Jose Rosa, a police officer in Passaic, responded to a call for emergency medical assistance for a sick employee at defendants' Dunkin' Donuts store in Passaic. On arriving at the store Officer Rosa found an unconscious employee. While he was carrying the unconscious employee on a stretcher to the police ambulance, Officer Rosa's left foot slipped on a white powdery substance (presumably confectioner's sugar or flour) on the kitchen floor of the donut shop. Officer Rosa recalls no conscious recognition of the powder's presence before his fall; however, there is no indication or insinuation that it was not present when he arrived at the scene.

Officer Rosa received unspecified injuries as a result of slipping while transporting the sick employee to the ambulance. His injuries form the basis of a workers' compensation claim. His injuries also form the basis of this lawsuit.

On July 21, 1984, Officer Rosa filed a lawsuit based on these unspecified injuries against defendants Dunkin' Donuts of Passaic and Carmel Aditya, the owner of the franchise. He alleged that the defendants had caused him to slip and fall by negligently allowing the white powdery substance to remain scattered on the kitchen floor, thereby creating a slippery floor. He contended that the white powdery substance on the floor created a foreseeable risk of avoidable future harm. His contention forms a classic, ordinary negligence claim.

    . . . .

In our view Rosa's fall was a risk inherent in the situation to which he responded (a rescue in the kitchen of a doughnut shop) and recovery was therein precluded under the "Fireman Rule."

II

The fireman's rule is followed throughout the country. . . .

In adopting the rule, we eschewed the technical formalistic classifications used to define varying duties of care landowners owe to trespassers, licensees, or invitees. We recognized that the officer's "status being *sui generis*, justice is not aided by appending an inappropriate label and then visiting consequences which flow from a status artificially imputed." *Krauth v. Geller, supra*, 31 N.J. [270,] 273, 157 A.2d 129 [1960].

In *Krauth*, Chief Justice Weintraub set forth the policy underlying the fireman's rule:

> The rationale of the prevailing rule is sometimes stated in terms of "assumption of risk" used doubtless in the so-called "primary" sense of the term and meaning that the defendant did not breach a duty owed, rather than that the fireman was guilty of contributory fault in responding to his public duty. Stated affirmatively, what is meant is that it is the fireman's business to deal with that very hazard and hence, perhaps by analogy to the contractor engaged as an expert to remedy dangerous situations, he cannot complain of negligence in the creation of the very occasion for his engagement. In terms of duty, it may be said there is none owed the fireman to exercise care so as not to require the special services for which he is trained and paid. Probably most fires are attributable to negligence and in the final analysis the policy decision is that it would be too burdensome to charge all who carelessly cause or fail to prevent fires with the injuries suffered by the expert retained with public funds to deal with those inevitable, although negligently created, occurrences. Hence, for that risk, the fireman should receive appropriate compensation from the public he serves, both in pay which reflects the hazard and in workmen's

compensation benefits for the consequences of the inherent risks of the calling. [31 N.J. at 273-74, 157 A.2d 129 (citations omitted).]

We continue to recognize the fundamental fairness of the *Krauth* public-policy rationale that supports the fireman's rule. In *Berko v. Freda, supra,* we held that the rule barred a police officer's suit against a car owner who negligently left keys in his car for the injuries inflicted on the officer by the youth who stole the car. In *Berko,* we stated:

> We perceive more than mere dollars-and-cents considerations underpinning the fundamental justice of the "fireman's rule." There is at work here a public policy component that strongly opposes the notion that an act of ordinary negligence should expose the actor to liability for injuries sustained in the course of a public servant's performance of necessary, albeit hazardous, public duties. In the absence of a legislative expression of contrary policy, a citizen should not have to run the risk of a civil judgment against him for negligent acts that occasion the presence of a firefighter at the scene of a carelessly-set fire or of a police officer at a disturbance or unlawful incident resulting from negligent conduct. [*Id.* at 88-89, 459 A.2d 663].

. . . .

The policies underlying the fireman's rule are simple, straightforward ones. The accidents and emergencies occasioning the presence of firefighters and police officers are a sad fact of life not soon to be eliminated. They are, however, also the very reason for the existence of the public forces of the "finest" and the "bravest." . . . A taxpayer who pays the fire and police departments to confront the risks should not have to pay again.

More significant, however, is the realization that the very nature of the profession that the officers have chosen embodies risks that the emergencies to which they will respond will neither be conveniently timed nor situated for rescuer, victim, or property-owner — they have assumed (and been trained to handle) those risks. Those professionals, whether firefighters or police officers, are charged with responding to a situation and effecting a rescue. They must measure the "situation" in the totality of the circumstances present at the scene. . . . It contravenes good sense and good policy to hold property owners liable to prepare for such unexpected arrivals.

> Ordinarily a firefighter or police officer is summoned in circumstances of emergency where the landowner has not had time to prepare the premises for his arrival. . . . A firefighter responding to such an emergency call has no reasonable expectation that the property has been made safe for his arrival. One engaged in this occupation does not determine whether to respond based on weather conditions. This is because a firefighter is likely to enter at unforeseeable times under emergent circumstances. In other words weather is one of the "inherent risks of (this) calling." [*Maryland Casualty Co. v. Heiot, supra,* 224 N.J. Super, at 444-45, 540 A.2d 920.]

The noted commentator Dean Prosser stated:

the most legitimate basis for [the firemen's rule] lies in the fact that firemen and policemen are likely to enter at unforeseeable times, upon unusual parts of the premises, and under circumstances of emergency where care in looking after the premises and in preparation for the visit, cannot reasonably be looked for. [W. Keeton, D. Dobbs, R. Keeton, D. Owen, Prosser and Keeton on the Law of Torts, § 61 at 431 (5th ed. 1984)].

We agree. Firefighters and police officers must be held to assume the risks that are to be expected in encountering the hazards and risks of their job. They are risks inherent and incidental to the performance of the duties of a firefighter and police officer. Such risks properly include an ordinary act of negligence that an officer may encounter at the scene of the incident. To hold otherwise creates artificial distinctions between the negligence that occasioned one's presence and the negligence defining the scene at which one arrives (and with which one has been commissioned and empowered to deal). Such distinctions serve neither the rationale underlying the public-policy considerations for the fireman's rule nor the assumption of risk.

The policy rationale underlying the fireman's rule fully supports its application in this case. The conditions and responsibilities that Officer Rosa faced when he entered Dunkin' Donuts were those of a type inherent in the performance of his duties. Officer Rosa entered the kitchen to render medical assistance to an unconscious female employee. He is paid, trained, and expected to confront such emergencies and to remove those in peril.

His duty compelled him to traverse the area sprinkled with powder. He could not have fulfilled his duty without passing over the area in question. In carrying out that duty, the plaintiff must take the premises as he found them. Indeed, the unconscious woman could herself have knocked over the powder while falling. The intervening medical emergency could have disrupted normal cleaning procedures. Such conditions define one's role as a paid protector of the public. "Poor housekeeping is a hazard inherent or inevitable in firefighting," *Jackson v. Velveray Corp.*, 82 N.J. Super. 469, 480, 198 A.2d 115 (App. Div. 1964), or police work, whether it compounds the difficulty of extinguishing the flames or extricating the fallen.

. . . .

The fireman's rule still allows recovery in situations of willful or intentional misconduct traditionally outside of the cloak of the rule's immunity. As we stated clearly in *Mahoney v. Carus Chemical Co., supra*, 102 N.J. at 576, 510 A.2d 4, willful and wanton misconduct is an appropriate exception to most general rules of immunity. In the case of the fireman's rule it is perhaps most appropriate because according "immunity to one who deliberately and maliciously creates the hazard that injures the firemen or policemen stretches the policy underlying the fireman's rule beyond the logic and justifiable limits of its principle." *Id.* at 574, 510 A.2d at 4. By contrast, today's decision is well within the limits of that principle.

. . . .

Of course, the fireman's rule only applies to bar suit by a police officer or firefighter injured in the performance of his or her duty. It does not apply when the officer is acting as a normal citizen. . . .

In conclusion, we find that the policies and goals that bar a firefighter and police officer from recovering for injuries sustained from an ordinary act of negligence that occasioned the officer's presence on the premises are equally applicable to bar liability for injuries that arise from an act of ordinary negligence posing a hazard that is incidental to and inherent in the performance of the officer's duties. Such a rule would bar recovery to an injured firefighter who slipped on icy steps while responding to an emergency medical call from the owner of the premises; to an injured police officer who slipped into a hole in the owner's yard while investigating a burglar alarm at the home; to an injured police officer who, while checking the rear doors of a building, fell down a stairway because the handrail was too wide; to a police officer who was injured when he fell on ice in the early morning hours while investigating the presence of a suspicious car in the shopping center's parking lot. All those injuries arose out of the officer's normal performance of his duties. The relationship among the injuries, their causes, and the officers' duties is neither attenuated nor artificial. The officers in those cases came to the scene to inspect the area or to carry out the injured. Their injuries arose out of their inspections or out of passing over the very area providing access to and exit for the injured person.

Similarly, when a police officer responds to a medical emergency, he or she must anticipate attending to the victim, removing the victim from the present location, and facilitating the victim's transportation to the hospital. Lifting a stretcher under less-than-ideal conditions is not unfathomable. Indeed, it is so likely as to be considered an inherent part of the performance of the officer's rescue duty.

Accordingly, the judgment of the Appellate Division is affirmed.

HANDLER, J., filed a separate dissenting opinion.

HANDLER, J., dissenting.

. . . .

I strongly believe we should abrogate the fireman's rule. The rule, as currently formulated, is obtuse and abstruse. It needlessly extends an immunity that has a dubious value. We have, except in the face of the most compelling countervailing reasons, eliminated and restricted common-law immunities.

. . . .

For affirmance — CHIEF JUSTICE WILENTZ and JUSTICES CLIFFORD, POLLOCK, O'HERN, GARIBALDI and STEIN — 6.

For reversal — JUSTICE HANDLER — 1.

---

1. Why do the courts not adopt a reasonableness approach to the problems presented by firefighters and police officers? Under such an approach, the firefighter could sue the landowner if the hazard were not one within the reasonable contemplation of a firefighter under the circumstances. If the hazard were not within the contemplation of the firefighter, the firefighter would be under no

obligation to protect him or herself from that hazard, and the landowner should be liable. Would such an approach fit the spirit of *Rowland*?

2. To what additional professions should the "firefighter's rule" apply? Should the rule apply only to professionals who are entering on the land to benefit the landowner? What about police officers executing a search warrant against the landowner, who are injured by a condition on the property while doing so? What if the police officer in *Rosa* had slipped on the sugar while arresting the owner of the Dunkin' Donuts?

It is clear that the firefighter's rule is not as uniformly applied as the *Rosa* majority thought. Indeed, New Jersey abrogated the *Rosa* result by statute, as follows:

> In addition to any other right of action or recovery otherwise available under law, whenever any law enforcement officer, firefighter, or member of a duly incorporated first aid, emergency, ambulance or rescue squad association suffers any injury, disease or death while in the lawful discharged of his official duties and that injury, disease or death is directly or indirectly the result of the neglect, willful omission, or willful or culpable conduct of any person or entity, other that that law enforcement officer, firefighter or first aid, emergency, ambulance or rescue squad member's employer or co-employee, the law enforcement officer, firefighter, or first aid emergency, ambulance or rescue squad member suffering that injury or disease, or, in the case of death, a representative of that law enforcement officer, firefighter or first aid, emergency, ambulance or rescue squad member's estate, may seek recovery and damages from the person or entity whose neglect, willful omission, or willful or culpable conduct resulted in that injury, disease for death.

N.J. Stat. § 2A:62A-21 (1993).

PROBLEM

The fire department receives an alarm from TLC Pet Stores, Inc., and proceeds to the site. Seeing smoke pouring from the shop, the firefighters appropriately use their axes and enter the shop. M, a firefighter, is injured by a Rottweiler, which is one of the dogs for sale in the shop. What result if M sues the shop owner?

Same facts as above, except that there is no visible smoke coming from the shop, and upon entering the shop, the firefighters discover that there is no fire, and that the fire alarm went off because of a short circuit caused by the electric company. What result?

What if the shop were an electronics store, and the dog that injured the firefighter were a guard dog stationed in the store by the owner? Would this change your analysis?

3. Landlords and Tenants

McCUTCHEON v. UNITED HOMES CORP.
Supreme Court of Washington, 1971 (en banc)
486 P.2d 1093

STAFFORD, ASSOCIATE JUSTICE.

The two cases involved herein were considered separately by the trial court. Since the issues presented are identical, they have been consolidated on appeal.

Plaintiff Norma McCutcheon, a tenant of defendant United Homes Corporation, was injured one evening when she fell down an unlighted flight of stairs leading from her apartment. She alleged the defendant was negligent because the lights at the top and bottom of the stairwell were not operative.

Plaintiff Douglas R. Fuller, also defendant's tenant, was injured as he descended the outside stairs of his apartment on his way to work. A step pulled loose causing him to fall. He, too, alleged negligence on the part of defendant.

Defendant's answer alleged each plaintiff had executed a form "Month to Month Rental Agreement" which contained the following exculpatory clause:

> neither the Lessor, nor his Agent, shall be liable for any injury to Lessee, his family, guests or employees or any other person entering the premises or the building of which the demised premises are a part.

In each case the trial court granted a summary judgment of dismissal.

The question is one of first impression. The issue is whether the lessor of a residential unit within a multi-family dwelling complex may exculpate itself from liability for personal injuries sustained by a tenant, which injuries result from the lessor's own negligence in maintenance of the approaches, common passageways, stairways and other areas under the lessor's dominion and control, but available for the tenants' use. (Hereinafter called the "common areas".)

Basic to the entire discussion is the common law rule that one who leases a portion of his premises but retains control over the approaches, common passageways, stairways and other areas to be used in common by the owner and tenants, has a duty to use reasonable care to keep them in safe condition for use of the tenant in his enjoyment of the demised premises. The landlord is required to do more than passively refrain from negligent acts. He has a duty of affirmative conduct, an affirmative obligation to exercise reasonable care to inspect and repair the previously mentioned portions of the premises for protection of the lessee.

It is readily apparent that the exculpatory clause was inserted in defendant's form "Month to Month Rental Agreement" to bar its tenants from asserting actions for personal injuries sustained through the landlord's own negligence. It was adopted to negative the result of the lessor's failure to comply with its affirmative duty to the tenants.

The defendant asserts that a lessor may contract, in a rental agreement, to exculpate itself from liability to its lessee, for personal injuries caused by lessor's own negligence. It contends such exculpatory clauses are not contrary to public policy because the landlord-tenant relationship *is not a matter of public interest, but relates exclusively to the private affairs of the parties concerned and that the two parties stand upon equal terms. Thus, there should be full freedom to contract.*

. . . .

The importance of "freedom of contract" is clear enough. However, the use of such an argument for avoiding the affirmative duty of a landlord to its residential tenant is no longer compelling in light of today's multi-family dwelling complex wherein a tenant merely rents some space with appurtenant rights to make it more usable or livable. Under modern circumstances the tenant is almost wholly dependent upon the landlord to provide reasonably for his safe use of the "common areas" beyond the four walls demised to him.

As early as 1938 Williston recognized that while such exculpatory clauses were recognized as "legal," many courts had shown a reluctance to enforce them. Even then, courts were disposed to interpret them strictly so they would not be effective to discharge liability for the consequences of negligence in making or failing to make repairs.

. . . .

The key to our problem is found in Restatement of Contracts § 574, p. 1079 (1932) which reads:

A bargain for exemption from liability for the consequences of negligence *not falling greatly below the standard established by law* for the protection of others against unreasonable risk of harm, is legal. . . .

(Italics ours.) In other words, such an exculpatory clause may be legal, when considered in the abstract. However, when applied to a specific situation, one may be exempt from liability for his own negligence *only when the consequences thereof do not fall greatly below the standard established by law.*

In the landlord-tenant relationship it is extremely meaningful to require that a landlord's attempt to exculpate itself, from liability for the result of its own negligence, *not fall greatly below the standard of negligence set by law.* As indicated earlier, a residential tenant who lives in a modern multi-family dwelling complex is almost wholly dependent upon the landlord for the reasonably safe condition of the "common areas." However, a clause which exculpates the lessor from liability to its lessee, for personal injuries caused by lessor's own acts of negligence, not only lowers the standard imposed by the common law, it effectively *destroys* the landlord's affirmative obligation or duty to keep or maintain the "common areas" in a reasonably safe condition for the tenant's use.

When a lessor is no longer liable for the failure to observe standards of affirmative conduct, or for *any* conduct amounting to negligence, by virtue of an exculpatory clause in a lease, *the standard ceases to exist.* In short, such a clause *destroys* the concept of negligence in the landlord-tenant relationship. Neither the standard nor negligence can exist in abstraction.

. . . .

[W]e are not faced merely with the theoretical duty of construing a provision in an isolated contract specifically bargained for by *one landlord and one tenant* as a ["]purely private affair." Considered realistically, we are asked to construe an exculpatory clause, the generalized use of which may have an impact upon thousands of potential tenants.

Under these circumstances it cannot be said that such exculpatory clauses are "purely a private affair" or that they are "not a matter of public interest." The real question is whether we should sanction a technique of immunizing lessors of residential units within a multi-family dwelling complex, from liability for personal injuries sustained by a tenant, which injuries result from the lessor's own negligence in maintaining the "common areas"; particularly when the technique employed destroys the concept of negligence and the standard of affirmative duty imposed upon the landlord for protection of the tenant.

An exculpatory clause of the type here involved contravenes long established common law rules of tort liability that exist in the landlord-tenant relationship. As so employed, it offends the public policy of the state and will not be enforced by the courts. It makes little sense for us to insist, on the one hand, that a workman have a safe place in which to work, but, on the other hand, to deny him a reasonably safe place in which to live.

The trial court is reversed and the cause is remanded for trial.

HAMILTON, C.J., and FINLEY, ROSELLINI, HUNTER, HALE, NEILL, and WRIGHT, JJ., concur.

SHARPE, J., did not participate.

———————

1. Would the courts uphold a contract in which the tenant agrees to assume the obligation of taking care of the common area surrounding his or her unit in exchange for a lower rent?

2. What is a real estate broker's responsibility for injury to potential buyers? Should a contract between the broker and the putative seller placing responsibility on the seller for any injuries to prospective buyers be valid?

3. What should be the relationship of tort and contract in cases like these?

4. Crime

TACO BELL, INC. v. LANNON
Supreme Court of Colorado, 1987 (en banc)
744 P.2d 43

Lohr, Justice.

This is a negligence case arising from an incident in which the plaintiff, John P. Lannon, was injured by a shot fired by a robber when Lannon tried to leave the premises of the defendant, Taco Bell, Inc. (Taco Bell), during the course of a robbery. . . . The appellate court held that Taco Bell had a legal duty to take reasonable measures to protect its patrons from the consequences of criminal acts on the part of unknown third persons in this case, and further held that the issue of whether it breached that duty by failing to employ one or more armed security guards was properly submitted to the jury. We granted certiorari but limited our review to the issue of duty. We agree with the holdings of the court of appeals with respect to that issue and therefore affirm the judgment of that court.

I.

At approximately 10:30 p.m. on January 28, 1979, the plaintiff, John P. Lannon, entered a Taco Bell restaurant located on East Colfax Avenue in Denver. When the plaintiff approached the service counter, he noticed that the employees were off to one side of the counter and that a man was crouched behind the counter holding a handgun and going through a floor safe. The plaintiff deduced that a robbery was in progress. He then retreated toward the door, whereupon he encountered another robber apparently acting as a lookout for the robber behind the counter. The plaintiff brushed past the second robber and ran out the door into the Taco Bell parking lot. At that point, the robber behind the counter went toward the door and shot at the plaintiff, hitting him on the ring finger of his left hand. The plaintiff ran to a nearby laundromat and called the police. Police officers arrived within minutes but the robbers had already fled.

The plaintiff filed suit against Taco Bell in Denver District Court, alleging that Taco Bell had a duty to take adequate measures to protect him from the foreseeable criminal acts of third persons and that Taco Bell was negligent in failing to take such measures. The plaintiff also alleged that Taco Bell's negligence was the proximate cause of his injury. . . . Taco Bell later filed a motion to dismiss the plaintiff's claim, alleging that the plaintiff had failed to state a claim upon which relief could be granted because Taco Bell owed no legal duty to the plaintiff to protect him from the consequences of criminal acts on the part of third persons. The trial court denied Taco Bell's motion to dismiss, and the case proceeded to trial.

At trial, the plaintiff established, in addition to the facts previously set forth, that ten armed robberies had taken place at this same Taco Bell restaurant in the three years prior to the robbery giving rise to this case. One of these armed robberies had occurred only two nights before the robbery during which the plaintiff was injured. Furthermore, Detective William Martin of the Denver Police Department testified, on behalf of the plaintiff, that it was his opinion that this particular Taco Bell restaurant is located in a "high crime area." Detective Martin and two other Denver police officers called by the plaintiff also testified concerning security measures, including the use of security guards, that could be taken by this kind of restaurant to reduce the possibility of armed robberies. A management employee of a fast food restaurant also located on East Colfax Avenue testified on behalf of the plaintiff concerning that restaurant's practices with respect to hiring armed security guards.

Taco Bell moved for a directed verdict at the close of the plaintiff's case. Taco Bell based its motion on arguments that it had no duty, as a matter of law, to protect its customers from the consequences of criminal acts on the part of unknown third persons and that even if such a duty did exist, any failure on its part to employ armed security guards could not have been the proximate cause of the plaintiff's injuries. The trial court denied the motion.

Taco Bell called Richard Parson, an employee of the Taco Bell restaurant that had been robbed, as its sole witness. Parson testified concerning the robbery itself and the security measures that the restaurant took to discourage such robberies. At the conclusion of Parson's testimony, Taco Bell made a motion for a directed verdict which incorporated the arguments it had made on the earlier directed verdict motion. The plaintiff also moved for a directed verdict in his favor on the issue of Taco Bell's liability. The trial court denied both motions.

The trial court instructed the jury on negligence, including an instruction that the owner of premises has a duty to operate his business in a reasonably safe manner in view of the foreseeability, if any, of injury to others. The court specifically instructed the jury that the criminal act of a third party that causes injuries to the plaintiff does not relieve the defendant of liability if the act of the third party is reasonably and generally foreseeable. No specific instruction was given relating to the use of armed guards.

The jury returned a verdict in the plaintiff's favor, awarding him $40,000 in damages. Taco Bell appealed. . . .

As relevant to the issues before us on certiorari review, the court [of appeals] first held that the evidence established a duty on the part of the defendant to take "reasonable measures to prevent or deter reasonably foreseeable acts, and to alleviate known dangerous conditions" — specifically, the risks associated with armed robberies. Second, the court held that it was for the jury to decide whether the defendant had breached its duty by failing to employ armed, uniformed security guards. Additionally, the court rejected the defendant's argument that proximate cause was not established because the criminal acts of the robbers were not foreseeable. The court held that this view of foreseeability was too restrictive and that the evidence that the restaurant was located in a high crime area and that previous armed robberies had occurred on the premises and at other nearby establishments was sufficient to present a jury question as to foreseeability. . . .

Both parties petitioned this court for a writ of certiorari. We denied the plaintiff's petition but, based on the defendant's petition, we granted certiorari on the issue of "[w]hether a fast food restaurant in a 'high crime area' has a legal duty to take security measures, possibly including the use of armed guards, to protect its patrons from the consequences of criminal acts on the part of unknown third persons." We turn now to the resolution of that issue.

II.

A.

"The question of whether a defendant owes a plaintiff a duty to act to avoid injury is a question of law to be determined by the court." . . .

On a few occasions, this court has considered the duty that owners or occupiers of land owe to those who enter on their premises. In *Safeway Stores, Inc. v. Smith*, 658 P.2d 255 (Colo. 1983), a case in which the plaintiff had slipped and fallen in the defendant's grocery store, we held that "[a] store operator has a duty to his customers to use ordinary care to keep the floors used by them in a reasonably safe condition." *Id.* at 256. More generally, we also stated that a "proprietor is guilty of negligence only if he fails to use reasonable care under the circumstances to discover the foreseeable dangerous condition and to correct it or to warn customers of its existence." *Id.* at 258.

In *Mile High Fence Co. v. Radovich*, 175 Colo. 537, 489 P.2d 308 (1971), a case in which the plaintiff had stepped in a posthole located on the defendant's property, we held that foreseeability, rather than the status of the plaintiff as a trespasser, licensee, or invitee, is the primary factor in determining whether an owner or occupier of land owes a duty to persons who enter on the premises. *Id.* at 547-48, 489 P.2d at 314. "[I]t is the *foreseeability* of harm from the failure by the possessor to carry on his activities with reasonable care for the safety of the entrants which determines liability." *Id.* at 547, 489 P.2d at 314 (emphasis in original). "[T]he occupant, in the management of his property, should act as a reasonable man in view of the probability or foreseeability of injury to others." *Id.* at 548, 489 P.2d at 314.

Together, *Safeway* and *Mile High Fence* stand for the proposition that owners or occupiers of land have a duty to exercise reasonable and ordinary care to make their premises safe for those who may enter upon them. However, this court has never decided whether this duty encompasses taking reasonable measures to protect business patrons from injuries caused by the criminal acts of unknown third persons.

Other courts that have considered this issue have almost uniformly held that while owners or occupiers of land held open for business purposes are not insurers of their customers' safety, a duty arises on the part of the owner or occupier to take reasonable measures to protect customers from injuries caused by the criminal acts of unknown third persons when such acts are generally foreseeable.

The Restatement (Second) of Torts § 344 (1965) also recognizes that an owner or occupier of property has a duty to protect customers from injury caused by criminal conduct in such circumstances. Section 344 provides:

Business Premises Open to Public: Acts of Third Persons or Animals

A possessor of land who holds it open to the public for entry for his business purposes is subject to liability to members of the public while they are upon the land for such a purpose, for physical harm caused by the accidental, negligent, or intentionally harmful acts of third persons or animals, and by the failure of the possessor to exercise reasonable care to

(a) discover that such acts are being done or are likely to be done, or

(b) give a warning adequate to enable the visitors to avoid the harm, or otherwise to protect them against it.

Comment f to section 344 makes clear that the existence of this duty depends, to a great extent, on the foreseeability of criminal conduct by third persons.

Duty to police premises. Since the possessor is not an insurer of the visitor's safety, he is ordinarily under no duty to exercise any care until he knows or has reason to know that the acts of the third person are occurring, or are about to occur. He may, however, know or have reason to know, from past experience, that there is a likelihood of conduct on the part of third persons in general which is likely to endanger the safety of the visitor, even though he has no reason to expect it on the part of any particular individual. If the place or character of his business, or his past experience, is such that he should reasonably anticipate careless or criminal conduct on the part of third persons, either generally or at some particular time, he *may* be under a duty to take precautions against it, and to provide a reasonably sufficient number of servants to afford a reasonable protection.

(Emphasis added.) We agree with the statement of the law contained in section 344 and comment f.

Turning to the facts of the present case, we conclude that the evidence of ten armed robberies at this particular Taco Bell restaurant in the three years prior to the incident at issue in this case sufficiently established that harm to customers as the result of criminal acts by third persons was foreseeable by Taco Bell.

Taco Bell argues, however, that the plaintiff's injury was not foreseeable since armed robberies of the type involved in this case occur randomly and without notice of the specific time and the specific manner in which they will take place. We reject this argument. The concept of foreseeability is simply not so limited. To establish that an incident is foreseeable, it is not necessary that an owner or occupier of land held open for business purposes be able to ascertain precisely when or how an incident will occur. Rather, foreseeability "includes whatever is likely enough in the setting of modern life that a reasonably thoughtful person would take account of it in guiding practical conduct." 3 F. Harper, F. James, & O. Gray, The Law of Torts § 18.2, at 658-59 (2d ed. 1986) (cited herein as "3 F. Harper"). The fact that ten armed robberies had occurred at the Taco Bell restaurant in a period of three years would certainly put a reasonable person on notice that such robberies would be likely to occur in the future and that the consequences of those robberies should be considered in determining how the restaurant should be run.

Taco Bell also argues that the plaintiff's injury was not foreseeable because none of the previous armed robberies at the restaurant had resulted in injury to any customer. This argument cannot withstand scrutiny. Simply because something has not yet happened does not mean that its happening is not foreseeable. Instead, foreseeability is based on common sense perceptions of the risks created by various conditions and circumstances. *See* Restatement (Second) of Torts § 289 (1965). We have little difficulty in concluding that armed robberies present a significant risk of injury to persons unfortunate enough to be present when one occurs. Therefore, the plaintiff's injury was foreseeable despite the absence of injuries from the previous armed robberies that had occurred at this particular Taco Bell restaurant.

We are satisfied that the risk of injury to the plaintiff was foreseeable in the present case. However, as noted earlier, foreseeability alone does not establish the existence of a duty. There are other considerations that we believe are relevant in helping to determine whether a duty arose in this case.

Armed robberies present a substantial degree of risk to the public. No evidence was presented in this case concerning the frequency of injuries to patrons resulting from armed robberies on business premises. However, we are persuaded that whatever the likelihood of armed robberies at this restaurant and of injuries resulting from those armed robberies may be, the gravity of the possible harm to patrons from such robberies is substantial. "As the gravity of the possible harm increases, the apparent likelihood of its occurrence need be correspondingly less to generate a duty of precaution." W. Keeton, § 31, at 171. *Accord* 3 F. Harper, § 16.2, at 471.

We also do not believe that imposition of a duty to take reasonable measures to protect patrons from the consequences of criminal acts on the part of unknown third persons would place an onerous burden on either Taco Bell or the community. . . .

Furthermore, we believe that it is equitable that the cost of taking reasonable measures to protect patrons from criminal activity be borne by the owner, operator, and, indirectly, the customers of the restaurant. As stated by the California Court of Appeals in *Cohen:*

> It is also not unfair that patrons pay a few cents more for items they purchase from such a store and gain the assurance of reasonable protection against criminal activity by shopping there, rather than allow the emotional and physical burden of a criminal attack to fall on the store patron who inadvertently finds himself or herself in the middle of a robbery invited by the store's failure to employ minimal crime deterrence measures.

Cohen, 703 Cal. Rptr. at 579. *See generally,* 3 F. Harper, § 16.9, at 475-80 (where cost of precautions is relatively low, social utility of not taking precautions is usually outweighed by the risk involved).

Taking all of these factors into consideration, we conclude that the court of appeals was correct in holding that Taco Bell had a legal duty, under the circumstances of this case, to take reasonable measures to protect its customers from the consequences of criminal acts on the part of unknown third persons.

. . . .

III.

In summary, we conclude that Taco Bell had a legal duty in this case to take reasonable measures to protect its patrons from the consequences of criminal acts on the part of unknown third persons. We further conclude that it was for the jury to decide whether Taco Bell breached its duty by failing to provide one or more armed security guards.

The judgment of the court of appeals is affirmed.

ERICKSON, J., dissents.

ROVIRA and VOLLACK, JJ., join in the dissent.

----

1. The court in *Taco Bell* follows those cases which reject classification of the cast of characters. It also departs from the old rule that intervening criminal acts are inherently unforeseeable, preferring to view the entire case from the perspective of foreseeability. What impact might such a decision have on the question of whether the plaintiff was negligent in entering a restaurant which the plaintiff knows to be subject to a high risk of crime? Is this the kind of argument a place of business would make?

2. What if the restaurant hired armed guards, and a customer were injured by a guard in the course of a robbery? What if the presence of armed guards caused gunfire at a robbery to be more likely to occur than if no armed guards were present?

3. How far should the obligation of a business to protect its patrons extend? What are the obligations of a bank towards patrons of its twenty-four hour ATM machine?

5. Business Establishments and Danger to the Public

F.W. WOOLWORTH v. KIRBY
Supreme Court of Alabama, 1974
302 So. 2d 67

HEFLIN, CHIEF JUSTICE.

Defendant, F.W. Woolworth Company, appeals from a judgment rendered against it in a personal injury action.

As a promotional scheme, the appellant-defendant's Woolco store on University Drive in Huntsville, Alabama, planned a ping-pong ball drop. The idea was to drop balls from a passing airplane into the back parking lot of the store, each ball containing a certificate entitling the finder to a prize. Prizes ranged from a color television and a stereo set to ice cream cones. The ping-pong ball drop was held on the morning of November 17, 1971, in conjunction with a sale at the store, and as the result of extensive advertising — some nine full-page ads in the Huntsville Times and 200 thirty-second radio spots advertising the sale and promotional activities — there were, in the estimation of the manager, some 4,500 people in the back parking lot (300' [by] 350') at 9:00 o'clock that morning to catch the ping-pong balls.

Mr. Dall Shady, a Huntsville pilot with 30 years' experience, contracted with appellant (defendant) to drop the balls. Shady had a television camera installed in the airplane so he could see what was directly under him, and then made practice drops. Just before the actual drops he passed over the parking lot and dropped toilet paper to check the wind. Pilot Shady told the defendant he could not control where the balls would fall, so Woolco should put some employees on the buildings to get those balls that might fall there. Woolco did station employees on the buildings to catch balls and throw them to the crowd in the parking lot.

Plaintiff, Mrs. Lona Pearl Kirby, 70 years old at the time, having heard and seen the sale advertising, went to the store that morning with other people, including her small grandson. Evidence indicates that, finding the door of the store locked, she took her grandson toward the rear parking lot to watch the airplane, which was then coming over at 1,000 feet to make the third drop. (There were 768 balls dropped — approximately ⅓ on each of three passes.) Mrs. Kirby took several steps into the parking lot and, within a very short time after arrival, the ping-pong balls began falling around her. The crowd came after the balls. Someone in the crowd knocked her down and some members of the crowd ran over her. She was carried by ambulance to a hospital and treated for injuries, the most serious being a broken right hip.

There was testimony from a former employee of Woolco that he watched the drop from the top of the building and that he saw a man "on the ground after the second drop," and perhaps "knocked down." Another witness testified that on the third drop she was knocked down and stepped on, suffering a slightly injured ankle. Evidence indicated that during all three drops the crowd would run, or hurry around chasing the falling balls, watching them shift direction with the wind.

Mrs. Kirby sued the defendant, alleging negligent acts causing her injuries. The jury gave a verdict for $52,500.00. The trial court ordered a remittitur of $17,500.00, reducing the judgment to $35,000.00.

This case arose and was tried before the implementation of the new Alabama Rules of Civil Procedure.

The plaintiff's amended complaint alleged, among other things, three negligent acts, in the alternative, and that "as a proximate consequence of the negligent act or acts, the mob of people in the said back parking lot in their effort to catch the balls ran into the Plaintiff knocking her down and trampling her" and causing injuries. The alternative averments of negligent acts were that "at said time and place Defendant, F.W. Woolworth Company, (1) negligently failed to police or control the crowd that said Defendant had amassed at said time and place or (2) the said Defendant negligently dropped balls in close proximity to and around the Plaintiff or (3) negligently had an independent contractor to drop balls which balls fell in close proximity to and around the Plaintiff."

The defendant contends that the trial court erred in refusing its written request for the affirmative charge and in overruling its demurrers to the complaint as last amended. These contentions relate to all three alternative allegations and involve the question of the duty owed on the part of the defendant to the plaintiff. This raises a case of first impression in this state concerning the liability of a proprietor for injury to a customer or patron caused by other patrons through pushing, shoving or crowding during a promotional activity.

In 62 Am. Jur. 2d Premises Liability § 201 the following appears:

> ". . . [I]n accord with the concept of foreseeability, a duty to prevent the crowding of a business establishment may arise in those situations where the proprietor can foresee that a customer may suffer injuries through the pressure of the crowd, and a storekeeper will be held liable if he has failed to exercise ordinary care to protect a customer from the actions of a crowd which he should have foreseen or anticipated, and the customer is injured by the pushing, crowding, or jostling of other persons. Specifically, a storekeeper will be liable for injuries to a customer where he carries on a promotional activity which foreseeably will cause crowds to gather and push, notwithstanding a disorder in the crowd contributed to the injuries.

> "In regard to children and elderly persons who may be injured by being pushed by others while visiting a business establishment, the proprietor's duty of care requires the taking of precautions commensurate with the increased likelihood of injury to persons in those classes."

The closest case to the present factual situation that this court has been able to locate is *Hicks v. M.H.A. Inc.*, 107 Ga. App. 290, 129 S.E.2d 817 (1963). This case involved an action against owners of a shopping center for injuries sustained by a patron who was knocked down by a crowd trying to get paper plates (redeemable for merchandise) which were being dropped onto a parking lot from an airplane. The Georgia Court of Appeals held that foreseeability of the conduct of a crowd competing for "merchandise prizes" dropped from an airplane was for jury solution and that actual notice by the defendants of the danger to the particular plaintiff need not be alleged.

In *Lee v. National League Baseball Club of Milwaukee Inc.*, 4 Wis. 2d 168, 89 N.W.2d 811 (1958), a jury verdict was upheld where the plaintiff was injured when pushed off her chair and trampled upon by other spectators who were attempting to recover a foul ball which had landed in front of her chair. The Supreme Court of Wisconsin, in an action against the baseball club, stated:

> "It has generally been held that one who invites the public to a public amusement place operated by him is liable for injury sustained by an invitee as a result of acts of third persons, if such operator has not taken reasonable and appropriate measures to restrict the conduct of such third parties, of which he should have been aware and should have realized was dangerous."

In Lane v. Fair Stores, Inc., 150 Tex. 566, 243 S.W.2d 683 (1951), a complaint was held sufficient which alleged that the defendant took no steps to police a crowd that had gathered at a store in response to advertising that ladies' hose would be given to the first 300 patrons on a particular morning where the plaintiff was injured when pushed by the crowd against the door and a glass showcase.

. . . .

Restatement, Second, Torts § 302 is as follows:

"§ 302. Risk of Direct or Indirect Harm

A negligent act or omission may be one which involves an unreasonable risk of harm to another through either

(a) the continuous operation of a force started or continued by the act or omission, or

(b) *the foreseeable action of the* other, *a third person*, an animal, or a force of nature." (Emphasis supplied)

Section 302 A of Restatement, Second, Torts recites:

"§ 302 A. Risk of Negligence or Recklessness of Others

An act or an omission may be negligent if the actor realizes or should realize that it involves an unreasonable risk of harm to another through the negligent or reckless conduct of the other or a third person."

In the case at hand the question arises as to whether or not the defendant should have foreseen or realized the probability of injury to the plaintiff or to a person similarly situated. Certainly it would be within the jury's province to determine that the defendant should have foreseen or realized that the crowd would run in unpredictable paths as the ping-pong balls were blown about with each gust of wind; that the crowd would push and shove in order to catch a ball and win a prize; and that dangerous conditions could develop for individuals in the crowd, including the elderly and children. Further the jury in this case had the right to determine that reasonable care under the circumstances required the defendant to take steps pertaining to the plaintiff and other persons similarly situated, including, but not limited to, giving warnings of the dangers involved, taking steps to control or police the crowd with supervisory personnel, and using loud speakers to warn the crowd not to run over people and to warn the elderly or children to stay out of the crowd.

. . . .

This court holds that when a proprietor or storekeeper causes a crowd of people to assemble pursuant to a promotional activity, then that person owes a duty to exercise reasonable care commensurate with foreseeable danger or injury to protect those assembled from injuries resulting from the pressure, pushing, shoving, jostling or other activities of the crowd or individuals within the crowd; that the foreseeability of danger or injury under such circumstances is for jury determination; and that reasonable care commensurate with the foreseeability of danger or injury may require greater precautions when children or the elderly are present.

. . . .

MERRILL, HARWOOD, BLOODWORTH, MADDOX, MCCALL, FAULKNER and JONES, JJ., concur.

COLEMAN, J., recuses himself.

JONES, JUSTICE (concurring specially).

. . . .

---

1. In *Walt Disney World Co. v. Goode*, 501 So. 2d 622 (Fla. Dist. Ct. App. 1986), the court applied ordinary rules of negligence to the question of the defendant's liability for the death of a child who had fallen into a moat in the amusement park. The doctrine of attractive nuisance was ruled inapplicable because the child had been a business invitee and not a trespasser.

2. Does a shopping mall have a duty to protect patrons using its parking lots? What if the mall parking area is full, and the patrons must park some distance away from the mall? How far does the mall-owner's duty extend?

3. Should a pizza establishment that promises delivery of any pizza within half an hour be liable when its delivery persons become involved in car accidents while rushing pizzas to its patrons?

4. Is there a problem for a radio station that promises prizes to the eighth listener to call with the correct answer to a question if someone who has heard this announcement on his or her car radio is involved in an accident while rushing to a telephone (or attempting to call in on a cell phone)? At what point does the radio station (or other entity) become exempt from responsibility, even for foreseeable responses to their advertisements or offers?

C. DEFENSES AND PLAINTIFF'S CONDUCT

1. Comparative Negligence

MATHIS v. MASSACHUSETTS ELECTRIC CO.
Supreme Judicial Court of Massachusetts, Norfolk, 1991
565 N.E.2d 1180

Before LIACOS, C.J., and WILKINS, ABRAMS, LYNCH AND GREANEY, JJ.

LIACOS, CHIEF JUSTICE.

During the evening of June 23, 1983, the plaintiff, Brian Mathis, sixteen years and eight months old, and three of his friends were gathered in front of the house located directly across from Brian's home in Franklin. Brian crossed the street and, to impress his friends, began climbing a utility pole, jointly owned by defendants

Massachusetts Electric Company (MEC) and New England Telephone and Telegraph Company (NET). The pole was located on the property of the plaintiff's parents. It was supported by two guy wires, the upper one installed and owned by MEC, the lower one installed and owned by NET. As Brian climbed the pole, he came in contact with several telephone, cable television, and electrical wires which did not harm him. When Brian reached the top of the utility pole, he grabbed the primary electrical wire and received an electrical shock. Brian fell to the ground. He sustained severe injuries and burns.

In March, 1984, the plaintiff filed suit in Superior Court alleging that MEC's negligence caused his injuries. . . .

The case proceeded to trial before a jury. . . . The jury found that MEC violated its duty toward foreseeable child trespassers. The jury also found that the plaintiff was comparatively negligent. The jury determined that the plaintiff was 75% at fault, while MEC was 25% at fault. Thus, the plaintiff was barred, under the comparative negligence statute, G.L. c. 231, § 85 (1988 ed.), from recovering any damages from MEC. The jury found that NET was not negligent. Judgment for the defendants was entered on November 30, 1988. MEC's third-party complaint and NET's cross claims against MEC were dismissed.

The plaintiff filed a motion for a new trial, and a motion to amend the judgment and for a new trial to assess damages. The judge denied both motions. The plaintiff appeals. He argues that (1) the lower court erred by denying his motion to amend the judgment and for a new trial on damages because the comparative negligence statute, G.L. c. 231, § 85, is inapplicable to an action brought under the child trespasser statute, G.L. c. 231, § 85Q[.]

1. *Comparative negligence.* The plaintiff claims that landowners who violate the child trespasser statute are strictly liable and therefore cannot avail themselves of the principle of comparative negligence. The child trespasser statute states:

. . . .

> "Any person who maintains an artificial condition upon his own land shall be liable for physical harm to children trespassing thereon if (a) the place where the condition exists *is one upon which the land owner knows or has reason to know* that children are likely to trespass, (b) the condition is one of which *the land owner knows or has reason to know and which he realizes or should realize will involve an unreasonable risk of death or serious bodily harm* to such children, (c) the children because of their youth do not discover the condition or realize the risk involved in intermeddling with it or in coming within the area made dangerous by it, (d) the utility to the land owner of maintaining the condition and the burden of eliminating the danger are slight as compared with the risk to children involved, and (e) *the land owner fails to exercise reasonable care* to eliminate the danger or otherwise to protect the children" (emphasis supplied). G.L. c. 231, § 85Q (1988).[6]

---

[6] The language of § 85Q is virtually identical to the language of § 339 of the Restatement (Second) of Torts (1965). We have previously recognized that the scope of § 85Q and § 339 of the Restatement is

The plaintiff argues that once the five statutory conditions are met, the owners are strictly liable, and therefore negligence principles are inapplicable.

Neither the statute nor the common law doctrine of *Soule v. Massachusetts Elec. Co.*, 378 Mass. 177, 390 N.E.2d 716 (1979), imposes liability on landowners or others irrespective of their degree of fault or knowledge of the risk involved.

Under the traditional common law rule, a landowner did not have a duty toward a child trespasser, except to refrain from wanton and wilful conduct. The child trespasser statute softened the "Draconian" common law rule. By enacting the statute, the Legislature followed the national trend towards imposing on landowners a uniform standard of care regardless of the status of the injured party.[7]

The child trespasser statute and the common law impose on landowners a duty of reasonable care, a negligence standard of liability.

Since the child trespasser statute, G.L. c. 231, § 85Q, imposes on landowners a duty of reasonable care, and creates liability based on negligence principles, the comparative negligence defense is available to defendants. "[T]he policy of negligence liability presumes that people will, or at least should, take reasonable measures to protect themselves and others from harm. . . . However, if the injured person's unreasonable conduct also has been a cause of his injury, his conduct will be accounted for in apportioning liability for damages." *Correia v. Firestone Tire & Rubber Co., supra*, 388 Mass, at 354, 446 N.E.2d 1033.

The plaintiff argues that a finding by a jury that children, because of their youth, did not "discover the condition or realize the risk involved in intermeddling" with the artificial condition, G.L. c. 231, § 85Q (c), is irreconcilable with the doctrine of comparative negligence. The plaintiff also argues that, even if such a finding by a jury is not irreconcilable with the doctrine of comparative negligence, the jury's answers to the special verdict questions in this case were inconsistent. The jury found that "the plaintiff, Brian Mathis, because of his youth, fail[ed] to appreciate the risk and danger involved or lack[ed] the understanding to evaluate the peril involved in intermeddling with the subject pole and its attachments." The jury also found that the plaintiff was negligent, and that his negligence was a proximate cause of his injuries. The plaintiff asks us to order a new trial because the jury's answers were inconsistent, and because they cannot be harmonized.

The child trespasser statute addresses a landowner's duty toward a child

---

identical. Although, in our view, § 85Q is not applicable because the plaintiff's injuries did not occur in the defendants' "own land," and therefore the defendants are not "landowners" within the meaning of the statute, the parties have assumed throughout that § 85Q applies to utility poles. Since the parties have made this the "law of the case," we shall make the same assumption. We believe, however, that this case should be governed by common law principles and not by § 85Q. *See* Soule v. Massachusetts Elec. Co., *supra*, 378 Mass, at 182, 390 N.E.2d 716 ("we hold that there is a common law duty of reasonable care by a landowner or occupier to prevent harm to foreseeable child trespassers" [emphasis supplied]).

[7] In Mounsey v. Ellard, 363 Mass. 693, 707, 297 N.E.2d 43 (1973), this court held that landowners owed the same duty of reasonable care to all lawful entrants regardless whether they were considered invitees or licensees at common law. Prior to *Mounsey*, landowners owed invitees a duty of reasonable care, while they owed licensees a duty not to inflict wanton or wilful harm. [Citations.] The court has refused, however, to extend the reasonable care standard to cases involving adult trespassers who are not helplessly trapped. [Citations.]

trespasser. In a case brought under the statute, a landowner's duty of reasonable care toward a foreseeable child trespasser will be breached only if the five conditions of the statute are satisfied. "[I]f the child is fully aware of the condition, understands the risk which it carries, and is quite able to avoid it, he stands in no better position than an adult with similar knowledge and understanding. This is not merely a matter of contributory negligence or assumption of risk, but of lack of duty to the child" (footnotes omitted). W. Prosser & W. Keeton, Torts, [§ 59] at 408-409. It is only after the jury determine that the landowner breached his or her duty toward the child that the child's possible negligence is taken into account.

The plaintiff is correct when he argues that an owner's liability under the child trespasser statute and a child's possible contributory negligence are two separate issues. "The question of the child's contributory negligence is a separate problem that must be carefully distinguished from that of the land occupier's duty." 5 F. Harper, F. James & O. Gray, Torts § 27.5 n. 60 (1986). The fact that they are two separate issues, however, does not make them irreconcilable.

The possible negligence of a child is "judged by the standard of behavior expected from a child of like age, intelligence, and experience." *Mann v. Cook*, 346 Mass. 174, 178, 190 N.E.2d 676 (1963). It is not inconsistent, therefore, for a jury to find that the landowner unreasonably created a dangerous condition, the risks of which would not ordinarily be discovered by children, while at the same time finding that even though the plaintiff failed to realize the risk, he or she acted without the degree of care expected from a child of similar age, intelligence, and experience. We cannot, as the plaintiff urges us, impose a judicially-created rule which would immunize child trespassers from their own negligence. The judge did not err in denying the plaintiff's motion to amend the judgment and for a new trial.

Judgment affirmed.

1.　Comparative negligence doctrine is a modern version of contributory negligence. Under contributory negligence doctrine, a plaintiff who was at all negligent in looking after his or her safety would be barred from any recovery for injuries caused by defendant. Comparative negligence assigns a percentage of responsibility for injury to a negligent plaintiff rather than barring recovery altogether. This subject is covered in the chapter on defenses.

2.　What sort of activity by a plaintiff should constitute contributory or comparative negligence? What should be the nature of the obligation of an institution of higher learning to intoxicated alumni wandering around the campus on reunion weekend? To intoxicated gate-crashers at a reunion party? What role do you think that the plaintiff's intoxication should play in the analysis? Should a defendant landowner have an obligation to protect intoxicated plaintiffs from themselves? Should intoxication ever be a defense against a charge of contributory or comparative negligence?

2. Assumption of Risk

GREENWOOD v. LOWE CHEMICAL CO.
Court of Civil Appeals of Texas, Houston (14th Dist.), 1968
428 S.W.2d 358

BARRON, JUSTICE.

This suit was brought by Rebecca Greenwood under the Texas Death and Survival Statutes for damages resulting from the death of her husband, Charles F. Greenwood. Greenwood was a construction worker employed by a Richard Greenwood (no relation), who in turn had a contract to do certain work for the defendant, Lowe Chemical Company. On the day of the accident made the basis of this suit, Charles F. Greenwood was placing an aluminum ladder between a scrubbing tower and an open scrubbing pit or vat containing about 95% Hot water and 5% Acid and chemicals. The space was narrow between the tower and the pit, and deceased suddenly stepped backward causing one of his legs to enter the pit. He could not maintain his balance and he foundered and fell completely into the pit. He was critically burned and his death resulted some four days later.

The principal business of Lowe Chemical Company, appellee-defendant, was the manufacture and regeneration of chemicals and acid. In the manufacturing process appellee maintained on its premises, in the normal operation of its business, covered and uncovered concrete pits or vats containing various types of corrosive liquids. Appellee also maintained on its premises a complex device denominated a scrubber. In conjunction with the scrubber, and located approximately three to four feet from it, the appellee maintained two open concrete pits which were used to hold and circulate scrubber water back into the scrubber. These scrubber pits did not have a railing or cover and were completely open and exposed. The scrubber water solution was composed of approximately 95% water as well as certain amounts of corrosive chemicals. The exact temperature of the scrubber water was unknown but it was very hot, and on cold days the pits would emit steam. On January 19, 1965, the deceased, while working on the scrubber with a carpenter, Eddie Hergert, backed and fell into one of these scrubber pits.

Charles F. Greenwood, the deceased, was in the employ of an independent contractor doing work for Lowe Chemical Company. On the date of the accident contractor Greenwood and his employees, including decedent, had been working on appellee's premises for several months. All employees on appellee's premises had been warned of the dangers of the pits, and it was common knowledge that they contained hot water and harmful chemical liquids. Contractor Greenwood testified that both he and the decedent had warned other employees to be careful around the scrubber pits. Between the sidewall of the scrubber and the edge of the vats is about three or four feet, and one could narrowly walk between the scrubber and the vats. Work was proceeding on the north side of the scrubber, and Hergert, a co-worker, told the deceased just before the incident causing his death, to bring a section of a 16-foot extension ladder around to the south side of the scrubber. At the time Hergert had walked off about 20 feet away from the vat and had his back to the area where Charles F. Greenwood was working. The vat into which Greenwood inadvertently stepped and fell was between seven and eight feet square and about 30 to 36 inches deep; the sides were made of concrete, extending about six inches above the ground, and curved all the way around — the top of the curbing was rounded. The curbing on the vats was about five inches thick at the point where it extended above the ground. These vats were not covered over, and there was no fence or railing or any other type of protective device around them or near them. There was no paint on the curbing, no reflectors, and no signs to remind workmen of the danger involved. The surface area between the scrubber and the vat was concrete with a rough finish. The distance between the two vats was four feet. On the premises of appellee there were several other uncovered vats of a similar nature and type. Some of the vats were covered.

Appellant, Mrs. Greenwood, alleged that appellee failed to exercise care commensurate with the risk of harm and extent of injury likely to occur and that such was negligence; that appellee failed to place a fence or rail around the vat in question which would have been adequate to prevent the accident, and that appellee failed to roof-over the top of the vat with a cover which would have been adequate to prevent a person in the position of Charles F. Greenwood from falling into the vat. Appellant further alleged that each failure was negligence and a proximate cause of the accident and resulting death of decedent, Greenwood. Appellant alleged that the open vats checkerboarding the premises constituted exceedingly dangerous instrumentalities for workmen on the premises, and that the appellee had an affirmative duty to protect invitees and other such as Charles F. Greenwood from the extra-hazardous and dangerous conditions on the premises regardless of general knowledge of the dangers.

The appellee, Lowe Chemical Company, pleaded in its answer that the occupier of the land owed an invitee no duty to warn or protect invitees against dangers which were open and obvious, and it further pleaded that the condition was open and obvious to the decedent and invoked the defense of volenti non fit injuria. Contributory negligence and unavoidable accident were also pleaded by appellee. On a hearing appellee's motion for summary judgment was granted by the trial court on the basis of depositions and affidavit submitted to the court, and the trial court rendered judgment that appellant, Mrs. Greenwood, take nothing of defendant, Lowe Chemical Company. Mrs. Greenwood has properly perfected her appeal from the trial court's summary judgment.

It is clear to us that the maintenance of premises in such a manner as Lowe Chemical Company maintained its premises at the time of and prior to the sustaining of injuries and the death of Charles F. Greenwood is near the ultimate in danger to workmen on the property. Men were called upon to work around several unprotected vats of deadly hot water and lethal chemicals. The only protection the vats contained was a six-inch curb around each vat, which was probably a hindrance rather than a help. No handrails or guardrails or other protective devices were installed by appellee, and no reason for not installing them was shown. Any workman on the premises was required daily to be constantly alert, and every moment of his attention was required to guard against what to us appears to be sudden death or serious bodily injury. Such attention was hardly possible to a man with work on his mind. At any moment a failure to heed the dangers of the open pits might have spelled disaster. That was exactly what happened here and which had almost happened only a short time before on these identical premises.

It is undisputed that decedent was employed by Richard H. Greenwood, the contractor employed by appellee, and that the contractor was on appellee's premises to perform a contract with appellee. Accordingly, the contractor and his employee, the decedent, were invitees on the premises of appellee.

The law is clear that the occupier of land or premises is required to keep his land or premises in a reasonably safe condition for his invitees. But the cases hold that the landowner's duty is to protect his invitees from hidden dangers of which the landowner knows, or of which he should know in the exercise of ordinary care. The general rule is that if there are open and obvious dangers of which the invitees know, or of which they are charged with knowledge, then the occupier owes them "no duty" to warn or to protect the invitees. This is said to be so because there is "no duty" to warn a person of things he already knows, or of dangerous conditions or activities which are so open and obvious that as a matter of law he will be charged with knowledge and full appreciation thereof.

Based upon the undisputed facts, it is manifest that decedent knew generally of the location of the pits, knew generally that they were uncovered and unguarded, and he knew that they were filled with a hot, noxious liquid. It is not clear, however, whether decedent knew the deadly effect of a fall into one of the pits, though he knew it would be to some extent dangerous. He had been working on the premises for several months. These facts may be also applicable to the defense of volenti non fit injuria. The requirements of the latter defense were recently set out in J. & W. Corp. v. Ball, 414 S.W.2d 143, 146 (Tex. Sup.):

> "(1) the plaintiff has knowledge of facts constituting a dangerous condition or activity; (2) he knows the condition or activity is dangerous; (3) he appreciates the nature or extent of the danger; and (4) he voluntarily exposes himself to this danger."

The final element is not necessary in "no duty" cases because if there is no duty owed to the plaintiff, he cannot create a duty by voluntarily exposing himself to a known and appreciated risk.

But the rules and authorities above cited are based upon facts which require that a plaintiff voluntarily and directly encounter the known risk with full appreciation of the nature or extent of the danger. It is not sufficient that the plaintiff have knowledge that there is some danger in the particular undertaking. Decedent was not working on the vat. He must have knowledge of the particular risk which he voluntarily incurs and a full appreciation of the danger which leads to his injury. There the plaintiff knew and appreciated the risk of falling down an unguarded elevator shaft but not of the danger which caused his injury, though it might have been presumed that all dangers in an elevator shaft should have been known and appreciated. In the present case, the decedent was placing a ladder in the space between the scrubber and the vat to work on the scrubber when he somehow lost his balance and could not avoid stepping backward and falling into the unguarded and open vat nearby. He did not encounter the vat willfully and directly. The open and unprotected vat gave rise to a situation which rendered the premises more than ordinarily dangerous for workmen on the premises. A guardrail or protective cover around the vat probably would have prevented the injury and death of Greenwood. . . .

We cannot say as a matter of law that decedent took a known risk by stumbling or falling into the open vat involuntarily. The risk he was voluntarily encountering at the time had to do with the ladder and the scrubber. He did not "voluntarily" back into a deadly vat of hot water and chemicals, nor was an intelligent choice necessarily involved. The vat was incidental to and apart from decedent's activities at the time. Decedent fell and was fatally injured by reason of a fact originating separately and unconnected with the vat. We hold that there are jury issues presented concerning these questions and the alleged negligence of appellee in failing to provide decedent a safe place to work, to-wit: whether failure to provide guard rails or protective covering around the vats was negligence proximately causing or cooperating to cause the accident and other similar issues. Appellee owed decedent a duty of care unless under the circumstances decedent had a full understanding and appreciation of the extent of the danger.

. . . .

From the facts in this record it is plain to us that the premises belonging to appellee were exceptionally dangerous and extra-hazardous to an invitee regardless of a general knowledge of danger. At the time and place in question the decedent was required to work where he did under his employer's contract with Lowe Chemical Company. To quit his job would have been an unreasonable requirement. The facts show that he thought he could work in safety. But when he lost his balance he backed into the open vat unintentionally and received a fatal injury. Section 343A, Restatement of the Law of Torts (2d Ed.), says:

> "(1) A possessor of land is not liable to his invitees for physical harm caused to them by any activity or condition on the land whose danger is known or obvious to them, *unless the possessor should anticipate the harm despite such knowledge or obviousness.*" (Emphasis added).

We think the possessor-appellee should have anticipated harm to an invitee on the premises despite general knowledge of the dangers caused by the vats. Especially is this true when the invitee's balance was lost while he was working on something else, when his fall into the deadly vat was beyond his control, and when he may not have had, under the circumstances, a full appreciation of the extent of the danger. We think appellee had some duty to provide ordinary safety to invitees on its premises under these circumstances.

Appellant's decedent did not of necessity willfully and intelligently expose himself to such danger. To say that a landowner is required to keep his premises in a reasonably safe condition for his invitees is an empty phrase unless some minimal duty of care is required of him when he clearly should anticipate harm, regardless of knowledge, in a dangerous condition of this kind. Failure to provide any type of safety devices against this type of extreme danger is clearly unreasonable.

. . . .

The judgment of the trial court is reversed and remanded.

TUNKS, CHIEF JUSTICE (dissenting).

I respectfully dissent. . . .

———————

1.   Does this case turn in any way upon the status of the plaintiff as an invitee? Should assumption of the risk doctrine look different in a workplace setting?

2.   Should the doctrine of assumption of risk ever truly apply in a case where the plaintiff has accidentally exposed him or herself to danger? Is assumption of risk doctrine designed for plaintiffs who negligently injure themselves, however known the danger may be?

3.   Can a court manipulate the assumption of risk doctrine in order to reach a given result? Does the doctrine lend itself to such manipulation?

PROBLEM

G takes the ferry from Manhattan to Hoboken, New Jersey. Upon his arrival on the ferry pier, he discovers that a train has been left standing on its track, blocking the exit from the pier to Hoboken. After waiting a few minutes for the train to move, G, who has an appointment in Hoboken, decides to crawl between two of the cars in order to leave the pier. Inevitably, as soon as he is between two cars, the train starts up, and G is severely injured.

G sues the railroad, which admits that the train should not have been left standing where it was. What arguments will the railroad make in its defense?

D.   THE TAXONOMY OF PLAINTIFFS: THE MODERN APPROACH

TANTIMONICO v. ALLENDALE MUTUAL INSURANCE CO.
Supreme Court of Rhode Island, 1994
637 A.2d 1056

SHEA, JUSTICE.

These consolidated cases are before the Supreme Court on the appeals of the plaintiffs from Superior Court orders granting the defendant's motions for summary judgment. For the reasons that follow we affirm.

The facts of this case are not in dispute. On May 5, 1985, Guy Tantimonico, Jr., and John McPhillips, Jr. (plaintiffs), were riding motorcycles on a piece of undeveloped property owned by Allendale Mutual Insurance Company (defendant) located near its corporate headquarters in Johnston, Rhode Island. While independently riding their motorcycles on the property, plaintiffs, both in their twenties, collided head on with each other. Neither plaintiff can recall the specifics of the accident, but both Tantimonico and McPhillips suffered severe injuries that required extensive hospitalization.

At the conclusion of the hearing on defendant's motions for summary judgment, the trial justice stated that he could find no legal duty that would support the actions against defendant and, that without a legal duty, no material facts were to be found because the question of law was dispositive of the entire matters.

The plaintiffs argue on appeal that in light of this court's holding in *Mariorenzi v. DiPonte, Inc.*, 114 R.I. 294, 333 A.2d 127 (1975), the trial justice erred in granting defendant's motions for summary judgment. In *Mariorenzi* a five-year-old trespasser at a construction site accidentally drowned in an excavation that had filled with water. On appeal, this court abolished the common-law distinctions between the duties owed to licensees, invitees, and trespassers and substituted the tort test of reasonableness. We now take this opportunity to depart from the holding in *Mariorenzi* as it pertains to trespassers.

Traditionally at common law the possessor of land owed a trespasser

> "no duty to discover, remedy, or warn of dangerous natural conditions. Perhaps if the possessor sees a trespasser about to encounter extreme danger from such a source, which is known to the possessor and perceptibly *not* known to the trespasser, there may be a duty to warn (as by shouting). That is about as far as the bystander's duty to a highway traveler would traditionally go, if indeed it would go that far." 4 Harper, James & Gray, The Law of Torts § 27.3 at 139 (2d ed. 1986).

Rhode Island followed the common law status categories, and in *Previte v. Wanskuck Co.*, 80 R.I. 1, 3, 90 A.2d 769, 770 (1952), this court stated that "in the ordinary case under the established law in this state no duty is owed a trespasser by a landowner except to refrain from injuring him wantonly or wilfully after discovering his peril."

Many jurisdictions carved out exceptions to the common-law status categories, and in 1957 Great Britain's Parliament enacted a statute abolishing the distinction between licensees and invitees.

In *Kermarec v. Compagnie Generate Transatlantique*, 358 U.S. 625, 79 S. Ct. 406, 3 L. Ed. 2d 550 (1959), the Supreme Court expressed its dissatisfaction with the common-law distinctions between licensees and invitees when it refused to extend them to maritime law. . . .

It was not until the Supreme Court of California issued its opinion in *Rowland v. Christian*, 69 Cal. 2d 108, 70 Cal. Rptr. 97, 443 P.2d 561 (1968), that the common-law categories were judicially abrogated in a United States jurisdiction.

. . . .

In the wake of *Rowland*, this court in *Mariorenzi* cited opinions from a limited number of jurisdictions that purportedly followed the California lead by totally abrogating the common-law status categories. *See* [cases from the United States Court of Appeals for the District of Columbia Circuit, Alaska, Colorado, Hawaii, Louisiana, New Hampshire, and New York]. As Justice Joslin pointed out in his dissent [in *Mariorenzi*], however, none of these cases involved an injury to a trespasser. . . .

Other jurisdictions repudiated the distinctions between licensee and invitee but retained limited-duty rules for trespassers. [Cases cited from Maine, Minnesota, North Dakota, and Wisconsin.]

Although repudiation or modification of the common-law status categories took effect in the above jurisdictions, by the late seventies an increasing number of courts had specifically rejected *Rowland. See* [cases from Alabama, Florida, Kansas, Maryland, Oklahoma, Texas, and Utah]. Others had postponed considering the repudiation of the categories, and still others simply reaffirmed the traditional classifications. *See* Page, The Law of Premises Liability at 139-40 (2d ed. 1988).

In *Mariorenzi* this court stated that it was giving a "final but fitting interment" to all three common-law categories. 114 R.I. at 307, 333 A.2d at 133. It also stated:

> "The time has come to extricate ourselves from a semantical quagmire that had its beginning in ancient and misleading phraseology. . . . The judiciary gave birth to the invitee, licensee, trespasser trio and the judiciary can lay this triptych to rest. Accordingly, we now give a final but fitting interment to the common-law categories of invitee, licensee, and trespasser as well as their extensions, exceptions, and extrapolations.
>
> "As we assign the trichotomy to the historical past, we substitute in its place the basic tort test of reasonableness. Hereafter, the common-law status of an entrant onto the land of another will no longer be determinative of the degree of care owed by the owner, but rather the question to be resolved will be whether the owner has used reasonable care for the safety of all persons reasonably expected to be upon his premises." *Id.* at 306-07, 333 A.2d at 133.

JUSTICE JOSLIN, however, dissented, stating:

> "[T]he majority have made, in effect, a value judgment that it is more acceptable to our society that the risk of loss due to foreseeable injury sustained by a trespasser while on another's land — in any event a slight and readily insurable risk — be shifted from him to the land possessor.
>
> "If that judgment were premised more upon legal analysis and persuasive precedent and less upon presumed public acceptability, I would abide by my concurring opinion in *Henry v. J. W. Eshelman & Sons,* 99 R.I. 518, 527, 209 A.2d 46, 51 (1965). There I said that '[w]hile a deferral to the Legislature in the initiation of changes in matters affecting public policy may often be appropriate, it is not required where the concept demanding change is judicial in its origins.' But the majority's decision is not so premised. Instead, it rests purely on what in their judgment is a socially desirable policy." 114 R.I. at 309-10, 333 A.2d at 134-35.

At the time the *Mariorenzi* accident occurred, there was no statutory or case law in this state that addressed the special concerns for the infant trespasser. The so-called attractive-nuisance or trespassing-child doctrine was not recognized in this state until [1971, when] this court adopted the standard set out in the Restatement (Second) Torts § 339 (1965). . . .

The case at bar is the incarnation of the worst fears of many opponents to the movement away from common-law status categories. In *Ouellette v. Blanchard*, 116 N.H. 552, 364 A.2d 631 (1976), the Supreme Court of New Hampshire abolished the distinction among invitees, licensees, and trespassers. Justice Grimes of that court, in a vigorous dissent, wrote:

> "I fear that the elimination of the trespasser distinction in the determination of the landowner's duty of care will result in unreasonable, unrealistic and unjust consequences. Every owner, lessee, and occupant of land will be faced with increased exposure to liability. If there are no good reasons for drawing a distinction between licensees and invitees, trespassers are in a fundamentally different position from those persons whom the landowner has expressly or by implication invited onto his property." *Id.* at 560, 364 A.2d at 636.

JUSTICE GRIMES continued:

> "One difficulty I have with the court's decision is that it casts aside a whole body of law, built up over the years, which clearly defines the rights and obligations of the property owner on the basis of the relationship he has with those who came upon his land. It is fundamental in tort law that the duty is created by the relationship. Under this law, the owner knows in advance what his duty is. In place of this well-settled and reasonable set of rules, the court now substitutes a single vague duty of reasonable care, under which the property owner acts at his peril with no standard by which he can judge his obligations in advance. The kinds of trespassers are many. The only thing they have in common is that they have no right on the land. And yet it is to be determined after the event what the owner's duty was before the event with regard to each of these various kinds of trespassers who enter upon his land.
>
> "Protesters who invade a company's property and are injured because of some condition of the premises will be able to have a jury decide after the event what duty the company owed to them. A burglar who is injured while scaling a fence in a high crime area where burglars are not unexpected would be able to put the owner to the risk of a jury decision on the question if he had used reasonable care toward the burglar. Such claims should of course be dismissed at the outset as they would be under our preexisting law." *Id.* at 561-62, 364 A.2d at 637.

Similarly, the Supreme Judicial Court of Massachusetts had stated in *Mounsey v. Ellard*, 363 Mass. 693, 297 N.E.2d 43 (1973):

> "We feel that there is [a] significant difference in the legal status of one who trespasses on another's land as opposed to one who is on the land under some color of right — such as a licensee or invitee. For this reason, among others, we do not believe they should be placed in the same legal category. For example, one who jumps over a six foot fence to make use of his neighbor's swimming pool in his absence does not logically belong in the same legal classification as a licensee or invitee." *Id.* at 708 n.7, 297 N.E.2d at 51-52 n.7.

The more recent trend in premises-liability law is to uphold the traditional common-law categories. In *Kirschner v. Louisville Gas & Electric Co.*, 743 S.W.2d 840 (Ky. 1988), the Supreme Court of Kentucky stated:

> "Historically, all tort law has been based on the theory of whether a defendant violated a duty owed to the injured party. There is nothing illogical or unfair in requiring violation of a duty before liability can be imposed, and we reject Kirschner's assertion that we should abolish the classifications of trespasser, licensee, and invitee." *Id.* at 844.

. . . .

Other recent cases that have upheld the common-law status categories are: [citing cases from Arizona, Maryland, Nebraska, New Jersey, and Oklahoma].

. . . .

In the case at bar we are presented with two adults who chose to ride their motorcycles on defendant's property without permission. Clearly plaintiffs were trespassers. . . . It is almost impossible to entertain the notion that anyone other than plaintiffs themselves is responsible for their injuries. To hold the property owner liable for injuries brought about by a plaintiff's negligent behavior would be patently ludicrous.

. . . .

Property owners have a basic right to be free from liability to those who engage in self-destructive activity on their premises without permission. The common-law rule developed over the centuries accomplishes this purpose clearly and without equivocation.

We conclude, therefore, that this landowner owed these plaintiffs no duty save to refrain from willful or wanton injury. To hold the defendant accountable would be tantamount to imposing strict liability upon every landowner in this jurisdiction. Consequently we depart from *Mariorenzi* as it applies to trespassers. We decline to comment on the other aspects of the holding in *Mariorenzi* as no issues involving invitees or licensees are before us.

For these reasons the plaintiffs' appeals are denied and dismissed, the judgments appealed from are affirmed, and the papers of the case are remanded to the Superior Court.

What does all this mean? Do you think that the courts which rejected the categories of plaintiff did not think through what their rejection would mean for landowners, particularly with respect to trespassers?

The Supreme Court of Iowa summarized the state of the law with respect to classifications of plaintiffs in *Alexander v. Medical Associates Clinic*, 646 N.W.2d 74, 77–78 (Iowa 2002), as follows:

> By the end of the 1970s, seven states had followed California's lead [in *Rowland*] and five states had not, the latter group choosing instead to retain the traditional rules based on the entrant's status. During that same period six states chose to abolish or modify the distinction made between

invitees and licensees, but did not take the same step with respect to trespassers. Thus, in the twelve years after *Rowland*, a total of eleven states rejected California's rule that the liability of property owners to trespassers should be judged by the same standard as their liability to persons legally on their land.

Since 1980, the rejection of California's one-rule-fits-all approach has been even more overwhelming. In Rhode Island, the Rhode Island Supreme Court [in *Tantimonico*] partially overruled its earlier decision that had followed *Rowland* and held that the traditional rules governing liability to trespassers should be retained. In addition, the state legislatures in California and Colorado abrogated or partially abrogated court decisions adopting a negligence standard for all premises liability actions. In Colorado, the legislature passed a statute that reinstated a classification-based system of liability for landowners. See Colo.Rev.Stat. § 13-21-115 (1997). In California, in response to cases in which trespassing criminals had recovered for injuries incurred during their unlawful intrusions, the state legislature enacted a law that limited landowners' liability to trespassers who were on the property to commit a crime, essentially reinstating the common law duty in such cases. *See* 1985 Cal. Stat. ch. 1541, § 1 (codified at Cal. Civil Code § 847 (West 2002)).

In addition to those jurisdictions retreating from a prior, wholesale adoption of negligence principles, eight states refused to change their conventional principles of trespasser liability, even though they judicially abolished or modified the distinction between an invitee and a licensee. Additionally, two states, Maryland and Oklahoma, decided to retain their common law rules governing liability to trespassers, but left open the question whether they would discard the invitee and licensee classifications. Finally, seven more states chose to maintain the common law rules making the duty owed by a landowner dependent on the status of the injured party.

In stark contrast to this widespread rejection of negligence principles in trespasser cases, only one state since the 1970s has joined the minority position, abandoning all classifications.

In summary, presently six states use a negligence standard to govern trespasser liability; twenty-nine states have declined the opportunity to change their rule in such cases; and two state legislatures have reinstated the common law trespasser rule after it had been abolished by court decision. Given the fact that only one court in the last twenty-seven years has abandoned the common law trespasser rule, the so-called "trend" to adopt a universal standard of care for premises liability has clearly lost momentum.

See also Singleton v. Sherer, 659 S.E.2d 196 (S.C. Ct. App. 2008) (South Carolina has four categories of plaintiffs: trespassers, invitees, licensees, and children).

Chapter 10

DAMAGES

In the introductory chapter we said that in many ways, Torts was a deceptively simple subject dealing with the question of who pays. The second most important question is, how much does the losing party pay? That is the subject of this chapter.

The basic theory of damages is to return the victim to the position that he or she was in just before the injury. Where the victim has suffered personal injury, dignitary harm (such as loss of reputation), or the loss of uniquely valuable property, that may not be actually possible, but the victim is nonetheless entitled to monetary compensation for his or her loss. Even when the defendant concedes liability, damages are sure to be challenged. The three types of damages that will be examined in this chapter are punitive damages (sometime called "exemplary" damages), pecuniary loss, and non-economic loss.

We have already studied some of the most challenging damage issues in the duty and proximate cause chapters. There we considered whether the actor had a duty to avoid the particular injury and whether the defendant's conduct was the proximate cause of the damage. Here we examine the Supreme Court's most important and most recent incursions into the punitive damage fray and some common damage questions.

A. PUNITIVE DAMAGES

Punitive damages are awarded by the jury to deter and punish intentional or malicious conduct by the defendant. The jury awards punitive damages in its discretion, although its decisions are subject to review by the courts, which often reduce the amount of a punitive award. Until recently there were few standards for the amount of the award other than the character of the misconduct, the nature of the plaintiff's injury, and perhaps the defendant's wealth. This vagueness and the size of a few awards have caused problems and attracted attention. Ultimately, they led to the "constitutionalization" of punitive damages law by the Supreme Court of the United States.

PROBLEM

In the crash of an economy car, the gas tank exploded; the driver was killed, and the passenger suffered severe burns. It was shown that the manufacturer was aware that the gas tank would explode in thirty mile per hour rear-end collisions.

The jury returned a verdict in favor of the plaintiff for $3.5 million compensatory damages and $125 million punitive damages. If you were the trial court judge, what, if anything, would you do with this verdict? As the appellate court judge, what would you do with the verdict, if the trial judge did nothing?

BMW OF NORTH AMERICA, INC. v. GORE
Supreme Court of the United States, 1996
517 U.S. 559

JUSTICE STEVENS delivered the opinion of the Court.

The Due Process Clause of the Fourteenth Amendment prohibits a State from imposing a "grossly excessive" punishment on a tortfeasor. *TXO Production Corp. v. Alliance Resources Corp.*, 509 U.S. 443, 454, 113 S. Ct. 2711, 125 L. Ed. 2d 366 (1993) (and cases cited). The wrongdoing involved in this case was the decision by a national distributor of automobiles not to advise its dealers, and hence their customers, of predelivery damage to new cars when the cost of repair amounted to less than 3 percent of the car's suggested retail price. The question presented is whether a $2 million punitive damages award to the purchaser of one of these cars exceeds the constitutional limit.

I

In January 1990, Dr. Ira Gore, Jr. (respondent), purchased a black BMW sports sedan for $40,750.88 from an authorized BMW dealer in Birmingham, Alabama. After driving the car for approximately nine months, and without noticing any flaws in its appearance, Dr. Gore took the car to "Slick Finish," an independent detailer, to make it look "snazzier than it normally would appear." 646 So. 2d 619, 621 (Ala. 1994). Mr. Slick, the proprietor, detected evidence that the car had been repainted.[1] Convinced that he had been cheated, Dr. Gore brought suit against petitioner BMW of North America (BMW), the American distributor of BMW automobiles.[2] Dr. Gore alleged, inter alia, that the failure to disclose that the car had been repainted constituted suppression of a material fact.[3] The complaint prayed for $500,000 in compensatory and punitive damages, and costs.

At trial, BMW acknowledged that it had adopted a nationwide policy in 1983 concerning cars that were damaged in the course of manufacture or transportation. If the cost of repairing the damage exceeded 3 percent of the car's suggested retail price, the car was placed in company service for a period of time and then sold as used. If the repair cost did not exceed 3 percent of the suggested retail price, however, the car was sold as new without advising the dealer that any repairs had

---

[1] The top, hood, trunk, and quarter panels of Dr. Gore's car were repainted at BMW's vehicle preparation center in Brunswick, Georgia. The parties presumed that the damage was caused by exposure to acid rain during transit between the manufacturing plant in Germany and the preparation center.

[2] Dr. Gore also named the German manufacturer and the Birmingham dealership as defendants.

[3] Alabama codified its common-law cause of action for fraud in a 1907 statute that is still in effect. H[a]ckmeyer v. Hackmeyer, 268 Ala. 329, 333, 106 So. 2d 245, 249 (Ala. 1958). The statute provides: "Suppression of a material fact which the party is under an obligation to communicate constitutes fraud. The obligation to communicate may arise from the confidential relations of the parties or from the particular circumstances of the case." Ala. Code § 6-5-102(1993); see Ala. Code § 4299 (1907).

been made. Because the $601.37 cost of repainting Dr. Gore's car was only about 1.5 percent of its suggested retail price, BMW did not disclose the damage or repair to the Birmingham dealer.

Dr. Gore asserted that his repainted car was worth less than a car that had not been refinished. To prove his actual damages of $4,000, he relied on the testimony of a former BMW dealer, who estimated that the value of a repainted BMW was approximately 10 percent less than the value of a new car that had not been damaged and repaired. To support his claim for punitive damages, Dr. Gore introduced evidence that since 1983 BMW had sold 983 refinished cars as new, including 14 in Alabama, without disclosing that the cars had been repainted before sale at a cost of more than $300 per vehicle. Using the actual damage estimate of $4,000 per vehicle, Dr. Gore argued that a punitive award of $4 million would provide an appropriate penalty for selling approximately 1,000 cars for more than they were worth.

The jury returned a verdict finding BMW liable for compensatory damages of $4,000. In addition, the jury assessed $4 million in punitive damages, based on a determination that the nondisclosure policy constituted "gross, oppressive or malicious" fraud. *See* Ala. Code §§ 6-11-20, 6-11-21 (1993).

. . . .

BMW filed a post-trial motion to set aside the punitive damages award. The company introduced evidence to establish that its nondisclosure policy was consistent with the laws of roughly 25 States defining the disclosure obligations of automobile manufacturers, distributors, and dealers. . . .

BMW also drew the court's attention to the fact that its nondisclosure policy had never been adjudged unlawful before this action was filed. [BMW further noted that it had altered its policy in Alabama after being found liable in a separate fraud action, and that it had discontinued its policy nationally after the verdict in this case.]

In response to BMW's arguments, Dr. Gore asserted that the policy change demonstrated the efficacy of the punitive damages award. He noted that while no jury had held the policy unlawful, BMW had received a number of customer complaints relating to undisclosed repairs and had settled some lawsuits. [Gore also challenged the evidence of legality by noting that BMW had failed to prove whether the statutes it cited "had supplanted, rather than supplemented, existing causes of action for common law fraud."]

The trial judge denied BMW's post-trial motion, holding, *inter alia*, that the award was not excessive. On appeal, the Alabama Supreme Court also rejected BMW's claim that the award exceeded the constitutionally permissible amount.

The Alabama Supreme Court did, however, rule in BMW's favor on one critical point: The court found that the jury improperly computed the amount of punitive damages by multiplying Dr. Gore's compensatory damages by the number of similar sales in other jurisdictions. . . . Having found the verdict tainted, the court held that "a constitutionally reasonable punitive damages award in this case is $2,000,000," . . . and therefore ordered a remittitur in that amount. The court's discussion of the amount of its remitted award expressly disclaimed any reliance on "acts that occurred in other jurisdictions"; instead, the court explained that it had used a "comparative analysis" that considered Alabama cases, "along with cases from other jurisdictions, involving the sale of an automobile where the seller misrepresented the condition of the vehicle and the jury awarded punitive damages to the purchaser." . . .

Because we believed that a review of this case would help to illuminate "the character of the standard that will identify constitutionally excessive awards" of punitive damages . . . we granted certiorari.

II

Punitive damages may properly be imposed to further a State's legitimate interests in punishing unlawful conduct and deterring its repetition. In our federal system, States necessarily have considerable flexibility in determining the level of punitive damages that they will allow in different classes of cases and in any particular case. Most States that authorize exemplary damages afford the jury similar latitude, requiring only that the damages awarded be reasonably necessary to vindicate the State's legitimate interests in punishment and deterrence. *See TXO*, 509 U.S. at 456; *Haslip*, 499 U.S. at 21, 22. Only when an award can fairly be categorized as "grossly excessive" in relation to these interests does it enter the zone of arbitrariness that violates the Due Process Clause of the Fourteenth Amendment. *Cf. TXO*, 509 U.S. at 456. For that reason, the federal excessiveness inquiry appropriately begins with an identification of the state interests that a punitive award is designed to serve. We therefore focus our attention first on the scope of Alabama's legitimate interests in punishing BMW and deterring it from future misconduct.

. . . .

We think it follows from . . . principles of state sovereignty and comity that a State may not impose economic sanctions on violators of its laws with the intent of changing the tortfeasors' lawful conduct in other States. Before this Court Dr. Gore argued that the large punitive damages award was necessary to induce BMW to change the nationwide policy that it adopted in 1983.[18] But by attempting to alter BMW's nationwide policy, Alabama would be infringing on the policy choices of other States. To avoid such encroachment, the economic penalties that a State such as Alabama inflicts on those who transgress its laws, whether the penalties take the form of legislatively authorized fines or judicially imposed punitive damages, must be supported by the State's interest in protecting its own consumers and its own economy. Alabama may insist that BMW adhere to a particular disclosure policy in

---

[18] Brief for Respondent 11-12, 23, 27-28; Tr. of Oral Arg. 50-54. Dr. Gore's interest in altering the nationwide policy stems from his concern that BMW would not (or could not) discontinue the policy in Alabama alone. *Id.*, at 11. "If Alabama were limited to imposing punitive damages based only on BMW's gain from fraudulent sales in Alabama, the resulting award would have no prospect of protecting Alabama consumers from fraud, as it would provide no incentive for BMW to alter the unitary, national policy of nondisclosure which yielded BMW millions of dollars in profits." *Id.*, at 23. The record discloses no basis for Dr. Gore's contention that BMW could not comply with Alabama's law without changing its nationwide policy.

that State. Alabama does not have the power, however, to punish BMW for conduct that was lawful where it occurred and that had no impact on Alabama or its residents. Nor may Alabama impose sanctions on BMW in order to deter conduct that is lawful in other jurisdictions.

. . . .

III

Elementary notions of fairness enshrined in our constitutional jurisprudence dictate that a person receive fair notice not only of the conduct that will subject him to punishment but also of the severity of the penalty that a State may impose. Three guideposts, each of which indicates that BMW did not receive adequate notice of the magnitude of the sanction that Alabama might impose for adhering to the nondisclosure policy adopted in 1983, lead us to the conclusion that the $2 million award against BMW is grossly excessive: the degree of reprehensibility of the nondisclosure; the disparity between the harm or potential harm suffered by Dr. Gore and his punitive damages award; and the difference between this remedy and the civil penalties authorized or imposed in comparable cases. We discuss these considerations in turn.

Degree of Reprehensibility

Perhaps the most important indicium of the reasonableness of a punitive damages award is the degree of reprehensibility of the defendant's conduct. . . . This principle reflects the accepted view that some wrongs are more blameworthy than others. Thus, we have said that "nonviolent crimes are less serious than crimes marked by violence or the threat of violence." *Solent v. Helm*, 463 U.S. 277, 292-293, 77 L. Ed. 2d 637, 103 S. Ct. 3001 (1983). Similarly, "trickery and deceit," *TXO*, 509 U.S. at 462, are more reprehensible than negligence. In *TXO*, both the West Virginia Supreme Court and the Justices of this Court placed special emphasis on the principle that punitive damages may not be "grossly out of proportion to the severity of the offense." *Id.*, at 453, 462. Indeed, for JUSTICE KENNEDY, the defendant's intentional malice was the decisive element in a "close and difficult" case. *Id.*, at 468.

In this case, none of the aggravating factors associated with particularly reprehensible conduct is present. The harm BMW inflicted on Dr. Gore was purely economic in nature. The presale refinishing of the car had no effect on its performance or safety features, or even its appearance for at least nine months after his purchase. BMW's conduct evinced no indifference to or reckless disregard for the health and safety of others. To be sure, infliction of economic injury, especially when done intentionally through affirmative acts of misconduct, *id.*, at 453, or when the target is financially vulnerable, can warrant a substantial penalty. But this observation does not convert all acts that cause economic harm into torts that are sufficiently reprehensible to justify a significant sanction in addition to compensatory damages.

. . . .

Dr. Gore's second argument for treating BMW as a recidivist is that the company should have anticipated that its actions would be considered fraudulent in some, if not all, jurisdictions. This contention overlooks the fact that actionable fraud requires a material misrepresentation or omission. This qualifier invites line drawing of just the sort engaged in by States with disclosure statutes and by BMW. We do not think it can be disputed that there may exist minor imperfections in the finish of a new car that can be repaired (or indeed, left unrepaired) without materially affecting the car's value. There is no evidence that BMW acted in bad faith when it sought to establish the appropriate line between presumptively minor damage and damage requiring disclosure to purchasers. For this purpose, BMW could reasonably rely on state disclosure statutes for guidance. In this regard, it is also significant that there is no evidence that BMW persisted in a course of conduct after it had been adjudged unlawful on even one occasion, let alone repeated occasions.

Finally, the record in this case discloses no deliberate false statements, acts of affirmative misconduct, or concealment of evidence of improper motive, such as were present in *Haslip* and *TXO*. *Haslip*, 499 U.S. at 5; *TXO*, 509 U.S. at 453. We accept, of course, the jury's finding that BMW suppressed a material fact which Alabama law obligated it to communicate to prospective purchasers of repainted cars in that State. But the omission of a material fact may be less reprehensible than a deliberate false statement, particularly when there is a good-faith basis for believing that no duty to disclose exists.

. . . Because this case exhibits none of the circumstances ordinarily associated with egregiously improper conduct, we are persuaded that BMW's conduct was not sufficiently reprehensible to warrant imposition of a $2 million exemplary damages award.

Ratio

The second and perhaps most commonly cited indicium of an unreasonable or excessive punitive damages award is its ratio to the actual harm inflicted on the plaintiff. *See TXO*, 509 U.S. at 459; *Haslip*, 499 U.S. at 23. The principle that exemplary damages must bear a "reasonable relationship" to compensatory damages has a long pedigree. Scholars have identified a number of early English statutes authorizing the award of multiple damages for particular wrongs. Some 65 different enactments during the period between 1275 and 1753 provided for double, treble, or quadruple damages. Our decisions in both *Haslip* and *TXO* endorsed the proposition that a comparison between the compensatory award and the punitive award is significant.

In *Haslip* we concluded that even though a punitive damages award of "more than 4 times the amount of compensatory damages," might be "close to the line," it did not "cross the line into the area of constitutional impropriety." *Haslip*, 499 U.S. at 23-24. *TXO*, following dicta in *Haslip*, refined this analysis by confirming that the proper inquiry is " 'whether there is a reasonable relationship between the punitive damages award and the harm likely to result from the defendant's conduct as well as the harm that actually has occurred.' " *TXO*, 509 U.S. at 460 (emphasis in original), quoting *Haslip*, 499 U.S. at 21. Thus, in upholding the $10 million award in *TXO*, we relied on the difference between that figure and the harm to the victim that would have ensued if the tortious plan had succeeded. That difference suggested that the relevant ratio was not more than 10 to 1.

The $2 million in punitive damages awarded to Dr. Gore by the Alabama Supreme Court is 500 times the amount of his actual harm as determined by the jury[35] Moreover, there is no suggestion that Dr. Gore or any other BMW purchaser was threatened with any additional potential harm by BMW's nondisclosure policy. The disparity in this case is thus dramatically greater than those considered in *Haslip* and *TXO*.

Of course, we have consistently rejected the notion that the constitutional line is marked by a simple mathematical formula, even one that compares actual and potential damages to the punitive award. *TXO*, 509 U.S. at 458. Indeed, low awards of compensatory damages may properly support a higher ratio than high compensatory awards, if, for example, a particularly egregious act has resulted in only a small amount of economic damages. A higher ratio may also be justified in cases in which the injury is hard to detect or the monetary value of noneconomic harm might have been difficult to determine. It is appropriate, therefore, to reiterate our rejection of a categorical approach. . . . We can say, however, that [a] general concern of reasonableness . . . properly enters into the constitutional calculus.' " *TXO*, 509 U.S. at 458 *(quoting Haslip*, 499 U.S., at 18). In most cases, the ratio will be within a constitutionally acceptable range, and remittitur will not be justified on this basis. When the ratio is a breathtaking 500 to 1, however, the award must surely "raise a suspicious judicial eyebrow." *TXO*, 509 U.S. at 482 (O'CONNOR, J., dissenting).

Sanctions for Comparable Misconduct

Comparing the punitive damages award and the civil or criminal penalties that could be imposed for comparable misconduct provides a third indicium of excessiveness. . . . In this case the $2 million economic sanction imposed on BMW is substantially greater than the statutory fines available in Alabama and elsewhere for similar malfeasance.

The maximum civil penalty authorized by the Alabama Legislature for a violation of its Deceptive Trade Practices Act is $2,000; other States authorize more severe sanctions, with the maxima ranging from $5,000 to $10,000. . . .

. . . In the absence of a history of noncompliance with known statutory requirements, there is no basis for assuming that a more modest sanction would not have been sufficient to motivate full compliance with the disclosure requirement imposed by the Alabama Supreme Court in this case.

. . . .

The fact that BMW is a large corporation rather than an impecunious individual

---

[35] Even assuming each repainted BMW suffers a diminution in value of approximately $4,000, the award is 35 times greater than the total damages of all 14 Alabama consumers who purchased repainted BMW's.

does not diminish its entitlement to fair notice of the demands that the several States impose on the conduct of its business. Indeed, its status as an active participant in the national economy implicates the federal interest in preventing individual States from imposing undue burdens on interstate commerce. While each State has ample power to protect its own consumers, none may use the punitive damages deterrent as a means of imposing its regulatory policies on the entire Nation.

As in *Haslip*, we are not prepared to draw a bright line marking the limits of a constitutionally acceptable punitive damages award. Unlike that case, however, we are fully convinced that the grossly excessive award imposed in this case transcends the constitutional limit. Whether the appropriate remedy requires a new trial or merely an independent determination by the Alabama Supreme Court of the award necessary to vindicate the economic interests of Alabama consumers is a matter that should be addressed by the state court in the first instance.

The judgment is reversed, and the case is remanded for further proceedings not inconsistent with this opinion.

It is so ordered.

JUSTICE SCALIA, with whom JUSTICE THOMAS joins, dissenting:

Today we see the latest manifestation of this Court's recent and increasingly insistent "concern about punitive damages that 'run wild.' " *Pacific Mut. Life Ins. Co. v. Haslip*, 499 U.S. 1, 18, 111 S. Ct. 1032, 113 L. Ed. 2d 1 (1991). Since the Constitution does not make that concern any of our business, the Court's activities in this area are an unjustified incursion into the province of state governments.

In earlier cases that were the prelude to this decision, I set forth my view that a state trial procedure that commits the decision whether to impose punitive damages, and the amount, to the discretion of the jury, subject to some judicial review for "reasonableness," furnishes a defendant with all the process that is "due." See *TXO Production Corp. v. Alliance Resources Corp.*, 509 U.S. 443, 470, 113 S. Ct. 2711, 125 L. Ed. 2d 366 (1993). . . .

[T]oday's judgment represents the first instance of this Court's invalidation of a state-court punitive assessment as simply unreasonably large. . . .

. . . .

One might understand the Court's eagerness to enter this field, rather than leave it with the state legislatures, if it had something useful to say. In fact, however, its opinion provides virtually no guidance to legislatures, and to state and federal courts, as to what a "constitutionally proper" level of punitive damages might be.

. . . .

In Part III of its opinion, the Court identifies "three guideposts" that lead it to the conclusion that the award in this case is excessive: degree of reprehensibility, ratio between punitive award and plaintiff's actual harm, and legislative sanctions provided for comparable misconduct. . . . The legal significance of these "guide-posts" is nowhere explored, but their necessary effect is to establish federal standards governing the hitherto exclusively state law of damages.

. . . .

These criss-crossing platitudes yield no real answers in no real cases. And it must be noted that the Court nowhere says that these three "guideposts" are the only guideposts; indeed, it makes very clear that they are not — explaining away the earlier opinions that do not really follow these "guideposts" on the basis of additional factors, thereby "reiterating our rejection of a categorical approach." . . . In other words, even these utter platitudes, if they should ever happen to produce an answer, may be overridden by other unnamed considerations. The Court has constructed a framework that does not genuinely constrain, that does not inform state legislatures and lower courts — that does nothing at all except confer an artificial air of doctrinal analysis upon its essentially ad hoc determination that this particular award of punitive damages was not "fair."

. . . .

JUSTICE GINSBURG, with whom the CHIEF JUSTICE [Rehnquist] joins, dissenting:

. . . The Court, I am convinced, unnecessarily and unwisely ventures into territory traditionally within the States' domain, and does so in the face of reform measures recently adopted or currently under consideration in legislative arenas. The Alabama Supreme Court, in this case, endeavored to follow this Court's prior instructions; and, more recently, Alabama's highest court has installed further controls on awards of punitive damages. . . . I would therefore leave the state court's judgment undisturbed, and resist unnecessary intrusion into an area dominantly of state concern.

---

1. If you were the trial court judge, how would you interpret *BMW v. Gore*? Does the opinion provide any more guidance than "yikes" or "that is too much"? What is the standard that the trial court must now use in evaluating the size of punitive damage awards?

2. What do you think of BMW's argument that its policy had never been judged unlawful? Was there "no deliberate false statement" here?

3. Should a state adopt a "safe harbor" policy that sets a maximum ratio of punitive to compensatory awards?

4. How do damages verdicts affect the defendant's business in other states? Was there a market failure here? Did BMW provide what the consumer wanted and expected? In regard to minor repairs, are the expectations of a BMW consumer different from those of a Chevrolet consumer?

5. In Justice Ginsburg's *Gore* dissent, she documented a great deal of activity by state legislatures intent on corralling punitive damages. In an appendix to her opinion, she identified pending or enacted measures in many states. These included various kinds of damages caps in 16 states, allocations of portions of a punitive award to state agencies in 13 states, and bifurcation of punitive damages from liability and compensatory damage proceedings in 12 states. State legislative

activity to curb punitive damages has continued since *Gore* was decided.

Does the variation in state answers to the punitive damage question suggest that something is fundamentally wrong, or does it manifest that there may be numerous acceptable solutions to the problem? Which reforms do you prefer, if any? Why?

STATE FARM MUTUAL AUTOMOBILE INS. CO. v. CAMPBELL
Supreme Court of the United States, 2003
538 U.S. 408

JUSTICE KENNEDY delivered the opinion of the Court.

We address once again the measure of punishment, by means of punitive damages, a State may impose upon a defendant in a civil case. The question is whether, in the circumstances we shall recount, an award of $145 million in punitive damages, where full compensatory damages are $1 million, is excessive and in violation of the Due Process Clause of the Fourteenth Amendment to the Constitution of the United States.

I

In 1981, Curtis Campbell (Campbell) was driving with his wife, Inez Preece Campbell, in Cache County, Utah. He decided to pass six vans traveling ahead of them on a two-lane highway. Todd Ospital was driving a small car approaching from the opposite direction. To avoid a head-on collision with Campbell, who by then was driving on the wrong side of the highway and toward oncoming traffic, Ospital swerved onto the shoulder, lost control of his automobile, and collided with a vehicle driven by Robert G. Slusher. Ospital was killed, and Slusher was rendered permanently disabled. The Campbells escaped unscathed.

In the ensuing wrongful death and tort action, Campbell insisted he was not at fault. Early investigations did support differing conclusions as to who caused the accident, but "a consensus was reached early on by the investigators and witnesses that Mr. Campbell's unsafe pass had indeed caused the crash." . . . Campbell's insurance company, petitioner State Farm Mutual Automobile Insurance Company (State Farm), nonetheless decided to contest liability and declined offers by Slusher and Ospital's estate (Ospital) to settle the claims for the policy limit of $50,000 ($25,000 per claimant). State Farm also ignored the advice of one of its own investigators and took the case to trial, assuring the Campbells that "their assets were safe, that they had no liability for the accident, that [State Farm] would represent their interests, and that they did not need to procure separate counsel." . . . To the contrary, a jury determined that Campbell was 100 percent at fault, and a judgment was returned for $185,849, far more than the amount offered in settlement.

At first State Farm refused to cover the $135,849 in excess liability. Its counsel made this clear to the Campbells: " 'You may want to put for sale signs on your property to get things moving.' " . . . Nor was State Farm willing to post a supersedeas bond to allow Campbell to appeal the judgment against him. Campbell obtained his own counsel to appeal the verdict. During the pendency of the appeal, in late 1984, Slusher, Ospital, and the Campbells reached an agreement whereby Slusher and Ospital agreed not to seek satisfaction of their claims against the Campbells. In exchange the Campbells agreed to pursue a bad-faith action against State Farm and to be represented by Slusher's and Ospital's attorneys.

. . . .

In 1989, the Utah Supreme Court denied Campbell's appeal in the wrongful-death and tort actions. *Slusher v. Ospital*, 777 P.2d 437. State Farm then paid the entire judgment, including the amounts in excess of the policy limits. The Campbells nonetheless filed a complaint against State Farm alleging bad faith, fraud, and intentional infliction of emotional distress. . . . At State Farm's request the trial court bifurcated the trial into two phases conducted before different juries. In the first phase the jury determined that State Farm's decision not to settle was unreasonable because there was a substantial likelihood of an excess verdict.

Before the second phase of the action against State Farm we decided *BMW of North America, Inc. v. Gore.* . . . The second phase addressed State Farm's liability for fraud and intentional infliction of emotional distress, as well as compensatory and punitive damages. The Utah Supreme Court aptly characterized this phase of the trial:

> "State Farm argued during phase II that its decision to take the case to trial was an 'honest mistake' that did not warrant punitive damages. In contrast, the Campbells introduced evidence that State Farm's decision to take the case to trial was a result of a national scheme [known as the "PP&R policy"] to meet corporate fiscal goals by capping payouts on claims company wide. . . . To prove the existence of this scheme, the trial court allowed the Campbells to introduce extensive expert testimony regarding fraudulent practices by State Farm in its nation-wide operations. Although State Farm moved prior to phase II of the trial for the exclusion of such evidence and continued to object to it at trial, the trial court ruled that such evidence was admissible to determine whether State Farm's conduct in the Campbell case was indeed intentional and sufficiently egregious to warrant punitive damages." 65 P. 3d, at 1143.

Evidence pertaining to the [PP&R scheme] concerned State Farm's business practices for over 20 years in numerous States. Most of these practices bore no relation to third party automobile insurance claims, the type of claim underlying the Campbells' complaint against the company. The jury awarded the Campbells $2.6 million in compensatory damages and $145 million in punitive damages, which the trial court reduced to $1 million and $25 million respectively. Both parties appealed.

The Utah Supreme Court sought to apply the three guideposts we identified in *Gore, supra,* . . . and it reinstated the $145 million punitive damages award. Relying in large part on the extensive evidence concerning the PP&R policy, the court concluded State Farm's conduct was reprehensible. The court also relied upon State Farm's "massive wealth" and on testimony indicating that "State Farm's actions, because of their clandestine nature, will be punished at most in one out of every 50,000 cases as a matter of statistical probability," 65 P. 3d, at 1153, and concluded that the ratio between punitive and compensatory damages was not unwarranted. Finally, the court noted that the punitive damages award was not excessive when compared to various civil and criminal penalties State Farm could have faced, including $10,000 for each act of fraud, the suspension of its license to conduct business in Utah, the disgorgement of profits, and imprisonment. *Id.*, at 1154–1155. We granted certiorari. . . .

II

We recognized in *Cooper Industries, Inc. v. Leatherman Tool Group, Inc.*, 532 U. S. 424 (2001), that in our judicial system compensatory and punitive damages, although usually awarded at the same time by the same decisionmaker, serve different purposes. *Id.*, at 432. Compensatory damages "are intended to redress the concrete loss that the plaintiff has suffered by reason of the defendant's wrongful conduct." *Ibid.* (citing Restatement (Second) of Torts § 903, pp. 453–454 (1979)). By contrast, punitive damages serve a broader function; they are aimed at deterrence and retribution. *Cooper Industries, supra*, at 432; see also *Gore, supra*, at 568. . . . While States possess discretion over the imposition of punitive damages, it is well established that there are procedural and substantive constitutional limitations on these awards. . . . The Due Process Clause of the Fourteenth Amendment prohibits the imposition of grossly excessive or arbitrary punishments on a tortfeasor. . . . The reason is that "[e]lementary notions of fairness enshrined in our constitutional jurisprudence dictate that a person receive fair notice not only of the conduct that will subject him to punishment, but also of the severity of the penalty that a State may impose." *Id.*, at 574. . . . To the extent an award is grossly excessive, it furthers no legitimate purpose and constitutes an arbitrary deprivation of property. . . .

Although these awards serve the same purposes as criminal penalties, defendants subjected to punitive damages in civil cases have not been accorded the protections applicable in a criminal proceeding. This increases our concerns over the imprecise manner in which punitive damages systems are administered. . . . Our concerns are heightened when the decisionmaker is presented, as we shall discuss, with evidence that has little bearing as to the amount of punitive damages that should be awarded. Vague instructions, or those that merely inform the jury to avoid "passion or prejudice," . . . do little to aid the decisionmaker in its task of assigning appropriate weight to evidence that is relevant and evidence that is tangential or only inflammatory.

In light of these concerns, in *Gore, supra*, we instructed courts reviewing punitive damages to consider three guideposts: (1) the degree of reprehensibility of the defendant's misconduct; (2) the disparity between the actual or potential harm suffered by the plaintiff and the punitive damages award; and (3) the difference between the punitive damages awarded by the jury and the civil penalties authorized or imposed in comparable cases. *Id.*, at 575. . . .

III

Under the principles outlined in *BMW of North America, Inc. v. Gore*, this case is neither close nor difficult. It was error to reinstate the jury's $145 million punitive damages award. We address each guidepost of *Gore* in some detail.

A

"[T]he most important indicium of the reasonableness of a punitive damages award is the degree of reprehensibility of the defendant's conduct." *Gore*, 517 U. S., at 575. We have instructed courts to determine the reprehensibility of a defendant by considering whether: the harm caused was physical as opposed to economic; the tortious conduct evinced an indifference to or a reckless disregard of the health or safety of others; the target of the conduct had financial vulnerability; the conduct involved repeated actions or was an isolated incident; and the harm was the result of intentional malice, trickery, or deceit, or mere accident. *Id.*, at 576–577. The existence of any one of these factors weighing in favor of a plaintiff may not be sufficient to sustain a punitive damages award; and the absence of all of them renders any award suspect. It should be presumed a plaintiff has been made whole for his injuries by compensatory damages, so punitive damages should only be awarded if the defendant's culpability, after having paid compensatory damages, is so reprehensible as to warrant the imposition of further sanctions to achieve punishment or deterrence. *Id.*, at 575.

Applying these factors in the instant case, we must acknowledge that State Farm's handling of the claims against the Campbells merits no praise. The trial court found that State Farm's employees altered the company's records to make Campbell appear less culpable. State Farm disregarded the overwhelming likelihood of liability and the near-certain probability that, by taking the case to trial, a judgment in excess of the policy limits would be awarded. State Farm amplified the harm by at first assuring the Campbells their assets would be safe from any verdict and by later telling them, postjudgment, to put a for-sale sign on their house. While we do not suggest there was error in awarding punitive damages based upon State Farm's conduct toward the Campbells, a more modest punishment for this reprehensible conduct could have satisfied the State's legitimate objectives, and the Utah courts should have gone no further. This case, instead, was used as a platform to expose, and punish, the perceived deficiencies of State Farm's operations throughout the country. The Utah Supreme Court's opinion makes explicit that State Farm was being condemned for its nationwide policies rather than for the conduct directed toward the Campbells. . . .

The Campbells contend that State Farm has only itself to blame for the reliance upon dissimilar and out-of-state conduct evidence. The record does not support this contention. From their opening statements onward the Campbells framed this case as a chance to rebuke State Farm for its nationwide activities. . . . This was a position maintained throughout the litigation. In opposing State Farm's motion to exclude such evidence under *Gore*, the Campbells' counsel convinced the trial court that there was no limitation on the scope of evidence that could be considered under our precedents. . . . A State cannot punish a defendant for conduct that may have been lawful where it occurred. *Gore, supra*, at 572. . . .

Nor, as a general rule, does a State have a legitimate concern in imposing punitive damages to punish a defendant for unlawful acts committed outside of the State's jurisdiction. Any proper adjudication of conduct that occurred outside Utah to other persons would require their inclusion, and, to those parties, the Utah courts, in the usual case, would need to apply the laws of their relevant jurisdiction. *Phillips Petroleum Co. v. Shutts*, 472 U. S. 797, 821–822 (1985). Here, the Campbells do not dispute that much of the out-of-state conduct was lawful where it occurred. They argue, however, that such evidence was not the primary basis for the punitive damages award and was relevant to the extent it demonstrated, in a general sense, State Farm's motive against its insured. . . . This argument misses the mark. Lawful out-of-state conduct may be probative when it demonstrates the deliberate-ness and culpability of the defendant's action in the State where it is tortious, but that conduct must have a nexus to the specific harm suffered by the plaintiff. A jury must be instructed, furthermore, that it may not use evidence of out-of-state conduct to punish a defendant for action that was lawful in the jurisdiction where it occurred. *Gore*, 517 U. S., at 572–573. . . . A basic principle of federalism is that each State may make its own reasoned judgment about what conduct is permitted or proscribed within its borders, and each State alone can determine what measure of punishment, if any, to impose on a defendant who acts within its jurisdiction. *Id.*, at 569.

For a more fundamental reason, however, the Utah courts erred in relying upon this and other evidence: The courts awarded punitive damages to punish and deter conduct that bore no relation to the Campbells' harm. A defendant's dissimilar acts, independent from the acts upon which liability was premised, may not serve as the basis for punitive damages. A defendant should be punished for the conduct that harmed the plaintiff, not for being an unsavory individual or business. Due process does not permit courts, in the calculation of punitive damages, to adjudicate the merits of other parties' hypothetical claims against a defendant under the guise of the reprehensibility analysis, but we have no doubt the Utah Supreme Court did that here. . . . Punishment on these bases creates the possibility of multiple punitive damages awards for the same conduct; for in the usual case nonparties are not bound by the judgment some other plaintiff obtains. *Gore, supra*, at 593 (Breyer, J., concurring) ("Larger damages might also 'double count' by including in the punitive damages award some of the compensatory, or punitive, damages that subsequent plaintiffs would also recover").

The same reasons lead us to conclude the Utah Supreme Court's decision cannot be justified on the grounds that State Farm was a recidivist. Although "[o]ur holdings that a recidivist may be punished more severely than a first offender recognize that repeated misconduct is more reprehensible than an individual instance of malfeasance," *Gore, supra*, at 577, in the context of civil actions courts must ensure the conduct in question replicates the prior transgressions. . . .

The Campbells have identified scant evidence of repeated misconduct of the sort that injured them. Nor does our review of the Utah courts' decisions convince us that State Farm was only punished for its actions toward the Campbells. Although evidence of other acts need not be identical to have relevance in the calculation of punitive damages, the Utah court erred here because evidence pertaining to claims that had nothing to do with a third-party lawsuit was introduced at length. . . . The reprehensibility guidepost does not permit courts to expand the scope of the case so that a defendant may be punished for any malfeasance, which in this case extended for a 20-year period. In this case, because the Campbells have shown no conduct by State Farm similar to that which harmed them, the conduct that harmed them is the only conduct relevant to the reprehensibility analysis.

B

Turning to the second *Gore* guidepost, we have been reluctant to identify concrete constitutional limits on the ratio between harm, or potential harm, to the plaintiff and the punitive damages award. . . . We decline again to impose a bright-line ratio which a punitive damages award cannot exceed. Our jurisprudence and the principles it has now established demonstrate, however, that, in practice, few awards exceeding a single-digit ratio between punitive and compensatory damages, to a significant degree, will satisfy due process. . . . Single-digit multipliers are more likely to comport with due process, while still achieving the State's goals of deterrence and retribution, than awards with ratios in range of . . . 145 to 1.

Nonetheless, because there are no rigid benchmarks that a punitive damages award may not surpass, ratios greater than those we have previously upheld may comport with due process where "a particularly egregious act has resulted in only a small amount of economic damages." . . .

The converse is also true, however. When compensatory damages are substantial, then a lesser ratio, perhaps only equal to compensatory damages, can reach the outermost limit of the due process guarantee. The precise award in any case, of course, must be based upon the facts and circumstances of the defendant's conduct and the harm to the plaintiff.

In sum, courts must ensure that the measure of punishment is both reasonable and proportionate to the amount of harm to the plaintiff and to the general damages recovered. In the context of this case, we have no doubt that there is a presumption against an award that has a 145-to-1 ratio. The compensatory award in this case was substantial; the Campbells were awarded $1 million for a year and a half of emotional distress. This was complete compensation. The harm arose from a transaction in the economic realm, not from some physical assault or trauma; there were no physical injuries; and State Farm paid the excess verdict before the complaint was filed, so the Campbells suffered only minor economic injuries for the 18-month period in which State Farm refused to resolve the claim against them. The compensatory damages for the injury suffered here, moreover, likely were based on a component which was duplicated in the punitive award. Much of the distress was caused by the outrage and humiliation the Campbells suffered at the actions of their insurer; and it is a major role of punitive damages to condemn such conduct. Compensatory damages, however, already contain this punitive element. See Restatement (Second) of Torts § 908, Comment c, p. 466 (1977) ("In many cases in which compensatory damages include an amount for emotional distress, such as humiliation or indignation aroused by the defendant's act, there is no clear line of demarcation between punishment and compensation and a verdict for a specified amount frequently includes elements of both").

. . . .

The remaining premises for the Utah Supreme Court's decision bear no relation to the award's reasonableness or proportionality to the harm. They are, rather, arguments that seek to defend a departure from well-established constraints on punitive damages. While States enjoy considerable discretion in deducing when punitive damages are warranted, each award must comport with the principles set forth in *Gore*. Here the argument that State Farm will be punished in only the rare case, coupled with reference to its assets (which, of course, are what other insured parties in Utah and other States must rely upon for payment of claims) had little to do with the actual harm sustained by the Campbells. The wealth of a defendant cannot justify an otherwise unconstitutional punitive damages award. *Gore*, 517 U. S., at 585 ("The fact that BMW is a large corporation rather than an impecunious individual does not diminish its entitlement to fair notice of the demands that the several States impose on the conduct of its business"); see also *id.*, at 591 (Breyer, J., concurring) ("[Wealth] provides an open-ended basis for inflating awards when the defendant is wealthy. . . . That does not make its use unlawful or inappropriate; it simply means that this factor cannot make up for the failure of other factors, such as 'reprehensibility,' to constrain significantly an award that purports to punish a defendant's conduct"). The principles set forth in *Gore* must be implemented with care, to ensure both reasonableness and proportionality.

C

The third guidepost in *Gore* is the disparity between the punitive damages award and the "civil penalties authorized or imposed in comparable cases." *Id.*, at 575. We note that, in the past, we have also looked to criminal penalties that could be imposed. *Id.*, at 583; *Haslip*, 499 U.S., at 23. The existence of a criminal penalty does have bearing on the seriousness with which a State views the wrongful action. When used to determine the dollar amount of the award, however, the criminal penalty has less utility. Great care must be taken to avoid use of the civil process to assess criminal penalties that can be imposed only after the heightened protections of a criminal trial have been observed, including, of course, its higher standards of proof. Punitive damages are not a substitute for the criminal process, and the remote possibility of a criminal sanction does not automatically sustain a punitive damages award.

Here, we need not dwell long on this guidepost. The most relevant civil sanction under Utah state law for the wrong done to the Campbells appears to be a $10,000 fine for an act of fraud, 65 P. 3d, at 1154, an amount dwarfed by the $145 million punitive damages award. The Supreme Court of Utah speculated about the loss of State Farm's business license, the disgorgement of profits, and possible imprisonment, but here again its references were to the broad fraudulent scheme drawn from evidence of out-of-state and dissimilar conduct. This analysis was insufficient to justify the award.

IV

An application of the Gore guideposts to the facts of this case, especially in light of the substantial compensatory damages awarded (a portion of which contained a punitive element), likely would justify a punitive damages award at or near the amount of compensatory damages. The punitive award of $145 million, therefore, was neither reasonable nor proportionate to the wrong committed, and it was an irrational and arbitrary deprivation of the property of the defendant. . . .

The judgment of the Utah Supreme Court is reversed, and the case is remanded for further proceedings not inconsistent with this opinion.

It is so ordered.

[JUSTICES SCALIA and THOMAS dissented]

JUSTICE GINSBURG, dissenting

. . . .

In *Gore*, I stated why I resisted the Court's foray into punitive damages "territory traditionally within the States' domain." 517 U. S., at 612 (dissenting opinion). I adhere to those views. . . . It was once recognized that "the laws of the particular State must suffice [to superintend punitive damages awards] until judges or legislators authorized to do so initiate system-wide change." *Haslip*, 499 U. S., at 42 (KENNEDY, J., concurring in judgment). I would adhere to that traditional view.

I

The large size of the award upheld by the Utah Supreme Court in this case indicates why damages-capping legislation may be altogether fitting and proper. Neither the amount of the award nor the trial record, however, justifies this Court's substitution of its judgment for that of Utah's competent decisionmakers. In this regard, I count it significant that, on the key criterion "reprehensibility," there is a good deal more to the story than the Court's abbreviated account tells.

Ample evidence allowed the jury to find that State Farm's treatment of the Campbells typified its "Performance, Planning and Review" (PP&R) program; implemented by top management in 1979, the program had "the explicit objective of using the claims-adjustment process as a profit center." . . . "[T]he Campbells presented considerable evidence," the trial court noted, documenting "that the PP&R program . . . has functioned, and continues to function, as an unlawful scheme . . . to deny benefits owed consumers by paying out less than fair value in order to meet preset, arbitrary payout targets designed to enhance corporate profits." . . . That policy, the trial court observed, was encompassing in scope; it "applied equally to the handling of both third-party and first-party claims." . . .

Evidence the jury could credit demonstrated that the PP&R program regularly and adversely affected Utah residents. Ray Summers, "the adjuster who handled the Campbell case and who was a State Farm employee in Utah for almost twenty years," described several methods used by State Farm to deny claimants fair benefits, for example, "falsifying or withholding of evidence in claim files." . . . A common tactic, Summers recounted, was to "unjustly attac[k] the character, reputation and credibility of a claimant and mak[e] notations to that effect in the claim file to create prejudice in the event the claim ever came before a jury." . . . State Farm manager Bob Noxon, Summers testified, resorted to a tactic of this order in the Campbell case when he "instruct[ed] Summers to write in the file that Todd Ospital (who was killed in the accident) was speeding because he was on his way to see a pregnant girlfriend." . . . In truth, "[t]here was no pregnant girlfriend." . . . Expert testimony noted by the trial court described these tactics as "completely improper." . . .

The trial court also noted the testimony of two Utah State Farm employees, Felix Jensen and Samantha Bird, both of whom recalled "intolerable" and "recurrent" pressure to reduce payouts below fair value. . . . When Jensen complained to top managers, he was told to "get out of the kitchen" if he could not take the heat; Bird was told she should be "more of a team player." . . . At times, Bird said, she "was forced to commit dishonest acts and to knowingly underpay claims." . . . Eventually, Bird quit. . . . Utah managers superior to Bird, the evidence indicated, were improperly influenced by the PP&R program to encourage insurance underpayments. For example, several documents evaluating the performance of managers Noxon and Brown "contained explicit preset average payout goals." . . .

Regarding liability for verdicts in excess of policy limits, the trial court referred to a State Farm document titled the "Excess Liability Handbook"; written before the Campbell accident, the handbook instructed adjusters to pad files with "self-serving" documents, and to leave critical items out of files, for example, evaluations of the insured's exposure. . . . Divisional superintendent Bill Brown used the handbook to train Utah employees. . . . While overseeing the Campbell case, Brown ordered adjuster Summers to change the portions of his report indicating that Mr. Campbell was likely at fault and that the settlement cost was correspondingly high. . . . The Campbells' case, according to expert testimony the trial court recited, "was a classic example of State Farm's application of the improper practices taught in the Excess Liability Handbook." . . .

The trial court further determined that the jury could find State Farm's policy "deliberately crafted" to prey on consumers who would be unlikely to defend themselves. . . . In this regard, the trial court noted the testimony of several former State Farm employees affirming that they were trained to target "the weakest of the herd" — "the elderly, the poor, and other consumers who are least knowledgeable about their rights and thus most vulnerable to trickery or deceit, or who have little money and hence have no real alternative but to accept an inadequate offer to settle a claim at much less than fair value." *Ibid.* (internal quotation marks omitted). The Campbells themselves could be placed within the "weakest of the herd" category. The couple appeared economically vulnerable and emotionally fragile. . . . At the time of State Farm's wrongful conduct, "Mr. Campbell had residuary effects from a stroke and Parkinson's disease."

To further insulate itself from liability, trial evidence indicated, State Farm made "systematic" efforts to destroy internal company documents that might reveal its scheme, . . . efforts that directly affected the Campbells. . . . For example, State Farm had "a special historical department that contained a copy of all past manuals on claim-handling practices and the dates on which each section of each manual was changed.". . . . Yet in discovery proceedings, State Farm failed to produce any claim-handling practice manuals for the years relevant to the Campbells' bad-faith case. . . .

State Farm's inability to produce the manuals, it appeared from the evidence, was not accidental. . . .

. . . State Farm admitted that it destroyed every single copy of claim-handling manuals on file in its historical department as of 1988, even though these documents could have been preserved at minimal expense. . . . Fortuitously, the Campbells obtained a copy of the 1979 PP&R manual by subpoena from a former employee. . . . Although that manual has been requested in other cases, State Farm has never itself produced the document. . . .

"As a final, related tactic," the trial court stated, the jury could reasonably find that "in recent years State Farm has gone to extraordinary lengths to stop damaging documents from being created in the first place." . . . State Farm kept no records at all on excess verdicts in third-party cases, or on bad-faith claims or attendant verdicts. . . . State Farm alleged "that it has no record of its punitive damage payments, even though such payments must be reported to the [Internal Revenue Service] and in some states may not be used to justify rate increases." . . . Regional Vice President Buck Moskalski testified that "he would not report a punitive damage verdict in [the Campbells'] case to higher management, as such reporting was not set out as part of State Farm's management practices." . . .

State Farm's "wrongful profit and evasion schemes," the trial court underscored, were directly relevant to the Campbells' case . . . : "The record fully supports the conclusion that the badfaith claim handling that exposed the Campbells to an excess verdict in 1983, and resulted in severe damages to them, was a product of the unlawful profit scheme that had been put in place by top management at State Farm years earlier. . . . There was ample evidence that the concepts taught in the Excess Liability Handbook, including the dishonest alteration and manipulation of claim files and the policy against posting any supersedeas bond for the full amount of an excess verdict, were dutifully carried out in this case. . . . There was ample basis for the jury to find that everything that had happened to the Campbells — when State Farm repeatedly refused in bad-faith to settle for the $50,000 policy limits and went to trial, and then failed to pay the 'excess' verdict, or at least post a bond, after trial — was a direct application of State Farm's overall profit scheme, operating through Brown and others." . . .

State Farm's "policies and practices," the trial evidence thus bore out, were "responsible for the injuries suffered by the Campbells," and the means used to implement those policies could be found "callous, clandestine, fraudulent, and dishonest." . . . The Utah Supreme Court, relying on the trial court's record-based recitations, understandably characterized State Farm's behavior as "egregious and malicious." . . .

II

The Court dismisses the evidence describing and documenting State Farm's PP&R policy and practices as essentially irrelevant, bearing "no relation to the Campbells' harm.". . . It is hardly apparent why that should be so. What is infirm about the Campbells' theory that their experience with State Farm exemplifies and reflects an overarching underpayment scheme, one that caused "repeated misconduct of the sort that injured them" . . . ? The Court's silence on that score is revealing: Once one recognizes that the Campbells did show "conduct by State Farm similar to that which harmed them," *ante*. . . . it becomes impossible to shrink the reprehensibility analysis to this sole case, or to maintain, at odds with the determination of the trial court . . . that "the adverse effect on the State's general population was in fact minor," *ante*. . . .

Evidence of out-of-state conduct, the Court acknowledges, may be "probative [even if the conduct is lawful in the State where it occurred] when it demonstrates the deliberateness and culpability of the defendant's action in the State where it is tortious. . . ." *Ante* . . . "Other acts" evidence concerning practices both in and out of State was introduced in this case to show just such "deliberateness" and "culpability." The evidence was admissible, the trial court ruled: (1) to document State Farm's "reprehensible" PP&R program; and (2) to "rebut [State Farm's] assertion that [its] actions toward the Campbells were inadvertent errors or mistakes in judgment.". . . Viewed in this light, there surely was "a nexus" between much of the "other acts" evidence and "the specific harm suffered by [the Campbells]." *Ante*. . . .

III

When the Court first ventured to override state-court punitive damages awards, it did so moderately. The Court recalled that "[i]n our federal system, States necessarily have considerable flexibility in determining the level of punitive damages that they will allow in different classes of cases and in any particular case." *Gore*, 517 U. S., at 568. Today's decision exhibits no such respect and restraint. No longer content to accord state-court judgments "a strong presumption of validity," *TXO*, 509 U. S., at 457, the Court announces that "few awards exceeding a single-digit ratio between punitive and compensatory damages, to a significant degree, will satisfy due process.". . . Moreover, the Court adds, when compensatory damages are substantial, doubling those damages "can reach the outermost limit of the due process guarantee." *Ibid*. . . . In a legislative scheme or a state high court's design to cap punitive damages, the handiwork in setting single-digit and 1-to-1 benchmarks could hardly be questioned; in a judicial decree imposed on the States by this Court under the banner of substantive due process, the numerical controls today's decision installs seem to me boldly out of order.

———————

1.   *Philip Morris USA, Inc. v. Williams*, 549 U.S. 346 (2007), held that a punitive damages award that is based on the conduct of the defendant toward nonparties to the litigation amounts to an unconstitutional taking of property without due process, although conduct toward others can be used to assess reprehensibility. The

case involved a suit alleging wrongful death of a smoker as a result of negligence and deceit by a tobacco manufacturer. In an opinion by Justice Breyer, the Court held that it was improper for the state courts to consider harm done to other smokers within the state in determining the amount of the punitive award. The Court reasoned that "to permit punishment for injuring a nonparty victim would add a near standardless dimension to the punitive damages equation." Justices Stevens, Scalia, Thomas, and Ginsburg dissented. In cases like *Gore, State Farm,* and *Philip Morris*, is the Court interpreting constitutional law or setting punitive damages policy?

2. Is there a punitive damages problem? In a watershed article, David G. Owen suggested that the problem, if any, has been overstated. For example, between 1960 and 1962, MER/29 was administered to 400,000 persons for the treatment of high levels of cholesterol. A side effect was that it allegedly caused injuries, such as cataracts, hair loss, and skin disorders, to a minimum of 5000 people. This led to 1500 suits against the manufacturer, Richardson-Merrell, for misrepresentation to the Food and Drug Administration. Only eleven suits resulted in jury verdicts, seven for the plaintiffs. Out of the 1500 suits there were only three awards of punitive damages, ranging from $100,000 to $250,000. One of these was set aside on appeal, leaving only two punitive damage awards standing. *See* David G. Owen, *Punitive Damages in Products Liability Litigation*, 74 Mich. L. Rev. 1257, 1329 (1976).

A later study of 220 federal cases found that punitive damages were awarded in only 2% of the cases. William Landes & Richard Posner, The Economic Structure of Tort Law 302–07 (1987).

3. A fundamental issue in punitive damages cases is whether the defendant must act with intent to harm the plaintiff. In *Taylor v. Superior Court*, involving a suit against a drunk driver, the California Supreme Court held:

Section 3294 of the Civil Code authorizes the recovery of punitive damages in noncontract cases "where the defendant has been guilty of oppression, fraud, or malice, express or implied. . . ."

Other authorities have amplified the foregoing principle. Thus it has been held that the "malice" required by section 3294 "implies an act conceived in a spirit of mischief or with criminal indifference towards the obligations owed to others." (. . . Prosser, Law of Torts (4th ed. 1971) § 2, at pp. 9-10.) In Dean Prosser's words: "Where the defendant's wrongdoing has been intentional and deliberate, and has the character of outrage frequently associated with crime, all but a few courts have permitted the jury to award in the tort action 'punitive' or 'exemplary' damages. . . . Something more than the mere commission of a tort is always required for punitive damages. There must be circumstances of aggravation or outrage, such as spite or 'malice,' or a fraudulent or evil motive on the part of the defendant, or such a conscious and deliberate disregard of the interests of others that his conduct may be called wilful or wanton." . . .

Defendant's successful demurrer to the complaint herein was based upon plaintiff's failure to allege any actual intent of defendant to harm plaintiff or others. Is this an essential element of a claim for punitive damages? . . .

We discern no valid reason whatever for immunizing the driver himself from the exposure to punitive damages given the demonstrable and almost inevitable risk visited upon the innocent public by his voluntary conduct as alleged in the complaint. Indeed, under another recent amendment enacted following our *Coulter* decision, the Legislature has expressly acknowledged that "the consumption of alcoholic beverages is the proximate cause of injuries inflicted upon another by an intoxicated person." (Civ. Code, § 1714, subd. (b).)

Since the filing of *Coulter* we have had the enactment of section 25602. There also has appeared a graphic illustration of the magnitude of the danger in question. In June 1978, the Secretary of Health, Education, and Welfare filed the Third Special Report to the U.S. Congress on Alcohol and Health. We take judicial notice of, and extract the following from, this extensive and very recent official study: "Traffic accidents are the greatest cause of violent death in the United States, and approximately one-third of the ensuing injuries and one-half of the fatalities are alcohol related. In 1975, as many as 22,926 traffic deaths involved alcohol. . . .

. . . .

It is crystal clear to us that courts in the formulation of rules on damage assessment and in weighing the deterrent function must recognize the severe threat to the public safety which is posed by the intoxicated driver. The lesson is self-evident and widely understood. Drunken drivers are extremely dangerous people.

24 Cal. 3d 890, 157 Cal. Rptr. 693, 598 P.2d 854 (1979).

4.   If malice is required for punitive damages, can one show malice in a products liability case resting on strict liability? In a suit by an injured asbestos worker for failure to warn of the danger, the New Jersey Supreme Court, in *Fischer v. Johns-Manville Corp.*, held that punitive damages could be recovered:

On this appeal Johns-Manville's position, succinctly stated, is that the punitive damages award against it is legally impermissible, ill-advised as a matter of public policy in litigation of this nature, and factually unwarranted.

. . . .

The "legally impermissible" argument rests on an asserted theoretical inconsistency between strict liability and punitive damages, which would preclude punitive damage claims when liability for compensatory damages is founded on strict products liability doctrine, if not in all situations at least in asbestos, strict liability lawsuits. We hold that there is no per se legal bar to pursuing a strict liability, failure-to-warn claim and a punitive damage claim in the same case. For this purpose there is no reason to distinguish asbestos litigation from other strict products liability actions. . . .

. . . .

. . . [A]lthough juries are asked in failure-to-warn cases to assess the reasonableness of a defendant's conduct, to prove a prima facie case of strict products liability a plaintiff need not introduce evidence relating to a manufacturer's or distributor's conduct, except to establish that the defendant did in fact put the offending article into the stream of commerce. This is in contrast to the quality of proofs required to establish a claim for punitive damages, in which a great deal must be shown about a defendant's conduct. "Punitive or exemplary damages are sums awarded apart from compensatory damages and are assessed when the wrongdoer's conduct is especially egregious." . . .

The type of conduct that will warrant an award of punitive damages has been described in various ways. The conduct must be "wantonly reckless or malicious. There must be an intentional wrongdoing in the sense of an 'evil-minded act' or an act accompanied by a wanton and willful disregard of the rights of another." *Nappe, supra,* 97 N.J. at 49 (citations omitted). "[T]he requirement may be satisfied upon a showing that there has been a deliberate act or omission with knowledge of a high degree of probability of harm and reckless indifference to consequences." *Berg v. Reaction Motors, supra,* 37 N.J. at 414, 181 A.2d 487. . . .

As should now be apparent, the proofs needed to establish a prima facie case of failure-to-warn, strict products liability differ markedly from the proofs that will support an award of punitive damages. Despite their differences — one going to the theory of liability, the other bearing on the form and extent of relief — they are not mutually exclusive nor even incompatible. There is no reason they cannot be litigated together. We agree with defendant's premises: strict products liability proofs center on the product; punitive damages proofs center on a defendant's conduct. We reject as wholly unwarranted the conclusion defendant draws — that these differences preclude punitive damages claims in failure-to-warn, strict product liability cases.

103 N.J. 643, 512 A.2d 466, 470–72 (1986).

5. Do punitive damage awards against corporations inappropriately punish shareholders?

[An] argument, which ignores the legal nature of corporations, is that punitive damages unfairly punish innocent shareholders. This argument has been rejected repeatedly. . . . It is the corporation, not the individual shareholders, that is recognized as an ongoing legal entity engaged in manufacturing and distributing products. True, payment of punitive damages claims will deplete corporate assets, which will possibly produce a reduction in net worth and thereby result in a reduction in the value of individual shares. But the same is true of compensatory damages. Both are possible legal consequences of the commission of harmful acts in the course of doing business. To the same extent that damages claims may affect shareholders adversely, so do profitable sales of harmful products redound to their benefit (at least temporarily). These are the risks and rewards that await investors. Also, we would not consider it harmful were shareholders to be encouraged by decisions such as this to give close scrutiny to corporate practices in making investment decisions.

Fischer v. Johns-Manville, 103 N.J. 643, 512 A.2d 466, 476 (1986). What can be said of investing in tobacco stocks today?

6. Is it against public policy for insurance to cover punitive damages (so the loss is spread among the public, rather than visited upon the actor)? Yes, in California, *J.C. Penney Cas. Ins. v. M.K.*, 52 Cal. 3d 1009, 278 Cal. Rptr. 64, 804 P.2d 689 (1991). Yes, in New York, *Home Ins. Co. v. American Home Prods. Corp.*, 75 N.Y.2d 196, 551 N.Y.S.2d 481, 550 N.E.2d 930 (1990).

7. For a further discussion of punitive damages, see James B. Sales & Kenneth B. Cole, Jr., *Punitive Damages: A Relic That Has Outlived Its Origins*, 37 Vand. L. Rev. 1117 (1984), and Johnston, *Punitive Liability: A New Paradigm of Efficiency in Tort Law*, 87 Colum. L. Rev. 1385 (1987).

8. Does the criminal prosecution of corporations make more sense than punitive damages? One author has concluded that punitive damages are better, because criminal prosecution is unlikely, unsuccessful, and expensive. Frank J. Vandall, *Criminal Prosecution of Corporations for Defective Products*, 12 Int'l Legal Prac. 66 (Sept. 1987).

9. Punitive damages are taxable as ordinary income. *O'Gilvie v. United States*, 519 U.S. 79 (1996).

B. PECUNIARY AND NONECONOMIC DAMAGES

PROBLEM

What would someone have to pay you in order to obtain your consent to breaking your little finger (without anesthesia)? Is your answer to that question relevant to determining what damages you should receive if someone negligently breaks your little finger?

SEFFERT v. LOS ANGELES TRANSIT LINES
Supreme Court of California, 1961
364 P.2d 337

PETERS, J.

Defendants appeal from a judgment for plaintiff for $187,903.75 entered on a jury verdict. Their motion for a new trial for errors of law and excessiveness of damages was denied.

At the trial plaintiff contended that she was properly entering defendants' bus when the doors closed suddenly catching her right hand and left foot. The bus started, dragged her some distance, and then threw her to the pavement. Defendants contended that the injury resulted from plaintiff's own negligence, that she was late for work and either ran into the side of the bus after the doors had closed or ran after the bus and attempted to enter after the doors had nearly closed.

The evidence supports plaintiff's version of the facts. Several eyewitnesses testified that plaintiff started to board the bus while it was standing with the doors wide open. Defendants do not challenge the sufficiency of the evidence. They do contend, however, that prejudicial errors were committed during the trial and that the verdict is excessive.

. . . .

One of the major contentions of defendants is that the damages are excessive, as a matter of law. There is no merit to this contention.

The evidence most favorable to the plaintiff shows that prior to the accident plaintiff was in good health, and had suffered no prior serious injuries. She was single, and had been self-supporting for 20 of her 42 years. The accident happened on October 11, 1957. The trial took place in July and August of 1959.

As already pointed out, the injury occurred when plaintiff was caught in the doors of defendants' bus when it started up before she had gained full entry. As a result she was dragged for some distance. The record is uncontradicted that her injuries were serious, painful, disabling and permanent.

The major injuries were to plaintiff's left foot. The main arteries and nerves leading to that foot, and the posterior tibial vessels and nerve of that foot, were completely severed at the ankle. The main blood vessel which supplies blood to that foot had to be tied off, with the result that there is a permanent stoppage of the main blood source. The heel and shin bones were fractured. There were deep lacerations and an avulsion[6] which involved the skin and soft tissue of the entire foot.

These injuries were extremely painful. They have resulted in a permanently raised left heel, which is two inches above the floor level, caused by the contraction of the ankle joint capsule. Plaintiff is crippled and will suffer pain for life.[7] Although this pain could, perhaps, be alleviated by an operative fusion of the ankle, the doctors considered and rejected this procedure because the area has been deprived of its normal blood supply. The foot is not only permanently deformed but has a persistent open ulcer on the heel, there being a continuous drainage from the entire area. Medical care of this foot and ankle is to be reasonably expected for the remainder of plaintiff's life.

Since the accident, and because of it, plaintiff has undergone nine operations and has spent eight months in various hospitals and rehabilitation centers. These operations involved painful skin grafting and other painful procedures. One involved the surgical removal of gangrenous skin leaving painful raw and open flesh exposed from the heel to the toe. Another involved a left lumbar sympathectomy in which plaintiff's abdomen was entered to sever the nerves affecting the remaining blood

---

[6] Defined in Webster's New International Dictionary (2d ed.) as a "tearing asunder; forcible separation."

[7] Her life expectancy was 34.9 years from the time of trial.

vessels of the left leg in order to force those blood vessels to remain open at all times to the maximum extent. Still another operation involved a cross leg flap graft of skin and tissue from plaintiff's thigh which required that her left foot be brought up to her right thigh and held at this painful angle, motionless, and in a cast for a month until the flap of skin and fat, partially removed from her thigh, but still nourished there by a skin connection, could be grafted to the bottom of her foot, and until the host site could develop enough blood vessels to support it. Several future operations of this nature may be necessary. One result of this operation was to leave a defective area of the thigh where the normal fat is missing and the muscles exposed, and the local nerves are missing. This condition is permanent and disfiguring.

Another operation called a debridement, was required. This involved removal of many small muscles of the foot, much of the fat beneath the skin, cleaning the end of the severed nerve, and tying off the severed vein and artery.

The ulcer on the heel is probably permanent, and there is the constant and real danger that osteomyelitis may develop if the infection extends into the bone. If this happens the heel bone would have to be removed surgically and perhaps the entire foot amputated.

Although plaintiff has gone back to work, she testified that she has difficulty standing, walking or even sitting, and must lie down frequently; that the leg is still very painful; that she can, even on her best days, walk not over three blocks and that very slowly; that her back hurts from walking; that she is tired and weak; that her sleep is disturbed; that she has frequent spasms in which the leg shakes uncontrollably; that she feels depressed and unhappy, and suffers humiliation and embarrassment.

Plaintiff claims that there is evidence that her total pecuniary loss, past and future, amounts to $53,903.75. This was the figure used by plaintiff's counsel in his argument to the jury, in which he also claimed $134,000 for pain and suffering, past and future. Since the verdict was exactly the total of these two estimates, it is reasonable to assume that the jury accepted the amount proposed by counsel for each item. . . .

The summary of plaintiff as to pecuniary loss, past and future, is as follows:

Doctor and Hospital Bills	$10,330.50	
Drugs and other medical expenses stipulated to in the amount of	2,273.25	
Loss of earnings from time of accident to time of trial	5,500.00	$18,103.75
Future Medical Expenses:		
$2,000 per year for next 10 years	20,000.00	
$200 per year for the 24 years thereafter	4,800.00	
Drugs for 34 years	1,000.00	25,800.00
		43,903.75
Possible future loss of earnings		10,000.00

Total Pecuniary Loss　　　　　　　　　　　　　　　　　　　$53,903.75

There is substantial evidence to support these estimates. The amounts for past doctor and hospital bills, for the cost of drugs, and for a past loss of earnings, were either stipulated to, evidence was offered on, or is a simple matter of calculation. These items totaled $18,103.75. While the amount of $25,800 estimated as the cost of future medical expense, for loss of future earnings and for the future cost of drugs, may seem high, there was substantial evidence that future medical expense is certain to be high. There is also substantial evidence that plaintiff's future earning capacity may be substantially impaired by reason of the injury. The amounts estimated for those various items are not out of line, and find support in the evidence.

This leaves the amount of $134,000 presumably allowed for the nonpecuniary items of damage, including pain and suffering, past and future. It is this allowance that defendants seriously attack as being excessive as a matter of law.

It must be remembered that the jury fixed these damages, and that the trial judge denied a motion for new trial, one ground of which was excessiveness of the award. These determinations are entitled to great weight. The amount of damages is a fact question, first committed to the discretion of the jury and next to the discretion of the trial judge on a motion for new trial. They see and hear the witnesses and frequently, as in this case, see the injury and the impairment that has resulted therefrom. As a result, all presumptions are in favor of the decision of the trial court. . . . The power of the appellate court differs materially from that of the trial court in passing on this question. An appellate court can interfere on the ground that the judgment is excessive only on the ground that the verdict is so large that, at first blush, it shocks the conscience and suggests passion, prejudice or corruption on the part of the jury. The proper rule was stated in *Holmes v. Southern Cal. Edison Co.*, 78 Cal. App. 2d 43, 51 [177 P.2d 32], as follows: "The powers and duties of a trial judge in ruling on a motion for new trial and of an appellate court on an appeal from a judgment are very different when the question of an excessive award of damages arises. The trial judge sits as a thirteenth juror with the power to weigh the evidence and judge the credibility of the witnesses. If he believes the damages awarded by the jury to be excessive and the question is presented it becomes his duty to reduce them. . . . When the question is raised his denial of a motion for new trial is an indication that he approves the amount of the award. An appellate court has no such powers. It cannot weigh the evidence and pass on the credibility of the witnesses as a juror does. To hold an award excessive it must be so large as to indicate passion or prejudice on the part of the jurors." In *Holder v. Key System*, 88 Cal. App. 2d 925, 940 [200 P.2d 98], the court, after quoting the above from the *Holmes* case added: "The question is not what this court would have awarded as the trier of the fact, but whether this court can say that the award is so high as to suggest passion or prejudice." In *Wilson v. Fitch*, 41 Cal. 363, 386, decided in 1871, there appears the oft-quoted statement that: "The Court will not interfere in such cases unless the amount awarded is so grossly excessive as to shock the moral sense, and raise a reasonable presumption that the jury was under the influence of passion or prejudice. In this case, whilst the sum awarded appears to be much larger than the facts demanded, the amount cannot be said to be so grossly excessive as to be reasonably imputed only to passion or prejudice in the jury. In such cases there is no accurate standard by which to compute the injury, and the jury must, necessarily, be left to the exercise of a wide discretion; to be restricted by the Court only when the sum awarded is so large that the verdict shocks the moral sense, and raises a presumption that it must have proceeded from passion or prejudice." This same rule was announced in *Johnston v. Long*, 30 Cal. 2d 54, 76 [181 P.2d 645], where it was stated that it "is not the function of a reviewing court to interfere with a jury's award of damages unless it is so grossly disproportionate to any reasonable limit of compensation warranted by the facts that it shocks the court's sense of justice and raises a presumption that it was the result of passion and prejudice." . . .

There are no fixed or absolute standards by which an appellate court can measure in monetary terms the extent of the damages suffered by a plaintiff as a result of the wrongful act of the defendant. The duty of an appellate court is to uphold the jury and trial judge whenever possible. . . . The amount to be awarded is "a matter on which there legitimately may be a wide difference of opinion". . . . In considering the contention that the damages are excessive the appellate court must determine every conflict in the evidence in respondent's favor, and must give him the benefit of every inference reasonably to be drawn from the record. . . .

While the appellate court should consider the amounts awarded in prior cases for similar injuries, obviously, each case must be decided on its own facts and circumstances. Such examination demonstrates that such awards vary greatly . . . Injuries are seldom identical and the amount of pain and suffering involved in similar physical injuries varies widely. These factors must be considered. . . . Basically, the question that should be decided by the appellate courts is whether or not the verdict is so out of line with reason that it shocks the conscience and necessarily implies that the verdict must have been the result of passion and prejudice.

In the instant case, the nonpecuniary items of damage include allowances for pain and suffering, past and future, humiliation as a result of being disfigured and being permanently crippled, and constant anxiety and fear that the leg will have to be amputated. While the amount of the award is high, and may be more than we would have awarded were we the trier of the facts, considering the nature of the injury, the great pain and suffering, past and future, and the other items of damage, we cannot say, as a matter of law, that it is so high that it shocks the conscience and gives rise to the presumption that it was the result of passion or prejudice on the part of the jurors.

Defendants next complain that it was prejudicial error for plaintiff's counsel to argue to the jury that damages for pain and suffering could be fixed by means of a mathematical formula predicated upon a per diem allowance for this item of damages. The propriety of such an argument seems never to have been passed upon in this state. In other jurisdictions there is a sharp divergence of opinion on the subject. . . . It is not necessary to pass on the propriety of such argument in the instant case because, when plaintiff's counsel made the argument in question, defendants' counsel did not object, assign it as misconduct or ask that the jury be admonished to disregard it. Moreover, in his argument to the jury, the defendants' counsel also adopted a mathematical formula type of argument. This being so, even if such argument were error (a point we do not pass upon), the point must be deemed to have been waived, and cannot be raised, properly, on appeal. *(State Rubbish etc. Assn. v. Siliznoff*, 38 Cal. 2d 330, 340 [240 P.2d 282].)

The judgment appealed from is affirmed.

TRAYNOR, J.

I dissent.

Although I agree that there was no prejudicial error on the issue of liability, it is my opinion that the award of $134,000 for pain and suffering is so excessive as to indicate that it was prompted by passion, prejudice, whim, or caprice.[1]

Before the accident plaintiff was employed as a file clerk at a salary of $375 a month. At the time of the trial she had returned to her job at the same salary and her foot had healed sufficiently for her to walk. At the time of the accident she was 42 years old with a life expectancy of 34.9 years.

During closing argument plaintiff's counsel summarized the evidence relevant to past and possible future damages and proposed a specific amount for each item. His total of $187,903.75 was the exact amount awarded by the jury.

Total Pecuniary Loss		53,903.75
Pain and Suffering:		
From time of accident to time of trial (660 days) at $100 a day	66,000.00	
For the remainder of her life (34 years) at $2,000 a year	68,000.00	134,000.00
Total proposed by counsel		$187,903.75

The jury and the trial court have broad discretion in determining the damages in a personal injury case . . . A reviewing court, however, has responsibilities not only to the litigants in an action but to future litigants and must reverse or remit when a jury awards either inadequate or excessive damages.

. . . .

The crucial question in this case, therefore, is whether the award of $134,000 for pain and suffering is so excessive it must have resulted from passion, prejudice, whim or caprice. "To say that a verdict has been influenced by passion or prejudice is but another way of saying that the verdict exceeds any amount justified by the evidence." . . .

---

[1] The award of $53,903.75 for pecuniary loss, past and future, is also suspect. The amount awarded for future medical expenses is $12,196.25 greater than the medical expenses incurred from the time of the accident to the time of trial, a period of nearly two years. The amount awarded for future loss of earnings is $4,500 greater than plaintiffs past loss of earnings. Yet the evidence indicates that plaintiff's medical care has been largely completed and that the future loss of earnings will not exceed the earnings lost by the prolonged stays in the hospital and the rehabilitation center.

There has been forceful criticism of the rationale for awarding damages for pain and suffering in negligence cases. (Morris, *Liability for Pain and Suffering*, 59 Columb. L. Rev. 476; Plant, *Damages for Pain and Suffering*, 19 Ohio L. J. 200; Jaffe, *Damages for Personal Injury: The Impact of Insurance*, 18 Law and Contemporary Problems 219; Zelermyer, *Damages for Pain and Suffering*, 6 Syracuse L. Rev. 27.) Such damages originated under primitive law as a means of punishing wrongdoers and assuaging the feelings of those who had been wronged. (Morris, *Liability for Pain and Suffering, supra,* 59 Columb. L. Rev. at p. 478; Jaffe, *Damages for Personal Injury: The Impact of Insurance, supra,* 18 Law and Contemporary Problems at pp. 222-223.) They become increasingly anomalous as emphasis shifts in a mechanized society from ad hoc punishment to orderly distribution of losses through insurance and the price of goods or of transportation. Ultimately such losses are borne by a public free of fault as part of the price for the benefits of mechanization. . . .

Nonetheless, this state has long recognized pain and suffering as elements of damages in negligence cases (*Zibbell v. Southern Pacific Co., supra,* 160 Cal. 237, 250; *Roedder v. Rowley, supra,* 28 Cal. 2d 820, 822); any change in this regard must await reexamination of the problem by the Legislature. Meanwhile, awards for pain and suffering serve to ease plaintiffs' discomfort and to pay for attorney fees for which plaintiffs are not otherwise compensated.

It would hardly be possible ever to compensate a person fully for pain and suffering. "No rational being would change places with the injured man for an amount of gold that would fill the room of the court, yet no lawyer would contend that such is the legal measure of damages." (*Zibbell v. Southern Pacific Co., supra,* 160 Cal. 237, 255; *see* 2 Harper and James, The Law of Torts 1322.) "Translating pain and anguish into dollars can, at best, be only an arbitrary allowance, and not a process of measurement, and consequently the judge can, in his instructions give the jury no standard to go by; he can only tell them to allow such amount as in their discretion they may consider reasonable. . . . The chief reliance for reaching reasonable results in attempting to value suffering in terms of money must be the restraint and common sense of the jury. . . ." (McCormick, Damages, § 88, pp. 318-319.) Such restraint and common sense were lacking here.

A review of reported cases involving serious injuries and large pecuniary losses reveals that ordinarily the part of the verdict attributable to pain and suffering does not exceed the part attributable to pecuniary losses. . . . The award in this case of $134,000 for pain and suffering exceeds not only the pecuniary losses but any such award heretofore sustained in this state even in cases involving injuries more serious by far than those suffered by plaintiff. . . . In *McNulty v. Southern Pacific Co., supra,* the court reviewed a large number of cases involving injuries to legs and feet, in each of which the total judgment, including both pecuniary loss and pain and suffering did not exceed $100,000[2] Although excessive damages is "an issue which is primarily factual and is not therefore a matter which can be decided upon the basis of awards made in other cases," . . . awards for similar injuries may be

---

[2] The verdicts in some of these cases were over $100,000 but in each case the award was reduced to $100,000 or less.

considered as one factor to be weighed in determining whether the damages awarded are excessive. . . .

The excessive award in this case was undoubtedly the result of the improper argument of plaintiff's counsel to the jury. Though no evidence was introduced, though none could possibly be introduced on the monetary value of plaintiff's suffering, counsel urged the jury to award $100 a day for pain and suffering from the time of the accident to the time of trial and $2,000 a year for pain and suffering for the remainder of plaintiff's life.

The propriety of counsel's proposing a specific sum for each day or month of suffering has recently been considered by courts of several jurisdictions. . . . The reasons for and against permitting "per diem argument for pain and suffering" are reviewed in *Ratner v. Arrington* (Fla. App.), 111 So. 2d 82, 85-90 [1959 Florida decision holding such argument is permissible] and *Botta v. Brunner*, 26 N.J. 82 [138 A.2d 713, 718-725, 60 A.L.R.2d 1331] [1958 New Jersey decision holding such argument to be an "unwarranted intrusion into the domain of the jury"].

The reason usually advanced for not allowing such argument is that since there is no way of translating pain and suffering into monetary terms, counsel's proposal of a particular sum for each day of suffering represents an opinion and a conclusion on matters not disclosed by the evidence, and tends to mislead the jury and result in excessive awards. The reason usually advanced for allowing "per diem argument for pain and suffering" is that it affords the jury as good an arbitrary measure as any for that which cannot be measured.

Counsel may argue all legitimate inferences from the evidence, but he may not employ arguments that tend primarily to mislead the jury. . . . A specified sum for pain and suffering for any particular period is bound to be conjectural. Positing such a sum for a small period of time and then multiplying that sum by the number of days, minutes or seconds in plaintiff's life expectancy multiplies the hazards of conjecture. Counsel could arrive at any amount he wished by adjusting either the period of time to be taken as a measure or the amount surmised for the pain for that period.

> "The absurdity of a mathematical formula is demonstrated by applying it to its logical conclusion. If a day may be used as a unit of time in measuring pain and suffering, there is no logical reason why an hour or a minute or a second could not be used, or perhaps even a heart-beat since we live from heart-beat to heart-beat. If one cent were used for each second of pain this would amount to $3.60 per hour, to $86.40 per twenty-four hour day, and to $31,536 per year. The absurdity of such a result must be apparent, yet a penny a second for pain and suffering might not sound unreasonable. . . . The use of the formula was prejudicial error." . . .

The misleading effect of the per diem argument was not cured by the use of a similar argument by defense counsel. Truth is not served by a clash of sophistic arguments. . . . Had defendant objected to the improper argument of plaintiff's counsel this error would be a sufficient ground for reversal whether or not the award was excessive as a matter of law. Defendant's failure to object, however, did not preclude its appeal on the ground that the award was excessive as a matter of law or preclude this court's reversing on that ground and ruling on the impropriety of counsel's argument to guide the court on the retrial. . . .

I would reverse the judgment and remand the cause for a new trial on the issue of damages.

---

1. Why is the jury verdict on damages entitled to "great weight"? What is the test for setting aside the jury's award? Is the test helpful? What is Justice Traynor's reasoning for casting aside the jury verdict? How is Traynor's view of the role of the appellate court different from the majority's view?

2. The majority of personal injury damages are awarded in lump-sum amounts, not on a weekly or monthly basis, although tort settlements sometimes provide for periodic payments from a fund established by the settling defendant(s). Compensatory damage awards can be divided into two subcategories: special damages and general damages. Special damages are pecuniary losses and are objectively calculated, while general damages are noneconomic and subjectively determined. General damages will be discussed below in connection with damages for pain and suffering and loss of enjoyment of life.

Past Pecuniary Losses. Included in pecuniary losses are both past and future losses. Past pecuniary losses are relatively easy to calculate because bills and receipts are available, documenting past losses, such as medical expenses, lost earnings, and funeral expenses.

Future Pecuniary Losses. In personal injury cases, future losses to the plaintiff are recoverable. These losses include such items as future medical expenses, future earnings, and future lost pension benefits. Lost future earnings and benefits are also recoverable in wrongful death actions. These future losses are more problematic to calculate and usually require an economist to give expert testimony. Without reliable expert evidence, any type of future losses estimate will likely be found too speculative.

Future losses vary according to the injured party's age, gender, type of injury, occupation, life expectancy, work life expectancy, any discount rate and inflation factor which may be applicable, the annual wage rate increase, probable future earning capacity, and the loss of future earning ability and capacity. *Andrews v. Mosley Well Serv.*, 514 So. 2d 491, 499 (La. Ct. App. 1987). "An award for the loss of future earnings requires first a determination of the underlying facts influencing future earning capacity, and then a calculation of the loss based upon those facts." *Id.* Economists often refer to life expectancy and mortality tables to determine how much longer the victim will live.

Discounting to Present Value. A dollar today is worth more than a dollar a year from now. That is the logic behind discounting lump sum damage awards for future losses to present value. Generally, only a plaintiff's future pecuniary losses are discounted to present value. "The rationale for reducing a lump-sum award to its present value is that: it is assumed that the plaintiff will invest the sum awarded and receive interest thereon. That interest accumulated over the number of relevant years will be available, in addition to the capital, to provide the plaintiff with his future support until the total is exhausted at the end of the period." *Kaczkowski v. Bolubasz*, 491 Pa. 561, 567 n.10, 421 A.2d 1027, 1030 n.10 (1980). The majority of courts do not discount damages for future pain and suffering because of the subjective character of those damages. *Friedman v. C & S Car Serv.*, 108 N.J. 72, 527 A.2d 871 (1987).

In order to reduce an award to present value, an economist generally testifies to the appropriate discount rate. The discount rate should be based on the rate of interest that would be earned on "the best and safest investments." *Jones & Laughlin Steel Corp. v. Pfeifer*, 462 U.S. 523, 537 (1983). *See* Restatement of the Law (Second) Torts § 913A; John G. Fleming, *The Impact of Inflation on Tort Compensation*, 26 Am. J. Comp. Law 51 (1977); John P. Henderson, *The Consideration of Increased Productivity and the Discounting of Future Earnings to Present Value*, 20 S.D. L. Rev. 307 (1975).

Allowing for Inflation. While the defendants' attorneys argue for present value of lump sum future earnings damages, the plaintiffs' attorneys argue for inflation, in terms of cost of living increases. Inflation plays two different roles. It determines the impact of inflation on the future earnings of the victim and the appropriate interest rate to discount the future damage award to its present value. *Kaczkowski v. Bolubasz*, 491 Pa. 561, 565 n.4, 421 A.2d 1027, 1029 n.4 (1980). The Fifth Circuit reviewed three possible methods for adjusting damage awards to account for inflation:

> In the case-by-case method, the fact-finder is asked to predict all of the wage increases a plaintiff would have received during each year that he could have been expected to work, but for his injury, including those attributable to price inflation. This prediction allows the fact-finder to compute the income stream the plaintiff has lost because of his disability. The fact-finder then discounts that income stream to present value, using the estimated after-tax market interest rate, and the resulting figure is awarded to the plaintiff. . . .

> In the below-market discount method, the fact-finder . . . estimates the wage increases the plaintiff would have received each year as a result of all factors other than inflation. The discount rate represents the estimated market interest rate, adjusted for the effect of any income tax and then offset by the estimated rate of general future price inflation. . . .

> The third method is the "total offset" method. In this calculation, future wage increases, including the effects of future price inflation, are legally presumed to offset exactly the interest a plaintiff would earn by investing the lump-sum damage award. Therefore, the fact-finder using this method awards the plaintiff the amount it estimates he would have earned, and neither discounts the award nor adjusts it for inflation.

Culver v. Odeco Drilling, 722 F.2d 114, 118 (5th Cir. 1983). Which is the best method? *See also Jones & Laughlin Steel Corp. v. Pfeifer*, 462 U.S. 523 (1983) (reviewing the various methods for adjusting damage awards to account for inflation, without imposing one particular method on the lower courts). For more discussion, see Steven L. Winer, *Adjusting Damage Awards for Future Inflation,*

1982 Wis. L. Rev. 397; William F. Landsea & David L. Roberts, *Inflation and the Present Value of Future Economic Damages*, 37 U. Miami L. Rev. 93 (1982); Alexander M. Waldrop, *Accounting for Inflation and Other Productivity Factors When Calculating Lost Future Earning Capacity*, 72 Ky. L.J. 951 (1984).

3. *Per Diem Argument.* A per diem argument is a tool of persuasion used by a plaintiff's attorney to suggest to the jury how it can quantify plaintiff's damages for pain and suffering, as based on the evidence. *Debus v. Grand Union Stores of Vermont*, 159 Vt. 537, 539, 621 A.2d 1288, 1290 (1993). Counsel generally presents a dollar amount per unit of time to assist the jury in its calculation of the extent of the pain. For example, in closing argument, counsel may argue to the jury that it should award the plaintiff ten dollars a day every day for the next twenty-five years of the plaintiff's life. With this mathematical formula, the numbers quickly accrue, but it gives the jury something concrete to comprehend the amount of pain and suffering the plaintiff will endure for the next twenty-five years. Opposing counsel is allowed to rebut these arguments and can easily do so if the plaintiff's numbers are unreasonable.

Jurisdictions are split regarding the use of such per diem arguments. Those against the per diem approach insist that per diem arguments are merely argument, having never been entered into evidence, but nonetheless relied on by the jury to generate a jury award. An "illusion of certainty" is created. The plaintiff presents an illusion that pain is "constant, uniform, and continuous." Some courts believe that the jury will be too easily misled by the per diem argument. *See Botta v. Brunner*, 26 N.J. 82, 138 A.2d 713 (1958).

The courts that allow per diem arguments sometimes do so with the safeguard of cautionary instructions to the jury. *See Giant Food, Inc. v. Satterfield*, 90 Md. App. 660, 603 A.2d 877 (1992). As long as the trial court instructs the jury that the plaintiff's per diem arguments are arguments, and not evidence, the appellate court will likely uphold the jury's award.

4. *Pain and Suffering.* General damages refer "to those damages which may not be fixed with any degree of exactitude, but which involve mental or physical pain or suffering, inconvenience, loss of gratification or intellectual or physical enjoyment, or other losses of lifestyle which cannot be measured definitively in terms of money." *Foster v. Trafalgar House Oil & Gas*, 603 So. 2d 284 (La. Ct. App. 1992). Included in general damages are damages for pain and suffering. These nonpecuniary damages serve to give the plaintiff a full recovery for his injury. The majority rule is that damages are recoverable only for pain and suffering that is consciously experienced.

For demonstrative purposes, some plaintiffs submit "day in the life" films to show the jury the effects of the injury on the plaintiff. These films are generally admissible as long as they are an "accurate representation of the victim," *Wagner v. York Hosp.*, 415 Pa. Super. 1, 608 A.2d 496 (1992), and are not unduly prejudicial to the defendant. Other forms of demonstrative evidence are photographs, charts, diagrams, and other visual aids. Demonstrative evidence is admissible as long as it does not mislead or confuse the jury.

What is the function of damages for pain and suffering? If they drive up the cost of goods and services, is that a good reason to limit them?

Many recent tort reform proposals focus on pain and suffering and other forms of "noneconomic" damages. In some states, statutory caps limit the amount of noneconomic damages a tort plaintiff may recover. *See, e.g., DRD Pool Serv. v. Freed*, 5 A.3d 45 (Md. 2010) (upholding constitutionality of Md. Code Ann., Cts. & Jud. Proc. § 11-108, which put a statutory cap on noneconomic damages in Maryland tort suits). See note 13, *infra*. When noneconomic damages are capped, which victims are most acutely affected?

5. *Contingent Fees*. Personal injury attorneys representing plaintiffs are generally paid on a contingent fee basis, as opposed to an hourly rate. A contingent fee arrangement means that the attorney contracts with his or her client to be paid a certain percentage of the proceeds from settlement or a successful judgment. Fee agreements often specify a lower percentage if the case is settled and a higher one if it goes to trial. If the plaintiff loses at trial, the attorney is paid nothing for his or her services. Three main reasons support the contingency fee basis: (1) it enables the poor plaintiff, who may not be able to afford an hourly rate attorney, to pursue a claim; (2) it allows the plaintiff to shift his economic risk to the attorney, who has greater resources and is better able to spread the risk; and (3) it aligns the interests of the plaintiff with those of the attorney. Bradley L. Smith, Note, *Three Attorney Fee-Shifting Rules and Contingency Fees: Their Impact on Settlement Incentives*, 90 Mich. L. Rev. 2154, 2163 (1992). Those opposing the contingency fee arrangement argue that it produces high fees, encourages excessive litigation, and creates incentives for lawyers to accept settlement offers when settlement is contrary to their clients' best interests. *Id.*

The contingent fee arrangement is banned in many foreign countries, and its presence in the United States has generated much criticism. In response, many state legislatures have enacted tort reform statutes imposing fixed or sliding scale maxima for contingent fees in medical malpractice suits. A few states, via statute or court rules, have limited the contingent fee system in all or most tort suits. Most of these rules have been held constitutional. Richard M. Birnholz, *The Validity and Propriety of Contingent Fee Controls*, 37 UCLA L. Rev. 949, 950–53 (1990). *See* Conn. Gen. Stat. § 52-251c (sliding scale for all personal injury, wrongful death, and property damage actions: an attorney's fee on a contingency fee arrangement may not exceed "(1) Thirty-three and one-third per cent of the first three hundred thousand dollars; (2) twenty-five per cent of the next three hundred thousand dollars; (3) twenty per cent of the next three hundred thousand dollars; (4) fifteen per cent of the next three hundred thousand dollars; and (5) ten per cent of any amount which exceeds one million two hundred thousand dollars.") and Mich. Gen. Ct. R. 8.121 (1996) (maximum allowable fee is one-third of the amount recovered).

6. Who pays the plaintiff's attorney? One explanation for an award for pain and suffering is that it pays the plaintiff's attorney. Without an award for pain and suffering, the plaintiff would not be put back in the position he or she was in before the injury, because the attorney's fee would be subtracted from the plaintiff's economic damages. *See* Michael Horowitz, *Making Ethics Real, Making Ethics Work: A Proposal for Contingency Fee Reform*, 44 Emory L.J. 173 (1995).

7. Is it accurate to say that no "rational being would change places with the injured man"? Could evidence have been introduced on the monetary value of plaintiff's suffering?

8. What do you think of the following argument by Judge Posner?

> We disagree with those students of tort law who believe that pain and suffering are not real costs and should not be allowable items of damages in a tort suit. No one likes pain and suffering and most people would pay a good deal of money to be free of them. If they were not recoverable in damages, the cost of negligence would be less to the tortfeasors and there would be more negligence, more accidents, more pain and suffering, and hence higher social costs.

Kwasny v. United States, 823 F.2d 194, 197 (7th Cir. 1987).

9. *Loss of Enjoyment of Life.* May a comatose person recover for an element of pain and suffering called "loss of enjoyment of life"? Loss of enjoyment of life damages, also known as hedonic damages, belong to the group of general damages. *See Thompson v. National R.R. Passenger Corp.*, 621 F.2d 814, 824 (6th Cir. 1980) (characterizing the types of damages as follows: "Permanent impairment compensates the victim for the fact of being permanently injured whether or not it causes any pain or inconvenience; pain and suffering compensates the victim for the physical and mental discomfort caused by the injury; and loss of enjoyment of life compensates the victim for the limitations on the person's life created by the injury.").

Courts vary in their approach to damages for the loss of enjoyment of life. Most courts place hedonic damages in the same group as pain and suffering, while others place them in a separate group, hedonic damages. A third category of courts completely disregards damages for the loss of enjoyment of life. Pamela J. Hermes, *Loss of Enjoyment of Life — Duplication of Damages Versus Full Compensation*, 63 N.D. L. Rev. 561 (1987). Unlike pain and suffering, courts may not require the victim to be conscious or aware of his or her loss of enjoyment of life. *See Holston v. Sisters of Third Order of St. Francis*, 247 Ill. App. 3d 985, 1005, 618 N.E.2d 334, 347 (1993) (holding that damages may be awarded for "the loss of enjoyment of life to a disabled person even if she was unaware of her loss because she had been deprived of her consciousness and therefore her ability to enjoy her life"). The award does not need to have any meaning or utility to the injured person. *But see McDougald v. Garber*, 73 N.Y.2d 246, 538 N.Y.S.2d 937, 536 N.E.2d 372 (1989) (requiring the plaintiff to have some level of cognitive awareness in order to recover for loss of enjoyment, because otherwise an award for such damages would be punitive and duplicative).

10. *Remittitur and Additur.* Remittitur and additur are procedural post-trial tools courts use to reduce appeals and to promote efficiency. Courts reduce jury awards through a remittitur. They increase a jury award through an additur. Before an additur or a remittitur is granted, however, the court examines the reasonableness of the jury verdict to see if it is against the clear weight of the evidence. The standards courts use are often dictated by statutes. However, a jury is given wide discretion in its award, and a trial court is also given much deference in granting or denying an additur or remittitur. One or both parties move for a new trial; then, if either party denies the additur or remittitur, a motion for a new trial may be granted. The new trial may be either a full-blown new trial or just a trial on the issue of damages.

Courts reduce jury awards considered excessive on the condition that the losing defendant will not be granted a new trial. *Honda Motor Co. v. Oberg*, 512 U.S. 415, 114 S. Ct. 2331 (1994). Neither side is required to accept the remittitur. Two principal objectives are considered when calculating the amount of the remittitur. "The first is to enable the parties to avoid the delay and expense of a new trial when the jury award is excessive. The second objective is to minimize the extent of the judicial interference with matter that is otherwise within the jury's domain." *Slade v. Whitco Corp.*, 811 F. Supp. 71, 77 (N.D.N.Y. 1993).

The *Slade* court described three possible methods for calculating a remittitur. The first method is to "reduce the verdict to the lowest amount that could reasonably be found by the jury." Second, the court can reduce the verdict only to the maximum amount not considered excessive and that would be upheld by the trial court. Third, the court can "reduce the jury award to what the trial court believes a properly functioning jury, acting free of suggestions by counsel will have awarded." *Slade*, 811 F. Supp. at 77. *See* Irene D. Sann, *Remittiturs (and Additurs) in the Federal Courts: An Evaluation with Suggested Alternatives*, 38 Case W. Res. L. Rev. 157 (1987).

Courts use additur to increase jury awards. However, the U.S. Supreme Court found additur to be unconstitutional in the federal courts. Finding additur to violate the Seventh Amendment right to a jury trial, the Court in *Dimick v. Schiedt*, 293 U.S. 474 (1935), held that additur invaded the jury's fact-finding authority. Some states allow additur, while others have found it unconstitutional under their state constitutions. The Supreme Court has not addressed the constitutional issue of remittiturs. *See* Fed. R. Civ. P. 59; David Baldus, John C. MacQueen, et al., *Improving Judicial Oversight of Jury Damages Assessments: A Proposal for the Comparative Additur/Remittitur Review of Awards for Nonpecuniary Harms and Punitive Damages*, 80 Iowa L. Rev. 1109 (1995).

11. *The Collateral Source Rule.* The plaintiff often has insurance that has paid his or her medical bills and property damage. Nevertheless, the plaintiff is entitled to recover the same damages in court. Under the common-law collateral source rule, evidence of a collateral source of compensation such as insurance is inadmissible at trial. The rule allows a successful plaintiff to make a double recovery, one from the defendant and one from insurance. Some collateral sources have the right of subrogation, or reimbursement, thereby denying the plaintiff this double recovery.

Many states have enacted legislation modifying or abolishing the collateral source rule. These statutes require courts to offset already paid or future collateral source benefits from the plaintiff[s] recovery. They reduce the defendant's liability toward the plaintiff, allowing the tortfeasor the windfall rather than the plaintiff. Restatement (Second) of Torts § 920A, cmt. b. For policy reasons that support retaining the collateral source rule, see Kenneth S. Abraham, *What Is a Tort Claim? An Interpretation of Contemporary Tort Reform*, 51 Md. L. Rev. 172, 190–93 (1992).

Besides all types of insurance, other funds considered as collateral source benefits are Social Security Disability Insurance, retirement benefits, welfare benefits, Medicare, workers' compensation, other employment benefits, and gratuities. *See* John G. Fleming, *The Collateral Source Rule and Loss Allocation in Tort Law*, 54 Cal. L. Rev. 1478 (1966).

12. *Substantial Damage Awards.* The fear of a "runaway jury" exists among many defendants today. Yet procedural devices exist to check the jury's discretion. Courts apply standards such as "unconscionable or outside reasonable bounds," "shock the judicial conscience," "so grossly excessive as to shock our sense of justice," and "tainted by passion or prejudice" in order to reduce or increase a jury's award. *See Wagner v. York Hosp.*, 415 Pa. Super. 1, 17, 608 A.2d 496, 504 (1992) (listing six factors used to determine excessiveness: (1) The severity of the injury; (2) whether plaintiff's injury is manifested by objective physical evidence instead of merely the subjective testimony of the plaintiff; (3) whether the injury will affect the plaintiff permanently; (4) whether the plaintiff can continue with his employment; (5) the size of the plaintiff's out-of-pocket expenses; and (6) the amount plaintiff demanded in the original complaint).

The Supreme Court has ruled that federal courts sitting in diversity in tort cases must apply state law when determining whether a jury award is excessive and a new trial is warranted. *Gasperini v. Center for Humanities, Inc.*, 518 U.S. 415 (1996).

13. *Tort Reform of Compensatory Damages.* Over the last two decades, numerous states have adopted statutes that limit or redefine the recovery of economic and noneconomic losses.

For example, Oregon adopted a $500,000 cap on pain and suffering:

> [I]n any civil action seeking damages arising out of bodily injury, including emotional injury or distress, death or property damage of any one person including claims for loss of care, comfort, companionship and society and loss of consortium, the amount awarded for noneconomic damages shall not exceed $500,000.

Or. Rev. Stat. § 560.

The purpose "of imposing a cap on noneconomic damages was to stabilize insurance premiums and to decrease the costs associated with tort litigation." *Tenold v. Weyerhaeuser Co.*, 127 Or. App. 511, 873 P.2d 413 (1994). What does that mean?

The $500,000 cap was held unconstitutional in common-law tort actions by *Lakin v. Senco Products, Inc.*, 329 Or. 62, 987 P.2d 463 (1999), although the same court upheld it as applied to wrongful death actions in *Greist v. Phillips*, 322 Or. 281, 906 P.2d 789 (1995). Why the different outcomes?

Kansas passed a statute limiting noneconomic loss to $250,000:

> In any personal injury action, the total amount recoverable by each party from all defendants for all claims for pain and suffering shall not exceed a sum total of $250,000.

Kan. Stat. Ann. § 60-19a01. It was upheld as constitutional in *Samsel v. Wheeler Transp. Servs.*, 246 Kan. 336, 789 P.2d 541 (1990).

Many of the caps on pain and suffering have passed constitutional muster. Others have not. For example, a cap of $875,000 on pain and suffering was held to violate the Equal Protection Clause in *Brannigan v. Usitalo*, 134 N.H. 50, 587 A.2d 1232 (1991):

> Although fewer tort plaintiffs would be affected by a $875,000 cap than a cap of $250,000, it seems to us even more "unfair and unreasonable to impose the burden of supporting the [insurance] industry solely upon those persons who are [even more] severely injured and therefore [even more] in need of compensation." *Carson*, 120 N.H. at 942, 424 A.2d at 837. . . . Finally, we note that society, through the courts, has developed a remedy to secure itself from the ills of a "run-away" jury that has imposed a disproportionally high award. That remedy is remittitur, to be exercised in the sound discretion of the trial court. *Hanlon v. Pomeroy*, 102 N.H. 407, 157 A.2d 646 (1960).
>
> RSA 508:4-d (Supp. 1990) is hereby declared unconstitutional. The case is remanded to the trial court.

Brannigan, 587 A.2d at 1236–37.

In *MacDonald v. City Hospital, Inc.*, 2011 W. Va. LEXIS 57 (June 22, 2011), the court upheld West Virginia's caps on noneconomic damages in medical malpractice cases. Collecting cases from other states, the court remarked that "our decision today is consistent with the majority of jurisdictions that have considered the constitutionality of caps on noneconomic damages in medical malpractice actions or in any personal injury action." It concluded that "now only a few states have declared such caps unconstitutional," and most of those decisions involved state constitutional provisions stating that "the right to trial by jury shall remain inviolate."

Some states have reformed compensatory damages by placing a cap on the total amount recovered. Virginia's one million dollar cap on the amount recovered in a medical malpractice case passed constitutional challenges. Va. Code Ann. § 8.01-581.15 provides:

> In any verdict returned against a health care provider in an action for malpractice . . . which is tried by a jury or in any judgment entered against a health care provider in such an action which is tried without a jury, the total amount recoverable for any injury . . . shall not exceed one million dollars.

The Supreme Court of Virginia, in *Fairfax Hosp. Sys. v. Nevitt*, held:

> Construing the language of the statutory recovery cap in a recent case, we said that "in a medical malpractice action, the total damages recoverable for injury to a 'patient' are limited to the statutory amount, regardless of the number of legal theories upon which the claims are based."

. . . .

We conclude that the plain meaning of the two statutes in issue, read together, is that where there is a verdict by a jury or a judgment by a court against a health care provider for "injury to . . . a patient" and the total amount recovered in that action and in all settlements related to the medical malpractice injury exceeds one million dollars, the total amount the plaintiff can recover for that injury is one million dollars. Accordingly, we hold that the trial court erred when it failed to apply the $600,000 credit for the PCA settlement against the $1,000,000 statutory recovery cap in determining the quantum of Nevitt's judgment.

457 S.E.2d 10, 14–15 (Va. 1995).

Other than the need to check the statutes in your state before advising a client, what do these legislative incursions into the law of tort damages suggest? *See* Michael J. Saks, *Do We Really Know Anything About the Behavior of the Tort Litigation System — And Why Not?*, 140 U. Pa. L. Rev. 1147 (1992).

Note that most of the successful tort reform has occurred at the state level, not the federal. *See* James A. Henderson & Theodore Eisenberg, *The Quiet Revolution in Products Liability: An Empirical Study of Legal Change*, 37 UCLA L. Rev. 479 (1990).

14. *The Role of Insurance in Tort Decisions.* Insurance, although often carried by both parties, is rarely mentioned in the opinions. There are two types of insurance: "first-party" and "third-party." First-party insurance, like property insurance, protects the owner from loss if his property is damaged. The owner's home burns, for example.

Third-party insurance, like automobile liability insurance, protects the insured from liability if he causes damage to a third party. Often, the insurance company has hired the attorney and is defending the insured in a suit brought by the injured third party. What conflicts might arise between the insurance company and the insured under third-party insurance? Would there be more such conflicts in a car crash case or a medical malpractice case?

Most of the cases in the book involve third-party insurance. The critical issue is the extent such insurance impacts the tort decision. Although barely mentioned by the courts before 1960, insurance has become a factor that affects judicial decisions and influences the structure of tort law. *See* Mark C. Rahdert, Covering Accident Costs: Insurance, Liability, and Tort Reform (1995).

The first case to mention insurance was *Ryan v. New York Central R.R. Co.*, 35 N.Y. 210, 91 Am. Dec. 49 (1866): "A man may insure his own house. . . . In a commercial country each man . . . runs the hazard of his neighbor's conduct, and each, by insurance against such hazard, is enabled to obtain a reasonable security against loss."

In a series of books and articles beginning in the late 1920's, Dean Leon Green argued that the ability to bear the loss and insurance were two of the key factors to be weighed by a court in deciding whether a duty extended to a particular plaintiff. *See* Green, *Proximate Cause in Texas Negligence Law*, 28 Tex. L. Rev. 471, 628, 755

(1950); Green, *The Duty Problem in Negligence Cases*, 28 Colum. L. Rev. 1034 (1928).

This theme was reflected by Justice Traynor in his often-cited concurring opinion in *Escola v. Coca-Cola Bottling Co.*, 24 Cal. 2d 453, 150 P.2d 436, 441 (1944): "The cost of an injury and the loss of time or health may be an overwhelming misfortune to the person injured, and a needless one, for the risk of injury can be insured by the manufacturer and distributed among the public as a cost of doing business."

In the famous case *Kinsman I*, Judge Friendly had insurance foremost in his mind when he defined the limits of proximate cause:

> [P]erhaps in the long run one returns to Judge Andrews' statement in *Palsgraf*, 248 N.Y. at 354-355, 162 N.E. at 104 (dissenting opinion). "It is all a question of expediency, . . . of fair judgment, always keeping in mind the fact that we endeavor to make a rule in each case that will be practical and in keeping with the general understanding of mankind." It would be pleasant if greater certainty were possible, . . . but the many efforts that have been made at defining the locus of the "uncertain and wavering line," 248 N.Y. at 354, 162 N.E. 99, are not very promising; what courts do in such cases makes better sense than what they, or others, say. Where the line will be drawn will vary from age to age; as society has come to rely increasingly on insurance and other methods of loss-sharing, the point may lie further off than a century ago.

Petition of Kinsman Transit Co., 338 F.2d 708, 725–26 (2d Cir. 1964).

Four years later, the California Supreme Court made clear that insurance played a critical role in its decision to discard the traditional theories of property owner liability:

> Without attempting to labor all of the rules relating to the possessor's liability, it is apparent that . . . the major factors which should determine whether immunity should be conferred upon the possessor of land . . . [include] the closeness of the connection between the injury and the defendant's conduct, the moral blame attached to the defendant's conduct, the policy of preventing future harm, and the prevalence and availability of insurance. . . .

Rowland v. Christian, 69 Cal. 2d 108, 70 Cal. Rptr. 97, 443 P.2d 561 (1968).

In *Kelly v. Gwinnell*, the New Jersey Supreme Court reflected on the limits of insurance in extending liability to the social host for the death caused by his intoxicated guest:

> Some fear has been expressed that the extent of the potential liability may be disproportionate to the fault of the host. A social judgment is therein implied to the effect that society does not regard as particularly serious the host's actions in causing his guests to become drunk, even though he knows they will thereafter be driving their cars. We seriously question that value judgment; indeed, we do not believe that the liability is disproportionate when the host's actions, so relatively easily corrected, may result in serious injury or death. The other aspect of this argument is that

the host's insurance protection will be insufficient. While acknowledging that homeowners' insurance will cover such liability, this argument notes the risk that both the host and spouse will be jointly liable. The point made is not that the level of insurance will be lower in relation to the injuries than in the case of other torts, but rather that the joint liability of the spouses may result in the loss of their home and other property to the extent that the policy limits are inadequate. . . . We observe, however, that it is common for both spouses to be liable in automobile accident cases. It may be that some special form of insurance could be designed to protect the spouses' equity in their homes in cases such as this one. In any event, it is not clear that the loss of a home by spouses who, by definition, have negligently caused the injury, is disproportionate to the loss of life of one who is totally innocent of any wrongdoing.

96 N.J. 538, 549–50, 476 A.2d 1219, 1225 (1984).

The Supreme Court of West Virginia concluded in 1991 that the loss-spreading effect of insurance was a critical factor in products liability cases:

> What is obvious from the . . . court's discussion is that product liability is concerned with spreading the cost of inevitable accidents. Inherent in this cost-spreading function is the collection of what amounts to insurance premiums from all the purchasers of products, and the purchase by manufacturers of commercial insurance or the creation of self insurance funds.
>
> The defendant before us, General Motors, is the largest producer of automobiles in the world. . . . In light of the fact that all of our sister states have adopted a cause of action for lack of crashworthiness, General Motors is *already* collecting a product liability premium every time it sells a car anywhere in the world, including West Virginia. . . . West Virginians, then, are already paying the product liability insurance premium when they buy a General Motors car, so this Court would be both foolish and irresponsible if we held that while West Virginians must pay the premiums, West Virginians can't collect the insurance after they're injured.

Blankenship v. General Motors Corp., 185 W. Va. 350, 406 S.E.2d 781 (1991). If you were an appellate court judge, how would you treat the issue of insurance?

Distinct from the treatment in the appellate courts, it may be reversible error to mention the defendant's insurance before the jury: "Evidence that a person was or was not insured against liability is not admissible upon the issue whether he acted negligently. . . ." Fed. R. Evid. 411. Why have this rule? May the trial court judge ask about your client's policy limits — in chambers? Why would the judge care?

For an instructive discussion of the role of insurance in the settlement of a car crash case, see H. Laurence Ross, Settled Out of Court (1970).

15. *Structured Settlements.* The usual award in a tort case is a lump sum. This has the advantage of administrative simplicity, but involves substantial speculation as to future damages. A solution is the structured settlement. This provides for periodic payments in place of a single judgment. There are two different approaches to structured settlements. First, the future payments will vary with the health of the plaintiff, and second, the payments are set at the time of the agreement. The first approach will obviously offer little incentive for the plaintiff to improve. What risks are involved in structured settlements? What administrative costs are involved?

The constitutionality of a structured settlement statute for medical malpractice was upheld in *Bernier v. Burris*, 113 Ill. 2d 219, 497 N.E.2d 763 (1986):

> The provisions, applicable to actions for healing-art malpractice *(see* 111. Rev. Stat. 1985, ch. 110, pars. 2-1701, 2-1704), change the traditional rule of lump-sum awards by permitting the payment of large awards of future damages in periodic installments. The provisions do not apply in a particular case, however, unless an effective election has been made by a party. In general terms, this requires that a party make a timely motion for application of the provisions; the election is effective if the parties agree to have the provisions apply or fail to object to them or, once an objection is made, if it appears that the amount of future damages will exceed $250,000.
> . . .
>
> If the procedures apply in a case, the trier of fact is to make several special findings regarding both past damages and future damages, and must further specify as future damages medical and other health-care costs, other economic losses, and noneconomic loss. Under these provisions, economic loss is defined in terms of pecuniary harm, and noneconomic loss includes loss of consortium and all nonpecuniary harm for which damages are recoverable, including damages for pain and suffering *(see* 111. Rev. Stat. 1985, ch. 110, par. 2-1702). Past damages are "damages that have accrued when the damages findings are made" . . . and future damages are ones that will accrue after that time.
>
> . . . .
>
> We do not believe that the provisions interfere with the right to trial by jury [nor do they violate due process].

Id. at 771.

For further discussion, see Roger C. Henderson, *Designing a Responsible Periodic-Payment System for Tort Awards*, 32 Ariz. L. Rev. 21 (1990); Samuel A. Rea, *Lump-Sum Versus Periodic Damage Awards*, 10 J. Legal Stud. 131 (1981) (defending the lump-sum approach).

16. *Expense of Litigation.* The American Rule in litigation is that each litigant bears its own attorney fees and other legal expenses. In contrast, the English Rule requires the losing party to pay the attorney fees for both sides. The English Rule has been widely accepted throughout the world. *See* Gregory E. Maggs & Michael D. Weiss, *Progress on Attorney's Fees: Expanding the "Loser Pays" Rule in Texas*, 30 Hous. L. Rev. 1915, 1920 (1994).

The American Rule may be varied by statute or contract. Otherwise, awarding attorney fees is within the discretion of the trial court. Many states have enacted statutes with a "loser pays" rule in some cases, while Alaska is the only state that has completely adopted the English Rule. *See* Alaska Stat. § 09.60.010 (2011); Alaska R. Civ. P. 82(a); Susanne Di Pietro & Teresa W. Cams, *Alaska's English Rule: Attorney's Fee Shifting in Civil Cases*, 13 Alaska L. Rev. 33 (1996). *See* John F. Vargo, *The American Rule on Attorney Fee Allocation: The Injured Person's Access to Justice*, 42 Am. U. L. Rev. 1567 (1993); Restatement of the Law (Second) Torts § 914.

17. *Taxation of Damage Awards.* Section 104(a)(2) of the Internal Revenue Code excludes personal injury awards from gross income. 26 U.S.C. § 104 (2009). Accordingly, some courts instruct juries about the tax-exempt status of these lump-sum awards. Defendants fear that a jury will assume that the plaintiff will have to pay taxes on the jury award, and that the jury needs to be prevented "from artificially inflating the award to compensate for what it anticipated would be the possible effects of taxation." *Spencer v. A-1 Crane Serv.*, 880 S.W.2d 938, 942 (Tenn. 1994). Many courts disagree and vary in their approaches. Some states require that the jury be instructed about the tax-exempt status, while the majority completely rejects such jury instructions. A third group of states leaves the tax jury instruction to the discretion of the trial judge. The Supreme Court, in *Norfolk & Western Ry. Co. v. Liepelt*, 444 U.S. 490 (1980), held that under the Federal Employers Liability Act, the jury must be instructed on the federal tax-exempt status of personal injury damages.

Often, a plaintiff's loss of past and future earnings is included in the damage award and will not be taxed. Should the portion of the award representing earnings be taxed? If not for the injury, the plaintiff would have had to pay taxes on his wages. Defendants argue that awards should be calculated according to the plaintiff's actual earnings or net income, not gross income. The award would be reduced by the amount of taxes the plaintiff would have been required to pay on his earnings. (Pain and suffering damages or other nonpecuniary losses are not taxed.) However, the majority of courts do not approve of this approach either, finding future income tax liability to be too speculative.

See Restatement (Second) of Torts § 914A: Effect of Taxation; Mark W. Cochran, *Should Personal Injury Damage Awards Be Taxed?*, 38 Case W. Res. L. Rev. 43 (1988) (arguing that IRS Code § 104 should be repealed and that personal injury awards should be taxed).

Punitive damage awards are taxable. *O'Gilvie v. United States*, 519 U.S. 79 (1996); 26 U.S.C. § 104(a)(2).

Chapter 11

THE WRONGFUL DEATH AND SURVIVAL STATUTES

Before 1846, a cause of action for personal injury died with the death of either the plaintiff or the defendant. There was no action for causing someone's death. It was therefore less expensive to take a person's life than to cause a minor injury.

In order to cure the problem and make clear that there was no public policy against allowing recovery for wrongful death, Lord Campbell's Act was passed in England. It granted a cause of action to the families of persons killed by tortious conduct. Lord Campbell's Act (Fatal Accidents Act), 1846, 9 & 10 Viet., ch. 93 (Eng.).

The history of the Wrongful Death Acts is summarized in *Moragne v. States Marine Lines*, 398 U.S. 375, 90 S. Ct. 1772 (1970):

> The first explicit statement of the common-law rule against recovery for wrongful death came in the opinion of Lord Ellenborough, sitting at *nisi prius*, in *Baker v. Bolton*, 1 Camp. 493, 170 Eng. Rep. 1033 (1808).
>
> . . . .
>
> It was suggested by some courts and commentators that the prohibition of . . . wrongful-death actions derived support from the ancient common-law rule that a personal cause of action in tort did not survive the death of its possessor. . . . However, it is now universally recognized that because this principle pertains only to the victim's own personal claims, such as for pain and suffering, it has no bearing on the question of whether a dependent should be permitted to recover for the injury he suffers from the victim's death. . . . [T]he legislatures both here and in England began to evidence unanimous disapproval of the rule against recovery for wrongful death.
>
> . . . .
>
> In the United States, every State today has enacted a wrongful-death statute. . . . The Congress has created actions for wrongful deaths of railroad employees, Federal Employers' Liability Act, 45 U.S.C. §§ 51-59; of merchant seamen, Jones Act, 46 U.S.C. § 688; and of persons on the high seas, Death on the High Seas Act, 46 U.S.C. §§ 761, 762. Congress has also, in the Federal Tort Claims Act, 28 U.S.C. § 1346(b), made the United States subject to liability in certain circumstances for negligently caused wrongful death to the same extent as a private person. *See, e.g., Richards v. United States*, 369 U.S. 1 (1962).

These . . . statutes, taken as a whole, make it clear that there is no present public policy against allowing recovery for wrongful death.

Moragne, 398 U.S. at 382–90, 90 S. Ct. at 1778–82.

In the United States two types of statutes, "survival acts" and "wrongful death acts," prevent the failure of an action because of the actor's or the victim's death. The "survival action" provides that the victim's action does not end with the death of the victim. It survives and is a continuation of the victim's claim. The "survival action" also provides that the victim's action survives the actor's death. The action is transferred to the victim's or actor's personal representative.

The "wrongful death" acts provide for a cause of action in the dependents or heirs of the victim. It is a new action and not a continuation of the victim's own claim.

Because many jurisdictions have both "survival" and "wrongful death" acts, there are problems of statutory interpretation dealing with pain and suffering, punitive damages, parties (who can sue), and statutes of limitations. The following materials are examples of these questions of statutory interpretation.

PROBLEM

A six-year-old child, whose mother was killed when a light fixture fell from the ceiling of an airport terminal and struck her, wishes to sue the manufacturer of the light fixture. The decedent's spouse/partner also wants to sue.

Consider the following:

1. Can a six-year-old child sue for the loss of consortium? Can the surviving spouse sue for the loss of consortium?

2. What if the decedent's male partner is a cohabitant with the decedent, rather than a spouse?

3. What if the decedent and the plaintiff were lesbian partners? Does it matter whether they were legally married, in a legal civil union, or simply living together? What if they were legally married in one state, but the accident occurred in another, where the state's constitution prohibits recognition of same-sex marriage? *See* Levin, *Resolving Interstate Conflicts over Same-Sex Non-Marriage*, 63 Fla. L. Rev. 47 (2011).

4. What result in each of the above if the parent, spouse, or partner was injured, but not killed?

LANGAN v. ST. VINCENT'S HOSPITAL OF NEW YORK
Supreme Court of New York, Appellate Division, 2005
802 N.Y.S.2d 476

LIFSON, J.

The underlying facts of this case are not in dispute. After many years of living together in an exclusive intimate relationship, Neil Conrad Spicehandler (hereinafter Conrad) and John Langan endeavored to formalize their relationship by traveling to Vermont in November 2000 and entering into a civil union. They returned to New York and continued their close, loving, committed, monogamous relationship as a family unit in a manner indistinguishable from any traditional marital relationship.

In February 2002 Conrad was hit by a car and suffered a severe fracture requiring hospitalization at the defendant St. Vincent's Hospital of New York. After two surgeries Conrad died. The plaintiff commenced the instant action which asserted, inter alia, a claim . . . to recover damages for the decedent's wrongful death. The defendant moved, inter alia, to dismiss that cause of action on the ground that the plaintiff and the decedent, being of the same sex, were incapable of being married and, therefore, the plaintiff had no standing as a surviving spouse to institute the present action. The Supreme Court, inter alia, denied that motion and the instant appeal ensued. For the reasons stated below, the Supreme Court's order must be reversed insofar as appealed from.

An action alleging wrongful death, unknown at common law, is a creature of statute requiring strict adherence to the four corners of the legislation (see Carrick v Cent. Gen. Hosp., 51 NY2d 242, 434 NYS2d 130, 414 NE2d 632 [1980]; Liff v Schildkrout, 49 NY2d 622, 427 NYS2d 746, 404 NE2d 1288 [1980]). The relevant portion of EPTL [Estates Powers & Trust Law] 5-4.1 provides as follows: "The personal representative, duly appointed in this state or any other jurisdiction, of a decedent *who is survived by distributees* may maintain an action to recover damages for a wrongful act, neglect or default which caused the decedent's death" (emphasis added). The class of distributees is set forth in EPTL 4-1.1. Included in that class is a surviving spouse. At the time of the drafting of these statutes, the thought that the surviving spouse would be of the same sex as the decedent was simply inconceivable and certainly there was no discriminatory intent to deny the benefits of the statute to a directed class. On the contrary, the clear and unmistakable purpose of the statute was to afford distributees a right to seek compensation for loss sustained by the wrongful death of the decedent (see Shu-Tao Lin v Mc Donnell Douglas Corp., 742 F2d 45 [1984]).

Like all laws enacted by the people through their elected representatives, EPTL 5-4.1 is entitled to a strong presumption that it is constitutional. . . . The plaintiff claims that application of the statute in such a manner as to preclude same-sex spouses as potential distributees is a violation of the Equal Protection Clauses of the Constitutions of the United States and the State of New York. However, any equal protection analysis must recognize that virtually all legislation entails classifications for one purpose or another which results in the advantage or disadvantage to the affected groups (see Romer v Evans, 517 US 620, 116 S Ct 1620, 134 L Ed 2d 855 [1996]). In order to survive constitutional scrutiny a law needs only to have a rational relationship to a legitimate state interest even if the law appears unwise or works to the detriment of one group or the other (see Romer v Evans, supra). Thus, the plaintiff must demonstrate that the denial of the benefits of EPTL 5-4.1 to same-sex couples is not merely unwise or unfair but serves no legitimate governmental purpose. The plaintiff has failed to meet that burden.

In the absence of any prior precedent, the court would have to analyze whether the statute imposes a broad and undifferentiated disadvantage to a particular group and if such result is motivated by an animus to that group (see Romer v Evans, supra). However, in this instance, it has already been established that confining marriage and all laws pertaining either directly or indirectly to the marital relationship to different sex couples is not offensive to the Equal protection clause of either the federal or state constitutions. In (Baker v Nelson, 291 Minn 310, 191 NW2d 185 [1971]), the Supreme Court of Minnesota held that the denial of marital status to same-sex couples did not violate the Fourteenth Amendment of the United States Constitution. The United States Supreme Court refused to review that result. . . . The plaintiff cannot meet his burden of proving the statute unconstitutional and does not refer this Court to any binding or even persuasive authority that diminishes the import of the Baker precedent.

On the contrary, issues concerning the rights of same-sex couples have been before the United States Supreme Court on numerous occasions since Baker and, to date, no justice of that Court has ever indicated that the holding in Baker is suspect. . . .

Similarly, this Court, in ruling on the very same issue in (Matter of Cooper, 187 AD2d 128, 592 NYS2d 797 [1993], *appeal dismissed*, 82 NY2d 801, 604 NYS2d 558, 624 NE2d 696 [1993]) not only held that the term "surviving spouse" did not include same-sex life partners, but expressly stated as follows: "Based on these authorities [including Baker, supra], we agree . . . that 'purported [homosexual] marriages do not give rise to any rights . . . pursuant to . . . EPTL 5-1.1 [and that] [n]o constitutional rights have been abrogated or violated in so holding' " (Matter of Cooper, id. at 134). Although issues involving same-sex spouses have been presented in various contexts since the perfection of this appeal, no court decision has been issued which undermines our obligation to follow our own precedents. Recently, in the somewhat analogous case of (Matter of Valentine v American Airlines, 17 AD3d 38, 791 NYS2d 217 [2005]), the Appellate Division, Third Department, in denying spousal status to same-sex couples for purposes of workers' compensation claims, cited both Baker and Cooper with approval. Thus, no cogent reason to depart from the established judicial precedent of both the courts of the United States and the courts of the State of New York has been demonstrated by the plaintiff or our dissenting colleagues.

The fact that since the perfection of this appeal the State of Massachusetts has judicially created such right for its citizens is of no moment here since the plaintiff and the decedent were not married in that jurisdiction. They opted for the most intimate sanctification of their relationship then permitted, to wit, a civil union pursuant to the laws of the State of Vermont. Although the dissenters equate civil union relationships with traditional heterosexual marriage, we note that neither the State of Vermont nor the parties to the subject relationship have made that jump in logic. In following the ruling of its Supreme Court in the case of (Baker v State of Vermont, 170 Vt 194, 744 A2d 864 [1999]) the Vermont Legislature went to great pains to expressly decline to place civil unions and marriage on an identical basis. While affording same-sex couples the same rights as those afforded married couples, the Vermont Legislature refused to alter traditional concepts of marriage (i.e., limiting the ability to marry to couples of two distinct sexes) (see Vt. Stat. Ann., tit. 15, §§ 8, 1201 [4]). The import of that action is of no small moment. The decedent herein, upon entering the defendant hospital, failed to indicate that he was married. Moreover, in filing the various probate papers in this action, the plaintiff likewise declined to state that he was married. In essence, this Court is being asked to create a relationship never intended by the State of Vermont in creating civil unions or by the decedent or the plaintiff in entering into their civil union. For the same reason, the theories of full faith and credit and comity have no application to the present fact pattern.

The circumstances of the present case highlight the reality that there is a substantial segment of the population of this state that is desirous of achieving state recognition and regulation of their relationships on an equal footing with married couples. There is also a substantial segment of the population of this state that wishes to preserve traditional concepts of marriage as a unique institution confined solely to one man and one woman. Whether these two positions are not so hopelessly at variance (to all but the extremists in each camp) to prevent some type of redress is an issue not for the courts but for the Legislature. Unlike the court, which can only rule on the issues before it, the Legislature is empowered to act on all facets of the issue including, but not limited to, the issues of the solemnization and creation of such relationships, the dissolution of such relationships and the consequences attendant thereto, and all other rights and liabilities that flow from such a relationship. Any contrary decision, no matter how circumscribed, will be taken as judicial imprimatur of same-sex marriages and would constitute a usurpation of powers expressly reserved by our Constitution to the Legislature. Accordingly, the order must be reversed insofar as appealed from.

FISHER, J. dissents and votes to affirm the order with the following memorandum, in which CRANE, J., concurs:

The majority's forceful defense of the Legislature's prerogative to define what constitutes a marriage in New York seems to me to miss the point. This case is not about marriage. The plaintiff does not claim to have been married to the decedent, and clearly he was not, either under the laws of New York or in the eyes of Vermont.

What this case is about is the operation of a single statute — New York's wrongful death statute — that controls access to the courts for those seeking compensation for the loss of a pecuniary expectancy created and guaranteed by law. The statute provides such access to a decedent's surviving spouse because the wrongful death of one spouse deprives the other of an expectation of continued support which the decedent would have been obligated by law to provide (see e.g. Family Ct. Act § 412; Social Services Law § 101). But, as applied here, the statute does not permit the surviving member of a Vermont civil union to sue for wrongful death, even though, like spouses, each member of the civil union is obligated by law to support the other (see Vt. Stat. Ann., tit. 15, § 1204 [c]). The principal question presented, therefore, is whether, as it currently operates to permit spouses but not partners in a Vermont civil union to sue for wrongful death, the law draws a distinction between similarly-situated persons on the basis of sexual orientation and, if so, whether the distinction bears some rational relationship to any conceivable governmental objective promoted by the statute. Because I conclude that the statute as applied here does classify similarly-situated persons on the basis of sexual orientation without a rational relationship to any conceivable governmental purpose furthered by the statute, I respectfully dissent.

. . . .

New York's Estates, Powers and Trusts Law (hereinafter EPTL) allows an action for the wrongful death of any individual who is survived by one or more distributees, with the recovery to provide compensation for economic injuries suffered as a result of the death (see EPTL 5-4.1 [1]; 5-4.4 [a]). A distributee is any person who may be entitled under law to take or share in the decedent's property not disposed of by will (see EPTL 1-2.5, 4-1.1). Distributees include certain of the decedent's blood relatives, his or her adopted children, and, unless disqualified, his or her "spouse" (see EPTL 4-1.1, 5-1.2).

The majority writes that it would have been inconceivable to the drafters of the wrongful death statute that the surviving spouse would be of the same sex as the decedent. I agree.

Although the term "spouse" is not defined in the EPTL, its use in several provisions in that chapter leaves no doubt that it was intended to include only those persons joined together in marriage.

. . . .

Indeed, even in more recent years, although New York's Legislature has provided same-sex couples with certain rights and benefits, it has not seen fit to include them in the class of persons entitled to assert a wrongful death claim . . .

. . . .

Because the wrongful death statute is in derogation of the common law, it must be strictly construed (see Gonzalez v New York City Hous. Auth., 77 NY2d 663, 667, 569 NYS2d 915, 572 NE2d 598 [1991]). Thus, I agree with the majority that the term "spouse" as used in EPTL 4-1.1 is limited to those persons who were married to a decedent at the time of death and cannot, through statutory construction, be interpreted expansively to include persons like the plaintiff and the decedent here who were partners in a Vermont civil union but were not joined in marriage (see Matter of Cooper, 187 AD2d 128, 592 NYS2d 797 [1993]).

. . . .

I turn, then, to the area of my disagreement with the majority's resolution of the appeal.

When a statute affords different treatment to similarly-situated persons on the basis of a constitutionally cognizable characteristic, the disparity of treatment must, at the least, bear some rational relationship to a legitimate governmental objective promoted by the statute. . . .

. . . .

The question to be addressed, therefore, is whether, considering the purpose and objective of the wrongful death statute, there is some ground of difference that rationally explains the different treatment the statute accords to spouses and partners in a Vermont civil union. . . .

The purpose of the wrongful death statute is well-defined and firmly established. It is not intended to recompense the survivor for the loss of companionship or consortium, or for the pain and anguish that accompanies the wrongful and unexpected loss of a loved one. It is instead designed solely to make a culpable tortfeasor liable for fair and just compensation to those who, by reason of their relationship to the decedent, suffer economic injury as a result of the decedent's death (see EPTL 5-4.3 [a]). A person suffers economic injury in this context when the death deprives him or her of a reasonable expectation of future financial assistance or support from the decedent (see Gonzalez v New York City Hous. Auth., supra at 667; Parilis v Feinstein, 49 NY2d 984, 429 NYS2d 165, 406 NE2d 1059 [1980]).

The plaintiff argues that, with respect to that objective, the wrongful death statute classifies similarly-situated persons on the basis of their sexual orientation. Sexual orientation is a constitutionally cognizable characteristic, and therefore when legislation is challenged on the ground that it classifies and treats persons differently on the basis of sexual orientation, courts will "insist on knowing the relation between the classification adopted and the object to be attained" (Romer v Evans, 517 US 620, 632, 116 S Ct 1620, 134 L Ed 2d 855 [1996]). . . .

. . . .

. . . [T]he classification here is not between unmarried opposite-sex couples who choose to live together in an informal arrangement, and unmarried same-sex couples who do the same. The classification at issue here is between couples who enter into a committed, formalized, and state-sanctioned relationship that requires state action to dissolve and, perhaps most important, makes each partner legally responsible for the financial support of the other. For opposite-sex couples, of course, the relationship is marriage, sanctioned and recognized by the State (see e.g. Domestic Relations Law § 14-a), requiring a divorce or annulment to dissolve (see e.g. Domestic Relations Law §§ 140, 170), and obligating each spouse to provide for the support of the other (see e.g. Family Court Act § 412; Social Services Law § 101 [1]). And, as relevant here, the relationship for same-sex couples is the Vermont civil union, sanctioned and recognized by the State (see Vt. Stat. Ann., tit. 15, § 1201), requiring a court proceeding to dissolve (see Vt. Stat Ann, tit. 15 § 1206), and obligating each party to provide for the support of the other (see Vt Stat Ann, tit. 15 § 1204 [c]).

With respect to the objectives of the wrongful death statute, spouses and parties to a Vermont civil union stand in precisely the same position. Marriage creates a legal and enforceable obligation of mutual support (see e.g. Family Court Act § 412; Social Services Law § 101 [1]), and therefore the death of one spouse causes economic injury to the other because it results in the loss of an expectancy of future support created and guaranteed by law. And, in exactly the same way, because the state-sanctioned Vermont civil union gives rise to a legal and enforceable obligation of mutual support (see Vt. Stat. Ann., tit. 15, § 1204 [c]), the death of one party to the union causes economic injury to the survivor because it results in the loss of an expectancy of future support also created and guaranteed by law. Because no statute or authoritative holding in New York now permits or recognizes a marriage except between opposite-sex couples, and because Vermont civil unions are open only to same-sex couples (see Vt. Stat. Ann., tit. 15, § 1202 [2]), the operation here of New York's wrongful death statute to authorize a party to a marriage to recover damages for the wrongful death of his or her spouse, but not to permit a party to a Vermont civil union to recover damages for the wrongful death of his or her partner, in effect, affords different treatment to similarly-situated persons on the basis of sexual orientation.

The question, then, is whether there is a rational relationship between that disparity of treatment and some legitimate governmental interest or purpose. . . . Ordinarily, when constitutional challenges are raised against laws prohibiting same-sex marriage, or laws favoring legal marriages over committed relationships between persons of the same sex, those who defend the challenged provisions do so on the basis of the traditional, religious, cultural, and legal understanding that marriage is the union of one man and one woman, and is the preferred environment for procreation and child-rearing. . . . The issue, therefore, is whether New York's interest in fostering traditional marriage, and in preferring it to any other relationship between unrelated adults, is in any conceivable way advanced or promoted by a law that authorizes a surviving spouse, but not a surviving member of a Vermont civil union, to sue for wrongful death. Two cases decided by the United States Supreme Court are instructive on this question, and both involve the right to sue for wrongful death.

In (Levy v Louisiana, 391 US 68, 88 S Ct 1509, 20 L Ed 2d 436 [1968]), the Supreme Court struck down a statute which, because it was construed to authorize only legitimate children to maintain an action for the wrongful death of a parent, precluded five illegitimate children from suing for the wrongful death of their mother. The Supreme Court wrote: "Legitimacy or illegitimacy of birth has no relation to the nature of the wrong allegedly inflicted on the mother. These children, though illegitimate, were dependent on her; she cared for them and nurtured them; they were indeed hers in the biological and in the spiritual sense; in her death they suffered wrong in the sense that any dependent would" (id. at 72).

And, in the companion case of (Glona v American Guar. & Liab. Ins. Co., 391 US 73, 88 S Ct 1515, 20 L Ed 2d 441 [1968]), the Supreme Court struck down the same statute insofar as it was construed to bar a mother from maintaining an action for the wrongful death of her illegitimate child killed in an automobile accident. Here the court pointedly observed: "[W]e see no possible rational basis for assuming that if the natural mother is allowed recovery for the wrongful death of her illegitimate child, the cause of illegitimacy will be served. It would, indeed, be farfetched to assume that women have illegitimate children so that they can be compensated in damages for their death. A law which creates an open season on illegitimates in the area of automobile accidents gives a windfall to tortfeasors. But it hardly has a causal connection with the 'sin,' which is, we are told, the historic reason for the creation of the disability" (id. at 75 [citation omitted]).

I recognize that "equal protection is not a license for courts to judge the wisdom, fairness, or logic of legislative choices . . . [and that, i]n areas of social and economic policy, a statutory classification that neither proceeds along suspect lines nor infringes fundamental constitutional rights must be upheld against equal protection challenge if there is any reasonably conceivable state of facts that could provide a rational basis for the classification" (FCC v. Beach Communications, Inc., 508 US 307, 313, 113 S Ct 2096, 124 L Ed 2d 211 [1993]; see also Port Jefferson Health Care Facility v Wing, 94 NY2d 284, 290, 704 NYS2d 897, 726 NE2d 449 [1999], cert. denied, 530 US 1276, 120 S Ct 2744, 147 L Ed 2d 1008 [2000]; Barklee Realty Co. v Pataki, 309 AD2d 310, 314, 765 NYS2d 599 [2003]).

But just as the Supreme Court could find no conceivable rational relationship between any governmental purpose promoted by a wrongful death law and a classification of wrongful death plaintiffs or victims according to their legitimacy, neither can I identify any reasonably conceivable rational basis for classifying similarly-situated wrongful death plaintiffs on the basis of their sexual orientation.

Stated otherwise, I simply cannot reasonably conceive of any way in which New York's interest in fostering and promoting traditional marriage is furthered by a law that determines, based on a person's sexual orientation, whether he or she may have access to our courts to seek compensation for the loss of a pecuniary expectancy created and guaranteed by law (cf. People v Onofre, supra at 491-492 [statute permitting consensual sodomy between married persons but banning same conduct between unmarried persons bears no rational relationship to society's interest in fostering and promoting marriage]). And, tellingly, the majority's rejection of the equal protection claim does not include any hint or suggestion of how preventing the plaintiff from asserting a wrongful death claim promotes the State's interest in fostering the institution of marriage, "thus leaving [its] constitutional analysis incomplete" (Trimble v Gordon, 430 US 762, 769, 97 S Ct 1459, 52 L Ed 2d 31 [1977]). Indeed, the only real effect of the majority's position is to provide a windfall to a potential tortfeasor.

Accordingly, I respectfully dissent and would hold that the application of New York's wrongful death statute to deny the right of a surviving member of a Vermont civil union to maintain an action to recover damages for the wrongful death of his or her partner is inconsistent with the right to equal protection of the laws. I would further hold that the proper remedy is to extend the benefit of EPTL 5-4.1 to include the plaintiff as a surviving member of a Vermont civil union. . . . In my judgment, therefore, the order appealed from should be affirmed insofar as appealed from.

In 2011, New York authorized same-sex marriage. See Marriage Equality Act, Laws 2011, ch. 95, §§ 1, 2, 5-a (June 24, 2011). Should that change the result in a civil-union situation such as Langan?

MAGEE v. ROSE

Superior Court of Delaware, 1979
405 A.2d 143

Tease, Judge.

Joann Magee and Marion P. Rose, Jr., lived together as husband and wife in a common-law marriage and a child of that union, Marion P. Magee, was born on December 26, 1973. Ms. Magee also had a daughter, Shauna, and all four lived together in the Roses' trailer at Angola, Sussex County, Delaware.

On August 20, 1976, a one-car accident occurred on County Route 275, about three miles west of Lewes, Delaware. The defendant, Marion Rose, was operating his 1969 Plymouth and in the car with him were Ms. Magee, her daughter, Shauna, and their son, Marion Magee. Joann Magee died as a result of the injuries she sustained in the accident.

The accident occurred at 6:15 p.m. and Joann was pronounced dead on arrival at the Beebe Hospital at 6:40 p.m. The death certificate issued by the medical examiner states that the cause of death was aspiration of blood due to skull fractures. She appeared lifeless at all times from the happening of the accident until she was officially pronounced dead on arrival at the hospital.

Since the accident the son has been cared for by the defendant and his parents and the daughter has been cared for by the decedent's parents. They have, in fact, adopted her.

The decedent's mother, Frances L. Magee, was appointed Administratrix of her estate and brought this wrongful death and survival action against the defendant.
. . .

The defendant has moved for summary judgment as to the following issues:

1. There can be no claim for survival action.

2. There can be no claim for punitive damages.

. . . .

Under the common law, a tort claim died with the person. Thus, the claim for damages — of whatever nature — could not be pursued and no claim could be asserted by virtue of the death.

Delaware's General Assembly has ameliorated this harsh situation by enacting two statutes that may be applicable to this lawsuit. They are commonly called the survival statute and the wrongful death statute, and they read as follows:

SURVIVAL STATUTE 10 Del. C. § 3701

"All causes of action, except action for defamation, malicious prosecution, or upon penal statutes, shall survive to and against the executors or administrators of the person to, or against whom, the cause of action accrued. Accordingly, all actions, so surviving, may be instituted or prosecuted by or against the executors or administrators of the person to or against whom the cause of action accrued. This section shall not affect the survivorship among the original parties to a joint cause of action."

WRONGFUL DEATH STATUTE 10 Del. C. § 3704(b)

"(b) Whenever death is occasioned by unlawful violence or negligence, and no suit is brought by the party injured to recover damages during his or her life, the widow or widower of any such deceased person, or, if there is no widow or widower, the personal representatives, may maintain an action for and recover damages for the death and loss thus occasioned."

Both statutes create a cause of action not recognized under the common law. Because both statutes are in derogation of the common law, both statutes must be strictly construed. . . .

Pain and Suffering

In Delaware, under the Wrongful Death Statute conscious pain and suffering is not a legally cognizable element of damages; in such actions recovery is limited to the pecuniary loss occasioned by death and not for the personal injuries suffered before death. . . .

However, under the Survival Statute conscious pain and suffering from the time of injury until death is a proper element of recovery, *Coulson v. Shirks Motor Express Corp.*, Del. Super., 48 Del. 561, 107 A.2d 922 (1954), provided that the plaintiff proves by a preponderance of the evidence that the decedent did not die instantaneously upon impact and that there was some appreciable interval of conscious pain and suffering after the injury. . . .

The plaintiff has the burden of proving the existence of conscious pain and suffering and a mere allegation that the decedent lived and suffered is insufficient where the only record supports a finding of almost instantaneous death. Proof of such pain and suffering as are substantially contemporaneous with death, or mere incidents to it, or as to a short period of insensibility intervening between fatal injuries and death, is not sufficient.

Plaintiff has not presented a sufficient factual basis for consideration of pain and suffering as a separate element of damages under the survival statute.

Moreover, pain and suffering is not cognizable as an element of damages under the wrongful death statute, under any factual setting, because recovery under the wrongful death statute is limited to pecuniary loss occasioned by the death. Pain and suffering is not a pecuniary loss. . . .

Punitive Damages

Plaintiff also seeks punitive damages under §§ 3701 and 3704(b). However, punitive damages, as a matter of law, are not recoverable under the Wrongful Death Statute. . . .

Under the Wrongful Death Statute . . . the administrator may "recover damages for the death and the loss thus occasioned" on behalf of the decedent's estate. 10 Del. C. § 3704(b); *Cann v. Mann Construction Co., supra.* The sole measure of damages under § 3704(b) for recovery by the administrator on the estate's behalf is a sum that the deceased would have probably earned in his business during his life and would have saved from his earnings and left as an estate and which would have gone to his next of kin. . . .

Likewise under the Survival Act, the sole damages recoverable by an administrator are limited to (a) pain and suffering from the time of injury to the time of death, (b) expenses incurred in endeavoring to be cured of such injuries and (c) loss of earnings resulting from such injuries from time of injury to the time of death. . . .

Since there is no basis for an award in this case of compensatory damages for conscious pain and suffering, there can be no award of punitive damages.

For the reasons set out above, the defendant's motion for summary judgment on the issues presented therein must be granted. *It is so ordered.*

---

1. What is the reason for permitting pain and suffering only under the survival act? Why does the plaintiff lose on that issue?

2. Why do the defamation and malicious prosecution actions not survive under the Delaware Survival Act?

3. What is "pecuniary loss" in a wrongful death situation? What are the reasons for rejecting punitive damages in this case?

4. Can the plaintiff recover for the pain and suffering endured before his or her death? Courts differ. *See Solomon v. Warren*, 540 F.2d 777 (5th Cir. 1976), *cert. dismissed*, 434 U.S. 801 (1977) (holding that jury could award damages for the few minutes prior to the plane crash even if the passengers died immediately upon impact). *But see DeYoung v. McDonnell Douglas Corp.*, 507 F. Supp. 21 (N.D. Ill. 1980) (barring recovery for claim that victims suffered emotional distress before plane crash; they recovered for the pain and suffering occurring after the crash, however).

5. For a further discussion of pain and suffering prior to death, see Leebron, *Final Moments: Damages for Pain and Suffering Prior to Death*, 64 N.Y.U. L. Rev. 256 (1989) (author argues that the primary justification for such awards must be deterrence and not compensation), and Fuchsberg, *Damages — Conscious Pain & Suffering Prior to Death*, 15 Trial L.Q. 66 (1983).

SELDERS v. ARMENTROUT
Supreme Court of Nebraska, 1973
207 N.W.2d 686

McCOWN, JUSTICE.

This is an action by Earl and Ila Selders to recover damages for the wrongful deaths of three of their minor children. The children were killed in an automobile accident. The jury found the defendants Charles and William Armentrout negligent and returned a verdict against them for the exact amount of the medical and funeral expenses of the three children. The parents have appealed.

The sole issue on this appeal involves the proper elements and measure of damages in a tort action in Nebraska for the wrongful death of a minor child. The court essentially instructed the jury that except for medical and funeral expenses, the damages should be the monetary value of the contributions and services which the parents could reasonably have expected to receive from the children less the reasonable cost to the parents of supporting the children.

The defendants contend that the measure of damages is limited to pecuniary loss and that the instructions to the jury correctly reflect the measure and elements of damage. The plaintiffs assert that the loss of the society, comfort, and companionship of the children are proper and compensable elements of damage, and that evidence of amounts invested or expended for the nurture, education, and maintenance of the children before death is proper.

. . . .

It is quite apparent from an examination of the judicial decisions and the legal literature in the field, that a broadening concept of the measure and elements of damages for the wrongful death of a minor child has been in the development stage for many years. . . . Following a discussion of the rigid common law rules limiting recovery for wrongful death to the loss of pecuniary benefits, Prosser states: "Recent years, however, have brought considerable modification of the rigid common law rules. It has been recognized that even pecuniary loss may extend beyond mere contributions of food, shelter, money or property; and there is now a decided tendency to find that the society, care and attention of the deceased are 'services' to the survivor with a financial value, which may be compensated. This has been true, for example, not only where a child has been deprived of a parent, . . . but also where the parent has lost a child. . . ." Prosser, Law of Torts (4th Ed.), § 127, p. 908.

The original pecuniary loss concept and its restrictive application arose in a day when children during minority were generally regarded as an economic asset to parents. Children went to work on farms and in factories at age 10 and even earlier. This was before the day of child labor laws and long before the day of extended higher education for the general population. A child's earnings and services could be generally established and the financial or pecuniary loss which could be proved became the measure of damages for the wrongful death of a child. Virtually all other damages were disallowed as speculative or as sentimental.

The damages involved in a wrongful death case even today must of necessity deal primarily with a fictitious or speculative future life, as it might have been had the wrongful death not occurred. . . . To limit damages for the death of a child to the monetary value of the services which the next of kin could reasonably have expected to receive during his minority less the reasonable expense of maintaining and educating him stamps almost all modern children as worthless in the eyes of the law. In fact, if the rule was literally followed, the average child would have a negative worth. . . . [T]he wrongful death of a child results in no monetary loss, except in the rare case, and the assumption that the traditional measure of damages is compensatory is a pure legal fiction.

Particularly in the last decade, a growing number of courts have extended the measure of damages to include the loss of society and companionship of the minor child, even under statutes limiting recovery to pecuniary loss or pecuniary value of services less the cost of support and maintenance, or similar limitations. . . .

In this state, the statute has not limited damages for wrongful death to pecuniary loss but this court has imposed that restriction. For an injury to the marital relationship, the law allows recovery for the loss of the society, comfort, and companionship of a spouse. This court has allowed such a recovery for the wrongful death of a wife. . . . There is no logical reason for treating an injury to the family relationship resulting from the wrongful death of a child more restrictively. It is no more difficult for juries and courts to measure damages for the loss of the life of a child than many other abstract concepts with which they are required to deal. We hold that the measure of damages for the wrongful death of a minor child should be extended to include the loss of the society, comfort, and companionship of the child. To the extent this holding is in conflict with prior decisions of this court, they are overruled.

. . . .

For the guidance of the court on retrial, we believe that evidence of expenses of birth, food, clothing, instruction, nurture, and shelter which have been incurred or were reasonably necessary to rear the child to the age he or she had attained on the date of death are not properly admissible. We conclude that the investment theory of measuring damages by the amounts expended in raising the child is inappropriate and improper.

The judgment of the trial court as to liability is affirmed, the judgment as to damages is reversed and the cause remanded for trial on the issue of damages only, consistent with our holding in this opinion.

———————

1. How would an economist critique *Selders*? How much have your parents invested in you at this point? How much will you pay back to them?

2. What do you think of the dissent's view that "the majority . . . throws open a death claim for a minor child to a sympathy and sentiment contest." *Selders*, 190 Neb. at 287–88, 207 N.W.2d at 693 (White, C.J., dissenting).

3. What is the reasoning underlying the trial court's opinion? What is the policy supporting the Nebraska Supreme Court's decision?

4. The size of the award in wrongful death cases has sometimes caused the courts to pause. The Supreme Court of Minnesota upheld the reduction of an award for the wrongful death of a one-month-old child from $428,000 to $100,000. *Ahrenholz v. Hennepin County*, 295 N.W.2d 645 (Minn. 1980). In contrast, the Georgia Court of Appeals upheld a $100 million punitive damage award against General Motors in a suit where a teenager was allegedly burned to death because of a defectively designed pick-up truck gas tank. *See General Motors Corp. v.*

Moseley, 213 Ga. App. 875, 447 S.E.2d 302 (1994).

5. Consortium compensates for loss of conjugal fellowship and sexual relations, and also includes love, companionship, society, and household services. *Borer v. American Airlines*, 19 Cal. 3d 441, 443, 138 Cal. Rptr. 302, 304, 563 P.2d 858, 860 (1977).

The husband or the wife may recover for the loss of consortium, depending on the language of the local wrongful death statute. *See Selders v. Armentrout*, 190 Neb. 275, 207 N.W.2d 686 (1973). In contrast, the Court of Appeals of New York held that a claim for loss of consortium could not be asserted under the wrongful death statute and there was no common-law cause of action on behalf of the surviving spouse for loss of consortium. *Liff v. Schildkrout*, 49 N.Y.2d 622, 427 N.Y.S.2d 746, 404 N.E.2d 1288 (1980).

Some courts require the plaintiff to be married to the decedent, *see Taylor v. Fields*, 178 Cal. App. 3d 653, 224 Cal. Rptr. 186 (1986), while others do not require marriage in order for the cohabitant to recover for loss of companionship. *See Bulloch v. United States*, 487 F. Supp. 1078 (D.N.J. 1980). *See also* Demidovich, *Loss of Consortium: Should Marriage Be Retained as a Prerequisite?*, 52 U. Cin. L. Rev. 842 (1983).

6. Children may be able to recover in a suit for the loss of society of their parents. Judicial decisions have permitted recovery by children for the value of the deceased parent's affection and society. *See* the cases cited in *Krouse v. Graham*, 19 Cal. 3d 59, 67–68, 137 Cal. Rptr. 863, 866, 562 P.2d 1022, 1025 (1977).

When the parent is injured, but not killed, the courts disagree on whether children can recover for loss of consortium. *Borer v. American Airlines*, 19 Cal. 3d 441, 138 Cal. Rptr. 302, 563 P.2d 858 (1977), refused to permit a recovery:

> Judicial recognition of a cause of action for loss of consortium, we believe, must be narrowly circumscribed. Loss of consortium is an intangible injury for which money damages do not afford an accurate measure or suitable recompense; recognition of a right to recover for such losses in the present context, moreover, may substantially increase the number of claims asserted in ordinary accident cases, the expense of settling or resolving such claims, and the ultimate liability of the defendants.

Id. at 444, 138 Cal. Rptr. at 304, 563 P.2d at 860. Michigan went the opposite way and held that a child has an independent cause of action for loss of parental society and companionship when the parent is negligently injured. *Berger v. Weber*, 411 Mich. 1, 303 N.W.2d 424 (1981).

7. In *Green v. Bittner*, 85 N.J. 1, 424 A.2d 210 (1980), a high school senior was killed in an automobile crash, and her parents sued under "wrongful death" for loss of consortium. The Supreme Court of New Jersey held:

> Companionship and advice in this context must be limited strictly to their pecuniary element. The command of the statute is too clear to allow compensation, directly or indirectly, for emotional loss. . . .

Companionship, lost by death, to be compensable must be that which would have provided services substantially equivalent to those provided by the "companions" often hired today by the aged or infirm, or substantially equivalent to services provided by nurses or practical nurses. And its value must be confined to what the marketplace would pay a stranger with similar qualifications for performing such services.

Id. at 12, 424 A.2d at 215–16. Do you agree? But note how the court permits a limited recovery for companionship.

CURTIS v. FINNERAN
Supreme Court of New Jersey, 1980
417 A.2d 15

POLLOCK, JUDGE.

The decedent, Ronald Paul Curtis, was killed instantly when the car in which he was a passenger struck a guardrail on a bridge on July 19, 1973. The accident occurred when the defendant, Robert A. Finneran, the owner and operator of the automobile, fell asleep at the wheel. Decedent's father, as the administrator ad prosequendum of the estate of his son, sued Finneran pursuant to the wrongful death statute, N.J.S.A. 2A:31-1 *et seq.* The complaint sought reimbursement for funeral expenses and for the net pecuniary loss suffered by decedent's surviving children, Ronald, Jr. and Paul.

At the conclusion of a non-jury trial, the court awarded damages of $1,894 for funeral expenses and, without providing findings of fact or reasons, set the amount of the loss suffered by Ronald, Jr. at $23,500 and the loss by Paul at $28,000, for a total of $53,394.

Thereafter the court denied plaintiff's motion for a new trial, but amended the judgment to add counsel fees to the amounts awarded to the children. In the amended judgment, the court awarded $29,375 to Ronald, Jr. and $35,000 to Paul, for a total of $66,269 including funeral expenses.

In an unreported opinion, the Appellate Division reversed the additur of the counsel fee and reinstated the original judgment of $53,394. We granted plaintiff's petition for certification. 81 N.J. 354 (1979). We reverse the judgment of the Appellate Division, except for the disallowance of the counsel fee, and remand the matter for trial on damages.

The trial centered on the financial loss suffered by the children because of their father's death. Evaluation of that loss requires a summary of the facts of the brief and tragic life of Ronald Paul Curtis. He was born on June 25, 1951, and after graduating from high school in 1969, attended Pennsylvania State University for one month. He served in the National Guard in California for seven months and remained an active member of the Guard until his death. In September, 1970, after returning from California, he began working with the North Eastern Telephone Company as a cable splicer. He also did maintenance work in the evening for the Federal City Manufacturing Company. Curtis took a correspondence course with the International Correspondence School to improve his technical knowledge.

On October 3, 1970, he married and bought a trailer home in Pennsylvania where he and his wife lived. His wife died nine days after the birth of their son, Ronald Paul Curtis, Jr., on October 14, 1972. In March, 1973, Curtis moved to his parents' house. His mother testified that he did about four hours of work a week around their home and that he made weekly contributions of $30 to his mother-in-law who shared the care of Ronald, Jr.

In early 1973, Curtis became engaged and planned to be married in September of that year. Because of his engagement, Curtis planned on relocating and found a job in New Jersey with the Continental Telephone Company as a frameman. He visited his fiancee frequently. She conceived his child some time in June, 1973. The child, Paul, was born on April 12, 1974.

Plaintiff offered as an expert witness Dr. Matiyahu Marcus, a professor of economics at Rutgers University, to estimate the present economic value of decedent's life to his two children. . . .

In calculating the loss, Dr. Marcus began with decedent's gross income for a base year, the year of the trial, and increased the base year income by 5% as an allowance for fringe benefits. He further increased the base income by the market value of decedent's services around his parents' house. Dr. Marcus did not include pension and retirement benefits in calculating decedent's base income, because the period of economic dependence of the two sons would end before decedent would have retired. Apparently Dr. Marcus did not consider either federal or state income tax liability. His final adjustment in calculating the base income was a deduction for the personal consumption expenses of the decedent if he had lived. Dr. Marcus set that allowance at 20% of base income until 1994, when he estimated the eldest son would attain economic independence, and at 40% from 1994 to 1996, when the youngest son would become economically independent.

He assumed that, because of inflation and increased productivity, the base income as adjusted would be subject to an annual growth rate of 6%. He then arrived at a total figure based on the number of years during which the children could have expected to receive their father's financial support. This period was assumed to run until the younger child graduated from college. The total figure, net of personal consumption, was discounted to present value by use of a 5.5% discount rate. Since the figure thus calculated was an estimate of future loss only, it was further increased by the base income, relevant fringe benefit amounts, and the estimated value of services from the date of the decedent's death to the time of trial. The sum of these two amounts, $199,048, was the gross amount of the lost income of the decedent and represented, in the expert's view, the net pecuniary loss of the surviving children.[1]

----

[1] The results of Dr. Marcus' calculations may be summarized as follows:

lost wages 1973-1975	23,493.00
present value wages etc. 1976-1996	252,719.00
personal consumption 1973-1975	6,273.00

The trial judge considered the expert's testimony too speculative to be a reliable guide in determining the net pecuniary loss to the surviving sons. The judge did not indicate where he differed with the assumptions and inferences of the expert. Furthermore, he recognized that Dr. Marcus had no alternative but to rely on general statistics, rather than specific information.

Without endorsing the testimony of the expert, we conclude that it conforms generally to the expectation that experts will provide the fact finder "with their analyses of trends of future wage increases and discount rates generally. . . ."

The problem on appellate review in this case is that the trial judge did not set forth how he estimated the projected earnings of the decedent. The record reflects that the trial court may have considered this wrongful death action like a support case and that he tacitly decided that the sons were entitled to a weekly allowance based on need. Recovery in a wrongful death action is based on the monetary contributions which the decedent reasonably might have been expected to make to the survivors and is not directly related to their needs. *Dubil, supra,* 52 N. J. at 259. However, an increase in a survivor's needs may be used to show that a decedent, within his financial ability, might reasonably be expected to have increased his contribution in light of greater need. *Id.* at n. 1.

In arriving at his own estimate, the trial court committed several mistakes that may have contributed to the amount of the award, which was characterized by the Appellate Division as "modest." For example, he stated that "[t]here was no contribution toward the maintenance and support by the decedent" of the decedent's first son, although decedent's mother gave uncontradicted testimony that decedent had made $30 weekly contributions for the support of his son. In evaluating the expert's estimate of net pecuniary loss, the judge commented that if the amount "were to be in the form of life insurance benefits payable as part of an automobile liability package, insurance package premium, it clearly would have been prohibitive." This consideration is clearly incorrect. As previously explained, the standard in a wrongful death action is the contribution decedent reasonably would have made to his infant sons, not the cost of insurance premiums for an amount equal to the net pecuniary loss. The trial court allowed the expert to project a gross amount of dollars to establish plaintiff's aggregate damages. That practice would be improper in a case tried before a jury. The reason is that "the projection of a gross figure before the jury submitted by an expert tends to exert an undue psychological impact leading to the danger of its uncritical acceptance by the jury in the place of its own function in evaluating the proofs." *Tenore,* supra, 67 N.J. at 482-483. However, in a non-jury case, as here, the admissibility of a "bottom line" figure can be left to the discretion of the trial judge. In a non-jury case, testimony about a gross dollar amount will be less prejudicial, particularly where the testimony is subject to vigorous cross-examination.

Apparently concerned about the adequacy of the award, the trial court granted an additur for counsel fees. However, there is no authority to award counsel fees in

---

personal consumption 1976-1996   70,891.00
Total wages minus total personal consumption   199,048.00.

a wrongful death action. Under our rules of practice, no fee for legal services shall be allowed except in certain specific instances which do not include wrongful death actions. . . .

Accordingly, we affirm that part of the judgment of the Appellate Division that disallowed counsel fees and otherwise reverse and remand to the trial court for a new trial as to damages.

---

1. Is the New Jersey Supreme Court's reasoning persuasive or arbitrary? Why?

2. In the absence of opposing testimony, is the court qualified to set aside the reasoning of a professor of economics, Dr. Marcus? On what basis?

3. Explain how the court's conclusion flows from the text of the wrongful death act. What is the relationship between policy and the language of the act?

4. If you were the clerk for the trial court judge, how would you advise him or her on remand of this case?

5. In *DeLong v. County of Erie*, 60 N.Y.2d 296, 469 N.Y.S.2d 611, 457 N.E.2d 717 (1983), the county was found to have a duty to respond to 911 calls in a reasonable manner. Because the decedent suffered twelve minutes of terror before being stabbed to death by a burglar, the court upheld a survival award of $200,000 for pain and suffering. It also upheld a wrongful death award of $600,000 for the decedent-mother, who was not employed outside the home. Expert testimony was held to be admissible:

> It is now apparent, as a majority of courts have held that qualified experts are available and may aid the jury in evaluating the housewife's services not only because jurors may not know the value of those services, but also to dispel the notion that what is provided without financial reward may be considered of little or no financial value in the marketplace. We conclude that it was not an abuse of discretion to allow the expert testimony in this case.

Id. at 307–08, 457 N.E.2d 723, 469 N.Y.S.2d 617–18.

6. *Defenses.* Under the survival and wrongful death actions, defenses are available that might have been used against the victim. There can be no recovery where, because of defenses, the decedent could not have maintained an action. There must have been a tort committed against the decedent.

Under a survival action, since the plaintiff steps into the shoes of the decedent, the defendant can assert the same defenses against the plaintiff that the defendant could have asserted against the decedent, had he or she been alive. In wrongful death actions, recovery for the plaintiff is barred if the decedent could never have sued the defendant. Such causes of action are usually denied because the defendant had not committed any tortious conduct against the decedent. Courts also deny recovery where the defendant can assert the defenses of contributory negligence, assumption of risk, consent, self-defense or the statute of limitations. There are variations depending on the language of the act, however.

What if a beneficiary is driving a car and negligently crashes and kills the decedent passenger? Do the defenses available against the beneficiary bar the beneficiary from recovery? Under a survival act, the suit is brought on behalf of the decedent and, therefore, the negligent beneficiary-driver may be permitted to recover.

If the action is brought under a wrongful death act, however, the negligent beneficiary may not be permitted to recover, because recovery is precluded by the beneficiary's contributory negligence, consent, or assumption of the risk, on the theory that these defenses would "bar any other plaintiff in interest." *See* W. Page Keeton et al., Prosser and Keeton on Torts 954–58 (5th ed. 1984).

Chapter 12

STRICT LIABILITY

The foundation of tort law is strict liability. The core of the concept is that the defendant will be liable without a showing of fault. Professor Malone argued that before the Middle Ages liability was absolute: if you invited someone to the circus and an animal escaped and mauled your guest, you were strictly liable. W. Malone, *Ruminations on the Role of Fault in the History of the Common Law of Torts*, 31 La. L. Rev. 1, 3 (1970).

In one of the earliest reported cases, decided in 1466, the court stated: "[I]f a man does a thing he is bound to do it in such a manner that by his deed no injury or damage is inflicted upon others." *Anonymous*, Y.B. 5 Edw. IV, fol. 7, pi. 18 (1466). If you kept a wild animal and it injured someone, you were strictly liable. *See May v. Burdett*, 9 Q.B. 101 (1846).

A study of early strict liability cases suggests that social policy has always driven the law. In the late 1800's, when great value was placed on cattle, farmers were required by statute to fence-in their property as a condition to recovery for crop damage from trespassing cattle. *See Buford v. Houtz*, 133 U.S. 320 (1890). Later, as more value was placed on farming, the cattle ranchers were forced to fence-in their animals or risk strict liability for the trespass of their cattle. *See* W. Page Keeton et al., Prosser and Keeton on Torts 539–41 (5th ed. 1984). For further discussion, see W. Malone, *supra*; C.H.S. Fifoot, History and Sources of the Common Law: Tort and Contract 189 (1949); R. Rabin, Perspectives on Tort Law 44 (2d ed. 1983); M. Horwitz, The Transformation of American Law, 1780-1860 (1977).

PROBLEM

Four years ago, Al purchased a large aboveground swimming pool and put it in his back yard. On numerous occasions Al has invited his next-door neighbor, Bob, to use the pool. Bob has often accepted the invitation.

Al lives on a hill. Bob's house is below and behind Al's house.

One day, Al's nine-year-old son, John, started Al's Ferrari and drove into the pool. The pool burst, and the water poured out. The water ran down the hill and into Bob's yard. In fact, it flooded Bob's living room and dining room. John was not injured.

In order to pump the water out of his house, Bob tried to start his portable gasoline water pump. Due to the exertion involved in trying to start the pump, Bob suffered a heart attack. As a result of his heart attack, Bob has lost the use of his right arm.

Discuss. Assume that, in purchasing, installing, and maintaining the pool, Al was not negligent.

FLETCHER v. RYLANDS
Exchequer Chamber, 1866
L.R. 1 Ex. 265

[The facts are taken from the opinion in the House of Lords, *infra.*

[I]n this case the Plaintiff . . . is the occupier of a mine and works under a close of land. The Defendants are the owners of a mill in his neighbourhood, and they proposed to make a reservoir for the purpose of keeping and storing water to be used about their mill upon another close of land, which, for the purposes of this case, may be taken as being adjoining to the close of the Plaintiff, although, in point of fact, some intervening land lay between the two. Underneath the close of land of the Defendants on which they proposed to construct their reservoir there were certain old and disused mining passages and works. There were five vertical shafts, and some horizontal shafts communicating with them. The vertical shafts had been filled up with soil and rubbish, and it does not appear that any person was aware of the existence either of the vertical shafts or of the horizontal works communicating with them. In the course of the working by the Plaintiff of his mine, he had gradually worked through the seams of coal underneath the close, and had come into contact with the old and disused works underneath the close of the Defendants.

In that state of things the reservoir of the Defendants was constructed. It was constructed by them through the agency and inspection of an engineer and contractor. Personally, the Defendants appear to have taken no part in the works. . . . As regards the engineer and the contractor, we must take it from the case that they did not exercise, as far as they were concerned, that reasonable care and caution which they might have exercised, taking notice, as they appear to have taken notice, of the vertical shafts filled up in the manner which I have mentioned. However, my Lords, when the reservoir was constructed, and filled, or partly filled, with water, the weight of the water bearing upon the disused and imperfectly filled-up verticle shafts, broke through those shafts. The water passed down them and into the horizontal workings, and from the horizontal workings under the close of the Defendants it passed on into the workings under the close of the Plaintiff, and flooded his mine, causing considerable damage, for which this action was brought.]

BLACKBURN, J.:

It appears from the statement in the case, that the plaintiff was damaged by his property being flooded by water, which, without any fault on his part, broke out of a reservoir constructed on the defendants' land by the defendants' orders, and maintained by the defendants.

It appears from the statement in the case, that the coal under the defendants' land had, at some remote period, been worked out; but this was unknown at the time when the defendants gave directions to erect the reservoir, and the water in the reservoir would not have escaped from the defendants' land, and no mischief would have been done to the plaintiff, but for this latent defect in the defendants' subsoil. And it further appears that the defendants selected competent engineers and contractors to make their reservoir, and themselves personally continued in total ignorance of what we have called the latent defect in the subsoil; but that these persons employed by them in the course of the work became aware of the existence of the ancient shafts filled up with soil, though they did not know or suspect that they were shafts communicating with old workings.

It is found that the defendants, personally, were free from all blame, but that in fact proper care and skill was not used by the persons employed by them, to provide for the sufficiency of the reservoir with reference to these shafts. The consequence was, that the reservoir when filled with water burst into the shafts, the water flowed down through them into the old workings, and thence into the plaintiff's mine, and there did the mischief. The plaintiff, though free from all blame on his part, must bear the loss, unless he can establish that it was the consequence of some default for which the defendants are responsible. The question of law therefore arises, what is the obligation which the law casts on a person who, like the defendants, lawfully brings on his land something which, though harmless whilst it remains there, will naturally do mischief if it escape out of his land. It is agreed on all hands that he must take care to keep in that which he has brought on the land and keeps there, in order that it may not escape and damage his neighbours, but the question arises whether the duty which the law casts upon him, under such circumstances, is an absolute duty to keep it in at his peril, or is, as the majority of the Court of Exchequer have thought, merely a duty to take all reasonable and prudent precautions, in order to keep it in, but no more. If the first be the law, the person who has brought on his land and kept there something dangerous, and failed to keep it in, is responsible for all the natural consequences of its escape. If the second be the limit of his duty, he would not be answerable except on proof of negligence, and consequently would not be answerable for escape arising from any latent defect which ordinary prudence and skill could not detect.

. . . .

We think that the true rule of law is, that the person who for his own purposes brings on his lands and collects and keeps there anything likely to do mischief if it escapes, must keep it in at his peril, and, if he does not do so, is prima facie answerable for all the damage which is the natural consequence of its escape. He can excuse himself by showing that the escape was owing to the plaintiff's default; or perhaps that the escape was the consequence of vis major, or the act of God; but as nothing of this sort exists here, it is unnecessary to inquire what excuse would be sufficient. The general rule, as above stated, seems on principle just. The person whose grass or corn is eaten down by the escaping cattle of his neighbour, or whose mine is flooded by the water from his neighbour's reservoir, or whose cellar is invaded by the filth of his neighbour's privy, or whose habitation is made unhealthy by the fumes and noisome vapours of his neighbour's alkali works, is damnified without any fault of his own; and it seems but reasonable and just that the neighbour, who has brought something on his own property which was not naturally there, harmless to others so long as it is confined to his own property, but which he

knows to be mischievous if it gets on his neighbour's, should be obliged to make good the damage which ensues if he does not succeed in confining it to his own property.
. . .

The case that has most commonly occurred, and which is most frequently to be found in the books, is as to the obligation of the owner of cattle which he has brought on his land, to prevent their escaping and doing mischief. The law as to them seems to be perfectly settled from early times; the owner must keep them in at his peril.
. . .

Judgment for the plaintiff.

---

1.   What was the holding in *Fletcher v. Rylands*?

2.   On what precedent does the case rest? Are the animal cases appropriate precedent here?

3.   Why not sue the defendant in negligence? Is the owner of the reservoir liable for the negligence of the contractor?

4.   Does Justice Blackburn believe that he is writing a radical and far-reaching decision?

5.   Before the case reached the Exchequer Chamber, the judge in the Exchequer held for the defendant, saying there was no trespass, because the damage was consequential and not immediate. A nuisance cause of action failed because the defendants were engaged in a lawful act. For liability under these facts, the defendant must be shown to have been negligent. *Fletcher v. Rylands*, 3 H. & C. 774, 159 Eng. Rep. 737 (1865).

RYLANDS v. FLETCHER
House of Lords, 1868
L.R. 3 H.L. 330

[The facts are presented in *Fletcher v. Rylands, supra.*]

THE LORD CHANCELLOR (LORD CAIRNS):

. . . .

The Court of Exchequer, when the special case stating the facts to which I have referred, was argued, was of opinion that the Plaintiff had established no cause of action. The Court of Exchequer Chamber, before which an appeal from this judgment was argued, was of a contrary opinion, and the Judges there unanimously arrived at the conclusion that there was a cause of action, and that the Plaintiff was entitled to damages.

My Lords, the principles on which this case must be determined appear to me to be extremely simple. The Defendants, treating them as the owners or occupiers of the close on which the reservoir was constructed, might lawfully have used that close for any purpose for which it might in the ordinary course of the enjoyment of land be used; and if, in what I may term the natural user of that land, there had been any accumulation of water, either on the surface or underground, and if, by the operation of the laws of nature, that accumulation of water had passed off into the close occupied by the Plaintiff, the Plaintiff could not have complained that that result had taken place.

On the other hand if the Defendants, not stopping at the natural use of their close, had desired to use it for any purpose which I may term a non-natural use, for the purpose of introducing into the close that which in its natural condition was not in or upon it, for the purpose of introducing water either above or below ground in quantities and in a manner not the result of any work or operation on or under the land, — and if in consequence of their doing so, the water came to escape and to pass off into the close of the Plaintiff, then it appears to me that that which the Defendants were doing they were doing at their own peril; and, if in the course of their doing it, the evil arose to which I have referred, the evil, namely, of the escape of the water and its passing away to the close of the Plaintiff and injuring the Plaintiff, then for the consequence of that, in my opinion, the Defendants would be liable. . . .

My Lords, these simple principles, if they are well founded, as it appears to me they are, really dispose of this case.

The same result is arrived at on the principles referred to by Mr. Justice Blackburn in his judgment, in the Court of Exchequer Chamber, where he states the opinion of that Court as to the law in these words: "We think that the true rule of law is. . . . "

My Lords, in that opinion, I must say I entirely concur. Therefore, I have to move your Lordships that the judgment of the Court of Exchequer Chamber be affirmed, and that the present appeal be dismissed with costs.

LORD CRANWORTH (concurring):

My Lords, I concur with my noble and learned friend in thinking that the rule of law was correctly stated by Mr. Justice Blackburn in delivering the opinion of the Exchequer Chamber. If a person brings, or accumulates, on his land anything which, if it should escape, may cause damage to his neighbour, he does so at his peril. If it does escape, and cause damage, he is responsible, however careful he may have been, and whatever precautions he may have taken to prevent the damage.

. . . The Plaintiff had a right to work his coal through the lands of Mr. Whitehead, and up to the old workings. If water naturally rising in the Defendants' land (we may treat the land as the land of the Defendants for the purpose of this case) had by percolation found its way down to the Plaintiffs mine through the old workings, and so had impeded his operations, that would not have afforded him any ground of complaint. . . . The Defendants, in order to effect an object of their own, brought on to their land, or on to land which for this purpose may be treated as being theirs, a large accumulated mass of water, and stored it up in a reservoir. The consequence of this was damage to the Plaintiff, and for that damage, however skillfully and carefully the accumulation was made, the Defendants, according to the principles and authorities to which I have adverted, were certainly responsible.

Judgment of the Court of Exchequer Chamber affirmed.

---

1. Something was added by the holding of Lord Cairns; what is it? What subjects are missing from the opinions?

2. Early cases in the United States relied on the opinion of the Exchequer Chamber to reject the concept of strict liability. *See Losee v. Buchanan*, 51 N.Y 476 (1873) (exploding steam boiler); *Brown v. Collins*, 53 N.H. 442 (1873) (a runaway horse).

3. What is a "natural use" of the land? Does the phrase refer to flowers, rocks, and trees, or is it a term of art to be given definition by the court for each case? Is there a difference between naturally occurring trees and planted ones?

TURNER v. BIG LAKE OIL CO.
Supreme Court of Texas, 1936
96 S.W.2d 221

CURETON, CHIEF JUSTICE.

The primary question for determination here is whether or not the defendants in error, without negligence on their part, may be held liable in damages for the destruction or injury to property occasioned by the escape of salt water from ponds constructed and used by them in the operation of their oil wells. . . .

The defendants in error in the operation of certain oil wells in Reagan County constructed large artificial earthen ponds or pools into which they ran the polluted waters from the wells. On the occasion complained of, water escaped from one or more of these ponds, and, passing over the grass lands of the plaintiffs in error, injured the turf, and after entering Garrison draw flowed down the same into Centralia draw. In Garrison draw there were natural water holes, which supplied water for the livestock of plaintiffs in error. The pond, or ponds, of water from which the salt water escaped were, we judge from the map, some six miles from the stock-water holes to which we refer. . . .

Upon both reason and authority we believe that the conclusion of the Court of Civil Appeals that negligence is a prerequisite to recovery in a case of this character is a correct one. There is some difference of opinion on the subject in American jurisprudence brought about by differing views as to the correctness or applicability of the decision of the English courts in *Rylands v. Fletcher*, L. R. 3 H. L. 330. . . .

In Texas we have conditions very different from those which obtain in England. A large portion of Texas is an arid or semi-arid region. West of the 98th meridian of longitude, where the rainfall is approximately 30 inches, the rainfall decreases until finally, in the extreme western part of the State, it is only about 10 inches. This land of decreasing rainfall is the great ranch or livestock region of the State, water for which is stored in thousands of ponds, tanks, and lakes on the surface of the ground. The country is almost without streams; and without the storage of water from rainfall in basins constructed for the purpose, or to hold waters pumped from the earth, the great live stock industry of West Texas must perish. No such condition obtains in England. With us the storage of water is a natural or necessary and common use of the land, necessarily within the contemplation of the State and its grantees when grants were made, and obviously the rule announced in *Rylands v. Fletcher*, predicated upon different conditions, can have no application here.

Again, in England there are no oil wells, no necessity for using surface storage facilities for impounding and evaporating salt waters therefrom. In Texas the situation is different. Texas has many great oil fields, tens of thousands of wells in almost every part of the State. Producing oil is one of our major industries. One of the by-products of oil production is salt water, which must be disposed of without injury to property or the pollution of streams. The construction of basins or pounds to hold this salt water is a necessary part of the oil business. . . .

The judgments of the Court of Civil Appeals and of the District Court are affirmed.

————

1. What does "natural use" of water mean in Texas?

2. What are the reasons for the decision in *Turner*?

3. What will be the result in Texas if the plaintiff sues in negligence? *See* L. Green, *Hazardous Oil and Gas Operations: Tort Liability*, 33 Tex. L. Rev. 574 (1955).

4. In a Florida case, the facts were:

> The appellant, Cities Service Company (Cities Service), operates a phosphate rock mine in Polk County. On December 3, 1971, a dam break occurred in one of Cities Service's settling ponds. As a result, approximately one billion gallons of phosphate slimes contained therein escaped into Whidden Creek and thence into the Peace River, thereby killing countless numbers of fish and inflicting other damage.

Faced with the question of whether strict liability *(Rylands)* should apply, the Florida court held:

> In early days it was important to encourage persons to use their land by whatever means were available for the purpose of commercial and industrial development. In a frontier society there was little likelihood that a dangerous use of land could cause damage to one's neighbor. Today our life has become more complex. Many areas are overcrowded, and even the non-negligent use of one's land can cause extensive damages to a neighbor's property. Though there are still many hazardous activities which are socially desirable, it now seems reasonable that they pay their own way. It is too much to ask an innocent neighbor to bear the burden thrust upon him as a consequence of an abnormal use of the land next door. The doctrine of *Rylands v. Fletcher* should be applied in Florida.

Cities Service Oil Co. v. Florida, 312 So. 2d 799 (Fla. Dist. Ct. App. 1975).

5. Why did Florida reach a decision different from Texas?

6. In *Cities Service*, the court considered the meaning of the term "non-natural" use:

> There have been many American cases which have passed upon the question of whether a particular use of the land was natural or non-natural for the purpose of applying the *Rylands v. Fletcher* doctrine. Thus, [W. Prosser, Law of Torts (4th ed. 1971)] states at page 510:
>
> > The conditions and activities to which the rule has been applied have followed the English pattern. They include water collected in quantity in a dangerous place, or allowed to percolate; explosives or inflammable liquids stored in quantity in the midst of a city; blasting; pile driving; . . . the fumigation of part of a building with cyanide gas; drilling oil wells or operating refineries in thickly settled communities; an excavation letting in the sea; factories emitting smoke, dust or noxious gases in the midst of a town; roofs so constructed as to shed snow into a highway; and a dangerous party wall.
> >
> > On the other hand the conditions and activities to which the American courts have refused to apply *Rylands v. Fletcher*, whether they purport to accept or to reject the case in principle, have been with few exceptions what the English courts would regard as a "natural" use of land, and not within the rule at all. They include water in household pipes, the tank of a humidity system or authorized utility mains; gas in a meter, electric wiring in a machine shop, and gasoline in a filling station; a dam in the natural bed of a stream; ordinary steam boilers; an ordinary fire in a factory; an automobile; Bermuda grass on a railroad right of way; a small quantity of dynamite kept for sale in a Texas hardware store; barnyard spray in a farmhouse; a division fence; the wall of a house left standing after a fire; coal mining operations regarded as usual and normal; vibrations from ordinary building construction; earth moving operations in grading a hillside; the construction of a railroad tunnel; and even a runaway horse.
>
> . . . .
>
> In the final analysis, we are impressed by the magnitude of the activity and the attendant risk of enormous damage. The impounding of billions of gallons of phosphatic slimes behind earthen walls which are subject to breaking even with the exercise of the best of care strikes us as being both "ultrahazardous" and "abnormally dangerous," as the case may be.

Cities Service Co. v. Florida, 312 So. 2d at 801–03.

YUKON EQUIPMENT, INC. v. FIREMAN'S FUND INSURANCE CO.
Supreme Court of Alaska, 1978
585 P.2d 1206

[Thieves broke into an explosives storage magazine located in the suburbs of Anchorage and ignited 80,000 pounds of explosives, damaging homes within a two-mile radius. Yukon's magazine which exploded was located 3,820 feet from the nearest building not used to store explosives and 4,330 feet from the nearest public highway. Partial judgment on the issue of liability was granted in favor of Fireman's Fund. Yukon Equipment argues that strict liability and absolute liability do not apply here.]

MATTHEWS, JUSTICE.

. . . .

I

The leading case on liability for the storage of explosives is *Exner v. Sherman Power Const. Co.*, 54 F.2d 510 (2d Cir. 1931). There dynamite stored by the defendant exploded causing personal injury and property damage to the plaintiffs who resided some 935 feet away from the storage site. A distinguished panel of the Circuit Court of Appeals for the Second Circuit held the defendant liable regardless of fault:

> Dynamite is of the class of elements which one who stores or uses in such a locality, or under such circumstances as to cause likelihood of risk to others, stores or uses at his peril. He is an insurer, and is absolutely liable if damage results to third persons, either from the direct impact of rocks thrown out by the explosion (which would be a common law trespass) or from concussion.

Id. at 512-13. The court pointed out that while the general principle of absolute liability expressed in the English case of *Rylands v. Fletcher* had been accorded a mixed reception at best in United States courts, there had been no such reluctance to impose absolute liability in blasting cases. The court then noted that some authorities had made a distinction between damage done by rocks or debris hurled by an explosion, as to which there would be absolute liability, and damage caused by a concussion, as to which a negligence standard applied. The court concluded that such a distinction was without a logical basis and rejected it. *Id.* at 514. The court also determined that there was no reason for attaching different legal consequences to the results of an explosion "whether the dynamite explodes when stored or when employed in blasting." The court expressed the policy behind the rule of absolute liability as follows:

> . . . . When, as here, the defendant, though without fault, has engaged in the perilous activity of storing large quantities of a dangerous explosive for use in his business, we think there is no justification for relieving it of

liability, and that the owner of the business, rather than a third party who has no relation to the explosion, other than that of injury, should bear the loss.

Id. at 514. *Exner* has been widely followed, and was based on many earlier authorities imposing absolute liability for explosions.

As *Exner* reflects, the particular rule of absolute liability for blasting damage received earlier and more general acceptance in the United States than the generalized rule of absolute liability for unusually dangerous activity which has its antecedents in *Rylands v. Fletcher.* . . .

The Restatement (Second) of Torts [Section 520] (1977), adopted by the ALI after the explosion in this case, does not reflect a *per se* rule of liability for the storage of explosives. Instead it lists six factors to be considered in determining whether an activity is "abnormally dangerous" and therefore subject to the rule of absolute liability. The factors are:

(a)   existence of a high degree of risk of some harm to the person, land or chattels of others;

(b)   likelihood that the harm that results from it will be great;

(c)   inability to eliminate the risk by the exercise of reasonable care;

(d)   extent to which the activity is not a matter of common usage;

(e)   inappropriateness of the activity to the place where it is carried on;

(f)   extent to which its value to the community is outweighed by its dangerous attributes.

Based in large part on the Restatement (Second), petitioners argue that their use was not abnormally dangerous. Specifically they contend that their use of the magazine for the storage of explosives was a normal and appropriate use of the area in question since the storage magazine was situated on lands set aside by the United States for such purposes and was apparently located in compliance with applicable federal regulations. They point out that the storage served a legitimate community need for an accessible source of explosives for various purposes. They contend that before absolute liability can be imposed in any circumstance a preliminary finding must be made as to whether or not the defendant's activity is abnormally dangerous, that such a determination involves the weighing of the six factors set out in section 520 of the Restatement (Second) of Torts, and that an evaluation of those factors in this case could not appropriately be done on motion for summary judgment.

The factors specified by section 520 of the Restatement (Second) of Torts are for consideration of the court, not the jury. . . .

If we were to apply the Restatement (Second)'s six factor test to the storage of explosives in this case we would be inclined to conclude that the use involved here was an abnormally dangerous one. Comment (f) to section 520 makes it clear that all of the factors need not be present for an activity to be considered abnormally dangerous:

In determining whether the danger is abnormal, the factors listed in clauses (a) to (f) of this Section are all to be considered, and are all of importance. Any one of them is not necessarily sufficient to itself in a particular case, and ordinarily several of them will be required for strict liability. On the other hand it is not necessary that each of them be present, especially if others weigh heavily.

The first three factors, involving the degree of risk, harm, and difficulty of eliminating the risk, are obviously present in the storage of 80,000 pounds of explosives in a suburban area. The fourth factor, that the activity not be a matter of common usage, is also met. Comment (i) states:

> Likewise the manufacture, storage, transportation and use of high explosives, although necessary to the construction of many public and private works, are carried on by only a comparatively small number of persons and therefore are not matters of common usage.

The fifth factor, inappropriateness of the activity, is arguably not present, for the storage did take place on land designated by the United States government for that purpose. However, the designation took place at a time when the area was less densely populated than it was at the time of the explosion. Likewise, the storage reserve was not entirely appropriate to the quantity of explosives stored because the explosion caused damage well beyond the boundaries of the reserve. The sixth factor, value to the community, relates primarily to situations where the dangerous activity is the primary economic activity of the community in question. Thus comment (k) states that such factor applies

> particularly when the community is largely devoted to the dangerous enterprise and its prosperity largely depends upon it. Thus the interests of a particular town whose livelihood depends upon such an activity as manufacturing cement may be such that cement plants will be regarded as a normal activity for that community notwithstanding the risk of serious harm from the emission of cement dust.

The comment further states that

> in Texas and Oklahoma, a properly conducted oil or gas well, at least in a rural area, is not regarded as abnormally dangerous, while a different conclusion has been reached in Kansas and Indiana. California, whose oil industry is far from insignificant, has concluded that an oil well drilled in a thickly settled residential area in the City of Los Angeles is a matter of strict liability.

Since five of the six factors required by section 520 of the Restatement (Second) are met and the sixth is debatable, we would impose absolute liability here if we were to use that approach.

However, we do not believe that the Restatement (Second) approach should be used in cases involving the use or storage of explosives. Instead, we adhere to the rule of *Exner v. Sherman Power Constr. Co.* and its progeny imposing absolute liability in such cases. The Restatement (Second) approach requires an analysis of degrees of risk and harm, difficulty of eliminating risk, and appropriateness of place, before absolute liability may be imposed. Such factors suggest a negligence standard. The six factor analysis may well be necessary where damage is caused by unique hazards and the question is whether the general rule of absolute liability applies, but in cases involving the storage and use of explosives we take that question to have been resolved by more than a century of judicial decisions.

The reasons for imposing absolute liability on those who have created a grave risk of harm to others by storing or using explosives are largely independent of considerations of locational appropriateness. We see no reason for making a distinction between the right of a homesteader to recover when his property has been damaged by a blast set off in a remote corner of the state, and the right to compensation of an urban resident whose home is destroyed by an explosion originating in a settled area. In each case, the loss is properly to be regarded as a cost of the business of storing or using explosives. Every incentive remains to conduct such activities in locations which are as safe as possible, because there the damages resulting from an accident will be kept to a minimum.

II

The next question is whether the intentional detonation of the storage magazine was a superseding cause relieving petitioners from liability. In *Sharp v. Fairbanks North Star Borough*, 569 P.2d 178 (Alaska 1977), a negligence case, we stated. . . .

> [w]here the defendant's conduct threatens a particular kind of result which will injure the plaintiff and an intervening cause which could not have been anticipated changes the situation but produces the same result as originally threatened, such a result is within the scope of the defendant's negligence.

Id. at 183 n. 9. The considerations which impel cutting off liability where there is a superseding cause in negligence cases also apply to cases of absolute liability.

Prior to the explosion in question the petitioners' magazines had been illegally broken into at least six times. Most of these entries involved the theft of explosives. Petitioners had knowledge of all of this.

Applying the standards set forth in *Sharp, supra,* to these facts we find there to have been no superseding cause. The incendiary destruction of premises by thieves to cover evidence of theft is not so uncommon an occurrence that it can be regarded as highly extraordinary. Moreover, the particular kind of result threatened by the defendant's conduct, the storage of explosives, was an explosion at the storage site. Since the threatened result occurred it would not be consistent with the principles stated in *Sharp, supra,* to hold there to have been a superseding cause. Absolute liability is imposed on those who store or use explosives because they have created an unusual risk to others. As between those who have created the risk for the benefit of their own enterprise and those whose only connection with the enterprise is to have suffered damage because of it, the law places the risk of loss on the former. When the risk created causes damage in fact, insistence that the precise details of the intervening cause be foreseeable would subvert the purpose of that rule of law.

The partial summary judgment is *affirmed.*

1. Is the Restatement (Second) of Torts Section 520 the same as the rule in *Rylands v. Fletcher*? If not, how is it different?

2. Why does the court reject the Restatement as a foundation of liability?

3. Argue that Section 520 of the Restatement (Second) is merely negligence. *See* W. Page Keeton et al., Prosser and Keeton on Torts 555 (5th ed. 1984).

4. The term "common usage" [Section 520(d)] cut off policy analysis and created problems for the plaintiff in *Wood v. United Air Lines*, 32 Misc. 2d 955, 223 N.Y.S.2d 692 (Sup. Ct. 1961). In *Wood*, two planes crashed into each other, and then one of them crashed into the plaintiff's apartment. She sued the airline, but the court rejected her argument of strict liability, stating:

> I am of the opinion, in light of the technical progress achieved in the design, construction, operation and maintenance of aircraft generally, that flying should no longer be deemed to be an ultra-hazardous activity, requiring the imposition of absolute liability for any damage or injury caused in the course thereof. This view is in accord with the current trend of the law. . . .

> It is to be noted that the Restatement (First), which was adopted and promulgated in 1938, rested its view of flying, as being an ultra-hazardous activity, upon the state of development of aviation existing at that time. It is indisputable that aviation has since made tremendous strides, both technically and in its use as a common mode of transportation.

Id. at 697.

What result under *Rylands v. Fletcher*? Is flying over a congested city non-natural? Who should bear the loss, the actor or the innocent victim?

5. For a blasting case that accepts the superseding cause defense, see *Bridges v. Kentucky Stone Co.*, 425 N.E.2d 125 (1981). The blast, set off by a thief, occurred three weeks after the theft, at a location 100 miles from the defendant's storage site. In *Yukon*, if thieves had never broken into the magazine previously, would the court have decided the case differently?

6. For a weaving of the lower court's strict liability decision into negligence, see Judge Posner's carefully crafted decision in *Indiana Harbor Belt R.R. Co. v. American Cyanamid Co.*, 916 F.2d 1174 (7th Cir. 1990). Judge Posner has long been an opponent of strict liability. *See* R.A. Posner, Tort Law: Cases and Economic Analysis 4, 5 (1982); Posner, *A Theory of Negligence*, 1 J. Legal Stud. 29, 32–34 (1972).

SPANO v. PERINI CORP.

Court of Appeals of New York, 1969
250 N.E.2d 31, *on remand,* 304 N.Y.S.2d 15 (1969)

FULD, CHIEF JUDGE.

The principal question posed on this appeal is whether a person who has sustained property damage caused by blasting on nearby property can maintain an action for damages without a showing that the blaster was negligent. Since 1893, when this court decided the case of *Booth v. Rome, W. & O. T. R. R. Co.*, 140 N.Y. 267 . . . , it has been the law of this State that proof of negligence was required unless the blast was accompanied by an actual physical invasion of the damaged property — for example, by rocks or other material being cast upon the premises. We are now asked to reconsider that rule.

The plaintiff Spano is the owner of a garage in Brooklyn which was wrecked by a blast occurring on November 27, 1962. There was then in that garage, for repairs, an automobile owned by the plaintiff Davis which he also claims was damaged by the blasting. Each of the plaintiffs brought suit against the two defendants who, as joint venturers, were engaged in constructing a tunnel in the vicinity pursuant to a contract with the City of New York. The two cases were tried together, without a jury, in the Civil Court of the City of New York, New York County, and judgments were rendered in favor of the plaintiffs. The judgments were reversed by the Appellate Term and the Appellate Division affirmed that order, granting leave to appeal to this court.

It is undisputed that, on the day in question (November 27, 1962), the defendants had set off a total of 194 sticks of dynamite at a construction site which was only 125 feet away from the damaged premises. Although both plaintiffs alleged negligence in their complaints, no attempt was made to show that the defendants had failed to exercise reasonable care or to take necessary precautions when they were blasting. Instead, they chose to rely, upon the trial, solely on the principle of absolute liability.
. . .

The concept of absolute liability in blasting cases is hardly a novel one. The overwhelming majority of American jurisdictions have adopted such a rule. . . .

We need not rely solely, however, upon out-of-state decisions in order to attain our result. Not only has the rationale of the *Booth* case (140 N.Y. 267, *supra*) been overwhelmingly rejected elsewhere but it appears to be fundamentally inconsistent with earlier cases in our own court which had held, long before *Booth* was decided, that a party was absolutely liable for damages to neighboring property caused by explosions. (*See, e.g., Hay v. Cohoes Co.*, 2 N.Y. 159; *Heeg v. Licht*, 80 N.Y. 579.) In the *Hay* case (2 N.Y. 159, *supra*), for example, the defendant was engaged in blasting an excavation for a canal and the force of the blasts caused large quantities of earth and stones to be thrown against the plaintiff's house, knocking down his stoop and part of his chimney. The court held the defendant absolutely liable for the damage caused, stating (2 N.Y., at pp. 160-161):

It is an elementary principle in reference to private rights, that every individual is entitled to the undisturbed possession and lawful enjoyment of his own property. . . .

Although the court in *Booth* drew a distinction between a situation — such as was presented in the *Hay* case — where there was "a physical invasion" of, or trespass on, the plaintiff's property and one in which the damage was caused by "setting the air in motion, or in some other unexplained way" (140 N.Y., at pp. 279, 280), it is clear that the court, in the earlier cases, was not concerned with the particular manner by which the damage was caused but by the simple fact that any explosion in a built-up area was likely to cause damage. Thus, in *Heeg v. Licht* (80 N.Y. 579, *supra*), the court held that there should be absolute liability where the damage was caused by the accidental explosion of stored gunpowder, even in the absence of a physical trespass (p. 581). . . .

Such reasoning should, we venture, have led to the conclusion that the *intentional* setting off of explosives — that is, blasting — in an area in which it was likely to cause harm to neighboring property similarly results in absolute liability. However, the court in the *Booth* case rejected such an extension of the rule for the reason that "[to] exclude the defendant from blasting . . . would not be a compromise between conflicting rights, but an extinguishment of the right of the one for the benefit of the other" (140 N.Y., at p. 281). The court expanded on this by stating, "This sacrifice, we think, the law does not exact. Public policy is promoted by the building up of towns and cities and the improvement of property. Any unnecessary restraint on freedom of action of a property owner hinders this."

This rationale cannot withstand analysis. The plaintiff in *Booth* was not seeking, as the court implied, to "exclude the defendant from blasting" and thus prevent desirable improvements to the latter's property. Rather, he was merely seeking compensation for the damage which was inflicted upon his own property as a result of that blasting. The question, in other words, was not whether it was lawful or proper to engage in blasting but who should bear the cost of any resulting damage — the person who engaged in the dangerous activity or the innocent neighbor injured thereby. Viewed in such a light, it clearly appears that *Booth* was wrongly decided and should be forthrightly overruled.

. . . .

Even though the proof was not insufficient as a matter of law, however, the Appellate Division affirmed on the sole ground that no negligence had been proven against the defendants and thus had no occasion to consider the question whether, in fact, the blasting caused the damage. That being so, we must remit the case to the Appellate Division so that it may pass upon the weight of the evidence. . . .

The order appealed from should be reversed, with costs, and the matter remitted to the Appellate Division for further proceedings in accordance with this opinion.

DYER v. MAINE DRILLING & BLASTING, INC.
Supreme Judicial Court of Maine, 2009
984 A.2d. 210

SILVER, J.

Vera E., Paul, and Robert Dyer appeal from a summary judgment entered in the Superior Court (Waldo County, Hjelm, J.) in favor of Maine Drilling & Blasting, Inc. (Maine Drilling). The Dyers argue that: (1) we should follow the weight of authority and adopt a common law rule of strict liability for abnormally dangerous activities. . . . [W]e adopt the Second Restatement's imposition of strict liability for abnormally dangerous activities, see Restatement (Second) of Torts §§ 519–520 (1977). . . .

I. CASE HISTORY

Vera Dyer and her sons, Paul and Robert, have a home in Prospect that the family has owned since the 1950s. The home, believed to be over seventy years old, has a cement foundation and floor. A stand-alone garage with a cement floor was constructed in the 1980s.

On September 22, 2004, Maine Drilling distributed a form notice that informed the Dyers that Maine Drilling would begin blasting rock near the home on or about October 1, 2004, in connection with a construction project to replace the Waldo – Hancock Bridge and bridge access roads. The notice stated that Maine Drilling uses "the most advanced technologies available . . . to measure the seismic effect to the area," and assured the Dyers "that ground vibrations associated with the blasting [would] not exceed the established limits that could potentially cause damage."

As offered in the notice, Maine Drilling provided a pre-blast survey of the Dyer home. The survey report recorded the surveyor's observation of "some concrete deterioration to [the] west wall" and "cracking to [the] concrete floor," and a slight tilt to a retaining wall behind the garage. Richard Dyer, another son of Vera, thoroughly documented the condition of the home and garage by videotape before blasting began.

Maine Drilling conducted over 100 blasts between October 2004 and early August 2005. The closest blast was approximately 100 feet from the Dyer home. Vera was inside the home for at least two of the blasts and felt the whole house shake. During other blasts, she was not in the home because Maine Drilling employees advised her to go outside. Vera visited Florida from approximately January through April 2005, and so was absent from her home when blasting occurred during that period. Paul, however, checked on the home several times a week while Vera was in Florida.

In the early spring of 2005, after the blasting work had begun and while Vera remained in Florida, both Paul and Richard observed several changes from the pre-blasting condition of the home and the garage: (1) the center of the basement floor had dropped as much as three inches; (2) the center beam in the basement that supported part of the first floor was sagging, and as a result the first floor itself was noticeably unlevel; (3) there was a new crack between the basement floor and the cement pad that formed the foundation of the chimney in the basement; (4) new or enlarged cracks radiated out across the basement floor from the chimney foundation; and (5) cracks that had previously existed in the garage floor were noticeably wider and more extensive. The brothers also noticed that a flowerbed retaining wall that helped to support the rear wall of the garage had "moved demonstrably."

When she returned to Maine, Vera observed the same changes in the condition of the property as her sons had reported and also noted larger or new cracks or separations on the back wall of the home's foundation.

The Dyers engaged an expert in ground engineering and environmental services, Mark Peterson, who testified at a deposition that the U.S. Bureau of Mines has established a "safe operating envelope" for seismic impact of blasts to minimize property damage. Under these guidelines, a blast is considered unlikely to cosmetically damage fragile structures in a building if its velocity falls below the established envelope. Where, however, a structure is underlain by "uncontrolled fill" as opposed to "engineered fill," damage can potentially result even if blasting is within the Bureau of Mines's envelope. Peterson testified that the Dyer home might be built on top of uncontrolled fill. Assuming this, Peterson stated that "there is not 100% certainty how the [Dyers'] floor would behave" in response to vibrations from blasting, and that settlement of uncontrolled fill could occur as a result of blasting.

Readings from a seismograph that Maine Drilling placed adjacent to the Dyer residence showed that six blasts produced vibrations that "slightly" exceeded the Bureau of Mines's envelope. . . .

Peterson testified that it is common for Maine homes to have cracking in foundations or basement floors that appear "over the course of the years," which could be caused by such things as vibrations, earth pressure, ground settlement, temperature, and ground water. Peterson opined that settlement under the Dyer home could have taken place for reasons unrelated to Maine Drilling's blasting, but that he would have expected such settlement to have occurred prior to blasting. Conversely, Peterson concluded that settlement due to the blasting was possible because: (1) the Dyers observed changes in floor settlement after blasting; (2) the pre-blast survey and the Dyers' observations did not indicate that the current basement settlement conditions existed before blasting began; (3) uncontrolled fill could consolidate and cause settlement from blasting vibrations; and (4) the most severe vibrations from blasting occurred prior to observations that the basement floor had settled.

The Dyers filed a three-count complaint, subsequently amended, alleging causes of action in strict liability and negligence. Maine Drilling filed a motion for summary judgment as to all counts in the Dyers' complaint. The Dyers opposed Maine Drilling's motion and filed a statement of additional material facts.

The court granted Maine Drilling's motion for a summary judgment and awarded costs to Maine Drilling. The court found in favor of Maine Drilling on the Dyers' claim for strict liability, citing *Reynolds v. W.H. Hinman Co.*, 145 Me. 343, 75 A.2d 802 (1950) and other Maine precedent in support of its ruling. [We reverse and remand.]

II. DISCUSSION

A. Standard of Review

We review a grant of a summary judgment de novo, considering the evidence in the light most favorable to the non-moving party. . . .

B. Strict Liability

We adopt today the Second Restatement's imposition of strict liability for abnormally dangerous activities, and remand to the court to determine if the blasting in this case was an abnormally dangerous activity under the Restatement's six-factor test. See Restatement (Second) of Torts §§ 519–520 (1977). In doing so, we overrule our prior opinions requiring proof of negligence in blasting cases.

1. History of Strict Liability

Strict liability doctrine originated in the English case *Rylands v. Fletcher*, (1868) 3 L.R. 330 (H.L.), where the court held that a defendant was liable regardless of negligence when he used his land in a way that was non-natural and likely to cause injury, and injury in fact resulted. *Id.* ("If a person brings, or accumulates, on his land anything which, if it should escape, may cause damage to his neighbour, he does so at his peril. If it does escape, and cause damage, he is responsible, however careful he may have been."). This Court rejected *Rylands* in the 1950s, deciding that proof of negligence would be required in blasting cases. *Reynolds*, 145 Me. at 362, 75 A.2d at 811.

In *Reynolds*, we noted that strict liability was the historic rule, but that the majority of states had switched to a negligence approach in abnormally dangerous activities cases. *Id.* at 347–48, 75 A.2d at 804–05. Additionally, the opinion quoted a law review article arguing against strict liability based in part on the "difficulty of drawing the line between the danger which calls for care and the extra hazard. There are, as yet[,] no unanimously approved rules or criteria as to this subject." *Id.* at 349, 75 A.2d at 805 (quotation marks omitted). Finally, our *Reynolds* decision was supported by the conclusions that blasting is a reasonable and lawful use of land, *id.* at 361, 75 A.2d at 811, and that plaintiffs would generally be able to recover under a negligence scheme. *Id.* at 351, 75 A.2d at 806 ("At the present time, in an action for blasting, if the courts apply the modern law as to negligence, a plaintiff who has a meritorious case can generally recover without calling in aid the old rule of absolute liability." (quotation marks omitted)).

2. Modern Strict Liability

These rationales have been undermined in the last half-century. Policy approaches have shifted nationwide, leading almost every other state to adopt strict liability in blasting and other abnormally dangerous activity cases, and leading Maine to apply strict liability in other contexts. Additionally, the Second Restatement has provided a scheme of clear criteria for delineating which activities require a strict liability approach. In light of these changes, we overturn *Reynolds* and its progeny and adopt strict liability under the Restatement's six factor test.

Reynolds operated on the assumption that negligence liability would allow most plaintiffs to recover in blasting cases. However, we have recognized that blasting is inherently dangerous, and most courts have recognized that this inherent danger cannot be eliminated by the exercise of care. The Dyers' expert testified that blasting may cause damage even when it is within the Bureau of Mines's guidelines. Consequently, although blasting is a lawful and often beneficial activity, the costs should fall on those who benefit from the blasting, rather than on an unfortunate neighbor. . . .

The negligence approach to abnormally dangerous activities initially taken by American courts was rooted in part in the idea that dangerous activities were essential to industrial development, "and it was considered that the interests of those in the vicinity of such enterprises must give way to them, and that too great a burden must not be placed upon them." But today, that attitude has changed, and strict liability seeks to encourage both cost-spreading and incentives for the utmost safety when engaging in dangerous activities. Additionally, blasters are already required by the rules of the Maine Department of Public Safety and by many town ordinances to have liability insurance covering damages that result from blasting. Thus, a strict liability scheme should not greatly increase costs for these businesses.

At least forty-one states have adopted some form of strict liability for blasting, with only two of those clearly limiting it to damage caused by debris. The other New England states are among those adopting strict liability, with the exception of New Hampshire, which has retained negligence liability for blasting damages . . .

Not only has the weight of authority shifted nationally, but we, acting pursuant to our common law authority, have applied forms of strict liability in certain circumstances. For example, we have adopted the Second Restatement approach to injuries caused by wild animals, analogizing those cases to blasting.

The Legislature has also been increasingly willing to apply strict liability in certain cases, imposing liability for explosions of natural gas, 14 M.R.S. § 165 (2008); for defective products, 14 M.R.S. § 221 (2008); and for oil spills and hazardous waste, 38 M.R.S. §§ 552(2), 1319–J (2008).

The Legislature has not, however, addressed the need for strict liability in abnormally dangerous activity cases. . . .

Under these circumstances, the application of strict liability or negligence to blasting "is a creation of our common law. . . . [I]ts applicability in Maine is controlled entirely by the precedents of this Court. It is therefore appropriate for this Court to continue to determine the scope of [the doctrine]." See *Picher v. Roman Catholic Bishop of Portland*, 974 A.2d 286, 295 (discussing doctrine of charitable immunity) (quotation marks omitted). . . .

We adopt the Second Restatement's approach to strict liability, imposing liability on defendants conducting an abnormally dangerous activity without requiring proof of negligence, although causation must still be proved. We believe that this approach strikes the right balance of policy interests by considering on a case-by-case basis which activities are encompassed by the rule, and by taking account of the social desirability of the activity at issue, see Restatement (Second) of Torts § 520(f) (1977), in contrast to the First Restatement approach, see Restatement (First) of Torts § 520 (1939).

Most jurisdictions have not adopted either the First or Second Restatement, and instead impose strict liability in blasting cases under a blanket rule that a blaster is always liable when causation is established. However, a number of courts that have re-examined the question since the adoption of the Second Restatement have chosen to apply the Restatement approach to abnormally dangerous activities. . . .

A person who creates a substantial risk of severe harm to others while acting for his own gain should bear the costs of that activity. Most of the courts of the nation have recognized this policy, and we now do as well. For these reasons we adopt strict liability and remand for a determination whether the activity in this case subjected Maine Drilling to liability under the Second Restatement approach.

---

1. What is the issue in *Spano* and *Dyer*? What are the holdings?

2. What is the policy underlying the *Booth v. Rome* decision? Why is *Booth* overruled?

3. Why did the plaintiffs abandon their negligence cause of action?

4. Compare the policy in *Spano* and *Rylands*, with the Restatement (Second) Section 520, with Fuld's argument that the question is "who should bear the cost of any resulting damage — the person who engaged in the dangerous activity or the innocent neighbor injured thereby." *Spano*, 250 N.E.2d at 34.

5. *Defenses to strict liability.* The following may be available as defenses to a suit in strict liability: proximate cause, *Foster v. Preston Mill Co.*, 44 Wash. 2d 440, 268 P.2d 645 (1954) (mother mink ate her kittens); Act of God, *Golden v. Amory*, 329 Mass. 484, 109 N.E.2d 131 (1952) (hurricane caused dike to overflow); assumption of risk, *Sandy v. Bushey*, 124 Me. 320, 128 A. 513 (1925) (plaintiff kicked by defendant's vicious horse). Contributory negligence is generally rejected as a defense to strict liability, Restatement (Second) of Torts § 524.

A NOTE ON ADDITIONAL APPLICATIONS OF STRICT LIABILITY

Strict liability applies in realms other than those specifically mentioned in this chapter. Recall *Langan v. Valicopters, Inc.*, 567 P.2d 218 (Wash. 1977), in which the court ruled that strict liability applied in a case involving crop dusting, and *Wrinkle v. Norman*, 242 P.3d 1216 (Kan. Ct. App. 2010), in which the court discussed statutes that impose strict liability for damage done by escaped animals. Liability for injuries caused by animals is further discussed in the Defenses chapter.

Strict liability may also have a new vitality in the realm of toxic torts. In *In re Hanford Nuclear Reservation Litigation, Phillips v. E.I. DuPont de Nemours & Co.*, 534 F.3d 986 (9th Cir.), *amended*, 521 F.3d 1028, *cert. denied*, 555 U.S. 1084

(2008), the Court of Appeals dealt with medical problems alleged to have been caused by emissions from a plutonium production facility in Washington. The Hanford facility had helped make the plutonium bomb that was dropped on Nagasaki in 1945. The emissions in question had been released into the area surrounding the facility as part of the production process.

The trial court decided that strict liability applied to the activity, and the Court of Appeals affirmed, stating that:

> We agree with the district court that Defendants' conduct at Hanford was an abnormally dangerous activity under factors [listed in the Restatement (Second) of Torts sections 519-520]. There was a high degree of risk to people and property associated with the Hanford facility and the gravity of any harm was likely to be great. Regardless of Defendants' efforts to exercise reasonable care, some [emissions] would be released, and developing plutonium is hardly an activity of common usage. While the value to the community at large, i.e., the nation, of developing an atomic bomb was perceived as high and there is pragmatically no very appropriate place to carry on such an activity, the [Section] 520 factors on balance support holding that Defendants' activities were abnormally dangerous.

The court rejected the argument that the defendants had been under a "public duty" to perform the work, ruling that the public duty exception to strict liability in Section 521 of the Restatement only applied to activities that the defendant was obligated to perform.

For more on this topic and on this case, please refer to the chapter on Toxic Torts.

Chapter 13

PRODUCTS LIABILITY

This chapter is intended as an introduction to this highly complex subject. Many law schools have separate courses on products liability, which is an area of the law perpetually in a state of turmoil. This is largely because the doctrine, a relative latecomer, was the product of a policy decision about who should be responsible for the costs when a product causes injury. Thus, the doctrine is subject to change when the prevailing view about who should pay for product-related injuries alters. Strict products liability is likely to thrive in a political climate which puts a priority on compensating plaintiffs for injuries caused by products. On the other hand, strict liability is likely to be curtailed when other goals — such as a perceived need for product innovation — take center stage. Courts were never entirely comfortable with the idea of imposing liability in the absence of negligence, and the susceptibility of the doctrine to change reflects this judicial reality as well.

A. FOOD AND DRINK

The history of strict liability for products begins with food and drink. From an early date, courts demonstrated that they did not care how an impurity got into the product, provided that the product was designed to be eaten or for other intimate bodily use (like hair dye) and that the responsibility for the presence of the impurity could be laid at the manufacturer's door. Courts eventually realized that the reasoning behind strict liability for impure (defective) food and drink readily applied to other types of products as well, and the doctrine of strict products liability for defects was born.

PILLARS v. R.J. REYNOLDS TOBACCO CO.
Supreme Court of Mississippi, 1918
78 So. 365

Cook, P.J.

The appellant sued the Corr-Williams Tobacco Company, distributors, and R.J. Reynolds Tobacco Company, distributors, and R.J. Reynolds Tobacco Company, manufacturer, of "Brown Mule Chewing Tobacco," for damages resulting to the appellant from chewing a piece of Brown Mule tobacco in which was concealed a decomposed human toe. The evidence disclosed that R.J. Reynolds Tobacco Company was the sole manufacturer of the tobacco. . . . It seems that appellant consumed one plug of his purchase, which measured up to representations, that it was tobacco unmixed with human flesh, but when appellant tackled the second plug it made him sick, but, not suspecting the tobacco, he tried another chew, and still another, until he bit into some foreign substance, which crumbled like dry bread, and caused him to foam at the mouth, while he was getting "sicker and sicker." Finally, his teeth struck something hard; he could not bite through it. After an examination he discovered a human toe, with flesh and nail intact. We refrain from detailing the further harrowing and nauseating details. The appellant consulted a physician, who testified that appellant exhibited all of the characteristic symptoms of ptomaine poison. The physician examined the toe and identified it as a human toe in a state of putrefaction, and said, in effect, that his condition was caused by the poison generated by the rotten toe. At the close of the evidence for the plaintiff the trial judge, at the request of the defendants, directed a verdict for the defendants, and from a judgment responsive to this instruction, an appeal is prosecuted to this court.

Generally speaking, the rule is that the manufacturer is not liable to the ultimate consumer for damages resulting from the defects and impurities of the manufactured article. This rule is generally based upon the theory that there is no contractual relation existing between the ultimate consumer and the manufacturer. From time to time, the courts have made exceptions to the rule. The manufacturers of food, beverages, drugs, condiments, and confections have been held liable to ultimate consumers for damages resulting from the negligent preparation of their products. The contention of the defendants here is that the limit has been reached by the courts, and that the facts of this case do not warrant an exception in favor of the plaintiff, and this view was adopted by the learned trial court. The exceptions already made were for the protection of the health of the people, and to insure a scrupulous care in the preparation of those articles of commerce so as to reduce to a minimum all danger to those using them.

If poisons are concealed in food, or in beverages, or in confections or in drugs, death or the impairment of health will be the probable consequence. We know that chewing tobacco is taken into the mouth, and that some, at least, of the juice or pulp will and does find its way into the alimentary canal, there to be digested and ultimately to become a part of the blood. Tobacco may be relatively harmless, but decaying flesh, we are advised, develops poisonous ptomaines, which are certainly dangerous and often fatal. Anything taken into the mouth there to be masticated should be free of those elements which may endanger the life or health of the user. No one would be so bold as to contend that the manufacturer would be free from liability if it should appear that he purposely mixed human flesh with chewing tobacco, or chewing gum. If the manufacturer would be liable for intentionally feeding putrid human flesh to any and all consumers of chewing tobacco, does it not logically follow that he would be liable for negligently bringing about the same result? It seems to us that this question must be answered in the affirmative.

The fact that the courts have at this time made only the exceptions mentioned to the general rule does not prevent a step forward for the health and life of the public. The principles announced in the cases which recognize the exceptions, in our opinion, apply, with equal force, to this case.

We believe that the way the tobacco is to be used furnishes the reason for great care in its preparation. If we eat food or drink beverages containing substances which under certain conditions may endanger our lives for obvious reasons, he who prepares the food or drink should be required to exercise great care to prevent the dangerous conditions. It appears sufficiently certain that chewing tobacco with poisonous ptomaines hidden in it is dangerous to the consumer, as was proven in this case.

We can imagine no reason why, with ordinary care, human toes could not be left out of chewing tobacco, and if toes are found in chewing tobacco, it seems to us that somebody has been very careless.

. . . .

Reversed in part and affirmed in part.

---

1.   The court in this case states that the manufacturer is liable for "negligent preparation." What is the evidence of negligence in this case? On what basis did the court conclude that "somebody has been very careless"?

2.   Was there any evidence that the manufacturer had acted unreasonably? Did the court conclude that the manufacturer had in fact been negligent?

PROBLEM

What would the analysis in *Pillars* have looked like if the plaintiff had introduced evidence that chewing tobacco, even in the absence of extraneous contaminants, causes tongue cancer?

MATTHEWS v. CAMPBELL SOUP CO.
United States District Court, S.D. Texas, Houston Division, 1974
380 F. Supp. 1061

MEMORANDUM AND ORDER:

SEALS, DISTRICT JUDGE.

This action is before the Court on a Motion for Summary Judgment filed by Defendant. In this diversity suit, 28 U.S.C. § 1332(a)(1), Plaintiff seeks to recover for injuries to his teeth and gums which were allegedly suffered while he was eating the contents of a can of Defendant's Oyster Stew Soup. Plaintiff claims that the injuries were caused by a small deleterious object in the soup. Plaintiff surrendered this object to Defendant for examination and it has been identified as a small irregularly shaped oyster pearl.

Plaintiff sets forth two theories of recovery: strict liability in tort and negligence in the manufacture and labeling of this product. Defendant contends that on the undisputed facts before the Court, Plaintiff cannot prevail on a theory of strict liability and that there is no evidence in the record to raise an issue of negligence. In ruling on Defendant's motion this Court is, of course, bound to apply those principles of products liability and negligence law which would be applied by the courts of this State. *Erie R.R. Co. v. Thompkins*, 304 U.S. 64, 58 S. Ct. 817, 82 L.

Ed. 1188 (1938).

Texas courts have long recognized that the manufacturers of food products warrant that they are wholesome and fit for human consumption. The warranty was imposed by operation of law as a matter of public policy:

> It seems to be the rule that where food products sold for human consumption are unfit for that purpose, there is such an utter failure of the purpose for which the food is sold, and the consequences of eating unsound food are so disastrous to human health and life, that the law imposes a warranty of purity in favor of the ultimate consumer as a matter of public policy.

Jacob E. Decker & Sons, Inc. v. Capps, [164 S.W.2d 828, 829 (Tex. 1942)].

In *McKisson v. Sales Affiliates, Inc.*, 416 S.W.2d 787 (Tex. 1967), this strict liability concept applicable to foodstuffs was extended to include consumer products generally. *See also, Putnam v. Erie City Manufacturing Company*, 338 F.2d 911 (5th Cir. 1964). The *McKisson* court adopted the Restatement, Second, Torts § 402A which provides as follows:

Special Liability of Seller of Product for Physical Harm to User or Consumer

1. One who sells any product in a defective condition unreasonably dangerous to the user or consumer or his property is subject to liability for physical harm thereby caused to the ultimate user or consumer, or to his property, if

(a) the seller is engaged in the business of selling such a product, and

(b) it is expected to and does reach the user or consumer without substantial change in the condition in which it is sold.

2. The rule stated in Subsection (1) applies although

(a) the seller has exercised all possible care in the preparation and sale of his product, and

(b) the user or consumer has not bought the product from or entered into any contractual relation with the seller.

[Comment:

a. This Section states a special rule applicable to sellers of products. The rule is one of strict liability, making the seller subject to liability to the user or consumer even though he has exercised all possible care in the preparation and sale of the product.]

In order to prevail under this strict liability standard Plaintiff must establish that: 1) the product in question was defective; 2) the defect existed at the time the products left the hands of the defendant; 3) that because of the defect the product was unreasonably dangerous to the user or consumer (plaintiff); 4) that the consumer was injured or suffered damages; 5) and that the defect (if proved) was the proximate cause of the injuries suffered.

Defendant argues that, as a matter of law, the can of Oyster Stew Soup at issue here was not unfit, unwholesome, defective, or unreasonably dangerous. As indicated in *Reyes v. Wyeth Laboratories, supra,* "defective condition" and "unreasonably dangerous" are essentially synonymous. Further, in light of the Texas Supreme Court's adoption of Section 402A of the Restatement in *McKisson, supra,* it is apparent that a food product is defective or unreasonably dangerous if it is unwholesome or unfit for human consumption and vice versa.

Defendant's position is bottomed on what may be labeled the "foreign-natural" doctrine. This doctrine, which has been neither accepted nor rejected by Texas courts, apparently first emerged in *Mix v. Ingersoll Candy Co.,* 6 Cal. 2d 674, 59 P.2d 144 (1936). There plaintiff brought suit for injuries caused by a fragment of chicken bone contained in a chicken pie. The court held that the chicken pie was not unfit for human consumption as a matter of law:

> "Although it may frequently be a question for a jury as the trier of facts to determine whether or not the particular defect alleged rendered the food not reasonably fit for human consumption, yet certain cases present facts from which the court itself may say, as a matter of law that the alleged defect does not fall within the terms of the statute. It is insisted that the court may so determine herein only if it is empowered to take judicial notice of the alleged fact that chicken pies usually contain chicken bones. It is not necessary to go so far as to hold that chicken pies usually contain chicken bones. It is sufficient if it may be said that as a matter of common knowledge chicken pies occasionally contain chicken bones. We have no hesitancy in so holding, and we are of the opinion that despite the fact that a chicken bone may occasionally be encountered in a chicken pie, such chicken pie, in the absence of some further defect, is reasonably fit for human consumption. *Bones which are natural to the type of meat served cannot legitimately be called a foreign substance, and a consumer who eats meat dishes ought to anticipate and be on his guard against the presence of such bones.* At least he cannot hold the restaurant keeper whose representation implied by law is that the meat dish is reasonably fit for human consumption, liable for any injury occurring as a result of the presence of a chicken bone in such chicken pie." At 148 (Emphasis supplied).

Probably a majority of jurisdictions having occasion to treat the problem have adopted the *Mix* rationale.

A relatively recent expression of the foreign-natural view is found in *Musso v. Picadilly Cafeterias, Inc.,* 178 So. 2d 421 (La. App. 1965). While eating at defendant's cafeteria, plaintiff encountered a cherry stone or pit in a slice of cherry pie. The court stated that vendors are strictly liable for injuries occasioned by the serving of food which is unwholesome or deleterious or which contains a vice or defect, but, held that a restauranteur is not liable for injuries resulting from substances natural to the food served and inadvertently left therein. The court's reasoning is attractively simple: if the food contains only natural substances it cannot be unfit or unwholesome. The essence of the foreign-natural rule and the rationale behind it is captured in the following passage from *Musso:*

The rationale of the majority rule as expressed in the cited authorities is that substances which are a natural part of the food served are not considered foreign matter or substances if inadvertently left therein. On this premise it is reasoned that the presence of substances natural to the ingredients or finished product does not constitute breach of the vendor's implied warranty that the food is wholesome and fit for human consumption. The cases further hold that the warranty implicit in the sale of food must be construed in the light of the common knowledge with reference to the nature and character of the food being served. In this respect it is further reasoned common experience dictates that one eating the meat of animals, fowl or fish should do so with the knowledge such foods may contain pieces of bone. At 426.

Not all jurisdictions have followed the foreign-natural view; it has been rejected by several courts in favor of a "reasonable expectation" test. In *Zabner u. Howard Johnson's Inc.*, 201 So. 2d 824 (Fla. App. 1967), a consumer was injured by a piece of walnut shell concealed in a dish of maple walnut ice cream. Following the foreign-natural test the trial court entered judgment for the defendant. After tracing the history of this doctrine and its application the appellate court opted in favor of a test of "reasonable expectation." "The test should be what is *'reasonably expected'* by the consumer in the food as served, not what might be natural to the ingredients of that food prior to preparation."

Observing that natural substances can often be as dangerous to the consumer as foreign objects such as a pebble or a piece of glass or wire, the *Zabner* court stated: "[The] naturalness of the substance to any ingredients in the food served is important only in determining whether the consumer may reasonably expect to find such substance in the particular type of dish or style of food served." The key question under the reasonable expectation test is whether the consumer ought to have anticipated the injury producing object in the final product not whether the object is foreign or natural. What the consumer might reasonably expect, the court noted, is a jury question in most cases.

The reasonable expectation view is also well stated in *Betehia v. Cape Cod Corp.*, 10 Wis. 2d 323, 103 N.E.2d 64 (1960):

The test should be what is reasonably expected by the consumer in the food as served, not what might be natural to the ingredients of that food prior to preparation. What is to be reasonably expected by the consumer is a jury question in most cases; at least, we cannot say as a matter of law that a patron of a restaurant must expect a bone in a chicken sandwich either because chicken bones are occasionally found there or are natural to chicken.

The test as applied to an action for breach of the implied warranty is keyed to what is "reasonably" fit. If it is found that the chicken bone the size alleged ought to be anticipated in a chicken sandwich and guarded against by the consumer plaintiff, then the sandwich was reasonably fit under the implied warranty. At 69.

Texas courts have never been in a position requiring an election between these two competing doctrines. A great number of cases involving harmful objects have been litigated but the objects were so obviously "foreign" that the issue did not arise.

Making an *Erie* educated guess, this Court holds that, if faced with the problem, Texas courts would follow the reasonable expectation rule as it is stated in *Zabner.* It is obvious that the "reasonable expectation" approach is considerably more compatible and consistent with Section 402A which has been adopted as the law of Texas in product liability cases. Section 402A makes the seller liable for injuries caused by defective or unreasonably dangerous products. "Defective condition" is defined in Comment (g) as " . . . a condition not contemplated by the ultimate consumer, which will be unreasonably dangerous to him." An article is "unreasonably dangerous" according to Comment (i) if it is " . . . dangerous to an extent beyond that which would be contemplated by the ordinary consumer who purchases it, with the ordinary knowledge common to the community as to its characteristics." These Comments have been viewed as persuasive if not controlling in the application of Section 402A. *Garcia v. Sky Climber, Inc.*, 470 S.W.2d 261 (Tex. Civ. App. 1971).

If Texas courts were to follow the "reasonable expectation" test they logically should reach a result consistent in every case with the Restatement definitions of "defective condition" and "unreasonably dangerous." This would not necessarily be true under the foreign-natural doctrine. It would be possible under that approach only if it is assumed that consumers *always* contemplate the presence of every species of object which might be categorized as natural to the food they are eating regardless of how infrequently the object might appear in common experience. That is obviously a faulty assumption which Texas courts are not at all likely to make.

Andrews, J., concurring in *Zabner, supra*, suggests that the difficulty with the foreign-natural test as a problem solving device lies not in its theory but in its artificial application. He contends that courts too often apply it at a preliminary stage of production focusing on a single ingredient rather than the final consumer product. "By moving the focus of the test to the consumable item the foreign-natural distinction as measured by the consumer's reasonable expectations becomes a valid and relevant standard."

If this analysis is correct, the only way of avoiding misapplication of the foreign-natural theory is to focus on what the consumer might reasonably expect to find in the final product. This being the case it would make even more sense to discard the foreign-natural distinction and go directly to the reasonable expectation issue. The use of these labels does not advance the inquiry and unnecessarily increases the possibility of confusion on the ultimate issue.

Loyacano v. Continental Insurance Company, 283 So. 2d 302 (La. App. 1973) is an example of the confusion which adherence to the foreign-natural distinction can create. There the plaintiff sued for injuries caused by a bone fragment concealed in a ground meat patty. The court first professed adherence to the foreign-natural distinction of *Musso, supra*, and then stated:

> In *Musso* there was ample evidence to show the probability of expectancy of cherry pits in pitted cherries, but unfortunately there is no evidence in

the present case concerning the probability of pieces of bone appearing in hamburger. Simply as a matter of general knowledge, we cannot say that we can take judicial notice that a hamburger patty should not contain any pieces of bone whatsoever . . . It may be said that a product can be considered defective if it does not meet the reasonable expectations of the ordinary consumer as to its safety. It is not the fact that a defect is a natural one which is important to this inquiry, but the fact that the ordinary consumer would expect that he might encounter it, and thus he would normally take his own precautions. A package of ground meat is not expected to be consumed from the sealed package as a bottle of soda water or milk, but is expected to be processed or otherwise altered before consumption by the purchaser. Therefore, it seems to us that the strict liability imposed upon vendors of sealed packages of that nature, cannot be imposed upon the vendor here, except insofar as a foreign object would be concerned. For a natural object, such as a bone, from the only evidence produced in this case, it appears that the inquiry should be directed to the size of the bone left in the ground meat. At 305.

The court went on to hold defendant liable for the injury stating that defendant had not presented sufficient evidence to prove its lack of negligence in handling the ground meat. Lemon, J., in a concurring opinion, indicates that *Musso* is the source of the problem and advocates a rethinking of the foreign-natural distinction, possibly portending changes to come in Louisiana jurisprudence. Texas courts have not descended into this quagmire and this Court is confident that they will not.

Having settled on the "reasonable expectation" standard the question before this Court can be restated. Can it be said, as a matter of law, that the consumer can reasonably expect to encounter a pearl in a can of Defendant's Oyster Stew Soup[?] This Court thinks not. It is clearly an issue for the jury to decide. With the undisputed facts reflected in the pleadings, interrogatories and affidavits on file herein it would be impossible for this Court to ascertain what the common consumer experience is with respect to pearls in canned oyster stew. Defendant's Motion For Summary Judgment on the issue of strict liability is therefore denied.

Defendant's motion going to Plaintiff's negligence theory of recovery is also denied. Even where there are no facts in dispute, it is usually for the jury to decide whether the conduct in question meets the reasonable man standard. *Cf.*, Wright & Miller, Federal Practice and Procedure, § 2729 at 572. On the facts reflected in this record the Court cannot say that Defendant was not negligent in the manufacture and labeling of this product as a matter of law.

––––––––––

1.   Is there any difference in result between the foreign/natural test and the reasonable expectation test? Wouldn't a consumer expect substances in food that naturally occur there? In what situations would the two tests produce different results? What role would a warning of possible bones serve?

2.   This case introduces the reader to the Restatement (Second) of Torts § 402A. What significance does Section 402A have in this case?

PROBLEM

B purchases a package of pork chops from a supermarket. He takes the pork chops home and prepares them for dinner by broiling them.

Some time later, B falls ill with trichinosis, a parasitic disease which results from eating pork which has not been thoroughly cooked. Cooking the meat thoroughly kills the trichinae and renders them unable to infest the person eating the pork. B's ailment was caused by the pork chops.

Assume that the supermarket is the appropriate entity for B to sue. What arguments would B make under the foreign/natural test? Under the reasonable expectation test? What do you think the supermarket will argue in response to either test?

B.   CONTRACT AND TORT IN STRICT PRODUCTS LIABILITY

Before strict products liability theory could establish its identity as a separate doctrine, courts needed to define the relationship (if any) between contract and tort law in the cases they were adjudicating. The following case, in which the Supreme Court of New Jersey definitively discussed the problem, appears in courses dealing with contracts, torts, sales, and products liability.

HENNINGSEN v. BLOOMFIELD MOTORS, INC.
Supreme Court of New Jersey, 1960
161 A.2d 69

FRANCIS, J.

Plaintiff Claus H. Henningsen purchased a Plymouth automobile, manufactured by defendant Chrysler Corporation, from defendant Bloomfield Motors, Inc. His wife, plaintiff Helen Henningsen, was injured while driving it and instituted suit against both defendants to recover damages on account of her injuries. Her husband joined in the action seeking compensation for his consequential losses. The complaint was predicated upon breach of express and implied warranties and upon negligence. At the trial the negligence counts were dismissed by the court and the cause was submitted to the jury for determination solely on the issues of implied warranty of merchantability. Verdicts were returned against both defendants and in favor of the plaintiffs. Defendants appealed and plaintiffs cross-appealed from the dismissal of their negligence claim. The matter was certified by this court prior to consideration in the Appellate Division.

The facts are not complicated, but a general outline of them is necessary to an understanding of the case.

On May 7, 1955 Mr. and Mrs. Henningsen visited the place of business of Bloomfield Motors, Inc., an authorized De Soto and Plymouth dealer, to look at a Plymouth. They wanted to buy a car and were considering a Ford or a Chevrolet as well as a Plymouth. They were shown a Plymouth which appealed to them and the purchase followed. The record indicates that Mr. Henningsen intended the car as a Mother's Day gift to his wife. He said the intention was communicated to the dealer. When the purchase order or contract was prepared and presented, the husband executed it alone. His wife did not join as a party.

The purchase order was a printed form of one page. On the front it contained blanks to be filled in with a description of the automobile to be sold, the various accessories to be included, and the details of the financing. The particular car selected was described as a 1955 Plymouth, Plaza "6," Club Sedan. The type used in the printed parts of the form became smaller in size, different in style, and less readable toward the bottom where the line for the purchaser's signature was placed. The smallest type on the page appears in the two paragraphs, one of two and one-quarter lines and the second of one and one-half lines, on which great stress is laid by the defense in the case. These two paragraphs are the least legible and the most difficult to read in the instrument, but they are most important in the evaluation of the rights of the contesting parties. They do not attract attention and there is nothing about the format which would draw the reader's eye to them. In fact, a studied and concentrated effort would have to be made to read them. De-emphasis seems the motive rather than emphasis. More particularly, most of the printing in the body of the order appears to be 12 point block type, and easy to read. In the short paragraphs under discussion, however, the type appears to be six point script and the print is solid, that is, the lines are very close together.

The two paragraphs are:

"The front and back of this Order comprise the entire agreement affecting this purchase and no other agreement or understanding of any nature concerning same has been made or entered into, or will be recognized. I hereby certify that no credit has been extended to me for the purchase of this motor vehicle except as appears in writing on the face of this agreement.

"I have read the matter printed on the back hereof and agree to it as a part of this order the same as if it were printed above my signature. I certify that I am 21 years of age, or older, and hereby acknowledge receipt of a copy of this order."

On the right side of the form, immediately below these clauses and immediately above the signature line, and in 12 point block type, the following appears:

"CASH OR CERTIFIED CHECK ONLY ON DELIVERY."

On the left side, just opposite and in the same style type as the two quoted clauses, but in eight point size, this statement is set out:

"This agreement shall not become binding upon the Dealer until approved by an officer of the company."

The two latter statements are in the interest of the dealer and obviously an effort is made to draw attention to them.

The testimony of Claus Henningsen justifies the conclusion that he did not read the two fine print paragraphs referring to the back of the purchase contract. And it is uncontradicted that no one made any reference to them, or called them to his attention. With respect to the matter appearing on the back, it is likewise uncontradicted that he did not read it and that no one called it to his attention.

The reverse side of the contract contains 8 1/2 inches of fine print. It is not as small, however, as the two critical paragraphs described above. The page is headed "Conditions" and contains ten separate paragraphs consisting of 65 lines in all. The paragraphs do not have headnotes or margin notes denoting their particular subject, as in the case of the "Owner Service Certificate" to be referred to later. In the seventh paragraph, about two-thirds of the way down the page, the warranty, which is the focal point of the case, is set forth. It is as follows:

> "7. It is expressly agreed that there are no warranties, express or implied, *made* by either the dealer or the manufacturer on the motor vehicle, chassis, of [sic] parts furnished hereunder except as follows.

> "The manufacturer warrants each new motor vehicle (including original equipment placed thereon by the manufacturer except tires), chassis or parts manufactured by it to be free from defects in material or workmanship under normal use and service. Its obligation under this warranty being limited to making good at its factory any part or parts thereof which shall, within ninety (90) days after delivery of such vehicle *to the original purchaser* or before such vehicle has been driven 4,000 miles, whichever event shall first occur, be returned to it with transportation charges prepaid and which its examination shall disclose to its satisfaction to have been thus defective; *this warranty being expressly in lieu of all other warranties expressed or implied, and all other obligations or liabilities on its part*, and it neither assumes nor authorizes any other person to assume for it any other liability in connection with the sale of its vehicles. . . ." (Emphasis ours.)

> After the contract had been executed, plaintiffs were told the car had to be serviced and that it would be ready in two days. . . .

. . . .

The new Plymouth was turned over to the Henningsens on May 9, 1955. . . . Thereafter, it was used for short trips on paved streets about the town. It had no servicing and no mishaps of any kind before the event of May 19. That day, Mrs. Henningsen drove to Asbury Park. On the way down and in returning the car performed in normal fashion until the accident occurred. She was proceeding north on Route 36 in Highlands, New Jersey, at 20-22 miles per hour. The highway was paved and smooth, and contained two lanes for northbound travel. She was riding in the right-hand lane. Suddenly she heard a loud noise "from the bottom, by the hood." It "felt as if something cracked." The steering wheel spun in her hands; the car veered sharply to the right and crashed into a highway sign and a brick wall. No other vehicle was in any way involved. A bus operator driving in the left-hand lane testified that he observed plaintiffs' car approaching in normal fashion in the opposite direction; "all of a sudden [it] veered at 90 degrees . . . and right into this wall." As a result of the impact, the front of the car was so badly damaged that it was impossible to determine if any of the parts of the steering wheel mechanism or workmanship or assembly were defective or improper prior to the accident. The condition was such that the collision insurance carrier, after inspection, declared the vehicle a total loss. It had 468 miles on the speedometer at the time.

The insurance carrier's inspector and appraiser of damaged cars, with 11 years of experience, advanced the opinion, based on the history and his examination, that something definitely went "wrong from the steering wheel down to the front wheels" and that the untoward happening must have been due to mechanical defect or failure; "something down there had to drop off or break loose to cause the car" to act in the manner described.

As has been indicated, the trial court felt that the proof was not sufficient to make out a *prima facie* case as to the negligence of either the manufacturer or the dealer. The case was given to the jury, therefore, solely on the warranty theory, with results favorable to the plaintiffs against both defendants.

I.

The Claim of Implied Warranty Against the Manufacturer.

In the ordinary case of sale of goods by description an implied warranty of merchantability is an integral part of the transaction. R.S. 46:30-20, N.J.S.A. . . . Th[is] type of warranty simply means that the thing sold is reasonably fit for the general purpose for which it is manufactured and sold.

. . . .

Of course . . . sales, whether oral or written, may be accompanied by an express warranty. Under the broad terms of the Uniform Sale of Goods Law any affirmation of fact relating to the goods is an express warranty if the natural tendency of the statement is to induce the buyer to make the purchase. R.S. 46:30-18, N.J.S.A. And over the years since the almost universal adoption of the act, a growing awareness of the tremendous development of modern business methods has prompted the courts to administer that provision with a liberal hand. Vold, Law of Sales, § 86, p. 429 (2d ed. 1959). Solicitude toward the buyer plainly harmonizes with the intention of the Legislature. That fact is manifested further by the later section of the act which preserves and continues any permissible implied warranty, despite an express warranty, unless the two are inconsistent. R.S. 46:30-21(6), N.J.S.A.

The uniform act codified, extended and liberalized the common law of sales. The motivation in part was to ameliorate the harsh doctrine *of caveat emptor,* and in some measure to impose a reciprocal obligation on the seller to beware. The transcendent value of the legislation, particularly with respect to implied warranties, rests in the fact that obligations on the part of the seller were imposed by operation of law, and did not depend for their existence upon express agreement of the parties. And of tremendous significance in a rapidly expanding commercial society was the recognition of the right to recover damages on account of personal injuries arising from a breach of warranty. The particular importance of this advance resides in the fact that under such circumstances strict liability is imposed upon the maker or seller of the product. Recovery of damages does not depend upon proof of negligence or knowledge of the defect.

As the Sales Act and its liberal interpretation by the courts threw this protective cloak about the buyer, the decisions in various jurisdictions revealed beyond doubt that many manufacturers took steps to avoid these ever increasing warranty obligations. Realizing that the act governed the relationship of buyer and seller, they undertook to withdraw from actual and direct contractual contact with the buyer. They ceased selling products to the consuming public through their own employees and making contracts of sale in their own names. Instead, a system of independent dealers was established; their products were sold to dealers who in turn dealt with the buying public, ostensibly solely in their own personal capacity as sellers. In the past in many instances, manufacturers were able to transfer to the dealers burdens imposed by the act and thus achieved a large measure of immunity for themselves. But, as will be noted in more detail hereafter, such marketing practices, coupled with the advent of large scale advertising by manufacturers to promote the purchase of these goods from dealers by members of the public, provided a basis upon which the existence of express or implied warranties was predicated, even though the manufacturer was not a party to the contract of sale.

The general observations that have been made are important largely for purposes of perspective. They are helpful in achieving a point from which to evaluate the situation now presented for solution. Primarily, they reveal a trend and a design in legislative and judicial thinking toward providing protection for the buyer. It must be noted, however, that the sections of the Sales Act, to which reference has been made, do not impose warranties in terms of unalterable absolutes. R.S. 46:30-3, N.J.S.A., provides in general terms that an applicable warranty may be negatived or varied by express agreement. As to disclaimers or limitations of the obligations that normally attend a sale, it seems sufficient at this juncture to say they are not favored, and that they are strictly construed against the seller.

With these considerations in mind, we come to a study of the express warranty on the reverse side of the purchase order signed by Claus Henningsen. At the outset we take notice that it was made only by the manufacturer and that by its terms it runs directly to Claus Henningsen. On the facts detailed above, it was to be extended to him by the dealer as the agent of Chrysler Corporation. The consideration for this warranty is the purchase of the manufacturer's product from the dealer by the ultimate buyer.

Although the franchise agreement between the defendants recites that the relationship of principal and agent is not created, in particular transactions involving third persons the law will look at their conduct and not to their intent or their words as between themselves but to their factual relation. Restatement (Second), Agency § 27 (1958). The normal pattern that the manufacturer-dealer relationship follows relegates the position of the dealer to the status of a way station along the car's route from maker to consumer. This is indicated by the language of the warranty. Obviously the parties knew and so intended that the dealer would not use the automobile for 90 days or drive it 4,000 miles. And the words "original purchaser," taken in their context, signify the purchasing member of the public. Moreover, the language of this warranty is that of the uniform warranty of the

Automobile Manufacturers Association, of which Chrysler is a member. And it is the form appearing in the Plymouth Owner Service Certificate mentioned in the servicing instruction guide sent with the new car from the factory. The evidence is overwhelming that the dealer acted for Chrysler in including the warranty in the purchase contract.

The terms of the warranty are a sad commentary upon the automobile manufacturers' marketing practices. Warranties developed in the law in the interest of and to protect the ordinary consumer who cannot be expected to have the knowledge or capacity or even the opportunity to make adequate inspection of mechanical instrumentalities, like automobiles, and to decide for himself whether they are reasonably fit for the designed purpose. But the ingenuity of the Automobile Manufacturers Association, by means of its standardized form, has metamorphosed the warranty into a device to limit the maker's liability. . . . The manufacturer agrees to replace defective parts for 90 days after the sale or until the car has been driven 4,000 miles, whichever is first to occur, *if the part is sent to the factory, transportation charges prepaid, and if examination discloses to its satisfaction that the part is defective.* It is difficult to imagine a greater burden on the consumer, or less satisfactory remedy. Aside from imposing on the buyer the trouble of removing and shipping the part, the maker has sought to retain the uncontrolled discretion to decide the issue of defectiveness. . . . [S]uppose, as in this case, a defective part or parts caused an accident and that the car was so damaged as to render it impossible to discover the precise part or parts responsible, although the circumstances clearly pointed to such fact as the cause of the mishap. Can it be said that the impossibility of performance deprived the buyer of the benefit of the warranty?

Moreover, the guaranty is against defective workmanship. That condition may arise from good parts improperly assembled. There being no defective parts to return to the maker, is all remedy to be denied? . . . Must the purchaser return the car, transportation charges prepaid, over a great distance to the factory? . . .

The matters referred to represent only a small part of the illusory character of the security presented by the warranty. Thus far the analysis has dealt only with the remedy provided in the case of a defective part. What relief is provided when the breach of the warranty results in personal injury to the buyer? (Injury to third persons using the car in the purchaser's right will be treated hereafter.) As we have said above, the law is clear that such damages are recoverable under an ordinary warranty. The right exists whether the warranty sued on is express or implied. And, of course, it has long since been settled that where the buyer or a member of his family driving with his permission suffers injuries because of negligent manufacture or construction the manufacturer's liability exists. But in this instance, after reciting that defective parts will be replaced at the factory, the alleged agreement relied upon by Chrysler provides that the manufacturer's "obligation under this warranty" is limited to that undertaking; further, that such remedy is "in lieu of all other warranties, express or implied, and all other obligations or liabilities on its part." The contention has been raised that such language bars any claim for personal injuries which may emanate from a breach of the warranty. Although not urged in this case, it has been successfully maintained that the exclusion "of all other obligations and liabilities on its part" precludes a cause of action for injuries based on negligence. *Shafer v. Reo Motors*, 205 F.2d 685 (3 Cir. 1953). Another Federal Circuit Court of Appeals holds to the contrary. *Doughnut Mach. Corporation v. Bibbey*, 65 F.2d 634 (1 Cir. 1933). There can be little doubt that justice is served only by the latter ruling.

Putting aside for the time being the problem of the efficacy of the disclaimer provisions contained in the express warranty, a question of first importance to be decided is whether an implied warranty of merchantability by Chrysler Corporation accompanied the sale of the automobile to Claus Henningsen.

Preliminarily, it may be said that the express warranty against defective parts and workmanship is not inconsistent with an implied warranty of merchantability. Such warranty cannot be excluded for that reason.

Chrysler points out that an implied warranty of merchantability is an incident of a contract of sale. It concedes, of course, the making of the original sale to Bloomfield Motors, Inc., but maintains that this transaction marked the terminal point of its contractual connection with the car. Then Chrysler urges that since it was not a party to the sale by the dealer to Henningsen, there is no privity of contract between it and the plaintiffs, and the absence of this privity eliminates any such implied warranty.

There is no doubt that under early common-law concepts of contractual liability only those persons who were parties to the bargain could sue for a breach of it. In more recent times a noticeable disposition has appeared in a number of jurisdictions to break through the narrow barrier of privity when dealing with sales of goods in order to give realistic recognition to a universally accepted fact. The fact is that the dealer and the ordinary buyer do not, and are not expected to, buy goods, whether they be foodstuffs or automobiles, exclusively for their own consumption or use. Makers and manufacturers know this and advertise and market their products on that assumption; witness, the "family" car, the baby foods, etc. The limitations of privity in contracts for the sale of goods developed their place in the law when marketing conditions were simple, when maker and buyer frequently met face to face on an equal bargaining plane and when many of the products were relatively uncomplicated and conducive to inspection by a buyer competent to evaluate their quality. With the advent of mass marketing, the manufacturer became remote from the purchaser, sales were accomplished through intermediaries, and the demand for the product was created by advertising media. In such an economy it became obvious that the consumer was the person being cultivated. Manifestly, the connotation of "consumer" was broader than that of "buyer." He signified such a person who, in the reasonable contemplation of the parties to the sale, might be expected to use the product. Thus, where the commodities sold are such that if defectively manufactured they will be dangerous to life or limb, then society's interests can only be protected by eliminating the requirement of privity between the maker and his dealers and the reasonably expected ultimate consumer. In that way the burden of losses consequent upon use of defective articles is borne by those who are in a position to either control the danger or make an equitable distribution of the losses when they do occur. As Harper & James put it, "The interest in consumer protection calls for warranties by the maker that *do* run with the goods, to reach all who are likely to be hurt by the use of the unfit commodity for a purpose ordinarily to be expected." 2 Harper & James, [Law of Torts] 1571, 1572 [(1956)]. As far back as 1932, in the well known case *of Baxter v. Ford Motor Co.*, 168 Wash. 456, 12 P.2d 409 (Sup. Ct. 1932), *affirmed* 15 P.2d 1118, 88 A.L.R. 521 (Sup. Ct. 1932), the Supreme Court of Washington gave recognition to the impact of then existing commercial practices on the strait jacket of privity, saying:

> "It would be unjust to recognize a rule that would permit manufacturers of goods to create a demand for their products by representing that they possess qualities which they, in fact, do not possess, and then, because there is no privity of contract existing between the consumer and the manufacturer, deny the consumer the right to recover if damages result from the absence of those qualities, when such absence is not readily noticeable." 12 P.2d at page 412.

. . . .

Although only a minority of jurisdictions have thus far departed from the requirement of privity, the movement in that direction is most certainly gathering momentum. Liability to the ultimate consumer in the absence of direct contractual connection has been predicated upon a variety of theories. Some courts hold that the warranty runs with the article like a covenant running with land; others recognize a third-party beneficiary thesis; still others rest their decision on the ground that public policy requires recognition of a warranty made directly to the consumer.

. . . .

Most of the cases where lack of privity has not been permitted to interfere with recovery have involved food and drugs. In fact, the rule as to such products has been characterized as an exception to the general doctrine. But more recently courts, sensing the inequity of such limitation, have moved into broader fields: home permanent wave set; soap detergent; inflammable cowboy suit (by clear implication); exploding bottle; defective emery wheel; defective wire rope; defective cinder blocks.

We see no rational doctrinal basis for differentiating between a fly in a bottle of beverage and a defective automobile. The unwholesome beverage may bring illness to one person, the defective car, with its great potentiality for harm to the driver, occupants, and others, demands even less adherence to the narrow barrier of privity. . . .

Under modern conditions the ordinary layman, on responding to the importuning of colorful advertising, has neither the opportunity nor the capacity to inspect or to determine the fitness of an automobile for use; he must rely on the manufacturer who has control of its construction, and to some degree on the dealer who, to the limited extent called for by the manufacturer's instructions, inspects and services it before delivery. In such a marketing milieu his remedies and those of persons who properly claim through him should not depend "upon the intricacies of the law of sales. The obligation of the manufacturer should not be based alone on privity of contract. It should rest, as was once said, upon "the demands of social justice." *Mazetti v. Armour & Co.*, 75 Wash. 622, 135 P. 633, 635, 48 L.R.A., N.S., 213 (Sup. Ct. 1913).

Accordingly, we hold that under modern marketing conditions, when a manufacturer puts a new automobile in the stream of trade and promotes its purchase by the public, an implied warranty that it is reasonably suitable for use as such accompanies it into the hands of the ultimate purchaser. Absence of agency between the manufacturer and the dealer who makes the ultimate sale is immaterial.

. . . .

IV.

Proof of Breach of the Implied Warranty of Merchantability.

Both defendants argue that the proof adduced by plaintiffs as to the happening of the accident was not sufficient to demonstrate a breach of warranty. Consequently, they claim that their motion for judgment should have been granted by the trial court. We cannot agree. In our view, the total effect of the circumstances shown from purchase to accident is adequate to raise an inference that the car was defective and that such condition was causally related to the mishap. Thus, determination by the jury was required.

The proof adduced by the plaintiffs disclosed that after servicing and delivery of the car, it operated normally during the succeeding ten days, so far as the Henningsens could tell. They had no difficulty or mishap of any kind, and it neither had nor required any servicing. It was driven by them alone. The owner's service certificate provided for return for further servicing at the end of the first 1,000 miles — less than half of which had been covered at the time of Mrs. Henningsen's injury.

The facts, detailed above, show that on the day of the accident, ten days after delivery, Mrs. Henningsen was driving in a normal fashion, on a smooth highway, when unexpectedly the steering wheel and the front wheels of the car went into the bizarre action described. Can it reasonably be said that the circumstances do not warrant an inference of unsuitability for ordinary use against the manufacturer and the dealer? Obviously there is nothing in the proof to indicate in the slightest that the most unusual action of the steering wheel was caused by Mrs. Henningsen's operation of the automobile on this day, or by the use of the car between delivery and the happening of the incident. Nor is there anything to suggest that any external force or condition unrelated to the manufacturing or servicing of the car operated as an inducing or even concurring factor.

. . . .

V.

The Defense of Lack of Privity Against Mrs. Henningsen.

Both defendants contend that since there was no privity of contract between them and Mrs. Henningsen, she cannot recover for breach of any warranty made by either of them. On the facts, as they were developed, we agree that she was not a party to the purchase agreement. Her right to maintain the action, therefore, depends upon whether she occupies such legal status thereunder as to permit her to take advantage of a breach of defendants' implied warranties.

For the most part the cases that have been considered dealt with the right of the buyer or consumer to maintain an action against the manufacturer where the contract of sale was with a dealer and the buyer had no contractual relationship with the manufacturer. In the present matter, the basic contractual relationship is between Claus Henningsen, Chrysler, and Bloomfield Motors, Inc. The precise issue presented is whether Mrs. Henningsen, who is not a party to their respective warranties, may claim under them. In our judgment, the principles of those cases and the supporting texts are just as proximately applicable to her situation. We are convinced that the cause of justice in this area of the law can be served only by recognizing that she is such a person who, in the reasonable contemplation of the parties to the warranty, might be expected to become a user of the automobile. Accordingly, her lack of privity does not stand in the way of prosecution of the injury suit against the defendant Chrysler.

The context in which the problem of privity with respect to the dealer must be considered, is much the same. Defendant Bloomfield Motors is chargeable with an implied warranty of merchantability to Claus Henningsen. There is no need to engage in a separate or extended discussion of the question. The legal principles which control are the same in quality. The manufacturer establishes the network of trade and the dealer is a unit utilized in that network to accomplish sales. He is the beneficiary of the same express and implied warranties from the manufacturer as he extends to the buyer of the automobile. If he is sued alone, he may implead the manufacturer. His understanding of the expected use of the car by persons other than the buyer is the same as that of the manufacturer. And so, his claim to the doctrine of privity should rise no higher than that of the manufacturer.

. . . .

It is important to express the right of Mrs. Henningsen to maintain her action in terms of a general principle. To what extent may lack of privity be disregarded in suits on such warranties? In that regard, the *Faber* case points the way. By a parity of reasoning, it is our opinion that an implied warranty of merchantability chargeable to either an automobile manufacturer or a dealer extends to the purchaser of the car, members of his family, and to other persons occupying or using it with his consent. It would be wholly opposed to reality to say that use by such persons is not within the anticipation of parties to such a warranty of reasonable suitability of an automobile for ordinary highway operation. Those persons must be considered within the distributive chain.

. . . .

VII.

Under all of the circumstances outlined above, the judgments in favor of the plaintiffs and against the defendants are affirmed.

For affirmance: CHIEF JUSTICE WEINTRAUB and JUSTICES BURLING, JACOBS, FRANCIS, PROCTOR and SCHETTINO — 6.

For reversal: None.

––––––––––

1. How does the court see the relationship between tort and contract law in cases involving defective products?

2. What was the product defect in *Henningsen*? How did the plaintiff prove that the automobile was defective?

3. It has long been settled law that the manufacturer that puts the fully assembled product into the stream of commerce is liable for any defects in the product, even when the defect lies in a component part of the product which the manufacturer did not make. *MacPherson v. Buick Motor Co.*, 111 N.E. 1050 (N.Y. 1916). The manufacturer may, of course, bring the producer of the component part into the lawsuit, but the injured consumer need not do so.

MacPherson, an extremely important opinion, involved a shattered wheel. In that case, the court rejected the idea that the plaintiff needed to be in some sort of privity with the seller, ruling that the consumer of the product (an automobile) could sue the manufacturer directly, even though there was no relationship between the manufacturer and the consumer.

C. STRICT PRODUCTS LIABILITY IN TORT

1. The Birth of the Doctrine

ESCOLA v. COCA COLA BOTTLING CO.
Supreme Court of California, 1944
150 P.2d 436

GIBSON, CHIEF JUSTICE.

Plaintiff, a waitress in a restaurant, was injured when a bottle of Coca Cola broke in her hand. She alleged that defendant company, which had bottled and delivered the alleged defective bottle to her employer, was negligent in selling "bottles containing said beverage which on account of excessive pressure of gas or by reason of some defect in the bottle was dangerous . . . and likely to explode." This appeal is from a judgment upon a jury verdict in favor of plaintiff.

Defendant's driver delivered several cases of Coca Cola to the restaurant, placing them on the floor, one on top of the other, under and behind the counter, where they remained at least thirty-six hours. Immediately before the accident, plaintiff picked up the top case and set it upon a near-by ice cream cabinet in front of and about three feet from the refrigerator. She then proceeded to take the bottles from the case with her right hand, one at a time, and put them into the refrigerator. Plaintiff testified that after she had placed three bottles in the refrigerator and had moved the fourth bottle about 18 inches from the case "it exploded in my hand." The bottle broke into two jagged pieces and inflicted a deep five-inch cut, severing blood vessels, nerves and muscles of the thumb and palm of the hand. Plaintiff further testified that when the bottle exploded, "It made a sound similar to an electric light bulb that would have dropped. It made a loud pop." Plaintiff's employer testified, "I was about twenty feet from where it actually happened and I heard the explosion." A fellow employee, on the opposite side of the counter, testified that plaintiff "had the bottle, I should judge, waist high, and I know that it didn't bang either the case or the door or another bottle . . . when it popped. It sounded just like a fruit jar would blow up. . . ." The witness further testified that the contents of the bottle "flew all over herself and myself and the walls and one thing and another."

The top portion of the bottle, with the cap, remained in plaintiff's hand, and the lower portion fell to the floor but did not break. The broken bottle was not produced at the trial, the pieces having been thrown away by an employee of the restaurant shortly after the accident. Plaintiff, however, described the broken pieces, and a diagram of the bottle was made showing the location of the "fracture line" where the bottle broke in two.

One of defendant's drivers, called as a witness by plaintiff, testified that he had seen other bottles of Coca Cola in the past explode and had found broken bottles in the warehouse when he took the cases out, but that he did not know what made them blow up.

Plaintiff then rested her case, having announced to the court that being unable to show any specific acts of negligence she relied completely on the doctrine of res ipsa loquitur.

Defendant contends that the doctrine of res ipsa loquitur does not apply in this case, and that the evidence is insufficient to support the judgment.

Many jurisdictions have applied the doctrine in cases involving exploding bottles of carbonated beverages. Other courts for varying reasons have refused to apply the doctrine in such cases. It would serve no useful purpose to discuss the reasoning of the foregoing cases in detail, since the problem is whether under the facts shown in the instant case the conditions warranting application of the doctrine have been satisfied.

Res ipsa loquitur does not apply unless (1) defendant had exclusive control of the thing causing the injury and (2) the accident is of such a nature that it ordinarily would not occur in the absence of negligence by the defendant.

Many authorities state that the happening of the accident does not speak for itself where it took place some time after defendant had relinquished control of the instrumentality causing the injury. Under the more logical view, however, the doctrine may be applied upon the theory that defendant had control at the time of the alleged negligent act, although not at the time of the accident, *provided* plaintiff first proves that the condition of the instrumentality had not been changed after it left the defendant's possession. As said in *Dunn v. Hoffman Beverage Co.*, 126 N.J.L. 556, 20 A.2d 352, 354, "defendant is not charged with the duty of showing affirmatively that something happened to the bottle after it left its control or management; . . . to get to the jury the plaintiff must show that there was due care during that period." Plaintiff must also prove that she handled the bottle carefully. The reason for this prerequisite is set forth in Prosser on Torts, *supra*, at page 300, where the author states: "Allied to the condition of exclusive control in the defendant is that of absence of any action on the part of the plaintiff contributing to the accident. Its purpose, of course, is to eliminate the possibility that it was the plaintiff who was responsible. If the boiler of a locomotive explodes while the plaintiff engineer is operating it, the inference of his own negligence is at least as great as that of the defendant, and res ipsa loquitur will not apply until he has accounted for his own conduct." It is not necessary, of course, that plaintiff eliminate every remote possibility of injury to the bottle after defendant lost control, and the requirement is satisfied if there is evidence permitting a reasonable inference that it was not accessible to extraneous harmful forces and that it was carefully handled by plaintiff or any third person who may have moved or touched it. *Cf* Prosser, *supra*, p. 300. If such evidence is presented, the question becomes one for the trier of fact, and, accordingly, the issue should be submitted to the jury under proper instructions.

In the present case no instructions were requested or given on this phase of the case, although general instructions upon res ipsa loquitur were given. Defendant, however, has made no claim of error with reference thereto on this appeal.

Upon an examination of the record, the evidence appears sufficient to support a reasonable inference that the bottle here involved was not damaged by any extraneous force after delivery to the restaurant by defendant. It follows, therefore, that the bottle was in some manner defective at the time defendant relinquished control, because sound and properly prepared bottles of carbonated liquids do not ordinarily explode when carefully handled.

The next question, then, is whether plaintiff may rely upon the doctrine of res ipsa loquitur to supply an inference that defendant's negligence was responsible for the defective condition of the bottle at the time it was delivered to the restaurant. Under the general rules pertaining to the doctrine, as set forth above, it must appear that bottles of carbonated liquid are not ordinarily defective without negligence by the bottling company. In 1 Shearman and Redfield on Negligence (Rev. Ed. 1941), page 153, it is stated that: "The doctrine . . . requires evidence which shows at least the probability that a particular accident could not have occurred without legal wrong by the defendant."

An explosion such as took place here might have been caused by an excessive internal pressure in a sound bottle, by a defect in the glass of a bottle containing a safe pressure, or by a combination of these two possible causes. The question is whether under the evidence there was a probability that defendant was negligent in any of these respects. If so, the doctrine of res ipsa loquitur applies.

The bottle was admittedly charged with gas under pressure, and the charging of the bottle was within the exclusive control of defendant. As it is a matter of common knowledge that an overcharge would not ordinarily result without negligence, it follows under the doctrine of res ipsa loquitur that if the bottle was in fact excessively charged an inference of defendant's negligence would arise. If the explosion resulted from a defective bottle containing a safe pressure, the defendant would be liable if it negligently failed to discover such flaw. If the defect were visible, an inference of negligence would arise from the failure of defendant to discover it. Where defects are discoverable, it may be assumed that they will not ordinarily escape detection if a reasonable inspection is made, and if such a defect is overlooked an inference arises that a proper inspection was not made. A difficult problem is presented where the defect is unknown and consequently might have been one not discoverable by a reasonable, practicable inspection. . . . In the present case . . . we are supplied with evidence of the standard methods used for testing bottles.

A chemical engineer for the Owens-Illinois Glass Company and its Pacific Coast subsidiary, maker of Coca Cola bottles, explained how glass is manufactured and the methods used in testing and inspecting bottles. . . .The witness stated that these tests are "pretty near" infallible.

It thus appears that there is available to the industry a commonly-used method of testing bottles for defects not apparent to the eye, which is almost infallible. Since Coca Cola bottles are subjected to these tests by the manufacturer, it is not likely that they contain defects when delivered to the bottler which are not discoverable by visual inspection. Both new and used bottles are filled and distributed by defendant. The used bottles are not again subjected to the tests referred to above, and it may be inferred that defects not discoverable by visual inspection do not develop in bottles after they are manufactured. Obviously, if such defects do occur in used bottles there is a duty upon the bottler to make appropriate tests before they are refilled, and if such tests are not commercially practicable the bottles should not be re-used. This would seem to be particularly true where a charged liquid is placed in the bottle. It follows that a defect which would make the bottle unsound could be discovered by reasonable and practicable tests.

Although it is not clear in this case whether the explosion was caused by an excessive charge or a defect in the glass there is a sufficient showing that neither cause would ordinarily have been present if due care had been used. Further, defendant had exclusive control over both the charging and inspection of the bottles. Accordingly, all the requirements necessary to entitle plaintiff to rely on the doctrine of res ipsa loquitur to supply an inference of negligence are present.

It is true that defendant presented evidence tending to show that it exercised considerable precaution by carefully regulating and checking the pressure in the bottles and by making visual inspections for defects in the glass at several stages during the bottling process. It is well settled, however, that when a defendant produces evidence to rebut the inference of negligence which arises upon application of the doctrine of res ipsa loquitur, it is ordinarily a question of fact for the jury to determine whether the inference has been dispelled.

The judgment is affirmed.

SHENK, CURTIS, CARTER, and SCHAUER, JJ., concurred.

TRAYNOR, JUSTICE.

I concur in the judgment, but I believe the manufacturer's negligence should no longer be singled out as the basis of a plaintiff's right to recover in cases like the present one. In my opinion it should now be recognized that a manufacturer incurs an absolute liability when an article that he has placed on the market, knowing that it is to be used without inspection, proves to have a defect that causes injury to human beings. *MacPherson v. Buick Motor Co.*, 217 N.Y. 382, 111 N.E. 1050, L.R.A. 1916F, 696, Ann. Cas. 1916C, 440 established the principle, recognized by this court, that irrespective of privity of contract, the manufacturer is responsible for an injury caused by such an article to any person who comes in lawful contact with it. In these cases the source of the manufacturer's liability was his negligence in the manufacturing process or in the inspection of component parts supplied by others. Even if there is no negligence, however, public policy demands that responsibility be fixed wherever it will most effectively reduce the hazards to life and health inherent in defective products that reach the market. It is evident that the manufacturer can anticipate some hazards and guard against the recurrence of others, as the public cannot. Those who suffer injury from defective products are unprepared to meet its consequences. The cost of an injury and the loss of time or health may be an overwhelming misfortune to the person injured, and a needless one, for the risk of injury can be insured by the manufacturer and distributed among the public as a cost of doing business. It is to the public interest to discourage the marketing of products having defects that are a menace to the public. If such products nevertheless find their way into the market it is to the public interest to place the responsibility for whatever injury they may cause upon the manufacturer, who, even if he is not negligent in the manufacture of the product, is responsible for its reaching the market. However intermittently such injuries may occur and however haphazardly they may strike, the risk of their occurrence is a constant risk and a general one. Against such a risk there should be general and constant protection and the manufacturer is best situated to afford such protection.

The injury from a defective product does not become a matter of indifference because the defect arises from causes other than the negligence of the manufacturer, such as negligence of a submanufacturer of a component part whose defects could not be revealed by inspection or unknown causes that even by the device of res ipsa loquitur cannot be classified as negligence of the manufacturer. The inference of negligence may be dispelled by an affirmative showing of proper care. If the evidence against the fact inferred is "clear, positive, uncontradicted, and of such a nature that it can not rationally be disbelieved, the court must instruct the jury that the nonexistence of the fact has been established as a matter of law." *Blank v. Coffin*, 20 Cal. 2d 457, 461, 126 P.2d 868, 870. An injured person, however, is not ordinarily in a position to refute such evidence or identify the cause of the defect, for he can hardly be familiar with the manufacturing process as the manufacturer himself is. In leaving it to the jury to decide whether the inference has been dispelled, regardless of the evidence against it, the negligence rule approaches the rule of strict liability. It is needlessly circuitous to make negligence the basis of recovery and impose what is in reality liability without negligence. If public policy demands that a manufacturer of goods be responsible for their quality regardless of negligence there is no reason not to fix that responsibility openly.

In the case of foodstuffs, the public policy of the state is formulated in a criminal statute. . . . The criminal liability under the statute attaches without proof of fault, so that the manufacturer is under the duty of ascertaining whether an article manufactured by him is safe. . . .

The statute may well be applicable to a bottle whose defects cause it to explode. In any event it is significant that the statute imposes criminal liability without fault, reflecting the public policy of protecting the public from dangerous products placed on the market, irrespective of negligence in their manufacture. While the Legislature imposes criminal liability only with regard to food products and their containers, there are many other sources of danger. It is to the public interest to prevent injury to the public from any defective goods by the imposition of civil liability generally.

The retailer, even though not equipped to test a product, is under an absolute liability to his customer, for the implied warranties of fitness for proposed use and merchantable quality include a warranty of safety of the product. This warranty is not necessarily a contractual one. . . . The courts recognize, however, that the retailer cannot bear the burden of this warranty, and allow him to recoup any losses by means of the warranty of safety attending the wholesaler's or manufacturer's sale to him. Such a procedure, however, is needlessly circuitous and engenders wasteful litigation. Much would be gained if the injured person could base his action directly on the manufacturer's warranty.

The liability of the manufacturer to an immediate buyer injured by a defective product follows without proof of negligence from the implied warranty of safety attending the sale. Ordinarily, however, the immediate buyer is a dealer who does not intend to use the product himself, and if the warranty of safety is to serve the purpose of protecting health and safety it must give rights to others than the dealer. In the words of Judge Cardozo in the *MacPherson* case [217 N.Y. 382, 111 N.E. 1053, L.R.A. 1916F, 696, Ann. Cas. 1916C, 440]: "The dealer was indeed the one person of whom it might be said with some approach to certainty that by him the car would not be used. Yet the defendant would have us say that he was the one person whom it was under a legal duty to protect. The law does not lead us to so inconsequent a conclusion." While the defendant's negligence in the *MacPherson* case made it unnecessary for the court to base liability on warranty, Judge Cardozo's reasoning recognized the injured person as the real party in interest and effectively disposed of the theory that the liability of the manufacturer incurred by his warranty should apply only to the immediate purchaser. It thus paves the way for a standard of liability that would make the manufacturer guarantee the safety of his product even when there is no negligence.

This court and many others have extended protection according to such a standard to consumers of food products, taking the view that the right of a consumer injured by unwholesome food does not depend "upon the intricacies of the law of sales" and that the warranty of the manufacturer to the consumer in absence of privity of contract rests on public policy. Dangers to life and health inhere in other consumers' goods that are defective and there is no reason to differentiate them from the dangers of defective food products.

In the food products cases the courts have resorted to various fictions to rationalize the extension of the manufacturer's warranty to the consumer. . . . They have also held the manufacturer liable on a mere fiction of negligence. . . . Such fictions are not necessary to fix the manufacturer's liability under a warranty if the warranty is severed from the contract of sale between the dealer and the consumer and based on the law of torts as a strict liability. Warranties are not necessarily rights arising under a contract. An action on a warranty "was, in its origin, a pure action of tort," and only late in the historical development of warranties was an action in assumpsit allowed. . . . As the court said in *Greco v. S. S. Kresge Co., supra* [277 N.Y. 26, 12 N.E.2d 561, 115 A.L.R. 1020], "Though the action may be brought solely for the breach of the implied warranty, the breach is a wrongful act, a default, and, in its essential nature, a tort." . . . "As an actual agreement to contract is not essential, the obligation of a seller in such a case is one imposed by law as distinguished from one voluntarily assumed. It may be called an obligation either on a quasi-contract or quasi-tort, because remedies appropriate to contract and also to tort are applicable." 1 Williston on Sales, 2d Ed. § 197.

As handicrafts have been replaced by mass production with its great markets and transportation facilities, the close relationship between the producer and consumer of a product has been altered. Manufacturing processes, frequently valuable secrets, are ordinarily either inaccessible to or beyond the ken of the general public. The consumer no longer has means or skill enough to investigate for himself the soundness of a product, even when it is not contained in a sealed package, and his erstwhile vigilance has been lulled by the steady efforts of manufacturers to build up confidence by advertising and marketing devices such as trade-marks. Consumers no longer approach products warily but accept them on faith, relying on the reputation of the manufacturer or the trade mark. Manufacturers have sought to justify that faith by increasingly high standards of inspection and a readiness to make good on defective products by way of replacements and refunds. The manufacturer's obligation to the consumer must keep pace with the changing relationship between them; it cannot be escaped because the marketing of a product has become so complicated as to require one or more intermediaries. Certainly there is greater reason to impose liability on the manufacturer than on the retailer who is but a conduit of a product that he is not himself able to test.

The manufacturer's liability should, of course, be defined in terms of the safety of the product in normal and proper use, and should not extend to injuries that cannot be traced to the product as it reached the market.

Rehearing denied; EDMONDS, J., dissenting.

———

1. What was the majority's basis for concluding that the manufacturer should be liable for the injury?

2. What is the difference between res ipsa loquitur and strict products liability? How do the differences between the two (if any) affect the proof a plaintiff must introduce? When would the two doctrines yield different results? Is there any evidence that the manufacturer could have introduced that would have resulted in a finding of nonliability?

GREENMAN v. YUBA POWER PRODUCTS, INC.
Supreme Court of California, 1963 (en banc)
377 P.2d 897

TRAYNOR, JUSTICE.

Plaintiff brought this action for damages against the retailer and the manufacturer of a Shopsmith, a combination power tool that could be used as a saw, drill, and wood lathe. He saw a Shopsmith demonstrated by the retailer and studied a brochure prepared by the manufacturer. He decided he wanted a Shopsmith for his home workshop, and his wife bought and gave him one for Christmas in 1955. In 1957 he bought the necessary attachments to use the Shopsmith as a lathe for turning a large piece of wood he wished to make into a chalice. After he had worked on the piece of wood several times without difficulty, it suddenly flew out of the machine and struck him on the forehead, inflicting serious injuries. About ten and a half months later, he gave the retailer and the manufacturer written notice of claimed breaches of warranties and filed a complaint against them alleging such breaches and negligence.

After a trial before a jury, the court ruled that there was no evidence that the retailer was negligent or had breached any express warranty and that the manufacturer was not liable for the breach of any implied warranty. Accordingly, it submitted to the jury only the cause of action alleging breach of implied warranties against the retailer and the causes of action alleging negligence and breach of express warranties against the manufacturer. The jury returned a verdict for the retailer against plaintiff and for plaintiff against the manufacturer in the amount of $65,000. The trial court denied the manufacturer's motion for a new trial and entered judgment on the verdict. The manufacturer and plaintiff appeal. Plaintiff seeks a reversal of the part of the judgment in favor of the retailer, however, only in the event that the part of the judgment against the manufacturer is reversed.

Plaintiff introduced substantial evidence that his injuries were caused by defective design and construction of the Shopsmith. His expert witnesses testified that inadequate set screws were used to hold parts of the machine together so that normal vibration caused the tailstock of the lathe to move away from the piece of wood being turned permitting it to fly out of the lathe. They also testified that there were other more positive ways of fastening the parts of the machine together, the use of which would have prevented the accident. The jury could therefore reasonably have concluded that the manufacturer negligently constructed the Shopsmith. The jury could also reasonably have concluded that statements in the manufacturer's brochure were untrue, that they constituted express warranties,[1]

---

[1] In this respect the trial court limited the jury to a consideration of two statements in the manufacturer's brochure. (1) "WHEN SHOPSMITH IS IN HORIZONTAL POSITION — Rugged construction of frame provides rigid support from end to end. Heavy centerless-ground steel tubing insures perfect alignment of components." (2) "SHOPSMITH maintains its accuracy because every

and that plaintiff's injuries were caused by their breach.

The manufacturer contends, however, that plaintiff did not give it notice of breach of warranty within a reasonable time and that therefore his cause of action for breach of warranty is barred by section 1769 of the Civil Code. Since it cannot be determined whether the verdict against it was based on the negligence or warranty cause of action or both, the manufacturer concludes that the error in presenting the warranty cause of action to the jury was prejudicial.

Section 1769 of the Civil Code provides: "In the absence of express or implied agreement of the parties, acceptance of the goods by the buyer shall not discharge the seller from liability in damages or other legal remedy for breach of any promise or warranty in the contract to sell or the sale. But, if, after acceptance of the goods, the buyer fails to give notice to the seller of the breach of any promise or warranty within a reasonable time after the buyer knows, or ought to know of such breach, the seller shall not be liable therefor."

Like other provisions of the uniform sales act (Civ. Code, §§ 1721-1800), section 1769 deals with the rights of the parties to a contract of sale or a sale. It does not provide that notice must be given of the breach of a warranty that arises independently of a contract of sale between the parties. Such warranties are not imposed by the sales act, but are the product of common-law decisions that have recognized them in a variety of situations. It is true that in many of these situations the court has invoked the sales act definitions of warranties (Civ. Code, §§ 1732, 1735) in defining the defendant's liability, but it has done so, not because the statutes so required, but because they provided appropriate standards for the court to adopt under the circumstances presented.

The notice requirement of section 1769, however, is not an appropriate one for the court to adopt in actions by injured consumers against manufacturers with whom they have not dealt. "As between the immediate parties to the sale [the notice requirement] is a sound commercial rule, designed to protect the seller against unduly delayed claims for damages. As applied to personal injuries, and notice to a remote seller, it becomes a booby-trap for the unwary. The injured consumer is seldom 'steeped in the business practice which justifies the rule,' [James, *Product Liability*, 34 Texas L. Rev. 44, 192, 197] and at least until he has had legal advice it will not occur to him to give notice to one with whom he has had no dealings." (Prosser, *Strict Liability to the Consumer*, 69 Yale L.J. 1099, 1130, footnotes omitted.). . . . We conclude . . . that even if plaintiff did not give timely notice of breach of warranty to the manufacturer, his cause of action based on the representations contained in the brochure was not barred.

Moreover, to impose strict liability on the manufacturer under the circumstances of this case, it was not necessary for plaintiff to establish an express warranty as defined in section 1732 of the Civil Code. A manufacturer is strictly liable in tort when an article he places on the market, knowing that it is to be used without inspection for defects, proves to have a defect that causes injury to a human being. Recognized first in the case of unwholesome food products, such liability has now

---

component has positive locks that hold adjustments through rough or precision work."

been extended to a variety of other products that create as great or greater hazards if defective.

Although in these cases strict liability has usually been based on the theory of an express or implied warranty running from the manufacturer to the plaintiff, the abandonment of the requirement of a contract between them, the recognition that the liability is not assumed by agreement but imposed by law, and the refusal to permit the manufacturer to define the scope of its own responsibility for defective products make clear that the liability is not one governed by the law of contract warranties but by the law of strict liability in tort. Accordingly, rules defining and governing warranties that were developed to meet the needs of commercial transactions cannot properly be invoked to govern the manufacturer's liability to those injured by their defective products unless those rules also serve the purposes for which such liability is imposed.

We need not recanvass the reasons for imposing strict liability on the manufacturer. They have been fully articulated in the cases cited above. *(See also* 2 Harper and James, Torts, §§ 28.15-28,16, pp. 1569-1574; Prosser, *Strict Liability to the Consumer,* 69 Yale L.J. 1099; *Escola v. Coca Cola Bottling Co.,* 24 Cal. 2d 453, 461, 150 P.2d 436, concurring opinion.) The purpose of such liability is to insure that the costs of injuries resulting from defective products are borne by the manufacturers that put such products on the market rather than by the injured persons who are powerless to protect themselves. Sales warranties serve this purpose fitfully at best. In the present case, for example, plaintiff was able to plead and prove an express warranty only because he read and relied on the representations of the Shopsmith's ruggedness contained in the manufacturer's brochure. Implicit in the machine's presence on the market, however, was a representation that it would safely do the jobs for which it was built. Under these circumstances, it should not be controlling whether plaintiff selected the machine because of the statements in the brochure, or because of the machine's own appearance of excellence that belied the defect lurking beneath the surface, or because he merely assumed that it would safely do the jobs it was built to do. It should not be controlling whether the details of the sales from manufacturer to retailer and from retailer to plaintiff's wife were such that one or more of the implied warranties of the sales act arose. (Civ. Code, § 1735.) "The remedies of injured consumers ought not to be made to depend upon the intricacies of the law of sales." *(Ketterer v. Armour & Co.,* D.C., 200 F. 322, 323.) To establish the manufacturer's liability it was sufficient that plaintiff proved that he was injured while using the Shopsmith in a way it was intended to be used as a result of a defect in design and manufacture of which plaintiff was not aware that made the Shopsmith unsafe for its intended use.

The manufacturer contends that the trial court erred in refusing to give three instructions requested by it. It appears from the record, however, that the substance of two of the requested instructions was adequately covered by the instructions given and that the third instruction was not supported by the evidence.

The judgment is affirmed.

GIBSON, C.J., and SCHAUER, MCCOMB, PETERS, TOBRINER and PEEK, JJ., concur.

---

1.   How does the court in *Greenman* define defect?

2.   Whom does the strict liability defined in *Greenman* protect? In other words, who may be a plaintiff?

PROBLEM

P undergoes spinal surgery at Mercy General Hospital. During the operation, the surgeon uses several clamps. P is injured when the point of one of these clamps breaks off in P's spine. P files suit against (1) the hospital, for negligently failing to inspect the instruments with which it provides its surgeons, (2) the surgeon, for failing to inspect the clamp before using it and for misuse of the clamp causing it to break, and (3) the manufacturer of the clamp in strict products liability for providing a defective clamp. The jury finds in favor of all three defendants.

P files an appeal. What arguments will P make? Is the jury verdict commensurate with the facts?

2.   Refining the Doctrine — Defining Defect

The central problem, once the courts had accepted the idea of liability without fault for defective products, was to define defect. Not all dangerous products are defective. A dangerous product is a product that causes injury. A defective product, on the other hand, is one that fails the applicable consumer expectation or risk/utility test. Classifying a product as defective means that the manufacturer will be liable for the injuries caused by that product. In other words, to classify a product as defective is to reach a legal conclusion about who pays for the injuries involved.

RESTATEMENT (SECOND) OF TORTS § 402A

402A. Special Liability of Seller of Product for Physical Harm to User or Consumer.

(1) One who sells any product in a defective condition unreasonably dangerous to the user or consumer or to his property is subject to liability for physical harm thereby caused to the ultimate user or consumer, or to his property, if

(a) the seller is engaged in the business of selling such a product, and

(b) it is expected to and does reach the user or consumer without substantial change in the condition in which it is sold.

(2) The rule stated in Subsection (1) applies although

(a) the seller has exercised all possible care in the preparation and sale of his product, and

(b) the user or consumer has not bought the product from or entered into any contractual relation with the seller.

As quoted in *Ex parte Chevron Chemical Co.*, 720 So. 2d 922, 927 (Ala. 1998).

---

1. How does Section 402A define defect?

2. Who may be a plaintiff under Section 402A?

3. What if the product could not be made safer? Should this have an impact upon the decision as to whether the product is defective?

4. One strict products liability arena in which the courts tend to be sloppy involves terminology. A dangerous product is a product which has attributes that may cause harm. To say that a product is dangerous is to make a factual statement about that product. A defective product, on the other hand, is a product for the dangers of which the manufacturer will be held responsible. In other words, to rule that a product is defective is to reach a legal conclusion about that product and the implications of its dangers for the manufacturer. Courts often refer to dangers as defects, even though the former is a fact and the latter a legal conclusion.

PHILLIPS v. KIMWOOD MACHINE CO.
Supreme Court of Oregon, 1974 (en banc)
525 P.2d 1033

HOLMAN, JUSTICE.

Plaintiff was injured while feeding fiberboard into a sanding machine during his employment with Pope and Talbot, a wood products manufacturer. The sanding machine had been purchased by Pope and Talbot from defendant. Plaintiff brought this action on a products liability theory, contending the sanding machine was unreasonably dangerous by virtue of defective design. At the completion of the testimony, defendant's motion for a directed verdict was granted and plaintiff appealed.

As is required in such a situation, the evidence is recounted in a manner most favorable to the plaintiff. The machine in question was a six-headed sander. Each sanding head was a rapidly moving belt which revolved in the direction opposite to that which the pieces of fiberboard moved through the machine. Three of the heads sanded the top of the fiberboard sheet and three sanded the bottom. The top half of the machine could be raised or lowered depending upon the thickness of the fiberboard to be sanded. The bottom half of the machine had powered rollers which moved the fiberboard through the machine as the fiberboard was being sanded. The top half of the machine had pinch rolls, not powered, which, when pressed down on the fiberboard by use of springs, kept the sanding heads from forcefully rejecting it from the machine.

On the day of the accident plaintiff was engaged in feeding the sheets of fiberboard into the sander. Because of the defective operation of a press, a large group of sheets of extra thickness was received for sanding. These sheets could not be inserted into the machine as it was set, so the top half of the sander was adjusted upwards to leave a greater space between the top and bottom halves to accommodate the extra thick fiberboard sheets. During the sanding of the extra thick sheets, a thin sheet of fiberboard, which had become mixed with the lot, was inserted into the machine. The pressure exerted by the pinch rolls in the top half of the machine was insufficient to counteract the pressure which the sanding belts were exerting upon the thin sheet of fiberboard and, as a result, the machine regurgitated the piece of fiberboard back at plaintiff, hitting him in the abdomen and causing him the injuries for which he now seeks compensation.

Plaintiff asserts in his complaint that the machine was defective in its design and unreasonably dangerous because (1) "it . . . could not be operated in the manner and for the purpose for which it was manufactured and sold without throwing back towards the operator panels of material being sanded . . . ," and (2) ". . . it did not . . . contain . . . any guards, catches, shields, barricades or similar devices to protect the operator of said machine from being struck by panels of material thrown back out of the sanding machine. . . ." The two allegations assert substantially the same thing, the first one in general terms, and the second one in particular terms. In effect, they allege the machine was defective and was unreasonably dangerous because there were no safety devices to protect the person feeding the machine from the regurgitation of sheets of fiberboard.

While we do not here attempt to recount all of the testimony presented by plaintiff concerning the defective design of the machine, there was evidence from which the jury could find that at a relatively small expense there could have been built into, or subsequently installed on, the machine a line of metal teeth which would point in the direction that the fiberboard progresses through the machine and which would press lightly against the sheet but which, in case of attempted regurgitation, would be jammed into it, thus stopping its backward motion. The evidence also showed that after the accident such teeth were installed upon the machine for that purpose by Pope and Talbot, whereupon subsequent regurgitations of thin fiberboard sheets were prevented while the efficiency of the machine was maintained. There was also evidence that defendant makes smaller sanders which usually are manually fed and on which there is such a safety device.

It was shown that the machine in question was built for use with an automatic feeder and that the one installed at Pope and Talbot is the only six-headed sander manufactured by defendant which is manually fed. There also was testimony that at the time of the purchase by Pope and Talbot, defendant had automatic feeders for sale but that Pope and Talbot did not purchase or show any interest in such a feeder. Pope and Talbot furnished a feeding device of their own manufacture for the machine which was partially automatic and partially manual but which, the jury could find, at times placed an employee in the way of regurgitated sheets.

There was testimony that at the time defendant's employee inspected the installation of the machine purchased by Pope and Talbot, which inspection was required by their contract, the inspecting employee became aware that the machine was being manually fed. There was no testimony of any warning given by defendant of the danger concerning regurgitated sheets to a person manually feeding the machine. Neither was there any evidence that Pope and Talbot was told that the machine was built for use with a fully automatic feeder and that it was not to be fed manually, nor was the recommendation made to plaintiff's employer that if the machine was to be used without a fully automatic feeder, some sort of safety device should be used for the protection of anyone who was manually feeding the machine. There was evidence that one of Pope and Talbot's representatives was told that the top of the machine should not be raised while sanding was taking place, but there was no evidence of the danger from doing so ever being mentioned.

. . . .

In defense of its judgment based upon a directed verdict, defendant contends there was no proof of a defect in the product, and therefore strict liability should not apply. This court and other courts continue to flounder while attempting to determine how one decides whether a product is "in a defective condition unreasonably dangerous to the user."[1] It has been recognized that unreasonably dangerous defects in products come from two principal sources: (1) mismanufacture and (2) faulty design.[2] Mismanufacture is relatively simple to identify because the item in question is capable of being compared with similar articles made by the same manufacturer. However, whether the mismanufactured article is dangerously defective because of the flaw is sometimes difficult to ascertain because not every such flaw which causes injury makes the article dangerously defective.[3]

The problem with strict liability of products has been one of limitation. No one wants absolute liability where all the article has to do is to cause injury. To impose liability there has to be something about the article which makes it dangerously defective without regard to whether the manufacturer was or was not at fault for such condition. A test for unreasonable danger is therefore vital.

A dangerously defective article would be one which a reasonable person would not put into the stream of commerce *if he had knowledge of its harmful character.* The test, therefore, is whether the seller would be negligent if he sold the article *knowing of the risk involved.* Strict liability imposed what amounts to constructive knowledge of the condition of the product.

On the surface such a test would seem to be different than the test of 2 Restatement (Second) of Torts § 402A, Comment i., of "dangerous to an extent beyond that which would be contemplated by the ordinary consumer who purchases

---

[1] 2 Restatement (Second) of Torts § 402A, at 347 (1965).

[2] Wade, *On the Nature of Strict Tort Liability for Products,* 44 Miss. L.J. 825, 830 (1973) (including failure to warn as a design defect).

[3] The California Supreme Court recognized this problem and attempted to eliminate it by requiring only a defect that causes injury, and not an unreasonably dangerous defect. In Cronin v. J. B. E. Olson Corp., 8 Cal. 3d 121, 104 Cal. Rptr. 433, 501 P.2d 1153 (1972), the court felt that requiring proof of an *unreasonably dangerous defect* would put an additional burden on plaintiff which the court deemed improper.

We, however, feel that regardless of whether the term used is "defective," as in *Cronin,* or "defective condition unreasonably dangerous," as in the Restatement, or "dangerously defective," as used here, or "not duly safe," as used by Professor Wade, the same considerations will necessarily be utilized in fixing liability on sellers; and, therefore, the supposedly different standards will come ultimately to the same conclusion. *See* Wade, *Strict Tort Liability of Manufacturers,* 19 Sw. L.J. 5, 14-15 (1965); Wade, *supra* note 2.

it." This court has used this test in the past. These are not necessarily different standards, however. As stated in Welch v. Outboard Marine Corp. [481 F.2d 252, 254 (5th Cir. 1973)], where the court affirmed an instruction containing both standards:

> "We see no necessary inconsistency between a seller-oriented standard and a user-oriented standard when, as here, each turns on foreseeable risks. They are two sides of the same standard. A product is defective and unreasonably dangerous when a reasonable seller would not sell the product if he knew of the risk involved or if the risks are greater than a reasonable buyer would expect."

To elucidate this point further, we feel that the two standards are the same because a seller acting reasonably would be selling the same product which a reasonable consumer believes he is purchasing. That is to say, a manufacturer who would be negligent in marketing a given product, considering its risks, would necessarily be marketing a product which fell below the reasonable expectations of consumers who purchase it. The foreseeable uses to which a product could be put would be the same in the minds of both the seller and the buyer unless one of the parties was not acting reasonably. The advantage of describing a dangerous defect in the manner of Wade and Keeton is that it preserves the use of familiar terms and thought processes with which courts, lawyers, and jurors customarily deal.

While apparently judging the seller's conduct, the test set out above would actually be a characterization of the product by a jury. If the manufacturer was not acting reasonably in selling the product, knowing of the risks involved, then the product would be dangerously defective when sold and the manufacturer would be subject to liability.

In the case of a product which is claimed to be dangerously defective because of misdesign, the process is not so easy as in the case of mismanufacture. All the products made to that design are the same. The question of whether the design is unreasonably dangerous can be determined only by taking into consideration the surrounding circumstances and knowledge at the time the article was sold, and determining therefrom whether a reasonably prudent manufacturer would have so designed and sold the article in question had he known of the risk involved which injured plaintiff. The issue has been raised in some courts concerning whether, in this context, there is any distinction between strict liability and negligence. The evidence which proves the one will almost always, if not always, prove the other. We discussed this matter recently in the case of *Roach v. Kononen*, 99 Or. Adv. Sh. 1092, 525 P.2d 125 (1974), and pointed out that there is a difference between strict liability for misdesign and negligence. We said:

> "However, be all this as it may, it is generally recognized that the basic difference between negligence on the one hand and strict liability for a design defect on the other is that in strict liability we are talking about the condition (dangerousness) of an article which is designed in a particular way, while in negligence we are talking about the reasonableness of the manufacturer's actions in designing and selling the article as he did. The article can have a degree of dangerousness which the law of strict liability will not tolerate even though the actions of the designer were entirely reasonable in view of what he knew at the time he planned and sold the

manufactured article. As Professor Wade points out, a way of determining whether the condition of the article is of the requisite degree of dangerousness to be defective (unreasonably dangerous; greater degree of danger than a consumer has a right to expect; not duly safe) is to assume that the manufacturer knew of the product's propensity to injury as it did, and then to ask whether, with such knowledge, something should have been done about the danger before it was sold. In other words, a greater burden is placed on the manufacturer than is the case in negligence because the law assumes he has knowledge of the article's dangerous propensity which he may not reasonably be expected to have, had he been charged with negligence." 99 Or. Adv. Sh. at 1099, 525 P.2d at 129.

To some it may seem that absolute liability has been imposed upon the manufacturer since it might be argued that no manufacturer could reasonably put into the stream of commerce an article which he realized might result in injury to a user. This is not the case, however. The manner of injury may be so fortuitous and the chances of injury occurring so remote that it is reasonable to sell the product despite the danger. In design cases the utility of the article may be so great, and the change of design necessary to alleviate the danger in question may so impair such utility, that it is reasonable to market the product as it is, even though the possibility of injury exists and was realized at the time of the sale. Again, the cost of the change necessary to alleviate the danger in design may be so great that the article would be priced out of the market and no one would buy it even though it was of high utility. Such an article is not dangerously defective despite its having inflicted injury.

In this case defendant contends it was Pope and Talbot's choice to purchase and use the sander without an automatic feeder, even though it was manufactured to be used with one, and, therefore, it was Pope and Talbot's business choice which resulted in plaintiff's injury and not any misdesign by defendant. However, it is recognized that a failure to warn may make a product unreasonably dangerous. Comment j, Section 402A, 2 Restatement (Second) of Torts, has the following to say:

"In order to prevent the product from being unreasonably dangerous, the seller may be required to give directions or warning, on the container, as to its use. The seller may reasonably assume that those with common allergies, as for example to eggs or strawberries, will be aware of them, and he is not required to warn against them. Where, however, the product contains an ingredient to which a substantial number of the population are allergic, and the ingredient is one whose danger is not generally known, or if known is one which the consumer would reasonably not expect to find in the product, the seller is required to give warning against it, if he had knowledge, or by the application of reasonable, developed human skill and foresight should have knowledge, of the presence of the ingredient and the danger. Likewise in the case of poisonous drugs, or those unduly dangerous for other reasons, warning as to use may be required."

Although the examples cited in the comment do not encompass machinery or such products, it has been recognized that a piece of machinery may or may not be dangerously defective, depending on the directions or warnings that may be given with it.

It is our opinion that the evidence was sufficient for the jury to find that a reasonably prudent manufacturer, knowing that the machine would be fed manually and having the constructive knowledge of its propensity to regurgitate thin sheets when it was set for thick ones, which the courts via strict liability have imposed upon it, would have warned plaintiff's employer either to feed it automatically or to use some safety device, and that, in the absence of such a warning, the machine was dangerously defective. It is therefore unnecessary for us to decide the questions that would arise had adequate warnings been given.

In *Anderson v. Klix Chemical*, 256 Or. 199, 472 P.2d 806 (1970), we came to the conclusion that there was no difference between negligence and strict liability for a product that was unreasonably dangerous because of failure to warn of certain characteristics. We have now come to the conclusion that we were in error. The reason we believe we were in error parallels the rationale that was expressed in the previously quoted material from *Roach v. Kononen, supra*, where we discussed the difference between strict liability for misdesign and negligence. In a strict liability case we are talking about the condition (dangerousness) of an article which is sold without any warning, while in negligence we are talking about the reasonableness of the manufacturer's actions in selling the article without a warning. The article can have a degree of dangerousness because of a lack of warning which the law of strict liability will not tolerate even though the actions of the seller were entirely reasonable in selling the article without a warning considering what he knew or should have known at the time he sold it. A way to determine the dangerousness of the article, as distinguished from the seller's culpability, is to assume the seller knew of the product's propensity to injure as it did, and then to ask whether, with such knowledge, he would have been negligent in selling it without a warning.

It is apparent that the language being used in the discussion of the above problems is largely that which is also used in *negligence* cases, i.e., "unreasonably dangerous," "have reasonably anticipated," "reasonably prudent manufacturer," etc. It is necessary to remember that whether the doctrine of negligence, ultrahazardousness, or strict liability is being used to impose liability, the same process is going on in each instance, i.e., weighing the utility of the article against the risk of its use. Therefore, the same language and concepts of reasonableness are used by courts for the determination of unreasonable danger in products liability cases.

. . . .

The case is reversed and remanded for a new trial.

———————

1. What is the *Phillips* definition of defect?

2. Under the *Phillips* test, what dangerous products are nondefective?

3. What if the manufacturer does not know and could not have discovered the danger in the product prior to marketing it? Is knowledge of the danger a factor in *Phillips*?

BARKER v. LULL ENGINEERING CO.
Supreme Court of California, 1978
573 P.2d 443

TOBRINER, ACTING CHIEF JUSTICE.

In August 1970, plaintiff Ray Barker was injured at a construction site at the University of California at Santa Cruz while operating a high-lift loader manufactured by defendant Lull Engineering Co. and leased to plaintiff's employer by defendant George M. Philpott Co., Inc. Claiming that his injuries were proximately caused, inter alia, by the alleged defective design of the loader, Barker instituted the present tort action seeking to recover damages for his injuries. The jury returned a verdict in favor of defendants, and plaintiff appeals from the judgment entered upon that verdict, contending primarily that in view of this court's decision in *Cronin v. J.B.E. Olson Corp.* (1972) 8 Cal. 3d 121, 104 Cal. Rptr. 433, 501 P.2d 1153, the trial court erred in instructing the jury "that strict liability for a defect in design of a product is based on a finding that the product was unreasonably dangerous for its intended use. . . ."

As we explain, we agree with plaintiff's objection to the challenged instruction and conclude that the judgment must be reversed. In *Cronin*, we reviewed the development of the strict product liability doctrine in California at some length, and concluded that, for a variety of reasons, the "unreasonably dangerous" element which section 402A of the Restatement Second of Torts had introduced into the definition of a defective product should not be incorporated into a plaintiff's burden of proof in a product liability action in this state. Although defendants maintain that our *Cronin* decision should properly be interpreted as applying only to "manufacturing defects" and not to the alleged "design defects" at issue here, we shall point out that the *Cronin* decision itself refutes any such distinction. Consequently, we conclude that the instruction was erroneous and that the judgment in favor of defendants must be reversed.

In addition, we take this opportunity to attempt to alleviate some confusion that our *Cronin* decision has apparently engendered in the lower courts. Although in *Cronin* we rejected the Restatement's "unreasonably dangerous" gloss on the defectiveness concept as potentially confusing and unduly restrictive, we shall explain that our *Cronin* decision did not dictate that the term "defect" be left undefined injury instructions given in all product liability cases.

As *Cronin* acknowledged, in the past decade and a half California courts have frequently recognized that the defectiveness concept defies a simple, uniform definition applicable to all sectors of the diverse product liability domain. Although in many instances as when one machine in a million contains a cracked or broken part the meaning of the term "defect" will require little or no elaboration, in other instances, as when a product is claimed to be defective because of an unsafe design or an inadequate warning, the contours of the defect concept may not be self-evident. In such a case a trial judge may find it necessary to explain more fully to the jury the legal meaning of "defect" or "defective." We shall explain that *Cronin* in no way precluded such elucidation of the defect concept, but rather contemplated that, in typical common law fashion, the accumulating body of product liability authorities would give guidance for the formulation of a definition.

As numerous recent judicial decisions and academic commentaries have recognized, the formulation of a satisfactory definition of "design defect" has proven a formidable task; trial judges have repeatedly confronted difficulties in attempting to devise accurate and helpful instructions in design defect cases. Aware of these problems, we have undertaken a review of the past California decisions which have grappled with the design defect issue, and have measured their conclusions against the fundamental policies which underlie the entire strict product liability doctrine.

As we explain in more detail below, we have concluded from this review that a product is defective in design either (1) if the product has failed to perform as safely as an ordinary consumer would expect when used in an intended or reasonably foreseeable manner, or (2) if, in light of the relevant factors discussed below, the benefits of the challenged design do not outweigh the risk of danger inherent in such design. In addition, we explain how the burden of proof with respect to the latter "risk-benefit" standard should be allocated.

This dual standard for design defect assures an injured plaintiff protection from products that either fall below ordinary consumer expectations as to safety, or that, on balance, are not as safely designed as they should be. At the same time, the standard permits a manufacturer who has marketed a product which satisfies ordinary consumer expectations to demonstrate the relative complexity of design decisions and the trade-offs that are frequently required in the adoption of alternative designs. Finally, this test reflects our continued adherence to the principle that, in a product liability action, the trier of fact must focus on the product, not on the manufacturer's conduct, and that the plaintiff need not prove that the manufacturer acted unreasonably or negligently in order to prevail in such an action.

1. *The facts of the present case*

Plaintiff Barker sustained serious injuries as a result of an accident which occurred while he was operating a Lull High-Lift Loader at a construction site. The loader, manufactured in 1967, is a piece of heavy construction equipment designed to lift loads of up to 5,000 pounds to a maximum height of 32 feet. The loader is 23 feet long, 8 feet wide and weighs 17,050 pounds; it sits on four large rubber tires which are about the height of a person's chest, and is equipped with four-wheel drive, an automatic transmission with no park position and a hand brake. Loads are lifted by forks similar to the forks of a forklift.

The loader is designed so that the load can be kept level even when the loader is being operated on sloping terrain. The leveling of the load is controlled by a lever located near the steering column, and positioned between the operator's legs. The lever is equipped with a manual lock that can be engaged to prevent accidental slipping of the load level during lifting.

The loader was not equipped with seat belts or a roll bar. A wire and pipe cage over the driver's seat afforded the driver some protection from falling objects. The cab of the loader was located at least nine feet behind the lifting forks.

On the day of the accident the regular operator of the loader, Bill Dalton, did not report for work, and plaintiff, who had received only limited instruction on the operation of the loader from Dalton and who had operated the loader on only a few occasions, was assigned to run the loader in Dalton's place. The accident occurred while plaintiff was attempting to lift a load of lumber to a height of approximately 18 to 20 feet and to place the load on the second story of a building under construction. The lift was a particularly difficult one because the terrain on which the loader rested sloped sharply in several directions.

Witnesses testified that plaintiff approached the structure with the loader, leveled the forks to compensate for the sloping ground and lifted the load to a height variously estimated between 10 and 18 feet. During the course of the lift plaintiff felt some vibration, and, when it appeared to several co-workers that the load was beginning to tip, the workers shouted to plaintiff to jump from the loader. Plaintiff heeded these warnings and leaped from the loader, but while scrambling away he was struck by a piece of falling lumber and suffered serious injury.

Although the above facts were generally not in dispute, the parties differed markedly in identifying the responsible causes for the accident. Plaintiff contended, inter alia, that the accident was attributable to one or more design defects of the loader. Defendant, in turn, denied that the loader was defective in any respect, and claimed that the accident resulted either from plaintiff's lack of skill or from his misuse of its product. We briefly review the conflicting evidence.

Plaintiff's principal expert witness initially testified that by reason of its relatively narrow base the loader was unstable and had a tendency to roll over when lifting loads to considerable heights; the witness surmised that this instability caused the load to tip in the instant case. The expert declared that to compensate for its instability, the loader should have been equipped with "outriggers," mechanical arms extending out from the sides of the machine, two in front and two in back, each of which could be operated independently and placed on the ground to lend stability to the loader. Evidence at trial revealed that cranes and some high lift loader models are either regularly equipped with outriggers or offer outriggers as optional equipment. Plaintiff's expert testified that the availability of outriggers would probably have averted the present accident.

The expert additionally testified that the loader was defective in that it was not equipped with a roll bar or seat belts. He stated that such safety devices were essential to protect the operator in the event that the machine rolled over. Plaintiff theorized that the lack of such safety equipment was a proximate cause of his injuries because in the absence of such devices he had no reasonable choice but to leap from the loader as it began to tip. If a seat belt and roll bar had been provided, plaintiff argued, he could have remained in the loader and would not have been struck by the falling lumber.

In addition, plaintiff's witnesses suggested that the accident may have been caused by the defective design of the loader's leveling mechanism. Several witnesses testified that both the absence of an automatic locking device on the leveling lever, and the placement of the leveling lever in a position in which it was extremely vulnerable to inadvertent bumping by the operator of the loader in the course of a lift, were defects which may have produced the accident and injuries in question.

Finally, plaintiff's experts testified that the absence of a "park" position on the loader's transmission, that could have been utilized to avoid the possibility of the loader's movement during a lift, constituted a further defect in design which may have caused the accident.

Defendants, in response, presented evidence which attempted to refute plaintiff's claims that the loader was defective or that the loader's condition was the cause of the accident. Defendants' experts testified that the loader was not unstable when utilized on the terrain for which it was intended, and that if the accident did occur because of the tipping of the loader it was only because plaintiff had misused the equipment by operating it on steep terrain for which the loader was unsuited. In answer to the claim that the high-lift loader was defective because of a lack of outriggers, defendants' expert testified that outriggers were not necessary when the loader was used for its intended purpose and that no competitive loaders with similar height lifting capacity were equipped with outriggers; the expert conceded, however, that a competitor did offer outriggers as optional equipment on a high-lift loader which was capable of lifting loads to 40, as compared to 32, feet. The expert also testified that the addition of outriggers would simply have given the loader the functional capability of a crane, which was designed for use on all terrain, and that an experienced user of a high-lift loader should recognize that such a loader was not intended as a substitute for a crane.

The defense experts further testified that a roll bar was unnecessary because in view of the bulk of the loader it would not roll completely over. The witnesses also maintained that seat belts would have increased the danger of the loader by impairing the operator's ability to leave the vehicle quickly in case of an emergency. With respect to the claimed defects of the leveling device, the defense experts testified that the positioning of the lever was the safest and most convenient for the operator and that the manual lock on the leveling device provided completely adequate protection. Finally, defendants asserted that the absence of a "park" position on the transmission should not be considered a defect because none of the transmissions that were manufactured for this type of vehicle included a park position.

In addition to disputing plaintiff's contention as to the defectiveness of the loader, defendants' witnesses testified that the accident probably was caused by the plaintiff's own inexperience and consequent dangerous actions. Defendants maintained that if the lumber had begun to fall during the lift it did so only because plaintiff had failed to lock the leveling device prior to the lift. Defendants alternatively suggested that although the workers thought they saw the lumber begin to tip during the lift, this tipping was actually only the plaintiff's leveling of the load during the lift. Defendants hypothesized that the lumber actually fell off the loader only after plaintiff had leaped from the machine and that plaintiff was responsible for his own injuries because he had failed to set the hand brake, thereby permitting the loader to roll backwards.

After considering the sharply conflicting testimony reviewed above, the jury by a 10 to 2 vote returned a general verdict in favor of defendants. Plaintiff appeals from the judgment entered upon that verdict.

2. *The trial court erred in instructing the jurors that "strict liability for a defect in*

design . . . is based on a finding that the product was unreasonably dangerous for its intended use."

Plaintiff principally contends that the trial court committed prejudicial error in instructing the jury "that strict liability for a defect in design of a product is based on a finding that the product was unreasonably dangerous for its intended use. . . ."

Plaintiff maintains that this instruction conflicts directly with this court's decision in *Cronin*, decided subsequently to the instant trial, and mandates a reversal of the judgment. Defendants argue, in response, that our *Cronin* decision should not be applied to product liability actions which involve "design defects" as distinguished from "manufacturing defects."

The plaintiff in *Cronin*, a driver of a bread delivery truck, was seriously injured when, during an accident, a metal hasp which held the truck's bread trays in place broke, permitting the trays to slide forward and propel plaintiff through the truck's windshield. Plaintiff brought a strict liability action against the seller, contending that his injuries were proximately caused by the defective condition of the truck. Evidence at trial established that the metal hasp broke during the accident "because it was extremely porous and had a significantly lower tolerance to force than a non-flawed aluminum hasp would have had" (8 Cal. 3d at p. 124, 104 Cal. Rptr. at p. 436, 501 P.2d at p. 1156), and, on the basis of this evidence, the jury returned a verdict in favor of plaintiff.

On appeal, defendant in *Cronin* argued that the trial court had erred "by submitting a definition of strict liability which failed to include, as defendant requested, the element that the defect found in the product be 'unreasonably dangerous.'" (8 Cal. 3d at pp. 127-128, 104 Cal. Rptr. at p. 438, 501 P.2d at p. 1158 (fns. omitted).) Relying upon section 402A of the Restatement Second of Torts and a number of California decisions which had utilized the "unreasonably dangerous" terminology in the product liability context, the defendant in *Cronin* maintained that a product's "unreasonable dangerousness" was an essential element that a plaintiff must establish in any product liability action.

After undertaking a thorough review of the origins and development of both California product liability doctrine and the Restatement's "unreasonably dangerous" criterion, we rejected the defendant's contention, concluding "that to require an injured plaintiff to prove not only that the product contained a defect but also that such defect made the product unreasonably dangerous to the user or consumer would place a considerably greater burden upon him than that articulated in *Greenman [v. Yuba Power Products, Inc.* (1963) 59 Cal. 2d 57, 27 Cal. Rptr. 697, 377 P.2d 897, California's seminal product liability decision]. . . . We are not persuaded to the contrary by the formulation of section 402A which inserts the factor of an 'unreasonably dangerous' condition into the equation of products liability." (8 Cal. 3d pp. 134-135, 104 Cal. Rptr. at p. 443, 501 P.2d at p. 1163.)

Plaintiff contends that the clear import of this language in *Cronin* is that the "unreasonably dangerous" terminology of the Restatement should not be utilized in defining defect in product liability actions, and that the trial court consequently erred in submitting an instruction which defined a design defect by reference to the "unreasonably dangerous" standard.

In attempting to escape the apparent force of *Cronin's* explicit language, defendants observe that the flawed hasp which rendered the truck defective in *Cronin* represented a manufacturing defect rather than a design defect, and they argue that *Cronin's* disapproval of the Restatement's "unreasonably dangerous" standard should be limited to the manufacturing defect context. Defendants point out that one of the bases for our rejection of the "unreasonably dangerous" criterion in *Cronin* was our concern that such language, when used in conjunction with the "defective product" terminology, was susceptible to an interpretation which would place a dual burden on an injured plaintiff to prove, first, that a product was defective and, second, that it was additionally unreasonably dangerous. (8 Cal. 3d at p. 133, 104 Cal. Rptr. 433, 501 P.2d 1153.) Defendants contend that the "dual burden" problem is present only in a manufacturing defect context and not in a design defect case.

In elaborating this contention, defendants explain that in a manufacturing defect case, a jury may find a product defective because it deviates from the manufacturer's intended result, but may still decline to impose liability under the Restatement test on the ground that such defect did not render the product unreasonably dangerous. In a design defect case, by contrast, defendants assert that a defect *is defined* by reference to the "unreasonably dangerous" standard and, since the two are equivalent, no danger of a dual burden exists. In essence, defendants argue that under the instruction which the trial court gave in the instant case, plaintiff was not required to prove both that the loader was defective and that such defect made the loader unreasonably dangerous, but only that the loader was defectively designed by virtue of its unreasonable dangerousness.

Although defendants may be correct, at least theoretically, in asserting that the so-called "dual burden" problem is averted when the "unreasonably dangerous" terminology is used in a design defect case simply as a definition of "defective condition" or "defect," defendants overlook the fact that our objection to the "unreasonably dangerous" terminology in *Cronin* went beyond the "dual burden" issue, and was based, more fundamentally, on a substantive determination that the Restatement's "unreasonably dangerous" formulation represented an undue restriction on the application of strict liability principles.

As we noted in *Cronin*, the Restatement draftsmen adopted the "unreasonably dangerous" language primarily as a means of confining the application of strict tort liability to an article which is "dangerous to an extent beyond that which would be contemplated by the ordinary consumer who purchases it, with the ordinary knowledge common to the community as to its characteristics." (Rest. 2d Torts, § 402A, com. i.) In *Cronin*, however, we flatly rejected the suggestion that recovery in a products liability action should be permitted *only* if a product is more dangerous than contemplated by the average consumer, refusing to permit the low esteem in which the public might hold a dangerous product to diminish the manufacturer's responsibility for injuries caused by that product. As we pointedly noted in *Cronin*, even if the "ordinary consumer" may have contemplated that Shopsmith lathes posed a risk of loosening their grip and letting a piece of wood strike the operator, "another Greenman" should not be denied recovery. (8 Cal. 3d at p. 133, 104 Cal. Rptr. 433, 501 P.2d 1153.) Indeed, our decision in *Luque v. McLean* (1972) 8 Cal. 3d 136, 104 Cal. Rptr. 443, 501 P.2d 1163 — decided the same day as *Cronin* — aptly reflects our disagreement with the restrictive implications of the Restatement formulation, for in *Luque* we held that a power rotary lawn mower with an unguarded hole could properly be found defective, in spite of the fact that the defect in the product was patent and hence in all probability within the reasonable contemplation of the ordinary consumer.

Thus, our rejection of the use of the "unreasonably dangerous" terminology in *Cronin* rested in part on a concern that a jury might interpret such an instruction, as the Restatement draftsman had indeed intended, as shielding a defendant from liability so long as the product did not fall below the ordinary consumer's expectations as to the product's safety.[7] As *Luque* demonstrates, the dangers posed by such a misconception by the jury extend to cases involving design defects as well as to actions involving manufacturing defects: indeed, the danger of confusion is perhaps more pronounced in design cases in which the manufacturer could frequently argue that its product satisfied ordinary consumer expectations since it was identical to other items of the same product line with which the consumer may well have been familiar.

Accordingly, contrary to defendants' contention, the reasoning of *Cronin* does not dictate that decision be confined to the manufacturing defect context. Indeed, in *Cronin* itself we expressly stated that our holding applied to design defects as well as to manufacturing defects (8 Cal. 3d at pp. 134-135, 104 Cal. Rptr. 433, 501 P.2d 1153), and in *Henderson v. Harnischfeger Corp.* (1974) 12 Cal. 3d 663, 670,117 Cal. Rptr. 1, 527 P.2d 353, we subsequently confirmed the impropriety of instructing a jury in the language of the "unreasonably dangerous" standard in a design defect case. *(See also Foglio v. Western Auto Supply* (1976) 56 Cal. App. 3d 470, 475, 128 Cal. Rptr. 545.)[8] Consequently, we conclude that the design defect instruction given in the instant case was erroneous.[9]

---

[7] This is not to say that the expectations of the ordinary consumer are irrelevant to the determination of whether a product is defective, for as we point out below we believe that ordinary consumer expectations are frequently of direct significance to the defectiveness issue. The flaw in the Restatement's analysis, in our view, is that it treats such consumer expectations as a "ceiling" on a manufacturer's responsibility under strict liability principles, rather than as a "floor." As we shall explain, past California decisions establish that at a *minimum* a product must meet ordinary consumer expectations as to safety to avoid being found defective.

[8] One commentator has observed that, in addition to the deficiencies in the "unreasonably dangerous" terminology noted in *Cronin*, the Restatement's language is potentially misleading because "[i]t may suggest an idea like ultrahazardous, or abnormally dangerous, and thus give rise to the impression that the plaintiff must prove that the product was unusually or extremely dangerous." (Wade, *On the Nature of Strict Tort Liability for Products* (1973) 44 Miss. L.J. 825, 832.) We agree with this criticism and believe it constitutes a further reason for refraining from utilizing the "unreasonably dangerous" terminology in defining a defective product.

[9] Indeed, the challenged instruction . . . was additionally erroneous because it suggested that in evaluating defectiveness, only the "intended use" of the product is relevant, rather than the product's "reasonably foreseeable use." In *Cronin*, we specifically held that the adequacy of a product must be determined in light of its reasonably foreseeable use, declaring that "[t]he design and manufacture of products should not be carried out in an industrial vacuum but with recognition of the realities of their everyday use." (8 Cal. 3d at p. 126, 104 Cal. Rptr. at p. 437, 501 P.2d at p. 1157.)

Because, in the instant case, the jury may have concluded that the use of the loader by a relatively inexperienced worker was not an "intended use" of the loader, but was a "reasonably foreseeable use," this aspect of the instruction may well have prejudiced the plaintiff.

3. A trial court may properly formulate instructions to elucidate the "defect" concept in varying circumstances. In particular, in design defect cases, a court may properly instruct a jury that a product is defective in design if (1) the plaintiff proves that the product failed to perform as safely as an ordinary consumer would expect when used in an intended or reasonably foreseeable manner, or (2) the plaintiff proves that the product's design proximately caused injury and the defendant fails to prove, in light of the relevant factors, that on balance the benefits of the challenged design outweigh the risk of danger inherent in such design.

Defendants contend, however, that if *Cronin* is interpreted as precluding the use of the "unreasonably dangerous" language in defining a design defect, the jury in all such cases will inevitably be left without any guidance whatsoever in determining whether a product is defective in design or not. Amicus California Trial Lawyer Association (CTLA) on behalf of the plaintiff responds by suggesting that the precise intent of our *Cronin* decision was to preclude a trial court from formulating any definition of "defect" in a product liability case, thus always leaving the definition of defect, as well as the application of such definition, to the jury. As we explain, neither of these contentions represents an accurate portrayal of the intent or effect of our *Cronin* decision.

In *Cronin*, we reaffirmed the basic formulation of strict tort liability doctrine set forth in *Greenman:* "A manufacturer is strictly liable in tort when an article he places on the market, knowing that it is to be used without inspection for defects, proves to have a defect that causes injury to a human being. . . ." We held in *Cronin* that a plaintiff satisfies his burden of proof under *Greenman*, in both a "manufacturing defect" and "design defect" context, when he proves the existence of a "defect" and that such defect was a proximate cause of his injuries. In reaching this conclusion, however, *Cronin* did not purport to hold that the term "defect" must remain undefined in all contexts, and did not preclude a trial court from framing a definition of defect, appropriate to the circumstances of a particular case, to guide the jury as to the standard to be applied in determining whether a product is defective or not.

As this court has recognized on numerous occasions, the term defect as utilized in the strict liability context is neither self-defining nor susceptible to a single definition applicable in all contexts. . . .

Resort to the numerous product liability precedents in California demonstrates that the defect or defectiveness concept has embraced a great variety of injury-producing deficiencies, ranging from products that cause injury because they deviate from the manufacturer's intended result (e.g., the one soda bottle in ten thousand that explodes without explanation), to products which, though "perfectly" manufactured, are unsafe because of the absence of a safety device (e.g., a paydozer without rear view mirrors), and including products that are dangerous because they lack adequate warnings or instructions (e.g., a telescope that contains inadequate instructions for assembling a "sun filter" attachment.)

Commentators have pointed out that in view of the diversity of product deficiencies to which the defect rubric has been applied, an instruction which requires a plaintiff to prove the existence of a product defect, but which fails to elaborate on the meaning of defect in a particular context, may in some situations prove more misleading than helpful. As Professor Wade has written: "[The] natural application [of the term 'defective'] would be limited to the situation in which something went wrong in the manufacturing process, so that the article was defective in the sense that the manufacturer had not intended it to be in that condition. To apply [the term 'defective'] also to the case in which a warning is not attached to the chattel or the design turns out to be a bad one or the product is likely to be injurious in its normal condition . . . [and] [t]o use it without defining it to the jury is almost to ensure that they will be misled." (Wade, *On the Nature of Strict Tort Liability for Products, supra*, 44 Miss. L.J. 825, 831-832 (fns. omitted)).

Our decision in *Cronin* did not mandate such confusion. Instead, by observing that the problem in defining defect might be alleviated by reference to the "cluster of useful precedents," we intended to suggest that in drafting and evaluating instructions on this issue in a particular case, trial and appellate courts would be well advised to consider prior authorities involving similar defective product claims.

Since the rendition of our decision in *Cronin*, a number of thoughtful Court of Appeal decisions have wrestled with the problem of devising a comprehensive definition of design defect in light of existing authorities. As these decisions demonstrate, the concept of defect raises considerably more difficulties in the design defect context than it does in the manufacturing or production defect context.

In general, a manufacturing or production defect is readily identifiable because a defective product is one that differs from the manufacturer's intended result or from other ostensibly identical units of the same product line. For example, when a product comes off the assembly line in a substandard condition it has incurred a manufacturing defect. A design defect, by contrast, cannot be identified simply by comparing the injury-producing product with the manufacturer's plans or with other units of the same product line, since by definition the plans and all such units will reflect the same design. Rather than applying any sort of deviation-from-the-norm test in determining whether a product is defective in design for strict liability purposes, our cases have employed two alternative criteria in ascertaining, in Justice Traynor's words, whether there is something "wrong, if not in the manufacturer's manner of production, at least in his product." (Traynor, *The Ways and Meanings of Defective Products and Strict Liability, supra*, 32 Tenn. L. Rev. 363, 366.)

First, our cases establish that a product may be found defective in design if the plaintiff demonstrates that the product failed to perform as safely as an ordinary consumer would expect when used in an intended or reasonably foreseeable manner. This initial standard, somewhat analogous to the Uniform Commercial Code's warranty of fitness and merchantability (Cal. U. Com. Code, § 2314), reflects the warranty heritage upon which California product liability doctrine in part rests. As we noted in *Greenman*, "implicit in [a product's] presence on the market . . . [is] a representation that it [will] safely do the jobs for which it was built." (59 Cal. 2d at p. 64, 27 Cal. Rptr. at p. 701, 377 P.2d at p. 901.) When a product fails to satisfy such ordinary consumer expectations as to safety in its intended or reasonably foreseeable operation, a manufacturer is strictly liable for resulting injuries. Under this standard, an injured plaintiff will frequently be able to demonstrate the defectiveness of a product by resort to circumstantial evidence, even when the accident itself precludes identification of the specific defect at fault.

As Professor Wade has pointed out, however, the expectations of the ordinary consumer cannot be viewed as the exclusive yardstick for evaluating design defectiveness because "[i]n many situations . . . the consumer would not know what to expect, because he would have no idea how safe the product could be made." (Wade, *On the Nature of Strict Tort Liability for Products, supra*, 44 Miss. L.J. 825, 829.) Numerous California decisions have implicitly recognized this fact and have made clear, through varying linguistic formulations, that a product may be found defective in design, even if it satisfies ordinary consumer expectations, if through hindsight the jury determines that the product's design embodies "excessive preventable danger," or, in other words, if the jury finds that the risk of danger inherent in the challenged design outweighs the benefits of such design.[10]

A review of past cases indicates that in evaluating the adequacy of a product's design pursuant to this latter standard, a jury may consider, among other relevant factors, the gravity of the danger posed by the challenged design, the likelihood that such danger would occur, the mechanical feasibility of a safer alternative design, the financial cost of an improved design, and the adverse consequences to the product and to the consumer that would result from an alternative design.

Although our cases have thus recognized a variety of considerations that may be relevant to the determination of the adequacy of a product's design, past authorities have generally not devoted much attention to the appropriate allocation of the burden of proof with respect to these matters. The allocation of such burden is particularly significant in this context inasmuch as this court's product liability decisions, from *Greenman* to *Cronin*, have repeatedly emphasized that one of the principal purposes behind the strict product liability doctrine is to relieve an injured plaintiff of many of the onerous evidentiary burdens inherent in a negligence cause of action. Because most of the evidentiary matters which may be relevant to the determination of the adequacy of a product's design under the "risk-benefit" standard — e.g., the feasibility and cost of alternative designs — are similar to issues typically presented in a negligent design case and involve technical matters peculiarly within the knowledge of the manufacturer, we conclude that once the plaintiff makes a prima facie showing that the injury was proximately caused by the product's design, the burden should appropriately shift to the defendant to prove, in light of the relevant factors, that the product is not defective. Moreover, inasmuch as this conclusion flows from our determination that the fundamental public policies embraced in *Greenman* dictate that a manufacturer who seeks to escape liability for an injury proximately caused by its product's design on a risk-benefit theory should bear the burden of persuading the trier of fact that its product should not be judged defective, the defendant's burden is one affecting the burden of proof, rather than

---

[10] In the instant case we have no occasion to determine whether a product which entails a substantial risk of harm may be found defective even if no safer alternative design is feasible. As we noted in *Jiminez v. Sears, Roebuck & Co., supra*, 4 Cal. 3d 379, 383, 93 Cal. Rptr. 769, 772, 482 P.2d 681, 684, Justice Traynor has "suggested that liability might be imposed as to products whose norm is danger." (Citing Traynor, *The Ways and Meaning of Defective Products and Strict Liability, supra*, 32 Tenn. L. Rev. 363, 367 *et seq.*).

simply the burden of producing evidence.

Thus, to reiterate, a product may be found defective in design, so as to subject a manufacturer to strict liability for resulting injuries, under either of two alternative tests. First, a product may be found defective in design if the plaintiff establishes that the product failed to perform as safely as an ordinary consumer would expect when used in an intended or reasonably foreseeable manner. Second, a product may alternatively be found defective in design if the plaintiff demonstrates that the product's design proximately caused his injury and the defendant fails to establish, in light of the relevant factors, that, on balance, the benefits of the challenged design outweigh the risk of danger inherent in such design.

Although past California decisions have not explicitly articulated the two-pronged definition of design defect which we have elaborated above, other jurisdictions have adopted a somewhat similar, though not identical, dual approach in attempting to devise instructions to guide the jury in design defect cases. As we have indicated, we believe that the test for defective design set out above is appropriate in light of the rationale and limits of the strict liability doctrine, for it subjects a manufacturer to liability whenever there is something "wrong" with its product's design — either because the product fails to meet ordinary consumer expectations as to safety or because, on balance, the design is not as safe as it should be — while stopping short of making the manufacturer an insurer for all injuries which may result from the use of its product. This test, moreover, explicitly focuses the trier of fact's attention on the adequacy of the product itself, rather than on the manufacturer's conduct, and places the burden on the manufacturer, rather than the plaintiff, to establish that because of the complexity of, and trade-offs implicit in, the design process, an injury-producing product should nevertheless not be found defective.

Amicus CTLA on behalf of the plaintiff, anticipating to some extent the latter half of the design defect standard articulated above, contends that any instruction which directs the jury to "weigh" or "balance" a number of factors, or which sets forth a list of completing considerations for the jury to evaluate in determining the existence of a design defect, introduces an element which "rings of negligence" into the determination of defect, and consequently is inconsistent with our decision in *Cronin*. (*Cf.* 8 Cal. 3d at p. 132, 104 Cal. Rptr. 433, 501 P.2d 1153.) As amicus interprets the decision, *Cronin* broadly precludes any consideration of "reasonableness" or "balancing" in a product liability action.

In the first place, however, in *Cronin* our principal concern was that the "unreasonably dangerous" language of the Restatement test had "burdened *the injured plaintiff* with proof of an element which rings of negligence" (italics added) (8 Cal. 3d at p. 132, 104 Cal. Rptr. at p. 442, 501 P.2d at p. 1162) and had consequently placed "a considerably greater burden upon [the injured plaintiff] than that articulated in *Greenman.*" (8 Cal. 3d at pp. 134-135, 104 Cal. Rptr. at p. 443, 501 P.2d at p. 1163.) By shifting the burden of proof to the manufacturer to demonstrate that an injury-producing product is not defective in design, the above standard should lighten the plaintiff's burden in conformity with our *Greenman* and *Cronin* decisions.

Secondly, past design defect decisions demonstrate that, as a practical matter, in many instances it is simply impossible to eliminate the balancing or weighing of competing considerations in determining whether a product is defectively designed or not. In *Self v. General Motors Corp., supra,* 42 Cal. App. 3d 1, 116 Cal. Rptr. 575, for example, an automobile passenger, injured when the car in which she was riding exploded during an accident, brought suit against the manufacturer claiming that the car was defective in that the fuel tank had been placed in a particularly vulnerable position in the left rear bumper. One issue in the case, of course, was whether it was technically feasible to locate the fuel tank in a different position which would have averted the explosion in question. But, as the *Self* court recognized, feasibility was not the sole issue, for another relevant consideration was whether an alternative design of the car, while averting the particular accident, would have created a greater risk of injury in other, more common situations. (*See* 42 Cal. App. 3d at pp. 7-8, 116 Cal. Rptr. 575.)

In similar fashion, weighing the extent of the risks and the advantages posed by alternative designs is inevitable in many design defect cases. As the *Self* court stated: "[W]e appreciate the need to balance one consideration against another in designing a complicated product so as to achieve reasonable and practical safety under a multitude of varying conditions." (42 Cal. App. 3d at p. 7, 116 Cal. Rptr. at p. 579.) Inasmuch as the weighing of competing considerations is implicit in many design defect determinations, an instruction which appears to preclude such a weighing process under all circumstances may mislead the jury.

Finally, contrary to the suggestion of amicus CTLA, an instruction which advises the jury that it may evaluate the adequacy of a product's design by weighing the benefits of the challenged design against the risk of danger inherent in such design is not simply the equivalent of an instruction which requires the jury to determine whether the manufacturer was negligent in designing the product. It is true, of course, that in many cases proof that a product is defective in design may also demonstrate that the manufacturer was negligent in choosing such a design. As we have indicated, however, in a strict liability case, as contrasted with a negligent design action, the jury's focus is properly directed to the condition of the product itself, and not to the reasonableness of the manufacturer's conduct.

Thus, the fact that the manufacturer took reasonable precautions in an attempt to design a safe product or otherwise acted as a reasonably prudent manufacturer would have under the circumstances, while perhaps absolving the manufacturer of liability under a negligence theory, will not preclude the imposition of liability under strict liability principles if, upon hindsight, the trier of fact concludes that the product's design is unsafe to consumers, users, or bystanders. *(See Foglio v. Western Auto Supply, supra,* 56 Cal. App. 3d 470, 477, 128 Cal. Rptr. 545.)

4. *Conclusion*

The technological revolution has created a society that contains dangers to the individual never before contemplated. The individual must face the threat to life and limb not only from the car on the street or highway but from a massive array of hazardous mechanisms and products. The radical change from a comparatively safe, largely agricultural, society to this industrial unsafe one has been reflected in the decisions that formerly tied liability to the fault of a tortfeasor but now are more concerned with the safety of the individual who suffers the loss. As Dean Keeton has written, "The change in the substantive law as regards the liability of makers of products and other sellers in the marketing chain has been from fault to defect. The plaintiff is no longer required to impugn the maker, but he is required to impugn the product." (Keeton, *Product Liability and the Meaning of Defect* (1973) 5 St. Mary's L.J. 30, 33.)

If a jury in determining liability for a defect in design is instructed only that it should decide whether or not there is "a defective design," it may reach to the extreme conclusion that the plaintiff, having suffered injury, should without further showing, recover; on the other hand, it may go to the opposite extreme and conclude that because the product matches the intended design the plaintiff, under no conceivable circumstance, could recover. The submitted definition eschews both extremes and attempts a balanced approach.

We hold that a trial judge may properly instruct the jury that a product is defective in design (1) if the plaintiff demonstrates that the product failed to perform as safely as an ordinary consumer would expect when used in an intended or reasonably foreseeable manner, or (2) if the plaintiff proves that the product's design proximately caused his injury and the defendant fails to prove, in light of the relevant factors discussed above, that on balance the benefits of the challenged design outweigh the risk of danger inherent in such design.

Because the jury may have interpreted the erroneous instruction given in the instant case as requiring plaintiff to prove that the high-lift loader was ultrahazardous or more dangerous than the average consumer contemplated, and because the instruction additionally misinformed the jury that the defectiveness of the product must be evaluated in light of the product's "intended use" rather than its "reasonably foreseeable use" *(see* fn. 9, *ante)*, we cannot find that the error was harmless on the facts of this case. In light of this conclusion, we need not address plaintiff's additional claims of error, for such issues may not arise on retrial.

The judgment in favor of defendants is reversed.

Mosk, Clark, Richardson, Wright (Retired Chief Justice of California assigned by the Acting Chairperson of the Judicial Council), and Sullivan (Retired Associate Justice of the Supreme Court sitting under assignment by the Chairperson of the Judicial Council), JJ., concur.

---

1. How did the *Cronin* court define defect? The *Barker* court? What kinds of dangerous products will *not* subject their manufacturer to strict liability under *Barker*? What role, if any, does manufacturer knowledge of the danger play in *Barker* and *Cronin*?

2. The *Barker* court deals with an additional question that has caused much court and commentator ink to be spilled: the question of to what kinds of uses strict product liability will apply. What does Section 402A say about this subject? *Barker*? When will consumer misuse constitute a defense in a strict products liability action? Or is an absence of misuse part of the plaintiff's case?

3. Defining Defect When the Basis for Products Liability is Failure to Warn

When it was written and adopted by courts, Section 402A and the courts treated all three types of defect — mismanufacture, design, and failure to warn — in an identical manner. This did not last long, and courts began dividing the three types of defect and applying different rules to each one. Failure to warn theory has proven to be by far the most complex of the three types of defect theory. Mismanufacture cases are relatively straightforward. In mismanufacture cases there is something wrong with the individual product that makes it differ from the product line, and that defect causes injury. The plaintiff's case consists of evidence that the product differed from the product line and that the difference caused the injury. Res ipsa loquitur works in these cases; often, the individual product is not itself available but the plaintiff can prove that it would not have behaved as it did if there had not been something the matter with it. Under a *Phillips* analysis, one can safely say that the manufacturer would not have sold the product in the form in which it was sold had the manufacturer known of the defect.

Design defect cases are more complex than mismanufacture cases. The stakes are much higher: in a mismanufacture case, the manufacturer will be liable for injury done by the one product unit. In a design defect case, on the other hand, the manufacturer might be liable for the injuries caused by a whole line of products. This has made courts more wary about finding manufacturers liable, with a concomitant increase in care about what the plaintiff must prove. A mismanufactured product by definition fails a risk/utility test. A product with an allegedly defective design might not.

Failure to warn cases introduce an added complexity. In design defect cases, the manufacturer can argue that the product was not defective because its utility outweighs its risks. This balancing test includes the feasibility of eliminating or reducing the danger by a change in design, the expense of doing so, any reduction in utility resulting from the design change, and the ability of the consumer to avoid the danger. In a design defect case, all of these factors can provide the defendant with viable arguments against liability. In a failure to warn case, on the other hand, the plaintiff is simply alleging that the product should have contained a warning of the danger, either informational (for dangers that cannot be avoided) or directional (for dangers that can be avoided if the product is used in accordance with the directions). Because warnings, unlike design changes, are cheap, it is much more difficult for a manufacturer to argue that a product without an adequate warning is not defective than it is for a manufacturer to argue that a design change would have been impractical or more expensive than it was worth. The particular scenario that has caused the most trouble in warnings cases involves a dangerous product with unknowable dangers. Such a product contains risks about which no one could have known at the time of manufacture or sale. The manufacturer is not negligent for failing to warn of the danger, because a reasonable manufacturer could not have known about it. Strict liability doctrine, at least as formulated, however, was not based on negligence. If one imputed knowledge of the danger to the manufacturer under a *Phillips v. Kimwood* test, the answer would be that a reasonable manufacturer, presumed to know of the danger, would not have sold the product without a warning. Thus, the manufacturer would be liable for failing to warn of a danger about which the manufacturer could not have known.

This happened in the unanimous opinion in *Beshada v. Johns-Manville Products Corp.*, 447 A.2d 539 (N.J. 1982). The court pointed out in that case that the difference between strict products liability and negligence-based liability was that in the former the manufacturer is irrebuttably presumed to know of the danger, and therefore can be liable for failing to warn about it. The manufacturer would not be allowed to introduce a so-called "state of the art" defense, pursuant to which the manufacturer would argue that it should not be liable because it could not have known of the danger.

The idea that a manufacturer could be held liable for failing to warn of dangers about which it could not have known caused massive consternation. While several courts continued to impute knowledge of all dangers to manufacturers, most did not. It took the Supreme Court of New Jersey only 23 months to back down from its decision in *Beshada*, which it did in the equally unanimous *Feldman v. Lederle Laboratories*, 479 A.2d 374 (N.J. 1984). In *Feldman*, the court ruled that a manufacturer of prescription pharmaceuticals had a duty to warn only of dangers about which the manufacturer could or should have known. Various other courts followed suit in various ways, ranging from exempting prescription pharmaceutical manufacturers from Section 402A altogether to holding that failure to warn law would be considered negligence-based, and not strict liability at all; thus, the manufacturer could only be liable for failing to warn of dangers about which a reasonable manufacturer could have known. The Third Restatement of Products Liability provides that manufacturers are only liable for design and warning defects where the dangers were foreseeable. This, by definition, excludes unknowable dangers from the scope of products liability altogether.

The following two cases illustrate alternative approaches to this issue.

STERNHAGEN v. DOW COMPANY
Supreme Court of Montana, 1997
935 P.2d 1139

JUSTICE JAMES C. NELSON delivered the Opinion of the Court.

The United States District Court for the District of Montana, Great Falls Division, has certified to this Court the following question:

> In a strict products liability case for injuries caused by an inherently unsafe product, is the manufacturer conclusively presumed to know the dangers inherent in his product, or is state-of-the-art evidence admissible to establish whether the manufacturer knew or through the exercise of reasonable human foresight should have known of the danger?

We conclude that Montana law precludes the admission of state-of-the-art evidence in products liability cases brought under the theory of strict liability.

FACTUAL AND PROCEDURAL BACKGROUND

The United States District Court for the District of Montana, Great Falls Division, found the following facts relevant to the question of law certified to this Court:

1. . . . [P]laintiff Marlene L. Sternhagen, as the personal representative of the estate of Charles J. Sternhagen, seeks recovery for injuries and damages allegedly sustained by Charles Sternhagen as a result of his exposure to the herbicide 2,4-D during the years 1948 through 1950. Plaintiff claims that the exposure of Charles Sternhagen to 2,4-D was the cause of the cancer that resulted in his death.

2. Plaintiff seeks recovery against the defendants under the doctrine of strict liability in tort. . . .

3. During the summer months of 1948, 1949 and 1950, Charles Sternhagen was employed by a crop spraying business in northeast Montana. Plaintiff claims that during that time, Charles Sternhagen was exposed to the herbicide, 2,4-D.

4. In 1981, Charles Sternhagen, a medical doctor specializing in radiology, was diagnosed as having a form of cancer which plaintiff claims was caused by his exposure to the herbicide 2,4-D during the years 1948 through 1950. Defendants dispute the claim that there is a causal link between the herbicide 2,4-D and the type of cancer from which Charles Sternhagen died.

5. The defendants claim neither they, nor medical science, knew or had reason to know of any alleged cancer-causing properties of the herbicide 2,4-D during the years 1948 through 1950.

DISCUSSION

. . . .

The Chemical Companies next argue that if Restatement (Second) of Torts § 402A (1965), is the applicable law, then state-of-the-art evidence is admissible because Montana law recognizes the state-of-the-art defense in failure to warn claims. The Chemical Companies contend that the certified question must be read in conjunction not only with Restatement (Second) of Torts § 402A (1965) but also with the comments to § 402A, including Comment j. Specifically, the Chemical Companies argue that the third sentence of Comment j applies, namely that "the seller is required to give warning . . . , if he has knowledge, or by the application of reasonably, developed human skill and foresight should have knowledge, of the presence of the . . . danger." . . .

Furthermore, the Chemical Companies contend that in *Tacke v. Vermeer Mfg. Co.* (1986), 220 Mont. 1, 713 P.2d 527, the plaintiff offered state-of-the-art evidence on the issue of the feasibility in a design defect case. The Chemical Companies assert that if a plaintiff is allowed to offer state-of-the-art evidence to prove feasibility in a design defect case, a defendant may also offer state-of-the-art evidence to rebut feasibility as part of its defense. Therefore, the Chemical Companies argue a defendant should also be allowed to offer state-of-the-art evidence to disprove the feasibility of a warning in a failure to warn case.

Sternhagen responds that the certified question must be answered based on the fundamental principles underlying strict products liability in Montana. Sternhagen asserts that when this Court . . . adopted strict liability in tort for defective products as defined in Restatement (Second) of Torts § 402A (1965), it did so based on substantial public interest and public policy grounds which included principles of fairness and economics, maximum protection for the consumer and placement of responsibility for injury on the manufacturer. Sternhagen asserts that over the past two-plus decades, this Court has consistently returned to and relied upon these core principles.

. . . .

Furthermore, Sternhagen contends that this Court has never adopted the state-of-the-art defense, but rather this Court has made it clear that even careful manufacturers may be strictly liable for unreasonably dangerous products which contained unforeseeable dangers. Therefore, Sternhagen argues that the critical question for this Court is "whether imposition of liability for undiscovered or even undiscoverable dangers of inherently unsafe products will advance the goals and policies sought to be achieved by Montana's adoption of strict liability." In answering the certified question, Sternhagen urges this Court to again return to the core principles underlying the doctrine of strict liability and thereby reject the state-of-the-art defense. We agree with Sternhagen that we have not previously adopted the state-of-the-art defense. Further, we expressly reject the state-of-the-art defense, as this defense is contrary to the doctrine of strict products liability as that body of law has developed in Montana. In reaching these conclusions, we emphasize that despite the Chemical Companies' assertion that the certified question involves a failure to warn cause of action, we note that the certified question is not so limited. Consequently, we address the certified question by addressing strict products liability law in Montana generally and without differentiating as among manufacturing defect, design defect, or failure to warn cases.

. . . The Chemical Companies assert that we have either previously adopted or should now adopt the language of Comment j to § 402A. However, after researching Montana law on strict products liability, we conclude that the language in Comment j, which the Chemical Companies contend supports the state-of-the-art defense, is inconsistent with our established law concerning strict products liability and we therefore decline to adopt that language. Rather, we conclude that the imputation of knowledge doctrine, as discussed below, is more consistent with existing Montana law.

Furthermore, the Chemical Companies rely on only one part of the third sentence of Comment j which, when considered in its entirety, indicates that this sentence is not applicable to the question certified to this Court. The Chemical Companies rely on the language, "the seller is required to give warning . . . , if he has knowledge, or by the application of reasonably developed human skill and foresight should have knowledge, of the presence of the . . . danger." However, the third sentence of Comment j, from which that language is extracted, states:

Where, however, the product contains **an ingredient to which a substantial number of the population are allergic**, *and the ingredient* is one whose danger is not generally known, or if known is one which the consumer would reasonably not expect to find in the product, the seller is required to give warning against *it* [the ingredient to which people are allergic], if he has knowledge, or by the application of reasonable, developed human skill and foresight should have knowledge, of the presence of *the ingredient* [to which people are allergic] and the danger. [Emphases [and parentheses] added [by the court in the original].]

The certified question before us involves an alleged cancer-causing ingredient, not one to which the decedent is alleged to have been allergic. Therefore, the third sentence of Comment j is not applicable to the certified question.

We adopted strict liability in torts for defective products based on important public policy considerations, to which we have consistently adhered for the past two-plus decades. "[T]he doctrine of strict liability was evolved to place liability on the party primarily responsible for the injury occurring, that is, the manufacturer of the defective product." *Brandenburger*, 513 P.2d at 273 (quoting *Lechuga, Inc. v. Montgomery* (1970), 12 Ariz. App. 32, 467 P.2d 256, 261 (Jacobson, J., concurring)). We, thereafter enumerated various public policy considerations supporting adoption of the strict liability doctrine:

1. The manufacturer can anticipate some hazards and guard against their recurrence, which the consumer cannot do.

2. The cost of injury may be overwhelming to the person injured while the risk of injury can be insured by the manufacturer and be distributed among the public as a cost of doing business.

3. It is in the public interest to discourage the marketing of defective products.

4. It is in the public interest to place responsibility for injury upon the manufacturer who was responsible for [the defective product] reaching the market.

5. That this responsibility should also be placed upon the retailer and wholesaler of the defective product in order that they may act as the conduit through which liability may flow to reach the manufacturer, where ultimate responsibility lies.

6. That because of the complexity of present day manufacturing processes and their secretiveness, the ability to prove negligent conduct by the injured plaintiff is almost impossible.

7. That the consumer does not have the ability to investigate for himself the soundness of the product.

8. That this consumer's vigilance has been lulled by advertising, marketing devices and trademarks.

Brandenburger, 513 P.2d at 273 (citations omitted). Furthermore, we stated:

> The essential rationale for imposing the doctrine of strict liability in tort is that such imposition affords the consuming public the maximum protection from dangerous defects in manufactured products by requiring the manufacturer to bear the burden of injuries and losses enhanced by such defects in its products.

Brandenburger, 513 P.2d at 275.

Subsequent to our adoption of strict liability, we identified three elements essential to the establishment of a prima facie case in strict liability pursuant to § 402A:

> (1) The product was in a defective condition, "unreasonably" dangerous to the user or consumer;
>
> (2) The defect caused the accident and injuries complained of; and
>
> (3) The defect is traceable to the defendant.

Brown, 576 P.2d at 716.

The Chemical Companies argue that if this Court recognizes the imputation of knowledge doctrine, rather than the state-of-the-art defense, we will eliminate all of the elements that a plaintiff must prove to establish a strict products liability cause of action. Specifically, the Chemical Companies assert that the imputation of knowledge doctrine removes a plaintiff's burden of proving that a defect in the product caused the injury. In effect, the Chemical Companies are arguing that adoption of the imputation of knowledge doctrine will transform strict liability into absolute liability. We disagree.

From the time we initially adopted strict products liability, we have reassured defendants that strict liability is not absolute liability:

> The adoption of the doctrine of strict liability does not relieve the plaintiff from the burden of proving his case. Vital to that proof is the necessity of proving the existence of a defect in the product and that such defect caused the injury complained of.

Brandenburger, 513 P.2d at 274. We explained again, in *Brown*, that by imposing upon a plaintiff the burden of proving a traceable defect, causation, and damage or injury, even with a flexible rule of evidence, we assured "an appropriate limitation to a manufacturer's liability." *Brown*, 576 P.2d at 717. This has not changed.

Under the imputation of knowledge doctrine, which is based on strict liability's focus on the product and not the manufacturer's conduct, knowledge of a product's undiscovered or undiscoverable dangers shall be imputed to the manufacturer. Our adoption of the imputation of knowledge doctrine, and concomitant rejection of the state-of-the-art defense, does not change the requirements of plaintiff's prima facie case; it only reinforces our commitment to provide the maximum protection for consumers, while still assuring "an appropriate limitation to a manufacturer's liability."

In fact, for the past two-plus decades, we have consistently adhered to the core public policy principles underlying strict products liability as set forth in both

Brandenburger and *Brown*. As stated in the certified question, state-of-the-art evidence is used to establish whether the manufacturer knew or through the exercise of reasonable human foresight should have known of the dangers inherent in his product. That is, the state-of-the-art defense raises issues of reasonableness and foreseeability — concepts fundamental to negligence law — to determine a manufacturer's liability. To recognize the state-of-the-art defense now would inject negligence principles into strict liability law and thereby sever Montana's strict products liability law from the core principles for which it was adopted — maximum protection for consumers against dangerous defects in manufactured products with the focus on the condition of the product, and not on the manufacturer's conduct or knowledge.

. . . .

Contrary to the Chemical Companies' assertion, our references to Comment j and our use of certain ambiguous language in previous case law does not support a conclusion that we have adopted the state-of-the-art defense. As discussed below, we conclude that in none of our prior cases was the state-of-the-art defense raised as an issue, much less adopted. Rather, these cases illustrate our strict adherence to the remedial policies underlying strict liability and our recognition of the basic differences between strict liability and negligence principles.

Attempting to demonstrate that we have adopted the state-of-the-art defense, the Chemical Companies cite to *Rost* and note that we referenced Comment j, and thereafter stated:

> Plaintiffs contend that this duty to warn is measured by an objective standard, the care which would be exercised by a reasonable seller or expected by the ordinary consumer. This standard focuses on the condition of the product and the degree of danger which would be tolerated by the reasonable manufacturer [who], ***apprised of the danger***, would not sell the product without a warning.

Rost, 616 P.2d at 385 (citing *Phillips v. Kimwood Machine Co.* (1974), 269 Or. 485, 525 P.2d 1033, 1036-37) (emphasis added) (other citations omitted). The Chemical Companies assert that this language is synonymous with the state-of-the-art defense, and, therefore, that we recognized the state-of-the-art defense in *Rost*. We disagree. Rather, in making this assertion, the Chemical Companies take the language in *Rost* out of context from the authority cited.

To explain the nature of the duty to warn standard that the plaintiffs in *Rost* asserted, we cited *Phillips*. The Oregon Supreme Court stated in *Phillips* that to prevent strict liability from becoming absolute liability, a test for unreasonable danger is necessary to show that something about a product makes it dangerously defective without regard to whether the manufacturer was at fault for the condition. *Phillips*, 525 P.2d at 1036.

> A dangerously defective article would be one which a reasonable person would not put into the stream of commerce *if he had knowledge of its harmful character*. The test, therefore, is whether the seller would be negligent if he sold the article *knowing of the risk involved*. Strict liability

imposes what amounts to constructive knowledge of the condition of the product.

Phillips, 525 P.2d at 1036. The Court in *Phillips* also explained that a difference exists between strict liability and negligence law because a product could be unreasonably dangerous even though the manufacturer's actions were reasonable in light of what he knew at the time he planned and sold the manufactured product. *Phillips*, 525 P.2d at 1037.

Furthermore, the Oregon Supreme Court explained that a way to determine if a product is unreasonably defective, is to assume that the manufacturer knew of the product's potential dangers and then ask whether a manufacturer with such knowledge should have done something about the danger before the product was sold. *Phillips*, 525 P.2d at 1037. When viewed in this context, it is apparent that this portion of the *Phillips* opinion to which we cited in *Rost* does not support the state-of-the-art defense, but rather describes the imputation of knowledge doctrine..

Moreover, after citing *Phillips*, we further distinguished strict liability from negligence law and reiterated the public policy supporting strict products liability:

This strict duty mandated by the theory of strict liability is warranted even though in some situations it may result in liability being imposed upon careful manufacturers. Unforeseeable product defects often cause severe physical injuries to members of the public. The manufacturer can distribute the risk from such accidents among the body of consumers, while the individual consumer must bear the financial burden alone. Placing the risk of loss on the manufacturer provides an incentive to design and produce fail-safe products which exceed reasonable standards of safety. *Phillips, supra*, 525 P.2d at 1041. Nor can we ignore the fact that a manufacturer with research capabilities can anticipate hazards better than unsophisticated purchasers. Strict liability has its underpinnings in public policy.

Rost, 616 P.2d at 386 (other citations omitted).

. . . .

Alternatively, the Chemical Companies argue that even if the cases, discussed above, do not show that Montana has adopted the rule allowing state-of-the-art evidence, we should do so now based on the experience of other jurisdictions which favor the adoption of the rule. After discussing numerous cases from other jurisdictions, the Chemical Companies contend that an overwhelming majority of jurisdictions that have adopted § 402A also admit state-of-the-art evidence. Additionally, the Chemical Companies argue that the Restatement (Third) of the Law of Torts: Products Liability (Proposed Final Draft, Preliminary Version) (Oct. 18, 1996) would also allow state-of-the-art evidence. Furthermore, the Chemical Companies assert that public policy supports adoption of the state-of-the-art defense.

Despite the adoption of the state-of-the-art defense in other jurisdictions, recognition of the defense in the Restatement (Third) of the Law of Torts: Products Liability (Proposed Final Draft, Preliminary Version) (Oct. 18, 1996) and the

Chemical Companies' assertion that public policy supports adoption of the defense, we choose to continue to adhere to the clear precedent we have heretofore established which focuses on the core principles and remedial purposes underlying strict products liability. Strict liability without regard to fault is the only doctrine that fulfills the public interest goals of protecting consumers, compensating the injured and making those who profit from the market bear the risks and costs associated with the defective or dangerous products which they place in the stream of commerce. As we discussed previously, no Montana case supports the Chemical Companies' position that state-of-the-art evidence is admissible when a product's inherent dangers are undiscovered or undiscoverable.

In fact, both our case law and statutory law make it clear that even careful manufacturers may be strictly liable for unreasonably dangerous products whose dangers could not be foreseen. Moreover, given strict liability's focus on the product and not on the manufacturer's conduct, knowledge of any undiscovered or undiscoverable dangers should be imputed to the manufacturer. That is, while a plaintiff must still prove the three prima facie elements set forth in *Brown*, evidence that a manufacturer knew or through the exercise of reasonable human foresight should have known of the dangers inherent in his product is irrelevant.

Accordingly, in answer to the question certified, we conclude that, in a strict products liability case, knowledge of any undiscovered or undiscoverable dangers should be imputed to the manufacturer. Furthermore, we conclude that, in a strict products liability case, state-of-the-art evidence is not admissible to establish whether the manufacturer knew or through the exercise of reasonable human foresight should have known of the danger.

TURNAGE, C.J., and GRAY, REGNIER, TRIEWEILER, LEAPHART and HUNT, JJ., concur.

POWERS v. TASER INTERNATIONAL, INC.
Court of Appeals of Arizona, 2007
174 P.3d 777

BARKER, JUDGE.

This Opinion addresses whether the hindsight test should be applied to a strict liability products claim alleging failure to warn as the defect. That test was adopted in *Dart v. Wiebe Manufacturing, Inc.* for strict liability products claims based on design defects. 147 Ariz. 242, 709 P.2d 876 (1985). The court expressly left open that issue as to strict liability products claims asserting a failure to warn. 147 Ariz. at 247 n. 2, 709 P.2d at 881 n. 2. For the reasons set forth below, we decline the invitation to adopt the hindsight test for such claims. . . .

I.

Plaintiff-Appellant Samuel E. Powers appeals a jury verdict in favor of Defendant-Appellee Taser International, Inc. ("Taser") on Powers' claim for strict products liability arising out of the alleged injury he suffered when shocked by the

Advanced Taser M-26 ("M-26").

Taser manufactures and sells conducted energy weapons, including the M-26, which employs electro-muscular disruption (EMD) technology to stimulate a person's motor nerves, causing an involuntary muscle contraction. The evidence at trial was that earlier electric weapon devices affected only the sensory nervous system and relied primarily on pain compliance, which can be overcome by the recipient through focus or when he or she is under the effects of drugs or alcohol. The M-26, however, is designed to affect the sensory and motor nervous systems, overriding the central nervous system and causing uncontrollable muscle contractions that make it physically impossible for a person exposed to the M-26 to not respond to its effects.

On July 16, 2002, Powers was a sixteen-year veteran of the Maricopa County Sheriff's Office ("MCSO"), where he worked as a deputy sheriff. That morning, he participated in a training and certification course offered by the MCSO that was a prerequisite to being certified to carry the M-26. During the course, Powers received training materials prepared by Taser and viewed a PowerPoint Presentation regarding the M-26.

The materials described the M-26 as a "less-lethal" weapon and represented that the M-26 had been (1) tested on animals and found to have no effect on heart rhythms and (2) deployed on more than 3000 persons with no long-term effects. The materials warned, however, that short-term injuries could result from a fall associated with exposure to the M-26, noting that the most significant injuries to date had been "cuts, bruises and abrasions." In addition, as part of the training course, Powers viewed several videos showing individuals being exposed to the M-26.

As part of the course and as a prerequisite for certification to carry the M-26, the MCSO required all officers to be exposed to the electrical force of the M-26. Powers agreed to be exposed to the M-26 and was struck by the device. As a result of his exposure to the M-26, Powers allegedly suffered a compression fracture of his T-7 spinal disc.

Powers' physician, Dr. Terry McLean, discovered while treating Powers for this injury that Powers had severe osteoporosis, a quantitative loss of bone mass that weakens the bones. As a result of his osteoporosis and his physician's orders restricting him to light duty, Powers was unable to continue to work as a deputy sheriff and resigned from the MCSO in June 2003.

Powers filed suit against Taser, alleging that the M-26 was unreasonably dangerous and defective because it lacked adequate instructions and warnings. He alleged that as a direct and proximate result of the defective and unreasonably dangerous condition of the M-26, he suffered severe and permanent injuries for which he sought compensation. Taser argued at trial that because it did not know that the muscle contractions produced by the M-26 were strong enough to cause a fracture, it was not required to warn Powers about such a danger and contested his claimed damages.

The jury returned a general verdict in favor of Taser. Powers moved for a new trial, which was denied. . . .

Powers timely appealed. . . .

II.

A.

Powers argues that Arizona has adopted a "hindsight" approach in strict liability cases involving alleged informational defects and claims the trial court erroneously failed to instruct the jury that it could impute to Taser knowledge of the danger of the M-26 that was revealed subsequent to Taser's distribution of the product. . . .

The trial court ruled before trial that Taser's "duty to warn under a product liability claim for relief is . . . a foresight test, i.e., what the manufacturer of the product knew or reasonably should have known when the product was introduced into the stream of commerce, and not a hindsight test." Consistent with this ruling, throughout the trial the court excluded evidence of subsequent testing of the M-26, except as it pertained to the feasibility of having performed that testing prior to Powers' injury. Despite the court's position, at the conclusion of trial Powers requested that the court instruct the jury that it could impute to Taser knowledge of dangers associated with the M-26 that only became known after Powers' injury. Specifically, Powers requested that the trial court instruct the jury based on alternative 2 set forth in Revised Arizona Jury Instruction-Product Liability 4 (January 2005) ("RAJI 4"). RAJI 4 states:

> [Name of plaintiff] claims that there was not (an) adequate [warning] [instruction] on/with the product. A product, even if faultlessly made, is defective and unreasonably dangerous if it would be unreasonably danger-ous for use in a reasonably foreseeable manner without (an) adequate [warning(s)] [instruction(s)].

[RAJI 4 (2005). The RAJI Committee then gave a choice of two alternatives to complete the instruction. Alternative 1 states]:

> A product is defective and unreasonably dangerous if a manufacturer or seller who knows or should know that a foreseeable use of its product may be unreasonably dangerous does not provide adequate [warning(s) of the danger] [instruction(s) for reasonably safe use].

Id. Alternative 2 provides:

> [A manufacturer or seller is presumed to have known at all relevant times the facts that this accident and this trial have revealed about the harmful characteristics of the product and the consequences of its reasonably foreseeable use, whether or not the manufacturer or seller actually knew those facts. If you find that it would not be reasonable for a manufacturer or seller, with such presumed knowledge, to have put this product on the market without providing (an) adequate [warning(s) of the danger][instruction(s) for reasonably safe use], then the product is defec-tive and unreasonably dangerous.]

Id. Taser objected to Powers' proposed instruction, arguing that because the court had already ruled that it would not apply the hindsight test, the court should instruct the jury based upon alternative 1 to RAJI 4].

In the notes to RAJI 4, the Committee suggests that the court give the first paragraph of the instruction and either the second paragraph or the third paragraph, depending on the circumstances of the case, explaining:

> The Committee was unable to determine, as a result of the Arizona Supreme Court's footnote 2 in *Dart v. Wiebe Manufacturing, Inc.*, 147 Ariz. 242, 709 P.2d 876 (1985), whether a hindsight test is applied in strict liability information defect cases. The court expressly reserved this question in *Dart*. Some members of the Committee hold to the view that *Gosewisch v. American Honda Motor Co.*, 153 Ariz. 400, 737 P.2d 376 (1987), resolves this issue in favor of using a hindsight test. Other members are of the view that until the Arizona Supreme Court actually addresses its reservation in *Dart*, it is reversible error to give a hindsight instruction in an information defect case. The [alternative 1] language is essentially a negligence instruction, but the Committee is unaware of any other alternatives to a hindsight instruction. If a hindsight test is not applicable, then the [alternative 1] language should be used. If a hindsight test is applicable, [alternative 2] language should be used.

RAJI 4, Use Note & Footnotes 1 & 2. The trial court gave a non-hindsight instruction similar to alternative 1, but included language that clarified what Taser should have known:

> Plaintiff claims that there was not an adequate warning on/with the product. A product, even if faultlessly made, is defective and unreasonably dangerous if it would be unreasonably dangerous for use in a reasonably foreseeable manner without an adequate warning(s).

> A product is defective and unreasonably dangerous if a manufacturer or seller who knows or should know that a foreseeable use of its product may be unreasonably dangerous does not provide adequate warning(s) of the danger for reasonably safe use.

> A seller of a product must warn of a particular risk that was known or knowable in light of the generally recognized and prevailing scientific and medical knowledge available at the time of its distribution.

Powers contends the trial court erred by refusing to instruct the jury to apply the hindsight test in this case, and by instead instructing the jury that it could only consider whether, at the time of the M-26's distribution, Taser knew or should have known that the M-26 was unreasonably dangerous unless accompanied by adequate warnings.

B.

The Arizona Supreme Court first adopted an imputed knowledge, or "hindsight," test in *Dart v. Wiebe Manufacturing, Inc.*, a case involving an alleged design defect. 147 Ariz. at 247, 709 P.2d at 881. In that case, the plaintiff sued the manufacturer of an industrial paper shredder after he was seriously injured by a shredding machine.

Id. at 243, 709 P.2d at 877. The plaintiff alleged that the shredder was defectively designed because it lacked safety guards that would have prevented the injury. *Id.* The trial court gave the jury a single instruction regarding the plaintiff's separate theories of negligence and strict liability. *Id.* The Arizona Supreme Court reversed, ruling that in order to preserve the difference between negligence and strict liability theories, the applicable standard for each claim must be different. *Id.*

The court wrote that to prove negligence, a plaintiff must prove that the manufacturer acted unreasonably at the time of manufacture or design of the product. *Id.* at 247, 709 P.2d at 881. However, in a strict liability analysis, "it is not the conduct of the manufacturer or designer which is primarily in question, but rather the quality of the end result; the product is the focus of the inquiry." *Id.* The court thus held that with regard to the plaintiff's claim for strict liability, the jury should have been instructed that the "quality of the product may be measured not only by the information available to the manufacturer at the time of design, *but also by the information available to the trier of fact at the time of trial.*" *Id.* (emphasis added).

The Arizona Supreme Court did not extend this holding to failure to warn cases, and, in fact, expressly declined to reach the issue whether a hindsight test should be applied in strict liability cases involving the failure to warn or those involving inherently dangerous products. *Id.* at 247 n. 2, 709 P.2d at 881 n. 2, ("We do not reach the issue of whether a 'hindsight test' is to be applied to strict liability cases involving failure to warn or those involving unavoidably unsafe products."). Subsequent Arizona cases have reiterated the fundamental difference between negligence and strict products liability theories discussed in *Dart*, but have not extended the hindsight test to failure to warn cases.

In the absence of Arizona law specifically addressing the court's reservation in *Dart*, we would ordinarily follow pre-*Dart* authority, in which Arizona courts applied a foreseeability test in warning cases. *Schneider v. Cessna Aircraft Co.*, 150 Ariz. 153, 158-59, 722 P.2d 321, 326-27 (App.1985) (reversing jury verdict because trial court erroneously refused to instruct jury that defendant could be held strictly liable for failing to warn of product dangers that manufacturer had "reason to foresee"); *Shell Oil Co. v. Gutierrez*, 119 Ariz. 426, 434, 581 P.2d 271, 279 (App.1978) (holding that whether a product is defective or unreasonably dangerous because of a failure to warn depends on foreseeability, seriousness, and the cost of preventing injury). Such an approach would also be consistent with the Restatement (Third) of Torts: Products Liability ("Restatement Third") § 2(c)(1998), which provides that a product:

> [I]s defective because of inadequate instructions or warnings when the foreseeable risks of harm posed by the product could have been reduced or avoided by the provision of reasonable instructions or warnings by the [manufacturer], . . . and the omission of the instructions or warnings renders the product not reasonably safe.[5]

---

[5] This standard further develops the view set forth in the Restatement (Second) of Torts ("Restatement Second") § 402A (1965), which required that a manufacturer give warnings to prevent a product from being unreasonably dangerous only, "if [the manufacturer] has knowledge, or by the

Absent controlling Arizona law to the contrary, we generally follow the Restatement, provided we deem it good legal authority. *In re Krohn*, 203 Ariz. 205, 210, 18, 52 P.3d 774, 779 (2002) (stating the Arizona Supreme Court has long followed the rule that it will follow the Restatement when not bound by previous decisions or legislative enactment); *Southwest Pet Prod., Inc., v. Koch Indus.*, 273 F. Supp. 2d 1041, 1052 n.17 (D.Ariz.2003) (stating reliance on Restatement Third is in keeping with "Arizona's long-standing policy to look to the Restatement absent contrary precedent."). However, we do not follow the Restatement blindly, *Barnes*, 192 Ariz. at 285, 6, 964 P.2d at 486, and will come to a contrary conclusion if Arizona law suggests otherwise. *Wilcox v. Waldman*, 154 Ariz. 532, 536, 744 P.2d 444, 448 (App.1987). Powers argues that we should not follow pre-*Dart* Arizona warning defect cases and the Restatement, and instead urges us to extend the Arizona Supreme Court's holding in *Dart* to warning defect cases, contending that the considerations the court relied on in *Dart* when adopting the hindsight test support the application of the same test in warning defect cases. We therefore consider whether the Restatement position is good legal authority under Arizona law, particularly in light of *Dart*.

C.

The court in *Dart* focused on the differences between the doctrine of negligence, which centers on the reasonableness of the manufacturer's conduct, and the doctrine of strict liability, which centers on the quality of the product. 147 Ariz. at 246-47, 709 P.2d at 880-81. The court ruled that by imposing on the manufacturer constructive knowledge of the condition of the product as revealed at trial, the inquiry would remain focused on the quality of the product, rather than on the reasonableness of the manufacturer's conduct in selecting the particular product design. *Id.* at 247, 709 P.2d at 881. In adopting this test, the court noted that it was "generally recommended by the commentators, and by precedent." *Id.* However, this circumstance has since changed, as the initial proponents of the hindsight doctrine later withdrew their support for the view, observing that a product's design should be measured in terms of the technology available at the time of manufacture. *See* Restatement Third § 2 cmt. m(1) (citing numerous academic articles taking issue with the validity of the hindsight approach).

Accordingly, the standard adopted by the Arizona Supreme Court in *Dart* is inconsistent with the recently adopted Restatement Third, which provides that a product is defective in design when "the *foreseeable* risks of harm posed by the product could have been reduced or avoided by the adoption of a reasonable alternative design." Restatement Third § 2(b) (emphasis added). In adopting this view, the American Law Institute expressly rejected the hindsight approach in design defect cases, citing widespread academic criticism of, and relatively thin judicial support for, the theory. Restatement Third § 2, note m.1 ("Given the criticism that has been leveled against the imputation of knowledge doctrine and the

---

application of reasonable, developed human skill and foresight should have knowledge, of the presence of the . . . danger." Restatement Second § 402A cmt. j. The Restatement Third § 2 approach to warning defects thus parallels the standard set forth for determining design defects. Restatement Third § 2, cmt. i.

relatively thin judicial support for it, it is here rejected as a doctrinal matter."). We are, of course, bound by the Arizona Supreme Court's holding in *Dart* as it applies to design defect cases, even though the authorities the court relied upon in *Dart* have been modified. *City of Phoenix v. Leroy's Liquors Inc.*, 177 Ariz. 375, 378, 868 P.2d 958, 961 (App.1993) (stating court of appeals is bound by decisions of the supreme court and may not "overrule, modify or disregard them"). Nevertheless, we give due regard to this recent criticism and authority when evaluating whether we should extend the holding in *Dart* to warning defect cases.

There are other reasons not to extend *Dart* to warning defect cases. The nature of a design defect case is fundamentally different than a failure to warn case. *See Anderson v. Owens-Corning Fiberglas Corp.*, 53 Cal.3d 987, 1002, 281 Cal.Rptr. 528, 810 P.2d 549, 558 (1991) (positing that the warning defect theory is "rooted in negligence" to a greater extent than manufacturing or design defect theories). Accordingly, the same analysis applied by the court in *Dart* cannot simply be imported wholesale to determine the proper standard in a warnings defect case. "The 'warning defect' relates to a failure extraneous to the product itself. Thus, while a manufacturing or design defect *can be* evaluated without reference to the conduct of the manufacturer, the giving of a warning cannot." *Id.* (emphasis in original) (internal citations omitted). The Arizona Supreme Court impliedly recognized this essential distinction in *Dart* when it refused to extend the hindsight test to warning defect claims, citing *Kearl v. Lederle Labs.*, 172 Cal.App.3d 812, 218 Cal.Rptr. 453 (1985).

The California Court of Appeal ruled in *Kearl* that a products liability claim based on a failure to warn about an unavoidably dangerous product could not be brought in strict liability, only negligence, because the adequacy of the manufacturer's warning must be based on a determination regarding what it knew or should have known. *Id.* at 832-33, 218 Cal.Rptr. 453. Although the California Supreme Court later overruled *Kearl* in *Brown v. Superior Court*, 44 Cal.3d 1049, 1069, 245 Cal.Rptr. 412, 751 P.2d 470, 482-83 (1988), holding that a claim may be brought in strict liability for failure to warn of unavoidably dangerous products, the court in *Brown* reiterated that the applicable standard is *foreseeability*, stating that a product must be "accompanied by warnings of its dangerous propensities that were either known or reasonably scientifically knowable at the time of distribution." 44 Cal.3d at 1068-69, 245 Cal.Rptr. 412, 751 P.2d at 483.[6]

Moreover, as the California Supreme Court has recognized, applying a foresight test does not eliminate the distinction between negligence and strict liability:

> [D]espite its roots in negligence, failure to warn in strict liability differs markedly from failure to warn in the negligence context. Negligence law in a failure-to-warn case requires a plaintiff to prove that a manufacturer or distributor did not warn of a particular risk for reasons which fell below the acceptable standard of care, i.e., what a reasonably prudent manufacturer would have known and warned about. Strict liability is not concerned with

---

[6] Both *Kearl* and *Brown* involved pharmaceutical products. In *Anderson*, the California Supreme Court extended its holding in *Brown* to cases not involving prescription drugs. 53 Cal.3d at 1000, 281 Cal.Rptr. 528, 810 P.2d at 557.

the standard of due care or the reasonableness of a manufacturer's conduct. The rules of strict liability require a plaintiff to prove only that the defendant did not adequately warn of a particular risk that was known or knowable in light of the generally recognized and prevailing best scientific and medical knowledge available at the time of manufacture and distribution. *Thus, in strict liability, as opposed to negligence, the reasonableness of the defendant's failure to warn is immaterial.*

Anderson, 53 Cal.3d at 1002-03, 281 Cal.Rptr. 528, 810 P.2d at 558-59 (emphasis added). Thus, applying a foresight test in failure to warn cases would not eliminate the distinction between negligence and strict liability as the court in *Dart* was concerned would happen in design defect cases.

Finally, it is our view that employing the hindsight test in warning defect cases would be tantamount to imposing a duty on manufacturers to warn of unknowable dangers. *Id.* at 998, 281 Cal.Rptr. 528, 810 P.2d at 555 ("To exact an obligation to warn the user of unknown and unknowable allergies, sensitivities and idiosyncrasies would be for the courts to recast the manufacturer in the role of an insurer. . . ."). As the Arizona Supreme Court recognized in *Dart*, however, the doctrine of strict liability does not impose liability for every injury caused by a product. 147 Ariz. at 244, 709 P.2d at 878. *See also Anderson*, 53 Cal.3d at 994, 281 Cal.Rptr. 528, 810 P.2d at 552 ("From its inception, . . . strict liability has never been, and is not now, *absolute* liability . . . [U]nder strict liability the manufacturer does not thereby become the insurer of the safety of the product's use.") (citations omitted); Restatement Third § 2, note M ("Unforeseeable risks arising from foreseeable product use or consumption by definition cannot specifically be warned against. . . . A seller is charged with knowledge of what reasonable testing would reveal."). For this reason, a majority of jurisdictions reject the approach in warning defect cases, instead requiring a manufacturer to warn only of risks that were known or should have been known to a reasonable manufacturer. *See, e.g., Anderson*, 53 Cal.3d at 999, 281 Cal.Rptr. 528, 810 P.2d at 557 (holding that "knowledge, actual or constructive, is a requisite for strict liability for failure to warn."); *Fibreboard Corp. v. Fenton*, 845 P.2d 1168, 1172 (Colo.1993) ("We agree with the petitioners that state-of-the-art evidence is properly admissible to establish that a product is not defective and unreasonably dangerous because of a failure-to-warn. A manufacturer cannot warn of dangers that were not known to it or knowable in light of the generally recognized and prevailing scientific and technical knowledge available at the time of manufacture and distribution."); *Woodill v. Parke Davis & Co.*, 79 Ill.2d 26, 37 Ill.Dec. 304, 402 N.E.2d 194, 198 (1980) ("requiring a plaintiff to plead and prove that the defendant manufacturer knew or should have known of the danger that caused the injury, and that the defendant manufacturer failed to warn plaintiff of that danger, is a reasonable requirement, and one which focuses on the nature of the product and the adequacy of the warning, rather than on the conduct of the manufacturer").

Accordingly, we decline to extend Arizona law to adopt the hindsight test from *Dart* in failure to warn strict liability cases. The trial court did not err by instructing the jury that it could only consider whether, at the time of the M-26's distribution, Taser knew or should have known that the M-26 was unreasonably dangerous unless accompanied by an adequate warning. . . .

1. In holding a manufacturer liable for failing to warn of an unknowable danger, is the court asking the manufacturer to do the impossible? Even if the answer to this question is "yes," does that mean that the manufacturer should not be liable? As between a non-negligent plaintiff and a non-negligent manufacturer, strict products liability at least in theory mandates that the loss should fall on the manufacturer, and not on the equally innocent plaintiff. Indeed, if the manufacturer is negligent in failing to warn of a knowable danger, the plaintiff will not need strict liability in order to prevail.

2. What does "state of the art" mean? There are several possibilities, including (but not limited to) "state of industry knowledge of the danger" and "state of industry knowledge of the cure." Industry knowledge of the cure has never been imputed under Section 402A. How satisfactory is the *Powers* Court's analysis of the two concepts?

3. What impact does abolishing the imputation of knowledge have on Section 402A? On strict products liability generally? Many courts have used comment j in the way that the *Powers* Court did. Compare the quotation from comment j in *Powers* with the full comment, included in *Sternhagen*.

4. The Third Restatement of the Law, Torts: Products Liability makes several changes to the Second. These changes have proven to be of fundamental importance, particularly in the realms of design and warning defects. Section 2(b) of the Third Restatement defines defective design as follows: "A product is defective in design when the foreseeable risks of harm posed by the product could have been reduced or avoided by the adoption of a reasonable alternative design . . . and the omission of the alternative design renders the product not reasonably safe." How is this different from the concept of design defect in the Second Restatement? It is worth noting that the Second Restatement does not make a reasonable alternative design a *sine qua non* of the plaintiff's case.

Section 2(c) of the Third Restatement defines defective warnings as follows: "A product is defective because of inadequate instructions or warnings when the foreseeable risks of harm posed by the product could have been reduced or avoided by the provision of reasonable instructions or warnings . . . and the omission of the instructions or warnings renders the product not reasonably safe." How does this differ from the Second Restatement concept of warning defect?

5. The Third Restatement leaves liability for mismanufacture basically intact: a plaintiff may use res ipsa loquitur doctrine in making his or her case that a product failed because the individual unit deviated from the norm for the particular product. The Third Restatement makes clear, however, that plaintiffs may no longer use res ipsa doctrine in proving that a product suffered from a design or warning defect. Reporters' Note 2 states that "Section 3 applies in most instances to manufacturing defects only."

6. There are products the dangers of which cannot be eliminated by the adoption of a reasonable alternative design, but which, unlike vaccines, fail any applicable risk/utility test. The most familiar such product is the cigarette. Could a manufacturer be liable for such a product under the Second Restatement? Under the Third?

PROBLEM

When C breaks his leg, the surgeons decide to attach the broken pieces together with a plate, which screws directly to the bone. Several months later, one of the screws fails, and C is seriously injured.

C files suit against the manufacturer of the screw. He cannot show why the screw failed. He can prove that he followed all the directions he was given after the surgery, and that he was not informed prior to surgery that the screw might fail. He can also prove that, under magnification, the screw contained "inclusions," microscopic bits of substances other than that metal of which the screw was made. The manufacturer can prove that all screws — indeed, all objects made of metal — contain inclusions.

What will C argue in a lawsuit filed under the Second Restatement? Under the Third Restatement? How will the manufacturer respond? What result under each of the Restatements?

4. Defining Defect Where the Product Is a Prescription Drug

FREEMAN v. HOFFMAN-LA ROCHE, INC.
Supreme Court of Nebraska, 2000
618 N.W.2d 827

CONNOLLY, J.

In this appeal, we reconsider our approach to products liability for defects in prescription drugs in light of changes in the law and the release of Restatement (Third) of Torts: Products Liability §§ 1 to 21 (1997) (Third Restatement). . . .

I. BACKGROUND

Freeman's operative petition alleged the following facts: On or about September 23, 1995, Freeman presented herself to her physician for treatment of chronic acne. After examination, her physician prescribed 20 milligrams daily of Accutane. Hoffman is the designer, manufacturer, wholesaler, retailer, fabricator, and supplier of Accutane.

Freeman took the Accutane daily from September 27 through October 2, 1995, and from October 4 through November 20, 1995. Hoffman alleged that as a result of taking the Accutane, she developed multiple health problems. These problems included ulcerative colitis, inflammatory polyarthritis, nodular episcleritis OS, and optic nerve head drusen. As a result, Freeman alleged that she sustained various damages. . . .

IV. ANALYSIS

Freeman contends that she has stated a cause of action for products liability under a variety of theories of recovery. Before proceeding, we believe it helpful to set forth a brief history of the general principles of products liability law and its development since the adoption of Restatement (Second) of Torts § 402 A (1965) (Second Restatement).

In products liability litigation, the notion of a defective product embraces two separate concepts. The first, commonly labeled as a manufacturing defect, is one in which the product differs from the specifications and plan of the manufacturer. The second concept of a defective product is one in which the product meets the specifications of the manufacturer but the product nonetheless poses an unreasonable risk of danger. This condition is generally characterized as a design defect. A manufacturer may also be liable for a failure to warn.

In products liability cases, there is a significant distinction between a manufacturer's liability as the result of negligent manufacture and its liability for the manufactured product on account of strict liability in tort. In a cause of action based on negligence, the question involves the manufacturer's conduct, that is, whether the manufacturer's conduct was reasonable in view of the foreseeable risk of injury; whereas in a cause of action based on strict liability in tort, the question involves the quality of the product, that is, whether the product was unreasonably dangerous.

For organizational purposes, we address Freeman's allegations of product defects in terms of the defects which she attempts to allege: design, manufacturing, and warning.

1. DESIGN DEFECT

In her operative petition, Freeman alleges that Hoffman is strictly liable for her injuries on the bases that Accutane was not fit for its intended purpose, that the risks inherent in the design outweighed the benefits of its use, and that Accutane was more dangerous to Freeman than was anticipated due to undisclosed side effects. As facts supporting her allegations, Freeman alleges that Accutane is sold as an acne medication and that the side effects of Accutane present life-threatening conditions. Thus, Freeman's petition asserts that Hoffman is liable on the basis of a design defect. Hoffman, however, alleges that because Accutane was approved by the FDA, it is exempted from liability for a design defect pursuant to our decision in *McDaniel v. McNeil Laboratories, Inc.*, 196 Neb. 190, 241 N.W.2d 822 (1976).

(a) Second Restatement § 402 A

In dealing with products other than prescription drugs, this court has recognized a manufacturer's liability in tort for design defects. Liability arises when an article a manufacturer has placed in the market, knowing that it is to be used without inspection for defects, proves to have a defect which causes an injury to a human being rightfully using the product. We have also adopted and applied the test set out in the Second Restatement § 402 A.

Section 402 A at 347-48 provides:

(1) One who sells any product in a defective condition unreasonably dangerous to the user or consumer or to his property is subject to liability for physical harm thereby caused to the ultimate user or consumer, or to his property, if

(a) the seller is engaged in the business of selling such a product, and

(b) it is expected to and does reach the user or consumer without substantial change in the condition in which it is sold.

(2) The rule stated in Subsection (1) applies although

(a) the seller has exercised all possible care in the preparation and sale of his product, and

(b) the user or consumer has not bought the product from or entered into any contractual relation with the seller.

Comment *i.* at 352 provides that the rule stated in § 402 A

applies only where the defective condition of the product makes it unreasonably dangerous to the user or consumer. . . . The article sold must be dangerous to an extent beyond that which would be contemplated by the ordinary consumer who purchases it, with the ordinary knowledge common to the community as to its characteristics.

This is commonly referred to as the "consumer expectations test."

In *Rahmig v. Mosley Machinery Co.*, 226 Neb. 423, 412 N.W.2d 56 (1987), we discussed criticisms of the consumer expectations test as embodied in § 402 A and the application in other jurisdictions of a risk-utility test in determining whether a product is unreasonably dangerous. We noted, however, that the issue of whether to adopt a risk-utility test was not before us. We then specifically overruled cases indicating that a plaintiff must present evidence of a reasonable alternative design in cases involving design defects.

Since *Rahmig*, we have applied the consumer expectations test for strict liability. See, e.g., *Haag v. Bongers*, 256 Neb. 170, 589 N.W.2d 318 (1999). Under this test, " '[u]nreasonably dangerous' means that a product has the propensity for causing physical harm beyond that which would be contemplated by the ordinary user or consumer who purchases it, with ordinary knowledge common to the foreseeable class of users as to its characteristics." *Id.* at 184, 589 N.W.2d at 329. Thus, in regard to nonprescription drug products, we have generally followed the rule as set out in § 402 A of the Second Restatement. Prescription drugs, however, have been treated differently both by this court and by the Second Restatement.

(i) Comment k. Exception for Unavoidably Unsafe Products

Under the Second Restatement, prescription drugs are treated specially under § 402 A, comment *k.* Comment *k.* at 353-54 provides an exception from strict liability when a product is deemed to be "unavoidably unsafe" and states:

There are some products which, in the present state of human knowledge, are quite incapable of being made safe for their intended and ordinary use.

These are especially common in the field of drugs. An outstanding example is the vaccine for the Pasteur treatment of rabies, which not uncommonly leads to very serious and damaging consequences when it is injected. Since the disease itself invariably leads to a dreadful death, both the marketing and the use of the vaccine are fully justified, notwithstanding the unavoidable high degree of risk which they involve. Such a product, properly prepared, and accompanied by proper directions and warning, is not defective, nor is it unreasonably dangerous. The same is true of many other drugs, vaccines, and the like, many of which for this very reason cannot legally be sold except to physicians, or under the prescription of a physician. It is also true in particular of many new or experimental drugs as to which, because of lack of time and opportunity for sufficient medical experience, there can be no assurance of safety, or perhaps even of purity of ingredients, but such experience as there is justifies the marketing and use of the drug notwithstanding a medically recognizable risk. The seller of such products, again with the qualification that they are properly prepared and marketed, and proper warning is given, where the situation calls for it, is not to be held to strict liability for unfortunate consequences attending their use, merely because he has undertaken to supply the public with an apparently useful and desirable product, attended with a known but apparently reasonable risk.

Application of comment *k.* has been justified under the law in some jurisdictions as a way to strike a balance between a manufacturer's responsibility and the encouragement of research and development of new products. Under certain instances, it is in the public interest to allow products to be marketed which are unsafe, because the benefits of the product justify its risks. See, *Hill v. Searle Laboratories*, 884 F.2d 1064 (8th Cir. 1989) (describing policy considerations); *Tansy v. Dacomed Corp.*, 890 P.2d 881 (Okla.1994).

We applied § 402 A, comment *k.*, to a products liability action involving a prescription drug in *McDaniel v. McNeil Laboratories, Inc.*, 196 Neb. 190, 241 N.W.2d 822 (1976). In *McDaniel*, a woman was rendered permanently comatose after being given doses of a prescription drug, Innovar, during surgery. At the time of her surgery, Innovar and the warnings and information contained in the package inserts had been approved for use by the FDA. At trial, it was contended that the manufacturer was negligent in failing to warn, strictly liable under § 402 A of the Second Restatement, and liable under a theory of either express or implied warranty. The trial court submitted the issue of negligence to the jury but did not submit the issue of strict liability or warranty to the jury. On appeal, we placed emphasis on FDA approval of the drug, and citing to § 402 A, comment *k.*, we held:

> An unavoidably unsafe drug which has been approved for marketing by the United States Food and Drug Administration, properly prepared, compounded, packaged, and distributed, and accompanied by proper approved directions and warnings, as a matter of law, is not defective nor unreasonably dangerous, in the absence of proof of inaccurate, incomplete, misleading, or fraudulent information furnished by the manufacturer in connection with such federal approval or later revisions thereof.

McDaniel, 196 Neb. at 201, 241 N.W.2d at 828. Under the evidence presented, we determined that it was not error for the trial court to refuse to submit the issue of strict liability or warranty either express or implied, to the jury.

(ii) Interpretation of Comment k. in Other Jurisdictions

Comment *k.*, however, has been interpreted in a variety of ways in other jurisdictions, and there has been a wide range of disagreement regarding its application.

Only a few jurisdictions have interpreted comment *k.* in a manner that strictly excepts all prescription drugs from strict liability. Under the minority view, a drug that is properly manufactured and accompanied by an adequate warning of the risks known to the manufacturer at the time of sale is not defectively designed as a matter of law. *Brown v. Superior Court (Abbott Laboratories)*, 44 Cal.3d 1049, 245 Cal.Rptr. 412, 751 P.2d 470 (1988); *Grundberg v. Upjohn Co.*, 813 P.2d 89 (Utah 1991); *Young v. Key Pharmaceuticals*, 130 Wash.2d 160, 922 P.2d 59 (1996) (en banc). These jurisdictions are commonly described by legal commentators as providing manufacturers with a "blanket immunity" from strict liability for design defects in prescription drugs. See, e.g., Winchester, *supra*. Our decision in *McDaniel, supra*, generally falls under this category of interpretation of comment *k.*

(iii) Cases Applying Risk-Utility Analysis Under Comment k.

An application of comment *k.* to provide a blanket immunity from strict liability is widely criticized. Comment *k.* has proved to be difficult to interpret and apply, thus, supporting the argument that it should not be applied so strictly. Further, it is said that an approach that entirely excepts manufacturers from [liability] limits the discretionary powers of the courts. Also, it is argued that a blanket immunity leads to patently unjust results. One court has stated:

> We believe that a more selective application [of comment *k.*] will encourage, rather than discourage, improvements in prescription products. Comment k was designed in part to protect new and experimental drugs. . . . "Comment k states: 'There are some products which, in the present state of human knowledge, are quite incapable of being made safe for their intended and ordinary use.' Obviously, for this to be true, the design must be as safe as the best available testing and research permits." . . . Thus, a product which is as safe as current testing and research permits should be protected. The reverse is also true; a product which is not as safe as current technology can make it should not be protected.

(Citation omitted.) *Adams v. G.D. Searle & Co., Inc.*, 576 So. 2d 728, 732 (Fla.App.1991).

The majority of jurisdictions that have adopted comment *k.* apply it on a case-by-case basis, believing that societal interests in ensuring the marketing and development of prescription drugs will be adequately served without the need to resort to a rule of blanket immunity. A few courts have not specifically adopted comment *k.* and have instead either fashioned their own rules or treated prescription drugs in the same manner as that of all other products.

Although a variety of tests are employed among jurisdictions that apply comment *k.* on a case-by-case basis, the majority apply the comment as an affirmative defense, with the trend toward the use of a risk-utility test in order to determine whether the defense applies. When a risk-utility test is applied, the existence of a reasonable alternative design is generally the central factor. Because the application of comment *k.* is traditionally viewed as an exception and a defense to strict liability, courts generally place the initial burden of proving the various risk utility factors on the defendant. Thus, under these cases, the plaintiff's burden of proof for his or her prima facie case remains the same as it is in any products liability case in the given jurisdiction.

At the time *McDaniel v. McNeil Laboratories, Inc.*, 196 Neb. 190, 241 N.W.2d 822 (1976), was decided, it reflected a minority view. Since that time, a clear majority of courts have decided on a case-by-case basis, through the application of a comment *k.* defense, the issue of liability of a manufacturer for a design defect in a prescription drug. On further reflection, we conclude that the rule of law expressed in *McDaniel* has not held up over time. We now believe that societal interests in ensuring the marketing and development of prescription drugs can be served without resorting to a rule which in effect amounts to a blanket immunity from strict liability for manufacturers. Accordingly, we overrule *McDaniel* to the extent it applies comment *k.* to provide a blanket immunity from strict liability for prescription drugs. Accordingly, we must address how, or if, comment *k.* should be applied, or whether we should consider adopting provisions of the Third Restatement. We next address those provisions in considering what test should be applied.

(b) Third Restatement

The provisions of the Second Restatement regarding products liability were changed dramatically in the Third Restatement, published by the American Law Institute in 1997. As stated in the introduction to the Third Restatement, the institute was required to answer questions that were not part of the products liability landscape when the Second Restatement was completed. Thus, the Third Restatement is a complete overhaul of the Second Restatement in the area of products liability.

Section 6 of the Third Restatement pertains specifically to prescription drugs, with § 6(c) applying to design defects. Section 6 at 144-45 states in part:

(a) A manufacturer of a prescription drug or medical device who sells or otherwise distributes a defective drug or medical device is subject to liability for harm to persons caused by the defect. A prescription drug or medical device is one that may be legally sold or otherwise distributed only pursuant to a health-care provider's prescription.

(b) For purposes of liability under Subsection (a), a prescription drug or medical device is defective if at the time of sale or other distribution the drug or medical device:

(1) contains a manufacturing defect as defined in § 2(a); or

(2) is not reasonably safe due to defective design as defined in Subsection (c); or

(3) is not reasonably safe due to inadequate instructions or warnings as defined in Subsection (d).

(c) A prescription drug or medical device is not reasonably safe due to defective design if the foreseeable risks of harm posed by the drug or medical device are sufficiently great in relation to its foreseeable therapeutic benefits that reasonable health-care providers, knowing of such foreseeable risks and therapeutic benefits, would not prescribe the drug or medical device for any class of patients.

In addition, § 6, comment *b.* at 146-47, states in part:

The traditional refusal by courts to impose tort liability for defective designs of prescription drugs and medical devices is based on the fact that a prescription drug or medical device entails a unique set of risks and benefits. What may be harmful to one patient may be beneficial to another. Under Subsection (c) a drug is defectively designed only when it provides no net benefit to any class of patients. Courts have concluded that as long as a drug or medical device provides net benefits to some persons under some circumstances, the drug or device manufacturer should be required to instruct and warn health-care providers of the foreseeable risks and benefits. Courts have also recognized that the regulatory system governing prescription drugs is a legitimate mechanism for setting the standards for drug design. In part, this deference reflects concerns over the possible negative effects of judicially imposed liability on the cost and availability of valuable medical technology. This deference also rests on two further assumptions: first, that prescribing health-care providers, when adequately informed by drug manufacturers, are able to assure that the right drugs and medical devices reach the right patients; and second, that governmental regulatory agencies adequately review new prescription drugs and devices, keeping unreasonably dangerous designs off the market.

Nevertheless, unqualified deference to these regulatory mechanisms is considered by a growing number of courts to be unjustified. An approved prescription drug or medical device can present significant risks without corresponding advantages. At the same time, manufacturers must have ample discretion to develop useful drugs and devices without subjecting their design decisions to the ordinary test applicable to products generally under § 2(b). Accordingly, Subsection (c) imposes a more rigorous test for defect than does § 2(b), which does not apply to prescription drugs and medical devices. . . .

. . .

. Subsections (c) and (d) recognize common-law causes of action for 'ective drug design and for failure to provide reasonable instructions or nings, even though the manufacturer complied with governmental lards.

Section 6, comment *f.* at 149, states in part:

> A prescription drug or device manufacturer defeats a plaintiff's design claim by establishing one or more contexts in which its product would be prescribed by reasonable, informed health-care providers. That some individual providers do, in fact, prescribe defendant's product does not in itself suffice to defeat the plaintiff's claim. Evidence regarding the actual conduct of health-care providers, while relevant and admissible, is not necessarily controlling. The issue is whether, objectively viewed, reasonable providers, knowing of the foreseeable risks and benefits of the drug or medical device, would prescribe it for any class of patients. Given this very demanding objective standard, liability is likely to be imposed only under unusual circumstances. The court has the responsibility to determine when the plaintiff has introduced sufficient evidence so that reasonable persons could conclude that plaintiff has met this demanding standard.

As of this writing, no state court has faced the issue of whether to adopt § 6(c). A few federal courts have discussed this section, but only to the extent of either predicting whether the applicable state court would adopt § 6(c) or declining to apply it in the absence of state precedent.

There are several criticisms of § 6(c), which will be briefly summarized. First, it does not accurately restate the law. It has been repeatedly stated that there is no support in the case law for the application of a reasonable physician standard in which strict liability for a design defect will apply only when a product is not useful for any class of persons. Rather, as illustrated by the discussion of the treatment of comment *k.* under the Second Restatement in other jurisdictions, the majority of courts apply some form of risk-utility balancing that focuses on a variety of factors, including the existence of a reasonable alternative design. The few cases that the Third Restatement cites to as support for the reasonable physician test also apply a risk-utility test. Thus, § 6(c) does not restate the law and instead seeks to formulate new law with no precedential support.

Second, the reasonable physician test is criticized as being artificial and difficult to apply. The test requires fact finders to presume that physicians have as much or more of an awareness about a prescription drug product as the manufacturer. The test also ignores concerns of commentators that physicians tend to prescribe drugs they are familiar with or for which they have received advertising material, even when studies indicate that better alternatives are available.

A third criticism of particular applicability to Freeman's case is that the test lacks flexibility and treats drugs of unequal utility equally. For example, a drug used for cosmetic purposes but which causes serious side effects has less utility than a drug which treats a deadly disease, yet also has serious side effects. In each case, the drugs would likely be useful to a class of patients under the reasonable physician standard for some class of persons. Consequently, each would be exempted from design defect liability. But under a standard that considers reasonable alternative design, the cosmetic drug could be subject to liability if a safer yet equally effective design was available. As a result, the reasonable physician standard of § 6(c) of the Third Restatement has been described as a standard that in effect will never allow liability. However, a standard applying a risk-utility test that focuses on the presence or absence of a reasonable alternative design, although also rarely allowing liability, at least allows the flexibility for liability to attach in an appropriate case.

Fourth, the test allows a consumer's claim to be defeated simply by a statement from the defense's expert witness that the drug at issue had some benefit for any single class of people. Thus, it is argued that application of § 6(c) will likely shield pharmaceutical companies from a wide variety of suits that could have been brought under comment *k.* of the Second Restatement. As the Third Restatement, § 6(c), comment *f.* at 149, states in part: "Given this very demanding objective standard, liability is likely to be imposed only under unusual circumstances." Thus, even though the rule is reformulated, any application of § 6(c) will essentially provide the same blanket immunity from liability for design defects in prescription drugs as did the application of comment *k.* in the few states that interpreted it as such.

We conclude that § 6(c) has no basis in the case law. We view § 6(c) as too strict of a rule, under which recovery would be nearly impossible. Accordingly, we do not adopt § 6(c) of the Third Restatement. . . .

We conclude that § 402 A, comment *k.*, of the Second Restatement should be applied on a case-by-case basis and as an affirmative defense in cases involving prescription drug products. Under this rule, an application of the comment does not provide a blanket immunity from strict liability for prescription drugs. Rather, the plaintiff is required to plead the consumer expectations test, as he or she would be required to do in any products liability case. The defendant may then raise comment *k.* as an affirmative defense. The comment will apply to except the prescription drug product from strict liability when it is shown that (1) the product is properly manufactured and contains adequate warnings, (2) its benefits justify its risks, and (3) the product was at the time of manufacture and distribution incapable of being made more safe.

In this case, because the application of comment *k.* is an affirmative defense, Freeman was only required to plead that the Accutane she took was unreasonably dangerous under a consumer expectations test. Freeman alleged that Accutane was unreasonably dangerous for use, that it was not fit for its intended purpose, that the risks inherent in the design outweighed the benefits of its use, and that Accutane was more dangerous to Freeman than was anticipated due to undisclosed side effects. As facts supporting her allegations, Freeman alleged that Accutane is sold as an acne medication and that the side effects of Accutane present life-threatening conditions. Thus, Freeman alleged facts that the Accutane was dangerous to an extent beyond that which would be contemplated by the ordinary consumer who purchases it, with the ordinary knowledge common to the community as to its characteristics. Accordingly, we conclude that Freeman has stated a theory of recovery based on a design defect. . . .

3. FAILURE TO WARN

Freeman alleges that Hoffman was negligent in failing to warn of dangers associated with the use of Accutane. Freeman also alleges that Hoffman failed to warn that Accutane was not adequately tested.

Under the Third Restatement § 2(c) at 14,

> [a product] is defective because of inadequate instructions or warnings when the foreseeable risks of harm posed by the product could have been reduced or avoided by the provision of reasonable instructions or warnings by the seller or other distributor, or a predecessor in the commercial chain of distribution, and the omission of the instructions or warnings renders the product not reasonably safe.

The Third Restatement reflects the same rule this court has applied in regard to a failure to warn. We have stated:

> In a products liability case based on negligence and the duty to warn: "A manufacturer or other seller is subject to liability for failing either to warn or adequately to warn about a risk or hazard inherent in the way a product is designed that is related to the intended uses as well as the reasonably foreseeable uses that may be made of the products it sells." . . . "[A] manufacturer's duty to produce a safe product, with appropriate warnings and instructions when necessary, is no different from the responsibility each of us bears to exercise due care to avoid unreasonable risks of harm to others. . . ."

Rahmig, 226 Neb. at 446, 412 N.W.2d at 72.

Pharmaceutical products have historically been treated differently in regard to a duty to warn. Although in ordinary product cases, a manufacturer's duty to warn runs directly to the consumer of the product, in cases involving prescription drugs, it is widely held that the duty to warn extends only to members of the medical profession and not to the consumer. This concept is known as the learned intermediary doctrine. . . .

The learned intermediary doctrine is provided for in § 6(d) of the Third Restatement. Section 6(d) at 145 states:

> A prescription drug or medical device is not reasonably safe due to inadequate instructions or warnings if reasonable instructions or warnings regarding foreseeable risks of harm are not provided to:
>
> (1) prescribing and other health-care providers who are in a position to reduce the risks of harm in accordance with the instructions or warnings; or
>
> (2) the patient when the manufacturer knows or has reason to know that health-care providers will not be in a position to reduce the risks of harm in accordance with the instructions or warnings.

We have not specifically adopted the learned intermediary doctrine as the applicable test for determining whether a manufacturer may be liable for a warning defect in prescription drug cases. However, with a few exceptions for instances where special facts require a direct warning to the consumer, the doctrine is followed in virtually all jurisdictions that have considered whether to adopt it. The doctrine as stated in the Third Restatement has also been adopted in other jurisdictions. We adopt § 6(d) of the Third Restatement. Accordingly, we apply the learned intermediary doctrine to Freeman's case.

The section of Freeman's petition devoted to factual allegations alleges that Hoffman failed to warn of Accutane's dangers in the package insert provided to physicians, including Freeman's physician. Freeman makes further allegations regarding Hoffman's failure to provide her with warnings under the section specifically devoted to her theory of recovery for a failure to warn. Thus, we conclude that Freeman has stated a theory of recovery for liability based on a warning defect. . . .

5. Alternative Feasible Designs in the Third Restatement

As was mentioned above, section 402A of the Second Restatement did not require an alternative feasible design in strict products liability cases based on design effects. The Third Restatement requires a reasonable alternative design in every case based upon defective design. The following case discusses this requirement.

MIKOLAJCZYK v. FORD MOTOR COMPANY
Supreme Court of Illinois, 2008
901 N.E.2d 329

JUSTICE GARMAN delivered the judgment of the court, with opinion:

James Mikolajczyk died of injuries sustained when the Ford Escort he was driving was struck from behind by another vehicle. His widow, as special administrator of his estate, sued the other driver, claiming negligence, and Ford Motor Company and Mazda Motor Corporation, claiming defective design of the driver's seat. Summary judgment was entered against the other driver. The claims against the other two defendants proceeded to a jury trial in the circuit court of Cook County. The jury found defendants liable. . . .

BACKGROUND

On February 4, 2000, William Timberlake shared two pints of gin with a friend before getting behind the wheel of his Cadillac. He was traveling approximately 60 miles per hour when he smashed into the rear of a 1996 Ford Escort that was stopped at a red light. The driver of the Escort, James Mikolajczyk, suffered severe, irreversible brain trauma and spent several days on life support before his death. His daughter, Elizabeth, then aged 10, who was asleep in the backseat at the time of the accident, suffered two broken legs. James was also survived by his wife, Connie, and son, Adam, then aged 14.

Plaintiff's negligence suit against defendant Timberlake resulted in the entry of summary judgment. Plaintiff's lawsuit against defendants Ford and Mazda alleged strict product liability premised on defective design of the driver's seat of the Escort. Specifically, she claimed that as a result of the defective design of the seat, it collapsed when the car was struck from behind, causing James to be propelled rearward and to strike his head on the backseat of the car. Plaintiff further alleged that the design of the seat was unreasonably dangerous and that the design defect proximately caused James's death. The Escort was manufactured by defendant Ford. The seat was designed by defendant Mazda; Ford had the authority to approve or disapprove the design.

The trial testimony is summarized in detail in the appellate court opinion. 374 Ill.App.3d at 650-53, 312 Ill.Dec. 441, 870 N.E.2d 885. For purposes of this appeal, it is necessary to note only that the evidence included testimony by expert witnesses for both parties regarding the risks and benefits posed by the "yielding" seat (referred to as the CT20 design), its compliance with federal safety requirements, the availability and feasibility of a rigid seat, the risks and benefits posed by the rigid seat design, and the seat designs employed in other makes and models of cars manufactured in 1996.

The trial court instructed the jury using plaintiff's tendered versions of Illinois Pattern Jury Instructions, Civil, Nos. 400.01.01 (setting out the plaintiff's claim of defective design and the defendants' denials), 400.02 (setting out the plaintiff's burden of proof and the elements of a claim for strict liability), and 400.06 (defining the expression "unreasonably dangerous"). Illinois Pattern Jury Instructions, Civil, Nos. 400.01.01, 400.02, 400.06 (2006) (hereinafter IPI Civil (2006)). The trial court rejected defendants' tendered nonpattern jury instructions that would have specifically instructed the jury to consider the "overall safety" of the design, whether the foreseeable risks of harm of the design outweighed its benefits, and whether the adoption of a feasible alternative design would have avoided or reduced the risks. Defendants argued unsuccessfully that this instruction should be given either instead of or in addition to instruction 400.06.

The jury answered the following special interrogatory in the affirmative: "Was the driver's seat of the Mikolajczyk car in an unreasonably dangerous condition that was a proximate cause of James Mikolajczyk's death?" The jury then returned a verdict in favor of the plaintiff and awarded $2 million in damages for loss of money, goods, and services and $25 million for loss of society. The jury assigned 60% of fault to Timberlake and 40% to Ford and Mazda.

The appellate court rejected defendants' argument that the jury was improperly instructed. . . .

Before this court, defendants argue that the appellate court "turned back the evolution of Illinois law" by applying the "outdated" consumer-expectation test rather than the risk-utility test that, they assert, is now the exclusive test for defective design of a complex product. In the alternative, they argue that even if this court has not expressly adopted risk-utility as the exclusive test in such cases, it should do so now. In effect, they argue that the trial court applied the wrong substantive law to plaintiff's claim, raising this issue in the context of the trial court's refusal to give their non-IPI jury instruction. Defendants also argue that a new trial must be granted in any event because the jury instructions that were given did not correspond to the evidence presented at trial. . . .

ANALYSIS

. . . .

(2)

Defendants argue that if we have not [rejected the consumer expectation test and adopted] the risk-utility test as the sole, exclusive test in design defect cases, we should do so now. They argue, in the alternative, that if we do not adopt the risk-utility test as the sole, exclusive test in all design defect cases, it should be the sole, exclusive test when the product is complex and the circumstances are not familiar to the ordinary consumer. This case, they insist, illustrates the need to restrict application of the consumer-expectation test to claims of defective manufacture or, at least, to design defects in simple products.

According to defendants, the consumer-expectation test evolved to evaluate claims of manufacturing defect where it is reasonable to believe that jurors, as ordinary consumers, can rely on their own experience and expectations to determine whether a manufacturing defect has rendered a product unreasonably dangerous. This, defendants assert, is a simple, straight-forward inquiry focused on one particular "unit" of the product and not on the product as a whole. Thus, there are no countervailing benefits to consider when a manufacturing defect is alleged.

The consumer-expectation test, defendants argue, does not make sense when a design defect is alleged because design decisions, by their very nature, involve considerations of the feasibility of alternative designs, cost, safety, and other factors with which the ordinary consumer is not familiar. In the context of the present case, defendants assert, the jurors could not have had reasonable expectations of their own regarding the proper degree of rigidity or flexibility in a car seat or how a seat should function in a wide range of potential accident conditions. According to defendants, the risk-utility test is specifically fashioned to evaluate this kind of claim and should be the sole measure of whether the product is unreasonably dangerous due to a design defect.

Plaintiff responds that defendants are proposing a "radical theory," adoption of which would overrule [prior Illinois cases]. Even if the proposed new rule were limited to cases involving complex products, plaintiffs claim, the distinction between simple and complex products is unworkable because there is no rational basis on which to distinguish them.

The rule advocated by defendants is contained in section 2(b) of the [Third] Products Liability Restatement, which would allow a finding of design defect only "when the foreseeable risks of harm posed by the product could have been reduced or avoided by the adoption of a reasonable alternative design * * * and the omission of the alternative design renders the product not reasonably safe." Restatement (Third) of Torts: Products Liability § 2(b), at 14 (1998).

If we were to accept defendants' invitation to adopt section 2(b) of the Products Liability Restatement, we would indeed overrule precedent, because section 2(b) would redefine the elements of a product liability claim based on alleged defective design.

Under Illinois law, the elements of a claim of strict liability based on a defect in the product are: (1) a condition of the product as a result of manufacturing or design, (2) that made the product unreasonably dangerous, (3) and that existed at the time the product left the defendant's control, and (4) an injury to the plaintiff, (5) that was proximately caused by the condition. The plaintiff has the burden of proof on each element.

Section 2(b) of the Products Liability Restatement would alter the "unreasonably dangerous" element in design defect cases in two significant ways. First, a plaintiff would be required to plead and prove the existence of a feasible alternative design in every case. Second, instead of proving that the defect rendered the product "unreasonably dangerous," the plaintiff would have the burden of proving that the product was "not reasonably safe."

The first of these new elements was briefly a part of Illinois law. In 1995, enactment of Public Act 89-7, the so-called "Tort Reform Act," added section 2-2104 to the Code of Civil Procedure. This section provided that in strict product liability actions, the design of a product is "presumed to be reasonably safe," unless the plaintiff proves that, "at the time the product left the control of the manufacturer, a practical and technically feasible alternative design was available that would have prevented the harm without significantly impairing the usefulness, desirability, or marketability of the product." 735 ILCS 5/2-2104 (West 1996) (declared unconstitutional).

In 1997, this court decided *Best v. Taylor Machine Works*, 179 Ill.2d 367, 467, 228 Ill.Dec. 636, 689 N.E.2d 1057 (1997), which held Public Act 89-7 unconstitutional in its entirety. Section 2-2104, standing alone, was not found unconstitutional, but this court held in *Best* that provisions of the act that were essential to the legislative purpose could not be severed from the rest of the act.

Our legislature has not reenacted this provision in the decade since *Best* was decided. We are reluctant to make a change that would so fundamentally alter the law of product liability in this state based solely on the suggestion that the drafters of the Restatement have a better idea of what the law should be than our own legislature. Such a change, if it is to be made, is a matter of public policy, better suited to legislative action than judicial decisionmaking. . . .

By urging adoption of the Products Liability Restatement's formulation of the elements of a strict product liability design defect claim, defendants seek a change in the substantive law of this state. This argument goes far beyond their assertion that the jury in this particular case was not properly instructed and would require our overruling [three prior cases], at least in part. We, therefore, decline defendants' invitation to adopt section 2(b) of the Products Liability Restatement. Thus, the existence of a feasible alternative design and the balancing of risks and benefits are relevant considerations in a strict product liability design defect case, but they are not elements of the claim that the plaintiff is required to plead and prove in every case.

[Reversed and remanded]

What products might be defective under a risk/utility test but escape strict products liability on the ground that there is no alternative feasible design? Does the utility of cigarettes outweigh their dangers (cost)? Can a cigarette ever be used safely?

Chapter 14

DEFENSES

This chapter deals with specific defenses in negligence-based, strict liability and strict products liability actions. These defenses are in addition to any arguments that defendants might make concerning missing or incompletely proven elements of the plaintiffs' case. For example, the argument that the defendant was not the proximate cause of the plaintiff's injury is not included in this chapter.

A. COMPARATIVE AND CONTRIBUTORY NEGLIGENCE AND ASSUMPTION OF RISK IN CASES WHERE THE BASIS OF LIABILITY IS NEGLIGENCE

1. Comparative Negligence: The Modern World

LI v. YELLOW CAB CO. OF CALIFORNIA
Supreme Court of California, 1975 (en banc)
532 P.2d 1226

SULLIVAN, JUSTICE.

In this case we address the grave and recurrent question whether we should judicially declare no longer applicable in California courts the doctrine of contributory negligence, which bars all recovery when the plaintiff's negligent conduct has contributed as a legal cause in any degree to the harm suffered by him, and hold that it must give way to a system of comparative negligence, which assesses liability in direct proportion to fault. As we explain in detail *infra*, we conclude that we should. In the course of reaching our ultimate decision we conclude that: (1) The doctrine of comparative negligence is preferable to the "all-or-nothing" doctrine of contributory negligence from the point of view of logic, practical experience, and fundamental justice; (2) judicial action in this area is not precluded by the presence of section 1714 of the Civil Code, which has been said to "codify" the "all-or-nothing" rule and to render it immune from attack in the courts except on constitutional grounds; (3) given the possibility of judicial action, certain practical difficulties attendant upon the adoption of comparative negligence should not dissuade us from charting a new course — leaving the resolution of some of these problems to future judicial or legislative action; (4) the doctrine of comparative negligence should be applied in this state in its so-called "pure" form under which the assessment of liability in proportion to fault proceeds in spite of the fact that the plaintiff is equally at fault as or more at fault than the defendant; and finally (5) this new rule should be given a limited retrospective application.

The accident here in question occurred near the intersection of Alvarado Street and Third Street in Los Angeles. At this intersection Third Street runs in a generally east-west direction along the crest of a hill, and Alvarado Street, running generally north and south, rises gently to the crest from either direction. At approximately 9 p.m. on November 21, 1968, plaintiff Nga Li was proceeding northbound on Alvarado in her 1967 Oldsmobile. She was in the inside lane, and about 70 feet before she reached the Third Street intersection she stopped and then began a left turn across the three southbound lanes of Alvarado, intending to enter the driveway of a service station. At this time defendant Robert Phillips, an employee of defendant Yellow Cab Company, was driving a company-owned taxicab southbound in the middle lane on Alvarado. He came over the crest of the hill, passed through the intersection, and collided with the right rear portion of plaintiff's automobile, resulting in personal injuries to plaintiff as well as considerable damage to the automobile.

The court, sitting without a jury, found as facts that defendant Phillips was traveling at approximately 30 miles per hour when he entered the intersection, that such speed was unsafe at that time and place, and that the traffic light controlling southbound traffic at the intersection was yellow when defendant Phillips drove into the intersection. It also found, however, that plaintiff's left turn across the southbound lanes of Alvarado "was made at a time when a vehicle was approaching from the opposite direction so close as to constitute an immediate hazard." The dispositive conclusion of law was as follows: "That the driving of Nga Li was negligent, that such negligence was a proximate cause of the collision, and that she is barred from recovery by reason of such contributory negligence." Judgment for defendants was entered accordingly.

I

"Contributory negligence is conduct on the part of the plaintiff which falls below the standard to which he should conform for his own protection, and which is a legally contributing cause cooperating with the negligence of the defendant in bringing about the plaintiff's harm." (Rest. 2d Torts, § 463.) Thus the American Law Institute, in its second restatement of the law, describes the kind of conduct on the part of one seeking recovery for damage caused by negligence which renders him subject to the doctrine of contributory negligence. What the effect of such conduct will be is left to a further section, which states the doctrine in its clearest essence: "Except where the defendant has the last clear chance, the plaintiff's contributory negligence *bars recovery* against a defendant whose negligent conduct would otherwise make him liable to the plaintiff for the harm sustained by him." (Rest. 2d Torts, § 467.) (Italics added.)

This rule, rooted in the long-standing principle that one should not recover from another for damages brought upon oneself, has been the law of this state from its beginning. Although criticized almost from the outset for the harshness of its operation, it has weathered numerous attacks, in both the legislative and the judicial arenas, seeking its amelioration or repudiation. We have undertaken a thorough reexamination of the matter, giving particular attention to the common law and statutory sources of the subject doctrine in this state. As we have indicated, this reexamination leads us to the conclusion that the "all-or-nothing" rule of contributory negligence can be and ought to be superseded by a rule which assesses liability in proportion to fault.

It is unnecessary for us to catalogue the enormous amount of critical comment that has been directed over the years against the "all-or-nothing" approach of the doctrine of contributory negligence. The essence of that criticism has been constant and clear: the doctrine is inequitable in its operation because it fails to distribute responsibility in proportion to fault.[3] Against this have been raised several arguments in justification, but none have proved even remotely adequate to the task.[4] The basic objection to the doctrine — grounded in the primal concept that in a system in which liability is based on fault, the extent of fault should govern the extent of liability — remains irresistible to reason and all intelligent notions of fairness.

Furthermore, practical experience with the application by juries of the doctrine of contributory negligence has added its weight to analyses of its inherent

---

[3] Dean Prosser states the kernel of critical comment in these terms: "It [the rule] places upon one party the entire burden of a loss for which two are, by hypothesis, responsible." (Prosser, Torts (4th ed. 1971) § 67, p. 433.) Harper and James express the same basic idea: "[T]here is no justification — in either policy or doctrine — for the rule of contributory negligence, except for the feeling that if one man is to be held liable because of his fault, then the fault of him who seeks to enforce that liability should also be considered. But this notion does not require the all-or-nothing rule, which would exonerate a very negligent defendant for even the slight fault of his victim. The logical corollary of the fault principle would be a rule of comparative or proportional negligence, not the present rule." (2 Harper & James, The Law of Torts (1956) § 22.3, p. 1207.)

[4] Dean Prosser, in a 1953 law review article on the subject which still enjoys considerable influence, addressed himself to the commonly advanced justificatory arguments in the following terms: "There has been much speculation as to why the rule thus declared found such ready acceptance in later decisions, both in England and in the United States. The explanations given by the courts themselves never have carried much conviction. Most of the decisions have talked about 'proximate cause,' saying that the plaintiff's negligence is an intervening, insulating cause between the defendant's negligence and the injury. But this cannot be supported unless a meaning is assigned to proximate cause which is found nowhere else. If two automobiles collide and injure a bystander, the negligence of one driver is not held to be a superseding cause which relieves the other of liability; and there is no visible reason for any different conclusion when the action is by one driver against the other. It has been said that the defense has a penal basis, and is intended to punish the plaintiff for his own misconduct; or that the court will not aid one who is himself at fault, and he must come into court with clean hands. But this is no explanation of the many cases, particularly those of the last clear chance, in which a plaintiff clearly at fault is permitted to recover. It has been said that the rule is intended to discourage accidents, by denying recovery to those who fail to use proper care for their own safety; but the assumption that the speeding motorist is, or should be, meditating on the possible failure of a lawsuit for his possible injuries lacks all reality, and it is quite as reasonable to say that the rule promotes accidents by encouraging the negligent defendant. Probably the true explanation lies merely in the highly individualistic attitude of the common law of the early nineteenth century. The period of development of contributory negligence was that of the industrial revolution, and there is reason to think that the courts found in this defense, along with the concepts of duty and proximate cause, a convenient instrument of control over the jury, by which the liabilities of rapidly growing industry were curbed and kept within bounds." (Prosser, *Comparative Negligence* (1953) 41 Cal. L. Rev. 1, 3-4; fhs. omitted. For a more extensive consideration of the same subject, see 2 Harper & James, [The Law of Torts (1956)], § 22.2, pp. 1199-1207.)

To be distinguished from arguments raised in justification of the "all or nothing" rule are practical considerations which have been said to counsel against the adoption of a fairer and more logical alternative. The latter considerations will be discussed in a subsequent portion of this opinion.

shortcomings: "Every trial lawyer is well aware that juries often do in fact allow recovery in cases of contributory negligence, and that the compromise in the jury room does result in some diminution of the damages because of the plaintiff's fault. But the process is at best a haphazard and most unsatisfactory one." (Prosser, *Comparative Negligence*, [(1953) 41 Cal. L. Rev. 1, 3-4,] p. 4; fn. omitted.) It is manifest that this state of affairs, viewed from the standpoint of the health and vitality of the legal process, can only detract from public confidence in the ability of law and legal institutions to assign liability on a just and consistent basis.

It is in view of these theoretical and practical considerations that to this date 25 states, have abrogated the "all or nothing" rule of contributory negligence and have enacted in its place general apportionment *statutes* calculated in one manner or another to assess liability in proportion to fault. In 1973 these states were joined by Florida, which effected the same result by *judicial* decision. *(Hoffman v. Jones* (Fla. 1973) 280 So. 2d 431.) We are likewise persuaded that logic, practical experience, and fundamental justice counsel against the retention of the doctrine rendering contributory negligence a complete bar to recovery — and that it should be replaced in this state by a system under which liability for damage will be borne by those whose negligence caused it in direct proportion to their respective fault.

The foregoing conclusion, however, clearly takes us only part of the way. It is strenuously and ably urged by defendants and two of the amici curiae that whatever our views on the relative merits of contributory and comparative negligence, we are precluded from making those views the law of the state by judicial decision. Moreover, it is contended, even if we are not so precluded, there exist considerations of a practical nature which should dissuade us from embarking upon the course which we have indicated. We proceed to take up these two objections in order.

II

It is urged that any change in the law of contributory negligence must be made by the Legislature, not by this court. Although the doctrine of contributory negligence is of judicial origin — its genesis being traditionally attributed to the opinion of Lord Ellenborough in *Butterfield v. Forrester* (KB. 1809) 103 Eng. Rep. 926 — the enactment of section 1714 of the Civil Code[7] in 1872 codified the doctrine as it stood at that date and, the argument continues, rendered it invulnerable to attack in the courts except on constitutional grounds. Subsequent cases of this court, it is pointed out, have unanimously affirmed that — barring the appearance of some constitutional infirmity — the "all-or-nothing" rule is the law of this state and shall remain so until the Legislature directs otherwise. The fundamental constitutional doctrine of separation of powers, the argument concludes, requires judicial abstention.

. . . .

---

[7] Section 1714 of the Civil Code has never been amended. It provides as follows: "Everyone is responsible, not only for the result of his willful acts, but also for an injury occasioned to another by his want of ordinary care or skill in the management of his property or person, *except so far as the latter has, willfully or by want of ordinary care, brought the injury upon himself.* The extent of liability in such cases is defined by the Title on Compensatory Relief." (Italics added.)

We have concluded that the foregoing argument, in spite of its superficial appeal, is fundamentally misguided. As we proceed to point out and elaborate below, it was not the intention of the Legislature in enacting section 1714 of the Civil Code, as well as other sections of that code declarative of the common law, to insulate the matters therein expressed from further judicial development; rather it was the intention of the Legislature to announce and formulate existing common law principles and definitions for purposes of orderly and concise presentation and with a distinct view toward continuing judicial evolution.

. . . .

[W]e hold that section 1714 of the Civil Code was not intended to and does not preclude present judicial action in furtherance of the purposes underlying it.

III

We are thus brought to the second group of arguments which have been advanced by defendants and the amici curiae supporting their position. Generally speaking, such arguments expose considerations of a practical nature which, it is urged, counsel against the adoption of a rule of comparative negligence in this state even if such adoption is possible by judicial means.

The most serious of these considerations are those attendant upon the administration of a rule of comparative negligence in cases involving multiple parties. One such problem may arise when all responsible parties are not brought before the court: it may be difficult for the jury to evaluate relative negligence in such circumstances, and to compound this difficulty such an evaluation would not be res judicata in a subsequent suit against the absent wrongdoer. Problems of contribution and indemnity among joint tortfeasors lurk in the background.

A second and related major area of concern involves the administration of the actual process of fact-finding in a comparative negligence system. The assigning of a specific percentage factor to the amount of negligence attributable to a particular party, while in theory a matter of little difficulty, can become a matter of perplexity in the face of hard facts. The temptation for the jury to resort to a quotient verdict in such circumstances can be great. These inherent difficulties are not, however, insurmountable. Guidelines might be provided the jury which will assist it in keeping focussed upon the true inquiry, and the utilization of special verdicts or jury interrogatories can be of invaluable assistance in assuring that the jury has approached its sensitive and often complex task with proper standards and appropriate reverence.

The third area of concern, the status of the doctrines of last clear chance and assumption of risk, involves less the practical problems of administering a particular form of comparative negligence than it does a definition of the theoretical outline of the specific form to be adopted. Although several states which apply comparative negligence concepts retain the last clear chance doctrine, the better reasoned position seems to be that when true comparative negligence is adopted, the need for last clear chance as a palliative of the hardships of the "all-or-nothing" rule disappears and its retention results only in a windfall to the plaintiff in direct contravention of the principle of liability in proportion to fault. As for assumption of risk, we have recognized in this state that this defense overlaps that of contributory negligence to some extent and in fact is made up of at least two distinct defenses. "To simplify greatly, it has been observed . . . that in one kind of situation, to wit, where a plaintiff *unreasonably* undertakes to encounter a specific known risk imposed by a defendant's negligence, plaintiff's conduct, although he may encounter that risk in a prudent manner, is in reality a form of contributory negligence. . . . Other kinds of situations within the doctrine of assumption of risk are those, for example, where plaintiff is held to agree to relieve defendant of an obligation of reasonable conduct toward him. Such a situation would not involve contributory negligence, but rather a reduction of defendant's duty of care." (*Grey v. Fibreboard Paper Products Co.* (1966) 65 Cal. 2d 240, 245-246, 53 Cal. Rptr. 545, 548, 418 P.2d 153, 156). We think it clear that the adoption of a system of comparative negligence should entail the merger of the defense of assumption of risk into the general scheme of assessment of liability in proportion to fault in those particular cases in which the form of assumption of risk involved is no more than a variant of contributory negligence.

Finally there is the problem of the treatment of willful misconduct under a system of comparative negligence. In jurisdictions following the "all-or-nothing" rule, contributory negligence is no defense to an action based upon a claim of willful misconduct, and this is the present rule in California. . . . The thought is that the difference between willful and wanton misconduct and ordinary negligence is one of kind rather than degree in that the former involves conduct of an entirely different order, and under this conception it might well be urged that comparative negligence concepts should have no application when one of the parties has been guilty of willful and wanton misconduct. It has been persuasively argued, however, that the loss of deterrent effect that would occur upon application of comparative fault concepts to willful and wanton misconduct as well as ordinary negligence would be slight, and that a comprehensive system of comparative negligence should allow for the apportionment of damages in all cases involving misconduct which falls short of being intentional. The law of punitive damages remains a separate consideration.

The existence of the foregoing areas of difficulty and uncertainty has not diminished our conviction that the time for a revision of the means for dealing with contributory fault in this state is long past due and that it lies within the province of this court to initiate the needed change by our decision in this case. Two of the indicated areas (i.e., multiple parties and willful misconduct) are not involved in the case before us, and we consider it neither necessary nor wise to address ourselves to specific problems of this nature which might be expected to arise. . . .

Our previous comments relating to the remaining two areas of concern (i.e., the status of the doctrines of last clear chance and assumption of risk, and the matter of judicial supervision of the finder of fact) have provided sufficient guidance to enable the trial courts of this state to meet and resolve particular problems in this area as they arise. As we have indicated, last clear chance and assumption of risk (insofar as the latter doctrine is but a variant of contributory negligence) are to be subsumed under the general process of assessing liability in proportion to fault, and the matter of jury supervision we leave for the moment within the broad discretion of the trial courts.

. . . .

It remains to identify the precise form of comparative negligence which we now adopt for application in this state. Although there are many variants, only the two basic forms need be considered here. The first of these, the so-called "pure" form of comparative negligence, apportions liability in direct proportion to fault in all cases. . . . The second basic form of comparative negligence, of which there are several variants, applies apportionment based on fault *up to the point* at which the plaintiff's negligence is equal to or greater than that of the defendant — when that point is reached, plaintiff is barred from recovery. Nineteen states have adopted this form or one of its variants by statute. The principal argument advanced in its favor is moral in nature: that it is not morally right to permit one more at fault in an accident to recover from one less at fault. Other arguments assert the probability of increased insurance, administrative, and judicial costs if a "pure" rather than a "50 percent" system is adopted, but this has been seriously questioned.

We have concluded that the "pure" form of comparative negligence is that which should be adopted in this state. In our view the "50 percent" system simply shifts the lottery aspect of the contributory negligence rule[21] to a different ground. As Dean Prosser has noted, under such a system "[i]t is obvious that a slight difference in the proportionate fault may permit a recovery; and there has been much justified criticism of a rule under which a plaintiff who is charged with 49 percent of a total negligence recovers 51 percent of his damages, while one who is charged with 50 percent recovers nothing at all."[22] Prosser, *Comparative Negligence, supra*, 41 Cal. L. Rev. 1, 25; fns. omitted.)

. . . .

For all of the foregoing reasons we conclude that the "all-or-nothing" rule of contributory negligence as it presently exists in this state should be and is herewith superseded by a system of "pure" comparative negligence, the fundamental purpose of which shall be to assign responsibility and liability for damage in direct proportion to the amount of negligence of each of the parties. Therefore, in all actions for negligence resulting in injury to person or property, the contributory negligence of the person injured in person or property shall not bar recovery, but the damages awarded shall be diminished in proportion to the amount of negligence attributable to the person recovering. The doctrine of last clear chance is abolished, and the defense of assumption of risk is also abolished to the extent that it is merely a variant of the former doctrine of contributory negligence; both of these are to be subsumed under the general process of assessing liability in proportion to negli-

---

[21] "The rule that contributory fault bars completely is a curious departure from the central principle of nineteenth century Anglo-American tort law — that wrongdoers should bear the losses they cause. Comparative negligence more faithfully serves that central principle by causing the wrongdoers to share the burden of resulting losses in reasonable relation to their wrongdoing, rather than allocating the heavier burden to the one who, as luck would have it, happened to be more seriously injured." (Comments on Maki v. Frelk, [21 Vand. L. Rev. 889], Comment by Keeton, pp. 912-913.)

[22] This problem is compounded when the injurious result is produced by the combined negligence of several parties. For example in a three-car collision a plaintiff whose negligence amounts to one-third or more recovers nothing; in a four-car collision the plaintiff is barred if his negligence is only one-quarter of the total.

gence. Pending future judicial or legislative developments, the trial courts of this state are to use broad discretion in seeking to assure that the principle stated is applied in the interest of justice and in furtherance of the purposes and objectives set forth in this opinion.

. . . .

CLARK, JUSTICE (dissenting).

. . . .

Contrary to the majority's assertions of judicial adequacy, the courts of other states — with near unanimity — have conceded their inability to determine the best system for replacing contributory negligence, concluding instead that the legislative branch is best able to resolve the issue.

. . . .

McComb, J., concurs.

———————

1. In many jurisdictions, contributory negligence no longer exists as a defense. Courts and legislatures have instead replaced contributory negligence with comparative negligence. Comparative negligence doctrine is often perceived as helping plaintiffs, because plaintiffs will no longer be barred from recovery even if they were negligent. A system of comparative negligence can also help defendants, however, because it removes any temptation for jurors to find that the plaintiff was not negligent in order to allow the plaintiff to recover. Thus, instead of paying for 100% of the damage done, the defendant will be held liable for the percentage of the injury actually caused by the defendant.

2. There are three basic types of comparative negligence doctrine. Pure comparative negligence doctrine assesses damages proportional to fault; a plaintiff who is 90% responsible will still collect 10% of his or her damages from the defendant (when, of course, the jury has assessed 10% of the blame against that defendant). Under the "less than 50%" type, a plaintiff may recover provided the plaintiff's negligence was less than the defendant's. If the plaintiff and the defendant were each responsible for 50% of the negligence, the plaintiff will be barred from recovery. Under the "equal to or less than" type, the plaintiff may recover as long as the blame attached to the plaintiff is not greater than the blame attached to the defendant. In this third type of comparative negligence, the plaintiff may recover even when the plaintiff's negligence is equal to the defendant's.

Various questions remain, particularly under the latter two types of comparative negligence. For example, what if a plaintiff is 40% at fault and two codefendants are 30% at fault each? Jurisdictions have various rules for the application of comparative negligence in cases involving multiple parties.

3. Are the courts really comparing fault? Aren't they really comparing causation? Blame is apportioned to the various parties depending upon what percentage of the damages the conduct at issue caused. In other words, a defendant is 10% at

fault if his or her conduct caused 10% of the damages. It is not the fault that is being divided; rather it is the causation of the damages. Viewing comparative negligence this way helps make the doctrine make sense as applied in strict liability or strict products liability cases, in which the defendant may not have been negligent at all. If the defendant has not been negligent, speaking of comparing the plaintiff's and the defendant's negligence makes no sense at all. But if the comparison is not between the negligence of the parties, but rather between the causative roles of the parties (or of the plaintiff and the product), applying what is somewhat misnamed as comparative negligence makes sense, even in the context of non-negligent defendants.

2. The Last Clear Chance Rule

DAVIES v. MANN
Exchequer, 1842
10 M.& W. 547, 152 Eng. Rep. 588

Exch. of Pleas. Nov. 4, 1842. — The general rule of law respecting negligence is, that, although there may have been negligence on the part of the plaintiff, yet unless he might by the exercise of ordinary care have avoided the consequences of the defendant's negligence, he is entitled to recover. Therefore, where the defendant negligently drove his horses and waggon against and killed an ass, which had been left in the highway fettered in the fore-feet, and thus unable to get out of the way of the defendant's waggon, which was going at a smartish pace along the road, it was held, that the jury were properly directed, that although it was an illegal act on the part of the plaintiff so to put the animal on the highway, the plaintiff was entitled to recover.

Case for negligence. The declaration stated, that the plaintiff theretofore, and at the time of the committing of the grievance thereinafter mentioned, to wit, on &c, was lawfully possessed of a certain donkey, which said donkey of the plaintiff was then lawfully in a certain highway, and the defendant was then possessed of a certain waggon and certain horses drawing the same, which said waggon and horses of the defendant were then under the care, government, and direction of a certain then servant of the defendant, in and along the said highway; nevertheless the defendant, by his said servant, so carelessly, negligently, unskillfully, and improperly governed and directed his said waggon and horses, that by and through the carelessness, negligence, unskillfulness, and improper conduct of the defendant, by his said servant, the said waggon and horses of the defendant then ran and struck with great violence against the said donkey of the plaintiff, and thereby then wounded, crushed, and killed the same.

The defendant pleaded not guilty.

At the trial, before Erskine, J., at the last Summer Assizes for the county of Worcester, it appeared that the plaintiff, having fettered the fore feet of an ass belonging to him, turned it into a public highway, and at the time in question the ass was grazing on the off side of a road about eight yards wide, when the defendant's waggon, with a team of three horses, coming down a slight descent, at what the witness termed a smartish pace, ran against the ass, knocked it down, and the wheels passing over it, it died soon after. The ass was fettered at the time, and it was proved that the driver of the waggon was some little distance behind the horses. The learned Judge told the jury, that though the act of the plaintiff, in leaving the donkey on the highway so fettered as to prevent his getting out of the way of carriages travelling along it, might be illegal, still, if the proximate cause of the injury was attributable to the want of proper conduct on the part of the driver of the waggon, the action was maintainable against the defendant; and his Lordship directed them, if they thought that the accident might have been avoided by the exercise of ordinary care on the part of the driver, to find for the plaintiff. The jury found their verdict for the plaintiff, damages 40s.

Godson now moved for a new trial, on the grounds of misdirection. The act of the plaintiff in turning the donkey into the public highway was an illegal one, and as the injury arose, principally from that act, the plaintiff was not entitled to compensation for that injury which, but for his own unlawful act, would never have occurred. [PARKE, B. The declaration states that the ass was lawfully on the highway, and the defendant has not traversed that allegation; therefore it must be taken to be admitted.] The principle of law, as deducible from the cases, is, that where an accident is the result of faults on both sides, neither party can maintain an action. Thus, in *Butterfield v. Forrester* (11 East, 60), it was held that one who is injured by an obstruction on a highway, against which he fell, cannot maintain an action, if it appear that he was riding with great violence and want of ordinary care, without which he might have seen and avoided the obstruction. So, in *Vennall v. Garner* (1 C. & M. 21), in case for running down a ship, it was held, that neither party can recover when both are in the wrong; and Bayley, B., there says, "I quite agree that if the mischief be the result of the combined negligence of the two, they must both remain in statu quo, and neither party can recover against the other." Here the plaintiff, by fettering the donkey, had prevented him from removing himself out of the way of accident; had his fore feet been free, no accident would probably have happened. *Pluckwell v. Wilson* (5 Carr. & P. 375), *Luxford v. Large (ibid.* 421) and *Lynch v. Nurdin* (1 Ad. & E. (N.S.), 29; 4 P. & D. 672), are to the same effect.

LORD ABINGER, C.B. I am of opinion that there ought to be no rule in this case. The defendant has not denied that the ass was lawfully there; but even were it otherwise, it would have made no difference, for as the defendant might, by proper care, have avoided injuring the animal, and did not, he is liable for the consequences of his negligence, though the animal may have been improperly there.

PARKE, B. This subject was fully considered by this Court in the case of *Bridge v. The Grand Junction Railway Company* (3 M. & W. 246), where, as appears to me, the correct rule is laid down concerning negligence, namely, that the negligence which is to preclude a plaintiff from recovering in an action of this nature, must be such as that he could, by ordinary care, have avoided the consequences of the defendant's negligence. I am reported to have said in that case, and I believe quite correctly, that "the rule of law is laid down with perfect correctness in the case of *Butterfield v. Forrester*, that, although there may have been negligence on the part of the plaintiff, yet unless he might, by the exercise of ordinary care, have avoided the consequences of the defendant's negligence, he is entitled to recover; if by ordinary care he might have avoided them he is the author of his own wrong." In that case of *Bridge v. Grand Junction Railway Company*, there was a plea imputing negligence on both sides; here it is otherwise; and the Judge simply told the jury, that the mere fact of negligence on the part of the plaintiff in leaving his donkey on the public highway, was no answer to the action, unless the donkey's being there was the immediate cause of the injury; and that, if they were of opinion that it was caused by the fault of the defendant's servant in driving too fast, or, which is the same thing, at a smartish pace, the mere fact of putting the ass upon the road would not bar the plaintiff of his action. All that is perfectly correct; for, although the ass may have been wrongfully there, still the defendant was bound to go along the road at such a pace as would be likely to prevent mischief. Were this not so, a man might justify the driving over goods left on a public highway, or even over a man lying asleep there, or the purposely running against a carriage going on the wrong side of the road.

GURNEY, B., and ROLFE, B., concurred.

Rule refused.

———————

In this case, the court deals with what came to be called the last clear chance rule. Under the last clear chance rule, a party, usually the defendant, is liable if that party fails to take reasonable steps to avoid the consequences of the negligent act of another (usually the plaintiff). In general, of course, a party is not entitled to recover for the consequences of another's negligence when those consequences could have been avoided. Avoidable consequences are caused not by the original negligence, but rather by the negligence of the party in failing to avoid them. Doesn't the last clear chance rule really represent the application of proximate causation principles in cases where both parties have been negligent, and the negligence of the injured party consists in failing to avoid the consequences of the negligence of the other party?

PROBLEMS

1. D is proceeding in her automobile down a quiet street and is approaching a stop light, which is green in her direction. E, approaching the crossroads from right angles, goes through the red light, and D and E make contact in the intersection. D saw E approaching the intersection before contact was made.

Assuming D could have stopped, what arguments will E make to avoid liability? Will E be able to avoid liability altogether? If so, would this be an appropriate result? What would the arguments of the parties be in a jurisdiction that had abolished the last clear chance rule by statute?

2. G negligently causes a car crash in which H is injured. The injury might have been cured if H's doctor had not been negligent in treating H; as it is, however, H has developed a permanent limp.

Do these facts lend themselves to a last clear chance analysis at all? Should G be exempt from liability for injuries caused by the doctor's negligence? Isn't it foreseeable, if one causes another to need medical attention, that the doctor administering that attention might be negligent?

3. The role that a plaintiff's non-use of an available, working seatbelt should play in a lawsuit where the defendant's negligent driving caused an accident has generated many cases and much statutory law. Should such non-use serve as a defense? If so, how should it be weighed against the negligent driving that caused the non-use to produce injuries? Failure to use an available seatbelt is, of course, not really a manifestation of the last clear chance rule. In a way, seatbelts are a "first clear chance" to reduce injuries from the foreseeable, albeit regrettable, risk of car accidents. Fastening one's seatbelt (or not) occurs before the accident, not after.

For a detailed and somewhat confusing discussion of this subject, see *Ridley v. Safety Kleen*, 693 So. 2d 934 (Fla. 1996). In that case, the court worked hard to reconcile the common law with various statutes enacted in Florida to try to resolve the problems posed in tort cases by non-use of seatbelts. In *Hodges v. Mack Trucks, Inc.*, 474 F.3d 188 (5th Cir. 2006), whether the plaintiff truck driver, who had been ejected from the vehicle, had been wearing a seatbelt at the time of the accident was in dispute. The court ruled that defendant Mack's evidence of the plaintiff's non-use of the seatbelt was admissible, despite the prohibition on such evidence imposed by the state statute in effect at the time. The court stated (at 202):

> Subsection (g) [of the statute] prohibits the introduction of seatbelt evidence to show the plaintiff was contributorily negligent. On the other hand, in secondary-collision product-liability actions, such evidence may be admissible to show, or, as in this action, rebut, the essential element of causation. Seatbelt evidence was necessary for Mack to rebut the essential element of causation — whether its door latch was the proximate cause of [plaintiff's] injuries, and, ultimately, to defeat a crashworthiness claim.

In many jurisdictions, non-use of seatbelts is a ticketable offense, which adds to the layers of complication. In such jurisdictions, the plaintiff who has failed to use an available seatbelt is guilty of at least a misdemeanor, which may mean that the plaintiff has acted unreasonably as a matter of law. Such unreasonableness may play a role in evaluating that plaintiff's comparative negligence in contributing to any injury caused by the crash and exacerbated by the seatbelt nonuse.

Many states have reduced the impact that the offense of failing to "click it" can have on any tort judgments that may result from the accident in question. For example, in *Lowe v. Estate Motors, Ltd.*, 410 N.W.2d 706 (Mich. 1987), the court cited Michigan's mandatory seatbelt statute. Under the statute, failure to use a seatbelt constituted evidence of negligence, but the plaintiff's recovery could be reduced by a maximum of 5%. Justice Levin, in a separate opinion, stated that, "A large majority of the statutes requiring adults to wear seatbelts provide either that a violation cannot be grounds for reducing an award on the basis of comparative or contributory negligence, or limit the possible reduction to a small percentage of the award." *Lowe*, 410 N.W.2d at 727–28 n.9 (Justice Levin, separate opinion).

Does it make sense to limit the reduction in damages for failure to wear a seatbelt? What if there would have been no injury had the plaintiff been wearing a seatbelt? One of the worst things that can happen in an accident is ejection from the vehicle, which cannot occur if the injured party is wearing a seatbelt. Why might a legislature adopt a statute limiting the effect of failure to wear a seat belt?

3.   Assumption of Risk

Assumption of risk doctrine is a complex network of competing concerns which arise, at least in part, out of the fact that assumption of the risk is a complete defense. Courts are reluctant to let negligent defendants avoid liability altogether. On the other hand, they are equally reluctant to allow plaintiffs to recover damages when the plaintiffs have taken on the risk themselves.

a.   The Elements

GOEPFERT v. FILLER
Supreme Court of South Dakota, 1997
563 N.W.2d 140

KONENKAMP, JUSTICE.

Michael Goepfert lost his life shortly after he jumped from a moving car. His parents sued the driver and others, and the circuit court granted summary judgment for the driver. Ordinarily, assumption of the risk is a question of fact for a jury, but under these circumstances, can it be decided as a matter of law? Because he voluntarily alighted from a moving vehicle without warning, we conclude Goepfert assumed the risk, and thus we uphold the summary judgment.

Facts

On Friday evening, October 29, 1993, several friends, including Chris Stethem and Michael Goepfert, began celebrating the annual "Hobo Day" homecoming at South Dakota State University in Brookings. After dinner and a few beers at a friend's home, the group of six left for downtown. Stethem drove. Goepfert was in the front passenger seat, another man sat between them, and the remaining three were in the backseat. As they neared their destination, the Chevy Lounge on Main Street, they approached an intersection with a red traffic light. Stethem slowed, but never stopped. About fifty feet from the intersection, a passenger in the back told Stethem, "Let us out. Let us out right here." Goepfert said nothing, but others joined in, wanting to be dropped off near the bar, so they would not have to walk back from where they would park. Stethem replied, "No, we'll all walk up there." One passenger persisted, and Stethem said, "If you want to get out, get out." They were still moving at approximately 10 to 15 miles per hour when the light turned green. Stethem began to accelerate normally. According to everyone in the car, at the moment of acceleration, Goepfert simultaneously, without a word, opened the car door and jumped out. When his feet hit the roadway, he flipped over backwards, causing his head to strike the pavement. He came to rest in the crosswalk where the car entered the intersection. Stethem pulled over on the other side, and all ran back to help their friend.

Goepfert was unconscious. He was taken by ambulance to Brookings Hospital, treated and released. Concerned friends watched him through the night to monitor his condition. In the morning, they took him back to the hospital when he became unresponsive. Doctors then discovered a skull fracture and intracranial hemorrhaging. Goepfert was rushed by air ambulance to a hospital in Sioux Falls, where he died the next day. His parents brought a wrongful death action against Stethem and certain medical providers. The malpractice claims are not part of this appeal. Stethem moved for summary judgment. Concluding as a matter of law Goepfert assumed the risk of injury by exiting a moving car, negating any duty Stethem owed to him, the circuit judge granted the motion.

Standard of Review

The framework for determining summary judgment questions is set forth in S.D.CL 15-6-56(c): "The judgment sought shall be rendered forthwith if the pleadings, depositions, answers to interrogatories, and admissions on file, together with the affidavits, if any, show that there is no genuine issue of material fact and that the moving party is entitled to a judgment as a matter of law." *Id.* (reproduced in part). . . .

Analysis and Decision

The circuit court ruled from the bench:

> [I]n looking at everything in the light most favorable to the plaintiff here, the scenario I get is that the driver of the car was driving by the Chevy Lounge, the passengers were saying, "Let us out here and so we don't have to walk all the way back to the Chevy Lounge after you find a place to park." The driver of the car said, "No," and then because he was getting badgered about it, he says, "Well, if you want to get out, get out now," but the car had not stopped; that is undisputed. It was going slow, but it had not stopped, and even looking at it from the perspective of the decedent here, that the defendant was slowing down and that he took the defendant's statement seriously, that "If you want to get out, get out now," that that was permission to exit the car, no reasonable person exits a moving car until it is stopped. I think that anytime somebody exits a moving vehicle, he is assuming a known risk. He is assuming there is a good chance that he is going to get injured. He has got to wait until it stops. And so to me, as a matter of law, I conclude that there was assumption of the risk here.

To learn whether the judge decided correctly, we now examine the concept of assumption of the risk with the facts viewed in a light most favorable to Goepfert. We review this question under the de novo standard. *Boever v. State Board of Accountancy*, 526 N.W.2d 747, 749 (S.D. 1995) (Boever I).

Assumption of the risk embodies three elements. It must be shown that Goepfert: (1) had actual or constructive knowledge of the risk; (2) appreciated its character; and (3) voluntarily accepted the risk, with the time, knowledge, and experience to make an intelligent choice. . . .

Though assumption of the risk is most often an issue for the jury, we have occasionally held summary judgment appropriate. . . . In *Myers v. Lennox Co-op. Ass'n*, 307 N.W.2d 863 (S.D. 1981), for example, we affirmed summary judgment on assumption of the risk against a plaintiff who was injured after stepping on an unstable pile of lumber while loading a garbage truck. No facts were in dispute; he had reasonable alternatives to stepping on the lumber; and reasonable persons could not differ over the risk the plaintiff assumed. "His decision to walk on the lumber was made under such circumstance that he must be held to have made an intelligent choice to encounter the risk presented by that course of action." *Id.* at 865. Has each required element been satisfied in this case?

First, to assume a risk, one must have actual or constructive knowledge of the peril involved. Constructive knowledge will be imputed if the risk is so plainly observable that "anyone of competent faculties [could be] charged with knowledge of it." *Westover [v. East River Elec. Power Co-op., Inc.*, [488 N.W.2d 892 (S.D. 1992)], at 901 (internal citations omitted). Risk is intrinsic to some acts. Considering these facts and exercising ordinary common sense, reasonable minds cannot differ on the jeopardy involved in stepping from a moving vehicle. *See Nix v. Williams*, 35 A.D.2d 188, 316 N.Y.S.2d 321, 324 (1970) (passenger who suddenly and unexpectedly jumped out of moving vehicle without saying anything barred from recovery as a matter of law); *Groshek v. Groshek*, 263 Wis. 515, 57 N.W.2d 704, 706 (1953) (where plaintiff driver allowed a passenger to drive while he reached into the backseat, it cannot be reasonably said that plaintiff did not know the danger in such activity).

Next, an individual will be hel *Bell*, 535 N.W.2d at 754d to have appreciated the danger undertaken if it was "a risk that no adult person of average intelligence can deny." *Bell*, 535 N.W.2d at 754; *Nelson*, 513 N.W.2d at 905. Obviously, "there are some risks to which no adult will be believed if he says he did not understand them." *Staats by Staats v. Lawrence*, 576 A.2d 663, 668 (Del. Super. Ct. 1990), *affd*, 582 A.2d 936 (Del. 1990). Michael Goepfert, a twenty-two year old college student, had to know and appreciate the hazard he faced in leaping from a moving car. "[One] may not close his eyes to obvious dangers, and cannot recover where he was in possession of facts from which he would be legally charged with appreciation of the danger." *Herod v. Grant*, 262 So. 2d 781, 783 (Miss. 1972) (quoting 57 Am. Jur. 2d *Negligence* § 282 (1971)). No testimony from anyone in the car suggests Goepfert was unaware of what he was doing or that he misperceived the car was moving.

Finally, assumption of the risk requires voluntarily acceptance, having had the time, knowledge, and experience to make an intelligent choice. As he leapt from the car, Goepfert may not have known the light had turned green and Stethem was just then accelerating. One passenger testified:

— **Q:**   After Chris said, "If you want to get out, get out," did you expect Chris to accelerate?

— **A:**   No.

— **Q:**   Then if you did not expect Chris to accelerate, would it not be reasonable that Mike would not have expected him to accelerate, too?

— **A:**   But Mike's focus wasn't on the green light is what I'm getting at.

Chris was watching the road. He was focused on the green light.

Mike's focus was thinking that if he stops, I'm going to jump out and get up there before everybody else does.

Consistent with the others, this same witness testified: Q. — "Were you surprised that Mike jumped out of the vehicle?" A. — "Yeah, I was very much so."

Everyone in the car felt Stethem spoke in jest or was acting the "smart aleck" when he said, "If you want to get out, get out." Even if Goepfert took this comment seriously, he still gave no sign of his intent, other than, as one passenger said, to glance at his friends in the backseat: "It was like he was joking like he was going to. Kind of acting like he was going to do it and then not really do it. Then he went ahead and did it." Automobile passengers have a duty of care for their own safety. *Glandon v. Fiala*, 261 Iowa 750, 156 N.W.2d 327, 331 (1968); *Atwood v. Holland*, 267 N.C. 722, 148 S.E.2d 851, 854 (N.C. 1966) ("A gratuitous passenger in an automobile is required to use that care for his own safety that a reasonably prudent person would employ under the same or similar circumstances."); *Rutz v. Iacono*, 229 Minn. 591, 40 N.W.2d 892, 895 (1949); *White v. Huffmaster*, 326 Mich. 108, 40 N.W.2d 87, 89 (1949).[*] Goepfert's decision surpassed mere negligence.

Acceptance of risk necessarily connotes attention to reasonable alternatives. Here "reasonable" refers to whether one had a fair opportunity to elect whether to subject oneself to danger. Acceptance is not voluntary if another's tortious conduct leaves no reasonable alternative to avert harm or to exercise or protect a right or privilege, which another has no right to deny. Everyone agreed Stethem drove normally. The car may have been moving faster than Goepfert anticipated when he jumped, but that cannot erase the reality that he still elected to jump while the car was moving. On this point the evidence is unrefuted. Goepfert's only reasonable alternative was to stay in the car until it reached a complete stop. No one's wrongful conduct forced him to make his fateful choice.

As a matter of law, Goepfert assumed the risk. We see no genuine issues of material fact for trial. By jumping from the car, Goepfert voluntarily and unfortunately accepted the peril inherent in such act, and, to the sorrow of his family and friends, his decision ended in tragedy.

Affirmed.

---

[*] Compare cases involving passengers engaged in horseplay in and around moving vehicles. *See, e.g.*, Brown v. Derry, 10 Wash. App. 459, 518 P.2d 251, 253 (Wash. Ct. App. 1974) (considering sixteen-year-old who rode on the trunk of a car, "The risk of harm in attempting to ride on the exterior of an automobile for even a short distance in such a fashion is plainly a foreseeable risk, and reasonable minds could not differ with respect to it"); Miller v. General Accident Fire & Life Assur. Corp., Ltd., 280 So. 2d 280, 282 (La. Ct. App. 1973) (man riding on a car fender, "The general rule when one is an outrider on a vehicle is that he only assumes such risks as are ordinarily incident to his position"); Vaughn v. Cortez, 180 So. 2d 796 (La. Ct. App. 1965) ("playing cowboy" while riding on the front of a moving car is so dangerous, a risk is assumed); Irwin v. Klaeren, 4 Ill. App. 2d 114, 123 N.E.2d 743, 744 (Ill. App. Ct. 1954) (holding as a matter of law and noting that "it is hard to conceive of a more reckless disregard for his own safety" than a man who holds his head and shoulders outside of the window of a moving car).

MILLER, CHIEF JUSTICE, and SABERS, AMUNDSON, and GILBERTSON, JUSTICES, concur.

RAY v. DOWNES
Supreme Court of South Dakota, 1998
576 N.W.2d 896

GILBERTSON, JUSTICE.

On October 16, 1995 Donald Ray (Ray) was injured in a farm accident when a semi-tractor/trailer rolled over his legs while he was attempting to position an auger under a trailer to unload crops into a large storage bin. Ray then brought a negligence action against his employer, the owner of the farm. He also sued the custom harvester hired by his employer and the custom harvester's driver. Ray's wife, Levena Ray, joined in the suit by submitting a loss of consortium claim. The trial court granted defendants' motion for summary judgment after finding, as a matter of law, that Ray had assumed the risk of his injuries. Ray appeals. We affirm as to his employer, Downes, and reverse as to the custom harvester, Wieczorek and his employee, Waldner.

FACTS AND PROCEDURE

Harold Downes (Downes), the owner of a farm near Pierre, South Dakota, hired Ray in May of 1995 as a farm laborer. Ray was 39 years old at the time and had many years of farm experience. As the fall 1995 harvest approached, Downes hired a custom harvester, John Wieczorek, to harvest his soybeans and corn. Wieczorek then assigned one of his employees to combine the fields and another, Phillip Waldner (Waldner), to drive a large 18-wheeled semi-tractor/trailer (semi) from the fields to the storage bins on Downes' farm and unload the crops into the bins. Wieczorek's two employees spent approximately one week harvesting soybeans. Ray was not directed by Downes to assist the harvesters but observed Waldner unloading the crops from the semi into the bins during the previous day's harvesting. During this process Waldner would drive the semi close to the bin, get out of the semi and position a swing-type auger directly underneath the openings in the bottom of the trailer. The crops would then fall through the bottom doors of the trailer into the auger to be transported into the bins.

On October 16, 1995, it became apparent that the ground near one of the bins was too high to allow sufficient clearance to get the auger under the semi trailer. Downes asked Ray to use a front-end loader to scrape smooth the ground near one of the bins so that the auger could be positioned. Downes did not direct Ray to assist Waldner in the actual unloading of the corn. After Ray scraped the ground, he volunteered to help Waldner position the auger under the trailer. Ray and Waldner agreed that Waldner would drive the truck and Ray would shove the auger underneath the trailer while the truck was moving. Ray would use hand signals and then "holler" for Waldner to stop when the auger was in place.

As Waldner was entering the truck Ray positioned himself three to four feet in front of the protruding rear set of wheels on the trailer. After the auger was in position Ray "hollered" for Waldner to stop. Either Ray did not signal or Waldner did not see Ray's signals or hear Ray "holler" and the wheels of the trailer caught Ray's left foot and ran over his left leg.[1] Downes was nearby and was alerted to the scene when he heard Ray urgently scream for Waldner to back up. Downes found Ray pinned under the trailer's wheels, got Waldner's attention, who then drove the trailer off of Ray.

Ray brought a personal injury suit against Waldner and Waldner's employer Wieczorek (under respondeat superior principles). Ray also alleged that Downes had maintained an unsafe workplace because the noise from the grain bin dryers prevented Waldner from hearing Ray's shouting to stop. Ray's wife, Levena, also filed a claim for loss of consortium. Downes brought a cross-claim against Waldner and Wieczorek. The circuit court granted summary judgment in favor of all defendants on the basis that Ray had assumed the risk of his injury based on his own admissions. The Rays appeal.

. . . .

ANALYSIS AND DECISION

. . . .

2. Whether summary judgment in favor of Waldner and Wieczorek was proper.

Although assumption of the risk is generally a jury issue, this Court has occasionally held summary judgment appropriate in those rare cases "where the essential elements are conclusively established that the plaintiff may be charged with assumption of the risk as a matter of law." *Goepfert*, 1997 S.D. 56 at ¶ 7, 563 N.W.2d at 142 (citation omitted). We examine the affirmative defense of assumption of the risk with the facts viewed in a light most favorable to Ray. This question is reviewed under the *de novo* standard.

Assumption of the risk is composed of three elements. It must be shown that Ray: (1) had actual or constructive knowledge of the risk; (2) appreciated its character; and (3) voluntarily accepted the risk, with the time, knowledge, and experience to make an intelligent choice. We have held that the failure to establish any of these elements will preclude summary judgment. At the pretrial hearing which addressed the motion for summary judgment, the circuit court held:

> [I]t's this court's reluctant view that this is one of those rare cases where [Ray's] own testimony establishes as a matter of law assumption of the risk. I don't believe there can be any reasonable dispute that when the deposition and the depositions of the other people are read together, even with the supplementary affidavit that was just filed by [Ray], I don't believe that reasonable people can disagree that the first two elements of the assump-

---

[1] The location was fairly noisy at the time because the engines of the semi and a tractor, which was used to power the auger, were running in addition to the grain bin dryers. Ray was aware that some of the truck's windows were rolled up prior to the accident.

tion of the risk doctrine were clearly satisfied and [Ray's] testimony, . . . in his deposition clearly establishes the voluntariness and the availability of reasonable alternatives.

b. Actual or Constructive Knowledge of the Risk

Generally, both knowledge and appreciation of danger are jury questions. However, "where it is clear that any person in [plaintiff's] position must have understood the danger, the issue may be decided by the court." W. Page Keeton Et Al., Prosser and Keeton on the Law of Torts § 68, at 481 (5th ed. 1984). Waldner argues that "[reasonable men could not differ that [Ray] had actual knowledge of the risk" of being run over by the rear wheels. *Mack*, 1996 S.D. 63 at ¶ 11, 548 N.W.2d at 814. Waldner cites Ray's deposition testimony to support his argument that Ray had *actual* knowledge of the risk of danger involved at the time he positioned himself near the rear wheels in his attempt to push the auger underneath the moving semi:

Q: You knew that the wheels on the rear of the semi-trailer extended out beyond the sides of the trailer?

A: I knew they extended out, yes.

Q: You could see them because they were a short distance behind you, weren't they?

A: Yes.

Q: In fact, they would have been less than three feet behind you?

A: Three or four, yes.

Q: And you knew that as the truck was being driven forward, that those wheels were getting closer and closer to you?

A: Yes.

Q: And you knew that if you didn't move, that the wheels on that trailer would drive over your leg?

A: Yes, I knew it. *But if he would have stopped when I motioned for him to stop, he wouldn't have got me.*

Q: But you knew you were in a position of danger?

A: Yes. There is danger anywhere on the farm.

Q: And you voluntarily put yourself in that position of danger, didn't you?

A: Yes, I guess I did.

Q: And you knew that you were taking the risk of injuring your legs or even your hip, as ultimately happened?

A: Yes.

(Emphasis added). "Risk is intrinsic to some acts." *Goepfert*, 1997 S.D. 56 at H8, 563 N.W.2d 140, 143. However this intrinsic risk is not unlimited. Certainly, Ray put himself in harm's way by standing in a position to be run over. He frankly admitted as much. Nonetheless, he did not consent to relieve the driver of his subsequent duty to act with reasonable care. In the words of Prosser, "This is a distinction which has baffled a great many law students, some judges, and unhappily a few very learned legal writers." Prosser & Keeton, The Law of Torts § 68, at 485.

It is here that there is the greatest misapprehension and confusion as to assumption of risk, and its most frequent misapplication. It is not true that in any case where the plaintiff voluntarily encounters a known danger he necessarily consents to any future negligence of the defendant. A pedestrian who walks across the street in the middle of a block, through a stream of traffic traveling at excessive speed, cannot by any stretch of the imagination be found to consent that the drivers shall not use care to watch for him and avoid running him down. On the contrary, he is insisting that they shall. This is contributory negligence pure and simple; it is not assumption of the risk. And if A leaves an automobile stopped at night on the traveled portion of the highway, and his passenger remains sitting in it, it can readily be found that there is consent to the prior negligence of A, whose control over the risk has terminated, but not to the subsequent negligence of B, who thereafter runs into the car from the rear.

Id.

Looking at the evidence in a light most favorable to Ray, as we must when reviewing summary judgments, Ray and Waldner had agreed upon certain "signals." According to Ray, Waldner so disregarded their understanding that he did not even realize he had run over Ray until Downes intervened. Nothing in the record even suggests that Ray anticipated Waldner would disregard his signals when moving the truck. Ray's awareness of danger was not consent to relieve Waldner of his duty of care. Not every acceptance of known danger may reasonably be interpreted as evidence of such consent. Prosser & Keeton, *supra* at 490. "[Although one may assume the risk of the negligence of another if he is fully informed of such negligence, one is not, under the doctrine of assumption of risk, bound to anticipate the negligent conduct of others." *Garcia v. City of South Tucson*, 131 Ariz. 315, 640 P.2d 1117, 1121 (Ct. App. 1981) rev'd on other grounds, *Garcia v. City of South Tucson*, 135 Ariz. 604, 663 P.2d 596 (Ct. App. 1983)).

. . . .

We . . . reverse and remand for trial as to Waldner and his employer, Wieczorek. In so doing, our disposition preserves the opportunity for Waldner and Wieczorek to pursue traditional tort defenses such as assumption of the risk at trial.

SABERS, AMUNDSON and KONENKAMP, JUSTICES, concur.

MILLER, CHIEF JUSTICE, concurs in part and dissents in part.

MILLER, CHIEF JUSTICE (concurring in part and dissenting in part).

I would affirm the circuit court's grant of summary judgment in its entirety.

. . . .

The majority grounds its holding, and ceases any further analysis of assumption of the risk, principally relying on secondary authority (a Prosser and Keeton hornbook) and an old decision by the intermediate court of appeals in Arizona. That simply is not an adequate analysis. I will next examine the three elements necessary to a proper assumption of the risk analysis.

A. Actual or Constructive Knowledge of the Risk.

A court must first look to see if a plaintiff had actual or constructive knowledge of the risk. Unlike the majority, I agree with Waldner and would hold that Ray's deposition clearly established that he had *actual* knowledge of the danger involved at the time he positioned himself near the rear wheels of the truck. . . .

B. Appreciation of the Character of the Risk.

A court must next examine the appreciation of the character of the risk. It is important to observe that although Ray had only worked for Downes for a short time, he did have considerable farm experience. Additionally, he had approximately ten years' experience driving and maneuvering heavy trucks with fellow co-workers in close proximity. Ray admitted that any adult person of average intelligence would understand the danger of getting in front of the wheels of a truck while it was moving.

Q: You didn't need to have anybody warn you or tell you you could get hurt if you got your feet and legs in front of the wheels on a semi-trailer, did you?

A: No. I [Ray] knew it was unsafe to be there.

See Bell v. East River Elec. Power Coop., Inc., 535 N.W.2d 750, 754 (S.D. 1995) (concluding a plaintiff will be held to have appreciated the danger undertaken if it was "a risk that no adult person of average intelligence can deny") (citation and internal quotations omitted). " 'One may not close his eyes to obvious dangers, and cannot recover where he was in possession of facts from which he would be legally charged with appreciation of the danger.' " *Goepfert*, 1997 S.D. 56, ¶9, 563 N.W.2d at 143 (citing *Herod v. Grant*, 262 So. 2d 781, 783 (Miss. 1972) (quoting 57 Am.Jur.2d *Negligence* § 282 (1971))).

C. Voluntary Acceptance of the Risk.

Finally, a plaintiff will be deemed to have assumed the risk if it can be said that the risk was voluntarily accepted, having had the time, knowledge, and experience to make an intelligent choice.

(1) A plaintiff does not assume a risk of harm unless he voluntarily accepts the risk.

(2) The plaintiff's acceptance of a risk is not voluntary if the defendant's tortious conduct has left him no reasonable alternative course in order to

(a) avert harm to himself or another, or

(b) exercise or protect a right or privilege of which the defendant has no right to deprive him.

Mack, 1996 S.D. 63, ¶ 15, 548 N.W.2d at 814-15 (citing with approval the Restatement (Second) of Torts § 496E (1965)).

As evidenced by the following testimony, Ray has conceded that he voluntarily put himself in a position of danger:

Q: And you voluntarily put yourself in that position of danger, didn't you?

A: Yes, I guess I did.

All individuals have a duty of care for their own safety. *See Goepfert,* 1997 S.D. 56, 111, 563 N.W.2d at 143.

Ray has testified that there were other, reasonable, alternatives available to him:

Q: You would agree that the accident would not have happened had you used other alternatives that were available to you?

A: Yes, I believe so.

Q: And one of the alternatives that was available to you, would have been to have the driver stop the truck, shut it off and get out; right?

A: Yes.

Q: And then the driver could have positioned the auger under the belly dump?

A: Yes.

Q: And that would have been a reasonable alternative to the one that you actually used wouldn't it?

A: Yes.

Ray admits that he was not compelled by Waldner to use the particular method he did. Rather, Ray felt the method of moving the auger that he employed was more convenient.[2] In utilizing this method, Ray was acting under no compulsion of

---

[2] There is no evidence in the record indicating that either Downes or Waldner gave Ray the impression that they were in a hurry. Setting up the auger took several minutes and it cannot be said that

circumstances created by Waldner. The Restatement (Second) of Torts § 496E cmt. b provides in part:

> The plaintiff's acceptance of the risk is to be regarded as voluntary even though he is acting under the compulsion of circumstances, not created by the tortious conduct of the defendant, which have left him no reasonable alternative. Where the defendant is under no independent duty to the plaintiff, and the plaintiff finds himself confronted by a choice of risks, or is driven by his own necessities to accept a danger, the situation is not to be charged against the defendant.

. . . .

Ray's reliance on *Stenholtz v. Modica*, 264 N.W.2d 514 (S.D. 1978), is misplaced. In *Stenholtz*, the plaintiff set up a scaffold underneath a canopy. The canopy was in poor condition and the plaintiff was aware of it. However, the owner/defendant assured the plaintiff the canopy was safe. The canopy collapsed, injuring the plaintiff. This Court held that plaintiff's knowledge of a potential danger and his appreciation of the risk were not established as they were offset " 'where the injured person surrenders his better judgment as a result of an assurance of safety' " of the canopy by the defendant. *Id.* at 518 (citing *McConnell v. Pic-Walsh Freight Co.*, 432 S.W.2d 292, 298 (Mo. 1968)). Here, there were no such assurances by any of the defendants, only Ray's repeated admissions that he was aware of the dangerousness of the situation he had voluntarily placed himself in.

Ray also contends that under *Nepstad v. Randall*, 82 S.D. 615, 152 N.W.2d 383 (1967), he should not have been held to have assumed the risk because of Waldner's alleged negligence in driving the semi. In other words, Ray argues that Waldner's alleged negligence was the proximate cause of his injury. Whether one adopts the majority or minority position in *Nepstad*, the present facts are clearly distinguishable. Ray has admitted he knew that it is difficult to move large vehicles short distances and that he was aware he might be injured. Simply put, Waldner's actions were not unforeseeable or unexpected as was the defendant's negligence of the unexpected accelerated turn in *Nepstad*. There is no allegation that Waldner suddenly turned or accelerated as in *Nepstad*. Upon Ray's command, Waldner drove the vehicle straight ahead only three or four feet. While the plaintiff in *Nepstad* did not anticipate a quick accelerated turn, Ray admits "I knew it was unsafe to be there" and that he was taking the risk of injuring his legs or hip.

Ray argues that Waldner failed to utilize his mirrors properly and failed to see his hand signals. Yet before Waldner entered the semi, Ray knew that he would be required to simultaneously use his hands to move the auger and signal Waldner. Furthermore, before the accident Ray knew that some of the windows were up in the semi and that there was a significant amount of noise which could have prevented Waldner from hearing him shout to stop. Where a plaintiff has impliedly consented to the negligence, and agrees to take his own chances, "[t]he legal result

---

Ray did not have a reasonable opportunity to reconsider his approach. *See Berg v. Sukup Mfg. Co.*, 355 N.W.2d 833, 835 (S.D. 1984) (in considering available alternatives, "reasonableness refers to whether the plaintiff had a reasonable opportunity to elect whether or not to subject himself to the danger."). Safer alternatives should not be held unreasonable merely because they entail duplicative effort.

is that the defendant is simply relieved of the duty which would otherwise exist." W. Page Keeton et al., *Prosser and Keeton on the Law of Torts* § 68, at 481 (5th ed. 1984).

Since I agree with the trial court that there exists no genuine issue of material fact as to whether Ray assumed the risk of his injury, I would affirm.

---

1.   In *Fred Harvey Corp. v. Mateas*, 170 F.2d 612 (9th Cir. 1948), the plaintiff was injured when he was thrown by an unusually rambunctious Grand Canyon tour mule named Chiggers. He argued (successfully) that he had assumed the risk of a well-behaved mule, not a fractious one. If a livery stable asks its customers about their skill, and assigns them horses to ride based on their answers, will they be protected from liability? What if it is a well-known phenomenon that people questioned about their skill at a given activity will tend to exaggerate their ability? How can a livery stable protect itself from liability? Should it be able to protect itself from liability for providing skittish horses to its customer?

As has been noted, express assumption of risk is usually a contractual matter. Whenever one goes horseback riding on a rented horse, uses a skateboard park, or participates in a rock-climbing class, the entity providing the resource will normally require that a release be signed before allowing access to the facilities. When one enters a city subway, there are certain risks that are tacitly accepted. When one is informed of the risks of a non-negligently performed medical procedure, one might be characterized as assuming those risks. There are, however, certain types of risk that one should not be able to accept, whether tacitly or by contract. In *Tunkl v. The Regents of the University of California*, 383 P.2d 441 (Cal. 1963) (In Bank), the Supreme Court of California ruled that a contract in which the plaintiff had released the defendants from the consequences of their own negligence was void as against public policy. The plaintiff in that case had been required to sign the release upon his admission to a hospital emergency room, and the court concluded that such a release was invalid as a matter of law.

2.   What kinds of risk are assumable? If you are teaching teenagers to drive, and are injured in an accident which occurs during a lesson, should you be able to sue the driver? Should a patient be able to exchange a promise not to sue a doctor, even for negligent treatment, for a reduced bill?

BASS v. AETNA INSURANCE CO.
Supreme Court of Louisiana, 1979
370 So. 2d 511

DIXON, JUSTICE.

Mr. and Mrs. Loyd Bass sued Aetna Insurance Company, insurer of Mr. Kenneth Fussell under a homeowner's policy, and Southern Farm Bureau Casualty Insurance Company, insurer of Shepard's Fold Church of God, seeking damages for personal injuries suffered by Mrs. Bass when Mr. Fussell, a member of the Shepard's Fold Church, ran down the church aisle and collided with Mrs. Bass, also a member of the church, who was in the aisle praying. The defendants denied all allegations of negligence on the part of their insureds, and, alternatively, pleaded the affirmative defenses of assumption of the risk and contributory negligence. After trial on the merits, the Twenty-Second Judicial District Court for the Parish of St. Tammany dismissed plaintiffs' suit and on appeal the First Circuit Court of Appeal affirmed the dismissal in an unpublished opinion. Upon plaintiffs' application we granted writs.

On the evening of February 12, 1974, during a revival service, the Shepard's Fold Church of God was very crowded with not enough seats to accommodate all the parishioners. Consequently, Mrs. Bass and other parishioners who could not find seats were standing in the aisles of the church. Reverend Rodney Jeffers, in the course of preaching to the congregation, stated that the doors of the church should be opened and referred to the possibility of "running." Immediately afterward, Mr. Fussell began running up the aisle and ran into Mrs. Bass, who was in the aisle praying with her head bowed. As a result, Mrs. Bass fell and was injured.

The issues are whether Mr. Fussell was negligent, whether the Shepard's Fold Church of God was negligent, and, if so, whether the plaintiffs' action is barred by either the defenses of assumption of the risk or contributory negligence. Although Mr. Fussell testified that he was "trotting" under the Spirit of the Lord and does not remember actually running into Mrs. Bass, another witness testified that she saw Mr. Fussell run into Mrs. Bass and knock her down. If Fussel's defense is that he was not in control of his actions, it can be compared to voluntary intoxication, which will not exonerate one from delictual responsibility. A worshiper in church has no more right to run over a fellow worshiper in the aisle than a passerby on the sidewalk. Mr. Fussell breached this duty and was negligent when he trotted or run [sic] down the aisle of the church without regard for the safety of other parishioners in the aisles.

Actionable negligence also results from the creation or maintenance of an unreasonable risk of injury to others. In determining whether the risk is unreasonable, not only the seriousness of the harm that may be caused is relevant, but also the likelihood that harm may be caused. In the instant case, according to both Mrs. Bass and Reverend Jeffers, there were approximately three hundred fifty to three hundred seventy-five parishioners in the church on the night of the accident, and many of the parishioners were standing in the aisles. Reverend Jeffers recognized the likelihood that harm might be caused by this crowded condition because he testified that he asked that the aisles be cleared, that he encouraged "open response to the Spirit," and that running or moving "in the Spirit" were common forms of religious expression in Shepard's Fold Church. Another defense witness testified that Reverend Jeffers, recognizing the crowded aisles, asked if somebody would run for him (which apparently is what Mr. Fussell did). Reverend Jeffers did not stop the service to clear the aisles, but continued to maintain an unreasonable risk of injury to the parishioners. The Shepard's Fold Church is responsible for the negligence of its pastor, Reverend Jeffers, under these circumstances. C.C. 2320.

Concluding that both Mr. Fussell and the church were negligent, we next consider the defenses of assumption of the risk and contributory negligence. The

Court of Appeal, in affirming the trial court, concluded that Mrs. Bass assumed the risk by remaining in the aisle with her eyes closed, and that she was contributorily negligent by remaining after having been alerted that running might occur.

Assumption of the risk and contributory negligence are affirmative defenses, C.C.P. 1005, and as we stated in *Langlois v. Allied Chemical Corp.*, 258 La. 1067, 249 So. 2d 133, 141 (1971):

> "The determination of whether a plaintiff has assumed a risk is made by subjective inquiry, whereas contributory negligence is determined objectively under the reasonable man standard. *See* Restatement (Second), Torts § 496 (1965); Symposium: *Assumption of Risk*, 22 La. L. Rev. 1-166. . . ."

Knowledge is the mainstay of this assumption of the risk defense, and this court will impute knowledge to a plaintiff, not because he was in a position to make certain observations, but only when the plaintiff *actually* made those observations and from those observations should reasonably have known that a risk was involved. Assumption of the risk therefore is properly applicable to those situations where the plaintiff, with knowledge of the peril, *voluntarily* enters into a relationship with defendant involving danger to himself because of defendant's contemplated conduct.

We cannot agree with the Court of Appeal's conclusion that Mrs. Bass assumed the risk. Although Mrs. Bass had belonged to the Church of God faith for approximately fifty-five years and the Shepard's Fold Church for approximately twenty-five years, neither she nor any other witness had seen or heard of any injury or collision in any Church of God church. Before the accident, no one, including Mrs. Bass, felt endangered by worshiping in this church. Mrs. Bass unequivocally testified that she had never seen anyone run in the church. The evidence fails to persuade us that Mrs. Bass actually, subjectively comprehended that by praying in the aisle she was incurring a risk of being run over, or that she could or should have known or understood that she was incurring such a risk.

The defense failed to prove that Mrs. Bass voluntarily assumed or exposed herself to this risk. Movement in the aisles was not an extraordinary condition in this church because worshipers frequently went to the altar, "the very central focal point in the church," for prayer. Heedless running in the aisle was an unusual and extraordinary hazard, to which plaintiff did not knowingly expose herself. *Rosenberger v. Central Louisiana District Livestock Show*, 312 So. 2d 300 (La. 1975).[4]

Contributory negligence is also an affirmative defense; the defendants bear the burden of proving contributory negligence by a preponderance of the evidence. Contributory negligence is objectively determined under the "reasonable [person]" standard. It is not contributory negligence to bow one's head when praying in a church, whether in the pew or in the aisle.

. . . .

For the reasons assigned, the judgments of the district court and of the Court of

---

[4] In *Rosenberger*, the plaintiff was injured in a bareback bronco riding contest when the horse ran the plaintiff into the gatepost of a gate in the arena negligently left open during the contest. This court found that the plaintiff had assumed the natural and ordinary risks ancillary to bronco riding but not the extraordinary risks created by negligent operation or maintenance of the rodeo premises.

Appeal are reversed; the case is remanded to the Court of Appeal, First Circuit, to fix the damages to which plaintiffs are entitled. All costs are taxed against the defendants.

MARCUS, J., concurs in part and dissents in part and assigns reasons.

SUMMERS, C.J., dissents.

BLANCHE, J., dissents and assigns reasons.

MARCUS, JUSTICE (concurring in part and dissenting in part).

I consider that Mr. Fussell was negligent and that his negligence was the sole proximate cause of the accident. Moreover, I do not feel that Mrs. Bass either assumed the risk or was contributorily negligent. I do not find that Reverend Jeffers was negligent; however, even assuming that he was, I do not consider that his negligence was a proximate cause of the accident. Hence, I concur in part and dissent in part.

BLANCHE, JUSTICE, dissenting.

I respectfully dissent.

I believe that Mrs. Bass assumed the risk of the injury which she suffered because she knew, or reasonably should have known, from her own personal experience the demonstrative nature of the church service which she understood and in which she was a willing participant.

PROBLEM

F, who was raised in the country and still lives there, decides to spend a day at a car race. He takes his seat in the stands, and the race begins. Fairly shortly thereafter, he begins to wheeze. He has so much trouble breathing that the paramedics at the track need to rescue him, and he is forced to spend some time in the hospital. It turns out that he is allergic to automobile exhaust in the large quantities that racing cars produce.

F files suit against the race track. What will he argue? What defenses will the track raise?

CASTELLO v. COUNTY OF NASSAU
Supreme Court, Appellate Division, Second Department, 1996
636 N.Y.S.2d 817

Before Bracken, J.P., and O'Brien, Ritter, Friedmann and Goldstein, JJ.

MEMORANDUM BY THE COURT.

In an action to recover damages for personal injuries, the plaintiff appeals from an order of the Supreme Court, Nassau County (Roberto, J.), dated July 29, 1994, which, upon reargument, granted the motion by the defendant Incorporated Village of Freeport to dismiss the complaint insofar as it is asserted against it.

ORDERED that the order is affirmed, with costs.

The plaintiff, an experienced softball player, was injured during the eighth inning of a softball game when he slid head-first into home plate and jammed his shoulder on a protruding corner of home plate. The plaintiff admitted that, prior to the accident, he had noticed that the third-base side of home plate was "being dug" by the batters.

It is well settled that those who voluntarily participate in a sporting activity "may be held to have consented, by their participation, to those injury-causing events which are known, apparent or reasonably foreseeable consequences of the participation" (*Turcotte v. Fell*, 68 N.Y.2d 432, 439, 510 N.Y.S.2d 49, 502 N.E.2d 964). "If the risks of the activity are fully comprehended or perfectly obvious, plaintiff has consented to them and defendant has performed its duty" (*Pascucci v. Town of Oyster Bay*, 186 A.D.2d 725, 726, 588 N.Y.S.2d 663). In the present case, the plaintiff admitted that he knew that the third-base side of home plate was "dug out". In addition, because the plaintiff, a right-handed batter, had batted several times during the game from that side of home plate, he had actually stood in the "ditch" next to the protruding corner of home plate. Under these circumstances, the risk presented by the "protruding home plate" was not a concealed one, and the plaintiff consciously assumed that risk by his voluntary participation in the game. Accordingly, the court properly dismissed the complaint insofar as it is asserted against the Incorporated Village of Freeport.

We have considered the plaintiff's remaining contentions and find them to be without merit.

Bracken, J.P., and O'Brien, Ritter, Friedmann and Goldstein, JJ., concur.

Was there any negligence on the part of the defendant in this case? Is the court even interested in the possibility?

PROBLEM

G visits a new zoo on its opening day to see the polar bears. She is particularly fond of polar bears and knows a good deal about them. The bear cage is made of an inner chain link fence and an outer iron fence. G climbs over the outer fence and reaches her arm into the cage under the chain link fence. One of the bears bites her arm severely. Whom may G sue, and for what? What defenses will be raised? Irrespective of the law, should G be able to recover anything?

b.   Assumption of Risk in the Context of Other Defenses

1.   Abolishing Assumption of Risk

BLACKBURN v. DORTA
Supreme Court of Florida, 1977
348 So. 2d 287

SUNDBERG, JUSTICE.

These three consolidated cases are before the Court under our conflict certiorari jurisdiction as provided by Article V, Section 3(b)(3), Florida Constitution, and Florida Appellate Rule 4.5(b). . . .

Since our decision in *Hoffman v. Jones*, [280 So. 2d 431 (Fla. 1973),] contributory negligence no longer serves as a complete bar to plaintiff's recovery but is to be considered in apportioning damages according to the principles of comparative negligence. We are now asked to determine the effect of the *Hoffman* decision on the common law doctrine of assumption of risk. If assumption of risk is equivalent to contributory negligence, then *Hoffman* mandates that it can no longer operate as a complete bar to recovery. However, if it has a distinct purpose apart from contributory negligence, its continued existence remains unaffected by *Hoffman*. This question was expressly reserved in *Hoffman* as being not ripe for decision. 280 So. 2d 431, 439.

At the outset, we note that assumption of risk is not a favored defense. There is a puissant drift toward abrogating the defense. The argument is that assumption of risk serves no purpose which is not subsumed by either the doctrine of contributory negligence or the common law concept of duty. It is said that this redundancy results in confusion and, in some cases, denies recovery unjustly. The leading case in Florida dealing with the distinction between the doctrines recognizes that "[a]t times the line of demarcation between contributory negligence and assumption of risk is exceedingly difficult to define." *Byers v. Gunn*, 81 So. 2d 723, 727 (Fla. 1955). The issue is most salient in states which have enacted comparative negligence legislation. Those statutes provide that the common law defense of contributory negligence no longer necessarily acts as a complete bar to recovery. The effect of these statutes upon the doctrine of assumption of risk has proved to be controversial. Joining the intensifying assault upon the doctrine, a number of comparative negligence jurisdictions have abrogated assumption of risk. Those jurisdictions hold that assumption of risk is interchangeable with contributory negligence and should be treated equivalently. Today we are invited to join this trend of dissatisfaction with the doctrine. For the reasons herein expressed, we accept the invitation.

At the commencement of any analysis of the doctrine of assumption of risk, we must recognize that we deal with a potpourri of labels, concepts, definitions, thoughts, and doctrines. The confusion of labels does not end with the indiscriminate and interchangeable use of the terms "contributory negligence" and "assumption of risk." In the case law and among text writers, there have developed categories of assumption of risk. Distinctions exist between *express* and *implied;* between *primary* and *secondary;* and between *reasonable* and *unreasonable* or, as sometimes expressed, *strict* and *qualified.* It will be our task to analyze these various labels and to trace the historical basis of the doctrine to unravel what has been in the law an "enigma wrapped in a mystery."

It should be pointed out that we are not here concerned with express assumption of risk which is a contractual concept outside the purview of this inquiry and upon which we express no opinion herein. Included within the definition of express assumption of risk are express contracts not to sue for injury or loss which may thereafter be occasioned by the covenantee's negligence as well as situations in which actual consent exists such as where one voluntarily participates in a contact sport.

The breed of assumption of risk with which we deal here is that which arises by implication or implied assumption of risk. Initially it may be divided into the categories of *primary* and *secondary.* The term primary assumption of risk is simply another means of stating that the defendant was not negligent, either because he owed no duty to the plaintiff in the first instance, or because he did not breach the duty owed. Secondary assumption of risk is an affirmative defense to an established breach of a duty owed by the defendant to the plaintiff.

The concept of primary assumption of risk is the basis for the historical doctrine which arose in the master-servant relationship during the late nineteenth century. The master was held not to be negligent if he provided a reasonably safe place to work; the servant was said to have assumed the inherent risks that remained. In this context assumption of risk was not an affirmative defense at all. Rather, it was another way of expressing that the master was not negligent, for the servant had the burden of proving that his injury resulted from a risk other than one inherent in a facility or location that was a reasonably safe place to work. As is often the case in the common law, however, the doctrine mutated into an affirmative defense, with the burden of pleading and proof upon the master. Consequently, even if the servant could show that the master owed and had breached a duty to provide a reasonably safe place to work, the master could escape liability if he could establish that the servant had voluntarily exposed himself to a risk negligently created by the master. Thus, two distinct concepts came to bear the same label with inevitable confusion which has persisted to the present.

It is apparent that no useful purpose is served by retaining terminology which expresses the thought embodied in primary assumption of risk. This branch (or trunk) of the tree of assumption of risk is subsumed in the principle of negligence itself. Under our Florida jury instructions, the jury is directed first to determine whether the defendant has been negligent, i.e., did he owe a duty to the plaintiff and, if so, did he breach that duty? To sprinkle the term assumption of risk into the equation can only lead to confusion of a jury. An example of this concept is presented in the operation of a passenger train. It can be said that a passenger assumes the risk of lurches and jerks which are ordinary and usual to the proper operation of the train, but that he does not assume the risk of extraordinary or unusual lurches and jerks resulting from substandard operation of the train. The same issue can be characterized in terms of the standard of care of the railroad. Thus, it can be said that the railroad owes a duty to operate its train with the degree of care of an ordinary prudent person under similar circumstances which includes some lurching and jerking while a train is in motion or commencing to move under ideal circumstances. So long as the lurching or jerking is not extraordinary due to substandard conduct of the railroad, there is no breach of duty and, hence, no negligence on the part of the railroad. The latter characterization of the issue clearly seems preferable and is consistent with the manner in which the jury is instructed under our standard jury instructions.

Having dispensed with *express* and *primary-implied* assumption of risk, we recur to *secondary-implied* assumption of risk which is the affirmative defense variety that has been such a thorn in the judicial side. The affirmative defense brand of assumption of risk can be subdivided into the type of conduct which is reasonable but nonetheless bars recovery (sometimes called *pure* or *strict* assumption of risk), and the type of conduct which is unreasonable and bars recovery (sometimes referred to as *qualified* assumption of risk). Application of pure or strict assumption of risk is exemplified by the hypothetical situation in which a landlord has negligently permitted his tenant's premises to become highly flammable and a fire ensues. The tenant returns from work to find the premises a blazing inferno with his infant child trapped within. He rushes in to retrieve the child and is injured in so doing. Under the pure doctrine of assumption of risk, the tenant is barred from recovery because it can be said he voluntarily exposed himself to a known risk. Under this view of assumption of risk, the tenant is precluded from recovery notwithstanding the fact that his conduct could be said to be entirely reasonable under the circumstances. There is little to commend this doctrine of implied-pure or strict assumption of risk, and our research discloses no Florida case in which it has been applied. Certainly, in light of *Hoffman v. Jones, supra,* there is no reason supported by law or justice in this state to give credence to such a principle of law.

There remains, then, for analysis only the principle of implied-qualified assumption of risk, and it can be demonstrated in the hypothetical recited above with the minor alteration that the tenant rushes into the blazing premises to retrieve his favorite fedora. Such conduct on the tenant's part clearly would be unreasonable. Consequently, his conduct can just as readily be characterized as contributory negligence. It is the failure to exercise the care of a reasonably prudent man under similar circumstances. It is this last category of assumption of risk which has caused persistent confusion in the law of torts because of the lack of analytic difference between it and contributory negligence. If the only significant form of assumption of risk (implied-qualified) is so readily characterized, conceptualized, and verbalized as contributory negligence, can there be any sound rationale for retaining it as a separate affirmative defense to negligent conduct which bars recovery altogether? In the absence of any historical imperative, the answer must be no. We are persuaded that there is no historical significance to the doctrine of implied-secondary assumption of risk. As pointed out earlier in this opinion, the affirmative defense developed from a misapplication of principles applicable to the standard of care imposed upon an employer in the master-servant relationship. The opinion of the United States Supreme Court in *Tiller v. Atlantic Coast Line R R*, 318 U.S. 54, 63 S. Ct. 444, 87 L. Ed. 610 (1943), demonstrates that the doctrine has not only been indiscriminately misapplied historically but also represents a morally unacceptable social policy which was calculated to advance the industrial revolution regardless of the cost in human suffering. . . .

We find no discernible basis analytically or historically to maintain a distinction between the affirmative defense of contributory negligence and assumption of risk. The latter appears to be a viable, rational doctrine only in the sense described herein as implied-qualified assumption of risk which connotes unreasonable conduct on the part of the plaintiff. This result comports with the definition of contributory negligence appearing in Restatement (Second) of Torts, § 466 (1965). Furthermore, were we not otherwise persuaded to elimination of assumption of risk as a separate affirmative defense in the context herein described, the decision of this Court in *Hoffman v. Jones, supra*, would dictate such a result. As stated therein:

> . . . . A primary function of a court is to see that legal conflicts are equitably resolved. In the field of tort law, the most equitable result that can ever be reached by a court is the equation of liability with fault. Comparative negligence does this more completely than contributory negligence, and we would be shirking our duty if we did not adopt the better doctrine. 280 So. 2d 431, 438.

Is liability equated with fault under a doctrine which would totally bar recovery by one who voluntarily, but reasonably, assumes a known risk while one whose conduct is unreasonable but denominated "contributory negligence" is permitted to recover a proportionate amount of his damages for injury? Certainly not. Therefore, we hold that the affirmative defense of implied assumption of risk is merged into the defense of contributory negligence and the principles of comparative negligence enunciated in *Hoffman v. Jones, supra*, shall apply in all cases where such defense is asserted.

. . . .

OVERTON, C.J., and ADKINS, BOYD, ENGLAND and HATCHETT, JJ., concur.

———————

What is the difference between assumption of risk and contributory or comparative negligence? Could a jurisdiction consistently maintain both an assumption of risk and a comparative negligence defense?

2. Retaining Assumption of Risk

PATTERSON v. SACRAMENTO CITY UNIFED SCHOOL DISTRICT

California Court of Appeal, 2007
66 Cal. Rptr. 3d 337

CANTIL-SAKAUYE, J.

Plaintiff James Patterson was injured while participating in a truck driver training course. Defendant Sacramento City Unified School District (District) offered the course as part of its adult education program. Patterson sued the District for negligent supervision. The trial court granted the District's motion for summary judgment, ruling that the doctrine of primary assumption of risk barred Patterson's negligence claim.

On appeal, Patterson contends judgment must be reversed because: (1) the court improperly overruled a finding of duty in the District's first summary judgment motion; (2) assumption of risk does not apply in the circumstances of this case; and (3) even if the assumption of risk doctrine applies, there are triable issues of fact on whether the District acted recklessly. We agree with plaintiff that assumption of the risk does not apply in these circumstances and shall reverse the judgment.

FACTUAL BACKGROUND

In spring 2003, Patterson enrolled in the District's California Heavy Duty Truck Driving Program. The truck driving course provided students with the training and hands-on experience they needed to become professional truck drivers. It consisted of three six-week segments: classroom instruction; hands-on training; and on-the-road experience. In order to pass the course, students were required to participate in community service projects as part of their hands-on training and on-the-road experience.

The District assigned credentialed heavy-duty truck driving instructors to teach each segment of the course. Joe Arcuri and Ward Allen taught the second and third segments. Allen also served as field instructor and supervisor for the community service projects.

On May 9, 2003, during the first week of the hands-on segment of the training course, Patterson and several other students participated in a community service project which involved picking up bleachers from several locations, loading them onto a flat bed trailer attached to a tractor, and transporting them to the site of a rugby tournament. The classroom curriculum covered freight loading in a basic sense, but did not cover the specifics of loading flat bed trucks or trailers. According to the instructors, a primary goal of the community service assignment was to teach students how to load the trailers safely. The instructors described the loading of cargo as a "hands-on kind of thing" that involved common sense. The instructors typically critiqued the students after they loaded the cargo.

Allen was responsible for instructing Patterson and the other students on loading the bleachers on the flat bed trailer. The bed of the trailer was between 96 and 102 inches wide and approximately five feet off the ground. Allen was present when the students picked up aluminum bleachers at the first location and loaded them on the trailer without incident. He told the students to pick up the bleachers at the second location on their own. Allen did not know how much prior training or experience his students had in loading trailers.

The bleachers at the second location were made of heavy wood. Allen had not seen the wooden bleachers before assigning the students to pick them up. Because there were no teachers present, and none of the students was considered to be in charge, the unsupervised students decided as a group how to load the wooden bleachers. It took six students to carry each section of wooden bleachers. Patterson and a student named Don Cruse stood on the trailer bed. Patterson had never climbed on the flat bed trailer before he and the other students arrived at the second pick-up location. Patterson and Cruse pulled on the wooden bleachers while the remaining students pushed the bleachers from below. Patterson cautioned the students who were pushing to slow down when he recognized that he was running out of room at the edge of the trailer. Instead, the students gave the bleachers "one big push," and Patterson fell backward off the trailer.

DISCUSSION

. . . .

III.

Duty of Care and Assumption of Risk

Patterson's complaint alleges that the District "had a duty to supervise, train, educate, instruct, and oversee the conduct of its [truck driver training] students" on proper techniques for loading and unloading flat bed trucks and trailers and "to exercise ordinary care to protect students from the type of injury" that Patterson suffered. The District maintains that under the doctrine of assumption of risk, it owed Patterson no duty of care.

Historically, the concept of duty developed in the late 19th century as a legal device was "designed to curtail the feared propensities of juries toward liberal awards." (*Dillon v. Legg* (1968) 68 Cal.2d 728, 734, 69 Cal.Rptr. 72, 441 P.2d 912 (*Dillon*).) The essential question in a duty analysis is " 'whether the plaintiff's interests are entitled to legal protection against the defendant's conduct. . . . [Duty] is a shorthand statement of a conclusion, rather than an aid to analysis in itself. . . . But it should be recognized that "duty" is not sacrosanct in itself, but only an expression of the sum total of those considerations of policy which lead the law to say that the particular plaintiff is entitled to protection.' [Citation.]" (*Ibid.*; accord, *Avila v. Citrus Community College Dist.* (2006) 38 Cal.4th 148, 160–161, 41 Cal.Rptr.3d 299, 131 P.3d 383 (*Avila*).)

In deciding whether to depart from the general principle that a person is liable for injuries caused by his or her failure to exercise reasonable care, courts balance the now classic list of policy considerations which include "the foreseeability of harm to the plaintiff, the degree of certainty that the plaintiff suffered injury, the closeness of the connection between the defendant's conduct and the injury suffered, the moral blame attached to the defendant's conduct, the policy of preventing future harm, the extent of the burden to the defendant and consequences to the community of imposing a duty to exercise care with resulting liability for breach, and the availability, cost, and prevalence of insurance for the risk involved." (*Rowland v. Christian* (1968) 69 Cal.2d 108, 113, 70 Cal.Rptr. 97, 443 P.2d 561; see *Stockinger v. Feather River Community College* (2003) 111 Cal.App.4th 1014, 1035, 4 Cal.Rptr.3d 385 (*Stockinger*).)

This case presents competing policy considerations. On one hand, as an adult student at a public school, is Patterson entitled to legal protection against the alleged negligence of the District employees in failing to supervise and instruct him on how to load wooden bleachers on a flat bed trailer? As we explained, the court denied the District's first summary judgment motion on grounds it owed Patterson a duty of care under statutory law. On the other hand, does the doctrine of assumption of risk relieve the District of any duty of care based on the nature of the class activity and the potentially chilling effect of imposing a duty of care on the District's truck driving instructors? Although this case may not fit neatly into either line of authority, we conclude that Patterson was not engaged in an inherently dangerous activity as a matter of law. Nor do policy considerations favor application of the doctrine of assumption of risk. Accordingly, the court erred in ruling that assumption of risk barred Patterson's negligence claims. . . .

B. *Primary and Secondary Assumption of Risk:*

In *Knight [v. Jewett,* 834 P.2d 696 (Cal. 1992) (en banc)] the Supreme Court reconciled the doctrine of assumption of risk, which completely bars a plaintiff's recovery in a negligence action, with comparative negligence principles announced in *Li v. Yellow Cab Co.* (1975) 13 Cal.3d 804, 119 Cal.Rptr. 858, 532 P.2d 1226 (*Li*). The discussion in *Knight* provides the necessary background for our decision that assumption of risk does not apply in this case. We quote *Knight* at length.

"In *Li,* our court undertook a basic reexamination of the common law doctrine of contributory negligence. As *Li* noted, contributory negligence generally has been defined as ' "conduct on the part of the plaintiff which falls below the standard to which he should conform for his own protection, and which is a legally contributing cause cooperating with the negligence of the defendant in bringing about the plaintiff's harm." ' (*Li, supra,* 13 Cal.3d at p. 809, 119 Cal.Rptr. 858, 532 P.2d 1226, quoting Rest.2d Torts, § 463.) Prior to *Li,* the common law rule was that ' "[e]xcept where the defendant has the last clear chance, the plaintiff's contributory negligence *bars recovery* against a defendant whose negligent conduct would otherwise make him liable to the plaintiff for the harm sustained by him." ' (*Li, supra,* at pp. 809–810, 119 Cal.Rptr. 858, 532 P.2d 1226, italics added, quoting Rest.2d Torts, § 467.)

"In *Li, supra,* 13 Cal.3d 804[, 119 Cal.Rptr. 858, 532 P.2d 1226], we observed that '[i]t is unnecessary for us to catalogue the enormous amount of critical comment that has been directed over the years against the "all-or-nothing" approach of the doctrine of contributory negligence. The essence of that criticism has been constant and clear: the doctrine is inequitable in its operation because it fails to distribute responsibility in proportion to fault. . . . *The basic objection to the doctrine — grounded in the primal concept that in a system in which liability is based on fault, the extent of fault should govern the extent of liability — remains irresistible to reason and all intelligent notions of fairness.*' (At pp. 810–811[, 119 Cal.Rptr. 858, 532 P.2d 1226], italics added.) After taking additional note of the untoward practical consequences of the doctrine in the litigation of cases and the increasing rejection of the doctrine in other jurisdictions, the *Li* court concluded that '[w]e are likewise persuaded that logic, practical experience, and fundamental justice counsel against the retention of the doctrine rendering contributory negligence a complete bar to recovery — and that it should be replaced in this state by a system under which liability for damage will be borne by those whose negligence caused it in direct proportion to their respective fault.' (At pp. 812–813[, 119 Cal.Rptr. 858, 532 P.2d 1226].)

"After determining that the 'all-or-nothing' contributory negligence doctrine should be replaced by a system of comparative negligence, the *Li* court went on to undertake a rather extensive discussion of the effect that the adoption of comparative negligence would have on a number of related tort doctrines, including the doctrines of last clear chance and assumption of risk. (*Li, supra,* 13 Cal.3d at pp. 823–826, 119 Cal.Rptr. 858, 532 P.2d 1226.)

"With respect to the effect of the adoption of comparative negligence on the assumption of risk doctrine — the issue before [the *Knight* court] — the *Li* decision, *supra,* 13 Cal.3d 804[, 119 Cal.Rptr. 858, 532 P.2d 1226], stated as follows: 'As for assumption of risk, we have recognized in this state that this defense overlaps that of contributory negligence to some extent and in fact is made up of at least two distinct defenses. "To simplify greatly, it has been observed . . . that in one kind of situation, to wit, where a plaintiff *unreasonably* undertakes to encounter a specific known risk imposed by a defendant's negligence, plaintiff's conduct, although he may encounter that risk in a prudent manner, is in reality a form of contributory negligence. . . . Other kinds of situations within the doctrine of assumption of risk are those, for example, where plaintiff is held to agree to relieve defendant of an obligation of reasonable conduct toward him. Such a situation would not involve contributory negligence, but rather a reduction of defendant's duty of care." [Citations.] We think it clear that the adoption of a system of comparative negligence should entail the merger of the defense of assumption of risk into the general scheme of assessment of liability in proportion to fault in those particular cases in which the form of assumption of risk involved is no more than a variant of contributory negligence. [Citation.]' (*Li, supra,* 13 Cal.3d at pp. 824–825, 119 Cal.Rptr. 858, 532 P.2d 1226, original italics.)

"As this passage indicates, the *Li* decision, *supra,* 13 Cal.3d 804[, 119 Cal.Rptr. 858, 532 P.2d 1226], clearly contemplated that the assumption of risk doctrine was to be *partially* merged or subsumed into the comparative negligence scheme. Subsequent Court of Appeal decisions have disagreed, however, in interpreting *Li,* as to what category of assumption of risk cases would be merged into the comparative negligence scheme.

"A number of appellate decisions, focusing on the language in *Li* indicating that assumption of risk is in reality a form of contributory negligence 'where a plaintiff *unreasonably* undertakes to encounter a specific known risk imposed by a defendant's negligence' (13 Cal.3d at p. 824[, 119 Cal.Rptr. 858, 532 P.2d 1226]), have concluded that *Li* properly should be interpreted as drawing a distinction between those assumption of risk cases in which a plaintiff 'unreasonably' encounters a known risk imposed by a defendant's negligence and those assumption of risk cases in which a plaintiff 'reasonably' encounters a known risk imposed by a defendant's negligence. (See, e.g., *Ordway v. Superior Court* [1988] 198 Cal.App.3d 98, 103–105[, 243 Cal.Rptr. 536].)

"In our view, these decisions — regardless whether they reached the correct result on the facts at issue — have misinterpreted *Li* by suggesting that our decision contemplated less favorable legal treatment for a plaintiff who reasonably encounters a known risk than for a plaintiff who unreasonably encounters such a risk. . . .

"Indeed, particularly when the relevant passage in *Li, supra,* 13 Cal.3d at pages 824–825, 119 Cal.Rptr. 858, 532 P.2d 1226, is read as a whole and in conjunction with the authorities it cites, we believe it becomes clear that the distinction in assumption of risk cases to which the *Li* court referred in this passage was not a distinction between instances in which a plaintiff unreasonably encounters a known risk imposed by a defendant's negligence and instances in which a plaintiff reasonably encounters such a risk. Rather, the distinction to which the *Li* court referred was between (1) those instances in which the assumption of risk doctrine embodies a legal conclusion that there is 'no duty' on the part of the defendant to protect the plaintiff from a particular risk — the category of assumption of risk that the legal commentators generally refer to as 'primary assumption of risk' — and (2) those instances in which the defendant does owe a duty of care to the plaintiff but the plaintiff knowingly encounters a risk of injury caused by the defendant's breach of that duty — what most commentators have termed 'secondary assumption of risk.' Properly interpreted, the relevant passage in *Li* provides that the category of assumption of risk cases that is not merged into the comparative negligence system and in which the plaintiff's recovery continues to be completely barred involves those cases in which the defendant's conduct did not breach a legal duty of care to the plaintiff, i.e., 'primary assumption of risk' cases, whereas cases involving 'secondary assumption of risk' properly are merged into the comprehensive comparative fault system adopted in *Li*.

"Although the difference between the 'primary assumption of risk'/'secondary assumption of risk' nomenclature and the 'reasonable implied assumption of risk'/'unreasonable implied assumption of risk' terminology embraced in many of the recent Court of Appeal decisions may appear at first blush to be only semantic, the significance extends beyond mere rhetoric. First, in 'primary assumption of risk' cases — where the defendant owes no duty to protect the plaintiff from a particular risk of harm — a plaintiff who has suffered such harm is not entitled to recover from the defendant, whether the plaintiff's conduct in undertaking the activity was reasonable *or unreasonable*. Second, in 'secondary assumption of risk' cases — involving instances in which the defendant has breached the duty of care owed to the plaintiff — the defendant is not entitled to be entirely relieved of liability for an injury proximately caused by such breach, simply because the plaintiff's conduct in encountering the risk of such an injury was *reasonable* rather than unreasonable. Third and finally, the question whether the defendant owed a legal duty to protect the plaintiff from a particular risk of harm does not turn on the reasonableness or unreasonableness of the plaintiff's conduct, but rather on the nature of the activity or sport in which the defendant is engaged and the relationship of the defendant and the plaintiff to that activity or sport. For these reasons, use of the 'reasonable implied assumption of risk'/unreasonable implied assumption of risk' terminology, as a means of differentiating between the cases in which a plaintiff is barred from bringing an action and those in which he or she is not barred, is more misleading than helpful." (*Knight, supra*, 3 Cal.4th at pp. 304–309, 11 Cal.Rptr.2d 2, 834 P.2d 696, fns. omitted.)

In our view, the case before us involves classic secondary assumption of risk — where the District owed a duty of care but, at most, Patterson may have unreasonably encountered the risk of climbing onto the flat bed truck to load the wooden bleachers. As we shall explain, the record and the policy reasons underlying primary assumption of risk demonstrate that the doctrine should not be applied in the circumstances of this case. Accordingly, Patterson's negligence claim survives the District's motion for summary judgment.

C. *Assumption of Risk Does Not Trump the District's Duty:*

The Supreme Court observed in *Knight* that, "the phrase 'assumption of risk' traditionally has been used in a number of very different factual settings involving analytically distinct legal concepts." (*Knight, supra*, 3 Cal.4th at p. 303, 11 Cal.Rptr.2d 2, 834 P.2d 696.) Two different species of assumption of risk are candidates for application in the case before us. One type of assumption of risk arose in the context of active sports and evolved to include similar activities in the school and employment setting. The other type of assumption of risk, more commonly known as the firefighter's rule, arose and developed in the context of the public service professions. As we shall explain, neither species of assumption of risk applies here.

1. The Firefighter's Rule:

The firefighter's rule is a variation on the doctrine of primary assumption of risk based on different policy concerns than those found in the sports context. "In its most classic form, the firefighter's rule involves the question whether a person who negligently has started a fire is liable for an injury sustained by a firefighter who is summoned to fight the fire; the rule provides that the person who started the fire is not liable under such circumstances. [Citation.] Although a number of theories have been cited to support this conclusion, the most persuasive explanation is that the party who negligently started the fire had no legal duty to protect the firefighter from the very danger that the firefighter is employed to confront. [Citations.]" (*Knight, supra*, 3 Cal.4th at p. 309, fn. 5, 11 Cal.Rptr.2d 2, 834 P.2d 696; see also, *Priebe v. Nelson* (2006) 39 Cal.4th 1112, 47 Cal.Rptr.3d 553, 140 P.3d 848 [employee of boarding kennel]; *Calatayud v. State of California* (1998) 18 Cal.4th 1057, 77 Cal.Rptr.2d 202, 959 P.2d 360 [police officer] (*Calatayud*).)

In *Calatayud*, the Supreme Court discussed the policies underlying the firefighter's rule. First, " ' "In terms of duty, it may be said there is none owed the fireman to exercise care so as not to require the special services for which he is trained and paid." ' [Citations.]" (*Calatayud, supra*, 18 Cal.4th at p. 1061, 77 Cal.Rptr.2d 202, 959 P.2d 360.) Second, "[t]he rule is equally grounded in considerations of public policy ' "distilled from the relevant factors involved upon an inquiry into what is fair and just. . . . [¶] [I]t is the fireman's business to deal with that very hazard [the fire] and hence, perhaps by analogy to the contractor engaged as an expert to remedy dangerous situations, he cannot complain of negligence in the creation of the very occasion for his engagement." ' [Citations.] Moreover, 'public safety employees receive special public compensation for confronting the dangers posed by the defendants' negligence.' [Citation.] 'Firemen and policemen are paid for the work they perform including preparation for facing the hazards of their professions and dealing with perils when they arise. When injury occurs, liberal compensation is provided. In addition to the usual medical and disability benefits ordinarily provided all employees covered by the Workers' Compensation Act, firemen and policemen are provided special benefits [including special statutory presumptions of industrial causation, special death benefits, optional paid leaves of absence, and fully paid disability benefits despite retirement].' [Citations.]" (*Id.* at pp. 1061–1062, 77 Cal.Rptr.2d 202, 959 P.2d 360.)

None of the policy reasons undergirding the firefighter's rule applies to a student like Patterson who attends adult education courses offered by a public school district. The student receives no advance training to deal with the danger; rather, he is attending the adult education class to obtain that training. The student receives no compensation in the form of wages; instead, he ordinarily pays fees to the district in order to participate in its educational program. Finally, the adult education student receives no special public benefits when he is injured. (See, e.g., *Land v. Workers' Comp. Appeals Bd.* (2002) 102 Cal.App.4th 491, 125 Cal.Rptr.2d 432 [university student injured during the field experience portion of a class in animal husbandry not entitled to workers' compensation benefits].) Because none of the policy reasons advanced for the firefighter's rule applies in the circumstances of the present case, we conclude the rule is inapplicable.

2. Assumption of Risk in the Sports Context:

The *Knight* court described primary assumption of risk as an exception to the general rule that people "have a duty to use due care to avoid injury to others, and may be held liable if their careless conduct injures another person." (*Knight, supra*, 3 Cal.4th at p. 315, 11 Cal.Rptr.2d 2, 834 P.2d 696.) As we explained earlier, the doctrine applies "where, by virtue of the nature of the activity and the parties' relationship to the activity, the defendant owes no legal duty to protect the plaintiff from the particular risk of harm that caused the injury. . . ." (*Id.* at pp. 314–315, 11 Cal.Rptr.2d 2, 834 P.2d 696.) *Knight* instructs that where "the careless conduct of others is treated as an 'inherent risk' of a sport" or activity, recovery is barred. (*Id.* at p. 316, 11 Cal.Rptr.2d 2, 834 P.2d 696.)

The classic assumption of risk cases arose in the active sports context where California courts ruled that the doctrine barred participants from suing coparticipants or coaches for their injuries. (See, e.g., *Avila, supra,* 38 Cal.4th 148, 41 Cal.Rptr.3d 299, 131 P.3d 383 [student baseball game]; *Cheong v. Antablin* (1997) 16 Cal.4th 1063, 68 Cal.Rptr.2d 859, 946 P.2d 817 [skier]; *Knight, supra,* 3 Cal.4th 296, 11 Cal.Rptr.2d 2, 834 P.2d 696 [touch football game]; *Fortier v. Los Rios Community College Dist.* (1996) 45 Cal.App.4th 430, 52 Cal.Rptr.2d 812 [football practice]; *Regents of the University of California v. Superior Court* (1996) 41 Cal.App.4th 1040, 48 Cal.Rptr.2d 922 [rock climbing class]; *Galardi v. Seahorse Riding Club* (1993) 16 Cal.App.4th 817, 20 Cal.Rptr.2d 270 [horse jumping instruction]; *Tan v. Goddard* (1993) 13 Cal.App.4th 1528, 17 Cal.Rptr.2d 89 [jockey school]; compare *Kahn v. East Side Union High School Dist.* (2003) 31 Cal.4th 990, 4 Cal.Rptr.3d 103, 75 P.3d 30 [primary assumption of risk applied to novice swimmer, but summary judgment reversed because the record established reckless conduct by the coach as a matter of law].)

Knight articulated the policy basis for applying the assumption of risk doctrine in the active sports setting. "In reaching the conclusion that a coparticipant's duty of care should be limited in this fashion, the cases have explained that, in the heat of an active sporting event like baseball or football a participant's normal energetic conduct often includes accidentally careless behavior. The courts have concluded that vigorous participation in such sporting events likely would be chilled if legal liability were to be imposed on a participant on the basis of his or her ordinary careless conduct. The cases have recognized that, in such a sport, even when a participant's conduct violates a rule of the game and may subject the violator to internal sanctions prescribed by the sport itself, imposition of *legal liability* for such conduct might well alter fundamentally the nature of the sport by deterring participants from vigorously engaging in activity that falls close to, but on the permissible side of, a prescribed rule." (*Knight, supra,* 3 Cal.4th at pp. 318–319, 11 Cal.Rptr.2d 2, 834 P.2d 696.)

If the assumption of risk doctrine were limited to the sports context, there would be little question that it is inapplicable in the circumstances of the present case. However, by expanding application of the doctrine to the school and employment setting, California courts have provided the District with a rationale to justify its argument that assumption of risk bars Patterson's negligence claim here. As we explain, the policy basis for applying the doctrine is still lacking.

3. Assumption of Risk in Other Contexts:

California courts have expanded the scope of the assumption of risk doctrine to encompass dangerous activities in other contexts where the activity is inherently dangerous. (See, e.g., *Saville, supra,* 133 Cal.App.4th 857, 36 Cal.Rptr.3d 515 [training in peace officer takedown maneuvers]; *Hamilton v. Martinelli & Associates* (2003) 110 Cal.App.4th 1012, 2 Cal.Rptr.3d 168 (*Hamilton*) [training on physical restraint methods]; *Aaris v. Las Virgenes* Unified School Dist. (1998) 64 Cal.App.4th 1112, 75 Cal.Rptr.2d 801 (*Aaris*) [cheerleader practice]; and *Bushnell v. Japanese–American Religious & Cultural Center* (1996) 43 Cal.App.4th 525, 50 Cal.Rptr.2d 671 (*Bushnell*) [practice of moves in judo class].) Two of these cases deserve special mention.

The first is *Hamilton.* In that case, plaintiff worked as a probation corrections officer (and peace officer) in a youth detention center. Her duties included supervising and counseling children between the ages of 10 and 18, including violent offenders. Plaintiff participated in an "Unarmed Defensive Tactics" training course taught by defendant Martinelli and Associates. She injured her neck and back when she performed a "maneuver . . . designed to teach [her how] to extricate herself if she was attacked, landed on her stomach, and was being choked by an assailant straddling her back." (*Hamilton, supra,* 110 Cal.App.4th at p. 1018, 2 Cal.Rptr.3d 168.) In holding that the doctrine of primary assumption of risk applied, the court found that the injuries plaintiff suffered in a training course for probation corrections officers were an inherent risk of performing the training maneuver. (*Id.* at pp. 1017–1018, 1023, 2 Cal.Rptr.3d 168.) "Moreover, plaintiff's employment duties entailed the very risk of injury of which she complains. Plaintiff's employment duties included restraining violent juvenile offenders. She was required to wear a uniform and carry pepper spray. And since 1997, her job philosophy emphasized physical restraint of juveniles. Thus, the ability to physically restrain juveniles was a necessary tool in plaintiff's employment. By continuing in this employment capacity, plaintiff assumed the risk that she would be injured by a violent juvenile offender. And by participating in an employer-required training course, she assumed the risk that she would be injured while training to restrain a violent juvenile offender." (*Id.* at p. 1023, 2 Cal.Rptr.3d 168.)

Unlike the activity described in *Hamilton,* which satisfied one requirement for applying assumption of risk, loading a flat bed trailer is not an inherently dangerous activity. We reject the District's suggestion, based on language in *Aaris, supra,* 64 Cal.App.4th at p. 1114, 75 Cal.Rptr.2d 801, that "[w]henever gravity is at play, . . . the risk of injury in inherent." This case involves standing on the bed of the trailer, albeit five feet above the ground. Gravity is similarly "at play" when a person climbs up a ladder, walks across a bridge or leans against a porch railing. The District cites no case that holds assumption of risk applies to such common, everyday work activities. We conclude that loading wooden bleachers on a flat bed trailer is not inherently dangerous as a matter of law.

Moreover, the court's rationale in *Hamilton* is really a mixture of the firefighter's rule and assumption of risk based on competitive or violent sports announced in *Knight.* Because plaintiff incurred the injury in connection with her employment, all the policy reasons supporting application of the firefighter's rule would apply, including the provision of care and treatment under the workers' compensation scheme. In the case before us, Patterson was not an employee who would be covered by workers' compensation or (so far as the record shows) by any other insurance. Patterson, a student, simply signed up for a truck driver training class. We conclude that the policy reasons for applying primary assumption of risk in *Hamilton* are completely absent here.

The second case deserving special mention is *Saville, supra,* 133 Cal.App.4th 857, 36 Cal.Rptr.3d 515, an opinion from this court. The plaintiff in *Saville* enrolled in a certified peace officer training class offered by the defendant community college. The course consisted of three parts: lectures, arrest and control methods, and firearms. Students were required to attend and pass all three parts of the course. (*Id.* at p. 861, 36 Cal.Rptr.3d 515.) They learned arrest and control methods from the local police chief "in as realistic an experience as possible . . . [by] 'modeling' the actions an actual police officer would take when performing a takedown in the field." (*Id.* at p. 862, 36 Cal.Rptr.3d 515.) Three police officers demonstrated four takedown maneuvers. (*Id.* at pp. 862–863, 36 Cal.Rptr.3d 515.) The officers then moved around the room to observe the students as they practiced the maneuvers. Plaintiff injured his back while practicing what was described as a forehead sweep. (*Id.* at p. 863, 36 Cal.Rptr.3d 515.) This court concluded that the takedown maneuvers bore "similar risks of injury inherent in many sports. The maneuvers are inherently dangerous. One person is intentionally throwing another to the ground. 'Whenever gravity is at play with the human body, the risk of injury is inherent.' " (*Ibid.*, quoting *Aaris, supra*, 64 Cal.App.4th at p. 1114, 75 Cal.Rptr.2d 801.) "Careless conduct by others is also an inherent risk in performing the maneuvers. Plaintiff acknowledged both he and his partner were inexperienced and had not learned or practiced these maneuvers before the class. Even with the steps taken by the officers to minimize the risk of injury — personal training, placing mats on the floors, demonstrating the moves, observing the students perform the moves — the risk of harm from participating in the actual maneuvers with an inexperienced person remained obvious, and plaintiff suffered injury from that particular risk. Grabbing someone's face from behind, pushing his head into his spine, and throwing him back and down to the ground with an elbow in his back, even at half speed, could hurt someone." (*Saville, supra*, at p. 867, 36 Cal.Rptr.3d 515.)

Once again, there is a vast difference between the activity described as inherently dangerous in *Saville* and the activity at issue in the present case. Driving a truck, or even loading a truck, does not involve the same risk of injury as the violent take-down maneuver at issue in that case. Inherent danger is measured by more than the number or inches or feet between the plaintiff and the ground. (Compare *Aaris, supra*, 64 Cal.App.4th at p. 1114, 75 Cal.Rptr.2d 801.)

We also concluded in *Saville* that "[i]mposing a duty to eliminate the risk of injury from the activity in [that] particular classroom situation would invariably chill vigorous participation in learning the maneuvers." (*Saville, supra*, 133 Cal.App.4th at p. 867, 36 Cal.Rptr.3d 515.) What the instructors allegedly did — or did not do — in the present case is conduct that we want to chill. As a matter of policy, we do not want truck driver training instructors to send inexperienced students out to load flat bed trailers without instruction and supervision.

In deciding that primary assumption of risk does not apply in the case before us, we cite *Knight* one last time: "It may be helpful at this point to summarize our general conclusions as to the current state of the doctrine of assumption of risk in light of the adoption of comparative fault principles in *Li, supra*, 13 Cal.3d 804, 119 Cal.Rptr. 858, 532 P.2d 1226, general conclusions that reflect the view of a majority of the justices of the court (i.e., the three justices who have signed this opinion and Justice Mosk (see conc. and dis. opn. by Mosk, J., *post*, p. 321, 11 Cal.Rptr.2d 2, 834 P.2d 696)). In cases involving 'primary assumption of risk' — where, by virtue of the nature of the activity and the parties' relationship to the activity, the defendant owes no legal duty to protect the plaintiff from the particular risk of harm that caused the injury — the doctrine continues to operate as a complete bar to the plaintiff's recovery. In cases involving 'secondary assumption of risk' — where the defendant does owe a duty of care to the plaintiff, but the plaintiff proceeds to encounter a known risk imposed by the defendant's breach of duty — the doctrine is merged into the comparative fault scheme, and the trier of fact, in apportioning the loss resulting from the injury, may consider the relative responsibility of the parties." (*Knight, supra,* 3 Cal.4th at pp. 314–315, 11 Cal.Rptr.2d 2, 834 P.2d 696.)

The wise and just rule to be applied in this case is one that imposes a duty of reasonable care upon the District to Patterson and apportions responsibility for damages between the District and Patterson according to their respective degrees of fault. Given the nature of the instructors' alleged breach of duty in this case, there is no reason in law, equity or policy to absolve the District entirely from liability for damages suffered by Patterson. Although it might be argued that the District will decline to provide truck driving classes in the future, that argument is speculative and therefore untenable on this record. (See *City of Santa Barbara v. Superior Court of Santa Barbara County* (2007) 41 Cal.4th 747, 773–776, 62 Cal.Rptr.3d 527, 161 P.3d 1095.) For all these reasons, we conclude the court erred in finding that the doctrine of assumption of risk applied.

Given this resolution of the case, we need not address Patterson's argument that even if primary assumption of risk applied in this case, the undisputed evidence suggests that the District's conduct recklessly increased the risks inherent in loading the flat bed trailer.

[Reversed.]

———————

Knight v. Jewett, 834 P.2d 696 (Cal. 1992) (en banc), from which the court quoted extensively in the preceding case, remains a leading analysis of assumption of the risk doctrine. *Knight* involved a touch football game played by the protagonists during the half-time break of the 1987 Super Bowl. During the game, the defendant ran into the plaintiff, who told him to stop playing so vigorously. On the next play, he ran into the plaintiff again, knocked her over, and stepped on her hand, an injury that led to three operations on and ultimately to the amputation of the plaintiff's little finger.

After a lengthy analysis, the Supreme Court of California ruled that a participant in an "active sport" only breaches a legal duty to a fellow participant if that participant intentionally or recklessly causes injury to the fellow participant. In other words, a person participating in an active sport has no duty not to be negligent; the only duty is not to cause injury recklessly or intentionally. Thus, those who engage in an active sporting activity assume the risk of all injury except injury caused by the intentional or reckless misconduct of a fellow participant.

What does *Knight* do to the rule that one cannot assume the risk of someone else's negligence? What does it do to the concept that one always has an obligation to act reasonably? If there are no consequences for unreasonable conduct that causes injury, is there any incentive to be reasonable? What social policies might (or might not) trump the obligation to act reasonably?

c. Assumption of Risk as a Duty Doctrine

VINIKOOR v. PEDAL PENNSYLVANIA, INC.
Commonwealth Court of Pennsylvania, 2009
974 A.2d 1233

OPINION BY Senior Judge Flaherty.

Paul M. Vinikoor (Vinikoor) appeals from an order of the Court of Common Pleas of Blair County (trial court) which denied the motion for summary judgment filed by the Department of Transportation (Department) but granted the motion for summary judgment filed by Pedal Pennsylvania, Inc. (Pedal). We affirm.

Vinikoor commenced this action by filing a writ of summons on July 17, 2006. In the negligence action, Vinikoor sought to recover damages resulting from a bicycle accident which occurred while he was participating in a tour organized by Pedal. Vinikoor alleged in his complaint that his bike's right front tire became locked in a groove on a public roadway. As a result, Vinikoor's bicycle was trapped and Vinikoor was unable to steer, causing him to fall from his bicycle. Vinikoor suffered injuries including a central dislocation of his right pelvis and a loss of cartilage in that joint.

Vinikoor asserts that Pedal was negligent, in that Pedal represented to Vinikoor that the route was safe when in fact there was a hidden danger, consisting of a curved groove on the roadway. Additionally, Vinikoor alleged that Pedal failed to make an inspection of the route, or alternatively, failed to notice the defect in the road during its inspection, and thus failed to provide a safe route. Vinikoor alleged that Pedal assured Vinikoor that it had inspected the route and that it was safe. Additionally, Vinikoor was provided a cue sheet and route description, which noted cautions at certain locations where there were dangers. A caution was not noted at the intersection where the incident occurred. Vinikoor also alleged that Department was negligent with respect to construction of the road in the area where the fall occurred.

Pedal filed an answer and new matter. In the new matter, Pedal asserted that Vinikoor's claims were released and discharged based upon a release signed by Vinikoor prior to the tour. Additionally, Pedal claimed that it had no duty to Vinikoor and that Vinikoor had voluntarily assumed the risk. Department also filed an answer and new matter. Vinikoor replied to all new matters.

Thereafter, both Pedal and Department filed motions for summary judgment. Pedal maintained that it was entitled to summary judgment because Vinikoor signed an exculpatory clause barring all claims against Pedal. Additionally, Pedal claimed that Vinikoor voluntarily assumed the risk and that it had no duty. Department filed a similar motion.

The trial court set the matter down for a hearing. According to Vinikoor's deposition, he was an experienced bicyclist who had been on numerous bicycle tours. The tour at issue, organized by Pedal, was a week long bike tour covering over four hundred miles. Vinikoor had previously been on a tour organized by Pedal. In his complaint and in his deposition testimony, Vinikoor claimed that he was assured by Pedal that the route had been inspected and was safe. Further, Pedal provided Vinikoor with a cue sheet and route description, which included detailed directions and noted cautions at various locations where there were dangers. No caution was noted at the intersection where the accident occurred. . . .

Although the trial court did not address the issue of whether Vinikoor's claim was barred under the voluntary assumption of the risk/no duty rule, which was raised in Pedal's motion for summary judgment, Pedal states that this court may, however, affirm on that basis. In *Howell v. Clyde*, 533 Pa. 151, 620 A.2d 1107 (1993), the defendant's grandfather had made a fireworks cannon. The plaintiff expressed an interest in firing the cannon and went to his house next door to retrieve black powder. The plaintiff held a flashlight while the defendant filled the cannon with powder. The plaintiff stood back while defendant ignited the cannon, which then exploded and injured both of them.

The court held that a non-suit in favor of defendant was proper because, as a matter of law, the plaintiff had assumed the risk of injury by voluntarily participating in a dangerous activity, as the ignition of gunpowder is inherently dangerous and might cause injury to oneself or others. A court may determine, as a matter of law, that a defendant owed plaintiff no duty of care where "reasonable minds could not disagree that the plaintiff deliberately and with the awareness of specific risks inherent in the activity nonetheless engaged in the activity that produced his injury." *Id.* at 162-163, 620 A.2d at 1113.

Similarly, in *Zachardy v. Geneva College*, 733 A.2d 648 (Pa.Super.1999), *appeal denied*, 561 Pa. 700, 751 A.2d 193 (2000), the court affirmed the granting of defendant's motion for summary judgment under the assumption of the risk analysis. Therein a baseball player voluntarily and knowingly proceeded to play on a baseball field which had depressions/unevenness and injured himself while stepping into a hole.

Here, Vinikoor knew that falling and encountering irregular road conditions were risks of bicycling. In fact, Vinikoor was involved in a bicycle accident in 1993, during which he injured his leg. Vinikoor nonetheless assumed the risks involved in bicycling.

The no-duty rule provides that a defendant owes no duty of care to warn, protect or insure against risks which are common, frequent, expected and inherent in an activity. *Craig v. Amateur Softball Association of America*, 951 A.2d 372 (Pa.Super.2008). In *Pakett v. The Phillies L.P.*, 871 A.2d 304 (Pa.Cmwlth.2005), the plaintiff attended a major league baseball game and was struck by a foul ball while sitting in the stands. The plaintiff had sat in the seat before and knew that foul balls reached that area. This court affirmed the grant of summary judgment determining that the risk of being hit by a foul ball during a baseball game was an inherent risk of attending a game. Additionally, the team did not assume additional duties by placing a protective screen behind home plate.

Likewise, in this case, even if Pedal engaged in actions such as planning the route, painting arrows on the road and warning of "rumble strips", these activities do not preclude application of the voluntary assumption of the risk/no duty rule with respect to the risk of falling from a bicycle or encountering an irregular surface.

In his reply brief, Vinikoor states that the doctrine of the assumption of the risk has been supplanted by the Pennsylvania General Assembly's adoption of a system of recovery based on comparative fault in the Comparative Negligence Act, 42 Pa.C.S. § 7102(a)-(b); *Hughes v. Seven Springs Farm, Inc.*, 563 Pa. 501, 762 A.2d 339 (2000). The doctrine of assumption of the risk is preserved only "in cases involving express assumption of risk, or cases brought pursuant to 402A (strict liability theory), or cases in which assumption of risk is specifically preserved by statute." *Duquesne Light Company v. Woodland Hills School District*, 700 A.2d 1038, 1054 (Pa.Cmwlth.1997), *appeal denied*, 555 Pa. 722, 724 A.2d 936 (1998) (citation omitted).

The issue of whether Vinikoor contractually waived his right to recover has been argued by the parties in terms of the exculpatory release at issue herein. Because this is not a strict liability case, nor has it been argued that any statutory exception applies, the only remaining question is whether Pedal owed a duty to Vinikoor. Here, the assertion by Pedal that it had no duty to Vinikoor is based solely on the claim that bicycling has inherent dangers. Vinikoor maintains that his acknowledgement that he was aware of the general risks of injury is not sufficient to grant summary judgment, unless it also appears that he consciously appreciated the specific risk that attended a certain endeavor, assumed the risk of injury by engaging in the endeavor despite the appreciation of the risk and that the injury sustained was the same risk of injury that was appreciated and assumed. *Hadar v. AVCO Corporation*, 886 A.2d 225, 229 (2005), *appeal denied*, 586 Pa. 758, 895 A.2d 550 (2006).

Here, we conclude that as acknowledged by Vinikoor, he was aware of the general risks of riding a bicycle, including uneven surfaces, voluntarily chose to participate, voluntarily signed a waiver releasing Pedal from all liability, and acknowledged by voluntarily signing the waiver that he was aware that riding a bicycle could result in serious bodily injury. Vinikoor deliberately engaged in the bicycle tour with knowledge and awareness of the specific risks inherent in riding a bicycle, including bodily injury.

In accordance with the above, the decision of the trial court is, therefore, affirmed.

----

1. Are the results in *Knight* and *Vinikoor* really different? Putting aside all legal analysis for a moment, what would a purely common-sense approach to the facts in these cases look like? What should be the goal of assumption of risk theory?

2. Assumption of risk doctrine clearly involves difficulties for the courts which must deal with it. Do you have any theory as to why this doctrine seems, more than others, to present problems? In reading the cases, the fact that plaintiffs sometimes do unbelievably stupid things forcibly strikes the reader. (Think about *Howell*, cited in *Vinikoor*, in which the plaintiff supplied the gunpowder.) Maybe this has something to do with the reaction of the courts in dealing with assumption of the risk: it is difficult to impose liability on the defendant when the plaintiff has done something surpassingly risky. On the other hand, the "defense" of lack of causation remains available to defendants, even where assumption of the risk has been abolished. At some point, the courts will sever the chain of causation from the defendant to the plaintiff. If the plaintiff has been appallingly stupid, the courts may rule that the defendant's act (or product) can no longer be considered the proximate cause of the injury to the plaintiff, and the defendant will not be liable.

3. To what extent has assumption of the risk doctrine really been abolished? Recall the cases in section A(3)(a) of this chapter. Many courts continue to apply the doctrine in its conventional form, as set forth in that section. See, for example, *Baker v. Harcon*, 694 S.E.2d 673 (Ga. Ct. App. 2010), in which a construction worker fell through an opening for a trash chute. See also *Ervin v. Continental Conveyor and Equipment Co.*, 674 F. Supp. 2d 709 (D.S.C. 2009), in which the court analyzed comparative negligence and assumption of the risk as two separate doctrines, with the conventional elements of assumption of the risk fully in effect.

B.   COMPARATIVE AND CONTRIBUTORY NEGLIGENCE AND ASSUMPTION OF RISK IN CASES WHERE THE BASIS OF LIABILITY IS STRICT LIABILITY

MARSHALL v. RANNE
Supreme Court of Texas, 1974
511 S.W.2d 255

Pope, Justice.

Paul Marshall instituted this suit against John C. Ranne seeking damages for injuries he sustained when Ranne's vicious hog attacked him and severely injured his hand. The jury made findings that plaintiff Marshall was contributorily negligent and also that he voluntarily assumed the risk of the hog. The trial court rendered judgment for the defendant on the verdict. The court of civil appeals ruled that the findings of the jury concerning the plaintiff's assumption of the risk supported the judgment and affirmed. 493 S.W.2d 533. We reverse the judgments of the courts below and render judgment for the plaintiff Marshall.

The opinion of the court of civil appeals correctly states these operative facts:

> The only witness to the occurrence was plaintiff. He and defendant both lived in Dallas, but they owned neighboring farms in Van Zandt County. Plaintiff's principal occupation was raising hogs. At the time of the injury he had about two hundred on his farm. The hog in question was a boar which had escaped from defendant's farm and had been seen on plaintiff's land during several weeks before the day of the injury. According to plaintiff, defendant's boar had charged him ten to twelve times before this occurrence, had held him prisoner in his outhouse several times, and had attacked his wife on four or five occasions. On the day of the injury plaintiff had hauled in several barrels of old bread in his pickup and had put it out for his hogs at the barn. At that time he saw defendant's boar about a hundred yards behind the barn, but it came no nearer. After feeding his hogs, he went into the house and changed clothes to get ready to go back

to Dallas. On emerging from the house, he looked for the boar because, as he testified, he always had to look before he made a move, but he did not see it. He started toward his pickup, and when he was about thirty feet from it, near the outhouse, he heard a noise behind him, turned around and saw the boar charging toward him. He put out his hand defensively, but the boar grabbed it and bit it severely.

Plaintiff testified that the first time the hog had jeopardized his safety was about a week or ten days before he was hurt. He did not shoot the hog because he did not consider that the neighborly thing to do, although he was an expert with a gun and had two available. He made no complaint about the hog to defendant until the day of the injury, when he wrote a note and put it on defendant's gate. The note read:

"John, your boar has gone bad. He is trying to chase me off the farm. He stalks us just like a cat stalks a mouse every time he catches us out of the house. We are going to have to get him out before he hurts someone."

This note did not come to defendant's attention until he came in late that afternoon, and the evidence does not reveal whether he saw it before plaintiff was injured. Plaintiff testified that he and defendant had previously discussed the hog's viciousness on several occasions.

The answers to the special issues were: (1) defendant's boar hog bit the plaintiff's right hand on January 21, 1970, (2) immediately prior to that date, the boar hog had vicious propensities and was likely to cause injury to persons, (3) [the jury] refused to find that at any time before plaintiff's injury, the defendant actually knew that the defendant's boar hog was vicious and was likely to cause injury to persons, (4) the defendant prior to plaintiff's injury in the exercise of ordinary care should have known that the boar hog was vicious and likely to cause injury to persons, (5) defendant permitted his boar hog to run at large after he knew or should have known that the hog was vicious and likely to cause injury to persons, (6) plaintiff, Paul Marshall, had knowledge of the vicious propensities of the defendant's boar hog and that it was likely to cause injury to persons at and prior to the time the hog bit him, (7) plaintiff, Paul Marshall, with knowledge of the nature of defendant's boar hog voluntarily exposed himself to the risk of attack by the animal, (8) plaintiff's failure to shoot the defendant's boar hog prior to the time the hog bit plaintiff was negligence, (9) which failure was a proximate cause of plaintiff's injuries, (10) plaintiff failed to maintain a fence about his premises sufficiently close to prevent hogs passing through, (11) which was negligence, and (12) a proximate cause of plaintiff's injuries, (13) plaintiff was damaged in the amount of $4,146.00.

The questions presented by this cause are (1) the true nature of an action for damages caused by a vicious animal, (2) whether contributory negligence is a defense to this action, and (3) whether plaintiff Marshall was, as a matter of law, deprived of a voluntary and free choice in confronting the risk.

Nature of Vicious Animal Cases

A correct classification of this case is important, since that decision also controls the nature of the acceptable defenses to the action. In Texas, actions for damages caused by vicious domestic animals have sometimes been cast as common law negligence cases, at other times as strict liability cases, and sometimes as either.

. . . .

We approve the rule expressed in *Moore v. McKay*, [55 S.W.2d 865 (Tex. Civ. App. 1933, no writ)], that suits for damages caused by vicious animals should be governed by principles of strict liability, and disapprove the cases which hold the contrary. The correct rule is expressed in Restatement of Torts §§ 507, 509 (1938):

> § 507. LIABILITY OF POSSESSOR OF WILD ANIMAL.
>
> Except as stated in §§ 505 and 517, a possessor of a wild animal is subject to liability to others, except trespassers on his land, for such harm done by the animal to their persons, lands or chattels as results from a dangerous propensity which is characteristic of wild animals of its class or of which the possessor has reason to know, although he has exercised the utmost care to confine the animal or otherwise prevent it from doing harm.
>
> § 509. HARM DONE BY ABNORMALLY DANGEROUS DOMESTIC ANIMALS.
>
> Except as stated in § 517, a possessor of a domestic animal which he has reason to know has dangerous propensities abnormal to its class, is subject to liability for harm caused thereby to others, except trespassers on his land, although he has exercised the utmost care to prevent it from doing the harm.

The jury in this case refused to find that the defendant actually knew that the hog was vicious and was likely to cause injury to persons, but it did find in answer to special issue four that the defendant prior to plaintiff's injury should have known that fact. Defendant Ranne does not challenge the finding to issue four.

The Restatement, quoted above, uses the phrase "has reason to know" and the fourth special issue submitted in this case used the phrase "should have known." There is no essential distinction between the two terms as explained in Restatement (Second) of Torts § 12 (1965):

> § 12. Reason to Know; Should Know
>
> (1) The words "reason to know" are used throughout the Restatement of this Subject to denote the fact that the actor has information from which a person of reasonable intelligence or of the superior intelligence of the actor would infer that the fact in question exists, or that such person would govern his conduct upon the assumption that such fact exists.
>
> (2) The words "should know" are used throughout the Restatement of this Subject to denote the fact that a person of reasonable prudence and intelligence or of the superior intelligence of the actor would ascertain the fact in question in the performance of his duty to another, or would govern his conduct upon the assumption that such fact exists.

Contributory Negligence is No Defense To Strict Liability

The trial court over plaintiff's objection, submitted contributory negligence issues and the jury found that plaintiff Marshall was negligent in several particulars. We hold that contributory negligence is not a defense to this action. The court in *Copley v. Wills*, 152 S.W. 830 (Tex. Civ. App. 1913, no writ), confronted this question and rejected contributory negligence as an applicable defense to an action for strict liability for keeping a vicious animal which one knew or had reason to know was vicious. This is also the view expressed in Restatement (Second) of Torts § 515, Comment b (Tent. Draft No. 10, 1964):

> *b.* Since the strict liability of the possessor of an animal is not founded on his negligence, the ordinary contributory negligence of the plaintiff is not a defense to such an action. The reason is the policy of the law which places the full responsibility for preventing the harm upon the defendant. Thus where the plaintiff merely fails to exercise reasonable care to discover the presence of the animal, or to take precautions against the harm which may result from it, his recovery on the basis of strict liability is not barred.

We conclude that the findings of plaintiff's contributory negligence as contained in the answers to special issues eight through twelve have no place in this case and did not bar the plaintiff from recovery. 2 F. Harper & F. James, The Law of Torts § 14.12, at 843 (1956). We do not hold that negligence and contributory negligence can never be a correct theory in a case which concerns animals. All animals are not vicious and a possessor of a non-vicious animal may be subject to liability for his negligent handling of such an animal.

Did Marshall Voluntarily Assume the Risk?

Plaintiff Marshall does not contend that voluntary assumption of risk is no defense to an action which asserts the defendant's strict liability. He alludes to the truth that it has been abolished as a defense in a number of states in actions grounded upon negligence. Marshall's argument is that he did not, as a matter of law voluntarily expose himself to the risk of the attack by the hog. The jury found that plaintiff Marshall had knowledge of the vicious propensities of the hog and that it was likely to cause injury to persons, and also found that plaintiff, with knowledge of the nature of defendant's boar hog, voluntarily exposed himself to the risk of attack by the animal. We hold that there was no proof that plaintiff had a free and voluntary choice, because he did not have a free choice of alternatives. He had, instead, only a choice of evils, both of which were wrongfully imposed upon him by the defendant. He could remain a prisoner inside his own house or he could take the risk of reaching his car before defendant's hog attacked him. Plaintiff could have remained inside his house, but in doing so, he would have surrendered his legal right to proceed over his own property to his car so he could return to his home in Dallas. The latter alternative was forced upon him against his will and was a choice he was not legally required to accept. W. Prosser, Law of Torts § 68, at 450-453 (4th ed. 1971). We approve and follow the rule expressed in Restatement (Second) of Torts § 496E (1965):

(1)   A plaintiff does not assume a risk of harm unless he voluntarily accepts the risk.

(2)   The plaintiff's acceptance of a risk is not voluntary if the defendant's tortious conduct has left him no reasonable alternative course of conduct in order to

(a) avert harm to himself or another, or

(b) exercise or protect a right or privilege of which the defendant has no right to deprive him.

The dilemma which defendant forced upon plaintiff was that of facing the danger or surrendering his rights with respect to his own real property, and that was not, as a matter of law the voluntary choice to which the law entitled him.

. . . .

Defendant Ranne argues also that the plaintiff Marshall had yet another alternative, that of shooting the hog. The proof showed that Marshall was an expert marksman and had a gun in his house with which he could have killed the hog. Plaintiff Marshall testified that he was reluctant to destroy his neighbor's animal because he did not know how Ranne would react. We do not regard the slaughter of the animal as a reasonable alternative, because plaintiff would have subjected himself arguably to charges under the provision of two criminal statutes.

We accordingly hold that contributory negligence is not a defense in a strict liability action. Voluntary assumption of risk, if established, would be a valid defense. In this case as a matter of law, the proof shows that plaintiff Marshall did not voluntarily encounter the vicious hog. We, therefore, reverse the judgments of the courts below and render judgment that plaintiff recover the sum of $4,146.00 the amount of damages found by the jury.

ON REHEARING

[Rehearing granted on ground of inadequate damages.]

---

1. How important is it that the plaintiff is on his own property when he is attacked? What if he had been on public property? What if he had been on the defendant's property for the purpose of complaining about the hog?

2. What if the hog had no prior history of viciousness?

3. The fact that liability for injuries caused by animals is strict does not exempt the plaintiff from any obligation to look after his or her own safety. In *Sandy v. Bushey*, 128 A. 513, 514 (Me. 1925), the court stated that a defendant would not be liable if "the injury is attributable, not to the keeping of the animal but to the injured party's unnecessarily and voluntarily putting himself in a way to be hurt knowing the probable consequences of his act, so that he may fairly be deemed to have brought the injury upon himself." The court also adopted the rule that the owner of an animal would not be liable when the plaintiff "knowingly" incites or provokes the animal. Negligence on the plaintiff's part would be insufficient to act as a defense.

C. COMPARATIVE AND CONTRIBUTORY NEGLIGENCE AND ASSUMPTION OF RISK IN CASES WHERE THE BASIS OF LIABILITY IS STRICT PRODUCTS LIABILITY

McCOWN v. INTERNATIONAL HARVESTER CO.
Supreme Court of Pennsylvania, 1975
342 A.2d 381

JONES, CHIEF JUSTICE.

Appellant, manufacturer of large over-the-road tractors, was held liable under Section 402A of Restatement (Second) of Torts (1965) for the injuries sustained by the appellee in a one-vehicle accident. The Superior Court affirmed and we granted allocatur limited to the issue of the availability of contributory negligence as a defense to a 402A action.

Appellee was injured while driving a tractor manufactured by appellant. The design of the steering mechanism of the tractor made the vehicle unusually difficult to maneuver. Specifically, twelve to fifteen percent more mechanical effort than that normally expended had to be applied to the steering wheel to accomplish any given turn. Appellee, after driving the vehicle for several hours, stopped for an equipment check on the blacktopped shoulder of the Pennsylvania Turnpike. After completing the inspection the appellee proceeded to reenter the Turnpike.

Unrelated to any steering difficulty appellee struck a guardrail adjoining the shoulder with the right front tire of the tractor. This collision caused the steering wheel to spin rapidly in the direction opposite to the turn. The spokes of the spinning steering wheel struck appellee's right arm, fracturing his wrist and forearm. Evidence adduced at trial indicated that the force and speed of the steering wheel's counterrotation were directly related to the design of the steering mechanism.

For the purposes of this appeal appellant concedes the defect in the steering system's design, but argues that appellee's contributory negligence in colliding with the guardrail should at least be considered in determining appellee's recovery. We disagree and affirm.

In *Webb v. Zern*, 422 Pa. 424, 220 A.2d 853 (1966), this Court adopted Section 402A of the Restatement and in *Ferraro v. Ford Motor Co.*, 423 Pa. 324, 223 A.2d 746 (1966), permitted the assertion of assumption of the risk as a defense to a 402A action, citing with approval comment *n* to Section 402A. Today, we complete our acceptance of the principles delineated in comment *n*[1] by rejecting contributory

---

[1] The portion of comment *n* relevant to this opinion is as follows:

negligence as an available defense in 402A cases.

Appellant's position that contributory negligence should affect 402A liability could have two possible applications. Either contributory negligence should serve to diminish any recovery in an amount adjudged equal to a plaintiff's lack of care or, as in most other tort actions, contributory negligence should be available as a complete defense to liability.

Acceptance of the appellant's first alternative would create a system of comparative assessment of damages for 402A actions. Neither the General Assembly by statute nor this Court by case law has established such a scheme of comparative negligence in other areas of tort law. Without considering the relative merits of comparative negligence, we think it unwise to embrace the theory in the context of an appeal involving Section 402A.[3]

Adoption of contributory negligence as a complete defense in 402A actions would defeat one theoretical basis for our acceptance of Section 402A. "Our courts have determined that a manufacturer by marketing and advertising his products [*sic*] impliedly represents that it is safe for its intended use." *Salvador v. Atlantic Steel Boiler Co.*, 457 Pa. 24, 32, 319 A.2d 903, 907 (1974). Based on that implied representation is the consumer's assumption that a manufacturer's goods are safe. Recognition of consumer negligence as a defense to a 402A action would contradict this normal expectation of product safety. One does not inspect a product for defects or guard against the possibility of product defects when one assumes the item to be safe. The law should not require such inspection or caution when it has accepted as reasonable the consumer's anticipation of safety. We reject contributory negligence as a defense to actions grounded in Section 402A.

Judgment affirmed.

MR. JUSTICE ROBERTS did not participate in the consideration or decision of this case.

MR. JUSTICE POMEROY filed a concurring opinion.

POMEROY, JUSTICE (CONCURRING).

I agree with the Court that negligence by the plaintiff should not necessarily bar recovery in a products liability action brought pursuant to Section 402A of the Restatement (Second) of Torts; I also agree that McCown's conduct in the instant case — misjudging whether the tractor he was driving would clear a guard rail as he was leaving the parking area — should not bar his recovery from the appellant. The purpose of this opinion is to place the Court's decision in what I perceive as its proper perspective.

"Contributory negligence of the plaintiff is not a defense when such negligence consists merely in a failure to discover the defect in the product, or to guard against the possibility of its existence."

[3] To initially apply a theory of comparative negligence to an area of the law in which liability is not premised on negligence seems particularly inappropriate.

Contrary to what the opinion of the Court seems to suggest, the answer to the question presented by this appeal is not to be found altogether in the language of Comment to Section 402A. Comment *n* provides, on the one hand, that the negligent failure to discover a defect in a product or to guard against the possibility of its existence is not defense to a strict liability action, and, on the other hand, that assumption of risk is a defense. But the conduct of John McCown, the appellee, fits into neither of the above categories. His negligence, if any, was the manner of his operation of an International Harvester tractor. Although Comment *n* is silent with regard to the consequences of negligent use of a product, it points to a resolution of the issue by referring to Section 524 of the Restatement (Second) of Torts. That section provides that in general "the contributory negligence of the plaintiff is not a defense to the strict liability of one who carries on an abnormally dangerous activity."[2] Neither the Comments to Section 524 nor Comment *n* to Section 402A offer a rationale for the application of this rule in products liability cases, but I am satisfied that the elimination of the defense of plaintiff's negligence is in accord not only with the weight of authority in other jurisdictions but also with the policy which underlies the concept of strict liability in tort.

The strict liability of Section 402A is founded in part upon the belief that as between the sellers of products and those who use them, the former are the better able to bear the losses caused by defects in the products involved. This greater loss-bearing capacity is unrelated to negligence in the manufacture or marketing of products. Indeed, retail and wholesale sellers of chattels are themselves often in no position to discover or avoid defects in their inventories, even by the exercise of a high degree of care. Thus, defendants in Section 402A actions are subjected to liability without regard to fault. It is a proper corollary to this principle that the lesser loss-bearing capacity of product users exists independently of their negligence or lack of it. It follows that such negligence should not ordinarily or necessarily operate to preclude recovery in a strict liability case. On the other hand, where assumption of risk is involved, the "loss-bearing" policy underlying Section 402A is outweighed by a countervailing policy, one which refuses recovery to persons who consciously expose themselves to known dangers. This policy is deemed stronger than the one, reflected in the normal law of contributory negligence, which denies recovery to individuals whose conduct is merely lacking in due care under the circumstances.

This is not to say, however, that evidence of ordinary negligence on the part of a plaintiff is never relevant in a Section 402A action; such evidence may bear directly upon the determination of whether the plaintiff has proved all the elements necessary to make out a cause of action. Thus, negligence in the use of a product may tend to show that the plaintiff caused a defect and therefore that the product

---

[2] In their treatise on the law of Torts, Professors Harper and James state as follows the rationale for the rule that contributory negligence is not a defense to the strict liability of one engaged in an extra-hazardous activity:

"Society has, in effect, permitted defendant's activity on the condition that he compensate those injured by its peculiar hazards and has thereby transferred some of the duty that protects potential victims from the victims themselves to the entrepreneur. In such a context ordinary questions of negligence on either side of the scale become irrelevant. Human failings like inadvertence are simply part of the setting that makes a toll of the enterprise inevitable." (Footnotes omitted). 2 F. Harper & F. James, The Law of Torts, § 22.7 at 1216-17 (1956).

was not defective when sold. See Comment g to Section 402A. Again, if the negligent use of a product amounts to abnormal use, it may be inferred that the product was not defective at all, for a product is not defective if it is safe for normal handling and use. See Comment h to Section 402A. Similarly, negligence in the use of a product may have a bearing on the question whether a defect in a product was the legal cause of the plaintiff's injury.

What has been said is not intended as an exhaustive listing of the purposes for which evidence of the plaintiff's negligence may be relevant in Section 402 A cases. It is intended merely to indicate that, although such negligence is not per se a bar to recovery, it may nevertheless have that effect in a proper case where it negates an essential element of the cause of action. I do not read the opinion of the Court as suggesting anything to the contrary.

---

1. Was the tractor safe for its intended use? What if the tractor had had a warning on it stating that the driver should avoid sudden turns?

2. Should a consumer's negligent use of a product be a defense when the claimed defect is the failure to prevent injury from just such a negligent use?

CULPEPPER v. HERMANN WEIHRAUCH KG
United States District Court for the Middle District of Alabama, 1997
991 F. Supp. 1397

MYRON H. THOMPSON, CHIEF JUDGE.

ORDER

Plaintiff Ann Culpepper brought this [diversity] action against defendant Hermann Weihrauch KG on August 12, 1996, seeking damages for injuries she sustained as a result of accidentally shooting herself with a handgun manufactured by Weihrauch. . . . The court now has before it Culpepper's motions for summary judgment, filed July 11, 1997, as to Weihrauch's three affirmative defenses: assumption of risk, misuse of the product, and contributory negligence. For the reasons set forth below, the court grants Culpepper's motions for summary judgment in their entirety.

I. STANDARD FOR SUMMARY JUDGMENT

Rule 56(c) of the Federal Rules of Civil Procedure provides that summary judgment is appropriate where "there is no genuine issue as to any material fact and . . . the moving party is entitled to a judgment as a matter of law." Once the party seeking summary judgment has informed the court of the basis for its motion, the burden shifts to the non-moving party to demonstrate why summary judgment would be inappropriate. . . . Because the court's jurisdiction is based on diversity of citizenship, the court must apply the law of the forum state.

II. FACTUAL BACKGROUND

Culpepper purchased a handgun, manufactured by Weihrauch, in 1968 as a gift for her then husband. After her divorce in 1977, she kept the gun for personal protection. In the early 1990's, after obtaining the necessary permit, she began carrying the gun to work in her automobile. She kept the gun in a leather zippered pouch; it was her custom to store the gun either in her bedside table when she was home or in the glove compartment of her car while she was at work.

On March 5, 1996, after going to work, to her parents' house, and to the supermarket, Culpepper returned home. She had placed the gun in the glove compartment of her car when she left for work in the morning and did not remove it until she came home in the afternoon. Culpepper does not remember how the accident occurred; she only remembers that she got out of the car, heard a shot, and felt pain. She does not remember how she attempted to carry the gun, along with her purse or her groceries, out of the car. When she was found by people who had heard the shot, her gun was lying on the ground out of its pouch, about one or two feet away from the driver's seat. One witness saw an indentation on the dirt in the driveway that looked as if it had been made by the hammer spur of the handgun. Culpepper was struck by the bullet in the lower right side of her abdomen; the injury required the removal of her right kidney, and parts of her small intestine and colon.

Culpepper brought this lawsuit against Weihrauch on August 12, 1996, under several different products liability theories, including allegations of design and manufacturing defects, warning defects, negligent assembly and sale, negligent failure to warn, wanton failure to warn, and breach of implied warranty. The crux of these claims is that the hammerblock safety, a device on the gun which prevents "drop fire" accidents such as the one described above, was improperly designed and manufactured. A hammerblock safety, according to Culpepper, is designed to "hold the hammer face off of the firing pin and prevent force applied to the back of the hammer spur from driving the hammer face into the firing pin and . . . eliminate the possibility of drop-fire except under extraordinary circumstances."

Weihrauch filed its answer on December 5, 1996, asserting general denials and seven affirmative defenses. Among these defenses, Weihrauch asserted the defenses of contributory negligence, assumption of risk, and misuse of the product.

On July 11, 1997, Culpepper filed motions for summary judgment on these three defenses. In its brief in opposition, filed August 21, 1997, Weihrauch conceded that summary judgment should be granted as to the assumption-of-risk and misuse-of-product defenses. Therefore, the only issue requiring this court's review is Culpepper's motions for summary judgment on the contributory-negligence defense.

III. DISCUSSION

Culpepper seeks to impose liability on Weihrauch under the Alabama Extended Manufacturer's Liability Doctrine (AEMLD). The AEMLD provides for such liability if "the defendant manufactured or designed or sold a defective product which, because of its unreasonably unsafe condition, injured the plaintiff or damaged his property when such product, substantially unaltered, was put to its intended use." *Atkins v. American Motors Corp.*, 335 So. 2d 134, 139 (Ala. 1976). The AEMLD is similar to a strict liability tort action under § 402(A) of the Restatement (Second) of Torts. However, the Alabama Supreme Court has rejected the Restatement's no-fault strict liability concept for products liability. *Atkins*, 335 So. 2d at 139. Rather, certain affirmative defenses and general denials are available to defendant manufacturers in an AEMLD action.

Contributory negligence is one such viable affirmative defense under the AEMLD. *Sears v. Waste Processing Equip., Inc.*, 695 So. 2d 51, 53 (Ala. Civ. App. 1997); *see also Hicks v. Commercial Union Ins. Co.*, 652 So. 2d 211 (Ala. 1994). A plaintiff is contributorily negligent when she fails to use reasonable care with regard to that product. *Williams v. Delta Int'l Machinery Corp.*, 619 So. 2d 1330 (Ala. 1993). Contributory negligence can be roughly divided into two categories: first, the plaintiff's negligence, or failure to use reasonable care, in actually using the product; second, the plaintiff's negligence in causing the accident in which the product is used. *Campbell v. Robert Bosch Power Tool Corp.*, 795 F. Supp. 1093, 1097 (M.D. Ala. 1992). In an AEMLD action, the contributory negligence defense is limited to acts within the first category. That is, the plaintiff's acts with regard to negligence or failure to use reasonable care in handling the product are admissible; the plaintiff's acts regarding the cause of the accident itself are not. *Dennis v. American Honda Motor Co.*, 585 So. 2d 1336, 1339 (Ala. 1991) ("To allow a plaintiff's negligence relating to accident causation to bar recovery would go against the purpose of the AEMLD, which is to protect consumers from defective products."); *see also Campbell v. Cutler Hammer, Inc.*, 646 So. 2d 573, 574 (Ala. 1994) (answering in the affirmative the Eleventh Circuit's certified question whether contributory negligence bars recovery if unreasonably dangerous condition of product was proximate cause of injury, but contributing proximate cause was plaintiff's failure to exercise reasonable care in using the product).

Failure to use reasonable care in the context of the contributory negligence defense is distinct from the separate affirmative defense of product misuse. *See General Motors Corp. v. Saint*, 646 So. 2d 564, 568 (Ala. 1994). In *Saint*, the court distinguished the two defenses by stating "A plaintiff misuses a product when he or she uses it in a manner not intended or foreseen by the manufacturer . . . A plaintiff is contributorily negligent in handling a defective product when he or she fails to use reasonable care with regard to that product." *Id.*

Culpepper argues that Weihrauch cannot avail itself of the contributory negligence defense because (1) there is no evidence to suggest that Culpepper was negligent in using the hammerblock safety on the gun, and (2) any evidence of negligence related to the causation of the accident cannot be used to support Weihrauch's defense pursuant to *Dennis*. Culpepper argues that in an AEMLD action involving a safety feature of a product, the only admissible evidence to support a finding of contributory negligence is the plaintiff's mishandling of the safety feature, rather than the product as a whole. Weihrauch admits that evidence of negligence related to accident causation is impermissible to support a claim of contributory negligence, but maintains that the issue is whether Culpepper failed to use due care in handling the gun, not the hammerblock safety. Because the law in Alabama is clear that only negligence related to use of the product, as opposed to negligence in accident causation, is admissible to prove contributory negligence, the only issues the court must decide on Culpepper's motions for summary judgment are (1) whether "product" refers to the hammerblock safety on the gun or the gun itself, and (2) whether Weihrauch has met its burden in demonstrating why summary judgment is inappropriate.

A.

Although contributory negligence serves as a total bar against recovery in AEMLD cases, the Alabama Supreme Court diminished its effect in *Dennis*, where the court held that contributory negligence related to accident causation was an invalid defense: "A plaintiff's mere inadvertence or carelessness in causing an accident should not be available as an affirmative defense to an AEMLD action." 585 So. 2d at 1339. In *Dennis*, the plaintiff brought suit against the manufacturer of a motorcycle helmet, alleging that the helmet was defective and not fit for its intended purpose. In charging the jury, the trial court gave instructions regarding the defendant's burden of proof for the defense of contributory negligence. The court stated that the defendant could meet its burden "by proving to [the jurors'] reasonable satisfaction that [plaintiff] violated a rule or rules of the road during the operation of the motorcycle at the time of the accident in question." 585 So. 2d at 1338. The Alabama Supreme Court rejected this instruction and stated that contributory negligence could be used as a defense to an AEMLD action only under certain circumstances, such as "plaintiff's misuse of the product." Id. at 1339. In *Saint*, which the court noted was "just the reverse of that in *Dennis*," 646 So. 2d at 566, the Alabama Supreme Court held that an automobile manufacturer was entitled to jury instructions regarding plaintiff's contributory negligence where the defendant contended plaintiff either did not wear or improperly wore a seatbelt at the time of a car accident. Culpepper interprets these two cases as holding that, in AEMLD cases involving safety devices, only mishandling of the safety feature can be used to support a contributory negligence defense. Culpepper cites two cases as supporting this interpretation: *Williams v. Delta Int'l Machinery Corp.*, 619 So. 2d 1330 (Ala. 1993), and *Gibson v. Norfolk Southern Corp.*, 878 F. Supp. 1455 (N.D. Ala. 1994), aff'd, 48 F.3d 536 (11th Cir. 1995) (table opinion). In *Williams*, the Alabama Supreme Court rejected application of the *Dennis* rule to a products liability case where the products, a table saw and dado blade, were not safety features and because "the only contributory negligence alleged in this case involved the use of the table saw and the dado blade." 619 So. 2d at 1332-33. In *Gibson*, the court held that contributory negligence could be asserted as a defense where the plaintiff failed to "stop, look, and listen" at the railroad's warning light and sign. 878 F. Supp. at 1461. Neither case directly supports the proposition of law Culpepper has advanced.

Arguing against Culpepper's interpretation, Weihrauch cites to *Haisten v. Kubota Corp.*, 648 So. 2d 561 (Ala. 1994). In *Haisten*, the plaintiff brought an AEMLD action against the manufacturer of a tractor alleging that the manufacturer's failure to include a rollover protection system rendered the tractor defective. The Alabama Supreme Court held that the trial judge correctly charged the jury with instructions to consider the plaintiff's contributory negligence as a defense to the AEMLD claim. *Haisten*, 648 So. 2d at 565. Weihrauch concludes that, since *Haisten* is factually analogous to the present case, the contributory negligence defense should be permitted. The court disagrees. The issue involved in *Haisten* was whether the tractor was defective for not having a rollover safety device, rather than a defect in the safety device rendering the product unreasonably dangerous, as was the case in *Dennis, Saint,* and the action presently before this court.

In grappling with the issue of whether misuse of the product for the purpose of proving contributory negligence refers to the handgun or the hammerblock safety, the court first notes that in her complaint, Culpepper alleges that "the handgun was unreasonably dangerous and therefore defective." The fact that Culpepper has alleged the product as a whole was unreasonably dangerous does not, however, end the court's inquiry. In *Saint*, the plaintiff brought an AEMLD action alleging that her automobile was unreasonably dangerous — because the seatbelt failed to protect her during the accident — and the court permitted evidence of only her negligence in misusing the seatbelt, rather than the automobile itself. The seatbelt in the automobile in *Saint* is sufficiently analogous to the hammerblock safety in the handgun here: both are designed to protect the user of the product in case of an accident. The court therefore concludes that Weihrauch may assert the contributory negligence defense only as to Culpepper's misuse of the hammerblock safety, rather than the handgun. To hold otherwise would permit Weihrauch to introduce evidence going to Culpepper's contributory negligence related to accident causation, and would directly contravene the Alabama Supreme Court's decision in *Dennis*.

B.

The second issue for the court to decide is whether Weihrauch has alleged sufficient facts to defeat Culpepper's motion for summary judgment. In order to find contributory negligence as a matter of law, there must be a finding that the plaintiff put herself in danger's way, a finding that the plaintiff appreciated the danger confronted, and that such appreciation of the danger was conscious at the moment the incident occurred. *Hicks v. Commercial Union Ins. Co.*, 652 So. 2d 211, 219 (Ala. 1994). A court may decide the issue of contributory negligence as a matter of law "only when the facts are such that all reasonable [people] must draw the same conclusion therefrom." *Caterpillar Tractor Co. v. Ford*, 406 So. 2d 854, 857 (Ala. 1981).

However, for the purposes of defeating Culpepper's motions for summary judgment, Weihrauch need only show that "specific facts, as opposed to general allegations, present a genuine issue worthy of trial." Wright & Miller, *Federal Practice and Procedure*, § 2727, at 148. "A mere 'scintilla' of evidence supporting the [nonmoving] party's position will not suffice; there must be enough of a showing that the jury could reasonably find for that party." *Walker v. Darby*, 911 F.2d 1573, 1577 (11th Cir. 1990) (citations omitted); *see also Jeffery v. Sarasota White Sox, Inc.*, 64 F.3d 590, 593-94 (11th Cir. 1995).

Weihrauch offers the following facts to support its argument that the jury should be able to decide whether Culpepper was contributorily negligent: Culpepper either had the gun in her hand or "under [her] arm," and Culpepper may have been trying to carry the gun, her purse, and her groceries at the same time. While these facts could support a conclusion that Culpepper failed to exercise due care in handling the gun, the facts do not support a conclusion that Culpepper failed to exercise due care in handling the hammerblock safety on the handgun. Moreover, these facts go directly to the issue of accident causation which, as discussed above, cannot be used to support a contributory negligence defense in an AEMLD case involving a safety device. Weihrauch has not provided evidence of the existence of any facts to support a finding of contributory negligence in Culpepper's use of the hammerblock safety. Culpepper's motions will therefore be granted in their entirety.

IV. CONCLUSION

For the above reasons, it is ORDERED that plaintiff Ann Culpepper's motions for summary judgment, filed July 11, 1997, regarding defendant Hermann Weihrauch KG's affirmative defenses of contributory negligence, misuse of the product, and assumption of risk, are granted.

---

1. What would a seatbelt defense argument look like under the AEMLD?

2. Does the contributing negligence described in part III(B) of the court's opinion really sound like contributory negligence?

DALY v. GENERAL MOTORS CORP.
Supreme Court of California, 1978
575 P.2d 1162

RICHARDSON, JUSTICE.

The most important of several problems which we consider is whether the principles of comparative negligence expressed by us in *Li v. Yellow Cab Co.* (1975) 13 Cal. 3d 804, 119 Cal. Rptr. 858, 532 P.2d 1226, apply to actions founded on strict products liability. We will conclude that they do. . . .

The Facts and the Trial

Although there were no eyewitnesses, the parties agree, generally, on the reconstruction of the accident in question. In the early hours of October 31, 1970, decedent Kirk Daly, a 36-year-old attorney, was driving his Opel southbound on the Harbor Freeway in Los Angeles. The vehicle, while travelling at a speed of 50-70 miles per hour, collided with and damaged 50 feet of metal divider fence. After the initial impact between the left side of the vehicle and the fence the Opel spun counterclockwise, the driver's door was thrown open, and Daly was forcibly ejected from the car and sustained fatal head injuries. It was equally undisputed that had the deceased remained in the Opel his injuries, in all probability, would have been relatively minor.

Plaintiffs, who are decedent's widow and three surviving minor children, sued General Motors Corporation, Boulevard Buick, Underwriter's Auto Leasing, and Alco Leasing Company, the successive links in the Opel's manufacturing and distribution chain. The sole theory of plaintiffs' complaint was strict liability for damages allegedly caused by a defective product, namely, an improperly designed door latch claimed to have been activated by the impact. It was further asserted that, but for the faulty latch, decedent would have been restrained in the vehicle and, although perhaps injured, would not have been killed. Thus, the case involves a so-called "second collision" in which the "defect" did not contribute to the original impact, but only to the "enhancement" of injury.

At trial the jury heard conflicting expert versions as to the functioning of the latch mechanism during the accident. Plaintiffs' principal witness testified that the Opel's door was caused to open when the latch button on the exterior handle of the driver's door was forcibly depressed by some protruding portion of the divider fence. It was his opinion that the exposed push button on the door constituted a design "defect" which caused injuries greatly in excess of those which Daly would otherwise have sustained. Plaintiffs also introduced evidence that other vehicular door latch designs used in production models of the same and prior years afforded substantially greater protection. Defendants' experts countered with their opinions that the force of the impact was sufficiently strong that it would have caused the door to open resulting in Daly's death even if the Opel had been equipped with door latches of the alternative designs suggested by plaintiffs.

Over plaintiffs' objections, defendants were permitted to introduce evidence indicating that: (1) the Opel was equipped with a seat belt-shoulder harness system, and a door lock, either of which if used, it was contended, would have prevented Daly's ejection from the vehicle; (2) Daly used neither the harness system nor the lock; (3) the 1970 Opel owner's manual contained warnings that seat belts should be worn and doors locked when the car was in motion for "accident security"; and (4) Daly was intoxicated at the time of collision, which evidence the jury was advised was admitted for the limited purpose of determining whether decedent had used the vehicle's safety equipment. After relatively brief deliberations the jury returned a verdict favoring all defendants, and plaintiffs appeal from the ensuing adverse judgment.

Strict Products Liability and Comparative Fault

In response to plaintiffs' assertion that the "intoxication-nonuse" evidence was improperly admitted, defendants contend that the deceased's own conduct contributed to his death. Because plaintiffs' case rests upon strict products liability based on improper design of the door latch and because defendants assert a failure in decedent's conduct, namely, his alleged intoxication and nonuse of safety equipment, without which the accident and ensuing death would not have occurred, there is thereby posed the overriding issue in the case, should comparative principles apply in strict products liability actions?

It may be useful to refer briefly to certain highlights in the historical development of the two principles — strict and comparative liability. Tort law has evolved from a legal obligation initially imposed without "fault," to recovery which, generally, was based on blameworthiness in a moral sense. For reasons of social policy and because of the unusual nature of defendants' acts, liability without fault continued to be prescribed in a certain restricted area, for example, upon keepers of wild animals, or those who handled explosives or other dangerous substances, or who engaged in ultrahazardous activities. Simultaneously, and more particularly, those who were injured in the use of personal property were permitted recovery on a contract theory if they were the purchasers of the chattel or were in privity. Subsequently, liability was imposed in negligence upon the manufacturer of personalty in favor of the general consumer. Evolving social policies designed to protect the ultimate consumer soon prompted the extension of legal responsibility beyond negligence to express or implied warranty. Thus, in the area of food and drink a form of strict liability predicated upon warranty found wide acceptance. Warranty actions, however, contained their own inherent limitations requiring a precedent notice to the vendor of a breach of the warranty, and absolving him from loss if he had issued an adequate disclaimer.

General dissatisfaction continued with the conceptual limitations which traditional tort and contract doctrines placed upon the consumers and users of manufactured products, this at a time when mass production of an almost infinite variety of goods and products was responding to a myriad of ever-changing societal demands stimulated by wide-spread commercial advertising. From an historic combination of economic and sociological forces was born the doctrine of strict liability in tort.

We, ourselves, were perhaps the first court to give the new principle judicial sanction. In *Greenman v. Yuba Power Products, Inc.* (1963) 59 Cal. 2d 57, 27 Cal. Rptr. 697, 377 P.2d 897, confronted with injury to an ultimate consumer caused by a defective power tool, we fastened strict liability on a manufacturer who placed on the market a defective product even though both privity and notice of breach of warranty were lacking. We rejected both contract and warranty theories, express or implied, as the basis for liability. Strict liability, we said, did not rest on a consensual foundation but, rather, on one created by law. The liability was created judicially because of the economic and social need for the protection of consumers in an increasingly complex and mechanized society, and because of the limitations in the negligence and warranty remedies. Our avowed purpose was "to insure that the costs of injuries resulting from defective products are borne by the manufacturer that put such products on the market rather than by the injured persons who are powerless to protect themselves." (*Id.*, at p. 63, 27 Cal. Rptr. at p. 701, 377 P.2d at p. 901.) Subsequently, the *Greenman* principle was incorporated in section 402A of the Restatement Second of Torts, and adopted by a majority of American jurisdictions. (Prosser, [Law of Torts (4th ed. 1971) § 96], at pp. 657-658.)

From its inception, however, strict liability has never been, and is not now, *absolute* liability. As has been repeatedly expressed, under strict liability the manufacturer does not thereby become the insurer of the safety of the product's user. On the contrary, the plaintiff's injury must have been caused by a "defect" in the product. Thus the manufacturer is not deemed responsible when injury results from an unforeseeable use of its product. Furthermore, we have recognized that though most forms of contributory negligence do not constitute a defense to a strict products liability action, plaintiff's negligence is a complete defense when it comprises assumption of risk. As will thus be seen, the concept of strict products liability was created and shaped judicially. In its evolution, the doctrinal encumbrances of contract and warranty, and the traditional elements of negligence, were stripped from the remedy, and a new tort emerged which extended liability for defective product design and manufacture beyond negligence but short of absolute liability.

In *Li v. Yellow Cab Co., supra*, 13 Cal. 3d 804, 119 Cal. Rptr. 858, 532 P.2d 1126, we introduced the other doctrine with which we are concerned, comparative negligence. We examined the history of contributory negligence, the massive criticism directed at it because its presence in the slightest degree completely barred plaintiff's recovery, and the increasing defection from the doctrine. We then weighed the two principal arguments against its removal from California law, namely, that such a sharp change in direction required legislative action, and that there existed a cluster of asserted practical obstacles relating to multiple parties, the apportionment burdens on a jury and the uncertain effect on the defenses of last clear chance, assumption of risk, and wilful misconduct. Concluding that none of the obstacles was insurmountable, we announced in *Li* the adoption of a "pure" form of comparative negligence which, when present, reduced but did not prevent plaintiff's recovery. (Pp. 828-829, 119 Cal. Rptr. 858, 532 P.2d 1126.) We held that the defense of assumption of risk, insofar as it is no more than a variant of contributory negligence, was merged into the assessment of liability in proportion to fault. (Pp. 824-825, 119 Cal. Rptr. 858, 532 P.2d 1126.) Within the broad guidelines therein announced, we left to trial court's discretion in the particular implementation of the new doctrine. (Pp. 826-827, 119 Cal. Rptr. 858, 532 P.2d 1126.)

We stand now at the point of confluence of these two conceptual streams, having been greatly assisted by the thoughtful analysis of the parties and the valuable assistance of numerous amici curiae. We are by no means the first to consider the interaction of these two developing principles. As with the litigants before us, responsible and respected authorities have reached opposing conclusions stressing in various degrees the different considerations which we now examine.

Those counseling against the recognition of comparative fault principles in strict products liability cases vigorously stress, perhaps equally, not only the conceptual, but also the semantic difficulties incident to such a course. The task of merging the two concepts is said to be impossible, that "apples and oranges" cannot be compared, that "oil and water" do not mix, and that strict liability, which is not founded on negligence or fault, is inhospitable to comparative principles. The syllogism runs, contributory negligence was only a defense to negligence, comparative negligence only affects contributory negligence, therefore comparative negligence cannot be a defense to strict liability. While fully recognizing the theoretical and semantic distinctions between the twin principles of strict products liability and traditional negligence, we think they can be blended or accommodated.

The inherent difficulty in the "apples and oranges" argument is its insistence on fixed and precise definitional treatment of legal concepts. In the evolving areas of both products liability and tort defenses, however, there has developed much conceptual overlapping and interweaving in order to attain substantial justice. The concept of strict liability itself, as we have noted, arose from dissatisfaction with the wooden formalisms of traditional tort and contract principles in order to protect the consumer of manufactured goods. Similarly, increasing social awareness of its harsh "all or nothing" consequences led us in *Li* to moderate the impact of traditional contributory negligence in order to accomplish a fairer and more balanced result.

We acknowledged an intermixing of defenses of contributory negligence and assumption of risk and formally effected a type of merger. "As for assumption of risk, we have recognized in this state that this defense overlaps that of contributory negligence to some extent. . . ." (Li, *supra*, 13 Cal. 3d at p. 824, 119 Cal. Rptr. at p. 872, 532 P.2d at p. 1240.) In *Li*, we further reaffirmed our observation in *Grey v. Fibreboard Paper Products Co.* (1966) 65 Cal. 2d 240, 245, 53 Cal. Rptr. 545, 418 P.2d 153. "[T]hat in one kind of situation, to wit, where a plaintiff unreasonably undertakes to encounter a specific known risk imposed by a defendant's negligence, plaintiff's conduct, although he may encounter that risk in a prudent manner, is in reality a form of contributory negligence. . . .' We think it clear that the adoption of a system of comparative negligence should entail the merger of the defense of assumption of risk into the general scheme of assessment of liability in proportion to fault in those particular cases in which the form of assumption of risk involved is no more than a variant of contributory negligence." (13 Cal. 3d at pp. 824-825, 119 Cal. Rptr. at pp. 872-873, 532 P.2d at pp. 1240-1241, quoting *Grey, supra*, 65 Cal. 2d at pp. 245-246, 53 Cal. Rptr. 545, 418 P.2d 153, italics in orig.)

Furthermore, the "apples and oranges" argument may be conceptually suspect. It has been suggested that the term "contributory negligence," one of the vital building blocks upon which much of the argument is based, may indeed itself be a misnomer since it lacks the first element of the classical negligence formula, namely, a duty of care owing to another. A highly respected torts authority, Dean William Prosser, has noted this fact by observing, "It is perhaps unfortunate that contributory negligence is called negligence at all. 'Contributory fault' would be a more descriptive term. Negligence as it is commonly understood is conduct which creates an undue risk of harm to others. Contributory negligence is conduct which involves an undue risk of harm to the actor himself. Negligence requires a duty, an obligation of conduct to another person. Contributory negligence involves no duty, unless we are to be so ingenious as to say that the plaintiff is under an obligation to protect the defendant against liability for the consequences of his own negligence." (Prosser, Law of Torts, *supra*, § 65, p. 418.)

We think, accordingly, the conclusion may fairly be drawn that the terms "comparative negligence," "contributory negligence" and "assumption of risk" do not, standing alone, lend themselves to the exact measurements of a micrometer-caliper, or to such precise definition as to divert us from otherwise strong and consistent countervailing policy considerations. Fixed semantic consistency at this point is less important than the attainment of a just and equitable result. The interweaving of concept and terminology in this area suggests a judicial posture that is flexible rather than doctrinaire.

We pause at this point to observe that where, as here, a consumer or user sues the manufacturer or designer alone, technically, neither fault nor conduct is really compared functionally. The conduct of one party in combination with the product of another, or perhaps the placing of a defective article in the stream of projected and anticipated use, may produce the ultimate injury. In such a case, as in the situation before us, we think the term "equitable apportionment or allocation of loss" may be more descriptive than "comparative fault."

Given all of the foregoing, we are, in the wake of *Li*, disinclined to resolve the important issue before us by the simple expedient of matching linguistic labels which have evolved either for convenience or by custom. Rather, we consider it more useful to examine the foundational reasons underlying the creation of strict products liability in California to ascertain whether the purposes of the doctrine would be defeated or diluted by adoption of comparative principles. We imposed strict liability against the manufacturer and in favor of the user or consumer in order to relieve injured consumers "from *problems of proof* inherent in pursuing negligence . . . and warranty . . . remedies, . . ." *(Cronin v. J.B.E. Olson Corp.,* 8 Cal. 3d at p. 133, 104 Cal. Rptr. at p. 442, 501 P.2d at p. 1162, italics added.) As we have noted, we sought to place the burden of loss on manufacturers rather than " . . . injured persons *who are powerless to protect themselves. . . ." (Greenman, supra,* 59 Cal.2d at p. 63, 27 Cal.Rptr. at p. 701, 377 P.2d at p. 901, italics added; see *Escola,* 24 Cal. 2d at p. 462, 150 P.2d 436; *Price v. Shell Oil Co.* (1970) 2 Cal. 3d 245, 251, 85 Cal. Rptr. 178, 182, 466 P.2d 722, 726 *["protection of otherwise defenseless victims of* manufacturing defects and the spreading throughout society of the cost of compensating them"] italics added.)

The foregoing goals, we think, will not be frustrated by the adoption of comparative principles. Plaintiffs will continue to be relieved of proving that the manufacturer or distributor was negligent in the production, design, or dissemination of the article in question. Defendant's liability for injuries caused by a defective product remains strict. The principle of protecting the defenseless is likewise preserved, for plaintiff's recovery will be reduced *only* to the extent that his own lack of reasonable care contributed to his injury. The cost of compensating the victim of a defective product, albeit proportionately reduced, remains on defendant manufacturer, and will, through him, be "spread among society." However, we do not permit plaintiff's own conduct relative to the product to escape unexamined, and as to that share of plaintiff's damages which flows from his own fault we discern no reason of policy why it should, following *Li,* be borne by others. Such a result would directly contravene the principle announced in *Li,* that loss should be assessed equitably in proportion to fault.

We conclude, accordingly, that the expressed purposes which persuaded us in the first instance to adopt strict liability in California would not be thwarted were we to apply comparative principles. What would be forfeit is a degree of semantic symmetry. However, in this evolving area of tort law in which new remedies are judicially created, and old defenses judicially merged, impelled by strong considerations of equity and fairness we seek a larger synthesis. If a more just result follows from the expansion of comparative principles, we have no hesitancy in seeking it, mindful always that the fundamental and underlying purpose of *Li* was to promote the equitable allocation of loss among all parties legally responsible in proportion to their fault.

A second objection to the application of comparative principles in strict products liability cases is that a manufacturer's incentive to produce safe products will thereby be reduced or removed. While we fully recognize this concern we think, for several reasons, that the problem is more shadow than substance. First, of course, the manufacturer cannot avoid its continuing liability for a defective product even when the plaintiff's own conduct has contributed to his injury. The manufacturer's liability, and therefore its incentive to avoid and correct product defects, remains; its exposure will be lessened only to the extent that the trier finds that the victim's conduct contributed to his injury. Second, as a practical matter a manufacturer, in a particular case, cannot assume that the user of a defective product upon whom an injury is visited will be blameworthy. Doubtless, many users are free of fault, and a defect is at least as likely as not to be exposed by an entirely innocent plaintiff who will obtain full recovery. In such cases the manufacturer's incentive toward safety both in design and production is wholly unaffected. Finally, we must observe that under the present law, which recognizes assumption of risk as a complete defense to products liability, the curious and cynical message is that it profits the manufacturer to make his product so defective that in the event of injury he can argue that the user had to be aware of its patent defects. To that extent the incentives are inverted. We conclude, accordingly, that no substantial or significant impairment of the safety incentives of defendants will occur by the adoption of comparative principles.

In passing, we note one important and felicitous result if we apply comparative principles to strict products liability. This arises from the fact that under present law when plaintiff sues in negligence his own contributory negligence, however denominated, may diminish but cannot wholly defeat his recovery. When he sues in strict products liability, however, his "assumption of risk" *completely bars* his recovery. Under *Li*, as we have noted, "assumption of risk" is merged into comparative principles. (13 Cal. 3d at p. 825, 119 Cal. Rptr. 858, 533 P.2d 1226.) The consequence is that after *Li* in a negligence action, plaintiff's conduct which amounts to "negligent" assumption of risk no longer defeats plaintiff's recovery. Identical conduct, however, in a strict liability case acts as a complete bar under rules heretofore applicable. Thus, strict products liability, which was developed to free injured consumers from the constraints imposed by traditional negligence and warranty theories, places a consumer plaintiff in a worse position than would be the case were his claim founded on simple negligence. This, in turn, rewards adroit pleading and selection of theories. The application of comparative principles to strict liability obviates this bizarre anomaly by treating alike the defenses to both negligence and strict products liability actions. In each instance the defense, if established, will reduce but not bar plaintiff's claim.

A third objection to the merger of strict liability and comparative fault focuses on the claim that, as a practical matter, triers of fact, particularly jurors, cannot assess, measure, or compare plaintiff's negligence with defendant's strict liability. We are unpersuaded by the argument and are convinced that jurors are able to undertake a fair apportionment of liability.

. . . .

We note that the majority of our sister states which have addressed the problem, either by statute or judicial decree, have extended comparative principles to strict products liability.

. . . .

Moreover, we are further encouraged in our decision herein by noting that the apparent majority of scholarly commentators has urged adoption of the rule which we announce herein.

. . . .

Having examined the principal objections and finding them not insurmountable, and persuaded by logic, justice, and fundamental fairness, we conclude that a system of comparative fault should be and it is hereby extended to actions founded on strict products liability. In such cases the separate defense of "assumption of risk," to the extent that it is a form of contributory negligence, is abolished. While, as we have suggested, on the particular facts before us, the term "equitable apportionment of loss" is more accurately descriptive of the process, nonetheless, the term "comparative fault" has gained such wide acceptance by courts and in the literature that we adopt its use herein.

In *Li*, we announced a system of pure comparative negligence "the fundamental purpose of which shall be to assign responsibility and liability for damage in direct proportion to the amount of negligence of each of the parties." *(Id.*, 13 Cal. 3d at p. 829, 119 Cal. Rptr. at p. 875, 532 P.2d at p. 1243.) Those same underlying considerations of policy which moved us judicially in *Li* to rescue blameworthy plaintiffs from a 100-year-old sanction against *all* recovery persuade us now to extend similar principles to the strict products liability area. Legal responsibility is thereby shared. We think that apportioning tort liability is sound, logical and capable of wider application than to negligence cases alone. To hold otherwise, in our view, would be to perpetuate a system which, as we noted in *Li*, Dean Prosser describes as placing " . . . upon one party the entire burden of a loss for which two are, by hypothesis, responsible." (Prosser, *supra*, § 67, p. 433.) We reiterate that our reason for extending a full system of comparative fault to strict products liability is because it is fair to do so. The law consistently seeks to elevate justice and equity above the exact contours of a mathematical equation. We are convinced that in merging the two principles what may be lost in symmetry is more than gained in fundamental fairness.

. . . .

By extending and tailoring the comparative principles announced in *Li, supra*, to the doctrine of strict products liability, we believe that we move closer to the goal of the equitable allocation of legal responsibility for personal injuries. We do so by relying on what Professor Schwartz aptly terms a "predicate of fairness." In making liability more commensurate with fault we undermine neither the theories nor the policies of the strict liability rule. In *Li* we took "a first step in what we deem to be a proper and just direction, . . ." (13 Cal. 3d at p. 826, 119 Cal. Rptr. at p. 874, 532 P.2d at p. 1242.) We are convinced that the principles herein announced constitute the next appropriate and logical step in the same direction.

The judgment is reversed.

TOBRINER, CLARK and MANUEL, JJ., concur.

CLARK, JUSTICE, concurring.

The reasoning of *Li v. Yellow Cab. Co.* (1975) 13 Cal. 3d 804, 119 Cal. Rptr. 858, 532 P.2d 1226, as the majority point out, is equally applicable to strict liability cases and compels applying comparative fault in those cases. Under the compulsion of *Li*, I have signed the majority opinion.

. . . .

Having undertaken the legislative function by repudiating contributory negligence and adopting comparative fault, we have abandoned our traditional deference to legislative province and to stare decisis. Having done so, we, like the Legislature, should reconsider our bold decisions from time to time, performing the legislative process to the best of our ability — until the Legislature awakens to reclaim and exercise its historic power.

JEFFERSON, [assigned], JUSTICE, concurring and dissenting.

I concur in part and dissent in part.

I agree with the majority's result that the judgment should be reversed because of the prejudicial error in admitting evidence of decedent's intoxication and of his failure to use available safety devices. Otherwise, I part company with the majority's views.

The majority rejects what I consider to be a sound criticism of its holding that it is illogical and illusory to compare elements or factors that are not reasonably subject to comparison. The majority states that it is convinced that jurors will be able to compare the noncomparables — plaintiff's negligence with defendant's strict liability for a defective product — and still reach a fair apportionment of liability.

I consider the majority conclusion a case of wishful thinking and an application of an impractical, ivory-tower approach. The majority's assumption that a jury is capable of making a fair apportionment between a plaintiff's negligent conduct and a defendant's defective product is no more logical or convincing than if a jury were to be instructed that it should add a quart of milk (representing plaintiff's negligence) and a metal bar three feet in length (representing defendant's strict liability for a defective product), and that the two added together equal 100 percent — the total fault for plaintiff's injuries; that plaintiff's quart of milk is then to be assigned its percentage of the 100 percent total and defendant's metal bar is to be assigned the remaining percentage of the total.

. . . .

BIRD, C.J., concurs.

MOSK, JUSTICE, dissenting.

I dissent.

This will be remembered as the dark day when this court, which heroically took the lead in originating the doctrine of products liability *(Greenman v. Yuba Power Products, Inc.* 59 Cal. 2d 57, 27 Cal. Rptr. 697, 377 P.2d 897 (1963)) and steadfastly resisted efforts to inject concepts of negligence into the newly designed tort *(Cronin v. J.B.E. Olson Corp.* 8 Cal. 121, 104 Cal. Rptr. 433, 501 P.2d 1153 (1972)), inexplicably turned 180 degrees and beat a hasty retreat almost back to square one. The pure concept of products liability so pridefully fashioned and nurtured by this court for the past decade and a half is reduced to a shambles.

. . . .

Transferring the liability, or part of the liability, from the party responsible for putting the article in the stream of commerce to the consumer is precisely what the majority propose to do. They do this by employing a euphemism: the victim's recovery is to be "proportionately reduced." The result, however delicately described, is to dilute the defect of the article by elevating the conduct of the wounded consumer to an issue of equal significance. We can be as certain as tomorrow's daylight that every defendant charged with marketing a defective product will hereafter assert that the injured plaintiff did something, anything, that conceivably could be deemed contributorily negligent: he drove the vehicle with a defective steering mechanism 56 miles an hour instead of 54; or he should have discovered a latent defect hidden in the machinery; or perhaps he should not have succumbed to the salesman's persuasion and purchased the defective object in the first instance. I need no crystal ball to foresee that the pleading of affirmative defenses alleging contributory negligence — or the currently approved substitute terminology will now become boilerplate.

. . . .

The best reasoned authorities decline to inject negligence, contributory or comparative, into strict products liability litigation. . . . In *Kirkland v. General Motors Corp.*, 521 P.2d 1353 (Okl. 1974), the Oklahoma Supreme Court refused to apply a comparative negligence statute to products liability because it consistently determined that "manufacturers' products liability is not negligence, nor is it to be treated as a negligence action" (*id.* at p. 1367). A similar result followed in *Melia v. Ford Motor Co.*, 534 F.2d 795, 802 (8th Cir. 1976), in which the court held application of a comparative negligence statute would be "inappropriate in a strict liability case." Even more emphatic was the court in *Kinard v. Coats Co., Inc.*, 553 P.2d 835, 837 (Colo. App. 1976): "Although some other jurisdictions have chosen to apply comparative negligence to products liability cases in our view the better-reasoned position is that comparative negligence has no application to products liability actions under § 402A. Products liability under § 402A does not rest upon negligence principles, but rather is premised on the concept of enterprise liability for casting a defective product into the stream of commerce. Thus, the focus is upon the nature of the product, and the consumer's reasonable expectations with regard to that product, rather than on the conduct either of the manufacturer or of the person injured because of the product." The Colorado Supreme Court completely eliminated negligence from products liability actions, declaring in such proceedings it " 'shifts the focus from the conduct of the manufacturer to the nature of the product.' " (*Hiigel v. General Motors Corp.*, 544 P.2d 983 (Colo. 1975)).

We also declared in *Ault v. International Harvester Co.*, 13 Cal. 3d 113 (1974), that the focus is not on the conduct of the defendant, but on the nature of the product. That being so, the majority create an impossible dilemma for trial courts. If comparative negligence is to be applied, how can the trier of fact rationally weigh the conduct of the plaintiff against the defective product? I know of no other instance in American jurisprudence in which the antagonists are the conduct of a human being versus an inanimate object.

. . . .

The majority note one "felicitous result" of adopting comparative negligence to products liability: the merger of assumption of risk — which they term a "bizarre anomaly" — into their innovative defense. I find that result neither felicitous nor tenable. In *Barker v. Lull Engineering Co.*, 20 Cal. 3d at page 429, 143 Cal. Rptr. 225, 573 P.2d 443, we defined a defective product as one which failed to perform safely when used in an intended or foreseeable manner. If a consumer elects to use a product patently defective when other alternatives are available, or to use a product in a manner clearly not intended or foreseeable, he assumes the risks inherent in his improper utilization and should not be heard to complain about the condition of the object. One who employs a power saw to trim his fingernails — and thereafter finds the number of his fingers reduced — should not prevail to any extent whatever against the manufacturer even if the saw had a defective blade. I would retain assumption of risk as a total defense to products liability, as it always has been.

The majority deny their opinion diminishes the therapeutic effect of products liability upon producers of defective products. It seems self-evident that procedures which evaluate the injured consumer's conduct in each instance, and thus eliminate or reduce the award against the producer or distributor of a defective product, are not designed as an effective incentive to maximum responsibility to consumers. The converse is more accurate: the motivation to avoid polluting the stream of commerce with defective products increases in direct relation to the size of potential damage awards.

In sum, I am convinced that since the negligence of the defendant is irrelevant in products liability cases, the negligence — call it contributory or comparative — of the plaintiff is also irrelevant. The majority, by considering the comparative negligence of a plaintiff in an action in which defendant's negligence is not an issue, apply an untenable double standard. Their error is grievously unsettling to the law of torts. More significantly, this decision seriously erodes the pattern of the law which up to now reflected a healthy concern for consumers victimized by defective products placed on the market in this mechanized age through the dynamics of mass production, national and international distribution, and psychologically subtle marketing.

. . . .

I would affirm the judgment.

Rehearing denied; BIRD, C.J., and MOSK, J., dissenting.

───────────

1. The concept of applying comparative negligence in strict products liability actions — where the defendant was not negligent at all — makes it all the more clear that the courts are in fact comparing causation and not negligence. But what about those products that are defective because they fail to prevent (or minimize the

effect of) negligent misuse? Can *Daly* be reconciled with *Culpepper*?

2. *Daly* is, in a way, a seatbelt case. It is unusual in that the driver, the plaintiff, caused the accident by reckless driving. Presumably, he was too intoxicated to fasten his seatbelt.

3. On the surface, *Daly* sounds like a pro-defendant opinion, because the court is opening the door to a new defense in strict products liability cases. In this connection, it is worth noting that the plaintiff had lost the case in the trial court.

4. *Culpepper, McCown,* and *Daly* are all "crashworthiness" cases, in which the issue is not whether the product caused the accident, but rather whether the product caused injuries from the accident to be exacerbated. Negligence in failing to use an available safety device or, as in *Culpepper,* misusing an available safety device, may become the issue. In other words, manufacturers have a duty to make a product that is safe in the face of foreseeable misuse, such as being crashed, whatever the cause of the crash. What about misuse of the safety device itself?

5. After *Daly,* how should a court handle the fact that a plaintiff's negligence was the sole cause of an accident? If the plaintiff in *Daly* had not negligently crashed his car, he would not have been injured at all. In this respect, his own negligence was the sole cause of the accident. If this fact bars recovery, how can safety devices included on a product to minimize the effects of user negligence, ever be challenged as defective in a jurisdiction that applies comparative negligence in products liability cases, when the plaintiff's own negligence has set the chain of events in motion?

Clearly, the Court in *Daly* did not intend this result, although the court fails to explain how the plaintiff's negligence should be treated in a crashworthiness case. What would a reasonable analysis of the relationship between causing an accident and causing the resulting injury to be exacerbated look like? It is perhaps worth noting here that courts have consistently held that user conduct that causes safety devices to be necessary is all too foreseeable.

FORD v. POLARIS INDUSTRIES, INC.
California Court of Appeal, 2006
43 Cal. Rptr. 3d 215

REARDON, J.

Susan Ford sustained severe orifice injuries after falling off the rear of a two-seater Polaris personal watercraft. The jet-powered nozzle propelled a high-pressure stream of water that tore apart her internal organs. Today she uses a colostomy bag, she urinates through a catheter, and her lower right torso and leg are numb from nerve damage. Susan and her husband sued the manufacturer and distributor of the watercraft on a strict products liability theory.

This appeal frames the question whether the doctrine of primary assumption of risk applies to the manufacturer of the personal watercraft so as to preclude the injured jet skier from raising a defective design claim. We conclude that the trial court properly ruled that primary assumption of the risk did not bar plaintiff's suit.

The appeal also addresses the propriety of instructions in a strict products liability case where the plaintiff alleges that the personal watercraft was defectively designed and caused her injury. We determine that the standard instructions on defective design were adequate.

Finally, defendant manufacturer insists that the court below erred in refusing to permit the jury to allocate fault to the watercraft operator for giving misleading instructions to the injured skier and to the owners and operator for failure to pass on safety warnings. This assertion begs the questions: Did the operator owe a duty not to deliver misleading instructions and did the owners and operator have a duty to convey the manufacturer's warnings? Finding no such duties, we reject these contentions as well and affirm the judgment.

I. FACTS AND PROCEDURE

A. *The Accident, Injuries and Aftermath*

In April 2001 Steve and Laura Nakamura bought two 2–seater Polaris SLH–700 personal watercraft.[3]

On September 9, 2001, the Fords and Nakamuras and various family members went to Lake Berryessa for a picnic. Laura took Susan for a ride on the watercraft. Susan was wearing a one-piece swimsuit and a life jacket. This was her first time riding a personal watercraft.

Susan held onto Laura's waist. After about five minutes, Laura stopped to tell Susan she was holding on too tight and to hold onto the grips behind her instead. Susan looked around; all she saw were the grab handles. She had to lean back and could only hook a couple fingers into each handle.

They started out again in a straight line. The jet ski was "bumping up and down." Susan lost her grip, was lifted off the seat and fell backward off the rear of the watercraft. As Susan hit the water she felt "a lot" of pain and vomited. Laura saw Susan floating in a pool of blood. Paramedics rushed Susan by helicopter to University of California Davis Medical Center.

Susan sustained a severe hernial and rectal injury. Her internal bleeding required multiple transfusions. Two surgeries were required to prepare and establish a colostomy. Medical records indicate she also required "massive resuscitation . . . from her initial operation."

Susan was in the hospital for 10 days, followed by a five-day postoperative stay at North Bay Medical Center.

Susan has no control over her bowels. She was evaluated for rectal-colon reconstructive surgery, but the specialist concluded there was no possibility of reconstruction. When Susan learned this, she "basically fell apart."

The injuries also created urological complications such that Susan must self-

---

[3] A personal watercraft is a small jet-propelled vessel. The sport of riding a personal watercraft is referred to as jet skiing.

catheterize in order to urinate. As well, Susan is numb from her right kneecap to her waist; her buttocks and pelvic area are also numb. She can no longer engage in such activities as playing softball and dancing. And, because of loss of sensation and the physical limitations she endures, Susan and Anthony's sex life has suffered. Susan used to work at Raley's Superstore but was unable to keep up with her responsibilities after she returned to work. She now takes care of her father-in-law.

B. *Cause of the Accident*

Michael Burleson, an industrial engineer and safety professional with extensive experience on personal watercraft concerns, testified that the jet nozzle is centrally positioned in back of the Polaris watercraft and protrudes two and five-eighths inches beyond the rear deck. The position of the jet increases the chance of high-pressure exposure should a passenger be ejected to the rear of the watercraft. Susan landed less than a foot from the back of the jet nozzle.

When a watercraft is accelerating and encounters a wave, the passenger can "get some lift" off the seat, and if the passenger is not well coupled to the craft he or she may lose balance and roll off. When there is a rearward ejection into the stream of water thrust by a jet nozzle such as occurred with Susan, the high pressure of the water penetrates the body, causing internal injuries.

C. *Design Defect*

1. *Plaintiffs' Case*

Burleson explained that because it is important that nothing interfere with the operator's ability to control a personal watercraft, a passenger cannot always hold onto the operator. Sometimes passengers pull more than is comfortable for the operator. In some situations it may not be feasible to hold on, for example if the operator stands up to move around. As well there may be social constraints to holding onto the operator. A significant difference in size may also militate against holding on.

In Burleson's opinion there was a defect in the design of the SLH Polaris watercraft because this particular craft lacked adequate design safeguards to protect against a rearward ejection injury. In other words, there was no easily identifiable alternative means for the passenger to hold on when it was not feasible to hold onto the operator.

Several feasible design features were available to Polaris to protect against rear ejections. A seatback is one alternative to prevent the passenger from "coming off" the back.[4]

Another solution would be recognizable and accessible handgrips that the passenger can "grasp completely." The grips Burleson proffered protruded from

---

[4] No originally equipped watercraft were sold with a seatback in 2001. Polaris offered evidence that a seatback would be in the way if installed on a two-person watercraft, and would increase the risk of back injuries.

the side of the craft. Many manufacturers have switched from protruding handles to the recessed handles that were on the Polaris craft.[5], [6]

For fifty cents at most, a simple seat strap that goes around the seat would provide a secure handhold for passenger stability. Several models in the Polaris manual for this machine had a seat strap, and there were bolt holes for such a strap on the craft but it had not been installed. Had the machine been equipped with a seat strap, Burleson did not think the accident would have occurred.[7]

Dr. Edward Karnes was the Fords' human factors engineer. That discipline concerns the evaluation of human factors involved in the design and use of products, including how people understand risks and respond to warnings. He described the hazard in this case as falling off the rear of the watercraft and being struck by the jet thrust. The manufacturer's job is to identify and evaluate hazards and make decisions about remedies according to a safety hierarchy. The first tier on the hierarchy is to design out the hazard. If that cannot be accomplished, the next tier would be to provide some type of guard to prevent access to the hazardous situation. Warning — the last tier — is an appropriate remedy only if the hazard cannot be eliminated by design or guard.

Polaris's solution to orifice injuries was to admonish participants to wear protective clothing. The rear and front on-craft labels for the SLH warned that the passenger must wear a wetsuit or equivalent protective clothing to avoid orifice injuries. The owner's manual reproduced the rear decal, in bigger typeface, as well as the front warning label, and instructed elsewhere to wear protective clothing for body or orifice protection. Susan did not notice the warning decal and, being a guest, she never saw the owner's manual.

In Dr. Karnes's opinion, warnings alone were not an appropriate remedy for the hazard that creates the risk of orifice injury. He regarded the cost of compliance — or the effort required to comply with warning — as high for wearing a wetsuit. First, they are not comfortable when worn in warm weather conditions. Second, the likelihood that owner-operators would have wetsuits on hand for recreational passengers such as friends or family members is "going to be about nil." Third, the person at greatest risk — the passenger — is also the person least likely to have read the vehicle warning label.

Moreover, although the Polaris decal warning provided correct basic risk factor information about the need to wear protective clothing, the forceful entry of water into orifices and the need for all riders to wear protective clothing, Karnes considered the warning inadequate because it did not identify the risk (falling off

---

[5] Polaris's expert testified that in 2001 there were not any personal watercraft marketed with protruding side handles. The purpose of recessed handles is "to minimize inadvertent contact with the handles."

[6] Apparently the Polaris watercraft was equipped with sculpted outside handles, also referred to as detents or fingerholds, with a rear grip handle primarily used for reboarding from the water. Susan reached for this grip handle.

[7] On cross-examination, Burleson stated that although the seat strap can provide a way to hold on, it was not the best solution for rearward ejection. The strap is an active device, meaning the passenger has to use it. On the other hand a seatback, for example, would provide passive safety that would be there all the time.

the rear of the craft) or pinpoint those who were at greatest risk, namely passengers. Additionally, had the decal been placed on the seat, it would be more conspicuous to the passenger. From the operators' perspective, the warning label fails to tell them directly not to give a ride to someone who is not wearing protective clothing, and why this is important. Further, the admonition to wear protective clothing was undermined by the safety video which did not discuss orifice injuries or the special risk to passengers, and indeed portrayed passengers in bathing suits, never in protective clothing.

3. Defendants' Case

Kevin Breen, Polaris's forensic engineer, concurred that it was likely Susan would not have been injured had she been holding onto a seat strap. The force required to dislodge a passenger holding onto a seat strap compares favorably with the force to dislodge the operator: It is the same or a bit greater. Indeed, the Polaris manual states that the passenger should hold onto the operator or seat strap.

Breen also stated that although orifice injuries are exceedingly rare, watercraft manufacturers cannot ignore them and have a responsibility to try to design features that would prevent or minimize the risk.

Breen tested different fabrics to determine whether other materials would have prevented Susan's injuries by reducing the water pressure behind the fabric below five pounds per square inch, the threshold for sphincter muscle tension. Both the neoprene wetsuit and blue jeans sufficiently reduced the water pressure. Susan wore denim shorts to the lake, but not when she boarded the watercraft.

Polaris designated Daniel Schroepher as the employee most qualified to address safety features on the SLH such as rear passenger seating, safety testing and safety studies. He testified that Polaris designed the SLH in-house. By the time of the 1996 model year, the label warned against orifice injuries. Polaris did not conduct tests to distinguish the risk of falling off the back of the craft as opposed to the side.

Schroepher identified several design features intended to prevent the passenger from sliding off the back. The driver's seat and handgrips were of nonslippery material so the driver could stay put as well as the passenger who was hanging on. The foot pad was also of grippy material, and there was a spot where the passenger could put his or her heels. Grab handles were an option to stay on board if there was discomfort with holding onto the operator. Schroepher testified that Polaris had been aware of the possibility of falling off the watercraft and the nature of injuries that could be sustained, and had done everything it could to address the situation.

Schroepher was not sure if Polaris ever provided seat straps for the two-person SLH. They were not offered as an optional feature because there was "no safety need" and "engineering got busy and was never able to get it done."

By 2001 Polaris was aware that the thrust of the jet pump would be dangerous to someone who fell off the rear of a moving watercraft. Yet the Polaris safety video did not refer to the risk of orifice injury. Schroepher offered as a rationale for this omission that Polaris "wanted to provide adequate information but not drag out the video so it's so long so people won't watch it." Therefore, the video "hit the highlights" such as wearing proper gear, avoiding collisions and the most common injuries. "And if you do those things, then it would avoid orifice injuries. . . ."

D. *The Nakamuras' Interaction with Polaris*

Prior to completing the purchase of the SLH–700 watercraft, Steve and Laura Nakamura watched a safety video at the dealership as required by Polaris. Neither the video nor representatives of the dealership mentioned the need to wear protective clothing or the risk of falling backward and sustaining orifice injuries. As described by Schroepher, the marketing product manager for Polaris, the safety video highlighted issues such as common injuries and how to avoid collisions.

The Polaris dealer went through the owner's manual with Steve Nakamura, pointing out all the warnings and stressing the importance of reading the manual. Polaris required Steve to sign a warranty registration certifying that he received and would read the owner's manual and warning labels before using the watercraft, and would ask anyone he allowed to use the craft to also read the labels and manual. Steve skimmed through the manual, focusing on maintenance issues. Prior to the accident he did not read the warning decals, including the decal advising "SEVERE INJURY or DEATH. . . . [¶] WEAR PROTECTIVE CLOTHING." Nor was it his practice to have guests read the manual and labels. The Nakamuras did not have any discussion with Susan about what to wear when riding the watercraft.

E. *Procedural History*

In September 2002 the Fords filed suit, alleging causes of action for "products liability" against Polaris and negligence against Laura Nakamura. Polaris cross-complained against Laura for equitable indemnity.

Laura moved for summary judgment asserting that the doctrine of primary assumption of risk barred the Fords' action against her. Laura argued that she owed no duty to eliminate, or protect Susan against, "the risk of falling while the water craft was engaged in its maneuvers[,] as those maneuvers constitute a risk inherent in, if not the very purpose of, the sport itself." The Fords did not oppose the motion but Polaris did, arguing that Laura failed to communicate to Susan the instructions and warnings provided by the company, and wrongfully instructed her to ride the watercraft in an unsafe manner.

Granting the motion and directing that judgment be entered in Laura's favor, the trial court concluded that the activity that Laura and Susan were engaged in was subject to the doctrine of primary assumption of the risk: "[T]his . . . personal water craft operation was being done for enjoyment or thrill. It does require physical exertion as well as elements of skill, and involves a challenge containing a potential risk of injury. [¶] And, in addition, even though there is no competition . . . or race going on with other operators of personal water craft, there was a kind of competition going on with the elements including waves [set up] by other boats and the testing of oneself against the challenges of speed and sudden turns." As to Polaris's claims, the court ruled that although Laura did not communicate to Susan the Polaris warning to wear protective clothing, and told her to hang onto the handles, contrary to Polaris instructions and warnings, these lapses at most amounted to mere negligence. Therefore under the doctrine of primary assumption of the risk Laura owed Susan no duty of care.

Polaris also moved for summary judgment, arguing that under principles of collateral estoppel, the court must apply primary assumption of the risk to the Fords' claims against it. Denying the motion, the trial court explained that reliance on the ruling in favor of Laura was misplaced because the Fords' allegations against Polaris concerned its duty to provide products free of design defects, a duty that did not attach to Laura. Moreover, while the court acknowledged that primary assumption of the risk may be applied to the activity of jet skiing, there was no finding that " 'rearward ejection jet thrust injuries' " were inherent in the sport.

At the close of evidence Polaris moved unsuccessfully for nonsuit, arguing that plaintiffs did not prove that Polaris increased the risks inherent in jet skiing. As well, Polaris proposed a special instruction to the effect that plaintiffs must prove "[t]hat the defects increased the risk of harm beyond those risks that are a normal part of the sport of jet skiing." The court denied the instruction, ruling that if plaintiffs prove a defect, "that ipso facto raises the risk beyond those normally inherent in jet skiing and, therefore, requiring the jury to return a finding on that would not only be a redundancy but would be a confusing factor." Polaris also proposed a special verdict that asked whether the design defect increased the risk of harm. The court rejected this verdict form.

Additionally, Polaris sought to allocate fault to the Nakamuras pursuant to Civil Code section 1431.2, proposing a verdict form permitting such allocation. The court declined this request.

The jury returned a special verdict against Polaris on the design defect claim, awarded Susan $382,024 in economic losses and $3,262,500 in noneconomic losses, and awarded Anthony $115,000 for loss of consortium. The jury also found that Susan was not comparatively negligent. This appeal followed.

II. DISCUSSION

A. *Assumption of the Risk Meets Strict Products Liability on a Recreational Equipment Design Defect Claim.*

1. *Introduction; Standards of Review*

Although Polaris frames the primary issue on appeal in terms of the court's failure to require Susan to prove not only that there was a design defect, but that the defect increased the inherent risks of jet skiing — an error manifest in denied instructions, denied nonsuit motion and rejected verdict form — the heart of its argument is that the court erred in deciding the lawsuit did not fall within the doctrine of primary assumption of the risk. We address both concerns.

The existence and scope of a defendant's duty of care in the context of primary assumption of the risk is a legal question to be decided by the court. (*Knight v. Jewett* (1992) 3 Cal.4th 296, 313, 11 Cal.Rptr.2d 2, 834 P.2d 696 (*Knight*); see *Kahn v. East Side Union High School Dist.* (2003) 31 Cal.4th 990, 1004, 4 Cal.Rptr.3d 103, 75 P.3d 30 (*Kahn*).) Therefore, we review, de novo, the trial court's decision denying Polaris's motion for summary judgment on primary assumption of the risk. (Code Civ. Proc., § 437c, subd. (p)(2); *American Golf Corp. v. Superior Court* (2000) 79 Cal.App.4th 30, 35, 93 Cal.Rptr.2d 683.) However, as we conclude that primary assumption of the risk does not bar the Fords' action, we next evaluate the nature of Polaris's duty as the manufacturer of recreational equipment, and whether the jury instructions on products liability/design defect were adequate in this context. The standard of review for a claim of instructional error of this type is also de novo because the question is one of law, involving the determination of the applicable legal principles. (*National Medical Transportation Network v. Deloitte & Touche* (1998) 62 Cal.App.4th 412, 427, 72 Cal.Rptr.2d 720.)

2. *Legal Framework*

Under the general umbrella of strict products liability, the case went to the jury on the risk-benefit test for design defect.[9] Pursuant to this test, a manufacturer is strictly liable in tort where "the plaintiff demonstrates that the product's design proximately caused his injury and the defendant fails to establish, in light of the relevant factors, that, on balance, the benefits of the challenged design outweigh the risk of danger inherent in such design." (*Barker v. Lull Engineering Co.* (1978) 20 Cal.3d 413, 432, 143 Cal.Rptr. 225, 573 P.2d 443.) Relevant factors pertinent to the risk-benefit analysis include "the gravity of the danger posed by the challenged design, the likelihood that such danger would occur, the mechanical feasibility of a safer alternative design, the financial cost of an improved design, and the adverse consequences to the product and to the consumer that would result from an alternative design." (*Id.* at p. 431, 143 Cal.Rptr. 225, 573 P.2d 443.)

In *Daly v. General Motors Corp.* (1978) 20 Cal.3d 725, 736, 144 Cal.Rptr. 380, 575 P.2d 1162, our Supreme Court reiterated that the purposes underlying the strict products liability doctrine are to relieve injured consumers from problems of proof inherent in pursuing negligence remedies, and to protect otherwise defenseless victims of manufacturing defects by spreading the cost of compensation throughout society. The court concluded that these purposes would not be diluted or frustrated by adoption of comparative fault principles and proceeded to extend these principles to actions founded on strict products liability. At the same time and with respect to such cases, it abolished the separate defense of assumption of the risk, to the extent it served as a form of contributory negligence. (*Id.* at p. 742, 144 Cal.Rptr. 380, 575 P.2d 1162.)

Years later in *Knight*, involving coparticipants in a game of touch football, our Supreme Court differentiated between cases involving primary assumption of the risk — where, in view of the nature of the activity and the parties' relationship to it, the defendant owes no legal duty to protect the plaintiff from a particular risk of harm — and those involving secondary assumption of the risk, in which the

---

[9] As a second strand, the Fords also pursued a defective warning theory. Since the jury found that there was a defect in the design of the watercraft that caused Susan's injuries, it did not reach the issue of the adequacy of warnings.

defendant owes a duty of care but the plaintiff knowingly encounters the risk. (*Knight, supra,* 3 Cal.4th at pp. 314–315, 11 Cal.Rptr.2d 2, 834 P.2d 696.) In the former situation, the absence of a duty operates as a complete bar to recovery whereas in the latter, the trier of fact apportions liability under comparative fault principles. (*Id.* at p. 315, 11 Cal.Rptr.2d 2, 834 P.2d 696.)

The determination whether the defendant owes a legal duty to protect the plaintiff from a particular risk of harm turns on the *nature of the activity in which the defendant is engaged and the relationship of the defendant and the plaintiff to that activity.* (*Knight, supra,* 3 Cal.4th at p. 309, 11 Cal.Rptr.2d 2, 834 P.2d 696.) As to any given active sport, "defendants generally have no legal duty to eliminate (or protect a plaintiff against) risks inherent in the sport itself, [although] defendants generally do have a duty to use due care not to increase the risks to a participant over and above those inherent in the sport." (*Id.* at pp. 315–316, 11 Cal.Rptr.2d 2, 834 P.2d 696.) As explained in *Kahn, supra,* 31 Cal.4th at page 1004, 4 Cal.Rptr.3d 103, 75 P.3d 30, this passage from *Knight* reflects a policy that in a sports setting it is not appropriate to "recognize a duty of care when to do so would require that an integral part of the sport be abandoned, or would discourage vigorous participation in sporting events." Further, because the duty question also hinges on the role of the defendant whose conduct is at issue, duties with respect to the same risk may vary depending on whether the defendant is a coparticipant, coach, recreation provider, manufacturer, and the like. (See *ibid.*)

Shortly after *Knight,* the reviewing court in *Milwaukee Electric Tool Corp. v. Superior Court* (1993) 15 Cal.App.4th 547, 19 Cal.Rptr.2d 24 (*Milwaukee Tool*), responding to the Supreme Court's direction to vacate and reconsider its prior opinion in light of *Knight,* applied the newly announced rules to a cause of action against a tool manufacturer sounding in strict products liability. (*Id.* at p. 550, 19 Cal.Rptr.2d 24.) The plaintiff in *Milwaukee Tool* was an experienced glazier who was injured while using a heavy-duty variable-speed drill. The manufacturer claimed he misused the tool.

The reasoning of *Milwaukee Tool* is instructive. Extensively reviewing the development of the strict product liability doctrine in California (*Milwaukee Tool, supra,* 15 Cal.App.4th at pp. 555–558, 19 Cal.Rptr.2d 24), the court concluded that although the doctrine is not pled in terms of classic negligence, unquestionably a manufacturer has a duty to provide consumers with defect-free products, and that duty is inherent in a strict liability cause of action (*id.* at p. 559, 19 Cal.Rptr.2d 24). Indeed, courts have viewed the doctrine of strict products liability theory — which focuses on the product itself rather than the conduct of the manufacturer — "as a 'short cut' to liability where negligence may be present but may be difficult to prove. [Citations.]" (*Id.* at pp. 556–557, 19 Cal.Rptr.2d 24.) Against this background, the *Milwaukee Tool* court did not hesitate to apply the duty analysis set forth in *Knight* to the question of whether the tool company in question could assert primary assumption of the risk as a complete defense to liability. (*Ibid.*)

First, the nature of the activity asserted in the action was the manufacturer's alleged production of a defective product. There was nothing "in the nature of the manufacturing activity to indicate that a finding of no duty on the manufacturer's part should be made. To the contrary, we believe there is a sound basis in the development of strict products liability doctrine to support analysis of a products liability case, even one involving an assertion of assumption of the risk, in terms of a duty on the part of the manufacturer to produce defect-free products." (*Milwaukee Tool, supra*, 15 Cal.App.4th at p. 562, 19 Cal.Rptr.2d 24.)

Second, looking at the relationship of the defendant and the plaintiff to the activity, namely the use of the tool, the court noted that the accident occurred in an employment setting. Therefore, the court examined the rationale of the firefighter's rule[10] and the related situation where a professional, such as a veterinary assistant, accepts employment involving a known risk of danger. In both cases, primary assumption of the risk has barred recovery. Notwithstanding parallels to the case at hand, the court concluded that an injury asserted to have been caused by a dangerously defective power tool is not " 'a risk that is inherent' in a worker's job." (*Milwaukee Tool, supra*, 15 Cal.App.4th at pp. 562–563, 19 Cal.Rptr.2d 24.) Moreover, "[i]n the relationship of the defendant and the plaintiff to the activity, the use of the tool, it cannot be said that the plaintiff user undertook to act as a product tester or guinea pig." (*Id.* at p. 563, 19 Cal.Rptr.2d 24.) In other words, the user of the tool which causes the injury is "not necessarily a professional employed to confront the very danger posed by the injury-causing agent." (*Ibid.*) Summing it up, the court stated: "[W]e believe that the purposes of strict products liability doctrine will be well served by a finding that a manufacturer owes a duty to a user of its product, thus making the primary assumption of the risk doctrine inapplicable, absent some extraordinary circumstance not reflected by this record." (*Id.* at p. 565, 19 Cal.Rptr.2d 24.)

More recently, the reviewing court in *Bunch v. Hoffinger Industries, Inc.* (2004) 123 Cal.App.4th 1278, 20 Cal.Rptr.3d 780 (*Bunch*) applied *Milwaukee Tool* in the context of a sports injury. There, a girl suffered catastrophic injuries when she dove into a shallow pool. She recovered against the manufacturer of the replacement pool liner on a product liability/failure to warn theory. (*Id.* at pp. 1281–1282, 1289–1290, 20 Cal.Rptr.3d 780.) The reviewing court recognized that under *Knight* and the rule of primary assumption of the risk, a participant in a sporting activity generally may not recover damages for injuries resulting from risks inherent in the sport. (*Id.* at p. 1300, 20 Cal.Rptr.3d 780.) However, the test for liability for equipment providers is different from that of coparticipant in a sport, and hence the doctrine of primary assumption of risk "does not insulate equipment suppliers from liability for injury from providing defective equipment." (*Ibid.*) Moreover, "under products liability, the manufacturer does owe a duty to produce defect-free products. [Citation.] In addition, in using a defective product, the user does not intend to confront a risk that is inherent in its use. [Citation.]" (*Id.* at p. 1301, 20 Cal.Rptr.3d 780.)

3. The Trial Court Correctly Ruled That Primary Assumption of the Risk Did Not Foreclose the Fords' Strict Products Liability Claim.

---

[10] The *Knight* court explained that this rule "involves the question whether a person who negligently has started a fire is liable for an injury sustained by a firefighter who is summoned to fight the fire; the rule provides that the person who started the fire is not liable under such circumstances. [Citation.] . . . [T]he most persuasive explanation [to support this conclusion] is that the party who negligently started the fire had no legal duty to protect the firefighter from the very danger that the firefighter is employed to confront." (*Knight, supra*, 3 Cal.4th at pp. 309–310, fn. 5, 11 Cal.Rptr.2d 2, 834 P.2d 696.)

Polaris's refrain on appeal, expressed in various ways throughout the briefs, is as follows: Falling off a watercraft and coming into contact with the surface of water are inherent risks of the sport of jet skiing. As well, suffering orifice injuries is an inherent, but rare, risk of the sport. Polaris owed Susan no duty to eliminate or protect against these risks and therefore primary assumption of the risk absolves it of any liability. Finally, *Milwaukee Tool* and *Bunch* "were wrongly decided" because products liability claims are not exempt from application of primary assumption of the risk principles.

a. *Polaris's Criticism of* Milwaukee Tool *and* Bunch

Milwaukee Tool and *Bunch* stand for the proposition that a manufacturer's duty to produce defect-free products is not obliterated by primary assumption of the risk, absent extraordinary circumstances. Polaris criticizes these decisions, asserting that they conflict with *Lipson v. Superior Court* (1982) 31 Cal.3d 362, 182 Cal.Rptr. 629, 644 P.2d 822, *Kelhi v. Fitzpatrick* (1994) 25 Cal.App.4th 1149, 31 Cal.Rptr.2d 182 and *Sanchez v. Hillerich & Bradsby Co.* (2002) 104 Cal.App.4th 703, 128 Cal.Rptr.2d 529. Polaris's authority does not undermine *Milwaukee Tool* and *Bunch.*

Lipson was a pre- *Knight* case entailing application of the firefighter's rule to a claim of strict liability for an ultrahazardous activity. The court focused on the petitioners' conduct, and did not engage in the analysis of duty set forth in *Knight.* (*Lipson v. Superior Court, supra,* 31 Cal.3d at pp. 375–376, 182 Cal.Rptr. 629, 644 P.2d 822.) *Kelhi* also involved the firefighter's rule. There, a highway patrol officer was injured by runaway tires while on duty and responding to the emergency created when the tires broke off a truck. Assuming that the manufacturer owed the general public a duty of care to manufacture a defect-free truck, the court explained that when the firefighter's rule applies as a matter of law, the case necessarily falls under the category of primary assumption of the risk in which the defendant owes no duty to the plaintiff. (*Kelhi v. Fitzpatrick, supra,* 25 Cal.App.4th at p. 1161, 31 Cal.Rptr.2d 182.) The present case does not involve the firefighter's rule and therefore the primary assumption of risk doctrine is not invoked automatically. Moreover, as emphasized in *Neighbarger v. Irwin Industries, Inc.* (1994) 8 Cal.4th 532, 546, 34 Cal.Rptr.2d 630, 882 P.2d 347, "[t]he most substantial justifications for the firefighter's rule are those based on the public nature of the service provided by firefighters and the relationship between the public and the public firefighter." Those concerns are not present here.

Nor does *Sanchez* aid Polaris. In *Sanchez* the injured college pitcher pursued negligence and products liability claims against a bat manufacturer. He alleged that the newly design[ed] bat, made of hollow aluminum alloy with a pressurized air bladder, significantly increased the inherent risk that a pitcher would be hit by a line drive. (*Sanchez v. Hillerich & Bradsby Co., supra,* 104 Cal.App.4th at p. 707, 128 Cal.Rptr.2d 529.) The reviewing court *rejected* primary assumption of the risk as shielding the manufacturer and *reversed* summary judgment because the plaintiff's evidence raised a triable issue whether the design increased the inherent risk. (*Id.* at p. 715, 128 Cal.Rptr.2d 529.) As the court further explained: "If it is ultimately determined primary assumption of the risk does not apply here, the issue then becomes one of secondary assumption of the risk." (*Ibid.*) Moreover, as pointed out in *Bunch, supra*, 123 Cal.App.4th at pages 1301–1302, 20 Cal.Rptr.3d 780, the court in *Sanchez* "did not discuss the interplay between products liability and primary assumption of risk. Nor did the court discuss or distinguish *Milwaukee* [*Tool*]." (*Id.* at p. 1302, 20 Cal.Rptr.3d 780.)

While we do not agree with Polaris that *Milwaukee Tool* and *Bunch* were "wrongly decided" and in conflict with the above opinions, we are mindful that these decisions are not exact templates for the instant case: *Milwaukee Tool* was not a sports case and thus there was no need for the court to address the issue of inherent risks in assessing the scope and existence of the defendant's duty. *Bunch* was a sports case, but the issue was inadequate warnings, not design defect. There was no charge in *Bunch* that imposing on the manufacturer a duty to provide effective and adequate warnings *would change* the nature of the sport or chill participation in it. The premise of these decisions is sound: Manufacturers have an independent duty to make nondefective products that as a general rule will withstand application of primary assumption of risk principles. However, in a recreational equipment defect case such as this, the *scope* of that duty may be at issue as when, for example, the defendant asserts that the purported defect is the very failure of the product to eliminate or provide protection against an inherent risk of the sport. Under such circumstances, the court must also assess the risks inherent in the sport as part and parcel of ascertaining the *scope* of the manufacturer's duty.

b. Analysis of Inherent Risks

To reiterate, in the context of an active sport, the "existence and scope of a defendant's duty of care . . . depends on *the nature of the sport or activity* in question and on the parties' general relationship to the activity. . . ." (*Knight, supra*, 3 Cal.4th at p. 313, 11 Cal.Rptr.2d 2, 834 P.2d 696, italics added.) Defining the risks inherent in a particular sport thus is integral to determining whether a particular defendant owes a duty of care. (*Staten v. Superior Court* (1996) 45 Cal.App.4th 1628, 1633, 1635, 53 Cal.Rptr.2d 657.) "Inherent" means "involved in the constitution or essential character of something: belonging by nature or habit: intrinsic." (Merriam–Webster's Collegiate Dict. (10th ed.2001) p. 600.) The court in *Freeman v. Hale* (1994) 30 Cal.App.4th 1388, 1394–1395, 36 Cal.Rptr.2d 418 articulated the test this way: An inherent risk is one that, if eliminated would fundamentally alter the nature of the sport or deter vigorous participation. (See also *Distefano v. Forester* (2001) 85 Cal.App.4th 1249, 1261, 102 Cal.Rptr.2d 813.)

Here, the general risk of falling and coming into contact with water is inherent in jet skiing. However, Polaris asks us to evaluate its potential for liability under a rubric that includes the specific risk of suffering orifice injuries within the inherent risks of jet skiing, thereby eliminating its duty of care. The trial court specifically declined to find that such injuries are inherent in the sport. We agree.

Orifice injuries and the conduct that causes them do not belong to the "fundamental nature or habit" of the sport. Such injuries occur by way of rearward ejection into a very dangerous, defined space, namely the high-pressure stream of water thrust by the jet nozzle of the watercraft. Polaris's role with respect to the sport of jet skiing is as the manufacturer and designer of the Polaris SLH–700 personal watercraft. The Fords asserted that the watercraft was defective because Polaris did not consider or utilize appropriate alternative designs that would reduce the chances of rearward ejection into the jet propulsion. *The norm in jet skiing is to hold on.* Providing an alternative to hanging on while jet skiing in circumstances where holding onto the operator is not feasible would not alter the fundamental nature of the sport or deter vigorous participation. The Fords submitted Burleson's declaration on summary judgment to the effect that the watercraft was defectively designed and substantially increased the risk of harm because "Polaris continue[d] to manufacture personal watercraft without passenger protection against rearward ejection injuries incorporated into the design of the machines."[11] Under these facts the trial court properly denied Polaris's motion for summary judgment on primary assumption of the risk.

Citing *American Golf Corp. v. Superior Court, supra,* 79 Cal.App.4th at page 37, 93 Cal.Rptr.2d 683, Polaris also maintains that what is standard in the industry defines the nature of the sport and its inherent risks. Since the designs of other watercraft are essentially the same as the Polaris craft, the standard is established and cannot be attacked without running afoul of the doctrine of primary assumption of the risk. This argument is not sustainable in the context of a strict product liability/design defect case. None of the cases cited by Polaris stand for the proposition that primary assumption of the risk will preclude a strict products liability/design defect claim against a recreational equipment manufacturer simply because its equipment is "essentially the same" in design as that of other manufacturers.[12] To reiterate, a risk is inherent if its absence would significantly change the sport or deter enthusiastic participation. Not all design features that are "essentially the same" throughout an industry would meet this definition. Moreover, the evidence does not support Polaris's proposition: Its own expert testified that "roughly half" of watercraft sold have seat straps, and roughly half do not!

---

[11] Specifically, Burleson referred to the alternative of a passenger seatback. At trial, three possible alternative designs were advanced. Polaris found fault with all three of them, but it is not the plaintiff's burden in a design defect case to prove the existence of a feasible alternative design. (*Bernal v. Richard Wolf Medical Instruments Corp.* (1990) 221 Cal.App.3d 1326, 1335, 272 Cal.Rptr. 41, overruled on another point in *Soule v. General Motors Corp.* (1994) 8 Cal.4th 548, 574, 34 Cal.Rptr.2d 607, 882 P.2d 298.) Nonetheless, seat straps, while perhaps not the best solution to rearward ejection into the high-pressure jet stream, are feasible and inexpensive, and do not alter the fundamental nature of the sport or deter active participation. Had Susan been able to grasp one, the evidence supports a finding that she would not have been injured.

[12] See *American Golf Corp. v. Superior Court, supra,* 79 Cal.App.4th at pages 38–39, 93 Cal.Rptr.2d 683 [primary assumption of risk foreclosed action against golf course for *negligent* design and placement of yardage markers: Errant shots are inherent risk of sport, yardage markers are integral to sport, and golf course as recreational provider did not increase risk of injury by its design and placement of yardage markers according to system standard]; *Ferrari v. Grand Canyon Dories* (1995) 32 Cal.App.4th 248, 256–257, 38 Cal.Rptr.2d 65 [plaintiff's negligence claim against commercial rafting trip sponsors and operators barred by primary assumption of risk: Defendants owed duty to provide customers with properly equipped raft made of materials adequate for intended purpose; rafts configured with exposed metal frames were standard in industry and defined sport such that significant change in watercraft to enhance safety would necessarily reduce challenge of whitewater rafting]; *Balthazor v. Little League Baseball, Inc.* (1998) 62 Cal.App.4th 47, 52, 72 Cal.Rptr.2d 337 [claim that league breached its duty not to increase risks inherent in baseball by failing to provide helmet with faceguard did not survive primary assumption of risk: Faceguard was not part of league's normal safety equipment and failure to require it did not increase risk of being struck by carelessly thrown ball].

c. Analysis of Defendant's Role

Polaris ignores a key principle of *Knight* and *Kahn*, namely that the examination of duty under a primary assumption of risk inquiry also takes into account the defendant's role in, or relationship to, the sport in question. (*Knight, supra,* 3 Cal.4th at pp. 317–318, 11 Cal.Rptr.2d 2, 834 P.2d 696; see *Kahn, supra,* 31 Cal.4th at p. 1004, 4 Cal.Rptr.3d 103, 75 P.3d 30.) The same risk may pose different duties according to the function of a particular defendant with respect to a particular sport. Thus, while a batter owes no duty to avoid carelessly throwing the bat after making a hit, a stadium owner has a duty to provide a reasonably safe stadium and may be held responsible "for its failure to provide the patron 'protection from flying bats, at least in the area where the greatest danger exists and where such an occurrence is reasonably to be expected.' " (*Knight, supra,* 3 Cal.4th at p. 317, 11 Cal.Rptr.2d 2, 834 P.2d 696, quoting *Ratcliff v. San Diego Baseball Club* (1938) 27 Cal.App.2d 733, 736, 81 P.2d 625 [spectator hit by accidentally thrown bat while walking in stands between home plate and first base].) The *Knight* court *approved* of *Ratcliff* and other cases which, in the process of analyzing the duty of proprietors of sports facilities, defined "the risks inherent in the sport not only by virtue of the nature of the sport itself, *but also by reference to the steps the sponsoring business entity reasonably should be obligated to take in order to minimize the risks without altering the nature of the sport.*" (*Knight, supra,* at p. 317, 11 Cal.Rptr.2d 2, 834 P.2d 696, italics added.)

A number of courts have taken their cue from this language in defining the duty of the owner or operator of a sporting venue. (See, for example, *Morgan v. Fuji Country USA, Inc.* (1995) 34 Cal.App.4th 127, 134–135, 40 Cal.Rptr.2d 249 [duty of golf course owner/operator to provide reasonably safe golf course requires owner to minimize risks without changing nature of game; owner thus has obligation to design course to minimize risk that players will be hit with golf balls and summary judgment was improper because golfer presented evidence that location where he was hit was particularly dangerous]; *Branco v. Kearny Moto Park, Inc.* (1995) 37 Cal.App.4th 184, 190, 193, 43 Cal.Rptr.2d 392 [operator of motocross bicycle course has duty to refrain from using jumps which by design create extreme risk of injury]; *Vine v. Bear Valley Ski Co.* (2004) 118 Cal.App.4th 577, 597–598, 13 Cal.Rptr.3d 370 [above passage from *Knight* articulated appropriate standard of care by which liability of ski resort charged with designing and constructing defective snowboard jump should be determined; jury should have been instructed to consider what steps resort reasonably should have taken to minimize risk that someone would be injured on jump, without altering nature of sport].)

While the above passage from *Knight* at first glance may seem at odds with the assertion that defendants have no duty to *protect against* inherent risks, it accurately acknowledges and articulates the appropriate standard for assessing liability of proprietors and operators of sports venues whose relationship to the sport is not that of coparticipant, trainer or coach. Indeed, it is the very existence of the independent duties of such entities with respect to the design and operation of sports venues that, if renounced, *would increase* the risks inherent in a particular sport. In other words, the scope of an inherent risk of a given sport does not incorporate the additional level of risk that would be accounted for within the duty of care of proprietors and operators of sports venues to take reasonable steps to minimize those risks without changing the nature of the sport. Thus, whether the standard is stated in terms of a duty not to increase the inherent risks, or in terms of taking reasonable steps to minimize risks while not altering the sport, the import is the same. And, it goes without saying that application of such a standard propels a case out of the purview of primary assumption of the risk.

We see no reason why the logic of the above cited cases would not apply equally to the role of manufacturing, supplying or distributing defective recreational equipment. Thus, by analogy to the duty of sports venue proprietors and operators, in a case such as this where the asserted design defect is the failure to incorporate protection against a serious injury into the design of the recreational equipment, the manufacturer's duty to design nondefective products could be rephrased as a duty to take reasonable steps to minimize inherent risks without altering the nature of the sport, at least under circumstances where the risk poses the gravest danger.

3. The Trial Court Did Not Err in Refusing to Deliver Polaris's Special Instructions or Granting Nonsuit in its Favor.

The question remains whether, once the trial court determined that primary assumption of the risk did not operate as a complete bar to the Fords' recovery, the court erred in refusing to instruct that in addition to proving a defective design that harmed her, Susan had to prove that the defect increased the risk of harm beyond those risks that are a normal part of the sport. Polaris's assertion of instructional error is based on the following rationale: Defendants generally have a duty to use due care not to *increase* the risks to a participant over and above those inherent in the sport. Therefore liability cannot attach to Polaris absent a finding, supported by substantial evidence, that the manufacturer's design of the watercraft increased the risk of harm. Plaintiffs offered no substantial evidence on this factor and, equally fatal, the jury was not instructed accordingly. Thus the judgment must be reversed and a new trial set.

Here, the trial court determined that a finding of a design defect would in itself establish that Polaris increased the risk of harm inherent in jet skiing, and therefore instructions also requiring plaintiffs to prove that the defect increased those risks would be redundant and confusing. We agree. The inherent risk is falling into the water. The Fords' theory was that the Polaris SLH–700 watercraft was defectively designed because it did not provide a way for the passenger to hang on securely when it was not feasible to hold onto the operator. We have concluded that the asserted design defect did not attack an inherent risk of the sport because protecting against rearward ejection into the jet stream, thereby preventing orifice injury, would not alter the sport or deter vigorous participation. The very nature of the defect necessarily increased the likelihood that a passenger would fall rearward and suffer the extreme harm of orifice injuries. Thus as a matter of law the defect escalated the risk of harm beyond the inherent risk of falling into the water.

Ferrari v. Grand Canyon Dories, supra, 32 Cal.App.4th at page 255, 38 Cal.Rptr.2d 65 is instructive. The plaintiff suffered injuries when her head struck the metal frame of a raft. The reviewing court applied primary assumption of the risk to bar the plaintiff's claim that the defendants owed a duty to provide rafts not configured with exposed metal frames, reasoning that metal frames were standard in the industry and a significant change in the watercraft to enhance safety would reduce the challenge of the sport. (*Id.* at p. 257, 38 Cal.Rptr.2d 65.) Nevertheless the court also observed that, given the inherent risks in whitewater rafting "it is readily apparent that providing a raft not equipped with grips or other mechanisms to help the passengers avoid ejection . . . would unreasonably increase the risk of injury." (*Id.* at p. 255, 38 Cal.Rptr.2d 65, fn. omitted; see also *Branco v. Kearny Moto Park, Inc., supra,* 37 Cal.App.4th at p. 193, 43 Cal.Rptr.2d 392 [jumps and falls are inherent to sport of motocross racing and although under doctrine of primary assumption of risk the race course operator has no duty to eliminate jumps or protect against injury arising from reasonably designed jumps, it does have duty not to design jumps that create extreme risk of injury].) Here, too, the absence of an alternative mechanism to help avoid rearward ejection increased the risk of serious injury. And again, while Susan did not have to prove a feasible alternative design, the seat strap was cheap, feasible and provided an alternative to holding onto the operator without any meaningful alteration of the watercraft.

To recap: With the jury's findings that the watercraft was defectively designed and that the defect caused Susan's injury, there was no need for Polaris's special instruction. The standard instructions on strict products liability/defective design were adequate, informing the jury that in deciding "whether or not a product possessed a defect in its design, if plaintiff proves that the design of the product was a cause of injury to plaintiff, Polaris then must prove that the benefits of the design outweigh the danger inherent in that design. [¶] In determining whether the benefits of the design outweigh its risks you may consider, among other things, the gravity of the danger posed by the design, the likelihood that the danger would cause damage, the mechanical feasibility of a safer alternate design at the time of manufacture, the financial cost of an improved design, and the adverse consequences to the product and the consumer that would result from an alternate design."

These criteria, stated in black-letter strict products liability terms, essentially encompass the criteria that would be assessed in determining whether a defendant breached the duty not to increase the inherent risks of a sport; or, stated in the more particular terms of the standard of care announced in *Knight* and its progeny for proprietors of sports venues, whether defendant breached the duty to pursue reasonable steps to minimize inherent risks without altering the nature of the sport. Determination of whether a particular design increased the inherent risks — or of what steps a manufacturer reasonably should take to minimize risks without altering the sport — would necessarily focus on the ingredients of a risk/benefit analysis, namely the feasibility and cost of an alternative design, the gravity and likelihood of the danger to be avoided by such alternative, and the consequences flowing from it. On this latter point, adverse consequences to the product and consumer would include changes that alter the nature of the sport or activity.

B. *The Trial Court Did Not Err in Precluding Allocation of Fault to Laura as Operator/Coparticipant and to the Nakamuras as Suppliers of the Watercraft.*

Polaris faults the trial court for rejecting a verdict form that would have permitted the jury to allocate some fault to Laura as operator/coparticipant and to the Nakamuras as the owners and suppliers of the personal watercraft. There was no basis to assign liability to them and therefore the trial court properly declined this request.

1. *Polaris Cannot Allocate Fault to Laura as Operator/Coparticipant.*

Notwithstanding that the trial court absolved Laura of liability under the doctrine of primary assumption of the risk, Polaris insists that the jury should have been allowed to assign fault to her as operator of the watercraft. Specifically, Polaris argues the jury could have apportioned some fault to her upon finding she negligently failed to relay the manufacturer's warnings to Susan and provided misleading instructions. Laura was not a tortfeasor and hence no fault could be allocated to her.

a. *Comparative Fault Principles*

Civil Code section 1431.2, subdivision (a) provides: "In any action for personal injury . . . based upon principles of comparative fault, the liability of each defendant for non-economic damages shall be several only and shall not be joint. Each defendant shall be liable only for the amount of non-economic damages allocated to that defendant in direct proportion to that defendant's percentage of fault, and a separate judgment shall be rendered against that defendant for that amount." Our Supreme Court has explained that this statute "neither states nor implies an exception for damages attributable to the fault of persons who are immune from liability or have no mutual joint obligation to pay missing shares. On the contrary, [the statute] expressly affords relief to every tortfeasor who *is* a liable 'defendant [ ]'. . . ." (*DaFonte v. Up–Right, Inc.* (1992) 2 Cal.4th 593, 601, 7 Cal.Rptr.2d 238, 828 P.2d 140 (*DaFonte*).) In *DaFonte*, a plaintiff ranch employee was injured by a harvester while on the job. The question was whether the manufacturer could limit its liability for noneconomic damages by the amount attributable to the employer's fault, notwithstanding that the employer was immune from tort damages for job-related injuries under our workers' compensation laws. (*Id.* at pp. 596–597, 7 Cal.Rptr.2d 238, 828 P.2d 140.) Rejecting the proposition that Civil Code section 1431.2 does not permit appointment of fault to absent or immune tortfeasors, the court held that "the only reasonable construction of section 1431.2 is that a 'defendant ['s]' liability for noneconomic damages cannot exceed his or her proportionate share of fault *as compared with all fault responsible for the plaintiff's injuries,* not merely that of 'defendant[s]' present in the lawsuit." (*DaFonte, supra,* at p. 603, 7 Cal.Rptr.2d 238, 828 P.2d 140; *Taylor v. John Crane, Inc.* (2003) 113 Cal.App.4th 1063, 1069, 6 Cal.Rptr.3d 695.)

DaFonte did not dictate the same result when the defendant asbestos manufacturer attempted to allocate fault to tobacco companies that were themselves protected from direct liability for providing an inherently unsafe product. Civil Code section 1714.45, as enacted at the time,[13] amounted to a legislative judgment that such companies had no legal fault or responsibility for harm caused by their products. (*Richards v. Owens–Illinois, Inc.* (1997) 14 Cal.4th 985, 988–989, 60

---

[13] The 1997 amendment to Civil Code section 1714.45, subdivision (a)(2) eliminated the reference to tobacco. (Stats.1997, ch. 570, § 1, No. 9 West's Cal. Legis. Service, pp. 2838-2839.)

Cal.Rptr.2d 103, 928 P.2d 1181 (*Richards*).)[14] The court in *Richards* concluded that under the conditions described in the statute, a tobacco supplier breaches no duty and commits no tort against knowing and voluntary smokers by making cigarettes available to them. (*Id.* at pp. 1000–1001, 60 Cal.Rptr.2d 103, 928 P.2d 1181.) On the other hand, as emphasized in *DaFonte*, an employer's immunity from tort damages for work-related injuries under the workers' compensation scheme does not imply an absence of legal fault in an employer whose act or omission contributed to the employee's injury. (*Id.* at p. 998, 60 Cal.Rptr.2d 103, 928 P.2d 1181.)

b. *Analysis*

Richards, not *DaFonte*, controls. Laura prevailed on summary judgment based on primary assumption of the risk. The judgment in her favor was a judgment that as a matter of law, Laura, as operator/coparticipant, owed no duty of care to Susan. Because Laura breached no duty and committed no tort, there is no legal fault to apportion to her.

Nonetheless, Polaris urges that the nature of the assumption of risk doctrine triggers a different rule. Specifically, Polaris posits that the negligence of Laura as a coparticipant is an inherent risk that Susan assumed and damages attributable to that negligence should rest with her, not the manufacturer. Polaris's proposal would eviscerate a central principle of *Knight* and *Kahn*, namely that in the context of an active sport, the question whether defendant has a legal duty to protect plaintiff from a particular risk of harm *does not depend* on the reasonableness or unreasonableness of plaintiff's conduct in subjecting him or herself to the risks of the game, including the risk of a coparticipant's conduct. Rather, the question of duty hinges on the nature of the sport and the relationship of plaintiff and defendant to that sport. (*Knight, supra*, 3 Cal.4th at pp. 309, 315, 11 Cal.Rptr.2d 2, 834 P.2d 696; see *Kahn, supra*, 31 Cal.4th at p. 1004, 4 Cal.Rptr.3d 103, 75 P.3d 30.)

Our reasoning does not run counter to Civil Code section 1431.2. Polaris has elected to engage in the industry of manufacturing recreational equipment for use in active sports. Because some risk of injury is inherent in active sports, our Supreme Court has recognized that it is inappropriate to hold coparticipants in sports activities liable for ordinary careless behavior. To do so would tend to deter vigorous participation in the sport or alter its fundamental character. (*Knight, supra*, 3 Cal.4th at pp. 315–316, 318–320, 11 Cal.Rptr.2d 2, 834 P.2d 696; see *Kahn, supra*, 31 Cal.4th at pp. 995–996, 1004, 4 Cal.Rptr.3d 103, 75 P.3d 30.) Thus liability will attach to a sports participant "only if the participant intentionally injures another player or engages in conduct that is so reckless as to be totally outside the range of the ordinary activity involved in the sport." (*Knight, supra*, 3 Cal.4th at p. 320, 11 Cal.Rptr.2d 2, 834 P.2d 696, fn. omitted.) The same general standard applies to sports instructors or coaches. (*Kahn, supra*, 31 Cal.4th at pp. 996, 1011, 4 Cal.Rptr.3d 103, 75 P.3d 30.) In the arena that Polaris operates, the standard of care

---

[14] *Richards* was an action by a smoker for asbestos-related lung injury. The defendant asbestos manufacturer attempted to establish that cigarette manufacturers also shared fault for these injuries because they supplied the harmful tobacco products the plaintiff consumed, and thus the defendant's liability for the plaintiff's noneconomic damages should have been reduced accordingly. (*Id.* at pp. 989–991, 60 Cal.Rptr.2d 103, 928 P.2d 1181.)

imposed on coparticipants, coaches and instructors is lower than the standard for ordinary negligence. There is a sound basis for this distinction. It would be anomalous if Laura could be assigned "fault" for her actions as a jet skiing coparticipant/watercraft operator in Susan's suit against Polaris, while as a matter of sound public policy she nevertheless has no direct liability to Susan for those actions. (See *Richards, supra*, 14 Cal.4th at pp. 1000–1001, 60 Cal.Rptr.2d 103, 928 P.2d 1181.)

2. The Nakamuras Had No Duty to Call Susan's Attention to the Manufacturer's Warnings.

As owners of the watercraft supplied for the family jet skiing activities on the day of the accident, the Nakamuras had a duty not to supply faulty equipment. (*Bjork v. Mason* (2000) 77 Cal.App.4th 544, 553–554, 92 Cal.Rptr.2d 49.) However, the Nakamuras played no role in the watercraft's defective condition and thus *Bjork* does not apply. They also had a duty to warn of the watercraft's defective condition if they had, or reasonably should have had, such knowledge. (*Yamaha Motor Corp. v. Paseman* (1990) 219 Cal.App.3d 958, 968, 268 Cal.Rptr. 514.) Again, they had no knowledge of the defective condition.

Nevertheless, Polaris asserts Steve Nakamura also had a duty to call to Susan's attention the warnings on the craft and in the owner's manual. Polaris maintains that a jury could find that Steve was on notice of the " 'SEVERE INJURY OR DEATH/WEAR PROTECTIVE CLOTHING' " warning, and knowing this was Susan's first time on the watercraft should reasonably have called her attention to it. The trial court determined that the law did not impose on the owner "a manufacturer's duty to warn."

Polaris first relies on the fact that Steve Nakamura signed a warranty registration form agreeing to ask anyone who used the watercraft to read the manual and labels. However, Polaris does not explain how any representation made in the warranty registration form could create a duty to third parties.

Polaris also cites section 388 of the Restatement Second of Torts (Restatement), which provides that a person who supplies "a chattel for another to use is subject to liability . . . for physical harm caused by the use of the chattel in the manner for which . . . it is supplied, if the supplier [¶] (a) knows or has reason to know that the chattel is or is likely to be dangerous for the use for which it is supplied, and [¶] (b) has no reason to believe that those for whose use the chattel is supplied will realize its dangerous condition, and [¶] (c) fails to exercise reasonable care to inform them of its dangerous condition or of the facts which make it likely to be dangerous."

Comment k to Restatement section 388 indicates that the supplier's duty to warn is limited, as follows: "One who supplies a chattel to others to use for any purpose is under a duty to exercise reasonable care to inform them of its dangerous character in so far as it is known to him, or of facts which to his knowledge make it likely to be dangerous, if, but only if, he has no reason to expect that those for whose use the chattel is supplied will discover its condition and realize the danger involved. It is not necessary for the supplier to inform those for whose use the chattel is supplied of a condition which a mere casual looking over will disclose, unless the circumstances under which the chattel is supplied are such as to make it likely that even so casual an inspection will not be made."

Here, the warning about the potential for orifice injuries and the need to wear protective clothing appeared on the body of the watercraft and in the owner's manual. There were two warning labels on the craft itself. One was located on the rear of the craft above the boarding platform where riders could board, and one was located in the front under the handlebars. The Nakamuras had not removed or altered the on-craft decals. Although Susan stepped onto the craft from the side and did not board from the rear, there were no special conditions that would have deterred her from casually taking notice of the labels as she approached and looked around the craft.

Oftentimes, as was the case here, those who supply the watercraft are also participating in the sport. The Nakamuras did not lend the watercraft to someone else to use and operate. In such a situation they might have been inclined to call the borrower's attention to the owner's manual. Instead, Laura and Susan went out on the craft together to have a good time. Polaris is attempting to foist onto suppliers/coparticipants the extra job of being the company's representative with the responsibility of nudging every passenger to read the label and owner's manual. This is unrealistic given the nature of the activity and the role of suppliers/coparticipants to that activity. As between the supplier/coparticipant and the manufacturer of the watercraft, the Nakamuras should be able to rely on the manufacturer's placement, design and content of warning labels to communicate its safety concerns to passengers. By not altering or removing the label, and in the absence of any special conditions, including any mental or physical limitations presented by the passenger, the supplier/coparticipant has no further duty with respect to the manufacturer warnings.

III. DISPOSITION

The judgment is affirmed.

PROBLEM

N decides to lay a new tile floor, and purchases a can of glue with which to fasten the tiles to the floor. The can sets forth a warning, in large letters, to the effect that the product will give off toxic fumes, and should only be used in a well-ventilated location or with a fan to dissipate the fumes.

N is laying the tile floor in the bathroom during the winter. Concerned about the risk that the pipes will freeze, N does not open the windows or ventilate the bathroom. N is injured by the fumes and sues the manufacturer of the glue.

Assume that the warning on the can is adequate. N contends that the glue is defective because it could have been made with a less toxic substance which would have reduced the risk of injury. Can this argument prevail? What defenses will the manufacturer raise?

A NOTE ON PREEMPTION

Preemption can be an important defense in products liability lawsuits. Under preemption doctrine, the defendant argues that it cannot be held liable under state tort law because it complied with the federal regulatory standards applicable to the particular aspect of whatever product or industry is involved. Federal standards, of course, preempt state law. When this defense arises, the court must decide whether the federal standards cover the claimed defect sufficiently to warrant dismissing the state tort suit. Most preemption cases involve prescription pharmaceuticals, medical devices, cigarettes, and automobiles.

Preemption is an extraordinarily difficult and complex area of the law. For those who want to investigate it more fully, see *Wyeth v. Levine*, 555 U.S. 555 (2009), and *PLIVA, Inc. v. Mensing*, 564 U.S. ___ (2011), both of which involved failures to warn in medical contexts. In *Wyeth*, the Court decided that the failure to warn lawsuit was not preempted by federal regulations. In *PLIVA*, the Court decided that the failure to warn lawsuit was preempted by federal regulations. This subject tends to be covered in courses on constitutional law, health law, and regulation.

D.   IMMUNITIES AND DEFENSES BASED UPON THE STATUS OF THE DEFENDANT

A variety of defenses have nothing to do with the conduct of the parties, but rather depend upon the nature of the defendant or upon the relationship between the plaintiff and the defendant. Many of the immunities, such as charitable immunity, have been abolished as antiquated and unnecessary to serve any valuable goal. It is a truism that an employee cannot sue his or her employer; the certainty of receiving workers' compensation replaces the right of action against the employer. In general, however, the doctrines which have developed around the willingness (or lack thereof) of the federal government and other sovereign bodies to give up their right not to be sued are highly complex.

1.   The Federal Government

LIVELY v. UNITED STATES OF AMERICA
United States Court of Appeals, Fifth Circuit, 1989
870 F.2d 296

Before THORNBERRY, GEE, and POLITZ, CIRCUIT JUDGES.

GEE, CIRCUIT JUDGE:

Plaintiffs in these actions were employed as Longshoremen working on the docks of the Baton Rouge Port Commission in Port Allen, Louisiana. During the period from 1959 through 1966 they were exposed to raw asbestos, which they helped to unload from ships traveling from South Africa. The asbestos was imported for stockpiling by the General Services Administration (G.S.A.) pursuant to the Strategic and Critical Materials Stockpiling Act (The Act), 50 U.S.C. § 98 *et seq.* The

Act authorizes the Secretaries of the Army, Navy & Interior to determine that some materials are of strategic importance and to determine that quantities of these materials should be stockpiled. The secretaries are authorized by the statute to direct the Administrator of the G.S.A. to make the purchases and provide for storage security and maintenance of the material. The Administrator is authorized, pursuant to 40 U.S.C. § 481, to prescribe policies and methods of procurement necessary to carry out his directive.

The plaintiffs allege that the United States is liable to them under the Federal Tort Claim Act (FTCA) for injuries resulting from their exposure to the asbestos. Their complaints assert that the United States negligently failed to warn them of the danger of exposure to asbestos and negligently failed to provide proper equipment to reduce that danger. The complaints further maintain that the United States is strictly liable for plaintiffs' injuries because stockpiling asbestos was an ultrahazardous activity.

The district court in *Lively* dismissed the complaint for lack of subject matter jurisdiction, holding that the plaintiffs' claims were within the discretionary function exemption to the FTCA. The court further held that plaintiffs could not assert a strict liability claim against the United States. In *Williams* the district court granted summary judgment for the United States, dismissing plaintiffs' claims with prejudice and adopting the opinion of the district court in *Lively*. We affirm the judgments of the district courts.

I. *The Discretionary Function Exception*

The discretionary function exception to the FTCA is found at 28 U.S.C. § 2680(a), stating that there shall be no liability under the FTCA for

> (a) *Any claim* based upon an act or omission of an employee of the Government, exercising due care, in the execution of a statute or regulation, whether or not such statute or regulation be valid, *or based upon the exercise or performance or the failure to exercise or perform a discretionary function or duty on the part of a federal agency or an employee of the Government, whether or not the discretion involved be abused* (emphasis added).

The plaintiffs, focusing upon the phrase "exercising due care" contend that the discretionary function exception is applicable only if the agency or employee exercised due care. This reading is incorrect. The subsection contains two clauses, separated by the disjunctive "or", which set forth two separate exceptions to the FTCA. The first clause, excepting claims based on the execution of a statute or regulation, requires for its application that the actor have exercised due care. The second clause, excepting claims based on the performance of a discretionary function, has no such requirement. These claims are excepted from the FTCA regardless of whether the actor exercised due care. The question which we must answer, therefore, is not whether the Government acted with due care but whether the Government's conduct was the result of the performance of a discretionary function.

It is impossible "to define with precision every contour of the discretionary function exception." *United States v. Varig Airlines*, 467 U.S. 797, 813, 104 S. Ct. 2755, 2764, 81 L. Ed. 2d 660 (1984).

> While all acknowledge that the important acts of high officials and the routine acts of their low level agents constitute the extremes of the discretionary-nondiscretionary function spectrum, all also recognize that there is no wholly satisfactory classification of those acts that fall near the midpoint of this spectrum.

Gordon v. Lykes Bros. S.S. Co., Inc., 835 F.2d 96 (5th Cir. 1988), *cert. denied*, [488] U.S. [825], 109 S. Ct. 73, 102 L. Ed. 2d 50 (1988). The Supreme Court has, however, set forth several factors which are helpful in determining whether conduct falls within the discretionary function exception. First, " . . . the basic inquiry . . . is whether the challenged acts . . . are of the nature and quality that Congress intended to shield from tort liability," *Varig Airlines*, 467 U.S. at 813, 104 S. Ct. at 2764. Second, " . . . it was plainly intended to encompass the discretionary acts of the government acting in its role as a regulator of the conduct of private individuals. . . ." *Varig Airlines* at 813, 104 S. Ct. at 2764. Third, "[w]here there is room for policy judgment and decision there is discretion."

Applying these criteria to the Government activities in this case we conclude that the district courts correctly held that the activities were within the discretionary function exception. The activities at issue in this case are the decision to stockpile the asbestos; the decisions regarding the manner of procuring the asbestos, including the decision not to place warnings on the bags; and the decision not to provide or require safety equipment or safety programs for the stevedores. The decision to stockpile asbestos was an administrative decision grounded in social, economic and public policy. The Secretaries of the Army, Navy and Interior base their decisions to stockpile a material on their determinations that the material is critical to the nation's industrial, military or naval needs. 50 U.S.C. § 98. When making the decision to stockpile, the Secretaries are exercising precisely the type of discretionary authority that Congress sought to immunize from judicial second-guessing in an FTCA action.

The G.S.A.'s choice of procurement policies also is within the exception. As we stated in *Ford v. American Motors Co.* : "Both the evaluation of actual or suspected hazards and the decision to proceed in a particular manner in light of those hazards, are protected discretionary acts not subject to tort claims . . ." 770 F.2d 465, 467 (5th Cir. 1985). Consequently, in *Ford* we held that the Government's decision to sell used United States Postal Service jeeps to the public without warning of the vehicles' propensity to roll over was a discretionary act exempted from FTCA liability. Like the Postal Service in *Ford*, the G.S.A. in this case chose to proceed with a program without warning of the hazards of the substance to which it was exposing the public. G.S.A. had the authority to promulgate specifications for purchasing asbestos, including specifications for packaging the material. When it exercised its authority, G.S.A. chose not to require a warning on the asbestos packages. Like the decision to stockpile the asbestos, the procurement policies are within the discretionary function exception.

. . . .

Although we agree with the Government that the activities at issue in this case are within the discretionary function exception, we reject the Government's offered interpretation of that exception: that if Government activity involves conduct that is rooted in policy, the discretionary function exception bars a cause of action based on that conduct unless the Government employee violated a mandatory regulation that restricts his discretion or judgment. Under this interpretation two types of activity would fall within the exception: violations of specific, mandatory regulations or statutes and ordinary, common law torts where the exercise of discretion is not based on policy considerations.

. . . .

The Government's position rests on tenuous grounds. Both the Supreme Court and our Circuit have said, time and again, that it is impossible to define the precise contours of the exception. . . . [T]he Government's construction would subsume the FTCA: Virtually any decision to act or not to act could be characterized as a decision grounded in economic, social or public policy and, thus, exempt. Although we construe the exception broadly, we have never construed it so that the exception swallows the rule. We therefore reaffirm our holding that in determining whether the discretionary function exception applies, we examine the nature and quality of the activity to determine if it is the type that Congress sought to protect. The activity in this case is of that type and is, therefore, within the discretionary function exception.

II. *Ultra-hazardous Activity And Strict Liability*

The plaintiffs contend that the FTCA permits suits against the Government based on strict liability, i.e., no fault. In support of this contention the plaintiffs cite 28 U.S.C. § 1346(b) which provides, in pertinent part:

> . . . the district court . . . shall have exclusive jurisdiction of civil actions on claims against the United States . . . for personal injury . . . *caused by the negligent or wrongful act or omission of any employee of the Government* . . . where the United States, if a private person, would be liable to the claimant in accordance with the law of the place where the act or omission occurred (emphasis added).

According to the plaintiffs, if this action were brought in Louisiana against a private person recovery would be permitted. Therefore, according to the plaintiffs, § 1346(b) permits such an action against the United States. In order to arrive at this conclusion the plaintiffs, in citing § 1346(b), emphasize the language "in accordance with the law of the place where the act or omission occurred." Further, in their quotation from this subsection the plaintiffs delete the language we emphasize, i.e., that the injury must be caused by a *negligent* or *wrongful* act. Under the plain language of the entire subsection, it is clear that strict liability "no fault" claims are not cognizable under the FTCA. Further, the Supreme Court has unequivocally stated that the FTCA does "not authorize suits against the Government on claims based on strict liability for ultrahazardous activity. . . ." *Laird v. Nelms*, 406 U.S. 797, 802-803, 92 S. Ct. 1899, 1902, 32 L. Ed. 2d 499 (1972). The district courts therefore correctly dismissed these claims.

. . . .

The judgments of the district courts are, therefore,

Affirmed.

---

1. Sovereign immunity is a judicial doctrine which precludes bringing suit against the government without its consent. Founded on the ancient principal that "the King can do no wrong," it bars holding the government or its political subdivisions liable for the torts of its officers or agents unless such immunity is expressly waived by statute or by necessary inference from legislative enactment. The Federal Tort Claims Act constitutes a limited statutory waiver of the sovereign immunity possessed by the federal government. The federal government waived its non-tort liability in the Tucker Act, 28 U.S.C. § 1346(a)(2).

2. *Discretionary acts.* The federal government has not waived its immunity for intentional torts committed by its employees or with respect to acts or omissions which fall within the "discretionary function or duty" of any federal agency or employee. Discretionary functions or acts are defined as "[t]hose acts wherein there is no hard and fast rule as to course of conduct that one must or must not take and, if there is clearly defined rule, such would eliminate discretion." *Elder v. Anderson,* 205 Cal. App. 2d 326 (1962). A discretionary act is an act "which requires exercise in judgement and choice and involves what is just and proper under the circumstances." *Burgdorf v. Funder,* 246 Cal. App. 2d 443 (1966). The opposite of a discretionary act is a ministerial act. "An act is 'ministerial' when its performance is positively commanded and so plainly prescribed as to be free from doubt." *J.E. Brenneman Co. v. Schramm,* 473 F. Supp. 1316, 1319 (E.D. Pa. 1979). "[An] [official's] duty is 'ministerial' when it is absolute, certain and imperative, involving merely execution of a specific duty arising from fixed and designated facts." *Long v. Seabrook,* 197 S.E.2d 659, 662 (S.C. 1973).

The government level at which the decision was made or the act performed is irrelevant in deciding whether the decision or act was ministerial or discretionary. In *United States v. S.A. Empresa de Viacao Aerea Rio Grandense (Varig Airlines),* 467 U.S. 797 (1984), the Supreme Court explicitly rejected distinctions based on the administrative level at which the challenged activity occurred. The Court emphasized that it is "the nature of the conduct, rather than the status of the actor, that governs whether the discretionary function exception applies in a given case." *Varig,* 467 U.S. at 813.

3. *Misrepresentation.* Under 28 U.S.C. § 2680(h), Congress has chosen not to allow the courts to consider "any claim arising out of . . . misrepresentation [whether negligent or intentional]. [Misrepresentation] must [be] construe[d] according to 'the traditional and commonly understood legal definition of tort.'" *Fitch v. United States,* 513 F.2d 1013, 1015 (6th Cir.), *cert. denied,* 423 U.S. 866 (1975), quoting *United States v. Neustadt,* 366 U.S. 696 (1961). Misrepresentation is broadly construed. In *Fitch v. United States,* 513 F.2d 1013(6th Cir.), *cert. denied,* 423 U.S. 866 (1975), in which the plaintiff had been incorrectly informed that he was subject to the draft, and drafted, the court rejected the plaintiff's claim of negligence and ruled that the mistake was a misrepresentation of the individual's draft status, and that the government was therefore immune. Should the government be liable for providing faulty information, such as flawed weather forecasts to commercial airline pilots?

4. *Intentional torts.* As was noted above (Note 2), the United States government has not waived its immunity from suits based on intentional torts committed by its employees. The Supreme Court has held that a plaintiff "cannot avoid the reach of § 2680(h) by framing [a] complaint in terms of negligent failure to prevent assault and battery. The 'sweeping language' of § 2680(h) of the FTCA not only excludes claims based on 'deliberate attacks by Government employees' but also 'excludes any claim *arising out of* assault and battery.' " *United States v. Shearer*, 473 U.S. 52, 55 (1985).

While the court in *Pottle v. United States*, 918 F. Supp. 843 (D.N.J. 1996), recognized that "premises liability may, under certain circumstances, be the basis of a negligence claim against the U.S., a theory of premises liability cannot be used as a subterfuge to mask . . . an assault and battery claim based on inadequate hiring, training, or supervision of the offending employee." *Id.* at 850.

5. One of the most important sovereign immunities is the so-called *Feres* doctrine. Under the *Feres* doctrine, "the Government is not liable under the Federal Tort Claims Act for injuries to [military personnel] where the injuries arise out of or are in the course of activity incident to service." *Feres v. United States*, 340 U.S. 135, 146 (1950). Application of the *Feres* doctrine and its precursors can be hard on plaintiffs:

— The plaintiff, while in the Army, was required to undergo an abdominal operation. About eight months later, after his discharge, the plaintiff underwent another operation, during the course of which the surgeon found a towel thirty inches by eighteen inches in the plaintiff's stomach. The towel was marked "Medical Department U.S. Army." No liability. *Jefferson v. United States*, 77 F. Supp. 706 (D. Md. 1948).

— The plaintiff was injured in an L.S.D. experiment conducted by the federal government without his consent. No liability. *United States v. Stanley*, 483 U.S. 669 (1987).

— Holding a recruit underwater until he died was within the bar of the *Feres* doctrine. *Kitowski v. United States*, 931 F.2d 1526 (11th Cir. 1991).

6. The federal government is not immune from suit in cases alleging constitutional torts. In *Bivens v. Six Unknown Named Agents of Fed. Bur. of Narcotics*, 403 U.S. 388 (1971), agents of the Federal Bureau subjected the plaintiff to an unconstitutional search, manacling, and threats. The Court ruled that the defendant agency was not entitled to immunity under the Federal Tort Claims Act, and that an individual may sue the federal government for damages when a federal official has violated that individual's constitutional rights, even in the absence of a federal statute specifically authorizing such constitutional tort actions.

PROBLEM

Sally, a civilian, is thrown from her startled horse and injured when an Air Force jet makes a loud bang as it breaks the sound barrier. What problems will face Sally if she sues the federal government?

2.   State Governments

States have a sovereign immunity similar to that possessed by the federal government. There are, however, arenas in which immunity is not available to state governments because such immunity would override the federal government's interest in making sure that all governmental officials, at whatever level, act in a constitutional manner.

CAMPBELL v. INDIANA
Supreme Court of Indiana, 1973
284 N.E.2d 733

ARTERBURN, CHIEF JUSTICE.

These cases were consolidated for the purposes of appeal. The facts in the two cases are somewhat different, but the outcome of both is dependent on the same question of law. The cases were decided separately in the Court of Appeals and were consolidated upon transfer to the Supreme Court. *See* opinions of the Appellate Court reported in 269 N.E.2d 765 and 274 N.E.2d 400.

In the *Campbell* case the appellants sustained personal injuries as a result of a head-on collision with an automobile traveling in appellants' lane of traffic upon a state-maintained highway. In their complaint appellants alleged negligence on the part of the state in that, after repaving the highway, it failed to: (a) mark with a yellow line the aforesaid State Road 221 where it is unsafe to pass; and (b) carelessly and negligently failed to install no passing signs along Road 221 or any other signs indicating to the traveling public that the public highway was unsafe for passing. Appellants also contended that the road as maintained constituted a nuisance.

In the *Knotts* case, the appellant sued the City of Indianapolis and the State of Indiana complaining that he sustained $100,000 in damages because of personal injuries incurred as the result of a fall on a crosswalk in Indianapolis. Appellant alleged that the injuries were the result of the negligent state of repair of the crosswalk. The fall occurred on the crosswalk at the intersection of Market Street and Monument Circle in Indianapolis. Monument Circle is a part of the state highway system and as such, the State of Indiana is responsible for its care and maintenance. In both *Campbell* and *Knotts* the state filed a motion to dismiss in the trial court alleging that there was no basis upon which relief could be granted premised upon the doctrine of sovereign immunity. In both cases the trial court sustained the motion and the Court of Appeals affirmed the rulings. Thereafter, both appellants petitioned this court for transfer to resolve the status of the doctrine of sovereign immunity in Indiana.

Both the *Campbell* and *Knotts* briefs raise the issue of whether the State of Indiana still recognizes the common law doctrine of sovereign immunity. The doctrine in its present form is a far cry from the original common law principle which exempted the sovereign from liability in court on the basis that "the king could do no wrong." The doctrine has been amended and eroded until the most that remains is an abstract and confusing principle which finds literally no continuity between jurisdictions. The purpose for which the doctrine was created has long since vanished and it is now time to finally reexamine the basis of the rule.

The original adoption of the doctrine in America following the Revolutionary War was founded on the premise that the new government was not financially secure enough to face claims of negligence in its governmental activities. Therefore, the English Common Law was adopted and the same immunity which protected the King from liability was adopted to protect the states. The first inroad in Indiana to limit the doctrine occurred in the case of *City of Goshen v. Myers* (1889), 119 Ind. 196, 21 N.E. 657, where the court held that:

> "In our opinion, it was the duty of the city of Goshen to keep the bridge under consideration in repair. The public bridges within the limits of the cities of the state, [are] located upon the streets and public highways of the cities . . . and such cities, where they take charge of the same, are liable to persons suffering injury or loss . . ." *Id.* at 199, 21 N.E. 658-659.

Out of early forms of municipal liability grew the current governmental-proprietary standard which has been applied to the state and its subdivisions. This is in essence a court-made distinction as to the types of activities which governmental bodies perform, created to ameliorate the harshness of total governmental immunity. It is generally held that if a governmental body is negligent in performing a proprietary function, it will be liable for its negligence; while, if its activity is classified as governmental, the defense of sovereign immunity shall apply.

Exactly what constitutes a proprietary function as opposed to a governmental function has never been clearly enunciated by the courts, and this failure to establish a criteria has led to the generally confused state of the bench and bar in the application of the doctrine of sovereign immunity. Deciding on useful guidelines between rather obscure, whimsical notions enunciated by the appellate courts throughout the country has caused enormous conflicts in the courts in the past decade. However, the fact that the doctrine is beyond the scope of explicit definition has not halted its application. In the case of *Flowers v. Board of Commissioners of County of Vanderburgh*, 240 Ind. 668, 168 N.E.2d 224 (1960), this court held, in regard to appellant recovering for injuries sustained in a skating rink operated by the county and for use of which admission was charged:

> [I]t is the well-settled general rule throughout the United States that while a county is not liable, in the absence of statute for torts committed by it in the exercise of its governmental functions, it is nevertheless liable for torts committed in a proprietary capacity. *Id.* at 671, 168 N.E.2d 225.

As to civil cities, there is numerous authority in this state distinguishing governmental functions from proprietary functions and holding civil cities liable for torts occurring in the performance of proprietary functions. *Id.*

[W]e see no valid reason why the well-settled rule holding civil cities liable for damages for torts occurring in the performance of their proprietary functions should not be applied to counties. *Id.* at 672, 168 N.E.2d 225.

Further erosion of the doctrine followed in the case of *Brinkman v. City of Indianapolis* (1967), 141 Ind. App. 662, 231 N.E.2d 169, *transfer denied*; in which the appellate court abolished the right of a city to claim the defense of sovereign immunity regardless of whether the nature of the act was governmental or proprietary. The court reasoned:

The governmental-proprietary rule, however, often produces legalistic distinctions that are only remotely related to the fundamental consider- ations of municipal tort responsibility. As for example, it does not seem to be good policy to permit the chance that a school building may or may not be producing rental income at the time, determine whether a victim may recover for a fall into a dark and unguarded basement stairway or elevator shaft. Neither does it seem to be good policy to find that a municipal garbage truck is engaged in a *nonimmune* proprietary function when enroute from a wash rack to the garage while the same truck is engaged in an *immune* governmental function when enroute to a garbage pickup. *Id.* at 665, 231 N.E.2d 171. The extent to which a municipal corporation should be held liable for torts committed by its officers or employees in the course of the employment is a perplexing problem that has been the subject of litigation on many occasions. There has been a general apprehension that fraud and excessive litigation would result in unbearable cost to the public in the event municipal corporations were treated as ordinary persons for purposes of tort liability. On the other hand the unfairness to the innocent victim of a principle of complete tort immunity and the social desirability of spreading the loss — a trend now evident in many fields — have been often advanced as arguments in favor of extending the scope of liability. It is doubtful whether the purposes of tort law are well served by either the immunity rule or its exceptions. After careful consideration we are of the opinion that *the doctrine of sovereign immunity has no proper place in the administration of a municipal corporation* (emphasis added). *Id.* at 666, 231 N.E.2d 172.

The next logical step was taken in the case of *Klepinger v. Board of Commissioners* (1968), 143 Ind. App. 155, 239 N.E.2d 160, *transfer denied*. The court abrogated immunity for all counties in Indiana. In the aftermath of *Klepinger* all that remained was immunity to the state. The court in *Klepinger* made it clear that the governmental-proprietary distinction was to be completely disregarded in cases involving city or county immunity.

In *Perkins v. State*, 252 Ind. 549, 251 N.E.2d 30 (1969), the Supreme Court utilized the governmental-proprietary function to limit the application of the doctrine on the state level. In *Perkins*, the appellants fell ill due to the contamina- tion of a lake with raw sewage. They had rented a lakeside cottage in a state park for which the maintenance thereof was the duty of the state. The trial court sustained the state's motion to dismiss on the ground that the court did not have jurisdiction due to the sovereign immunity of the state. The Supreme Court reversed, holding that such operation was a proprietary activity, and, therefore, the state could not avail itself of the immunity privilege. Following the holding in *Perkins*, all that remained of sovereign immunity was immunity on the part of the state from negligent acts occurring while the state was in performance of a solely "governmental function." Exactly what a governmental function constituted was not yet clearly defined. However, this court in *Perkins* recognized that municipal corporations and county governments had been eliminated from the scope of sovereign immunity as to tortious acts.

With only a mere fraction of the original doctrine remaining, we are faced with the task of attempting to eliminate the confusion surrounding the doctrine.

The argument has been presented that elimination of the doctrine of sovereign immunity will impose a disastrous financial burden upon the state. Assuming there is any relevancy to this contention, we point out that the abrogation of sovereign immunity on the state level is consistent with conditions already existing in cities and counties in this state. If city and county governments can withstand the consequences of such liability, where traffic hazards seemingly are greater, the state should be able to also bear such burden.

We may also add that the elimination of sovereign immunity means a more equitable distribution of losses in society caused by the government unto members of society, rather than forcing individuals to face the total loss of the injury.

The state argues that abolition of sovereign immunity will result in a great number of problems for the state. Inability to collect payment for claims against the state, inability of the state to secure adequate insurance, and prospective legal chaos are cited as examples of some of these problems. The arguments which the state presents are questions which properly belong to the legislature in facing and solving the problems of liability. Such arguments do not apply to the doctrine in its present state. We are only concerned with the common law justification of the doctrine. This court has spoken as to its view on the fabrication of new grounds for outmoded concepts in *Troue v. Marker* (1969), 253 Ind. 284, 252 N.E.2d 800; where Holmes, The Common Law at 5 (1881), was quoted with approval as follows:

> The customs, beliefs, or needs of a primitive time establish a rule or a formula. In the course of centuries the customs, belief, or necessity disappear, but the rule remains. The reason which gave rise to the rule has been forgotten, and ingenious minds set themselves to inquire how it is to be accounted for. Some ground of policy is thought of, which seems to explain it and to reconcile it with the present state of things; and then the rule adapts itself to the new reasons which have been found for it, and centers on a new career. The old form receives a new content, and in time even the form modifies itself to fit the meaning which it has received. *Id.* at 290, 252 N.E.2d at 804.

The court in *Troue*, in answer to the arguments for the continued existence of an archaic theory based on new principles, stated:

> Here we have the type of reasoning and attempted analysis, such as Holmes points out above, resorted to when an ancient doctrine has lost its underpinning by social changes. The courts frequently attempt to shore up

the doctrine by offering reasons for its existence inconsistent with its origin. The reasoning here appears to us to be obviously specious. *Id.*, at 291, 252 N.E.2d at 804, 805.

We feel that the above quotes are on point to the issues presented to this court by the state. The proper forum for such argument is in the legislature on the topic. The existence and application of the doctrine of sovereign immunity is a judicial question.

We do not mean to say by this opinion that all governmental units can be held liable for any and all acts or omissions which might cause damage to persons. For example, one may not claim a recovery because a city or state failed to provide adequate police protection to prevent crime. *Simpson's Food Fair, Inc. v. City of Evansville* (1971), Ind. App., 272 N.E.2d 871, *transfer denied.* Nor may one recover damages because a state official made an appointment of an individual whose incompetent performance gives rise to a suit alleging negligence on the part of the state official for making such an appointment. Likewise the United States Supreme Court has recognized a judicial immunity. *Pierson v. Ray* (1967) 386 U.S. 547, 87 S. Ct. 1213, 18 L. Ed. 2d 288. On this subject matter Professor Prosser, in his treatise, stated the following:

> At the very outset it was more or less obvious that some vestige of the governmental immunity must be retained. It was, for example unthinkable that either state [or] a municipality should be held liable for a wrong decision of its courts, for an erroneous evaluation of property by a tax assessor. In several of the decisions abrogating the immunities, there was language used which reserved the possibility that there might still be immunity as to "legislative" or "judicial" functions, or as to acts or omissions of government employees which were "discretionary." Prosser, Law of Torts § 131, at 986 (4th ed. 1971.)

Therefore, it appears that in order for one to have standing to recover in a suit against the state there must have been a breach of duty owed to a private individual.

Finding no basis for the continuation of the doctrine of sovereign immunity as applicable to the state any more than it is applicable to municipal corporations and counties, we hold that such a defense by the state is not available to any greater extent than it is now available to municipal corporations and counties of this state. Judgment of the trial court is reversed with directions to vacate by ruling on the motion to dismiss in each case and to enter an order overruling such motion and for further proceedings in conformity with this opinion.

All JUSTICES concur.

---

1.   Most states have waived immunities to at least some extent. State and local government bodies may also have had their immunity waived for them by the federal courts, which have held that state and local governments are not immune from suit based on constitutional violations. *Monell v. Department of Social Servs. of the City of New York*, 436 U.S. 658 (1978) (no immunity in suit challenging City of New York Department of Social Services and Board of Education policy requiring

pregnant employees to take unpaid not-medically-necessary leaves of absence). *See* Chapter 23, below.

2. There are several other types of government-related immunity which apply to various officials. *See Stump v. Sparkman*, 435 U.S. 349 (1978) (judicial immunity); *Imbler v. Pachtman*, 424 U.S. 409 (1976) (prosecutorial immunity); *Tenney v. Brandhove*, 341 U.S. 367 (1951) (discussing legislative immunity); *Briscoe v. LaHue*, 460 U.S. 325 (1983) (witness immunity from defamation suits). These immunities have tended to remain intact (especially judicial immunity).

3. Many immunities are statutory, and statutory interpretation will thus play a role in their application.

3. Charitable Immunity

There are other forms of immunity in addition to sovereign immunity. Many of these have been discarded as outmoded, unnecessary, and generally senseless. Some of the factors in this change include the availability of insurance and the realities of everyday life.

ALBRITTON v. NEIGHBORHOOD CENTERS ASSOCIATION FOR CHILD DEVELOPMENT
Supreme Court of Ohio, 1984
466 N.E.2d 867

Syllabus by the Court

The doctrine of charitable immunity is hereby abolished. A charitable organization is subject to liability in tort to the same extent as any other person or corporation.

This is an action brought by Alfreda Albritton, on behalf of herself and her minor child, against the Neighborhood Centers Association for Child Development ("NCA") and the Eleanor B. Rainey Memorial Institute, Inc. ("Rainey Institute"), both nonprofit corporations. The child was injured while participating in a Head Start day care program run by NCA and housed at the Rainey Institute.

NCA operated this program pursuant to an arrangement with the Council for Economic Opportunities In Greater Cleveland, Inc. The program was federally funded and NCA was required to conform to federal guidelines and comply with all applicable state and local laws, ordinances and codes. The child attended the program and participated at no cost.

In March 1981, NCA moved for summary judgment on the ground that it was immune from liability under the doctrine of charitable immunity. NCA's motion was granted on May 1, 1981. Albritton then moved for relief from judgment pending submission of further pleadings. This motion was granted. On April 15, 1982 the trial court again granted NCA summary judgment. Albritton entered into a covenant not to sue with the Rainey Institute and her claim against Rainey was dismissed. The court of appeals affirmed the grant of summary judgment for NCA.

This cause is now before the court pursuant to the allowance of a motion to certify the record.

WILLIAM B. BROWN, JUSTICE.

The issue presented by this case is whether an organization enjoys immunity from liability for damages in tort merely because it is organized for charitable purposes. Because this court can no longer discover any valid, rational reasons for retaining charitable immunity this doctrine is hereby abolished.

. . . .

The critical question is whether the doctrine of charitable immunity retains any validity in Ohio today. The origin of the doctrine in the United States is well documented and needs no repetition here. Suffice it to say that the rule was originally erroneously adopted in that it derived from *dicta* in two English cases which had already been overruled. Despite such a tenuous inception, the doctrine of charitable immunity spread until it became a concept firmly embedded in American jurisprudence, although not one universally accepted.

However, the "rule" of charitable immunity is, in reality, not a rule at all. In the first place, charitable immunity is an exception to the general principle of liability for tortious conduct. Individuals and entities are ordinarily held responsible for their own legally careless action and for negligent harms inflicted by their agents and employees. The form of legal organization may affect where liability is ultimately placed. But, in general, it does not nullify liability altogether and does not leave the burden of negligent injury to be borne exclusively by the victim.

Moreover, the "rule" of charitable immunity has itself been devoured by exceptions. . . . In light of these exceptions it is apparent that the doctrine of charitable immunity is not an ironclad, sacrosanct rule but has been severely limited in its actual application. Indeed, the very existence of these manifold exceptions militates strongly against all of the policy arguments advanced in favor of retention of the doctrine.

Furthermore, charitable immunity does not, and has not, existed as a "rule" in the nation as a whole. In other jurisdictions charitable immunity survived only in a welter of conflict founded on a kaleidoscope of result and reasoning. There is, consequently, no compelling precedential reason for retention of this doctrine.

This court has previously founded its acceptance of charitable immunity on the theory of public policy. This theory reasons that charities are good and that their purpose, to provide services for intended beneficiaries, should not be defeated by indemnification of tort claimants. As NCA has characterized the rationale, it has been determined that the benefit to society as a whole from protecting charitable organizations outweighs the detriment to any one particular injured individual.

. . . [R]esolution of such a question involves a balancing of two rights. On the one hand is the right of charitable organizations to any benefit and assistance which society can justly allow them. On the other hand is the right of an individual, injured by the negligence of another, to seek compensation. . . . A careful review of the competing policies underlying the present question convinces this court that [charitable immunity should now be abolished].

In the first place, it is certainly true that a personal injury is no less painful, disabling, costly, or damage producing simply because it was inflicted by a charitable institution rather than by any other party or entity. Indeed, it is almost contradictory to hold that an institution organized to dispense charity shall be charitable and give aid to others but shall not compensate or aid those individuals who have been injured by it.

As has previously been noted by this court, when an individual is injured or killed through the negligence of a charitable institution there is a strong likelihood that the individual or his or her family will become dependent upon outside support unless recovery may be had. Such support may be met by governmental assistance or may have to be assumed by another charity.

In addition, a policy exempting a charitable organization from having to compensate for harm caused by it is equivalent to requiring an injured individual to make an unwilling contribution to that organization in the amount of the compensation which would be due him had he been injured by a noncharitable entity. Such coerced donations are inimical to the whole concept of charitable donation and service. They are, to say the least, distinctly uncharitable.

At its heart, the whole policy behind charitable immunity rests upon the idea that we do not want to discourage charitable activities or force charities out of business by subjecting them to tort liability. However, as was aptly stated in *Flagiello v. Pennsylvania Hospital*, 417 Pa. 486, 503, 208 A.2d 193, 201 (1965):

"If havoc and financial chaos were inevitably to follow the abrogation of the immunity doctrine, as the advocates for its retention insist, this would certainly have become apparent in the states where that doctrine is no longer a defense."

As Dean Prosser has indicated, this argument appears to have been concocted in some defense counsel's imagination rather than having been based on experience. Prosser, Law of Torts (4th Ed. 1971) 994, Section 133. Nowhere is there the slightest evidence that the role of charities has been repressed in the overwhelming majority of jurisdictions which have abolished the rule as opposed to the handful which retain some form of immunity. This reality is independent of the existence of liability insurance. In short, charities continue to operate with very little regard as to whether they are immune from tort liability or not.

In 1956, this court observed that the law on charitable immunity was unsettled. In 1984, that is no longer the case. . . . Jurisdictions which have totally abolished charitable immunity now number well over thirty. Apparently, no state continues to grant absolute immunity to charities. Opinion among legal scholars is virtually unanimous that charitable immunity no longer has any valid reason for existence and must go. The Restatement of the Law, Torts 2d (1979), 420, Section 895E, would have the law be that "[o]ne engaged in a charitable, educational, religious or benevolent enterprise or activity is not for that reason immune from tort liability." Prosser saw the immunity in full retreat and predicted, with his approval, its rapid disappearance from American law. Thus, to continue to hold in favor of charitable immunity is out of step not just with the trend but with the reality of the law in this country.

Lastly, NCA contends that if charitable immunity is to be abolished it should be done by the General Assembly and not by the courts. This argument has repeatedly been demolished in other contexts. There is no doubt that charitable immunity was judicially created in Ohio. . . . It is, therefore, the proper province of this court to correct judicially created doctrines if they are no longer grounded in good morals and sound law.

For these reasons, this court now concludes that the doctrine of charitable immunity is hereby abolished. A charitable organization is subject to liability in tort to the same extent as individuals and corporations. The judgment of the court of appeals is reversed and the cause remanded to the trial court for further proceedings.

Judgment reversed and cause remanded,

FRANK D. CELEBREZZE, C.J., and SWEENEY, CLIFFORD F. BROWN and JAMES P. CEL- EBREZZE, JJ., concur.

LOCHER and HOLMES, JJ., dissent.

LOCHER [and HOLMES], JUSTICE[s], dissenting [in two opinions].

---

1.   The Restatement (Second) of Torts Section 895E does not recognize charitable immunity.

2.   One of the reasons often given for abolishing charitable immunity is the availability of insurance. If a state has a doctrine of charitable immunity, however, the charities within that state may well not purchase insurance. What happens when the court abolishes charitable immunity in the context of a particular case? Who will pay for the injuries involved, in light of the fact that the defendant had no insurance? Should the courts abolish charitable immunity prospectively only? Is that fair to the individual in the context of whose case the doctrine is eliminated?

4.   Interspousal Tort Immunity

Under the doctrine of interspousal tort immunity, the persons in a married couple could not sue each other in tort. As one court pointed out, however, immunities are generally disfavored "as conflicting exceptions to the general principle that there should be reparation for wrongful injury." *Merenoff v. Merenoff*, 388 A.2d 951 (N.J. 1978) (abolishing interspousal tort immunity). Immunities are also archaic in a society which has come to support the idea that all members should be responsible for the injuries they cause to others.

HEINO v. HARPER

Supreme Court of Oregon, 1988

759 P.2d 253

In Banc Gillette, J.

We are asked in this case to reconsider the rule of law in Oregon that a person is immune from liability for negligent torts committed against his or her spouse. . . . [W]e now agree with the overwhelming number of jurisdictions which have concluded that the public policy rationale traditionally asserted in favor of a doctrine of interspousal immunity for negligent torts does not support the rule. Accordingly, we hold that the common-law rule of interspousal immunity is no longer available in this state to bar negligence actions between spouses.

The facts, as alleged in plaintiff's complaint, present a typical case of interspousal negligence. On May 5, 1982, plaintiff Dorothy Heino (wife) was riding as a passenger in an automobile driven by her husband, defendant Arno Heino (husband). At an intersection in north Portland, husband turned left into the path of an oncoming automobile driven by defendant Harper. The resulting collision injured wife. Wife filed a complaint alleging, *inter alia*, that husband was negligent in failing to keep a proper lookout, in failing to keep his automobile under proper control, and in failing to yield the right-of-way. In his answer, husband asserted the defense of interspousal immunity. Based on that defense, he filed a motion for summary judgment. The trial court allowed the motion and entered final judgment in husband's favor. The Court of Appeals affirmed, citing *Moser v. Hampton, supra. Heino v. Harper*, 81 Or. App. 106, 723 P.2d 1082 (1986) (per curiam). We reverse.

. . .

IDENTIFICATION AND ANALYSIS OF KEY ELEMENTS FAVORING AND OPPOSING INTERSPOUSAL IMMUNITY FOR NEGLIGENT TORTS

[We here] set forth the principal competing theoretical arguments advanced for and against retention of the doctrine of interspousal immunity for negligent torts. We do so here in outline form in order to facilitate further discussion and analysis:

A. Factors Favoring Retention of the Immunity Doctrine:

1. Maintenance of peace in the marital relationship;

2. Prevention of collusion between parties in litigation;

3. Practical difficulties in applying fully tort principles to a relationship as close and intimate as the marital relationship;

4. The doctrine should be abolished by the legislature, if at all.

B. Factors Favoring Abolition of the Immunity Doctrine:

1. Where the tort is intentional, marital harmony is already lost; the same is probably true whenever one spouse is prepared to sue the other;

2. Litigation between spouses on every other kind of legal theory presently is permissible; saving out only negligent torts is neither symmetrical nor otherwise rational;

3. Almost every other jurisdiction has abolished the doctrinee. . . .

B. The Policy Analysis. . . .

1. The rule fosters marital harmony

This argument assumes that abolition of [inter-spousal tort immunity] would encourage enmity between spouses. Would the abolition of common-law inter-spousal immunity for negligent torts have that effect? There are no studies or other sources or authorities that provide us with a definitive answer to this question, and its answer is one that this court is ill-equipped to posit on its own.

2. Prevention of collusion

The fear of collusion is entirely a product of the relatively recent phenomenon of widely available insurance. But, as this court already has held, the presence or absence of insurance has nothing to do with the substantive obligations one party may have toward another apart from the contract of insurance itself. This factor is not relevant.

3. Practical difficulties

Much is made of the fact that husband and wife live in a relationship so close and so intimate that it guarantees that there will be incidents of negligence by the spouses on a scale unparalleled in any other relationship of life. . . .

The Restatement rule regarding interspousal torts parallels the rule adopted by this court in the case of parent-child torts. Restatement (Second) Torts § 895F. Because of the nature of the marital relationship, conduct that would be tortious as against a stranger might not be tortious as against one's spouse; considerations similar to such doctrines as consent and privilege may render conduct between spouses nontortious. We think that resort to these doctrines sufficiently alleviates any practical difficulties.

4. Other reasons

It also can be argued (although our previous cases did not) that, if the doctrine of interspousal immunity for negligent torts is to be abolished, that action should be taken by the legislature. We reject this argument for the reasons that follow.

Of course, the legislature could abolish interspousal immunity, or change it, or reenact it if changed. Common law decisions do not preclude legislative reaction; they often invite it. Moreover, the legislature has entered the field in a significant way — the statutes contain comprehensive laws relating to marriage, divorce, children and related matters. But this is not a matter in which the legislature has purported to pre-empt the field. Both the legislative and judicial branches remain competent to act.

And, while we have competence, we should not hide from our responsibilities on the ground that someone else shares them. The rule we consider today is judge-made. If it is no longer valid or appropriate, it is our responsibility to say so. It must be remembered that any answer we give has substantive effect — deferring to the legislature leaves the present rule in place just as fully as if we had affirmatively declared it for the first time.

Based on essentially the same considerations that motivated this court [earlier] to conclude that the rule of parental immunity for negligent personal injury to children should be abolished, we now conclude that the rule of interspousal immunity for negligent personal injury to a spouse also should be abolished. Restatement (Second) Torts § 895F correctly states the law of Oregon.

The decision of the Court of Appeals is reversed; the judgment of the trial court is reversed and the case is remanded to the trial court for further proceedings consistent with this opinion.

What entity do you think represented the husband in this case? Do you think insurance played a role? Is immunity really more likely to foster marital harmony than liability?

E. STATUTES OF LIMITATION AND REPOSE

1. The Discovery Rule

In the distant past when statutes of limitation were born, there was no particular problem about setting a time limit within which the plaintiff had to file his or her suit. The horse ran over the pedestrian: the injury was known from the start, and the time limit placed no burden on the plaintiff. But as the relationships between people grew more complex, it grew increasingly possible that an injury might be inflicted and the plaintiff not know about it for years. The classic example of this is the surgeon who leaves a sponge behind in the patient. If the limitations period begins to run on the date of the surgery, and if the patient does not have any ill effects for years, it is possible that the limitations period would have run before the plaintiff has found out about the negligent act of the surgeon. The discovery rule was developed in response to such cases, to protect the plaintiff from being cut off from access to the courts before he or she even knew such access was needed.

HARIG v. JOHNS-MANVILLE PRODUCTS CORP.
Court of Appeals of Maryland, 1978
394 A.2d 299

Argued before MURPHY, C.J., and SMITH, DIGGES, LEVINE, ELDRIDGE, ORTH and COLE, JJ.

Murphy, Chief Judge.

Pursuant to the Uniform Certification of Questions of Law Act, Maryland Code (1974), §§ 12-601 to 12-609 of the Courts and Judicial Proceedings Article, the United States District Court for the District of Maryland has certified for our consideration two questions of law:

> 1. At what time does a plaintiff's cause of action for negligence accrue when plaintiff developed a disease in late 1975 or early 1976, allegedly as a result of exposure during the period 1940-55 to a deleterious substance allegedly occasioned by defendant's negligence?

> 2. At what time does a plaintiff's cause of action for strict liability accrue when plaintiff developed a disease in late 1975 or early 1976, allegedly as a result of exposure during the period 1940-55 to a deleterious substance emanating from defendant's products?

For reasons that follow, we hold that a plaintiff's cause of action for latent disease, whether framed in terms of negligence or strict liability, accrues when he discovers, or through the exercise of reasonable care and diligence should have discovered, the nature and cause of his disability or impairment. Our decision in this matter is premised upon an analysis of the rationale underlying the applicable statute of limitations considered in conjunction with authoritative case law construing when a cause of action accrues.

Frances Harig, the designated appellant in this proceeding, instituted a civil action in the United States District Court for the District of Maryland on May 23, 1977 against the appellee Johns-Manville Products Corporation (Johns-Manville), alleging that she developed a disease in late 1975 or early 1976 as a result of exposure to the appellee's asbestos products from 1940 through 1955. During the period 1940-55 (except for a short period as a federal employee in Washington, D.C.), Mrs. Harig was employed as a secretary for Reid-Hayden, Inc. (Reid-Hayden), a Baltimore firm engaged in the purchasing, fabrication, sale and installation of asbestos products.

Johns-Manville mines, processes and sells products containing asbestos to independent fabricators who then shape, cut and otherwise create a finished product for their customers' needs. During the period 1940-55, Johns-Manville sold products containing asbestos to Reid-Hayden, which fabricated them into finished products.

Most of these products were fabricated and some were warehoused two stories above the office where Mrs. Harig was employed as a secretary. In addition, Reid-Hayden also warehoused other products containing asbestos in other buildings on its premises.

Mrs. Harig alleged in her complaint that part of her secretarial duties with Reid-Hayden required her to enter areas where employees of the firm were working with products containing asbestos, as well as handling files that had been exposed to asbestos dust. It was during the course of this employment that Mrs. Harig alleges that she was exposed to Johns-Manville's asbestos products. It is alleged that exposure directly and proximately caused her to develop a malignant mesothelioma, described as a cancer of the pleura and pericardium.

Mrs. Harig left the employ of Reid-Hayden in January of 1955 and since that date has had no known asbestos exposure. At no time during the course of her employment with Reid-Hayden or subsequent thereto, did Mrs. Harig ever purchase or work directly with any of Johns-Manville's products. After leaving Reid-Hayden, Mrs. Harig was employed by the Western Maryland Railway Co. She retired on June 1, 1977.

Until November, 1975, Mrs. Harig claimed to be in good health. But soon thereafter she developed a cough. In 1976, she was hospitalized on three occasions. On October 27, 1976 her condition was diagnosed as malignant mesothelioma, and she was so advised by her physicians. Mrs. Harig alleges that she did not suffer any consequential damages from her exposure to products containing asbestos until after 1975.

The complaint filed in the District Court consisted of three counts and sought both compensatory and punitive damages. Count I alleged negligence; Count II alleged a breach of warranty; and Count III alleged strict liability due to Johns-Manville's sale of its products in a defective and dangerous condition. Johns-Manville raised the defense that the claim was barred by limitations. On March 2, 1978 the District Court dismissed Count II and the punitive damage claim as to Count III. It concluded, however, that with regard to the applicable statute of limitations "there are involved in this case two questions of law of the State of Maryland, the answers to which may be determinative of this case." Finding that "there are no controlling precedents among the decisions of the Court of Appeals of Maryland as to those questions," the District Court certified the two questions previously set forth concerning the time at which a cause of action accrues in situations involving the latent development of disease.

Code, § 5-101 of the Courts Article provides: "A civil action at law shall be filed within three years from the date it accrues unless another provision of the Code provides a different period." Mrs. Harig contends that because of the latent nature of her illness, her cause of action, whether framed in terms of traditional negligence concepts or in terms of strict liability, did not accrue until she knew or reasonably should have known of the injury — at the earliest when the cough developed in 1975. She urges that we so construe the statute and thereby apply the "discovery rule," previously recognized in Maryland, but heretofore limited to cases of professional malpractice. In the alternative, Mrs. Harig argues that her cause of action did not accrue until she suffered consequential damages because, until that time, she could not have maintained either her negligence or strict liability action to a successful result.

Johns-Manville contends that the statute of limitations began to run, at the latest, when Mrs. Harig was last exposed to its asbestos products. It characterizes Mrs. Harig's latent disease as "[l]ater injurious developments . . . merely elements of damage . . . not in and of themselves individual causes of action." Under this construction, Mrs. Harig's cause of action would have been time-barred three years after she left Reid-Hayden.

I

In a case in which limitations is an issue, it is necessary to ascertain the date from which the cause of action accrues. The certified questions involve the determination of when a cause of action accrues in situations in which the occurrence of a wrong (exposure to a deleterious substance) and the subsequent development and discovery of a latent disease are not contemporaneous. Judge Finan, speaking for the Court in *Mattingly v. Hopkins*, 254 Md. 88, 92-93, 253 A.2d 904, 907 (1969), underscored the complexities of such issues in these words:

"Like most general rules of law, those pertaining to 'limitations' become less than profound when an attempt is made to apply them to specific cases. Much has been written as to when 'limitations' should start to run. Some courts have held the cause of action accrues when the defendant commits his wrong, others when the plaintiff discovers the wrong, and still others have held that it does not accrue until the maturation of harm. Sometimes the happening of the wrong, the knowledge of it and the maturation of the harm are simultaneous. When this occurs the recognition of the accrual of the cause of action is simple, when these elements happen sequentially it can become complex. Furthermore, there are nuances of difference in the accrual of the cause of action in cases arising out of actions *ex contractu*, as distinguished from actions *ex delicto*, and a further hybridization of actions arising out of professional malpractice and otherwise."

While § 5-101 mandates when suit on a civil action at law is foreclosed, it does not define the word "accrues" and thus does not indicate when the three-year time period is triggered. Absent such statutory definition, the question of when a cause of action accrues is left to judicial determination. The determination is properly made with reference to the rationale underlying statutes of limitations. These purposes include encouraging promptness in instituting actions, suppressing stale or fraudulent claims, and avoiding inconvenience which may stem from delay when it is practicable to assert rights. The chief consideration is fairness to the defendant — providing assurance that no ancient obligations remain, and relieving him of defending against a claim after "evidence has been lost, memories have faded, and witnesses have disappeared." *Order of R.R. Telegraphers v. Railway Express Agency*, 321 U.S. 342, 349, 64 S. Ct. 582, 88 L. Ed. 788 (1944). Our own cases emphasize that the adoption of statutes of limitations reflect a policy decision regarding what constitutes an "adequate period of time" for "a person of ordinary diligence" to pursue his claim. *Walko Corp. v. Burger Chef Systems, Inc.*, 281 Md. 207, 215, 378 A.2d 1100 (1977).

In Maryland, the general rule is that limitations against a right or cause of action begin to run from the date of the alleged wrong and not from the time the wrong is discovered. The legislature has promulgated exceptions to this general rule. None of these exceptions [is] applicable to the present case. Our predecessors have recognized two other departures from the general rule: the continuation of events theory and the discovery rule. Only the latter exception concerns us here.

Ordinarily, a potential tort plaintiff is immediately aware that he has been wronged. He therefore is put on notice that the statute of limitations begins to run from the date of the alleged wrong. Our predecessors recognized, however, that in professional malpractice cases, the fact that a tort has been committed may go unnoticed for years, because the plaintiff is unqualified to ascertain the initial wrong and could not reasonably be expected to know of the tort until actual injury is experienced. The inherently unknowable character of this type of cause of action, coupled with the peculiarly harsh consequences of adherence to the general rule of accrual from the date of the "wrong," prompted our predecessors to recognize the discovery principle in determining when a cause of action accrues for latent injury resulting from professional malpractice.

Other jurisdictions have applied the discovery rule, in various factual situations, for similar or analogous reasons. One such theory is that a cause of action simply cannot exist until there has been an injury or consequential damage which is discoverable by a reasonably prudent plaintiff. Other courts simply emphasize that a contrary result does violence to the purpose of statutes of limitation, because a plaintiff who could not have known of his cause of action cannot be accused of slumbering on his rights. In this regard, one commentator has stated that "[a]s between the duly diligent plaintiff and the wrongdoer, the courts have been unnecessarily sympathetic towards the latter, in shortening the period in which it is likely that the plaintiff will bring an action or in entirely depriving the plaintiff of a practical remedy." *Developments in the Law*, 63 Harv. L. Rev. at 1205. Those courts applying the discovery rule consider any unfairness to the defendant as either outweighed by, or at least to be measured against, the unfairness of depriving a reasonably prudent plaintiff of an opportunity to present his claim.

Maryland first recognized the discovery rule in *Hahn v. Claybrook*, 130 Md. 179, 100 A. 83 (1917), a medical malpractice case. Although the plaintiff's recovery in *Hahn* was barred by the limitations statute, because she had, in fact, discovered her injury more than three years prior to the filing of suit, the Court enunciated the rule as follows:

> "The ground of the cause of action in this case was the discoloration of the plaintiff's skin by the use of the drug called argentum oxide, and the statute began to run from the time of the discovery of the alleged injury therefrom." *Id.* at 187, 100 A. at 86.

. . . .

In the period from 1969 to 1972, we extended the applicability of the discovery rule to all cases of professional malpractice.

. . . .

In our judgment, the critical factor, which precipitated our adoption of the discovery rule in the professional malpractice cases, is equally present in the instant case. We noted in a professional malpractice case against an accounting firm that the rule "gives to the individual exercising reasonable diligence the full benefit of the statutory period in which to file suit, while at the same time protecting the defendant from 'stale claims,' as was intended by the statute." *Feldman v. Granger*, [255 Md. 288, 257 A.2d 421 (1969)], 255 Md. at 297, 257 A.2d at 426. The same rationale calls for application of the discovery rule in cases of latent disease. If the construction of § 5-101 urged upon us by Johns-Manville were adopted, "a person of ordinary diligence" would have an "[in]adequate period of time" to pursue his claim.

Walko Corp. v. Burger Chef Systems, Inc., 281 Md. at 215, 378 A.2d 1100. Like the victim of undiscoverable malpractice a person incurring disease years after exposure cannot have known of the existence of the tort until some injury manifests itself. In neither case can the tort victim be charged with slumbering on his rights, for there was no notice of the existence of a cause of action. This feature distinguishes these situations from ordinary tort cases, which require no exception to the general rule that knowledge of the wrong is immaterial, because usually some harm will be apparent to a reasonably diligent plaintiff. In cases where the initial injury is inherently unknowable, however, the statute of limitations should not begin to run until the plaintiff should reasonably learn of the cause of action. Avoiding possible injustice in such cases outweighs the desire for repose and administrative expediency, which are the primary underpinnings of the limitations statute.

In construing statutes of limitation worded similarly to § 5-101 of the Courts Article, the clearly discernible trend of recent decisions in state and federal courts favors application of the discovery rule in latent disease cases. Moreover, recognition of the discovery principle in these types of cases has gained favor in the commentaries.

. . . .

It is thus clear that authorities from other jurisdictions recognize the applicability of the discovery rule in contexts other than professional malpractice. We think our earlier decisions applying the discovery rule to professional malpractice actions are properly to be extended to cases involving, as here, latent disease. Both classes of tort plaintiffs may, in appropriate circumstances, be "blamelessly ignorant" of the fact that a tort has occurred and thus, ought not be charged with slumbering on rights they were unable to ascertain. Therefore, in situations involving the latent development of disease, a plaintiff's cause of action accrues when he ascertains, or through the exercise of reasonable care and diligence should have ascertained, the nature and cause of his injury.

II

We think Mrs. Harig's strict liability action should be treated the same under § 5-101 as her negligence action.

In *Phipps v. General Motors Corp.*, 278 Md. 337, 363 A.2d 955 (1976), we stated that "[a]n action under the theory of strict liability . . . [is] governed by the general tort limitations period . . . which is three years but may begin to run at a later time." *Id.* at 350, 363 A.2d at 962. Implicit in this statement is our recognition that the theory of strict liability does not mark a "radical departure" from established tort concepts. Rather, "the major distinction between an action in strict liability in tort and one founded on traditional negligence theory relates to the proof which must be presented by the plaintiff." *Id.* at 350-51, 363 A.2d at 962. Bearing this distinction in mind, the limitations statute presumably serves the same purposes and is premised upon the same rationale whether an action is framed in negligence or strict liability. Hence, the statute ought to be applied consistently. Consequently, our holding today with regard to the discovery doctrine in latent disease cases, applies to a strict liability action to the same extent it applies to an action sounding in negligence.

Questions of law answered as herein set forth; costs to abide the result.

2.   Statutes of Repose

Statutes of repose set an absolute time limit within which a suit must be filed. They override the discovery rule: under a statute of repose, the fact that the infliction of the injury was unknown until after the repose period has run will not protect the plaintiff.

CRAVEN v. LOWNDES COUNTY HOSPITAL AUTHORITY
Supreme Court of Georgia, 1993
437 S.E.2d 308

CLARKE, CHIEF JUSTICE.

In August, 1986, when he was fifteen years old, Appellant (Craven) had a mole on his back examined. Appellee (Santos) performed a biopsy and diagnosed it as noncancerous. From August, 1986, until September, 1991, Craven experienced no pain or other symptoms of cancer. In September, 1991, however, a physician advised Craven that the growth on his back was cancerous. Subsequent investigations showed that the biopsy done in 1986 revealed a malignant melanoma which was misdiagnosed as benign.

Craven filed this medical malpractice complaint on September 3, 1992, naming Dr. Santos and Lowndes County Hospital Authority as defendants. The trial court granted summary judgment to the defendants concluding that the claim was barred by OCGA § 9-3-71(b), the medical malpractice statute of repose. Craven appealed on two grounds: first, that OCGA § 9-3-71(b) denies him equal protection of the law; second, that defendants are estopped from relying on the statute because their misrepresentation to him hid the injury until the claim was time barred.

1. The statute in question does two things. It imposes a statute of limitations and superimposes on that a statute of repose. As originally enacted, the act of the legislature simply provided for a statute of limitations for malpractice actions and read as follows:

> "Except as otherwise provided in this article, an action for medical malpractice shall be brought within two years after the date on which the negligent or wrongful act or omission occurred." OCGA § 9-3-71.

In 1985, the legislature amended the statute by dividing it into four subsections. Subsection (a) of the amended statute is similar to the above language and reads as follows:

> "(a) Except as otherwise provided in this article, an action for medical malpractice shall be brought within two years after the date on which an injury or death arising from a negligent or wrongful act or omission occurred." OCGA § 9-3-71(a).

Subsections (b), (c) and (d) were added to the statute and read as follows:

> "(b) Notwithstanding subsection (a) of this Code section, in no event may an action for medical malpractice be brought more than five years after the date on which the negligent or wrongful act or omission occurred.

> (c) Subsection (a) of this Code section is intended to create a two-year statute of limitations. Subsection (b) of this Code section is intended to create a five-year statute of ultimate repose and abrogation.

> (d) Nothing contained in subsection (a) or (b) of this Code section shall be construed to repeal Code Section 9-3-73, which shall be deemed to apply either to the applicable statutes of limitation or repose." OCGA § 9-3-71(b)-(d).

Relying on *Clark v. Singer*, 250 Ga. 470, 298 S.E.2d 484 (1983), and *Shessel v. Stroup*, 253 Ga. 56, 316 S.E.2d 155 (1984), appellant contends that OCGA § 9-3-71(b) creates an arbitrary classification of plaintiffs in medical malpractice cases. The first classification is those victims of medical malpractice who discover bodily harm within five years of the date of the negligent act or omission. The second classification includes those persons who discover their injuries more than five years after the date of the negligent act or omission. The statute allows the first group to bring an action against the defendant. The second group has no cause of action because the statute says it is abrogated and is in a state of ultimate repose. Appellant argues these classifications are "arbitrary and not based on some difference having a fair and substantial relation to the object of the legislation." He concedes that the legislature has the power to establish statutes of repose, but he contends that the legislature may not impose a time-triggered abrogation of a cause of action to some groups of claimants but not for others. The parties agree the plaintiff is not a member of a suspect class and is not entitled to strict scrutiny. Therefore, we apply the rational basis test.

Under this test, the court will uphold the statute if, under any conceivable set of facts, the classification bears a rational relationship to a legitimate end of government not prohibited by the Constitution. Those challenging the statute bear the responsibility to "convince the court that the legislative facts on which the classification is apparently based could not reasonably be conceived to be true by the governmental decision maker." *Vance v. Bradley*, 440 U.S. 93, 111, 99 S. Ct. 939, 59 L. Ed. 2d 171 (1979).

In *Clark v. Singer, supra*, we identified the interest behind OCGA § 9-3-71 as eliminating stale claims. Indeed, that justification still applies to the statute of limitations, but the amended version of OCGA § 9-3-71 is directed toward other interests as well. Because of the nature of the practice of medicine, uncertainty over the causes of illness and injury makes it difficult for insurers to adequately assess premiums based on known risks. Furthermore, the passage of time makes it more difficult to determine the cause of injury, particularly in diseases where medical science cannot pinpoint the exact cause. Therefore, we conclude that the purpose of the statute of repose is rational. Our decisions in both *Clark v. Singer, supra*, and *Shessel v. Stroup, supra*, support this finding.

2. *Clark* and *Shessel* invalidated the pre-1985 statute of limitations because the

statute barred the cause of action before it accrued. *Shessel* found no "substantial relation in this . . . classification to the object of a limitation statute." 253 Ga. at 59, 316 S.E.2d 155. This case deals with a different situation. The pre-1985 statute was a statute of limitation. As such, its clear purpose is to eliminate stale claims. A special concurrence noted that although a statute of limitation should not bar a claim before it accrued, a statute of repose could abolish a claim before its accrual. *Shessel*, 253 Ga. at 60, 316 S.E.2d 155 (Clarke, J., concurring specially). The distinction between the statute of limitation and the statute of repose is clear.

> "A statute of limitation is a procedural rule limiting the time in which a party may bring an action for a right which has already accrued. A statute of ultimate repose delineates a time period in which a right may accrue. If the injury occurs outside that period, it is not actionable."

Hill v. Fordham, 186 Ga. App. 354, 357, 367 S.E.2d 128 (1988). This amounts to a recognition that the legislature may conclude that the time may arrive when past transgressions are no longer actionable. The long history of such conclusions emphasizes their rationality. From the biblical time of the Year of Jubilee to the present day, policymakers have exercised the right to "wipe the slate clean" after a fixed period of time. In doing this, there is the clear distinction between a statute of limitation "barring" an action, and a statute of repose providing for the abolition of a cause of action after the passage of the time provided. We cannot say that the legislature acted irrationally when it amended the statute in question. . . .

Judgment affirmed

All the JUSTICES concur, except BENHAM, SEARS-COLLINS and HUNSTEIN, JJ., who dissent.

BENHAM, JUSTICE, dissenting.

Because I am persuaded that OCGA § 9-3-71(b) denies equal protection of the law to those victims of medical malpractice whose injuries do not manifest before five years after the act of malpractice, I must dissent to the affirmance of the grant of summary judgment to appellees. Since the rights involved in this case are too substantial to be considered under the extremely relaxed "rational basis" test, I offer in this opinion an intermediate level of scrutiny which I believe this court should apply in equal protection cases involving such rights.

. . . .

I am authorized to state that JUSTICE HUNSTEIN joins in this dissent.

KENNEDY v. CUMBERLAND ENGINEERING CO.
Supreme Court of Rhode Island, 1984
471 A.2d 195

SHEA, JUSTICE.

The plaintiff appeals from the order for summary judgment entered against him in the Superior Court. The appeal raises the issue of the validity of G.L. 1956 (1969 Reenactment) § 9-1-13(b), as amended by P.L. 1978, ch. 299, § 2, under the Federal and State Constitutions. We reverse the order for summary judgment and remand the case to the Superior Court for further proceedings.

The plaintiff, Charles Kennedy, filed a complaint in Superior Court on October 6, 1981, alleging that on or about October 16, 1978, three fingers on his right hand were amputated and a fourth finger fractured while he was using a machine manufactured by defendant, Cumberland Engineering. The machine was first sold for use by defendant in November 1969, and later was obtained by Service Color Corporation, plaintiff's employer.

In 1978 the General Assembly amended § 9-1-13 to require that claims for recovery of damages involving injury-causing products must be commenced "within ten (10) years after the date the product was first purchased for use or consumption." Section 9-l-13(b) reads:

> "Notwithstanding the provisions of subsection (a) of this section, an action for the recovery of damages for personal injury, death or damage to real or personal property, including any action based upon implied warranties arising out of an alleged design, inspection, listing or manufacturing defect, or any other alleged defect of whatsoever kind or nature in a product, or arising out of any alleged failure to warn regarding a product, or arising out of any alleged failure to properly instruct in the use of a product, shall be commenced within ten (10) years after the date the product was first purchased for use or consumption."

The defendant filed a motion for summary judgment and an affidavit from Stanley T. Gotham, a vice president of Cumberland Engineering, claiming that § 9-1-13(b) barred the action because plaintiff's complaint was filed more than ten years after the machine was first purchased. The Attorney General intervened in support of the motion for summary judgment because the constitutionality of a state statute was called into question by plaintiff in his objection to the motion. The trial judge granted the motion, and plaintiff appealed, alleging violations of the equal-protection and due-process guarantees of the Fourteenth Amendment to the United States Constitution and access to the courts protected by art. I, sec. 5, of the Rhode Island Constitution. Two amicus curiae briefs were filed in support of plaintiff's appeal.

I

Applicability of Article I, Section 5, of the Rhode Island Constitution

Article I, sec. 5, of the Rhode Island Constitution states:

"§ 5. Remedies for wrongs — Right to justice. — Every person within this state ought to find a certain remedy, by having recourse to the laws, for all injuries or wrongs which he may receive in his person, property, or character. He ought to obtain right and justice freely and without purchase, completely and without denial; promptly and without delay; conformably to the laws."

The defendant claims that this section is limited to a prohibition of the purchase and sale of justice. This interpretation, however, is too narrow and ignores the clear command contained in the first sentence.

. . . .

We therefore conclude that an analysis of the present issue under R.I. Const. art. I, sec. 5, is appropriate.

Analysis

Clearly, art. I, sec. 5, of the Rhode Island Constitution should not be interpreted to bar the Legislature from enacting any laws that may limit a party from bringing a claim in our courts. There are instances in which the Legislature permissibly placed reasonable limits or burdens on the parties' right to have their claims adjudicated by the courts. Statutes of limitation have been upheld as reasonable legislative determination of when to cut off a plaintiff's right to bring an existing claim. Reasonable filing fees also have been sustained as a permissible condition to a party's seeking to have his or her existing claim adjudicated.

The total denial of access to the courts for adjudication of a claim even before it arises, however, most certainly "flies in the face of the constitutional command found in art. 1, § 5," *Lemoine v. Martineau*, 115 R.I. at 240, 342 A.2d at 621, and to hold otherwise would be to render this constitutional protection worthless. To prohibit court access absolutely for a generally recognized claim to a class of plaintiffs merely because they were injured by a product more than ten years old not only is irrational, in our opinion, but also flies in the face of even minimal constitutional protection mandated by art. I, sec. 5. As we stated in *Boucher v. Sayeed*, R.I., 459 A.2d 87, 93 (1983), in which we struck down a statute that treated medical-malpractice plaintiffs differently from tort plaintiffs as a whole, "The statute constitutes special class legislation enacted solely for the benefit of specially defined defendant(s). . . ." Even where this court has upheld reasonable limitations, it has stopped short of allowing absolute bars to court access.

. . . .

This statute . . . completely denies products-liability claimants of their day in court, notwithstanding the merits of their claims and the direct liability of the potential defendants. Products-liability claimants injured by products more than ten years old are left with no forum in which to bring their claims. If the constitutional guarantee of right of access to the courts is to have any meaning, this statute must be struck down.

In the present case, plaintiff alleges that he was injured on October 16, 1978, by a machine approximately nine years after it was first sold for use by defendant. The applicable statute of limitations (three years for personal injuries, § 9-1-14) gave defendant until October 16, 1981, to file his complaint, which he complied with by filing October 6, 1981. Yet, unknown to him, his right to bring the claim ceased in November 1979 (ten years after the purchase of the injury-causing machine), because of the provision of § 9-1-13(b).

The plaintiff was not even aware that his suit was barred until he filed suit and learned through answers to interrogatories and from affidavits the date of the sale of the injury-causing machine. Parties in the future who wish to ensure their right to redress for injuries would be forced to file suit the day of the injury, but even then they may be too late. They would be totally unaware of when the clock began to run or even if it had already run out.

This court has invalidated bars to claims until the injured party at least discovered, or should have discovered, his or her injury.

> "It would, in our opinion, be manifestly unjust to bar the enforcement of injury claims brought by a plaintiff who was not, nor could not have known that he was, the victim of tortious conduct because the consequent harm was unknowable within two years of the negligent act.
>
> . . . .
>
> "[T]o preclude a person from obtaining a remedy simply because the wrong of which he was the victim did not manifest itself for at least two years from the time of the negligent conduct, is *clearly inconsistent with the concept of fundamental justice. To require a man to seek a remedy before he knows of his rights, is palpably unjust.*" (Emphasis added.) *Wilkinson v. Harrington*, 104 R.I. 224, 237-38, 243 A.2d 745, 752-53 (1968). *See* Prosser, Handbook of the Law of Torts § 30 at 144 (4th ed. 1971).
>
> . . . .

[I]n the instant case Charles Kennedy's right of access to the court is absolutely barred before the running of the applicable statute of limitation. The plaintiff was barred from bringing his action before he was able to discover the time frame that was applicable to his rights. It would be manifestly unjust and inconsistent with art. I, sec. 5, to bar plaintiff's right to access to the courts absolutely.

The harshness of § 9-1-13(b) is further highlighted and intensified when one hypothesizes about its application in other similar situations. Plaintiffs may be absolutely barred from court through no carelessness or fault of their own because they were injured by products that did not manifest their defects until after they were ten years old. Furthermore, plaintiffs would be barred from recovery because they were injured by products that continually injured people because of defective designs or construction when the manufacturers determine it more economical to allow the product to stay in the field of commerce until the ten-year bar applies than to correct the defect. Finally, as may be the case in this instance, a product with a life expectancy much greater than ten years can unfairly enjoy a total immunity from the effect of its defect for a great part of the product's useful life. The application of this statute to this plaintiff is no less harsh and unjust.

States with similar constitutional provisions have also struck down this type of statute.

. . . .

Although we recognize the Legislature's wide scope of discretion to balance interests and enact laws accordingly, we believe that the Rhode Island Constitution forbids absolute bars to recovery for a recognized claim before the full tolling of the applicable statute of limitations. The plaintiff should have his day in court to show whether he is entitled to relief. The question of whether he will prevail must await a hearing on the merits in a court of proper jurisdiction.

Because we find that § 9-1-13(b) is inconsistent with art. I, sec. 5, of the Rhode Island Constitution, we need not address the remainder of the plaintiff's contentions concerning the validity of the statute under the Federal Constitution.

The plaintiff's appeal is sustained, and the papers in the case are remanded to the Superior Court for further proceedings.

MURRAY, JUSTICE, dissenting.

While recognizing the legitimate concern of my colleagues in upholding a statute that effectively denies redress to the injured plaintiff, I must respectfully dissent upon the ground that G.L. 1956 (1969 Reenactment) § 9-l-13(b), as amended by P.L. 1978, ch. 299, § 2, is well within the legislative power as defined by our constitution.

––––––––––

Whether a statute is one of repose or limitation can be crucial. Statutes of limitation are procedural, and the court therefore applies the limitation period of the forum state. Statutes of repose are substantive, which means that the court applies the repose period of the state the substantive law of which is applicable. For a discussion of this issue, see *President and Directors, Etc. v. Madden*, 505 F. Supp. 557, 571 (D. Md. 1980), *aff'd in part and appeal dismissed in part*, 660 F.2d 91 (4th Cir. 1981). Since states have different repose periods, this choice of law principle may be determinative of a plaintiff's right to bring suit at all. For this reason, courts fairly frequently are compelled to deal with whether the particular statute at issue is one of limitation or repose.

Chapter 15

TOXIC TORTS

A. INTRODUCTION

This chapter is included in the casebook because of the size of the toxic tort problem and because the issues presented test the limits of existing doctrines. There are six connecting links in most of these cases: First is the enormous difficulty in proving that the defendant's act caused in fact the claimed injury. A second element is the substantial delay in the onset of the injury or disease. Often the period is fifteen or twenty years after exposure. Third, the cases often have large numbers of victims and tortfeasors as well as huge potential damages. These problems challenge the very fabric of the courts. Fourth, resolving the issues often requires an interpretation of scientific principles, and this forces the court and the jury to rely upon expert testimony. The courts have therefore been required to consider when such testimony is admissible. Fifth, the actor has usually been engaged in lawful activities such as manufacturing chemicals, cigarettes, or drugs, nuclear testing, or guarding prisoners. Finally, toxic tort cases are often without precedent, and this has required the courts to carefully examine policy issues concerning the role of tort compensation in society.

B. CAUSE IN FACT

PROBLEM

A large number of residents of a town that manufactures steel would like to sue owners of the mills for lung cancer, liver damage, mental distress, and property damage they feel were brought about from steel mill emissions over the last fifty years. What issues will you have to research before you decide whether to represent them?

FEREBEE v. CHEVRON CHEMICAL CO.
United States Court of Appeals for the District of Columbia Circuit, 1984
736 F.2d 1529, *cert. denied*, 469 U.S. 1062

MIKVA, CIRCUIT JUDGE:

This is an appeal by Chevron Chemical Company from a judgment rendered against it after a jury trial in a suit brought by the minor children and the estate of Richard Ferebee. Ferebee, an agricultural worker at the Beltsville Agricultural Research Center (BARC), an installation of the United States Department of

Agriculture located in Beltsville, Maryland, allegedly contracted pulmonary fibrosis as a result of long-term skin exposure to dilute solutions of paraquat, a herbicide distributed in the United States solely by Chevron. The jury returned a verdict on the wrongful death count for $60,000 against Chevron. The verdict was based on the theory that Chevron's failure to label paraquat in a manner which adequately warned that long-term skin exposure to paraquat could cause serious lung disease made Chevron strictly liable for Ferebee's injuries.

We . . . affirm the district court's judgment upholding the jury verdict.

Paraquat is an important agricultural herbicide that has been sold in the United States since 1966. Paraquat is known to be toxic and to cause acute injury if directly absorbed into the body. For this reason, the sale and labelling of paraquat has been extensively regulated since 1966 by the federal government, first by the Department of Agriculture and currently by the Environmental Protection Agency (EPA).

Mr. Ferebee began spraying paraquat in the summer of 1977. He ordinarily sprayed six or seven times a month for between one and three hours. He used the product regularly during the outdoor growing seasons of 1977, 1978, and 1979.

When Mr. Ferebee sprayed paraquat in the fields, he frequently got the dilute spray on his skin. Mr. Ferebee described two incidents of more extensive exposure to paraquat. The first occurred soon after he began spraying the compound. On that day, Ferebee spent several hours walking behind a tractor that was spraying paraquat. His head and bare arms became drenched with spray. At the end of the day, he began to feel dizzy and exhausted. When he went home, he was too tired to wash or change his clothes and fell asleep instantly. The dizziness and other symptoms did not persist, however, and he later returned to work.

Mr. Ferebee's second major exposure to paraquat also occurred during the 1977 growing season. On that occasion, he was spraying paraquat with a hand-held sprayer for some time when he noticed that the sprayer was defective and had leaked paraquat solution all over his pants. He stopped spraying and cleaned up as much as possible, but was not able to change his clothes until he went home.

Even before 1977, Mr. Ferebee was not a picture of perfect health. He was overweight, suffered from high blood pressure, and had a life-long sinus problem. Nonetheless, in late 1977, according to Mr. Ferebee's testimony, he began to notice a marked change in his physical condition, most notably increasing shortness of breath. Mr. Ferebee's lung condition continued to degenerate, and on March 18, 1982 he died.

. . . [A]ppellees presented both of Mr. Ferebee's treating physicians as expert witnesses. Both Dr. Yusuf and Dr. Crystal testified that, in their opinion, paraquat had caused Mr. Ferebee's pulmonary fibrosis. To support this view, they relied not only upon their own observation of Mr. Ferebee and the medical tests performed on him, but also upon medical studies which, they asserted, suggested that dermal absorption of paraquat can lead to chronic lung abnormalities of the sort characterized as pulmonary fibrosis. Appellees then argued to the jury that Chevron had not adequately labelled paraquat to warn against the possibility that chronic skin exposure could lead to lung disease and death and that this failure was a proximate cause of Mr. Ferebee's illness and death.

. . . Under that law as interpreted by the trial judge, appellees had the burden of proving, by a preponderance of the evidence, the following elements:

(1)   That paraquat proximately caused Mr. Ferebee's illness and death;

(2)   That paraquat is inherently dangerous;

(3)   That Chevron knew, or should have known, at the time it sold the paraquat used by Mr. Ferebee, that the chemical was inherently dangerous;

(4)   That the resulting duty to provide an adequate warning of the danger was not met;

(5)   That the inadequacy of the warning proximately caused Mr. Ferebee's illness and death.

Chevron does not dispute that this is a correct statement of the elements necessary to recover under Maryland strict liability principles in a failure-to-warn suit. Nonetheless, Chevron seeks to overturn the jury's verdict on the theory that, with the exception of the second element, the jury could not reasonably have inferred from the conflicting testimony the existence of any of these elements.

I. *The Jury Verdict*

A. *Standard of Review*

. . . .

. . . Judges, both trial and appellate, have no special competence to resolve the complex and refractory causal issues raised by the attempt to link low-level exposure to toxic chemicals with human disease. On questions such as these, which stand at the frontier of current medical and epidemiological inquiry, if experts are willing to testify that such a link exists, it is for the jury to decide whether to credit the testimony.

B. *Causation*

Chevron first argues that the jury was obligated to reject appellee's theory that long-term exposure to paraquat caused Ferebee's illness and death. Chevron acknowledges that paraquat is known to be toxic, but argues that it is only acutely toxic — that is, that any injuries resulting from exposure to paraquat occur within a very short time of exposure, such as days or weeks, and that when exposure ceases, so too does the injury. In this case, Ferebee did not experience any of the symptoms of pulmonary fibrosis until late 1978, at which point it had been ten months since he last sprayed paraquat, and his chronic inflammatory lung disease continued to worsen long after his final use of paraquat in August of 1979. Chevron argues that there has never been any evidence nor any suggestion that paraquat can cause chronic injury of this sort and that, in any event, Ferebee could not have been exposed to enough paraquat to injure him in this fashion.

The short answer to Chevron's argument is that two expert witnesses refuted it and that the jury was entitled to believe those experts. Both Drs. Crystal and Yusuf, who are eminent specialists in pulmonary medicine and who were Ferebee's treating physicians, testified that paraquat poisoning was the cause of Ferebee's illness and death. Both admitted that cases like Ferebee's were rare. . . . Chevron of course introduced its own experts who were of the view that Ferebee's illness was not caused by paraquat, but the testimony of those witnesses, who did not treat Mr. Ferebee or examine him, can hardly be deemed so substantial that the jury had no choice but to accept it. The experts on both sides relied on essentially the same diagnostic methodology; they differed solely on the conclusions they drew from the test results and other information. The case was thus a classic battle of the experts, a battle in which the jury must decide the victor.

Chevron seeks to avoid this conclusion by asserting that expert opinion testimony must be generally accepted in the scientific community before it can be introduced as evidence and that the views of Drs. Crystal and Yusuf, while not rejected by the medical community, are sufficiently novel at this point as to be inadmissible. As support for this proposition, Chevron cites the Maryland Court of Appeal's statement in the criminal case of *Reed v. State*, 283 Md. 374, 391 A.2d 364, 368 (1978): "before a scientific opinion will be received as evidence at trial, the basis of that opinion must be shown to be generally accepted as reliable within the expert's particular scientific field." The court in *Reed*, however, was referring to the introduction of evidence based on novel scientific techniques or methodologies, *see id.* at 367-68, and carefully distinguished the test applied to such evidence from that involved in the admission of scientific opinion testimony that, while controversial in its conclusions, is based on well-founded methodologies. As long as the basic methodology employed to reach such a conclusion is sound, such as use of tissue samples, standard tests, and patient examination, products liability law does not preclude recovery until a "statistically significant" number of people have been injured or until science has had the time and resources to complete sophisticated laboratory studies of the chemical. In a courtroom, the test for allowing a plaintiff to recover in a tort suit of this type is not scientific certainty but legal sufficiency; if reasonable jurors could conclude from the expert testimony that paraquat more likely than not caused Ferebee's injury, the fact that another jury might reach the opposite conclusion or that science would require more evidence before conclusively considering the causation question resolved is irrelevant.

C. *Foreseeability and Duty to Warn*

Chevron next argues that, even if Ferebee's pulmonary fibrosis was caused by paraquat exposure, Chevron had no knowledge until this case that long-term dermal absorption of paraquat could induce pulmonary fibrosis; accordingly, Chevron claims, it cannot have been charged with a duty to warn against a danger that was not foreseeable at the time Ferebee was exposed to paraquat. Chevron is correct that its duty to warn is limited to dangers that it knew or should have known about during the time Ferebee was exposed to paraquat. The conclusion which Chevron would have us draw from this principle, however, is not correct. The jury could have found that, as of July 1979, the last date on which Ferebee sprayed paraquat, Chevron's knowledge of the link between dermal paraquat exposure and lung disease was sufficient to require a more detailed label than that which the company provided.

In assessing Chevron's argument, it is necessary to consider the label which Chevron did provide. That label contains several warnings about the danger of skin exposure to paraquat.

The label thus does inform the user that spilling paraquat on the skin may cause immediate and perhaps severe skin irritation. Yet nowhere does the label persuasively suggest that users whose skin comes into contact with the herbicide should be concerned about other possible consequences of skin exposure — particularly the specter of long-term lung disease culminating, perhaps, in death. The jury certainly could have concluded that, absent a more specific warning about the relationship between skin exposure and lung disease, the average reader of the label who got paraquat onto his skin would presume that, once no immediate and acute injury occurred, the user was safe and need not take further precautions — such as seeing a doctor, having x-rays taken, or ceasing use of the pesticide.

Moreover, there can be no doubt that Chevron did by 1979 have sufficient information regarding the general link between dermal paraquat exposure and lung disease that the company could have been charged with a duty to provide this more specific warning. First, Chevron does not dispute the fact that, since the early 1960's, it has been known that paraquat exposure can lead to fibrotic lung disease. Second, expert witnesses for both sides agreed at trial that, once paraquat enters the body, it selectively attacks the lungs. Finally, the medical literature and the company's own incident reports catalogued cases in which dermal exposure to paraquat in some cases caused almost immediate death and in other cases caused rather immediate lung problems.

. . . Chevron argues that it had no information that prolonged exposure to paraquat could cause a chronic illness like Ferebee's or that such illness could continue long after exposure to paraquat had ceased. But the fact that the injuries of which Chevron knew occurred much more quickly than the prolonged illness through which Ferebee suffered is no answer to Chevron's complete failure to warn that any such injuries, whether immediate or latent, could result from dermal exposure to paraquat. The label gave no indication at all that skin exposure could produce lung disease of any sort, a failing upon which the jury could ground liability.

Chevron next argues that, if Ferebee indeed died from chronic paraquat exposure of his skin, his case is so unique as to make him a hypersensitive plaintiff against whose injuries Chevron is not obligated to guard. Once again, however, Chevron has attempted to define its duty at too specific a level. If paraquat caused Mr. Ferebee's illness, and the jury could reasonably conclude that it did, there is nothing to suggest that another individual in Ferebee's position would not also have been likely to contract the disease. The jury was entitled to find it reasonably foreseeable that illness of the general type from which Mr. Ferebee suffered — fibrotic lung disease leading to death — could be caused by dermal exposure to paraquat. As a matter of law, we cannot hold it so unforeseeable that dermal paraquat exposure could lead to serious lung disease and death that Chevron was insulated from any duty to warn against such a possibility.

. . . .

D. *Inadequate Labeling as the Proximate Cause of Mr. Ferebee's Pulmonary Fibrosis*

On appeal Chevron argues that the evidence overwhelmingly suggests that Mr. Ferebee did not read the label that was provided and that a more detailed label thus would have done nothing to prevent Ferebee's injuries.

It is true that the plaintiff's failure to read a warning actually provided may at times absolve a manufacturer of liability. . . . [W]e hold that satisfaction of the proximate cause requirement does not depend entirely on whether Mr. Ferebee read the label. Instead, if the jury could reasonably have found that the information on an adequately labelled paraquat bottle would have been communicated to Mr. Ferebee — even if he personally did not read the warning — the failure to provide such a warning could validly be treated as a proximate cause of Mr. Ferebee's pulmonary fibrosis.

We live in an organizational society in which traditional common-law limitations on an actor's duty must give way to the realities of society. *See, e.g., MacPherson v. Buick Motor Co.*, 217 N.Y. 382 (1916) (eliminating "privity" requirement for tort suits). The requirement that an improper warning proximately "cause" the injury should be elaborated against this background. We believe Maryland would construe its tort law in this case to require only that someone in the workplace have read the label, not that Mr. Ferebee personally have read it. Because there is no dispute that one or more employees at BARC did read the label, we hold that the jury could properly have inferred that, had a warning about the danger of disease from dermal exposure been included on the label, the warning would have been communicated to Mr. Ferebee and that he would as a result have acted differently. Alternatively, the jury could have inferred that an adequate warning would have led Ferebee's employers to undertake steps that would have protected him from paraquat poisoning — for example, provision of showers for use after spraying.

---

1. What did the judge mean when he said: "Judges . . . have no special competence to resolve the complex . . . causal issues raised by the attempt to link low-level exposure to toxic chemicals with human disease"? Was he correct? Did he overstate?

2. Is the jury always entitled to believe the experts? Was too much discretionary power given to the jury? When should the judge get involved in deciding a "classic battle of the experts"?

3. Why would the fact that the doctor had treated Ferebee increase the weight of his testimony? Does it follow that the testimony of a nontreating doctor would be of less weight?

4. When would the testimony of an expert not be "generally accepted in the scientific community"? What limitation does this requirement place on products' cases?

5. What problems are raised for the court when the case is the "first of its exact type"? What factors does the court consider in deciding "there was sufficient evidence of causation to justify submission of that issue to the jury"?

6. In *Bates v. Dow Agrosciences LLC*, 544 U.S. 431 (2005), the Supreme Court considered whether the Federal Insecticide, Fungicide, and Rodenticide Act (FIFRA), 7 U.S.C. § 136 *et seq.* , which regulates the branding and labeling of pesticides, pre-empted state tort claims. The Court held that claims for defects in design, negligent testing, and mismanufacture, among others, are not pre-empted, but that claims for fraud and failure to warn are pre-empted. Justices Scalia and Thomas dissented in part, arguing that all tort claims should be pre-empted by FIFRA.

RUBANICK v. WITCO CHEMICAL CORP.

Supreme Court of New Jersey, 1991

593 A.2d 733

HANDLER, JUSTICE.

In this case, the Court must determine the standard governing the admissibility of expert evidence relating to the causation of cancer in toxic-tort litigation. The survivors of two men who had worked at a chemical plant where they had been exposed to a toxic substance, polychlorinated biphenyls (PCBs), claim that their decedents' fatal colon cancer was caused by that exposure. Applying the conventional rule for determining the admissibility of such testimony, the court found that the expert's theory of causation was not sufficiently reliable because it had not been "accepted by at least a substantial minority of the applicable scientific community," and granted summary judgment for defendants.

A divided panel of the Appellate Division reversed the trial court. It determined that the conventional "general acceptance" test of reliability for theories of causation that are novel and controversial is inadequate in toxic-tort cases. It concluded that a different test of testimonial reliability, one focusing on the soundness of the foundation for the novel scientific theory of causation, is required in toxic-tort litigation. Finding plaintiffs' expert testimony admissible under that standard, it remanded the case to trial.

Ronald G. Rubanick worked for the Witco Chemical Corporation (Witco) at its plant in Perth Amboy from 1974 through 1979. In 1979 he was diagnosed as suffering from colon cancer. He died of the cancer on July 23, 1980, at the age of twenty-nine. About three-and-one half years after Rubanick's death, Anthony DeMaio, a thirty-year Witco employee, was also diagnosed as suffering from colon cancer. He died of the disease on June 29, 1984, at the age of fifty-two.

Plaintiffs, survivors of Rubanick and DeMaio, brought separate actions, which were heard together in the Appellate Division. Each complaint alleged that the individual decedent's exposure to PCBs caused the decedent's colon cancer and ultimate death. Defendant Monsanto Company (Monsanto) had sold Witco PCB fluids, under the trade-name Therminal, beginning in 1969 and continuing until some time prior to 1976.

Dr. Balis then testified as plaintiff's sole witness. . . . Dr. Balis never personally examined Rubanick. This was the first time that Dr. Balis had testified as an expert witness (he told the court he hoped it would be his last).

Dr. Balis's opinion that exposure to PCBs caused Rubanick's colon cancer was essentially based on the following factors: (1) the extremely low incidence of cancer in males under thirty; (2) Rubanick's personal history, e.g., his diet, the fact that he was a non-smoker, and that he did not come from a "cancer family" (i.e., a family whose members are at a high risk of cancer due to genetic predisposition to the disease); (3) the fact that 5 out of 105 employees at Witco developed some kind of cancer during the relevant period; (4) "a very large body of evidence" showing that PCBs produce cancer in experimental animals; and (5) thirteen articles on the effects of exposure to PCBs on animals and human beings that, according to Dr. Balis, supported his opinion that PCBs are human carcinogens.

The trial court asked Dr. Balis whether his theory that PCBs cause cancer in human beings finds support in the scientific community. Answering that most of the scientific community "pays [no] attention to PCBs whatsoever," Dr. Balis noted that thirteen of the thirty-nine papers he had reviewed on the subject supported his opinion.

. . . At the close of the hearing, the court determined that the expert testimony of Dr. Balis was inadmissible. It made the following findings: (1) that Dr. Balis was qualified to offer an opinion on human carcinogenesis generally; (2) that as a non-physician he was not qualified to offer an opinion on a specific patient's cancer and its possible causal relationship to PCBs; and (3) that the theory of causation Dr. Balis offered had not been generally accepted by the scientific community.

The Appellate Division, in reversing the trial court, issued three separate opinions. All three of the Appellate Division judges agreed, however, that the conventional standard for admissibility of evidence of causation applied by the trial court was too strict.

Resolution of the issues in this case is dictated by our rules governing the admissibility of expert evidence. Evidence Rule 56(2) provides:

> A witness qualified pursuant to Rule 19 as an expert by knowledge, skill, experience, training or education may testify in the form of opinion or otherwise as to matters requiring scientific, technical or other specialized knowledge if such testimony will assist the trier of fact to understand the evidence or determine a fact in issue. The facts or data in the particular case upon which an expert bases an opinion or inference may be those perceived by or made known to him at or before the hearing. If of a type reasonably relied upon by experts in the particular field in forming opinions or inferences upon the subject, the facts or data need not be admissible in evidence.

"There are," we stated in *Windmere, Inc. v. International Ins. Co.*, "generally three ways in which a proponent of expert testimony or scientific results can prove the required reliability in terms of its general acceptance within the scientific community: (1) the testimony of knowledgeable experts; (2) authoritative scientific literature; (3) persuasive judicial decisions which acknowledge such general acceptance of expert testimony."

The trial court, here, relying primarily on *Windmere, Inc.*, determined that plaintiff's theory of causation was inadmissible because it had not been accepted by "at least a substantial minority of the applicable scientific community." All three Appellate Division judges, however, thought that the conventional "general acceptance" test of reliability is too stringent for determining the reliability of expert theories of causation in toxic-tort litigation because scientific knowledge of carcinogenesis is still evolving.

We do not easily depart from the traditional test governing the admissibility of expert testimony. We have recognized the dangers of allowing the jury to consider expert testimony the reliability of which has not been sufficiently demonstrated. "When unreliable evidence is labeled 'expert' juries might not accurately assess its weight." At the same time, we have recognized the extraordinary and unique burdens facing plaintiffs who seek to prove causation in toxic-tort litigation. *See Ayers v. Jackson Twp.* 106 N.J. 557, 580-87 (1987). In *Ayers*, for example, a large class of plaintiffs had been exposed to toxic pollutants due to the township's negligent operation of a landfill. In toxic tort cases, the task of proving causation is invariably made more complex because of the long latency period of illnesses caused by carcinogens or other toxic chemicals. The fact that ten or twenty years or more may intervene between the exposure and the manifestation of disease highlights the practical difficulties encountered in the effort to prove causation. Moreover, the fact that segments of the entire population are afflicted by cancer and other toxically-induced diseases requires plaintiffs, years after their exposure, to counter the argument that other intervening exposures or forces were the "cause" of their injury.

We recognize, too, that because of the extremely high level of proof required before scientists will accept a new theory, and particularly because of the current inability of science to fully comprehend carcinogenesis, plaintiffs in toxic-tort litigation, despite strong and indeed compelling indicators that they have been tortiously harmed by toxic exposure, may never recover if required to await general acceptance by the scientific community of a reasonable, but as yet not certain, theory of causation.

In recent years, a number of commentators have suggested that a broadened standard for determining the admissibility of causation theories in toxic-tort litigation is needed. . . . Those authorities agree that both the delayed effects in toxic-tort cases — effects that may not manifest themselves for years after the occurrence of the responsible act or events — as well as the inability of current science to identify precisely the causes of cancer, create the need for a reasonable alternative to the traditional requirement of general acceptance as the primary measure of reliability of scientific knowledge for use in the tort system.

Recovery in toxic-tort cases has typically been granted "only after a statistically significant number of deaths and injuries were incurred, allowing experts to quantify the hazard." In the words of Dr. Harbison [Monsanto's witness], "without that rigorous form of evaluation one has not used the scientific method, and the importance of the scientific method is to make certain that the observations that we make as scientists aren't in error." The scientific method, however, fails to address or accommodate the needs and goals of the tort system.

Expressing similar concerns, several courts have taken a more flexible approach to the admission of causation theories in toxic-tort litigation. Those courts have looked not to whether the theories have been generally accepted by the scientific community, but rather to whether the scientific knowledge is sufficiently founded or based on a sound methodology, leaving the decision to credit the theory to the finder of fact.

. . . .

. . . [W]e hold that in toxic-tort litigation, a scientific theory of causation that has not yet reached general acceptance may be found to be sufficiently reliable if it is based on a sound, adequately-founded scientific methodology involving data and information of the type reasonably relied on by experts in the scientific field. The evidence of such scientific knowledge must be proffered by an expert who is sufficiently qualified by education, knowledge, training, and experience in the specific field of science. The expert must possess a demonstrated professional capability to assess the scientific significance of the underlying data and information, to apply the scientific methodology, and to explain the bases for the opinion reached.

We appreciate that the process for determining the admissibility of such scientific evidence will be complicated and the ultimate decision difficult. In determining if the scientific methodology is sound and well-founded, courts should consider whether others in the field use similar methodologies. As reflected in our own rule, Evid. R. 56(2), it is not essential that there be general agreement with the opinions drawn from the methodology used. There must merely be some expert consensus that the methodology and the underlying data are generally followed by experts in the field.

The trial court in this case did not apply this methodology-based standard. Without deciding the matter, we note that the record suggests that Dr. Balis's methodology could be found to be sound and well-founded. Dr. Balis explained his methodology. He relied on his review of Rubanick's personal and family histories, articles and studies on the effects, in both animals and human, of exposure to PCBs and the extremely low incidence of cancer in males under thirty. Dr. Balis also considered circumstantial evidence, such as the extent to which Rubanick was exposed to PCBs and the relatively high incidence of cancer at Witco during the relevant period of time.

. . . The qualifications of the expert proffering relatively new scientific knowledge must be factored into the determination of the soundness of the methodology used. The trial court believed that, as a non-physician, Dr. Balis was not qualified to testify to the specific cause of Rubanick's colon cancer. However, plaintiff's expert indisputably was possessed of "extraordinary expertise."

The necessary inquiry into the expert's qualifications implicates an additional concern relating to "the hired gun phenomenon," i.e., that "an expert can be found to testify to the truth of almost any factual theory, no matter how frivolous." "Juries can be misled by highly paid experts who will find at least some support in the voluminous scientific literature for any position, even when that position is repudiated by the majority of scientists." (courts can "lose control of scientific evidence" "when courts accept qualified, willing testifiers."). The "hired gun" argument, however, cuts both ways.

Well-funded defense attorneys can afford to hire expensive and prestigious experts who will find error in even the best epidemiological studies and discount any adverse evidence. Plaintiffs' attorneys can identify a small cadre of well-versed toxicologists who will testify that a causal connection exists even when there is no evidence at all.

The answer to the problem should . . . consist of greater judicial vigilance in scrutinizing the status of the expert and in directing the factfinder to those factors that bear relevantly on the expert's credibility.

. . . .

As earlier noted, the judgment of the Appellate Division was that the testimony of plaintiffs' expert was admissible and to remand the matter for trial. We conclude that the admissibility of expert testimony in the context of this case must be determined under the standard herein adopted. Accordingly, we modify the judgment of the Appellate Division and remand the matter for proceedings consistent with this opinion.

----

1. What is the meaning of New Jersey Rule 56(2)? How does causation of cancer by PCBs test the rule? What is the impact of the "general acceptance by the scientific community" test upon toxic tort plaintiffs?

2. Should the admissibility standard for scientific evidence be different for pharmaceutical products and chemical products? How does the court deal with the "hired gun phenomenon"?

NEAL v. DOW AGROSCIENCES LLC
Texas Court of Appeals, Fifth District, 2002
74 S.W.3d 468

Opinion by JUSTICE WHITTINGTON.

Stephen Tim Neal, Sr. and Laura Neal, as the surviving parents of Stephen Tim Neal, Jr., appeal the summary judgment granted in favor of Dow Agrosciences LLC [and other defendants] (collectively, "Dow"). In one issue on appeal, the Neals contend the trial judge abused his discretion in granting Dow's motion to strike the Neals' medical causation expert and causation evidence. We affirm the trial court's judgment.

BACKGROUND

The Neals lived in an apartment from September 1993 to February 1995. During that time, the apartment unit became infested with ants. In response to the Neals' numerous complaints, the management of the complex requested the apartment be sprayed. During the five-month period from September 1993 until January 1994, the apartment was sprayed several times for ants. Laura was pregnant at the time and later gave birth to Neal, Jr. Several months after his birth, Neal, Jr. was diagnosed with malignant ependymoma (a malignant brain tumor) and subsequently died.

The Neals sued Dow, Intercity Investments, Inc. d/b/a Green Valley Apartments, and Scott Rackley d/b/a Mustang Pest Control for negligence, strict products liability, violations of the Texas Deceptive Trade Practices Act, intentional infliction of emotional distress, fraud, fraudulent concealment, and wrongful death. The Neals alleged (i) their apartment was sprayed repeatedly with Dursban, a pesticide containing chlorpyrifos, (ii) Dow manufactured, distributed, and/or supplied Dursban, and (iii) the repeated exposure to chlorpyrifos caused Laura's and Neal, Jr.'s alleged injuries, including Neal, Jr.'s malignant brain tumor. After the Neals designated their expert witnesses, including Dr. John Midtling, Rackley filed a motion to strike the expert report and any of Midtling's subsequent testimony. Dow joined in the motion. After a hearing, the trial judge orally granted the motion to strike Midtling's report and testimony regarding a causal connection between ependymoma and chlorpyrifos, but denied the motion with respect to Laura's alleged injuries.

Dow filed a no-evidence motion for summary judgment, alleging there was no evidence that Neal, Jr.'s brain tumor resulted from exposure to Dursban. In response, the Neals filed a motion to reconsider and vacate the prior ruling striking their witness's testimony. The trial judge later signed an order striking "Plaintiffs' experts' opinions that Dursban caused [Neal, Jr.] to suffer personal injury, including the development of [a brain tumor]." He then granted Dow's no-evidence summary judgment motion and severed all claims involving Neal, Jr.'s injuries into a separate cause number. After the Neals filed motions to nonsuit Intercity and Rackley, the trial judge signed orders dismissing the claims against both. This appeal followed.

EXPERT WITNESS'S CONCLUSION ON CAUSATION

In their sole issue on appeal, the Neals contend the trial judge abused his discretion in striking Midtling's testimony regarding causation. Under this issue, the Neals claim Midtling's testimony and expert report met the requirements of Texas Rule of Evidence 702, as well as those set forth in *E.I. du Pont de Nemours & Co. v. Robinson*, 923 S.W.2d 549 (Tex. 1995) and *Merrell Dow Pharmaceuticals, Inc. v. Havner*, 953 S.W.2d 706 (Tex. 1997). After reviewing the record in this case, we cannot agree.

We review a trial judge's decision to exclude an expert witness's testimony under an abuse of discretion standard. . . . A trial judge does not abuse his discretion in excluding expert testimony when (i) the testimony was not based on a reliable foundation, (ii) no testing was conducted to exclude other possible causes, (iii) the expert's methodology was suspect, (iv) the expert's research was conducted for litigation, or (v) the expert's methodology had not been subjected to peer review or publication. *Jarrell*, 53 S.W.3d at 902 (citing *Robinson*, 923 S.W.2d at 558-59).

To admit expert testimony, Rule 702 requires (i) the witness be qualified, (ii) the proposed testimony be "scientific . . . knowledge," and (iii) the testimony "assist the trier of fact to understand the evidence or to determine a fact in issue." *Robinson*, 923 S.W.2d at 556. To constitute scientific knowledge that will "assist the trier of fact," the proposed testimony must be both relevant and reliable. *Robinson*, 923 S.W.2d at 556. The trial judge's role is to make the initial determination of whether an expert's opinion is relevant and whether the methods and research upon which it is based are reliable. *Robinson*, 923 S.W.2d at 558. Relevant testimony is that which is "sufficiently tied to the facts of the case that it will aid the jury in resolving a factual dispute." *Robinson*, 923 S.W.2d at 556 (quoting *United States v. Downing*, 753 F.2d 1224, 1242 (3d Cir. 1985)). "In addition to being relevant, the underlying scientific technique or principle must be reliable. Scientific evidence which is not grounded 'in the methods and procedures of science' is no more than 'subjective belief or unsupported speculation.' " *Robinson*, 923 S.W.2d at 557 (quoting *Daubert v. Merrell Dow Pharm., Inc.*, 509 U.S. 579, 590, 125 L. Ed. 2d 469, 113 S. Ct. 2786 (1993)); see *Havner*, 953 S.W.2d at 711-14 (expert's bare opinion is not sufficient; trial judge must examine expert's methodology and underlying studies or data to determine whether opinion is reliable). Evidence that is either irrelevant or unreliable is inadmissible. *Robinson*, 923 S.W.2d at 557.

In toxic tort litigation, causation is often discussed in terms of general and specific causation:

> General causation is whether a substance is capable of causing a particular injury or condition in the general population, while specific causation is whether a substance caused a particular individual's injury. In some cases, controlled scientific experiments can be carried out to determine if a substance is capable of causing a particular injury or condition, and there will be objective criteria by which it can be determined with reasonable certainty that a particular individual's injury was caused by exposure to a given substance. However, in many toxic tort cases, direct experimentation cannot be done, and there will be no reliable evidence of specific causation.

> In the absence of direct, scientifically reliable proof of causation, claimants may attempt to demonstrate that exposure to the substance at issue increases the risk of their particular injury. The finder of fact is asked to infer that because the risk is demonstrably greater in the general population due to exposure to the substance, the claimant's injury was more likely than not caused by that substance. Such a theory concedes that science cannot tell us what caused a particular plaintiff's injury. It is based on a policy determination that when the incidence of a disease or injury is sufficiently elevated due to exposure to a substance, someone who was exposed to that substance and exhibits the disease or injury can raise a fact question on causation. *Havner*, 953 S.W.2d at 714-15.

Here, it is clear that direct, scientific experimentation to determine whether exposure to chlorpyrifos causes ependymoma cannot be performed. Therefore, to establish general causation, Midtling relied upon articles and studies published in the medical literature. We first determine whether Midtling's conclusion that Dursban, or more specifically chlorpyrifos, is capable of causing ependymoma in the general population has a reliable basis.

In his expert report, Midtling opined that "the development of [Neal, Jr.'s] brain cancer . . . was from his in utero exposure and/or from his postnatal exposure to chlorpyrifos." Rackley, joined by Dow, filed a motion to strike Midtling's testimony because it did not meet the requirements of Rule 702, *Robinson*, and *Havner*. The Neals filed a response, attaching Midtling's affidavit. In his affidavit, Midtling testified he concluded Neal, Jr.'s "exposure to Dursban (chlorpyrifos) was more likely than not a cause or a contributing cause of the development of his ependymoma." Midtling based his conclusion, in part, on the "medical and scientific literature which was cited in the reference section of [his expert] report." Specifically, Midtling discussed four studies "reporting on exposure to pesticides and the risk of childhood brain cancer" which, according to Midtling, showed a significant association between the "extermination for insects" and the risk of brain cancer. The motion was set for a hearing.

During the hearing, Midtling stated his opinion that the effects of Laura's "acute and chronic exposure to chlorpyrifos would, in fact, be a likely cause or would more likely than not be a contributing factor to the development of [Neal, Jr.'s] brain tumor." He testified he rendered his opinion after reviewing the medical records, interviewing Laura, obtaining her history and a physical exam, "reviewing the medical literature regarding the effects of the organophosphate chlorpyrifos," consulting with other experts, and doing a differential diagnosis.[3]

Although Midtling identified various medical articles on which he based his conclusion that Neal, Jr.'s brain tumor was caused by his and Laura's exposures to chlorpyrifos, the articles Midtling relied upon do not conclude that chlorpyrifos "causes" ependymoma, nor do they conclude that such exposure will result in a statistically significant risk of developing ependymoma. One of the studies noted:

> Most epidemiological research done to date on pesticides and pediatric brain tumor risk has focused on nonspecific pesticide use, and findings from these studies have been inconclusive. Some investigators have noted increased risk of brain tumor among children generally exposed to pesticides but several studies, including ours, have not supported this observation. . . . Several pesticide exposures during childhood were associated with increased risk, including general pesticides for nuisance pests, pest strips, termite treatment, lice treatment, garden and orchard insecticides (specifically carbaryl and diazinon), and herbicides. We found no risk increases for any of these exposures during childhood. . . . The only exposure we studied that produced a significantly increased risk of pediatric brain tumor was prenatal exposure to flea/tick products, especially among children diagnosed at younger ages (less than 5 years).

Janice M. Pogoda and Susan Preston-Martin, Household Pesticides and Risk of Pediatric Brain Tumors, 105 ENV'T HEALTH PERSPECTIVES 1214, 1217-18 (Nov. 1997) ("POGODA STUDY") (emphasis added). The study noted the risk "appeared to be primarily confined to sprays/foggers" and that chlorpyrifos was "relatively common only in sprays." POGODA STUDY at 1218. However, it concluded only that "there appeared to be enough evidence to warrant further investigation." POGODA STUDY at 1219.

---

[3] Differential diagnosis is a "patient-specific process of elimination that medical practitioners use to identify the 'most likely' cause of a set of signs and symptoms from a list of possible causes." *Minn. Mining & Mfg. Co. v. Atterbury*, 978 S.W.2d 183, 194 n.9 (Tex. App.-Texarkana 1998, pet. denied) (citing *Pick v. Am. Med. Sys., Inc.*, 958 F. Supp. 1151, 1162-63 (E.D. La. 1997)).

According to Midtling, another study "reported that the risk factor 'extermination for insects' in the household prior to diagnosis of the index child was significantly associated with the risk of brain cancer." However, the study's own authors concluded:

> Regarding chemical carcinogenic exposures that the children may have had, the findings remain inconclusive. There was a marked tendency for more children with brain tumors to have had exposures to insecticides when compared to normal children [i.e., children without cancer or brain tumors], but no such differences were observed when the comparison was made to children with other cancers. The finding that exposure to insecticides is greater in both children with brain tumors and cancer controls than in normal children may be suggestive of selective recall on the part of parents of seriously ill children in an attempt to somehow explain their childrens' [sic] illnesses. However, it is also possible that insecticides may contain nonspecific chemical carcinogens which may induce not only brain tumors in children but cancers in general. Further information regarding particular insecticide agents would be of interest in this regard.

Ellen Gold, Leon Gordis, James Tonascia, and Moyses Szklo, Risk Factors for Brain Tumors in Children, 109 AM. J. OF EPIDEMIOLOGY 309, 317 (1979) ("GOLD STUDY"). The study concluded by stating that "several intriguing observations [had] been made with regard to possible etiologic facts associated with brain tumors in children." GOLD STUDY at 318.

Neither of these studies nor their "conclusions" show a statistically significant association, much less evidence of general causation sufficient to meet the *Robinson* and *Havner* requirements. Similarly, the other studies Midtling cited do not establish any statistically significant association between the exposure to chlorpyrifos and ependymoma. Because Midtling's opinion that Neal, Jr.'s ependymoma was more likely than not caused by his exposure to chlorpyrifos is not supported by reliable evidence of general causation, we cannot conclude the trial judge abused his discretion in excluding Midtling's testimony. We overrule the Neals' sole issue.

We affirm the trial court's judgment.

---

1.   The United States Supreme Court's decision in *Daubert v. Merrell Dow Pharmaceuticals, Inc.*, 509 U.S. 579 (1993), *infra*, which set standards for admissibility of expert testimony under the Federal Rules of Evidence, has also had a substantial influence on standards in state court. This is partly due to the fact that many state systems have modeled their rules of evidence after the Federal Rules.

2.   Do the standards for admissibility of expert testimony on causation effectively guarantee that some victims will not be compensated — those who experience harm at early stages of scientific investigation into the potential dangers of a toxic substance? Is that an appropriate result?

IN RE "AGENT ORANGE" PRODUCT LIABILITY LITIGATION
United States District Court, Eastern District of New York, 1984
597 F. Supp. 740

WEINSTEIN, C.J.

Preface and Summary

In 1979 a class action was commenced charging the United States government and a major portion of the chemical industry with deaths and dreadful injuries to tens of thousands of Vietnam veterans who came in contact with herbicides used in the war in Southeast Asia. The suit also claimed that as a result of the veterans' exposure, their children suffer severe birth defects. After five years of numerous motions and extensive discovery a tentative settlement was reached on the eve of trial.

The sole question before this court is whether the case against the chemical companies should now be settled. Eleven days of nationwide hearings were conducted to give the class members themselves an opportunity to be heard on the merits of the settlement. After weighing the uncertainties and legal obstacles that would accompany years of protracted litigation were the case to go to trial, the court has concluded that the settlement should be approved.

Pursuant to the stipulation of settlement, defendants have agreed to pay to the class $180 million plus interest in a manner directed by the court. Interest began accruing from May 7, 1984, at the rate of some $60,000 per day.

Defendants have not admitted any liability in connection with plaintiffs' claims.

. . . For the reasons indicated at greater length below, the settlement must be tentatively approved as reasonable under the law. There are many considerations that make this settlement desirable from the plaintiffs' viewpoint. First, the scientific data available to date make it highly unlikely that, except perhaps for those who have or have had chloracne, any plaintiff could legally prove any causal relationship between Agent Orange and any other injury, including birth defects. Second, the law that would need to be established is unique and would almost certainly result in repeated trials and appeals, with the likely ultimate result being no recovery by any plaintiff. Third, the suit was being financed by plaintiffs' lawyers who had already expended millions of dollars in disbursements and time; a full trial, appeals and retrials would have lasted years and would have required the expenditure of many more millions of dollars with serious doubts about the plaintiffs' attorneys' ability to finance the litigation properly. Fourth, benefit to plaintiffs from an ultimate recovery, if any, would not be available for many years. And, fifth, a result adverse to the plaintiffs in the litigation might have an unfavorable impact on evaluation of the Agent Orange claims by Congress and the responsible executive departments which, in the final analysis, must take responsibility for the medical and other care of servicepersons and their families.

From the defendants' point of view the settlement is reasonable: First, defending the case would have cost more tens of millions of dollars in legal fees and expenses plus the time of employees and executives who could be doing more productive work. Second, though slight, there was a possibility of an ultimate finding of liability with claims totalling billions of dollars. Third, an ongoing emotional trial would have created adverse publicity (whether or not unfair), perhaps causing a spillover effect against defendants' other products. Fourth, continued litigation and the possibility of an adverse result has a negative influence on the financial community, causing greater financing expenses as the companies become less attractive to investors. And, fifth, representatives of the defendants, like other Americans, have a sense of compassion and respect for veterans of the Vietnam War and their families who, because of circumstances beyond their control, have been treated with less favor and respect than they should have been. This is a matter of concern to all citizens, including those responsible for defendants' decisions.

. . . This has been one of the most complex litigations ever brought. Some 600 separate cases have been sent to this district from all over the country with an estimated fifteen thousand named plaintiffs.

. . . On February 19, 1979, plaintiffs filed a 162-page complaint in this district on behalf of named and unnamed Vietnam veterans and members of their families who claimed to have been injured as a result of the veterans' exposure to various phenoxy herbicides, including Agent Orange. Plaintiffs alleged, among other things, that defendants negligently manufactured and sold to the government for use in Vietnam herbicides that contained dioxin, thought to be one of the most toxic substances known to man. Plaintiffs also based their claims on theories of strict liability, breach of warranty, intentional tort and nuisance.

. . . .

Need to Settle Now to Get on With Life

A veteran from Pennsylvania voiced his desire to bring the litigation to a close:

> I too would like to see the chemical companies admit that they knew what the herbicides would do, but I do not, nor do the veterans and their families, have the time to continue to fight this out in a court of law.

Many veterans spoke about how the Agent Orange controversy continues the Vietnam war for them. They feel that the government refuses to recognize that there is a problem, they feel slighted by the VA, they feel that no one appreciates the fact that they, like all veterans, fought for their country in time of need. For them, Agent Orange is part of the remaining unfinished business of the Vietnam war.

Plaintiffs' Evidence of Causality

The critical problem for the plaintiffs is to establish that the relatively small quantities of dioxin to which servicepersons were exposed in Vietnam caused their present disabilities. Here adequate proof is lacking.

A central problem under plaintiffs' theory would be establishing a causal relationship between exposure and discrete diseases. As yet little if any scientific support for plaintiffs' views has been developed.

Even if we assume that chloracne in veterans was caused by exposure to Agent Orange, plaintiffs concede that the government contract defense . . . represents a substantial impediment to recovery for this disease. It was well known in the 1960's that workers' exposure to dioxin in herbicides caused chloracne, so that the government's knowledge of this fact was probably as great as that of the manufacturers.

. . . The evidence with respect to birth defects is even more tenuous. Male mediated birth defects might theoretically result from exposure of the father to Agent Orange, but no supporting data associating dioxin exposure of males with birth defects of children has been made available.

. . . .

The Problem of the Indeterminate Defendant

(1) *Introduction*

This case illustrates the inapplicability of burden of proof rules designed for simple two-party cases to mass toxic torts where injury was allegedly caused, but the question of which manufacturer created the harm cannot be answered with precision. Under "traditional" product liability law, to establish a prima facie case against any given manufacturer of Agent Orange, a plaintiff would have to prove, by a preponderance of the evidence, the following material propositions: (1) he was injured, (2) the injury was caused by Agent Orange, (3) a defendant had violated some legal duty owed to the plaintiff (as by negligent manufacture of Agent Orange), and (4) the particular Agent Orange causing injury to the plaintiff was manufactured by that defendant.

Plaintiffs concede that because of the way the defendants' herbicides were mixed by the government in Vietnam before spraying no plaintiff would be able to establish the fourth material proposition. As will be seen, this inability is not fatal to their case. Instead, a class of plaintiffs would be able to establish a prima facie case by showing, in addition to the first three material propositions, that the manufacturer knew or should have known about the dangers of Agent Orange as it was to be used in Vietnam and that the manufacturer failed to warn the government of those dangers.

. . . .

Applicable Law

While it can be shown that defendants injured some of a large group of plaintiffs, it is impossible to determine which of the plaintiffs were injured. This could happen, for example, if defendants exposed plaintiffs to a toxic substance that caused the incidence of cancer among the plaintiffs to rise significantly above the "background" level of cancers, but it is impossible to determine if the cancer in a particular plaintiff is due to the toxic substance or is part of the "background" cancers.

. . . .

The Problem of the Indeterminate Plaintiff

The preceding discussion assumed that although a plaintiff would be unable to identify the manufacturer of the Agent Orange to which the veteran was exposed he or she would be able to prove, by a preponderance of the evidence, that the specific injuries he or she suffers from were caused by Agent Orange. It is likely, however, that even if plaintiffs as a class could prove that they were injured by Agent Orange, no individual class member would be able to prove that his or her injuries were caused by Agent Orange. For example, plaintiffs as a class may be able to show that statistically, X% of the population not exposed to Agent Orange could have been expected to develop soft-tissue sarcoma, but that among those veterans who were exposed to Agent Orange, X - Y% suffer from soft-tissue sarcoma. If Y is equal to or less than X and there is no meaningful "particularistic" or anecdotal proof as to the vast majority of plaintiffs, virtually no plaintiff would be able to show by a preponderance of the evidence that his or her cancer is attributable to the Agent Orange rather than being part of the "background" level of cancer in population as a whole. The probability of specific cause would necessarily be less than 50% based upon the evidence submitted.

. . . In two of the largest and most widely publicized mass tort litigations, those involving DES and asbestos, the problem outlined above does not pose a serious obstacle since at least some of the damage caused by the harmful substance was, it has been claimed, unique to that substance. Adenosis and clear cell adenocarcinoma of the vagina and uterus, the conditions associated with DES, are, it is said, almost unknown among women whose mothers had not taken DES. The situation is similar, in the asbestos litigation, albeit to a lesser extent. Although lung cancer is associated with cigarette smoking and other factors as well as asbestos exposure and mesothelioma may have causes other than asbestos, asbestosis is alleged to be uniquely associated with asbestos exposure.

. . . .

Preponderance Rule

Despite the near certainty as to general causation and the significant uncertainty as to individual causation, traditional tort principles dictate that causation may be determined on a case-by-case basis using the preponderance-of-the-evidence rule. The rule provides an "all or nothing" approach, whereby [assuming all other elements of the cause of action are proven], the plaintiff becomes entitled to full compensation for those . . . damages that are proved to be "probable" (a greater than 50 percent chance), but it is not entitled to any compensation if the proof does not establish a greater than 50 percent chance." . . .

Under the "strong" version of the preponderance rule, statistical correlations alone indicating that the probability of causation exceeds fifty percent are insufficient; some "particularistic" or anecdotal evidence, that is, "proof that can provide direct and actual knowledge of the causal relationship between the defendant's tortious conduct and the plaintiff's injury," is required.

. . . The "weak" version of the preponderance rule would allow a verdict solely on statistical evidence; the "all-or-nothing" approach converts the statistical probability into a legally absolute finding that the causal connection did or did not exist in the case. The justification for not requiring "particularistic" or anecdotal evidence is trenchantly and accurately stated by Professor Rosenberg:

> "Particularistic" evidence, however, is in fact no less probabilistic than is the statistical evidence that courts purport to shun. . . . "Particularistic" evidence offers nothing more than a basis for conclusions about a perceived balance of probabilities.

Rosenberg, *supra* , 97 Harv. L. Rev. at 870.

. . . A simple hypothetical will illustrate why too heavy a burden should not be placed on plaintiffs by requiring a high percentage or incidence of a disease to be attributable to a particular product. Let us assume that there are 10 manufacturers and a population of 10 million persons exposed to their product. Assume that among this population 1,000 cancers of a certain type could be expected, but that 1,100 exist, and that this increase is "statistically significant," permitting a reasonable conclusion that 100 cancers are due to the product of the manufacturers. In the absence of other evidence, it might be argued that as to any one of the 1100 there is only a chance of about 9% (100/1100) that the product caused the cancer. Under traditional tort principles no plaintiff could recover.

Any attempt to resolve the problem on a plaintiff-by-plaintiff basis cannot be fully satisfactory.

. . . .

Conclusion Concerning Fairness of Settlement

Based on all the information presently available, the procedural posture of the litigation, the difficulty any plaintiff would have in establishing a case against any one or more of the defendants, the uncertainties associated with a trial, and the unacceptable burdens on plaintiffs' and defendants' legal staffs and the courts, the proposed settlement appears to be reasonable. It appears to be in the public's as well as the parties' interest.

. . . .

Conclusion

In conclusion it is well to remind ourselves of President Lincoln's admonition which is as relevant now, almost fifteen years after the end of the Vietnam war, as it was six score years ago. In his Second Inaugural Address he urged us "to bind up the nation's wounds; to care for him who shall have borne the battle and for his widow, and his orphan — to do all which may achieve and cherish a just and lasting peace among ourselves. . . ." It is time for the government to join with plaintiffs and defendants in even greater efforts toward this noble goal.

. . . The settlement is approved subject to hearings of fees and preliminary consideration of plans for distribution. This order is not final.

---

1. What would motivate the defendants to pay $180 million when cause in fact cannot be proven? Why would a plaintiff's attorney bring a case when he or she cannot prove cause in fact?

2. Why do plaintiffs favor a settlement? Defendant? Under what circumstances would you counsel your client (plaintiff) not to settle? Should plaintiffs with chloracne have formed their own class action?

3. Do the facts of class-action toxic tort cases (15,000 plaintiffs, etc.) argue for some forum other than the courts? What forum would you suggest? Professor Rabin suggests four alternatives: the black lung compensation scheme, the Japanese Environmental Liability Act, CERCLA (Superfund, a tax on hazardous chemicals and fuels), a New Zealand-type comprehensive no-fault scheme covering all accidental personal injuries. Rabin, *Environmental Liability and the Tort System*, 24 Hous. L. Rev. 27, 45–51 (1987). To these models, one might add the various means (charitable donations, workers' compensation, governmental compensation funds, and insurance) used to compensate victims and responders harmed as a result of the 9/11/2001 attacks, including the federal September 11 Victims' Compensation Fund. *See* Howard, *The World Trade Center Disaster: Health Effects and Compensation Mechanisms*, 16 J.L. & Pol'y 69 (2007). What are the problems with each model? What is the cost of each? Although thousands of victims have accepted compensation settlements, many tort suits were filed as a result of the World Trade Center disaster. *See In re World Trade Center Disaster Site Litigation*, 521 F.3d 169 (2d Cir. 2008); *In re World Trade Center Disaster Site Litigation*, 456 F. Supp. 2d 520 (S.D.N.Y. 2006).

4. Are class actions the most efficient means to end cases like *Agent Orange*? Do too many people recover? What is the proper role for the court in settling such cases?

5. Is it better for a manufacturer to settle or to fight the causation issue? *See Malcolm v. National Gypsum Co.*, 995 F.2d 346 (2d Cir. 1993) (discussing the benefits and burdens of a class action suit for the defendant, the manufacturer of asbestos).

6. Before accepting the settlement, should the judge require the defendant to admit liability? How would the defendant respond? What causes of action would the plaintiffs argue? Why doesn't the specific cause of action matter very much in many toxic tort cases?

7. Why can't plaintiffs prove cause in fact? In cases like this, should the burden shift to the defendant to prove the absence of causation? What is the difference between the "strong" version and the "weak" version of the preponderance rule? Do you agree that the settlement appears fair? Cause in fact was equally challenging in a suit brought by victims of nuclear testing:

> The complaint in this action alleges that each plaintiff, or his predecessor, has suffered injury or death as a proximate result of exposure to radioactive

fallout that drifted away from the Nevada Test Site and settled upon communities and isolated populations in southern Utah, northern Arizona and southeastern Nevada. Each of the plaintiffs or their decedents resided in that area. Each claims serious loss due to radiation-caused cancer or leukemia. Each asserts that the injury suffered resulted from the negligence of the United States in conducting open-air nuclear testing, in monitoring testing results, in failing to inform persons at hazard of attendant dangers from such testing and in failing to inform such persons how to avoid or minimize or mitigate such dangers.

Allen v. United States, 588 F. Supp. 247, 257–58 (D. Utah 1984).

This verdict for the victims was reversed in *Allen v. United States*, 816 F.2d 1417 (10th Cir. 1987), because the decision to engage in nuclear testing fell under the discretionary function exception to the Federal Tort Claim Act, 28 U.S.C. § 2680(a).

C.   CAUSE OF ACTION

PROBLEMS

1. A chemical plant releases toxic substances into a nearby river. How would you deal with each of the following as the attorney for the victims? You represent: (a) the owner of a cattle ranch located on the banks of the river five miles below the plant, (b) a restaurant, serving fresh trout, located ten miles downstream from the plant, (c) seven pregnant women from a nearby town that takes its water from the river at a point below the plant, (d) fifteen adults from the same town, who now fear they will develop cancer.

2. Fifteen years ago, Ace Corp. stored PCBs on property near the river. Some have leaked into the river. Ace Corp. sold the property ten years ago. What result?

T & E INDUSTRIES v. SAFETY LIGHT CORP.
Supreme Court of New Jersey, 1991
123 N.J. 371, 587 A.2d 1249

CLIFFORD, JUSTICE.

This appeal takes us once again over the unsettled waters of toxic-tort litigation. At the storm center of this case is a radium-contaminated site that is now owned by plaintiff, T & E Industries, Inc. (T & E), but was once owned by United States Radium Corporation (USRC), the predecessor corporation of all the defendant corporations. The primary issue is whether an owner of radium-contaminated property can hold a distant predecessor in title that is responsible for the contamination strictly liable for damages caused by its abnormally-dangerous activity. We hold that it can.

Until 1943 USRC owned an industrial site on Alden Street in Orange. From around 1917 to 1926 it processed radium at that site. It extracted the radium from carnotite ore. It could, however, recover successfully only eighty percent of the radium from the ore. The unextracted radium was contained in "tailings," the solid by-products of the extraction process, which USRC discarded onto the unimproved portions of the Alden Street site.

Carnotite ore consists primarily of Uranium 238, radium, and vanadium. As the nucleus disintegrates, Uranium 238 decays into other elements, one of which is Radium 226. In turn Radium 226 emits gamma rays and decays into Radon 222, which is a naturally-occurring radioactive gas. Radon then decays into radon progeny or radon "daughters," which can adhere to walls, ceilings, dust particles, and, if inhaled, the tissue of the lungs. Gamma-ray exposure can cause bone cancer and leukemia, while radon inhalation can cause lung cancer.

It was not until the mid-1950s, however, that the scientific community engaged in any serious study of the epidemiological risks associated with radon. It did not generally accept the link between radon and lung cancer until the 1960s, and it was not aware of the problems generated by radioactive tailings until the late 1960s. The federal government, reflecting an unfortunate lag time, did not regulate the disposition of tailings until 1978.

Nevertheless, both the scientific community and USRC had suspicions about the hazards of radium at a much earlier date. In 1917 Florence Wall, an employee of USRC, calculated the amount of radium extracted from ore and measured its radioactivity. For protection at work she wore a full-length lead-lined apron, much like a "mummy case."

Others too were concerned about handling radium. Wall recalled an incident involving Dr. Von Sochocky, the president of USRC, when radium lodged beneath his fingernail: he immediately "hacked" off his fingertip because he feared the effects of radium.

In the early 1920s, USRC acquired still more evidence of the dangers of radium. Some of its employees applied the luminous paint to watch and instrument dials. After dipping their brushes into the paint, the dial-painters often sharpened the tip of the brush in their mouths, thereby ingesting a small amount of radium. Many of those employees eventually developed cancer. After discovering the problems associated with ingesting radium, USRC posted warnings cautioning its employees against sharpening the brushes in that fashion.

Radium processing at the Orange facility ceased in 1926, and USRC vacated the premises.

. . . In 1943, USRC sold the Orange property to Arpin, a plastics manufacturer. Despite its suspicions about the harmful effects of radium, as recited above, USRC did not remove the discarded tailings from the site.

Arpin, unaware of the potential risks associated with the tailings, added to the plant a new section that rested on the discarded tailings. Since then the property has changed hands several times. Plaintiff, T & E, a manufacturer of electronic components, began leasing the premises in 1969 and purchased it in 1974.

The Uranium Mill Tailings Radiation Control Act, 42 U.S.C. § 7901 to § 7942 (1978), calls for the evaluation of inactive mill-tailing sites. In accordance with that Act, Jeanette Eng, a supervisor in the New Jersey Department of Environmental Protection (DEP), visited plaintiff's plant in March 1979.

Tests on air and soil samples verified that the levels of radon, radon progeny, and gamma radiation exceeded State regulations. The radon level of the soil samples taken from beneath the building exceeded federal standards as well. The most severe problem existed in the oven room, the portion of the building added by Arpin. DEP instructed plaintiff "to begin immediate remedial action." It also informed plaintiff that such remedial action would serve only as an interim measure. DEP suggested that if funding for a full decontamination of the site could not be found quickly, plaintiff's options would be "limited to undertaking the cost of decontamination or consider[ing] abandoning the site."

Despite plaintiff's interim efforts, in 1981 the Environmental Protection Agency (EPA), at DEP's request, placed the property on the National Priorities List, consisting of those sites posing the most significant potential threats to human health because of their known or suspected toxicity. Although DEP did not order plaintiff to abandon the site, T & E moved its operations to another building in Orange and closed the Alden Street plant. Under the Environmental Cleanup and Responsibility Act (ECRA), T & E cannot sell the property until cleanup has been effected.

In March 1981 T & E sued Safety Light Corporation; USR Industries; USR Chemical Products, Inc.; USR Lighting Products, Inc.; USR Metals, Inc.; U.S. Natural Resources, Inc.; GAF Corporation; and Mitsubishi Chemical Industries, all successor corporations of USRC. The suit is based on nuisance, negligence, misrepresentation and fraud, and strict liability for an abnormally-dangerous activity. The trial court ordered separate trials and designated Safety Light Corporation as the defendant in the first trial. Thereafter the other defendants stipulated that any damages awarded against Safety Light would be binding on any defendant found liable in the second trial. "Defendant" as used hereafter in this opinion refers to Safety Light.

Finding that USRC had "placed hazardous wastes in the form of radium ore tailings" on the Alden Street property in Orange, the court granted plaintiff's motion for partial summary judgment.

. . . When plaintiff's case concluded, the court reversed itself and granted defendant's motion to dismiss plaintiff's strict-liability claims. It ruled that strict liability arising from an abnormally dangerous activity may be imposed only if the defendant knew at the time of performance that its activity was in fact abnormally dangerous. . . .

. . . The court then granted judgment n.o.v. in favor of all defendants, ruling that the doctrine of caveat emptor barred plaintiff's recovery. The Appellate Division granted leave to appeal and reversed.

. . . The Appellate Division also rejected the contention that strict liability applies only to interference with the property rights of a neighbor, not those of a successor in title. It concluded that there is "no practical or legal distinction between the rights of a successor in title to use and enjoy its land and the rights of a neighboring property owner. Both have rights and both can suffer injury through the acts of a prior owner."

Nor did the court below believe that the doctrine of caveat emptor insulated defendant from liability. Finding that doctrine outdated, the Appellate Division concluded that a "party who creates [an abnormally-dangerous] condition is absolutely liable and cannot avoid that responsibility unless a purchaser knowingly accepts that burden."

We granted defendant's petition for certification. . . .

. . . At the outset we must determine whether a property owner can assert against a predecessor in title a cause of action sounding in strict liability for abnormally-dangerous activities. Defendant suggests that only neighboring property owners, not successors in title, can maintain such a suit, and that successors in title must rely on contract law to recover from a prior owner.

. . . In *Philadelphia Electric Co.* the court considered whether a property owner could recover damages for toxic-waste contamination from its predecessor in title. Relying on the doctrine of caveat emptor and the historical role of private-nuisance law, the court concluded that the property owner could not bring a private-nuisance claim against its former owner and could not recover damages.

Defendant stresses that a successor in title, unlike an innocent neighbor, could have inspected the property or demanded a warranty deed. We are not persuaded, however, that a landowner who engages in abnormally-dangerous activities should be liable only to neighboring property owners.

. . . The [strict liability] rule reflects a policy determination that such "enterprise[s] should bear the costs of accidents attributable to highly dangerous [or unusual activities]."

. . . The rule recognizes an additional policy consideration: such enterprises are in "a better position to administer the unusual risk by passing it onto the public." Prosser, *supra*, § 75, at 537. Because of that opportunity, the enterprise can better bear the loss.

Neither policy rests on notions of property rights. Rather, the first serves to induce certain businesses to "internalize" the external costs of business, while the second seeks to shift a seemingly-inevitable loss onto the party deemed best able to shoulder it. Because the former owner of the property whose activities caused the hazard might have been in the best position to bear or spread the loss, liability for the harm caused by abnormally-dangerous activities does not necessarily cease with the transfer of property.

. . . Defendant complains that holding a predecessor in title strictly liable for its abnormally-dangerous activities "would destroy the real estate market." [We think that is] [n]ot likely. A buyer can assume the risk of harm from an abnormally-dangerous activity.

. . . We focus now on the elements of the abnormally-dangerous-activity doctrine. That doctrine is premised on the principle that "one who carries on an abnormally dangerous activity is subject to liability for harm to the person, land or chattels of another resulting from the activity, although he has exercised the utmost care to prevent the harm." Restatement (Second) of Torts, *supra*, § 519. The Restatement sets forth six factors that a court should consider in determining whether an activity is "abnormally dangerous." They are:

(a)   existence of a high degree of risk of some harm to the person, land or chattels of others;

(b)   likelihood that the harm that results from it will be great;

(c)   inability to eliminate the risk by the exercise of reasonable care;

(d)   extent to which the activity is not a matter of common usage;

(e)   inappropriateness of the activity to the place where it is carried on; and

(f)   extent to which its value to the community is outweighed by its dangerous attributes.

[Restatement (Second) of Torts, *supra* , § 520.]

. . . Defendant adds that knowledge, or the ability to acquire such knowledge, must be assessed as of the time the enterpriser engaged in the activity, not at a later time — that is, if the risk of harm from the activity was scientifically unknowable at that time, an enterpriser should not be held liable.

. . . Defendant's argument poses an interesting question concerning the availability of a state-of-the-art defense — that is, the risk of the activity was scientifically unknowable at the time — to a strict-liability claim for abnormally-dangerous activities. It is a question we need not resolve here, however, because state-of-the-art becomes an issue only if we agree that knowledge is a prerequisite for strict-liability claims and if we accept defendant's narrow view of the "knowledge" inquiry.

. . . But requirements such as "knowledge" and "foreseeability" smack of negligence and may be inappropriate in the realm of strict liability.

. . . We need not, however, determine whether knowledge is a requirement in the context of a strict-liability claim predicated on an abnormally-dangerous activity. Even if the law imposes such a requirement, we are convinced, for the reasons set forth more fully below, that defendant should have known about the risks of its activity, and that its constructive knowledge would fully satisfy any such requirement.

. . . Furthermore, although the risks involved in the processing and disposal of radium might be curtailed, one cannot safely dispose of radium by dumping it onto the vacant portions of an urban lot. Because of the extraordinarily-hazardous nature of radium, the processing and disposal of that substance is particularly inappropriate in an urban setting. We conclude that despite the usefulness of radium, defendant's processing, handling, and disposal of that substance under the facts of this case constituted an abnormally-dangerous activity. . . .

The judgment below is modified and as modified, affirmed. The cause is remanded for further proceedings consistent with this opinion.

---

1.   What is at stake in *T. & E. Industries*? What are the risks from radium tailings? When did the defendant know of these risks? What is the impact of the government's regulation in 1978? What is the point of the Von Sochocky story? Is the

court suggesting that the defendant should have removed the tailings in 1943?

2. In regard to abnormally dangerous activities, how does the court deal with the "knowledge" and the "successor in title" defense? The state-of-the-art defense? For a different take on the liability of successors in title, see *Rosenblatt v. Exxon Co.*, 335 Md. 58, 642 A.2d 180 (1994) (concluding the successor strict liability for abnormally dangerous activities is inconsistent with policies behind Restatement (Second) of Torts § 519).

3. Do you agree with the court's treatment of the destruction of the market theory? What burden does this place on the purchaser? Consider the purchase of an old gas station property by a buyer who plans to convert the property to a different business. What should the parties discuss during the purchase negotiations?

4. If "common usage" is a defense, could the defendant argue that a substantial number of companies in the community discarded hazardous wastes on their property?

5. *See* Jones, *Strict Liability for Hazardous Enterprise*, 92 Colum. L. Rev. 1705, 1705–79 (1992); Comment, *Absolute Liability for Ultrahazardous Activities: An Appraisal of the Restatement Doctrine*, 37 Cal. L. Rev. 269 (1969).

6. In *Indiana Harbor Belt R.R. Co. v. American Cyanamid Co.*, 916 F.2d 1174 (7th Cir. 1990), about 5,000 gallons of acrylontrile, a highly toxic and carcinogenic substance, leaked from a leased tank car into the plaintiff's switching yard. The plaintiff paid a clean-up cost of $981,022.75 and sought to recover that from the manufacturer of acrylontrile, American Cyanamid Company. The district court held that strict liability applied, but (in an opinion by Judge Posner) the court of appeals reversed, finding that only negligence applied.

IN RE HANFORD NUCLEAR RESERVATION LITIGATION
PHILLIPS v. E.I. DUPONT DE NEMOURS & CO.
United States Court of Appeals for the Ninth Circuit, 2008
534 F.3d 986, *amended,* 521 F.3d 1028, *cert. denied,* 555 U.S. 1084

SCHROEDER, Circuit Judge.

Introduction.

The origins of this case trace back more than sixty years to the height of World War II when the federal government solicited Appellants E.I. DuPont de Nemours & Co., Inc., General Electric Co., UNC Nuclear Industries, Inc., Atlantic Richfield Co., and Rockwell International Corp. (collectively "Defendants") to operate the Hanford Nuclear Weapons Reservation ("Hanford") in southeastern Washington. The Hanford Reservation was a plutonium-production facility that helped make the atomic bomb that dropped on Nagasaki, Japan in World War II.

A regrettable Hanford byproduct was the radioiodine emitted into the surrounding area. The plaintiffs in this litigation are over two thousand residents who now claim that these emissions, known as 1-131, caused various cancers and other life-threatening diseases. . . . After almost two decades of litigation, which already has included two appeals to this court, the parties in 2005 agreed to a bellwether trial. The trial was designed to produce a verdict that would highlight the strengths and weaknesses of the parties' respective cases and thus focused on six plaintiffs ("Plaintiffs") who were representative of the larger group. The purpose of the trial was to promote settlement and bring long-overdue resolution to this litigation.

Before us on appeal is a litany of issues stemming from the bellwether trial. A threshhold [sic] issue is whether Defendants may seek complete immunity under the common law government contractor defense, because they were operating Hanford at the request of the federal government. We hold that the defense is inapplicable as a matter of law, because Congress enacted the PAA before the courts recognized the government contractor defense, and the PAA provides a comprehensive liability scheme that precludes Defendants' reliance on such a defense.

In the alternative, Defendants argue that even if they are not immune, they are not strictly liable for any 1-131 emissions, because the amounts of the emissions were within federally-authorized levels; the plutonium-production process was not an abnormally dangerous activity that would create strict liability; and even if it were, Defendants qualify for the "public duty" exception to strict liability. The district court held that none of Defendants' contentions were sufficient to relieve them of strict liability for the injuries they caused. We agree.

With respect to the trial itself, the district court with admirable diligence ruled on many issues of first impression. We hold that under Washington law, the district court properly instructed the jury that to impose liability, it had to find Hanford was the "but for" cause of Plaintiffs' diseases and not just a contributing cause under the more lenient "substantial factor" test. The court also made a host of evidentiary rulings that are before us on appeal. We hold that three of these rulings constitute reversible error with respect to three of the Bellwether Plaintiffs.

. . . .

Lastly, we hold that the district court properly dismissed any medical monitoring claims as not cognizable under the PAA. This is consistent with our decision in Berg, 293 F.3d 1127.

II. Background.

The United States government constructed Hanford during World War II to manufacture plutonium for military purposes. The facility was a component of the Army Corps of Engineer's secret Manhattan Project, with the primary objective of developing an atomic bomb. In 1942, the Army Corps began hiring civilian contractors to help build and operate the Hanford facility. It first recruited the University of Chicago Metallurgical Laboratory ("Met Lab") to design the process and equipment to produce plutonium. It then solicited E.I. DuPont de Nemours & Co. ("DuPont") to actually run the facility. It is apparent the government itself did not have the expertise or resources to operate Hanford.

DuPont initially refused. The government, however, persisted and implored

DuPont to run the plutonium-production facility, because, as the government provided in DuPont's contract, the project was of the "utmost importance" and was "necessary in facilitating the prosecution of the war." DuPont eventually acquiesced, stating it would run the facility out of patriotic considerations. It accepted only one dollar as payment for its services. Several years later, the Hanford facility successfully produced the plutonium that was used in 1945 to drop the atomic bomb on Nagasaki and effectively end World War II. (The bomb dropped on Hiroshima was uranium-based, not plutonium-based).

As part of the plutonium-production process, the Hanford facility emitted 1-131, a fission byproduct known as radioiodine. I-131 was known at the time to have potential adverse health effects on humans. Accordingly, the Met Lab scientists set tolerance doses for human exposure. For example, the Met Lab determined that the human thyroid should not absorb more than one rad per day for those individuals subject to continuous exposure in the area. A rad is a measurement of the amount of radioiodine absorbed into an organ or tissue. On the basis of these safe exposure limit estimates, the Met Lab approved a detailed operating procedure that would ensure that the plutonium was produced within those emission limits. The key to decreasing 1-131 emissions was to allow for longer cooling times of the uranium slugs used to produce the plutonium. This strategy, however, often conflicted with the federal government's orders to increase plutonium production.

On September 1, 1946, DuPont transferred its duties to General Electric ("GE"), which also agreed to earn no profit from its work. GE ran the Hanford facility through the Cold War. During the period of its operation, GE asked the federal government to increase cooling times to allow for lower emissions of 1-131. By this time, Congress had established the Atomic Energy Commission ("AEC"), see 42 U.S.C. §§ 2011-2013 (1946), and GE was bound by its determinations. The AEC denied the request for longer cooling times, and GE continued to produce plutonium consistent with government demands. By the 1950s, however, significant improvements were made to the production process, and I-131 emission levels dropped.

In 1987, the United States Department of Energy ("DOE") created the Hanford Environmental Dose Reconstruction Project ("HEDR"), overseen by the Center for Disease Control and Prevention. The underlying purpose of the HEDR was to estimate and reconstruct all radionuclide emissions from Hanford from 1944 to 1972 in order to ascertain whether neighboring individuals and animals had been exposed to harmful doses of radiation. Of particular concern to the HEDR were the estimated doses of 1-131 received by the thyroid glands of humans, principally through consumption of milk from cows that ingested contaminated vegetation on neighboring farms and pastures. The HEDR concluded that 1-131 emissions peaked during the period from 1944 to 1946, when an estimated 88% of Hanford's total iodine emissions occurred. HEDR explained that in later years, emissions declined because of technological advances. In 1990, the Technical Steering Panel of HEDR released a report entitled Initial Hanford Radiation Dose Estimates that publicly disclosed for the first time that large quantities of radioactive and non-radioactive substances had been released from Hanford, beginning in the 1940s.

This disclosure sparked a blaze of litigation. Thousands of plaintiffs filed suit pursuant to the Price-Anderson Act, 42 U.S.C. § 2210(n)(2), which had been amended in 1988 to provide exclusive federal jurisdiction over all claims arising from a nuclear incident, otherwise known as public liability actions. The PAA allowed the plaintiffs to sue private parties, such as DuPont, and to consolidate the claims in federal district court. Id. While Congress wanted to ensure that victims of nuclear incidents recovered compensation, it also included government indemnification provisions in the PAA to give private parties an incentive to participate in the nuclear industry. See, e.g., S. REP. No. 100-70, at 14 (1988), reprinted in 1988 U.S.C.C.A.N. 1424, 1425-26.

The PAA provides that although federal courts have exclusive and original jurisdiction over claims stemming from nuclear incidents, the substantive rules of decision are provided by the law of the state in which the nuclear incident occurs. See 42 U.S.C. § 2014(hh). Plaintiffs therefore brought tort claims under Washington law, asserting that because Defendants were engaged in an abnormally dangerous activity, they were strictly liable for any Hanford-caused radiation illness.

On August 6, 1990, a group of plaintiffs filed a joint consolidated complaint in the Eastern District of Washington, alleging a class action against Defendants. In 1991, the district court consolidated any and all Hanford-related actions pending in various courts, directed preparation of one consolidated complaint, and designated specific lead counsel for all parties. In an order dated September 22, 1994, the district court addressed the issue of class certification and decided to reserve decision under Federal Rule of Civil Procedure 23(b)(3) pending further discovery on causation issues.

Accordingly, pending class certification, the litigation proceeded as a consolidated action.

. . . .

After [various preliminary matters] . . . Judge William Fremming Nielsen steered the case toward resolution. The parties agreed to proceed with a bellwether trial, hoping it would reveal the strengths and weaknesses of their respective cases and thus pave the way for a settlement. The parties eventually agreed on twelve bellwether plaintiffs. Six of these plaintiffs had their claims dismissed on dispositive, pre-trial motions. The remaining six plaintiffs went to trial in April 2005.

The Bellwether Plaintiffs represent plaintiffs who suffer from various thyroid diseases they claim were caused by radiation emanating from Hanford [including thyroid cancer, hypothyroidism, "Hashimoto's disease," Hurthle cell thyroid cancer and lung cancer].

Prior to trial, the Bellwether Plaintiffs made several motions to strike Defendants' affirmative defenses. Defendants first claimed that the government contractor defense insulated them from all liability. The district court, in an unpublished 2003 order, struck the defense under Federal Rule of Civil Procedure 12(b), holding that the PAA displaced any such defense as a matter of law. In a published order, the court also ruled that plutonium production at Hanford was an abnormally dangerous activity warranting strict liability under Washington law. In re Hanford Nuclear Res. Litig., 350 F. Supp. 2d 871, 888 (E.D. Wash. 2004). It then limited the issues at trial to causation and damages. Id.

The primary dispute at trial was whether the amount of radiation to which each plaintiff was exposed was sufficient to be the cause-in-fact of his or her thyroid disease. There was extensive testimony that 1-131 radiation causes Hashimoto's disease, a cause of hypothyroidism, and that 1-131 can also be a contributing factor to thyroid cancer. The testimony revealed, however, that to date epidemiological studies can establish only that radiation of at least 100 rads is a contributing factor to thyroid illness. Some epidemiological studies hypothesize that 40 rads might cause Hashimoto's disease, but there are no data beyond that threshold.

Because many Plaintiffs were not exposed to radiation above 40 rads, and no Plaintiff was exposed to radiation above 100 rads, Plaintiffs had to present expert testimony that scientific extrapolation permitted a finding of causation below 40 rads. . . .

After fourteen days of trial and four days of deliberations, the jury found in favor of two plaintiffs . . . ; the jury hung with respect to one plaintiff . . . ; and it found in favor of Defendants with respect to the remaining three plaintiffs. . . . As damages for prevailing plaintiffs, the jury awarded Stanton $227,508 and Wise $317,251. Because the jury could not reach a verdict with respect to Plaintiff Rhodes, the district court declared a mistrial. Rhodes re-tried her claims in front of a second jury in November 2005, and the jury entered a defense verdict on all counts.

Rhodes, along with the three non-prevailing plaintiffs in the first trial, appeal a variety of evidentiary rulings, as well as the district court's jury instruction that under Washington law Plaintiffs had to prove "but-for" causation, rather than "substantial factor" causation. Defendants appeal the judgments entered in favor of the two prevailing plaintiffs, claiming the district court erred as a matter of law in striking the government contractor defense. In the alternative, Defendants argue that Plaintiffs may not proceed under a strict liability theory, because the 1-131 emissions were within federally-authorized levels. They also contend the plutonium-production process was not an abnormally dangerous activity under Washington law and, even if it were, that Defendants qualify for the narrow "public duty" exception to strict liability.

. . . Apart from the issues relating to the Bellwether Plaintiffs, Plaintiffs Pamela Durfey, Paulene Echo Hawk, and Dorothy George, who do not yet have symptoms of any thyroid disease, sued Defendants for the costs of medical monitoring. The district court, following this court's decision in Berg, 293 F.3d at 1132-33, held that the PAA precluded any medical monitoring claims that were unaccompanied by physical injury. Rather than remanding those claims to state court, however, the district court held that the PAA bestowed exclusive jurisdiction in the federal courts for claims arising from a nuclear incident, and that therefore the PAA's provisions preempted any state-derived medical monitoring claim. Accordingly, it directed entry of final judgment for DuPont under Federal Rule of Civil Procedure 54(b). The plaintiffs appeal this dismissal.

III. The Government Contractor Defense.

The overarching issue before us is Defendants' contention that the government contractor defense is available to them as a matter of law and that it provides complete immunity from liability if its substantive requirements are satisfied. The district court held that the affirmative defense was inapplicable as a matter of law because the provisions of the PAA cannot be reconciled with the defense and implicitly displace it. We . . . reach the same conclusion.

The government contractor defense is by now an established component of federal common law, but it was first recognized by the Supreme Court less than twenty years ago in Boyle v. United Techs. Corp., 487 U.S. 500, 108 S. Ct. 2510, 101 L. Ed. 2d 442 (1988). The defense is intended to implement and protect the discretionary function exception of the Federal Tort Claims Act ("FTCA"), 28 U.S.C. § 2680(a), which was enacted after World War II. The defense allows a contractor-defendant to receive the benefits of sovereign immunity when a contractor complies with the specifications of a federal government contract. Boyle, 487 U.S. at 511-12. As the Court said in Boyle, "[i]t makes little sense to insulate the Government against financial liability for the judgment that . . . equipment is necessary when the Government produces the equipment itself, but not when it contracts for the production." Id. at 512.

As a threshold matter, we agree with Defendants that the government contractor defense applies not only to claims challenging the physical design of a military product, but also to the process by which such equipment is produced. Accordingly, a contractor who agrees to operate a production facility pursuant to government specifications may qualify for the defense.

The issue here, however, is whether the PAA preempts reliance on the common law doctrine, either because the defense contradicts the federal statute or because the statute predates the defense. Congress is presumed to "legislate against a background of common-law adjudicatory principles." Astoria Fed. Savings & Loan Ass'n v. Solimino, 501 U.S. 104, 108, 111 S. Ct. 2166, 115 L. Ed. 2d 96 (1991). A federal statute enacted after a common law doctrine has been established will not therefore abrogate the federal common law rule unless the statute speaks directly to the question addressed by common law. United States v. Texas, 507 U.S. 529, 534, 113 S. Ct. 1631, 123 L. Ed. 2d 245 (1993). This is because "where a common law principle is well established . . . the courts may take it as given that Congress has legislated with an expectation that the principle will apply except when a statutory purpose to the contrary is evident." Astoria, 501 U.S. at 108 (internal quotations and citations omitted).

Whether the PAA preempts the government contractor defense is therefore a two-step inquiry. We must first determine whether the government contractor defense was well-established at the time Congress enacted the operative version of the PAA. If so, we must determine whether a statutory purpose contrary to the government contractor defense is evident. The defense fails the first inquiry. Defendants are not entitled to the government contractor defense, because the statute predates clear judicial recognition of any such defense. In addition, the statute's comprehensive liability scheme is patently inconsistent with the defense and precludes its operation in this case.

. . . .

. . . The defense is . . . inconsistent with Congressional purpose . . . .

Congress enacted the PAA with twin goals in mind: to provide an incentive to contractors to participate in the nuclear industry by limiting their liability, and to compensate victims of nuclear accidents. See, e.g., Pub. L. No. 100-408, 102 Stat. 1066 (1988); S. REP. No. 100-218, at 4-13 (1987), reprinted in 1988 U.S.C.C.A.N. 1476, 1479-88. The Act placed Plaintiffs' state law claims in federal court and provided indemnification of Defendants from the federal government for any liability to victims of nuclear incidents. See 42 U.S.C. § 2210; S. REP. No. 100-218, at 13, reprinted in 1988 U.S.C.C.A.N. at 1484, 1488. To allow those entitled to indemnity as government contractors to disclaim any liability because they are government contractors would be inconsistent with the goal of the PAA to provide compensation to victims of nuclear incidents. We will not assume that in enacting the PAA's comprehensive scheme, Congress intended, yet failed to state in the Act, that victims of nuclear incidents cannot recover tort damages from nuclear operators when the operators were pursuing government goals. Accordingly, we hold that the government contractor defense is inapplicable as a matter of federal law and affirm the district court's ruling on this key issue.

IV. Strict Liability.

Defendants next argue that the district court erred as a matter of Washington state law in holding Defendants strictly liable for any 1-131 emissions from the Hanford facility. Defendants challenge that ruling on three grounds: (1) that strict liability pursuant to Washington state law may not be imposed under the PAA if Defendants released 1-131 within federally-authorized emission levels; (2) even if state liability law applies, the Hanford activity did not meet the "abnormally dangerous activity" test that warrants strict liability; and (3) even if Washington courts would apply a strict liability regime, Defendants would be exempted under the "public duty" exception that applies generally to heavily regulated entities doing potentially hazardous work. For the reasons below, we affirm the district court's imposition of strict liability.

A. Federally-Authorized Emissions.

It is not disputed that the federal government is in charge of nuclear safety. "[T]he safety of nuclear technology [is] the exclusive business of the Federal Government," which has "occupied the entire field of nuclear safety concerns." Koller v. Pinnacle West Capital Corp., 2007 U.S. Dist. LEXIS 9186 (D. Ariz. Feb. 7, 2007) (second alteration in original) (quoting Pac. Gas Elec. Co. v. State Energy Res. Conservation & Dev. Comm'n, 461 U.S. 190, 208, 212, 103 S. Ct. 1713, 75 L. Ed. 2d 752 (1983)). Every federal circuit that has considered the appropriate standard of care under the PAA has concluded that nuclear operators are not liable unless they breach federally-imposed dose limits. See, e.g., O'Conner, 13 F.3d at 1105; In re TMI Litig., 940 F.2d at 859; Roberts v. Fla. Power & Light Co., 146 F.3d 1305, 1308 (11th Cir. 1998); Nieman v. NLO, Inc., 108 F.3d 1546, 1553 (6th Cir. 1997).

Defendants are thus correct insofar as they point out that the clear weight of authority supports the principle that federal law preempts states from imposing a more stringent standard of care than federal safety standards. Strict liability may not be imposed for 1-131 releases within federally-authorized limits, because any federal authorization would preempt state-derived standards of care. To allow a jury to decide on the basis of a state's reasonableness standard of care would "put juries in charge of deciding the permissible levels of radiation exposure and, more generally, the adequacy of safety procedures at nuclear plants — issues that have explicitly been reserved to the federal government." In re TMI Gen. Publ. Utils. Corp., 67 F.3d 1103, 1115 (3d Cir. 1995) (citing Pacific Gas, 461 U.S. at 212). This result would undermine the purpose of a comprehensive and exclusive federal scheme for nuclear incident liability.

Defendants then go further, however, and argue that the district court in this case permitted the jury to substitute its view of a reasonable emission standard for a government standard. The problem with Defendants' argument is that no federal standards governing emission levels existed at the time of the 1-131 emissions. Defendants try to remedy this problem by pointing to "tolerance doses" recommended and implemented by military and government scientists working on the Hanford project and ask us to equate such recommendations with federally-authorized emission levels. They are not the same.

These tolerance doses, although established under the aegis of the United States Army, did not carry the force of law and thus cannot provide the basis for a safe harbor from liability. They amounted to no more than site-specific safety rules. The United States Army instructed the Manhattan Engineering District to set forth standard, internal operating procedures for the plutonium-production process at Hanford. The tolerance doses were part of these procedures. The Met Lab scientists calculated what they thought were the outer limits of safe exposure at the plant. These internal guidelines were, however, exactly and only what they claimed to be: internal. They were not comprehensive, federal standards governing emission levels on which Defendants could rely to relieve them from liability for harm they caused.

Defendants are correct that it would not have been possible for an agency to establish emission levels in the early 1940s, because the Atomic Energy Act was not enacted until 1954 and the Nuclear Regulatory Commission was created in 1974. In fact, the emissions occurred even prior to the enactment of the Administrative Procedure Act in 1946. This history, however, undermines Defendants' position, because it highlights the absence of any federal machinery to promulgate legal standards on which Defendants could have reasonably relied to insulate them from liability to those living and breathing twenty-four hours a day in the area surrounding Hanford. The need for such standards was not recognized until many years later.

B. Abnormally Dangerous Activity.

Defendants next argue that even if state law standards apply in this case, the district court erred by holding that Washington tort law would impose strict liability. Specifically, Defendants contend that operating the Hanford facility does not constitute an "abnormally dangerous activity" under Washington law. We review de novo the question of whether an activity is abnormally dangerous, Langan v. Valicopters, Inc., 88 Wn.2d 855, 567 P.2d 218, 221 (Wash. 1977), and we affirm.

Washington has adopted the Restatement (Second) of Torts, sections 519 and 520, which outline the strict liability regime for abnormally dangerous activities. Klein v. Pyrodyne Corp., 117 Wn.2d 1, 810 P.2d 917, 920 (Wash. 1991); New Meadows Holding Co. v. Wash. Water Power Co., 102 Wn.2d 495, 687 P.2d 212, 215 (Wash. 1984). Section 519 provides:

> (1) One who carries on an abnormally dangerous activity is subject to liability for harm to the person, land, or chattels of another resulting from the activity, although he has exercised the utmost care to prevent such harm.

> (2) Such strict liability is limited to the kind of harm, the risk of which makes the activity abnormally dangerous.

Section 520 lists the factors to be used when determining what constitutes an abnormally dangerous activity . . . A court does not have to weigh each of the elements listed in § 520 equally. Langan, 567 P.2d at 221. One factor, alone, however, is generally not sufficient to find an activity abnormally dangerous. Id.

Defendants argue that at the time of the emissions in the 1940s, they did not know the risks that were attributable to radioiodine exposure, and therefore § 520's factors (a)-(c) cannot be weighed against them. Any possible injury from radiation, however, need not have been actually known by Defendants at the time of exposure in order to impose strict liability. Under Washington law, if the actual harm fell within a general field of danger which should have been anticipated, strict liability may be appropriate. Whether an injury should have been anticipated does not depend on whether the particular harm was actually expected to occur. Koker v. Armstrong Cork, Inc., 60 Wn. App. 466, 804 P.2d 659, 667-68 (Wash. Ct. App. 1991). It is sufficient that "the risk created [be] so unusual, either because of its magnitude or because of the circumstances surrounding it. . . ." Langan, 567 P.2d at 221.

There is no question that Defendants should have anticipated some of the many risks associated with operating a nuclear facility, creating plutonium, and releasing 1-131 into the atmosphere. It is exactly because of these risks, and the potential exposure to liability arising from them, that the government contracted with Defendants to limit liability in case of an accident. For these, same reasons, the Met Lab scientists recommended dosage limits.

We agree with the district court that Defendants' conduct at Hanford was an abnormally dangerous activity under the § 520 factors. There was a high degree of risk to people and property associated with the Hanford facility and the gravity of any harm was likely to be great. See RESTATEMENT (SECOND) OF TORTS § 520. Regardless of Defendants' efforts to exercise reasonable care, some 1-131 would be released, and developing plutonium is hardly an activity of common usage. While the value to the community at large, i.e., the nation, of developing an atomic bomb was perceived as high and there is pragmatically no very appropriate place to carry on such an activity, the § 520 factors on balance support holding that Defendants' activities were abnormally dangerous.

C. Public Duty Exception to Strict Liability.

Defendants' final defense is that even if their conduct constituted an abnormally dangerous activity, they are exempted from strict liability under Washington law pursuant to the "public duty" exception. See RESTATEMENT (SECOND) OF TORTS § 521. While this issue presents a close question, we conclude that Defendants do not qualify for the exception.

Section 521 of the Restatement provides:

> The rules as to strict liability for abnormally dangerous activities do not apply if the activity is carried on in pursuance of a public duty imposed upon the actor as a public officer or employee or as a common carrier.

Id. As a threshold matter, Washington courts have not yet adopted § 521. We must therefore decide what the Washington Supreme Court would likely do if confronted with the issue. See NLRB v. Calkins, 187 F.3d 1080, 1089 (9th Cir. 1999). We hold that the court would likely adopt the public duty exception.

. . . .

Although widely adopted, the courts that have applied the public duty exception have generally done so only to the extent a defendant was legally required to perform the ultrahazardous activity. See RESTATEMENT (SECOND) OF TORTS, § 521, cmt. a. The Washington Supreme Court's decision in Siegler v. Kuhlman, 81 Wn.2d 448, 502 P.2d 1181 (Wash. 1972), supports such an application of the public duty doctrine here. The defendants in Siegler were a trucking company for Texaco and its driver, and the company was not legally obligated as a common carrier to carry materials that eventually caused an explosive, fatal accident on a highway. The Washington court held that the activity was abnormally dangerous and that the defendants could be held strictly liable for the accident. It is therefore most likely that the Washington Supreme Court would apply strict liability when the defendant was performing a dangerous activity for "his own purpose," and would apply the public duty exception only in the appropriate case when the defendant was engaged in a legally-obligated activity, such as a regulated common carrier bound to carry hazardous substances.

Defendants argue that in light of the exceptional and patriotic circumstances under which they operated Hanford, we should treat them as analogous to public employees who would qualify for the exception. Although Defendants are correct that we generally do not parse the language of a restatement as meticulously as that of a statute, and we will apply it "when the purposes it seeks to serve dictate its application," McKay, 704 F.2d at 447, Defendants do not satisfy the exception's purpose in this case. Defendants are not public officers or employees or common carriers, see Restatement (Second) of Torts § 521, and they were not legally obligated to operate Hanford.

The prototypical example of a defendant entitled to the public duty exception is a utility company that is legally required to transport an ultrahazardous good, such as electricity, and causes injury to someone during transport. Courts have recognized a public duty exception in such cases, because common carriers must accept, carry, and deliver all goods offered to them for transport within the scope of the operating authority set forth in their permits. See, e.g., 16 U.S.C. § 824 et. seq. (granting the Federal Energy Regulatory Commission authority to establish guidelines for common carriers of electricity in interstate commerce); United States v. W. Processing Co., 756 F. Supp. 1416, 1421 (W.D. Wash. 1991). They cannot discriminate against customers or refuse to accept commodities that may be dangerous for transport. Id.

The case law therefore illustrates that the duty involved is the legal obligation to perform the abnormally dangerous activity in accordance with government orders. See, e.g., EAC Timberlane v. Pisces, Ltd, 745 F.2d 715, 721 n.12 (1st Cir. 1984) (noting that the public duty must be one imposed on the actor) (citing Actiesselskabet Ingrid v. Central R.R. Co. of New Jersey, 216 F. 72 (2d Cir. 1914); Town of East Troy v. Soo Line R.R. Co., 409 F. Supp. 326, 329 (E.D. Wis. 1976) (no strict liability for spillage of carbolic acid by derailment of common carrier train); Christ Church Parish v. Cadet Chem. Corp., 25 Conn. Supp. 191, 199 A.2d 707, 708-09 (Conn. Super. Ct. 1964) (transportation of twenty tons of various chemical substances); Pecan Shoppe of Springfield v. Tri-State Motor Transit Co., 573 S.W.2d 431, 438-39 (Mo. Ct. App. 1978) (transporter of explosives); Pope v. Edward M Rude Carrier Corp., 138 W. Va. 218, 75 S.E.2d 584, 595-96 (W. Va. 1953) (transporter of explosives). Qualifying entities must be operating pursuant to the mandate and control of the government; they must have little discretion over the manner in which they conduct their activities. See Actiesselskabet Ingrid, 216 F. at 78 ("It certainly would be an extraordinary doctrine for courts . . . to say that a common carrier is under legal obligation to transport dynamite and is an insurer against any damage which may result in the course of transportation, even though it has been guilty of no negligence which occasioned the explosion which caused the injury."); Pope, 75 S.E. 2d at 591-92 (holding no strict liability for common carrier transport of explosives); but see Lamb v. Martin Marietta Energy Sys., Inc., 835 F. Supp. 959 (W.D. Ky. 1993) (applying the public duty exception to a nuclear facility because under Kentucky law the public duty exception includes entities engaged in activities of public necessity even when there is no legal duty to perform them).

There was no government mandate here. The events giving rise to this litigation occurred before the government developed rules or the ability to control nuclear facilities. The government was relying on the expertise of defendants and not vice versa.

We should not confuse the legal concept of a public duty with popular notions of patriotic duty taken at personal sacrifice. Defendants may well have been acting at the government's urging during wartime. The public duty exception, however, was developed under state law in recognition of the need to protect private actors who are legally required to engage in ultrahazardous activities. No matter how strongly Defendants may have felt a patriotic duty, they had no legal duty to operate Hanford, and they are, therefore, not entitled to the public duty exception. The district court correctly found defendants subject to strict liability.

. . . .

VI. Medical Monitoring Claims.

Plaintiffs Pamela Durfey, Paulene Echo Hawk, and Dorothy George's only claim on appeal is for medical monitoring. They do not yet have any diseases attributable to Hanford radiation. Because in all relevant respects Plaintiffs are analogous to the plaintiffs who requested medical monitoring in 2002 in Berg, 293 F.3d 1127, Plaintiffs' claims were originally stayed pending this court's decision in that case.

We then decided Berg, in which we held that claims for medical monitoring are not compensable under the PAA, because they do not constitute claims of "bodily injury, sickness, disease, or death . . ." Berg, 293 F.3d at 1132-33 (citing 42 U.S.C. § 2014(q)). After our decision, Plaintiffs in this case asked the district court to remand their medical monitoring claims to state court. They claimed that Berg abrogated subject matter jurisdiction in federal court for all medical monitoring claims. Defendants opposed remand, arguing that Berg did not remove the district court's subject matter jurisdiction, but held only that a medical monitoring claim was not cognizable under the PAA.

. . . .

The PAA is the exclusive means of compensating victims for any and all claims arising out of nuclear incidents. Berg, 293 F.3d at 1132; In re TMI Litig., 940 F.2d at 854; see also 42 U.S.C. § 2014(hh), (w) (federal courts have jurisdiction over public liability actions, defined as "any suit asserting . . . any legal liability arising out of or resulting from a nuclear accident") (emphasis added). This result is consistent with Congress's explicit intent in enacting the 1988 Amendments and avoiding piecemeal litigation arising from nuclear incidents. We therefore affirm the district court's exercise of jurisdiction over Plaintiffs' medical monitoring claims and its conclusion pursuant to our decision in Berg that they were not compensable under the Act. The district court properly denied Plaintiffs' request for a remand to state court.

VII. First Bellwether Trial.

The remaining issues on appeal stem from a variety of legal and evidentiary rulings in the two trials. Three of the six Bellwether Plaintiffs, Goldbloom, Buckner, and Carlisle, lost at the first trial. Three of their evidentiary challenges constitute reversible error; the remaining arguments are meritless.

A. Causation.

We first decide whether under Washington law the district court properly instructed the jury in the bellwether trial on "but-for," and not "substantial factor," causation. Plaintiffs contend that the more lenient substantial factor test should apply because other factors could have contributed to their illnesses, such as smoking and genetics. We review the district court's application of Washington law de novo, Ostad v. Or. Health Scis. Univ., 327 F.3d 876, 883 (9th Cir. 2003), and we affirm the district court's instruction on but-for causation.

Under the PAA, Washington state law controls the standard of causation to be used in this case. See 42 U.S.C. § 2014(hh). . . . Washington courts will depart from the standard but-for causation instruction in favor of the substantial factor test only in three rare circumstances: (1) the plaintiff was excusably ignorant of the identity of the tortfeasor who caused his injury; (2) the plaintiff probably would have been injured anyway, but lost a significant chance of avoiding the injury; or (3) the plaintiff has been injured by multiple independent causes, each of which would have been sufficient to cause the injury. Gausvik v. Abbey, 126 Wn. App. 868, 107 P.3d 98, 108 (Wash. Ct. App. 2005); see also Daugert v. Pappas, 104 Wn.2d 254, 704 P.2d 600, 605-06 (Wash. 1985).

The parties agree that the first and second exceptions are not at issue here. . . .

Plaintiffs therefore appear to rely on the third type of substantial factor causation, which applies when there have been "multiple, independent causes," each of which alone is sufficient to cause the injury. Gausvik, 107 P.3d at 108. There are two requirements they must satisfy (1) there must have been multiple causes of the injury; and (2) any one cause alone was sufficient to cause the injury. Id. Plaintiffs can not satisfy the second requirement. Plaintiffs instead ask us to expand the substantial factor doctrine and apply the test when there are potentially multiple causes of each plaintiff's injury, such as radiation, smoking, genetics, or pregnancy, even though Plaintiffs cannot show that Hanford radiation alone would have been sufficient to cause the injury. Their reading of Washington law would allow the substantial factor test to supplant but-for causation in virtually all toxic tort cases. Such a result is inconsistent with existing Washington law, which applies the substantial factor test in very limited circumstances. See also RESTATEMENT (THIRD) OF TORTS § 26 cmt. j (Proposed Final Draft 2005) (eliminating the substantial factor test). We therefore hold that the district court properly instructed the jury on but-for causation.

B. Evidentiary Rulings Constituting Reversible Error.

. . . .

[The court found that several trial court evidentiary rulings constituted reversible error]

IX. Conclusion.

We are mindful of the time and resources both the district court and the parties have expended in this protracted litigation. We also realize that resolution is needed. We affirm the district court's major rulings. These relate to the government contractor defense, strict liability, and causation. We also affirm the district court's ruling on the medical monitoring claims and the judgment against Plaintiff Rhodes, as well as the judgments in favor of Plaintiffs Stanton and Wise. We reverse, on evidentiary grounds, the judgments against Plaintiffs Buckner, Carlisle, and Goldbloom. We remand those matters for further proceedings. . . . .

AFFIRMED IN PART; REVERSED AND REMANDED IN PART.

D. GOVERNMENT REGULATION

Over the past half-century, there has been a huge expansion in federal and state regulation of dangerous activities and substances. As a consequence, governmental regulation often plays a significant role in toxic tort litigation. Federal law regulating and requiring cleanup of hazardous substances under the Comprehensive Environmental Response, Compensation, and Liability Act of 1980 ("CERCLA") is one of many examples.

3550 STEVENS CREEK ASSOCIATES v. BARCLAYS BANK OF CALIFORNIA
United States Court of Appeals for the Ninth Circuit, 1990
915 F.2d 1355

RYMER, CIRCUIT JUDGE.

3550 Stevens Creek Associates appeals the entry of judgment on the pleadings in its action for recovery of costs incurred in the voluntary removal of asbestos during remodeling of a commercial building against Barclays Bank of California, a predecessor-in-interest who owned the building at the time materials containing asbestos were installed. The United States as Amicus Curiae has filed a brief on behalf of Stevens Creek. The question on appeal is whether a private party may recover its response costs for clean-up of asbestos installed in a commercial building under section 107(a)(2)(B) of the Comprehensive Environmental Response, Compensation, and Liability Act of 1980, 42 U.S.C. § 9607 (CERCLA). We hold that CERCLA does not permit such an action, and affirm.

In 1963, First Valley Corporation constructed a building, located at 3550 Stevens Creek Boulevard in San Jose, California, which contained asbestos insulation and fire retardants. In 1969, Barclays Bank acquired First Valley's assets. First Valley Corporation was dissolved in 1971, when Barclays acquired title to the property. Barclays sold the property to Stevens Creek in 1984. From 1984 through 1986, Stevens Creek remodeled the building, spending more than $100,000.00 in removing asbestos.

Stevens Creek brought this suit in district court under CERCLA, 42 U.S.C. §§ 9601-9657.

. . . CERCLA was enacted to "provide for liability, compensation, cleanup, and emergency response for hazardous substances released into the environment and the cleanup of inactive hazardous waste disposal sites." Pub. L. No. 96-510, 94 Stat. 2767 (1980). It generally imposes strict liability on owners and operators of facilities at which hazardous substances were disposed. 42 U.S.C. § 9607(a); *Hanna*, 882 F.2d at 394. To promote these objectives, Congress created a private claim for certain "response costs" against "various types of persons who contributed to the dumping of hazardous waste at a site." *Ascon Properties, Inc. v. Mobil Oil Co.*, 866 F.2d 1149, 1152 (9th Cir. 1989) (citations omitted).

Through the creation of Superfund, the federal government is empowered to respond to hazardous waste disposal. 42 U.S.C. §§ 9604-05, 9611-12. The statute also authorizes private parties to institute civil actions to recover the costs involved in the cleanup of hazardous wastes from those responsible for their creation. 42 U.S.C. § 9607(a) (1-4).

. . . A private party may recover its "response costs" for cleanup of hazardous wastes from a liable party under Section 107(a) of CERCLA, 42 U.S.C. § 9607(a).

. . . To prevail in a private cost recovery action, a plaintiff must establish that (1) the site on which the hazardous substances are contained is a "facility" under CERCLA's definition of that term, Section 101(9), 42 U.S.C. § 9601(9); (2) a "release" or "threatened release" of any "hazardous substance" from the facility has occurred, 42 U.S.C. § 9607(a)(4); (3) such "release" or "threatened release" has caused the plaintiff to incur response costs that were "necessary" and "consistent with the national contingency plan," 42 U.S.C. §§ 9607(a)(4) and (a)(4)(B); and (4) the defendant is within one of four classes of persons subject to the liability provisions of Section 107(a). *Ascon Properties*, 866 F.2d at 1152.

Stevens Creek argues that it has sufficiently pleaded all the allegations necessary for a claim under section 107, and that its cause of action is properly brought under the actual language of that section. Barclays contends that its predecessors-in-interest did not "dispose" of a hazardous substance within the meaning of section 107, and that the response limitations in section 104 are persuasive authority that removal of building materials containing asbestos is outside the scope of CERCLA.

. . . Stevens Creek argues that CERCLA is to be broadly construed and that private remedies were intended to supplement, indeed supplant, governmental response to environmental threats. We agree that the Act is to be given a broad interpretation to accomplish its remedial goals. *See First United Methodist Church*, 882 F.2d 862; *see also Wickland Oil Terminals v. Asarco*, 792 F.2d 887, 891, 892 (9th Cir. 1986). However we must reject a construction that the statute on its face does not permit, and the legislative history does not support.

CERCLA was designed to deal with the problem of inactive and abandoned hazardous waste disposal sites. U.S. Code Cong. & Admin. News 1980, at 6119, 6125. Necessarily it was the product of many compromises. *Shore Realty*, 759 F.2d at 1040. Section 107 could have, but did not, explicitly provide for the problem of the release of asbestos fibers from materials that are part of the structure of a building.

The legislative history shows that Congress intended just what CERCLA provides on its face. *Id.*

. . . To recognize a private cause of action under Section 107(a)(2) for the voluntary removal of asbestos from a commercial building would have substantial and far-reaching legal, financial, and practical consequences. As the Fourth Circuit has observed:

> to extend CERCLA's strict liability scheme to all past and present owners of buildings containing asbestos as well as to all persons who manufactured, transported, and installed asbestos products into buildings, would be to shift literally billions of dollars of removal cost liability based on nothing

more than an improvident interpretation of a statute that Congress never intended to apply in this context. Certainly, if Congress had intended for CERCLA to address the monumental asbestos problem, it would have said so more directly when it passed [the 1986 "Superfund" amendments to CERCLA].

Affirmed.

PREGERSON, J., dssenting

. . . The widespread use of asbestos in private building structures presents an extensive problem for which there is no common law remedy. Precisely because of the widespread nature of the problem, government Superfund resources are not sufficient to deal with these clean-up costs. Thus, without recognition of a statutory remedy of a private cause of action under section 107(a)(2), there will be no effective remedy for the damage and injury caused by the existence of asbestos in private structures.

---

1. What does CERCLA provide in regard to the private removal of hazardous wastes? Does CERCLA not go far enough in its regulatory impact?

2. Why does the court reject holding the bank liable for clean-up costs? If the bank were held liable, what would be the impact on the lending market? How could the plaintiff have protected itself? What would you argue against the dissent?

KALIK v. GENERAL ELECTRIC CO.
United States District Court, Western District Pennsylvania, 1987
658 F. Supp. 631

TEITELBAUM, DISTRICT JUDGE

This is an action by the owners of a site contaminated by hazardous substances against the manufacturers and suppliers of the products containing the hazardous substances to recover clean-up costs and damages under the Comprehensive Environmental Response Compensation and Liability Act of 1980 (CERCLA) and under state law.

The action was brought by the Kaliks, the owners of a site from which plaintiff Ben Kalik operated the Swissvale Auto Surplus Parts Company (SASPC), a scrap metal business. There are 27 defendants: 3 manufacturers of electrical components containing PCB's, a hazardous substance . . . , 23 suppliers of junk electrical components containing PCB's, and 1 defendant which is both a manufacturer of electrical components containing PCB's and a supplier of junk electrical components containing PCB's.

The complaint makes the following allegations. Between 1970 and 1984 SASPC purchased junk electrical components for use as scrap. The junk electrical components contained PCB's, a hazardous substance. During the course of storage, handling and dismantling of the junk electrical components, PCB contaminated oil spilled or leaked onto the site. The combustion of PCB's under certain circumstances may produce dioxins, a highly toxic substance. As a furnace was used in dismantling and processing the junk electrical components, dioxins polluted the site. The United States Environmental Protection Agency (EPA) has spent $1.9 million to clean up the site; the plaintiffs have spent $22,000 to remove PCB contaminated oil from the site.

Plaintiffs seek recovery of clean-up costs, damages for injuries to the site and to the business, and a declaration of rights.

. . . The complaint identifies GE as a manufacturer of electrical components containing PCB's. GE is named as a defendant in two counts: Count 1 sets forth a products liability claim under § 402A of the Restatement (2d) of Torts, Count 5 sets forth a claim for a negligent failure to warn.

. . . GE moves to dismiss for failure to state a claim. GE's position derives from the fact that it manufactured new electrical components, but that SASPC dealt in junk electrical components. Based on these facts, GE makes a three part argument.

First, GE argues that the plaintiffs are not within the class of persons protected under § 402A or the duty to warn. Specifically, GE contends that the allegations of the complaint that SASPC dealt in junk electrical components establishes as a matter of law that the plaintiffs are not "users" of the new electrical components manufactured by GE entitled to the protection of § 402A or to warnings.

Second, GE argues that it is not a person subject to liability under § 402A. Specifically, GE contends that there are no allegations that it sold junk electrical components which would be necessary to impose liability under § 402A.

Third, GE argues that its product has been substantially changed precluding liability under § 402A. Specifically, GE contends that there are no allegations that the new electrical components it manufactured were not substantially changed and, in fact, the allegations that SASPC dealt in junk electrical components suggest that GE's product was substantially changed, thereby precluding liability under § 402A.

Although GE has framed its argument in three parts focusing on the persons protected, the persons subject to liability, and the product, these three parts can all be subsumed within the broader inquiry of whether plaintiffs' use of defendant's product was reasonably foreseeable by defendant manufacturer. It is to this question that the Court now turns.

Liability exists under § 402A or for a negligent failure to warn — only if there was a use of the product reasonably foreseeable to the manufacturer. Under § 402A a product is defective if it lacks any element necessary to make it safe for its intended use or contains any condition that makes it unsafe for its intended use.

. . . Nevertheless, it has been held, as a matter of law, that the recycling of a product, after it has been destroyed, is not a use of the product reasonably foreseeable to the manufacturer. *Johnson v. Murph Metals, Inc.*, 562 F. Supp. 246 (N.D. TX 1983). In *Johnson* the defendant manufactured automotive batteries. After the useful life of the batteries, the batteries were often resold in order to recycle the lead in the batteries. In the recycling process, the batteries were first destroyed, then the lead was extracted, and then the lead was introduced into a lead smelting process. The plaintiffs, employees of lead smelting companies, alleged that during the lead smelting process, they were exposed to harmful lead fumes and lead dust. It was stipulated that the employees did not sustain any harm while the batteries were intact or while the batteries were being destroyed. The employees asserted the battery manufacturer was liable under § 402A and for a negligent failure to warn. The Court held, as a matter of law, that it was "untenable to find that the creation of dangerous gases due to the smelting of scrap metal is a 'use' of defendant's automotive batteries." 562 F. Supp. at 249.

It has also been held, as a matter of law, that the destruction of a product is not a use of the product reasonably foreseeable to the manufacturer.

. . . In the present case the plaintiffs allege injuries sustained during the course of storage and handling of junk electrical components, and also injuries sustained during the course of dismantling and processing junk electrical components. . . . [T]hese decisions do provide a persuasive basis for concluding, as a matter of law, that the dismantling and processing of junk electrical components was not a reasonably foreseeable use of GE's product, and the Court so finds. Accordingly, the allegations of injury as a result of the dismantling and processing of junk electrical components will be dismissed.

---

1. What "law" does the court use in applying CERCLA to these facts? What is the source of the "foreseeable use" concept?

2. Argue that GE could foresee Swissvale's "use" of the product. If so, what is the real reason for the decision? According to *Monsanto Co. v. Reed*, 950 S.W.2d 811 (Ky. 1997), "many jurisdictions . . . have declined to find a duty of care running from the supplier of the goods to salvage yard workers who allege injury during the scrapping and dismantling of chattels." Why is this the case?

3. Why is the burden placed upon the suppliers of junk electrical components but not upon the manufacturers of electrical components? How can the suppliers of the junk components protect themselves in situations like this case?

BURLINGTON NORTHERN AND SANTA FE RAILWAY COMPANY v. UNITED STATES
Supreme Court of the United States, 2009
129 S. Ct. 1870, 173 L. Ed. 2d 812

JUSTICE STEVENS delivered the opinion of the Court.

In 1980, Congress enacted the Comprehensive Environmental Response, Compensation, and Liability Act (CERCLA), 94 Stat. 2767, as amended, 42 U.S.C. §§ 9601-9675, in response to the serious environmental and health risks posed by industrial pollution. *See United States v. Bestfoods*, 524 U.S. 51, 55, 118 S.Ct. 1876, 141 L.Ed.2d 43 (1998). The Act was designed to promote the " 'timely cleanup of hazardous waste sites' " and to ensure that the costs of such cleanup efforts were borne by those responsible for the contamination. *Consolidated Edison Co. of N.Y.*

v. UGI Util., Inc., 423 F.3d 90, 94 (C.A.2 2005); see also *Meghrig v. KFC Western, Inc.*, 516 U.S. 479, 483, 116 S.Ct. 1251, 134 L.Ed.2d 121 (1996); *Dedham Water Co. v. Cumberland Farms Dairy, Inc.*, 805 F.2d 1074, 1081 (C.A.1 1986). These cases raise the questions whether and to what extent a party associated with a contaminated site may be held responsible for the full costs of remediation.

I

In 1960, Brown & Bryant, Inc. (B & B) began operating an agricultural chemical distribution business, purchasing pesticides and other chemical products from suppliers such as Shell Oil Company (Shell). Using its own equipment, B & B applied its products to customers' farms. B & B opened its business on a 3.8 acre parcel of former farmland in Arvin, California, and in 1975, expanded operations onto an adjacent.9 acre parcel of land owned jointly by the Atchison, Topeka & Santa Fe Railway Company, and the Southern Pacific Transportation Company (now known respectively as the Burlington Northern and Santa Fe Railway Company and Union Pacific Railroad Company) (Railroads). Both parcels of the Arvin facility were graded toward a sump and drainage pond located on the southeast corner of the primary parcel. *See* Appendix, *infra*. Neither the sump nor the drainage pond was lined until 1979, allowing waste water and chemical runoff from the facility to seep into the ground water below.

During its years of operation, B & B stored and distributed various hazardous chemicals on its property. Among these were the herbicide dinoseb, sold by Dow Chemicals, and the pesticides D-D and Nemagon, both sold by Shell. Dinoseb was stored in 55-gallon drums and 5-gallon containers on a concrete slab outside B & B's warehouse. Nemagon was stored in 30-gallon drums and 5-gallon containers inside the warehouse. Originally, B & B purchased D-D in 55-gallon drums; beginning in the mid-1960's, however, Shell began requiring its distributors to maintain bulk storage facilities for D-D. From that time onward, B & B purchased D-D in bulk. 1 When B & B purchased D-D, Shell would arrange for delivery by common carrier, f.o.b. destination. When the product arrived, it was transferred from tanker trucks to a bulk storage tank located on B & B's primary parcel. From there, the chemical was transferred to bobtail trucks, nurse tanks, and pull rigs. During each of these transfers leaks and spills could — and often did — occur. Although the common carrier and B & B used buckets to catch spills from hoses and gaskets connecting the tanker trucks to its bulk storage tank, the buckets sometimes overflowed or were knocked over, causing D-D to spill onto the ground during the transfer process. Aware that spills of D-D were commonplace among its distributors, in the late 1970's Shell took several steps to encourage the safe handling of its products. Shell provided distributors with detailed safety manuals and instituted a voluntary discount program for distributors that made improvements in their bulk handling and safety facilities.

Later, Shell revised its program to require distributors to obtain an inspection by a qualified engineer and provide self-certification of compliance with applicable laws and regulations. B & B's Arvin facility was inspected twice, and in 1981, B & B certified to Shell that it had made a number of recommended improvements to its facilities. Despite these improvements, B & B remained a " '[s]loppy' [o]perator."

. . . Over the course of B & B's 28 years of operation, delivery spills, equipment failures, and the rinsing of tanks and trucks allowed Nemagon, D-D and dinoseb to seep into the soil and upper levels of ground water of the Arvin facility. In 1983, the California Department of Toxic Substances Control (DTSC) began investigating B & B's violation of hazardous waste laws, and the United States Environmental Protection Agency (EPA) soon followed suit, discovering significant contamination of soil and ground water. Of particular concern was a plume of contaminated ground water located under the facility that threatened to leach into an adjacent supply of potential drinking water.

Although B & B undertook some efforts at remediation, by 1989 it had become insolvent and ceased all operations. That same year, the Arvin facility was added to the National Priority List, *see* 54 Fed.Reg. 41027, and subsequently, DTSC and EPA (Governments) exercised their authority under 42 U.S.C. § 9604 to undertake cleanup efforts at the site. By 1998, the Governments had spent more than $8 million responding to the site contamination; their costs have continued to accrue.

In 1991, EPA issued an administrative order to the Railroads directing them, as owners of a portion of the property on which the Arvin facility was located, to perform certain remedial tasks in connection with the site. The Railroads did so, incurring expenses of more than $3 million in the process. Seeking to recover at least a portion of their response costs, in 1992 the Railroads brought suit against B & B in the United States District Court for the Eastern District of California. In 1996, that lawsuit was consolidated with two recovery actions brought by DTSC and EPA against Shell and the Railroads.

The District Court conducted a 6-week bench trial in 1999 and four years later entered a judgment in favor of the Governments. In a lengthy order supported by 507 separate findings of fact and conclusions of law, the court held that both the Railroads and Shell were potentially responsible parties (PRPs) under CERCLA — the Railroads because they were owners of a portion of the facility, see 42 U.S.C. §§ 9607(a)(1)-(2), and Shell because it had "arranged for" the disposal of hazardous substances through its sale and delivery of D-D, see § 9607(a)(3).

Although the court found the parties liable, it did not impose joint and several liability on Shell and the Railroads for the entire response cost incurred by the Governments. The court found that the site contamination created a single harm but concluded that the harm was divisible and therefore capable of apportionment. Based on three figures — the percentage of the total area of the facility that was owned by the Railroads, the duration of B & B's business divided by the term of the Railroads' lease, and the Court's determination that only two of three polluting chemicals spilled on the leased parcel required remediation and that those two chemicals were responsible for roughly two-thirds of the overall site contamination requiring remediation — the court apportioned the Railroads' liability as 9% of the Governments' total response cost. Based on estimations of chemicals spills of Shell products, the court held Shell liable for 6% of the total site response cost.

The Governments appealed the District Court's apportionment, and Shell cross-appealed the court's finding of liability. The Court of Appeals acknowledged that Shell did not qualify as a "traditional" arranger under § 9607(a)(3), insofar as it had not contracted with B & B to directly dispose of a hazardous waste product.

520 F.3d 918, 948 (C.A.9 2008). Nevertheless, the court stated that Shell could still be held liable under a " 'broader' category of arranger liability" if the "disposal of hazardous wastes [wa]s a foreseeable byproduct of, but not the purpose of, the transaction giving rise to" arranger liability. *Ibid.* Relying on CERCLA's definition of "disposal," which covers acts such as "leaking" and "spilling," 42 U.S.C. § 6903(3), the Ninth Circuit concluded that an entity could arrange for "disposal" "even if it did not intend to dispose" of a hazardous substance. 520 F.3d, at 949.

Applying that theory of arranger liability to the District Court's findings of fact, the Ninth Circuit held that Shell arranged for the disposal of a hazardous substance through its sale and delivery of D-D:

> "Shell arranged for delivery of the substances to the site by its subcontractors; was aware of, and to some degree dictated, the transfer arrangements; knew that some leakage was likely in the transfer process; and provided advice and supervision concerning safe transfer and storage. Disposal of a hazardous substance was thus a necessary part of the sale and delivery process." *Id.*, at 950.

Under such circumstances, the court concluded, arranger liability was not precluded by the fact that the purpose of Shell's action had been to transport a useful and previously unused product to B & B for sale.

On the subject of apportionment, the Court of Appeals found "no dispute" on the question whether the harm caused by Shell and the Railroads was capable of apportionment. *Id.*, at 942. The court observed that a portion of the site contamination occurred before the Railroad parcel became part of the facility, only some of the hazardous substances were stored on the Railroad parcel, and "only some of the water on the facility washed over the Railroads' site." *Ibid.* With respect to Shell, the court noted that not all of the hazardous substances spilled on the facility had been sold by Shell. Given those facts, the court readily concluded that "the contamination traceable to the Railroads and Shell, with adequate information, would be allocable, as would be the cost of cleaning up that contamination." *Ibid.* Nevertheless, the Court of Appeals held that the District Court erred in finding that the record established a reasonable basis for apportionment. Because the burden of proof on the question of apportionment rested with Shell and the Railroads, the Court of Appeals reversed the District Court's apportionment of liability and held Shell and the Railroads jointly and severally liable for the Governments' cost of responding to the contamination of the Arvin facility.

The Railroads and Shell moved for rehearing en banc, which the Court of Appeals denied over the dissent of eight judges. *See id.*, at 952 (Bea, J., dissenting). We granted certiorari to determine whether Shell was properly held liable as an entity that had "arranged for disposal" of hazardous substances within the meaning of § 9607(a)(3), and whether Shell and the Railroads were properly held liable for all response costs incurred by EPA and the State of California. . . . Finding error on both points, we now reverse.

II

CERCLA imposes strict liability for environmental contamination upon four broad classes of PRPs:

"(1) the owner and operator of a vessel or a facility,

"(2) any person who at the time of disposal of any hazardous substance owned or operated any facility at which such hazardous substances were disposed of,

"(3) any person who by contract, agreement, or otherwise arranged for disposal or treatment, or arranged with a transporter for transport for disposal or treatment, of hazardous substances owned or possessed by such person, by any other party or entity, at any facility or incineration vessel owned or operated by another party or entity and containing such hazardous substances, and

"(4) any person who accepts or accepted any hazardous substances for transport to disposal or treatment facilities, incineration vessels or sites selected by such person, from which there is a release, or a threatened release which causes the incurrence of response costs, of a hazardous substance. . . ." 42 U.S.C. § 9607(a).

Once an entity is identified as a PRP, it may be compelled to clean up a contaminated area or reimburse the Government for its past and future response costs. *See Cooper Industries, Inc. v. Aviall Services, Inc.*, 543 U.S. 157, 161, 125 S.Ct. 577, 160 L.Ed.2d 548 (2004). In these cases, it is undisputed that the Railroads qualify as PRPs under both §§ 9607(a)(1) and 9607(a)(2) because they owned the land leased by B & B at the time of the contamination and continue to own it now. The more difficult question is whether Shell also qualifies as a PRP under § 9607(a)(3) by virtue of the circumstances surrounding its sales to B & B.

To determine whether Shell may be held liable as an arranger, we begin with the language of the statute. As relevant here, § 9607(a)(3) applies to an entity that "arrange[s] for disposal . . . of hazardous substances." It is plain from the language of the statute that CERCLA liability would attach under § 9607(a)(3) if an entity were to enter into a transaction for the sole purpose of discarding a used and no longer useful hazardous substance. It is similarly clear that an entity could not be held liable as an arranger merely for selling a new and useful product if the purchaser of that product later, and unbeknownst to the seller, disposed of the product in a way that led to contamination. *See Freeman v. Glaxo Wellcome, Inc.*, 189 F.3d 160, 164 (C.A.2 1999); *Florida Power & Light Co. v. Allis Chalmers Corp.*, 893 F.2d 1313, 1318 (C.A.11 1990). Less clear is the liability attaching to the many permutations of "arrangements" that fall between these two extremes — cases in which the seller has some knowledge of the buyers' planned disposal or whose motives for the "sale" of a hazardous substance are less than clear. In such cases, courts have concluded that the determination whether an entity is an arranger requires a fact-intensive inquiry that looks beyond the parties' characterization of the transaction as a "disposal" or a "sale" and seeks to discern whether the arrangement was one Congress intended to fall within the scope of CERCLA's strict-liability provisions. . . .

Although we agree that the question whether § 9607(a) (3) liability attaches is fact intensive and case specific, such liability may not extend beyond the limits of the statute itself. Because CERCLA does not specifically define what it means to "arrang[e] for" disposal of a hazardous substance . . . we give the phrase its ordinary meaning. . . . In common parlance, the word "arrange" implies action directed to a specific purpose. See Merriam-Webster's Collegiate Dictionary 64 (10th ed.1993) (defining "arrange" as "to make preparations for; plan[;] . . . to bring about an agreement or understanding concerning"); *see also Amcast Indus. Corp.,* 2 F.3d, at 751 (words " 'arranged for' . . . imply intentional action"). Consequently, under the plain language of the statute, an entity may qualify as an arranger under § 9607(a)(3) when it takes intentional steps to dispose of a hazardous substance. . . .

The Governments do not deny that the statute requires an entity to "arrang[e] for" disposal; however, they interpret that phrase by reference to the statutory term "disposal," which the Act broadly defines as "the discharge, deposit, injection, dumping, spilling, leaking, or placing of any solid waste or hazardous waste into or on any land or water." 42 U.S.C. § 6903(3); see also § 9601(29) (adopting the definition of "disposal" contained in the Solid Waste Disposal Act). The Governments assert that by including unintentional acts such as "spilling" and "leaking" in the definition of disposal, Congress intended to impose liability on entities not only when they directly dispose of waste products but also when they engage in legitimate sales of hazardous substances knowing that some disposal may occur as a collateral consequence of the sale itself. Applying that reading of the statute, the Governments contend that Shell arranged for the disposal of D-D within the meaning of § 9607(a)(3) by shipping D-D to B & B under conditions it knew would result in the spilling of a portion of the hazardous substance by the purchaser or common carrier. . . . Because these spills resulted in wasted D-D, a result Shell anticipated, the Governments insist that Shell was properly found to have arranged for the disposal of D-D.

While it is true that in some instances an entity's knowledge that its product will be leaked, spilled, dumped, or otherwise discarded may provide evidence of the entity's intent to dispose of its hazardous wastes, knowledge alone is insufficient to prove that an entity "planned for" the disposal, particularly when the disposal occurs as a peripheral result of the legitimate sale of an unused, useful product. In order to qualify as an arranger, Shell must have entered into the sale of D-D with the intention that at least a portion of the product be disposed of during the transfer process by one or more of the methods described in § 6903(3). Here, the facts found by the District Court do not support such a conclusion.

Although the evidence adduced at trial showed that Shell was aware that minor, accidental spills occurred during the transfer of D-D from the common carrier to B & B's bulk storage tanks after the product had arrived at the Arvin facility and had come under B & B's stewardship, the evidence does not support an inference that Shell intended such spills to occur. To the contrary, the evidence revealed that Shell took numerous steps to encourage its distributors to reduce the likelihood of such spills, providing them with detailed safety manuals, requiring them to maintain adequate storage facilities, and providing discounts for those that took safety precautions. Although Shell's efforts were less than wholly successful, given these facts, Shell's mere knowledge that spills and leaks continued to occur is insufficient grounds for concluding that Shell "arranged for" the disposal of DD within the meaning of § 9607(a)(3). Accordingly, we conclude that Shell was not liable as an arranger for the contamination that occurred at B & B's Arvin facility.

III

Having concluded that Shell is not liable as an arranger, we need not decide whether the Court of Appeals erred in reversing the District Court's apportionment of Shell's liability for the cost of remediation. We must, however, determine whether the Railroads were properly held jointly and severally liable for the full cost of the Governments' response efforts.

The seminal opinion on the subject of apportionment in CERCLA actions was written in 1983 by Chief Judge Carl Rubin of the United States District Court for the Southern District of Ohio. *United States v. Chem-Dyne Corp.*, 572 F.Supp. 802. After reviewing CERCLA's history, Chief Judge Rubin concluded that although the Act imposed a "strict liability standard," *id.*, at 805, it did not mandate "joint and several" liability in every case. *See id.*, at 807. Rather, Congress intended the scope of liability to "be determined from traditional and evolving principles of common law[.]" Id., at 808. The *Chem-Dyne* approach has been fully embraced by the Courts of Appeals. *See, e.g., In re Bell Petroleum Services, Inc.*, 3 F.3d 889, 901-902 (C.A.5 1993); *United States v. Alcan Aluminum Corp.*, 964 F.2d 252, 268 (C.A.3 1992); *O'Neil v. Picillo*, 883 F.2d 176, 178 (C.A.1 1989); *United States v. Monsanto Co.*, 858 F.2d 160, 171-173 (C.A.4 1988).

Following *Chem-Dyne*, the courts of appeals have acknowledged that "[t]he universal starting point for divisibility of harm analyses in CERCLA cases" is § 433A of the Restatement (Second) of Torts. *United States v. Hercules, Inc.*, 247 F.3d 706, 717 (C.A.8 2001); *Chem-Nuclear Systems, Inc. v. Bush*, 292 F.3d 254, 259 (C.A.D.C.2002); *United States v. R.W. Meyer, Inc.*, 889 F.2d 1497, 1507 (C.A.6 1989). Under the Restatement,

> "when two or more persons acting independently caus[e] a distinct or single harm for which there is a reasonable basis for division according to the contribution of each, each is subject to liability only for the portion of the total harm that he has himself caused. Restatement (Second) of Torts, §§ 433A, 881 (1976); Prosser, Law of Torts, pp. 313-314 (4th ed.1971). . . . But where two or more persons cause a single and indivisible harm, each is subject to liability for the entire harm. Restatement (Second) of Torts, § 875; Prosser, at 315-316." *Chem-Dyne Corp.*, 572 F.Supp., at 810.

In other words, apportionment is proper when "there is a reasonable basis for determining the contribution of each cause to a single harm." Restatement (Second) of Torts § 433A(1)(b), p. 434 (1963-1964).

Not all harms are capable of apportionment, however, and CERCLA defendants seeking to avoid joint and several liability bear the burden of proving that a reasonable basis for apportionment exists. *See Chem-Dyne Corp.*, 572 F.Supp., at 810 (citing Restatement (Second) of Torts § 433B (1976)) (placing burden of proof on party seeking apportionment). When two or more causes produce a single, indivisible harm, "courts have refused to make an arbitrary apportionment for its own sake, and each of the causes is charged with responsibility for the entire harm." Restatement (Second) of Torts § 433A, Comment i, p. 440 (1963-1964).

Neither the parties nor the lower courts dispute the principles that govern apportionment in CERCLA cases, and both the District Court and Court of Appeals agreed that the harm created by the contamination of the Arvin site, although singular, was theoretically capable of apportionment. The question then is whether the record provided a reasonable basis for the District Court's conclusion that the Railroads were liable for only 9% of the harm caused by contamination at the Arvin facility.

The District Court criticized the Railroads for taking a " 'scorched earth,' all-or-nothing approach to liability," failing to acknowledge any responsibility for the release of hazardous substances that occurred on their parcel throughout the 13-year period of B & B's lease. According to the District Court, the Railroads' position on liability, combined with the Governments' refusal to acknowledge the potential divisibility of the harm, complicated the apportioning of liability. . . . Yet despite the parties' failure to assist the court in linking the evidence supporting apportionment to the proper allocation of liability, the District Court ultimately concluded that this was "a classic 'divisible in terms of degree' case, both as to the time period in which defendants' conduct occurred, and ownership existed, and as to the estimated maximum contribution of each party's activities that released hazardous substances that caused Site contamination." . . . Consequently, the District Court apportioned liability, assigning the Railroads 9% of the total remediation costs.

The District Court calculated the Railroads' liability based on three figures. First, the court noted that the Railroad parcel constituted only 19% of the surface area of the Arvin site. Second, the court observed that the Railroads had leased their parcel to B & B for 13 years, which was only 45% of the time B & B operated the Arvin facility. Finally, the court found that the volume of hazardous-substance-releasing activities on the B & B property was at least 10 times greater than the releases that occurred on the Railroad parcel, and it concluded that only spills of two chemicals, Nemagon and dinoseb (not D-D), substantially contributed to the contamination that had originated on the Railroad parcel and that those two chemicals had contributed to two-thirds of the overall site contamination requiring remediation. The court then multiplied.19 by.45 by.66 (two-thirds) and rounded up to determine that the Railroads were responsible for approximately 6% of the remediation costs. "Allowing for calculation errors up to 50%," the court concluded that the Railroads could be held responsible for 9% of the total CERCLA response cost for the Arvin site. . . .

The Court of Appeals criticized the evidence on which the District Court's conclusions rested, finding a lack of sufficient data to establish the precise proportion of contamination that occurred on the relative portions of the Arvin facility and the rate of contamination in the years prior to B & B's addition of the Railroad parcel. The court noted that neither the duration of the lease nor the size of the leased area alone was a reliable measure of the harm caused by activities on the property owned by the Railroads, and — as the court's upward adjustment confirmed — the court had relied on estimates rather than specific and detailed records as a basis for its conclusions.

Despite these criticisms, we conclude that the facts contained in the record reasonably supported the apportionment of liability. The District Court's detailed findings make it abundantly clear that the primary pollution at the Arvin facility was contained in an unlined sump and an unlined pond in the southeastern portion of the facility most distant from the Railroads' parcel and that the spills of hazardous chemicals that occurred on the Railroad parcel contributed to no more than 10% of the total site contamination, . . . some of which did not require remediation. With those background facts in mind, we are persuaded that it was reasonable for the court to use the size of the leased parcel and the duration of the lease as the starting point for its analysis. Although the Court of Appeals faulted the District Court for relying on the "simplest of considerations: percentages of land area, time of ownership, and types of hazardous products," 520 F.3d, at 943, these were the same factors the court had earlier acknowledged were relevant to the apportionment analysis. *See id.*, at 936, n. 18 ("We of course agree with our sister circuits that, if adequate information is available, divisibility may be established by 'volumetric, chronological, or other types of evidence,' including appropriate geographic considerations" (citations omitted)).

The Court of Appeals also criticized the District Court's assumption that spills of Nemagon and dinoseb were responsible for only two-thirds of the chemical spills requiring remediation, observing that each PRP's share of the total harm was not necessarily equal to the quantity of pollutants that were deposited on its portion of the total facility. Although the evidence adduced by the parties did not allow the court to calculate precisely the amount of hazardous chemicals contributed by the Railroad parcel to the total site contamination or the exact percentage of harm caused by each chemical, the evidence did show that fewer spills occurred on the Railroad parcel and that of those spills that occurred, not all were carried across the Railroad parcel to the B & B sump and pond from which most of the contamination originated. The fact that no D-D spills on the Railroad parcel required remediation lends strength to the District Court's conclusion that the Railroad parcel contributed only Nemagon and dinoseb in quantities requiring remediation.

The District Court's conclusion that those two chemicals accounted for only two-thirds of the contamination requiring remediation finds less support in the record; however, any miscalculation on that point is harmless in light of the District Court's ultimate allocation of liability, which included a 50% margin of error equal to the 3% reduction in liability the District Court provided based on its assessment of the effect of the Nemagon and dinoseb spills. . . . Because the District Court's ultimate allocation of liability is supported by the evidence and comports with the apportionment principles outlined above, we reverse the Court of Appeals' conclusion that the Railroads are subject to joint and several liability for all response costs arising out of the contamination of the Arvin facility.

IV

For the foregoing reasons, we conclude that the Court of Appeals erred by holding Shell liable as an arranger under CERCLA for the costs of remediating environmental contamination at the Arvin, California facility. Furthermore, we conclude that the District Court reasonably apportioned the Railroads' share of the site remediation costs at 9%. The judgment is reversed, and the cases are remanded for further proceedings consistent with this opinion.

It is so ordered.

JUSTICE GINSBURG, dissenting.

Although the question is close, I would uphold the determinations of the courts below that Shell qualifies as an arranger within the compass of the Comprehensive Environmental Response, Compensation and Liability Act (CERCLA). . . .

E.   THE NATURE OF INJURY

ANDERSON v. W.R. GRACE & CO.
United States District Court, District of Massachusetts, 1986
628 F. Supp. 1219

SKINNER, J.

This case arises out of the defendants' alleged contamination of the ground-water in certain areas of Woburn, Massachusetts, with chemicals, including trichloroethylene and tetrachloroethylene. Plaintiffs allege that two of Woburn's water wells, Wells G and H, drew upon the contaminated water until the wells were closed in 1979 and that exposure to this contaminated water caused them to suffer severe injuries.

Of the 33 plaintiffs in this action, five are the administrators of minor[s] who died of leukemia allegedly caused by exposure to the chemicals. They bring suit for wrongful death and conscious pain and suffering. Sixteen of the 28 living plaintiffs are members of the decedents' immediate families. These plaintiffs seek to recover for the emotional distress caused by witnessing the decedents' deaths. Three of the living plaintiffs also contracted leukemia and currently are either in remission or treatment for the disease. The 25 non-leukemic plaintiffs allege that exposure to the contaminated water cause[d] a variety of illnesses and damaged their bodily systems. All of the living plaintiffs seek to recover for their illnesses and other damage, increased risk of developing future illness, and emotional distress.

. . . .

Claims for Emotional Distress.

Defendants move for summary judgment on plaintiffs' claims of emotional distress on the grounds that the non-leukemic plaintiffs' distress was not caused by any physical injury. They also move for summary judgment on the emotional distress claims of plaintiffs who witnessed a family member die of leukemia, arguing that Massachusetts law does not recognize such a claim. Some plaintiffs are in both of these separate categories.

1. *Physical Injury.*

In seeking summary judgment on the non-leukemic plaintiffs' claims for emotional distress, defendants rely on *Payton v. Abbott Labs*, 386 Mass. 540, 437 N.E.2d 171 (1982). In *Payton*, the Supreme Judicial Court answered a certified question as follows:

> [I]n order for . . . plaintiffs to recover for negligently inflicted emotional distress, [they] must allege and prove [they] suffered physical harm as a result of the conduct which caused the emotional distress. We answer, further, that a plaintiffs physical harm must either cause or be caused by the emotional distress alleged, and that the physical harm must be manifested by objective symptomatology and substantiated by expert medical testimony.

Id. at 437 N.E.2d 181. Defendants attack plaintiffs' claims of emotional distress at three points: they argue that plaintiffs did not suffer physical harm as a result of defendants' allegedly negligent conduct; that, if the plaintiffs did suffer any harm, it was not "manifested by objective symptomatology"; and that any manifest physical harm did not cause the claimed emotional distress.

The Third Amended Complaint alleges only that "each plaintiff has suffered a direct adverse physical affect [sic]. . . ." Plaintiffs make a slightly more specific claim to physical injury in their answers to interrogatories. Each plaintiff states that exposure to contaminants in the water drawn from Wells G and H

> affected my body's ability to fight disease, [and] caused harm to my body's organ systems, including my respiratory, immunological, blood, central nervous, gastro-intestinal, urinary-renal systems. . . .

Plaintiffs' Further Answers to Interrogatories Propounded by Beatrice Foods Co., Answer 8(a).

This alleged harm is sufficient to maintain plaintiffs' claims for emotional distress under *Payton*. As used in that opinion, the term "physical harm" denotes "harm to the bodies of the plaintiffs." 437 N.E.2d at 175 n.4. In requiring physical harm rather than mere "injury" as an element of proof in a claim for emotional distress, the court required that a plaintiff show some actual physical damage as a predicate to suit. *See Leardi v. Brown*, 394 Mass. 151, 474 N.E.2d 1094, 1101 (1985) (distinguishing between "injury" and "harm").

Defendants argue that plaintiffs' alleged harm is "subcellular" and therefore not the type of harm required to support a claim for emotional distress under *Payton*. I disagree. The Supreme Judicial Court requires that plaintiffs' physical harm be "manifested by objective symptomatology and substantiated by expert medical testimony." 437 N.E.2d at 181. In setting forth this requirement, the court did not distinguish between gross and subcellular harm. Instead, the court drew a line between harm which can be proven to exist through expert medical testimony based on objective evidence and harm which is merely speculative or based solely on a plaintiff's unsupported assertions. The phrase "manifested by objective symptomatology" does not indicate that the necessary harm need be immediately apparent but that its existence must be objectively evidenced. Where, as in this case, the harm is not obvious to the layman, its existence may not be demonstrated solely by the complaints of the alleged victim; it must also be "substantiated by expert medical testimony." Upon review of the pleadings and the affidavits of plaintiffs' expert, I cannot say as a matter of law that this standard will not be met at trial.

. . . Under *Payton*, of course, injury is not sufficient. The harm allegedly caused by defendants' conduct must either have caused or been caused by the emotional distress. 437 N.E.2d at 181; *see DiGiovanni v. Latimer*, 390 Mass. 265, 454 N.E.2d 483, 486 (1983). The Complaint does not state that plaintiffs' emotional distress was caused by any physical harm. Plaintiffs only allege that "[a]s a result of the knowledge that they . . . have consumed hazardous chemicals, the plaintiffs have suffered and will continue to suffer great emotional distress." Third Amended Complaint ¶ 65.

. . . [C]ertain elements of plaintiffs' emotional distress stem from the physical harm to their immune systems allegedly caused by defendants' conduct and are compensable. Plaintiffs have stated that the illnesses contributed to by exposure to the contaminated water have caused them anxiety and pain. Plaintiffs' Further Answers to Interrogatories Propounded by Beatrice Foods Co., Answer (d). The excerpts from plaintiffs' depositions appended to defendants' motion indicate that plaintiffs are also worried over the increased susceptibility to disease which results from the alleged harm to their immune systems and exposure to carcinogens. As these elements of emotional distress arise out of plaintiffs' injuries, plaintiffs may seek to recover for them.

. . . Accordingly, defendants' motion for summary judgment on the non-leukemic plaintiffs' claims for emotional distress is *denied.*

. . . .

Claims for Increased Risk of Future Illness.

Plaintiffs seek to recover damages for the increased risk of serious illness they claim resulted from consumption of and exposure to contaminated water. Defendants argue that Massachusetts does not recognize a claim for increased risk of future harm, regardless of whether plaintiffs have suffered physical harm. This issue has not been directly addressed by the Massachusetts courts. It was not decided in *Payton*. . . .

Plaintiffs view their claim as merely an element of damages, compensation for the risk of probable future consequences stemming from negligently inflicted present harm.

. . . To view the risk of a future illness as part of damages is to ignore the question of whether a cause of action has accrued. Defendants argue that the cause of action for any future serious illness, including leukemia and other cancers, has not yet accrued because the injury has not yet occurred.[1] This is the rationale of the discovery rule applied to latent disease cases in Massachusetts under which the

---

[1] The weight of authority would deny plaintiffs a cause of action solely for increased risk because no "injury" has occurred. . . .

injury is equated with the manifestation of the disease. *Olsen v. Bell Telephone Laboratories, Inc.*, 388 Mass. 171, 445 N.E.2d 609, 612 (1983) (cause of action accrues when insidious disease manifests itself). The question thus becomes whether, upon the manifestation of one or more diseases, a cause of action accrues for all prospective diseases so that a plaintiff may seek to recover for physically distinct and separate diseases which may develop in the future.

The answer to this question depends on the connection between the illnesses plaintiffs ha[ve] suffered and fear they will suffer in the future. Unfortunately, the nature of plaintiffs' claim for increased risk of future illness is unclear on two counts. Nothing in the present record indicates the magnitude of the increased risk or the diseases which plaintiffs may suffer. Paragraph 63 of the Third Amended Complaint only alleges the plaintiffs face an "increased risk of serious illness," and the affidavits of plaintiffs' expert only state the exposure to the chemicals "can induce" cancer and result in an "increased susceptibility to disease" including an "increased propensity to serious illnesses as well as cancer." . . . Insofar as plaintiffs seek to recover for their probable future costs and suffering due to ailments of the types they already claim to have endured, they may seek damages in this action. However, plaintiffs also claim an increased risk of leukemia or other cancers. These diseases seem at least qualitatively different from the illnesses plaintiffs have actually suffered. The record is insufficient to determine whether leukemia and other cancers are part of the same disease process as the other illnesses alleged to have resulted from exposure to the contaminated water. If they are part of the same disease process, then plaintiffs may seek recovery for the future illness in this action by showing a "reasonable probability" that they will occur. *See Wilson v. Johns-Manville Sales Corp.*, 684 F.2d 111, 119, 221 U.S. App. D.C. 337 & n.44 (D.C. Cir. 1982) (noting traditional American rule requires proof that damage is more likely than not to occur); *Ayers v. Township of Jackson*, 201 N. J. Super. 106, 493 A.2d 1314, 1323, 1324 (App. Div. 1985) (requiring that increased risk be quantified to determine whether future cancer is "reasonably probable"). If, however, they are distinct diseases, then plaintiffs must wait until the disease has manifested itself to sue.

The policies which advise against holding that a cause of action for a disease accrues at the time plaintiff sustains some injury other than the illness were stated in *Gore v. Daniel O'Connell's Sons, Inc.*, 17 Mass. App. 645, 461 N.E.2d 256, 259 (1984):

> Not only does it offend fairness to require of claimants the gift of prophecy, but it is unsound judicial policy to encourage the initiation of lawsuits in anticipation that a grave disease will manifest itself pendente lite. (citations omitted).

Although *Gore* concerned the application of the discovery rule in an attempt to avoid a statute of limitations instead of a claim for future damage, the described policy of avoiding speculative claims applies equally in this situation.

Gore indicates that Massachusetts could apply the discovery rule to permit suit for a disease even where an earlier injury had occurred if a claim for the disease would have been speculative at the time of the earlier injury.

A further reason for denying plaintiffs' damages for the increased risk of future harm in this action is the inevitable inequity which would result if recovery were allowed. "To award damages based on a mere mathematical probability would significantly undercompensate those who actually develop cancer and would be a windfall to those who do not." *Arnett v. Dow Chemical Corp.*, No. 729586, slip op. at 15 (Cal. Super. Ct. Mar. 21, 1983); *see also Wilson*, 684 F.2d at 120 n.45. In addition, if plaintiffs could show that they were more likely than not [to] suffer cancer or other future illness, full recovery would be allowed for all plaintiffs, even though only some number more than half would actually develop the illness. In such a case, the defendant would overcompensate the injured class. *See Jackson*, 727 F.2d at 520.

Accordingly, action on plaintiffs' claims for the increased risk of serious future illness, including cancer, must be delayed. If the future illnesses stem from the same disease process as the illnesses plaintiffs presently complain of, recovery must be sought in this action. If the disease processes are different, however, the cause of action for the future illness will not accrue until the illness manifests itself.

———————

1. What are the alleged injuries? What is the purpose of the physical injury test for emotional distress? Is it a valid test? Have you ever suffered severe emotional distress without a resulting physical injury?

2. For what future injuries does the court permit recovery? What would happen if all negligently caused emotional injuries were compensable?

3. Is it fair to force the plaintiff to "wait until the disease has manifested itself to sue"?

4. How does the court deal with the statute of limitations problem?

AYERS v. TOWNSHIP OF JACKSON
Supreme Court of New Jersey, 1987
525 A.2d 287

STEIN, JUSTICE

In this case we consider the application of the New Jersey Tort Claims Act (the Act), N.J.S.A. 59:1-1 to 12-3, to the claims asserted by 339 residents of Jackson Township against that municipality.

The litigation involves claims for damages sustained because plaintiffs' well water was contaminated by toxic pollutants leaching into the Cohansey Aquifer from a landfill established and operated by Jackson Township. After an extensive trial, the jury found that the township had created a "nuisance" and a "dangerous condition" by virtue of its operation of the landfill, that its conduct was "palpably unreasonable," — a prerequisite to recovery under N.J.S.A. 59:4-2 — and that it was the proximate cause of the contamination of plaintiffs' water supply. The jury verdict resulted in an aggregate judgment of $15,854,392.78, to be divided among the plaintiffs in varying amounts. The jury returned individual awards for each of the plaintiffs that varied in accordance with such factors as proximity to the landfill, duration and extent of the exposure to contaminants, and the age of the claimant.

The verdict provided compensation for three distinct claims of injury: $2,056,480 was awarded for emotional distress caused by the knowledge that they had ingested water contaminated by toxic chemicals for up to six years; $5,396,940 was awarded for the deterioration of their quality of life during the twenty months when they were deprived of running water; and $8,204,500 was awarded to cover the future cost of annual medical surveillance that plaintiffs' expert testified would be necessary because of plaintiffs' increased susceptibility to cancer and other diseases. The balance of the verdict, approximately $196,500, represented miscellaneous expenses not involved in this appeal.

The evidence at trial provided ample support for the jury's conclusion that the township had operated the Legler landfill in a palpably unreasonable manner, a finding that the township did not contest before the Appellate Division. Briefly summarized, the proof showed that prior to 1971 the township operated another landfill that was the subject of complaints by neighboring residents and at least one citation for violation of state regulations. When the prior landfill's capacity was exhausted, the township opened the Legler landfill in 1972.

Quality of Life

. . . The trial court charged the jury that plaintiffs' claim for "quality of life" damages encompassed "inconveniences, aggravation, and unnecessary expenditure of time and effort related to the use of the water hauled to their homes, as well as to other disruption in their lives, including disharmony in the family unit."

. . . We agree. The Tort Claims Act's ban against recovery of damages for "pain and suffering resulting from any injury" is intended to apply to the intangible, subjective feelings of discomfort that are associated with personal injuries. It was not intended to bar claims for inconvenience associated with the invasion of a property interest. As the trial court's charge explained, plaintiffs sought damages to compensate them for the multiple inconveniences associated with a lack of running water. Although the disruption of plaintiffs' water supply is an "injury" under the Act, N.J.S.A. 59:1-3, the interest invaded here, the right to obtain potable running water from plaintiffs' own wells, is qualitatively different from "pain and suffering" related to a personal injury.

As the Appellate Division acknowledged, plaintiffs' claim for quality of life damages is derived from the law of nuisance. 202 N.J. Super, at 117-18. It has long been recognized that damages for inconvenience, annoyance, and discomfort are recoverable in a nuisance action. The Restatement (Second) of Torts § 929 (1977) sets out three distinct categories of compensation with respect to invasions of an interest in land:

(a)   the difference between the value of the land before the harm and the value after the harm, or at [plaintiff's] election in an appropriate case, the cost of restoration that has been or may be reasonably incurred;

(b)   the loss of use of the land, and

(c)   discomfort and annoyance to him as occupant.

While the first two of these components constitute damages for the interference with plaintiff's use and enjoyment of his land, the third category compensates the plaintiff for his personal losses flowing directly from such an invasion. . . . As such, damages for inconvenience, discomfort, and annoyance constitute "distinct grounds of compensation for which in ordinary cases the person in possession is entitled to recover in addition to the harm to his proprietary interests." Restatement Second of Torts § 929 comment e (1977).

Accordingly, we conclude that the quality of life damages represent compensation for losses associated with damage to property, and agree with the Appellate Division that they do not constitute pain and suffering under the Tort Claims Act. We therefore sustain the judgment for quality of life damages.

Emotional Distress

. . . Many of the plaintiffs testified about their emotional reactions to the knowledge that their well-water was contaminated. Most of the plaintiffs' testimony on the issue of emotional distress was relatively brief and general. Typically, their testimony did not indicate that the emotional distress resulted in physical symptoms or required medical treatment. No treating physicians testified regarding plaintiffs' emotional distress claims. Nevertheless, the consistent thrust of the testimony offered by numerous witnesses was that they suffered anxiety, stress, fear, and depression, and that these feelings were directly and causally related to the knowledge that they and members of their family had ingested and been exposed to contaminated water for a substantial time period.

. . . We cannot conceive how plaintiffs' concern that their exposure to toxic wastes might have precipitated a serious illness can be characterized as anything other than pain and suffering. It is a measure of their entirely subjective responses to a situation which, though threatening, never materialized into objective manifestations of injury. Under the circumstances, we conclude that although damages for these intangible harms might be recoverable from a non-governmental entity, as consequential to a nuisance, the language of N.J.S.A. 59:9-2(d), barring damages from a public entity "for pain and suffering resulting from any injury," clearly precludes recovery herein.

. . . .

Claims for Enhanced Risk and Medical Surveillance

No claims were asserted by plaintiffs seeking recovery for specific illnesses caused by their exposure to chemicals. Rather, they claim damages for the enhanced risk of future illness attributable to such exposure. They also seek to recover the expenses of annual medical examinations to monitor their physical health and detect symptoms of disease at the earliest possible opportunity.

. . . Our evaluation of the enhanced risk and medical surveillance claims requires that we focus on a critical issue in the management of toxic tort litigation: at what stage in the evolution of a toxic injury should tort law intercede by requiring the responsible party to pay damages?

In addition to the staggering problem of removing — or at least containing — the hazardous remnants of past practices, there remains the moral and legal problem of compensating the human victims of past misuse of chemical products. Governmental response to the problem of compensation has been slow. In enacting the Comprehensive Environmental Response, Compensation and Liability Act of 1980 (CERCLA), 42 U.S.C.A. §§ 9601-9657 (West 1983), more commonly called the Superfund legislation, Congress deliberately made no provision for the recovery of damages for personal injury and property damage resulting from exposure to hazardous waste. Instead, Congress provided for the creation of a Study Group to propose solutions to the problem of victims' compensation. 42 U.S.C.A. § 9651(e). The Superfund Study Group, recognizing the difficulty in adapting traditional legal doctrines to redress the grievances of the toxic tort victim, recommended a no-fault victims' compensation fund similar in structure to the workers' compensation laws in place in the states. Under the Study Group's recommendations, victims compensated by the fund would maintain their right to sue under traditional tort principles, assuming they could overcome the numerous problems of proving injury and causation. *Id.* at 464-65. To date, none of the Study Group's recommendations regarding victims' compensation has been adopted. Without a comprehensive governmental response to the problem of compensating victims of toxic exposure, the only available remedy lies within the legal system.

. . . .

. . . A variety of factors are cited to demonstrate that judicial resolution of mass exposure claims is unworkable. Among the obstacles cited are practical difficulties endemic to mass exposure litigation, including the identification of the parties responsible for environmental damage; the risk that responsible parties are judgment-proof; the expense of compensating expert witnesses in specialized fields such as toxicology and epidemiology; and the strong temptation for premature settlement because of the cost and complexity of protracted multi-party litigation.

. . . Because of the long latency period typical of illnesses caused by chemical pollutants, victims often discover their injury and the existence of a cause of action long after the expiration of the personal-injury statute of limitations, where the limitations period is calculated from the date of the exposure. Most jurisdictions have remedied this problem by adopting a version of the "discovery rule" that tolls the statute until the injury is discovered. However, we note that CERCLA now pre-empts state statutes of limitation where they provide that the limitations period for personal-injury or property-damage suits prompted by exposure to hazardous substances starts on a date earlier than the "federally required commencement date." That term is defined as "the date plaintiff knew (or reasonably should have known) that the personal injury or property damages . . . were caused or contributed to by the hazardous substance . . . concerned." Superfund Amendments and Authorization Act of 1986, Pub. L. No. 99-499, 100 Stat. 1613, 1695-96 (codified at 42 U.S.C.A. § 9658 (West Supp. 1987).

. . . .

Accordingly, we concur with the principle advanced by the trial court, 189 N.J. Super. at 568, and endorsed by other federal and state courts, that . . . the statute of limitations should [not] bar timely causes of action in toxic-tort cases instituted after discovery of a disease or injury related to tortious conduct, although there has been prior litigation between the parties of different claims based on the same tortious conduct.

Another commonly identified obstacle to judicial resolution of mass exposure tort claims is the difficulty encountered by plaintiffs in proving negligence. . . .

It is frequently argued that a negligence standard unfairly imposes on plaintiffs the difficult burden of establishing by a cost-benefit analysis that the cost to defendant of taking precautionary measures is outweighed by the probability and gravity of harm. A frequent proposal involves the substitution of strict liability doctrine in place of a negligence standard.

By far the most difficult problem for plaintiffs to overcome in toxic tort litigation is the burden of proving causation.

. . . The legal issue we must resolve, in the context of the jury's determination of defendant's liability under the Act, is whether the proof of an unqualified enhanced risk of illness or a need for medical surveillance is sufficient to justify compensation under the Tort Claims Act.

. . . Although both the enhanced risk and medical surveillance claims are based on Dr. Highland's testimony, supplemented by Dr. Daum's testimony in the case of the surveillance claim, these claims seek redress for the invasion of distinct and different interests. The enhanced risk claim seeks a damage award, not because of any expenditure of funds, but because plaintiffs contend that the unquantified injury to their health and life expectancy should be presently compensable, even though no evidence of disease is manifest.

By contrast, the claim for medical surveillance does not seek compensation for an unquantifiable injury, but rather seeks specific monetary damages measured by the cost of periodic medical examinations.

A preliminary question is whether a significant exposure to toxic chemicals resulting in an enhanced risk of disease is an "injury" for the purposes of the Tort Claims Act. The Act defines injury to include "damage to or loss of property or any other injury that a person may suffer that would be actionable if inflicted by a private person." N.J.S.A. 59:1-3.

In our view, an enhanced risk of disease caused by significant exposure to toxic chemicals is clearly an "injury" under the Act. In this case, neither the trial court nor the Appellate Division challenged the contention that the enhanced risk of disease was a tortiously inflicted injury, but both concluded that the proof quantifying the likelihood of disease was insufficient to submit the issue to the jury. We discern no way to compensate one for enhanced risk without knowing in some way the degree of enhancement. Additionally, the recoverability of damages for enhanced risk in this state has not been decided. *See Euers v. Dollinger*, 95 N.J. 399, 406 (1984). [202 N.J. Super. at 125-26.]

. . . Other courts have acknowledged the propriety of the enhanced risk cause of action, but have emphasized the requirement that proof of future injury be reasonably certain. *See Hagerty v. L & L Marine Servs., supra,* 788 F.2d at 319 ("[A] plaintiff can recover [damages for enhanced risk] only where he can show that the toxic exposure more probably than not will lead to cancer.").

Additionally, several courts have permitted recovery for increased risk of disease, but only where the plaintiff exhibited some present manifestation of disease.

. . . .

. . . In our view, the speculative nature of an unquantified enhanced risk claim, the difficulties inherent in adjudicating such claims, and the policies underlying the Tort Claims Act argue persuasively against the recognition of this cause of action. Accordingly, we decline to recognize plaintiffs' cause of action for the unquantified enhanced risk of disease.

. . . The claim for medical surveillance expenses stands on a different footing from the claim based on enhanced risk. It seeks to recover the cost of periodic medical examinations intended to monitor plaintiffs' health and facilitate early diagnosis and treatment of disease caused by plaintiffs' exposure to toxic chemicals.

This point is well-illustrated by the hypothetical case discussed in the opinion of the Court of Appeals in *Friends For All Children v. Lockheed Aircraft Corp.,* 746 F.2d 816 (D.C. Cir. 1984): Jones is knocked down by a motorbike when Smith is riding through a red light. Jones lands on his head with some force. Understandably shaken, Jones enters a hospital where doctors recommend that he undergo a battery of tests to determine whether he has suffered any internal head injuries. The tests prove negative, but Jones sues Smith solely for what turns out to be the substantial cost of the diagnostic examinations.

From our example, it is clear that even in the absence of physical injury Jones ought to be able to recover the cost for the various diagnostic examinations proximately caused by Smith's negligent action. A cause of action allowing recovery for the expense of diagnostic examinations recommended by competent physicians will, in theory, deter misconduct, whether it be negligent motorbike riding or negligent aircraft manufacture. The cause of action also accords with commonly shared intuitions of normative justice which underlie the common law of tort. The motorbike rider, through his negligence, caused the plaintiff, in the opinion of medical experts, to need specific medical services — a cost that is neither inconsequential nor of a kind the community generally accepts as part of the wear and tear of daily life. Under these principles of tort law, the motorbiker should pay.

. . . Recognition of pre-symptom claims for medical surveillance serves other important public interests. . . . [P]ermitting recovery for reasonable pre-symptom, medical-surveillance expenses subjects polluters to significant liability when proof of the causal connection between the tortious conduct and the plaintiffs' exposure to chemicals is likely to be most readily available. The availability of a substantial remedy before the consequences of the plaintiffs' exposure are manifest may also have the beneficial effect of preventing or mitigating serious future illnesses and thus reduce the overall costs to the responsible parties.

. . . Accordingly, we hold that the cost of medical surveillance is a compensable item of damages where the proofs demonstrate, through reliable expert testimony predicated upon the significance and extent of exposure to chemicals, the toxicity of the chemicals, the seriousness of the diseases for which individuals are at risk, the relative increase in the chance of onset of disease in those exposed, and the value of early diagnosis, that such surveillance to monitor the effect of exposure to toxic chemicals is reasonable and necessary.

HANDLER, J., concurring in part and dissenting in part.

This case involves a municipality that operated a landfill over a long period of time in a palpably unreasonable way, directly subjecting its own residents to carcinogenic and otherwise toxic chemicals. These chemicals caused medical injury in the residents, creating a significant risk that they would develop cancer and other diseases equally grave. The risk of disease to these residents is indisputably greater than the risk of disease experienced by the general population. Because of limitations in current scientific knowledge and because of the number and variety of toxic chemicals involved, the victims of this toxic exposure were unable to measure or quantify the enhancement of their risk of disease. The Court focuses on this inability to measure the risk, rather than on the fact of contamination, and rules that these residents cannot therefore recover any damages referable to that enhanced risk. Further, while the majority does recognize a claim for medical monitoring that is clearly referable to the enhanced risk of disease, it rules that in the future the award of this limited item of special damages is not to be treated as compensation paid directly to aggrieved plaintiffs, but will be used only to reimburse actual expenses through a court-supervised fund. In effect, the Court's holding leaves these grievously wronged persons uncompensated for the injuries caused by the defendant's palpably unreasonable conduct. The Court thus affords the victims of tortious toxic exposure significantly less protection than it would plaintiffs in other tort actions. While in some respects the Court is influenced by the provisions of the New Jersey Tort Claims Act, N.J.S.A. 59:1-1 to 59:12-3, and the status of defendant as a governmental entity covered by the Act, these considerations do not require or justify the unfairness to plaintiffs. Accordingly, I dissent in part from the majority's reasoning and holding.

---

1. What factors did the jury consider in returning awards? On what bases does this court reverse the awards for emotional distress? How is the "right to obtain potable water" different from "pain and suffering"?

2. How does the court deal with the claims for enhanced risk of future illness? "At what stage in the evolution of a toxic injury should tort law intercede by requiring the responsible party to pay damages?" Can a clear line be drawn? Where?

3. Why did CERCLA omit recovery of damages for personal injury resulting from exposure to hazardous wastes? What is the answer to those who say leave it to the legislature? What factors suggest that judicial resolution of toxic exposure claims is unworkable? Why, then, does this court proceed?

4. How do CERCLA and the states treat the statute of limitations problem?

5. Why do the majority of courts not permit recovery for an enhanced risk of disease caused by exposure to toxic chemicals? Would the outcome regarding the claim for enhanced risk be different in this case if the plaintiffs could demonstrate that the onset of the disease is reasonably probable?

6. What do you think of the court awarding expenses for medical surveillance? What is the impact of this holding on polluters? Why does the dissent suggest that people who fear cancer and other diseases should be able to recover now?

7. In *Laxton v. Orkin Exterminating Co.*, 639 S.W.2d 431 (Tenn. 1982), Orkin was held liable for mental distress as well as property damage resulting from Orkin's negligence in allowing chlordane to contaminate plaintiffs' water supply. Orkin had treated plaintiffs' house for termites.

8. *Preemption.* In *Pedraza v. Shell Oil Co.*, 942 F.2d 48 (1st Cir. 1991), the issue was whether the plaintiff's claim for respiratory ailments from workplace exposure to Epichlorohydrin manufactured by Shell was preempted by the federal Occupational Safety and Health Act (OSHA). The court held that the plaintiff's claim was not preempted.

9. *Constitutional issues. McKinney v. Anderson*, 924 F.2d 1500 (9th Cir. 1991), upheld a prisoner's claim that he was being injured by cigarette smoke to such an extent that it constituted a violation of the Eighth Amendment prohibition of cruel and unusual punishment. The claim for damages was rejected, but the injunctive relief claim was remanded to consider evidence on the level and degree of exposure to cigarette smoke. *Contra, Oliver v. Deen*, 77 F.3d 156 (7th Cir. 1996).

F. JOINT LIABILITY

NEW JERSEY DEPARTMENT OF ENVIRONMENTAL PROTECTION v. VENTRON CORP.
Supreme Court of New Jersey, 1983
468 A.2d 150

Pollock, Justice.

This appeal concerns the responsibility of various corporations for the cost of the cleanup and removal of mercury pollution seeping from a forty-acre tract of land into Berry's Creek, a tidal estuary of the Hackensack River that flows through the Meadowlands. The plaintiff is the State of New Jersey, Department of Environmental Protection (DEP); the primary defendants are Velsicol Chemical Corporation (Velsicol), its former subsidiary, Wood Ridge Chemical Corporation (Wood Ridge), and Ventron Corporation (Ventron), into which Wood Ridge was merged. Other defendants are F.W. Berk and Company, Inc. (Berk), which no longer exists, United States Life Insurance Company, which was dismissed by the lower courts in an unappealed judgment, and Robert M. and Rita W. Wolf (the Wolfs), who purchased part of the polluted property from Ventron.

Beneath its surface, the tract is saturated by an estimated 268 tons of toxic waste, primarily mercury. For a stretch of several thousand feet, the concentration of mercury in Berry's Creek is the highest found in fresh water sediments in the world. The waters of the creek are contaminated by the compound methyl mercury, which continues to be released as the mercury interacts with other elements. Due to depleted oxygen levels, fish no longer inhabit Berry's Creek, but are present only when swept in by the tide and, thus, irreversibly toxified.

The contamination at Berry's Creek results from mercury processing operations carried on at the site for almost fifty years. In March, 1976, DEP filed a complaint against Ventron, Wood Ridge, Velsicol, Berk, and the Wolfs, charging them with violating the "New Jersey Water Quality Improvement Act of 1971," N.J.S.A. 58:10-23.1 to -23.10, and N.J.S.A. 23:5-28, and further, with creating or maintaining a nuisance. Velsicol and Ventron counterclaimed against DEP, which amended its complaint to allege the violation of the "Spill Compensation and Control Act" (Spill Act), N.J.S.A. 58:10-23.11 to -23.11z (repealing N.J.S.A. 58:10-23.1 to -23.10), enacted in 1977. The Spill Compensation Fund (Fund), created by the Spill Act to provide funds to abate toxic nuisances, N.J.S.A. 58:10-23.11, intervened.

Because of issues related to the liability of the Fund, a number of its contributors (Mobil Oil Corporation; Chevron U.S.A., Inc.; Texaco, Inc.; and Exxon Company, U.S.A.) filed a complaint, later consolidated with the present action, seeking a declaratory judgment that the Spill Act not be retroactively applied to discharges of toxic wastes occurring before the effective date of the act.

After a fifty-five-day trial, the trial court determined that Berk and Wood Ridge were jointly liable for the cleanup and removal of the mercury; that Velsicol and Ventron were severally liable for half of the costs; that the Wolfs were not liable; and that, while the Spill Act liability provisions did not apply retroactively, monies from the Fund should be made available.

The Appellate Division substantially affirmed the judgment, but modified it in several respects, including the imposition of joint and several liability on Ventron and Velsicol for all costs incurred in the cleanup and removal of the mercury pollution in Berry's Creek. 182 N.J. Super. 210, 224-26 (1981). Because of an amendment to the Spill Act after the trial, the Appellate Division further modified the judgment by imposing retroactive liability under the act on Wood Ridge, Velsicol, and Ventron. *Id.* at 219-22. Furthermore, the Appellate Division precluded payments from the Fund if other sources were available to pay for the cleanup, *id.* at 228, and approved the future monitoring of Berry's Creek at the expense of Velsicol and Ventron. *Id.* at 229.

. . . We believe it is time to recognize expressly that the law of liability has evolved so that a landowner is strictly liable to others for harm caused by toxic wastes that are stored on his property and flow onto the property of others. Therefore, we overrule *Marshall v. Welwood* and adopt the principle of liability originally declared in *Rylands v. Fletcher.* The net result is that those who use, or permit others to use, land for the conduct of abnormally dangerous activities are strictly liable for resultant damages. Comprehension of the relevant legal principles, however, requires a more complete explanation of their development.

. . . The disposal of mercury is particularly inappropriate in the Hackensack Meadowlands, an environmentally sensitive area where the arterial waterways will disperse the pollution through the entire ecosystem. Finally, the dumping of untreated hazardous waste is a critical societal problem in New Jersey, which the Environmental Protection Agency estimates is the source of more hazardous waste than any other state. J. Zazzali and F. Grad, *Hazardous Wastes: New Rights and Remedies?*, 13 Seton Hall L. Rev. 446, 449 n. 12 (1983). From the foregoing, we conclude that mercury and other toxic wastes are "abnormally dangerous," and the disposal of them, past or present, is an abnormally dangerous activity. We recognize that one engaged in the disposing of toxic waste may be performing an activity that is of some use to society. Nonetheless, "the unavoidable risk of harm that is inherent in it requires that it be carried on at his peril, rather than at the expense of the innocent person who suffers harm as a result of it." Restatement (Second), *supra*, comment h at 39.

. . . Further, as a result of a 1979 amendment, the Spill Act expressly applies to a discharge of a hazardous substance that occurred prior to May 1, 1977, the effective date of the act, "if such discharge poses a substantial risk of imminent damage to the public health or safety or imminent and severe damage to the environment." N.J.S.A. 58:10-23.llf(b)(3) (as amended, L. 1979, c. 346, § 4; L. 1981, c. 25, § 1).

Not only has the Legislature granted DEP the power to clean up preexisting spills, but it has also established retroactive strict liability:

> Any person who has discharged a hazardous substance or is in any way responsible for any hazardous substance which the department has removed or is removing pursuant to subsection b. of section 7 of this act shall be strictly liable, jointly and severally without regard to fault, for all cleanup and removal costs. [N.J.S.A. 58:10-23.llg(c), as amended, L.1976, c. 141, § 8].

. . . Further, the Spill Act does not so much change substantive liability as it establishes new remedies for activities recognized as tortious both under prior statutes and the common law. . . . A statute that gives retrospective effect to essentially remedial changes does not unconstitutionally interfere with vested rights.

. . . Given the extended liability of the Spill Act, we conclude that the Legislature intended that the privilege of incorporation should not, under the circumstances that obtain here, become a device for avoiding statutory responsibility. A contrary result would permit corporations, merely by creating wholly-owned subsidiaries, to pollute for profit under circumstances when the Legislature intended liability to be imposed.

. . . Pursuant to the mandate of the Spill Act, *see* N.J.S.A. 58:10-23.llg(c), Berk, Wood Ridge, Velsicol, and Ventron are jointly and severally liable without regard to fault. Only Ventron and Velsicol remain in existence, and we affirm that portion of the Appellate Division judgment that holds them jointly and severally liable for the cleanup and removal of mercury from the Berry's Creek area. . . .

1. What policies support making the statutory liability for pollution retroactive? If the polluter was not liable, who would pay for the clean-up?

2. What is the historical basis for the strict liability adopted by the legislature?

3. Why would a court find retroactive liability for pollution to be constitutional? Argue that it is unconstitutional.

4. What does joint and several liability mean for the defendants in this case? States that have eliminated joint and several liability have often retained it for toxic torts. Why? Joint liability under CERCLA is now governed by the Supreme Court's decision in *Burlington Northern, supra*.

5. In 1999 the American Law Institute embarked on a project to evaluate and redesign joint and several liability, apparently because corporate defendants often pay more that their share of the damages. This has resulted in promulgation of the Restatement (Third) of Torts: Apportionment of Liability (2003). For an examination of the A.L.I. project, see F.J. Vandall, A *Critique of the Restatement (Third), Apportionment as It Affects Joint and Several Liability*, 49 Emory L.J. 565 (2000).

G.   EXPERT TESTIMONY

DAUBERT v. MERRELL DOW PHARMACEUTICALS, INC.
Supreme Court of the United States, 1993
509 U.S. 579

JUSTICE BLACKMUN delivered the opinion of the Court

In this case we are called upon to determine the standard for admitting expert scientific testimony in a federal trial.

I

Petitioners Jason Daubert and Eric Schuller are minor children born with serious birth defects. They and their parents sued respondent in California state court, alleging that the birth defects had been caused by the mothers' ingestion of Bendectin, a prescription anti-nausea drug marketed by respondent.

After extensive discovery, respondent moved for summary judgment, contending that Bendectin does not cause birth defects in humans and that petitioners would be unable to come forward with any admissible evidence that it does. In support of its motion, respondent submitted an affidavit of Steven H. Lamm, physician and epidemiologist, who is a well-credentialed expert on the risks from exposure to various chemical substances. Doctor Lamm stated that he had reviewed all the literature on Bendectin and human birth defects — more than 30 published studies involving over 130,000 patients. No study had found Bendectin to be a human teratogen (i.e., a substance capable of causing malformations in fetuses). On the basis of this review, Doctor Lamm concluded that maternal use of Bendectin during the first trimester of pregnancy has not been shown to be a risk factor for human birth defects.

Petitioners did not (and do not) contest this characterization of the published record regarding Bendectin. Instead, they responded to respondent's motion with the testimony of eight experts of their own, each of whom also possessed impressive credentials. These experts had concluded that Bendectin can cause birth defects.

The court stated that scientific evidence is admissible only if the principle upon which it is based is " 'sufficiently established to have general acceptance in the field to which it belongs.' " 727 F. Supp. 570, 572 (S.D. Cal. 1989). The court concluded that petitioners' evidence did not meet this standard.

The United States Court of Appeals for the Ninth Circuit affirmed. 951 F.2d 1128 (1991). Citing *Frye v. United States*, 293 F. 1013, 1014, 54 App. D.C. 46, 47 (1923), the court stated that expert opinion based on a scientific technique is inadmissible unless the technique is "generally accepted" as reliable in the relevant scientific community. The court declared that expert opinion based on a methodology that diverges "significantly from the procedures accepted by recognized authorities in the field . . . cannot be shown to be 'generally accepted as a reliable technique.' "

II

A

In the 70 years since its formulation in the *Frye* case, the "general acceptance" test has been the dominant standard for determining the admissibihty of novel scientific evidence at trial. Although under increasing attack of late, the rule continues to be followed by a majority of courts, including the Ninth Circuit.

The *Frye* test has its origin in a short and citation-free 1923 decision concerning the admissibihty of evidence derived from a systolic blood pressure deception test, a crude precursor to the polygraph machine.

. . . The merits of the *Frye* test have been much debated, and scholarship on its proper scope and application is legion. Petitioners' primary attack, however, is not on the content but on the continuing authority of the rule. They contend that the *Frye* test was superseded by the adoption of the Federal Rules of Evidence. We agree.

Rule 402 provides the baseline:

> "All relevant evidence is admissible, except as otherwise provided by the Constitution of the United States, by Act of Congress, by these rules, or by other rules prescribed by the Supreme Court pursuant to statutory authority. Evidence which is not relevant is not admissible."

"Relevant evidence" is defined as that which has "any tendency to make the existence of any fact that is of consequence to the determination of the action more probable or less probable than it would be without the evidence." Rule 401. The Rule's basic standard of relevance thus is a liberal one.

Frye, of course, predated the Rules by half a century. In *Bourjaily v. United States*, 483 U.S. 171 (1987), on the other hand, the Court was unable to find a particular common-law doctrine in the Rules, and so held it superseded.

Here there is a specific Rule that speaks to the contested issue. Rule 702, governing expert testimony, provides:

> "If scientific, technical, or other specialized knowledge will assist the trier of fact to understand the evidence or to determine a fact in issue, a witness qualified as an expert by knowledge, skill, experience, training, or education, may testify thereto in the form of an opinion or otherwise."

Nothing in the text of this Rule establishes "general acceptance" as an absolute prerequisite to admissibility. Nor does respondent present any clear indication that Rule 702 or the Rules as a whole were intended to incorporate a "general acceptance" standard. The drafting history makes no mention of *Frye*, and a rigid "general acceptance" requirement would be at odds with the "liberal thrust" of the Federal Rules and their "general approach of relaxing the traditional barriers to 'opinion' testimony." Given the Rules' permissive backdrop and their inclusion of a specific rule on expert testimony that does not mention "general acceptance," the assertion that the Rules somehow assimilated *Frye* is unconvincing. *Frye* made "general acceptance" the exclusive test for admitting expert scientific testimony. That austere standard, absent from and incompatible with the Federal Rules of Evidence, should not be applied in federal trials.

B

That the *Frye* test was displaced by the Rules of Evidence does not mean, however, that the Rules themselves place no limits on the admissibility of purportedly scientific evidence. Nor is the trial judge disabled from screening such evidence. To the contrary, under the Rules the trial judge must ensure that any and all scientific testimony or evidence admitted is not only relevant, but reliable.

The primary locus of this obligation is Rule 702, which clearly contemplates some degree of regulation of the subjects and theories about which an expert may testify. The subject of an expert's testimony must be "scientific . . . knowledge." The adjective "scientific" implies a grounding in the methods and procedures of science. Similarly, the word "knowledge" connotes more than subjective belief or unsupported speculation. The term "applies to any body of known facts or to any body of ideas inferred from such facts or to any body of ideas inferred from such facts or accepted as truths on good grounds." Webster's Third New International Dictionary 1252 (1986). Of course, it would be unreasonable to conclude that the subject of scientific testimony must be "known" to a certainty; arguably, there are no certainties in science. But, in order to qualify as "scientific knowledge," an inference or assertion must be derived by the scientific method. Proposed testimony must be supported by appropriate validation — i.e., "good grounds," based on what is known. In short, the requirement that an expert's testimony pertain to "scientific knowledge" establishes a standard of evidentiary reliability.

Rule 702 further requires that the evidence or testimony "assist the trier of fact to understand the evidence or to determine a fact in issue." This condition goes primarily to relevance. "Expert testimony which does not relate to any issue in the case is not relevant and, ergo, non-helpful." 3 Weinstein & Berger § 702[02], p. 702-18. The consideration has been aptly described by Judge Becker as one of "fit."

"Fit" is not always obvious, and scientific validity for one purpose is not necessarily scientific validity for other, unrelated purposes. The study of the phases of the moon, for example, may provide valid scientific "knowledge" about whether a certain night was dark, and if darkness is a fact in issue, the knowledge will assist the trier of fact. However (absent creditable grounds supporting such a link), evidence that the moon was full on a certain night will not assist the trier of fact in determining whether an individual was unusually likely to have behaved irrationally on that night. Rule 702's "helpfulness" standard requires a valid scientific connection to the pertinent inquiry as a precondition to admissibility.

That these requirements are embodied in Rule 702 is not surprising. Unlike an ordinary witness, *see* Rule 701, an expert is permitted wide latitude to offer opinions, including those that are not based on first-hand knowledge — a rule which represents "a 'most pervasive manifestation' of the common law insistence upon 'the most reliable sources of information,' " Advisory Committee's Notes on Fed. Rule Evid. 602, 28 U.S.C. App. p. 755 (citation omitted) — is premised on an assumption that the expert's opinion will have a reliable basis in the knowledge and experience of his discipline.

C

Faced with a proffer of expert scientific testimony, then, the trial judge must determine at the outset, pursuant to Rule 104(a), whether the expert is proposing to testify to (1) scientific knowledge that (2) will assist the trier of fact to understand or determine a fact in issue. This entails a preliminary assessment of whether the reasoning or methodology underlying the testimony is scientifically valid and of whether that reasoning or methodology properly can be applied to the facts in issue. We are confident that federal judges possess the capacity to undertake this review. Many factors will bear on the inquiry, and we do not presume to set out a definitive checklist or test. But some general observations are appropriate.

Ordinarily, a key question to be answered in determining whether a theory or technique is scientific knowledge that will assist the trier of fact will be whether it can be (and has been) tested. "Scientific methodology today is based on generating hypotheses and testing them to see if they can be falsified; indeed, this methodology is what distinguishes science from other fields of human inquiry." Green, at 645.

Another pertinent consideration is whether the theory or technique has been subjected to peer review and publication. Publication (which is but one element of peer review) is not a sine qua non of admissibility; it does not necessarily correlate with reliability, and in some instances well-grounded but innovative theories will not have been published. Some propositions, moreover, are too particular, too new, or of too limited interest to be published. But submission to the scrutiny of the scientific community is a component of "good science," in part because it increases the likelihood that substantive flaws in methodology will be detected. The fact of publication (or lack thereof) in a peer-reviewed journal thus will be a relevant, though not dispositive, consideration in assessing the scientific validity of a particular technique or methodology on which an opinion is premised.

Additionally, in the case of a particular scientific technique, the court ordinarily should consider the known or potential rate of error, and the existence and maintenance of standards controlling the technique's operation.

Finally, "general acceptance" can yet have a bearing on the inquiry. A "reliability assessment does not require, although it does permit, explicit identification of a relevant scientific community and an express determination of particular degree of acceptance within that community." *United States v. Downing*, 753 F.2d, at 1238. Widespread acceptance can be an important factor in ruling particular evidence admissible, and "a known technique that has been able to attract only minimal support within the community," *Downing, supra*, at 1238, may properly be viewed with skepticism.

The inquiry envisioned by Rule 702 is, we emphasize, a flexible one. Its overarching subject is the scientific validity — and thus the evidentiary relevance and reliability — of the principles that underlie a proposed submission. The focus, of course, must be solely on principles and methodology, not on the conclusions that they generate.

We conclude by briefly addressing what appear to be two underlying concerns of the parties and amici in this case. Respondent expresses apprehension that abandonment of "general acceptance" as the exclusive requirement for admission will result in a "free-for-all" in which befuddled juries are confounded by absurd and irrational pseudoscientific assertions. In this regard respondent seems to us to be overly pessimistic about the capabilities of the jury, and of the adversary system generally. Vigorous cross-examinations, presentation of contrary evidence, and careful instruction on the burden of proof are the traditional and appropriate means of attacking shaky but admissible evidence. Additionally, in the event the trial court concludes that the scintilla of evidence presented supporting a position is insufficient to allow a reasonable juror to conclude that the position more likely than not is true, the court remains free to direct a judgment, Fed. Rule Civ. Proc. 50(a), and likewise to grant summary judgment, Fed. Rule Civ. Proc. 56. These conventional devices, rather than wholesale exclusion under an uncompromising "general acceptance" test, are the appropriate safeguards where the basis of scientific testimony meets the standards of Rule 702.

Petitioners and, to a greater extent, their amici exhibit a different concern. They suggest that recognition of a screening role for the judge that allows for the exclusion of "invalid" evidence will sanction a stifling and repressive scientific orthodoxy and will be inimical to the search for truth. Yet there are important differences between the quest for truth in the courtroom and the quest for truth in the laboratory. Scientific conclusions are subject to perpetual revision. Law, on the other hand, must resolve disputes finally and quickly. The scientific project is advanced by broad and wide-ranging consideration of a multitude of hypotheses, for those that are incorrect will eventually be shown to be so, and that in itself is an advance. Conjectures that are probably wrong are of little use, however, in the project of reaching a quick, final, and binding legal judgment — often of great consequence — about a particular set of events in the past. We recognize that in practice, a gatekeeping role for the judge, no matter how flexible, inevitably on occasion will prevent the jury from learning of authentic insights and innovations. That, nevertheless is the balance that is struck by Rules of Evidence designed not for the exhaustive search for cosmic understanding but for the particularized resolution of legal disputes.

IV

To summarize: "general acceptance" is not a necessary precondition to the admissibility of scientific evidence under the Federal Rules of Evidence, but the Rules of Evidence — especially Rule 702 — do assign to the trial judge the task of ensuring that an expert's testimony both rests on a reliable foundation and is relevant to the task at hand. Pertinent evidence based on scientifically valid principles will satisfy those demands.

The inquiries of the District Court and the Court of Appeals focused almost exclusively on "general acceptance," as gauged by publication and the decisions of other courts. Accordingly, the judgment of the Court of Appeals is vacated and the case is remanded for further proceedings consistent with this opinion.

It is so ordered.

CHIEF JUSTICE REHNQUIST, with whom JUSTICE STEVENS joins, concurring in part and dissenting in part.

. . . .

I do not doubt that Rule 702 confides to the judge some gatekeeping responsibility in deciding questions of the admissibility of proffered expert testimony. But I do not think it imposes on them either the obligation or the authority to become amateur scientists in order to perform that role. I think the Court would be far better advised in this case to decide only the questions presented, and to leave the further development of this important area of the law to future cases.

---

1. On remand, the court of appeals concluded that the plaintiffs failed to meet the requirements of Rule 702:

> Under *Daubert*, we must engage in a difficult, two-part analysis. First, we must determine nothing less than whether the experts' testimony reflects "scientific knowledge," whether their findings are "derived by the scientific method," and whether their work product amounts to "good science." Second, we must ensure that the proposed expert testimony is "relevant to the task at hand," i.e., that it logically advances a material aspect of the proposing party's case.

The court concluded that the testimony of the plaintiff's experts was inadmissible under the second prong of Rule 702. Summary judgment for the defendant was affirmed. *Daubert v. Merrell Dow Pharmaceuticals, Inc.*, 43 F.3d 1311 (9th Cir. 1995).

2. Law professors argued in an amicus brief:

> The matter of judges becoming effective screeners of scientific information is not merely an academic matter. There are substantial costs associated with judges continuing to fail to impose some principle on the admissibility

of scientific information. The costs in court time alone to litigate cases involving shoddy science is staggering. The increasing tendency in the lower courts to adopt more stringent rules is undoubtedly a response to this phenomenon. In addition there are enormous costs to society when defendants are forced to litigate claims that are premised upon little more than the alignment of tealeaves.

Daubert v. Merrell Dow Pharmaceuticals, Inc., Brief for a Group of American Law Professors as Amicus Curiae in Support of Neither Party, Certiorari to U.S. Ct. App. (9th Cir. Dec. 2, 1992).

3. *General Electric Co. v. Joiner*, 522 U.S. 136 (1997), held that "abuse of discretion" is the appropriate standard of review under *Daubert*. The Court further held that a district judge did not abuse his discretion in rejecting expert testimony that exposure to PCB's contributed to an electrical worker's cancer. The Court held that it was within the district court's authority to reject expert testimony of a causal link that had been based solely on animal and epidemiological studies.

4. In *Merrell Dow Pharmaceuticals, Inc. v. Havner*, 907 S.W.2d 535, 557 (Tex. Ct. App. 1994), the trial court found for the plaintiff, and this was affirmed on appeal after applying *Daubert*: "The Havners produced evidence that Bendectin is a human teratogen and that it caused Kelly's birth defect." However, in *Le Blanc v. Merrell Dow Pharmaceuticals, Inc.*, 932 F. Supp. 782 (E.D. La. 1996) (en banc), the U.S. District Court applied *Daubert* and granted Merrell Dow's motion for summary judgment.

5. *Breast implants.* In *Hopkins v. Dow Corning Corp.*, 33 F.3d 1116 (9th Cir. 1994), *cert. denied*, 513 U.S. 1082 (1995), the court followed *Daubert* and allowed plaintiff's expert to introduce evidence where plaintiff sued Dow Corning Corp. to recover for injuries suffered as a result of two sets of breast implants. The jury award of $840,000 compensatory and $6.5 million in punitive damages was upheld.

6. Over 440,000 women joined in a massive class action suit against Dow Corning and other companies over the defective manufacture of silicone breast implants. In April 1994, the court approved a settlement of $4.25 billion. Dow Corning, after having pledged to contribute $2 billion to the award, filed for bankruptcy. By filing for protection, Dow Corning left the class action claimants without any foreseeable chance of payment. Dow Corning followed the lead of other companies who have faced mass tort lawsuits — for example, Johns Manville Corp. in asbestos suits and A.H. Robins Co. in the Dalkon Shield birth control cases. Is it appropriate for corporations to seek protection in bankruptcy court from tort suits? *See* Pitt & Groskaufmanis, *When Bad Things Happen to Good Companies: A Crisis Management Primer*, 15 Cardozo L. Rev. 951 (1994); Weinstein, *Ethical Dilemmas in Mass Tort Litigation*, 88 Nw. U. L. Rev. 469 (1994); Roe, *Bankruptcy and Mass Tort*, 84 Colum. L. Rev. 846 (1984).

In the late 1990s, new evidence raised doubts about the connection between silicone breast implants and connective-tissue disease. A "Harvard's Nurses' Health Study, released in 1995 . . . found 'no association between silicone breast implants and connective-tissue diseases. . . .' " Austin American Statesman, *It's Time for Women to Consult Science on Breast-Implant Issues*, July 16, 1996, at A9. *See*

Pozefsky v. Baxter Healthcare Corp., 2001 U.S. Dist. LEXIS 11813 (N.D.N.Y Aug. 16, 2001) (ruling plaintiff's expert testimony linking silicone breast implants with connective tissue disease was inadmissible because a "multitude of scientific studies and reports" had determined that there was no causal connection). If you were a plaintiff's lawyer, would you be willing to take a breast implant case today?

Would some scientific evidence cases be decided differently if men were the predominant victims, or if more women were judges? *See* Steinman, A *Legal Sampler: Women, Medical Care, and Mass Tort Litigation*, 68 Chi.-Kent L. Rev. 409 (1992) (discussing the regulatory structures, judicial system, and corporations which have failed to maintain safe health treatment for women).

7.   *Class actions.* One of the largest class actions ever attempted, consisting of all nicotine-dependent persons, their spouses and children, was decertified as a class by the court of appeals. Suit had been brought against numerous tobacco companies and the Tobacco Institute. *Castano v. American Tobacco Co.*, 84 F.3d 734 (5th Cir. 1996).

On the other hand, in *Broin v. Philip Morris Cos.*, 641 So. 2d 888 (Fla. Dist. Ct. App. 1994), thirty nonsmoking flight attendants filed a class action against numerous tobacco manufacturers. The attendants alleged that they suffered injuries caused by the inhalation of second-hand cigarette smoke in airplane cabins. The appellate court reversed the dismissal of the class action and held that the fact that class members resided in different states and countries and that alleged injuries varied in degree and severity did not foreclose the class action.

Issues of class certification are better addressed in courses on civil procedure, but the ability to secure class action treatment is often critical for plaintiffs in toxic tort cases. Why?

Chapter 16

DEFAMATION

PROBLEM

Bertha edits a newsletter that she posts on her website and sends free by email to 50 families in Pigskin County. All the families have children who play on the public Pigskin High School football team. In her newsletter (called *The Squeeeel*), Bertha wrote in regard to the Friday night football game "the coach was a 'weenie.' " Coach Chuckie has come to you for advice. He wants to know whether he can sue Bertha for defamation, and if so with what prospects for success. In addition to being the coach of the Pigskin H.S. football team, he ran for mayor of Pigskin County five years ago.

Libel and Slander have their roots in the middle ages and England's Star Chamber, where they were used to protect the Crown and government from criticism. Both are concerned with protection from injury to reputation by false or misleading statements. Until 1964, defamation was a very technical tort dealing with the subtle issues involved in whether the statement was "libel" or "slander," what damages must be shown and what privileges were available as defenses. Roughly, libel applied to "published" defamation, while slander applied to spoken defamation. Although technically an intentional tort, defamation rested effectively on strict liability since publication or utterance of the defamatory statement itself proved intent. Damages, often "presumed," were determined by the whim of the jury. In many jurisdictions, truth of the statements in question was an affirmative defense that had to be proved by the defendant.

The Supreme Court's decision in *New York Times v. Sullivan*, 376 U.S. 254 (1964), fundamentally changed the nature of defamation. The Court held that actions for defamation are subject to constitutional limitation under the First Amendment's protections for freedom of speech and press. The issues shifted to whether the plaintiff was a public official or a public figure and whether "actual malice," the constitutionally required standard for liability in public official and public figure cases, had been shown. Different standards have developed for private persons. The Court also held that plaintiffs must prove the falsehood of the statements in question as part of their case, and that they must prove "actual damages." The Court has extended analogous constitutional limitations to actions for "false light" invasions of privacy and to actions for infliction of emotional distress, when they are based on constitutionally protected speech or publication. *See Time, Inc. v. Hill*, 385 U.S. 374 (1967); *Hustler Magazine, Inc. v. Falwell*, 485 U.S. 46 (1988), *supra*. All these changes have been driven by the importance of free speech and the media in the United States. Collectively they have effectively transformed defamation into a tort-based branch of federal constitutional law.

The chapter will reflect these changes in defamation doctrine. We will first consider the historic torts of libel and slander. Then we will view some of the changes wrought by the Supreme Court after 1964.

A.   WHAT CONSTITUTES A DEFAMATORY STATEMENT?

ROMAINE v. KALLINGER
Supreme Court of New Jersey, 1988
109 N.J. 282

HANDLER, J.

More than ten years ago Joseph Kallinger and his son went on a criminal rampage in Pennsylvania and New Jersey. The offenses were vicious, involving physical threats and sexual abuse of victims during the course of robberies of suburban homes. Kallinger murdered his victims on three occasions. In 1983, approximately eight years after Kallinger and his son had been apprehended, the defendant Simon & Schuster Publishing Inc. published a book entitled "The Shoemaker," written by the defendant Flora Rheta Schreiber, depicting the life and crimes of Joseph Kallinger. The book gave rise to this litigation.

The plaintiffs . . . were victims of Kallinger, whose criminal acts against them resulted in the murder of a young woman, Maria Fasching. Plaintiffs sued the defendants Kallinger, Elizabeth Kallinger, his wife, Schreiber, Simon & Schuster, and Paul J. Giblin, claiming to have been legally injured by defamatory and offensively intrusive statements relating to these crimes contained in "The Shoemaker." Plaintiffs sought in separate counts the award of compensatory and punitive damages based respectively on libel and invasion of privacy by being cast in a false light; they also claimed that their privacy had been invaded through the unreasonable publication of private facts. . . .

Defendants Simon & Schuster and Schreiber filed motions for summary judgment seeking dismissal of the action. . . . The trial court granted defendants' motion for summary judgment with respect to the defamation and privacy claims. . . .

Plaintiffs filed a notice of appeal. . . .

I

The factual context of this litigation is important. Ms. Schreiber, the author of "The Shoemaker," is a professor at the City University of New York, John Jay College of Criminal Justice. . . .

According to defendants, Professor Schreiber's work is an in-depth study of the psychological make-up of a killer. Specifically, the book explores the relationship between the abuse suffered by Kallinger as a child and the psychotic behavior that led to his criminal acts. *The Shoemaker* received a significant amount of critical praise and Schreiber was named "Author of the Year" by the American Society of Journalists and Authors in 1985 in recognition of her work.

The complaint focuses on a chapter of "The Shoemaker" called "The Hunting Knife." The chapter . . . describes the murder of Maria Fasching on January 8, 1975, in Leonia, New Jersey. The chapter relates that Kallinger and his son broke into the home of Mr. and Mrs. DeWitt Romaine. . . . While this was occurring, Maria Fasching, a friend of one of the victims, the plaintiff Randi Romaine, came into the house. She was also captured by Kallinger. He directed Ms. Fasching, a nurse, to perform an act of sexual mutilation on plaintiff Frank Welby, who was tied up and helpless. When she refused to do so, he killed her by slashing her throat several times. . . .

On the second page of "The Hunting Knife" chapter this passage appears relating the circumstances leading up to Maria Fasching's visit to the Romaine house:

> . . . .
>
> A militant women's libber, Maria Fasching was famous among her friends for her battles on behalf of the weak and downtrodden. She would always try to rescue someone a bully had attacked, and she could not tolerate racists.
>
> Maria thought of herself as a "free spirit." She resisted anything that she considered a restriction on her freedom. She cared for cats that had been hit by cars and for birds with broken wings.
>
> Today, Maria Fasching was on the four-to-midnight shift at Hackensack Hospital, and she wore her nurse's uniform under her coat. In the morning Maria's friend Randi Romaine, who lived in the stucco house, had called Maria and asked her to drop over for coffee. The two women had not seen each other for a long time, for, between hospital duties and preparations for her wedding, Maria's schedule was full.
>
> At first Maria said that she couldn't visit because she had to go to a wake. The wake, however, was only for an acquaintance. Randi and her twin sister, Retta, had been Maria's friends since they were all in the first grade. Besides, Maria was eager for news from Randi about a junkie they both knew who was doing time in prison. . . .

According to plaintiffs, one sentence in the passage falsely depicts the reason for Ms. Fasching's visit: "Besides, Maria was eager for news from Randi about a junkie they both knew who was doing time in prison." This sentence, it is claimed, is defamatory as a matter of law and constitutes a false-light invasion of privacy.[1] The chapter's general narration of the criminal events, from which this passage is taken,

---

[1] The trial court dismissed the defamation claims of plaintiffs Edwin Wiseman, Retta Romaine Welby, and Frank Welby, finding that the statement did not concern these individuals. Plaintiffs Wiseman, Welby, and Welby conceded before the Appellate Division that this ruling was correct, hence the only remaining defamation claim is that of Randi Romaine. All plaintiffs, however, continue to press the false-light invasion of privacy claim caused by this same statement.

is in turn the basis for plaintiffs' invasion of privacy by unreasonable publication of private facts claim.

II

Plaintiff Randi Romaine asserts that the particular sentence is defamatory as a matter of law, or alternatively, that the statement's defamatory content was at least a question for the jury. She claims this sentence falsely accuses her of criminality or associations with criminals. Plaintiff also contends that the false accusation was particularly damaging because it injured Ms. Romaine's professional reputation as a drug counsellor and a social worker, interfering with her ability to obtain future employment.

A defamatory statement is one that is false and "injurious to the reputation of another" or exposes another person to "hatred, contempt or ridicule" or subjects another person to "a loss of the good will and confidence" in which he or she is held by others. *Leers v. Green*, 24 N.J. 239, 251 (1957); *see* W. Keeton, D. Dobbs, R. Keeton & D. Owen, Prosser and Keeton on the Law of Torts, para. III at 773-78 (5th ed. 1984); *see also* Restatement (Second) of Torts § 559 (1977) (a defamatory communication is one that "tends so to harm the reputation of another so as to lower him in the estimation of the community or to deter third persons from associating or dealing with him.").

The threshold issue in any defamation case is whether the statement at issue is reasonably susceptible of a defamatory meaning. *Kotlikoff v. The Community News*, 89 N.J. 62, 67 (1982); *Mosler v. Whelan*, 28 N.J. 397, 404 (1958). This question is one to be decided first by the court. In making this determination, the court must evaluate the language in question "according to the fair and natural meaning which will be given it by reasonable persons of ordinary intelligence." In assessing the language, the court must view the publication as a whole and consider particularly the context in which the statement appears.

If a published statement is susceptible of one meaning only, and that meaning is defamatory, the statement is libelous as a matter of law. *See Mosler v. Whelan, supra*, 28 N.J. at 40; *Herrmann v. Newark Morning Ledger Co., supra*, 48 N.J. Super, at 430. Conversely, if the statement is susceptible of only a non-defamatory meaning, it cannot be considered libelous, justifying dismissal of the action. *See Pierce v. Capital Cities Communications Inc.*, 576 F.2d 495, 501-04 (3d Cir.) (applying Pennsylvania law), *cert. denied*, 439 U.S. 861, 99 S. Ct. 181, 58 L. Ed. 2d 170 (1978); *Cibenko v. Worth Publishers, supra*, 510 F. Supp. at 764-65. However, in cases where the statement is capable of being assigned more than one meaning, one of which is defamatory and another not, the question of whether its content is defamatory is one that must be resolved by the trier of fact.

Certain kinds of statements denote such defamatory meaning that they are considered defamatory as a matter of law. A prime example is the false attribution of criminality. *See Hoagburg v. Harrah's Marina Hotel Casino*, 585 F.Supp. 1167, 1170 (D.N.J.1984); *Karnell v. Campbell, supra*, 206 N.J. Super. at 88-89; *cf. Lawrence v. Bauer Publishing & Printing Ltd., supra*, 89 N.J. at 459-60 (statement that plaintiff might be charged with criminal conduct defamatory as a matter of law). Relying essentially on this example of defamation, plaintiff Randi Romaine contends in this case that the published offending statement must be considered libelous *per se*. According to Ms. Romaine, the sentence has only a defamatory meaning, in that it accuses her of having engaged in criminal conduct or having associated with criminals relating to drugs.

The trial court concluded, and the Appellate Division agreed, that only the most contorted reading of the offending language could lead to the conclusion that it accuses plaintiff of illegal drug use or criminal associations. We concur in the determinations of the courts below. "[A]ccording to the fair and natural meaning which will be given [this statement] by reasonable persons of ordinary intelligence," *Herrmann v. Newark Morning Ledger Co., supra*, 48 N.J. Super, at 431, it does not attribute any kind of criminality to plaintiff. A reasonable and fair understanding of the statement simply does not yield an interpretation that the plaintiff was or had been in illegal possession of drugs or otherwise engaging in any illegal drug-related activity. . . .

At most, the sentence can be read to imply that plaintiff knew a junkie. Even if we assume that a commonly accepted and well-understood meaning of the term "junkie" is "a narcotics peddler or addict," Webster's Third New International Dictionary 1227 (1981), *see also* Dictionary of American Slang 300 (2d ed. 1975) (defining "junkie" as a "drug addict"), the statement still does not suggest either direct or indirect involvement by plaintiff herself in any criminal drug-related activities. Absent exceptional circumstances, the mere allegation that plaintiff knows a criminal is not defamatory as a matter of law. . . .

Beyond the language itself, we are satisfied that the statement in its contextual setting cannot fairly and reasonably be invested with any defamatory meaning. Maria Fasching, we note, is described in the chapter as a person who had compassion for others and who would care for less fortunate persons. The reasonable meaning of the critical sentence that is implied from this context is that Ms. Fasching's interest in the "junkie" stemmed from sympathy and compassion, not from any prediliction toward or involvement in criminal drug activity. As extended to Randi Romaine, the only fair inference to be drawn from the larger context is that Ms. Romaine shared her friend's feelings, attitudes and interests, and that her own interest in the junkie was similar to that of Ms. Fasching's.

We note the further contention that this statement had a defamatory meaning because it implied that the only reason for Ms. Fasching's visit to the Romaine home was her "interest" in news about a "junkie." A review of the full text, however, indicates that there were several reasons for the visit, only one of which was Ms. Fasching's interest in the "junkie." The lower courts soundly rejected this contention.

We conclude that the statement is not defamatory as a matter of law and accordingly uphold the ruling of the lower court on this point.

. . . .

1. Where a published statement is defamatory on its face, it is sometimes called libel *per se*. Where the published statement is capable of more than one meaning, it is sometimes called libel *per quod* and special damages must be shown. Special damages will be considered *infra*. *Gertz v. Robert Welch, infra*, by requiring the showing of actual damages and fault, reduces the importance of special damages.

2. In *Belli v. Orlando Daily Newspapers*, 389 F.2d 579 (5th Cir. 1967), *cert. denied*, 393 U.S. 825 (1968), the court defined libel as "a false and unprivileged publication by letter . . . which exposes a person to distrust, hatred, contempt, ridicule . . . or which has a tendency to injure such person in his office, occupation, business, or employment." The court held: "It is for the court in the first instance to determine whether the words are reasonably capable of a particular interpretation . . . it is then for the jury to say whether they were in fact understood as defamatory. If the language used is open to two meanings . . . it is for the jury to determine whether the defamatory sense was the one conveyed."

MATHERSON v. MARCHELLO
Supreme Court of New York, Appellate Division, 1984
473 N.Y.S.2d 998

TITONE, JUSTICE presiding

On October 28, 1980, radio station WBAB conducted an interview with the members of a singing group called "The Good Rats". Following a commercial which advertised a Halloween party at an establishment known as "OBI", a discussion ensued in which various members of the group explained that they are no longer permitted to play at OBI South because:

"Good Rat #1:	Well, you know, we had that law suit with Mr. Matherson.
"A Good Rat:	And we used to fool around with his wife.
"Good Rat #1:	And we won.
"A Good Rat:	One of us used to fool around with his wife. He wasn't into that too much.
"D.J."	Oh yea.
"Good Rat #1: (interrupted and joined by another Good Rat)	We used to start off our gigs over there with the National Anthem, and he was very upset about that, now all of a sudden he's very patriotic and he's using it in his commercials.
"A Good Rat:	I don't think it was his wife that he got so upset about, I think it was when somebody started messing round with his boyfriend that he really freaked out. Really. (Laughter) That did it man."

Plaintiffs, who are husband and wife, subsequently commenced this action against "The Good Rats" (as individuals and against their record company), alleging that the words "we used to fool around with his wife" and "I don't think it was his wife that he got upset about, I think it was when somebody started messing around with his boyfriend that he really freaked out," were defamatory. They seek compensatory and punitive damages for humiliation, mental anguish, loss of reputation and injury to their marital relationship as well as for the loss of customers, business opportunities and good will allegedly suffered by Mr. Matherson. . . .

Preliminarily, we observe that if special damages are a necessary ingredient of plaintiffs' cause of action, Special Term properly found the allegations of the complaint to be deficient.

Special damages consist of "the loss of something having economic or pecuniary value" (Restatement, Torts 2d, § 575, Comment *b*) which "must flow directly from the injury to reputation caused by the defamation; not from the effects of defamation" (Sack, Libel, Slander, and Related Problems, § VII.2.2, 345-346; see, also, 1 Harper and James, The Law of Torts, § 5.14) and it is settled law that they must be fully and accurately identified "with sufficient particularity to identify actual losses" *(Lincoln First Bank v. Siegel*, 60 A.D.2d 270, 280). When loss of business is claimed, the persons who ceased to be customers must be named and the losses itemized *(Reporters' Assn. v. Sun Print. & Pub. Assn.*, 186 N.Y. 437; *Continental Air Ticketing Agency v. Empire Int. Travel*, 51 A.D.2d 104, 108). "Round figures" or a general allegation of a dollar amount as special damages do not suffice *(Drug Research Corp. v. Curtis Pub. Co.*, 7 N.Y.2d 435, 440; *Continental Air Ticketing Agency v. Empire Int. Travel, supra*, p. 108). Consequently, plaintiffs' nonspecific conclusory allegations do not meet the stringent requirements imposed for pleading special damages *(Zausner v. Fotochrome*, 18 A.D.2d 649; Fuchsberg, 9 Encyclopedia of N.Y. Law, Damages, § 243).

We must, therefore, determine whether an allegation of special damages is necessary. In large measure, this turns on which branch of the law of defamation is involved. As a result of historical accident, which, though not sensibly defensible today, is so well settled as to be beyond our ability to uproot it *(Ostrowe v. Lee*, 256 N.Y. 36, 39), there is a schism between the law governing slander and the law governing libel (see Restatement, Torts 2d, § 568, Comment *b;* see, also, *Gurtler v. Union Parts Mfg. Co.*, 1 N.Y.2d 5; 2 N.Y. PJI 84 [1983 Supp]).[1]

A plaintiff suing in slander must plead special damages unless the defamation falls into any one of four per se categories (see Prosser, Torts [4th ed], § 112, pp. 751-760; Restatement, Torts 2d, § 570). Those categories consist of allegations (1) that the plaintiff committed a crime, (2) that tend to injure the plaintiff in his or her trade, business or profession, (3) that plaintiff has contracted a loathsome disease, and (4) that impute unchastity to a woman.[2]

---

[1] The historical development is traced in Franklin, *Cases and Materials on Tort Law and Alternatives* (pp. 884-886), and Veeder, *The History and Theory of the Law of Defamation* (3 Col. L. Rev. 546; 4 Col. L. Rev 33). The distinction has, moreover, not gone unchallenged. As early as 1812, a defendant urged that a libel read by one person should not be treated more harshly than a slander spoken to hundreds in a crowd. While the Judge conceded the merits of the argument, he refused to overturn the firmly rooted contrary precedents (Thorley v. Lord Kerry, 128 Eng. Rep. 367; see 1 Harper and James, The Law of Torts, § 5.9, p 372; Comment, *The Pre-Thorley v. Kerry Case Law of The Libel-Slander Distinction*, 23 U Chi. L. Rev 132).

[2] The first three categories were established relatively early. The fourth is of more recent vintage,

The exceptions were established apparently for no other reason than a recognition that by their nature the accusations encompassed therein would be likely to cause material damage (Prosser, Torts [4th ed], § 112, p. 754).

On the other hand, a plaintiff suing in libel need not plead or prove special damages if the defamatory statement "'tends to expose the plaintiff to public contempt, ridicule, aversion or disgrace, or induce an evil opinion of him in the minds of right-thinking persons, and to deprive him of their friendly intercourse in society.' "[3] Thus, unlike the law of slander, in the law of libel the existence of damage is conclusively presumed from the publication itself and a plaintiff may rely on general damages (compare Restatement, Torts 2d, § 569 with § 570; but see Excessiveness or Inadequacy of Damages for Defamation, Ann., 35 A.L.R.2d 218, which suggests, by its scheme of classification, how relatively few cases of libel actually do arise which are not more or less easily referrable to the categories of slander per se).

On the question of whether the allegedly defamatory statements are actionable, our scope of review is limited. "If the contested statements are reasonably susceptible of a defamatory connotation, then 'it becomes the jury's function to say whether that was the sense in which the words were likely to be understood by the ordinary and average reader' "(*James v. Gannett Co.* 40 N.Y.2d 415, 419, quoting

---

having first been put into effect in England by the Slander of Women Act of 1891 (54 & 55 Viet, ch 51); similar statutory additions to the common law were made in this country (e.g., Civil Rights Law, § 77, derived from L 1871, ch 219, § 1; see, generally, 1 Harper and James, The Law of Torts, §§ 5.10-5.13; Prosser, Torts [4th ed], pp. 754-760). We do not view these categories as fixed or rigid and, in appropriate circumstances, a new category may be judicially established (see, e.g., Privitera v. Town of Phelps, 79 A.D.2d 1, 3; 2 N.Y. PJI 85-86, 101-102 [1983 Supp], listing the imputation of homosexual behavior as a separate category of per se slander; contra, Stein v. Trager, 36 Misc. 2d 227).

[3] We have avoided the use of the terms libel per se and libel per quod because, as explained in this footnote, the cases and commentators are divided on the question of whether any meaningful distinction exists between the two.

It is clear that when the defamatory import is apparent from the face of the publication itself without resort to any other source, the libel, often referred to as libel per se, is actionable without proof of special harm (2 NY PJI *86* [1983 Supp]). Libel per quod, on the other hand, has been traditionally defined as an encompassing libel in which the defamatory import can only be ascertained by reference to facts not set forth in the publication (Prosser, Libel Per Quod, 46 Va. L. Rev. 839).

In the view of some writers, libel per quod does not exist in New York. Under their reasoning, special harm is a necessary component only under the so-called "single instance" rule, i.e., where the statement charges the plaintiff with a single dereliction in connection with his or her trade or profession (*see* Lyons v. New Amer. Lib., 78 A.D.2d 723, app withdrawn 53 N.Y.2d 704). They read Hinsdale v. Orange County Pub. (17 N.Y.2d 284) as establishing that all other libel, whether defamatory on its face or by extrinsic fact, is actionable without proof of special harm (see Prosser, Torts [4th ed], § 112, p 762; 2 N.Y. PJI 706-707).

Other commentators decline to interpret Hinsdale *(supra)* as obliterating the special harm requirements in extrinsic fact cases, viewing the pleading and proof of special damages as necessary both under the "single instance" rule and in extrinsic fact cases unless, with respect to extrinsic fact cases, it is "reasonably likely" that the plaintiff's reputation will be impaired among readers who are aware of the extrinsic facts (2 N.Y. PJI 95-96 [1983 Supp]; see, e.g., Samore, *New York Libel Per Quod: Enigma Still?*, 31 Albany L. Rev. 250).

The cases simply state that if a libel is not per se, a plaintiff must plead and prove special damages as part of the prima facie case, without drawing a line of demarcation between them. Since neither the single instance rule nor extrinsic fact libel is involved, we have no opportunity to resolve the conflict.

Mencher v. Chesley, 297 N.Y. 94, 100; *cf. Gurda v. Orange County Pub. Div.*, 81 A.D.2d 120, 130 [dissenting opn of MOLLEN, P.J., and TITONE, J.], *revd* 56 N.Y.2d 705 on dissent at App. Div.). We must accord the words their natural meaning and we cannot strain to interpret them in their mildest and most inoffensive sense in order to render them nondefamatory (e.g., *November v. Time Inc.*, 13 N.Y.2d 175, 178-179; *Schermerhorn v. Rosenberg*, 73 A.D.2d 276, 283-284; *Nowark v. Maguire*, 22 A.D.2d 901). Unless we can say, as a matter of law, that the statements could not have had a defamatory connotation, it is for the jury to decide whether or not they did (*Schermerhorn v. Rosenberg, supra; Greenberg v. CBS Inc.*, 69 A.D.2d 693).

Taken in the context of a rock and roll station's interview with musicians, and taking note of contemporary usage, we have no difficulty in concluding that the words "fooling around with his wife" could have been interpreted by listeners to mean that Mrs. Matherson was having an affair with one of the defendants. Such charges are clearly libelous on their face, thus obviating any need to and prove special damages (see Civil Rights Law, § 77; *James v Gannett Co.*, supra, p 419). While it may be possible to construe the words in an inoffensive manner, since they are susceptible of a defamatory connotation, the cause of action should stand (*cf. Schermerhorn v. Rosenberg, supra; Greenberg v. CBS Inc., supra; Jordon v. Lewis*, 20 A.D.2d 773, 774).

The second comment — "I don't think it was his wife that he got upset about, I think it was when somebody started messing around with his boyfriend that he really freaked out" — presents a far more subtle and difficult question (see Imputation of Homosexuality as Defamation, Ann., 3 A.L.R. 4th 752). It is plaintiffs' contention that this statement constitutes an imputation of homosexuality which should be recognized as defamatory. Defendants, on the other hand, basically do not deny that such reading is plausible. Rather, they claim that many public officials have acknowledged their homosexuality and, therefore, no social stigma may be attached to such an allegation. We are constrained to reject defendants' position at this point in time.

It cannot be said that social opprobrium of homosexuality does not remain with us today. Rightly or wrongly, many individuals still view homosexuality as immoral (*see Newsweek*, Aug. 8, 1983, p. 33, containing the results of a Gallup poll; *cf. People v Onofre*, 51 N.Y.2d 476, 488, n. 3, *cert. den*, 451 U.S. 987). Legal sanctions imposed upon homosexuals in areas ranging from immigration (*Matter of Longstaff*, 716 F.2d 1439) to military service (*Watkins v. United States Army*, 721 F.2d 687) have recently been reaffirmed despite the concurring Judge's observation in *Watkins* (p. 691) that it "demonstrates a callous disregard for the progress American law and society have made toward acknowledging that an individual's choice of life style is not the concern of government, but a fundamental aspect of personal liberty."

In short, despite the fact that an increasing number of homosexuals are publicly expressing satisfaction and even pride in their status, the potential and probable harm of a false charge of homosexuality, in terms of social and economic impact, cannot be ignored. Thus, on the facts of this case, where the plaintiffs are husband and wife, we find, given the narrow scope of review, that the imputation of homosexuality is "reasonably susceptible of a defamatory connotation" (*James v. Gannett Co.*, 40 N.Y.2d 415, 419, *supra*) and is actionable without proof of special damages (*cf. Nowark v. Maguire*, 22 AD2d 901, *supra*).

For these reasons, the order should be reversed insofar as appealed from, with costs, the defendants' motion to dismiss should be denied and the complaint should be reinstated.

---

1. Note the court's treatment of defamation, libel, slander, slander *per se*, and libel *per quod*.

2. Is it slander *per se* to call a secretary a coward? What about calling a soldier a coward?

3. Is it slander *per se* to say that someone has AIDS? What about mono?

4. The special damage rule arose from *Terwilliger v. Wands*, 17 N.Y. 54 (1858), which held that the plaintiff could not recover for slander because his only damage was to his health and ability to work. Neither mental nor physical injury constitutes special damage. Special damages are essentially a loss of business.

5. Can a statue be defamatory? What test do you apply?

6. In *Agnant v. Shakur*, 30 F. Supp. 2d 420 (S.D.N.Y. 1998), the plaintiff alleged that Tupac Shakur's rap song had libeled him. The district court held for the defendant's estate that the statement the plaintiff had worked as a federal undercover informant was not defamatory, the lyrics did not constitute libel *per se* and plaintiff failed to plead and prove special damages.

7. If the statement is not defamatory on its face, plaintiff must plead extrinsic facts in order to prove the defamatory meaning of the statement. See *Barter v. Wilson*, 512 N.E.2d 816 (Ill. App. Ct. 1987), where defendant said in regard to developer's application for a permit, "the fix was in." The court held that the reasonable interpretation of the statement was not defamatory.

8. In deciding whether a statement is defamatory, who is the relevant public to consider? Should a court take into consideration widely shared attitudes, even if they are unfair or prejudiced? What if a defendant writes that the plaintiff is gay, or that the plaintiff reported being the victim of a crime? In *Stern v. Cosby*, 645 F. Supp. 2d 258 (S.D.N.Y. 2009), in a defamation suit brought by the attorney of controversial television personality Anna Nicole Smith, the court refused to follow *Matherson's* conclusion that imputation of homosexuality can be defamatory. Among other factors, the court reasoned that the conclusion was questionable after the Supreme Court's decision in *Lawrence v. Texas*, 539 U.S. 558 (2003), establishing constitutional protection for same-sex intimate relations.

9. For a gender-neutral approach, perhaps "serious sexual misconduct" should replace "chastity." *See Nazeri v. Missouri Valley College*, 860 S.W.2d 303 (Mo. 1993).

10. The defamatory statement must be published. This is a term of art and means that the statement must be communicated to someone other than the plaintiff. In *Economopoulos v. A. G. Pollard Co.*, 218 Mass. 294, 105 N.E. 896 (1914), liability failed because although the statement was communicated to a third party, that person did not understand English.

11.   Dictating a letter to a secretary is often considered to be a publication. *Rickbeil v. Grafton Deaconess Hosp*, 74 N.D. 525, 23 N.W.2d 247 (1946). Sending the defamatory statement on a postcard is presumed to be publication. *Ostro v. Safir*, 165 Misc. 647, 1 N.Y.S.2d 377 (Sup. Ct. 1937). Sending a sealed letter to the plaintiff, however, is not a publication. *Barnes v. Clayton House Motel*, 435 S.W.2d 616 (Tex. Civ. App. 1968). What forms of electronic communication involve a publication?

B.   THE DEFAMATORY STATEMENT MUST BE UNDERSTOOD TO HAVE BEEN MADE "OF AND CONCERNING" THE PLAINTIFF

NEIMAN-MARCUS CO. v. LAIT
United States District Court for the Southern District of New York, 1952
13 F.R.D. 311

Irving R. Kaufman, District Judge

The defendants are authors of a book entitled "U.S.A. Confidential." The plaintiffs are the Neiman-Marcus Company, a Texas corporation operating a department store at Dallas, Texas, and three groups of its employees. They allege that the following matter libeled and defamed them:

. . . .

"He [Stanley Marcus, president of plaintiff Neiman-Marcus Company] may not know that some Neiman models are call girls — the top babes in town. The guy who escorts one feels in the same league with the playboys who took out Ziegfeld's glorified. Price, a hundred bucks a night."

"The salesgirls are good, too — pretty, and often much cheaper — twenty bucks on the average. They're more fun, too, not as snooty as the models. We got this confidential, from a Dallas wolf."

"Neiman-Marcus also contributes to the improvement of the local breed when it imports New York models to make a flash at style shows. These girls are the cream of the crop. Oil millionaires toss around thousand-dollar bills for a chance to take them out."

"Neiman's was a women's specialty shop until the old biddies who patronized it decided their husbands should get class, too. So Neiman's put in a men's store. Well, you should see what happened."

"Houston is faced with a serious homosexual problem. It is not as evident as Dallas', because there are no expensive imported faggots in town like those in the Neiman-Marcus set." . . .

The individual plaintiffs . . . state that they were employed by the Neiman-Marcus Company at the time the alleged libel was published and that the groups of individual plaintiffs are composed as follows:

(1) Nine individual models who constitute the entire group of models at the time of the publication . . . ;

(2) Fifteen salesmen of a total of twenty-five suing on their own behalf and on behalf of the others pursuant to Rule 23(a)(3) of the Federal Rules of Civil Procedure . . . ;

(3) Thirty saleswomen of a total of 382 suing on their own behalf and on behalf of the others . . .

The first part of defendants' motion is to dismiss the amended complaint as to the salesmen and saleswomen for failure to state a cause of action for libel since, it is alleged, no ascertainable person is identified by the words complained of.

. . . .

An examination of the case and text law of libel reveals that the following propositions are rather widely accepted:

(1) Where the group or class libeled is large, none can sue even though the language used is inclusive.

(2) Where the group or class libeled is small, and each and every member of the group or class is referred to, then any individual member can sue.

Conflict arises when the publication complained of libels *some* or *less than all* of a designated small group. Some courts say no cause of action exists in any individual of the group. Other courts in other states would apparently allow such an action.

. . . .

The Court of Appeals for this Circuit has referred to the Restatement of Torts for the "general law." *Mattox v. News Syndicate Co., supra,* 176 F.2d at page 901. If we do so in this instance, we find that Illustration 2 of § 564, Comment (c) reads as follows:

"A newspaper publishes the statement that some member of B's household has committed murder. In the absence of any circumstances indicating that some particular member of B's household was referred to, the newspaper has defamed each member of B's household."

Thus the Restatement of Torts would authorize suit by each member of a small group where the defamatory publication refers to but a portion of the group. This result seems to find support in logic and justice, as well as the case law mentioned above. See Riesman, *Group Libel,* 42 Col. Law Review 727, 768 (1942). An imputation of gross immorality to *some* of a small group casts suspicion upon all, where no attempt is made to exclude the innocent.[1]

Applying the above principles to the case at bar, it is the opinion of this Court that the plaintiff salesmen, of whom it is alleged that "most . . . are fairies" have a

---

[1] It should be noted that defendants have not moved to dismiss as to the plaintiff models. If this is a concession of a valid cause of action on the part of the models, it is difficult to perceive a legalistic distinction between the statements that 'some Neiman models are call girls' and 'most of the sales staff are fairies.'

cause of action in New York and most likely other states; . . . . Defendants' motion to dismiss as to the salesmen for failure to state a claim upon which relief can be granted is denied.

The plaintiff saleswomen are in a different category. The alleged defamatory statement in defendants' book speaks of the saleswomen generally. While it does not use the word "all" or similar terminology, yet it stands unqualified. However, the group of saleswomen is extremely large, consisting of 382 members at the time of publication. No specific individual is named in the alleged libelous statement. I am not cited to a single case which would support a cause of action by an individual member of any group of such magnitude.

. . . .

[W]here the group or class disparaged is a large one, absent circumstances pointing to a particular plaintiff as the person defamed, no individual member of the group or class has a cause of action. Restatement of Torts, § 564(c); Gatley, Libel and Slander (3rd Ed. 1938) pp. 123-124. . . .

Giving the plaintiff saleswomen the benefit of all legitimate favorable inferences, the defendants' alleged libel cannot reasonably be said to concern more than the saleswomen as a class. There is no language referring to some ascertained or ascertainable person. Nor is the class so small that it follows that defamation of the class infects the individual of the class. This Court so holds as a matter of law since it is of the opinion that no reasonable man would take the writers seriously and conclude from the publication a reference to any individual saleswoman. *Weston v. Commercial Advertiser Ass'n, supra,* 184 N.Y. at page 485, 77 N.E. 660; *Watts-Wagner Co. v. General Motors Corp., supra.*

While it is generally recognized that even where the group is large, a member of the group may have a cause of action if some particular circumstances point to the plaintiff as the person defamed, no such circumstances are alleged in the amended complaint. This further exception is designed to apply only where a plaintiff can satisfy a jury that the words referred solely or especially to himself. Odgers, Libel and Slander (6th Ed.) p. 128. The plaintiffs' general allegation that the alleged libellous and defamatory matter was written "of and concerning . . . each of them" is insufficient to satisfy this requirement. *Cf. Noral v. Hearst Publications, supra.*

Accordingly it is the opinion of this Court that as a matter of law the individual saleswomen do not state a claim for libel upon which relief can be granted and the motion to dismiss their cause of action is granted.

———————

1.   The plaintiff must show that the statement was made "of and concerning" her. What if the statement is: "She burned her car."?

2.   One of the problems with common law defamation is that if the defendant intended to make the statement and it is defamatory, she is strictly liable, regardless of whether she intended to defame the plaintiff. For example, in *Hutton v. Jones,* [1920] A.C. 20, the defendant Newspaper published: "[T]here is Artemus Jones with a woman who is not his wife, who must be the other thing." The name was invented by the author without realizing that there actually was such a man.

The true Artemus Jones, an attorney, came forward, sued, and won.

In *New York Times v. Sullivan, infra,* a newspaper advertisement refers to the chief of police, but does not name him, and makes some trivial factual errors. Because of strict liability, the commissioner of police won $500,000 before the Alabama courts.

PRING v. PENTHOUSE INTERNATIONAL
United States Court of Appeals for the Tenth Circuit, 1982
695 F.2d 438, *cert. denied,* 462 U.S. 1132 (1983)

SETH, CHIEF JUDGE.

This defamation case concerns an article which appeared in defendant's magazine *Penthouse.* It was written about a "Charlene," a Miss Wyoming at the Miss America contest and about the contest. The defendants argue that the story is a spoof of the contest, ridicule, an attempt to be humorous, "black humor," a complete fantasy which could not be taken literally.

The basic question which had to be resolved at the trial was in two parts — whether the publication was about the plaintiff, that is, whether it was of and concerning her as a matter of identity; and secondly, whether the story must reasonably be understood as describing actual facts or events about plaintiff or actual conduct of the plaintiff.

. . . .

[T]he story must reasonably be understood as describing actual facts about the plaintiff or her actual conduct. . . . In some opinions it is treated as part of the "of and concerning" requirement. It is really part of the basic ingredient of any defamation action; that is, a false representation of fact. In the case before us this requirement that the story must reasonably be understood to describe actual facts about the plaintiff has become the central issue.

. . . .

The article had its setting at a Miss America contest and described Charlene, a Miss Wyoming at the contest, who was a baton twirler. The article began with a description of Charlene with other contestants at a bar during the course of the contest. It quotes a conversation between Charlene and her coach, a man referred to as Corky. The story then switches to the contest as Charlene is about to perform her talent as a baton twirler. She is about to go on stage and her thoughts are described. She thinks of Wyoming and an incident there when she was with a football player from her school. It describes an act of fellatio whereby she causes him to levitat. . . .

The complaint, as amended, refers to these incidents and limits the consequences to:

"The net effect of the aforementioned article was to create the impression throughout the United States, Wyoming and the world that the Plaintiff committed fellatio on one Monty Applewhite and also upon her coach,

Corky Corcoran, in the presence of a national television audience at the Miss America Pageant. The article also creates the impression that Plaintiff committed fellatio like acts upon her baton at the Miss America contest."

. . . .

The author of the article was the defendant Cioffari, a Ph.D. who was a professor of English at a university in New Jersey.

. . . Here, the underlying event described was the Miss America Pageant, but it was readily apparent, with the extended description of thoughts of Charlene and other indications, that it was all fanciful and did not purport to be a factual account. In this context there are the particular three incidents which are in themselves fantasy and present levitation as the central theme and as a device to "save the world." We have impossibility and fantasy within a fanciful story. Also of significance is the fact that some of the incidents were described as being on national television and apparently before the audience at the pageant or part of the audience. This in itself would seem to provide a sufficient signal that the story could not be taken literally, and the portions charged as defamatory could not reasonably be understood as a statement of fact. . . .

The test is not whether the story is or is not characterized as "fiction," "humor," or anything else in the publication, but whether the charged portions in context could be reasonably understood as describing actual facts about the plaintiff or actual events in which she participated. If it could not be so understood, the charged portions could not be taken literally. . . .

All the testimony from plaintiff's lay witnesses was that it could not be about the plaintiff. An "expert" witness testified that some individuals might attach a broader subliminal meaning of sexual permissiveness, but this does not represent an applicable standard and cannot be regarded as much more than a contradiction of the testimony of her witnesses.

The charged portions of the story described something physically impossible in an impossible setting. In these circumstances we must reach the same conclusion . . . that it is simply impossible to believe that a reader would not have understood that the charged portions were pure fantasy and nothing else. It is impossible to believe that anyone could understand that levitation could be accomplished by oral sex before a national television audience or anywhere else. The incidents charged were impossible. The setting was impossible.

This does not leave, on the record before us, any alternative but to decide as a matter of law . . . "even the most careless reader must have perceived that" the descriptions were "no more than rhetorical hyperbole." Here, they were obviously a complete fantasy.

. . . .

The judgment must be reversed with directions to set aside the verdict of the jury and to dismiss the action.

IT IS SO ORDERED.

BREITENSTEIN, CIRCUIT JUDGE, dissenting:

The majority holds that as a matter of law this defamation action must be dismissed because the publication was pure fantasy protected by the First Amendment. I do not agree.

On overwhelming evidence the jury found that the plaintiff Pring was the "Miss Wyoming" about whom the Penthouse article was written. The majority accept that jury finding. The question is whether Penthouse can escape liability by the claim that the article was fiction and fantasy.

The article contains both fact and fiction. The article says that Miss Wyoming performed fellatio with a male companion and caused him to levitate. . . . I consider levitation, dreams, and public performance as fiction. Fellatio is not. It is a physical act, a fact, not a mental idea. . . .

Penthouse cannot escape liability by relying on the fantasy used to embellish the fact. Penthouse did not present the article as fiction. It did not make the usual disclaimer of reference to no person living or dead. In the table of contents, the article is characterized as "Humor."

---

1. If Ms. Pring were a married woman with children, would she likely have suffered shame and humiliation? Why then did the court refuse to provide a remedy? How would you have decided the case?

2. Hyperbole has been discussed earlier in *Hustler Magazine v. Falwell*, Chapter 2, *supra*.

C. DEFENSES TO DEFAMATION

1. Truth

An action for defamation cannot be maintained for truthful statements. Absolute truth is not required and substantial truth is sufficient. *See Kilian v. Doubleday & Co.*, 367 Pa. 117, 79 A.2d 657 (Pa. 1951). In *Kilian*, which involved an account of alleged mistreatment of American soldiers in a camp in England during World War II, the defendant lost because he failed to prove that the statements were substantially true. In many jurisdictions, truth used to be an affirmative defense, but it is now established that the First Amendment usually requires the plaintiff to prove the falsehood of the statements in question. *See Masson v. New Yorker Magazine* and *Philadelphia Newspapers v. Hepps, infra*.

2. Privileges

CARRADINE v. MINNESOTA
Supreme Court of Minnesota, 1994
511 N.W.2d 733

COYNE, JUSTICE.

We agreed to review this case, which has not yet been tried, in order to address whether a state trooper enjoys an absolute privilege that affords him or her absolute immunity from a defamation suit for anything said in preparing an arrest report or in responding to press inquiries about the arrest.

On July 9, 1987, plaintiff, Robert Reed Carradine, was stopped and arrested by a state trooper, defendant Patrick Chase, as he was driving to the airport to catch a flight. In his arrest report and in statements to jail personnel, to prosecutors and to a reporter, Chase said that Carradine's conduct involved speeding, reckless driving, fleeing an officer, and impersonating an officer. Carradine was booked, finger printed, strip-searched and held in custody for 10 hours before being released. News accounts of Carradine's alleged conduct appeared in newspapers throughout the county and on television because Carradine, in addition to "racing" cars professionally, is an actor who has appeared in a number of movies, the most well-known being "Revenge of the Nerds."

. . . .

Carradine then filed suit against Chase and his employer, the State of Minnesota, claiming unreasonable search and seizure, denial of due process, assault and battery, false imprisonment, excessive use of force, negligent infliction of emotional distress, defamation, malicious prosecution, negligence, trespass to personal property, conversion, and vicarious liability.

. . . .

The trial court granted summary judgment to the defendants on all of Carradine's federal claims and all of his state claims except for three: negligent infliction of emotional distress, defamation and vicarious liability. Defendants appealed from the denial of summary judgment as to those three claims. Carradine noticed review of the award of partial summary judgment.

The court of appeals, in affirming, said, inter alia, that Chase lacked an absolute privilege to make defamatory statements in preparing the arrest report and in subsequently talking with the press about the arrest. *Carradine v. State*, 494 N.W.2d 77, 81 (Minn. App. 1992).

The history of absolute privilege for defamatory statements made by public officials in the course of duty is "a story of uneven development." *Barr v. Matteo*, 360 U.S. 564, 579, 79 S. Ct. 1335, 3 L. Ed. 2d 1434 (1959) (Warren, C.J., dissenting). Absolute legislative privilege "dates back to at least 1399." Id., citing Van Vechten Veeder, *Absolute Immunity in Defamation: Legislative and Executive Proceedings*, 10 Colum. L. Rev. 131, 132 (1910). "The Constitution itself gives an absolute privilege to members of both Houses of Congress in respect to any speech, debate, vote, report, or action done in session." *Barr v. Matteo*, 360 U.S. at 569 (Harlan, J.), citing U.S. Const., Art. I, § 6. Moreover, the privilege is given by our state constitution to the legislative branch. Minn. Const., Art. IV, § 10.

Absolute immunity for defamatory statements made by participants in the course of a judicial proceeding dates back at least to the sixteenth century. Van Vechten Veeder, *Absolute Immunity in Defamation: Judicial Proceedings*, 9 Colum. L. Rev. 463, 474 (1909). The United States Supreme Court "early held that judges of courts of superior or general authority are absolutely privileged as respects civil suits to recover for actions taken by them in the exercise of their judicial functions, irrespective of the motives with which those acts are alleged to have been performed," *Bradley v. Fisher*, 80 U.S. 335, 20 L. Ed. 646, 13 Wall 335, and that a like immunity extends to other officers of government whose duties are related to the judicial process.

Barr v. Matteo, 360 U.S. 564, 79 S. Ct. 1335, 3 L. Ed. 2d 1434, is the leading case recognizing absolute privilege in the executive branch. The officer there, Acting Director of the Office of Rent Stabilization, issued a press release announcing his intention to suspend certain employees because of the part they had played in formulating a controversial plan for the use of certain agency funds. The employees sued the Acting Director for libel, alleging malice. The United States Supreme Court, by a split decision, held that the statements in the press release were absolutely privileged.

There is now considerable agreement among state courts that "high level" executive officers have absolute immunity from suit for defamatory statements made in the course of their duties. . . .

It is no answer to the question whether an executive branch employee has absolute immunity to say that the employee is not a "high level" employee but a "low level" employee. Immunity "is not a badge or emolument of exalted office, but an expression of a policy designed to aid in the effective functioning of government. The complexities and magnitude of governmental activity have become so great that there must of necessity be a delegation and redelegation of authority as to many functions, and we cannot say that these functions become less important simply because they are exercised by officers of lower rank in the executive hierarchy." *Barr v. Matteo*, 360 U.S. at 572-73.

In other words, the purpose of extending absolute immunity to an officer performing a certain governmental function is not primarily to protect the officer personally from civil liability (although that is the effect of absolute immunity). Rather, the rationale is that unless the officer in question is absolutely immune from suit, the officer will timorously, instead of fearlessly, perform the function in question and, as a result, government — that is, the public — will be the ultimate loser. *Barr v. Matteo*, 360 U.S. at 571. . . .

Whether an executive officer is absolutely immune from defamation liability depends on many factors, including the nature of the function assigned to the officer and the relationship of the statements to the performance of that function.

The issue in this case, therefore, is not whether police officers have absolute immunity from civil suit for all allegedly defamatory statements made in the performance of their duties. Instead, we address two much more specific issues: (a) whether Trooper Chase has absolute immunity from civil suit for allegedly defamatory statements made in an arrest report; and (b) whether this officer has absolute immunity from civil suit for allegedly defamatory statements made in response to press inquiries about the arrest. We believe that the proper answers are "yes" to the first question and "no, with qualification" to the second.

In answering "yes" to the first question, we attach great significance to the following factors: (a) It is a key part of an arresting officer's job to prepare a written arrest report accurately summarizing the circumstances leading to and surrounding the arrest; (b) the report typically is useful not only to the officer's departmental superiors but also to the prosecutor in determining whether to charge the arrestee and, if so, what offenses to charge; (c) moreover, the police report often plays a significant role in the trial of a criminal defendant, with the prosecutor using the report to refresh the officer's recollection and with defense counsel using the report to cross-examine and attempt to impeach the officer; and (d) the knowledge that making statements in the report subjects the officer to possible civil liability in a defamation or similar action may well deter the honest officer from fearlessly and vigorously preparing a detailed, accurate report and increase the likelihood that the officer will hesitate to prepare anything more than a bland report that will be less useful within the department and in any subsequent prosecution and trial. . . . Given these and other factors, we conclude that Trooper Chase has absolute immunity from a civil suit in defamation for the statements made in the written police report.[2]

Whether Chase has absolute immunity from civil suit for allegedly defamatory statements made in response to press inquiries is another matter. An arresting officer's freedom of expression in making an arrest report is essential to the performance of his function as an officer, whereas it is not at all essential to the officer's performance of his duties as an officer that he respond to press inquiries about the circumstances leading up to and surrounding an arrest. . . . It appears that there is evidence that statements to the media by state troopers are "allowed" by state patrol policy but that officers are not required to give statements when requested. In fact, there is evidence that state troopers are encouraged to refer questions to a public affairs officer in well-publicized cases.

Since we must presume on this record that responding to press inquiries was not one of the officer's duties and because of the greater risk of publication to a large number of people that accompanies the making of public statements about the arrestee, we conclude that not all statements made to the press by an arresting officer such as Trooper Chase are absolutely privileged.

To the extent, however, that Chase's statements to the press merely amounted to an exact repetition or a substantial repetition, without amplification or comment, of the statements made in the arrest report, which is a matter of public record available to the press pursuant to Minn. Stat. § 13.82 (1993 Supp.), the statements

---

[2] For similar reasons, we conclude that, on the facts as we understand them, Chase also has absolute immunity from civil suit for any other intradepartmental statements he made in the course of his duties.

to the press may not support liability. *Johnson v. Dirkswager*, 315 N.W.2d at 222. Plaintiff Carradine argues that Chase's statements to the press did not merely amount to a substantial repetition of the statements in the arrest report. We believe that the trial court is in a better position at this time than we are to determine whether this is so. If it is so and if a jury properly might find that the additional statements significantly added to any injury sustained by plaintiff over and above any injury sustained as a result of the absolutely privileged statements, then plaintiff should be allowed to proceed to trial against Chase;[3] otherwise, not.

The only remaining issue is whether any absolute immunity of the officer also extends to protect the state in its capacity as the officer's employer. We hold that, in this context, the immunity enjoyed by the officer extends to the state. *Pletan v. Gaines*, 494 N.W.2d 38, 41-43 (Minn. 1992).

Affirmed in part and reversed in part; remanded to trial court for further proceedings.

---

1.   Absolute immunity extends to the judge, the attorney, and witnesses as long as the statements are relevant to the case. *See Irwin v. Ashurst*, 158 Or. 61, 74 P.2d 1127 (1938).

2.   Some states would not extend absolute immunity to a low ranking official, such as a police officer. She would receive a qualified immunity instead. *See Chamberlain v. Mathis*, 151 Ariz. 551, 729 P.2d 905 (1986).

3.   Although Senator William Proxmire had an absolute privilege under the Speech or Debate Clause to speak on the Senate floor, he lost it by speaking to the press outside the Senate. He defamed a scientist by giving him the "Golden Fleece Award" (a device Proxmire used to ridicule wasteful government spending) for his research on emotional behavior. *Hutchinson v. Proxmire*, 443 U.S. 111 (1979).

LIBERMAN v. GELSTEIN
Court of Appeals of New York, 1992
605 N.E.2d 344

KAYE, J.

In this action for slander, we consider whether the plaintiff has stated a viable claim without any showing of special damages, whether the alleged slander is protected by qualified privilege, and whether there is a triable issue of fact as to malice. We conclude that plaintiff's claims were correctly dismissed on summary judgment.

---

[3] Moreover, in order to be entitled to proceed to trial on the basis of any significantly different statements made to the press, plaintiff must first satisfy the trial court that he has evidence to establish actual malice by the officer in the making of the statements, because, to the extent the statements by the officer are not protected by an absolute privilege, they are protected by a qualified privilege. Plaintiff must therefore establish that he has actual evidence of malice; it is not enough for him to argue that malice may be inferred from the mere making of the statements in question. We also leave this determination to the trial court at this time.

I

Before us is one of eight actions, consolidated for disposition by the motion court, centering on a luxury apartment building in Manhattan. Plaintiff, Barnet L. Liberman, is the building's landlord. Defendant, Leonard Gelstein (a tenant), is on the board of governors of the tenants' association. . . .

This defamation action against Gelstein is one of three suits brought by Liberman against individual members of the tenant association's board of governors. . . .

The present complaint alleged five causes of action sounding in slander. Only two — the second and fifth — are pressed by plaintiff on this appeal. . . .

In his second cause of action, plaintiff alleged that in July 1986, the following conversation took place between defendant and another tenant of the building, Robert Kohler.

> "Gelstein: Can you find out from your friend at the precinct which cop is on the take from Liberman?

> "Kohler: What are you talking about?

> "Gelstein: There is a cop on the take from Liberman. That's why none of the building's cars ever get tickets — they can park anywhere because Liberman's paid them off. He gives them a hundred or two hundred a week."

The fifth cause of action alleged that in May 1986 defendant made the following statement in the presence of employees of the building:

> "Liberman threw a punch at me. He screamed at my wife and daughter. He called my daughter a slut and threatened to kill me and my family."

Plaintiff claimed $5 million damages on each cause of action for injury to his reputation and emotional distress. . . .

II

We next consider whether the courts below properly concluded that defendant's conversation with Kohler was conditionally privileged and that plaintiff failed to raise an issue of fact on malice.

Courts have long recognized that the public interest is served by shielding certain communications, though possibly defamatory, from litigation, rather than risk stifling them altogether (*see, Bingham v Gaynor*, 203 NY 27, 31). When compelling public policy requires that the speaker be immune from suit, the law affords an absolute privilege, while statements fostering a lesser public interest are only conditionally privileged.

One such conditional, or qualified, privilege extends to a "communication made by one person to another upon a subject in which both have an interest" (*Stillman v Ford*, 22 N.Y.2d 48, 53). This "common interest" privilege (*see*, Restatement § 596) has been applied, for example, to employees of an organization (*see, Loughry v*

Lincoln First Bank, 67 N.Y.2d 369, 376), members of a faculty tenure committee *(Stukuls v. State of New York*, 42 N.Y.2d 272) and constituent physicians of a health insurance plan *(Shapiro v. Health Ins. Plan*, 7 N.Y.2d 56, 60-61). The rationale for applying the privilege in these circumstances is that so long as the privilege is not abused, the flow of information between persons sharing a common interest should not be impeded.

We thus agree with the motion court and Appellate Division that defendant's conversation with Kohler was conditionally privileged *(see,* Restatement § 596, comment *d* ["Tenants in common . . . are included within the rule stated in this Section as being conditionally privileged to communicate among themselves matter defamatory of others which concerns their common interests"]). Gelstein and Kohler were members of the governing body of an association formed to protect the tenants' interests. If Liberman was in fact bribing the police so that his cars could occupy spaces in front of the building, that would be inimical to those interests. Thus, Gelstein had a qualified right to communicate his suspicions — though defamatory of Liberman — to Kohler.

The shield provided by a qualified privilege may be dissolved if plaintiff can demonstrate that defendant spoke with "malice." Under common law, malice meant spite or ill will. In *New York Times Co. v. Sullivan* (376 U.S. 254), however, the Supreme Court established an "actual malice" standard for certain cases governed by the First Amendment: "knowledge that [the statement] was false or . . . reckless disregard of whether it was false or not." Consequently, the term "malice" has become somewhat confused. . . . Indeed, as the Supreme Court itself recently acknowledged:

> "Actual malice under the *New York Times* standard should not be confused with the concept of malice as an evil intent or a motive arising from spite or ill will . . . We have used the term actual malice as a shorthand to describe the First Amendment protections for speech injurious to reputation and we continue to do so here. But the term can confuse as well as enlighten. In this respect, the phrase may be an unfortunate one."

Nevertheless, malice has now assumed a dual meaning, and we have recognized that the constitutional as well as the common-law standard will suffice to defeat a conditional privilege.

Under the *Times* malice standard, the plaintiff must demonstrate that the "statements [were] made with [a] high degree of awareness of their probable falsity" *(Garrison v. Louisiana*, 379 U.S. 64, 74). In other words, there "must be sufficient evidence to permit the conclusion that the defendant in fact entertained serious doubts as to the truth of [the] publication" *(St. Amant v. Thompson*, 390 U.S. 727, 731; *see also,* Restatement § 600, comment *b*).

Applying these principles, we conclude that there is no triable malice issue under the *Times* standard. Although the dissenter below suggested that Gelstein's admission that he did not know whether the bribery charge was true raised a triable issue on malice, there is a critical difference between not knowing whether something is true and being highly aware that it is probably false. Only the latter establishes reckless disregard in a defamation action. Moreover, as the motion court correctly observed, plaintiff's mere characterization of Gelstein's informants as "disgruntled" is insufficient to raise a triable issue. Although plaintiff criticizes defendant for not producing affidavits from the informants — arguing that "it has never been factually established that Gelstein had any source" — it was plaintiff's burden to raise a factual issue on malice, and he did not seek to depose the employees either. In sum, this record is insufficient to raise a triable issue of fact under the *Times* standard of malice.

Similarly, there is insufficient evidence of malice under the common-law definition. A jury could undoubtedly find that, at the time Gelstein discussed his bribery suspicions with Kohler, Gelstein harbored ill will toward Liberman. In this context, however, spite or ill will refers not to defendant's general feelings about plaintiff, but to the speaker's motivation for making the defamatory statements (*see*, Restatement § 603, and comment *a*). If the defendant's statements were made to further the interest protected by the privilege, it matters not that defendant *also* despised plaintiff. Thus, a triable issue is raised only if a jury could reasonably conclude that "malice was the one and only cause for the publication."

Plaintiff has not sustained that burden. Significantly, Gelstein did not make a public announcement of his suspicions — from which an inference could be drawn that his motive was to defame Liberman — but relayed them to a colleague who was in a position to investigate. As noted, the conversation was within the common interest of Gelstein and Kohler, and there is nothing in this record from which a reasonable jury could find that Gelstein was not seeking to advance that common interest.

Thus, the courts below properly concluded that defendant's conversation with Kohler was qualifiedly privileged, and plaintiff failed to raise a fact issue on malice.

Accordingly, the order of the Appellate Division should be affirmed, with costs.

---

1. *Liberman* defines the concept of qualified privilege and how it may be lost.

2. A common application of the qualified privilege is an employer's reply to an inquiry from a prospective employer regarding the qualifications of a job applicant. *Erickson v. Marsh & McLennan*, 569 A.2d 793 (N.J. 1990), suggests a three-part test for whether the qualified privilege applies:

> The critical elements of this test are the appropriateness of the occasion on which the defamatory information is published, the legitimacy of the interest thereby sought to be protected or promoted, and the pertinence of the receipt of that information by the recipient.

Applying that test *Erickson* held that a qualified privilege extended to statements made to Erickson's prospective employers where they "were made in response to inquiries . . . [and] not simply volunteered," the "prospective employers had a legitimate and obvious interest in the professional qualifications, skill, and experience" of the plaintiff "including the reasons for his termination," and the information provided "specifically addressed the questions posed" making it "directly relevant to their inquiry."

3. Some jurisdictions recognize a qualified privilege for reports to the police of potentially criminal behavior. *See Kennedy v. Sheriff of E. Baton Rouge*, 935 So. 2d 669 (La. 2006) (report to sheriff by fast-food outlet's employees erroneously claiming that plaintiff was using counterfeit money held subject to qualified privilege).

BROWN & WILLIAMSON TOBACCO CORPORATION v. JACOBSON AND CBS
United States Court of Appeals for the Seventh Circuit, 1983
713 F.2d 262

POSNER, CIRCUIT JUDGE.

This diversity suit brought by Brown & Williamson, the manufacturer of Viceroy cigarettes, charges CBS and Walter Jacobson with libel and other violations of Illinois law. Jacobson is a news commentator for WBBM-TV, a Chicago television station owned by CBS. . . .

In 1975, Ted Bates, the advertising agency that had the Viceroy account, hired the Kennan market-research firm to help develop a new advertising strategy for Viceroy. Kennan submitted a report which stated that for "the young smoker," "a cigarette, and the whole smoking process, is part of the illicit pleasure category. . . . In the young smoker's mind a cigarette falls into the same category with wine, beer, shaving, wearing a bra (or purposely not wearing one), declaration of independence and striving for self-identity. . . . To the best of your ability, (considering some legal constraints), relate the cigarette to 'pot', wine, beer, sex, etc. *Don't* communicate health or health-related points." Ted Bates forwarded the report to Brown & Williamson. According to the allegations of the complaint, which on this appeal we must accept as true, Brown & Williamson rejected the "illicit pleasure strategy" proposed in the report, and fired Ted Bates primarily because of displeasure with the proposed strategy.

Years later the Federal Trade Commission conducted an investigation of cigarette advertising, and in May 1981 it published a report of its staff on the investigation. The FTC staff report discusses the Kennan report, correctly dates it to May 1975, and after quoting from it the passages we have quoted states that "B&W adopted many of the ideas contained in this report in the development of a Viceroy advertising campaign." . . .

Walter Jacobson's "Perspective" on the tobacco industry was broadcast on November 11 and rebroadcast on November 12 and again on March 5, 1982. In the broadcast, Jacobson, after stating that "pushing cigarettes on television is prohibited," announces his theme: "Television is off limits to cigarettes and so the business, the killer business, has gone to the ad business in New York for help, to the slicksters on Madison Avenue with a billion dollars a year for bigger and better ways to sell cigarettes. Go for the youth of America, go get'em guys. . . . Hook'em while they are young, make'em start now — just think how many cigarettes they'll be smoking when they grow up." Various examples of how cigarette marketing attempts "to addict the children to poison" are given. The last and longest concerns Viceroy.

. . . .

Under contemporary as under traditional Illinois law, Jacobson's broadcast is libelous per se. Accusing a cigarette company of what many people consider the immoral strategy of enticing children to smoke — enticing them by advertising that employs themes exploitive of adolescent vulnerability — is likely to harm the company. It may make it harder for the company to fend off hostile government regulation and may invite rejection of the company's product by angry parents who smoke but may not want their children to do so. These harms cannot easily be measured, but so long as some harm is highly likely the difficulty of measurement is an additional reason, under the modern functional approach of the Illinois courts, for finding libel per se rather than insisting on proof of special damage. . . .

The defendants . . . argue and the district court also found that the libel was privileged as a fair and accurate summary of the Federal Trade Commission staff's report on cigarette advertising. The parties agree as they must that Illinois recognizes a privilege for fair and accurate summaries of, or reports on, government proceedings and investigations. They agree that the privilege extends to a public FTC staff report on an investigation. But they disagree over whether Jacobson's summary of the FTC staff report was "fair," that is, whether the overall impression created by the summary was no more defamatory than that created by the original. See Restatement (Second) of Torts § 611, Comment f (1977). Since this is a question of fact . . . and the case was dismissed on the pleadings, all we need decide is whether the fairness of the Jacobson summary emerges so incontrovertibly from a comparison of the FTC staff report with the broadcast that no rational jury considering these documents with the aid of whatever additional evidence Brown & Williamson might introduce could consider the summary unfair.

. . . .

The fact that there are discrepancies between a libel and the government report on which it is based need not defeat the privilege of fair summary. Unless the report is published verbatim it is bound to convey a somewhat different impression from the original, no matter how carefully the publisher attempts to summarize or paraphrase or excerpt it fairly and accurately. An unfair summary in the present context is one that amplifies the libelous effect that publication of the government report verbatim would have on a reader who read it carefully — that carries a "greater sting," . . . The Jacobson broadcast conveys the following message: Brown & Williamson currently is advertising cigarettes in a manner designed to entice children to smoke by associating smoking with drinking, sex, marijuana, and other illicit pleasures of youth. So at least a rational jury might interpret the source and the summary, and if it did it would be entitled to conclude that the summary carried a greater sting and was therefore unfair.

————————

1. Aren't there always going to be "discrepancies" between the media report and the government record? How does a court determine whether those discrepancies "amplif[y] the libelous effect"? Won't a media report almost always carry more "sting"?

2. Why was the CBS report libelous? Why didn't CBS argue truth? Is the tobacco industry viewed differently today?

3. Other Defenses

A full and fair retraction by the newspaper may reduce the amount of damages. *See Burnett v. National Enquirer, Inc.*, 144 Cal. App. 3d 991, 193 Cal. Rptr. 206 (1983). The California Code provides:

> Section 48a:
>
> 1. In any action for damages for the publication of a libel in a newspaper, or of a slander by radio broadcast, plaintiff shall recover no more than special damages unless a correction be demanded and be not published or broadcast, as hereinafter provided. Plaintiff shall serve upon the publisher, at the place of publication or broadcaster at the place of broadcast, a written notice specifying the statements claimed to be libelous and demanding that the same be corrected. Said notice and demand must be served within 20 days after knowledge of the publication or broadcast of the statements claimed to be libelous.

A defamatory statement cannot be enjoined because to do so would involve a "prior restraint" violating the defendant's right to free speech, protected by the First Amendment. *Near v. Minnesota*, 283 U.S. 697 (1931); *New York Times v. United States*, 403 U.S. 713 (1971).

Sometimes a defendant argues that the plaintiff's reputation is so bad (*e.g.*, if the plaintiff were a mass murderer) that he is libel-proof and cannot be defamed. *See Jackson v. Long-Cope*, 476 N.E.2d 617 (Mass. 1985). However, it may still be possible to defame bad people, on the theory that "[t]he law . . . proceeds upon the optimistic premise that there is a little bit of good in all of us — or perhaps upon the pessimistic assumption that no matter how bad someone is, he can always be worse." *Liberty Lobby v. Anderson*, 746 F.2d 1563 (D.C. Cir. 1984) (Scalia, J.)

The single publication rule is now widely accepted: "The publication of a book, periodical, or newspaper containing defamatory matter gives rise to one cause of action for libel which accrues at the time of the original publication." The previous rule that each sale gives rise to a separate cause of action is no longer followed. *Ogden v. Association of the United States Army*, 177 F. Supp. 498 (D.D.C. 1959).

A vendor or distributor of newspapers, magazines, or books is known as a "secondary publisher" and is not liable unless it can be shown that the distributor knew of the defamatory material in the publication. *See Balabanoff v. Fossani*, 81 N.Y.S.2d 732 (Sup. Ct. 1948). Under federal law, internet providers are similarly immune from suits based on the content of information they transmit. The Communications Decency Act, 47 U.S.C. § 230(c)(1), states: "No provider of an interactive computer service shall be treated as the publisher or speaker of information provided by another content provider."

In recent years, some jurisdictions have experienced a phenomenon known as "SLAPP" suits (Strategic Lawsuits Against Public Participation). These are actions, frequently claiming defamation, that are brought against individuals, not with the expectation of success on the merits, but to deter plaintiffs (or others like them) from seeking legal redress or engaging in various forms of public criticism of an individual or entity. They are sometimes brought as a counterclaim, sometimes as an original action. In an attempt to counteract these suits, some jurisdictions have established procedures for summary dismissal of SLAPP suits and have allowed successful defendants to recover attorneys' fees and costs from the plaintiffs or counterclaimants who bring them. For cases applying California's anti-SLAPP legislation, see *Simpson Strong-Tie Co., Inc. v. Gore*, 49 Cal. 4th 12 (2010) (finding defamation suit brought against individual who questioned safety of plaintiff's products within scope of anti-SLAPP legislation); *Kibler v. Northern Inyo County Local Hospital Dist.*, 39 Cal. 4th 192 (2006) (applying anti-SLAPP legislation to suit by doctor suspended by hospital for abusive behavior). For general discussion, see Kathryn Tate, *California's Anti-SLAPP Legislation: A Summary of and Commentary on Its Operation and Scope*, 33 Loy. L.A. L. Rev. 801 (2000).

D. CONSTITUTIONAL ISSUES

In 1964, an action was brought in Alabama against the *New York Times* and numerous civil rights leaders, based on an advertisement carried in the *Times* that criticized police handling of civil rights protests in Montgomery, Alabama. The libel action, resting on strict liability, led to a $500,000 jury verdict, based on assumed damages. The defendants argued constitutional freedom of speech as a defense, and the Supreme Court's decision in their favor changed the nature of defamation law.

1. Public Officials

NEW YORK TIMES CO. v. SULLIVAN
Supreme Court of the United States, 1964
376 U.S. 254

MR. JUSTICE BRENNAN delivered the opinion of the Court.

We are required in this case to determine for the first time the extent to which the constitutional protections for speech and press limit a State's power to award damages in a libel action brought by a public official against critics of his official conduct.

Respondent L. B. Sullivan is one of the three elected Commissioners of the City of Montgomery, Alabama. He testified that he was "Commissioner of Public Affairs and the duties are supervision of the Police Department, Fire Department, Department of Cemetery and Department of Scales." He brought this civil libel action against the four individual petitioners, who are Negroes and Alabama clergymen, and against petitioner the New York Times Company, a New York corporation which publishes the *New York Times*, a daily newspaper. A jury in the

Circuit Court of Montgomery County awarded him damages of $500,000, the full amount claimed, against all the petitioners, and the Supreme Court of Alabama affirmed. 273 Ala. 656, 144 So. 2d 25.

Respondent's complaint alleged that he had been libeled by statements in a full-page advertisement that was carried in the *New York Times* on March 29, 1960. Entitled "Heed Their Rising Voices," the advertisement began by stating that "As the whole world knows by now, thousands of Southern Negro students are engaged in widespread non-violent demonstrations in positive affirmation of the right to live in human dignity as guaranteed by the U.S. Constitution and the Bill of Rights." It went on to charge that "in their efforts to uphold these guarantees, they are being met by an unprecedented wave of terror by those who would deny and negate that document which the whole world looks upon as setting the pattern for modern freedom. . . ."

The text appeared over the names of 64 persons, many widely known for their activities in public affairs, religion, trade unions, and the performing arts. Below these names, and under a line reading "We in the South who are struggling daily for dignity and freedom warmly endorse this appeal," appeared the names of the four individual petitioners and of 16 other persons, all but two of whom were identified as clergymen in various Southern cities. The advertisement was signed at the bottom of the page by the "Committee to Defend Martin Luther King and the Struggle for Freedom in the South," and the officers of the Committee were listed.

Of the 10 paragraphs of text in the advertisement, the third and a portion of the sixth were the basis of respondent's claim of libel. They read as follows:

Third paragraph:

"In Montgomery, Alabama, after students sang 'My Country/Tis of Thee' on the State Capitol steps, their leaders were expelled from school, and truckloads of police armed with shotguns and tear-gas ringed the Alabama State College Campus. When the entire student body protested to state authorities by refusing to re-register, their dining hall was padlocked in an attempt to starve them into submission."

Sixth paragraph:

"Again and again the Southern violators have answered Dr. King's peaceful protests with intimidation and violence. They have bombed his home almost killing his wife and child. They have assaulted his person. They have arrested him seven times — for 'speeding,' 'loitering' and similar 'offenses.' And now they have charged him with 'perjury' — a *felony* under which they could imprison him for *ten years.* . . ."

Although neither of these statements mentions respondent by name, he contended that the word "police" in the third paragraph referred to him as the Montgomery Commissioner who supervised the Police Department, so that he was being accused of "ringing" the campus with police. He further claimed that the paragraph would be read as imputing to the police, and hence to him, the padlocking of the dining hall in order to starve the students into submission. As to the sixth paragraph, he contended that since arrests are ordinarily made by the police, the statement "They have arrested [Dr. King] seven times" would be read as referring to him; he further contended that the "They" who did the arresting would be equated with the "They" who committed the other described acts and with the "Southern violators." Thus, he argued, the paragraph would be read as accusing the Montgomery police, and hence him, of answering Dr. King's protests with "intimidation and violence," bombing his home, assaulting his person, and charging him with perjury. Respondent and six other Montgomery residents testified that they read some or all of the statements as referring to him in his capacity as Commissioner.

It is uncontroverted that some of the statements contained in the two paragraphs were not accurate descriptions of events which occurred in Montgomery. Although Negro students staged a demonstration on the State Capitol steps, they sang the National Anthem and not "My Country, 'Tis of Thee." Although nine students were expelled by the State Board of Education, this was not for leading the demonstration at the Capitol, but for demanding service at a lunch counter in the Montgomery County Courthouse on another day. Not the entire student body, but most of it, had protested the expulsion, not by refusing to register, but by boycotting classes on a single day; virtually all the students did register for the ensuing semester. The campus dining hall was not padlocked on any occasion, and the only students who may have been barred from eating there were the few who had neither signed a preregistration application nor requested temporary meal tickets. Although the police were deployed near the campus in large numbers on three occasions, they did not at any time "ring" the campus, and they were not called to the campus in connection with the demonstration on the State Capitol steps, as the third paragraph implied. Dr. King had not been arrested seven times, but only four; and although he claimed to have been assaulted some years earlier in connection with his arrest for loitering outside a courtroom, one of the officers who made the arrest denied that there was such an assault.

On the premise that the charges in the sixth paragraph could be read as referring to him, respondent was allowed to prove that he had not participated in the events described. Although Dr. King's home had in fact been bombed twice when his wife and child were there, both of these occasions antedated respondent's tenure as Commissioner, and the police were not only not implicated in the bombings, but had made every effort to apprehend those who were. Three of Dr. King's four arrests took place before respondent became Commissioner. Although Dr. King had in fact been indicted (he was subsequently acquitted) on two counts of perjury, each of which carried a possible five-year sentence, respondent had nothing to do with procuring the indictment.

Respondent made no effort to prove that he suffered actual pecuniary loss as a result of the alleged libel. . . .

The manager of the Advertising Acceptability Department testified that he had approved the advertisement for publication because he knew nothing to cause him to believe that anything in it was false, and because it bore the endorsement of "a number of people who are well known and whose reputation" he "had no reason to question." Neither he nor anyone else at the Times made an effort to confirm the accuracy of the advertisement, either by checking it against recent Times news stories relating to some of the described events or by any other means.

. . . .

The trial judge submitted the case to the jury under instructions that the statements in the advertisement were "libelous per se" and were not privileged, so that petitioners might be held liable if the jury found that they had published the advertisement and that the statements were made "of and concerning" respondent. . . . The judge rejected petitioners' contention that his rulings abridged the freedoms of speech and of the press that are guaranteed by the First and Fourteenth Amendments.

. . . [T]he Supreme Court of Alabama sustained the trial judge's rulings and instructions in all respects. . . . [T]he court said that malice could be inferred from the Times' "irresponsibility" in printing the advertisement while "the Times in its own files had articles already published which would have demonstrated the falsity of the allegations in the advertisement"; from the Times' failure to retract for respondent while retracting for the Governor, whereas the falsity of some of the allegations was then known to the Times and "the matter contained in the advertisement was equally false as to both parties"; and from the testimony of the Times' Secretary that, apart from the statement that the dining hall was padlocked, he thought the two paragraphs were "substantially correct." . . .

II

Under Alabama law as applied in this case, a publication is "libelous per se" if the words "tend to injure a person . . . in his reputation" or to "bring [him] into public contempt"; the trial court stated that the standard was met if the words are such as to "injure him in his public office, or impute misconduct to him in his office, or want of official integrity, or want of fidelity to a public trust. . . ." The jury must find that the words were published "of and concerning" the plaintiff, but where the plaintiff is a public official his place in the governmental hierarchy is sufficient evidence to support a finding that his reputation has been affected by statements that reflect upon the agency of which he is in charge. Once "libel per se" has been established, the defendant has no defense as to stated facts unless he can persuade the jury that they were true in all their particulars. *Alabama Ride Co. v. Vance*, 235 Ala. 263, 178 So. 438 (1938); *Johnson Publishing Co. v. Davis*, 271 Ala. 474, 494-495, 124 So. 2d 441, 457-458 (1960). His privilege of "fair comment" for expressions of opinion depends on the truth of the facts upon which the comment is based. *Parsons v. Age-Herald Publishing Co.*, 181 Ala. 439, 450, 61 So. 345, 350 (1913). Unless he can discharge the burden of proving truth, general damages are presumed, and may be awarded without proof of pecuniary injury. A showing of actual malice is apparently a prerequisite to recovery of punitive damages, and the defendant may in any event forestall a punitive award by a retraction meeting the statutory requirements. Good motives and belief in truth do not negate an inference of malice, but are relevant only in mitigation of punitive damages if the jury chooses to accord them weight.

The question before us is whether this rule of liability, as applied to an action brought by a public official against critics of his official conduct, abridges the freedom of speech and of the press that is guaranteed by the First and Fourteenth Amendments.

Respondent relies heavily, as did the Alabama courts, on statements of this Court to the effect that the Constitution does not protect libelous publications. Those statements do not foreclose our inquiry here. None of the cases sustained the use of libel laws to impose sanctions upon expression critical of the official conduct of public officials.

. . . .

The general proposition that freedom of expression upon public questions is secured by the First Amendment has long been settled by our decisions. The constitutional safeguard, we have said, "was fashioned to assure unfettered interchange of ideas for the bringing about of political and social changes desired by the people." . . . The First Amendment, said Judge Learned Hand, "presupposes that right conclusions are more likely to be gathered out of a multitude of tongues, than through any kind of authoritative selection. To many this is, and always will be, folly; but we have staked upon it our all."

. . . .

Thus we consider this case against the background of a profound national commitment to the principle that debate on public issues should be uninhibited, robust, and wide-open, and that it may well include vehement, caustic, and sometimes unpleasantly sharp attacks on government and public officials. The present advertisement, as an expression of grievance and protest on one of the major public issues of our time, would seem clearly to qualify for the constitutional protection. The question is whether it forfeits that protection by the falsity of *some* of its factual statements and by its alleged defamation of respondent.

Authoritative interpretations of the First Amendment guarantees have consistently refused to recognize an exception for any test of truth — whether administered by judges, juries, or administrative officials — and especially one that puts the burden of proving truth on the speaker. *Cf. Speiser v. Randall*, 357 U.S. 513, 525-526. The constitutional protection does not turn upon "the truth, popularity, or social utility of the ideas and beliefs which are offered." *NAACP v. Button*, 371 U.S. 415, 445. As Madison said, "Some degree of abuse is inseparable from the proper use of every thing; and in no instance is this more true than in that of the press."

. . . .

[E]rroneous statement is inevitable in free debate, and . . . it must be protected if the freedoms of expression are to have the "breathing space" that they "need . . . to survive," *NAACP v. Button*. . . .

Injury to official reputation affords no more warrant for repressing speech that would otherwise be free than does factual error. . . . Criticism of their official conduct does not lose its constitutional protection merely because it is effective criticism and hence diminishes their official reputations.

If neither factual error nor defamatory content suffices to remove the constitutional shield from criticism of official conduct, the combination of the two elements is no less inadequate. This is the lesson to be drawn from the great controversy over the Sedition Act of 1798, 1 Stat. 596, which first crystallized a national awareness of the central meaning of the First Amendment. See Levy, Legacy of Suppression (1960), at 258 *et seq.;* Smith, Freedom's Fetters (1956), at 426, 431, and *passim.* That statute made it a crime, punishable by a $5,000 fine and five years in prison, "if any person shall write, print, utter or publish . . . any false, scandalous and malicious writing or writings against the government of the United States, or either house of the Congress . . . , or the President . . . , with intent to defame . . . or to bring them, or either of them, into contempt or disrepute; or to excite against them, or either or any of them, the hatred of the good people of the United States." The Act allowed the defendant the defense of truth, and provided that the jury were to be judges both of the law and the facts. Despite these qualifications, the Act was vigorously condemned as unconstitutional in an attack joined in by Jefferson and Madison. . . .

Madison prepared the Report in support of the protest. His premise was that the Constitution created a form of government under which "The people, not the government, possess the absolute sovereignty." The structure of the government dispersed power in reflection of the people's distrust of concentrated power, and of power itself at all levels. This form of government was "altogether different" from the British form, under which the Crown was sovereign and the people were subjects. "Is it not natural and necessary, under such different circumstances," he asked, "that a different degree of freedom in the use of the press should be contemplated?" *Id.,* pp. 569-570. . . . On this footing the freedom of the press has stood; on this foundation it yet stands. . . ." 4 Elliot's Debates, *supra,* p. 570. The right of free public discussion of the stewardship of public officials was thus, in Madison's view, a fundamental principle of the American form of government.

Although the Sedition Act was never tested in this Court [the Act expired by its terms in 1801], the attack upon its validity has carried the day in the court of history. . . . These views reflect a broad consensus that the Act, because of the restraint it imposed upon criticism of government and public officials, was inconsistent with the First Amendment.

The constitutional guarantees require, we think, a federal rule that prohibits a public official from recovering damages for a defamatory falsehood relating to his official conduct unless he proves that the statement was made with "actual malice" — that is, with knowledge that it was false or with reckless disregard of whether it was false or not. . . .

III

We hold today that the Constitution delimits a State's power to award damages for libel in actions brought by public officials against critics of their official conduct. Since this is such an action, the rule requiring proof of actual malice is applicable. While Alabama law apparently requires proof of actual malice for an award of punitive damages, where general damages are concerned malice is "presumed." Such a presumption is inconsistent with the federal rule. . . .

Since respondent may seek a new trial, we deem that considerations of effective judicial administration require us to review the evidence in the present record to determine whether it could constitutionally support a judgment for respondent. This Court's duty is not limited to the elaboration of constitutional principles; we must also in proper cases review the evidence to make certain that those principles have been constitutionally applied. . . .

Applying these standards, we consider that the proof presented to show actual malice lacks the convincing clarity which the constitutional standard demands, and hence that it would not constitutionally sustain the judgment for respondent under the proper rule of law. . . .

As to the *Times*, we similarly conclude that the facts do not support a finding of actual malice. The statement by the *Times'* Secretary that . . . he thought the advertisement was "substantially correct," affords no constitutional warrant for the Alabama Supreme Court's conclusion that it was a "cavalier ignoring of the falsity of the advertisement" . . . "[E]ven if the advertisement was not "substantially correct" — although respondent's own proofs tend to show that it was — that opinion was at least a reasonable one, and there was no evidence to impeach the witness' good faith in holding it. The Times' failure to retract upon respondent's demand . . . is likewise not adequate evidence of malice for constitutional purposes. . . .

Finally, there is evidence that the Times published the advertisement without checking its accuracy against the news stories in the Times' own files. The mere presence of the stories in the files does not, of course, establish that the Times "knew" the advertisement was false, since the state of mind required for actual malice would have to be brought home to the persons in the Times' organization having responsibility for the publication of the advertisement. With respect to the failure of those persons to make the check, the record shows that they relied upon their knowledge of the good reputation of many of those whose names were listed as sponsors of the advertisement, and upon the letter from A. Philip Randolph, known to them as a responsible individual, certifying that the use of the names was authorized. . . . We think the evidence against the Times supports at most a finding of negligence in failing to discover the misstatements, and is constitutionally insufficient to show the recklessness that is required for a finding of actual malice.

We also think the evidence was constitutionally defective in another respect: it was incapable of supporting the jury's finding that the allegedly libelous statements were made "of and concerning" respondent. Respondent relies on the words of the advertisement and the testimony of six witnesses to establish a connection between it and himself. . . .

There was no reference to respondent in the advertisement, either by name or official position. A number of the allegedly libelous statements — the charges that the dining hall was padlocked and that Dr. King's home was bombed, his person assaulted, and a perjury prosecution instituted against him — did not even concern the police; despite the ingenuity of the arguments which would attach this significance to the word "They," it is plain that these statements could not reasonably be read as accusing respondent of personal involvement in the acts in question. . . . Although the statements may be taken as referring to the police, they did not on their face make even an oblique reference to respondent as an individual. Support for the asserted reference must, therefore, be sought in the testimony of respondent's witnesses. But none of them suggested any basis for the belief that respondent himself was attacked in the advertisement beyond the bare fact that he was in overall charge of the Police Department and thus bore official responsibility for police conduct . . .

The judgment of the Supreme Court of Alabama is reversed and the case is remanded to that court for further proceedings not inconsistent with this opinion.

Reversed and remanded.

MR. JUSTICE BLACK, with whom MR. JUSTICE DOUGLAS joins, concurring.

I concur in reversing this half-million-dollar judgment against the New York Times Company and the four individual defendants. In reversing the Court holds that "the Constitution delimits a State's power to award damages for libel in actions brought by public officials against critics of their official conduct." . . . I base my vote to reverse on the belief that the First and Fourteenth Amendments not merely "delimit" a State's power to award damages to "public officials against critics of their official conduct" but completely prohibit a State from exercising such a power. The Court goes on to hold that a State can subject such critics to damages if "actual malice" can be proved against them. "Malice," even as defined by the Court, is an elusive, abstract concept, hard to prove and hard to disprove. The requirement that malice be proved provides at best an evanescent protection for the right critically to discuss public affairs and certainly does not measure up to the sturdy safeguard embodied in the First Amendment. Unlike the Court, therefore, I vote to reverse exclusively on the ground that the Times and the individual defendants had an absolute, unconditional constitutional right to publish in the Times advertisement their criticisms of the Montgomery agencies and officials. . . .

We would, I think, more faithfully interpret the First Amendment by holding that at the very least it leaves the people and the press free to criticize officials and discuss public affairs with impunity. . . . An unconditional right to say what one pleases about public affairs is what I consider to be the minimum guarantee of the First Amendment.

I regret that the Court has stopped short of this holding indispensable to preserve our free press from destruction.

---

1. As the Court struggled to define the scope *of New York Times*, it was faced with a case brought by a University of Georgia football coach and athletic director (*Curtis Publishing Co. v. Butts*) and a retired Army General (*Associated Press v. Walker*) for libel. The cases were consolidated for decision. The opinions offer several different tests for liability. An important point is that both Butts and Walker were held to be public figures who should be treated the same as public officials for purposes of "actual malice." *Curtis Publishing Co. v. Butts*, 388 U.S. 130 (1967).

2. *Malice.* A great deal of caution must be exercised in using the word "malice." At common law, malice was imputed if the statement was intended. *Bromage v.*

Prosser, (1825) 4 B. & C. 247, 107 Eng. Rep. 1051 (K.B.). Often "malice" means spite or ill will and may be used to defeat a privilege. *New York Times* presents and defines the term "actual malice" in a way that is quite different from spite and ill will. It focuses instead on whether the defendant either knew of a statement's falsehood or showed "reckless disregard" of the truth.

The Supreme Court later moved away from this position in *Gertz, infra.*

3.   What is the scope of *New York Times*? If "actual malice" applies to public officials and public figures, should it apply to all matters of "public interest"? In 1971, a plurality of the Supreme Court answered in the affirmative in *Rosenbloom v. Metromedia, Inc.*, 403 U.S. 29 (1971):

> The instant case presents the question whether the *New York Times'* knowing-or-reckless-falsity standard applied in a state civil libel action brought not by a "public official" or a "public figure" but by a private individual for a defamatory falsehood uttered in a news broadcast by a radio station about the individual's involvement in an event of public or general interest. The Court of Appeals for the Third Circuit held that the *New York Times* standard did apply and reversed the judgment for damages awarded to petitioner by the jury. We granted certiorari. We agree with the Court of Appeals and affirm that court's judgment.

4.   *Public Officials.* A public (county) recreation supervisor was held to be a public official in *Rosenblatt v. Baer*, 383 U.S. 75 (1966). What about a high school athletic coach? *See O'Connor v. Burningham*, 165 P.3d 1214 (Utah 2007) (distinguishing *Butts* and holding that coach of a high school girls' basketball team was not a public official because he was "not likely to influence matters of public policy in the civil, as distinguished from the cultural, educational or sports realms").

5.   Police officers are considered public officials, *Rotkiewicz v. Sadowsky*, 730 N.E.2d 282 (Mass. 2000), but not firefighters, *Jones v. Palmer Communications*, 440 N.W.2d 884 (Iowa 1989). Why not? Should the treatment of firefighters change after 9/11/2001?

6.   *Kassel v. Gannett Co.*, 875 F.2d 935 (1st Cir. 1989), presents a three part test for public official:

> Read together, the Court's defamation opinions reveal that the "public official" rule rests on a tripodal base. The trio of policy concerns which undergirds the caselaw can be instructive in attempting to assess the rule's range and reach.
>
> . . . The Three-Legged Stool.
>
> The first leg of the stool is a frank recognition that the First Amendment requires maximum latitude for "uninhibited, robust, and wide-open" discourse on issues of public importance. That philosophy necessarily implies "a strong interest in debate about those persons who are in a position significantly to influence the resolution of [such] issues." The public official doctrine provides an extra measure of protection for speakers who dare to voice "[c]riticism of those responsible for government operations." Id. Policymakers, upper-level administrators, and supervisors are caught up in

the "public official" net for that reason: such plenipotentiaries occupy niches of "apparent importance" sufficient to give the public "an independent interest in the qualifications and performances of the person[s] who hold[] [them], beyond the general public interest in the qualifications and performance of all government employees."

. . . .

The second leg of the stool implicates communication. Those who hold public office are frequently able to defend themselves in the media. That ability is tantamount to the ability to engage in self-help. When the need arises to respond to charges, such officeholders "usually enjoy significantly greater access to the channels of effective communication and hence have a more realistic opportunity to counteract false statements than private individuals normally enjoy."

. . . .

The last leg of the stool recognizes the reality of assumed risks. Persons who actively seek positions of influence in public life do so with the knowledge that, if successful in attaining their goals, diminished privacy will result. The classic case, of course, is the aspirant to elective office: a candidate is on fair notice that adverse, even negligent, press coverage is a "necessary consequence [] of that involvement in public affairs." The same can be said of individuals who accept appointments to powerful government positions.

2.   The Actual Malice Standard

ST. AMANT v. THOMPSON
Supreme Court of the United States, 1968
390 U.S. 727

MR. JUSTICE WHITE delivered the opinion of the Court.

The question presented by this case is whether the Louisiana Supreme Court, in sustaining a judgment for damages in a public official's defamation action, correctly interpreted and applied the rule of *New York Times Co. v. Sullivan*, 376 U.S. 254 (1964), that the plaintiff in such an action must prove that the defamatory publication "was made with 'actual malice' — that is, with knowledge that it was false or with reckless disregard of whether it was false or not." 376 U.S., at 279-280.

On June 27, 1962, petitioner St. Amant, a candidate for public office, made a televised speech in Baton Rouge, Louisiana. In the course of this speech, St. Amant read a series of questions which he had put to J. D. Albin, a member of a Teamsters Union local, and Albin's answers [in an affidavit] to those questions. The exchange concerned the allegedly nefarious activities of E. G. Partin, the president of the local, and the alleged relationship between Partin and St. Amant's political opponent. . . .

Thompson promptly brought suit for defamation, claiming that the publication had "impute[d] . . . gross misconduct" and "infer[red] conduct of the most nefarious nature." The case was tried prior to the decision in *New York Times Co. v. Sullivan, supra.* The trial judge ruled in Thompson's favor and awarded $5,000 in damages. Thereafter, in the course of entertaining and denying a motion for a new trial, the Court considered the ruling in *New York Times*, finding that rule no barrier to the judgment already entered. The Louisiana Court of Appeal reversed because the record failed to show that St. Amant had acted with actual malice. . . . The Supreme Court of Louisiana reversed the intermediate appellate court. . . . In its view, there was sufficient evidence that St. Amant recklessly disregarded whether the statements about Thompson were true or false. We granted a writ of certiorari. . . .

For purposes of this case we accept the determinations of the Louisiana courts that the material published by St. Amant charged Thompson with criminal conduct, that the charge was false, and that Thompson was a public official and so had the burden of proving that the false statements about Thompson were made with actual malice as defined in *New York Times Co. v. Sullivan* and later cases. We cannot, however, agree with either the Supreme Court of Louisiana or the trial court that Thompson sustained this burden.

Purporting to apply the *New York Times* malice standard, the Louisiana Supreme Court ruled that St. Amant had broadcast false information about Thompson recklessly, though not knowingly. . . . St. Amant had no personal knowledge of Thompson's activities; he relied solely on Albin's affidavit although the record was silent as to Albin's reputation for veracity; he failed to verify the information with those in the union office who might have known the facts; he gave no consideration to whether or not the statements defamed Thompson and went ahead heedless of the consequences; and he mistakenly believed he had no responsibility for the broadcast because he was merely quoting Albin's words.

These considerations fall short of proving St. Amant's reckless disregard for the accuracy of his statements about Thompson. "Reckless disregard," it is true, cannot be fully encompassed in one infallible definition. . . . Our cases, however, have furnished meaningful guidance for the further definition of a reckless publication. In *New York Times, supra,* the plaintiff did not satisfy his burden because the record failed to show that the publisher was aware of the likelihood that he was circulating false information. . . . Mr. Justice Harlan's opinion in *Curtis Publishing Co. v. Butts,* 388 U.S. 130, 153 (1967), stated that evidence of either deliberate falsification or reckless publication "despite the publisher's awareness of probable falsity" was essential to recovery by public officials in defamation actions. These cases are clear that reckless conduct is not measured by whether a reasonably prudent man would have published, or would have investigated before publishing. There must be sufficient evidence to permit the conclusion that the defendant in fact entertained serious doubts as to the truth of his publication. Publishing with such doubts shows reckless disregard for truth or falsity and demonstrates actual malice.

It may be said that such a test puts a premium on ignorance, encourages the irresponsible publisher not to inquire, and permits the issue to be determined by the defendant's testimony that he published the statement in good faith and unaware of its probable falsity. Concededly the reckless disregard standard may permit recovery in fewer situations than would a rule that publishers must satisfy the standard of the reasonable man or the prudent publisher. But *New York Times* and succeeding cases have emphasized that the stake of the people in public business and the conduct of public officials is so great that neither the defense of truth nor the standard of ordinary care would protect against self-censorship and thus adequately implement First Amendment policies. . . . But to insure the ascertainment and publication of the truth about public affairs, it is essential that the First Amendment protect some erroneous publications as well as true ones. We adhere to this view and to the line which our cases have drawn between false communications which are protected and those which are not.

The defendant in a defamation action brought by a public official cannot, however, automatically insure a favorable verdict by testifying that he published with a belief that the statements were true. The finder of fact must determine whether the publication was indeed made in good faith. Professions of good faith will be unlikely to prove persuasive, for example, where a story is fabricated by the defendant, is the product of his imagination, or is based wholly on an unverified anonymous telephone call. Nor will they be likely to prevail when the publisher's allegations are so inherently improbable that only a reckless man would have put them in circulation. Likewise, recklessness may be found where there are obvious reasons to doubt the veracity of the informant or the accuracy of his reports.

By no proper test of reckless disregard was St. Amant's broadcast a reckless publication about a public officer. Nothing referred to by the Louisiana courts indicates an awareness by St. Amant of the probable falsity of Albin's statement about Thompson. Failure to investigate does not in itself establish bad faith. *New York Times Co. v. Sullivan, supra,* at 287-288. St. Amant's mistake about his probable legal liability does not evidence a doubtful mind on his part. . . .

Because the state court misunderstood and misapplied the actual malice standard which must be observed in a public official's defamation action, the judgment is reversed and the case remanded for further proceedings not inconsistent with this opinion.

Reversed and remanded.

---

1. *Westmoreland v. CBS,* 601 F. Supp. 66 (S.D.N.Y. 1984), held that the presentation of "one-sided attacks" does not constitute actual malice, if the publisher honestly believes in the truth of his statements:

> The fairness of the broadcast is not at issue in the libel suit. Publishers and reporters do not commit a libel in a public figure case by publishing unfair one-sided attacks. The issue in the libel suit is whether the publisher recklessly or knowingly published false material. The fact that a commentary is one sided and sets forth categorical accusations has no tendency to prove that the publisher believed it to be false. The libel law does not require the publisher to grant his accused equal time or fair reply. It requires only that the publisher not slander by known falsehoods (or reckless ones). A publisher who honestly believes in the truth of his accusations (and can point to a non-reckless basis for his beliefs) is under

no obligation under the libel law to treat the subject of his accusations fairly or evenhandedly.

MASSON v. NEW YORKER MAGAZINE, INC.
Supreme Court of the United States, 1991
501 U.S. 496

JUSTICE KENNEDY delivered the opinion of the Court.

In this libel case, a public figure claims he was defamed by an author who, with full knowledge of the inaccuracy, used quotation marks to attribute to him comments he had not made. The First Amendment protects authors and journalists who write about public figures by requiring a plaintiff to prove that the defamatory statements were made with what we have called "actual malice," a term of art denoting deliberate or reckless falsification. We consider in this opinion whether the attributed quotations had the degree of falsity required to prove this state of mind, so that the public figure can defeat a motion for summary judgment and proceed to a trial on the merits of the defamation claim.

I

Petitioner Jeffrey Masson trained at Harvard University as a Sanskrit scholar, and in 1970 became a professor of Sanskrit & Indian Studies at the University of Toronto. . . . Through his professional activities, he came to know Dr. Kurt Eissler, head of the Sigmund Freud Archives, and Dr. Anna Freud, daughter of Sigmund Freud and a major psychoanalyst in her own right. The Sigmund Freud Archives . . . serves as a repository for materials about Freud, including his own writings, letters, and personal library. The materials, and the right of access to them, are of immense value to those who study Freud and his theories, life, and work.

In 1980, Eissler and Anna Freud hired petitioner as projects director of the archives. After assuming his post, petitioner became disillusioned with Freudian psychology. In a 1981 lecture before the Western New England Psychoanalytical Society in New Haven, Connecticut, he advanced his theories of Freud. Soon after, the board of the archives terminated petitioner as projects director.

Respondent Janet Malcolm is an author and a contributor to respondent *The New Yorker*, a weekly magazine. She contacted petitioner in 1982 regarding the possibility of an article on his relationship with the archives. He agreed, and the two met in person and spoke by telephone in a series of interviews. Based on the interviews and other sources, Malcolm wrote a lengthy article. One of Malcolm's narrative devices consists of enclosing lengthy passages in quotation marks, reporting statements of Masson, Eissler, and her other subjects.

During the editorial process, Nancy Franklin, a member of the fact-checking department at *The New Yorker*, called petitioner to confirm some of the facts underlying the article. According to petitioner, he expressed alarm at the number of errors in the few passages Franklin discussed with him. Petitioner contends that he asked permission to review those portions of the article which attributed quotations or information to him, but was brushed off with a never-fulfilled promise to "get back to [him]." . . .

The New Yorker published Malcolm's piece in December 1983, as a two-part series. In 1984, with knowledge of at least petitioner's general allegation that the article contained defamatory material, respondent Alfred A. Knopf, Inc., published the entire work as a book, entitled In the Freud Archives.

Malcolm's work received complimentary reviews. But this gave little joy to Masson, for the book portrays him in a most unflattering light. According to one reviewer:

> "Masson the promising psychoanalytic scholar emerges gradually, as a grandiose egotist — mean-spirited, self-serving, full of braggadocio, impossibly arrogant and, in the end, a self-destructive fool. But it is not Janet Malcolm who calls him such: his own words reveal this psychological profile — a self-portrait offered to us through the efforts of an observer and listener who is, surely, as wise as any in the psychoanalytic profession." Coles, Freudianism Confronts Its Malcontents, Boston Globe, May 27, 1984, pp. 58, 60.

Petitioner brought an action for libel under California law in the United States District Court for the Northern District of California. . . .

Each passage before us purports to quote a statement made by petitioner during the interviews. Yet in each instance no identical statement appears in the more than 40 hours of taped interviews. Petitioner complains that Malcolm fabricated all but one passage; with respect to that passage, he claims Malcolm omitted a crucial portion, rendering the remainder misleading.

Malcolm submitted to the District Court that not all of her discussions with petitioner were recorded on tape, in particular conversations that occurred while the two of them walked together or traveled by car, while petitioner stayed at Malcolm's home in New York, or while her tape recorder was inoperable. She claimed to have taken notes of these unrecorded sessions, which she later typed, then discarding the handwritten originals. Petitioner denied that any discussion relating to the substance of the article occurred during his stay at Malcolm's home in New York, that Malcolm took notes during any of their conversations, or that Malcolm gave any indication that her tape recorder was broken.

Respondents moved for summary judgment. The parties agreed that petitioner was a public figure and so could escape summary judgment only if the evidence in the record would permit a reasonable finder of fact, by clear and convincing evidence, to conclude that respondents published a defamatory statement with actual malice as defined by our cases. The District Court analyzed each of the passages and held that the alleged inaccuracies did not raise a jury question. The court found that the allegedly fabricated quotations were either substantially true, or were " 'one of a number of possible rational interpretations' of a conversation or event that 'bristled with ambiguities,' " and thus were entitled to constitutional protection. The court also ruled that the "he had the wrong man" passage involved an exercise of editorial judgment upon which the courts could not intrude. 686 F. Supp. at 1403-1404.

The Court of Appeals affirmed, with one judge dissenting. 895 F.2d 1535 (CA9 1989). The court assumed for much of its opinion that Malcolm had deliberately altered each quotation not found on the tape recordings, but nevertheless held that petitioner failed to raise a jury question of actual malice, in large part for the reasons stated by the District Court. . . .

The dissent argued that any intentional or reckless alteration would prove actual malice, so long as a passage within quotation marks purports to be a verbatim rendition of what was said, contains material inaccuracies, and is defamatory. 895 F.2d at 1562-1570. We granted certiorari, 498 U.S. 808 (1990), and now reverse.

II

A

Under California law, "libel is a false and unprivileged publication by writing . . . which exposes any person to hatred, contempt, ridicule, or obloquy, or which causes him to be shunned or avoided, or which has a tendency to injure him in his occupation." Cal. Civ. Code Ann. § 45 (West 1982). False attribution of statements to a person may constitute libel, if the falsity exposes that person to an injury comprehended by the statute. It matters not under California law that petitioner alleges only part of the work at issue to be false. "The test of libel is not quantitative; a single sentence may be the basis for an action in libel even though buried in a much longer text," though the California courts recognize that "while a drop of poison may be lethal, weaker poisons are sometimes diluted to the point of impotency."

B

In general, quotation marks around a passage indicate to the reader that the passage reproduces the speaker's words verbatim. They inform the reader that he or she is reading the statement of the speaker, not a paraphrase or other indirect interpretation by an author. By providing this information, quotations add authority to the statement and credibility to the author's work. Quotations allow the reader to form his or her own conclusions and to assess the conclusions of the author, instead of relying entirely upon the author's characterization of her subject.

A fabricated quotation may injure reputation in at least two senses, either giving rise to a conceivable claim of defamation. First, the quotation might injure because it attributes an untrue factual assertion to the speaker. An example would be a fabricated quotation of a public official admitting he had been convicted of a serious crime when in fact he had not.

Second, regardless of the truth or falsity of the factual matters asserted within the quoted statement, the attribution may result in injury to reputation because the manner of expression or even the fact that the statement was made indicates a negative personal trait or an attitude the speaker does not hold. John Lennon once was quoted as saying of the Beatles, "We're more popular than Jesus Christ now." Time, Aug. 12, 1966, p. 38. Supposing the quotation had been a fabrication, it appears California law could permit recovery for defamation because, even without regard to the truth of the underlying assertion, false attribution of the statement could have injured his reputation. Here, in like manner, one need not determine whether petitioner is or is not the greatest analyst who ever lived in order to determine that it might have injured his reputation to be reported as having so proclaimed.

. . . .

Of course, quotations do not always convey that the speaker actually said or wrote the quoted material. "Punctuation marks, like words, have many uses. Writers often use quotation marks, yet no reasonable reader would assume that such punctuation automatically implies the truth of the quoted material." . . .

The work at issue here, however, as with much journalistic writing, provides the reader no clue that the quotations are being used as a rhetorical device or to paraphrase the speaker's actual statements. To the contrary, the work purports to be nonfiction, the result of numerous interviews. At least a trier of fact could so conclude. The work contains lengthy quotations attributed to petitioner, and neither Malcolm nor her publishers indicate to the reader that the quotations are anything but the reproduction of actual conversations. Further, the work was published in *The New Yorker*, a magazine which at the relevant time seemed to enjoy a reputation for scrupulous factual accuracy. These factors would, or at least could, lead a reader to take the quotations at face value. A defendant may be able to argue to the jury that quotations should be viewed by the reader as nonliteral or reconstructions, but we conclude that a trier of fact in this case could find that the reasonable reader would understand the quotations to be nearly verbatim reports of statements made by the subject.

C

The constitutional question we must consider here is whether, in the framework of a summary judgment motion, the evidence suffices to show that respondents acted with the requisite knowledge of falsity or reckless disregard as to truth or falsity. . . . We must consider whether the requisite falsity inheres in the attribution of words to the petitioner which he did not speak.

In some sense, any alteration of a verbatim quotation is false. But writers and reporters by necessity alter what people say, at the very least to eliminate grammatical and syntactical infelicities. If every alteration constituted the falsity required to prove actual malice, the practice of journalism, which the First Amendment standard is designed to protect, would require a radical change, one inconsistent with our precedents and First Amendment principles.

. . . .

We reject the idea that any alteration beyond correction of grammar or syntax by itself proves falsity in the sense relevant to determining actual malice under the First Amendment. An interviewer who writes from notes often will engage in the task of attempting a reconstruction of the speaker's statement. That author would, we may assume, act with knowledge that at times she has attributed to her subject words other than those actually used.

. . . .

Even if a journalist has tape-recorded the spoken statement of a public figure, the full and exact statement will be reported in only rare circumstances. The existence of both a speaker and a reporter; the translation between two media, speech and the printed word; the addition of punctuation; and the practical necessity to edit and make intelligible a speaker's perhaps rambling comments, all make it misleading to suggest that a quotation will be reconstructed with complete accuracy. The use or absence of punctuation may distort a speaker's meaning, for example, where that meaning turns upon a speaker's emphasis of a particular word. In other cases, if a speaker makes an obvious misstatement, for example by unconscious substitution of one name for another, a journalist might alter the speaker's words but preserve his intended meaning. And conversely, an exact quotation out of context can distort meaning, although the speaker did use each reported word.

In all events, technical distinctions between correcting grammar and syntax and some greater level of alteration do not appear workable, for we can think of no method by which courts or juries would draw the line between cleaning up and other changes, except by reference to the meaning a statement conveys to a reasonable reader. To attempt narrow distinctions of this type would be an unnecessary departure from First Amendment principles of general applicability, and, just as important, a departure from the underlying purposes of the tort of libel as understood since the latter half of the 16th century. From then until now, the tort action for defamation has existed to redress injury to the plaintiff's reputation by a statement that is defamatory and false. See *Milkovich v. Lorain Journal Co.*, 497 U.S. 1, 11, 110 S. Ct. 2695, 111 L. Ed. 2d 1 (1990). As we have recognized, "the legitimate state interest underlying the law of libel is the compensation of individuals for the harm inflicted on them by defamatory falsehood." *Gertz v. Robert Welch, Inc.*, 418 U.S. 323, 341, 94 S. Ct. 2997, 41 L. Ed. 2d 789 (1974). If an author alters a speaker's words but effects no material change in meaning, including any meaning conveyed by the manner or fact of expression, the speaker suffers no injury to reputation that is compensable as a defamation.

. . . .

The common law of libel takes but one approach to the question of falsity, regardless of the form of the communication. See Restatement (Second) of Torts § 563, Comment *c* (1977); W. Keeton, D. Dobbs, R. Keeton, & D. Owen, Prosser and Keeton on Law of Torts 776 (5th ed. 1984). It overlooks minor inaccuracies and concentrates upon substantial truth. As in other jurisdictions, California law permits the defense of substantial truth and would absolve a defendant even if she cannot "justify every word of the alleged defamatory matter; it is sufficient if the substance of the charge be proved true, irrespective of slight inaccuracy in the details." 5 B. Witkin, Summary of California Law § 495 (9th ed. 1988) (citing cases). . . . Minor inaccuracies do not amount to falsity so long as "the substance, the gist, the sting, of the libelous charge be justified." Put another way, the statement is not considered false unless it "would have a different effect on the mind of the reader from that which the pleaded truth would have produced." R. Sack, Libel, Slander, and Related Problems 138 (1980); see, *e.g., Wehling v. Columbia Broadcasting System*, 721 F.2d 506, 509 (CA5 1983); see generally R. Smolla, Law of Defamation § 5.08 (1991). Our definition of actual malice relies upon this historical understanding.

We conclude that a deliberate alteration of the words uttered by a plaintiff does not equate with knowledge of falsity for purposes of *New York Times Co. v. Sullivan*, 376 U.S. at 279-280, and *Gertz v. Robert Welch, Inc., supra*, at 342, unless the alteration results in a material change in the meaning conveyed by the statement. The use of quotations to attribute words not in fact spoken bears in a most important way on that inquiry, but it is not dispositive in every case . . .

III

. . . .

Because of the Court of Appeals' disposition with respect to Malcolm, it did not have occasion to address petitioner's argument that the District Court erred in granting summary judgment to The New Yorker Magazine, Inc., and Alfred A. Knopf, Inc., on the basis of their respective relations with Malcolm or the lack of any independent actual malice. These questions are best addressed in the first instance on remand.

The judgment of the Court of Appeals is reversed, and the case is remanded for further proceedings consistent with this opinion.

It is so ordered.

JUSTICE WHITE, with whom JUSTICE SCALIA joins, concurring in part and dissenting in part.

I join Parts I, II-A, II-D, and III-A, but cannot wholly agree with the remainder of the opinion. My principal disagreement is with the holding . . . that "a deliberate alteration of the words uttered by a plaintiff does not equate with knowledge of falsity . . . unless the alteration results in a material change in the meaning conveyed by the statement."

. . . .

[T]he Court states that deliberate misquotation does not amount to *New York Times* malice unless it results in a material change in the meaning conveyed by the statement. This ignores the fact that, under *New York Times*, reporting a known falsehood — here the knowingly false attribution — is sufficient proof of malice. The falsehood, apparently, must be substantial; the reporter may lie a little, but not too much.

This standard is not only a less manageable one than the traditional approach, but it also assigns to the courts issues that are for the jury to decide. For a court to ask whether a misquotation substantially alters the meaning of spoken words in a defamatory manner is a far different inquiry from whether reasonable jurors could find that the misquotation was different enough to be libelous. In the one case, the court is measuring the difference from its own point of view; in the other it is asking how the jury would or could view the erroneous attribution.

Does *Masson* introduce a constitutional definition of truth or is it *sui generis*? Does it set the standard for accuracy in quotation too high? Too low? Could the author and publisher avoid liability by putting a disclaimer regarding quotations at the front of a book or article? If so, what should the disclaimer say?

3.   Private Plaintiffs

GERTZ v. ROBERT WELCH, INC.
Supreme Court of the United States, 1974
418 U.S. 323

Mr. Justice Powell delivered the opinion of the Court.

. . . We granted certiorari to reconsider the extent of a publisher's constitutional privilege against liability for defamation of a private citizen. . . .

I

In 1968 a Chicago policeman named Nuccio shot and killed a youth named Nelson. The state authorities prosecuted Nuccio for the homicide and ultimately obtained a conviction for murder in the second degree. The Nelson family retained petitioner Elmer Gertz, a reputable attorney, to represent them in civil litigation against Nuccio.

Respondent publishes *American Opinion*, a monthly outlet for the views of the John Birch Society. Early in the 1960's the magazine began to warn of a nationwide conspiracy to discredit local law enforcement agencies and create in their stead a national police force capable of supporting a Communist dictatorship. As part of the continuing effort to alert the public to this assumed danger, the managing editor *of American Opinion* commissioned an article on the murder trial of Officer Nuccio. . . . In March 1969 respondent published the resulting article under the title "FRAME-UP: Richard Nuccio And The War On Police." The article purports to demonstrate that the testimony against Nuccio at his criminal trial was false and that his prosecution was part of the Communist campaign against the police.

In his capacity as counsel for the Nelson family in the civil litigation, petitioner attended the coroner's inquest into the boy's death and initiated actions for damages, but he neither discussed Officer Nuccio with the press nor played any part in the criminal proceeding. Notwithstanding petitioner's remote connection with the prosecution of Nuccio, respondent's magazine portrayed him as an architect of the "frame-up." According to the article, the police file on petitioner took "a big, Irish cop to lift." The article stated that petitioner had been an official of the "Marxist League for Industrial Democracy, originally known as the Intercollegiate Socialist Society, which has advocated the violent seizure of our government." It labeled Gertz a "Leninist" and a "Communist-fronter." It also stated that Gertz had been an officer of the National Lawyers Guild, described as a Communist organization that "probably did more than any other outfit to plan the Communist attack on the Chicago police during the 1968 Democratic Convention."

These statements contained serious inaccuracies. The implication that petitioner had a criminal record was false. Petitioner had been a member and officer of the National Lawyers Guild some 15 years earlier, but there was no evidence that he or that organization had taken any part in planning the 1968 demonstrations in Chicago. There was also no basis for the charge that petitioner was a "Leninist" or a "Communist-fronter." And he had never been a member of the "Marxist League for Industrial Democracy" or the "Intercollegiate Socialist Society."

The managing editor of *American Opinion* made no effort to verify or substantiate the charges against petitioner. Instead, he appended an editorial introduction stating that the author had "conducted extensive research into the Richard Nuccio Case." And he included in the article a photograph of petitioner and wrote the caption that appeared under it: "Elmer Gertz of Red Guild harrasses Nuccio." Respondent placed the issue of American Opinion containing the article on sale at newsstands throughout the country and distributed reprints of the article on the streets of Chicago.

Petitioner filed a diversity action for libel in the United States District Court for the Northern District of Illinois. He claimed that the falsehoods published by respondent injured his reputation as a lawyer and a citizen. . . .

After answering the complaint, respondent filed a pretrial motion for summary judgment, claiming a constitutional privilege against liability for defamation. It asserted that petitioner was a public official or a public figure and that the article concerned an issue of public interest and concern. For these reasons, respondent argued, it was entitled to invoke the privilege enunciated in *New York Times Co. v. Sullivan*, 376 U.S. 254 (1964). Under this rule respondent would escape liability unless petitioner could prove publication of defamatory falsehood "with 'actual malice' — that is, with knowledge that it was false or with reckless disregard of whether it was false or not." *Id.*, at 280. . . .

The District Court denied respondent's motion for summary judgment in a memorandum opinion of September 16, 1970. . . . After all the evidence had been presented but before submission of the case to the jury, the court ruled in effect that petitioner was neither a public official nor a public figure. It added that, if he were, the resulting application of the *New York Times* standard would require a directed verdict for respondent. Because some statements in the article constituted libel *per se* under Illinois law, the court submitted the case to the jury under instructions that withdrew from its consideration all issues save the measure of damages. The jury awarded $50,000 to petitioner.

Following the jury verdict and on further reflection, the District Court concluded that the *New York Times* standard should govern this case even though petitioner was not a public official or public figure. It accepted respondent's contention that that privilege protected discussion of any public issue without regard to the status of a person defamed therein. Accordingly, the court entered judgment for respondent notwithstanding the jury's verdict. . . .

Petitioner appealed to contest the applicability of the *New York Times* standard to this case. Although the Court of Appeals for the Seventh Circuit doubted the correctness of the District Court's determination that petitioner was not a public figure, it did not overturn that finding. It agreed with the District Court that respondent could assert the constitutional privilege because the article concerned a matter of public interest . . . After reviewing the record, the Court of Appeals endorsed the District Court's conclusion that petitioner had failed to show by clear and convincing evidence that respondent had acted with "actual malice" as defined by *New York Times*. . . . The Court of Appeals therefore affirmed, 471 F.2d 801 (1972). For the reasons stated below, we reverse.

II

The principal issue in this case is whether a newspaper or broadcaster that publishes defamatory falsehoods about an individual who is neither a public official nor a public figure may claim a constitutional privilege against liability for the injury inflicted by those statements. . . .

Three years after *New York Times*, a majority of the Court agreed to extend the constitutional privilege to defamatory criticism of "public figures." This extension was announced in *Curtis Publishing Co. v. Butts* and its companion, *Associated Press v. Walker*, 388 U.S. 130, 162 (1967). . . .

III

We begin with the common ground. Under the First Amendment there is no such thing as a false idea. However pernicious an opinion may seem, we depend for its correction not on the conscience of judges and juries but on the competition of other ideas. But there is no constitutional value in false statements of fact. Neither the intentional lie nor the careless error materially advances society's interest in "uninhibited, robust, and wide-open" debate on public issues. *New York Times Co. v. Sullivan*, 376 U.S., at 270. . . .

Although the erroneous statement of fact is not worthy of constitutional protection, it is nevertheless inevitable in free debate. . . . Our decisions recognize that a rule of strict liability that compels a publisher or broadcaster to guarantee the accuracy of his factual assertions may lead to intolerable self-censorship. Allowing the media to avoid liability only by proving the truth of all injurious statements does not accord adequate protection to First Amendment liberties. . . .

The legitimate state interest underlying the law of libel is the compensation of individuals for the harm inflicted on them by defamatory falsehood. We would not lightly require the State to abandon this purpose, for, as Mr. Justice Stewart has reminded us, the individual's right to the protection of his own good name

"reflects no more than our basic concept of the essential dignity and worth of every human being — a concept at the root of any decent system of ordered liberty. The protection of private personality, like the protection of life itself, is left primarily to the individual States under the Ninth and Tenth Amendments. But this does not mean that the right is entitled to any

less recognition by this Court as a basic of our constitutional system."
Rosenblatt v. Baer, 383 U.S. 75, 92 (1966) (concurring opinion).

Some tension necessarily exists between the need for a vigorous and uninhibited press and the legitimate interest in redressing wrongful injury. . . . To that end this Court has extended a measure of strategic protection to defamatory falsehood.

The *New York Times* standard defines the level of constitutional protection appropriate to the context of defamation of a public person. Those who, by reason of the notoriety of their achievements or the vigor and success with which they seek the public's attention, are properly classed as public figures and those who hold governmental office may recover for injury to reputation only on clear and convincing proof that the defamatory falsehood was made with knowledge of its falsity or with reckless disregard for the truth. This standard administers an extremely powerful antidote to the inducement to media self-censorship of the common-law rule of strict liability for libel and slander. And it exacts a correspondingly high price from the victims of defamatory falsehood. Plainly many deserving plaintiffs, including some intentionally subjected to injury, will be unable to surmount the barrier of the *New York Times* test. Despite this substantial abridgment of the state law right to compensation for wrongful hurt to one's reputation, the Court has concluded that the protection of the *New York Times* privilege should be available to publishers and broadcasters of defamatory falsehood concerning public officials and public figures. *New York Times Co. v. Sullivan, supra; Curtis Publishing Co. v. Butts, supra.* We think that these decisions are correct, but we do not find their holdings justified solely by reference to the interest of the press and broadcast media in immunity from liability. Rather, we believe that the *New York Times* rule states an accommodation between this concern and the limited state interest present in the context of libel actions brought by public persons. For the reasons stated below, we conclude that the state interest in compensating injury to the reputation of private individuals requires that a different rule should obtain with respect to them.

Theoretically, of course, the balance between the needs of the press and the individual's claim to compensation for wrongful injury might be struck on a case-by-case basis. . . . Because an *ad hoc* resolution of the competing interests at stake in each particular case is not feasible, we must lay down broad rules of general application. Such rules necessarily treat alike various cases involving differences as well as similarities. . . .

With that caveat we have no difficulty in distinguishing among defamation plaintiffs. The first remedy of any victim of defamation is self-help — using available opportunities to contradict the lie or correct the error and thereby to minimize its adverse impact on reputation. Public officials and public figures usually enjoy significantly greater access to the channels of effective communication and hence have a more realistic opportunity to counteract false statements than private individuals normally enjoy. Private individuals are therefore more vulnerable to injury, and the state interest in protecting them is correspondingly greater.

More important than the likelihood that private individuals will lack effective opportunities for rebuttal, there is a compelling normative consideration underlying the distinction between public and private defamation plaintiffs. An individual who decides to seek governmental office must accept certain necessary consequences of that involvement in public affairs. He runs the risk of closer public scrutiny than might otherwise be the case. And society's interest in the officers of government is not strictly limited to the formal discharge of official duties. As the Court pointed out in *Garrison v. Louisiana*, 379 U.S., at 77, the public's interest extends to "anything which might touch on an official's fitness for office. . . . Few personal attributes are more germane to fitness for office than dishonesty, malfeasance, or improper motivation, even though these characteristics may also affect the official's private character."

Those classed as public figures stand in a similar position. Hypothetically, it may be possible for someone to become a public figure through no purposeful action of his own, but the instances of truly involuntary public figures must be exceedingly rare. For the most part those who attain this status have assumed roles of special prominence in the affairs of society. Some occupy positions of such persuasive power and influence that they are deemed public figures for all purposes. More commonly, those classed as public figures have thrust themselves to the forefront of particular public controversies in order to influence the resolution of the issues involved. In either event, they invite attention and comment.

Even if the foregoing generalities do not obtain in every instance, the communications media are entitled to act on the assumption that public officials and public figures have voluntarily exposed themselves to increased risk of injury from defamatory falsehood concerning them. No such assumption is justified with respect to a private individual. He has not accepted public office or assumed an "influential role in ordering society." *Curtis Publishing Co. v. Butts*, 388 U.S., at 164 (Warren, C. J., concurring in result). He has relinquished no part of his interest in the protection of his own good name, and consequently he has a more compelling call on the courts for redress of injury inflicted by defamatory falsehood. Thus, private individuals are not only more vulnerable to injury than public officials and public figures; they are also more deserving of recovery.

For these reasons we conclude that the States should retain substantial latitude in their efforts to enforce a legal remedy for defamatory falsehood injurious to the reputation of a private individual. . . . The "public or general interest" test for determining the applicability of the *New York Times* standard to private defamation actions inadequately serves both of the competing values at stake. On the one hand, a private individual whose reputation is injured by defamatory falsehood that does concern an issue of public or general interest has no recourse unless he can meet the rigorous requirements *of New York Times*. This is true despite the factors that distinguish the state interest in compensating private individuals from the analogous interest involved in the context of public persons. On the other hand, a publisher or broadcaster of a defamatory error which a court deems unrelated to an issue of public or general interest may be held liable in damages even if it took every reasonable precaution to ensure the accuracy of its assertions. And liability may far exceed compensation for any actual injury to the plaintiff, for the jury may be permitted to presume damages without proof of loss and even to award punitive damages.

We hold that, so long as they do not impose liability without fault, the States may define for themselves the appropriate standard of liability for a publisher or broadcaster of defamatory falsehood injurious to a private individual. This approach provides a more equitable boundary between the competing concerns involved here. It recognizes the strength of the legitimate state interest in compensating private individuals for wrongful injury to reputation, yet shields the press and broadcast media from the rigors of strict liability for defamation. At least this conclusion obtains where, as here, the substance of the defamatory statement "makes substantial danger to reputation apparent." . . .

IV

Our accommodation of the competing values at stake in defamation suits by private individuals allows the States to impose liability on the publisher or broadcaster of defamatory falsehood on a less demanding showing than that required by *New York Times.* This conclusion is not based on a belief that the considerations which prompted the adoption of the *New York Times* privilege for defamation of public officials and its extension to public figures are wholly inapplicable to the context of private individuals. Rather, we endorse this approach in recognition of the strong and legitimate state interest in compensating private individuals for injury to reputation. But this countervailing state interest extends no further than compensation for actual injury. For the reasons stated below, we hold that the States may not permit recovery of presumed or punitive damages, at least when liability is not based on a showing of knowledge of falsity or reckless disregard for the truth.

The common law of defamation is an oddity of tort law, for it allows recovery of purportedly compensatory damages without evidence of actual loss. Under the traditional rules pertaining to actions for libel, the existence of injury is presumed from the fact of publication. Juries may award substantial sums as compensation for supposed damage to reputation without any proof that such harm actually occurred. The largely uncontrolled discretion of juries to award damages where there is no loss unnecessarily compounds the potential of any system of liability for defamatory falsehood to inhibit the vigorous exercise of First Amendment freedoms. Additionally, the doctrine of presumed damages invites juries to punish unpopular opinion rather than to compensate individuals for injury sustained by the publication of a false fact. More to the point, the States have no substantial interest in securing for plaintiffs such as this petitioner gratuitous awards of money damages far in excess of any actual injury.

We would not, of course, invalidate state law simply because we doubt its wisdom, but here we are attempting to reconcile state law with a competing interest grounded in the constitutional command of the First Amendment. It is therefore appropriate to require that state remedies for defamatory falsehood reach no farther than is necessary to protect the legitimate interest involved. It is necessary to restrict defamation plaintiffs who do not prove knowledge of falsity or reckless disregard for the truth to compensation for actual injury. We need not define "actual injury," as trial courts have wide experience in framing appropriate jury instructions in tort actions. Suffice it to say that actual injury is not limited to out-of-pocket loss. Indeed, the more customary types of actual harm inflicted by defamatory falsehood include impairment of reputation and standing in the community, personal humiliation, and mental anguish and suffering. Of course, juries must be limited by appropriate instructions, and all awards must be supported by competent evidence concerning the injury, although there need be no evidence which assigns an actual dollar value to the injury.

We also find no justification for allowing awards of punitive damages against publishers and broadcasters held liable under state-defined standards of liability for defamation. In most jurisdictions jury discretion over the amounts awarded is limited only by the gentle rule that they not be excessive. Consequently, juries assess punitive damages in wholly unpredictable amounts bearing no necessary relation to the actual harm caused. And they remain free to use their discretion selectively to punish expressions of unpopular views. Like the doctrine of presumed damages, jury discretion to award punitive damages unnecessarily exacerbates the danger of media self-censorship, but, unlike the former rule, punitive damages are wholly irrelevant to the state interest that justifies a negligence standard for private defamation actions. They are not compensation for injury. Instead, they are private fines levied by civil juries to punish reprehensible conduct and to deter its future occurrence. In short, the private defamation plaintiff who establishes liability under a less demanding standard than that stated by *New York Times* may recover only such damages as are sufficient to compensate him for actual injury.

V

Notwithstanding our refusal to extend the *New York Times* privilege to defamation of private individuals, respondent contends that we should affirm the judgment below on the ground that petitioner is either a public official or a public figure. There is little basis for the former assertion. Several years prior to the present incident, petitioner had served briefly on housing committees appointed by the mayor of Chicago, but at the time of publication he had never held any remunerative governmental position. Respondent admits this but argues that petitioner's appearance at the coroner's inquest rendered him a "de facto public official." Our cases recognize no such concept. Respondent's suggestion would sweep all lawyers under the *New York Times* rule as officers of the court and distort the plain meaning of the "public official" category beyond all recognition. We decline to follow it.

Respondent's characterization of petitioner as a public figure raises a different question. That designation may rest on either of two alternative bases. In some instances an individual may achieve such pervasive fame or notoriety that he becomes a public figure for all purposes and in all contexts. More commonly, an individual voluntarily injects himself or is drawn into a particular public controversy and thereby becomes a public figure for a limited range of issues. In either case such persons assume special prominence in the resolution of public questions.

Petitioner has long been active in community and professional affairs. He has served as an officer of local civic groups and of various professional organizations, and he has published several books and articles on legal subjects. Although petitioner was consequently well known in some circles, he had achieved no general fame or notoriety in the community. . . . We would not lightly assume that a citizen's participation in community and professional affairs rendered him a public figure for all purposes. Absent clear evidence of general fame or notoriety in the community, and pervasive involvement in the affairs of society, an individual should not be deemed a public personality for all aspects of his life. It is preferable to reduce the public-figure question to a more meaningful context by looking to the nature and extent of an individual's participation in the particular controversy giving rise to the defamation.

In this context it is plain that petitioner was not a public figure. He played a minimal role at the coroner's inquest, and his participation related solely to his representation of a private client. He took no part in the criminal prosecution of Officer Nuccio. Moreover, he never discussed either the criminal or civil litigation with the press and was never quoted as having done so. He plainly did not thrust himself into the vortex of this public issue, nor did he engage the public's attention in an attempt to influence its outcome. We are persuaded that the trial court did not err in refusing to characterize petitioner as a public figure for the purpose of this litigation.

We therefore conclude that the *New York Times* standard is inapplicable to this case and that the trial court erred in entering judgment for respondent. Because the jury was allowed to impose liability without fault and was permitted to presume damages without proof of injury, a new trial is necessary. We reverse and remand for further proceedings in accord with this opinion.

It is so ordered.

MR. JUSTICE BLACKMUN, concurring.

. . . .

The Court today refuses to apply *New York Times* to the private individual, as contrasted with the public official and the public figure. . . . It thereby fixes the outer boundary of the *New York Times* doctrine and says that beyond that boundary, a State is free to define for itself the appropriate standard of media liability so long as it does not impose liability without fault. As my joinder in *Rosenbloom's* plurality opinion would intimate, I sense some illogic in this.

. . . Although the Court's opinion in the present case departs from the rationale of the *Rosenbloom* plurality, . . . I am willing to join, and do join, the Court's opinion and its judgment for two reasons:

1. By removing the specters of presumed and punitive damages in the absence of *New York Times* malice, the Court eliminates significant and powerful motives for self-censorship that otherwise are present in the traditional libel action. . . . What the Court has done, I believe, will have little, if any, practical effect on the functioning of responsible journalism.

. . . .

Mr. Chief Justice Burger, dissenting.

. . . In today's opinion the Court abandons the traditional thread so far as the ordinary private citizen is concerned and introduces the concept that the media will be liable for negligence in publishing defamatory statements with respect to such persons. . . . I am frank to say I do not know the parameters of a "negligence" doctrine as applied to the news media. Conceivably this new doctrine could inhibit some editors, as the dissents of Mr. Justice Douglas and Mr. Justice Brennan suggest. But I would prefer to allow this area of law to continue to evolve as it has up to now with respect to private citizens rather than embark on a new doctrinal theory which has no jurisprudential ancestry.

. . . .

I would reverse the judgment of the Court of Appeals and remand for reinstatement of the verdict of the jury and the entry of an appropriate judgment on that verdict.

Mr. Justice Douglas, dissenting.

. . . .

With the First Amendment made applicable to the States through the Fourteenth, I do not see how States have any more ability to "accommodate" freedoms of speech or of the press than does Congress. . . . Like Congress, States are without power "to use a civil libel law or any other law to impose damages for merely discussing public affairs." *Id., at 295* (Black, J., concurring).

Continued recognition of the possibility of state libel suits for public discussion of public issues leaves the freedom of speech honored by the Fourteenth Amendment a diluted version of First Amendment protection. . . .

Since in my view the First and Fourteenth Amendments prohibit the imposition of damages upon respondent for this discussion of public affairs, I would affirm the judgment below.

TIME, INC. v. FIRESTONE
Supreme Court of the United States, 1976.
424 U.S. 448

Mr. Justice Rehnquist delivered the opinion of the Court.

Petitioner is the publisher of *Time,* a weekly news magazine. . . .

I

Respondent, Mary Alice Firestone, married Russell Firestone, the scion of one of America's wealthier industrial families, in 1961. In 1964, they separated, and respondent filed a complaint for separate maintenance in the Circuit Court of Palm Beach County, Fla. Her husband counterclaimed for divorce on grounds of extreme cruelty and adultery. After a lengthy trial the Circuit Court issued a judgment granting the divorce requested by respondent's husband. In relevant part the court's final judgment read:

    . . . .

> "According to certain testimony in behalf of the defendant, extramarital escapades of the plaintiff were bizarre and of an amatory nature which would have made Dr. Freud's hair curl. Other testimony, in plaintiff's behalf, would indicate that defendant was guilty of bounding from one bed partner to another with the erotic zest of a satyr. The court is inclined to discount much of this testimony as unreliable. Nevertheless, it is the conclusion and finding of this court that neither party is domesticated within the meaning of that term as used by the Supreme Court of Florida.

    . . .

> "In the present case, it is abundantly clear from the evidence of marital discord that neither of the parties has shown the least susceptibility to domestication, and that the marriage should be dissolved.

    . . . .

Time's editorial staff, headquartered in New York, was alerted by a wire service report and an account in a New York newspaper to the fact that a judgment had been rendered in the Firestone divorce proceeding. The staff subsequently received further information regarding the Florida decision from *Time's* Miami bureau chief and from a "stringer" working on a special assignment basis in the Palm Beach area. On the basis of these four sources, *Time's* staff composed the following item, which appeared in the magazine's "Milestones" section the following week:

> "DIVORCED. By Russell A. Firestone Jr., 41, heir to the tire fortune: Mary Alice Sullivan Firestone, 32, his third wife; a onetime Palm Beach schoolteacher; on grounds of extreme cruelty and adultery; after six years of marriage, one son; in West Palm Beach, Fla. The 17-month intermittent trial produced enough testimony of extramarital adventures on both sides, said the judge, 'to make Dr. Freud's hair curl.' "

Within a few weeks of the publication of this article respondent demanded in writing a retraction from petitioner, alleging that a portion of the article was "false, malicious and defamatory." Petitioner declined to issue the requested retraction.[1]

Respondent then filed this libel action against petitioner in the Florida Circuit Court. Based on a jury verdict for respondent, that court entered judgment against petitioner for $100,000, and after review in both the Florida District Court of Appeal and the Supreme Court of Florida the judgment was ultimately affirmed. 305 So. 2d 172 (1974). . . .

---

[1] Under Florida law the demand for retraction was a prerequisite for filing a libel action, and permits defendants to limit their potential liability to actual damages by complying with the demand. Fla. Stat. Ann. §§ 770.01-770.02 (1963).

II

Petitioner initially contends that it cannot be liable for publishing any falsehood defaming respondent unless it is established that the publication was made "with actual malice," as that term is defined in *New York Times Co. v. Sullivan*, 376 U.S. 254 (1964). Petitioner advances two arguments in support of this contention: that respondent is a "public figure" within this Court's decisions extending New York Times to defamation suits brought by such individuals, see, e.g., *Curtis Publishing Co. v. Butts*, 388 U.S. 130 (1967); and that the *Time* item constituted a report of a judicial proceeding, a class of subject matter which petitioner claims deserves the protection of the "actual malice" standard even if the story is proved to be defamatorily false or inaccurate. We reject both arguments.

Respondent did not assume any role of especial prominence in the affairs of society, other than perhaps Palm Beach society, and she did not thrust herself to the forefront of any particular public controversy in order to influence the resolution of the issues involved in it.

Petitioner contends that because the Firestone divorce was characterized by the Florida Supreme Court as a "cause celebre," it must have been a public controversy and respondent must be considered a public figure. But in so doing petitioner seeks to equate "public controversy" with all controversies of interest to the public. Were we to accept this reasoning, we would reinstate the doctrine advanced in the plurality opinion in *Rosenbloom v. Metromedia, Inc.*, 403 U.S. 29 (1971), which concluded that the *New York Times* privilege should be extended to falsehoods defamatory of private persons whenever the statements concern matters of general or public interest. In *Gertz*, however, the Court repudiated this position, stating that "extension of the *New York Times* test proposed by the *Rosenbloom* plurality would abridge [a] legitimate state interest to a degree that we find unacceptable." 418 U.S., at 346.

. . . .

Dissolution of a marriage through judicial proceedings is not the sort of "public controversy" referred to in *Gertz*, even though the marital difficulties of extremely wealthy individuals may be of interest to some portion of the reading public. Nor did respondent freely choose to publicize issues as to the propriety of her married life. She was compelled to go to court by the State in order to obtain legal release from the bonds of matrimony. We have said that in such an instance "[r]esort to the judicial process . . . is no more voluntary in a realistic sense than that of the defendant called upon to defend his interests in court." *Boddie v. Connecticut*, 401 U.S. 371, 376-377 (1971). Her actions, both in instituting the litigation and in its conduct, were quite different from those of General Walker in *Curtis Publishing Co., supra.*[3] She assumed no "special prominence in the resolution of public

---

[3] Nor do we think the fact that respondent may have held a few press conferences during the divorce proceedings in an attempt to satisfy inquiring reporters converts her into a "public figure." Such interviews should have had no effect upon the merits of the legal dispute between respondent and her husband or the outcome of that trial, and we do not think it can be assumed that any such purpose was intended. Moreover, there is no indication that she sought to use the press conferences as a vehicle by which to thrust herself to the forefront of some unrelated controversy in order to influence its resolution.

questions." *Gertz, supra,* at 351. We hold respondent was not a "public figure" for the purpose of determining the constitutional protection afforded petitioner's report of the factual and legal basis for her divorce.

It may be argued that there is still room for application of the *New York Times* protections to more narrowly focused reports of what actually transpires in the courtroom. But even so narrowed, the suggested privilege is simply too broad. Imposing upon the law of private defamation the rather drastic limitations worked by *New York Times* cannot be justified by generalized references to the public interest in reports of judicial proceedings. The details of many, if not most, courtroom battles would add almost nothing toward advancing the uninhibited debate on public issues thought to provide principal support for the decision in *New York Times. See* 376 U.S., at 270; *cf. Rosenblatt v. Baer,* 383 U.S. 75, 86 (1966). And while participants in some litigation may be legitimate "public figures," either generally or for the limited purpose of that litigation, the majority will more likely resemble respondent, drawn into a public forum largely against their will in order to attempt to obtain the only redress available to them or to defend themselves against actions brought by the State or by others. There appears little reason why these individuals should substantially forfeit that degree of protection which the law of defamation would otherwise afford them simply by virtue of their being drawn into a courtroom. . . .

III

Petitioner's theory seems to be that the only compensable injury in a defamation action is that which may be done to one's reputation, and that claims not predicated upon such injury are by definition not actions for defamation. But Florida has obviously decided to permit recovery for other injuries without regard to measuring the effect the falsehood may have had upon a plaintiff's reputation. This does not transform the action into something other than an action for defamation as that term is meant in *Gertz.* In that opinion we made it clear that States could base awards on elements other than injury to reputation, specifically listing "personal humiliation, and mental anguish and suffering" as examples of injuries which might be compensated consistently with the Constitution upon a showing of fault. Because respondent has decided to forgo recovery for injury to her reputation, she is not prevented from obtaining compensation for such other damages that a defamatory falsehood may have caused her.

The trial court charged, consistently with *Gertz,* that the jury should award respondent compensatory damages in "an amount of money that will fairly and adequately compensate her for such damages," and further cautioned that "[i]t is only damages which are a direct and natural result of the alleged libel which may be recovered." App. 509. There was competent evidence introduced to permit the jury to assess the amount of injury. Several witnesses[6] testified to the extent of

---

See Gertz v. Robert Welch, Inc., 418 U.S. 323, 345 (1974).

[6] These included respondent's minister, her attorney in the divorce proceedings, plus several friends and neighbors, one of whom was a physician who testified to having to administer a sedative to respondent in an attempt to reduce discomfort wrought by her worrying about the article.

respondent's anxiety and concern over Time's inaccurately reporting that she had been found guilty of adultery, and she herself took the stand to elaborate on her fears that her young son would be adversely affected by this falsehood when he grew older. The jury decided these injuries should be compensated by an award of $100,000. We have no warrant for re-examining this determination. *Cf. Lincoln v. Power*, 151 U.S. 436 (1894).

IV

. . . .

It may well be that petitioner's account in its "Milestones" section was the product of some fault on its part, and that the libel judgment against it was, therefore, entirely consistent with *Gertz*. But in the absence of a finding in some element of the state-court system that there was fault, we are not inclined to canvass the record to make such a determination in the first instance. *Cf. Rosenblatt v. Baer*, 383 U.S., at 87-88. Accordingly, the judgment of the Supreme Court of Florida is vacated and the case remanded for further proceedings not inconsistent with this opinion.

So ordered.

---

1. Why wasn't Mrs. Firestone held to be a public figure? What must she prove as a private person in order to recover?

2. While the Court refused to recognize a constitutional privilege for reporting judicial proceedings, in many jurisdictions a "fair report" privilege is recognized under state law for reasonably accurate reports of various official proceedings, including court matters. The privilege "extends to publication of defamatory matter concerning another in a report of an official action or proceeding, or of a meeting open to the public that deals with a matter of public concern." It is based on "the right of the public, in a democratic society, to be informed about a wide variety of official matters" and "attaches where the report is accurate and complete or a fair abridgement of the occurrence that is recounted." *Salzano v. North Jersey Media Group, Inc.*, 993 A.2d 778 (N.J. 2010) (applying privilege to report on complaint filed in bankruptcy proceedings).

4. The Limited Purpose Public Figure

WALDBAUM v. FAIRCHILD PUBLICATIONS, INC.
United States Court of Appeals, District of Columbia Circuit, 1980
627 F.2d 1287, *cert. denied*, 449 U.S. 898

Tamm, Circuit Judge:

In this action we must determine when an individual not a public official has left the relatively safe harbor that the law of defamation provides for private persons and has become a public figure within the meaning of the Supreme Court's decision in *Gertz v. Robert Welch, Inc.*, 418 U.S. 323, 94 S. Ct. 2997, 41 L. Ed. 2d 789 (1974). . . . [T]he United States District Court for the District of Columbia concluded that the plaintiff was a limited public figure under Gertz. Because the plaintiff admitted that he could not prove "actual malice" on the part of the defendant, which Gertz requires public figures to do, [the court] entered summary judgment for the defendant. Having reviewed the facts in light of the criteria that govern the status of a defamation plaintiff, we . . . affirm.

I

Although the parties in this case differ over how to classify the plaintiff, they fundamentally agree on the underlying facts. Eric Waldbaum, the plaintiff, became president and chief executive officer of Greenbelt Consumer Services, Inc. (Greenbelt) in January of 1971. Greenbelt is a diversified consumer cooperative that, during Waldbaum's tenure, ranked as the second largest cooperative in the country.[1]

While serving as Greenbelt's president, Waldbaum played an active role not only in the management of the cooperative but also in setting policies and standards within the supermarket industry. He battled the traditional practices in the industry and fought particularly hard for the introduction of unit pricing and open dating in supermarkets. He held several meetings, to which press and public were invited, on topics varying from supermarket practices to energy legislation and fuel allocation. He pursued a vigorous policy of consolidating Greenbelt's operations to eliminate unprofitable outlets. These actions generated considerable comment on both Greenbelt and Waldbaum in trade journals and general-interest publications.

On March 16, 1976, Greenbelt's board of directors dismissed Waldbaum as the cooperative's president and chief executive officer. *Supermarket News*, a trade publication owned by the defendant, Fairchild Publications, Inc. (Fairchild), ran an item on Waldbaum's ouster on page 35 of its March 22 issue. The five-sentence article stated at one point that Greenbelt "has been losing money the past year and retrenching."[5]

On September 27, 1976, Waldbaum filed a libel action in the district court based upon this comment in the article. He contended that in fact Greenbelt had not been losing money or retrenching and that this allegedly false report damaged his reputation as a businessman. Waldbaum sought actual and exemplary damages totalling $75,000.

---

[1] When Waldbaum left as Greenbelt's president, the cooperative had approximately 38,500 members. The company owns retail supermarkets (Co-op Supermarkets), furniture and gift outlets (SCAN stores), and automobile service stations (Exval stations).

[5] The story in its entirety read:

GREENBELT OUSTS ERIC WALDBAUM

WASHINGTON Eric Waldbaum has been replaced as president of Greenbelt Consumer Services. Rowland Burnstan will serve as acting chief executive office(r) until a new president is named. Burnstan, an independent management consultant and economist, has worked for various Government agencies and businesses.

Greenbelt said part of his interim job will be to locate a new president for the co-op, which has been losing money the past year and retrenching.

After discovery, Fairchild moved for summary judgment. It argued that Wald-baum was a public figure and, because he had admitted the absence of "actual malice," he could not recover damages for defamation. Waldbaum countered that he was not a public figure and thus would have to prove only negligence on the part of Fairchild in researching and publishing the article. On February 15, 1979, Judge Corcoran granted Fairchild's motion. He concluded that although Waldbaum could not be considered a public figure for all purposes, he was a public figure for the limited range of issues concerning "Greenbelt's unique position within the super-market industry and Waldbaum's efforts to advance that position."

. . . .

In Gertz, decided in 1974, the Court focused on the public or private status of the plaintiff. . . . It therefore held that a state may allow a private person to recover for defamation under any standard, as long as that standard does not impose liability without fault.

. . . .

In trying to define who is a public figure, the Court in Gertz created two subclassifications, persons who are public figures for all purposes and those who are public figures for particular public controversies. An individual may have attained a position "of such persuasive power and influence," id., and of "such pervasive fame or notoriety," *id.* at 351, 94 S. Ct. at 3013, that he has become a public figure in all situations. This test is a strict one. The Court stated flatly that "(a)bsent clear evidence of general fame or notoriety in the community, and pervasive involvement in the affairs of society, an individual should not be deemed a public personality for all aspects of his life."

The Court in Gertz acknowledged freely that under this definition the general public figure is a rare creature. More common are persons who "have thrust themselves to the forefront of particular public controversies in order to influence the resolution of the issues involved." 418 U.S. at 345, 94 S. Ct. at 3009. Put slightly differently, this limited-purpose public figure is "an individual (who) voluntarily injects himself or is drawn into a particular public controversy and therefore becomes a public figure for a limited range of issues." *Id.* at 351, 94 S. Ct. at 3013. The relevant examination turns on "the nature and extent of an individual's participation in the particular controversy giving rise to the defamation." *Id.* at 352, 94 S. Ct. at 3013.

III

. . . From analyzing Gertz and more recent defamation cases, we believe that a person can be a general public figure only if he is a "celebrity[,]" his name a "household word" whose ideas and actions the public in fact follows with great interest. We also conclude that a person has become a public figure for limited purposes if he is attempting to have, or realistically can be expected to have, a major impact on the resolution of a specific public dispute that has foreseeable and substantial ramifications for persons beyond its immediate participants. In under-taking this examination, a court must look through the eyes of a reasonable person at the facts taken as a whole.

B

Given these considerations, a court[12] analyzing whether a given plaintiff is a public figure must look at the facts, taken as a whole, through the eyes of a reasonable person. This objective approach should enable both the press and the individual in question to assess the individual's status, in advance, against the same yardstick. . . . Resolving these questions based upon what a reasonable person, looking at the entire situation, would conclude allows the press and the individual to evaluate public-figure status against a single, discoverable norm and from there to act as they see fit, understanding the consequences of their conduct under *New York Times*.

C

. . . A court first must ask whether the plaintiff is a public figure for all purposes. . . . In other words, a general public figure is a well-known "celebrity," his name a "household word." The public recognizes him and follows his words and deeds, either because it regards his ideas, conduct, or judgment as worthy of its attention or because he actively pursues that consideration.

. . . .

In determining whether a plaintiff has achieved the degree of notoriety and influence necessary to become a public figure in all contexts, a court may look to several factors.[19] The judge can examine statistical surveys, if presented, that concern the plaintiff's name recognition. Previous coverage of the plaintiff in the press also is relevant. . . .

. . . .

Newsworthiness alone will not suffice, for the alleged defamation itself indicates that someone in the press believed the matter deserved media coverage. Moreover, a court may not question the legitimacy of the public's concern; such an approach would turn courts into censors of " 'what information is relevant to self-government.' " A vital part of open public debate is deciding what should be debated. No arm of the government, including the judiciary, should be able to set society's agenda.

Trivial or tangential participation is not enough. The language of Gertz is clear that plaintiffs must have "thrust themselves to the forefront" of the controversies so as to become factors in their ultimate resolution. The plaintiff either must have been purposely trying to influence the outcome or could realistically have been expected, because of his position in the controversy, to have an impact on its resolution. . . .

---

[12] Whether the plaintiff is a public figure is a question of law for the court to resolve.

[19] The court must examine these factors as they existed before the defamation was published. Otherwise, the press could convert a private individual into a general public figure simply by publicizing the defamation itself and creating a controversy surrounding it and, perhaps, litigation arising out of it. *See* Hutchinson v. Proxmire, 443 U.S. Ill, 99 S. Ct. 2675, 2688, 61 L. Ed. 2d 411 (1979) ("those charged with defamation cannot, by their own conduct, create their own defense by making the claimant a public figure").

Finally, the alleged defamation must have been germane to the plaintiff's participation in the controversy. His talents, education, experience, and motives could have been relevant to the public's decision whether to listen to him. Misstatements wholly unrelated to the controversy, however, do not receive the *New York Times* protection.

Those who attempt to affect the result of a particular controversy have assumed the risk that the press, in covering the controversy, will examine the major participants with a critical eye. Occasionally, someone is caught up in the controversy involuntarily and, against his will, assumes a prominent position in its outcome. . . . In short, the court must ask whether a reasonable person would have concluded that this individual would play or was seeking to play a major role in determining the outcome of the controversy and whether the alleged defamation related to that controversy.

IV

With the foregoing analysis in mind, we now must determine whether Judge Corcoran correctly concluded that Waldbaum was a public figure. As noted above, Fairchild concedes that he was not a general-purpose public figure, and Waldbaum concedes that he cannot prove "actual malice" within the meaning of *New York Times.* . . . After examining the facts, we do agree and, therefore, affirm.

Evidence submitted with Fairehild's motion for summary judgment indicates clearly that Greenbelt was an innovative company often the subject of news reports. As the second largest cooperative in the nation it attracted attention, and its pathbreaking marketing policies . . . became the subject of public debate with the supermarket industry and beyond.. . .

Waldbaum was known as a leading advocate of certain precedent-breaking policies before coming to Greenbelt. . . .

Being an executive within a prominent and influential company does not by itself make one a public figure.[36]. . . . [Waldbaum's] own deposition indicates that he was the mover and shaper of many of the cooperative's controversial actions. He made it a leader in unit pricing and open dating. . . .

Thus, it would appear to a reasonable person that Waldbaum had thrust himself into the public controversies concerning unit pricing, open dating, the cooperative form of business, and other issues. . . . Looking at the overall picture, we conclude that Waldbaum was a public figure for the limited purpose of comment on Greenbelt's and his own innovation policies and that the article giving rise to this action was within the protected sphere of reporting. Because Fairchild concededly did not act with "actual malice," it was entitled to summary judgment.

---

[36] Sometimes position alone can make one a public figure.

V

. . . Nevertheless, when one assumes a position of great influence within a specific area and uses that influence to advocate and practice controversial policies that substantially affect others, he becomes a public figure for that debate. Waldbaum was such a person, and comment on his termination as president and chief executive officer of Greenbelt falls within the range of reports protected under *New York Times*. Therefore, the judgment of the district court is

Affirmed.

FORETICH v. CAPITAL CITIES/ABC, INC.
United States Court of Appeals for the Fourth Circuit, 1994
37 F.3d 1541

MURNAGHAN, CIRCUIT JUDGE

Vincent and Doris Foretich filed a defamation action against the producers and broadcasters of an ABC docudrama in which a character apparently referred to one or both of them as "abusers" of their granddaughter, Hilary A. Foretich, who had been the subject of a prolonged and highly publicized child-custody dispute.

. . .

On November 29, 1992, American Broadcasting Companies, Inc. aired, as its "ABC Sunday Night Movie," a 91-minute docudrama entitled "A Mother's Right: The Elizabeth Morgan Story." . . . In the scene, Hilary is initially agitated, gradually warms to her grandparents, and eventually climbs into her grandfather's lap after joining in the singing of "Row, Row, Row Your Boat." There immediately follows a conversation between Dr. Morgan and her friend, as they are leaving Washington by car. The friend had brought Hilary to the psychiatrist's office and had remained in an adjacent room during the visit. He describes to Dr. Morgan what he heard: "It was like a circus pony going through her tricks. You know, she even giggled on cue." Dr. Morgan responds, "It's just like the therapist said. . . . Classic response. She's being kind to her abusers so she won't be hurt again" (emphasis added).

. . . Plaintiffs' entire case is based on the utterance of a single sound — the "s" in the word "abusers," which allegedly indicated that Hilary was being abused not only by her father but also by one or both of her paternal grandparents. At the present stage of the litigation, it is undisputed that the "s" that converted the singular "abuser" into the plural "abusers" was included unintentionally.. . . .

II

Because the question of whether a defamation plaintiff is a "limited-purpose public figure" is an issue of law, we review de novo. In conducting our review, we "must look through the eyes of a reasonable person at the facts taken as a whole."

. . . .

In *Fitzgerald* [*v. Penthourse Int'l, Ltd.*, 691 F.2d 666 (4th Cir. 1982), *cert. denied*, 460 U.S. 1024 (1983)] and again in our en banc opinion in *Reuber* [v. Food Chemical News, 925 F.2d 703 (4th Cir.), cert. denied, 501 U.S. 1212 (1991)], we set forth five requirements that the defamation defendant must prove before a court can properly hold that the plaintiff is a public figure for the limited purpose of comment on a particular public controversy: (1) the plaintiff had access to channels of effective communication; (2) the plaintiff voluntarily assumed a role of special prominence in the public controversy; (3) the plaintiff sought to influence the resolution or outcome of the controversy; (4) the controversy existed prior to the publication of the defamatory statement; and (5) the plaintiff retained public-figure status at the time of the alleged defamation.

. . . .

IV

The first question we must address is whether there was a particular public controversy that gave rise to the alleged defamation.

Gertz provided no express definition of a "public controversy," but the Court's subsequent decisions on limited-purpose public figure status provide some useful guidance. . . .

In 1980, after carefully sifting through the Supreme Court cases, the United States Court of Appeals for the District of Columbia Circuit enunciated an express definition of a "public controversy":

A public controversy is not simply a matter of interest to the public; it must be a real dispute, the outcome of which affects the general public or some segment of it in an appreciable way. . . . Essentially private concerns or disagreements do not become public controversies simply because they attract attention. . . . Rather, a public controversy is a dispute that in fact has received public attention because its ramifications will be felt by persons who are not direct participants.

. . . .

. . . Dr. Morgan's prolonged contempt incarceration for refusing to divulge Hilary's whereabouts raised a special set of public policy issues. . . . The public discussion of those issues ultimately prompted Congress and the President to secure Dr.Morgan's release through federal legislation limiting the power of the District of Columbia courts to impose contempt in child custody cases. . . .

V

Having concluded that there was indeed a public controversy that gave rise to the alleged defamation, we must next examine "the nature and extent of [Vincent Foretich's and Doris Foretich's] participation in [that] controversy." . . . Because we find that neither Vincent nor Doris Foretich voluntarily assumed a role of special prominence in the Morgan-Foretich controversy in order to influence its outcome, we need not consider the other elements of the *Fitzgerald/Reuber* test. *See Reuber*,

925 F. 2d at 708-09 . . . ; *Fitzgerald*, 691 F. 2d at 668.

The bare words of the legal test — whether the plaintiff "voluntarily assumed a role of special prominence in a public controversy in order to influence its outcome" can best be illuminated by reference to *Gertz* and subsequent Supreme Court cases . . .

. . . ABC has argued that Vincent and Doris Foretich voluntarily participated in the public controversy when they chose to support their son by publicly criticizing Dr.Morgan, by speaking with news reporters, and by appearing on television, at press conferences, and at public gatherings. . . . ABC has argued, both Vincent and Doris Foretich voluntarily assumed special roles of prominence in the Morgan-Foretich controversy in order to influence its outcome, and they may not now claim the protections of purely "private" persons.

We reject ABC's argument because it pays inadequate attention to the context . . . The resultant publicity doubtless had the potential to destroy Vincent Foretich's and Doris Foretich's reputations, and that potential may well have been realized.

The common law of defamation has long recognized that charges such as those leveled against the Foretich grandparents are so obviously and materially harmful to reputational interests that they must be deemed defamatory per se. We, too, recognize the devastation that public accusations of child sexual abuse can wreak, and we are extremely reluctant to attribute public-figure status to otherwise private persons merely because they have responded to such accusations in a reasonable attempt to vindicate their reputations.

In determining the reasonableness of a reply, we need not plow entirely new ground: the common law on the conditional (or qualified) privilege of reply, also known as the privilege to speak in self-defense or to defend one's reputation, can help guide our discussion. . . .

Because the Foretiches' public responses to Dr.Morgan's accusations were responsive, proportionate, and not excessively published, they were "reasonable." . . . [W]e conclude that the Foretiches' primary motive was to defend their own good names against Dr.Morgan's accusations and that their public statements can most fairly be characterized as measured defensive replies to her attacks, rather than as efforts to thrust themselves to the forefront of a public controversy in order to influence its outcome. Therefore, we hold that Vincent and Doris Foretich were private individuals, not limited-purpose public figures.

. . . At first blush, one might characterize our decision today as favoring [reputation] over [free expression]. But such a characterization would miss the point. We see no good reason "why someone dragged into a controversy should be able to speak publicly only at the expense of foregoing a private person's protection from defamation." *Clyburn*, 903 F.2d at 32. By allowing the Foretiches to defend their good names without succumbing to public-figure status, we protect not only their own interests in reputation, but also society's interest in free speech. . . . By freely permitting the Foretiches to respond to Dr.Morgan's charges against them — charges that have never been proved in any court of law — we foster both the individual interest in self-expression and the social interest in the discovery and dissemination of truth — the very goals that animate our First Amendment jurisprudence.

. . . .

Affirmed and remanded.

---

1. Why do the Foretiches escape the "public figure" classification?

2. Is this a situation in which the *Rosenbloom* test ("matter in the public interest") would be helpful?

3. In *Mzamane v. Winfrey*, 693 F. Supp. 2d 442 (E.D. Pa. 2010), the headmistress of the Oprah Winfrey Leadership Academy for Girls (OWLAG) in South Africa sued television celebrity and OWLAG founder Winfrey for defamation, based on statements Winfrey made to parents of students at the academy, and later at a press conference, in response to allegations of student abuse by some OWLAG staff members. The court distinguished *Foretich* and held that the headmistress was a limited purpose public figure. She "voluntarily held a significant position in a high-profile public institution" so that "even before she went public with her version of the facts, she was already a limited purpose public figure."

4. *Erickson v. Jones Street Publishers, LLC*, 629 S.E.2d 653 (S.C. 2006), held that an individual serving as a private guardian *ad litem* assigned by the court to represent the interests of a minor child in a divorce/custody proceeding is not a limited purpose public figure. Do you agree?

5. The Nonmedia Defendant

GREENMOSS BUILDERS, INC. v. DUN & BRADSTREET, INC.
Supreme Court of Vermont, 1983
461 A.2d 414

HILL, J.

Plaintiff, a residential and commercial building contractor, brought this defamation action against defendant as a result of an erroneous credit report issued to defendant's subscribers (plaintiff's creditors). The credit report alleged that plaintiff had filed a voluntary petition in bankruptcy and, in addition, grossly misrepresented plaintiff's assets and liabilities. The false nature of the report's allegations has never been disputed.

In its complaint, plaintiff asserted that the consequences of defendant's report, which it insisted was published with reckless disregard for truth and accuracy, were a damaged business reputation, loss of company profits, and loss of money expended to correct the error. In response, defendant claimed both a constitutional and common law qualified privilege against defamation actions, and on that basis contended that since its report was published in good faith, it could not be held liable.

After a trial by jury, a verdict was returned in favor of plaintiff for $50,000 in compensatory or actual damages, and $300,000 in punitive damages. Thereafter, defendant filed timely motions for judgment notwithstanding the verdict, V.R.C.P. 50, and for new trial, V.R.C.P. 59, on the issues of liability and damages. The trial court, persuaded that the evidence was sufficient as a matter of law to create issues of fact for the jury as to both liability and damages, denied defendant's motions for judgment notwithstanding the verdict. Upon reviewing its jury instructions, however, the trial court concluded that it had incorrectly charged those standards of liability enunciated in *Gertz v. Robert Welch, Inc.*, 418 U.S. 323 (1974), and granted defendant's motions for new trial on all issues.

This action is before us pursuant to an interlocutory order by the Washington Superior Court, V.R.A.P. 5(b)(1), certifying five questions of law for our resolution.
. . .

We begin with a review of the record. Defendant operates a business in which factual and financial reports about individual business enterprises are issued exclusively to subscribers of defendant's service. These subscribers, usually creditors of the reported enterprises, may contract for "continuous service reports" which enable them to receive all report updates about a particular business over a year's time from the subscriber's initial inquiry. The reports are based on information solicited from the business itself, the business' banking and credit sources, from trade suppliers, and from public records such as annual reports filed with the Secretary of State and reports of bankruptcy petitions.

On or about July 26, 1976, plaintiff's president met with a representative of its principal creditor, a bank, to discuss the possibility of future financing. During the meeting, the bank's representative informed plaintiff's president that he had just received a credit report issued by defendant indicating that plaintiff had recently filed a voluntary petition in bankruptcy. Plaintiff's president testified that he was both shocked and confused when confronted with the report, since plaintiff had never filed such a petition and, at the time the report was published, plaintiff's business was steadily expanding. In fact, plaintiff's president later testified that prior to the issuance of the credit report, plaintiff had never suffered a major economic reversal and its financial condition was sound. Nevertheless, despite the bank representative's trial testimony that he never really believed the report, the bank put off any future consideration of credit to plaintiff until the discrepancy was cleared up. The bank later terminated plaintiff's credit allegedly for reasons unrelated to the report.

. . . .

The basis of the error was established at trial: a former employee of plaintiff, and not plaintiff, had filed a voluntary petition in bankruptcy. Defendant's employee, a seventeen-year-old high school student, paid $200 annually to review Vermont's bankruptcy petitions, had inadvertently attributed the former employee's bankruptcy petition to plaintiff itself, and reported the information as such to defendant. A representative of defendant testified that prior to the issuance of a credit report indicating a bankrupt business, it was defendant's routine practice first to check the report's accuracy with the business itself. No prepublication verification was ever attempted in the present case.

On or about August 3, 1976, having satisfied itself that its credit report on plaintiff was wrong, defendant issued a corrective notice to the five subscribers who had received the initial report. In substance, the corrective notice stated that it was a former employee of plaintiff, not plaintiff itself, who had filed the petition in bankruptcy, and that plaintiff "continued in business as usual." Plaintiff informed defendant that it was dissatisfied with the corrective notice, since it implied that the initial mistake was attributable to plaintiff, not defendant. Plaintiff again demanded a list of subscribers who had seen the report, but its request was once again denied.

Thereafter, plaintiff refused to provide defendant with any further financial data, and requested that defendant inform anyone seeking such data that they were being withheld pending the outcome of plaintiff s defamation action against defendant. Instead, defendant issued plaintiff a "blank rating," indicating that plaintiff's circumstances were "difficult to classify" within defendant's rating system, and such information was distributed to those creditors who requested a current indication of plaintiff's financial status. A short while later, plaintiff commenced its defamation action.

I

. . . Although *Gertz* permitted a "private individual" to recover actual damages, presumed or punitive damages were not permitted absent proof of the *New York Times* standard "of knowledge of falsity or reckless disregard for the truth." *Id.* at 348.

The critical issue underlying the certified questions presented, a matter of first impression for this Court, is whether the First and Fourteenth Amendments to the United States Constitution require that the qualified protections afforded the media in "private" defamation actions, as set forth in *Gertz*, be extended to actions involving nonmedia defendants.

. . . .

[I]n carefully surveying the decisions of those jurisdictions which have specifically addressed the issue of whether *Gertz* should be applied to non-media defendants, we note that the majority have refused such an extension. Although we are not bound by these decisions, their reasoning is both persuasive and compelling. In nonmedia defamation actions, "[the] crucial elements . . . which brought the United States Supreme Court into the field of defamation law are missing. There is no threat to the free and robust debate of public issues; there is no potential interference with a meaningful dialogue of ideas concerning self-government; and there is no threat of liability causing a reaction of self-censorship by the press."

. . . .

In light of the above, we are convinced that the balance must be struck in favor of the private plaintiff defamed by a nonmedia defendant. "Neither the intentional lie nor the careless error materially advances society's interest in 'uninhibited, robust, and wide-open' debate on public issues." *Gertz v. Robert Welch, Inc., supra,*

418 U.S. at 340 (quoting *New York Times Co. v. Sullivan, supra,* 376 U.S. at 270). Accordingly, we hold that as a matter of federal constitutional law, the media protections outlined in *Gertz* are inapplicable to nonmedia defamation actions.

. . . .

III

With regard to the question of damages, we note that "the availability of both general and punitive damages in libel actions has not been rejected as a matter of constitutional law." "When the defamation is actionable per se the plaintiff can recover general damages without proof of loss or injury, which is conclusively presumed to result from the defamation, but he is not required to rely solely upon the implications that are applicable and may present any evidence of a competent character that is authorized by his pleadings, for the purpose of showing the extent of the injury and the amount of the compensation that should be awarded."

Likewise, in accordance with this Court's belief that "[punitive] damages are awarded to 'stamp the condemnation of the jury upon the acts of defendant on account of their malicious character,' " . . . we have indicated that malice "may be shown by conduct manifesting personal ill will or carried out under circumstances evidencing insult or oppression, or even by conduct showing a reckless or wanton disregard of one's rights."

Since "punitive damages are incapable of precise determination, their assessment is 'largely discretionary with the jury' " . . .

IV

. . . .

We are not persuaded that the trial court abused its discretion in denying defendant's motion to set aside the verdict as to the issue of punitive damages. There was ample evidence in the record to enable the jury to conclude that defendant's conduct was insulting, reckless, and in total disregard of plaintiff s rights. . . .

---

1. Why doesn't *Gertz* apply?

2. What damages may Plaintiff recover? What proof of these damages is required?

DUN & BRADSTREET v. GREENMOSS BUILDERS, INC.
Supreme Court of the United States, 1985
472 U.S. 749

JUSTICE POWELL announced the judgment of the Court and delivered an opinion, in which JUSTICE REHNQUIST and JUSTICE O'CONNOR joined.

In *Gertz v. Robert Welch, Inc.,* 418 U.S. 323 (1974), we held that the First

Amendment restricted the damages that a private individual could obtain from a publisher for a libel that involved a matter of public concern. More specifically, we held that in these circumstances the First Amendment prohibited awards of presumed and punitive damages for false and defamatory statements unless the plaintiff shows "actual malice," that is, knowledge of falsity or reckless disregard for the truth. The question presented in this case is whether this rule of *Gertz* applies when the false and defamatory statements do not involve matters of public concern.

I

Petitioner Dun & Bradstreet, a credit reporting agency, provides subscribers with financial and related information about businesses. All the information is confidential; under the terms of the subscription agreement the subscribers may not reveal it to anyone else. On July 26, 1976, petitioner sent a report to five subscribers indicating that respondent, a construction contractor, had filed a voluntary petition for bankruptcy. This report was false and grossly misrepresented respondent's assets and liabilities. That same day, while discussing the possibility of future financing with its bank, respondent's president was told that the bank had received the defamatory report. He immediately called petitioner's regional office, explained the error, and asked for a correction. In addition, he requested the names of the firms that had received the false report in order to assure them that the company was solvent. Petitioner promised to look into the matter but refused to divulge the names of those who had received the report.

After determining that its report was indeed false, petitioner issued a corrective notice on or about August 3, 1976, to the five subscribers who had received the initial report. The notice stated that one of respondent's former employees, not respondent itself, had filed for bankruptcy and that respondent "continued in business as usual." Respondent told petitioner that it was dissatisfied with the notice, and it again asked for a list of subscribers who had seen the initial report. Again petitioner refused to divulge their names.

Respondent then brought this defamation action in Vermont state court. It alleged that the false report had injured its reputation and sought both compensatory and punitive damages. The trial established that the error in petitioner's report had been caused when one of its employees, a 17-year-old high school student paid to review Vermont bankruptcy pleadings, had inadvertently attributed to respondent a bankruptcy petition filed by one of respondent's former employees. Although petitioner's representative testified that it was routine practice to check the accuracy of such reports with the businesses themselves, it did not try to verify the information about respondent before reporting it.

After trial, the jury returned a verdict in favor of respondent and awarded $50,000 in compensatory or presumed damages and $300,000 in punitive damages. Petitioner moved for a new trial. It argued that in *Gertz v. Robert Welch, Inc., supra,* at 349, this Court had ruled broadly that "the States may not permit recovery of presumed or punitive damages, at least when liability is not based on a showing of knowledge of falsity or reckless disregard for the truth," and it argued that the judge's instructions in this case permitted the jury to award such damages on a lesser showing. The trial court indicated some doubt as to whether *Gertz* applied to "non-media cases," but granted a new trial "[because] of . . . dissatisfaction with its charge and . . . conviction that the interests of justice [required]" it. App. 26.

The Vermont Supreme Court reversed. 143 Vt. 66, 461 A. 2d 414 (1983). Although recognizing that "in certain instances the distinction between media and nonmedia defendants may be difficult to draw," the court stated that "no such difficulty is presented with credit reporting agencies, which are in the business of selling financial information to a limited number of subscribers who have paid substantial fees for their services." . . . Relying on this distinguishing characteristic of credit reporting firms, the court concluded that such firms are not "the type of media worthy of First Amendment protection as contemplated by *New York Times [Co. v. Sullivan*, 376 U.S. 254 (1964),] and its progeny." . . . It held that the balance between a private plaintiff's right to recover presumed and punitive damages without a showing of special fault and the First Amendment rights of "nonmedia" speakers "must be struck in favor of the private plaintiff defamed by a nonmedia defendant." . . . Accordingly, the court held "that as a matter of federal constitutional law, the media protections outlined in *Gertz* are inapplicable to nonmedia defamation actions."

Recognizing disagreement among the lower courts about when the protections *of Gertz* apply, we granted certiorari. . . . We now affirm, although for reasons different from those relied upon by the Vermont Supreme Court.

. . . .

In Gertz, we held that the fact that expression concerned a public issue did not by itself entitle the libel defendant to the constitutional protections *of New York Times*. These protections, we found, were not "justified solely by reference to the interest of the press and broadcast media in immunity from liability." 418 U.S., at 343. Rather, they represented "an accommodation between [First Amendment] [concerns] and the limited state interest present in the context of libel actions brought by public persons." *Ibid.* In libel actions brought by private persons we found the competing interests different. Largely because private persons have not voluntarily exposed themselves to increased risk of injury from defamatory statements and because they generally lack effective opportunities for rebutting such statements, *id.*, at 345, we found that the State possessed a "strong and legitimate . . . interest in compensating private individuals for injury to reputation." *Id.*, at 348-349. Balancing this stronger state interest against the same First Amendment interest at stake in *New York Times*, we held that a State could not allow recovery of presumed and punitive damages absent a showing of "actual malice." Nothing in our opinion, however, indicated that this same balance would be struck regardless of the type of speech involved.

IV

We have never considered whether the *Gertz* balance obtains when the defamatory statements involve no issue of public concern. To make this determination, we must employ the approach approved in *Gertz* and balance the State's interest in compensating private individuals for injury to their reputation against the First Amendment interest in protecting this type of expression. This state interest is identical to the one weighed in *Gertz.* There we found that it was "strong and legitimate." . . .

The First Amendment interest, on the other hand, is less important than the one weighed in *Gertz.* We have long recognized that not all speech is of equal First Amendment importance. It is speech on " 'matters of public concern' " that is "at the heart of the First Amendment's protection." . . . In contrast, speech on matters of purely private concern is of less First Amendment concern. . . .

While such speech is not totally unprotected by the First Amendment, its protections are less stringent. In *Gertz,* we found that the state interest in awarding presumed and punitive damages was not "substantial" in view of their effect on speech at the core of First Amendment concern. 418 U.S., at 349. This interest, however, *is* "substantial" relative to the incidental effect these remedies may have on speech of significantly less constitutional interest. The rationale of the common-law rules has been the experience and judgment of history that "proof of actual damage will be impossible in a great many cases where, from the character of the defamatory words and the circumstances of publication, it is all but certain that serious harm has resulted in fact." W. Prosser, Law of Torts § 112, p. 765 (4th ed. 1971); accord, *Rowe v. Metz, supra,* at 425-426, 579 P. 2d, at 84; Note, Developments in the Law — Defamation, 69 Harv. L. Rev. 875, 891-892 (1956). As a result, courts for centuries have allowed juries to presume that some damage occurred from many defamatory utterances and publications. This rule furthers the state interest in providing remedies for defamation by ensuring that those remedies are effective. In light of the reduced constitutional value of speech involving no matters of public concern, we hold that the state interest adequately supports awards of presumed and punitive damages — even absent a showing of "actual malice.

V

The only remaining issue is whether petitioner's credit report involved a matter of public concern. In a related context, we have held that "[whether] . . . speech addresses a matter of public concern must be determined by [the expression's] content, form, and context . . . as revealed by the whole record." *Connick v. Myers, supra,* at 147-148. These factors indicate that petitioner's credit report concerns no public issue. It was speech solely in the individual interest of the speaker and its specific business audience. Cf. *Central Hudson Gas & Elec. Corp. v. Public Service Comm'n of New York,* 447 U.S. 557, 561 (1980). This particular interest warrants no special protection when — as in this case — the speech is wholly false and clearly damaging to the victim's business reputation. Cf. *id.,* at 566; *Virginia Pharmacy Bd. v. Virginia Citizens Consumer Council, Inc.,* 425 U.S. 748, 771-772 (1976). Moreover, since the credit report was made available to only five subscribers, who, under the terms of the subscription agreement, could not disseminate it further, it cannot be said that the report involves any "strong interest in the free flow of commercial information." *Id.,* at 764. There is simply no credible argument that this type of credit reporting requires special protection to ensure that "debate on public issues [will] be uninhibited, robust, and wide-open." *New York Times Co. v. Sullivan,* 376 U.S., at 270.

In addition, the speech here, like advertising, is hardy and unlikely to be deterred by incidental state regulation. . . . Arguably, the reporting here was also more objectively verifiable than speech deserving of greater protection. See *ibid.* In any case, the market provides a powerful incentive to a credit reporting agency to be accurate, since false credit reporting is of no use to creditors. Thus, any incremental "chilling" effect of libel suits would be of decreased significance.[9]

VI

We conclude that permitting recovery of presumed and punitive damages in defamation cases absent a showing of "actual malice" does not violate the First Amendment when the defamatory statements do not involve matters of public concern. Accordingly, we affirm the judgment of the Vermont Supreme Court.

It is so ordered.

CHIEF JUSTICE BURGER, concurring in the judgment.

. . . .

I dissented in *Gertz* because I believed that, insofar as the "ordinary private citizen" was concerned, 418 U.S., at 355, the Court's opinion "[abandoned] the traditional thread," *id.*, at 354-355, that had been the theme of the law in this country up to that time. I preferred "to allow this area of law to continue to evolve as it [had] up to [then] with respect to private citizens rather than embark on a new doctrinal theory which [had] no jurisprudential ancestry." *Ibid. Gertz*, however, is now the law of the land, and until it is overruled, it must, under the principle of *stare decisis*, be applied by this Court.

The single question before the Court today is whether *Gertz* applies to this case. . . . I agree that *Gertz* is limited to circumstances in which the alleged defamatory expression concerns a matter of general public importance, and that the expression in question here relates to a matter of essentially private concern. I therefore agree with the plurality opinion to the extent that it holds that *Gertz* is inapplicable in this case for the two reasons indicated. No more is needed to dispose of the present case.

---

1. What is the difference between matters of "public concern" and matters of "public interest," *Rosenbloom v. Metromedia*?

2. What defamation rules apply to private persons when the matter is not of "public concern"?

---

[9] The Court of Appeals for the Fifth Circuit has noted that, while most States provide a qualified privilege against libel suits for commercial credit reporting agencies, in those States that do not there is a thriving credit reporting business and commercial credit transactions are not inhibited.

6.   The Burden of Proving Truth

PHILADELPHIA NEWSPAPERS, INC. v. HEPPS
Supreme Court of the United States, 1986
475 U.S. 767

JUSTICE O'CONNOR delivered the opinion of the Court.

This case requires us once more to "[struggle] . . . to define the proper accommodation between the law of defamation and the freedoms of speech and press protected by the First Amendment." *Gertz v. Robert Welch, Inc.*, 418 U.S. 323, 325 (1974). In *Gertz*, the Court held that a private figure who brings a suit for defamation cannot recover without some showing that the media defendant was at fault in publishing the statements at issue. *Id.*, at 347. Here, we hold that, at least where a newspaper publishes speech of public concern, a private-figure plaintiff cannot recover damages without also showing that the statements at issue are false.

I

Maurice S. Hepps is the principal stockholder of General Programming, Inc. (GPI), a corporation that franchises a chain of stores — known at the relevant time as "Thrifty" stores — selling beer, soft drinks, and snacks. Mr. Hepps, GPI, and a number of its franchisees are the appellees here. Appellant Philadelphia Newspapers, Inc., owns the Philadelphia Inquirer (Inquirer). The Inquirer published a series of articles, . . . containing the statements at issue here. The general theme of the five articles, which appeared in the Inquirer between May 1975 and May 1976, was that appellees had links to organized crime and used some of those links to influence the State's governmental processes, both legislative and administrative. The articles discussed a state legislator, described as "a Pittsburgh Democrat and convicted felon," . . . whose actions displayed "a clear pattern of interference in state government by [the legislator] on behalf of Hepps and Thrifty," . . . The stories reported that federal "investigators have found connections between Thrifty and underworld figures," . . . ; that "the Thrifty Beverage beer chain . . . had connections . . . with organized crime" . . . ; and that Thrifty had "won a series of competitive advantages through rulings by the State Liquor Control Board". . . . A grand jury was said to be investigating the "alleged relationship between the Thrifty chain and known Mafia figures," and "[whether] the chain received special treatment from the [state Governor's] administration and the Liquor Control Board." . . .

Appellees brought suit for defamation against appellants in a Pennsylvania state court. Consistent with *Gertz, supra*, Pennsylvania requires a private figure who brings a suit for defamation to bear the burden of proving negligence or malice by the defendant in publishing the statements at issue. 42 Pa. Cons. Stat. § 8344 (1982). As to falsity, Pennsylvania follows the common law's presumption that an individual's reputation is a good one. Statements defaming that person are therefore presumptively false, although a publisher who bears the burden of proving the truth of the statements has an absolute defense. . . .

After all the evidence had been presented by both sides, the trial court concluded that Pennsylvania's statute giving the defendant the burden of proving the truth of the statements violated the Federal Constitution. . . .. The trial court therefore instructed the jury that the plaintiffs bore the burden of proving falsity. . . .

. . . The jury ruled for appellants and therefore awarded no damages to appellees.

[T]he appellees here brought an appeal directly to the Pennsylvania Supreme Court. That court viewed *Gertz* as simply requiring the plaintiff to show fault in actions for defamation. It concluded that a showing of fault did not require a showing of falsity, held that to place the burden of showing truth on the defendant did not unconstitutionally inhibit free debate, and remanded the case for a new trial. 506 Pa., at 318-329, 485 A. 2d, at 382-387. We noted probable jurisdiction, 472 U.S. 1025 (1985), and now reverse.

II

In *New York Times Co. v. Sullivan*, 376 U.S. 254 (1964), the Court "[determined] for the first time the extent to which the constitutional protections for speech and press limit a State's power to award damages in a libel action brought by a public official against critics of his official conduct." . . .

The Court therefore held that the Constitution "prohibits a public official from recovering damages for a defamatory falsehood relating to his official conduct unless he proves that the statement was made with 'actual malice' — that is, with knowledge that it was false or with reckless disregard of whether it was false or not." *Id.*, at 279-280. That showing must be made with "convincing clarity," *id.*, at 285-286, or, in a later formulation, by "clear and convincing proof," *Gertz*, 418 U.S., at 342. The standards of *New York Times* apply not only when a public official sues a newspaper, but also when a "public figure" sues a magazine or news service.

A decade after *New York Times*, the Court examined the constitutional limits on defamation suits by private-figure plaintiffs against media defendants. . . . *Gertz*, *supra*, at 344-345, the Court held that the Constitution "allows the States to impose liability on the publisher or broadcaster of defamatory falsehood on a less demanding showing than that required by *New York Times*," 418 U.S., at 348: "[So] long as they do not impose liability without fault, the States may define for themselves the appropriate standard of liability for a publisher or broadcaster of defamatory falsehood injurious to a private individual." *Id.*, at 347. . . . In addition, the Court in *Gertz* expressly held that, although a showing of simple fault sufficed to allow recovery for actual damages, even a private-figure plaintiff was required to show actual malice in order to recover presumed or punitive damages. *Id.*, at 348-350.

The Court most recently considered the constitutional limits on suits for defamation in *Dun & Bradstreet, Inc. v. Greenmoss Builders, Inc.*, 472 U.S. 749 (1985). In sharp contrast to *New York Times*, *Dun & Bradstreet* involved not only a private-figure plaintiff, but also speech of purely private concern. 472 U.S., at 751-752. A plurality of the Court in *Dun & Bradstreet* was convinced that . . . the showing of actual malice needed to recover punitive damages under either *New York Times* or *Gertz* was unnecessary.

. . . .

One can discern in these decisions two forces that may reshape the common-law landscape to conform to the First Amendment. The first is whether the plaintiff is a public official or figure, or is instead a private figure. The second is whether the speech at issue is of public concern. When the speech is of public concern and the plaintiff is a public official or public figure, the Constitution clearly requires the plaintiff to surmount a much higher barrier before recovering damages from a media defendant than is raised by the common law. When the speech is of public concern but the plaintiff is a private figure, as in *Gertz*, the Constitution still supplants the standards of the common law, but the constitutional requirements are, in at least some of their range, less forbidding than when the plaintiff is a public figure and the speech is of public concern. When the speech is of exclusively private concern and the plaintiff is a private figure, as in *Dun & Bradstreet*, the constitutional requirements do not necessarily force any change in at least some of the features of the common-law landscape.

Our opinions to date have chiefly treated the necessary showings of fault rather than of falsity. Nonetheless, as one might expect given the language of the Court in *New York Times*, see *supra*, at 772-773, a public-figure plaintiff must show the falsity of the statements at issue in order to prevail in a suit for defamation. . . .

Here, as in *Gertz*, the plaintiff is a private figure and the newspaper articles are of public concern. . . . We believe that the common law's rule on falsity — that the defendant must bear the burden of proving truth — must similarly fall here to a constitutional requirement that the plaintiff bear the burden of showing falsity, as well as fault, before recovering damages.

. . . .

We recognize that requiring the plaintiff to show falsity will insulate from liability some speech that is false, but unprovably so. Nonetheless, the Court's previous decisions on the restrictions that the First Amendment places upon the common law of defamation firmly support our conclusion here with respect to the allocation of the burden of proof. . . . We therefore do not break new ground here in insulating speech that is not even demonstrably false.

We note that our decision adds only marginally to the burdens that the plaintiff must already bear as a result of our earlier decisions in the law of defamation. The plaintiff must show fault. A jury is obviously more likely to accept a plaintiff's contention that the defendant was at fault in publishing the statements at issue if convinced that the relevant statements were false. As a practical matter, then, evidence offered by plaintiffs on the publisher's fault in adequately investigating the truth of the published statements will generally encompass evidence of the falsity of the matters asserted. See Keeton, *Defamation and Freedom of the Press*, 54 Texas L. Rev. 1221, 1236 (1976). See also Franklin & Bussel, *The Plaintiff's Burden in Defamation: Awareness and Falsity*, 25 Wm. & Mary L. Rev. 825, 856-857 (1984).

. . . .

For the reasons stated above, the judgment of the Pennsylvania Supreme Court is reversed, and the case is remanded for further proceedings not inconsistent with this opinion.

It is so ordered.

JUSTICE BRENNAN, with whom JUSTICE BLACKMUN joins, concurring.

I believe that where allegedly defamatory speech is of public concern, the First Amendment requires that the plaintiff, whether public official, public figure, or private individual, prove the statements at issue to be false, and thus join the Court's opinion. Cf. *Rosenbloom v. Metromedia, Inc.*, 403 U.S. 29 (1971). I write separately only to note that, while the Court reserves the question whether the rule it announces applies to nonmedia defendants, *ante*, at 779, n. 4, I adhere to my view that such a distinction is "irreconcilable" with the fundamental First Amendment principle that " '[the] inherent worth of . . . speech in terms of its capacity for informing the public does not depend upon the identity of the source, whether corporation, association, union, or individual.' "

JUSTICE STEVENS, with whom THE CHIEF JUSTICE, JUSTICE WHITE, and JUSTICE REHNQUIST join, dissenting.

The issue the Court resolves today will make a difference in only one category of cases — those in which a private individual can prove that he was libeled by a defendant who was at least negligent. For unless such a plaintiff can overcome the burden imposed by *Gertz v. Robert Welch, Inc.*, 418 U.S. 323, 347 (1974), he cannot recover regardless of how the burden of proof on the issue of truth or falsity is allocated. By definition, therefore, the only litigants — and the only publishers — who will benefit from today's decision are those who act negligently or maliciously.

The Court . . . decides to override "the common-law presumption" retained by several States that "defamatory speech is false" because of the need "[to] ensure that true speech on matters of public concern is not deterred." . . . I do not agree that our precedents require a private individual to bear the risk that a defamatory statement — uttered either with a mind toward assassinating his good name or with careless indifference to that possibility — cannot be proven false. By attaching no weight to the State's interest in protecting the private individual's good name, the Court has reached a pernicious result.

7. Opinion

MR. CHOW OF NEW YORK v. STE. JOUR AZUR S.A.
United States Court of Appeals for the Second Circuit, 1985
759 F.2d 219

MESKILL, CIRCUIT JUDGE:

On February 19, 1982 Mr. Chow of New York, the joint venture that owns Mr. Chow, commenced the instant action. In the complaint, Ste. Jour, Gault and Millau were named as defendants and jurisdiction was based on diversity of citizenship.

The complaint alleged that the review [in the defendants' restaurant guide] contained false and defamatory statements and sought compensatory damages in excess of $10,000 and punitive damages in excess of $250,000.

. . . .

The district court submitted six statements to the jury. It instructed the jury that, as a matter of law, these were statements of fact and that if any one of them was false, defamatory and made with malice it would support a finding that the review had libeled Mr. Chow. The six statements submitted were:

(1)   "It is impossible to have the basic condiments . . . on the table."

(2)   "The sweet and sour pork contained more dough . . . than meat."

(3)   "The green peppers . . . remained still frozen on the plate."

(4)   The rice was "soaking . . . in oil."

(5)   The Peking Duck "was made up of only one dish (instead of the traditional three)."

(6)   The pancakes were "the thickness of a finger."

The jury returned a general verdict, finding that the review was libelous. It awarded $20,000 in compensatory and $5 in punitive damages. Appellants' motion for judgment notwithstanding the verdict was denied without opinion.

DISCUSSION

On appeal, appellants raise a host of grounds for reversal. Among them are a claim that the statements submitted to the jury are opinion and thus protected speech and a claim that the evidence on the issue of malice is insufficient to support the jury's findings. Because we find these two claims dispositive of this appeal, we do not consider appellants' other claims.

A. *Opinion*

Appellants' initial argument is that the district court erred when it failed to hold that the statements submitted to the jury were opinion and thus privileged. Appellants' argument stems from the Supreme Court's decision in *Gertz v. Robert Welch, Inc.*, 418 U.S. 323, 94 S. Ct. 2997, 41 L. Ed. 2d 789 (1974), . . .

We begin with the common ground. Under the First Amendment there is no such thing as a false idea. However pernicious an opinion may seem, we depend for its correction not on the conscience of judges and juries but on the competition of other ideas. But there is no constitutional value in false statements of fact. *Id*, at 339-40 (footnote omitted). We have recognized that *Gertz* made crucial the distinction between statements of fact and opinions. And, we have held that generally one cannot be liable simply for expressing an opinion. The Supreme Court has also made clear that the constitutional protection afforded statements of opinion is not lost simply because the opinion is expressed through the use of figurative or hyperbolic language. . . .

Although it is clear that expressions of opinion are constitutionally protected, the determination of whether a specific statement is one of opinion or fact is difficult. As an initial matter, the inquiry into whether a statement should be viewed as one of fact or one of opinion must be made from the perspective of an "ordinary reader" of the statement. *Buckley v. Littell*, 539 F.2d at 894. It is also clear that the determination of whether a statement is opinion or rhetorical hyperbole as opposed to a factual representation is a question of law for the court. . . .

. . . .

Although none of [our prior] decisions can be said to establish an actual test for determining if a statement is protected opinion or unprotected fact, they do provide guidance. Thus, it is clear that we must examine both the context in which the statements are made and the circumstances surrounding the statements. . . . We must also look at the language itself to determine if it is used in a precise, literal manner or in a loose, figurative or hyperbolic sense. . . . Related to this inquiry, we must examine the statements to determine if they are objectively capable of being proved true or false. . . . Finally, if the above analysis indicates that the statement is opinion, we must determine if it implies the allegation of undisclosed defamatory facts as the basis for the opinion. . . .

In the recent en banc decision of the D.C. Circuit in *Ollman v. Evans*, 750 F.2d 970, 242 U.S. App. D.C. 301 (D.C. Cir. 1984), Judge Starr, writing for the court, developed a similar guide to aid in the determination of whether the average reader would view a statement as one of fact or one of opinion.

. . . .

Turning to the instant case, we believe that application of the guidelines culled from our previous opinions and Judge Starr's opinion in *Ollman* mandates a holding that five of the six statements submitted to the jury were opinion rather than fact. Only the statement that Mr. Chow served Peking Duck in one dish rather than the traditional three can be considered factual.

1. Context

As indicated earlier, both the immediate and broader context in which a statement occurs can indicate that what appears to be a statement of fact is in reality protected opinion. . . .

Restaurant reviews are also the well recognized home of opinion and comment. Indeed, "by its very nature, an article commenting upon the quality of a restaurant or its food, like a review of a play or movie, constitutes the opinion of the reviewer." *Greer v. Columbus Monthly Publishing Corp.*, 4 Ohio App. 3d 235, 238, 448 N.E.2d 157, 161 (1982). The natural function of the review is to convey the critic's opinion of the restaurant reviewed: the food, the service, the decor, the atmosphere, and so forth. Such matters are to a large extent controlled by personal tastes. The average reader approaches a review with the knowledge that it contains only one person's views of the establishment. And importantly, "as is essential in aesthetic criticism . . . the object of the judgment is available to the critic's audience." *Myers*, 380 Mass. at 341, 403 N.E.2d at 379. Appellee does not cite a single case that has found a restaurant review libelous. Appellants and *amici*, on the other hand, cite numerous decisions that have refused to do so. Although the rationale underlying each of these decisions is different, they all recognize to some extent that reviews, although they may be unkind, are not normally a breeding ground for successful libel actions.

2. Language Used

Recognizing that reviews are normally conveyors of opinion, we turn to the language in the review before us to see if it makes factual representations. Examining the language in the review itself, we cannot say that it would cause the average reader to believe that the writer in five of the six contested remarks had gone beyond statements of opinion. . . .

The average reader would understand the author's statements to be attempts to express his opinions through the use of metaphors and hyperbole. Because the average reader would understand the statements involved to be opinion, the statements are entitled to the same constitutional protection as a straight-forward expression of opinion would receive.

3. Truth/Falsity

The final factor that our previous decisions indicate should be examined is whether the statement is objectively capable of being proved true or false. As Judge Starr stated in *Ollman*, "a reader cannot rationally view an unverifiable statement as conveying actual facts."

. . . .

When viewed in the entire context and given a reasonable rather than a literal reading, only the statement that Mr. Chow served Peking Duck in one dish instead of the traditional three can be viewed as an assertion of fact. The statement is not metaphorical or hyperbolic; it clearly is laden with factual content. . . .

. . . .

CONCLUSION

We conclude that five of the six statements submitted to the jury were statements of opinion and thus constitutionally protected. Plaintiff has failed to prove by clear and convincing evidence that the sixth statement, even if false and defamatory, was made with actual malice. Moreover, Mr. Chow points to no statements that could support a jury verdict in a new trial. Therefore, the judgment below is vacated and the case is remanded to the district court with instructions to dismiss the complaint.

---

1. The common law recognized a privilege known as fair comment to allow critique of the arts, restaurants, candidates for public office, anything presented to the public. As you see in *Mr. Chow*, the Second Circuit believes this has changed into a constitutional privilege to comment. Both rest on protected opinion.

2. Did *Gertz* establish that the Constitution protects all opinions?

MILKOVICH v. LORAIN JOURNAL CO.
Supreme Court of the United States, 1990
497 U.S. 1

CHIEF JUSTICE REHNQUIST delivered the opinion of the Court.

Respondent J. Theodore Diadiun authored an article in an Ohio newspaper implying that petitioner Michael Milkovich, a local high school wrestling coach, lied under oath in a judicial proceeding about an incident involving petitioner and his team which occurred at a wrestling match. Petitioner sued Diadiun and the newspaper for libel, and the Ohio Court of Appeals affirmed a lower court entry of summary judgment against petitioner. This judgment was based in part on the grounds that the article constituted an "opinion" protected from the reach of state defamation law by the First Amendment to the United States Constitution. We hold that the First Amendment does not prohibit the application of Ohio's libel laws to the alleged defamations contained in the article.

This lawsuit is before us for the third time in an odyssey of litigation spanning nearly 15 years. Petitioner Milkovich, now retired, was the wrestling coach at Maple Heights High School in Maple Heights, Ohio. In 1974, his team was involved in an altercation at a home wrestling match with a team from Mentor High School. Several people were injured. In response to the incident, the Ohio High School Athletic Association (OHSAA) held a hearing at which Milkovich and H. Don Scott, the Superintendent of Maple Heights Public Schools, testified. Following the hearing, OHSAA placed the Maple Heights team on probation for a year and declared the team ineligible for the 1975 state tournament. OHSAA also censured Milkovich for his actions during the altercation. Thereafter, several parents and wrestlers sued OHSAA in the Court of Common Pleas of Franklin County, Ohio, seeking a restraining order against OHSAA's ruling on the grounds that they had been denied due process in the OHSAA proceeding. Both Milkovich and Scott testified in that proceeding. The court overturned OHSAA's probation and ineligibility orders on due process grounds.

The day after the court rendered its decision, respondent Diadiun's column appeared in the News-Herald, a newspaper which circulates in Lake County, Ohio, and is owned by respondent Lorain Journal Co. The column bore the heading "Maple beat the law with the 'big lie,'" beneath which appeared Diadiun's photograph and the words "TD Says." The carryover page headline announced ". . . Diadiun says Maple told a lie." The column contained the following passages:

". . . [A] lesson was learned (or relearned) yesterday by the student body of Maple Heights High School, and by anyone who attended the Maple-Mentor wrestling meet of last Feb. 8."

"A lesson which, sadly, in view of the events of the past year, is well they learned early."

"It is simply this: If you get in a jam, lie your way out."

"If you're successful enough, and powerful enough, and can sound sincere enough, you stand an excellent chance of making the lie stand up, regardless of what really happened."

"The teachers responsible were mainly head Maple wrestling coach, Mike Milkovich, and former superintendent of schools H. Donald Scott."

". . . ."

"Anyone who attended the meet, whether he be from Maple Heights, Mentor, or impartial observer, knows in his heart that Milkovich and Scott lied at the hearing after each having given his solemn oath to tell the truth."

"But they got away with it."

"Is that the kind of lesson we want our young people learning from their high school administrators and coaches?"

"I think not."

Petitioner commenced a defamation action against respondents . . . alleging that the headline of Diadun's article and the nine passages quoted above "accused plaintiff of committing the crime of perjury. . . ."

Meanwhile, Superintendent Scott had been pursuing a separate defamation action through the Ohio courts. [In the *Scott* case], the Ohio Supreme Court . . . [concluded] that the column was "constitutionally protected opinion." *Scott v. News-Herald*, 25 Ohio St. 3d 243, 254, 496 N.E.2d 699, 709 (1986). Consequently, the court upheld a lower court's grant of summary judgment against Scott.

The *Scott* court decided that the proper analysis for determining whether utterances are fact or opinion was set forth in the decision of the United States Court of Appeals for the District of Columbia Circuit in *Ollman v. Evans* (1985). . . . Under that analysis, four factors are considered to ascertain whether, under the "totality of circumstances," a statement is fact or opinion. These factors are: (1) "the specific language used"; (2) "whether the statement is verifiable"; (3) "the general context of the statement"; and (4) "the broader context in which the statement appeared." . . . The court found that application of the first two factors to the column militated in favor of deeming the challenged passages actionable assertions of fact. . . . That potential outcome was trumped, however, by the court's consideration of the third and fourth factors. With respect to the third factor, the general context, the court explained that "the large caption 'TD Says' . . . would indicate to even the most gullible reader that the article was, in fact, opinion." . . . As for the fourth factor, the "broader context," the court reasoned that because the article appeared on a sports page — "a traditional haven for cajoling, invective, and hyperbole" — the article would probably be construed as opinion.

Subsequently, considering itself bound by the Ohio Supreme Court's decision in *Scott*, the Ohio Court of Appeals in the instant proceedings affirmed a trial court's grant of summary judgment in favor of respondents, concluding that "it has been decided, as a matter of law, that the article in question was constitutionally protected opinion." . . . The Supreme Court of Ohio dismissed petitioner's ensuing appeal for want of a substantial constitutional question. . . . We granted certiorari

. . . to consider the important questions raised by the Ohio courts' recognition of a constitutionally required "opinion" exception to the application of its defamation laws. We now reverse.

. . . Defamation law developed not only as a means of allowing an individual to vindicate his good name, but also for the purpose of obtaining redress for harm caused by such statements. . . . As the common law developed in this country, apart from the issue of damages, one usually needed only allege an unprivileged publication of false and defamatory matter to state a cause of action for defamation. . . . The common law generally did not place any additional restrictions on the type of statement that could be actionable. Indeed, defamatory communications were deemed actionable regardless of whether they were deemed to be statements of fact or opinion. See, e. g., Restatement of Torts, *supra*, §§ 565-567. As noted in the 1977 Restatement (Second) of Torts § 566, Comment *a:*

> "Under the law of defamation, an expression of opinion could be defamatory if the expression was sufficiently derogatory of another as to cause harm to his reputation, so as to lower him in the estimation of the community or to deter third persons from associating or dealing with him. . . . The expression of opinion was also actionable in a suit for defamation, despite the normal requirement that the communication be false as well as defamatory. . . . This position was maintained even though the truth or falsity of an opinion — as distinguished from a statement of fact — is not a matter that can be objectively determined and truth is a complete defense to a suit for defamation."

However, due to concerns that unduly burdensome defamation laws could stifle valuable public debate, the privilege of "fair comment" was incorporated into the common law as an affirmative defense to an action for defamation. "The principle of 'fair comment' afforded legal immunity for the honest expression of opinion on matters of legitimate public interest when based upon a true or privileged statement of fact." 1 F. Harper & F. James, Law of Torts § 5.28, p. 456 (1956) (footnote omitted). As this statement implies, comment was generally privileged when it concerned a matter of public concern, was upon true or privileged facts, represented the actual opinion of the speaker, and was not made solely for the purpose of causing harm. See Restatement of Torts, *supra*, § 606. "According to the majority rule, the privilege of fair comment applied only to an expression of opinion and not to a false statement of fact, whether it was expressly stated or implied from an expression of opinion." . . .

Respondents would have us recognize, in addition to the established safeguards discussed above, still another First-Amendment-based protection for defamatory statements which are categorized as "opinion" as opposed to "fact." For this proposition they rely principally on the following dictum from our opinion in *Gertz:*

> "Under the First Amendment there is no such thing as a false idea. However pernicious an opinion may seem, we depend for its correction not on the conscience of judges and juries but on the competition of other ideas. But there is no constitutional value in false statements of fact."

. . . Read in context, though, the fair meaning of the passage is to equate the word "opinion" in the second sentence with the word "idea" in the first sentence. Under this view, the language was merely a reiteration of Justice Holmes' classic "marketplace of ideas" concept. . . .

Thus, we do not think this passage from *Gertz* was intended to create a wholesale defamation exemption for anything that might be labeled "opinion." Not only would such an interpretation be contrary to the tenor and context of the passage, but it would also ignore the fact that expressions of "opinion" may often imply an assertion of objective fact.

If a speaker says, "In my opinion John Jones is a liar," he implies a knowledge of facts which lead to the conclusion that Jones told an untruth. Even if the speaker states the facts upon which he bases his opinion, if those facts are either incorrect or incomplete, or if his assessment of them is erroneous, the statement may still imply a false assertion of fact. Simply couching such statements in terms of opinion does not dispel these implications; and the statement, "In my opinion Jones is a liar," can cause as much damage to reputation as the statement, "Jones is a liar." As Judge Friendly aptly stated: "[It] would be destructive of the law of libel if a writer could escape liability for accusations of [defamatory conduct] simply by using, explicitly or implicitly, the words 'I think.' " See *Cianci, supra,* at 64. It is worthy of note that at common law, even the privilege of fair comment did not extend to "a false statement of fact, whether it was expressly stated or implied from an expression of opinion." Restatement (Second) of Torts, § 566, Comment *a* (1977).

Apart from their reliance on the *Gertz* dictum, respondents do not really contend that a statement such as, "In my opinion John Jones is a liar," should be protected by a separate privilege for "opinion" under the First Amendment. But they do contend that in every defamation case the First Amendment mandates an inquiry into whether a statement is "opinion" or "fact," and that only the latter statements may be actionable. They propose that a number of factors developed by the lower courts (in what we hold was a mistaken reliance on the *Gertz* dictum) be considered in deciding which is which. But we think the " 'breathing space' " which " 'freedoms of expression require in order to survive,' " *Hepps,* 475 U.S. at 772 (quoting *New York Times,* 376 U.S. at 272), is adequately secured by existing constitutional doctrine without the creation of an artificial dichotomy between "opinion" and fact.

Foremost, we think *Hepps* stands for the proposition that a statement on matters of public concern must be provable as false before there can be liability under state defamation law, at least in situations, like the present, where a media defendant is involved. Thus, unlike the statement, "In my opinion Mayor Jones is a liar," the statement, "In my opinion Mayor Jones shows his abysmal ignorance by accepting the teachings of Marx and Lenin," would not be actionable. *Hepps* ensures that a statement of opinion relating to matters of public concern which does not contain a provably false factual connotation will receive full constitutional protection.

. . . .

The *New York Times-Butts-Gertz* culpability requirements further ensure that debate on public issues remains "uninhibited, robust, and wide-open." *New York Times,* 376 U.S. at 270. Thus, where a statement of "opinion" on a matter of public concern reasonably implies false and defamatory facts regarding public figures or officials, those individuals must show that such statements were made with knowledge of their false implications or with reckless disregard of their truth. Similarly, where such a statement involves a private figure on a matter of public concern, a plaintiff must show that the false connotations were made with some level of fault as required by *Gertz*.

. . . .

We are not persuaded that, in addition to these protections, an additional separate constitutional privilege for "opinion" is required to ensure the freedom of expression guaranteed by the First Amendment. The dispositive question in the present case then becomes whether a reasonable factfinder could conclude that the statements in the Diadiun column imply an assertion that petitioner Milkovich perjured himself in a judicial proceeding. We think this question must be answered in the affirmative. . . . This is not the sort of loose, figurative, or hyperbolic language which would negate the impression that the writer was seriously maintaining that petitioner committed the crime of perjury. Nor does the general tenor of the article negate this impression.

We also think the connotation that petitioner committed perjury is sufficiently factual to be susceptible of being proved true or false. A determination whether petitioner lied in this instance can be made on a core of objective evidence by comparing, *inter alia*, petitioner's testimony before the OHSAA board with his subsequent testimony before the trial court. . . .

We believe our decision in the present case holds the balance true. The judgment of the Ohio Court of Appeals is reversed, and the case is remanded for further proceedings not inconsistent with this opinion.

Reversed.

JUSTICE BRENNAN, with whom JUSTICE MARSHALL joins, dissenting.

. . . .

[W]hile the Court today dispels any misimpression that there is a so-called opinion privilege *wholly in addition* to the protections we have already found to be guaranteed by the First Amendment, it determines that a protection for statements of pure opinion is dictated by *existing* First Amendment doctrine. As the Court explains, "full constitutional protection" extends to any statement relating to matters of public concern "that cannot 'reasonably [be] interpreted as stating actual facts' about an individual."

---

1.   The Court refuses to recognize a blanket exemption for all opinion. Why?

2.   *Sullivan v. Conway*, 157 F.3d 1092 (7th Cir. 1998), holds that the statement he is a "very poor lawyer" is protected opinion, not a verifiable fact:

It is one thing to say that a lawyer is dishonest, or has falsified his credentials, or has lost every case he has tried, or can never file suit within the statute of limitations. These are all readily verifiable statements of fact. But to say that he is a very poor lawyer is to express an opinion that is so difficult to verify or refute that it cannot feasibly be made a subject to inquiry by a jury. It is true that prefacing a defamatory statement with the qualification, "In my opinion," does not shield a defendant from liability for defamation. The test is whether a reasonable listener would take him to be basing his "opinion" on knowledge of facts of the sort that can be evaluated in a defamation suit. Here the answer is "no." Legal representation is attended by a great deal of uncertainty. Excellent lawyers may lose most of their cases because they are hired only in the most difficult ones, while poor lawyers may win cases because they turn away all the ones that would challenge their meager abilities. Many lawyers are good at some things and poor at others, so that the evaluation of them will depend on what the evaluator is interested in. It would be unmanageable to ask a court, in order to determine the validity of the defendants' defense of truth, to determine whether "in fact" Sullivan is a poor lawyer.

3. Courts continue to distinguish between fact and opinion. In *Flamm v. American Assoc. of Univ. Women*, 201 F.3d 144 (2d Cir. 2000), the court held that statements in a nonprofit organization's directory of lawyers willing to accept referrals, where at least one client had described the attorney as an "ambulance chaser" who was interested only in "slam dunk" cases was not necessarily opinion and could support an action in defamation. By contrast, in *Imperial Apparel, Ltd. v. Cosmo's Designer Direct, Inc.*, 882 N.E.2d 1011 (Ill. 2008), the court held that an advertisement which disparaged a commercial rival by claiming that "they brazenly attempt pulling polyester over their customer's eyes by conjuring up a low rent imitation [to the defendant's 3-for-1 promotion] that has the transparency of a hooker's come on" amounted to constitutionally protected opinion because the reasonable reader would recognize the ad as nothing more than "colorful hyperbole" meant only to attract the reader's attention. And in *State v. Carpenter*, 171 P.3d 41 (Alaska, 2007), the court ruled that sexually explicit derogatory comments made on air by a radio talk show personality about a complaining listener "were pure insults that were not factually verifiable" and hence not defamatory as a matter of law.

Chapter 17

PRIVACY

PROBLEM

Sally, a college student, attended the festivities in New Orleans during Mardi Gras. When a young man with a video camera said "lift your top," she obliged. He then gave her a string of beads. Sally was surprised to find that she is being pictured on a TV ad for a video called, "Naked Ladies of Mardi Gras" (price $19.95) produced by One Night Production and that she is pictured in the video with her top lifted.

Sally acknowledges that she had a lot to drink, many other cameras were there, and other women were lifting their tops. Discuss Sally's suit against One Night Productions.

The development of a common law right of privacy was heralded at the end of the 19th century by an influential article in *Harvard Law Review* by Professor Samuel Warren and future Supreme Court Justice Louis Brandeis:

> This development of the law was inevitable. The intense intellectual and emotional life, and the heightening of sensations which came with the advance of civilization, made it clear to men that only a part of the pain, pleasure, and profit of life lay in physical things. Thoughts, emotions, and sensations demanded legal recognition, and the beautiful capacity for growth which characterizes the common law enabled the judge to afford the requisite protection, without the interposition of the legislature.

> Recent inventions and business methods call attention to the next step which must be taken for the protection of the person, and for securing to the individual what Judge Cooley calls the right "to be let alone." Instantaneous photographs and newspaper enterprise have invaded the sacred precincts of private and domestic life; and numerous mechanical devices threaten to make good the prediction that "what is whispered in the closet shall be proclaimed from the house-tops." For years there has been a feeling that the law must afford some remedy for the unauthorized circulation of portraits of private persons; and the evil of the invasion of privacy by the newspapers, long keenly felt, has been but recently discussed by an able writer. The alleged facts of a somewhat notorious case brought before an inferior tribunal in New York a few months ago directly involved the consideration of the right of circulating portraits; and the question whether our law will recognize and protect the right to privacy in

this and in other respects must soon come before our courts for consideration.

Of the desirability — indeed of the necessity — of some such protection, there can, it is believed, be no doubt. The press is overstepping in every direction the obvious bounds of propriety and decency. Gossip is no longer the resource of the idle and of the vicious, but has become a trade, which is pursued with industry as well as effrontery. To satisfy a prurient taste the details of sexual relations are spread broadcast in the columns of the daily papers. To occupy the indolent, column upon column is filled with idle gossip, which can only be procured by intrusion upon the domestic circle. The intensity and complexity of life, attendant upon advancing civilization, have rendered necessary some retreat from the world, and man, under the refining influence of culture, has become more sensitive to publicity, so that solitude and privacy have become more essential to the individual; but modern enterprise and invention have, through invasions upon his privacy, subjected him to mental pain and distress, far greater than could be inflicted by mere bodily injury. Nor is the harm wrought by such invasions confined to the suffering of those who may be made the subjects of journalistic or other enterprise. In this, as in other branches of commerce, the supply creates the demand. Each crop of unseemly gossip, thus harvested, becomes the seed of more, and, in direct proportion to its circulation, results in a lowering of social standards and of morality. Even gossip apparently harmless, when widely and persistently circulated, is a potent for evil. It both belittles and perverts. It belittles by inverting the relative importance of things, thus dwarfing the thoughts and aspirations of a people. . . .

It is our purpose to consider whether the existing law affords a principle which can properly be invoked to protect the privacy of the individual; and, if it does, what the nature and extent of such protection is.

S. Warren & L. Brandeis, The Right to Privacy, 4 Harv. L. Rev. 193 (1890).

As with most of torts, Dean William Prosser has done much to organize and classify the subject of privacy:

[The] law of privacy comprises four distinct kinds of invasion of four different interests of the plaintiff, which are tied together by the common name, but otherwise have almost nothing in common. . . . [T]hese four torts may be described as follows:

1. Intrusion upon the plaintiff's seclusion or solitude, or into his private affairs.

2. Public disclosure of embarrassing private facts about the plaintiff.

3. Publicity which places the plaintiff in a false light in the public eye.

4. Appropriation, for the defendant's advantage, of the plaintiff's name or likeness.

. . . .

W. Prosser, Privacy, 48 Cal. L. R. 383, 389, 407 (1960).

A.   INTRUSION

NADER v. GENERAL MOTORS CORPORATION
Court of Appeals of New York, 1970
255 N.E.2d 765

Fuld, Chief Judge

On this appeal, taken by permission of the Appellate Division on a certified question, we are called upon to determine the reach of the tort of invasion of privacy as it exists under the law of the District of Columbia.

The complaint, in this action by Ralph Nader, pleads four causes of action against the appellant, General Motors Corporation, and three other defendants allegedly acting as it agents. The first two causes of action charge an invasion of privacy, the third is predicated on the intentional infliction of severe emotional distress and the fourth on interference with the plaintiff's economic advantage. This appeal concerns only the legal sufficiency of the first two causes of action, which were upheld in the courts below as against the appellant's motion to dismiss. . . .

The plaintiff, an author and lecturer on automotive safety, has, for some years, been an articulate and severe critic of General Motors' products from the standpoint of safety and design. According to the complaint — which, for present purposes, we must assume to be true — the appellant, having learned of the imminent publication of the plaintiff's book "Unsafe at any Speed," decided to conduct a campaign of intimidation against him in order to "suppress plaintiff's criticism of and prevent his disclosure of information" about its products. To that end, the appellant authorized and directed the other defendants to engage in a series of activities which, the plaintiff claims in his first two causes of action, violated his right to privacy.

Specifically, the plaintiff alleges that the appellant's agents (1) conducted a series of interviews with acquaintances of the plaintiff, "questioning them about, and casting aspersions upon [his] political, social . . . racial and religious views . . . ; his integrity; his sexual proclivities and inclinations; and his personal habits" (Complaint, par. 9[b]); (2) kept him under surveillance in public places for an unreasonable length of time (par. 9 [c]); (3) caused him to be accosted by girls for the purpose of entrapping him into illicit relationships (par. 9[d]); (4) made threatening, harassing and obnoxious telephone calls to him (par. 9[e]); (5) tapped his telephone and eavesdropped, by means of mechanical and electronic equipment, on his private conversations with others (par. 9[f]); and (6) conducted a "continuing" and harassing investigation of him (par. 9[g]). . . .

Turning, then, to the law of the District of Columbia, it appears that its courts have not only recognized a common-law action for invasion of privacy but have broadened the scope of that tort beyond its traditional limits. Thus, in the most recent of its cases on the subject, *Pearson v. Dodd* (410 F. 2d 701, *supra*), the Federal Court of Appeals for the District of Columbia declared (p. 704):

"We approve the extension of the tort of invasion of privacy to instances of *intrusion*, whether by physical trespass or not, into spheres from which an ordinary man in a plaintiff's position could reasonably expect that the particular defendant should be excluded." (Italics supplied.) It is this form of invasion of privacy — initially termed "intrusion" by Dean Prosser in 1960 (*Privacy*, 48 Cal. L. Rev. 383, 389 *et seq.*; Torts, § 112) — on which the two challenged causes of action are predicated.

Quite obviously, some intrusions into one's private sphere are inevitable concomitants of life in an industrial and densely populated society, which the law does not seek to proscribe even if it were possible to do so. "The law does not provide a remedy for every annoyance that occurs in everyday life." (*Kelley v. Post Pub. Co.*, 327 Mass. 275, 278.) However, the District of Columbia courts have held that the law should and does protect against certain types of intrusive conduct, and we must, therefore, determine whether the plaintiff's allegations are actionable as violations of the right to privacy under the law of that jurisdiction. To do so, we must, in effect, predict what the judges of that jurisdiction's highest court would hold if this case were presented to them.

. . . .

The classic article by Warren and Brandeis (*The Right to Privacy*, 4 Harv. L. Rev. 193) — to which the court in the *Pearson* case referred as the source of the District's common-law action for invasion of privacy (410 F. 2d, at p. 703) — was premised, to a large extent, on principles originally developed in the field of copyright law. The authors thus based their thesis on a right granted by the common law to "each individual . . . of determining, ordinarily, to what extent his thoughts, sentiments and emotions shall be communicated to others" (4 Harv. L. Rev., at p. 198). Their principal concern appeared to be not with a broad "right to be let alone" (Cooley, Torts [2d ed.], p. 29) but, rather, with the right to protect oneself from having one's private affairs known to others and to keep secret or intimate facts about oneself from the prying eyes or ears of others.

In recognizing the existence of a common-law cause of action for invasion of privacy in the District of Columbia, the Court of Appeals has expressly adopted this latter formulation of the nature of the right. (See, e.g., *Afro-American Pub. Co. v. Jaffe*, 366 F. 2d 649, 653, *supra.*) Quoting from the Restatement, Torts (§ 867), the court in the *Jaffe* case (366 F. 2d at p. 653) has declared that "[liability] attaches to a person who 'unreasonably and seriously interferes with another's interest in *not having his affairs known to others*' " (Emphasis supplied.) And, in *Pearson*, where the court extended the tort of invasion of privacy to instances of "intrusion," it again indicated . . . that the interest protected was one's right to keep knowledge about oneself from exposure to others, the right to prevent *"the obtaining of the information* by improperly intrusive means" 410 F. 2d, at p. 704; emphasis supplied. . . .

It should be emphasized that the mere gathering of information about a particular individual does not give rise to a cause of action under this theory. Privacy is invaded only if the information sought is of a confidential nature and the defendant's conduct was unreasonably intrusive. Just as a common-law copyright is lost when material is published, so, too, there can be no invasion of privacy where the information sought is open to public view or has been voluntarily revealed to others. (Restatement, 2d, Torts, Tent. Draft No. 13, § 652B, comment c.) In order to sustain a cause of action for invasion of privacy, therefore, the plaintiff must show that the appellant's conduct was truly "intrusive" and that it was designed to elicit information which would not be available through normal inquiry or observation.

. . . At most, only two of the activities charged to the appellant are, in our view, actionable as invasions of privacy under the law of the District of Columbia (*infra*, pp. 568-571). However, since the first two counts include allegations which are sufficient to state a cause of action, we could — as the concurring opinion notes (p. 571) — merely affirm the order before us without further elaboration. To do so, though, would be a disservice both to the judge who will be called upon to try this case and to the litigants themselves. In other words, we deem it desirable, nay essential, that we go further and, for the guidance of the trial court and counsel, indicate the extent to which the plaintiff is entitled to rely on the various allegations in support of his privacy claim.

. . . .

Turning, then, to the particular acts charged in the complaint, we cannot find any basis for a claim of invasion of privacy, under District of Columbia law, in the allegations that the appellant, through its agents or employees, interviewed many persons who knew the plaintiff, asking questions about him and casting aspersions on his character. Although those inquiries may have uncovered information of a personal nature, it is difficult to see how they may be said to have invaded the plaintiff's privacy. Information about the plaintiff which was already known to others could hardly be regarded as private to the plaintiff. Presumably, the plaintiff had previously revealed the information to such other persons, and he would necessarily assume the risk that a friend or acquaintance in whom he had confided might breach the confidence. If, as alleged, the questions tended to disparage the plaintiff's character, his remedy would seem to be by way of an action for defamation, not for breach of his right to privacy. (*Cf. Morrison v. National Broadcasting Co.*, 19 N Y 2d 453, 458-459.)

Nor can we find any actionable invasion of privacy in the allegations that the appellant caused the plaintiff to be accosted by girls with illicit proposals, or that it was responsible for the making of a large number of threatening and harassing telephone calls to the plaintiff's home at odd hours. Neither of these activities, howsoever offensive and disturbing, involved intrusion for the purpose of gathering information of a private and confidential nature.

As already indicated, it is manifestly neither practical nor desirable for the law to provide a remedy against any and all activity which an individual might find annoying. On the other hand, where severe mental pain or anguish is inflicted through a deliberate and malicious campaign of harassment or intimidation, a remedy is available in the form of an action for the intentional infliction of emotional distress — the theory underlying the plaintiff's third cause of action. But the elements of such an action are decidedly different from those governing the tort of invasion of privacy, and just as we have carefully guarded against the use of the prima facie tort doctrine to circumvent the limitations relating to other established tort remedies (*see Morrison v. National Broadcasting Co.*, 19 N.Y.2d 453, 458-459, *supra*), we should be wary of any attempt to rely on the tort of invasion of privacy as a means of avoiding the more stringent pleading and proof requirements for an action for infliction of emotional distress. (*See, e.g., Clark v. Associated Retail Credit Men*, 105 F. 2d 62, 65 [Ct. App., D.C.].)

Apart, however, from the foregoing allegations which we find inadequate to spell out a cause of action for invasion of privacy under District of Columbia law, the complaint contains allegations concerning other activities by the appellant or its agents which do satisfy the requirements for such a cause of action. The one which most clearly meets those requirements is the charge that the appellant and its codefendants engaged in unauthorized wiretapping and eavesdropping by mechanical and electronic means. The Court of Appeals in the *Pearson* case expressly recognized that such conduct constitutes a tortious intrusion (410 F. 2d 701, 704, *supra)*, and other jurisdictions have reached a similar conclusion. In point of fact, the appellant does not dispute this, acknowledging that, to the extent the two challenged counts charge it with wiretapping and eavesdropping, an actionable invasion of privacy has been stated.

There are additional allegations that the appellant hired people to shadow the plaintiff and keep him under surveillance. In particular, he claims that, on one occasion, one of its agents followed him into a bank, getting sufficiently close to him to see the denomination of the bills he was withdrawing from his account. From what we have already said, it is manifest that the mere observation of the plaintiff in a public place does not amount to an invasion of his privacy. But, under certain circumstances, surveillance may be so "overzealous" as to render it actionable. Whether or not the surveillance in the present case falls into this latter category will depend on the nature of the proof. A person does not automatically make public everything he does merely by being in a public place, and the mere fact that Nader was in a bank did not give anyone the right to try to discover the amount of money he was withdrawing. On the other hand, if the plaintiff acted in such a way as to reveal that fact to any casual observer, then, it may not be said that the appellant intruded into his private sphere. In any event, though, it is enough for present purposes to say that the surveillance allegation is not insufficient as a matter of law.

. . . .

We would but add that the allegations concerning the interviewing of third persons, the accosting by girls and the annoying and threatening telephone calls, though insufficient to support a cause of action for invasion of privacy, are pertinent to the plaintiff's third cause of action — in which those allegations are reiterated — charging the intentional infliction of emotional distress. . . .

———————

1.   Restatement (Second) of Torts § 652B (Intrusion) provides:

One who intentionally intrudes, physically or otherwise, upon the solitude or seclusion of another or his private affairs or concerns, is subject to liability to the other for invasion of his privacy, if the intrusion would be highly offensive to a reasonable person.

2. *Pavesich v. New England Life Ins. Co.*, 50 S.E. 68 (Ga. 1905), involved an unauthorized use of plaintiff's picture in an advertisement and was the first case to recognize the privacy cause of action:

> In *Pavesich*, the Georgia Supreme Court determined that the "right of privacy has its foundation in the instincts of nature," and is therefore an "immutable" and "absolute" right "derived from natural law." The court emphasized that the right of privacy was not new to Georgia law, as it was encompassed by the well-established right to personal liberty.

Lake v. Wal-Mart, 582 N.W.2d 231 (Minn. 1998).

PEARSON v. DODD

United States Court of Appeals for the District of Columbia Circuit, 1969
410 F.2d 701, *cert. denied*, 395 U.S. 947

J. Skelly Wright, Circuit Judge:

This case arises out of the exposure of the alleged misdeeds of Senator Thomas Dodd of Connecticut by newspaper columnists Drew Pearson and Jack Anderson. . . . [T]he court denied partial summary judgment on the theory of invasion of privacy. . . . We affirm the District Court's denial of summary judgment for invasion of privacy . . .

The undisputed facts in the case were stated by the District Court as follows:

> ". . . On several occasions in June and July, 1965, two former employees of the plaintiff, at times with the assistance of two members of the plaintiff's staff, entered the plaintiff's office without authority and unbeknownst to him, removed numerous documents from his files, made copies of them, replaced the originals, and turned over the copies to the defendant Anderson, who was aware of the manner in which the copies had been obtained. The defendants Pearson and Anderson thereafter published articles containing information gleaned from these documents."

I

The District Court ruled that appellants' six newspaper columns concerning appellee, which were attached to appellee's complaint, did not establish liability for the tort of invasion of privacy. That tort, whose historical origin lies in the famous Warren and Brandeis article of 1890, is recognized in the District of Columbia. It has always been considered a defense to a claim of invasion of privacy by publication, however, that the published matter complained of is of general public interest. The columns complained of here gave appellants' version of appellee's relationship with certain lobbyists for foreign interests, and gave an interpretive biographical sketch of appellee's public career. They thus clearly bore on appellee's qualifications as a United States Senator, and as such amounted to a paradigm example of published speech not subject to suit for invasion of privacy.

Indeed, appellee has not urged with any vigor on appeal the theory that appellants' publications in themselves tortiously invaded his privacy. Rather he has argued that the District Court misapprehended his privacy claim, which went rather to the manner in which the information in the columns was obtained than to the matter contained in them.

Appellee proceeds under a branch of privacy theory which Dean Prosser has labeled "intrusion," and which has been increasingly recognized by courts and commentators in recent years. Thus it has been held that unauthorized bugging of a dwelling, tapping a telephone, snooping through windows, and overzealous shadowing amount to invasions of privacy, whether or not accompanied by trespasses to property.

Unlike other types of invasion of privacy, intrusion does not involve as one of its essential elements the publication of the information obtained. The tort is completed with the obtaining of the information by improperly intrusive means.

"Intrusion" has not been either recognized or rejected as a tort in the District of Columbia. It has been recognized by a number of state courts. . . .

We approve the extension of the tort of invasion of privacy to instances of intrusion, whether by physical trespass or not, into spheres from which an ordinary man in a plaintiff's position could reasonably expect that the particular defendant should be excluded. . . . The protection should not turn exclusively on the question of whether the intrusion involves a technical trespass under the law of property. The common law, like the Fourth Amendment, should "protect people, not places."

The question then becomes whether appellants Pearson and Anderson improperly intruded into the protected sphere of privacy of appellee Dodd in obtaining the information on which their columns were based. In determining this question, we may assume, without deciding, that appellee's employees and former employees did commit such an improper intrusion when they removed confidential files with the intent to show them to unauthorized outsiders.[19]

Although appellee's complaint charges that appellants aided and abetted in the removal of the documents, the undisputed facts . . . established only that appellants received copies of the documents knowing that they had been removed without authorization. If we were to hold appellants liable for invasion of privacy on these facts, we would establish the proposition that one who receives information from an intruder, knowing it has been obtained by improper intrusion, is guilty of a tort. In an untried and developing area of tort law, we are not prepared to go so far. A person approached by an eavesdropper with an offer to share in the information gathered through the eavesdropping would perhaps play the nobler part should he

---

[19] Appellants have argued that appellee's employees and former employees committed neither conversion nor trespass nor invasion of privacy, because their actions are privileged by a public policy in favor of exposing wrongdoing. See Restatement (Second) of Agency § 395, Comment f (1958):

> "An agent is privileged to reveal information confidentially acquired by him in the course of his agency in the protection of a superior interest of himself or of a third person. Thus, if the confidential information is to the effect that the principal is committing or is about to commit a crime, the agent is under no duty not to reveal it. . . ."

And compare Code of Ethics for Government Service, House Doc. No. 103, 86th Cong., 1st Sess. (1958): "Any person in government service should: . . . (IX) Expose corruption wherever discovered."

spurn the offer and shut his ears. However, it seems to us that at this point it would place too great a strain on human weakness to hold one liable in damages who merely succumbs to temptation and listens.

Of course, appellants did more than receive and peruse the copies of the documents taken from appellee's files; they published excerpts from them in the national press. But in analyzing a claimed breach of privacy, injuries from intrusion and injuries from publication should be kept clearly separate. Where there is intrusion, the intruder should generally be liable whatever the content of what he learns. An eavesdropper to the marital bedroom may hear marital intimacies, or he may hear statements of fact or opinion of legitimate interest to the public; for purposes of liability that should make no difference. On the other hand, where the claim is that private information concerning plaintiff has been published, the question of whether that information is genuinely private or is of public interest should not turn on the manner in which it has been obtained. . . .

Here we have separately considered the nature of appellants' publications concerning appellee, and have found that the matter published was of obvious public interest. The publication was not itself an invasion of privacy. Since we have also concluded that appellants' role in obtaining the information did not make them liable to appellee for intrusion, their subsequent publication, itself no invasion of privacy, cannot reach back to render that role tortious.

. . . .

1.   In *Pinkerton National Detective Agency, Inc. v. Stevens*, 132 S.E.2d 119 (Ga. Ct. App. 1963), the surveillance employed by the insurance company was sufficiently intrusive to be "highly offensive to the reasonable person." However, in *I.C.U. Investigations v. Jones*, 780 So. 2d 685 (Ala. 2000), the videotaping of a worker's compensation claimant urinating in his front yard was held not sufficiently offensive or objectionable to constitute intrusion.

2.   In *Bartnicki v. Vopper*, 532 U.S. 514 (2000), the Supreme Court held that the First Amendment barred liability for a media defendant that accurately broadcast the contents of a private conversation between a union official and union members about a teacher's strike that had been illegally obtained by others.

3.   In *Vernars v. Young*, 539 F.2d 966 (3d Cir. 1976), liability for intrusion was imposed on a corporate executive who opened and read employees' personal mail that had arrived at the office.

4.   The cause of action for invasion of privacy need not involve a physical trespass. *See Roach v. Harper*, 105 S.E.2d 564 (W. Va. 1958).

5.   The wide availability of tiny, unobtrusive, and remotely operable cameras and recording instruments has vastly increased the potential for surreptitious video and audio surveillance of others. How should these developments affect tort liability? *See Hernandez v. Hillsides, Inc.*, 97 Cal. Rptr. 3d 274, 211 P.3d 1063 (2009) (employer's surreptitious video surveillance of employees in workplace to discover who was using employer's computers to access pornography was not "highly offensive").

GALELLA v. ONASSIS
United States Court of Appeals for the Second Circuit, 1973
487 F.2d 986

J. Joseph Smith, Circuit Judge:

Galella is a free-lance photographer specializing in the making and sale of photographs of well-known persons. Defendant Onassis is the widow of the late President, John F. Kennedy, mother of the two Kennedy children, John and Caroline, and is the wife of Aristotle Onassis, widely known shipping figure and reputed multimillionaire. John Walsh, James Kalafatis and John Connelly are U.S. Secret Service agents assigned to the duty of protecting the Kennedy children. . . .

Galella fancies himself as a "paparazzo" (literally a kind of annoying insect, perhaps roughly equivalent to the English "gadfly.") Paparazzi make themselves as visible to the public and obnoxious to their photographic subjects as possible to aid in the advertisement and wide sale of their works.

Some examples of Galella's conduct brought out at trial are illustrative. Galella took pictures of John Kennedy riding his bicycle in Central Park across the way from his home. He jumped out into the boy's path, causing the [secret service] agents concern for John's safety. The agents' reaction and interrogation of Galella led to Galella's arrest and his action against the agents; Galella on other occasions interrupted Caroline at tennis, and invaded the children's private schools. At one time he came uncomfortably close in a power boat to Mrs. Onassis swimming. He often jumped and postured around while taking pictures of her party, notably at a theater opening but also on numerous other occasions. He followed a practice of bribing apartment house, restaurant and nightclub doormen as well as romancing a family servant to keep him advised of the movements of the family.

After detention and arrest following complaint by the Secret Service agents protecting Mrs. Onassis' son and his acquittal in the state court, Galella filed suit in state court against the agents and Mrs. Onassis. Galella claimed that under orders from Mrs. Onassis, the three agents had falsely arrested and maliciously prosecuted him, and that this incident in addition to several others described in the complaint constituted an unlawful interference with his trade.

Mrs. Onassis answered denying any role in the arrest or any part in the claimed interference with his attempts to photograph her, and counterclaimed for damages and injunctive relief, charging that Galella had invaded her privacy, assaulted and battered her, intentionally inflicted emotional distress and engaged in a campaign of harassment.

. . . .

Certain incidents of photographic coverage by Galella, subsequent to an agreement among the parties for Galella not to so engage, resulted in the issuance of a temporary restraining order to prevent further harassment of Mrs. Onassis and the children. Galella was enjoined from "harassing, alarming, startling, tormenting, touching the person of the defendant . . . or her children . . . and from blocking their movements in the public places and thoroughfares, invading their immediate zone of privacy by means of physical movements, gestures or with photographic equipment and from performing any act reasonably calculated to place the lives and safety of the defendant . . . and her children in jeopardy." Within two months, Galella was charged with violation of the temporary restraining order; a new order was signed which required that the photographer keep 100 yards from the Onassis apartment and 50 yards from the person of the defendant and her children. Surveillance was also prohibited.

. . . .

After a six-week trial the court dismissed Galella's claim and granted relief to both the defendant and the intervenor. Galella was enjoined from (1) keeping the defendant and her children under surveillance or following any of them; (2) approaching within 100 yards of the home of defendant or her children, or within 100 yards of either child's school or within 75 yards of either child or 50 yards of defendant; (3) using the name, portrait or picture of defendant or her children for advertising; (4) attempting to communicate with defendant or her children except through her attorney.

. . . .

Discrediting all of Galella's testimony the court found the photographer guilty of harassment, intentional infliction of emotional distress, assault and battery, commercial exploitation of defendant's personality, and invasion of privacy. Fully crediting defendant's testimony, the court found no liability on Galella's claim. Evidence offered by the defense showed that Galella had on occasion intentionally physically touched Mrs. Onassis and her daughter, caused fear of physical contact in his frenzied attempts to get their pictures, followed defendant and her children too closely in an automobile, endangered the safety of the children while they were swimming, water skiing and horseback riding. Galella cannot successfully challenge the court's finding of tortious conduct.

Finding that Galella had "insinuated himself into the very fabric of Mrs. Onassis' life . . ." the court framed its relief in part on the need to prevent further invasion of the defendant's privacy. Whether or not this accords with present New York law, there is no doubt that it is sustainable under New York's proscription of harassment.

Of course legitimate countervailing social needs may warrant some intrusion despite an individual's reasonable expectation of privacy and freedom from harassment. However the interference allowed may be no greater than that necessary to protect the overriding public interest. Mrs. Onassis was properly found to be a public figure and thus subject to news coverage. Nonetheless, Galella's action went far beyond the reasonable bounds of news gathering. When weighed against the *de minimis* public importance of the daily activities of the defendant, Galella's constant surveillance, his obtrusive and intruding presence, was unwarranted and unreasonable. If there were any doubt in our minds, Galella's inexcusable conduct toward defendant's minor children would resolve it.

Galella does not seriously dispute the court's finding of tortious conduct. Rather, he sets up the First Amendment as a wall of immunity protecting newsmen from any liability for their conduct while gathering news. There is no such scope to the

First Amendment right. Crimes and torts committed in news gathering are not protected. . . .

What do you think of the solution adopted by the court? Under what circumstances should individuals be able to seek injunctive relief (as opposed to the typical tort remedy of damages) to prevent invasions of privacy? Note the court's reliance on New York law proscribing harassment as support for its decision.

SHULMAN v. GROUP W PRODUCTIONS, INC.
Supreme Court of California, 1998
955 P.2d 469

WERDEGAR, JUSTICE.

In the present case, we address the balance between privacy and press freedom in the commonplace context of an automobile accident. . . .

FACTS AND PROCEDURAL HISTORY

On June 24, 1990, plaintiffs Ruth and Wayne Shulman, mother and son, were injured when the car in which they and two other family members were riding on interstate 10 in Riverside County flew off the highway and tumbled down an embankment into a drainage ditch on state-owned property, coming to rest upside down. Ruth, the most seriously injured of the two, was pinned under the car. Ruth and Wayne both had to be cut free from the vehicle by the device known as "the jaws of life."

A rescue helicopter operated by Mercy Air was dispatched to the scene. The flight nurse, who would perform the medical care at the scene and on the way to the hospital, was Laura Carnahan. Also on board were the pilot, a medic and Joel Cooke, a video camera operator employed by defendants Group W Productions, Inc., and 4MN Productions. Cooke was recording the rescue operation for later broadcast.

Cooke roamed the accident scene, videotaping the rescue. Nurse Carnahan wore a wireless microphone that picked up her conversations with both Ruth and the other rescue personnel. Cooke's tape was edited into a piece approximately nine minutes long, which, with the addition of narrative voice-over, was broadcast on September 29, 1990, as a segment of *On Scene: Emergency Response.*

The segment begins with the Mercy Air helicopter shown on its way to the accident site. The narrator's voice is heard in the background, setting the scene and describing in general terms what has happened. The pilot can be heard speaking with rescue workers on the ground in order to prepare for his landing. As the helicopter touches down, the narrator says: "[F]our of the patients are leaving by ground ambulance. Two are still trapped inside." (The first part of this statement was wrong, since only four persons were in the car to start.) After Carnahan steps from the helicopter, she can be seen and heard speaking about the situation with various rescue workers. A firefighter assures her they will hose down the area to prevent any fire from the wrecked car.

The videotape shows only a glimpse of Wayne, and his voice is never heard. Ruth is shown several times, either by brief shots of a limb or her torso, or with her features blocked by others or obscured by an oxygen mask. She is also heard speaking several times. Carnahan calls her "Ruth," and her last name is not mentioned on the broadcast.

While Ruth is still trapped under the car, Carnahan asks Ruth's age. Ruth responds, "I'm old." On further questioning, Ruth reveals she is 47, and Carnahan observes that "it's all relative. You're not that old." During her extrication from the car, Ruth asks at least twice if she is dreaming. At one point she asks Carnahan, who has told her she will be taken to the hospital in a helicopter: "Are you teasing?" At another point she says: "This is terrible. Am I dreaming?" She also asks what happened and where the rest of her family is, repeating the questions even after being told she was in an accident and the other family members are being cared for. While being loaded into the helicopter on a stretcher, Ruth says: "I just want to die." Carnahan reassures her that she is "going to do real well," but Ruth repeats: "I just want to die. I don't want to go through this."

Ruth and Wayne are placed in the helicopter, and its door is closed. The narrator states: "Once airborne, Laura and [the flight medic] will update their patients' vital signs and establish communications with the waiting trauma teams at Loma Linda." Carnahan, speaking into what appears to be a radio microphone, transmits some of Ruth's vital signs and states that Ruth cannot move her feet and has no sensation. The video footage during the helicopter ride includes a few seconds of Ruth's face, covered by an oxygen mask. Wayne is neither shown nor heard.

The helicopter lands on the hospital roof. With the door open, Ruth states while being taken out: "My upper back hurts." Carnahan replies: "Your upper back hurts. That's what you were saying up there." Ruth states: "I don't feel that great." Carnahan responds: "You probably don't."

Finally, Ruth is shown being moved from the helicopter into the hospital. The narrator concludes by stating: "Once inside both patients will be further evaluated and moved into emergency surgery if need be. Thanks to the efforts of the crew of Mercy Air, the firefighters, medics and police who responded, patients' lives were saved." As the segment ends, a brief, written epilogue appears on the screen, stating: "Laura's patient spent months in the hospital. She suffered severe back injuries. The others were all released much sooner."

The accident left Ruth a paraplegic. When the segment was broadcast, Wayne phoned Ruth in her hospital room and told her to turn on the television because "Channel 4 is showing our accident now." Shortly afterward, several hospital workers came into the room to mention that a videotaped segment of her accident was being shown. Ruth was "shocked, so to speak, that this would be run and I would be exploited, have my privacy invaded, which is what I felt had happened." She did not know her rescue had been recorded in this manner and had never consented to the recording or broadcast. . . . Asked at deposition what part of the broadcast material she considered private, Ruth explained: "I think the whole scene was pretty private. It was pretty gruesome, the parts that I saw, my knee sticking out of the car. I certainly did not look my best, and I don't feel it's for the public to see. I was not at my best in what I was thinking and what I was saying and what was being shown, and it's not for the public to see this trauma that I was going through."

Ruth and Wayne sued the producers of *On Scene: Emergency Response*. . . . The first amended complaint included two causes of action for invasion of privacy, one based on defendants' unlawful intrusion by videotaping the rescue in the first instance and the other based on the public disclosure of private facts, i.e., the broadcast.

Defendants moved for summary judgment, contending primarily that their conduct was protected by the First Amendment because of the broadcast's newsworthy content. . . .

The trial court granted the media defendants' summary judgment motion, basing its ruling on plaintiffs' admissions that the accident and rescue were matters of public interest and public affairs. Those admissions, in the trial court's view, showed as a matter of law that the broadcast material was newsworthy, thereby vesting the media defendants' conduct with First Amendment protection. The court entered judgment for defendants on all causes of action.

The Court of Appeal reversed and remanded for further proceedings, but on limited grounds and as to some causes of action only. First, the Court of Appeal held plaintiffs had no reasonable expectation of privacy in the events at the accident scene itself. According to the lower court, "Appellants' accident occurred on a heavily traveled public highway. . . . The videotape itself shows a crowd of onlookers peering down at the rescue scene below. Appellants could be seen and heard by anyone at the accident site itself and could not have had a reasonable expectation of privacy at the scene in regard to what they did or said. Their statements or exclamations could be freely heard by all who passed by and were thus public, not private." Once inside the helicopter, however, the court next reasoned, plaintiffs *did* have a reasonable expectation of privacy; the helicopter was essentially an airborne ambulance, and an ambulance in emergency medical use is considered a private space, both by social tradition and by analogy to a hospital room, which was deemed private *in Noble v. Sears, Roebuck & Co.* (1973) 33 Cal. App. 3d 654 [109 Cal. Rptr. 269, 73 A.L.R.3d 1164].

As to Ruth's cause of action for publication of private facts (limited to the broadcast of events recorded inside the helicopter), the Court of Appeal concluded triable issues of fact existed on the element of offensiveness and on a defense of newsworthiness. With regard to plaintiffs' claims of intrusion, also as related to the recording of events in the helicopter, the Court of Appeal, citing *Hill v. National Collegiate Athletic Assn.* (1994) 7 Cal. 4th 1 [26 Cal. Rptr. 2d 834, 865 P.2d 633], held the trial court . . . should have conducted an analysis balancing plaintiffs' privacy rights against defendants' First Amendment interest in recording the rescue. The Court of Appeal therefore remanded for further proceedings as to both plaintiffs' cause of action for intrusion and as to Ruth's cause of action for publication of private facts.

We conclude the Court of Appeal's judgment should be affirmed except insofar as it remanded for further proceedings on Ruth's private facts claim. . . . Summary judgment thus was proper as to both plaintiffs on the private facts cause of action.

As to intrusion, the Court of Appeal correctly found triable issues exist as to whether defendants invaded plaintiffs' privacy by accompanying plaintiffs in the helicopter. Contrary to the holding below, we also hold triable issues exist as to whether defendants tortiously intruded by listening to Ruth's confidential conversations with Nurse Carnahan at the rescue scene without Ruth's consent. Moreover, we hold defendants had no constitutional privilege so to intrude on plaintiffs' seclusion and private communications.

DISCUSSION

. . . California courts have recognized both of the privacy causes of action pleaded by plaintiffs here: (1) public disclosure of private facts, and (2) intrusion into private places, conversations or other matters.

We shall review the elements of each privacy tort, as well as the common law and constitutional privilege of the press as to each, and shall apply in succession this law to the facts pertinent to each cause of action.

I. Publication of Private Facts

. . . .

A few words are in order at this point regarding the right of privacy secured by article I, section 1 of the California Constitution. The Court of Appeal, citing *Hill v. National Collegiate Athletic Assn., supra*, 7 Cal. 4th at pages 37-38 *(Hill)*, equated the judicial balancing undertaken in delineation of the common law right of privacy to the balancing of interests this court has prescribed for evaluating claims raised under our state's constitutional right of privacy. Defendants attack the Court of Appeal's adoption of *Hill's* balancing test in the common law tort context, arguing that under the *federal* Constitution newsworthiness is a complete bar to liability, rather than merely an interest to be balanced against private or state-protected interests.

We agree with defendants that the publication of truthful, lawfully obtained material of legitimate public concern is constitutionally privileged and does not create liability under the private facts tort. As discussed above, however, a certain amount of interest-balancing *does* occur in deciding whether material is of legitimate public concern, or in formulating rules for that decision. To that extent, the Court of Appeal's analogy to *Hill* was not in error.

. . . .

II. Intrusion

Of the four privacy torts identified by Prosser, the tort of intrusion into private places, conversations or matter is perhaps the one that best captures the common understanding of an "invasion of privacy." It encompasses unconsented-to physical intrusion into the home, hospital room or other place the privacy of which is legally recognized, as well as unwarranted sensory intrusions such as eavesdropping, wiretapping, and visual or photographic spying. (See Rest. 2d Torts, § 652B, com. b., pp. 378-379, and illustrations.) It is in the intrusion cases that invasion of privacy is most clearly seen as an affront to individual dignity. "[A] measure of personal isolation and personal control over the conditions of its abandonment is of the very essence of personal freedom and dignity, is part of what our culture means by these concepts. A man whose home may be entered at the will of another, whose conversations may be overheard at the will of another, whose marital and familial intimacies may be overseen at the will of another, is less of a man, has less human dignity, on that account." . . .

[T]he intrusion tort has received less judicial attention than the private facts tort, and its parameters are less clearly defined. The leading California decision is *Miller v. National Broadcasting Co., supra*, 187 Cal. App. 3d 1463 *(Miller). Miller*, which like the present case involved a news organization's videotaping the work of emergency medical personnel, adopted the Restatement's formulation of the cause of action: "One who intentionally intrudes, physically or otherwise, upon the solitude or seclusion of another or his private affairs or concerns, is subject to liability to the other for invasion of his privacy, if the intrusion would be highly offensive to a reasonable person." (Rest. 2d Torts, § 652B; *Miller, supra*, 187 Cal. App. 3d at p. 1482.)

As stated in *Miller* and the Restatement, therefore, the action for intrusion has two elements: (1) intrusion into a private place, conversation or matter, (2) in a manner highly offensive to a reasonable person. We consider the elements in that order.

We ask first whether defendants "intentionally intrude[d], physically or otherwise, upon the solitude or seclusion of another," that is, into a place or conversation private to Wayne or Ruth. (Rest. 2d Torts, § 652B; *Miller, supra*, 187 Cal. App. 3d at p. 1482). "[T]here is no liability for the examination of a public record concerning the plaintiff, . . . [or] for observing him or even taking his photograph while he is walking on the public highway. . . ." (Rest. 2d Torts, § 652B, com. c, pp. 379-380; . . .). To prove actionable intrusion, the plaintiff must show the defendant penetrated some zone of physical or sensory privacy surrounding, or obtained unwanted access to data about, the plaintiff. The tort is proven only if the plaintiff had an objectively reasonable expectation of seclusion or solitude in the place, conversation or data source. (Rest. 2d Torts, § 652B, com. c, p. 379; . . .).

Cameraman Cooke's mere presence at the accident scene and filming of the events occurring there cannot be deemed either a physical or sensory intrusion on plaintiffs' seclusion. Plaintiffs had no right of ownership or possession of the property where the rescue took place, nor any actual control of the premises. Nor could they have had a reasonable expectation that members of the media would be excluded or prevented from photographing the scene; for journalists to attend and record the scenes of accidents and rescues is in no way unusual or unexpected. *(Cf. Pen. Code, § 409.5*, subd. (d), *409.6*, subd. (d) [exempting press representatives from certain emergency closure orders].)

Two aspects of defendants' conduct, however, raise triable issues of intrusion on seclusion. First, a triable issue exists as to whether both plaintiffs had an objectively reasonable expectation of privacy in the interior of the rescue helicopter, which served as an ambulance. Although the attendance of reporters and photographers at the scene of an accident is to be expected, we are aware of no law or custom permitting the press to ride in ambulances or enter hospital rooms during treatment without the patient's consent. (See *Noble v. Sears, Roebuck & Co., supra,* 33 Cal. App. 3d at p. 660 [accepting, subject to proof at trial, intrusion plaintiff's theory she had "an exclusive right of occupancy of her hospital room" as against investigator]; *Miller, supra,* 187 Cal. App. 3d at pp. 1489-1490. . . . Other than the two patients and Cooke, only three people were present in the helicopter, all Mercy Air staff. As the Court of Appeal observed, "[i]t is neither the custom nor the habit of our society that any member of the public at large or its media representatives may hitch a ride in an ambulance and ogle as paramedics care for an injured stranger." (See also *Green v. Chicago Tribune Co., supra,* 675 N.E.2d at p. 252 [hospital room not public place]; *Barber v. Time, Inc., supra,* 159 S.W.2d at p. 295 ["Certainly, if there is any right of privacy at all, it should include the right to obtain medical treatment at home or in a hospital . . . without personal publicity."].)

Second, Ruth was entitled to a degree of privacy in her conversations with Carnahan and other medical rescuers at the accident scene, and in Carnahan's conversations conveying medical information regarding Ruth to the hospital base. Cooke, perhaps, did not intrude into that zone of privacy merely by being present at a place where he could hear such conversations with unaided ears. But by placing a microphone on Carnahan's person, amplifying and recording what she said and heard, defendants may have listened in on conversations the parties could reasonably have expected to be private.

The Court of Appeal held plaintiffs had no reasonable expectation of privacy at the accident scene itself because the scene was within the sight and hearing of members of the public. The summary judgment record, however, does not support the Court of Appeal's conclusion. . . . The videotapes (broadcast and raw footage) show the rescue did not take place "on a heavily traveled highway," as the Court of Appeal stated, but in a ditch many yards from and below the rural superhighway, which is raised somewhat at that point to bridge a nearby crossroad. From the tapes it appears unlikely the plaintiffs' extrication from their car and medical treatment at the scene could have been observed by any persons who, in the lower court's words, "passed by" on the roadway. Even more unlikely is that any passersby on the road could have heard Ruth's conversation with Nurse Carnahan or the other rescuers.

Whether Ruth expected her conversations with Nurse Carnahan or the other rescuers to remain private and whether any such expectation was reasonable are, on the state of the record before us, questions for the jury. We note, however, that several existing legal protections for communications could support the conclusion that Ruth possessed a reasonable expectation of privacy in her conversations with Nurse Carnahan and the other rescuers. A patient's conversation with a provider of medical care in the course of treatment, including emergency treatment, carries a traditional and legally well-established expectation of privacy.

. . . .

Ruth's claim, of course, does not require her to prove a statutory violation, only to prove that she had an objectively reasonable expectation of privacy in her conversations. Whether the circumstances of Ruth's extrication and helicopter rescue would reasonably have indicated to defendants, or to their agent, Cooke, that Ruth would desire and expect her communications to Carnahan and the other rescuers to be confined to them alone, and therefore not to be electronically transmitted and recorded, is a triable issue of fact in this case. As observed earlier, whether anyone present (other than Cooke) was a mere observer, uninvolved in the rescue effort, is unclear from the summary judgment record. Also unclear is who, if anyone, could overhear conversations between Ruth and Carnahan, which were transmitted by a microphone on Carnahan's person, amplified and recorded by defendants. We cannot say, as a matter of law, that Cooke should not have perceived he might be intruding on a confidential communication when he recorded a seriously injured patient's conversations with medical personnel.

We turn to the second element of the intrusion tort, offensiveness of the intrusion. In a widely followed passage, the *Miller* court explained that determining offensiveness requires consideration of all the circumstances of the intrusion, including its degree and setting and the intruder's "motives and objectives." The *Miller* court concluded that reasonable people could regard the camera crew's conduct in filming a man's emergency medical treatment in his home, without seeking or obtaining his or his wife's consent, as showing "a cavalier disregard for ordinary citizens' rights of privacy" and, hence, as highly offensive. (*Miller, supra*, 187 Cal. App. 3d at p. 1484.)

We agree with the *Miller* court that all the circumstances of an intrusion, including the motives or justification of the intruder, are pertinent to the offensiveness element. Motivation or justification becomes particularly important when the intrusion is by a member of the print or broadcast press in the pursuit of news material. . . . the First Amendment does not immunize the press from liability for torts or crimes committed in an effort to gather news the constitutional protection of the press does reflect the strong societal interest in effective and complete reporting of events, an interest that may — as a matter of tort law — justify an intrusion that would otherwise be considered offensive. . . .

In deciding, therefore, whether a reporter's alleged intrusion into private matters (i.e., physical space, conversation or data) is "offensive" and hence actionable as an invasion of privacy, courts must consider the extent to which the intrusion was, under the circumstances, justified by the legitimate motive of gathering the news. Information-collecting techniques that may be highly offensive when done for socially unprotected reasons — for purposes of harassment, blackmail or prurient curiosity, for example — may not be offensive to a reasonable person when employed by journalists in pursuit of a socially or politically important story. . . .

The mere fact the intruder was in pursuit of a "story" does not, however, generally justify an otherwise offensive intrusion; offensiveness depends as well on the particular method of investigation used. At one extreme, "routine . . . reporting techniques" such as asking questions of people with information ("including those with confidential or restricted information") could rarely, if ever, be deemed an actionable intrusion. At the other extreme, violation of well-established legal areas of physical or sensory privacy — trespass into a home or tapping a personal telephone line, for example — could rarely, if ever, be justified by a reporter's need to get the story. Such acts would be deemed highly offensive even if the information sought was of weighty public concern; they would also be outside any protection the Constitution provides to newsgathering.

. . . .

On this summary judgment record, we believe a jury could find defendants' recording of Ruth's communications to Carnahan and other rescuers, and filming in the air ambulance, to be "highly offensive to a reasonable person." With regard to the depth of the intrusion . . . , a reasonable jury could find highly offensive the placement of a microphone on a medical rescuer in order to intercept what would otherwise be private conversations with an injured patient. In that setting, as defendants could and should have foreseen, the patient would not know her words were being recorded and would not have occasion to ask about, and object or consent to, recording. Defendants, it could reasonably be said, took calculated advantage of the patient's "vulnerability and confusion." . . . Arguably, the last thing an injured accident victim should have to worry about while being pried from her wrecked car is that a television producer may be recording everything she says to medical personnel for the possible edification and entertainment of casual television viewers.

For much the same reason, a jury could reasonably regard entering and riding in an ambulance — whether on the ground or in the air — with two seriously injured patients to be an egregious intrusion on a place of expected seclusion. Again, the patients, at least in this case, were hardly in a position to keep careful watch on who was riding with them, or to inquire as to everyone's business and consent or object to their presence. A jury could reasonably believe that fundamental respect for human dignity requires the patients' anxious journey be taken only with those whose care is solely for them and out of sight of the prying eyes (or cameras) of others.

Nor can we say as a matter of law that defendants' motive — to gather usable material for a potentially newsworthy story — necessarily privileged their intrusive conduct as a matter of common law tort liability. A reasonable jury could conclude the producers' desire to get footage that would convey the "feel" of the event — the real sights and sounds of a difficult rescue — did not justify either placing a microphone on Nurse Carnahan or filming inside the rescue helicopter. Although defendants' purposes could scarcely be regarded as evil or malicious (in the colloquial sense), their behavior could, even in light of their motives, be thought to show a highly offensive lack of sensitivity and respect for plaintiffs' privacy. (*Miller, supra*, 187 Cal. App. 3d at p. 1484.) . . .

CONCLUSION

. . . .

The intrusion claim calls for a much less deferential analysis. In contrast to the broad privilege the press enjoys for publishing truthful, newsworthy information in its possession, the press has *no* recognized constitutional privilege to violate generally applicable laws in pursuit of material. Nor, even absent an independent crime or tort, can a highly offensive intrusion into a private place, conversation, or source of information generally be justified by the plea that the intruder hoped thereby to get good material for a news story. Such a justification *may* be available when enforcement of the tort or other law would place an impermissibly severe burden on the press, but that condition is not met in this case.

In short, the state may not intrude into the proper sphere of the news media to dictate what they should publish and broadcast, but neither may the media play tyrant to the people by unlawfully spying on them in the name of newsgathering. Summary judgment for the defense was proper as to plaintiffs' cause of action for publication of private facts (the second cause of action), but improper as to the cause of action for invasion of privacy by intrusion (the first cause of action).

DISPOSITION

The judgment of the Court of Appeal is affirmed except insofar as the Court of Appeal reversed and remanded for further proceedings on Ruth Shulman's cause of action for publication of private facts.

GEORGE, C. J., and KENNARD, J., concurred.

KENNARD, JUSTICE, concurring.

    . . . .

The free flow of truthful information, however, is also a fundamental value of our society, embodied in the First Amendment to the federal Constitution. As the plurality opinion notes, the United States Supreme Court has not yet attempted to fashion a general rule striking a balance between our competing interests in preserving a sphere of personal privacy and in unfettered publication of truthful information. Because of the complexities of the problem, crafting a general rule in this area would not be an easy task. The authors of two prominent constitutional law treatises, for example, take opposite views on whether the First Amendment permits a cause of action for truthful publication of private facts. Professors Rotunda and Nowak would not allow the cause of action: "[I]n light of later constitutional cases, and given the general [First Amendment] rationale articulated by the Supreme Court over the years, the state should always recognize that truth is a defense in a defamation or right of privacy action. . . ." Professor Tribe, on the other hand, takes the view that the First Amendment permits the cause of action: "[W]hen government acts to limit the untrammeled gathering, recording, or dissemination of data or statements about an individual, of course it inhibits speech — but it also vindicates the individual's ability to control what others are told about his or her life. Such control constitutes a central part of the right to shape the 'self that any individual presents to the world." (Tribe, American Constitutional Law (2d ed. 1988) § 12-14, p. 887.)

Mosk, J., concurred.

Chin, Justice, concurring and dissenting.

. . . .

I dissent . . . from the plurality's holding that plaintiffs' "intrusion" cause of action should be remanded for trial. The critical question is whether defendants' privacy intrusion was " '*highly* offensive to a reasonable person.' " . . . As the plurality explains, "the constitutional protection of the press does reflect the strong societal interest in effective and complete reporting of events, an interest that may — as a matter of law — justify an intrusion that *would otherwise be considered offensive*". . . . I also agree with the plurality that "Information-collecting techniques that *may be highly offensive* when done for socially unprotected reasons — for purposes of harassment, blackmail or prurient curiosity, for example — *may not be offensive to a reasonable person* when employed by journalists in pursuit of a socially or politically important story" . . . (italics added.)

. . . .

Ruth's expectations notwithstanding, I do not believe that a reasonable trier of fact could find that defendants' conduct in this case was "highly offensive to a reasonable person," the test adopted by the plurality. Plaintiffs do not allege that defendants, though present at the accident rescue scene and in the helicopter, interfered with either the rescue or medical efforts, elicited embarrassing or offensive information from plaintiffs, or even tried to interrogate or interview them. Defendants' news team evidently merely recorded newsworthy events "of legitimate public concern" . . . as they transpired. Defendants' apparent motive in undertaking the supposed privacy invasion was a reasonable and nonmalicious one: to obtain an accurate depiction of the rescue efforts from start to finish. The event was newsworthy, and the ultimate broadcast was both dramatic and educational, rather than tawdry or embarrassing.

. . . .

Is this a valid case of intrusion or should plaintiff be asked to develop a thicker skin? Should truth be a defense?

DESNICK v. AMERICAN BROADCASTING COMPANIES, INCORPORATED
United States Court of Appeals for the Seventh Circuit, 1995
44 F.3d 1345

Posner, Chief Judge.

The plaintiffs — an ophthalmic clinic known as the "Desnick Eye Center" after its owner, Dr. Desnick, and two ophthalmic surgeons employed by the clinic, Glazer and Simon — appeal from the dismissal of their suit against the ABC television network, a producer of the ABC program *PrimeTime Live* named Entine, and the program's star reporter, Donaldson. The suit is for trespass, defamation, and other torts arising out of the production and broadcast of a program segment of *PrimeTime Live* that was highly critical of the Desnick Eye Center. . . .

In March of 1993 Entine telephoned Dr. Desnick and told him that *Prime-Time Live* wanted to do a broadcast segment on large cataract practices. The Desnick Eye Center has 25 offices in four midwestern states and performs more than 10,000 cataract operations a year, mostly on elderly persons whose cataract surgery is paid for by Medicare. . . . Entine told Desnick that the segment would not be about just one cataract practice, that it would not involve "ambush" interviews or "undercover" surveillance, and that it would be "fair and balanced." Thus reassured, Desnick permitted an ABC crew to videotape the Desnick Eye Center's main premises in Chicago, to film a cataract operation "live," and to interview doctors, technicians, and patients. Desnick also gave Entine a videotape explaining the Desnick Eye Center's services.

Unbeknownst to Desnick, Entine had dispatched persons equipped with concealed cameras to offices of the Desnick Eye Center in Wisconsin and Indiana. Posing as patients, these persons — seven in all — requested eye examinations. Plaintiffs Glazer and Simon are among the employees of the Desnick Eye Center who were secretly videotaped examining these "test patients."

The program aired on June 10. Donaldson introduces the segment by saying, "We begin tonight with the story of a so-called 'big cutter,' Dr. James Desnick. . . . In our undercover investigation of the big cutter you'll meet tonight, we turned up evidence that he may also be a big charger, doing unnecessary cataract surgery for the money." Brief interviews with four patients of the Desnick Eye Center follow. One of the patients is satisfied ("I was blessed"); the other three are not — one of them says, "If you got three eyes, he'll get three eyes." Donaldson then reports on the experiences of the seven test patients. The two who were under 65 and thus not eligible for Medicare reimbursement were told they didn't need cataract surgery. Four of the other five were told they did. Glazer and Simon are shown recommending cataract surgery to them. Donaldson tells the viewer that *PrimeTime Live* has hired a professor of ophthalmology to examine the test patients who had been told they needed cataract surgery, and the professor tells the viewer that they didn't need it — with regard to one he says, "I think it would be near malpractice to do surgery on him." Later in the segment he denies that this could just be an honest difference of opinion between professionals.

An ophthalmic surgeon is interviewed who had turned down a job at the Desnick Eye Center because he would not have been "able to screen who I was going to operate on." He claims to have been told by one of the doctors at the Center (not Glazer or Simon) that "as soon as I reject them [i.e., turn down a patient for cataract surgery], they're going in the next room to get surgery." A former marketing executive for the Center says Desnick took advantage of "people who had Alzheimer's, people who did not know what planet they were on, people whose quality of life wouldn't change one iota by having cataract surgery done." Two patients are interviewed who report miserable experiences with the Center — one claiming that the doctors there had failed to spot an easily visible melanoma, another that as a result of unnecessary cataract surgery her "eye ruptured," producing "running pus." A former employee tells the viewer that Dr. Desnick alters patients' medical records to show they need cataract surgery — for example, changing the record of one patient's vision test from 20/30 to 20/80 — and that he instructs all members of his staff to use pens of the same color in order to facilitate the alteration of patients' records.

One symptom of cataracts is that lights of normal brightness produce glare. . . . Donaldson tells the viewer that "the Desnick Center uses a very interesting machine, called an auto-refractor, to determine whether there are glare problems." Donaldson demonstrates the machine, then says that "Paddy Kalish is an optometrist who says that when he worked at the Desnick clinic from 1987 to 1990, the machine was regularly rigged. He says he watched a technician tamper with the machine, this way" — and then Kalish gives a demonstration, adding, "This happened routinely for all the older patients that came in for the eye exams." . . .

The second class of claims in this case concerns, as we said, the methods that the defendants used to create the broadcast segment. There are four such claims: that the defendants committed a trespass in insinuating the test patients into the Wisconsin and Indiana offices of the Desnick Eye Center, that they invaded the right of privacy of the Center and its doctors at those offices (specifically Glazer and Simon), that they violated federal and state statutes regulating electronic surveillance, and that they committed fraud by gaining access to the Chicago office by means of a false promise that they would present a "fair and balanced" picture of the Center's operations and would not use "ambush" interviews or undercover surveillance.

. . . .

No embarrassingly intimate details of anybody's life were publicized in the present case. There was no eavesdropping on a private conversation; the testers recorded their own conversations with the Desnick Eye Center's physicians. There was no violation of the doctor-patient privilege. There was no theft, or intent to steal trade secrets; no disruption of decorum, of peace and quiet; no noisy or distracting demonstrations. Had the testers been undercover FBI agents, there would have been no violation of the Fourth Amendment, because there would have been no invasion of a legally protected interest in property or privacy. "Testers" who pose as prospective home buyers in order to gather evidence of housing discrimination are not trespassers even if they are private persons not acting under color of law. . . . The situation of the defendants' "testers" is analogous. Like testers seeking evidence of violation of antidiscrimination laws, the defendants' test patients gained entry into the plaintiffs' premises by misrepresenting their purposes (more precisely by a misleading omission to disclose those purposes). But the entry was not invasive in the sense of infringing the kind of interest of the plaintiffs that the law of trespass protects; it was not an interference with the ownership or possession of land. . . .

What we have said largely disposes of two other claims — infringement of the right of privacy, and illegal wiretapping. The right of privacy embraces several distinct interests, but the only ones conceivably involved here are the closely related interests in concealing intimate personal facts and in preventing intrusion into legitimately private activities, such as phone conversations. As we have said already, no intimate personal facts concerning the two individual plaintiffs (remember that Dr. Desnick himself is not a plaintiff) were revealed; and the only conversations that were recorded were conversations with the testers themselves.

. . . The defendants did not order the camera-armed testers into the Desnick Eye Center's premises in order to commit a crime or tort. Maybe the program as it was eventually broadcast was tortious, for we have said that the defamation count was dismissed prematurely. But there is no suggestion that the defendants sent the testers into the Wisconsin and Illinois offices for the purpose of defaming the plaintiffs by charging tampering with the glare machine. The purpose, by the plaintiffs' own account, was to see whether the Center's physicians would recommend cataract surgery on the testers. By the same token it was not to injure the Desnick Eye Center, unless the public exposure of misconduct is an "injurious act" within the meaning of the Wisconsin statute. Telling the world the truth about a Medicare fraud is hardly what the framers of the statute could have had in mind in forbidding a person to record his own conversations if he was trying to commit an "injurious act."

------

1. Was the defamation count prematurely dismissed?

2. *Sanders v. ABC*, 978 P.2d 67 (Cal. 1999), makes clear that the use of technology may "contribute to the offensiveness of an intrusion." Employees of a telepsychic marketing company, whose workplace conversations had been covertly videotaped by an undercover television news reporter, who had secretly taken position with company, sued the reporter and broadcaster after the video tapes were aired. The court held that an "employee who lacks a reasonable expectation of complete privacy in a workplace conversation, because it could be seen and overheard by coworkers (but not the general public) may nevertheless have a claim for invasion of privacy by intrusion based on a television reporter's covert videotaping of that conversation."

3. In *Food Lion v. Capital Cities/ABC*, 194 F.3d 505 (4th Cir. 1999):

Two ABC television reporters, after using false resumes to get jobs at Food Lion, Inc., supermarkets, secretly videotaped what appeared to be unwholesome food handling practices. Some of the video footage was used by ABC in a Prime Time Live broadcast that was sharply critical of Food Lion. The grocery chain sued Capital Cities/ABC . . . for the program. . . . Food Lion did not sue for defamation, but focused on how ABC gathered its information through claims for fraud, breach of duty of loyalty, trespass, and unfair trade practices. Food Lion won at trial.

The Court of Appeals held:

(1) alleged acts of fraud by undercover reporters who obtained jobs with chain did not proximately cause damages; (2) reporters breached duty of loyalty owed to chain under North Carolina and South Carolina law by using hidden cameras; (3) breach of duty of loyalty vitiated reporters' consent to enter chain's stores, so that they could be held liable for

trespass; (4) misrepresentations could not support claim under North Carolina Unfair and Deceptive Trade Practices Act; (5) First Amendment did not bar recovery for fraud and breach of duty of loyalty; but (6) chain could not recover for damages resulting from broadcast of news programs.

The award of $2.00 for trespass by the two reporters was upheld. Other damages were reversed.

B.   PUBLIC DISCLOSURE OF PRIVATE FACTS

SIDIS v. F-R PUB. CORPORATION
United States Court of Appeals for the Second Circuit, 1940
113 F.2d 806

CLARK, CIRCUIT JUDGE.

William James Sidis was the unwilling subject of a brief biographical sketch and cartoon printed in *The New Yorker* weekly magazine for August 14, 1937. . . . He brought an action in the district court against the publisher, F-R Publishing Corporation. His complaint stated three "causes of action": The first alleged violation of his right of privacy. . . . Defendant's motion to dismiss the first two "causes of action" was granted, and plaintiff has filed an appeal from the order of dismissal. Since a majority of this court believe that order appealable, for reasons referred to below, we may consider the merits of the case.

William James Sidis was a famous child prodigy in 1910. His name and prowess were well known to newspaper readers of the period. At the age of eleven, he lectured to distinguished mathematicians on the subject of Four-Dimensional Bodies. When he was sixteen, he was graduated from Harvard College, amid considerable public attention. Since then, his name has appeared in the press only sporadically, and he has sought to live as unobtrusively as possible. Until the articles objected to appeared in The New Yorker, he had apparently succeeded in his endeavor to avoid the public gaze.

Among The New Yorker's features are brief biographical sketches of current and past personalities. In the latter department, which appears haphazardly under the title of "Where Are They Now?" the article on Sidis was printed with subtitle "April Fool." The author describes his subject's early accomplishments in mathematics and the wide-spread attention he received, then recounts his general breakdown and the revulsion which Sidis thereafter felt for his for his former life of fame and study. The unfortunate prodigy is traced over the years that followed, through his attempts to conceal his identity, through his chosen career as an insignificant clerk who would not need to employ unusual mathematical talents, and through the bizarre ways in which his genius flowered, as in his enthusiasm for collecting streetcar transfers and in his proficiency with an adding machine. The article closes with an account of an interview with Sidis at his present lodgings, "a hall bedroom of Boston's shabby south end." The untidiness of his room, his curious laugh, his manner of speech, and other personal habits are commented upon at length, as is his present interest in the lore of the Okamakammessett Indians. The subtitle is explained by the closing sentence, quoting Sidis as saying "with a grin" that it was strange, "but, you know, I was born on April Fool's Day." Accompanying the biography is a small cartoon showing the genius of eleven years lecturing to a group of astounded professors.

It is not contended that any of the matter printed is untrue. Nor is the manner of the author unfriendly; Sidis today is described as having "a certain childlike charm." But the article is merciless in its dissection of intimate details of its subject's personal life, and this in company with elaborate accounts of Sidis' passion for privacy and the pitiable lengths to which he has gone in order to avoid public scrutiny. The work possesses great reader interest, for it is both amusing and instructive; but it may be fairly described as a ruthless exposure of a once public character, who has since sought and has now been deprived of the seclusion of private life.

. . . .

1. . . . Under the first "cause of action" we are asked to declare that this exposure transgresses upon plaintiff's right of privacy. . . .

All comment upon the right of privacy must stem from the famous article by Warren and Brandeis on *The Right of Privacy* in 4 Harv. L. Rev. 193. The learned authors of that paper were convinced that some limits ought to be imposed upon the privilege of newspapers to publish truthful items of a personal nature. "The press is overstepping in every direction the obvious bounds of propriety and of decency." . . . Warren and Brandeis, supra at page 196.

Warren and Brandeis realized that the interest of the individual in privacy must inevitably conflict with the interest of the public in news. Certain public figures, they conceded, such as holders of public office, must sacrifice their privacy and expose at least part of their lives to public scrutiny as the price of the powers they attain. But even public figures were not to be stripped bare. "In general, then, the matters of which the publication should be repressed may be described as those which concern the private life, habits, acts, and relations of an individual, and have no legitimate connection with his fitness for a public office. . . . Some things all men alike are entitled to keep from popular curiosity, whether in public life or not, while others are only private because the persons concerned have not assumed a position which makes their doings legitimate matters of public investigation." Warren and Brandeis, supra at page 216.

It must be conceded that under the strict standards suggested by these authors plaintiff's right of privacy has been invaded. Sidis today is neither politician, public administrator, nor statesman. Even if he were, some of the personal details revealed were of the sort that Warren and Brandeis believed "all men alike are entitled to keep from popular curiosity."

But despite eminent opinion to the contrary, we are not yet disposed to afford to all of the intimate details of private life an absolute immunity from the prying of the press. Everyone will agree that at some point the public interest in obtaining information becomes dominant over the individual's desire for privacy. Warren and Brandeis were willing to lift the veil somewhat in the case of public officers. We would go further, though we are not yet prepared to say how far. At least we would permit limited scrutiny of the "private" life of any person who has achieved, or has had thrust upon him, the questionable and indefinable status of a "public figure."

William James Sidis was once a public figure. As a child prodigy, he excited both admiration and curiosity. Of him great deeds were expected. In 1910, he was a person about whom the newspapers might display a legitimate intellectual interest, in the sense meant by Warren and Brandeis, as distinguished from a trivial and unseemly curiosity. But the precise motives of the press we regard as unimportant. And even if Sidis had loathed public attention at that time, we think his uncommon achievements and personality would have made the attention permissible. Since then Sidis has cloaked himself in obscurity, but his subsequent history, containing as it did an answer to the question of whether or not he had fulfilled his early promise, was still a matter of public concern. The article in *The New Yorker* sketched the life of an unusual personality, and it possessed considerable popular news interest.

We express no comment on whether or not the news worthiness of the matter printed will always constitute a complete defense. Revelations may be so intimate and so unwarranted in view of the victim's position as to outrage the community's notions of decency. But when focused upon public characters, truthful comments upon dress, speech, habits, and the ordinary aspects of personality will usually not transgress this line. Regrettably or not, the misfortunes and frailties of neighbors and "public figures" are subjects of considerable interest and discussion of the rest of the population. And when such are the mores of the community, it would be unwise for a court to bar their expression in the newspapers, books, and magazines of the day.

. . . .

---

1. The Restatement 2d § 652D (Publicity) provides:

One who gives publicity to a matter concerning the private life of another is subject to liability to the other for invasion of his privacy, if the matter publicized is of a kind that

(a) would be highly offensive to a reasonable person, and

(b) is not of legitimate concern to the public.

2. In *Sidis*, why did the public need to know of the facts which were so painful to the plaintiff? Why was there a "legitimate intellectual interest" as opposed to "trivial and unseemly curiosity"?

HAYNES v. ALFRED A. KNOPF, INCORPORATED
United States Court of Appeals for the Seventh Circuit, 1993
8 F.3d 1222

POSNER, CHIEF JUDGE.

Luther Haynes and his wife, Dorothy Haynes nee Johnson, appeal from the dismissal on the defendants' motion for summary judgment of their suit against

Nicholas Lemann, the author of a highly praised, best-selling book of social and political history called *The Promised Land: The Great Black Migration and How It Changed America* (1991), and Alfred A. Knopf, Inc., the book's publisher. The plaintiffs' claim that the book libels Luther Haynes and invades both plaintiffs' right of privacy. Federal jurisdiction is based on diversity, and the common law of Illinois is agreed to govern the substantive issues. The appeal presents difficult issues at the intersection of tort law and freedom of the press.

Between 1940 and 1970, five million blacks moved from impoverished rural areas in the South to the cities of the North in search of a better life. Some found it, and after sojourns of shorter or greater length in the poor black districts of the cities moved to middle-class areas. Others, despite the bally-hooed efforts of the federal government, particularly between 1964 and 1972, to erase poverty and racial discrimination, remained mired in what has come to be called the "urban ghetto." *The Promised Land* is a history of the migration. It is not history as a professional historian, a demographer, or a social scientist would write it. Lemann is none of these. He is a journalist and has written a journalistic history, in which the focus is on . . . the actual migrants. Foremost among these is Ruby Lee Daniels. Her story is the spine of the book.

. . . .

When we meet her, it is the early 1940s and she is a young woman picking cotton on a plantation in Clarksdale, Mississippi. . . . Ruby had married young, but after her husband had been inducted into the army on the eve of World War II she had fallen in love with a married man, by whom she had had a child. The man's wife died and Ruby married him, but they broke up after a month. Glowing reports from an aunt who had moved to Chicago persuaded Ruby Daniels to move there in 1946. She found a job doing janitorial work, but eventually lost the job and went on public aid. She was unmarried, and had several children, when in 1953 she met "the most important man in her life." Luther Haynes, born in 1924 or 1925, a sharecropper from Mississippi, had moved to Chicago in an effort to effect a reconciliation with his wife. The effort had failed. When he met Ruby Daniels he had a well-paying job in an awning factory. They lived together, and had children. But then "Luther began to drink too much. When he drank he got mean, and he and Ruby would get into ferocious quarrels. He was still working, but he wasn't always bringing his paycheck home." Ruby got work as a maid. They moved to a poorer part of the city. The relationship went downhill. "It got to the point where [Luther] would go out on Friday evenings after picking up his paycheck, and Ruby would hope he wouldn't come home, because she knew he would be drunk. On the Friday evenings when he did come home . . . he would walk into the apartment, put on a record and turn up the volume, and saunter into their bedroom, a bottle in one hand and a cigarette in the other, in the mood for love. On one such night, Ruby's last child, Kevin, was conceived. Kevin always had something wrong with him — he was very moody, he was scrawny, and he had a severe speech impediment. Ruby was never able to find out exactly what the problem was, but she blamed it on Luther; all that alcohol must have gotten into his sperm, she said."

Ruby was on public aid, but was cut off when social workers discovered she had a man in the house. She got a night job. Luther was supposed to stay with the children while she was at work, especially since they lived in a dangerous neighborhood; but often when she came home, at 3:00 a.m. or so, she would "find the older children awake, and when she would ask them if Luther had been there, the answer would be, 'No, ma'am.' ". . . After only a few months, Luther ruined everything by going out and buying a brand-new 1961 Pontiac. It meant more to him than the house did, and when they couldn't make the house payment, he insisted on keeping the car" even though she hadn't enough money to buy shoes for the children. The family was kicked out of the house. . . .

Meanwhile Luther had lost his job in the awning factory "that he had for a decade, and then bounced around a little. He lost jobs because of transportation problems, because of layoffs, because of a bout of serious illness, because of his drinking, because he had a minor criminal record (having been in jail for disorderly conduct following a fight with Ruby), and because creditors were after him." He resumed "his old habit of not returning from work on Fridays after he got his paycheck." One weekend he didn't come home at all. In a search of his things Ruby discovered evidence that Luther was having an affair with Dorothy Johnson, a former neighbor. "Luther was not being particularly careful; he saw in Dorothy, who was younger than Ruby, who had three children compared to Ruby's eight, who had a job while Ruby was on public aid, the promise of an escape from the ghetto, and he was entranced." The children discovered the affair. Kermit tried to strangle Luther. In 1965 Luther moved out permanently, and eventually he and Ruby divorced.

. . . .

After divorcing Ruby, Luther Haynes married Dorothy Johnson. He is still married to her, "owns a home on the far South Side of Chicago, and has worked for years as a parking-lot attendant; only recently have he and Ruby found that they can speak civilly to each other on the phone."

. . . .

The major claim in the complaint, and the focus of the appeal . . . is invasion of the right of privacy. . . .

Even people who have nothing rationally to be ashamed of can be mortified by the publication of intimate details of their life. Most people in no wise deformed or disfigured would nevertheless be deeply upset if nude photographs of themselves were published in a newspaper or a book. They feel the same way about photographs of their sexual activities, however "normal," or about a narrative of those activities, or about having their medical records publicized. . . . The desire for privacy illustrated by these examples is a mysterious but deep fact about human personality. It deserves and in our society receives legal protection. The nature of the injury shows, by the way, that the defendants are wrong to argue that this branch of the right of privacy requires proof of special damages.

But this is not the character of the depictions of the Hayneses in *The Promised Land*. Although the plaintiffs' claim that the book depicts their "sex life" and "ridicules" Luther Haynes's lovemaking (the reference is to the passage we quoted in which the author refers to Ruby's "devastating imitation" of Luther's manner when he would come home Friday nights in an amorous mood), these characterizations are misleading. No sexual act is described in the book. No intimate details are revealed. Entering one's bedroom with a bottle in one hand and a cigarette in the other is not foreplay. Ruby's speculation that Kevin's problems may have been due to Luther's having been a heavy drinker is not the narration of a sexual act.

. . . .

The branch of privacy law that the Hayneses invoke in their appeal is not concerned with, and is not a proper surrogate for legal doctrines that are concerned with, the accuracy of the private facts revealed. It is concerned with the propriety of stripping away the veil of privacy with which we cover the embarrassing, the shameful, the tabooed, truths about us. . . . The revelations in the book are not about the intimate details of the Hayneses' life. They are about misconduct, in particular Luther's. (There is very little about Dorothy in the book, apart from the fact that she had had an affair with Luther while he was still married to Ruby and that they eventually became and have remained lawfully married.) The revelations are about his heavy drinking, his unstable employment, his adultery, his irresponsible and neglectful behavior toward his wife and children. So we must consider cases in which the right of privacy has been invoked as a shield against the revelation of previous misconduct.

Two early cases illustrate the range of judicial thinking. In *Melvin v. Reid*, 112 Cal. App. 285, 297 P. 91 (Cal. App. 1931), the plaintiff was a former prostitute, who had been prosecuted but acquitted of murder. She later had married and (she alleged) for seven years had lived a blameless respectable life in a community in which her lurid past was unknown — when all was revealed in a movie about the murder case which used her maiden name. The court held that these allegations stated a claim for invasion of privacy. The Hayneses' claim is similar although less dramatic. They have been a respectable married couple for two decades. Luther's alcohol problem is behind him. He has steady employment as a doorman. His wife is a nurse, and in 1990 he told Lemann that the couple's combined income was $60,000 a year. He is not in trouble with the domestic relations court. He is a deacon of his church. He has come a long way from sharecropping in Mississippi and public housing in Chicago and he and his wife want to bury their past just as Mrs. Melvin wanted to do and in *Melvin v. Reid* was held entitled to do. Cf. *Briscoe v. Reader's Digest Ass'n*, 4 Cal. 3d 529, 93 Cal. Rptr. 866, 483 P.2d 34, 43 (Cal. 1971). In Luther Haynes's own words, from his deposition, "I know I haven't been no angel, but since almost 30 years ago I have turned my life completely around. I stopped the drinking and all this bad habits and stuff like that, which I deny, some of [it] I didn't deny, because I have changed my life. It take me almost 30 years to change it and I am deeply in my church. I look good in the eyes of my church members and my community. Now, what is going to happen now when this public reads this garbage which I didn't tell Mr. Lemann to write? Then all this is going to go down the drain. And I worked like a son of a gun to build myself up in a good reputation and he has torn it down."

. . . .

Luther Haynes did not aspire to be a representative figure in the great black migration from the South to the North. People who do not desire the limelight and do not deliberately choose a way of life or course of conduct calculated to thrust them into it nevertheless have no legal right to extinguish it if the experiences that have befallen them are newsworthy, even if they would prefer that those experiences be kept private. The possibility of an involuntary loss of privacy is recognized in the modern formulations of this branch of the privacy tort, which require not only that the private facts publicized be such as would make a reasonable person deeply offended by such publicity but also that they be facts in which the public has no legitimate interest.

The two criteria, offensiveness and newsworthiness, are related. An individual, and more pertinently perhaps the community, is most offended by the publication of intimate personal facts when the community has no interest in them beyond the voyeuristic thrill of penetrating the wall of privacy that surrounds a stranger. The reader of a book about the black migration to the North would have no legitimate interest in the details of Luther Haynes's sex life; but no such details are disclosed. Such a reader does have a legitimate interest in the aspects of Luther's conduct that the book reveals. For one of Lemann's major themes is the transposition virtually intact of a sharecropper morality characterized by a family structure "matriarchal and elastic" and by an "extremely unstable" marriage bond to the slums of the northern cities, and the interaction, largely random and sometimes perverse, of that morality with governmental programs to alleviate poverty. Public aid policies discouraged Ruby and Luther from living together; public housing policies precipitated a marriage doomed to fail. No detail in the book claimed to invade the Hayneses' privacy is not germane to the story that the author wanted to tell, a story not only of legitimate but of transcendent public interest.

The Hayneses question whether the linkage between the author's theme and their private life really is organic. They point out that many social histories do not mention individuals at all, let alone by name. That is true. . . . But it would be absurd to suggest that cliometric or other aggregative, impersonal methods of doing social history are the only proper way to go about it and presumptuous to claim even that they are the best way. Lemann's book has been praised to the skies by distinguished scholars, among them black scholars covering a large portion of the ideological spectrum. . . . Lemann's methodology places the individual case history at center stage. If he cannot tell the story of Ruby Daniels without waivers from every person who she thinks did her wrong, he cannot write this book.

Well, argue the Hayneses, at least Lemann could have changed their names. But the use of pseudonyms would not have gotten Lemann and Knopf off the legal hook. The details of the Hayneses' lives recounted in the book would identify them unmistakably to anyone who has known the Hayneses well for a long time (members of their families, for example), or who knew them before they got married; and no more is required for liability either in defamation law. . . . Lemann would have had to change some, perhaps many, of the details. But then he would no longer have been writing history. He would have been writing fiction. The nonquantitative study of living persons would be abolished as a category of scholarship, to be replaced by the sociological novel. . . . Reporting the true facts about real people is necessary to "obviate any impression that the problems raised in the [book] are remote or hypothetical." *Gilbert v. Medical Economics Co., supra,* 665 F.2d at 308. And surely a composite portrait of ghetto residents would be attacked as racial stereotyping.

The Promised Land does not afford the reader a titillating glimpse of tabooed activities. The tone is decorous and restrained. Painful though it is for the Hayneses to see a past they would rather forget brought into the public view, the public needs the information conveyed by the book, including the information about Luther and Dorothy Haynes, in order to evaluate the profound social and political questions that the book raises. . . .

Does it follow, as the Hayneses' lawyer asked us rhetorically at oral argument, that a journalist who wanted to write a book about contemporary sexual practices could include the intimate details of named living persons' sexual acts without the persons' consent? Not necessarily, although the revelation of such details in the memoirs of former spouses and lovers is common enough and rarely provokes a lawsuit even when the former spouse or lover is still alive. The core of the branch of privacy law with which we deal in this case is the protection of those intimate physical details the publicizing of which would be not merely embarrassing and painful but deeply shocking to the average person subjected to such exposure. The public has a legitimate interest in sexuality, but that interest may be outweighed in such a case by the injury to the sensibilities of the persons made use of by the author in such a way. Restatement (Second) of Torts, *supra* 652D, comment *h.* At least the balance would be sufficiently close to preclude summary judgment for the author and publisher.

The judgment for the defendants is

AFFIRMED.

---

1. In *Doe v. Berkeley Pub.*, 496 S.E.2d 636 (S.C. 1998), plaintiff sued a newspaper after it ran a truthful report that the plaintiff was sexually assaulted while in jail. The court held that "the commission of a violent crime between inmates of a county jail is a matter of public significance, as a matter of law."

2. In *Gilbert v. Medical Economics Co.*, 665 F.2d 305 (10th cir. 1981), plaintiff anesthesiologist accused of causing two serious injuries sued defendant after an article reported her history of psychiatric and related personal problems. Even though she conceded that the event itself was newsworthy, plaintiff claimed the intrusions were actionable. The court held for defendant; the facts were connected to the article by the "rational inference that plaintiff's personal problems were the underlying cause of the malpractice."

3. In *Sipple v. Chronicle Publishing Co.*, 201 Cal. Rptr. 665 (Ct. App. 1984), plaintiff thwarted an assassination attempt on President Ford and received a great deal of media coverage including stories that disclosed his homosexuality. The court held for the defendants, finding that the article was "prompted by 'legitimate political considerations,' i.e., to dispel the false public opinion that gays were timid, weak and unheroic figures and to raise the equally important political question whether the President of the United States entertained a discriminatory attitude or bias against a minority group such as homosexuals."

In a non-media case, *Ozer v. Borquez*, 940 P.2d 371 (Colo. 1997), plaintiff associate brought suit against a partner of his law firm who told everyone in the entire firm that plaintiff had AIDS; plaintiff, who was gay, had not disclosed his homosexuality to anyone in his firm, and he had asked the partner to keep his sensitive medical condition in confidence. Verdict for plaintiff.

C.   CONSTITUTIONAL PRIVILEGE

THE FLORIDA STAR v. B. J. F.
Supreme Court of the United States, 1989
491 U.S. 524

JUSTICE MARSHALL delivered the opinion of the Court.

Florida Stat. § 794.03 (1987) makes it unlawful to "print, publish, or broadcast . . . in any instrument of mass communication" the name of the victim of a sexual offense. Pursuant to this statute, appellant The Florida Star was found civilly liable for publishing the name of a rape victim which it had obtained from a publicly released police report. The issue presented here is whether this result comports with the First Amendment. We hold that it does not.

I

The Florida Star is a weekly newspaper which serves the community of Jacksonville, Florida, and which has an average circulation of approximately 18,000 copies. A regular feature of the newspaper is its "Police Reports" section. That section, typically two to three pages in length, contains brief articles describing local criminal incidents under police investigation.

On October 20,1983, appellee B. J. F. reported to the Duval County, Florida, Sheriff's Department (Department) that she had been robbed and sexually assaulted by an unknown assailant. The Department prepared a report on the incident which identified B. J. F. by her full name. The Department then placed the report in its pressroom. The Department does not restrict access either to the pressroom or to the reports made available therein.

A Florida Star reporter-trainee sent to the pressroom copied the police report verbatim, including B. J. F.'s full name, on a blank duplicate of the Department's forms. A Florida Star reporter then prepared a one-paragraph article about the crime, derived entirely from the trainee's copy of the police report. The article included B. J. F.'s full name. It appeared in the "Robberies" subsection of the "Police Reports" section on October 29, 1983, one of 54 police blotter stories in that day's edition. . . . In printing B. J. F.'s full name, The Florida Star violated its internal policy of not publishing the names of sexual offense victims.

On September 26, 1984, B. J. F. filed suit in the Circuit Court of Duval County against the Department and The Florida Star, alleging that these parties negligently violated § 794.03. . . . Before trial, the Department settled with B. J. F. for $2,500. The Florida Star moved to dismiss, claiming, *inter alia*, that imposing civil sanctions on the newspaper pursuant to § 794.03 violated the First Amendment. The trial judge rejected the motion. . . .

At the ensuing daylong trial, B. J. F. testified that she had suffered emotional distress from the publication of her name. She stated that she had heard about the article from fellow workers and acquaintances; that her mother had received several threatening phone calls from a man who stated that he would rape B. J. F. again; and that these events had forced B. J. F. to change her phone number and residence, to seek police protection, and to obtain mental health counseling. In defense, The Florida Star put forth evidence indicating that the newspaper had learned B. J. F.'s name from the incident report released by the Department, and that the newspaper's violation of its internal rule against publishing the names of sexual offense victims was inadvertent.

At the close of B. J. F.'s case, and again at the close of its defense, The Florida Star moved for a directed verdict. On both occasions, the trial judge denied these motions. He ruled from the bench that § 794.03 was constitutional because it reflected a proper balance between the First Amendment and privacy rights, as it applied only to a narrow set of "rather sensitive . . . criminal offenses." App. 18-19 (rejecting first motion); see *id.*, at 32-33 (rejecting second motion). At the close of the newspaper's defense, the judge granted B. J. F.'s motion for a directed verdict on the issue of negligence, finding the newspaper *per se* negligent based upon its violation of § 794.03. *Id.*, at 33. This ruling left the jury to consider only the questions of causation and damages. The judge instructed the jury that it could award B. J. F. punitive damages if it found that the newspaper had "acted with reckless indifference to the rights of others." *Id.*, at 35. The jury awarded B. J. F. $75,000 in compensatory damages and $25,000 in punitive damages. Against the actual damages award, the judge set off B. J. F.'s settlement with the Department.

The First District Court of Appeal affirmed in a three-paragraph per *curiam* opinion. 499 So. 2d 883 (1986). In the paragraph devoted to The Florida Star's First Amendment claim, the court stated that the directed verdict for B. J. F. had been properly entered because, under § 794.03, a rape victim's name is "of a private nature and not to be published as a matter of law." *Id.*, at 884, citing Doe *v. Sarasota-Bradenton Florida Television Co.*, 436 So. 2d 328, 330 (Fla. App. 1983) (footnote omitted). . . .

II

The tension between the right which the First Amendment accords to a free press, on the one hand, and the protections which various statutes and common-law doctrines accord to personal privacy against the publication of truthful information, on the other, is a subject we have addressed several times in recent years. Our decisions in cases involving government attempts to sanction the accurate dissemination of information as invasive of privacy, have not, however, exhaustively considered this conflict. On the contrary, although our decisions have without exception upheld the press' right to publish, we have emphasized each time that we were resolving this conflict only as it arose in a discrete factual context.

The parties to this case frame their contentions in light of a trilogy of cases which have presented, in different contexts, the conflict between truthful reporting and state-protected privacy interests. In *Cox Broadcasting Corp. v. Cohn*, 420 U.S. 469 (1975), we found unconstitutional a civil damages award entered against a television station for broadcasting the name of a rape-murder victim which the station had obtained from courthouse records. In *Oklahoma Publishing Co. v. Oklahoma County District Court*, 430 U.S. 308 (1977), we found unconstitutional a state court's pretrial order enjoining the media from publishing the name or photograph of an 11-year-old boy in connection with a juvenile proceeding involving that child which reporters had attended. Finally, in *Smith v. Daily Mail Publishing Co.*, 443 U.S. 97 (1979), we found unconstitutional the indictment of two newspapers for violating a state statute forbidding newspapers to publish, without written approval of the juvenile court, the name of any youth charged as a juvenile offender. The papers had learned about a shooting by monitoring a police band radio frequency and had obtained the name of the alleged juvenile assailant from witnesses, the police, and a local prosecutor.

. . . .

We conclude that imposing damages on appellant for publishing B. J. F.'s name violates the First Amendment, although not for either of the reasons appellant urges. Despite the strong resemblance this case bears to *Cox Broadcasting*, that case cannot fairly be read as controlling here. The name of the rape victim in that case was obtained from courthouse records that were open to public inspection. . . . Significantly, one of the reasons we gave in *Cox Broadcasting* for invalidating the challenged damages award was the important role the press plays in subjecting trials to public scrutiny and thereby helping guarantee their fairness. *Id.*, at 492-493. That role is not directly compromised where, as here, the information in question comes from a police report prepared and disseminated at a time at which not only had no adversarial criminal proceedings begun, but no suspect had been identified.

Nor need we accept appellant's invitation to hold broadly that truthful publication may never be punished consistent with the First Amendment. Our cases have carefully eschewed reaching this ultimate question, mindful that the future may bring scenarios which prudence counsels our not resolving anticipatorily. . . . Respecting the fact that press freedom and privacy rights are both "plainly rooted in the traditions and significant concerns of our society," we instead focused on the less sweeping issue "whether the State may impose sanctions on the accurate publication of the name of a rape victim obtained from public records — more specifically, from judicial records which are maintained in connection with a public prosecution and which themselves are open to public inspection." *Ibid.* We continue to believe that the sensitivity and significance of the interests presented in clashes between First Amendment and privacy rights counsel relying on limited principles that sweep no more broadly than the appropriate context of the instant case.

In our view, this case is appropriately analyzed with reference to such a limited First Amendment principle. It is the one, in fact, which we articulated in *Daily Mail* in our synthesis of prior cases involving attempts to punish truthful publication: "[I]f a newspaper lawfully obtains truthful information about a matter of public significance then state officials may not constitutionally punish publication of the information, absent a need to further a state interest of the highest order." 443 U.S., at 103 . . . .

Applied to the instant case, the *Daily Mail* principle clearly commands reversal.

The first inquiry is whether the newspaper "lawfully obtain[ed] truthful information about a matter of public significance." 443 U.S., at 103. It is undisputed that the news article describing the assault on B. J. F. was accurate. In addition, appellant lawfully obtained B. J. F.'s name. Appellee's argument to the contrary is based on the fact that under Florida law, police reports which reveal the identity of the victim of a sexual offense are not among the matters of "public record" which the public, by law, is entitled to inspect. Brief for Appellee 17-18, citing Fla. Stat. § 119.07(3)(h) (1983). But the fact that state officials are not required to disclose such reports does not make it unlawful for a newspaper to receive them when furnished by the government. Nor does the fact that the Department apparently failed to fulfill its obligation under § 794.03 not to "cause or allow to be . . . published" the name of a sexual offense victim make the newspaper's ensuing receipt of this information unlawful. Even assuming the Constitution permitted a State to proscribe *receipt* of information, Florida has not taken this step. It is, clear, furthermore, that the news article concerned "a matter of public significance," 443 U.S., at 103, in the sense in which the *Daily Mail* synthesis of prior cases used that term. That is, the article generally . . . involved a matter of paramount public import: the commission, and investigation, of a violent crime which had been reported to authorities.

. . . .

When a State attempts the extraordinary measure of punishing truthful publication in the name of privacy, it must demonstrate its commitment to advancing this interest by applying its prohibition evenhandedly, to the smalltime disseminator as well as the media giant. Where important First Amendment interests are at stake, the mass scope of disclosure is not an acceptable surrogate for injury. A ban on disclosures effected by "instrument[s] of mass communication" simply cannot be defended on the ground that partial prohibitions may effect partial relief. Without more careful and inclusive precautions against alternative forms of dissemination, we cannot conclude that Florida's selective ban on publication by the mass media satisfactorily accomplishes its stated purpose.

III

Our holding today is limited. We do not hold that truthful publication is automatically constitutionally protected, or that there is no zone of personal privacy within which the State may protect the individual from intrusion by the press, or even that a State may never punish publication of the name of a victim of a sexual offense. We hold only that where a newspaper publishes truthful information which it has lawfully obtained, punishment may lawfully be imposed, if at all, only when narrowly tailored to a state interest of the highest order, and that no such interest is satisfactorily served by imposing liability under § 794.03 to appellant under the facts of this case. The decision below is therefore

Reversed.

---

1.   Compare the constitutional privilege presented in *The Florida Star* with "fair comment" found in the defamation chapter.

2. What rule do you gather from *Cox, Florida Star* and *Oklahoma Publishing*? How is your conclusion different from the holding in *Florida Star*?

D. FALSE LIGHT

CANTRELL v. FOREST CITY PUBLISHING CO.
Supreme Court of the United States, 1974
419 U.S. 245

MR. JUSTICE STEWART delivered the opinion of the Court.

Margaret Cantrell and four of her minor children brought this diversity action in a Federal District Court for invasion of privacy against the Forest City Publishing Co., publisher of a Cleveland newspaper, the *Plain Dealer*, and against Joseph Eszterhas, a reporter formerly employed by the *Plain Dealer*, and Richard Conway, a *Plain Dealer* photographer. The Cantrells alleged that an article published in the *Plain Dealer Sunday Magazine* unreasonably placed their family in a false light before the public through its many inaccuracies and untruths. The District Judge struck the claims relating to punitive damages as to all the plaintiffs and dismissed the actions of three of the Cantrell children in their entirety, but allowed the case to go to the jury as to Mrs. Cantrell and her oldest son, William. The jury returned a verdict against all three of the respondents for compensatory money damages in favor of these two plaintiffs.

The Court of Appeals for the Sixth Circuit reversed, holding that, in the light of the First and Fourteenth Amendments, the District Judge should have granted the respondents' motion for a directed verdict as to all the Cantrells' claims. 484 F.2d 150. We granted certiorari, 418 U.S. 909.

In December 1967, Margaret Cantrell's husband Melvin was killed along with 43 other people when the Silver Bridge across the Ohio River at Point Pleasant, W. Va., collapsed. The respondent Eszterhas was assigned by the *Plain Dealer* to cover the story of the disaster. He wrote a "news feature" story focusing on the funeral of Melvin Cantrell and the impact of his death on the Cantrell family.

Five months later, after conferring with the Sunday Magazine editor of the *Plain Dealer*, Eszterhas and photographer Conway returned to the Point Pleasant area to write a follow-up feature. The two men went to the Cantrell residence, where Eszterhas talked with the children and Conway took 50 pictures. Mrs. Cantrell was not at home at any time during the 60 to 90 minutes that the men were at the Cantrell residence.

Eszterhas' story appeared as the lead feature in the August 4, 1968, edition of the *Plain Dealer Sunday Magazine*, The article stressed the family's abject poverty; the children's old, ill-fitting clothes and the deteriorating condition of their home were detailed in both the text and accompanying photographs. As he had done in his original, prize-winning article on the Silver Bridge disaster, Eszterhas used the Cantrell family to illustrate the impact of the bridge collapse on the lives of the people in the Point Pleasant area.

It is conceded that the story contained a number of inaccuracies and false statements. Most conspicuously, although Mrs. Cantrell was not present at any time during the reporter's visit to her home, Eszterhas wrote, "Margaret Cantrell will talk neither about what happened nor about how they are doing. She wears the same mask of non-expression she wore at the funeral. She is a proud woman. Her world has changed. She says that after it happened, the people in town offered to help them out with money and they refused to take it." Other significant misrepresentations were contained in details of Eszterhas' descriptions of the poverty in which the Cantrells were living and the dirty and dilapidated conditions of the Cantrell home.

The case went to the jury on a so-called "false light" theory of invasion of privacy. In essence, the theory of the case was that by publishing the false feature story about the Cantrells and thereby making them the objects of pity and ridicule, the respondents damaged Mrs. Cantrell and her son William by causing them to suffer outrage, mental distress, shame, and humiliation.

II

In *Time, Inc. v. Hill*, 385 U.S. 374, the Court considered a similar false-light, invasion-of-privacy action. The New York Court of Appeals had interpreted New York Civil Rights Law §§ 50-51 to give a "newsworthy person" a right of action when his or her name, picture or portrait was the subject of a "fictitious" report or article. Material and substantial falsification was the test for recovery. 385 U.S., at 384-386. Under this doctrine the New York courts awarded the plaintiff James Hill compensatory damages based on his complaint that Life Magazine had falsely reported that a new Broadway play portrayed the Hill family's experience in being held hostage by three escaped convicts. This Court, guided by its decision in *New York Times Co. v. Sullivan*, 376 U.S. 254, which recognized constitutional limits on a State's power to award damages for libel in actions brought by public officials, held that the constitutional protections for speech and press precluded the application of the New York statute to allow recovery for "false reports of matters of public interest in the absence of proof that the defendant published the report with knowledge of its falsity or in reckless disregard of the truth." 385 U.S., at 388. Although the jury could have reasonably concluded from the evidence in the *Hill* case that Life had engaged in knowing falsehood or had recklessly disregarded the truth in stating in the article that "the story re-enacted" the Hill family's experience, the Court concluded that the trial judge's instructions had not confined the jury to such a finding as a predicate for liability as required by the Constitution. *Id.*, at 394.

The District Judge in the case before us, in contrast to the trial judge in *Time, Inc. v. Hill*, did instruct the jury that liability could be imposed only if it concluded that the false statements in the Sunday Magazine feature article on the Cantrells had been made with knowledge of their falsity or in reckless disregard of the truth. No objection was made by any of the parties to this knowing-or-reckless-falsehood instruction. Consequently, this case presents no occasion to consider whether a State may constitutionally apply a more relaxed standard of liability for a publisher or broadcaster of false statements injurious to a private individual under a false-light theory of invasion of privacy, or whether the constitutional standard announced in *Time, Inc. v. Hill* applies to all false-light cases. *Cf. Gertz v. Robert Welch, Inc.*, 418 U.S. 323. Rather, the sole question that we need decide is whether the Court of Appeals erred in setting aside the jury's verdict.

III

At the close of the petitioners' case-in-chief, the District Judge struck the demand for punitive damages. He found that Mrs. Cantrell had failed to present any evidence to support the charges that the invasion of privacy "was done maliciously within the legal definition of that term." The Court of Appeals interpreted this finding to be a determination by the District Judge that there was no evidence of knowing falsity or reckless disregard of the truth introduced at the trial. Having made such a determination, the Court of Appeals held that the District Judge should have granted the motion for a directed verdict for respondents as to all the Cantrells' claims. 484 F.2d, at 155.

The Court of Appeals appears to have assumed that the District Judge's finding of no malice "within the legal definition of that term" was a finding based on the definition of "actual malice" established by this Court in *New York Times Co. v. Sullivan*, 376 U.S., at 280: "with knowledge that [a defamatory statement] was false or with reckless disregard of whether it was false or not." As so defined, of course, "actual malice" is a term of art, created to provide a convenient shorthand expression for the standard of liability that must be established before a State may constitutionally permit public officials to recover for libel in actions brought against publishers. As such, it is quite different from the common-law standard of "malice" generally required under state tort law to support an award of punitive damages. In a false-light case, common-law malice — frequently expressed in terms of either personal ill will toward the plaintiff or reckless or wanton disregard of the plaintiff's rights — would focus on the defendant's attitude toward the plaintiff's privacy, not toward the truth or falsity of the material published. See *Time, Inc. v. Hill*, 385 U.S., at 396 n. 12. See generally W. Prosser, Law of Torts 9-10 (4th ed.).

Although the verbal record of the District Court proceedings is not entirely unambiguous, the conclusion is inescapable that the District Judge was referring to the common-law standard of malice rather than to the *New York Times* "actual malice" standard when he dismissed the punitive damages claims. For at the same time that he dismissed the demands for punitive damages, the District Judge refused to grant the respondents' motion for directed verdicts as to Mrs. Cantrell's and William's claims for compensatory damages. And, as his instructions to the jury made clear, the District Judge was fully aware that the *Time, Inc. v. Hill* meaning of the *New York Times* "actual malice" standard had to be satisfied for the Cantrells to recover actual damages. Thus, the only way to harmonize these two virtually simultaneous rulings by the District Judge is to conclude, contrary to the decision of the Court of Appeals, that in dismissing the punitive damages claims he was not determining that Mrs. Cantrell had failed to introduce any evidence of knowing falsity or reckless disregard of the truth. This conclusion is further fortified by the District Judge's subsequent denial of the respondents' motion for judgment *n. o. v.* and alternative motion for a new trial.

Moreover, the District Judge was clearly correct in believing that the evidence introduced at trial was sufficient to support a jury finding that the respondents Joseph Eszterhas and Forest City Publishing Co. had published knowing or reckless falsehoods about the Cantrells. There was no dispute during the trial that Eszterhas, who did not testify, must have known that a number of the statements in the feature story were untrue. In particular, his article plainly implied that Mrs. Cantrell had been present during his visit to her home and that Eszterhas had observed her "[wearing] the same mask of non-expression she wore [at her husband's] funeral." These were "calculated falsehoods," and the jury was plainly justified in finding that Eszterhas had portrayed the Cantrells in a false light through knowing or reckless untruth.

The Court of Appeals concluded that there was no evidence that Forest City Publishing Co. had knowledge of any of the inaccuracies contained in Eszterhas' article. However, there was sufficient evidence for the jury to find that Eszterhas' writing of the feature was within the scope of his employment at the *Plain Dealer* and that Forest City Publishing Co. was therefore liable under traditional doctrines of respondeat superior. Although Eszterhas was not regularly assigned by the *Plain Dealer* to write for the *Sunday Magazine*, the editor of the magazine testified that as a staff writer for the Plain Dealer Eszterhas frequently suggested stories he would like to write for the magazine. When Eszterhas suggested the follow-up article on the Silver Bridge disaster, the editor approved the idea and told Eszterhas the magazine would publish the feature if it was good. From this evidence, the jury could reasonably conclude that Forest City Publishing Co., publisher of the Plain Dealer, should be held vicariously liable for the damage caused by the knowing falsehoods contained in Eszterhas' story.

It is so ordered.

Mr. Justice Douglas, dissenting.

. . . Freedom of the press is "abridged" in violation of the First and Fourteenth Amendments by what we do today. . . .

A bridge accident catapulted the Cantrells into the public eye and their disaster became newsworthy. To make the First Amendment freedom to report the news turn on subtle differences between common-law malice and actual malice is to stand the Amendment on its head. Those who write the current news seldom have the objective, dispassionate point of view — or the time — of scientific analysts. They deal in fast-moving events and the need for "spot" reporting. The jury under today's formula sits as a censor with broad powers — not to impose a prior restraint, but to lay heavy damages on the press. The press is "free" only if the jury is sufficiently disenchanted with the Cantrells to let the press be free of this damages claim. That regime is thought by some to be a way of supervising the press which is better than not supervising it at all. But the installation of the Court's regime would require a constitutional amendment. Whatever might be the ultimate reach of the doctrine Mr. Justice Black and I have embraced, it seems clear that in matters of public import such as the present news reporting, there must be freedom from damages lest the press be frightened into playing a more ignoble role than the Framers visualized.

---

1. The Restatement 2d § 652E (False Light) provides:

One who gives publicity to a matter concerning another that places the other before the public in a false light is subject to liability to the other for invasion of his privacy, if

    (a)   the false light in which the other was placed would be highly offensive to a reasonable person, and

    (b)   the actor had knowledge of or acted in reckless disregard as to the falsity of the publicized matter and the false light in which the other would be placed.

2. What does the Court say about "malice" as applied to privacy?

LAKE v. WAL-MART STORES, INC.
Supreme Court of Minnesota, 1998
582 N.W.2d 231

BLATZ, CHIEF JUSTICE

Elli Lake and Melissa Weber appeal from a dismissal of their complaint for failure to state a claim upon which relief may be granted. The district court and court of appeals held that Lake and Weber's complaint alleging intrusion upon seclusion, appropriation, publication of private facts, and false light publicity could not proceed because Minnesota does not recognize a common law tort action for invasion of privacy. We reverse as to the claims of intrusion upon seclusion, appropriation, and publication of private facts, but affirm as to false light publicity.

Nineteen-year-old Elli Lake and 20-year-old Melissa Weber vacationed in Mexico in March 1995 with Weber's sister. During the vacation, Weber's sister took a photograph of Lake and Weber naked in the shower together. After their vacation, Lake and Weber brought five rolls of film to the Dilworth, Minnesota Wal-Mart store and photo lab. When they received their developed photographs along with the negatives, an enclosed written notice stated that one or more of the photographs had not been printed because of their "nature."

In July 1995, an acquaintance of Lake and Weber alluded to the photograph and questioned their sexual orientation. Again, in December 1995, another friend told Lake and Weber that a Wal-Mart employee had shown her a copy of the photograph. By February 1996, Lake was informed that one or more copies of the photograph were circulating in the community.

Lake and Weber filed a complaint against Wal-Mart Stores, Inc. and one or more as-yet unidentified Wal-Mart employees on February 23, 1996, alleging the four traditional invasion of privacy torts — intrusion upon seclusion, appropriation, publication of private facts, and false light publicity. Wal-Mart denied the allegations and made a motion to dismiss the complaint under Minn. R. Civ. P. 12.02, for failure to state a claim upon which relief may be granted. The district court granted Wal-Mart's motion to dismiss, explaining that Minnesota has not recognized any of the four invasion of privacy torts. The court of appeals affirmed.

Whether Minnesota should recognize any or all of the invasion of privacy causes of action is a question of first impression in Minnesota. . . .

Today we join the majority of jurisdictions and recognize the tort of invasion of privacy. The right to privacy is an integral part of our humanity; one has a public persona, exposed and active, and a private persona, guarded and preserved. The heart of our liberty is choosing which parts of our lives shall become public and which parts we shall hold close.

Here Lake and Weber allege in their complaint that a photograph of their nude bodies has been publicized. One's naked body is a very private part of one's person and generally known to others only by choice. This is a type of privacy interest worthy of protection. Therefore, without consideration of the merits of Lake and Weber's claims, we recognize the torts of intrusion upon seclusion, appropriation, and publication of private facts. Accordingly, we reverse the court of appeals and the district court and hold that Lake and Weber have stated a claim upon which relief may be granted and their lawsuit may proceed.

. . . .

We decline to recognize the tort of false light publicity at this time. We are concerned that claims under false light are similar to claims of defamation, and to the extent that false light is more expansive than defamation, tension between this tort and the First Amendment is increased.

False light is the most widely criticized of the four privacy torts and has been rejected by several jurisdictions. Most recently, the Texas Supreme Court refused to recognize the tort of false light invasion of privacy because defamation encompasses most false light claims and false light "lacks many of the procedural limitations that accompany actions for defamation, thus unacceptably increasing the tension that already exists between free speech constitutional guarantees and tort law." Citing "numerous procedural and substantive hurdles" under Texas statutory and common law that limit defamation actions, such as privileges for public meetings, good faith, and important public interest and mitigation factors, the court concluded that these restrictions "serve to safeguard the freedom of speech." Thus to allow recovery under false light invasion of privacy, without such safeguards, would "unacceptably derogate constitutional free speech." The court rejected the solution of some jurisdictions — application of the defamation restrictions to false light — finding instead that any benefit to protecting nondefamatory false speech was outweighed by the chilling effect on free speech.

We agree with the reasoning of the Texas Supreme Court. Defamation requires a false statement communicated to a third party that tends to harm a plaintiff's reputation. False light requires publicity, to a large number of people, of a falsity that places the plaintiff in a light that a reasonable person would find highly offensive. The primary difference between defamation and false light is that defamation addresses harm to reputation in the external world, while false light protects harm to one's inner self. Most false light claims are actionable as defamation claims; because of the overlap with defamation and the other privacy torts, a case has rarely succeeded squarely on a false light claim.

Additionally, unlike the tort of defamation, which over the years has become subject to numerous restrictions to protect the interest in a free press and discourage trivial litigation, the tort of false light is not so restricted. Although many jurisdictions have imposed restrictions on false light actions identical to those for defamation, we are not persuaded that a new cause of action should be recognized if little additional protection is afforded plaintiffs.

We are also concerned that false light inhibits free speech guarantees provided by the First Amendment. As the Supreme Court remarked in *New York Times Co. v. Sullivan:* "Whatever is added to the field of libel is taken from the field of free debate." Accordingly, we do not want to:

> create a grave risk of serious impairment of the indispensable service of a free press in a free society if we saddle the press with the impossible burden of verifying to a certainty the facts associated in news articles with a person's name, picture or portrait, particularly as related to nondefamatory matter.

Although there may be some untrue and hurtful publicity that should be actionable under false light, the risk of chilling speech is too great to justify protection for this small category of false publication not protected under defamation.

Thus we recognize a right to privacy present in the common law of Minnesota, including causes of action in tort for intrusion upon seclusion, appropriation, and publication of private facts, but we decline to recognize the tort of false light publicity. This case is remanded to the district court for further proceedings consistent with this opinion.

Affirmed in part, reversed in part.

----

1. What about consent or assumption of risk by the plaintiffs that the photographs would be shown to others? What if they forgot these pictures were on the roll of film?

2. Was the plaintiffs' assumption that the pictures would not be passed around reasonable? Do individuals who engage in "sexting" (electronic transmission of sexually suggestive or revealing messages or images) have a reasonable expectation that the recipients of their "sexts" will not retransmit them to others?

3. How does the court draw the distinction between defamation and false light? Is it valid?

E. APPROPRIATION

ZACCHINI v. SCRIPPS-HOWARD BROADCASTING CO.
Supreme Court of the United States, 1977
433 U.S. 562

MR. JUSTICE WHITE delivered the opinion of the Court.

Petitioner, Hugo Zacchini, is an entertainer. He performs a "human cannon-ball" act in which he is shot from a cannon into a net some 200 feet away. Each performance occupies some 15 seconds. In August and September 1972, petitioner was engaged to perform his act on a regular basis at the Geauga County Fair in Burton, Ohio. He performed in a fenced area, surrounded by grandstands, at the fair grounds. Members of the public attending the fair were not charged a separate admission fee to observe his act.

On August 30, a free-lance reporter for Scripps-Howard Broadcasting Co., the operator of a television broadcasting station and respondent in this case, attended the fair. He carried a small movie camera. Petitioner noticed the reporter and asked him not to film the performance. The reporter did not do so on that day; but on the instructions of the producer of respondent's daily newscast, he returned the following day and videotaped the entire act. This film clip, approximately 15 seconds in length, was shown on the 11 o'clock news program that night, together with favorable commentary.

Petitioner then brought this action for damages, alleging that he is "engaged in the entertainment business," that the act he performs is one "invented by his father and . . . performed only by his family for the last fifty years," that respondent "showed and commercialized the film of his act without his consent," and that such conduct was an "unlawful appropriation of plaintiff's professional property." App. 4-5. Respondent answered and moved for summary judgment, which was granted by the trial court.

The Court of Appeals of Ohio reversed. The majority held that petitioner's complaint stated a cause of action for conversion and for infringement of a common-law copyright, and one judge concurred in the judgment on the ground that the complaint stated a cause of action for appropriation of petitioner's "right of publicity" in the film of his act. All three judges agreed that the First Amendment did not privilege the press to show the entire performance on a news program without compensating petitioner for any financial injury he could prove at trial.

Like the concurring judge in the Court of Appeals, the Supreme Court of Ohio rested petitioner's cause of action under state law on his "right to publicity value of his performance." 47 Ohio St. 2d 224, 351 N.E. 2d 454, 455 (1976). The opinion syllabus, to which we are to look for the rule of law used to decide the case, declared first that one may not use for his own benefit the name or likeness of another, whether or not the use or benefit is a commercial one, and second that respondent would be liable for the appropriation, over petitioner's objection and in the absence of license or privilege, of petitioner's right to the publicity value of his performance.

Ibid. The court nevertheless gave judgment for respondent because, in the words of the syllabus:

> "A TV station has a privilege to report in its newscasts matters of legitimate public interest which would otherwise be protected by an individual's right of publicity, unless the actual intent of the TV station was to appropriate the benefit of the publicity for some non-privileged private use, or unless the actual intent was to injure the individual." *Ibid.*

We granted certiorari . . . to consider an issue unresolved by this Court: whether the First and Fourteenth Amendments immunized respondent from damages for its alleged infringement of petitioner's state-law "right of publicity." Insofar as the Ohio Supreme Court held that the First and Fourteenth Amendments of United States Constitution required judgment for respondent, we reverse the judgment of that court.

I

. . . .

There is no doubt that petitioner's complaint was grounded in state law and that the right of publicity which petitioner was held to possess was a right arising under Ohio law. It is also clear that respondent's claim of constitutional privilege was sustained. The source of this privilege was not identified in the syllabus. It is clear enough from the opinion of the Ohio Supreme Court . . . that in adjudicating the crucial question of whether respondent had a privilege to film and televise petitioner's performance, the court placed principal reliance on *Time, Inc. v. Hill*, 385 U.S. 374 (1967), a case involving First Amendment limitations on state tort actions. It construed the principle of that case, along with that *of New York Times Co. v. Sullivan*, 376 U.S. 254 (1964), to be that "the press has a privilege to report matters of legitimate public interest even though such reports might intrude on matters otherwise private," and concluded, therefore, that the press is also "privileged when an individual seeks to publicly exploit his talents while keeping the benefits private." 47 Ohio St. 2d, at 234, 351 N.E. 2d, at 461. The privilege thus exists in cases "where appropriation of a right of publicity is claimed." The court's opinion also referred to Draft 21 of the relevant portion of Restatement (Second) of Torts (1975), which was understood to make room for reasonable press appropriations by limiting the reach of the right of privacy rather than by creating a privileged invasion. The court preferred the notion of privilege over the Restatement's formulation, however, reasoning that "since the gravamen of the issue in this case is not whether the degree of intrusion is reasonable, but whether First Amendment principles require that the right of privacy give way to the public right to be informed of matters of public interest and concern, the concept of privilege seems the more useful and appropriate one."

II

The Ohio Supreme Court held that respondent is constitutionally privileged to include in its newscasts matters of public interest that would otherwise be protected by the right of publicity, absent an intent to injure or to appropriate for some nonprivileged purpose. If under this standard respondent had merely reported that petitioner was performing at the fair and described or commented on his act, with or without showing his picture on television, we would have a very different case. But petitioner is not contending that his appearance at the fair and his performance could not be reported by the press as newsworthy items. His complaint is that respondent filmed his entire act and displayed that film on television for the public to see and enjoy. This, he claimed, was an appropriation of his professional property. The Ohio Supreme Court agreed that petitioner had "a right of publicity" that gave him "personal control over commercial display and exploitation of his personality and the exercise of his talents." This right of "exclusive control over the publicity given to his performances" was said to be such a "valuable part of the benefit which may be attained by his talents and efforts" that it was entitled to legal protection. It was also observed, or at least expressly assumed, that petitioner had not abandoned his rights by performing under the circumstances present at the Geauga County Fair Grounds.

The Ohio Supreme Court nevertheless held that the challenged invasion was privileged, saying that the press "must be accorded broad latitude in its choice of how much it presents of each story or incident, and of the emphasis to be given to such presentation. No fixed standard which would bar the press from reporting or depicting either an entire occurrence or an entire discrete part of a public performance can be formulated which would not unduly restrict the 'breathing room' in reporting which freedom of the press requires." 47 Ohio St. 2d, at 235, 351 N.E. 2d, at 461. Under this view, respondent was thus constitutionally free to film and display petitioner's entire act.

The Ohio Supreme Court relied heavily on *Time, Inc. v. Hill*, 385 U.S. 374 (1967), but that case does not mandate a media privilege to televise a performer's entire act without his consent. Involved in *Time, Inc. v. Hill* was a claim under the New York "Right of Privacy" statute that *Life Magazine*, in the course of reviewing a new play, had connected the play with a long-past incident involving petitioner and his family and had falsely described their experience and conduct at that time. The complaint sought damages for humiliation and suffering flowing from these nondefamatory falsehoods that allegedly invaded Hill's privacy. The Court held, however, that the opening of a new play linked to an actual incident was a matter of public interest and that Hill could not recover without showing that the Life report was knowingly false or was published with reckless disregard for the truth — the same rigorous standard that had been applied in *New York Times Co. v. Sullivan*, 376 U.S. 254 (1964).

Time, Inc. v. Hill, which was hotly contested and decided by a divided Court, involved an entirely different tort from the "right of publicity" recognized by the Ohio Supreme Court. As the opinion reveals in *Time, Inc. v. Hill*, the Court was steeped in the literature of privacy law and was aware of the developing distinctions and nuances in this branch of the law. The Court, for example, cited W. Prosser, Law of Torts 831-832 (3d ed. 1964), and the same author's well-known article, *Privacy*, 48 Calif. L. Rev. 383 (1960), both of which divided privacy into four distinct branches. The Court was aware that it was adjudicating a "false light" privacy case involving a matter of public interest, not a case involving "intrusion," 385 U.S., at 384-385, n. 9, "appropriation" of a name or likeness for the purposes of trade, *id.*, at 381, or "private details" about a non-newsworthy person or event, *id.*, at 383 n. 7. It is also abundantly clear that *Time, Inc. v. Hill* did not involve a performer, a person with a name having commercial value, or any claim to a "right of publicity." This discrete kind of "appropriation" case was plainly identified in the literature cited by the Court and had been adjudicated in the reported cases.

The differences between these two torts are important. First, the State's interests in providing a cause of action in each instance are different. "The interest protected" in permitting recovery for placing the plaintiff in a false light "is clearly that of reputation, with the same overtones of mental distress as in defamation." Prosser, supra, 48 Calif. L. Rev., at 400. By contrast, the State's interest in permitting a "right of publicity" is in protecting the proprietary interest of the individual in his act in part to encourage such entertainment. . . . Second, the two torts differ in the degree to which they intrude on dissemination of information to the public. In "false light" cases the only way to protect the interests involved is to attempt to minimize publication of the damaging matter, while in "right of publicity" cases the only question is who gets to do the publishing. An entertainer such as petitioner usually has no objection to the widespread publication of his act as long as he gets the commercial benefit of such publication. Indeed, in the present case petitioner did not seek to enjoin the broadcast of his act; he simply sought compensation for the broadcast in the form of damages.

. . . .

There is no doubt that entertainment, as well as news, enjoys First Amendment protection. It is also true that entertainment itself can be important news. *Time, Inc. v. Hill.* But it is important to note that neither the public nor respondent will be deprived of the benefit of petitioner's performance as long as his commercial stake in his act is appropriately recognized. Petitioner does not seek to enjoin the broadcast of his performance; he simply wants to be paid for it. Nor do we think that a state-law damages remedy against respondent would represent a species of liability without fault contrary to the letter or spirit of *Gertz v. Robert Welch, Inc.*, 418 U.S. 323 (1974). Respondent knew that petitioner objected to televising his act but nevertheless displayed the entire film.

We conclude that although the State of Ohio may as a matter of its own law privilege the press in the circumstances of this case, the First and Fourteenth Amendments do not require it to do so.

Reversed.

———————

1. Many television news shows, in addition to reporting the day's events, have features on various local activities, coming television attractions, lives of celebrities, and the like. Are they news or entertainment?

2. How should the court treat the fact that Zacchini had asked defendant not to film his performance?

3. The Restatement 2d § 652C (Appropriation) provides:

One who appropriates to his own use or benefit the name or likeness of another is subject to liability to the other for invasion of his privacy.

MIDLER v. FORD MOTOR COMPANY
United States Court of Appeals for the Ninth Circuit, 1988
849 F.2d 460

JOHN T. NOONAN, CIRCUIT JUDGE:

This case centers on the protectibility of the voice of a celebrated chanteuse from commercial exploitation without her consent. Ford Motor Company and its advertising agency, Young & Rubicam, Inc., in 1985 advertised the Ford Lincoln Mercury with a series of nineteen 30 or 60 second television commercials in what the agency called "The Yuppie Campaign." The aim was to make an emotional connection with Yuppies, bringing back memories of when they were in college. Different popular songs of the seventies were sung on each commercial. The agency tried to get "the original people," that is, the singers who had popularized the songs, to sing them. Failing in that endeavor in ten cases the agency had the songs sung by "sound alikes." Bette Midler, the plaintiff and appellant here was done by a sound alike.

Midler is a nationally known actress and singer. She won a Grammy as early as 1973 as the Best New Artist of that year. Records made by her since then have gone Platinum and Gold. She was nominated in 1979 for an Academy award for Best Female Actress in *The Rose*, in which she portrayed a pop singer. *Newsweek* in its June 30, 1986 issue described her as an "outrageously original singer/comedian." *Time* hailed her in its March 2, 1987 issue as "a legend" and "the most dynamic and poignant singer-actress of her time."

When Young & Rubicam was preparing the Yuppie Campaign it presented the commercial to its client by playing an edited version of Midler singing "Do You Want To Dance," taken from the 1973 Midler album, "The Divine Miss M." After the client accepted the idea and form of the commercial, the agency contacted Midler's manager, Jerry Edelstein. The conversation went as follows: "Hello, I am Craig Hazen from Young and Rubicam. I am calling you to find out if Bette Midler would be interested in doing . . . ?" Edelstein: "Is it a commercial?" "Yes." "We are not interested."

Undeterred, Young & Rubicam sought out Ula Hedwig whom it knew to have been one of "the Harlettes" a backup singer for Midler for ten years. Hedwig was told by Young & Rubicam that "they wanted someone who could sound like Bette Midler's recording of [Do You Want To Dance]." She was asked to make a "demo" tape of the song if she was interested. She made an a capella demo and got the job.

At the direction of Young & Rubicam, Hedwig then made a record for the commercial. The Midler record of "Do You Want To Dance" was first played to her. She was told to "sound as much as possible like the Bette Midler record," leaving out only a few "aahs" unsuitable for the commercial. Hedwig imitated Midler to the best of her ability.

After the commercial was aired Midler was told by "a number of people" that it "sounded exactly" like her record of "Do You Want To Dance." Hedwig was told by "many personal friends" that they thought it was Midler singing the commercial. Ken Fritz, a personal manager in the entertainment business not associated with Midler, declares by affidavit that he heard the commercial on more than one occasion and thought Midler was doing the singing.

Neither the name nor the picture of Midler was used in the commercial; Young & Rubicam had a license from the copyright holder to use the song. At issue in this case is only the protection of Midler's voice. The district court described the defendants' conduct as that "of the average thief." They decided, "If we can't buy it, we'll take it." The court nonetheless believed there was no legal principle preventing imitation of Midler's voice and so gave summary judgment for the defendants. Midler appeals.

The First Amendment protects much of what the media do in the reproduction of likenesses or sounds. A primary value is freedom of speech and press. *Time, Inc. v. Hill*, 385 U.S. 374, 388, 87 S. Ct. 534, 17 L. Ed. 2d 456 (1967). The purpose of the media's use of a person's identity is central. If the purpose is "informative or cultural" the use is immune; "if it serves no such function but merely exploits the individual portrayed, immunity will not be granted." Felcher and Rubin, *"Privacy, Publicity and the Portrayal of Real People by the Media"* 88 Yale L.J. 1577, 1596 (1979). Moreover, federal copyright law preempts much of the area. "Mere imitation of a recorded performance would not constitute a copyright infringement even where one performer deliberately sets out to simulate another's performance as exactly as possible." Notes of Committee on the Judiciary, 17 U.S.C.A. § 114(b). It is in the context of these First Amendment and federal copyright distinctions that we address the present appeal.

Nancy Sinatra once sued Goodyear Tire and Rubber Company on the basis of an advertising campaign by Young & Rubicam featuring "These Boots Are Made For Walkin'," a song closely identified with her; the female singers of the commercial were alleged to have imitated her voice and style and to have dressed and looked like her. The basis of Nancy Sinatra's complaint was unfair competition; she claimed that the song and the arrangement had acquired "a secondary meaning" which, under California law, was protectible. This court noted that the defendants "had paid a very substantial sum to the copyright proprietor to obtain the license for the use of the song and all of its arrangements." To give Sinatra damages for their use of the song would clash with federal copyright law. Summary judgment for the defendants was affirmed. If Midler were claiming a secondary meaning to "Do You Want To Dance" or seeking to prevent the defendants from using that song, she would fail like Sinatra. But that is not this case. Midler does not seek damages for Ford's use of "Do You Want To Dance," and thus her claim is not preempted by federal copyright law. Copyright protects "original works of authorship fixed in any tangible medium of expression." 17 U.S.C. § 102(a). A voice is not copyright-able. The sounds are not "fixed." What is put forward as protectible here is more personal than any work of authorship.

Bert Lahr once sued Adell Chemical Co. for selling Lestoil by means of a commercial in which an imitation of Lahr's voice accompanied a cartoon of a duck.

Lahr alleged that his style of vocal delivery was distinctive in pitch, accent, inflection, and sounds. The First Circuit held that Lahr had stated a cause of action for unfair competition, that it could be found "that defendant's conduct saturated plaintiff's audience, curtailing his market." That case is more like this one. But we do not find unfair competition here. One-minute commercials of the sort the defendants put on would not have saturated Midler's audience and curtailed her market. Midler did not do television commercials. The defendants were not in competition with her.

California Civil Code section 3344 is also of no aid to Midler. The statute affords damages to a person injured by another who uses the person's "name, voice, signature, photograph or likeness, in any manner." The defendants did not use Midler's name or anything else whose use is prohibited by the statute. The voice they used was Hedwig's, not hers. The term "likeness" refers to a visual image not a vocal imitation. The statute, however, does not preclude Midler from pursuing any cause of action she may have at common law; the statute itself implies that such common law causes of action do exist because it says its remedies are merely "cumulative." *Id.* § 3344(g).

The companion statute protecting the use of a deceased person's name, voice, signature, photograph or likeness states that the rights it recognizes are "property rights." *Id.* § 990(b). By analogy the common law rights are also property rights. Appropriation of such common law rights is a tort in California. *Motschenbacher v. R.J. Reynolds Tobacco Co.*, 498 F.2d 821 (9th Cir. 1974). In that case what the defendants used in their television commercial for Winston cigarettes was a photograph of a famous professional racing driver's racing car. The number of the car was changed and a wing-like device known as a "spoiler" was attached to the car; the car's features of white pinpointing, an oval medallion, and solid red coloring were retained. The driver, Lothar Motschenbacher, was in the car but his features were not visible. Some persons, viewing the commercial, correctly inferred that the car was his and that he was in the car and was therefore endorsing the product. The defendants were held to have invaded a "proprietary interest" of Motschenbacher in his own identity. *Id.* at 825.

Midler's case is different from Motschenbacher's. He and his car were physically used by the tobacco company's ad; he made part of his living out of giving commercial endorsements. But, as Judge Koelsch expressed it in *Motschenbacher*, California will recognize an injury from "an appropriation of the attributes of one's identity." *Id.* at 824. It was irrelevant that Motschenbacher could not be identified in the ad. The ad suggested that it was he. The ad did so by emphasizing signs or symbols associated with him. In the same way the defendants here used an imitation to convey the impression that Midler was singing for them.

Why did the defendants ask Midler to sing if her voice was not of value to them? Why did they studiously acquire the services of a sound-alike and instruct her to imitate Midler if Midler's voice was not of value to them? What they sought was an attribute of Midler's identity. Its value was what the market would have paid for Midler to have sung the commercial in person.

A voice is more distinctive and more personal than the automobile accouterments protected in *Motschenbacher.* A voice is as distinctive and personal as a face. The human voice is one of the most palpable ways identity is manifested. We are all aware that a friend is at once known by a few words on the phone. At a philosophical level it has been observed that with the sound of a voice, "the other stands before me." D. Ihde, Listening and Voice 77 (1976). A fortiori, these observations hold true of singing, especially singing by a singer of renown. The singer manifests herself in the song. To impersonate her voice is to pirate her identity. *See* W. Keeton, D. Dobbs, R. Keeton, D. Owen, Prosser & Keeton on Torts 852 (5th ed. 1984).

We need not and do not go so far as to hold that every imitation of a voice to advertise merchandise is actionable. We hold only that when a distinctive voice of a professional singer is widely known and is deliberately imitated in order to sell a product, the sellers have appropriated what is not theirs and have committed a tort in California. Midler has made a showing, sufficient to defeat summary judgment, that the defendants here for their own profit in selling their product did appropriate part of her identity.

REVERSED AND REMANDED FOR TRIAL.

———————

1. Why no recovery in copyright? Why did Nancy Sinatra lose her case? Does the California Statute preclude Midler's suit?

2. If damages are the market value of Midler's voice, who won? Does this make a case for punitive damages?

3. What are the reasons for allowing an action for using pictures of Motschenbacher's racing car?

4. When are videos circulated on YouTube actionable?

WHITE v. SAMSUNG ELECTRONICS AMERICA, INC.
United States Court of Appeals for the Ninth Circuit, 1991
971 F.2d 1395, *amended*, 1992 U.S. App. LEXIS 19253 (9th Cir. Aug. 19, 1992), *cert. denied*, 508 U.S. 951 (1993)

GOODWIN, SENIOR CIRCUIT JUDGE:

This case involves a promotional "fame and fortune" dispute. In running a particular advertisement without Vanna White's permission, defendants Samsung Electronics America, Inc. (Samsung) and David Deutsch Associates, Inc. (Deutsch) attempted to capitalize on White's fame to enhance their fortune. White sued, alleging infringement of various intellectual property rights, but the district court granted summary judgment in favor of the defendants. We affirm in part, reverse in part, and remand.

Plaintiff Vanna White is the hostess of "Wheel of Fortune," one of the most popular game shows in television history. An estimated forty million people watch the program daily. Capitalizing on the fame which her participation in the show has bestowed on her, White markets her identity to various advertisers.

The dispute in this case arose out of a series of advertisements prepared for

Samsung by Deutsch. The series ran in at least half a dozen publications with widespread, and in some cases national, circulation. Each of the advertisements in the series followed the same theme. Each depicted a current item from popular culture and a Samsung electronic product. Each was set in the twenty-first century and conveyed the message that the Samsung product would still be in use by that time. By hypothesizing outrageous future outcomes for the cultural items, the ads created humorous effects. . . .

The advertisement which prompted the current dispute was for Samsung video-cassette recorders (VCRs). The ad depicted a robot, dressed in a wig, gown, and jewelry which Deutsch consciously selected to resemble White's hair and dress. The robot was posed next to a game board which is instantly recognizable as the Wheel of Fortune game show set, in a stance for which White is famous. The caption of the ad read: "Longest-running game show. 2012 A.D." Defendants referred to the ad as the "Vanna White" ad. Unlike the other celebrities used in the campaign, White neither consented to the ads nor was she paid.

Following the circulation of the robot ad, White sued Samsung and Deutsch in federal district court under: (1) California Civil Code § 3344; (2) the California common law right of publicity; and (3) § 43(a) of the Lanham Act, *15 U.S.C. § 1125(a)*. The district court granted summary judgment against White on each of her claims. White now appeals.

I. *Section 3344*

. . . Section 3344(a) provides, in pertinent part, that "any person who knowingly uses another's name, voice, signature, photograph, or likeness, in any manner, . . . for purposes of advertising or selling, . . . without such person's prior consent . . . shall be liable for any damages sustained by the person or persons injured as a result thereof."

White argues that the Samsung advertisement used her "likeness" in contravention of section 3344. In *Midler v. Ford Motor Co.*, 849 F.2d 460 (9th Cir. 1988), this court rejected Bette Midler's section 3344 claim concerning a Ford television commercial in which a Midler "sound-alike" sang a song which Midler had made famous. In rejecting Midler's claim, this court noted that "the defendants did not use Midler's name or anything else whose use is prohibited by the statute. The voice they used was [another person's], not hers. The term likeness' refers to a visual image not a vocal imitation." *Id.* at 463.

In this case, Samsung and Deutsch used a robot with mechanical features, and not, for example, a manikin molded to White's precise features. Without deciding for all purposes when a caricature or impressionistic resemblance might become a "likeness," we agree with the district court that the robot at issue here was not White's "likeness" within the meaning of section 3344. Accordingly, we affirm the court's dismissal of White's section 3344 claim.

II. *Right of Publicity*

White next argues that the district court erred in granting summary judgment to defendants on White's common law right of publicity claim. In *Eastwood v. Superior Court*, 149 Cal. App. 3d 409, 198 Cal. Rptr. 342 (1983), the California court of appeal stated that the common law right of publicity cause of action "may be pleaded by alleging (1) the defendant's use of the plaintiff's identity; (2) the appropriation of plaintiff's name or likeness to defendant's advantage, commercially or otherwise; (3) lack of consent; and (4) resulting injury." *Id.* at 417 (citing Prosser, Law of Torts (4th ed. 1971) § 117, pp. 804-807). The district court dismissed White's claim for failure to satisfy *Eastwood's* second prong, reasoning that defendants had not appropriated White's "name or likeness" with their robot ad. We agree that the robot ad did not make use of White's name or likeness. However, the common law right of publicity is not so confined.

. . . .

The "name or likeness" formulation referred to in *Eastwood* originated not as an element of the right of publicity cause of action, but as a description of the types of cases in which the cause of action had been recognized. The source of this formulation is Prosser, *Privacy*, 48 Cal.L.Rev. 383, 401-07 (1960), one of the earliest and most enduring articulations of the common law right of publicity cause of action. In looking at the case law to that point, Prosser recognized that right of publicity cases involved one of two basic factual scenarios: name appropriation, and picture or other likeness appropriation. *Id.* at 401-02, nn. 156-57.

Even though Prosser focused on appropriations of name or likeness in discussing the right of publicity, he noted that "it is not impossible that there might be appropriation of the plaintiff's identity, as by impersonation, without the use of either his name or his likeness, and that this would be an invasion of his right of privacy." *Id.* at 401, n.155. At the time Prosser wrote, he noted however, that "no such case appears to have arisen." *Id.*

Since Prosser's early formulation, the case law has borne out his insight that the right of publicity is not limited to the appropriation of name or likeness. In *Motschenbacher v. R.J. Reynolds Tobacco Co.*, 498 F.2d 821 (9th Cir. 1974), the defendant had used a photograph of the plaintiff's race car in a television commercial. Although the plaintiff appeared driving the car in the photograph, his features were not visible. Even though the defendant had not appropriated the plaintiff's name or likeness, this court held that plaintiff's California right of publicity claim should reach the jury.

In *Midler*, this court held that, even though the defendants had not used Midler's name or likeness, Midler had stated a claim for violation of her California common law right of publicity because "the defendants . . . for their own profit in selling their product did appropriate part of her identity" by using a Midler sound-alike. *Id.* at 463-64.

In *Carson v. Here's Johnny Portable Toilets, Inc.*, 698 F.2d 831 (6th Cir. 1983), the defendant had marketed portable toilets under the brand name "Here's Johnny" — Johnny Carson's signature "Tonight Show" introduction — without Carson's permission. The district court had dismissed Carson's Michigan common law right of publicity claim because the defendants had not used Carson's "name or likeness." *Id.* at 835. In reversing the district court, the sixth circuit found "the district court's conception of the right of publicity . . . too narrow" and held that the right was implicated because the defendant had appropriated Carson's identity by using, *inter alia*, the phrase "Here's Johnny." *Id.* at 835-37.

. . . .

Viewed separately, the individual aspects of the advertisement in the present case say little. Viewed together, they leave little doubt about the celebrity the ad is meant to depict. The female-shaped robot is wearing a long gown, blond wig, and large jewelry. Vanna White dresses exactly like this at times, but so do many other women. The robot is in the process of turning a block letter on a game-board. Vanna White dresses like this while turning letters on a game-board but perhaps similarly attired Scrabble-playing women do this as well. The robot is standing on what looks to be the Wheel of Fortune game show set. Vanna White dresses like this, turns letters, and does this on the Wheel of Fortune game show. She is the only one. Indeed, defendants themselves referred to their ad as the "Vanna White" ad. We are not surprised.

Television and other media create marketable celebrity identity value. Considerable energy and ingenuity are expended by those who have achieved celebrity value to exploit it for profit. The law protects the celebrity's sole right to exploit this value whether the celebrity has achieved her fame out of rare ability, dumb luck, or a combination thereof. We decline Samsung and Deutch's invitation to permit the evisceration of the common law right of publicity through means as facile as those in this case. Because White has alleged facts showing that Samsung and Deutsch had appropriated her identity, the district court erred by rejecting, on summary judgment, White's common law right of publicity claim.

. . . .

IV. *The Parody Defense*

In defense, defendants cite a number of cases for the proposition that their robot ad constituted protected speech. The only cases they cite which are even remotely relevant to this case are *Hustler Magazine v. Falwell*, 485 U.S. 46, 108 S. Ct. 876, 99 L. Ed. 2d 41 (1988) and *L.L. Bean, Inc. v. Drake Publishers, Inc.*, 811 F.2d 26 (1st Cir. 1987). Those cases involved parodies of advertisements run for the purpose of poking fun at Jerry Falwell and L.L. Bean, respectively. This case involves a true advertisement run for the purpose of selling Samsung VCRs. The ad's spoof of Vanna White and Wheel of Fortune is subservient and only tangentially related to the ad's primary message: "buy Samsung VCRs." Defendants' parody arguments are better addressed to non-commercial parodies. The difference between a "parody" and a "knock-off is the difference between fun and profit.

V. *Conclusion*

In remanding this case, we hold only that White has pleaded claims which can go to the jury for its decision.

AFFIRMED IN PART, REVERSED IN PART, and REMANDED.

---

1.   Where is the privacy case if the robot was "not in White's likeness"?

2.   What is the problem with the parody defense?

3.   In *Cardtoons v. Major League Baseball Players Ass'n*, 95 F.3d 959 (10th Cir. 1996):

> Cardtoons . . . brought this action to obtain a declaratory judgment that its parody trading cards featuring active major league baseball players do not infringe on the publicity rights of members of the Major League Baseball Players Association ("MLBPA"). The district court held that the trading cards constitute expression protected by the First Amendment and therefore read a parody exception into Oklahoma's statutory right of publicity. MLBPA appeals, arguing that . . . Cardtoons does not have a First Amendment right to market its trading cards. . . . Because Cardtoons' First Amendment right to free expression outweighs MLBPA's proprietary right of publicity, we affirm.

> Cardtoons [was] formed in late 1992 to produce parody trading cards featuring caricatures of major league baseball players. Cardtoons contracted with a political cartoonist, a sports artist, and a sports author and journalist, who designed a set of 130 cards. The majority of the cards, 71, have caricatures of active major league baseball players on the front and humorous commentary about their careers on the back. The balance of the set is comprised of 20 "Big Bang Bucks" cards (cartoon drawings of currency with caricatures of the most highly paid players on the front, yearly salary statistics on the back), 10 "Spectra" cards (caricatures of active players on the front, nothing on the back), 10 retired player cards (caricatures of retired players on the front, humorous commentary about their careers on the back), 10 "Politics in Baseball" cards (cartoons featuring caricatures of political and sports figures on the front, humorous text on the back), 7 standing cards (caricatures of team logos on the front, humorous text on the back), and 1 checklist card. Except for the Spectra cards, the back of each card bears the Cardtoons logo and the following statement: "Cardtoons baseball is a parody and is NOT licensed by Major League Baseball Properties or Major League Baseball Players Association."

>   . . . .

> Cardtoons' parody trading cards receive full protection under the First Amendment. The cards provide social commentary on public figures, major league baseball players, who are involved in a significant commercial enterprise and major league baseball. While not core political speech (the cards do not, for example, adopt a position on the Ken Griffey, Jr., for President campaign), this type of commentary on an important social institution constitutes protected expression.

Why is the "parody" protected in *Cardtoons*, but not in *White*? Aren't both commercial?

4. In *ETW Corp. v. Jireh Publishing, Inc.*, 332 F.3d 915 (6th Cir. 2003), the court held that defendant's marketing of an artistic print featuring the likeness of professional golfer Tiger Woods at the Masters golf tournament was protected by the First Amendment from a right of publicity claim. The court reasoned that the artist's rendition contained "significant transformative elements" which made it "especially worthy of First Amendment protection and also less likely to interfere with the economic interest protected by Woods' right of publicity." Over a strong dissent, the court both distinguished and noted its disagreement with much of the reasoning in *White*.

Chapter 18

MISREPRESENTATION

The tort of misrepresentation ranges from intentional misrepresentation (fraud) through negligent misrepresentation to innocent misrepresentation, in which the defendant has acted neither fraudulently nor negligently. Issues include the affirmative duty (if any) to disclose information, the obligation of the buyer in a business transaction to look after his or her own interests (caveat emptor), and the general aura of the transactions involved. Courts are reluctant to assist litigants in conduct that looks suspicious, and misrepresentation is a useful tool to combat unethical sellers.

BORTZ v. NOON
Supreme Court of Pennsylvania, 1999
729 A.2d 555

NEWMAN, JUSTICE.

This is an appeal by Coldwell Banker Real Estate (Coldwell Banker) from an Order of the Superior Court, which affirmed the determination of the Court of Common Pleas of Allegheny County (Chancellor). Coldwell Banker was held liable to the buyer of residential property for a misrepresentation made by its agent relating to a third party's repairs of the on-site sewage disposal system (septic system) located on the property. Coldwell Banker raises the sole issue of whether the actions of its agent amounted to fraudulent misrepresentation. For the reasons that follow, we reverse the Superior Court and hold that a real estate broker cannot be liable for the misrepresentation of its agent, innocently made, under circumstances where the agent had no reason to know that her statement was false, and the agent had no duty to verify the accuracy of the third party report.

I. FACTS

On July 27, 1986, Albert M. Bortz (the Buyer) and his former wife entered into an Agreement of Sale with Patrick J. Noon and Virginia R. Noon (collectively Sellers), to buy the Sellers' home on Woodland Road in Pittsburgh, Pennsylvania. Coldwell Banker, through its agent, Renee Valent (the Agent), was the selling agent for the property. The Buyer had used the Agent as a selling agent for his previous home, and testified at the hearing of this matter that he considered the Agent as his representative for the Woodland Road transaction. For the purchase of the Woodland Road home, the Agent referred the Buyer to a lender, Coldwell Banker Residential Mortgage Services, Inc. (the Lender). There is no evidence to suggest that the Lender was affiliated with Coldwell Banker. For the Buyer to receive a mortgage commitment from the Lender, the septic system had to pass a dye test before closing, and the Agent informed the Buyer that the septic system needed to pass this test before the closing. The Agent referred the Buyer to a contractor to conduct the test. On August 14, 1986, the contractor performed the dye test, and the septic system failed. The contractor told the Agent that the septic system failed the dye test and the Agent then informed the Buyer. The Agent did not give the Buyer a copy of this report, and apparently, the Buyer did not ask for one.

Following the failed dye test, the Agent told the Buyer that the Sellers had the option of repairing the septic system, and they had chosen another contractor, J.J. Nolte (Nolte), to do the work. There is no evidence that the Agent had any dealings with Nolte nor played any part in the selection of Nolte as a contractor. The Agent informed the Buyer that settlement would be delayed until a dye test was successful. The Buyer argues that the Agent represented to him that the problem with the septic system would be repaired. During the period that Nolte was working on the septic system, the Buyer and his father-in-law went to the home, observed Nolte, and seemingly had the opportunity to ask questions about the repairs to the septic system.

At some point in September of 1986, a woman from Suburban Settlement Services, Inc. (the Title Company) told the Agent that "the dye test passed and now we can set closing." The Agent conveyed this information to the Buyer, and then set a settlement closing date. Neither the Agent nor the Buyer reviewed a written Nolte report evidencing a satisfactory dye test. The closing on the house was on September 26, 1986, at the offices of the Title Company, but apparently, the proceedings were delayed for ten to twenty minutes. The Agent believed that the closing was delayed because of "Mr. Nolte's inspection — you know, everything was supposed to be fine a week before the closing, so I assume they had this paperwork." In addition, the Agent testified that she believed that the County was inspecting Nolte's work on the day of closing, and she in turn told the Buyer that the County would inspect the septic system.

When the closing finally occurred, the settlement officer from the Title Company, Christopher Abernathy, told everyone present, including the Agent and the Buyer, that the dye test on the septic system had passed. Apparently, however, neither the Agent nor the Buyer was given any written materials to verify this statement, and neither asked to review the report. Following the closing, the Buyer and his former wife discovered that the septic tank had not actually passed a dye test. In fact, the former wife of the Buyer testified that she received a call from the Title Company and was advised that it had "forgotten to do the dye test." (7/5/94 N.T. at 106) The Title Company then scheduled a new dye test for October 22, 1986. The septic system failed the test and the system could not be repaired. The only alternative was to connect into the public sewer system at a cost of more than $15,000.

In an equity proceeding, the Buyer then sued Coldwell Banker, the Title Company, and the Sellers seeking monetary damages and recision [sic] of the Agreement of Sale. The Buyer claimed that all defendants made affirmative misstatements regarding repairs on the septic system and reported that the septic system was functioning properly. The Sellers joined Nolte. After a hearing in the matter, the Chancellor entered an order in favor of the Buyer, and against Coldwell Banker, concluding that Coldwell Banker, "through [its agent], made material misrepresentations to [the Buyer] by failing to disclose the conflicting septic test results and making affirmative representations that the septic system was repaired and properly functioning." The Chancellor denied a recision [sic] of the sale, but entered a decree nisi in favor of the Buyer and against Coldwell Banker for $15,300 plus pre-judgment interest. The Chancellor held that neither Nolte nor the Title Company owed a duty to the Buyer and thus could not be liable for misrepresentation. Coldwell Banker filed motions for post-trial relief, alleging that it could not be liable for misrepresentation, which the trial court denied. Coldwell Banker then filed an appeal to the Superior Court.

On the appeal of Coldwell Banker, the Superior Court affirmed in part and reversed in part the decision of the Chancellor. The Superior Court agreed with the conclusion of the Chancellor that Coldwell Banker was liable to the Buyer for misrepresentation because the Agent had a duty to ascertain whether the septic system had actually passed the dye test, and her failure to do so constituted a misrepresentation under the circumstances of this case. However, the Superior Court reversed the finding of the Chancellor regarding Nolte and the Title Company, and held that both could be liable to the Buyer for misrepresentation. Judge Johnson dissented. While Judge Johnson agreed that Nolte and the Title Company were liable to the Buyer for misrepresentation, he disagreed that Coldwell Banker was liable.

We granted allocatur limited to the question of whether the Superior Court was correct in its conclusions that the Agent had a duty to ascertain whether the septic system had actually passed the dye test and if her failure to do so amounted to a misrepresentation to the Buyer. There is no appeal docketed regarding the determination of the Superior Court that Nolte and the Title Company owed a duty to the Buyer, and we do not address that portion of the Superior Court's opinion in this appeal.

II. ANALYSIS

Coldwell Banker argues that it cannot be liable for fraudulent misrepresentation because the Agent made no affirmative misrepresentation, she had no duty to disclose Nolte's reports, and she had no knowledge that the septic system was not working properly. Coldwell Banker further asserts that at most the Agent made a statement concerning a future event that the septic system *would be* repaired, a statement that can not support a cause of action for fraudulent misrepresentation.

The Buyer counters that the Agent indeed misrepresented material facts when she misrepresented that the dye test was clear, *coupled with* a promise of a future event that the septic system would pass a dye test and function properly before closing. Moreover, she scheduled and attended the closing; failed to advise the Buyer that she was unaware of whether the original representation was actually true; and failed to ascertain whether the facts originally represented continued to be true. Thus, the Agent is liable for misrepresenting a material fact on which the Buyer relied in closing on the property. Therefore, she had a duty both to correct this misrepresentation and to disclose the report of Nolte to the Buyer.

. . . .

[T]he issues before us concern whether the record reasonably reflects the Chancellor's finding that the Agent made an affirmative misrepresentation and whether the Chancellor correctly determined that Coldwell Banker could be legally liable, under the circumstances of this case. We will analyze this matter first to determine whether the record supports the Chancellor's conclusion that the Agent made affirmative statements and second to decide whether Coldwell Banker is legally liable for any misrepresentation of the Agent, including whether she had a duty to disclose the written report of Nolte.

A. FACT FINDING OF THE CHANCELLOR:

After a hearing in this matter, the Chancellor found that the Agent made "affirmative misrepresentations that the septic system was repaired and properly functioning." A review of the record reasonably reflects this conclusion. In particular, the Agent testified that in the days preceding the closing, she told the Buyer that the septic system had passed the dye test. This representation was not accurate, and was followed by conduct that reinforced the affirmative statement that the septic system had passed the dye test. The Agent set up the closing date, which strengthened the perception that the septic system was acceptable because the mortgage could not be approved without such a test. Additionally, at the closing, the proceedings were delayed on the assumption the dye test information was delivered to the closing. These acts, together with the affirmative statement of the Agent before the closing, support the determination of the Chancellor that the Agent made an affirmative misrepresentation. We now turn to the question of whether, under the facts presented here, the Agent had a duty to disclose the written report and whether the law in this Commonwealth allows the Buyer to recover against Coldwell Banker for the Agent's affirmative misrepresentation regarding the dye test.

B. LEGAL LIABILITY FOR MISREPRESENTATION:

Generally, a misrepresentation may be actionable pursuant to three theories: Intentional Misrepresentation, Negligent Misrepresentation, and Innocent Misrepresentation.

1. Intentional Misrepresentation:

The elements of intentional misrepresentation are as follows:

(1) A representation;

(2) which is material to the transaction at hand;

(3) made falsely, with knowledge of its falsity or recklessness as to whether it is true or false;

(4) with the intent of misleading another into relying on it;

(5) justifiable reliance on the misrepresentation; and,

(6) the resulting injury was proximately caused by the reliance.

Gibbs v. Ernst, 538 Pa. 193, 207, 647 A.2d 882, 889 (1994), *citing*, Restatement (Second) of Torts § 525 (1977). The tort of intentional non-disclosure has the same elements as intentional misrepresentation "except in the case of intentional non-disclosure, the party intentionally conceals a material fact rather than making an affirmative misrepresentation." *Id.* We have recognized the tort of intentional misrepresentation and intentional concealment in the context of real estate broker liability to the buyer of residential property. *See, e.g., Aiello v. Ed Saxe Real Estate, Inc.*, 508 Pa. 553, 499 A.2d 282 (1985) (Real estate broker may be liable for intentional misrepresentation). *See also Highmont Music Corp. v. J.M. Hoffmann Co.*, 397 Pa. 345, 155 A.2d 363 (1959) (recision [sic] of sale appropriate where the agent intentionally failed to disclose latent defects in real estate).

Here, there is no evidence supporting a conclusion that the Agent intentionally misrepresented any facts to the Buyer, nor intended to deceive the Buyer by failing to give him copies of the septic system reports, which she herself did not have. While the Agent made an affirmative misrepresentation that the dye test was clear, there is no finding that the Agent made any misrepresentation with knowledge that it was false. Instead, the Agent was giving information to the Buyer that she received from the Title Company, an apparently reputable company, so that she could schedule the closing. The Agent had no agency relationship with the Title Company or Nolte, and she had not selected Nolte to perform the septic tank repairs nor asked him to do the dye test. The Chancellor did not find that the Agent acted with knowledge that the septic tank had not passed the dye test, nor that she acted recklessly. Moreover, there was no evidence in the record that the Agent intended to mislead the Buyer in any way, a required element of intentional misrepresentation. *Gibbs*, 538 Pa. at 207, 647 A.2d at 889; *Reichert's Estate*, 356 Pa. 269, 271, 51 A.2d 615, 616 (1947) ("fraud consists in anything calculated to deceive"). Thus, the Record does not support any conclusion that the Agent could be liable to the Buyer for an intentional fraudulent misrepresentation or concealment.

2. Negligent Misrepresentation:

Negligent misrepresentation requires proof of: (1) a misrepresentation of a material fact; (2) made under circumstances in which the misrepresenter ought to have known its falsity; (3) with an intent to induce another to act on it; and; (4) which results in injury to a party acting in justifiable reliance on the misrepresentation. *See, e.g., Gibbs*, 538 Pa. at 210, 647 A.2d at 890, *citing*, Restatement (Second) Torts § 552. The elements of negligent misrepresentation differ from intentional misrepresentation in that the misrepresentation must concern a material fact and the speaker need not know his or her words are untrue, but must have failed to make a reasonable investigation of the truth of these words. *Id.* Moreover, like any action in negligence, there must be an existence of a duty owed by one party to another. *Id.* This Court has not specifically recognized this cause of action in the situation of a real estate broker, but the Superior Court has applied a negligence standard in a number of cases. *See, e.g., Sevin v. Kelshaw*, 417 Pa. Super. 1, 611 A.2d 1232 (1992);[5]

---

[5] In *Kelshaw*, the court held that a real estate broker was not liable for negligent misrepresentation

Smith v. Renaut, 387 Pa. Super. 299, 564 A.2d 188 (1989);[6] *Slaybaugh v. Newman*, 330 Pa. Super. 216, 479 A.2d 517 (1984);[7] *Long v. Brownstone Real Estate Co.*, 335 Pa. Super. 268, 484 A.2d 126 (1984);[8] *Glanski v. Ervine*, 269 Pa. Super. 182, 409 A.2d 425 (1979).[9]

Moreover, many other states recognize that a real estate broker may be liable for negligent misrepresentations when the broker fails to use reasonable care in ascertaining the truth of a representation. *See, e.g., Mahler v. Keenan Real Estate, Inc.*, 255 Kan. 593, 876 P.2d 609 (1994); *Teter v. Old Colony Company*, 190 W. Va. 711, 441 S.E.2d 728 (1994); *Hoffman v. Connall*, 108 Wash. 2d 69, 736 P.2d 242 (1987); *Menzel v. Morse*, 362 N.W.2d 465 (Iowa 1985); *Gauerke v. Rozga*, 112 Wis. 2d 271, 332 N.W.2d 804 (1983); *Hagar u. Mobley*, 638 P.2d 127 (Wyo. 1981); *Prigge v. South Seventh Realty*, 97 Nev. 640, 637 P.2d 1222 (1981); *Berryman v. Riegert*, 286 Minn. 270, 175 N.W.2d 438 (1970). Generally, these courts have expanded liability of real estate brokers for failing independently to verify facts that the seller represents to the broker, and which the broker then passes on to the buyer. In these cases, the courts have found that because of the relationship among the buyer, seller, and broker, the broker is in a better position to verify the statements of the seller than is the buyer. *See, e.g., Hoffman v. Connall*, 736 P.2d at 245.

Here, neither the Chancellor nor the Superior Court specifically articulated the exact legal theory supporting their ultimate finding of liability. However, although not specifically labeled, it appears that both the Chancellor and the Superior Court found Coldwell Banker liable based upon either a negligent or innocent misrepresentation, for the Agent's misstatement to the Buyer that the septic system passed the dye test and for negligently failing to provide him with Nolte's written reports. In his Adjudication of the matter, the Chancellor discussed Section 323 of the Restatement (Second) of Torts, apparently concluding that the Agent had assumed a duty to the Buyer. In denying post-trial motions, the Chancellor opined that the Agent "so positioned [herself] as to be liable to the Buyer in money damages" and

---

for failing to disclose non-material facts about easement.

[6] In *Renaut*, the Superior Court held that "where a broker employed to sell real estate misrepresents or conceals a material fact, he may be found liable to the purchaser in damages." The issue in *Renaut* was whether the real estate broker was liable to the buyer of the property for misrepresenting the extent of termite damage in a home, and caused the buyer not to conduct an inspection of the premises. Also at issue was the existence of a carcinogen in the well. The Superior Court held that the broker could be liable for the failure to disclose termite damage, but not for the carcinogen. It appears from the facts presented in that opinion that the real estate broker was charged with knowing that the termite damage was actually more extensive than represented, and that the broker failed to disclose known damage. The broker could not have known about the carcinogen in the well, and was not liable for his failure to disclose it.

[7] In *Slaybaugh*, the court held that a real estate broker and salesmen owe a duty of candor towards buyers and other third parties and may be held accountable in damages by a third party purchaser for misrepresentation including the failure to disclose material information.

[8] In *Long*, a real estate broker was held liable to the purchaser for stating that the property was not subject to flooding, when there was evidence of previous flooding on the property.

[9] In *Glanski*, the Superior Court found that a real estate broker can be liable to the purchaser of real estate where the broker made a material misrepresentation regarding the lack of termite damage and the broker was duty bound to determine otherwise, where the seller admitted that seller knew of termite damage.

"had the duty to be sure that when the closing of title occurred the circumstances conformed with the Buyer's expectations or risk the consequences." He also determined that the Agent:

> took no action to be sure that the Nolte report was, in fact, a 'clear septic test'. . . . It was careless (or worse) of Valent to either rely wholly on Abernathy's interpretation of the report, and not to examine it herself . . . At the very least, Valent should have seen to it that Bortz had both the Ross and Nolte reports available for his review. Valent did none of the above and proceeded in reckless disregard of the expectations and attendant rights of Bortz.

The Superior Court essentially agreed with the Chancellor and determined that the Agent and Coldwell Banker were liable to the Buyer because the Agent had a duty to make an independent inquiry to determine whether the septic tank actually had passed the dye test, by reviewing either the report herself, or checking County records.

While we recognize that there is no reason to *per se* omit a real estate broker or its agent from liability for negligence or misrepresentations negligently made, a reasonable review of the record in this matter does not support the conclusion that the Agent made a negligent misrepresentation, or negligently failed to disclose the Nolte report, because there is not an adequate record of evidence to support a conclusion that the Agent had a duty to investigate the accuracy of the dye test, or that she had a duty to provide the Buyer with a written copy of Nolte's report. First, there was no testimony or introduction of other evidence to establish that in 1986, the standard of care in the real estate brokerage business required an agent independently to verify or disclose test results that the broker had not ordered and were not part of the sales purchase agreement. Second, under the circumstances of this case, the Agent would have no reason to know that the representatives from the Title Company failed to confirm that the dye test was properly executed, before telling her that the test was clean. Third, there was no special relationship among the Buyer, the Agent, the Title Company and the Lender that would require the Agent to undertake such investigation, or that would place the Agent in a superior position to the Buyer in verifying the accuracy of the third party reports of the dye test. *See, e.g., Morena v. South Hills Health System*, 501 Pa. 634, 462 A.2d 680 (1983) (predicating duty on relationship between parties at relevant time, which necessarily requires some degree of knowledge). The dye test was part of the requirement of the Lender's mortgage and it was the Title Company that on two occasions misrepresented facts to both the Agent and the Buyer that the dye test was clear.

The Agent was not acting as a source of information from Sellers or other entity with whom she had an agency relationship and which might then trigger a duty to physically transfer the reports to the Buyer and verify the accuracy of statements that were material to the sales transaction. *See, e.g., Aiello v. Ed Saxe Real Estate*, 508 Pa. at 557-59, 499 A.2d at 284-85 (discussing generally liability of principal and agents in context of real estate agency). She had not assumed the duty of arranging, verifying or investigating the test, and did not act with the pretense of knowledge that the dye test was in fact clear. Instead, the Agent acted as the innocent conduit of information from an apparently reliable source, who said that the dye test was "clear," and the Agent repeated this statement solely in the context of scheduling the closing.

While the Agent did state to the Buyer that there was a clean septic dye test, she had no knowledge to the contrary and she did not know that the representative from the Title Company was providing misinformation. There was nothing in the relationship among the parties that would place the Agent on notice that the information was incorrect and she had no duty to engage in any independent inquiry. There is no record evidence that the Agent had specialized knowledge of septic systems, that she pretended to have such knowledge, or that she assumed the obligation of guaranteeing or providing this information to the Buyer.

We believe that imposing upon the Agent the duty to investigate, in the unique circumstance of this case, would place too high a burden on real estate agents. It would be an unreasonable burden on them because it would make it their responsibility to guarantee the accuracy of pre-closing tests done by persons with whom they have no relationship. Thus, we hold that a real estate broker has no duty to make an independent investigation of a contractor's report, where the real estate broker did not have any agency or contractual relationship with the third party.

3. Innocent Misrepresentation:

A claim for an "innocent" misrepresentation has been recognized in this Commonwealth in order to rescind a real estate transaction that is based upon a material misrepresentation, even if the misrepresentation is innocently made. However, we have found no cases in which this Court adopted this theory as a basis to award monetary damages for tort recovery. *See, e.g., De Joseph v. Zambelli*, 392 Pa. 24, 139 A.2d 644 (1958); *La Course v. Kiesel*, 366 Pa. 385, 77 A.2d 877 (1951). In *De Joseph*, we set aside a sale because of termite infestation that was concealed from the purchaser. We formulated the cause of action for fraud as follows:

> Where a party is induced to enter into a transaction with another by means of the latter's fraud or material misrepresentation; such a transaction can be avoided by the innocent party. Fraud arises where the misrepresentation is knowingly false, where there is concealment calculated to deceive, or where there is non-privileged failure to disclose. Fraud renders a transaction voidable even where the misrepresentation is not material; *on the other hand, a misrepresentation made innocently is not actionable unless it is material, and in such case there must be a right to reliance.*

139 A.2d at 647 (Emphasis added).

In *La Course v. Kiesel*, 366 Pa. 385, 77 A.2d 877(1951), we also set aside a sale, although neither the seller nor the real estate broker intentionally misrepresented facts to the buyer. In *La Course*, the sellers of real estate engaged an auction company to act as their agent in advertising and selling real estate. One of the sellers told the broker that the property was zoned R-5, which permitted apartments, and the broker advertised the property as "splendid for apartments." Prospective buyers entered an agreement of sale for the property and then learned that the building lot was not appropriately zoned for apartments. They thus sought an action in equity to cancel the agreement of sale and for a return of their deposit money. The Chancellor entered an Order in favor of the buyers. This Court affirmed although there was no evidence that either the brokers or the owners knew of the restriction on the zoning. We held that:

> whether the auctioneer or owners knew that the representation was false has been repeatedly held in this jurisdiction to be a matter of no consequence. A vendor has no right to make a statement of which he has no knowledge.
>
> . . . .
>
> A material misrepresentation of an existing fact confers on the party who relies on it the right to rescind whether the defendant here actually knew the truth or not, especially where as here, they had means of knowledge from which they were bound to ascertain the truth before making the representation.

366 Pa. at 388, 389, 77 A.2d at 879, 880. *See also, Boyle v. Odell*, 413 Pa. Super. 562, 605 A.2d 1260 (1992).[11]

A claim for a misrepresentation, innocently made, to the extent recognized in this Commonwealth, is an equitable doctrine based upon contract principles supporting equitable recision [sic] to make a contract voidable by the innocent party, where appropriate, as set forth in *De Joseph, supra* and *La Course, supra.* Here, we have not been asked to address the issue of whether this doctrine was viable here, because the Chancellor denied recision [sic], and that determination was not appealed. However, we decline to extend these equitable principles to establish legal tort liability for an innocent misrepresentation of the Agent, where she had no duty to ascertain the accuracy of test results of a third party with whom she had no agency or other relationship. Such strict liability would place too high a burden on the real estate broker.

III. CONCLUSION

For the reasons set forth in this Opinion, we reverse the Superior Court's determination and hold that Coldwell Banker is not liable to the Buyer for the affirmative misrepresentations of the Agent. The remainder of the Superior Court's Opinion governing the liability of the Title Company and Nolte was not at issue in this appeal.

---

[11] In *Boyle*, a right of first refusal had been granted by seller's mother to neighboring property owners. After the seller's mother was deceased, seller sold property to the buyers, without knowledge of the right of refusal to the third party. The Superior Court determined that even though seller did not know of a right of first refusal, the buyers were entitled to recision of the sale because "fraud may be established where there is a misrepresentation, innocently made, but relating to a matter material to the transaction involved."

SAYLOR, JUSTICE, concurring.

I agree with the majority that the factual findings made by the trial court in this case do not support imposition of liability upon Coldwell Banker and therefore concur in the result. I am unable, however, to subscribe to the majority's broad holding that, absent a contractual relationship, a real estate broker has no legal duty to verify factual representations made to a purchaser. In the typical residential real estate transaction, the selling broker, having a pecuniary interest in the consummation of a sale, frequently cultivates reliance by the purchaser upon its professional expertise, representing itself as an accurate source of vital information. *See generally* P. Murray, *The Real Estate Broker and the Buyer: Negligence and the Duty to Investigate*, Vill. L. Rev. 939, 984 (Sep. 1987). It would seem unjust to permit brokers to profit from such arrangements, yet escape any accountability to the purchaser for negligent conduct for the sole reason that their relationship with the buyer is not based in contract. Indeed, as the majority acknowledges, many jurisdictions authorize a cause of action for negligent misrepresentation against a real estate broker without requiring a demonstration of privity. *See, e.g., Mahler v. Keenan Real Estate, Inc.*, 255 Kan. 593, 876 P.2d 609, 616-17 (Kan. 1994). *See generally* Restatement (Second) of Torts § 552 (providing that one who, in the course of his business, profession or employment supplies false information for the guidance of others in their business transactions, is subject to liability for pecuniary loss caused to them by their justifiable reliance upon the information, if he fails to exercise reasonable care or competence in obtaining or communicating the information); Annotation, "Real-Estate Broker's Liability to Purchaser for Misrepresentation or Nondisclosure of Physical Defects in Property Sold," 46 A.L.R. 4th 546 (Supp. 1998); Prosser & Keeton on the Law of Torts, § 107, at 746 (5th ed. 1984) (stating that "[n]o doubt virtually all courts today would recognize the existence of some situations where the nature of a representer's activity or a pre-existing relationship between the representer and the representee or the two factors together will constitute the basis for the imposition of a duty to exercise reasonable care to avoid harm from reasonable and expectable reliance on what is said at least about certain matters related to the subject matter of the transaction").

Thus, I would not foreclose a cause of action against a broker that negligently provides false material information to a purchaser, represents such information to be true, and induces the purchaser to rely upon the information to his detriment.

––––––––––

1.   What is the duty of the seller's real estate agent (the listing agent) to the buyer? Historically, the listing agent has been viewed as working for the seller, and as having no duty to the buyer. How can confusion in this respect be avoided?

2.   *Bilt-Rite Contractors, Inc. v. Architectural Studio*, 866 A.2d 270 (Pa. 2005), held that a general contractor on a public construction project could sue the project's architect for economic loss based on negligent misrepresentation, despite the absence of contract privity between the architect and the general contractor. How is this different from the real estate setting in *Bortz*?

RAMSDEN v. FARM CREDIT SERVICES OF NORTH CENTRAL WISCONSIN ACA
Court of Appeals of Wisconsin, 1998
590 N.W.2d 1

Before EICH, VERGERONT and ROGGENSACK, J.

ROGGENSACK, J.

Mark, Raelynn and Milton Ramsden appeal an order of the circuit court dismissing their complaint as to Thomas Hass, an agent of Agribank, FCB and Farm Credit Services of North Central Wisconsin, ACA (FCS). The circuit court concluded that the Ramsdens did not state a claim against Hass for negligent misrepresentation in connection with the sale of a dairy farm to the Ramsdens, because absent a special duty of care, agents are not liable to third persons under theories of negligence. We conclude that under certain circumstances agents may be liable to third persons for both their untrue statements of material fact and for failing to disclose material facts concerning the condition of property and that the Ramsdens stated claims for intentional and negligent misrepresentation. Therefore, we reverse and remand for further proceedings consistent with this opinion.

BACKGROUND

According to the complaint[2] on March 19, 1996, the Ramsdens were the high bidders on a dairy farm sold at public auction by Agribank. FCS, who had financed the prior owners, Triple L Dairy, also financed the Ramsdens' purchase, which closed on April 17, 1996. Hass, an Agribank employee and an agent of both Agribank and FCS, was the auctioneer and he also handled the details of the Ramsdens' purchase from Agribank.

While Triple L Dairy was the owner of the property, it had complained to Hass, Agribank and FCS that its cattle were sick and dying. After investigation and prior to selling the property to the Ramsdens, Agribank, FCS, and Hass learned that an underground gasoline storage tank on the property was leaking and contaminating the soil. On June 15, 1995, Hass reported to the Department of Natural Resources that groundwater on the property was contaminated. Thereafter, Agribank was directed to remove the underground storage tank and to remedy the contamination to the property, in both the soil and in the groundwater. Agribank removed the tank, but it did not remedy the contamination. Notwithstanding their knowledge of the contamination and its effect on dairy cows, Agribank and Hass sought to sell the property as a dairy farm.

At the auction, Hass told the Ramsdens, who said they were considering buying

---

[2] Because the Ramsdens' appeal arises from a motion to dismiss for failure to state a claim, for purposes of this appeal, we assume that all statements of fact and the reasonable inferences therefrom set forth in the complaint are true. Heinritz v. Lawrence Univ., 194 Wis. 2d 606, 610, 535 N.W.2d 81, 83 (Ct. App. 1995).

the property for a dairy farm, that: (1) Agribank would be responsible for any contamination, cleanup or problems associated with an underground storage tank that had leaked; (2) the property was suitable for use as a dairy farm; and (3) there was plenty of good, clean water available for the cattle. Hass did not mention that the groundwater had been contaminated or that Triple L's cattle had died. Based on Hass's factual representations and the failure of Hass, Agribank and FCS to disclose that the groundwater was not fit for consumption and that the prior owner's cattle had died, the Ramsdens bought the property.

On April 18, 1996, the Ramsdens moved their cattle onto the property. By April 20, 1996, the cows began to appear depressed, ceased producing milk, and exhibited sunken eyes, general weakness, bellowing, and a lack of appetite. By April 23, 1996, four of the cows had died. Mark Ramsden also became ill. To determine the cause of these problems, the Ramsdens submitted water samples to the University of Wisconsin at Stevens Point. The samples showed benzene contamination from the underground storage tank that had leaked. The Ramsdens also had a local toxicologist perform a necropsy on one of the dead cows. The toxicologist determined that the cow had died of benzene poisoning.

As a result of the benzene poisoning, the Ramsdens suffered the loss of 186 head of cattle and the loss of profits from the operation of their dairy. Additionally, Mark Ramsden suffered personal injuries, both physical and emotional, due to benzene poisoning. On February 17, 1997, the Ramsdens filed a *pro se* complaint alleging thirteen claims for relief against Agribank, FCS, and Hass. Hass moved to dismiss the complaint for failure to state a claim upon which relief can be granted, pursuant to § 802.06(2)(a)6., STATS. On June 16, 1997, the circuit court granted Hass's motion to dismiss because Hass made the representations as an agent. This appeal followed.

DISCUSSION

Standard of Review.

Whether a complaint states a claim upon which relief can be granted is a question of law, which we review *de novo. Heinritz v. Lawrence Univ.*, 194 Wis. 2d 606, 610, 535 N.W.2d 81, 83 (Ct. App. 1995). A motion to dismiss for failure to state a claim tests the legal sufficiency of the claim. *Ollerman v. O'Rourke Co., Inc.*, 94 Wis. 2d 17, 24, 288 N.W.2d 95, 98 (1980). Therefore, we admit as true all facts pleaded and all reasonable inferences from the pleadings, but only for the purpose of testing the legal sufficiency of the claim, not for the purpose of trial. *Id.* A complaint does not need to state all the ultimate facts constituting each cause of action, and we will not affirm the dismissal of a complaint as legally insufficient unless "it is quite clear that under no conditions can the plaintiff recover." *Id.* at 24, 288 N.W.2d at 98-99.

Ramsdens' Complaint.

. . . .

[O]f the thirteen claims presented in the complaint, only the eleventh claim, which is directed at Hass and is based on representations he made, will be the focus of our discussion. In this claim, which incorporates all allegations previously made, it is asserted that Hass told the Ramsdens that Agribank would remedy the contamination from an underground storage tank that had leaked; that the property was suitable for use as a dairy farm; and that the property had plenty of clean water for the cattle. The Ramsdens also allege that: (1) Hass failed to disclose that the cattle of the previous dairy farmer had died over the last several years; (2) the groundwater was contaminated and that Agribank had been ordered to remedy the contamination and it had not done so; (3) Hass had a duty to disclose the true condition of the property; (4) if facts about the property had not been misrepresented by the defendants' false statements and their failures to disclose the true condition of the property, the Ramsdens would not have purchased it; and (5) the misrepresentations caused them to suffer economic loss and personal injuries, both physical and emotional.

Misrepresentation.

There are three types of misrepresentation: strict liability for misrepresentation, negligent misrepresentation, and intentional misrepresentation. *Whipp v. Iverson*, 43 Wis.2d 166, 169, 168 N.W.2d 201, 203 (1969). The development of the law of misrepresentation in regard to each of these three types of claims has divided into two lines of cases. One line of cases is based on claims that arise from the failure to disclose a material fact and the other line is bottomed on the statement of a material fact which is untrue. *Southard v. Occidental Life Ins. Co.*, 31 Wis. 2d 351, 359, 142 N.W.2d 844, 848 (1966).

For example, in *Ollerman*, 94 Wis. 2d at 51-52, 288 N.W.2d at 112, the supreme court concluded that a claim for intentional misrepresentation exists for intentionally failing to disclose a material fact,[3] when there is a duty to speak, but it left open the question of whether a claim for negligent misrepresentation can be based on the failure to disclose.[4] In Wisconsin, negligence is based on the breach of a duty of care. It is the duty of each person to exercise ordinary care to refrain from any act which will cause foreseeable harm to another. *Id.* at 46, 288 N.W.2d at 109. Therefore, in order to state a claim for negligent misrepresentation it must be reasonably foreseeable, based on an objective standard, that harm will result from one's action or failure to act. *Id.* at 47, 288 N.W.2d at 109. Whether the harm is "reasonably foreseeable" depends to some degree on whether the claimed injury is commercial or personal. *Id.* at 50-51, 288 N.W.2d at 111. This is so because the range of personal injuries are generally more limited and therefore more reasonable to foresee, but purely economic harms may be much farther reaching and therefore not as reasonable to foresee. *Id.* at 51, 288 N.W.2d at 111. Public policy concerns may further limit when claims for relief exist, if they are based on purely economic injuries. *Citizens State Bank v. Timm, Schmidt & Co., S.C.*, 113 Wis. 2d 376, 385-86, 335 N.W.2d 361, 365-66 (1983).

The Ramsdens contend they have pled claims for both negligent and intentional

---

[3] If there is a duty to disclose a fact, the failure to disclose that fact is treated under the law as a representation that the fact does not exist. *Ollerman v. O'Rourke Co., Inc.*, 94 Wis. 2d 17, 26-27, 288 N.W.2d 95, 99-100 (1980) (citing *Southard v. Occidental Life Ins. Co.*, 31 Wis. 2d 351, 359, 142 N.W.2d 844, 848 (1966)).

[4] In *Grube v. Daun*, 173 Wis. 2d 30, 496 N.W.2d 106 (Ct. App. 1992), we concluded that negligent failure to disclose may give rise to a claim for relief, if there is a duty to speak.

misrepresentation, based on both Hass's failure to disclose and on his untrue factual statements. They claim economic and personal injuries and their claims present the additional complication of allegations made against an agent. It was because Hass made the representations as an agent that the circuit court dismissed the complaint against him.

In *Grube v. Daun*, 173 Wis. 2d 30, 496 N.W.2d 106 (Ct. App. 1992), we examined whether a seller's agent who makes a representation of fact which he did not know was untrue could be held liable for the representation when the property was sold in an "as is" condition. We restated the general rule that an agent who does an act that would be a tort if he were not then acting as an agent for another is not relieved from liability to an injured third party, simply because he was acting as an agent when he caused the injury. *Id.* at 51, 496 N.W.2d at 113 (citing *Purtell v. Tehan*, 29 Wis. 2d 631, 639, 139 N.W.2d 655, 659 (1966)). We concluded that one can make a claim against a seller's agent in a real estate sale for both negligent misrepresentation and intentional misrepresentation, grounded on either a material factual statement which was untrue or on the failure to disclose a material fact when there was a duty to speak. *Grube*, 173 Wis. 2d at 55-56, 496 N.W.2d at 115.

In *Greenberg v. Stewart Title Guaranty Co.*, 171 Wis. 2d 485, 492 N.W.2d 147 (1992), the supreme court carefully examined the obligations of both the principal (Stewart Title, the issuer of title insurance) and its agent (Southwestern, who searched the title) to Greenberg, who had purchased a policy of title insurance from Stewart Title. The court concluded that Stewart Title had contracted to provide a policy of insurance that would pay Greenberg up to a stated amount if there were a defect in the title that had not been excepted from coverage under the policy. It also concluded that Stewart Title did not assume a duty to search the title for Greenberg's benefit by selling him a title insurance policy. In other words, if Stewart Title had chosen to issue the policy without examining the title, it was free to do so under its agreement to indemnify Greenberg. The court further concluded that any title search done by Southwestern was only for the benefit of Stewart Title, in order to lower its potential risk when issuing the policy of insurance; and therefore, Southwestern owed no duty to Greenberg. In order for Southwestern to be liable to Greenberg, Southwestern would have had to have had an independent duty to Greenberg. Since it did not, there could have been no breach of duty by Southwestern, even if it negligently conducted the title search. *Id.* at 495, 492 N.W.2d at 151-52. The supreme court's opinion in *Greenberg* did not change the liability rules in regard to potential negligence claims against agents. It simply explained why Southwestern had no duty to Greenberg, and it reaffirmed that without a duty of care owed to Greenberg, Southwestern could not be liable to him for its acts.

We reviewed *Greenberg* when we decided *Krawczyk v. Bank of Sun Prairie*, 203 Wis. 2d 556, 553 N.W.2d 299 (Ct. App. 1996), on which the circuit court relied in dismissing the complaint as to Hass. In *Krawczyk*, the Bank of Sun Prairie contracted to act as the trustee of trusts used to maintain two Wisconsin cemeteries. Livingston was the vice-president in charge of the trust funds. When a significant portion of the funds were lost through what was contended to be negligent management by Livingston, Krawczyk, a special trustee, sued the bank, Livingston and the bank's insurer. The insurer paid Krawczyk for the lost funds and obtained an assignment of Krawczyk's claims against Livingston. It was the bank's insurer who then attempted to proceed against Livingston. In concluding that Livingston had no duty of care to Krawczyk when he performed services for the bank, we relied on *Greenberg* because Livingston had provided no services to Krawczyk, just as Southwestern had provided no services to Greenberg. *Id.* at 567, 553 N.W.2d at 303. We acknowledged that losses can, at times, be recouped for negligent conduct in a commercial context[8] such as was presented in *Krawczyk. Id.* at 566, 553 N.W.2d at 303. However, we concluded there must first have been a reasonably foreseeable injury that would result from Livingston's transferring funds to licensed brokerage houses, before an independent duty would arise between Krawczyk and Livingston. *Id.* at 567, 553 N.W.2d at 303. Although unstated in our opinion, but apparent in the reasoning that underlies our decision, we concluded that Krawczyk's commercial injury, which resulted from the mismanagement of the funds by the agents of the brokerage houses, was too remote to have been reasonably foreseeable by Livingston when he facilitated the transfer of funds to the brokerage houses on behalf of the bank. Therefore, Livingston had no independent duty to Krawczyk; and, even if he had been negligent in the provision of services to the bank, Krawczyk's claim against him was properly dismissed. The Ramsdens contend they have stated claims against Hass for both intentional and negligent misrepresentation.

1. *Intentional Misrepresentation.*

To state a claim for intentional misrepresentation,[9] a complaint must allege that: (1) the defendant made a factual representation; (2) which was untrue; (3) the defendant either made the representation[10] knowing it was untrue or made it recklessly without caring whether it was true or false; (4) the defendant made the representation with intent to defraud and to induce another to act upon it; and (5) the plaintiff believed the statement to be true and relied on it to his/her detriment. *Grube*, 173 Wis. 2d at 53-54, 496 N.W.2d at 114.

There is no insulation from liability under the law for making untrue factual statements about the condition of property during the course of a sale. An agent who makes factual statements that are untrue may incur liability, just as a principal does when he/she makes such statements. *Appleton Chinese Food Serv., Inc. v. Murken Ins., Inc.*, 185 Wis. 2d 791, 804, 519 N.W.2d 674, 678 (Ct. App. 1994) (citing *Ford v. Wisconsin Real Estate Exam. Bd.*, 48 Wis. 2d 91, 102, 179 N.W.2d 786, 792 (1970)). Therefore, Hass may be liable, provided that the Ramsdens have properly pled the elements of intentional misrepresentation.

---

[8] *See also* A.E. Investment Corp. v. Link Builders, Inc., 62 Wis. 2d 479, 214 N.W.2d 764 (1974) (architect who negligently constructs building may be liable to a third party with whom the architect has no privity of contract, if liability is not precluded by public policy considerations); Citizens State Bank v. Timm, Schmidt & Co., S.C., 113 Wis. 2d 376, 335 N.W.2d 361 (1983) (certified public accounting firm may be liable to third person with whom the firm had no privity of contract for an audit report the firm prepared in preparation for the firm's client obtaining a loan).

[9] Intentional misrepresentation is another term for fraudulent misrepresentation.

[10] A claim of intentional misrepresentation also may be based on the failure to disclose a material fact, when there is a duty to disclose.

The Ramsdens alleged that Hass made factual representations about the suitability of the property for a dairy farm when they listed Hass's three material, affirmative statements. Second, they alleged that those statements were untrue, by noting that the groundwater was contaminated with benzene. Third, they pled his knowledge by stating that Hass was aware of the problems with the property due to his contact with the prior owners. Fourth, the Ramsdens pled the element of intent to defraud when they alleged that Hass "induced Plaintiffs to purchase the subject real property by concealing from Plaintiffs the true condition of the property" and when they alleged that Hass intentionally failed to disclose known defects in order to sell the property to the Ramsdens. Finally, the Ramsdens alleged that they relied on Hass's misstatements to their detriment by stating that they would not have purchased the property and suffered the loss of their cattle, the loss of profits, and personal injury from the contamination, but for Hass's statements and failures to disclose. Therefore, because they have properly pled all the elements of intentional misrepresentation, the Ramsdens have stated a claim against Hass, even though he was an agent of Agribank.[12]

2. Negligent misrepresentation.

In order to plead a claim sounding in negligence, one must allege: "1) a duty of care on the part of the defendant; 2) a breach of that duty; 3) a causal connection between the conduct and the injury; and 4) an actual loss or damage as a result of the injury." *Robinson v. Mount Sinai Med. Ctr.*, 137 Wis. 2d 1, 15, 402 N.W.2d 711, 717 (1987). A claim for negligent misrepresentation has been described as requiring that: (1) defendant made a factual representation; (2) which was untrue; (3) which plaintiff believed to be true and relied on to his/her detriment; and (4) defendant breached his duty of care to plaintiff in making the representation at issue. *Grube*, 173 Wis. 2d at 55, 496 N.W.2d at 115. Reliance, in a negligent misrepresentation claim, is equivalent to the causation element set forth in *Robinson*. Additionally, when we review whether a claim has been stated, pleadings must be liberally construed in favor of the plaintiff. *Robinson*, 137 Wis. 2d at 16, 402 N.W.2d at 717.

The Ramsdens pled that Hass's untrue statements and failures to disclose were the proximate causes of their harm and that Hass had a duty not to misrepresent material facts. As explained in footnote 12 above, Hass, as an agent, may not have had an initial duty to disclose his knowledge of the property to the Ramsdens because any disclosure may have been contrary to the interests of his principal, Agribank. However, once Hass made factual statements about the leaky underground storage tank and its contamination of the property, he assumed a duty to the Ramsdens to make truthful statements. Additionally, he then was not free to omit material facts about that condition of the property on which he had spoken, which omissions would have foreseeably affected the Ramsdens' decision about whether to purchase the property for use as a dairy farm. Therefore, we conclude that the

---

[12] The reader should note that we do not decide whether Hass, as the agent of Agribank and FCS, had a duty to the Ramsdens to disclose his knowledge about the condition of the property *before* he made the untrue statements at issue here. However, once he made factual representations to the Ramsdens about the condition of the property relative to the leak from the gasoline storage tank, he was not free to omit material facts about that condition that could have affected their decision to purchase.

Ramsdens have also pled a claim for negligent misrepresentation.

CONCLUSION

The holdings in *Krawczyk* and *Greenberg* do not preclude a finding of liability when an agent affirmatively misstates the condition of property to a potential buyer because he assumes a duty to speak truthfully, if he speaks at all. And, once he has spoken, he may not omit material facts relevant to the same condition of the property on which he has spoken, which omissions would foreseeably affect a potential buyer's decision about whether to purchase or not. Because the Ramsdens alleged that Hass made affirmative statements about the property in regard to its contamination from the leakage of the underground storage tank, and because they properly pled the elements of intentional and negligent misrepresentation under our liberal pleading rules, the Ramsdens have stated claims against Hass and their complaint should not have been dismissed as to him.

By the Court. — Order reversed and cause remanded.

Cases in which a tank of some toxic substance has leaked into the water table are all too common in today's world. Such spills can be virtually impossible to clean up, and can, of course, spread vastly beyond property lines. How can an innocent buyer of real estate, one who had no idea there was a potential problem, protect him or herself from liability to neighboring properties for such leaks? Property and government land use regulation courses cover this topic in some depth.

WINTER v. G. P. PUTNAM'S SONS
United States Court of Appeals for the Ninth Circuit, 1991
938 F.2d 1033

Sneed, Circuit Judge.

Plaintiffs are mushroom enthusiasts who became severely ill from picking and eating mushrooms after relying on information in *The Encyclopedia of Mushrooms*, a book published by the defendant. Plaintiffs sued the publisher and sought damages under various theories. The district court granted summary judgment for the defendant. We affirm.

I.

FACTS AND PROCEEDINGS BELOW

The Encyclopedia of Mushrooms is a reference guide containing information on the habitat, collection, and cooking of mushrooms. It was written by two British authors and originally published by a British publishing company. Defendant Putnam, an American book publisher, purchased copies of the book from the British publisher and distributed the finished product in the United States. Putnam neither wrote nor edited the book.

Plaintiffs purchased the book to help them collect and eat wild mushrooms. In 1988, plaintiffs went mushroom hunting and relied on the descriptions in the book in determining which mushrooms were safe to eat. After cooking and eating their harvest, plaintiffs became critically ill. Both have required liver transplants.

Plaintiffs allege that the book contained erroneous and misleading information concerning the identification of the most deadly species of mushrooms. In their suit against the book publisher, plaintiffs allege liability based on products liability, breach of warranty, negligence, negligent misrepresentation, and false representations. Defendant moved for summary judgment asserting that plaintiffs' claims failed as a matter of law because 1) the information contained in a book is not a product for the purposes of strict liability under products liability law; and 2) defendant is not liable under any remaining theories because a publisher does not have a duty to investigate the accuracy of the text it publishes. The district court granted summary judgment for the defendant. Plaintiffs appeal. We affirm.[1]

II.

DISCUSSION

A book containing Shakespeare's sonnets consists of two parts, the material and print therein, and the ideas and expression thereof. The first may be a product, but the second is not. The latter, were Shakespeare alive, would be governed by copyright laws; the laws of libel, to the extent consistent with the First Amendment; and the laws of misrepresentation, negligent misrepresentation, negligence, and mistake. These doctrines applicable to the second part are aimed at the delicate issues that arise with respect to intangibles such as ideas and expression. Products liability law is geared to the tangible world.

A. *Products Liability*

The language of products liability law reflects its focus on tangible items. In describing the scope of products liability law, the Restatement (Second) of Torts lists examples of items that are covered,[2] All of these are tangible items, such as tires, automobiles, and insecticides.[3] The American Law Institute clearly was

---

[1] This court has jurisdiction through diversity. 28 U.S.C. § 1332 (1988). California tort law applies. Sherman v. Mutual Benefit Life Ins. Co., 633 F.2d 782, 784 (9th Cir. 1980).

[2] The California courts look to the Restatement (Second) of Torts, § 402A for guidance on products liability law. *See* Brooks v. Eugene Burger Management Corp., 215 Cal. App. 3d 1611, 1624-25, 264 Cal. Rptr. 756, 763-64 (1989).

[3] The relevant comment states:

> The rule stated in this Section is not limited to the sale of food for human consumption, or other products for intimate bodily use, although it will obviously include them. It extends to any product sold in the condition, or substantially the same condition, in which it is expected to reach the ultimate user or consumer. Thus the rule stated applies to an automobile, a tire, an airplane, a grinding wheel, a water heater, a gas stove, a power tool, a riveting machine, a chair, and an insecticide. It applies also to products which, if they are defective, may be expected to and do cause only "physical harm" in the form of damage to the user's land or

concerned with including all physical items but gave no indication that the doctrine should be expanded beyond that area.

The purposes served by products liability law also are focused on the tangible world and do not take into consideration the unique characteristics of ideas and expression. Under products liability law, strict liability is imposed on the theory that "[t]he costs of damaging events due to defectively dangerous products can best be borne by the enterprisers who make and sell these products." Prosser & Keeton on The Law of Torts, § 98, at 692-93 (W. Keeton ed. 5th ed. 1984). Strict liability principles have been adopted to further the "cause of accident prevention . . . [by] the elimination of the necessity of proving negligence." *Id.* at 693. Additionally, because of the difficulty of establishing fault or negligence in products liability cases, strict liability is the appropriate legal theory to hold manufacturers liable for defective products. *Id.* Thus, the seller is subject to liability "even though he has exercised all possible care in the preparation and sale of the product." Restatement § 402A comment a. It is not a question of fault but simply a determination of how society wishes to assess certain costs that arise from the creation and distribution of products in a complex technological society in which the consumer thereof is unable to protect himself against certain product defects.

Although there is always some appeal to the involuntary spreading of costs of injuries in any area, the costs in any comprehensive cost/benefit analysis would be quite different were strict liability concepts applied to words and ideas. We place a high priority on the unfettered exchange of ideas. We accept the risk that words and ideas have wings we cannot clip and which carry them we know not where. The threat of liability without fault (financial responsibility for our words and ideas in the absence of fault or a special undertaking or responsibility) could seriously inhibit those who wish to share thoughts and theories. As a New York court commented, with the specter of strict liability, "[w]ould any author wish to be exposed . . . for writing on a topic which might result in physical injury? e.g. How to cut trees; How to keep bees?" *Walter v. Bauer*, 109 Misc. 2d 189, 191, 439 N.Y.S.2d 821, 823 (Sup. Ct. 1981) (student injured doing science project described in textbook; court held that the book was not a product for purposes of products liability law), *aff'd in part & rev'd in part on other grounds*, 88 A.D.2d 787, 451 N.Y.S.2d 533 (1982). One might add: "Would anyone undertake to guide by ideas expressed in words either a discrete group, a nation, or humanity in general?"

Strict liability principles even when applied to products are not without their costs. Innovation may be inhibited. We tolerate these losses. They are much less disturbing than the prospect that we might be deprived of the latest ideas and theories.

Plaintiffs suggest, however, that our fears would be groundless were strict liability rules applied only to books that give instruction on how to accomplish a physical activity and that are intended to be used as part of an activity that is inherently dangerous. We find such a limitation illusory. Ideas are often intimately linked with proposed action, and it would be difficult to draw such a bright line. While "How To" books are a special genre, we decline to attempt to draw a line that

---

chattels, as in the case of animal food or a herbicide. Restatement (Second) of Torts § 402A comment d (1965).

puts "How To Live A Good Life" books beyond the reach of strict liability while leaving "How To Exercise Properly" books within its reach.

Plaintiffs' argument is stronger when they assert that *The Encyclopedia of Mushrooms* should be analogized to aeronautical charts. Several jurisdictions have held that charts which graphically depict geographic features or instrument approach information for airplanes are "products" for the purpose of products liability law. *See Brocklesby v. United States*, 767 F.2d 1288,1294-95 (9th Cir. 1985) (applying Restatement for the purpose of California law), *cert. denied*, 474 U.S. 1101, 106 S. Ct. 882, 88 L. Ed. 2d 918 (1986); *Saloomey v. Jeppesen & Co.*, 707 F.2d 671, 676-77 (2d Cir. 1983) (applying Restatement for the purpose of Colorado Law); *Aetna Casualty & Surety Co. v. Jeppesen & Co.*, 642 F.2d 339, 342-43 (9th Cir. 1981) (applying Nevada law); *Fluor Corp. v. Jeppesen & Co.*, 170 Cal. App. 3d 468, 475, 216 Cal. Rptr. 68, 71 (1985) (applying California law). Plaintiffs suggest that *The Encyclopedia of Mushrooms* can be compared to aeronautical charts because both items contain representations of natural features and both are intended to be used while engaging in a hazardous activity. We are not persuaded.

Aeronautical charts are highly technical tools. They are graphic depictions of technical, mechanical data. The best analogy to an aeronautical chart is a compass. Both may be used to guide an individual who is engaged in an activity requiring certain knowledge of natural features. Computer software that fails to yield the result for which it was designed may be another. In contrast, *The Encyclopedia of Mushrooms* is like a book on how to *use* a compass or an aeronautical chart. The chart itself is like a physical "product" while the "How to Use" book is pure thought and expression.[4]

Given these considerations, we decline to expand products liability law to embrace the ideas and expression in a book.[5] We know of no court that has chosen

---

[4] In reversing a lower court opinion that aeronautical charts are not products, the *Fluor* court made the following comments:

> [The trial court] explained that it believed strict liability principles are applicable only to items whose physical properties render them innately dangerous, e.g., mechanical devices, explosives, combustible or flammable materials, etc. This belief was erroneous.
>
> . . . [A]lthough a sheet of paper might not be dangerous, per se, it would be difficult indeed to conceive of a salable commodity with more inherent lethal potential than an aid to aircraft navigation that, contrary to its own design standards, fails to list the highest land mass immediately surrounding a landing site.

Fluor Corp. v. Jeppesen & Co., 170 Cal. App. 3d 468, 475-76, 216 Cal. Rptr. 68, 71-72 (1985).

Plaintiffs argue that this language shows that California courts would not draw a line between physical products and intangible ideas.

The *Fluor* language, however, cannot be stretched that far. The court was simply discussing the fact that under products liability law, the injury does not have to be caused by impact from the physical properties of the item. In other words, the injury does not have to result because a compass explodes in your hand, but can result because the compass malfunctions and leads you over a cliff. *Cf* Vandermark v. Ford Motor Co., 61 Cal. 2d 256, 261, 37 Cal. Rptr. 896, 899, 391 P.2d 168, 171 (1964) (in bank) (negligence action allowed against manufacturer for injuries that resulted when automobile brakes malfunctioned causing accident). This is quite different from saying that liability can be imposed for such things as ideas which have no physical properties at all.

[5] Plaintiffs also have brought a claim under Restatement (Second) § 402B for false representation. This section provides strict liability for misrepresentations concerning the character or quality of

the path to which the plaintiffs point.[6]

B. *The Remaining Theories*

As discussed above, plaintiffs must look to the doctrines of copyright, libel, misrepresentation, negligent misrepresentation, negligence, and mistake to form the basis of a claim against the defendant publisher. Unless it is assumed that the publisher is a guarantor of the accuracy of an author's statements of fact, plaintiffs have made no case under any of these theories other than possibly negligence. Guided by the First Amendment and the values embodied therein, we decline to extend liability under this theory to the ideas and expression contained in a book.

In order for negligence to be actionable, there must be a legal duty to exercise due care. 6 B. Witkin, *Summary of California Law*, Torts § 732 (9th ed. 1988). The plaintiffs urge this court that the publisher had a duty to investigate the accuracy of *The Encyclopedia of Mushrooms'* contents. We conclude that the defendants have no duty to investigate the accuracy of the contents of the books it publishes. A publisher may of course assume such a burden,[7] but there is nothing inherent in the role of publisher or the surrounding legal doctrines to suggest that such a duty should be imposed on publishers. Indeed the cases uniformly refuse to impose such a duty.[8] Were we tempted to create this duty, the gentle tug of the First

---

"chattels" sold. To the extent that it is inappropriate to apply § 402A because strict liability should not be applied to the transmission of ideas, the same logic would apply to § 402B which also imposes strict liability.

[6] *See* Jones v. J.B. Lippincott Co., 694 F. Supp. 1216, 1217-18 (D. Md. 1988) (nursing student injured treating self with constipation remedy listed in nursing textbook; court held that Restatement § 402A does not extend to dissemination of an idea of knowledge); Herceg v. Hustler Magazine, Inc., 565 F. Supp. 802, 803-04 (S.D. Tex. 1983) (person died after imitating "autoerotic asphyxiation" described in magazine article; court held that contents of magazines are not within meaning of Restatement § 402A); Walter v. Bauer, 109 Misc. 2d 189, 190-91, 439 N.Y.S.2d 821, 822-23 (Sup. Ct. 1981) (student injured doing science project described in textbook; court held that the book was not a defective product for purposes of products liability law because the intended use of a book is reading and the plaintiff was not injured by reading), *affd in part & rev'd in part on other grounds*, 88 A.D.2d 787, 451 N.Y.S.2d 533 (1982); Smith v. Linn, 386 Pa. Super. 392, 398, 563 A.2d 123, 126 (1989) (reader *of Last Chance Diet* book died from diet complications; court held that book is not a product under Restatement § 402A), *affd*, 526 Pa. 447, 587 A.2d 309 (1991); *cf.* Cardozo v. True, 342 So. 2d 1053, 1056-57 (Fla. Dist. Ct. App.) (transmission of words is not the same as selling items with physical properties so that where a bookseller merely passes on a book without inspection, the thoughts and ideas within the book do not constitute a "good" for the purposes of a breach of implied warranty claim under the UCC), *cert. denied*, 353 So. 2d 674 (1977).

[7] *See* Hanberry v. Hearst Corp., 276 Cal. App. 2d 680, 683-84, 81 Cal. Rptr. 519, 521 (1969) (Good Housekeeping held liable for defective product because it had given the product its "Good Housekeeping's Consumer's Guaranty Seal"). In *Hanberry*, the defendant had made an independent examination of the product and issued an express, limited warranty. The defendant here has done nothing similar.

[8] *See* First Equity Corp. v. Standard & Poor's Corp., 869 F.2d 175, 179-80 (2d Cir. 1989) (investors who relied on inaccurate financial publications to their detriment may not recover their losses); Jones v. J. B. Lippincott Co., 694 F. Supp. 1216, 1216-17 (D. Md. 1988) (publisher not liable to nursing student injured in treating self with remedy described in nursing textbook); Lewin v. McCreight, 655 F. Supp. 282, 283-84 (E.D. Mich. 1987) (publisher not liable to plaintiffs injured in explosion while mixing a mordant according to a book on metalsmithing); Aim v. Van Nostrand Reinhold Co., 134 Ill. App. 3d 716, 721, 480 N.E.2d 1263, 1267, 89 Ill. Dec. 520 (1985) (publisher not liable to plaintiff injured following instructions in book on how to make tools); Roman v. City of New York, 110 Misc. 2d 799, 802, 442 N.Y.S.2d 945, 948 (Sup. Ct. 1981) (Planned Parenthood not liable for misstatement in contraceptive

Amendment and the values embodied therein would remind us of the social costs.[9]

Finally, plaintiffs ask us to find that a publisher should be required to give a warning 1) that the information in the book is not complete and that the consumer may not fully rely on it or 2) that this publisher has not investigated the text and cannot guarantee its accuracy. With respect to the first, a publisher would not know what warnings, if any, were required without engaging in a detailed analysis of the factual contents of the book. This would force the publisher to do exactly what we have said he has no duty to do — that is, independently investigate the accuracy of the text. We will not introduce a duty we have just rejected by renaming it a "mere" warning label. With respect to the second, such a warning is unnecessary given that *no* publisher has a duty as a guarantor.

For the reasons outlined above, the decision of the district court is AFFIRMED.

---

1.   Liability for innocent misrepresentation is, of course, a form of strict liability, because the defendant has acted neither intentionally nor negligently. *Winter* involves a recurring issue: the responsibility of a publisher for the accuracy of the materials he or she publishes. Note the intersection between the issues here and the First Amendment issues addressed in Chapter 16.

2.   The following case moves into a very different type of misrepresentation. The misrepresentation is far from innocent, but the issue of damages looms large.

---

pamphlet); Gutter v. Dow Jones, Inc., 22 Ohio St. 3d 286, 291, 490 N.E.2d 898, 902 (1986) (Wall Street Journal not liable for inaccurate description of certain corporate bonds); Smith v. Linn, 386 Pa. Super. 392, 396, 563 A.2d 123, 126 (1989) (publisher of diet book not liable for death caused by complications arising from the diet), *aff'd*, 526 Pa. 447, 587 A.2d 309 (1991); *see also* Herceg v. Hustler Magazine, Inc., 565 F. Supp. 802, 803 (S.D. Tex. 1983) (finding magazine publisher not liable to family of youth who died emulating "autoerotic asphyxiation" as described in article but granting leave to amend incitement claim); *cf.* Libertelli v. Hoffman-La Roche, 7 Media L. Rptr. (BNA) 1734,1736 (S.D.N.Y. 1981) (publisher of Physician's Desk Reference not liable for failure to include drug warning because the work was like a published advertisement of products rather than a reference work); Yuhas v. Mudge, 129 N.J. Super. 207, 209-10, 322 A.2d 824, 825 (1974) (magazine publisher not liable for injury caused by advertised product); Beasock v. Dioguardi Enters., Inc., 130 Misc. 2d 25, 30-31, 494 N.Y.S.2d 974, 979 (Sup. Ct. 1985) (truck association not liable for injuries caused by products manufactured in adherence to industry standards adopted, approved and published by association).

   The *Weirum* case, cited by the plaintiffs, is inapposite. Weirum v. RKO General, Inc., 15 Cal. 3d 40, 123 Cal. Rptr. 468, 539 P.2d 36 (1975) (in bank). In *Weirum*, a radio station ran a promotional contest for teenagers encouraging them to pursue a travelling disc jockey. The station broadcast periodic updates on the disc jockey's location and encouraged teenagers to scramble to the next place. Two teens, who were speeding after the disc jockey, caused a fatal traffic accident. The radio station was held liable. In upholding the jury verdict, the *Weirum* court carefully limited its holding to the facts of the case, which the court described as "a competitive scramble in which the thrill of the chase to be the one and only victor was intensified by the live broadcasts which accompanied the pursuit." Id. at 48, 539 P.2d at 41, 123 Cal. Rptr. at 473; *see also* id. at 46 n.4, 539 P.2d at 39 n.4,123 Cal. Rptr. at 471 n.4 (noting that duty determinations must be made case by case). A publisher's role in bringing ideas and information to the public bears no resemblance to the *Weirum* scenario.

[9]   A stronger argument might be made by a plaintiff alleging libel or fraudulent, intentional, or malicious misrepresentation, but such is not contended in this case. Gutter v. Dow Jones, Inc., 490 N.E.2d at 902 n.4.

C.A.M. v. R.A.W.
Superior Court of New Jersey, Appellate Division, 1990
568 A.2d 556

O'Brien, J.A.D.

Plaintiff appeals from a summary judgment in favor of defendant. In her complaint, she asserted a variety of claims against defendant arising out of his false representation to her that he had had a vasectomy, on the basis of which she engaged in sexual intercourse with him resulting in the birth of a normal, healthy child. In granting summary judgment to defendant the trial judge ruled that, except for a paternity claim pursuant to N.J.S.A. 9:17-38 *et seq.*, and *R.* 5:14-1 *et seq.*, plaintiff had no independent cause of action for damages in this State. We agree and affirm.

On December 5, 1987, plaintiff gave birth to a normal, healthy child. By order of October 17, 1988, the Family Part of the Chancery Division declared defendant the father of that child (by agreement on the record in open court under oath). Defendant was ordered to pay $95 per week support for the child, to obtain Blue Cross, Blue Shield and Major Medical coverage, to be paid 80% by defendant and 20% by plaintiff, to pay one-half of the child's uncovered medical expenses, and to obtain a $25,000 whole life or term insurance policy for the child with plaintiff mother as trustee. Defendant was also ordered to pay the sum of $5,000 in full payment of all outstanding arrears for support and uncovered medical expenses.

Meanwhile, on April 28, 1988, plaintiff filed a separate action against defendant. Despite her acknowledgement in a later certification that she engaged in voluntary sexual relations with defendant while using a contraceptive sponge form of birth control, in her complaint, as amended on May 23, 1988, plaintiff alleged that she engaged in a "personal relationship" with defendant in reliance upon his representations that "he was single and incapable of impregnating" her because he had undergone a vasectomy. She sought relief for negligent misrepresentation, tortious interference with prospective economic advantage or contractual relationship, equitable and legal fraud, and negligent and intentional infliction of emotional distress. She sought damages for physical pain and suffering during her pregnancy and post delivery recuperation and loss of income from her business. She also sought punitive damages on some of the counts. In his answer, defendant admitted telling plaintiff he had undergone a vasectomy, but claimed it was said in jest. By way of separate defense, defendant claimed plaintiff's complaint failed to state a cause of action, was duplicative of the paternity action then pending in the Family Part, and was barred by the equitable doctrines of unclean hands, laches and waiver.

Defendant moved for summary judgment, supported by his certification. In her responding certification, plaintiff alleged that the first time she engaged in sexual intercourse with defendant was in March 1987 while they were in Mexico together. She said the first several times they engaged in sexual intercourse she used a contraceptive sponge for birth control. However, when she informed defendant of her use of this device, he told her she did not have to use any birth control because he had had a vasectomy. Because of her belief that he was telling the truth,[2] plaintiff engaged in sexual intercourse with defendant without any form of birth control. Although defendant did not entirely agree with plaintiff's version of the facts, he conceded that for purposes of his summary judgment motion plaintiff's version of the facts must be accepted as true. *Judson v. Peoples Bank & Trust Co. of Westfield*, 17 N. J. 67, 73-75, 110 A.2d 24 (1954); *Pierce v. Ortho Pharmaceutical Corp.*, 84 N.J. 58, 65, 417 A.2d 505 (1980).

In a short oral opinion delivered on October 28, 1988, the trial judge granted summary judgment to defendant. The judge found no legal precedent in this state on the issue presented, but noted the existence of some out-of-state cases dealing with the subject. He relied in particular upon *Stephen K. v. Roni L.*, 105 Cal. App. 3d 640, 164 Cal. Rptr. 618 (Cal. Ct. App., 2d Dist. 1980), and *L. Pamela P. v. Frank S.*, 88 A.D.2d 865, 451 N.Y.S.2d 766 (App. Div. 1982), *aff'd* 59 N.Y.2d 1, 462 N.Y.S.2d 819, 449 N.E.2d 713 (Ct. App. 1983).

Since the issue is one of first impression in this state it requires a policy determination. In making that decision we are greatly aided by the California court. In *Stephen K. v. Roni L., supra*, a mother and her minor child brought a paternity suit against Stephen K., who, after admitting paternity, filed a cross-claim [counterclaim] "for fraud, negligent misrepresentation and negligence" seeking compensatory and punitive damages for the "wrongful birth" of his child. 164 Cal. Rptr. at 619. He claimed the child's mother had falsely represented to him that she was taking birth control pills and that, in reliance upon her representation, he engaged in sexual intercourse with her, eventually resulting in the birth of the child. The court found that such claims arise from conduct so intensely private that the court should not be asked, nor attempt to resolve them. Concluding that, although the mother may have lied and betrayed the personal confidence reposed in her by Stephen, the circumstances and the highly intimate nature of the relationship wherein the false representations may have occurred, are such that a court should not define any standard of conduct therefor. The court continued:

> The claim of Stephen is phrased in the language of the tort of misrepresentation. Despite its legalism, it is nothing more than asking the court to supervise the promises made between two consenting adults as to the circumstances of their private sexual conduct. To do so would encourage unwarranted governmental intrusion into matters affecting the individual's right to privacy. In *Stanley v. Georgia* (1969) 394 U.S. 557, 564, 89 S. Ct. 1243, 1247, 22 L. Ed. 2d 542, the high court recognized the right to privacy as the most comprehensive of rights and the right most valued in our civilization. Courts have long recognized a right of privacy in matters relating to marriage, family and sex *(see e.g. People v. Belous,* (1969) 71 Cal. 2d 954, 963, 80 Cal. Rptr. 354, 458 P.2d 194, regarding the right of a woman to bear children; *Griswold v. Connecticut* (1965) 381 U.S. 479, 485-486, 85 S. Ct. 1678, 1682, 14 L. Ed. 2d 510, concerning state law forbidding use of contraceptives by married couples; *Eisenstadt v. Baird* (1972) 405 U.S. 438,

---

[2] Since both parties were adults and consented to the relationship, an issue of reasonable reliance might well arise in these circumstances. Plaintiff also said she first learned defendant was married after she became pregnant with his child.

453-455, 92 S. Ct. 1029, 1038-1039, 31 L. Ed. 2d 349, regarding state law prohibiting distribution of contraceptives to unmarried persons).

We reject Stephen's contention that tortious liability should be imposed against Roni, and conclude that as a matter of public policy the practice of birth control, if any, engaged in by two partners in a consensual sexual relationship is best left to the individuals involved, free from any governmental interference. [164 Cal. Rptr. at 620-621.]

We agree with these expressions by the California court. These principles have also been followed by our sister states of New York and Pennsylvania. In *L. Pamela P. v. Frank S., supra*, the New York Court of Appeals affirmed the Appellate Division's decision that the deliberate misrepresentation by the mother concerning her use of contraception had no bearing on the father's obligation to support his child. In reaching that conclusion, the court conceded that the father had a constitutionally protected right to decide for himself whether to father a child, which involved the freedom to decide for oneself without unreasonable governmental interference whether to avoid procreation through the use of contraception. However, the court concluded:

This aspect of the right of privacy has never been extended so far as to regulate the conduct of private actors as between themselves. Indeed, as the Appellate Division recognized, judicial inquiry into so fundamentally private and intimate conduct as is required to determine the validity of respondent's assertions may itself involve impermissible State interference with the privacy of these individuals *(see, also, Stephen K v. Roni L.,* 105 Cal. App. 3d 640, 164 Cal. Rptr. 618). [462 N.Y.S.2d at 822.]

The Supreme Court of Pennsylvania reached a similar conclusion in *Hughes v. Hutt,* 500 Pa. 209, 455 A.2d 623, 625 (Pa. 1983), in which a father sought to raise as a defense or counterclaim an allegation that the mother deceived him into believing she was practicing birth control when in fact she was not. In a footnote, the court noted that its conclusions were shared by the courts of California and New York, citing *Stephen K. v. Roni L., supra,* and *L. Pamela P. v. Frank S., supra.*

We recognize that in all three of these out-of-state cases the issue arose by way of a father's counterclaim to a suit seeking to establish paternity and support for the child, whereas, in this case, it is the mother who seeks a personal recovery from the father, the questions of paternity and support having been resolved in a separate proceeding. However, the courts of California were again called upon to address this issue in a suit by a female against a male for fraud and deceit, and intentional infliction of emotional distress arising out of their sexual relationship. In *Perry v. Atkinson,* 195 Cal. App. 3d 14, 240 Cal. Rptr. 402 (Cal. Ct. App. 4th Dist.1987), Perry alleged that she terminated her pregnancy by abortion based upon Atkinson's promise that he would impregnate her the following year either through sexual intercourse or artificial insemination. She alleged the representation was false, and that he had no intention of impregnating her again and made these statements to deceive her into aborting her pregnancy. The trial court concluded that public policy prohibits a cause of action for fraud and deceit concerning intimate matters involving procreation. It further found that to adjudicate the promises of the parties by legal action constituted an unwarranted governmental intrusion into matters affecting the individuals' right to privacy and would violate public policy. However, it denied Atkinson's motion for summary judgment as to Perry's claim for intentional infliction of emotional distress. In affirming the trial court, the appellate court found the reasoning in *Stephen K. v. Roni L., supra*, persuasive as applied to the facts. The court held:

> Although Atkinson may have deliberately misrepresented his intentions to Perry in order to persuade her to have an abortion, their procreative decisions were so intensely private that we decline to intervene. Tort liability cannot apply to the choice, however motivated, of whether to conceive or bear a child. [240 Cal. Rptr. at 404.]

The *Perry* court then noted that the California Legislature had recognized that certain sexual conduct in interpersonal decisions are, on public policy grounds, outside the realm of tort liability, citing *inter alia*, a statutory provision that no cause of action exists for alienation of affections.[6] The court continued:

> If no cause of action can exist in tort for a fraudulent promise to fulfill the rights, duties and obligations of a marriage relationship, then logically no cause of action can exist for a fraudulent promise by a married man to impregnate a woman not his wife. [240 Cal.Rptr. at 405.]

The *Perry* court made reference to two decisions since *Stephen K v. Roni L.*, which appeared to have reached a different result. In *Barbara A. v. John G.*, 145 Cal. App. 3d 369, 193 Cal. Rptr. 422 (Cal. Ct. App. 1 Dist. 1983), the court was confronted with the issue of whether a woman who has suffered injuries from an ectopic pregnancy has a cause of action in tort against the man responsible for his misrepresentations of infertility. The court held the plaintiff had stated a cause of action for battery and deceit because the right to privacy does not insulate sexual relations from judicial scrutiny when that right is used as a shield from liability at the expense of the other party. In *Barbara A.*, the court attempted to distinguish *Stephen K.* on both factual and public policy grounds, saying:

> In essence, Stephen was seeking damages for the 'wrongful birth' of his child [footnote omitted] resulting in support obligations and alleged damages for mental suffering. Here, no child is involved; appellant is seeking damages for severe injury to her own body.

> Although the *Stephen K* court alluded to Stephen's claim as separate and apart from the issue of either parent's obligation to raise and support the child, it reached its decision without attempting to resolve the problem of the mother's reduced financial ability to support the child if she were required to pay damages to the father. We think this concern over the child, and not governmental intrusion into private sexual matters, . . . is the central issue in *Stephen K.* and compels different public policy considerations. [193 Cal. Rptr. at 429.]

The *Perry* court disagreed with that conclusion, finding that instead, *Stephen K. v. Roni L.* had been based "on the public policy consideration that 'the practice of

---

[6] We have a similar statute in New Jersey abolishing suits for damages for alienation of affections, criminal conversation, seduction or breach of contract to marry. N.J.S.A. 2A:23-1.

birth control, if any, engaged in by two partners in a consensual sexual relationship is best left to the individuals involved, free from any governmental interference'" and it chose to follow the "sound reasoning" of *Stephen K*, 240 Cal. Rptr. at 406.

The *Perry* court also referred to *Kathleen K. v. Robert B.*, 150 Cal. App. 3d 992, 198 Cal. Rptr. 273 (Cal. Ct. App. 2d Dist. 1984). There, a woman brought an action against a man because she had contracted genital herpes from sexual intercourse with him. The court in *Kathleen K.* concluded that the constitutional right of privacy did not protect the defendant from his tortious conduct in failing to inform the plaintiff he was infected with venereal disease. The court concluded, "The right of privacy is not absolute, and in some cases is subordinate to the state's fundamental right to enact laws which promote public health, welfare and safety, even though such laws may invade the offender's right of privacy." 198 Cal. Rptr. at 276. That court also reasoned, ". . . as in *Barbara A.*, there is no child involved, and the public policy consideration with respect to parental obligations are absent." 198 Cal. Rptr. at 275. A similar result was reached in New Jersey by the Family Part of our Chancery Division in *G.L. v. M.L.*, 228 N.J. Super. 566, 550 A.2d 525 (Ch. Div. 1988). The *Perry* court went on to distinguish the *Kathleen K.* decision, noting that:

> The tortious transmission of a contagious disease implicates policy considerations beyond the sexual conduct and procreative decisions of two consenting adults. The state's interest 'in the prevention and control of contagious and dangerous disease, [citation omitted] is sufficient to allow a cause of action for fraudulent concealment of the risk of infection with venereal disease. The absence of such policy considerations here compels a different result. [240 Cal. Rptr. at 406.]

The same reasoning distinguishes the instant case from the result reached here in New Jersey in *G.L. v. M.L.*

Most recently a California court dealt with this problem in *Richard P. v. Gerald B.*, 202 Cal. App. 3d 1089, 249 Cal. Rptr. 246 (Cal. App. 1st Dist. 1988). Gerald B. sued Richard P. for fraud and intentional infliction of emotional distress, alleging that Richard fathered two children born to Linda B. while she was Gerald's wife. In various counts of the complaint it was alleged that Richard misrepresented that Gerald was the father. In reversing a trial judge's denial of a demurrer to the complaint, the Court of Appeals for the 1st District in California, said:

> We agree with real parties in interest that they have alleged words which normally would suffice to state tort causes of action for fraud and intentional infliction of emotional distress. We feel that the subject matter of the action, however, is not one in which it is appropriate for the courts to intervene. 'Broadly speaking, the word "tort" means a civil wrong, other than a breach of contract, for which the law will provide a remedy in the form of an action for damages. It does not lie within the power of any judicial system, however, to remedy all human wrongs. There are many wrongs which in themselves are flagrant. For instance, such wrongs as betrayal, brutal words, and heartless disregard of the feelings of others are beyond any effective legal remedy in any practical administration of law.' (Prosser [& Keeton], Torts (3d ed. 1964) ch. 1 §§ 1 and 4, pp. 1-2, 18, 21.) To attempt to correct such wrongs or give relief from their effects 'may do

more social damage than if the law leaves them alone.' (Ploscowe, *An Action for 'Wrongful Life* (1963), 38 N.Y. Univ. Law Review, 1078, 1080) *(Stephen K v. Roni L.* (1980), 105 Cal. App. 3d 640, 642-643, 164 Cal. Rptr. 618). [249 Cal. Rptr. at 249.]

The *Richard* P. court distinguished both *Barbara A.* and *Kathleen K.* on the ground that those cases involved physical injury to plaintiff and had no potential for harming innocent children. The court noted that the *Kathleen K.* court had said, quoting from the *Barbara A.* court:

> . . . [W]e think it is not sound social policy to allow one parent to sue the other over the wrongful birth of their child. Using the child as the damage element in a tortious claim of one parent against the other could seldom, if ever, result in benefit to the child. [198 Cal. Rptr. at 275.]

We agree with the various sentiments expressed by the California courts, although we recognize that in *Perry* the court permitted plaintiff's claim for intentional infliction of emotional distress. However, in that case there was no allegation of the wrongful birth of a child. Where there is a normal, healthy child, as in this case, the California courts have said it is not sound social policy to allow one parent to sue the other over the wrongful birth of their child, and that using the child as the damage element in a tortious claim of one parent against the other could seldom, if ever, result in benefit to a child. Those principles are clearly applicable in this case.

We conclude that the birth of a normal, healthy child as a consequence of a sexual relationship between consenting adults precludes inquiry by the courts into representations that may have been made before or during that relationship by either of the partners concerning birth control. We recognize the seeming applicability of traditional tort principles to a misrepresentation such as that in this case, resulting in the birth of a child to a woman with resultant labor pain attendant to the birth, followed by expense, inconvenience, and loss of income because of the birth and existence of the child. We further recognize that we have specifically authorized recovery of some of these expenses in a medical malpractice suit by a husband and wife against a doctor for his negligence in connection with a sterilization procedure, where a normal, healthy child was born in *P. v. Portadin*, 179 N.J.Super. 465, 432 A.2d 556 (App. Div. 1981).[8] We also recognize that in *M. and wife v. Schmid Laboratories, Inc.*, 178 N.J.Super. 122, 428 A.2d 515 (App. Div.

---

[8] Based upon *Berman v. Allan*, 80 N.J. 421 (1979), in *Portadin* we precluded recovery for the future expense which the parents will incur in raising, educating and supervising the child. Quoting the Wisconsin Supreme Court in *Rieck v. Medical Protective Co. of Fort Wayne, Ind.*, 64 Wis.2d 514, 219 N.W.2d 242 (Sup.Ct. 1974), we said:

> To permit the parents to keep their child and shift the entire cost of its upbringing to a physician who failed to determine or inform them of the fact of pregnancy would be to create a new category of surrogate parent. Every child's smile, every bond of love and affection, every reason for parental pride in a child's achievements, every contribution by the child to the welfare and well-being of the family and parents, is to remain with the mother and father. For the most part, these are intangible benefits, but they are nonetheless real. On the other hand, every financial cost or detriment-what the complaint terms "hard money damages"-including the cost of food, clothing and education, would be shifted to the physician who allegedly failed to timely diagnose the fact of pregnancy. We hold that such result would be wholly out of proportion to the culpability involved, and that the allowance of recovery would place too

1981), a suit by a husband and wife against a condom manufacturer alleging that normal, healthy twins were born as a result of the negligent manufacture of a condom, we authorized the defendant manufacturer to maintain its counterclaim for contribution against the husband for his negligent use of the contraceptive device. We reached this conclusion, in spite of the husband's argument that he was having intercourse with his wife in the privacy of their bedroom when the defective product failed to prevent impregnation and resultant damages. We also concluded defendant could not cloak his actions with interspousal immunity, because

> While some matters or proceedings between a husband and wife within the privacy of the bedroom may remain within the protection of interspousal immunity, it is clear plaintiffs have lifted the veil of secrecy here and place squarely in issue all the facts surrounding their use or misuse of the alleged defective product. [178 N.J.Super. at 125.]

In contrast to those cases, the recovery sought in this case by the mother is against the father of the child, and not against a third party, such as a physician for malpractice or a condom manufacture for product liability. Nor is this a case in which the resultant child suffers from some abnormality as in *Berman v. Allan, supra, Schroeder v. Perkel,* 87 N.J. 53, 432 A.2d 834 (1981), or *Procanik by Procanik v. Cillo,* 97 N.J. 339, 478 A.2d 755 (1984).

As we view this case, plaintiff seeks to recover damages for the wrongful birth of her normal, healthy child. She alleges as damages, in addition to the labor pain attendant upon the birth of the child, her inability to work while pregnant and during recuperation, and damage to her business. If normal tort principles are applicable to plaintiff's claim, it would seem that normal defenses should be available to defendant. One defense might be whether there was reasonable reliance on defendant's status; another might be mitigation of damages. It is well settled that injured parties have a duty to take reasonable steps to mitigate their damages. *McDonald v. Mianecki,* 79 N.J. 275, 299, 398 A.2d 1283 (1979). The requirement that plaintiffs mitigate damages prevails as much in the case of damages arising out of tort as it does in the case of breach of contract. *McGraw v. Johnson,* 42 N.J.Super. 267, 274, 126 A.2d 203 (App. Div. 1956).[9] We discussed this question in *Comras v. Lewin,* 183 N.J.Super. 42, 443 A.2d 229 (App. Div. 1982). There, a woman sued a doctor for wrongful birth of a defective child, and the trial judge dismissed the action because plaintiff could have had an abortion at the time she found out she was pregnant. We reversed the trial judge's decision concluding that the enhanced risks of an abortion delayed to the second trimester, because of defendant's

---

unreasonable a burden upon physicians, under the facts and circumstances here alleged. [179 N.J.Super. at 471.]

We do not know whether plaintiff in this case offered defendant custody of the child or what, if any, visitation arrangements have been made.

[9] We recognize that in this case defendant has not asserted in his answer plaintiff's duty to mitigate her damages. Mitigation of damages has been referred to as an affirmative defense. *See* Roselle v. La Fera Contracting Co., 18 N.J. Super. 19, 28, 86 A.2d 449 (Ch. Div. 1952); *but see* Becker v. Kelsey, 9 N.J. Misc. 1265, 1273, 157 A. 177 (Sup. Ct. 1931). However, in McGraw v. Johnson, *supra,* we said at 42 N.J. Super. 273, 126 A.2d 203, the "law requires" an injured party to mitigate damages. Moreover, in her brief plaintiff correctly argues that she alone has the right to decide whether to terminate her pregnancy by abortion, citing Roe v. Wade, 410 U.S. 113, 93 S. Ct. 705, 35 L. Ed. 2d 147 (1973).

negligent failure to make a timely diagnosis of her pregnancy, were of such a nature and magnitude that, even though abortion remains lawfully available, she was effectively denied a meaningful opportunity to decide whether the fetus should be aborted. The theory of that plaintiff's case was that, had her pregnancy been confirmed in the first trimester, she would have aborted it because of the peculiar and known risks of bearing a defective child arising from her age and history of diabetes, but defendant's negligence had delayed a diagnosis until the second trimester.

In this case, according to plaintiff's contentions, the child was unwanted from the beginning. At the time plaintiff first became aware she was pregnant, she had the legal right to safely abort the fetus. Thus a claim might be made that plaintiff should have mitigated her damages. We recognize there are a variety of reasons why a woman may decide not to undergo an abortion. However, we question whether a plaintiff in a tort action for the wrongful birth of a normal, healthy child may decide to have the child and then look to defendant for damages of the type sought by plaintiff in this case.

Our dissenting colleague recognizes that the trial judge and the jury may have to face some extremely difficult issues relating to the question of damages sustained by plaintiff. As to mitigation of damages he appropriately cites *In re University of Ariz. v. Superior Court*, 136 Ariz. 579, 667 P.2d 1294 (Ariz. 1983). In that case the court addressed the question of the appropriate rule of damages where a normal, healthy child was born to a couple after an unsuccessful vasectomy undergone by the husband because they did not want any more children. The couple sued for malpractice and the court decided upon a full damage rule with offsets for the benefits of the parent/child relationship. However, as to mitigation of damages, the court said, in a footnote, it did not mean that parents should be forced to mitigate damages by choosing abortion or adoption or that the failure to do so may be considered an offset. However, that case does not involve a suit by one parent against the other, but rather is a malpractice case similar to *P. v. Portadin, supra*, where we noted the intangible benefits of having a child. *See* footnote 8.

Although we do not decide whether the father in this case can assert mitigation of damages (or an offset for the intangible benefits of having a normal, healthy child), the potential for such a defense underscores our conclusion that courts should not intrude into this manifestly private relationship between consenting adults by inquiring into the circumstances resulting in conception and the damages resulting from the alleged wrongful birth, beyond the recognized obligation of the parents to provide complete support for that child and the father to pay some or all of the medical expenses. The specter of the mother claiming as her damages the wrongful existence of her normal, healthy child in addition to her claim for labor pain attendant upon the child's birth, and the father potentially arguing that the mother should have mitigated her damages by aborting their child, clearly support the conclusion of the California courts and our sister states that we should not embark upon the resolution of such a dispute.

While there is facial logic to the conclusion of our dissenting colleague that dismissal at this stage is premature, we conclude that the very public policy reasons which dictate that such causes of action should not lie would be defeated if the matter proceeded to trial, even if it were dismissed on the grounds we state after presentation of some or all of the evidence. If the causes of action alleged in the complaint fall within the invasion of privacy concept espoused by the California court and adopted by us herein, the action should be dismissed before the presentation of any evidence. Summary judgment was clearly appropriate.

We conclude, for the reasons stated, that plaintiff's claims against defendant are not cognizable in the State of New Jersey on public policy grounds. This is particularly so since defendant has been ordered to support the child and compensate plaintiff for her expenses attendant upon the child's birth. We conclude that compensatory or punitive damages may not be recovered by plaintiff individually on the causes of action pled by her where the alleged wrong resulted in the birth of a normal, healthy child.

Affirmed.

STERN, J.A.D., dissenting.

The issue before us is not whether plaintiff has alleged sufficient facts to satisfy the elements of the various claims she asserts. Rather, the question is only whether that issue and others related to her claims can be addressed in the courts of New Jersey. The trial judge dismissed the complaint only because there is "a clear jurisdictional reluctance to support a cause of action based on fraudulent misrepresentation of one's ability to have or not have a child." He concluded that "the Court's reluctance extends from an unwillingness to introduce state authority into this area."

I cannot join the majority in affirming that conclusion in this case. I agree wholeheartedly with my colleagues that what occurs in the bedroom between consenting adults is protected by a constitutional right of privacy and should not be cognizable in our courts. However, this case is premised on the assertion that plaintiff's "consent" to having sex with defendant and not taking her normal birth control precautions was based on his fraudulent misrepresentation. In other contexts our judges and juries frequently review factual disputes and decide if sexual relationships involve nonconsensual or otherwise unlawful conduct. *See* N.J.S.A. 2C:14-2, 2C.14-3, 2C.14-5. More significantly, with respect to civil claims, our courts have held that even a spouse can bring a personal injury action "based on transmittal of a sexual disease." *G.L. v. M.L.*, 228 N.J.Super. 566, 571, 550 A.2d 525 (Ch. Div. 1988). *G.L.* quoted from *Kathleen K. v. Robert B.*, 150 Cal. App. 3d 992, 198 Cal. Rptr. 273, 277 (Cal. App. 2 Dist. 1984), which held that a woman could recover damages stemming from a man's failure to inform her before intercourse that he had contracted genital herpes. The court found that the right to privacy did not prevent recovery where the "[c]onsent to sexual intercourse [was] vitiated by one partner's fraudulent concealment of the risk of infection with venereal disease . . . , whether or not the partners involved are married to each other." *Kathleen K. v. Robert B., supra*, 150 Cal. App. 3d at 997, 198 Cal. Rptr. at 277.

If physical injury premised on the failure of a spouse or nonspouse sexual partner to disclose a contagious disease is actionable, *see also B.N. v. K.K.*, 312 Md. 135, 152, 538 A.2d 1175, 1184 (Md. 1988), I fail to see why another type of fraud resulting in the "unprotected" sexual relationship should not be cognizable at least where the sexual activity has impact on plaintiff's physical condition. *Cf. Frame v. Kothari*, 115 N.J. 638, 560 A.2d 675 (1989); *Giardina v. Bennett*, 111 N.J. 412, 545 A.2d 139 (1988) with respect to the emotional distress claim. *See also Alice D. v. William M.*, 113 Misc. 2d 940, 450 N.Y.S.2d 350 (N.Y. City Civ. Ct. 1982) (cause of action for negligent misrepresentation resulting in pregnancy sustained).

The plaintiff here alleges that she engaged in "unprotected" sexual intercourse based upon a knowing misrepresentation. But more than mere intercourse is involved. *Compare, State v. Saunders*, 75 N.J. 200, 381 A.2d 333 (1977). Plaintiff became pregnant and gave birth. She claims that she had to reduce work, if not abandon her profession, at least during pregnancy, and independent of the time she was out of work during pregnancy, she will be diverted from her chosen profession and social activities because of the time, effort and attention it will take to raise and care for the child. Further, she will have expenses in this regard independent of those provided in the support order and the medical expenses which defendant must reimburse for the childbirth.

Plaintiff may have a difficult time proving that she justifiably relied on the misrepresentation that defendant had a vasectomy and could not impregnate her. She may also have difficulty meeting her burden of proving that his misrepresentation caused her to engage in sexual intercourse without taking her usual birth control precautions and was thus a "proximate cause" of the pregnancy. And, if the case goes that far, the trial judge and jury may have to face some extremely difficult issues relating to the question of damages sustained by *plaintiff*. These issues simply are not now before us in this case, and our concern with the policies and difficulties flowing from these questions, should they be reached, cannot form an underlying basis for affirming on the premise that the judiciary should not consider them at all.

There is much to be said for the position articulately developed by my colleagues. I, too, am concerned about a "potential for harming innocent children" and recognize that "using the child as the damage element in a tortious claim of one parent against the other could seldom, if ever, result in benefit to a child." But the majority concludes that the birth of a normal, healthy child in effect precludes all damages, and does so notwithstanding the misrepresentation of one partner to the sexual act. And it so holds in a case where the mitigation issue was neither raised, briefed nor argued. Moreover, the holding of the majority is essentially based on cases which, as the majority notes, understandably and appropriately reject defenses to paternity and support actions. However, here, the right of privacy is being used as "a shield from liability." *See Barbara A. v. John G., supra.*

Further, the damages claimed in this case transcend the impact of childbirth.[4] Plaintiff seeks damages from the consequences of her pregnancy, a claim which, as I understand it, is in addition to those stemming from the resulting birth itself.

---

[4] It is hard to take issue with the majority's suggestion that no damages flow from the birth of a happy, normal child. But there may be economic or non-economic consequences in a given case which flow from the decision to give birth even to a loved child, such as the pain which flows from the "stigma," at least in some areas, of being a single parent. Thus, the mother may sustain damages well beyond that provided in a support order for the child.

Finally, the issues posed by this case are difficult and troublesome. Like my colleagues I have agonized over them. However, I must dissent from their conclusion which, in essence, precludes review of these questions by dismissing the complaint altogether.

Accordingly, I dissent.

Should a wife be able to sue her husband for negligent (unknowing and unintentional) transmission of a sexually transmitted disease as a result of an undisclosed extramarital affair, on the theory that the husband misrepresented his lack of marital fidelity? *See McPherson v. McPherson*, 712 A.2d 1043 (Me. 1998) (rejecting claim).

Chapter 19

NUISANCE

Although related to trespass to land, the tort of nuisance is an entirely separate cause of action with different elements and goals. Some of these were introduced in Chapters 2 and 9; this chapter covers the tort in more depth.

The tort of nuisance developed out of a perceived need to allow property owners to sue those who interfered with their enjoyment of their own land but whose conduct fell short of a physical invasion of their property. Nuisance suits must balance various competing interests, including the interests of the respective landowners in using their own property and the interest of society in controlling land use that might have an adverse impact on more than just the landowners involved. Nuisance suits often involve far more than neighborly conflict, and the cases can implicate powerful public interest concerns as well, pursuant to which the courts must weigh the impact upon a landowner of ruling in favor of the plaintiffs against the injury to the plaintiffs in the use and enjoyment in their land. The remedy sought in these cases is often injunctive, which brings concerns of equity into the mix.

The cases included here range from the ringing of church bells through barking dogs and the odors produced by cattle feed lots to air pollution and the regional impact of enjoining the operation of the relevant factory. You should think about what factors outside those in the cases themselves might have an impact upon the court's decision. What other remedies might creative litigants propose when the public interest is involved? What role should general state concerns play in the decisions?

ROGERS v. ELLIOTT
Supreme Judicial Court of Massachusetts, 1888
15 N.E. 768

KNOWLTON, J.

The defendant was the custodian and authorized manager of property of the Roman Catholic Church used for religious worship. The acts for which the plaintiff seeks to hold him responsible were done in the use of this property, and the sole question before us is whether or not that use was unlawful. The plaintiff's case rests upon the proposition that the ringing of the bell was a nuisance. The consideration of this proposition involves an inquiry into what the defendant could properly do in the use of the real estate which he had in charge, and what was the standard by which his rights were to be measured. It appears that the church was built upon a public street, in a thickly-settled part of the town; and if the ringing of the bell on Sundays had materially affected the health or comfort of all in the vicinity, whether residing or passing there, this use of the property would have been a public nuisance, for which there would have been a remedy by indictment. Individuals suffering from it in their persons or their property could have recovered damages for a private nuisance. *Wesson v. Iron Co.*, 13 Allen, 95. In an action of this kind, a fundamental question is, by what standard, as against the interests of a neighbor, is one's right to use his real estate to be measured. In densely populated communities the use of property in many ways which are legitimate and proper necessarily affects in greater or less degree the property or persons of others in the vicinity. In such cases the inquiry always is, when rights are called in question, what is reasonable under the circumstances. If a use of property is objectionable solely on account of the noise which it makes, it is a nuisance, if at all, by reason of its effect upon the health or comfort of those who are within hearing. The right to make a noise for a proper purpose must be measured in reference to the degree of annoyance which others may reasonably be required to submit to. In connection with the importance of the business from which it proceeds, that must be determined by the effect of noise upon people generally, and not upon those, on the one hand, who are peculiarly susceptible to it, or those, on the other, who by long experience have learned to endure it without inconvenience; not upon those whose strong nerves and robust health enable them to endure the greatest disturbances without suffering, nor upon those whose mental or physical condition makes them painfully sensitive to everything about them. That this must be the rule in regard to public nuisances is obvious. It is the rule as well, and for reasons nearly, if not quite, as satisfactory, in relation to private nuisances. Upon a question whether one can lawfully ring his factory bell, or run his noisy machinery, or whether the noise will be a private nuisance to the occupant of a house near by, it is necessary to ascertain the natural and probable effect of the sound upon ordinary persons in that house, — not how it will affect a particular person who happens to be there to-day, or who may chance to come to-morrow. *Fay v. Whitman*, 100 Mass. 76; *Davis v. Sawyer*, 133 Mass. 289; *Walter v. Selfe*, 4 De Gex & S. 323; *Soltau v. De Held*, 2 Sim. (N. S.) 133; *Smelting Co. v. Tipping*, 11 H. L. Cas. 642. In *Walter v. Selfe*, Vice-Chancellor Knight Bruce, after elaborating his statement of the rule, concludes as follows: "They have I think established that the defendant's intended proceeding will, if prosecuted, abridge and diminish seriously and materially the ordinary comfort of existence to the occupier and inmates of the plaintiff's house, whatever their rank or station, whatever their age or state of health." It is said by Lord Romilly, Master of the Rolls, in *Crump v. Lambert*, L. R. 3 Eq. 408, that "the real question in all the cases is the question of fact, viz., whether the nuisance is such as materially to interfere with the ordinary comfort of human existence." In the opinion in *Sparhawk v. Railway Co.*, 54 Pa. St. 401, these words are used: "It seems to me that the rule expressed in the cases referred to is the only true one in judging of injury from alleged nuisances, viz., such as naturally and necessarily result to all alike who come within their influence." In the case of *Westcott v. Middleton*, 43 N. J. Eq. 478, 11 Atl. Rep. 490, (decided Dec. 9, 1887) it appeared that the defendant carried on the business of an undertaker, and the windows of the plaintiff's house looked out upon his yard, where boxes which had been used to preserve the bodies of the dead were frequently washed, and where other objects were visible and other work was going on, which affected the tender sensibilities of the plaintiff, and caused him great discomfort. Vice-Chancellor Bird, in dismissing the bill for an injunction against carrying on the business there, said: "The inquiry inevitably arises, if a decision is rendered in Mr. Westcott's favor because he is so morally or mentally constituted that the particular business complained of is an offence or a nuisance to him, or destructive to his comfort or his enjoyment of his home, — how many other cases will arise and claim the benefit of the same principle, however different the facts may be, or whatever may be the mental condition of the party complaining. . . . A wide range has indeed been given to courts of equity, in dealing with these matters, but I can find no case where the court has extended aid, unless the act complained of was, as I have above said, of a nature to affect all reasonable persons, similarly situated, alike." If one's right to use his property were to depend upon the effect of the use upon a person of peculiar temperament or disposition, or upon one suffering from an uncommon disease, the standard for measuring it would be so uncertain and fluctuating as to paralyze industrial enterprises. The owner of a factory containing noisy machinery, with dwelling-houses all about it, might find his business lawful as to all but one of the tenants of the houses, and as to that one, who dwelt no nearer than the others, it might be a nuisance. The character of his business might change from legal to illegal, or illegal to legal, with every change of tenants of an adjacent estate, or with an arrival or departure of a guest or boarder at a house near by; or even with the wakefulness or the tranquil repose of an invalid neighbor on a particular night. Legal rights to the use of property cannot be left to such uncertainty. When an act is of such a nature as to extend its influence to those in the vicinity, and its legal quality depends upon the effect of that influence, it is as important that the rightfulness of it should be tried by the experience of ordinary people, as it is, in determining a question as to negligence, that the test should be the common care of persons of ordinary prudence, without regard to the peculiarities of him whose conduct is on trial.

In the case at bar it is not contended that the ringing of the bell for church services in the manner shown by the evidence materially affected the health or comfort of ordinary people in the vicinity, but the plaintiff's claim rests upon the injury done him on account of his peculiar condition. However his request should have been treated by the defendant upon considerations of humanity, we think he could not put himself in a place of exposure to noise, and demand as of legal right that the bell should not be used. The plaintiff, in his brief, concedes that there was no evidence of express malice on the part of the defendant, but contends that malice was implied in his acts. In the absence of evidence that he acted wantonly, or with express malice, this implication could not come from his exercise of his legal rights. How far, and under what circumstances, malice may be material in cases of this kind, it is unnecessary to consider. Exceptions overruled.

What if the bell is rung very early in the morning, when most nearby residents are asleep? *See* "Too loud too early for Manayunk church bell, neighbor complains," Philadelphia Inquirer, Sept. 9, 2010, http://articles.philly.com/2010-09-09/news/ 24975796_1_bell-clock-tower-noise-law (complaint filed with city's Department of Licenses and Inspections complaining of bell ringing at 7:00 AM).

TICHENOR v. VORE
Court of Appeals of Missouri, 1997
953 S.W.2d 171

BARNEY, JUDGE.

This action was brought by Charles Wayne Tichenor, Shirley Jean Tichenor, Donald Cooper, Judy Cooper, Charles Murphy, Daniel David Dunigan, Sr., Karen Ann Dunigan, R.E. White and Mosell White (Plaintiffs), five separate land owners in Barry County, Missouri. Plaintiffs sought to enjoin James L. Vore, Patricia M. Vore and Carl Vore (Defendants) from keeping and maintaining a large dog kennel on Defendants' property because Plaintiffs alleged that the noise from the barking dogs was a private nuisance which unreasonably interfered with Plaintiffs' use and enjoyment of their property. Following a court-tried case, the trial court permanently enjoined Defendants' "operating, maintaining or having a dog kennel or otherwise keeping or maintaining more than two dogs" on their property.

Defendants appeal, assigning one point of trial court error. Defendants maintain that the trial court's judgment was against the manifest weight of the evidence because the Defendants' dog kennel did not substantially interfere with the rights of Plaintiffs to use and enjoy their property. Specifically, Defendants aver that the trial court erred in granting the permanent injunction because (1) the location of the property where the nuisance was alleged to exist is semi-rural in nature, (2) the dog kennel is well-constructed and is a considerable distance from Plaintiffs' homes, (3) the dogs barked only during daytime hours, and (4) because most of the Plaintiffs did not lose any sleep or develop health problems due to the barking dogs.

I

This being a court-tried case, this Court will sustain the judgment of the trial court unless there is no substantial evidence to support it, unless it is against the weight of the evidence, unless it erroneously declares the law, or unless it erroneously applies the law. . . .

We note that the trial court's judgment does not contain specific findings of fact and conclusions of law. When, as here, specific findings of fact and conclusions of law were not requested and none were entered, this Court will affirm the trial court's judgment if it is supported under any legal theory . . .

II

Defendants' parcel of land, purchased in February 1995, is located approximately three-quarters of a mile north of Wheaton, Barry County, Missouri, near Missouri Highway 86.[1]

---

[1] The record shows that all but one of the Plaintiffs purchased and recorded their deeds to their respective properties prior to Defendants' purchase and recording of Defendants' deed to their property. Plaintiffs Tichenors began constructing their home in 1995, prior to Defendants constructing their dog kennel.

. . . .

In June 1995, Defendants constructed a dog kennel to house their Australian Shepard [sic] show dogs. The kennel is an insulated building, constructed of cinder block and a wood shingle roof. The kennel contains sixteen pens/runs. No dogs were sold from the kennel.

Generally, Defendants would maintain sixteen Australian Shepard [sic] dogs, more or less, in the kennel. The dogs remained in the indoor/outdoor portion of the kennel during daytime hours. Defendants would move the dogs inside the kennel usually between 6:00 p.m. and 9:00 p.m.

There was detailed testimony from each of the five Plaintiffs regarding the noise generated by Defendants' barking dogs. Each of the Plaintiffs testified that Defendants' dogs barked in a fairly constant and annoying manner.

Plaintiffs Tichenors testified that Defendants' barking dogs were a constant source of aggravation. The Plaintiffs Tichenors noted that Defendants' dogs would bark as much as twenty hours per day, with "[n]ot a breath between barks." They both testified that they would often lose sleep from hearing the dogs barking. Plaintiff Charles Tichenor testified that Defendants' dogs would "[b]e barking hard enough, constant enough, you can't go back to sleep . . . you lay there and listen to them dogs." Plaintiff Charles Tichenor also testified that when the dogs were inside the kennel at night, barking, that the kennel structure created a "megaphone effect" and that he was forced to wear ear plugs when he slept at night. Plaintiff Charles Tichenor further testified that "I've been a royal grouch total for the last year . . . [t]he dogs has finally just got me — my nerves shook. There ain't no place to get away from it." He testified that they would often leave their residence and travel to "Cassville, Monett, Joplin, anywhere to just get away . . . for a few hours and let the dogs just go crazy. . . ."

The Plaintiffs Tichenors also testified that they were often unable to perform yard work, plant flowers, work in the garage or enjoy their back porch because of the constant "roar" of dog barking.

As additional evidence of the nuisance created by Defendants' barking dogs, Plaintiffs Tichenors presented a videotape and audiotape at trial, both of which recorded the level of noise generated by the dog barking. Also admitted in evidence was a diary maintained by Plaintiff Shirley Jean Tichenor that recorded their daily aggravation from hearing the dogs barking for some thirteen consecutive months. This diary was a detailed, fifty page, type-written document that chronicled when the Plaintiffs Tichenors were awakened by the dogs, when the dogs would stop barking and when they would resume barking.

Plaintiff Donald Cooper testified that the dog barking is "annoying — nerve

---

Although the issue of "prior occupation" was not expressly raised in Defendants' point relied on, we note that ["w]hile the weight of authority is that priority of occupation is not a defense as to one maintaining a nuisance, some courts have expressed the view that it is a factor to be considered in determining the character of the locality." Clinic & Hosp., Inc. v. McConnell, 241 Mo. App. 223, 236 S.W.2d 384, 391 (1951) (disapproved on other grounds in Frank v. Envir. Sanitation Mgt., Inc., 687 S.W.2d 876, 879-80 (Mo. banc 1985)); see also 58 Am. Jur. 2d Nuisances § 108 (1989).

racking." He further testified that often he and his wife would go outside of their home, "but sometimes we get tired of it and go in the house." Plaintiff Donald Cooper testified that he heard the dogs barking every day and agreed that the noise makes him physically upset.

Plaintiff Charles Murphy testified that sometimes he would go outside and you "don't hear them, but most of the time you do." He testified that even in his house he could easily hear the dogs barking. He testified that Defendants' barking dogs have had an adverse effect on his sleeping and his nerves.

Plaintiff Robert White testified that from where he lives he could easily hear the dogs barking. He testified that occasionally the barking dogs have been particularly annoying, in one instance disturbing his family reunion.

Plaintiff Daniel Dunigan testified that he and his wife often worked in their yard and that they could hear the dogs barking on and off all day long. He testified that "after two or three hours . . . you get annoyed with them."

On the other hand, Defendant Carl Vore denied that his dogs barked at night "to such a point that [he] had to go out — inside the kennel." Additionally, a neighbor, Tina Burns, testified that she had never been wakened by the dogs barking and had never had a problem entertaining guests or staying outside and enjoying the use of her property. Likewise, Patricia Utter testified that although she heard the dogs barking, it was not loud and would not bother her daily routine; neither was her sleep disturbed by the barking from the dog kennel. Mr. Douglas Hughes, a pet distributor/broker, who lived about three-fourths of a mile from the dog kennel, testified that he occasionally heard barking in the mornings but not on a regular basis. He acknowledged, however, that the "dogs [were] going to be louder on the Tichenor property than on [his] property" because of the closer location of the Tichenor property to the dog kennel. Lastly, Defendants presented the testimony of Kenneth Herrington. Mr. Herrington was hired by Defendants to check "for the noise in and around the kennel." He generally testified about going to the homes of the Plaintiffs to ascertain if he could hear dogs barking from these locations. He heard none.

The trial court granted a permanent injunction against Defendants and ordered Defendants to cease operation of their dog kennel. The judgment allowed Defendants to maintain no more than two dogs on their property.

III

An action for "private nuisance" rests on tort liability. *Vermillion v. Pioneer Gun Club*, 918 S.W.2d 827, 831 (Mo. App. 1996). A private nuisance is the unreasonable, unusual or unnatural use of one's property which substantially impairs the right of another to peacefully enjoy his property. *Frank v. Envir. Sanitation Mgt., Inc.*, 687 S.W.2d 876, 880 (Mo. banc 1985); *McCombs*, 925 S.W.2d at 950. The focus is on a defendant's unreasonable interference with the use and enjoyment of a plaintiff's land. *Frank*, 687 S.W.2d at 880.

The law of nuisance recognizes two conflicting rights: (1) property owners have a right to control their land and use it to benefit their best interests; and (2) the public and neighboring land owners have a right to prevent unreasonable use that substantially impairs the peaceful use and enjoyment of other land. *Id.* The *unreasonable use* element of nuisance balances the rights of adjoining property owners. *Id.* The crux, then, of a nuisance case is unreasonable land use. *Id.*

The easiest way to show a nuisance is to prove that a defendant's land use is unreasonable as a matter of law, "a nuisance per se."[2] *Id.* However, "the keeping of a dog or dogs *is not* nuisance per se since the dog is traditionally deemed to be one of the beasts friendliest to man. . . . "[3] *City of Fredericktown v. Osborn*, 429 S.W.2d 17, 23 (Mo. App. 1968) (emphasis added). Therefore, where the particular nuisance may not be considered a nuisance per se, the following is to be observed:

> There is no exact rule or formula by which the existence of a nuisance or the nonexistence of a nuisance may be determined. Necessarily each case must stand upon its own special circumstances, and no definite rule can be given that is applicable in all cases, but when an appreciable interference with the ordinary enjoyment of property, physically, is clearly made out as the result of a nuisance, a court of equity will never refuse to interfere.

Frank, 687 S.W.2d at 881 (citation omitted).

Further, as noted above, for a private nuisance to exist, the alleged harm to a land owner must be substantial. *See id.* at 880. In determining whether harm is substantial, we recognize that "the law does not concern itself with trifles. . . ." *McCombs*, 925 S.W.2d at 950.

> By significant harm is meant harm of importance, involving more than slight inconvenience or petty annoyance, determined by the standard of normal persons or property in the particular locality. If normal persons living in the community would regard the invasion as definitely oppressive, seriously annoying or intolerable, it is significant. If normal persons in the locality would not be substantially annoyed or disturbed, the invasion is not significant, even though the idio-syncracies [*sic*] of the particular plaintiff may make it unendurable to him.

---

[2] The court in *Rae* noted the following:

That mere noise may be so great at certain times and under certain circumstances as to amount to an actionable nuisance and entitle the party subjected to it to the preventative remedy of the court of equity is thoroughly established. The reason why a certain amount of noise is or may be a nuisance is that it is not only disagreeable but it also wears upon the nervous system and produces that feeling which we call "tired." That the subjection of a human being to a continued hearing of loud noises tends to shorten life, I think, is beyond all doubt. Another reason is that mankind needs both rest and sleep, and noise tends to prevent both. Rae v. Flynn, 690 So. 2d 1341, 1342 n.1 (Fla. App. 1997). Generally, maliciously designing to harm a neighbor, acts forbidden by statute, and activities openly carried on that a court considers flagrantly against accepted moral standards are considered a nuisance per se. Roger A. Cunningham, et al., The Law of Property § 7.2, at 414-15 (1984).

[3] "Noise is not a nuisance per se but may be of such a character or so excessive as to become one, even though it arises from operation of a lawful business." Racine v. Glendale Shooting Club, Inc., 755 S.W.2d 369, 372 (Mo. App. 1988). The following factors are relevant in determining whether a particular noise has risen to the level of a nuisance: (1) locality, (2) character of the neighborhood, (3) nature of use, (4) extent and frequency of injury, and (5) the effect upon enjoyment of life, health, and property of those affected. *Id.*

Id. (citation omitted).

Finally, we note that trial courts have the authority to issue an injunction enjoining the use of property if such use constitutes a nuisance injuring another or his property. *Osborn*, 429 S.W.2d at 22. Nevertheless, "[a]n injunction is an extraordinary and harsh remedy and should not be employed where there is an adequate remedy at law." *Farm Bureau Town & Country Ins. Co. of Missouri v. Angoff* 909 S.W.2d 348, 354 (Mo. en banc 1995).

Here, Defendants maintain that viewing the totality of the evidence adduced at trial, the annoyance caused to the Plaintiffs by Defendants' barking dogs was not substantial enough to conclude that the use and enjoyment of Plaintiffs' property was significantly impaired so as to warrant the issuance of a permanent injunction. Further, Defendants aver that they rebutted Plaintiffs' evidence and testimony, as outlined above, by presenting testimony from other neighbors in the surrounding area that they were not exasperated by Defendants' dogs.

However, "although there is no exact rule or formula for ascertaining when barking dogs rise to the level of a nuisance, relief will be granted where plaintiffs show they are substantially and unreasonably disturbed notwithstanding proof that others living in the vicinity are not annoyed." *Rae v. Flynn*, 690 So. 2d 1341, 1343 (Fla. App. 1997). Further, appellate courts defer to trial courts on the choice between conflicting evidence. *Warren*, 946 S.W.2d at 757.

We note that in *Rae*, the court stated that "in these types of cases even meager or uncorroborated evidence will support the [trial court's] findings if the evidence is of record and properly before the court." *Rae*, 690 So. 2d at 1343.

We conclude, given the nature of the Plaintiffs' neighborhood, the Defendants' maintenance of a dog kennel to house at least sixteen dogs that periodically but consistently barked day and night, thereby disturbing the peace and tranquility of Plaintiffs, constituted an unreasonable interference with Plaintiffs' use and enjoyment of their property. *See Frank*, 687 S.W.2d at 880. Further, the testimony and evidence adduced during the trial, particularly from the Plaintiffs Tichenors, established that the Plaintiffs' peaceful enjoyment of their property was significantly impaired by the Defendants' barking dogs and that Plaintiffs' complaints did not stem from "petty annoyances." *See McCombs*, 925 S.W.2d at 950; *Osborn*, 429 S.W.2d at 23.

The trial court's judgment issuing a permanent injunction was supported by substantial evidence.

The judgment is affirmed.

MONTGOMERY, C.J. and SHRUM, J., concur.

Was it necessary for the court to order the defendants permanently to cease all operation of a dog kennel? What other remedies might the court have considered? Note that many communities address such issues through local zoning ordinances.

CARPENTER v. THE DOUBLE R CATTLE COMPANY, INC. (CARPENTER I)
Court of Appeals of Idaho, 1983
669 P.2d 643

On Rehearing

Burnett, Judge

Dean William Prosser once observed, "There is perhaps no more impenetrable jungle in the entire law than that which surrounds the word 'nuisance'." W. Prosser, Handbook of the Law of Torts, § 86, at 571 (4th ed. 1971). Today we review a case that has thrust us into the jungle of nuisance law. We are asked to define the legal test for determining whether an intended use of property, which incidentally produces adverse effects upon neighboring properties, constitutes a nuisance.

This lawsuit was filed by a group of homeowners who alleged that expansion of a nearby cattle feedlot had created a nuisance. The homeowners claimed that operation of the expanded feedlot had caused noxious odors, air and water pollution, noise and pests in the area. The homeowners sought damages and injunctive relief. The issues of damages and injunctive relief were combined in a single trial, conducted before a jury. Apparently it was contemplated that the jury would perform a fact-finding function in determining whether a nuisance existed and whether the homeowners were entitled to damages, but would perform an advisory function on the question of injunctive relief. The district judge gave the jury a unified set of instructions embracing all of these functions. The jury returned a verdict simply finding that no nuisance existed. The court entered judgment for the feedlot proprietors, denying the homeowners any damages or injunctive relief. This appeal followed. For reasons appearing below, we vacate the judgment and remand the case for a new trial.

The homeowners contend that the jury received improper instructions on criteria for determining the existence of a nuisance. The jury was told to weigh the alleged injury to the homeowners against the "social value" of the feedlot, and to consider "the interests of the community as a whole," in determining whether a nuisance existed. In Part I of this opinion we consider the adequacy of the record upon which to review the jury instructions. In Part II we establish an historical framework for reviewing the instructions, by examining the development of American nuisance law. In Part III we turn to pertinent sections from the nuisance chapter of the Restatement (Second) of Torts (1977). We explain how these sections limit the utilization of such concepts as "social value" and "the interests of the community as a whole" in determining whether a nuisance exists. We discuss the implications of these sections; and we adopt them. Finally, in Part IV, we return to the jury instructions in this case, holding them to be erroneous and offering guidance to the trial court upon remand.

. . . .

II

The concept of nuisance originated in the law of property. At common law, a distinction was maintained between two encroachments upon property rights — interference with possession of land, and interference with the use and enjoyment of land. The first type of encroachment was subject to an "assize of novel disseisen," a remedy for trespass. The latter form of encroachment was subject to an "assize of nuisance," a remedy for a variety of invasions which diminished the owner's enjoyment of his property without dispossessing him of it. Thus, nuisance and trespass have common roots in property law, and occasionally it is difficult to distinguish between them. But where an invasion of property is merely incidental to the use of adjoining property, and does not physically interfere with possession of the property invaded, it generally has been classified as a nuisance rather than as a trespass. *See* cases collected in 58 Am. Jur. 2d *Nuisances*, § 2, 556-57 (1971).

The early concepts of nuisance and trespass shared the common law's reverence for property rights. Invasions of property were deemed wrongful per se, and the parties responsible for such invasions were subject to a form of strict liability. Thus, in the famous case of *Rylands v. Fletcher*, L.R. 1 Ex. 265 (1866), *aff'd* L.R. 3 H.L. 330 (1868), an English court held that the owner of a reservoir would be liable to the owner of adjacent property for any injury caused by escaping water. The court stated:

> We think that the true rule of law is, that the person who for his own purposes brings on his lands and collects and keeps there anything likely to do mischief if it escapes, must keep it in at his peril, and, if he does not do so, is prima facie answerable for all the damage which is the natural consequence of its escape. [L.R. 1 Ex. at 279.]

Although a physical intrusion by water might have been viewed as a trespass, rather than as a nuisance, the court noted that the result would have been the same regardless of whether the mischief was caused by "beasts, or water, or filth, or stenches." *Id.* at 280. Thus, the English concept of nuisance was broad, and it carried remedies similar to those available for trespass.

The property-oriented, English concept of a nuisance had its analogue in early American law. In one illustrative case of the nineteenth century, an American court held that title to land gave the owner the right to impregnate the air with odors, dust and smoke, pollute his own water and make noises, provided that he did not substantially interfere with the comfort of others or injure the use or enjoyment of their property. *Pennoyer v. Allen*, 56 Wis. 502, 14 N.W. 609 (1883).

This broad description of nuisance was incorporated into Idaho law. Idaho Code § 52-101, which has antecedents dating to 1881, defines a nuisance as "[a]nything which is injurious to health or morals, or is indecent, or offensive to the senses, or an obstruction to the free use of property, so as to interfere with the comfortable enjoyment of life or property." The statutory remedies are similarly broad. Idaho Code § 52-111 empowers "any person whose property is injuriously affected, or whose personal enjoyment is lessened by the nuisance [to bring an action] . . . and by the judgment the nuisance may be enjoined or abated, as well as damages recovered." Both private and public nuisances in Idaho may be the subjects of such actions brought by affected individuals, and the available remedies are the same in both categories. *See* I.C. §§ 52-102, 107, 111.

However, as the English concept of nuisance was assimilated into American law, it underwent a transformation. It ceased to be solely a creature of property law. As exemplified by the Idaho statutes, nuisance law came to protect life and health, as well as property. A nuisance signified not merely an infringement of property rights, but a wrong against both person and property — a tort.

American tort law in the nineteenth and early twentieth centuries was founded upon the rock of "fault." As the notion of fault burrowed into the concept of nuisance, the strict liability which had attended nuisance in property law began to deteriorate. American courts stressed that liability for nuisance would arise only from "unreasonable" uses of property. In some cases, the courts began to treat nuisance as a form of conduct rather than as a condition affecting the enjoyment of property. *E.g., Francisco v. Furry*, 82 Neb. 754, 118 N.W. 1102 (1908). This position later fell into disfavor. *E.g., Riter v. Keokuk Electro-Metals Co.*, 248 Iowa 710, 82 N.W.2d 151 (1957); *Smith v. City of Ann Arbor*, 303 Mich. 476, 6 N.W.2d 752 (1942).

However, American emphasis upon the element of reasonableness persisted. Our courts also underscored the distinction between conditions which are inherently nuisances (nuisances per se) and those conditions which may or may not constitute nuisances, depending upon the surrounding circumstances (nuisances per accidens). Of cases in the latter category, it became customary for the courts to say that whether an invasion of another's enjoyment of property was unreasonable would depend upon all circumstances in the case. These circumstances typically would include the location of the claimed nuisance, the character of the neighborhood, the nature of the offending activity, the frequency of the intrusion, and the effect upon the enjoyment of life, health and property. *E.g., York v. Stallings*, 217 Or. 13, 341 P.2d 529 (1959); *Reber v. Ill. Cent. R.R.*, 161 Miss. 885, 138 So. 574 (1932).

Moreover, the American transformation resulted in diminished application of the principle — derived from property law — that where property rights were substantially impaired by a nuisance, the complaining party was entitled to an injunction. This principle, which had complemented the property-based concept of strict liability, entitled a property owner to block an offensive activity on neighboring property, regardless of disparate economic consequences. American courts apparently found this approach ill-suited to the demands of a developing nation.

There evolved two lines of American response to the problem of injunctions. One response was to narrow the scope of cases in which injunctions would be granted, while continuing to recognize an entitlement to damages for injury to property rights. Thus, in *Clifton Iron Co. v. Dye*, 87 Ala. 468, 6 So. 192 (1889), the Alabama Supreme Court held that a mining company would not be enjoined from washing its ores simply because the operation polluted a stream below. The court held that the aggrieved parties' recourse was in damages. Similarly, in *New York City v. Pine*, 185 U.S. 93, 22 S.Ct. 592, 46 L.Ed. 820 (1902), the United States Supreme Court held that two farmers would not be entitled to an absolute injunction against construction of a dam designed to enhance the water supply of the city, even though it adversely affected their properties. However, the Supreme Court held that a conditional injunction would issue unless the farmers were compensated in damages. Other illustrative cases from that era, in which injunctive relief was withheld, but the availability of damages was affirmed, include *Bartel v. Ridgefield Lumber Co.*, 131 Wash. 183, 229 P. 306 (1924), and *Galveston H. & S.A. Ry. v. DeGroff*, 102 Tex. 433, 118 S.W. 134 (1909).

Ultimately, the approach exemplified by these cases developed into the "comparative injury" doctrine. Under this doctrine, the comparative benefits and hardships of discontinuing one activity for the protection of another would be weighed in determining whether injunctive relief or damages represented the more appropriate remedy for a nuisance. The Idaho Supreme Court adopted the comparative injury doctrine in *Koseris v. J.R. Simplot Co.*, 82 Idaho 263, 352 P.2d 235 (1960). As explained later in this opinion, our Supreme Court in *Koseris* acknowledged the right to recover damages for the invasion of one's property, even where the comparative injury doctrine might bar injunctive relief.

The second line of American response to the injunction problem was to narrow the scope of cases in which nuisances were found to exist. This was achieved by incorporating the social value — the "utility" — of the offending activity into the litany of circumstances to be weighed in determining whether a particular use of property was "unreasonable." Thus, the utility of an offending activity militated not merely against the issuance of an injunction, but also against a determination that the offending activity was a nuisance at all. This second line of response found expression in the general ("black letter") principles set forth by the Restatement of Torts (1932) (herein cited as the First Restatement). Section 826 of the First Restatement declared that an invasion of another's enjoyment of property would be deemed unreasonable, and therefore a nuisance, *unless* the utility of the actor's conduct outweighed the gravity of the harm.

The Idaho Supreme Court never explicitly adopted the First Restatement. However, in *McNichols v. J.R. Simplot Co., supra*, the Court may have intimated a similar approach. In that case, emissions from a large phosphate plant were alleged to have adversely affected a small neighboring business. Both damages and injunctive relief were sought. As noted earlier in this opinion, the Supreme Court in *McNichols* found certain jury instructions to be incomplete; and the Court reversed a judgment for the phosphate plant. However, the Court also mentioned, without disapproval, other instructions stating that existence of a nuisance should be determined in light of "all circumstances," and outlining the factors to be weighed. These factors included "inconsequentialness of the relative size or importance of the respective businesses (relative benefit or loss is a pertinent factor). . . ." 74 Idaho at 324, 262 P.2d at 1014. This ambiguous language later was deemed to support a pattern jury instruction stating that "the interests of the community as a whole" should be considered in determining whether a nuisance exists. *See* Idaho Jury Instructions (IDJI) 491 (1st ed. 1974 & 2d ed. 1982).

Thus, when confronted with a choice between the two American lines of response to the problem of injunctions in nuisance cases, Idaho appeared to choose both. *Koseris* adopted the "comparative injury" doctrine, restricting the cases qualifying for injunctions without narrowing the scope of nuisance cases in which an aggrieved party was entitled to be compensated in damages. However, *McNichols* and IDJI 491 allowed the offending activity's value to the community to be considered in determining whether any nuisance existed at all.

Idaho's uncertain direction reflected a national confusion which led Dean Prosser to deliver his characterization of nuisance law as a "jungle." Indeed, Dean Prosser's treatise on torts, in its 1964 edition, reflected the ambivalence of the time. Prosser expounded the black letter test of the First Restatement, balancing the gravity of harm against the utility of the offending activity, for determining existence of a nuisance. However, he further noted that "[i]n an action for damages, the relative hardship upon the plaintiff and the defendant is not material, once the nuisance is found to exist." W. Prosser, Handbook of the Law of Torts 621 (3d ed. 1964). In the 1971 edition of his treatise, Prosser further observed that in a case where the balancing test would preclude an injunction, nevertheless, "the defendant's conduct may be found to be so unreasonable that he should pay for the harm. . . ." W. Prosser, Handbook of the Law of Torts 604 (4th ed. 1971).

Dissatisfaction with the First Restatement also was expressed by the courts. In *Boomer v. Atlantic Cement Co.*, 26 N.Y.2d 219, 309 N.Y.S.2d 312, 257 N.E.2d 870 (1970), the New York Court of Appeals held that parties adversely affected by dust from a cement plant would be entitled to recover damages for the harm, although the value of the cement plant to the community was so great that its operation would not be enjoined. The Oregon Supreme Court also refused to follow the First Restatement's test for determining existence of a nuisance. In *Furrer v. Talent Irr. Dist*, 258 Or. 494, 466 P.2d 605 (1970), the Court rejected the contention:

> that in every case the jury has the power to exonerate the defendant from liability because it feels that the social value of the defendant's conduct outweighs the harm which the defendant has visited upon the plaintiff. . . . [I]f the plaintiff's land is harmed by the conduct of the defendant, the latter cannot escape compensating the plaintiff for the harm simply by showing that the defendant's use had a greater social value than the plaintiff's. [466 P.2d at 613.]

Similarly, *Jost v. Dairyland Power Coop.*, 45 Wis. 2d 164, 172 N.W.2d 647 (1970), upheld compensation for crop damage caused by sulfur fumes from an electrical power generating plant. On appeal, the power company contended that the trial court erred by not allowing it to prove its economic importance to the region, as a defense against the damage claim. The Wisconsin Supreme Court replied:

> We . . . conclude that the court properly excluded all evidence that tended to show the utility of the [power company's] enterprise. Whether its economic or social importance dwarfed the claim of a small farmer is of no consequence in this lawsuit. It will not be said that, because a great and socially useful enterprise will be liable in damages, an injury small by comparison should go unredressed. We know of no acceptable rule of jurisprudence that permits those who are engaged in important and desirable enterprises to injure with impunity those who are engaged in enterprises of lesser economic significance. [172 N.W.2d at 653.]

Thus, it was clear by 1970 that the First Restatement's black letter test for existence of a nuisance had ceased to be —if, indeed, it ever was — an adequate expression of case law. The days were drawing to a close when an economic activity could escape all liability under nuisance law for harm caused to its neighbors, simply because a large measure of social utility was ascribed to it.

III

The seeds of reform had been sown. They took root in fertile soil when the American Law Institute (ALI), which had begun to write a new restatement of the law of torts, turned its attention to the subject of nuisances in 1970.

A. *The ALI Proceedings*

The first pertinent draft of the new restatement, Tentative Draft No. 16, echoed § 826 of the First Restatement. It reiterated the test of balancing utility against gravity of the harm. However, in a memorandum to ALI participants, Professor Fleming James, Jr., argued that this test was no longer sufficient. At the 1970 Proceedings of the American Law Institute (herein cited as the 1970 Proceedings), Professor Robert Keeton moved that the Tentative Draft be amended so that "in the black letter of one of the appropriate sections this proposition be stated:

> "[E]ven though one's conduct is reasonable in the sense that its social utility outweighs the harms and risks it causes, he is subject to liability for a private nuisance if the resulting interference with another's use and enjoyment of land is greater than it is reasonable to require the other to bear under the circumstances without compensation." [1970 Proceedings at 312.]

Dean Prosser, who was then serving as the reporter of the Proceedings, acknowledged that the cases had come to disagree with the First Restatement's test for existence of a nuisance. . . . Nevertheless, Prosser opposed Keeton's motion to amend the black letter of the Tentative Draft. Prosser argued that in determining whether an interference is greater than it is reasonable to expect the other to bear under the circumstances without compensation, the courts should continue to examine all circumstances including the utility of the offending activity. . . .

However, several other participants, including Professor James, supported Keeton's motion. They urged a fundamental principle that, regardless of the balance between utility and harm, there should be liability in damages if a plaintiff's injury is more than he should bear without compensation. Professor Keeton, again taking the floor, emphasized that an ordinary reader, looking at the black letter of § 826, would be led to think that an invasion is deemed reasonable, and therefore gives rise to no liability for nuisance, if the utility exceeds the harm. Keeton urged that this was an erroneous conclusion, and that the black letter should be amended. Ultimately, Keeton's motion was put to vote, and the presiding officer declared that it had "plainly carried." 1970 Proceedings at 325.

This amendment of Tentative Draft No. 16 in 1970 led to preparation of Tentative Draft No. 17 in 1971. Dean John W. Wade succeeded Dean Prosser as reporter of the Proceedings and wrote the new draft. Wade viewed Keeton's 1970 motion as "having two ideas in it.

(1) [T]hat the activity may be a very useful one in general so that it should not be abated and yet be one which should "pay its own way" (i.e., compensate for the damage it caused), and (2) that the damage to the injured party may be so substantial that payment should be made regardless of the utility of the conduct.

Wade, *Environmental Protection, The Common Law of Nuisance and The Restatement of Torts*, 8 Forum 165, 170 (1972).

Wade cautiously incorporated these ideas into Tentative Draft No. 17. In response to the first idea, he retained the balancing test between gravity of the harm and utility of the conduct but added a new factor for determining the gravity of the harm — "[w]hether it is impractical to maintain the activity if it is required to bear the cost of compensating for the invasion." As to the second idea, Wade did not change the black letter of the new restatement, but added pertinent comments. 1971 Proceedings of the American Law Institute (herein cited as 1971 Proceedings) at 74.

Wade's cautious method of dealing with Keeton's motion was criticized in the 1971 Proceedings. Professor Keeton noted that Tentative Draft No. 17 still contained a conflict between the black letter of § 826, which recited that an invasion would be deemed reasonable if the utility exceeded the harm, and those other sections or comments which said there could be liability for damages in some circumstances even though the utility exceeded the harm. Keeton urged that the black letter of § 826 itself be amended to set forth an additional, alternative test of nuisance — that despite its utility, an activity would be liable in damages if the harm it created were greater than others should be required to bear without compensation. 1971 Proceedings at 83. Reporter Wade then offered a proposal to that general effect. 1971 Proceedings at 85.

The only significant resistance to this proposal came not from any speakers who would have returned to the simple balancing test set forth in the First Restatement, but from those who felt the proposal did not go far enough in protecting against harm caused by activities with great social utility. . . .

Professor Dennis Hynes also emphasized the importance of changing § 826. He argued that liability in damages must not turn narrowly upon the balance of utility against harm. Rather, damages serve the important function of forcing an enterprise to bear the societal costs ("externalities") which its activity imposes upon neighboring land uses. 1971 Proceedings at 76-79. Such externalities, when not internalized by a mechanism such as damage awards, understate the cost of economic activity, creating an involuntary subsidy of the enterprise.

Dean Wade's proposal was not further amended during the 1971 Proceedings. It spawned Tentative Draft No. 18, prepared by Wade in 1972. This draft contained both the traditional balancing test and an alternative test — explained in greater detail below — for determining liability in damages. The concept of utility itself was also modified to indicate that the utility of an activity would be diminished if it did not pay its way in society.

B. *The Second Restatement*

Ultimately, the provisions of Tentative Draft No. 18 were approved and incorporated into the private nuisance sections of chapter 40, Restatement (Second) of Torts (1977) (herein cited as the Second Restatement). The Second Restatement, like its predecessor, divides such nuisances into two groups: (a) "intentional and unreasonable" invasions of another's interest in the use and enjoyment of property, and (b) invasions which are "unintentional" but otherwise actionable under general tort principles. Second Restatement at § 822.

The first category is broader than the term "intentional" at first glance might suggest. Section 825 of the Second Restatement explains that an invasion is "intentional" if the actor knows that the invasion is resulting, or is substantially certain to result, from his activity. Thus, the purpose of an activity, such as a feedlot, may not be to invade its neighbors' interests in the use and enjoyment of their property; but the invasion is "intentional" within the meaning of the Second Restatement if the proprietors of the activity know that such an invasion is resulting — or is substantially certain to result — from the intended operation of their business. We focus upon "intentional" invasion, in this sense, because it is the type of nuisance alleged to exist in the present case.

The Second Restatement treats such an "intentional" invasion as a nuisance if it is "unreasonable." Section 826 of the Second Restatement now provides two sets of criteria for determining whether this type of nuisance exists:

> An intentional invasion of another's interest in the use and enjoyment of land is unreasonable if
>
> (a) the gravity of the harm outweighs the utility of the actor's conduct, or
>
> (b) the harm caused by the conduct is serious and the financial burden of compensating for this and similar harm to others would not make the continuation of the conduct not feasible.

The present version of § 826, unlike its counterpart in the First Restatement, recognizes that liability for damages caused by a nuisance may exist regardless of whether the utility of the offending activity exceeds the gravity of the harm it has created. This fundamental proposition now permeates the entire Second Restatement. The commentary to § 822, which distinguishes between "intentional" and "unintentional" invasions, and which serves as the gateway for all succeeding sections, emphasizes that the test for existence of a nuisance no longer depends solely upon the balance between the gravity of harm and utility of the conduct. Comment d to § 822 states that, for the purpose of determining liability for damages, an invasion may be regarded as unreasonable even though the utility of the conduct is great and the amount of harm is relatively small. Comment g to the same section reemphasizes that damages are appropriate where the harm from the invasion is greater than a party should be required to bear, "at least without compensation."

The distinction between damages and injunctive relief is carried over in the commentary to § 826. Comment e recognizes that the utility of an activity may be greatly reduced if it does not compensate those whom it harms. Comment f stresses that an intentional invasion, for which damages may be sought, is unreasonable where the harm can be compensated even if the gravity of the harm does not outweigh the utility of the conduct.

C. *Evaluation of The Second Restatement*

The Second Restatement clearly has rejected the notion that if an activity's utility exceeds the harm it creates, the activity is not a nuisance and therefore is free from all liability in damages or for injunctive relief. *See Pendergrast v. Aiken*, 293 N.C. 201, 236 S.E.2d 787 (1977) (adopting Tentative Draft 18 of the Second Restatement). It discards those earlier authorities which had responded to the problem of disparate economic consequences of injunctions by narrowing the concept of nuisance. Thus, the Second Restatement today is inconsistent with the Idaho Supreme Court's decision in *McNichols, supra*, insofar as that decision is said to support IDJI 491. As noted earlier, this pattern instruction would require a jury to consider "the interest of the community as a whole" in determining whether a nuisance exists. IDJI 491 enunciates a single test for existence of a nuisance — regardless of whether damages or an injunction are sought — and obliquely incorporates the utility of the offending activity into the unified test. The pattern instruction perpetuates a discredited line of authority rejected by the Second Restatement.

In contrast, the Idaho Supreme Court's decision in *Koseris, supra*, is entirely consistent with — and in some respects might be said to have presaged — the Second Restatement. In that case, a plaintiff sought injunctive relief, but claimed no damages, from fumes emitted by the same phosphate plant involved in *McNichols*. The phosphate plant offered to prove, among other things, that its facility was important to the economies and tax bases of certain counties in southeastern Idaho. The trial court disallowed the proof. On appeal our Supreme Court said:

> We are constrained to hold that the trial court erred in sustaining objections to those offers of proof, since they were relevant as bearing upon the issue whether respondents, in seeking *injunctive relief*, were pursuing the proper remedy; nevertheless, on the theory of *damages* which respondents had waived, the ruling was correct. [82 Idaho at 270, 352 P.2d at 239. Emphasis added.]

Both the Second Restatement and *Koseris* recognize that utility of the activity alleged to be a nuisance is a proper factor to consider in the context of injunctive relief; but that damages may be awarded regardless of utility. Evidence of utility does not constitute a defense against recovery of damages where the harm is serious and compensation is feasible. Were the law otherwise, a large enterprise, important to the local economy, would have a lesser duty to compensate its neighbors for invasion of their rights than would a smaller business deemed less essential to the community. In our view, this is not, and should not be, the law in Idaho.

Koseris and the Second Restatement also share a recognition of the fundamental difference between making an activity compensate those whom it harms, and forcing the activity to discontinue or to modify its operations. The damage question goes to a person's basic right in tort law to recover for harm inflicted by another. The injunction question is broader; it brings into play the interest of other persons who may benefit from the activity. Comparative benefits and hardships must be weighed in determining whether injunctive relief is appropriate. Thus, the Second Restatement is consistent with the "comparative injury" standard adopted in *Koseris. See also Hansen v. Indep. School Dist. No. 1*, 61 Idaho 109, 98 P.2d 959 (1939).

We believe that *Koseris* and the Second Restatement furnish better guidance than IDJI 491 for the future path of nuisance law in Idaho. The law of nuisance profoundly affects the quality of life enjoyed by all Idahoans. It should be broad in coverage, as our statutes provide, and fair in its application. It should not contain blind spots for large or important enterprises.

However, our view is not based simply upon general notions of fairness; it is also grounded in economics. The Second Restatement deals effectively with the problem of "externalities" identified in the ALI proceedings. Where an enterprise externalizes some burdens upon its neighbors, without compensation, our market system does not reflect the true cost of products or services provided by that enterprise. Externalities distort the price signals essential to the proper functioning of the market.

This problem affects two fundamental objectives of the economic system. The first objective, commonly called "efficiency" in economic theory, is to promote the greatest aggregate surplus of benefits over the costs of economic activity. The second objective, usually termed "equity" or "distributive justice," is to allocate these benefits and costs in accordance with prevailing societal values. The market system best serves the goal of efficiency when prices reflect true costs; and the goal of distributive justice is best achieved when benefits are explicitly identified to the correlative costs.

Although the problem of externalities affects both goals of efficiency and distributive justice, these objectives are conceptually different and may imply different solutions to a given problem. In theory, if there were no societal goal other than efficiency, and if there were no impediments to exchanges of property or property rights, individuals pursuing their economic self-interests might reach the most efficient allocation of costs and benefits by means of exchange, without direction by the courts. *See* Coase, *The Problem of Social Cost*, 3 J.L. & Econ. 1 (1960). However, the real world is not free from impediments to exchanges, and our economic system operates within the constraints of a society which is also concerned with distributive justice. Thus, the courts often are the battle-grounds upon which campaigns for efficiency and distributive justice are waged.

Our historical survey of nuisance law, in Part II of this opinion, has reflected the differing emphases upon efficiency and distributive justice. As noted, the English system of property law placed a preeminent value upon property rights. It was thus primarily concerned with distributive justice in accord with those rights. For that reason the English system favored the injunction as a remedy for a nuisance, regardless of disparate economic consequences. However, when the concept of nuisance was incorporated into American law, it encountered a different value system. Respect for property rights came to be tempered by the tort-related concept of fault, and the demands of a developing nation placed greater emphasis upon the economic objective of efficiency relative to the objective of distributive justice. The injunction fell into disfavor. The reaction against the injunction, as embodied in the First Restatement, so narrowed the concept of nuisance itself that it rendered the courts impotent to deal with externalities generated by enterprises of great utility. This reaction was excessive; neither efficiency nor distributive justice has been well served.

In order to address the problem of externalities, the remedies of damages and injunctive relief must be carefully chosen to accommodate the often competing goals of efficiency and distributive justice. *See generally* Polinsky, *Resolving Nuisance Disputes: The Simple Economics of Injunctive and Damage Remedies*, 32 Stan. L. Rev. 1075 (1980); Ellickson, *Alternatives to Zoning: Covenants, Nuisance Rules, and Fines as Land Use Controls*, 40 U. Chi. L. Rev. 681 (1973). *Koseris* and the Second Restatement recognize the complementary functions of injunctions and damages. Section 826(a) of the Second Restatement allows both injunctions and damages to be employed where the harm created by an economic activity exceeds its utility. Section 826(b) allows the more limited remedy of damages alone to be employed where it would not be appropriate to enjoin the activity but the activity is imposing harm upon its neighbors so substantial that they cannot reasonably be expected to bear it without compensation.

We follow *Koseris* and adopt § 826 of the Second Restatement. To the extent that IDJI 491 is inconsistent with our decision today, we urge that it be modified. In any event, IDJI 491 is merely recommendatory in nature; it is not mandatory. I.R.C.P. 51(a)(2).

D. *Implications of the Second Restatement*

Each of the parties in the present case has viewed the Second Restatement with some apprehension. We now turn to those concerns.

The homeowners, echoing an argument made during the ALI proceedings, have contended that the test of nuisance set forth in § 826 grants large enterprises a form of private eminent domain. They evidently fear that if the utility of a large enterprise exceeds the gravity of the harm it creates — insulating it from an injunction and subjecting it to liability only in damages — the enterprise might interfere at will with the enjoyment and use of neighboring property, upon penalty only of paying compensation from time to time. Such a result might be consistent with the economic goal of efficiency, but it may conflict with the goal of distributive justice insofar as it violates a basic societal value which opposes forced exchanges of property rights. *See* Calabresi, *Some Thoughts on Risk Distribution and the Law of Torts*, 70 Yale L.J. 499, 536 (1961).

Even those legal scholars who advocate the most limited role for injunctions as a remedy against nuisances acknowledge that damages may be inadequate, and injunctions may be necessary, where the harm in question relates to personal health and safety, or to one's fundamental freedom of action within the boundaries of his own property. Ellickson, *supra*, 40 U. Chi. L. Rev. at 740-41. Ordinarily, plaintiffs in such cases would prevail on the test which balances utility against gravity of the harm. Moreover, in the exceptional cases, the offending activity might be modified or eliminated through legislative or administrative controls such as environmental protection laws or zoning. Therefore, we expect that few cases would remain in need of a judicial remedy. However, we do not today close the door on the possibility that an injunction might lie, to protect personal health and safety or fundamental freedoms, in cases missed by the balancing test and by non-judicial controls. To this extent, our adoption of the Second Restatement's test of nuisance stops short of being absolute.

The Second Restatement also has encountered a host of objections from the feedlot proprietors and from the amicus curiae. These objections reflect genuine, legitimate concerns of Idaho business, particularly the agricultural community. The concerns have been eloquently presented by able counsel. We recognize that business is an anchor of our state. We believe that Idaho business will find that it can operate responsibly and profitably within the contours of nuisance liability defined by the Second Restatement. Every business person is someone else's neighbor. Business people are as much benefited by protecting our quality of life as are other Idaho residents. We further note that business enterprises which do not depend for their viability upon an asserted right to impose serious harm upon their neighbors will not be threatened by the nuisance tests articulated in the Second Restatement.

Beyond these general observations, we address several particular objections to the Second Restatement. First, our attention has been invited to the Idaho "Right to Farm Act," I.C. §§ 22-4501 et seq. This Act recites the Legislature's concern that agricultural activities conducted on farmland in urbanizing areas often are subjected to nuisance lawsuits. The Act imposes restrictions upon such lawsuits. However, we find that these restrictions are inapposite to the present case. The Act does not apply to lawsuits commenced before March 31, 1981. See I.C. § 22-4504. The homeowners' complaint in the instant case was filed on March 28, 1978.

More fundamentally, even assuming, without deciding, that a feedlot constitutes an "agricultural operation" within the meaning of the Act, the Act precludes a finding of nuisance only with respect to an activity which would not have been a nuisance but for a change in surrounding non-agricultural uses more than one year after the activity began. See I.C. § 22-4503. In contrast, the pleadings in the present case disclose that the feedlot is alleged to be a nuisance, not because of changes in surrounding non-agricultural uses, but because of an expansion of the feedlot itself.

The proprietors and amicus curiae recognize that the Act does not strictly apply in this case, but they suggest that it is a legislative statement of policy which should inhibit our adoption of the Second Restatement. However, the Act in essence represents a statutory adaptation of the common law doctrine of "coming to the nuisance." This doctrine does not conflict with the Second Restatement.

At early common law, the doctrine of "coming to the nuisance" was thus expressed:

> If my neighbor makes a tan-yard so as to annoy and render less salubrious the air of my house or gardens, the law will furnish me with a remedy; but

> if he is first in possession of the air, and I fix my habitation near him, the nuisance is of my own seeking, and may continue.

2 W. Blackstone, Commentaries on the Laws of England, 402 (17th ed. 1830). This rigid doctrine later was changed to provide that coming to the nuisance was not an absolute bar to the finding of a nuisance, but was merely one factor to be considered. *E.g., Kellogg v. Village of Viola*, 67 Wis.2d 345, 227 N.W.2d 55 (1975); *Spencer Creek Pollution Control Ass'n v. Organic Fertilizer Co.*, 264 Or. 557, 505 P.2d 919 (1973). This change stemmed from recognition that an absolute bar to a finding of nuisance would, in effect, give the offending activity a perpetual servitude upon the land of its neighbors without the payment of any compensation.

In keeping with this case law development, the Second Restatement recites, at § 840D, that coming to the nuisance is not a total bar to relief, but is a factor to be considered. When this section of the Second Restatement is considered in relation to the tests of nuisance set forth in § 826, we believe that coming to the nuisance is a factor which a jury may consider in evaluating the seriousness of the harm later claimed by the plaintiffs. We conclude that the Act affords no basis to view the Second Restatement as contrary to legislative policy.

The feedlot proprietors and amicus curiae also contend that the Second Restatement should be rejected because it assertedly contains a rule of absolute liability, making an enterprise liable in damages to anyone adversely affected by its operations. However, this argument overlooks the requirement in § 826(b) that the harm be "serious." A plaintiff who fails to demonstrate harm exceeding the utility of a defendant's conduct will fail to establish a nuisance under § 826(a). The plaintiff also will fail under § 826(b) unless the trier of fact is persuaded that the harm shown is "serious." Long before the Second Restatement, it had been well established by case law that an activity would not be deemed a nuisance unless the harm attributed to it was more injurious to the normal use and enjoyment of land than the harm attributed to other types of activities customarily encountered in the relevant area. *E.g., Amphitheaters, Inc. v. Portland Meadows*, 184 Or. 336, 198 P.2d 847 (1948); *The Shelburne, Inc. v. Crossan Corp.*, 95 N.J.Eq. 188, 122 A. 749 (1923). Moreover, "[a]n interference is not a nuisance unless, among other things, it *substantially* interferes with the use and enjoyment of neighboring land." Rabin, *Nuisance Law: Rethinking Fundamental Assumptions*, 63 Va. L. Rev. 1299, 1319 (1977) (emphasis in original). In our view, unless the harm claimed by a plaintiff is substantial, and more injurious than that caused by other types of activities customary to the area, it would not be deemed "serious" within the meaning of § 826(b).

In determining seriousness, the factors for evaluating gravity of harm, as set forth in § 827, may be utilized. They include the extent and character of the harm, the suitability of the particular use or enjoyment invaded to the character of the locality, the burden on the injured person to avoid such harm, and the value which the law attaches to the type of use or enjoyment invaded. The last factor — the value attached to the type of use or enjoyment invaded — obviously relates to its intrinsic value when applied under § 826(b); its relative value, in comparison with the utility of the offending activity, should be considered only when applying § 826(a).

Moreover, comment g to § 822 makes it clear that the Second Restatement does not create a rule of absolute liability. The comment states, in part, the following:

Not every intentional and significant invasion of a person's interest in the use and enjoyment of land is actionable. . . . Life in organized society and especially in populous communities involves an unavoidable clash of individual interests. Practically all human activities unless carried on in a wilderness interfere to some extent with others or involve some risk of interference, and these interferences range from mere trifling annoyances to serious harms. . . . Liability for damages is imposed in those cases in which the harm or risk to one is greater than he ought to be required to bear under the circumstances, at least without compensation.

The feedlot proprietors and amicus curiae also assert that the Second Restatement will prove uneven in its application, because damages may be awarded only in those cases where the payment of such compensation is "feasible." They contend that the element of feasibility subjects a profitable enterprise to greater potential liability than that which would attend a similar activity conducted by a marginal business. However, we believe this contention misperceives the thrust of the feasibility requirement.

As used in § 826(b), the term "feasible" does not refer to the financial condition of the business conducting the activity, but refers to the activity itself. Section 826(b) merely recognizes that if the burden of paying compensation in damages would make it unfeasible to continue the activity, the effect of a damage award would be to discontinue operation of the activity. In those circumstances, the result would be the same as an injunction. In order to qualify for injunctive relief under § 826(a), a plaintiff would be required to show that the gravity of the harm exceeded the utility of the defendant's conduct. Thus, as noted in comment f to § 826, "[i]f imposition of this financial burden would make continuation of the activity not feasible, the weighing process for determining unreasonableness is similar to that in a suit for injunction." Comment f to the same section further notes that the feasibility requirement may limit the scope of plaintiffs who can recover:

[I]n the case of a factory emitting smoke and odors, the granting of compensation for annoyance and inconvenience to all persons located in the general vicinity may create a burden so heavy as to make it not feasible to continue to operate the factory. Compensation may therefore be granted only to those in closer vicinity to the plant whose annoyance is more severe, and not to those farther away whose annoyance is less. . . . Cases involving airport noise [also] illustrate this principle.

The element of feasibility illustrates the interrelationship between § 826(a) and § 826(b). If a plaintiff suffers serious harm from an intentional invasion of the use and enjoyment of his property, he is entitled to injunctive relief or damages — or a mix of these remedies — if the trier of fact determines that the gravity of the harm exceeds the utility of the defendant's conduct. If the harm does not outweigh the utility, but remains serious, the plaintiff's remedy is limited to damages — subject, however, to the further limitation that if the nature of the activity (not the particular enterprise conducting it) is such that payment of compensation in damages would cause the activity to be discontinued, then the damage award will be viewed as having the same impact as an injunction. In those circumstances, full compensation will not be awarded unless the gravity of the harm has been found to exceed the utility of the defendant's conduct.

IV

We now resume our focus upon the instant case. The feeding of large congregations of animals within the confined area of a feedlot may create problems that affect the use and enjoyment of neighboring properties. *See generally* Recker, *Animal Feeding Factories and the Environment: A Summary of Feedlot Pollution, Federal Controls, and Oklahoma Law*, 30 S.W.L.J. 556 (1976). In general, feedlots are subject to the same principles of nuisance law which apply to other economic activities. *Botsch v. Leigh Land Co.*, 195 Neb. 509, 239 N.W.2d 481 (1976). General nuisance instructions were given to the jury in this case.

The actual instructions need not be set forth at length. In summary . . . the district judge gave the jury a set of instructions which did not conform precisely to, but were consistent with, the First Restatement and IDJI 491. The court took no account of *Koseris*, nor of the dual criteria for determining the existence of a nuisance under § 826 of the Second Restatement. The jury was given no instruction on damage liability comparable to § 826(b) of the Second Restatement. We conclude that the jury was improperly instructed, in light of our adoption today of the Second Restatement's criteria for determining existence of a nuisance.

The feedlot proprietors argue that even if the instructions failed adequately to state the entire standard contained in the Second Restatement, nevertheless, the instructions sufficiently stated the test of balancing harm against utility under § 826(a). Accordingly, the proprietors urge us not to disturb that part of the district court's judgment which denied injunctive relief. They contend that any remand in this case should be limited to a determination of damage liability — that is, whether the harm claimed by the plaintiff was "serious" and the payment of compensation was "feasible" under § 826(b). This argument is attractive because it comports with a surface reading of the tests set forth in the two subsections of § 826. However, we believe the argument overlooks the deeper interrelationships between these subsections, and between the remedies of damages and injunctive relief.

As noted earlier, the questions of existence of a nuisance and of liability for damages under § 826(b) turn, in part, upon the feasibility of compensation. If the nature of the activity itself is found to be such that payment of compensation would not be feasible, then the trier of fact could not find a nuisance to exist, and could not make a damage award, unless the gravity of the plaintiffs' harm were determined to exceed the utility of the defendants' conduct under § 826(a). This clearly would overlap with the issue framed in the first trial.

No two trials in the same action are identical. A second trial in this case might involve more or less evidence, or different emphases upon the evidence, than the first trial. We believe it would be unsound to preclude the trier of fact in a second trial from reaching an issue governed by § 826(a) if that issue were central to the outcome of the case under § 826(b). . . .

Further, we believe that a rigid separation of § 826(a) from § 826(b) would be inconsistent with the nexus between the remedies of damages and injunc-tive relief in nuisance cases. A nuisance may be alleviated by no fewer than four possible remedies: (1) an injunction; (2) damages; (3) a conditional injunction, which may be dissolved or modified upon payment of damages; or (4) in unusual circumstances, the "purchased injunction" which is imposed upon condition that a plaintiff may make some offsetting payment to the defendant. Calabresi & Malamed, *Property Rules, Liability Rules, and Inalienability: One View of the Cathedral*, 85 Harv. L. Rev. 1089 (1972). Moreover, where a nuisance can be abated, and the harm is not permanent but would stop when the nuisance is abated, a plaintiff would not necessarily be entitled to permanent damages. Rather, he could receive temporary or conditionally continuing damages, until the abatement occurs.

Thus, in a nuisance case, the remedies may not be simplistically differentiated between damages and injunctive relief. Some mixture of the remedies may be appropriate. Because the two tests for existence of a nuisance under § 826 carry direct implications for the types of remedies available, the possible mixture of remedies makes it conceptually unsound for different triers of fact, upon different presentations of evidence, to determine the existence of a nuisance under §§ 826(a) and 826(b), separately.

We conclude that the entire judgment of the district court, entered upon the verdict of a jury which had been improperly instructed, must be vacated. The case must be remanded for a new trial to determine whether a nuisance exists under the full criteria set forth in § 826 of the Second Restatement.

Because a remand is necessary, we will also address an issue, raised by the homeowners, as to whether the district court should have instructed the jury that they could consider "standards and practices in the feedlot business." Because this case involves an alleged "intentional" invasion, it would have been inappropriate to give the jury any "standards and practices" instruction which suggested that negligence was an issue in the case. The concept of negligence has no application to "intentional" invasions under the Second Restatement. An issue of negligence may arise only in connection with "unintentional" invasions. *See* Second Restatement at § 822, comment i; *compare Preston v. Schrenk*, 77 Idaho 481, 295 P.2d 272 (1956). The district court safeguarded the instruction on this point by informing the jury that the plaintiffs were "not required to show negligence . . . in order to establish a nuisance."

However, there is a further limitation upon the use of a "standards and practices" instruction. In *Koseris*, the phosphate plant's offer to prove the utility of its operation had been coupled with a companion offer to prove its use of modern pollution control procedures. Our Supreme Court referred to both of these offers of proof when it said that the evidence could be allowed on a question of injunctive relief, but would have been improper on an issue of damages. Similarly, the Second Restatement refers to the skill or care with which an activity is conducted as a factor to be considered only in measuring the utility of the conduct. *See* § 828, comment h. Thus, it falls within the balancing test set forth in § 826(a), but would not apply to a determination of nuisance under § 826(b). We instruct upon remand that if the district court again elects to give a "standards and practices" instruction, it should inform the jury that such "standards and practices" are germane only to a determination under § 826(a) and are not to be considered among the criteria applied to a determination of nuisance under § 826(b).

The judgment of the district court is vacated. The case is remanded for further proceedings consistent with this opinion. Costs to appellants. No attorney fees on appeal.

WALTERS, C.J., and SWANSTROM, J., concur.

CARPENTER v. THE DOUBLE R CATTLE COMPANY, INC. (CARPENTER II)
Supreme Court of Idaho, 1985
701 P.2d 222

BAKES, JUSTICE.

Plaintiffs appealed a district court judgment based upon a court and jury finding that defendant's feedlot did not constitute a nuisance. The Court of Appeals, 105 Idaho 320, 669 P.2d 643, reversed and remanded for a new trial. On petition for review, we vacate the decision of the Court of Appeals and affirm the judgment of the district court.

Plaintiff appellants are homeowners who live near a cattle feedlot owned and operated by respondents. Appellants filed a complaint in March, 1978, alleging that the feedlot had been expanded in 1977 to accommodate the feeding of approximately 9,000 cattle. Appellants further alleged that "the spread and accumulation of manure, pollution of river and ground water, odor, insect infestation, increased concentration of birds, . . . dust and noise" allegedly caused by the feedlot constituted a nuisance. After a trial on the merits a jury found that the feedlot did not constitute a nuisance. The trial court then also made findings and conclusions that the feedlot did not constitute a nuisance.

Appellants assigned as error the jury instructions which instructed the jury that in the determination of whether a nuisance exists consideration should be given to such factors as community interest, utility of conduct, business standards and practices, gravity of harm caused, and the circumstances surrounding the parties' movement to their locations. On appeal, appellants chose not to provide an evidentiary record, but merely claimed that the instructions misstated the law in Idaho.

The case was assigned to the Court of Appeals which reversed and remanded for a new trial. The basis for this reversal was that the trial court did not give a jury instruction based upon subsection (b) of Section 826 of the Restatement (Second) of Torts. That subsection allows for a finding of a nuisance even though the gravity of harm is outweighed by the utility of the conduct if the harm is "serious" and the payment of damages is "feasible" without forcing the business to discontinue.

This Court granted defendant's petition for review. We hold that the instructions which the trial court gave were not erroneous, being consistent with our prior case law and other persuasive authority. We further hold that the trial court did not err in not giving an instruction based on subsection (b) of Section 826 of the Second Restatement, which does not represent the law in the State of Idaho, as pointed out in Part III. Accordingly, the decision of the Court of Appeals is vacated, and the judgment of the district court is affirmed.

. . . .

III

The Law of Nuisance

The Court of Appeals adopted subsection (b) of Section 826 of the Restatement Second, that a defendant can be held liable for a nuisance regardless of the utility of the conduct if the harm is "serious" and the payment of damages is "feasible" without jeopardizing the continuance of the conduct. We disagree that this is the law in Idaho.

At the outset, it is important to again note that appellants neither requested such an instruction nor assigned as error the failure of the trial court to give an instruction consistent with the new rule stated above. In fact, the appellants initially argued both at trial and on appeal that the Second Restatement should not apply and objected to giving any instructions based on the Restatement. It is therefore not surprising that the trial court did not give an instruction on the new rule in Section 826(b), Restatement (Second). Further, the instructions given were consistent with both the First Restatement and Section 826(a) of the Second Restatement, and also our decisions in *McNichols v. J.R. Simplot Co.*, 74 Idaho 321, 262 P.2d 1012 (1953) (action for damages and injunction), and *Koseris v. J.R. Simplot Co.*, 82 Idaho 263, 352 P.2d 235 (1960) (action for injunction only).

The Court of Appeals, without being requested by appellant, adopted the new subsection (b) of Section 826 of the Second Restatement partially because of language in *Koseris* which reads:

> "We are constrained to hold that the trial court erred in sustaining objections to those offers of proof [evidence of utility of conduct], since they were relevant as bearing upon the issue whether respondents, in seeking injunctive relief, were pursuing the proper remedy; nevertheless, on the theory of damages which respondents had waived, the ruling was correct." 82 Idaho at 270, 352 P.2d at 239.

The last phrase of the quote, relied on by the Court of Appeals, is clearly *dictum*, since the question of utility of conduct in a nuisance action for damages was not at issue in *Koseris*. It is very doubtful that this Court's *dictum* in *Koseris* was intended to make such a substantial change in the nuisance law. When the isolated statement of *dictum* was made in 1960, there was no persuasive authority for such a proposition. Indeed, no citation of authority was given. The three cases from other jurisdictions which the Court of Appeals relied on for authority did not exist until 1970. *See Boomer v. Atlantic Cement Co.*, 26 N.Y.2d 219, 309 N.Y.S.2d 312, 257 N.E.2d 870 (1970); *Jost v. Dairyland Power Co-op.*, 45 Wis. 2d 164, 172 N.W.2d 647 (1970). The third case from Oregon, *Furrer v. Talent Irr. Dist*, 258 Or. 494, 466 P.2d 605 (1970), was not even a nuisance case. Rather, it was an action in "negligence." The Second Restatement, which proposed the change in the law by adding subsection (b) to Section 826, was also not in existence until 1970. Therefore, we greatly discount this Court's *dictum* in the 1960 *Koseris* opinion as authority for such a substantial change in the nuisance law. The case of *McNichols v. J.R. Simplot Co.*, 74 Idaho 321, 262 P.2d 1012 (1953) should be viewed as the law in Idaho that in a nuisance action seeking damages the interests of the community, which would include the utility of the conduct, should be considered in the determination of the existence of a nuisance. The trial court's instructions in the present case were entirely consistent with *McNichols*. A plethora of other modern cases are in accord. *E.g., Nissan Motor Corp. v. Maryland Shipbuilding & Dry dock Co.*, 544 F.Supp. 1104 (D. Md. 1982) (utility of defendant's conduct is factor to be considered in determining existence of nuisance in damages action); *Little Joseph Realty, Inc. v. Town of Babylon*, 41 N.Y.2d 738, 395 N.Y.S.2d 428, 363 N.E.2d 1163 (N.Y.Ct.App.1977) (indicating that New York still adheres to balancing of risk and utility, requiring that harm to plaintiff must outweigh social usefulness of defendant's activity); *Pendergrast v. Aiken*, 293 N.C. 201, 236 S.E.2d 787 (1977) (balancing of harm versus utility retained, despite change of section 826 Restatement (Second) of Torts); *Pate v. City of Martin*, 614 S.W.2d 46 (Tenn.1981) (determination of existence of nuisance in action for damages and injunction cannot be determined by exact rules, but depends on circumstances of each case, including locality and character of surroundings, as well as utility and social value of defendant's conduct).

The State of Idaho is sparsely populated and its economy depends largely upon the benefits of agriculture, lumber, mining and industrial development. To eliminate the utility of conduct and other factors listed by the trial court from the criteria to be considered in determining whether a nuisance exists, as the appellant has argued throughout this appeal, would place an unreasonable burden upon these industries. We see no policy reasons which should compel this Court to accept appellant's argument and depart from our present law. Accordingly, the judgment of the district court is affirmed and the Court of Appeals decision is set aside.

Costs to respondents. No attorney fees.

DONALDSON, C.J., and SHEPARD, J., concur.

BISTLINE, JUSTICE, dissenting.

We have before us today a most remarkable event: two appellate courts, each obviously unaware of its true appellate function. The Court of Appeals, in reviewing the instant case, acted as a court of law, while the Idaho Supreme Court functioned as a court of error correction. In my mind, the roles have been reversed — I always understood that the Court of Appeals was a court of error correction, and it was our function to act as a court of law. I applaud the efforts of the Court of Appeals to modernize the law of nuisance in this state. I am not in the least persuaded to join the majority with its narrow view of nuisance law as expressed in the majority opinion.

The majority today continues to adhere to ideas on the law of nuisance that should have gone out with the use of buffalo chips as fuel. We have before us today homeowners complaining of a nearby feedlot — not a small operation, but rather a feedlot which accommodates 9,000 cattle. The homeowners advanced the theory that after the expansion of the feedlot in 1977, the odor, manure, dust, insect infestation and increased concentration of birds which accompanied all of the foregoing, constituted a nuisance. If the odoriferous quagmire created by 9,000 head of cattle is *not* a nuisance, it is difficult for me to imagine what is. However, the real question for us today is the legal basis on which a finding of nuisance can be made.

The Court of Appeals adopted subsection (b) of § 826 of the Restatement (Second) of Torts.[1] The majority today rejects this Restatement section, reasoning that the Court of Appeals improperly relied upon dictum in *Koseris v. J.R. Simplot Co.*, 82 Idaho 263, 352 P.2d 235 (1960). *See infra*, at 227. Instead, the majority holds that the 1953 case of *McNichols v. J.R. Simplot Co.*, 74 Idaho 321, 262 P.2d 1012 (1953) espoused the correct rule of law for Idaho: in a nuisance action seeking damages, the interests of the community, which includes the utility of the conduct, should be considered in determining the existence of a nuisance. I find nothing immediately wrong with this statement of the law and agree wholeheartedly that the interests of the community should be considered in determining the existence of a nuisance. However, where this primitive rule of law fails is in recognizing that in our society, while it may be desirable to have a serious nuisance continue because the utility of the operation causing the nuisance is great, at the same time, those directly impacted by the serious nuisance deserve some compensation for the invasion they suffer as a result of the continuation of the nuisance. This is exactly what the more progressive provisions of § 826(b) of the Restatement (Second) of Torts addresses [*sic*]. Clearly, § 826(b) recognizes that the continuation of the serious harm must remain feasible. *See especially* comment on clause (b), subpart f of § 826 of the Restatement. What § 826(b) adds is a method of compensating those who must suffer the invasion without putting out of business the source or cause of the invasion. This does not strike me as a particularly adventuresome or far-reaching rule of law. In fact, the fairness of it is overwhelming.

The majority's rule today overlooks the option of compensating those who suffer a nuisance because the interests of the community outweigh the interests of those afflicted by the nuisance. This unsophisticated balancing overlooks the possibility that it is not necessary that one interest be ignored when the community interest is strong. We should not be adopting a rule of preference which suggests that if the community interest is preferred any other interest must be disregarded. Instead, § 826(b) accommodates adverse interests by contemplating continuation of the facility which creates the nuisance while compensating those who suffer the direct impact of the nuisance — in the instant case the homeowners who live in the vicinity of the feedlot.

The majority's rule today suggests that part of the cost of industry, agriculture or development must be borne by those unfortunate few who have the fortuitous

---

[1] § 826. Unreasonableness of Intentional Invasion. An intentional invasion of another's interest in the use and enjoyment of land is unreasonable if

    (a) the gravity of the harm outweighs the utility of the actor's conduct, or

    (b) the harm caused by the conduct is serious and the financial burden of compensating for this and similar harm to others would not make the continuation of the conduct not feasible.

luck to live in the immediate vicinity of a nuisance producing facility. Frankly, I think this naive economic view is ridiculous in both its simplicity and its outdated view of modern economic society. The "cost" of a product includes not only the amount it takes to produce such a product but also includes the external costs: the damage done to the environment through pollution of air or water is an example of an external cost. In the instant case, the nuisance suffered by the homeowners should be considered an external cost of operating a feedlot and producing beef for public consumption. I do not believe that a few should be required to pay this extra cost of doing business by going uncompensated for a nuisance of this sort. If a feedlot wants to continue, I say fine, providing compensation is paid for the serious invasion (the odors, flies, dust, etc.) of the homeowner's interest. My only qualification is that the financial burden of compensating for this harm should not be such as to force the feedlot (or any other industry) out of business. The true cost can then be shifted to the consumer who rightfully should pay for the *entire* cost of producing the product he desires to obtain.

The majority today blithely suggests that because the State of Idaho is sparsely populated and because our economy is largely dependent on agriculture, lumber, mining and industrial development, we should forego compensating those who suffer a serious invasion. If humans are such a rare item in this state, maybe there is all the more reason to protect them from the discharge of industry. At a minimum, we should compensate those who suffer a nuisance at the hands of industry and agriculture. What the majority overlooks is that the cost of development should not be absorbed by [a] few, but rather should be spread out and paid by all. I am not convinced that agriculture or industry will be put out of business by requiring compensation for the nuisance they generate. Let us look at the case before us. The owners of the feedlot will not find themselves looking for new jobs if they are required to compensate the homeowners for the stench and dust and flies attendant with 9,000 head of cattle. Rather, meat prices at the grocery store will undoubtedly go up. But, in my view it is far better that the cost of the nuisance be carried by the consumer of a product than by the unfortunate homeowners currently suffering under adverse conditions. Some compensation should be paid the homeowners for suffering the burden from which we all benefit.

The decision of the Court of Appeals is an outstanding example of a judicial opinion which comes from a truly exhaustive and analytical review. *See* 105 Idaho 320, 669 P.2d 643 (1983). I see no need to reiterate the authority cited therein. The Court of Appeals clarified the standard for determining the existence of a nuisance. Because the jury instructions were inconsistent with this Idaho law, the Court of Appeals properly vacated the lower court judgment.

[HUNTLEY, J. concurred in the dissent.]

SPUR INDUSTRIES, INC. v. DEL E. WEBB DEVELOPMENT CO.

Supreme Court of Arizona, 1972
494 P.2d 700

In Banc.

CAMERON, VICE CHIEF JUSTICE

From a judgment permanently enjoining the defendant, Spur Industries, Inc., from operating a cattle feedlot near the plaintiff Del E. Webb Development Company's Sun City, Spur appeals. Webb cross-appeals. Although numerous issues are raised, we feel that it is necessary to answer only two questions. They are:

1. Where the operation of a business, such as a cattle feedlot is lawful in the first instance, but becomes a nuisance by reason of a nearby residential area, may the feedlot operation be enjoined in an action brought by the developer of the residential area?

2. Assuming that the nuisance may be enjoined, may the developer of a completely new town or urban area in a previously agricultural area be required to indemnify the operator of the feedlot who must move or cease operation because of the presence of the residential area created by the developer?

The facts necessary for a determination of this matter on appeal are as follows. The area in question is located in Maricopa County, Arizona, some 14 to 15 miles west of the urban area of Phoenix, on the Phoenix-Wickenburg Highway, also known as Grand Avenue. About two miles south of Grand Avenue is Olive Avenue which runs east and west. 111th Avenue runs north and south as does the Agua Fria River immediately to the west.

Farming started in this area about 1911. In 1929, with the completion of the Carl Pleasant Dam, gravity flow water became available to the property located to the west of the Agua Fria River, though land to the east remained dependent upon well water for irrigation. By 1950, the only urban areas in the vicinity were the agriculturally related communities of Peoria, El Mirage, and Surprise located along Grand Avenue. Along 111th Avenue, approximately one mile south of Grand Avenue and 1 1/2 miles north of Olive Avenue, the community of Youngtown was commenced in 1954. Youngtown is a retirement community appealing primarily to senior citizens.

In 1956, Spur's predecessors in interest, H. Marion Welborn and the Northside Hay Mill and Trading Company, developed feedlots, about 1/2 mile south of Olive Avenue, in an area between the confluence of the usually dry Agua Fria and New Rivers. The area is well suited for cattle feeding and in 1959, there were 25 cattle feeding pens or dairy operations within a 7 mile radius of the location developed by Spur's predecessors. In April and May of 1959, the Northside Hay Mill was feeding between 6,000 and 7,000 head of cattle and Welborn approximately 1,500 head on a combined area of 35 acres.

In May of 1959, Del Webb began to plan the development of an urban area to be known as Sun City. For this purpose, the Marinette and the Santa Fe Ranches, some 20,000 acres of farmland, were purchased for $15,000,000 or $750.00 per acre. This price was considerably less than the price of land located near the urban area of Phoenix, and along with the success of Youngtown was a factor influencing the decision to purchase the property in question.

By September 1959, Del Webb had started construction of a golf course south of Grand Avenue and Spur's predecessors had started to level ground for more feedlot area. In 1960, Spur purchased the property in question and began a rebuilding and expansion program extending both to the north and south of the original facilities. By 1962, Spur's expansion program was completed and had expanded from approximately 35 acres to 114 acres.

Accompanied by an extensive advertising campaign, homes were first offered by Del Webb in January 1960 and the first unit to be completed was south of Grand Avenue and approximately 2 1/2 miles north of Spur. By 2 May 1960, there were 450 to 500 houses completed or under construction. At this time, Del Webb did not consider odors from the Spur feed pens a problem and Del Webb continued to develop in a southerly direction, until sales resistance became so great that the parcels were difficult if not impossible to sell. . . .

By December 1967, Del Webb's property had extended south to Olive Avenue and Spur was within 500 feet of Olive Avenue to the north. Del Webb filed its original complaint alleging that in excess of 1,300 lots in the southwest portion were unfit for development for sale as residential lots because of the operation of the Spur feedlot.

Del Webb's suit complained that the Spur feeding operation was a public nuisance because of the flies and the odor which were drifting or being blown by the prevailing south to north wind over the southern portion of Sun City. At the time of the suit, Spur was feeding between 20,000 and 30,000 head of cattle, and the facts amply support the finding of the trial court that the feed pens had become a nuisance to the people who resided in the southern part of Del Webb's development. The testimony indicated that cattle in a commercial feedlot will produce 35 to 40 pounds of wet manure per day, per head, or over a million pounds of wet manure per day for 30,000 head of cattle, and that despite the admittedly good feedlot management and good housekeeping practices by Spur, the resulting odor and flies produced an annoying if not unhealthy situation as far as the senior citizens of southern Sun City were concerned. There is no doubt that some of the citizens of Sun City were unable to enjoy the outdoor living which Del Webb had advertised and that Del Webb was faced with sales resistance from prospective purchasers as well as strong and persistent complaints from the people who had purchased homes in that area.

Trial was commenced before the court with an advisory jury. The advisory jury was later discharged and the trial was continued before the court alone. Findings of fact and conclusions of law were requested and given. The case was vigorously contested, including special actions in this court on some of the matters. In one of the special actions before this court, Spur agreed to, and did, shut down its operation without prejudice to a determination of the matter on appeal. On appeal the many questions raised were extensively briefed.

It is noted, however, that neither the citizens of Sun City nor Youngtown are represented in this lawsuit and the suit is solely between Del E. Webb Development Company and Spur Industries, Inc.

MAY SPUR BE ENJOINED?

The difference between a private nuisance and a public nuisance is generally one of degree. A private nuisance is one affecting a single individual or a definite small number of persons in the enjoyment of private rights not common to the public, while a public nuisance is one affecting the rights enjoyed by citizens as a part of the public. To constitute a public nuisance, the nuisance must affect a considerable number of people or an entire community or neighborhood. *City of Phoenix v. Johnson*, 51 Ariz. 115, 75 P.2d 30 (1938).

Where the injury is slight, the remedy for minor inconveniences lies in an action for damages rather than in one for an injunction. *Kubby v. Hammond*, 68 Ariz. 17, 198 P.2d 134 (1948). Moreover, some courts have held, in the "balancing of conveniences" cases, that damages may be the sole remedy. See *Boomer v. Atlantic Cement Co.*, 26 N.Y.2d 219, 309 N.Y.S.2d 312, 257 N.E.2d 870, 40 A.L.R.3d 590 (1970), and annotation comments, 40 A.L.R.3d 601.

Thus, it would appear from the admittedly incomplete record as developed in the trial court, that, at most, residents of Youngtown would be entitled to damages rather than injunctive relief.

We have no difficulty, however, in agreeing with the conclusion of the trial court that Spur's operation was an enjoinable public nuisance as far as the people in the southern portion of Del Webb's Sun City were concerned.

§ 36-601, subsec. A reads as follows:

"§ 36-601. Public nuisances dangerous to public health

"A. The following conditions are specifically declared public nuisances dangerous to the public health:

"1. Any condition or place in populous areas which constitutes a breeding place for flies, rodents, mosquitoes and other insects which are capable of carrying and transmitting disease-causing organisms to any person or persons."

By this statute, before an otherwise lawful (and necessary) business may be declared a public nuisance, there must be a "populous" area in which people are injured:

". . . [I]t hardly admits a doubt that, in determining the question as to whether a lawful occupation is so conducted as to constitute a nuisance as a matter of fact, the locality and surroundings are of the first importance, (citations omitted) A business which is not per se a public nuisance may become such by being carried on at a place where the health, comfort, or convenience of a populous neighborhood is affected. . . . What might amount to a serious nuisance in one locality by reason of the density of the population, or character of the neighborhood affected, may in another place and under different surroundings be deemed proper and unobjectionable. . . ." *MacDonald v. Perry*, 32 Ariz. 39, 49-50, 255 P. 494, 497 (1927).

It is clear that as to the citizens of Sun City, the operation of Spur's feedlot was both a public and a private nuisance. They could have successfully maintained an action to abate the nuisance. Del Webb, having shown a special injury in the loss of sales, had standing to bring suit to enjoin the nuisance. *Engle v. Clark*, 53 Ariz. 472, 90 P.2d 994 (1939); *City of Phoenix v. Johnson, supra.* The judgment of the trial court permanently enjoining the operation of the feedlot is affirmed.

MUST DEL WEBB INDEMNIFY SPUR?

A suit to enjoin a nuisance sounds in equity and the courts have long recognized a special responsibility to the public when acting as a court of equity:

§ 104. Where public interest is involved.

"Courts of equity may, and frequently do, go much further both to give and withhold relief in furtherance of the public interest than they are accustomed to go when only private interests are involved. Accordingly, the granting or withholding of relief may properly be dependent upon considerations of public interest. . . ."

27 Am. Jur. 2d, Equity, page 626.

In addition to protecting the public interest, however, courts of equity are concerned with protecting the operator of a lawfully, albeit noxious, business from the result of a knowing and willful encroachment by others near his business.

In the so-called "coming to the nuisance" cases, the courts have held that the residential landowner may not have relief if he knowingly came into a neighborhood reserved for industrial or agricultural endeavors and has been damaged thereby:

"Plaintiffs chose to live in an area uncontrolled by zoning laws or restrictive covenants and remote from urban development. In such an area plaintiffs cannot complain that legitimate agricultural pursuits are being carried on in the vicinity, nor can plaintiffs, having chosen to build in an agricultural area, complain that the agricultural pursuits carried on in the area depreciate the value of their homes. The area being *primarily agricultural*, any opinion reflecting the value of such property must take this factor into account. The standards affecting the value of residence property in an urban setting, subject to zoning controls and controlled planning techniques, cannot be the standards by which agricultural properties are judged.

"People employed in a city who build their homes in suburban areas of the county beyond the limits of a city and zoning regulations do so for a reason. Some do so to avoid the high taxation rate imposed by cities, or to avoid special assessments for street, sewer and water projects. They usually build on improved or hard surface highways, which have been built either at state or county expense and thereby avoid special assessments for these improvements. It may be that they desire to get away from the congestion of traffic, smoke, noise, foul air and the many other annoyances of city life. But with all these advantages in going beyond the area which is zoned and restricted to protect them in their homes, they must be prepared to take the disadvantages." *Dill v. Excel Packing Company*, 183 Kan. 513, 525, 526, 331 P.2d 539, 548, 549 (1958). See also *East St. Johns Shingle Co. v. City of Portland*, 195 Or. 505, 246 P.2d 554, 560-562 (1952).

And:

> ". . . a party cannot justly call upon the law to make that place suitable for his residence which was not so when he selected it. . . ." *Gilbert v. Showerman*, 23 Mich. 448, 455, 2 Brown 158 (1871).

Were Webb the only party injured, we would feel justified in holding that the doctrine of "coming to the nuisance" would have been a bar to the relief asked by Webb, and, on the other hand, had Spur located the feedlot near the outskirts of a city and had the city grown toward the feedlot, Spur would have to suffer the cost of abating the nuisance as to those people locating within the growth pattern of the expanding city:

> "The case affords, perhaps, an example where a business established at a place remote from population is gradually surrounded and becomes part of a populous center, so that a business which formerly was not an interference with the rights of others has become so by the encroachment of the population. . . ." *City of Ft. Smith v. Western Hide & Fur Co.*, 153 Ark. 99, 103, 239 S.W. 724, 726 (1922).

We agree, however, with the Massachusetts court that:

> "The law of nuisance affords no rigid rule to be applied in all instances. It is elastic. It undertakes to require only that which is fair and reasonable under all the circumstances. In a commonwealth like this, which depends for its material prosperity so largely on the continued growth and enlargement of manufacturing of diverse varieties, 'extreme rights' cannot be enforced. . . ." *Stevens v. Rockport Granite Co.*, 216 Mass. 486, 488, 104 N.E. 371, 373 (1914).

There was no indication in the instant case at the time Spur and its predecessors located in western Maricopa County that a new city would spring up, full-blown, alongside the feeding operation and that the developer of that city would ask the court to order Spur to move because of the new city. Spur is required to move not because of any wrongdoing on the part of Spur, but because of a proper and legitimate regard of the courts for the rights and interests of the public.

Del Webb, on the other hand, is entitled to the relief prayed for (a permanent injunction), not because Webb is blameless, but because of the damage to the people who have been encouraged to purchase homes in Sun City. It does not equitably or legally follow, however, that Webb, being entitled to the injunction, is then free of any liability to Spur if Webb has in fact been the cause of the damage Spur has sustained. It does not seem harsh to require a developer, who has taken advantage of the lesser land values in a rural area as well as the availability of large tracts of land on which to build and develop a new town or city in the area, to indemnify those who are forced to leave as a result.

Having brought people to the nuisance to the foreseeable detriment of Spur, Webb must indemnify Spur for a reasonable amount of the cost of moving or shutting down. It should be noted that this relief to Spur is limited to a case wherein a developer has, with foreseeability, brought into a previously agricultural or industrial area the population which makes necessary the granting of an injunction against a lawful business and for which the business has no adequate relief.

It is therefore the decision of this court that the matter be remanded to the trial court for a hearing upon the damages sustained by the defendant Spur as a reasonable and direct result of the granting of the permanent injunction. Since the result of the appeal may appear novel and both sides have obtained a measure of relief, it is ordered that each side will bear its own costs.

Affirmed in part, reversed in part, and remanded for further proceedings consistent with this opinion.

HAYS, C.J., STRUCKMEYER and LOCKWOOD, JJ., and UDALL, RETIRED JUSTICE.

———————

Does the result in *Spur Industries* seem fair? In an era in which cities are sprawling and suburbs are transforming former farmlands, how should a court handle the inevitable conflicts? How important should a public priority — either developing or preserving farmlands — be in a court's analysis? What happens to the "coming to the nuisance" doctrine in *Spur Industries*? Didn't the homeowners, as well as Del Webb, come to the nuisance?

HANES v. CONTINENTAL GRAIN CO.
Court of Appeals of Missouri, 2001
58 S.W.3d 1

SULLIVAN, JUDGE.

Continental Grain Co. (Appellant) appeals from the trial court judgment entered upon a jury verdict awarding Respondents $100,000 each on temporary nuisance claims arising from Appellant's operation of hog farms in northwest Missouri. We affirm.

In this case, 108 residents in five counties in northwest Missouri sued Appellant for nuisance arising out of Appellant's operation of four hog farms in northwest Missouri. The residents claimed that odor, flies and/or contaminated water emanating from Appellant's operations unreasonably impaired the use and enjoyment of their properties. After a three and one-half month trial, a jury returned a verdict awarding 52 out of 108 plaintiffs $100,000 each on their nuisance claims. Respondents are 51 of those 52 prevailing plaintiffs. Appellant timely filed this appeal.

Appellant claims the trial court erred in denying its motion for judgment notwithstanding the verdict with respect to compensatory damages because

Respondents failed to make a submissible case in that (1) Respondents failed to present any evidence that the alleged nuisance was abatable, as required to establish a temporary nuisance, and (2) Respondents failed to present any evidence of diminished property value, which is the only type of damages recoverable for a permanent nuisance.

The denial of a motion for judgment notwithstanding the verdict presents the same issue as a denial of a motion for directed verdict. . . . [W]e view the evidence and all reasonable inferences therefrom in the light most favorable to the jury's verdict, disregarding all evidence and inferences to the contrary. . . . A motion for judgment notwithstanding the verdict should be granted only when the evidence and reasonable inferences to be drawn therefrom are so strong against the prevailing party that there is no room for reasonable minds to differ. . . .

Nuisance is the unreasonable, unusual or unnatural use of one's property so that it substantially impairs the right of another to peacefully enjoy his or her property. *Snelling v. Land Clearance for Redev. Authority*, 793 S.W.2d 232, 232 (Mo. App. E.D. 1990). Appellant does not maintain that a nuisance per se was not established in this case. Rather, Appellant contends that Respondents failed to establish that the nuisance was temporary. The distinguishing feature between a permanent and a temporary nuisance is the abatability of the nuisance. *Vermillion v. Pioneer Gun Club*, 918 S.W.2d 827, 831 (Mo. App. W.D. 1996). A nuisance is temporary if it may be abated, and it is permanent if abatement is impracticable or impossible. *Id.* It is the character of the source of the injury, rather than the character of the injury, which distinguishes a temporary from a permanent nuisance. *Racine v. Glendale Shooting Club, Inc.*, 755 S.W.2d 369, 374 (Mo. App. E.D. 1988). A permanent nuisance must result from a permanent construction which is necessarily injurious as installed and not from one which becomes injurious through its use. *Id.*

We note initially that prior to opening its hog farming facility, Appellant made several representations to the public that the hog farms would not produce odors noticeable beyond one quarter of a mile. Appellant also represented in a recorded radio interview as well as to neighbors of its proposed hog farm facility and government officials that it would employ the latest available technology in order to prevent pervasive odors. Against this factual backdrop, we now address Appellant's argument that Respondents failed to present any evidence that the nuisance caused by its hog farms was abatable.

Respondents presented substantial evidence of scientifically possible management practices and technologies available to abate the odor, water contamination, and insect infestation associated with Appellant's hog farm operations. Accordingly, Respondents presented substantial evidence that the nuisance created by Appellant's hog farms was abatable.

In regards to the odor nuisance, these practices and technologies included: using a proper amount of water in the start-up of an anaerobic lagoon; starting lagoons only at the beginning of warm weather; maintaining proper lagoon volumes; removing dead pigs and afterbirth from the lagoons on a timely basis; using lagoon covers, solid-liquid separators, aeration devices, and anaerobic digesters. Respondents also provided evidence that the odor associated with spreading waste material over farmland could be abated by using soil injection technology instead of travelling guns. Injection would put the waste into the ground as opposed to spreading it over the top. Respondents presented testimony that Appellant had recently built walls outside the exhaust fans positioned to disperse the odor from the hogs' buildings, and that the walls successfully abated the odors. There was evidence that such air dispersion techniques had been known for years. Respondents argued that Appellant could have had its dumpsters, filled to the brim with dead pigs such that the lids would not close, picked up and emptied more frequently by its rendering service. Respondents also argued that Appellant could have used more dumpsters, so that they would close completely.

Large wastewater spills at Appellant's hog farms also caused water contamination. Respondents presented evidence that these spills could have been prevented by better maintenance and inspection procedures, such as collecting construction debris and conducting periodic checks. Appellant had prevented damage from further wastewater spills by constructing new underground piping, installing automatic controls, and building numerous containment ponds.

Insect infestation also comprised part of the nuisance. Respondents presented evidence that the slope of the lagoons, the fluctuation in the lagoons' levels and the composition of the lagoons and their open exposure, without covers, served as a breeding ground for flies. Dead animal carcasses also attracted flies. As discussed above, lagoon covers and more frequent disposal or covering of dead pigs would have abated this nuisance.

Respondents presented substantial evidence that it was economically feasible for Appellant to employ these methods and technologies to abate the nuisance created by its hog farms. Accordingly, we find that Respondents established that the nuisance in this case was a temporary nuisance, capable of scientifically possible and reasonably practical abatement.

We disagree with Appellant's contention that in order to show a nuisance can be abated, it must be shown that the entire nuisance can be eliminated, and a reduction or lessening of the nuisance is insufficient. This contention has no basis in Missouri law. Further it is not a logical argument. A nuisance is a substantial interference with the use and enjoyment of one's property. Substantial is a term of degree. A nuisance can be abated to the degree where it is no longer a substantial interference. Although in some cases cited by Appellant a nuisance may have been completely eliminated, that does not mean that a nuisance has to be completely eliminated in order to be abated. *See, e.g., Racine*, 755 S.W.2d at 372-373 ("Noise is not a nuisance per se but may be of such a character or so excessive as to become one, even though it arises from operation of a lawful business." . . . "The trial court's relief was an effort to restrict the club's activities to a level which did not constitute a substantial impairment of plaintiffs' peaceful enjoyment of their property."). As illustrated in *Racine*, Appellant could reduce the odor, flies and wastewater spills emanating from its hog farms to the point where they do not constitute a substantial interference with Respondents' use and enjoyment of their property. Respondents demonstrated that such abatement was reasonably practicable and economically feasible. Accordingly, Respondents established a temporary nuisance by substantial evidence. Since we find that Respondents established a temporary nuisance, we need not address the part of Appellant's point on appeal concerning Respondents' failure to present any evidence of damages recoverable for a permanent nuisance.

In its second point on appeal, Appellant maintains that the trial court erred in denying Appellant's motion for judgment notwithstanding the verdict with respect to the claims of Mandy Patton-Stahl, Denise Turner, and Les Turner because those Respondents failed to make a submissible case of nuisance in that their evidence showed that they did not have any ownership or possessory rights in any property affected by the nuisance, an essential element of a nuisance claim.

Denise and Les Turner lived in their own house on Les Turner's father's land, with his consent. The Turners farmed the property, built improvements and repaired existing structures, repaired fences, and owned adjacent farmland. With her mother Juanita Patton's consent, Mandy Patton-Stahl lived with a young child in a separate dwelling on property owned by her mother.

Appellant maintains that to prevail in a nuisance case, a plaintiff must establish that the alleged nuisance impairs the use of property in which he has an interest. Respondents contend that the occupants of a home who suffer interference with the enjoyment of the premises from a temporary nuisance may recover for any actual inconvenience or physical discomfort which materially affects their comfort or health.

We find that a person who rightfully occupies but does not own a home may sue for injuries caused by a temporary nuisance. In a temporary nuisance action, the damages are for personal injuries inflicted upon the person occupying the property. *See, e.g., McCracken v. Swift & Co.*, 265 S.W. 91, 92 (Mo. 1924). By contrast, the damages for a permanent nuisance involve the diminution in value of the residence, thereby necessitating that the one seeking damages from a permanent nuisance have an interest in the property. The two cases cited by Appellant do not aid its argument. In *Ellis v. Kansas City, St. J. & C.B.R. Co.*, 63 Mo. 131 (1876), the Court found that the husband, who happened to be in possession of the house, could bring a nuisance cause of action against a railroad company for the illness caused to his wife by a dead horse that the railroad company's train had hit and allowed to remain outside the plaintiff's house. We do not read this case as mandating a possessory or ownership interest in a property in order to bring a cause of action for temporary nuisance. Appellant also relies on *Frank v. Environmental Sanitation Management, Inc.*, 687 S.W.2d 876, 880 (Mo. 1985), simply for its language that "Nuisance is the unreasonable, unusual, or unnatural use of one's property so that it substantially impairs the right of another to peacefully enjoy *his* property." This sentence does not, by itself, make possessory or ownership interest in property a prerequisite to maintaining a temporary nuisance claim. For the foregoing reasons, Appellant's second point on appeal is denied.

The judgment of the trial court is affirmed.

MOONEY, P.J., and SIMON, J., concur.

The following is a classic case dealing with air pollution and the public interest.

Much of this area is now governed by federal and state environmental law and regulation. What role should state tort doctrine continue to play?

BOOMER v. ATLANTIC CEMENT CO.
Court of Appeals of New York, 1970
257 N.E.2d 870

BERGAN, JUDGE.

Defendant operates a large cement plant near Albany. These are actions for injunction and damages by neighboring land owners alleging injury to property from dirt, smoke and vibration emanating from the plant. A nuisance has been found after trial, temporary damages have been allowed; but an injunction has been denied.

The public concern with air pollution arising from many sources in industry and in transportation is currently accorded ever wider recognition accompanied by a growing sense of responsibility in State and Federal Governments to control it. Cement plants are obvious sources of air pollution in the neighborhoods where they operate.

But there is now before the court private litigation in which individual property owners have sought specific relief from a single plant operation. The threshold question . . . is whether the court should resolve the litigation between the parties now before it as equitably as seems possible; or whether, seeking promotion of the general public welfare, it should channel private litigation into broad public objectives.

A court performs its essential function when it decides the rights of parties before it. Its decision of private controversies may sometimes greatly affect public issues. Large questions of law are often resolved by the manner in which private litigation is decided. But this is normally an incident to the court's main function to settle controversy. It is a rare exercise of judicial power to use a decision in private litigation as a purposeful mechanism to achieve direct public objectives greatly beyond the rights and interests before the court.

Effective control of air pollution is a problem presently far from solution even with the full public and financial powers of government. In large measure adequate technical procedures are yet to be developed and some that appear possible may be economically impracticable.

It seems apparent that the amelioration of air pollution will depend on technical research in great depth; on a carefully balanced consideration of the economic impact of close regulation; and of the actual effect on public health. It is likely to require massive public expenditure and to demand more than any local community can accomplish and to depend on regional and interstate controls.

A court should not try to do this on its own as a by-product of private litigation and it seems manifest that the judicial establishment is neither equipped in the limited nature of any judgment it can pronounce nor prepared to lay down and implement an effective policy for the elimination of air pollution. This is an area beyond the circumference of one private lawsuit. It is a direct responsibility for government and should not thus be undertaken as an incident to solving a dispute between property owners and a single cement plant — one of many — in the Hudson River valley.

The cement making operations of defendant have been found by the court at Special Term to have damaged the nearby properties of plaintiffs in these two actions. That court, as it has been noted, accordingly found defendant maintained a nuisance and this has been affirmed at the Appellate Division. The total damage to plaintiffs' properties is, however, relatively small in comparison with the value of defendant's operation and with the consequences of the injunction which plaintiffs seek.

The ground for the denial of injunction, notwithstanding the finding both that there is a nuisance and that plaintiffs have been damaged substantially, is the large disparity in economic consequences of the nuisance and of the injunction. This theory cannot, however, be sustained without overruling a doctrine which has been consistently reaffirmed in several leading cases in this court and which has never been disavowed here, namely that where a nuisance has been found and where there has been any substantial damage shown by the party complaining an injunction will be granted.

The rule in New York has been that such a nuisance will be enjoined although marked disparity be shown in economic consequence between the effect of the injunction and the effect of the nuisance.

The problem of disparity in economic consequence was sharply in focus in *Whalen v. Union Bag & Paper Co.*, 208 N. Y. 1, 101 N.E. 805. A pulp mill entailing an investment of more than a million dollars polluted a stream in which plaintiff, who owned a farm, was "a lower riparian owner." The economic loss to plaintiff from this pollution was small. This court, reversing the Appellate Division, reinstated the injunction granted by the Special Term against the argument of the mill owner that in view of "the slight advantage to plaintiff and the great loss that will be inflicted on defendant" an injunction should not be granted (p. 2, 101 N.E. p.805). "Such a balancing of injuries cannot be justified by the circumstances of this case," Judge Werner noted (p. 4, 101 N.E. p. 805). He continued: "Although the damage to the plaintiff may be slight as compared with the defendant's expense of abating the condition, that is not a good reason for refusing an injunction" (p. 5, 101 N.E. p.806).

Thus the unconditional injunction granted at Special Term was reinstated. The rule laid down in that case, then, is that whenever the damage resulting from a nuisance is found not "unsubstantial," viz., $100 a year, injunction would follow. This states a rule that had been followed in this court with marked consistency (*McCarty v. Natural Carbonic Gas Co.*, 189 N. Y. 40, 81 N.E. 549; *Strobel v. Kerr Salt Co.*, 164 N.Y. 303, 58 N.E. 142; *Campbell v. Seaman*, 63 N. Y. 568).

There are cases where injunction has been denied. *McCann v. Chasm Power Co.*, 211 N. Y. 301, 105 N.E. 416 is one of them. There, however, the damage shown by plaintiffs was not only unsubstantial, it was non-existent. Plaintiffs owned a rocky bank of the stream in which defendant had raised the level of the water. This had no economic or other adverse consequence to plaintiffs, and thus injunctive relief was denied. Similar is the basis for denial of injunction in *Forstmann v. Joray Holding Co.*, 244 N.Y. 22, 154 N.E. 652 where no benefit to plaintiffs could be seen from the injunction sought (p. 32, 154 N.E. 655). Thus if, within *Whalen* v. *Union Bag & Paper Co., supra*, which authoritatively states the rule in New York, the damage to plaintiffs in these present cases from defendant's cement plant is "not unsubstantial," an injunction should follow.

Although the court at Special Term and the Appellate Division held that injunction should be denied, it was found that plaintiffs had been damaged in various specific amounts up to the time of the trial and damages to the respective plaintiffs were awarded for those amounts. The effect of this was, injunction having been denied, plaintiffs could maintain successive actions at law for damages thereafter as further damage was incurred.

The court at Special Term also found the amount of permanent damage attributable to each plaintiff, for the guidance of the parties in the event both sides stipulated to the payment and acceptance of such permanent damage as a settlement of all the controversies among the parties. The total of permanent damages to all plaintiffs thus found was $185,000. This basis of adjustment has not resulted in any stipulation by the parties.

This result at Special Term and at the Appellate Division is a departure from a rule that has become settled; but to follow the rule literally in these cases would be to close down the plant at once. This court is fully agreed to avoid that immediately drastic remedy; the difference in view is how best to avoid it.

One alternative is to grant the injunction but postpone its effect to a specified future date to give opportunity for technical advances to permit defendant to eliminate the nuisance; another is to grant the injunction conditioned on the payment of permanent damages to plaintiffs which would compensate them for the total economic loss to their property present and future caused by defendant's operations. For reasons which will be developed the court chooses the latter alternative.

If the injunction were to be granted unless within a short period — e.g., 18 months — the nuisance be abated by improved methods, there would be no assurance that any significant technical improvement would occur.

The parties could settle this private litigation at any time if defendant paid enough money and the imminent threat of closing the plant would build up the pressure on defendant. If there were no improved techniques found, there would inevitably be applications to the court at Special Term for extensions of time to perform on showing of good faith efforts to find such techniques.

Moreover, techniques to eliminate dust and other annoying by-products of cement making are unlikely to be developed by any research the defendant can undertake within any short period, but will depend on the total resources of the cement industry nationwide and throughout the world. The problem is universal wherever cement is made.

For obvious reasons the rate of the research is beyond [the] control of defendant. If at the end of 18 months the whole industry has not found a technical solution a court would be hard put to close down this one cement plant if due regard be given to equitable principles.

On the other hand, to grant the injunction unless defendant pays plaintiffs such permanent damages as may be fixed by the court seems to do justice between the contending parties. All of the attributions of economic loss to the properties on which plaintiffs' complaints are based will have been redressed.

The nuisance complained of by these plaintiffs may have other public or private consequences, but these particular parties are the only ones who have sought remedies and the judgment proposed will fully redress them. The limitation of relief granted is a limitation only within the four corners of these actions and does not foreclose public health or other public agencies from seeking proper relief in a proper court.

It seems reasonable to think that the risk of being required to pay permanent damages to injured property owners by cement plant owners would itself be a reasonable effective spur to research for improved techniques to minimize nuisance.

The power of the court to condition on equitable grounds the continuance of an injunction on the payment of permanent damages seems undoubted. (*See, e.g.*, the alternatives considered in *McCarty v. Natural Carbonic Gas Co., supra*, as well as *Strobel v. Kerr Salt Co., supra.*)

The damage base here suggested is consistent with the general rule in those nuisance cases where damages are allowed. "Where a nuisance is of such a permanent and unabatable character that a single recovery can be had, including the whole damage past and future resulting therefrom, there can be but one recovery" (66 C. J. S., Nuisances, § 140, p. 947). It has been said that permanent damages are allowed where the loss recoverable would obviously be small as compared with the cost of removal of the nuisance (*Kentucky-Ohio Gas Co. v. Bowling*, 264 Ky. 470, 477, 95 S.W. 2d 1).

The present cases and the remedy here proposed are in a number of other respects rather similar to *Northern Indiana Public Serv. Co. v. W.J. and M.S. Vesey*, 210 Ind. 338, 200 N.E. 620, decided by the Supreme Court of Indiana. The gases, odors, ammonia and smoke from the Northern Indiana Company's gas plant damaged the nearby Vesey greenhouse operation. An injunction and damages were sought, but an injunction was denied and the relief granted was limited to permanent damages "present, past, and future" (p. 371, 200 N.E. 620).

Denial of injunction was grounded on a public interest in the operation of the gas plant and on the court's conclusion "that less injury would be occasioned by requiring the appellant [Public Service] to pay the appellee [Vesey] all damages suffered by it . . . than by enjoining the operation of the gas plant; and that the maintenance and operation of the gas plant should not be enjoined" (p. 349, 200 N.E. p.625).

The Indiana Supreme Court opinion continued: "When the trial court refused injunctive relief to the appellee upon the ground of public interest in the continuance of the gas plant, it properly retained jurisdiction of the case and awarded full compensation to the appellee. This is upon the general equitable principle that equity will give full relief in one action and prevent a multiplicity of suits" (pp. 353-354, 200 N.E. p.627).

It was held that in this type of continuing and recurrent nuisance permanent damages were appropriate. *See also, City of Amarillo v. Ware*, 120 Tex. 456, 40 S.W. 2d 57 where recurring overflows from a system of storm sewers were treated as the kind of nuisance for which permanent depreciation of value of affected property would be recoverable.

There is some parallel to the conditioning of an injunction on the payment of permanent damages in the noted "elevated railway cases" (*Pappenheim v. Metropolitan El. Ry. Co.*, 128 N.Y. 436, 28 N.E. 518, and others which followed). Decisions in these cases were based on the finding that the railways created a nuisance as to adjacent property owners, but in lieu of enjoining their operation, the court allowed permanent damages.

Judge Finch, reviewing these cases in *Ferguson v. Village of Hamburg*, 272 N.Y. 234, 239-240, 5 N.E. 2d 801, 803, said: "The courts decided that the plaintiffs had a valuable right which was being impaired, but did not grant an absolute injunction or require the railway companies to resort to separate condemnation proceedings. Instead they held that a court of equity could ascertain the damages and grant an injunction which was not to be effective unless the defendant failed to pay the amount fixed as damages for the past and permanent injury inflicted." (*See also, Lynch v. Metropolitan El. Ry. Co.*, 129 N.Y. 274, 29 N.E. 315; *Van Allen v. New York El. R. R. Co.*, 144 N.Y. 174, 38 N.E. 997; *Cox v. City of New York*, 265 N.Y. 411, 193, N.E. 251, and similarly, *Westphal v. City of New York*, 177 N.Y. 140, 69 N.E. 369.)

Thus it seems fair to both sides to grant permanent damages to plaintiffs which will terminate this private litigation. The theory of damage is the "servitude on land" of plaintiffs imposed by defendant's nuisance. (See *United States v. Causby*, 328 U.S. 256, 261, 262, 267, 66 S.Ct. 1062, 90 L.Ed. 1206, where the term "servitude" addressed to the land was used by Justice Douglas relating to the effect of airplane noise on property near an airport.)

The judgment, by allowance of permanent damages imposing a servitude on land, which is the basis of the actions, would preclude future recovery by plaintiffs or their grantees (see *Northern Indiana Public Serv. Co. v. W.J. and M.S. Vesey, supra*, p. 351, 200 N.E. 620).

This should be placed beyond debate by a provision of the judgment that the payment by defendant and the acceptance by plaintiffs of permanent damages found by the court shall be in compensation for a servitude on the land.

Although the Trial Term has found permanent damages as a possible basis of settlement of the litigation, on remission the court should be entirely free to re-examine this subject. It may again find the permanent damage already found; or make new findings.

The orders should be reversed, without costs, and the cases remitted to Supreme Court, Albany County to grant an injunction which shall be vacated upon payment by defendant of such amounts of permanent damage to the respective plaintiffs as shall for this purpose be determined by the court.

JASEN, JUDGE (dissenting).

I agree with the majority that a reversal is required here, but I do not subscribe to the newly enunciated doctrine of assessment of permanent damages, in lieu of an injunction, where substantial property rights have been impaired by the creation of a nuisance.

It has long been the rule in this State, as the majority acknowledges, that a nuisance which results in substantial continuing damage to neighbors must be enjoined. (*Whalen v. Union Bag & Paper Co.*, 208 N. Y. 1; 101 N.E. 805; *Campbell v. Seaman*, 63 N. Y. 568; see, also, *Kennedy v. Moog Servocontrols*, 21 N.Y. 2d 966, 290 N.Y. S.2d 193, 237 N.E. 2d 356.) To now change the rule to permit the cement company to continue polluting the air indefinitely upon the payment of permanent damages is, in my opinion, compounding the magnitude of a very serious problem in our State and Nation today.

In recognition of this problem, the Legislature of this State has enacted the Air Pollution Control Act (Public Health Law, Consol. Laws. C. 45 §§ 1264 to 1299-m) declaring that it is the State policy to require the use of all available and reasonable methods to prevent and control air pollution (Public Health Law, § 1265).

The harmful nature and widespread occurrence of air pollution have been extensively documented. Congressional hearings have revealed that air pollution causes substantial property damage, as well as being a contributing factor to a rising incidence of lung cancer, emphysema, bronchitis and asthma.

The specific problem faced here is known as particulate contamination because of the fine dust particles emanating from defendant's cement plant. The particular type of nuisance is not new, having appeared in many cases for at least the past 60 years. (*See Hulbert v. California Portland Cement Co.*, 161 Cal. 239, 118 P.928 [1911].) It is interesting to note that cement production has recently been identified as a significant source of particulate contamination in the Hudson Valley. This type of pollution, wherein very small particles escape and stay in the atmosphere, has been denominated as the type of air pollution which produces the greatest hazard to human health. We have thus a nuisance which not only is damaging to the plaintiffs, but also is decidedly harmful to the general public.

I see grave dangers in overruling our long-established rule of granting an injunction where a nuisance results in substantial continuing damage. In permitting the injunction to become inoperative upon the payment of permanent damages, the majority is, in effect, licensing a continuing wrong. It is the same as saying to the cement company, you may continue to do harm to your neighbors so long as you pay a fee for it. Furthermore, once such permanent damages are assessed and paid, the incentive to alleviate the wrong would be eliminated, thereby continuing air pollution of an area without abatement.

It is true that some courts have sanctioned the remedy here proposed by the majority in a number of cases, but none of the authorities relied upon by the majority are analogous to the situation before us. In those cases, the courts, in denying an injunction and awarding money damages, grounded their decision on a showing that the use to which the property was intended to be put was primarily for the public benefit. Here, on the other hand, it is clearly established that the cement company is creating a continuing air pollution nuisance primarily for its own private interest with no public benefit.

This kind of inverse condemnation (*Ferguson v. Village of Hamburg*, 272 N. Y. 234, 5 N.E. 2d 801) may not be invoked by a private person or corporation for private gain or advantage. Inverse condemnation should only be permitted when the public is primarily served in the taking or impairment of property. (*Matter of New York City Housing Auth. v. Muller*, 270 N. Y. 333, 343, 1 N.E. 2d 153, 156, *Pocantico Water Works Co. v. Bird*, 130 N. Y. 249, 258, 29 N.E. 246, 248.) The promotion of the interests of the polluting cement company has, in my opinion, no public use or benefit.

Nor is it constitutionally permissible to impose servitude on land, without consent of the owner, by payment of permanent damages where the continuing impairment of the land is for a private use. (*See Fifth Ave. Coach Lines v. City of New York*, 11 N.Y. 2d 342, 347, 229 N.Y. 2d 400, 403, 183 N.E. 2d 684, 686; *Walker v. City of Hutchinson*, 352 U.S. 112, 77 S.Ct. 200, 1 L.Ed. 2d 178.) This is made clear by the State Constitution (art. I, § 7, subd. [a]) which provides that "[p]rivate property shall not be taken for *public use* without just compensation" (emphasis added). It is, of course, significant that the section makes no mention of taking for a *private* use.

In sum, then, by constitutional mandate as well as by judicial pronouncement, the permanent impairment of private property for private purposes is not authorized in the absence of clearly demonstrated public benefit and use.

I would enjoin the defendant cement company from continuing the discharge of dust particles upon its neighbors' properties unless, within 18 months, the cement company abated this nuisance.

It is not my intention to cause the removal of the cement plant from the Albany area, but to recognize the urgency of the problem stemming from this stationary source of air pollution, and to allow the company a specified period of time to develop a means to alleviate this nuisance.

I am aware that the trial court found that the most modern dust control devices available have been installed in defendant's plant, but, I submit, this does not mean that *better* and more effective dust control devices could not be developed within the time allowed to abate the pollution.

Moreover, I believe it is incumbent upon the defendant to develop such devices, since the cement company, at the time the plant commenced production (1962), was well aware of the plaintiffs' presence in the area, as well as the probable consequences of its contemplated operation. Yet, it still chose to build and operate the plant at this site.

In a day when there is a growing concern for clean air, highly developed industry should not expect acquiescence by the courts, but should, instead, plan its operations to eliminate contamination of our air and damage to its neighbors.

Accordingly, the orders of the Appellate Division, insofar as they denied the injunction, should be reversed, and the actions remitted to Supreme Court, Albany County to grant an injunction to take effect 18 months hence, unless the nuisance is abated by improved techniques prior to said date.

FULD, C.J., and BURKE and SCILEPPI, JJ., concur with BERGAN, J.

JASEN, J., dissents in part and votes to reverse in a separate opinion.

BREITEL and GIBSON, JJ., taking no part.

ARMORY PARK NEIGHBORHOOD ASSOCIATION v. THE EPISCOPAL COMMUNITY SERVICES IN ARIZONA
Supreme Court of Arizona, 1985 (En Banc)
712 P.2d 914

FELDMAN, JUSTICE.

On December 11, 1982, defendant Episcopal Community Services in Arizona (ECS) opened the St. Martin's Center (Center) in Tucson. The Center's only purpose is to provide one free meal a day to indigent persons. Plaintiff Armory Park Neighborhood Association (APNA) is a non-profit corporation organized for the purpose of "improving, maintaining and insuring the quality of the neighborhood known as Armory Park Historical Residential District." The Center is located on Arizona Avenue, the western boundary of the Armory Park district. On January 10, 1984, APNA filed a complaint in Pima County Superior Court, seeking to enjoin ECS from operating its free food distribution program. The complaint alleged that the Center's activities constituted a public nuisance and that the Armory Park residents had sustained injuries from transient persons attracted to their neighborhood by the Center.

The superior court held a hearing on APNA's application for preliminary injunction on March 6 and 7, 1984. At the commencement of the hearing, the parties stipulated that

> . . . . there is no issue concerning any State, County, or Municipal zoning ordinance, or health provision, before the Court. And, the Court may find that defendants are in compliance with the same.

The residents then testified about the changes the Center had brought to their neighborhood. Before the Center opened, the area had been primarily residential with a few small businesses. When the Center began operating in December 1982, many transients crossed the area daily on their way to and from the Center. Although the Center was only open from 5:00 to 6:00 p.m., patrons lined up well before this hour and often lingered in the neighborhood long after finishing their meal. The Center rented an adjacent fenced lot for a waiting area and organized neighborhood cleaning projects, but the trial judge apparently felt these efforts were inadequate to control the activity stemming from the Center. Transients frequently trespassed onto residents' yards, sometimes urinating, defecating, drinking and littering on the residents' property. A few broke into storage areas and unoccupied homes, and some asked residents for handouts. The number of arrests in the area increased dramatically. Many residents were frightened or annoyed by the transients and altered their lifestyles to avoid them.

Following the hearing, ECS filed a motion to dismiss the complaint based on three grounds: 1) that compliance with all applicable zoning and health laws constituted a complete defense to a claim of public nuisance; 2) that there had been no allegation or evidence of a violation of a criminal statute or ordinance, which it argues is a prerequisite to a finding of public nuisance; and 3) that APNA lacked standing to bring an action to abate a public nuisance because it had neither pled nor proved any special injury differing in kind and degree from that suffered by the public generally.

Based on the hearing testimony, the trial court granted the preliminary injunction and denied ECS' motion to dismiss. In its order, the court noted that ECS could be enjoined because its activities constituted both a public and a private nuisance. After its motion for reconsideration was denied, ECS filed a special action in the court of appeals, and shortly thereafter filed a notice of appeal from the order granting the injunction. The court of appeals consolidated the proceedings and stayed enforcement of the trial court's order pending a final decision.

A divided court of appeals reversed the trial court's order. In the view of the majority, a criminal violation was a prerequisite to a finding of public nuisance; because plaintiff had alleged no criminal violation, the injunction was improperly granted. The majority also concluded that the trial court abused its discretion by finding both a public and a private nuisance when the plaintiff had not alleged a private nuisance. Finally, the court held that compliance with zoning provisions was a complete defense. The court vacated the order for preliminary injunction and remanded the matter to the trial court with directions to grant ECS' motion to dismiss. We have jurisdiction pursuant to Rule 23, Ariz. R. Civ. App. P., 17A A.R.S., A.R.S. § 12-120.24, and Rule 8(b), Ariz. R. P. Sp. Act; 17A A.R.S. We granted review in this case because of the importance of the following questions:

1) When does a voluntary association have standing to bring an action for public nuisance on behalf of its members?

2) May a lawful business be enjoined for acts committed off its premises by clients who are not under its control or direction?

3) Is it necessary to plead and prove a zoning or criminal violation by the defendant, or may a lawful activity be enjoined because the manner in which it is conducted is unreasonable and therefore constitutes a public nuisance?

THE CONCEPT OF "NUISANCE"

Now considered a tort, a public nuisance action originated in criminal law. Early scholars defined public nuisance as "an act or omission 'which obstructs or causes inconvenience or damage to the public in the exercise of rights common to all her Majesty's subjects.'" Prosser, W. and W.P. Keetons, Handbook on the Law of Torts, § 90, at 643 (5th ed. 1984), quoting Stephen, General View of the Criminal Law in England 105 (1890). The sole remedy was criminal prosecution. Prosser, *supra* § 86, at 618.

Historically, the remedy for a private nuisance was an action "upon the case," as it was an injury consequential to the act done and found its roots in civil law. Pearce, E. and D. Meston, Handbook on the Law Relating to Nuisances 2 (1926). A private nuisance is strictly limited to an interference with a person's interest in the enjoyment of real property. The Restatement defines a private nuisance as "a nontrespassory invasion of another's interest in the private use and enjoyment of land." Restatement (Second) of Torts § 821D. A public nuisance, to the contrary, is not limited to an interference with the use and enjoyment of the plaintiff's land. It encompasses any unreasonable interference with a right common to the general public. Restatement, *supra* § 821B. *Accord*, Prosser, *supra* § 86, at 618.

We have previously distinguished public and private nuisances. In *City of Phoenix v. Johnson*, 51 Ariz. 115, 75 P.2d 30 (1938), we noted that a nuisance is public when it affects rights of "citizens as a part of the public, while a private nuisance is one which affects a single individual or a definite number of persons in the enjoyment of some private right which is not common to the public." *Id.* at 123, 75 P.2d 34. A public nuisance must also affect a considerable number of people. *Id. See also Spur Industries v. Del Webb Development Co.*, 108 Ariz. 178, 494 P.2d 700 (1972). The legislature has adopted a similar requirement for its criminal code, defining a public nuisance as an interference "with the comfortable enjoyment of life or property by an entire community or neighborhood, or by a considerable number of persons. . . ." A.R.S. § 13-2917[3]

The defendant contends that the trial court erred in finding both public and private nuisances when the plaintiff had not asserted a private nuisance claim. The defendant has read the trial court's minute entry too strictly. While we acknowledge that public and private nuisances implicate different interests, we recognize also that the same facts may support claims of both public and private nuisance. As Dean Prosser explained:

> When a public nuisance substantially interferes with the use or enjoyment of the plaintiff's rights in land, it never has been disputed that there is a particular kind of damage, for which the private action will lie. Not only is every plot of land traditionally unique in the eyes of the law, but in the ordinary case the class of landowners in the vicinity of the alleged nuisance will necessarily be a limited one, with an interest obviously different from that of the general public. The interference itself is of course a private nuisance; but is none the less particular damage from a public one, and the action can be maintained upon either basis, or upon both. (Citations omitted.)

Prosser, *Private Action for Public Nuisance*, 52 Va. L. Rev. 997, 1018 (1966).

Thus, a nuisance may be simultaneously public and private when a considerable number of people suffer an interference with their use and enjoyment of land. *See Spur Industries*, 108 Ariz, at 184, 494 P.2d at 706. The torts are not mutually exclusive. Some of plaintiff's members in this case have suffered an injury to the use and enjoyment of their land. Any reference to both a public and a private nuisance

---

[3] This statute was neither raised nor argued by the plaintiff; in fact, the plaintiff expressly denied any statutory violation by the defendant.

by which the trial court was, we believe, merely a recognition of this well-accepted rule and not error. However, both because plaintiff did not seek relief under the theory of private nuisance and because that theory might raise standing issues not addressed by the parties, we believe plaintiff's claim must stand or fall on the public nuisance theory alone.

1. Do the residents have standing?

Defendant argues that the Association has no standing to sue and that, therefore, the action should be dismissed. The trial court disagreed and defendant claims it erred in so doing. Two standing questions are before us. The first pertains to the right of a private person, as distinguished from a public official, to bring a suit to enjoin the maintenance of a public nuisance. The original rule at common law was that a citizen had no standing to sue for abatement or suppression of a public nuisance since such inconvenient or troublesome offences [sic], as annoy the whole community in general, and not merely some particular persons; and therefore are indictable only, and not actionable; as it would be unreasonable to multiply suits, by giving every man a separate right of action, by what damnifies him in common only with the rest of his fellow subjects." IV Blackstone Commentaries 167 (1966). It was later held that a private individual might have a tort action to recover personal damages arising from the invasion of the public right. Y.B. 27 Hen. VIII, Mich, pi. 10, *cited in* Restatement, *supra* § 821C comment a. However, the individual bringing the action was required to show that his damage was different in kind or quality from that suffered by the public in common. Prosser, *supra* § 90, at 646; Harper & James, The Law of Torts § 1.23, at 64-5 (1956).

The rationale behind this limitation was two-fold. First, it was meant to relieve defendants and the courts of the multiple actions that might follow if every member of the public were allowed to sue for a common wrong. Second, it was believed that a harm which affected all members of the public equally should be handled by public officials. Restatement, *supra* § 821C comment a. *See also Engle v. Clark*, 53 Ariz. 472, 90 P.2d 994 (1939). Considerable disagreement remains over the type of injury which the plaintiff must suffer in order to have standing to bring an action to enjoin a public nuisance. However, we have intimated in the past that an injury to plaintiff's interest in land is sufficient to distinguish plaintiff's injuries from those experienced by the general public and to give the plaintiff-landowner standing to bring the action. *See, e.g., Tucson Community Development and Design Center v. City of Tucson*, 131 Ariz. 454, 457, 641 P.2d 1298, 1302 (1981) (plaintiffs denied standing to challenge city's redevelopment plan because they neither lived nor held property in the area affected by the plan); *Folk v. City of Phoenix*, 27 Ariz.App. 146, 551 P.2d 595 (1976) (plaintiff had standing sufficient to withstand a motion to dismiss by alleging ownership of a prescriptive right in the land affected). This seems also to be the general rule accepted in the United States. *See* Prosser, *supra* § 90, at 651; Restatement, *supra* § 821C comment d.

We hold, therefore, that because the acts allegedly committed by the patrons of the neighborhood center affected the residents' use and enjoyment of their real property, a damage special in nature and different in kind from that experienced by the residents of the city in general, the residents of the neighborhood could bring an action to recover damages for or enjoin the maintenance of a public nuisance.

2. May the Association bring the action on behalf of its members?

We have not previously decided whether an association or other organization has standing to assert the claims of its members in a representational capacity. . . .

We hold, therefore, that APNA has standing to bring the action as the representative of its members.

DEFENDANT'S DERIVATIVE RESPONSIBILITY

Defendant claims that its business should not be held responsible for acts committed by its patrons off the premises of the Center. It argues that since it has no control over the patrons when they are not on the Center's premises, it cannot be enjoined because of their acts. We do not believe this position is supported either by precedent or theory.

In *Shamhart v. Morrison Cafeteria Co.*, 159 Fla. 629, 32 So. 2d 727 (1947), the defendant operated a well frequented cafeteria. Each day customers waiting to enter the business would line up on the sidewalk, blocking the entrances to the neighboring establishments. The dissenting justices argued that the defendant had not actually caused the lines to form and that the duty to prevent the harm to the plaintiffs should be left to the police through regulation of the public streets. The majority of the court rejected this argument, and remanded the case for a determination of the damages. *See, also, Reid v. Brodsky*, 397 Pa. 463, 156 A.2d 334 (1959) (operation of a bar enjoined because its patrons were often noisy and intoxicated; they frequently used the neighboring properties for toilet purposes and sexual misconduct); *Barrett v. Lopez*, 57 N.M. 697, 262 P.2d 981, 983 (1953) (operation of a dance hall enjoined, the court finding that "mere possibility of relief from another source [police] does not relieve the courts of their responsibilities"); *Wade v. Fuller*, 12 Utah 2d 299, 365 P.2d 802 (1961) (operation of drive-in cafe enjoined where patrons created disturbances to nearby residents); *McQuade v. Tucson Tiller Apartments*, 25 Ariz. App. 312, 543 P.2d 150 (1975) (music concerts at mall designed to attract customers enjoined because of increased crowds and noise in residential area).

Under general tort law, liability for nuisance may be imposed upon one who sets in motion the forces which eventually cause the tortious act; liability will arise for a public nuisance when "one person's acts set in motion a force or chain of events resulting in the invasion." Restatement, *supra* § 824 comment b. We hold, therefore, that defendant's activity may be enjoined upon the showing of a causal connection between that activity and harm to another.

The testimony at the hearing establishes that it was the Center's act of offering free meals which "set in motion" the forces resulting in the injuries to the Armory Park residents. Several residents testified that they saw many of the same transients passing through the neighborhood and going in and out of the Center. We find the testimony sufficient to support the trial judge's finding of a causal link between the acts of ECS and the injuries suffered by the Armory Park residents.

The court of appeals thus erred by holding that there was no evidence from which the trial court could have concluded that ECS had engaged in conduct which would render it causally responsible for the interferences. The question is not whether defendant directly caused each improper act, but whether defendant's business operation frequently attracted patrons whose conduct violated the rights of residents to peacefully use and enjoy their property.

REASONABLENESS OF THE INTERFERENCES

Since the rules of a civilized society require us to tolerate our neighbors, the law requires our neighbors to keep their activities within the limits of what is tolerable by a reasonable person. However, what is reasonably tolerable must be tolerated; not all interferences with public rights are public nuisances. As Dean Prosser explains, "[t]he law does not concern itself with trifles, or seek to remedy all of the petty annoyances and disturbances of everyday life in a civilized community even from conduct committed with knowledge that annoyance and inconvenience will result." Prosser, *supra* § 88, at 626. Thus, to constitute a nuisance, the complained-of interference must be substantial, intentional and unreasonable under the circumstances. Restatement, *supra* § 826 comment c and § 821F. Our courts have generally used a balancing test in deciding the reasonableness of an interference. *See McQuade v. Tucson Tiller Apartments, supra.* The trial court should look at the utility and reasonableness of the conduct and balance these factors against the extent of harm inflicted and the nature of the affected neighborhood. We noted in the early case of *MacDonald v. Perry:*

> What might amount to a serious nuisance in one locality by reason of the density of the population, or character of the neighborhood affected, may in another place and under different surroundings be deemed proper and unobjectionable. What amount of annoyance or inconvenience caused by others in the lawful use of their property will constitute a nuisance depends upon varying circumstances and cannot be precisely defined.

32 Ariz. 39, 50, 255 P. 494 (1927). *See, also, Spur Industries, supra.*

The trial judge did not ignore the balancing test and was well aware of the social utility of defendant's operation. His words are illuminating:

> It is distressing to this Court that an activity such as defendants [sic] should be restrained. Providing for the poor and the homeless is certainly a worthwhile, praisworthy [sic] activity. It is particularly distressing to this Court because it [defendant] has no control over those who are attracted to the kitchen while they are either coming or leaving the premises. However, the right to the comfortable enjoyment of one's property is something that another's activities should not affect, the harm being suffered by the Armory Park Neighborhood and the residents therein is irreparable and substantial, for which they have no adequate legal remedy.

Minute Entry, 6/8/84, at 8. We believe that a determination made by weighing and balancing conflicting interests or principles is truly one which lies within the discretion of the trial judge. *State v. Chappie*, 135 Ariz. 281, 660 P.2d 1208 (1983). We defer to that discretion here. The evidence of the multiple trespasses upon and defacement of the residents' property supports the trial court's conclusion that the interference caused by defendant's operation was unreasonable despite its charitable cause.

The common law has long recognized that the usefulness of a particular activity may outweigh the inconveniences, discomforts and changes it causes some persons to suffer. We, too, acknowledge the social value of the Center. Its charitable purpose, that of feeding the hungry, is entitled to greater deference than pursuits of lesser intrinsic value. It appears from the record that ECS' purposes in operating the Center were entirely admirable. However, even admirable ventures may cause unreasonable interferences. *See e.g., Assembly of God Church of Tahoka v. Bradley*, 196 S.W.2d 696 (Tex. Civ. App. 1946). We do not believe that the law allows the costs of a charitable enterprise to be visited in their entirety upon the residents of a single neighborhood. The problems of dealing with the unemployed, the homeless and the mentally ill are also matters of community or governmental responsibility.

ZONING

ECS argues that its compliance with City of Tucson zoning regulations is a conclusive determination of reasonableness. We agree that compliance with zoning provisions has some bearing in nuisance cases. We would hesitate to find a public nuisance, if, for example, the legislature enacted comprehensive and specific laws concerning the manner in which a particular activity was to be carried out. *Accord* Restatement, *supra* § 821B comment f. We decline, however, to find that ECS' compliance with the applicable zoning provisions precludes a court from enjoining its activities. The equitable power of the judiciary exists independent of statute. Although zoning and criminal provisions are binding with respect to the type of activity, they do not limit the power of a court acting in equity to enjoin an unreasonable, albeit permitted, activity as a public nuisance. *Accord State ex rel. Carlson v. Hatfield*, 183 Neb. 157, 158 N.W.2d 612 (1968); *Monroe City v. Arnold*, 22 Utah 2d 291, 452 P.2d 321 (1969).

The determination of the type of business to be permitted in a particular neighborhood, therefore, may be left to administrative agencies or legislative bodies. However, the judgment concerning the manner in which that business is carried out is within the province of the judiciary. Restatement, *supra* § 821B comment f. *See also* J. Joyce, Treatise on the Law of Governing Nuisances § 73, at 115 (1906). Zoning provisions may permit one's neighbor to operate a business. This does not give him license to use one's yard, nor permit his customers to do so.

In so far as *Desruisseau v. Isley*, 27 Ariz. App. 257, 553 P.2d 1242 (1976) is contrary to this principle, it is disapproved.

CRIMINAL VIOLATION

Occasionally we have indicated that conduct which violates a specific criminal statute is an element of public nuisance for civil tort claims. *See, e.g., State v. B Bar Enterprises, Inc.; Spur Industries, supra; State ex rel. Sullivan v. Phoenix Savings Bank & Trust Co.*, 68 Ariz. 42, 198 P.2d 1018 (1948); *MacDonald v. Perry, supra; Cactus Corp. v. State ex rel. Murphy*, 14 Ariz. App. 38, 480 P.2d 375 (1971). These cases did not face the issue whether a tort claim for public nuisance exists independent of statute. ECS argued that there is no criminal violation and that a tort claim for nuisance must be based on such a violation. The trial court did find that the consequences of ECS' activities fit within A.R.S. § 13-2917, which defines a criminal nuisance as an interference with the "comfortable enjoyment of life or property." We need not reach this issue nor need we rule on the constitutionality of the statute. We do not find it fatal that the plaintiff failed to allege a statutory violation. The statute in question adds little to APNA's claim. It does not proscribe specific conduct nor define what conduct constitutes a public nuisance, but only declares, in effect, that a public nuisance is a crime. We are squarely faced, therefore, with the issue of whether a public nuisance may be found in the absence of a statute making specific conduct a crime.

In *MacDonald v. Perry, supra*, we indicated that the inquiry in a nuisance claim is not whether the activity allegedly constituting the nuisance is lawful but whether it is reasonable under the circumstances. The Restatement states that a criminal violation is only one factor among others to be used in determining reasonableness. That section reads:

(1) A public nuisance is an unreasonable interference with a right common to the general public.

(2) Circumstances that may sustain a holding that an interference with a public right is unreasonable include the following:

(a) Whether the conduct involves a significant interference with the public health, the public safety, the public peace, the public comfort or the public convenience, *or*

(b) whether the conduct is proscribed by a statute, ordinance or administrative regulation, *or*

(c) whether the conduct is of a continuing nature or has produced a permanent or long-lasting effect, and, as the actor knows or has reason to know, has a significant effect upon the public right. (*Emphasis supplied.*)

Restatement, *supra* § 821B. Comment d to that section explains:

It has been stated with some frequency that a public nuisance is always a criminal offense. This statement is susceptible of two interpretations. The first is that in order to be treated as a public nuisance, conduct must have been already proscribed by the state as criminal. This is too restrictive. . . . [T]here is clear recognition that a defendant need not be subject to criminal responsibility.

Restatement, *supra* § 821B comment d, at 89.

Our earlier decisions indicate that a business which is lawful may nevertheless be a public nuisance. For example, in *Spur Industries, supra*, we enjoined the defendant's lawful business. We explained that "Spur is required to move not because of any wrongdoing on the part of Spur, but because of a proper and legitimate regard of the courts for the rights and interests of the public." 108 Ariz, at 186, 494 P.2d at 708. *See also City of Phoenix v. Harlan*, 75 Ariz. 290, 255 P.2d

609 (1953). This rule is widely accepted. Joyce, *supra* § 99 at 146; Harper and James, § 1.30 at 90.

We hold, therefore, that conduct which unreasonably and significantly interferes with the public health, safety, peace, comfort or convenience is a public nuisance within the concept of tort law, even if that conduct is not specifically prohibited by the criminal law.

. . . .

CONCLUSION

The trial court's order granting the preliminary injunction is affirmed. By affirming the trial court's preliminary orders, we do not require that he close the center permanently. It is of course, within the equitable discretion of the trial court to fashion a less severe remedy, if possible. The opinion of the court of appeals is vacated. The case is remanded for further proceedings.

————

1. A perennial problem in land use planning and social services is the "Not In My Back Yard" (NIMBY) issue. Are there better ways to handle this issue than through nuisance suits? Communities must deal with trash and sewage disposal, with caring for their less fortunate members, with industry, and animals. How should decisions be made when public concerns clash with private wishes?

2. What sorts of unconventional use can create a nuisance? *See Rankin v. FPL Energy, LLC*, 266 S.W.3d 506 (Tex. Civ. App. 2008), *review denied*, 2009 Tex. LEXIS 138 (Apr. 17, 2009) (windfarm is not a nuisance); *Rattigan v. Wile*, 841 N.E.2d 680 (Mass. 2006) (construction debris purposefully placed where it will annoy a neighbor is a nuisance); *Mark v. State Dep't of Fish and Wildlife*, 84 P.3d 155 (Or. Ct. App. 2004) (nude beach is a nuisance).

Chapter 20

ABUSE OF PROCESS AND MALICIOUS PROSECUTION

These torts, while distinct from each other, are often paired. The elements of a lawsuit for malicious prosecution are:

(1) the previous commencement of a lawsuit against the plaintiff; (2) that was instigated by the defendant; (3) that terminated in favor of the plaintiff; (4) due to a lack of probable cause for the instigation of the suit; (5) because the defendant's conduct was motivated by malice; and (6) the plaintiff sustained damages as a result.

The elements of a lawsuit for abuse of process are:

(1) the defendant made an illegal, improper, perverted use of process, which was neither warranted nor authorized by the process; (2) the defendant had an improper purpose in exercising such illegal, perverted, or improper use of process; and (3) the plaintiff sustained damages as a result.

Diehl v. Fred Weber, Inc., 309 S.W.3d 309, 318, 320 (Mo. Ct. App. 2010). A few courts, such as New Mexico's, have combined the two torts into one, but most seem intent on keeping their identities and roles separate.

Courts seem reluctant to allow the recovery of damages in suits for abuse of process and malicious prosecution, particularly when the defendant is the attorney who represented a client in what is now alleged to be a frivolous or malicious lawsuit. As you work your way through these cases, you should think about why this might be the case.

Many of the unsuccessful suits underlying abuse of process claims are medical malpractice cases. One common perception about medical malpractice is that attorneys are overly enthusiastic about filing malpractice suits. Whether this perception is accurate or not, the torts of abuse of process and malicious prosecution come into play as part of the response. In this context, any reluctance by courts to award damages to those aggrieved by meritless lawsuits may itself contribute to hostility between the medical and legal professions. Many jurisdictions now have statutory requirements that a medical malpractice complaint must meet before it is filed; to some extent, these requirements eliminate the need to use tort law to solve the perceived problem of excessive litigation in the medical area.

GRELL v. POULSEN

Supreme Court of Iowa, 1986

389 N.W.2d 661

REYNOLDSON, C.J., and HARRIS, CARTER, WOLLE, and LAVORATO, JJ.

WOLLE, J.

A disagreement concerning the unwritten terms of a business relationship between Paul E. Poulsen, now deceased, and plaintiff William Grell mushroomed into the present several-party multiple-count lawsuit. The case was submitted to a jury on four damage claims: the Grells' quantum meruit claim against the Poulsen estate; the estate's counterclaims for abuse of process and defamation; and defendant John Underwood's counterclaim against the Grells for abuse of process. The jury found no merit in the Grells' quantum meruit claim and also rejected the defamation counterclaim of the Poulsen estate. On the abuse of process claims which are the subject of this appeal, however, the estate and Underwood recovered damages from the Grells on the theory that [the] Grells had initiated the litigation for the purpose of gaining a competitive business advantage. The Grells contend they were entitled to a directed verdict and judgment notwithstanding the verdict on the counterclaims because the evidence did not satisfy one element of abuse of process. We agree and therefore reverse.

I. *Background Facts.*

In determining whether the evidence was sufficient to satisfy the elements of abuse of process and engender a jury question, we view the evidence in the light most favorable to the counterclaimants who received a favorable jury verdict. We focus on the business relationships between the parties. The counterclaimants seek to uphold their favorable jury verdicts on the theory that [the] Grells sued Poulsen and Underwood not to recover damages but solely to disrupt the counterclaimants' businesses and business relationship.

William Grell first went to work for Poulsen as a distributor in Las Vegas, Nevada, for Poulsen's line of marguerita mixes. Poulsen did not manufacture his own drink mixes but obtained them from Bar None, Inc., a bottling company located in Tustin, California which Underwood owned and operated. When the Las Vegas venture was unsuccessful, William Grell returned to Iowa but continued working in Poulsen's bar mix business. His wife Mary and he also performed bookwork and other duties in connection with Poulsen's several Iowa City enterprises. The good business relationship between Poulsen and his supplier Underwood survived the unsuccessful Las Vegas venture; they continued their joint enterprise involving the production and sale of bar mixes in Iowa.

[The] Grells worked for Poulsen in the Iowa City area from April of 1982 until March of 1983 when their business relationship ended in harsh words and bitter disagreements. Poulsen rejected the Grells' contention that he had orally agreed to provide them a partnership interest in his business enterprise. Within three weeks after the employment relationship terminated, the Grells commenced this lawsuit as a damage action against Poulsen. They contended he had committed intentional business torts by inducing them to work for him and then forcing them out of the business. Subsequently the Grells added Underwood as a defendant and alleged that he had "usurped [William Grell's] partnership position with Poulsen." By the time the jury received and rejected those damage claims against the Poulsen estate and Underwood, the Grells had scaled down their theories for recovery to a simple quantum meruit claim for damages.

In the meantime, however, Poulsen counterclaimed for damages alleging abuse of process and defamation, and when Underwood was joined as a defendant he too alleged in a counterclaim that [the] Grells had abused process in filing their damage action. Because the jury rejected Poulsen's defamation counterclaim, we need not relate the evidence on which it was based. The abuse of process counterclaims were premised on the theory that the Grells had filed their lawsuit solely to gain a competitive business advantage over Poulsen and Underwood. The evidence, viewed in the light most favorable to the counterclaimants, disclosed that William Grell's brother was involved in a bar mix business that was in direct competition with that of Poulsen and Underwood. The brother's business had also received financial assistance from certain relatives of the attorney who initially filed the Grells' lawsuit. Against that backdrop of the Grells' motive to gain a competitive advantage over the bar mix business of Poulsen and Underwood, the counterclaimants highlighted three events which occurred after Poulsen and the Grells had parted company. First, William Grell declared shortly after the breakup that he had set out to find "the meanest lawyer in the country" and he was going to "tear Paul Poulsen's . . . head right off his shoulders." Second, William Grell acknowledged that he considered Underwood an innocent bystander; Underwood contends this proved the Grells joined him as a lawsuit defendant solely to destroy his business relationship with Poulsen by driving a wedge between them.[1] Finally, the counterclaimants emphasized that in preparation for trial the Grells requested that Poulsen disclose to them his customer lists and other data concerning the bar mix business.

We must decide whether the evidence satisfied all of the elements of abuse of process or whether, as the Grells contend, the evidence was insufficient to support submission of those counterclaims to the jury.

II. *Elements of Abuse of Process.*

We have most recently defined the elements of an abuse of process claim in *Schmidt v. Wilkinson*, 340 N.W.2d 282, 284-85 (Iowa 1983), drawing upon earlier discussions of abuse of process in *Mills County State Bank v. Roure*, 291 N.W.2d 1, 4 (Iowa 1980), and *Sarvold v. Dodson*, 237 N.W.2d 447, 448-49 (Iowa 1976). *Schmidt*

---

[1] After this action was filed and tried, we amended Iowa R. Civ. P. 80 to discourage the filing of frivolous actions. The amended rule now provides that appropriate sanctions can be imposed upon any lawyer who signs frivolous pleadings and also upon the party for whom frivolous pleadings are filed.

adopted the definition contained in section 682 of the Restatement (Second) of Torts (1977):

> One who uses a legal process, whether criminal or civil, against another primarily to accomplish a purpose for which it is not designed, is subject to liability to the other for harm caused by the abuse of process.

In *Schmidt*, we quoted with approval comment b to that Restatement section, an important comment on why the restrictive word "primarily" had been added to the original Restatement definition. The comment provides in pertinent part:

> "Primarily." The significance of this word is that there is no action for abuse of process when the process is used for the purpose for which it is intended, but there is an incidental motive of spite or an ulterior purpose or benefit . . .

> For abuse of process to occur there must be use of the process for an immediate purpose other than that for which it was designed and intended. The usual case of abuse of process is one of some form of extortion, using the process to put pressure upon the other to compel him to pay a different debt or to take some other action or refrain from it.

We also specifically adopted the following quoted commentary from the Restatement which our *Schmidt* case (340 N.W.2d at 284) describes as an attempt to "crystalize the essence of abuse of process":

> Some act or threat directed to an immediate objective not legitimate in the use of the process is required, and the defendant is not liable if he has done no more than carry the process to its authorized conclusion, even with bad intentions.

Restatement (Second), Torts § 682 app. (1981).

Two Iowa abuse of process decisions cited in *Schmidt* focus on the element which is in question here — whether [the] Grells committed any irregular act in their use of court process. In *Brody v. Ruby*, 267 N.W.2d 902, 906 (Iowa 1978), we held that a lawsuit commenced solely in the expectation of settlement could not be classified as an abuse of process. Subsequently, in *Froning & Deppe, Inc. v. South Story Bank & Trust Co.*, 327 N.W.2d 214, 215 (Iowa 1982), we rejected a counterclaim for abuse of process which alleged that the plaintiff had commenced a damage action to intimidate and embarrass defendants knowing it was not entitled to recover the full amount set forth in the prayer. In both the *Brody* and *Froning & Deppe* cases, we relied on *Holiday Magic, Inc. v. Scott*, 4 Ill. App. 3d 962, 969, 282 N.E.2d 452, 456-57 (1972), which held that an act which is proper in the regular prosecution of a proceeding cannot be relied upon as a basis for an abuse of process claim.

We distill from these authorities one element of an abuse of process claim which is missing in this case. A prerequisite for recovery is evidence that the person committed some act in the use of process that was not proper in the regular prosecution of the proceeding. This element has been identified and described, though in somewhat differing language, in several federal and state court decisions. *See, e.g., Sage International Ltd. v. Cadillac Gauge Co.*, 556 F. Supp. 381, 388-90 (E.D. Mich. 1982) (some irregular act in the use of process must be plead to state an abuse of process claim); *The Savage Is Loose Co. v. United Artists Theatre Circuit, Inc.*, 413 F. Supp. 555, 562 (S.D.N.Y. 1976) (abuse of process action is not supported by post-lawsuit events interfering with use of property since they were "a concomitant of any lawsuit"); *Unit, Inc. v. Kentucky Fried Chicken Corp.*, 304 A. 2d 320, 331-32 (Del. Super. Ct. 1973) (abuse of process claimant must demonstrate "a threat or act in the use of process not proper in the regular conduct of a lawsuit"); *Melton v. Rickman*, 225 N.C. 700, 703, 36 S.E.2d 276, 278 (1945) (an element of abuse of process is use of the process to secure "a result not lawfully or properly attainable under it"); *Martin v. Trevino*, 578 S.W.2d 763, 769 (Tex. Civ. App. 1978) (first element of abuse of process claim is "that the defendant made an illegal, improper, or perverted use of the process, a use neither warranted nor authorized by the process").

Neither the Poulsen estate nor Underwood introduced evidence to support this element of abuse of process — an act not proper in the regular prosecution of the proceeding. Proof of an improper motive by the person filing a lawsuit, even a malicious purpose, does not satisfy that element. The Grells took no specific action in connection with their use of process which can be characterized as unlawful or irregular. They did attempt during discovery to obtain lists of the counterclaimants' drink mix customers. Discovery of that type, however, is routine in civil actions and a concomitant of much business litigation. The request was authorized by Iowa Rule of Civil Procedure 129. The counterclaimants had the right to request, and in this case they received, a protective order authorized by Iowa Rule of Civil Procedure 123. *See Farnum v. G.D. Searle & Co.*, 339 N.W.2d 384, 389-90 (Iowa 1983) (discussing factors the trial court may consider in determining whether to restrict or prevent disclosure of confidential information pursuant to Iowa R. Civ. P. 123). The Grells never did receive the customer lists through any legal process. Moreover, the Grells persuasively argue that they had ready access to the same lists while working for Poulsen just three weeks before they commenced the lawsuit.

In ruling on the Grells' motion for judgment notwithstanding the verdict, the trial court wrote that William Grell had used the legal process against the counterclaimants "to help his brother's business, as opposed to collecting damages." That finding does not provide the element missing here — proof of an irregular misuse of the process itself. We conclude that neither the Grells' filing of a damage lawsuit nor their request for production of customer lists constituted an irregular act in the use of process on which an actionable claim could be founded.

The Grells were entitled to a directed verdict and judgment notwithstanding the verdict on the counterclaims of the Poulsen estate and Underwood. We overturn the counterclaimants' judgments against the Grells.

REVERSED.

MOZZOCHI v. BECK

Supreme Court of Connecticut, 1987

529 A.2d 171

PETERS, C. J., SHEA, CALLAHAN, GLASS and COVELLO, JS.

PETERS, C.J.

The principal issue in this case is whether a cause of action for abuse of process may be brought to recover damages from attorneys who allegedly pursued litigation despite their discovery that their client's claim lacked merit. The plaintiff, Charles J. Mozzochi, filed a five count complaint charging the defendants, attorneys Bruce S. Beck and Kathleen Eldergill and the law firm of Beck & Pagano, with unlawful conduct in the nature of vexatious litigation, abuse of process and malpractice. The trial court, concluding that the plaintiff had failed to state any cause of action, granted the defendants' motion to strike the complaint and subsequently, at the plaintiff's request, rendered judgment in favor of the defendants. The plaintiff's appeal to the appellate court was transferred to this court. We find no error.

In an appeal challenging a ruling on a motion to strike, we must take the facts to be those alleged in the plaintiff's complaint, and must construe the complaint in the manner most favorable to the plaintiff. According to the complaint, at some time prior to May 7, 1982, the defendants instituted an action on behalf of Walter Muszynski against the present plaintiff. An amended complaint in the Muszynski action, filed on August 13, 1982, alleged that the plaintiff had falsely and maliciously accused Muszynski of having falsified his original job application with the Glastonbury police department and of having been arrested by federal agents for a felony. A subsequent amendment to the Muszynski complaint alleged that the plaintiff had falsely and maliciously accused Muszynski of having wrongfully obtained unemployment compensation benefits. The defendants persisted in filing these amended complaints and otherwise continued to pursue the Muszynski action despite the fact that they had learned that the plaintiff's statements about Muszynski were true and that the Muszynski action was without merit. The defendants pursued this course of conduct for the unlawful, ulterior purpose of inflicting injury upon the plaintiff and enriching themselves and their client, Muszynski.

The trial court determined that these allegations did not suffice to state a cause of action. With respect to a possible claim for vexatious litigation, the court determined that the complaint was defective for failure to allege that the underlying action "was initiated maliciously, without probable cause, and terminated in the plaintiff's favor." *Blake v. Levy*, 191 Conn. 257, 263, 464 A.2d 52 (1983); *Vandersluis v. Weil*, 176 Conn. 353, 356, 407 A.2d 982 (1978). The court held that the complaint did not state a claim for abuse of process because it failed to allege that the defendants had engaged in overt acts for a collateral purpose unrelated to the lawsuit that they were prosecuting. *Varga v. Pareles*, 137 Conn. 663, 667, 81 A.2d 112 (1951). Finally, the court concluded that the plaintiff's complaint could not support an action for legal malpractice grounded in the provisions of the Code of Professional Responsibility, because it did not allege that the plaintiff had ever been the foreseeable beneficiary of the legal services rendered by the defendants for their client, Muszynski.

The plaintiff's appeal does not contest the trial court's ruling on vexatious litigation. The plaintiff maintains, however, that the trial court erred in holding that his complaint failed to state a claim either for abuse of process or for legal malpractice. These claims of error warrant separate consideration.

I

The plaintiff asserts that he has stated a cause of action for abuse of process by alleging, in his complaint, that the defendants: (1) filed amendments to the pleadings in the Muszynski action when the defendants knew that the allegations of those amendments were false; and (2) refused to withdraw the Muszynski action after learning that it was utterly without merit. This conduct constituted abuse of process, according to the plaintiff, because it was allegedly undertaken for "an unlawful ulterior purpose, to wit: to inflict injury upon the plaintiff and to enrich themselves and their said client although they knew that their said lawsuit was without merit."

In our assessment of the viability of this complaint, it is useful to note at the outset what the complaint does not allege. There is no claim that the defendants undertook any action outside of the normal course of proceedings in the Muszynski case itself. For example, there is no claim that the defendants used the pleadings or the process in the Muszynski case as leverage to coerce the plaintiff to pay a debt or surrender property unrelated to that litigation. Similarly, there is no claim that the defendants used unreasonable force, excessive attachments or extortionate methods to enforce the right of action asserted in the Muszynski case. Finally, there is no claim that the defendants' purpose in pursuing the Muszynski case was to gain any collateral advantage extraneous to its merits. The only injury of which the plaintiff complains is that the defendants improperly continued to pursue the Muszynski case in order to enrich themselves and Muszynski at the plaintiff's expense.

An action for abuse of process lies against any person using "a legal process against another in an improper manner or to accomplish a purpose for which it was not designed." *Varga v. Pareles, supra*, 667; *Schaefer v. O.K. Tool Co.*, 110 Conn. 528, 532-33, 148 A. 330 (1930). Because the tort arises out of the accomplishment of a result that could not be achieved by the proper and successful use of process, the Restatement Second (1977) of Torts, § 682, emphasizes that the gravamen of the action for abuse of process is the use of "a legal process . . . against another *primarily* to accomplish a purpose for which it is not designed. . . ." (Emphasis added.) Comment b to § 682 explains that the addition of "primarily" is meant to exclude liability "when the process is used for the purpose for which it is intended, but there is an incidental motive of spite or an ulterior purpose of benefit to the defendant." See also 1 F. Harper, F. James & O. Gray, Torts (2d Ed. 1986) § 4.9; R. Mallen & V. Levit, Legal Malpractice (2d Ed. 1981) § 61; W. Prosser & W. Keeton, Torts (5th Ed. 1984) § 121.

We have not previously considered the scope of the potential liability of an attorney for abuse of process arising out of the attorney's professional representation of the interests of his or her clients. Such a cause of action must be reconciled with our responsibility to assure unfettered access to our courts. Because litigants cannot have such access without being assured of the unrestricted and undivided loyalty of their own attorneys, we have afforded to attorneys, as officers of the court, absolute immunity from liability for allegedly defamatory communications in the course of judicial proceedings. For other causes of action, however, the exigencies of the adversary system have not been deemed to require absolute immunity for attorneys. We have assumed, without discussion, that an attorney may be sued in an action for vexatious litigation, arguably because that cause of action has built-in restraints that minimize the risk of inappropriate litigation.[1] Other courts have held that immunity from libel actions should not carry over to provide an attorney with an absolute defense to liability for abuse of process. Accordingly, we conclude that an attorney may be sued for misconduct by those who have sustained a special injury because of an unauthorized use of legal process. In permitting such a cause of action, we must, however, take care "not to adopt rules which will have a chilling and inhibitory effect on would-be litigants of justiciable issues." *Morowitz v. Marvel*, 423 A.2d 196, 197-98 (D.C. App. 1980).

State courts in other jurisdictions have undertaken the process of balancing these competing interests, principally in cases arising out of medical malpractice litigation. The factual setting of these cases is a suit by a physician seeking vindication from an attorney after a malpractice claim brought on behalf of the physician's patient has ended in withdrawal, dismissal or settlement. Courts have struggled to determine under what circumstances such a complaint states a cause of action for abuse of process. The existing case law demonstrates that there is no bright line that clearly distinguishes between the ends ordinarily associated with litigation and the ulterior purpose that the tort of abuse of process is intended to sanction. Much turns on the specificity of the pleadings. In many of the cases, the complaints have alleged generally that a physician has incurred costs to defend against the underlying malpractice suit, or that the malpractice suit has injured his professional reputation, or that the malpractice suit was initiated in the hopes of procuring a favorable settlement. Ruling in favor of the attorney defendants, courts have held such complaints to be legally insufficient because they do not allege conduct showing the use of process to accomplish a purpose for which it was not designed. When, however, such allegations are buttressed by specific claims of egregious misconduct, such as utter failure to investigate the validity of the underlying action, or unwarranted pursuit of inappropriate motions, some courts have sustained liability for abuse of process.

Accordingly, we conclude that although attorneys have a duty to their clients and to the judicial system not to pursue litigation that is utterly groundless, that duty does not give rise to a third party action for abuse of process unless the third party can point to specific misconduct intended to cause specific injury outside of the normal contemplation of private litigation. Any other rule would ineluctably

---

[1] One such restraint is the requirement that the action that is the subject of the vexatious litigation suit have terminated in the plaintiff's favor. See Vandersluis v. Weil, 176 Conn. 353, 356, 407 A.2d 982 (1978).

interfere with the attorney's primary duty of robust representation of the interests of his or her client.

Our appraisal of the plaintiff's complaint in light of this holding leads us to conclude that the complaint does not state a cause of action for abuse of process. Its key allegation is that the defendants continued to pursue litigation "for an unlawful ulterior purpose, to wit: to inflict injury upon the plaintiff and to enrich themselves and their said client although they knew that their said lawsuit was without merit." So general an allegation of abuse does not satisfy the requirement of showing the use of legal process *"primarily* to accomplish a purpose for which it is not designed. . . ." (Emphasis added.) 3 Restatement (Second), supra, § 682. The complaint in no way distinguishes between the costs and benefits ordinarily associated with the pursuit of litigation and the burdens that the defendants in this case allegedly improperly inflicted upon the plaintiff. We agree with the trial court that the plaintiff failed to state a cause of action for abuse of process.

. . . .

There is no error.

DETENBECK v. KOESTER
Court of Appeals of Texas, 1994
886 S.W.2d 477

HUTSON-DUNN, JUSTICE.

Before HUTSON-DUNN, COHEN, and O'CONNER, JJ.

The issue in this case is whether a doctor may maintain a cause of action for abuse of process against his former patient and her attorney for bringing a frivolous malpractice suit in an attempt to coerce a settlement.

In 1981, appellee, Winifred Koester, filed a malpractice suit against appellant, Dr. Detenbeck, arising out of a knee surgery he performed on her in 1978. In 1990, Koester dismissed the suit against Dr. Detenbeck with prejudice. After the malpractice case was dismissed, Dr. Detenbeck filed this abuse of process suit against Koester and her attorney, appellee, Charles Houssiere. Koester and Houssiere filed special exceptions that were sustained by the trial court, claiming that Dr. Detenbeck's pleading failed to state a cause of action. Dr. Detenbeck chose not to amend his pleadings, and the trial court dismissed his case with prejudice. In his sole point of error, Dr. Detenbeck contends the trial court erred in sustaining appellees' special exceptions and dismissing his case. We affirm.

. . . .

BACKGROUND

The facts set forth in Dr. Detenbeck's pleadings, which we are obliged to accept as true, are as follows. In 1980, Winifred Koester had mounting medical bills from numerous surgeries to her knee. In an effort to meet these expenses, Koester sought legal advice from Gus J. Zgourides to determine whether she could bring a medical malpractice claim against Dr. Detenbeck, who had performed a knee replacement on her in 1978. Zgourides obtained the records from Dr. Detenbeck's 1978 surgery, and a subsequent surgery performed by Dr. Bruce Cameron in 1979, and forwarded them to Dr. Sam Yates for review. After reviewing the records, Dr. Yates concluded that there had been no negligence on the part of Dr. Detenbeck. Thereafter, Zgourides informed Koester that there was not much of a chance of establishing liability against Dr. Detenbeck, and withdrew his representation.

Koester then hired Charles Houssiere to represent her. She also gave Houssiere copies of the opinions by Zgourides and Dr. Yates. On January 19, 1981, the day before the statute of limitations ran on Koester's claim, Houssiere filed suit against Dr. Detenbeck on Koester's behalf.

Four years later, with little or no discovery, Houssiere designated Dr. Bruce Cameron as an expert, even though Dr. Cameron testified that in his opinion the surgery had been performed by Dr. Detenbeck in the standard and accepted manner for orthopedic surgeons.

Dr. Detenbeck further alleges that seven years after the malpractice suit was filed, Houssiere began trying to coerce a settlement of the case by threatening to try the case, and forcing Dr. Detenbeck to take considerable time away from his practice. In an attempt to support the malpractice claim, Houssiere obtained an affidavit from Dr. John Bunting, an internist, stating his opinion that Dr. Detenbeck was negligent in his treatment of Koester.

Two years later, now nine years after the malpractice suit was filed, Houssiere again began trying to coerce a settlement by threatening to keep Dr. Detenbeck tied up for two weeks in trial. After this attempt at settlement, Houssiere's expert, Dr. John Bunting, signed a second affidavit stating that he had not read the previous affidavit, nor had an opportunity to review it after he signed it. He further stated that he had no opinion as to the standard of care applicable to orthopedic surgeons, and that the surgery performed by Dr. Detenbeck exceeded his scope of knowledge. He concluded that he had no criticism of Dr. Detenbeck, and did not feel that he was negligent.

On September 11, 1990, over nine years after the malpractice suit was filed, Houssiere and Koester decided to dismiss the action with prejudice. Dr. Detenbeck then brought this action against Koester and Houssiere for abuse of process.

ABUSE OF PROCESS

The sole issue to be resolved by this Court is whether the factual allegations set forth in Dr. Detenbeck's pleading will support a cause of action for abuse of process. The elements of a cause of action for abuse of process are: (1) that the defendant made an illegal, improper, perverted use of the process; (2) that the defendant had an ulterior motive or purpose in exercising such illegal, perverted, or improper use of process; and (3) that damage resulted to the plaintiff from the irregularity. *J. C. Penney Co. v. Gilford*, 422 S.W.2d 25, 31 (Tex. Civ. App. — Houston [1st Dist.] 1967, writ refd n.r.e.). To constitute an abuse of process, the process must be used to accomplish an end which is beyond the purview of the process, and which compels a party to do a collateral thing which he would not be compelled to do. *Blanton v. Morgan*, 681 S.W.2d 876, 878 (Tex. App. — El Paso 1984, writ refd n.r.e.). When the process is used for the purpose for which it is intended, even though accompanied by an ulterior motive, no abuse of process occurs. *Baubles & Beads v. Louis Vuitton*, 766 S.W.2d 377, 378-79 (Tex. App. — Texarkana 1989, no writ).

The clearest explanation of abuse of process is found in *Blackstock v. Tatum*, 396 S.W.2d 463, 468 (Tex. App. — Houston [1st Dist.] 1965, no writ), *(quoting, Prosser on Torts*, 3rd Ed., Section 115):

> "The essential elements of abuse of process . . . have been stated to be: first, an ulterior purpose, and second, a wilful act in the use of the process not proper in the regular conduct of the proceeding. Some definite act or threat not authorized by the process, or aimed at an objective not legitimate in the use of the process, is required; and there is no liability where the defendant has done nothing more than carry out the process to its authorized conclusion, even though with bad intentions. The improper purpose usually takes the form of coercion to obtain a collateral advantage, not properly involved in the proceeding itself, such as the surrender of property or the payment of money, by the use of the process as a threat or a club. There is, in other words, a form of extortion, and it is what is done in the course of negotiation, rather than the issuance or any formal use of the process itself, which constitutes the tort."

ANALYSIS

Several Texas cases have addressed the issue of whether a doctor may recover from former patients and their attorneys because of prior malpractice suits. All of these cases, regardless of the cause of action asserted, have been unsuccessful. *See Kale v. Palmer*, 791 S.W.2d 628 (Tex. App. — Beaumont 1990, writ denied) (fraud and conspiracy); *Blanton v. Morgan*, 681 S.W.2d 876 (Tex. App. — El Paso 1985, writ ref d n.r.e.) (malicious prosecution and abuse of process); *Butler v. Morgan*, 590 S.W.2d 543 (Tex. App. — Houston [1st Dist.] 1979, writ refd n.r.e.) (malicious prosecution); *Martin v. Trevino*, 578 S.W.2d 763 (Tex. Civ. App. — Corpus Christi 1978, writ ref d n.r.e.) (malicious prosecution, abuse of process, prima facie tort, and breach of Texas Code of Professional Responsibility); *Moiel v. Sandlin*, 571 S.W.2d 567 (Tex. Civ. App. — Corpus Christi 1978, no writ) (malicious prosecution, barratry, abuse of process, and negligence); *Wolfe v. Arroyo*, 543 S.W.2d 11 (Tex. Civ. App. — San Antonio 1976, no writ) (constructive contempt).

In *Martin v. Trevino*, 578 S.W.2d at 768-69, the plaintiff-physician brought an action against his former patient and her attorney alleging they had negligently filed a medical malpractice suit against him without just cause or proper investigation. The court held that the plaintiff's pleadings failed to state a cause of action for abuse of process because "they fail to allege an improper use of the process other than the mere institution of the civil action. There were no damages other than that necessarily incident to filing a lawsuit." *Id.* at 769.

Dr. Detenbeck argues that *Martin* is distinguishable because in that case there was no evidence that the patient and her attorney ever actually attempted to coerce a settlement, whereas in this case, Houssiere allegedly threatened to tie up Dr. Detenbeck for two weeks by taking the case to trial if the doctor refused to settle. We find this argument unpersuasive. Evidence of an actual attempt to coerce a settlement would go to proving the element of malice. However, the mere procurement or issuance of process with a malicious intent, or without probable cause, is not actionable; there must be an improper use of the process after its issuance. *Id.* at 769. "[T]here is no liability where the defendant has done nothing more than carry out the process to its authorized conclusion, even though with bad intentions." *Blackstock* at 468. Where the only process issued is a citation, and no allegations are made that there was any abuse in the execution or service of this process, no cause of action for abuse of process is stated. *Morris v. Blangger*, 423 S.W.2d 133, 134 (Tex. Civ. App. — Austin 1968, writ ref d n.r.e.).

In *Blanton*, 681 S.W.2d at 877-78, the plaintiff-physician alleged that his former patient and her attorney asserted a claim for punitive damages in their malpractice suit and attempted to use the punitive damages claim to extort a settlement of the case. When the attempt at settlement failed, the attorneys dropped their punitive damages claim. The court held that the plaintiff's petition failed to allege a cause of action for abuse of process because the process was used only for its intended purpose, i.e., to compel the doctor to answer the petition. The court followed the *Martin* case in holding that the suit failed to allege an improper use of the process. *Id.*

In *Blackstock*, 396 S.W.2d at 467-468, the appellants alleged that the appellees filed a frivolous suit against them in an attempt to coerce appellants into dismissing an action that was already pending between the parties. In rejecting appellants' abuse of process claim, the court stated:

> As we understand it, *abuse of process consists not in the filing and maintenance of a civil action*, but rather in the perversion of some process issued in the suit after its issuance. The process referred to in the cases is not in the filing and maintenance of a civil action, but in the wrongful use of a writ issued in the suit. The writ or process must be used in a manner or for a purpose for which it is not by law intended and the use must interfere with the person or property of another.

Id. at 467 (emphasis added).

Based on these cases, we conclude that Dr. Detenbeck's cause of action for abuse of process must fail. Even if we were to assume that Koester and Houssiere instituted the malpractice suit without probable cause, and with the malicious intent of coercing a settlement, Dr. Detenbeck's pleadings remain defective because they do not allege an improper use of the process. The only process involved in this case was the citation issued when the cause was filed. The citation was used only for its intended purpose of compelling an answer to the lawsuit. The mere maintenance of a civil action, even if done with malicious intent, will not support a cause of action for abuse of process.

Furthermore, an attempt to coerce a settlement is not an attempt to obtain a collateral advantage not properly involved in the proceeding itself. The purpose of every lawsuit is to obtain either a settlement or a judgment. Therefore, an attempt to use a citation, and the resulting lawsuit, to coerce a settlement, is not an attempt to obtain a collateral advantage, but merely an attempt to carry out the process to its natural conclusion.

This is not to say that doctors have no remedy for frivolous, or "bad faith" lawsuits filed by former patients. When the Medical Liability and Insurance Improvement Act was enacted in 1977, subchapter H of the statute allowed a health care professional to file a separate suit against a patient who brought a lawsuit in "bad faith," or "with reckless disregard as to whether or not reasonable grounds exist for asserting the claim." However, by its own terms, subchapter H *never became effective* because the State Bar of Texas certified to the Supreme Court that it had adopted rules for appropriate disciplinary measures against an attorney who filed a claim in bad faith.

Disciplinary rules alone proved to be an unsatisfactory remedy, because physicians who suffered damages as a result of a breach of the Code of Professional Responsibility had no cause of action for that breach. *Blanton*, 681 S.W.2d at 878-79.

However, in 1988 the Supreme Court enacted Tex. R. Civ. P. 13, which allows the trial court to impose sanctions against an attorney or party for lawsuits that are groundless, and brought in bad faith or for purposes of harassment. A lawsuit is "groundless" if it has "no basis in law or fact and not warranted by good faith argument for the extension, modification, or reversal of existing law." Tex. R. Civ. P. 13. Therefore, the proper remedy for a physician seeking compensation for damages as a result of a "bad faith" malpractice action, is to seek rule 13 sanctions in the malpractice action; a separate lawsuit for abuse of process is inappropriate.

The judgment is affirmed.

ROBERTS v. FEDERAL EXPRESS CORP.
Supreme Court of Tennessee, 1992
842 S.W.2d 246

DROWOTA, JUSTICE

This malicious prosecution action involves the question of whether Defendant had probable cause to institute criminal proceedings against Plaintiff. The trial court granted Defendant's motion for summary judgment, finding, on the undisputed facts, that Defendant had probable cause for instituting prosecution. In so holding, the trial court recognized that, under existing precedent, the ultimate determination of probable cause is a question of law for the court. We conclude that the existence of probable cause is a question (1) unrelated to a prosecutor's subjective belief, and (2) properly decided by a jury.

Plaintiff Richard Roberts worked for Defendant Federal Express Corporation for nine years, compiling an exemplary job record. As a maintenance mechanic, his duties included working on Defendant's concealed security cameras.

Defendant's sorting process sometimes results in contents being spilled from mutilated packages. Plaintiff had often picked up spilled contents and turned them in, although not necessarily on the same day. On one occasion he turned in a box of

13 diamond rings. Defendant has also experienced problems with employee theft. Plaintiff had, in the past, helped Defendant uncover employee dishonesty.

On February 1, 1988, while at work, Plaintiff was taking medication for severe back pain. Although fellow employees urged him to go home, he continued to work. At some point while on the job, Plaintiff discovered a gold ring, an aerosol can, a videotape, a silver spoon, chocolate candy, and a dildo on Defendant's premises. He placed the videotape in a sleeve, and the other articles in the pockets, of his jacket.

Sometime later that day, apparently affected by the medication, Plaintiff had a fellow employee take him to a break area. On the way there, Plaintiff told this employee of the items in his jacket and that he needed to turn them in. Upon reaching the break area, Plaintiff slept for the remainder of his shift.

At approximately 5:00 p.m. at the end of his shift, Plaintiff was awakened by another employee. Plaintiff, still drowsy, was then driven to an employee exit that contained an electronic screening device. Plaintiff went to this exit despite holding special permission to leave the premises via locations not equipped with surveillance devices.

As Plaintiff was passing through one of these screening devices the alarm sounded. Plaintiff backed up and removed a set of keys and returned through the device. The alarm sounded a second time. Plaintiff then removed his jacket and a knife he had in his possession and passed back through the screening device. The alarm did not sound. Allegedly, that's when Plaintiff realized that he had left certain items that he had picked up from mutilated packages in his pockets. Plaintiff contends that he was disoriented and forgot the items were in his jacket due to medication he had been taking. Plaintiff appeared drowsy to the security guard.

Plaintiff explained to the security officers that he had found the items and forgot to turn them in and had no intention of stealing them. Plaintiff was detained for approximately four hours and questioned for about 30 to 45 minutes. The officers took Plaintiff's statement concerning the incident during this period. In addition, they discussed the valium tablets and Plaintiff took two security officers over to the location where he found the items. Thereafter, Plaintiff was released and given a suspension.

On February 10, 1988, Defendant caused an arrest warrant to be issued charging Plaintiff with grand larceny. A Shelby County Grand Jury later returned a no true bill.

When Plaintiff brought this action for malicious prosecution, the trial court granted summary judgment for Defendant, finding Defendant had probable cause to institute the criminal proceedings. This finding was made in procedural conformance with existing precedent mandating that the ultimate determination of probable cause is a question of law for the court. The Court of Appeals affirmed.

I.

In order to establish the essential elements of malicious prosecution, a plaintiff must prove that (1) a prior suit or judicial proceeding was instituted without probable cause, (2) defendant brought such prior action with malice, and (3) the prior action was finally terminated in plaintiff's favor. *See Christian v. Lapidus*, 833 S.W.2d 71, 73 (Tenn. 1992); *Lewis v. Allen*, 698 S.W.2d 58, 59 (Tenn. 1985). The present case concerns the element of probable cause.

Probable cause is established where "facts and circumstances [are] sufficient to lead an ordinarily prudent person to believe the accused was guilty of the crime charged." *See Logan v. Kuhn's Big K Corp.*, 676 S.W.2d 948, 951 (Tenn. 1984); *Lewis v. Williams*, 618 S.W.2d 299, 303 (Tenn. 1981). However, this Court has also stated that "[t]he prosecutor must in good faith have honestly believed the accused was guilty of the crime charged." See *Logan*, 676 S.W.2d at 951; *Lewis*, 618 S.W.2d at 303. We now conclude that the existence of probable cause does not depend on the subjective mental state of the prosecutor.

A malicious prosecution is one brought in the absence of probable cause, and with malice. These two elements are distinct. Whereas malice concerns the subjective mental state of the prosecutor, appraisal of probable cause necessitates an objective determination of the reasonableness of the prosecutor's conduct in light of the surrounding facts and circumstances. *Accord Sheldon Appel Co. v. Albert & Oliker*, 47 Cal. 3d 863, 254 Cal. Rptr. 336, 765 P.2d 498, 506 (1989); Dobbs, *Belief and Doubt in Malicious Prosecution and Libel*, 21 Ariz. L. Rev. 607 (1979) (rejecting Restatement (Second) of Torts § 662 comment c (1977)).

Properly defined, probable cause requires only the existence of such facts and circumstances sufficient to excite in a reasonable mind the belief that the accused is guilty of the crime charged. While a mind "beclouded by prejudice, passion, hate and malice" is not "reasonable," see *Poster v. Andrews*, 183 Tenn. 544, 554, 194 S.W.2d 337, 341 (1946), the question whether a particular prosecutor is so motivated goes only to the element of malice. Probable cause is to be determined solely from an objective examination of the surrounding facts and circumstances.

II.

We now review whether the question of probable cause should be decided by the court or jury.

The existence of probable cause has long been characterized as a mixed question of law and fact:

> The facts from which probable cause is to be deduced are to be found by the jury; the deduction, as matter of law, is to be made by the court. The rule by which the court determines whether there is probable cause or not, is to look at the facts as found by the jury, and from these determine whether a reasonable man, in view of the facts so found, would have instituted the suit.

Memphis Gayoso Gas Co. v. Williamson, 56 Tenn. 314, 343 (1872). The ultimate determination is thus taken from the jury, even though "the existence of probable cause, which involves only the conduct of a reasonable man under the circumstances, . . . does not differ essentially from the determination of negligence." W. Keeton, *Prosser and Keeton on the Law of Torts*, § 119, at 882 (5th ed. 1984).

Justification for this anomaly has been attributed to "the apprehension of the courts that if the question of probable cause were left to juries, they might not sufficiently safeguard the rights of defendants, and thus might discourage the performance of a public duty of bringing complaints against persons they believe to have committed offenses." Annotation, *Probable Cause or Want Thereof, In Malicious Prosecution Action, As Question of Law for Court or of Fact for Jury*, 87 A.L.R.2d 183, 186-87 (1963). However, our jury system "occupies so firm a place in our history and jurisprudence that any seeming curtailment of the right to a jury trial should be scrutinized with the utmost care." *Dimick v. Schiedt*, 293 U.S. 474, 486, 55 S. Ct. 296, 301, 79 L. Ed. 603 (1935). This historical "apprehension" does not withstand such scrutiny; accordingly, the determination of the reasonableness of a defendant's conduct should be made by a jury. To the extent our cases hold to the contrary, *e.g.*, *Logan*, 676 S.W.2d at 951; *Lewis*, 618 S.W.2d at 300; *Cohen v. Cook*, 224 Tenn. 729, 731, 462 S.W.2d 499, 500 (1970); and *Memphis Gayoso*, 56 Tenn. at 343, they are overruled.

Under the facts presented, reasonable minds could differ as to whether probable cause existed for bringing charges against Plaintiff. The trial court, in line with existing procedural precedent, resolved the issue against Plaintiff and granted summary judgment for Defendant. The Court of Appeals affirmed. Because we now hold that where reasonable minds can differ as to the existence of probable cause a jury is to decide the issue, the judgments of the lower courts must be reversed.

Two final points must be addressed. First, Plaintiff asserts that a reasonable preprosecution investigation would have revealed certain exculpatory facts. Where such an allegation is made and there is evidence to support it, the jury is to determine the facts a reasonable investigation would have disclosed, and then base its probable cause determination considering those facts.

Second, Plaintiff asserts that the grand jury's refusal to indict creates a presumption that the prosecution was initiated without probable cause. We disagree. Termination of the prior proceeding in Plaintiff's favor has no bearing on whether probable cause existed at the time prosecution was initiated, and, where relevant, the jury shall be specifically so instructed.

The judgments below are reversed and the case remanded for proceedings consistent with this opinion. Costs of this appeal are taxed to Defendant. REID, C.J., and O'BRIEN, DAUGHTRY and ANDERSON, JJ., concur.

DUTT v. KREMP
Supreme Court of Nevada, 1995
894 P.2d 354

SHEARING, J.:

This appeal arises from a jury verdict and judgment against attorney Virgil Dutt ("Dutt") in favor of respondent physicians in an action for malicious prosecution and abuse of process. Dutt had filed a malpractice action against the physicians on behalf of Jack Rentnelli ("Rentnelli"), which Rentnelli later voluntarily dismissed. This dismissed malpractice action formed the basis of the physicians' allegations of malicious prosecution and abuse of process against both Dutt and Rentnelli. At trial, at the close of the physicians' case, the district court dismissed the action against Rentnelli and awarded him costs. The case against Dutt was submitted to a jury, which returned a verdict against Dutt. Dutt appeals the judgment against him. The physicians cross-appeal on the issue of costs.

The issues on appeal are whether the court rather than the jury should have decided certain issues, and whether there was sufficient evidence to support a verdict of malicious prosecution or abuse of process against Dutt.

FACTS

In February and March, 1985, respondent physicians treated Rentnelli at a local hospital for an ailment that was eventually diagnosed as tuberculous meningitis and hydrocephalus. Rentnelli was given medication, and after approximately two weeks was discharged from the hospital. Rentnelli's son ("John"), testified that after treatment Rentnelli's condition continued to deteriorate, that John tried to reach one of the physicians by telephone, but was only allowed to speak with the staff and not with the doctor. Rentnelli's condition deteriorated to the point that after ten days John decided to seek new physicians and flew Rentnelli to a Santa Barbara hospital where a new doctor surgically implanted a shunt to relieve pressure on his brain. Immediately after this treatment, Rentnelli improved markedly. The Santa Barbara doctor told Rentnelli's son that if he had not brought Rentnelli in when he did, Rentnelli might not have lived.

Based on this series of events, Rentnelli and his family believed that he had not received proper care by respondent physicians and consulted Rentnelli's attorney, Virgil Dutt. Dutt interviewed Rentnelli and John, and obtained the medical records from the physicians in Reno and Santa Barbara. Dutt reviewed the records and researched both medical literature on meningitis and hydrocephalus and legal authorities regarding malpractice actions. Based on this review and research, Dutt filed a malpractice action against the physicians on December 30, 1985. After the action was filed, Dutt continued his factual investigation and research. Upon learning of the Medical Quality Foundation in Virginia, Dutt agreed with one of physicians' counsel that he would submit the Rentnelli records to that foundation for evaluation; if the Foundation supported his claims, he would continue to prosecute the action, if not, Dutt would dismiss it. The Medical Quality Foundation concluded that given Rentnelli's condition, the one-month between Rentnelli's initial admission in Reno and the eventual shunt placement in Santa Barbara "would not produce significant brain damage," and that there was no provable negligence apparent from the records. On January 30, 1987, Dutt dismissed the malpractice action.

On December 29, 1987, the physicians filed their complaint for malicious prosecution and abuse of process against Rentnelli and Dutt. The court granted Rentnelli's motion for a directed verdict at the close of the physicians' case. The case against Dutt was tried before a jury which returned a verdict in the total amount of $40,000 in favor of the physicians against Dutt.

DISCUSSION

The questions presented in this appeal are: (1) whether the issue of probable cause should have been determined by the court rather than submitted to the jury, and (2) whether there was sufficient evidence to support the jury's verdict that Dutt was guilty of malicious prosecution or abuse of process.

The court instructed the jury on both malicious prosecution and abuse of process but the jury did not specify on which cause of action it based its verdicts. This court has held that the difference between the two torts is that the action for abuse of process hinges on the misuse of regularly issued process, in contrast to malicious prosecution, which rests upon the wrongful issuance of process. *Nevada Credit Rating Bur. v. Williams*, 88 Nev. 601, 606, 503 P.2d 9, 12 (1972). Malice and want of probable cause are necessary elements for recovering in an action for malicious prosecution, but they are not essential to recovery for abuse of process. *Id.* The fundamental elements of abuse of process are an ulterior purpose and a willful act in the use of process not proper in the regular conduct of the proceeding. *Id.* Because the jury did not specify which it found, both causes of action will be discussed.

Malicious Prosecution

The elements that must be proved in a malicious prosecution action in addition to the filing of a prior action against the plaintiffs are: (1) a lack of probable cause to commence the prior action; (2) malice; (3) favorable termination of the prior action; and (4) damages. See *Chapman v. City of Reno*, 85 Nev. 365, 369, 455 P.2d 618, 620 (1969). The first question presented in this appeal is whether, as appellant contends, the trial court erred by refusing to rule on the issue of probable cause.

When there is no dispute concerning the facts upon which an attorney acted in filing the prior action, the question of whether there was probable cause to institute the prior action is purely a legal question to be answered by the court. *Bonamy v. Zenoff,* 11 Nev. 250, 252, 362 P.2d 445, 447 (1961). Here, the trial court submitted the question of probable cause to the jury. We hold that this was error, because the facts upon which Dutt relied in filing the malpractice action are essentially undisputed.[2] The existence of probable cause was a legal question which, under *Bonamy*, the district court should have decided.

In *Sheldon Appel Co. v. Albert & Oliker*, 47 Cal. 3d 863, 254 Cal. Rptr. 336, 765 P.2d 498, 504 (Cal. 1989), the California Supreme Court offered a persuasive rationale for the requirement that the court, rather than the jury, determine the existence of probable cause:

> The question whether, on a given set of facts, there was probable cause to institute an action requires a sensitive evaluation of legal principles and precedents, a task generally beyond the ken of lay jurors, and courts have recognized that there is a significant danger that jurors may not sufficiently appreciate the distinction between a merely unsuccessful and a legally

---

[2] Even where the facts are disputed, the jury should be given the opportunity to find the facts, after which the court makes the legal determination of probable cause.

untenable claim. To avoid improperly deterring individuals from resorting to the courts for the resolution of disputes, the common law affords litigants the assurance that tort liability will not be imposed for filing a lawsuit unless *a court* subsequently determines that the institution of the action was without probable cause.

There is a division of authority in other jurisdictions as to whether the existence of probable cause in a malicious prosecution action should be judged by a strictly objective standard or by a combination of an objective and a subjective standard. In other words, in addition to whether a reasonable attorney would have found probable cause to file the action, must the filing attorney also have had an honest belief that the cause of action was meritorious? It appears that the result in this case would have been the same regardless of which standard was used, since there is no evidence in the record that the subjective standard is not met, i.e., that Dutt lacked an honest belief that his cause of action was meritorious. However, the standard affects the evidence required and allowed to be presented. Therefore, this court must decide which standard applies.

Clearly, there is a societal interest in providing an opportunity for peaceable redress for people who believe they have been wronged. However, society also has an interest in protecting people from unjustifiable and unreasonable litigation. That is the policy behind the tort of malicious prosecution. Attorneys have the role of facilitating access to our judicial system. Attorneys are charged with what may appear to be conflicting ethical obligations — not to file unwarranted suits and to represent their clients' interests diligently. In *Wong v. Tabor*, 422 N.E.2d 1279, 1286 (Ind. Ct. App. 1981), the court described these considerations as follows:

> While an attorney is under an ethical duty to avoid suit where its only purpose is to harass or injure, if a balance must be struck between the desire of an adversary to be free from unwarranted accusations and the need of the client for undivided loyalty, the client's interests must be paramount. . . . [T]he very nature of our adversary system of law mandates that the most useful and meaningful tests in this area must be derived from an attorney's ethical and professional obligations to his client.
>
> . . .
>
> We thus emphasize that any standard of probable cause must insure that the attorney's duty to his client to present his case vigorously in a manner as favorable to the client as the rules of law and professional ethics will permit is preserved.

(Citations omitted.)

We conclude that the objective test set forth by the California Supreme Court in *Sheldon Appel Co.*, is most appropriate to maintain the balance between these interests. Under this test, the court must determine whether, on the basis of the facts known to the attorney, a reasonable attorney would have believed that the institution of the prior action was legally tenable. *Sheldon Appel Co.*, 765 P.2d at 511. The standard is objective rather than subjective. The degree of expertise and the belief of the attorney are not relevant.

This court may determine whether Dutt had probable cause for filing the malpractice action in this case since the material facts were fully developed at trial and are essentially undisputed.

Dutt had information from Rentnelli's medical records, the description of events by Rentnelli and his son, John, and medical literature on meningitis and hydrocephalus. Judging Dutt's filing of the malpractice action under the objective standard, we conclude that a reasonable attorney would have believed that the action against the Reno doctors was legally tenable. The very fact that Rentnelli's condition continued to deteriorate after treatment by the Reno doctors but immediately improved after the Santa Barbara doctors' treatment would lead a reasonable person to believe that the first doctors did not adequately treat Rentnelli's ailments. A Santa Barbara doctor even told John that Rentnelli would have died if he had not brought Rentnelli in to them when he did. Dutt had no reason to believe that any of this information was unreliable. In fact, the medical records corroborated his client's statement of events.

There is no absolute requirement that an attorney obtain an expert medical opinion before filing a malpractice lawsuit. Whether enough information exists for a reasonable attorney to file a malpractice suit remains discretionary. In some situations the facts related by the patient may provide a sufficient basis to file suit, such as where a doctor amputates the wrong leg. In other situations, where the medical situation is more complex, more extensive research may be required, including consultation with medical experts. In the instant case, we hold that a reasonable attorney would have believed that he or she had sufficient information to justify filing a malpractice action.

It has never been the law that every piece of evidence necessary to prevail at trial must be available to the attorney before suit is filed. That is one of the functions of discovery.

The objectively reasonable standard set out above already applies in a malpractice suit against a physician. Physicians routinely make diagnoses and provide treatment based on the initial information given by the patient, even while planning further tests. When the doctor obtains additional information a different treatment may be indicated, but no one would suggest that taking preliminary action on the basis of the initial examination and history constitutes malpractice. Each professional may take objectively reasonable actions on the basis of information available at the time.

Just as an action for malicious prosecution will lie where a person commences an action without an objectively reasonable basis, an action will also lie where a person wrongfully continues a civil proceeding without probable cause. *Nelson v. Miller*, 227 Kan. 271, 607 P.2d 438, 443 (Kan. 1980). This theory was presented to the jury below, and respondents contend that the jury's verdict can be sustained on this basis. We disagree. The evidence adduced below does not support a finding against Dutt on this theory. Dutt received the Medical Quality Foundation's report on September 16, 1986, and he prepared a stipulation for dismissal the very next day. Moreover, after receiving the report, Dutt neither initiated further proceedings in the case nor conveyed any formal settlement demands to respondents. In our view, this evidence conclusively shows that Dutt discontinued the proceedings once he learned that a medical expert concluded that the delay in treatment did not cause significant damage, and that there was no probable negligence apparent from the medical records.

Since we have determined that Dutt had probable cause to file a complaint, no further inquiry is required as to the other elements of an action for malicious prosecution.

Abuse of Process

At the close of trial, Dutt moved for a directed verdict and for judgment notwithstanding the verdict or, in the alternative, for a new trial on the grounds that there was no evidence to support a verdict in favor of the physicians on their abuse of process claim. The trial court denied these motions, and Dutt contends that this was error. We agree.

An abuse of process claim consists of two elements: (1) an ulterior purpose other than resolving a legal dispute, and (2) a willful act in the use of process not proper in the regular conduct of the proceeding. *Kovacs v. Acosta*, 106 Nev. 57, 59, 787 P.2d 368, 369 (1990). An "ulterior purpose" includes any "improper motive" underlying the issuance of legal process. See *Laxalt v. McClatchy*, 622 F. Supp. 737, 751 (D. Nev. 1985). At trial, the physicians assigned two improper motives to appellant Dutt.

The physicians first argued that Dutt and Rentnelli filed the malpractice action in an effort to avoid paying the bill for medical services provided by respondents. Even if Rentnelli was motivated by a desire not to pay respondents, Dutt clearly was not. Nothing in the record supports such a claim where Dutt is concerned.

Second, the physicians asserted that Dutt filed the malpractice action to coerce a nuisance settlement. According to the physicians, this improper motive was demonstrated by Dutt's attempt to negotiate a settlement with the lawyer for one of the respondents after he had obtained the Medical Quality Foundation's report. The record does not support a finding of such improper motive. While the physicians attempted to analogize to *Bull v. McCuskey*, 96 Nev. 706, 615 P.2d 957 (1980), this case is readily distinguishable. In *Bull*, a jury award for a doctor in an abuse of process suit was supported by substantial evidence that the attorney filed a medical malpractice suit for the ulterior purpose of coercing a nuisance settlement. The attorney examined no medical records, conferred with no one, and then offered to settle the case for $750. *Id.* at 708, 615 P.2d at 959. This court held that this evidence was sufficient to sustain the verdict for abuse of process against the attorney. *Id.* at 709, 615 P.2d at 960. Unlike the defendant attorney in *Bull*, Dutt examined all the medical records, consulted medical and legal authorities, made no formal demand for settlement, and dismissed the complaint shortly after receiving the Medical Quality Foundation's report. Thus, we conclude that there is insufficient evidence to support a finding that appellant filed the malpractice action to coerce a nuisance settlement.

There is no evidence that appellant Dutt harbored an ulterior motive; because he was apparently merely attempting to resolve Rentnelli's apparent malpractice dispute with respondents, we need not consider the second element of an abuse of process claim, namely, whether appellant engaged in a willful act in the use of process not proper in the regular conduct of the proceeding.

CONCLUSION

For the reasons set forth above, we reverse the judgment entered below, and we remand this case to the district court for entry of judgment in favor of the appellant. Our decision renders the physicians' cross-appeal moot.

We concur: SPRING, J., YOUNG, J.

STEFFEN, C.J., with whom ROSE, J., agrees, dissenting:

In this court's opinion in *Dutt v. Kremp*, 109 Nev. 397, 848 P.2d 1073 (1993), we granted rehearing and ordered that the original opinion issued on December 22, 1992 (*Butt v. Kremp*, 108 Nev. 1076, 844 P.2d 786 (1992)) (Dutt I) be withdrawn. The majority opinion issued today again reverses the judgment entered pursuant to jury verdicts in the district court. I remain convinced that the record provides substantial evidence to support the factual findings by the jury and sound legal support for the district court's post-trial rulings denying Dutt relief from the judgment entered pursuant to the jury's verdicts favoring the respondent physicians. I am therefore again forced to dissent. In large measure, the dissent set forth herein constitutes a restatement of my earlier dissent in Dutt I.

If we were reviewing a judgment against a member of the medical profession for medical malpractice on equivalent facts, there is little doubt that the judgment would be upheld. Consider the hypothetical physician who, after listening to the complaints of a patient, reaches a diagnosis in an area outside his or her area of expertise without even performing a meaningful medical evaluation. Moreover, the hypothetical physician disdains a consultation, forging ahead on the basis of an unconfirmed diagnosis derived almost entirely from the verbalized complaints of the patient. Finally, the uninformed physician performs unnecessary and unsuccessful surgery. Accountability for medical malpractice under those circumstances would be both predictable and justified.

In the instant case, attorney Dutt filed a thoroughly inadequate complaint against numerous doctors and a hospital two days before the effective date of a statute that would have required Dutt to file a complaint with a medical-legal screening panel. The purpose for which the screening panel procedure was enacted is to discourage or minimize the filing of medical malpractice actions that are lacking in merit. The benefits of such a screening procedure are obvious: lower medical malpractice insurance rates (insurance costs are always passed on to the patients), less diversion of limited medical resources to defend against unwarranted litigation, enlightenment to attorneys inexperienced in complex medical malpractice cases, and a decreased toll on physicians and their reputations that would otherwise result from unmeritorious malpractice actions, to name but a few. According to attorney Dutt, the instant action was the first time he had ever filed a civil complaint for medical malpractice.

The majority concludes that a reasonable attorney "would have thought that the action against the Reno doctors was legally tenable" based upon the following factors: (1) Dutt had information from Rentnelli's medical records; (2) the description of events by Rentnelli and his son; and (3) medical literature on meningitis and hydrocephalus. Moreover, after reaching the conclusion that a reasonable attorney would have endorsed the sufficiency of the meager efforts itemized above, the majority added two additional observations: (1) that Rentnelli's condition continued to deteriorate after treatment by the Reno doctors and improved after treatment in Santa Barbara; and (2) the Rentnelli's son was informed by "the Santa Barbara doctor" that "his father would have died if he had not brought him in to them when he did."

The foregoing factors constitute the sum and substance of the majority's conclusion supporting a reasonable attorney's belief that a malpractice action was "legally tenable." I suggest that both the medical and legal professions have much to fear if the majority's evaluation continues to prevail. I also suggest that the foregoing recital of what the majority finds adequate under an objective standard is woefully inadequate under any standard. This was Dutt's first venture into the complex world of medical malpractice. Medical records and treatises left unanalyzed by medical professionals are of little value to persons untrained in medicine or attorneys who have not developed either an expertise in medical malpractice, or paid the price to fully inform themselves of the proper requisites for handling such a complex area of the law. To conclude, as the majority obviously does, that a tyro in medical malpractice litigation can translate highly technical medical records and treatises into a reasoned determination of malpractice without even consulting a knowledgeable health care provider, let alone the physician who provided later care to the patient/client and who allegedly had knowledge of professional negligence by the treating physicians, is worrisome to the extreme.

Remembering that a jury heard the evidence and observed the witnesses, it is revealing to outline a number of the operative facts which, I submit, strongly support the verdicts reached by the jury. Relevant factors include: (1) prior to filing the complaint, the inexperienced Dutt assigned a law school graduate who worked for him to read the medical records and evaluate them with him; (2) Dutt relied on the law school graduate's "opinions and recommendations as to what was in the [medical] records and how to interpret them;" (3) Dutt contacted no physicians or medical experts of any kind prior to filing the complaint; (4) Dutt did not even bother to contact the physicians who succeeded the respondent physicians in caring for his client; (5) at no time prior to filing the complaint did Dutt have any health care provider or physician review the medical records to determine whether a cause of action for medical malpractice existed; (6) after receiving a letter from Dr. Johnson, one of the physicians sued by Dutt, the latter responded to Dr. Johnson's attorney that the physician's letter "caused him to look at the case much more critically;" (7) almost nine months after Dutt filed his complaint against the Reno physicians, The Medical Quality Foundation ("Foundation"), with whom Dutt had at last corresponded in order to obtain a professional, medical evaluation of Rentnelli's treatment by the Reno physicians, informed Dutt that with respect to Rentnelli's condition, "once diagnosis is reached based on clinical features and laboratory studies, treatment is instituted at the earliest convenience, since without treatment an invariably fatal outcome occurs within 4 to 8 weeks of the onset." Continuing with its lengthy analysis, the Foundation concluded "after thorough review and research we can find no provable negligence in this case[;]" (8) On November 17, 1986, Dutt wrote to Dr. Johnson's attorney, observing in part:

[Y]ou stated that Dr. Johnson is very upset. I can understand his feelings. Determining that the problem was tuberculosis related clearly was *brilliant*.

Our problem was the failure to relieve the pressure within the skull. It now seems apparent that the pressure could have remained for an indefinite period of time without serious damage and that a shunt was only a matter of personal preference. *The fact that Mr. Rentnelli was on the proper medicine was apparently the only important factor.*

We now have Dr. Domz' deposition and clearly no reason exists for delaying the inevitable. *It is very clear that I would be unable to carry the burden of the proof* and therefore request dismissal of this matter (emphasis added);

(9) Rentnelli did not keep his follow-up appointments with the Reno physicians; (10) Dutt irresponsibly denied a request to admit that he had no expert witness "known or believed to be willing to testify under oath as a physician that the [Reno physicians] had breached the standard of care;" (11) in an answer to an interrogatory, Dutt identified Santa Barbara physician Dr. Domz "as a witness who would state that the CT Scans in Reno were not properly interpreted;" (12) two months after Dutt had received the Foundation report indicating no provable negligence, and even as he praised the Reno physicians' diagnosis as "brilliant," Dutt explained to Dr. Johnson's counsel that he had told attorney Osborne, who also represented certain of the defendants in the medical malpractice action, that he, Dutt, would not dismiss the action "until after the depositions came back in the event that Dr. Domz did suggest that the treatment did not meet the standard of care that one should expect from this area;" (13) Dutt, having stated in the answer to interrogatory referred to above that Dr. Domz would, as a witness, testify that the CT Scans taken in Reno were not interpreted properly, did not even bother to appear in California at the taking of his "witness'" deposition; (14) at no time did Dutt even speak to Dr. Domz, the Santa Barbara physician upon whom Dutt was allegedly going to rely for proving his case of medical negligence on the part of the Reno physicians; (15) Dr. Domz, in fact, found no fault with the treatment provided by the Reno physicians, a fact which prompted Dutt to admit in his letter of November 17, 1986, to attorney Pagni that "we now have Dr. Domz' deposition *and clearly no reason exists for delaying the inevitable*"; (16) it was clear that by forcing counsel for the Reno physicians to depose Dr. Domz, Dutt "hoped" that the Santa Barbara physician might say something, anything, that might provide a liability peg upon which to hang his hat, but his "hope" was not sufficiently strong to warrant the expenditure of his time and money to prepare for and attend the deposition of his critical "witness;" and (17) even after all of the foregoing factors and events, Dutt still attempted to exact a nuisance settlement out of attorney Osborne.

The majority tells us that despite all the afore-mentioned factors, attorney Dutt's efforts represented a basis for a reasonable attorney to believe that there was probable cause to file this action against the Reno physicians! Moreover, the majority notes that it is not always necessary to obtain the opinion of a medical expert before filing a complaint for medical malpractice. In support of the proposition, the majority cites *Badell v. Beeks*, 115 Idaho 101, 765 P.2d 126 (Idaho

1988), a case involving a dentist who had ruined a model's career by filing her teeth without the patient's permission. The result of the dentist's work, demonstrated by before and after photographs, aptly portrayed why he was sued. Most likely, a medical expert would also be unnecessary to prove negligence in situations where a surgeon leaves a sponge in a patient's abdomen or removes a wrong appendage. *See* NRS 41A.100. Incredibly, with respect to the underlying area of medical negligence in the instant case, the majority observes that "in other situations when the medical situation is more complex, more extensive research may be required, including consulting with medical experts. In the instant case, we find that a reasonable attorney would have believed that he or she had sufficient information to justify filing a malpractice action."

In Nevada, the importance and necessity of expert medical testimony or applicable medical literature demonstrating negligence under the circumstances at issue, is provided by statute:

> Liability for personal injury or death is not imposed upon any provider of medical care based on alleged negligence in the performance of that care unless evidence consisting of expert medical testimony, material from recognized medical texts or treatises or the regulations of the licensed medical facility wherein the alleged negligence occurred is presented to demonstrate the alleged deviation from the accepted standard of care in the specific circumstances of the case and to prove causation of the alleged personal injury or death. . . .

NRS 41A.100.

. . . I suggest that even lay persons will understand, as did the jury in the instant case, that the Reno physicians provided Rentnelli with life-saving expertise and treatment, properly characterized even by Dutt as "brilliant," and that the requisites of diagnosis and treatment were so complex that no action should have been contemplated, let alone filed, without first obtaining a thorough, professional medical analysis of the care provided by the Reno physicians. Unfortunately, their efforts were rewarded by the trauma and embarrassment of an ill-advised, precipitous and decidedly unenlightened lawsuit.

. . . .

I also find it doubly troubling that Rentnelli's Reno physicians, who were demonstrably vigilant and effective in their treatment and care of Dutt's client, were not only subjected to an unwarranted lawsuit, but were further demeaned at trial by Dutt's flippant and contradictory testimony ascribing the physicians' successful and difficult diagnosis to luck.

On these facts, it is little wonder that the respondent physicians insisted on having their efforts and their reputations vindicated in a trial against their uninformed, precipitant tormentor, attorney Dutt. I suggest that there is also little cause to wonder why the jury provided the respondent physicians with the vindication they sought from the civil justice system.

If society is to have any confidence in the legal system and the administration of justice within our courts, there must be an accountability for derelict lawyers that is equal to the level of accountability we impose on derelict physicians and other professionals. As I view this record, the evidence strongly supports the jury's findings against Dutt. Plainly stated, the jury, by its verdict, announced that lawyers are not privileged to assail the reputation of physicians in court and subject them to the enervating trauma, time and cost of a lawsuit with its concomitant attenuation of professional standing without reasonable cause.

Turning now to certain aspects of the majority's legal analysis, I note first my disagreement with the majority's conclusions regarding probable cause and the role it played in this case. The majority endorses for adoption in Nevada the probable cause rule announced in *Sheldon Appel Co. v. Albert & Oliker*, 47 Cal. 3d 863, 254 Cal. Rptr. 336, 765 P.2d 498 (Cal. 1989). With due respect to the California Supreme Court, I do not find its reasoning either sound or persuasive on the point. In adopting an "objectively tenable" standard for determining probable cause, the *Sheldon Appel Co.* court concluded that "the adequacy of an attorney's research is not relevant to the probable cause determination." *Id.* at 510. In so ruling, the California court disapproved dictum in *Tool Research & Engineering Corp. v. Henigson*, 46 Cal. App. 3d 675, 120 Cal. Rptr. 291 (Ct. App. 1975), to the effect that "an attorney's reasonable investigation and industrious search of legal authority is an essential component of probable cause." *Id. at* 509.

It appears to me that the *Sheldon Appel Co.* rule is in essence a rule of happenstance. In other words, if, in evaluating the issue of probable cause, a court concludes that the action was objectively tenable when filed, then there is a proper basis for finding probable cause for filing the action despite a provable condition of complete ignorance on the part of the plaintiff's attorney regarding the merits of the action when the complaint was filed. I am of the opinion that the "objectively tenable" rule adopted in *Sheldon Appel Co.* tends to reward indolence, ignorance, indifference or exploitiveness by focusing on the ability of the defendant attorney and his counsel to produce, *after the fact*, a semblance of objective tenability that would satisfy the probable cause standard of the California court. This is a backward-looking rule that seeks to find and interject a rational basis for filing an action when an objective analysis of the conditions surrounding the action at the time it was filed would reveal none.

I am persuaded that the rule embraced by the Supreme Court of Arizona in *Bradshaw v. State Farm Mut. Auto. Ins.*, 157 Ariz. 411, 758 P.2d 1313 (1988), is more appropriate. Holding that the test for probable cause is both subjective and objective, the *Bradshaw* court stated that "the initiator of the action must honestly *believe* in its possible merits; and, in light of the facts, that *belief must be objectively reasonable*." *Id.* at 417, 758 P.2d at 1319 (citing *Haswell v. Liberty Mutual Insurance Co.*, 557 S.W.2d 628, 633 (Mo. 1977); Restatement (Second) of Torts § 675 cmt. c (1977); Prosser & Keeton on the Law of Torts § 120, at 893 (5th ed. 1984)) (emphasis in original text).

Under the *Bradshaw* view, an inexperienced attorney's failure to research, consult, interview and meaningfully prepare before filing a complaint would be relevant in determining whether the attorney could have entertained an honest belief in the possible merits of his or her client's cause of action. Moreover, the second prong of the *Bradshaw* test requires that the attorney's honest belief be objectively reasonable. The latter test thus becomes a form of validation of the former.

Assuming the attorney has a modicum of legal ability that has been adequately focused on meaningful research and evaluation, it is logical to expect that the attorney's honest belief regarding the merits of the client's cause of action will be endowed with an aspect of objective reasonability.[4]

Moreover, at least in the more esoteric and complex areas of litigation, such as most instances of alleged medical malpractice, I disagree with both the majority and the *Sheldon Appel Co.* court in concluding that an attorney is entitled to rely entirely on what the client has said in determining whether there is probable cause to file an action. A client may, without any knowledge of the adequacy of his or her medical treatment, tell the attorney that the physician negligently treated him, describing the basis for his or her opinion. An attorney inexperienced in medical malpractice litigation may be as ignorant as the client with respect to the quality of the medical services actually provided by the client's physician. Under the view espoused by the majority, the uninformed attorney need not look beyond the client's perspective in determining whether there is probable cause to file a lawsuit. I believe such a view denigrates both the legal profession and the lawyers within the profession who are expected to apply enlightened understanding and analysis to a client's problems and concerns. *See Nelson v. Miller*, 227 Kan. 271, 607 P.2d 438, 448 (Kan. 1980).

If a client describes a simple battery to his or her attorney, it could be argued that the attorney may have probable cause to file an action against the alleged tortfeasor on the basis of what appears to be an honest factual recital by the client. In such a case, it is at least arguable that the rule adopted by the majority might be justified. In most medical malpractice cases, however, research and diligent inquiry and preparation are essential to an honest conclusion that probable cause exists for the filing of a complaint. I therefore take issue with the blanket rule adopted by the majority in the instant case.[5] I fully agree with both the *Sheldon Appel Co.* and *Bradshaw* courts that when the operative facts are not in dispute, the issue of probable cause is an issue of law to be decided by the court. I also agree with the *Bradshaw* ruling that when the operative facts are in dispute, the trial court may, by special verdict form or by a hypothetical jury instruction, provide guidance to the jury as to what facts will constitute probable cause. *Bradshaw*, 157 Ariz, at 419, 758 P.2d at 1321.

---

[4] I note, as did the *Bradshaw* court with regard to the Arizona rule, that the subjective-objective test is consonant with NRCP 11, which forbids the filing of groundless actions by requiring an attorney to certify, by his or her signature, that

> he or she has read the pleading . . . [and] that to the best of his or her knowledge, information and belief, formed after reasonable inquiry under the circumstances obtaining at the time of the signature, that it is well grounded in fact and is warranted by existing law . . . and that it is not interposed for any improper purpose.

[5] *NRS 41A.016* now requires all medical malpractice complaints to be filed in the first instance with a screening panel for a determination on the merits. The complaint so filed must contain a clear and concise statement of the facts and other circumstances relevant to the alleged malpractice. As a salutary consequence, the prospects for recurring actions of the type presented by the instant case should be minimized.

The operative facts in this case are not in dispute and the district court should have ruled on the issue of probable cause as a matter of law. Based upon my review of the record, however, I must agree with respondents that the district court impliedly ruled in their favor on the issue of probable cause. The issue was fully discussed by the parties at trial, and the trial judge refused to grant an NRCP 41(b) motion to dismiss at the conclusion of plaintiffs' case, ruling that plaintiffs had "made out a prima facie case." The trial judge also rejected Dutt's motion for a directed verdict at the conclusion of the evidence. In any event, my review of the record leads me to conclude, contrary to the majority's determination, that as a matter of law, Dutt did not have probable cause to file the lawsuit even under the *Sheldon Appel Co.* standard. I have previously recounted the numerous derelictions surrounding the filing of the complaint and will only observe here that if, as the majority concludes, there was probable cause for Dutt's lawsuit, there would appear to be little basis for ever holding attorneys legally accountable for the filing of frivolous medical malpractice claims.

Needless to say, I also disagree with the majority's ruling on the issue of malice. A jury may infer malice from an absence of probable cause, *Nelson*, 607 P.2d at 445, and as previously observed, I find ample evidence in the record undermining the majority's recognition of probable cause. Moreover, I again emphasize that in my view, there is no basis for concluding that Dutt's pre-filing behavior and preparation were reasonable. In any event, the record as I read it provides ample support for the jury's finding of malice.

I suggest that the record also provides a factual basis for liability resulting from abuse of process. Dutt's attempt to secure a settlement after he was thoroughly disabused of the possibility of negligence on the part of respondents is discounted by the majority because the settlement attempt was unadorned by a "formal demand." I am unable to discern in the majority's characterization of the evidence any basis for casting aside the jury's verdict. Moreover, I find entirely unpersuasive the majority's attempt to distinguish the instant case from that of *Bull v. McCuskey*, 96 Nev. 706, 615 P.2d 957 (1980). In *Bull*, this court affirmed an award against the attorney who filed a medical malpractice action based upon a determination that substantial evidence in the record supported the finding that the action was filed for the ulterior purpose of coercing a nuisance settlement. By way of contrast, the majority concludes that Dutt's (uninformed) examination of "all the medical records," and his after-the-fact, belated consultation with medical and legal authorities, coupled with a lack of "formal" settlement demand, eventuating in the dismissal of the complaint, justified Dutt's traumatizing efforts against the respondent physicians. I disagree and so did the jury who heard the evidence.

For the reasons abbreviated above, I would endorse the jury's verdict and affirm the judgment entered pursuant thereto. I therefore respectfully dissent.

The preceding decision deals, as do many others in this arena, with a meritless medical malpractice suit and a subsequent tort action against the client and attorney who filed that action. In what ways might one perceive the legal system as treating attorneys and doctors differently when they are defendants? How do abuse of process actions differ from malpractice suits? Absent some change in the law, a doctor who was a defendant in a frivolous lawsuit cannot sue the attorney who filed it against him or her in malpractice. Should a physician be able to argue that an attorney owes a duty to a physician defendant to represent the plaintiff client in an ethical manner? The medical profession is often perceived as having a profoundly negative view of attorneys. What ideas does *Dutt* give you about why this might be the case?

Chapter 21

TORTIOUS INTERFERENCE WITH CONTRACT

A. TORTIOUS INTERFERENCE WITH EXISTING CONTRACT

PROBLEM

Chucky has constructed a restaurant one block from the one owned by his ex-wife, Bertha. One of his stated goals is to drive her into bankruptcy and he therefore sells his hamburgers at ten cents less than hers. Chucky's food is very good.

Chucky has been negotiating with Red Pup Cola to stop selling to Bertha and to only sell to him. Red Pup is the leading soft drink in the region. Chucky now sells Yellow Drool Cola.

Bertha has asked you for advice.

———

Certainly the largest and perhaps the most important case on this subject is *Pennzoil v. Texaco*. Because the reports dealing with the case are voluminous, a summary follows:

PENNZOIL CO. v. TEXACO, INC.*

This extraordinary case arose out of a prospective merger between the Pennzoil Company and the "Getty Oil" entities (the Getty Oil Company, the J. Paul Getty Museum, and the Sarah C. Getty Trust) that was set to take place in January, 1984. Pennzoil had been following the well-publicized dissention that commenced between the Getty Oil entities and director Gordon Getty in late 1983. Beginning in 1983, Pennzoil had remained in close contact with Gordon Getty and representatives of the J. Paul Getty Museum, and had made repeated public offerings in an attempt to gain control of stock in Getty Oil. In January of 1984, after reaching an agreement with Museum authorities to purchase all of its existing shares of Getty Oil, Pennzoil contacted Gordon Getty (as former director of Getty Oil and the named trustee of the Sarah C. Getty Trust) in an effort to strengthen its merger potential and solidify its ownership in Getty Oil.

In January of 1984, Pennzoil representatives, Gordon Getty (on behalf of the Trust) and the President of the Getty Museum, drafted and signed a "Memorandum

———

* *See Texaco v. Pennzoil*, 729 S.W.2d 768 (Tex. Ct. App. 1987) (subsequent history omitted).

of Agreement" which provided that the requested stocks would be sold to Pennzoil at a purchase price of $110 per share. Ownership interests in the stock were to be divided (the Trust would own 4/7 of the shares and Pennzoil would own 3/7). The memo provided that Pennzoil and the Trust would form a partnership to own and operate Getty Oil. Gordon Getty was to become the Chairman of the Board of Getty Oil, and the CEO of Pennzoil was to sit as the new CEO. If the companies could not agree on a satisfactory restructuring plan by December of 1984, the memo provided that the assets of Getty Oil would be divided, based on ownership percentage, between the two.

The Pennzoil-Getty Oil merger proposal was first brought before the Board of Getty Oil in New York on January 3, 1984. While the board initially rejected some of the terms of Pennzoil's original offer, a satisfactory counter-offer was quickly accepted by Pennzoil and approved by the Board. On January 4, both parties issued press releases announcing the upcoming merger.

On January 5, following the press releases, representatives from Texaco, Inc. allegedly contacted Museum representatives and offered to acquire its shares of Getty Oil "at any cost." Following a successful negotiation with the Museum, Texaco contacted Gordon Getty and offered $125 per share for his shares, exceeding the $110 purchase price previously offered by Pennzoil and ostensibly accepted its soon-to-be partners in Getty Oil. Once Getty had agreed to accept Texaco's offer, the Board of Getty Oil held a meeting on January 6, 1984, where it unanimously agreed to reject its previous proposal to Pennzoil and accept that proposed by Texaco. Texaco immediately issued a press release announcing the successful merger negotiations, and a formal merger agreement was signed between these parties on January 6, 1984.

After receiving a cease and desist letter from Pennzoil, Getty Oil filed a declaratory judgment action claiming that any contract it may have had with Pennzoil was not binding or legally enforceable. Pennzoil defended, claiming that Texaco had tortiously interfered with Pennzoil's contract for a stock purchase and merger with Getty Oil. After a four and one-half month trial in a Texas State court, a jury found that:

1) at the end of the board meeting on January 3, 1984, the Getty entities intended to bind themselves to an agreement with Pennzoil providing for Pennzoil's purchase of stock in Getty Oil;

2) Texaco had actual knowledge of the pending merger and stock purchase agreement between Pennzoil and the Getty Oil entities; and

3) Texaco interfered with this pending agreement intentionally, willfully, and in wanton disregard of Pennzoil's rights.

Based on the jury's special findings, Judge Casseb of the 151st Judicial District of Texas entered a judgment on December 10, 1985, entitling Pennzoil to $7.53 billion in compensatory damages, $3 billion in punitive damages, and $624,753,662 in prejudgment interest. The order also provided that post-judgment interest would be recoverable at 10% per annum until the judgment was paid in full.

Following entry of the judgment, Texaco was granted a preliminary injunction barring Pennzoil's enforcement of the judgment pending appeal. Under Texas procedural law, Texaco would have been required to post a supersedeas bond in order to secure an appeal. Texaco argued that posting a bond in excess of $12 billion would force it into bankruptcy, and that the bond requirements were so prohibitive in this case that to uphold them would effectively deny Texaco the right to appeal. Based on Texaco's due process and equal protection arguments, the preliminary injunction was granted.

---

1.   Was there a legally binding contract here? Is this really a case of tortious interference with prospective economic relations? On appeal, the court found that myriad possible inferences prevented it from questioning the jury's findings of fact that the entities did intend to be bound and that an enforceable contract did exist.

2.   Is this an arbitrary and unfair amount of damages for this type of tort considering the tenuous nature of the business relationship in the first place? These are sophisticated, economically savvy business players operating in a system allowing freedom of contract — does this violate normal (albeit shrewd) business practices in our society?

3.   How would *Pennzoil Co. v. Texaco, Inc.* be decided under *Della Penna, infra*?

LUMLEY v. GYE
Queens Bench, 1853
2 E. & B. 216, 118 E.R. 749

[The contract was between Plaintiff, manager of the Queen's Theatre, London, and Johanna Wagner, a well-known opera star. The Defendant allegedly enticed and procured Ms. Wagner to refuse to perform. The third count alleged that the defendant maliciously enticed her to depart from her employment. The contract contained a condition that she not sing elsewhere.]

ERIE, J. The question raised upon this demurrer is whether an action will lie by the proprietor of a theatre against a person who maliciously procures an entire abandonment of a contract to perform exclusively at that theatre for a certain time, whereby damage was sustained? It seems to me that it will. The authorities are numerous and uniform that an action will lie by a master against a person who procures that a servant should unlawfully leave his service. The principle involved in these cases comprises the present, for, there, the right of action in the master arises from the wrongful act of the defendant in procuring that the person hired should break his contract by putting an end to the relation of employer and employed, and the present case is the same.

If it is objected that this class of actions for procuring a breach of contract of hiring rests upon no principle and ought not to be extended beyond the cases heretofore decided, . . . the answer appears to me to be that the class of cases referred to rests upon the principle that the procurement of the violation of the right is a cause of action, and that when this principle is applied to a violation of a right arising upon a contract of hiring, the nature of the service contracted for is immaterial. It is clear that the procurement of the violation of a right is a cause of action in all instances where the violation is an actionable wrong, as in violations of a right to property, whether real or personal, or to personal security. He who procures the wrong is a joint wrongdoer, and may be sued, either alone or jointly with the agent, in the appropriate action for the wrong complained of. Where a right to the performance of a contract has been violated by a breach thereof, the remedy is upon the contract against the contracting party. If he is made to indemnify for such breach, no further recourse is allowed, and, as in the case of the procurement of a breach of contact the action is for a wrong and cannot be joined with the action on the contract, and as the act itself is not likely to be of frequent occurrence nor easy of proof, therefore, the action for this wrong, in respect of other contracts than those of hiring, are not numerous, but still they seem to me sufficient to show that the principle has been recognized.

. . . .

This principle is supported by good reason. He who maliciously procures a damage to another by violation of his right ought to be made to indemnify, and that whether he procures an actionable wrong or a breach of contract. He who procures the non-delivery of goods according to contract may inflict an injury, the same as he who procures the abstraction of goods after delivery, and both ought on the same ground to be made responsible. The remedy on the contract may be inadequate, as where the measures of damages is restricted. . . . In such cases, he who procures the damage maliciously might justly be made responsible beyond the liability of the contractor.

With respect to the objection that the contracting party had not begun the performance of the contract, I do not think it a tenable ground of defence. The procurement of the breach of the contract may be equally injurious, whether the service has begun or not, and, in my judgment, ought to be equally actionable as the relation of employer and employed is constituted by the contract alone and no act of service is necessary thereto. The result is that there ought to be, in my opinion, judgment for the plaintiff.

---

1. What are the problems with the plaintiff's suit in contract? What is the role of the tort cause of action?

2. In the related case of *Lumley v. Wagner*, 21 L.J. Ch. 898, 42 E.R. 687 (1852), the Court was asked to enjoin Ms. Wagner from singing elsewhere. The court granted the injunction and said:

It was objected that the operation of the injunction in the present case was mischievous, excluding the defendant Johanna Wagner from performing at any other theatre while this court had no power to compel her to perform at Her Majesty's Theatre. It is true that I have not the means of compelling her to sing, but she has no cause of complaint if I compel her to abstain from the commission of an act which she has bound herself not to do, and thus possibly cause her to fulfill her engagement. The jurisdiction which I now exercise is wholly within the power of the court, and, being of opinion that it is a proper case for interfering, I shall leave nothing unsatisfied by the judgment I pronounce.

IMPERIAL ICE COMPANY v. ROSSIER
Supreme Court of California, 1941
18 Cal. 2d 33, 112 P.2d 631

TRAYNOR, JUSTICE.

The California Consumers Company purchased from S. L. Coker an ice distributing business, inclusive of good will, located in territory comprising the city of Santa Monica and the former city of Sawtelle. In the purchase agreement Coker contracted as follows: "I do further agree in consideration of said purchase and in connection therewith, that I will not engage in the business of selling and or distributing ice, either directly or indirectly, in the above described territory so long as the purchasers, or anyone deriving title to the good will of said business from said purchasers, shall be engaged in a like business therein." Plaintiff, the Imperial Ice Company, acquired from the successor in interest of the California Consumers Company full title to this ice distributing business, including the right to enforce the covenant not to compete. Coker subsequently began selling in the same territory, in violation of the contract, ice supplied to him by a company owned by W. Rossier, J. A. Matheson, and Fred Matheson. Plaintiff thereupon brought this action in the superior court for an injunction to restrain Coker from violating the contract and to restrain Rossier and the Mathesons from inducing Coker to violate the contract. The complaint alleges that Rossier and the Mathesons induced Coker to violate his contract so that they might sell ice to him at a profit. The trial court sustained without leave to amend a demurrer to the complaint of the defendants Rossier and Mathesons and gave judgment for those defendants. Plaintiff has appealed from the judgment on the sole ground that the complaint stated a cause of action against the defendants Rossier and the Mathesons for inducing the breach of contract.

The question thus presented to this court is under what circumstances may an action be maintained against a defendant who has induced a third party to violate a contract with the plaintiff.

It is universally recognized that an action will lie for inducing breach of contract by a resort to means in themselves unlawful such as libel, slander, fraud, physical violence, or threats of such action. Most jurisdictions also hold that an action will lie for inducing a breach of contract by the use of moral, social, or economic pressures, in themselves lawful, unless there is sufficient justification for such inducement.

Such justification exists when a person induces a breach of contract to protect an interest that has greater social value than insuring the stability of the contract. (Rest., Torts, sec. 767.) Thus, a person is justified in inducing the breach of a contract the enforcement of which would be injurious to health, safety, or good morals. (*Brimelow v. Casson*, 1 Ch. 302 (1924); *Legris v. Marcotte*, 129 Ill. App. 67; Rest., Torts, sec. 767 (d).) The interest of labor in improving working conditions is of sufficient social importance to justify peaceful labor tactics otherwise lawful, though they have the effect of inducing breaches of contracts between employer and employee or employer and customer. In numerous other situations justification exists (see Rest., Torts, sees. 766 to 774) depending upon the importance of the interest protected. The presence or absence of ill-will, sometimes referred to as "malice", is immaterial, except as it indicates whether or not an interest is actually being protected.

It is well established, however, that a person is not justified in inducing a breach of contract simply because he is in competition with one of the parties to the contract and seeks to further his own economic advantage at the expense of the other. (See cases cited in 84 A. L. R. 83; 24 Cal. L. Rev. 208, 211; see Rest., Torts, sec. 768 (2).) Whatever interest society has in encouraging free and open competition by means not in themselves unlawful, contractual stability is generally accepted as of greater importance than competitive freedom. Competitive freedom, however, is of sufficient importance to justify one competitor in inducing a third party to forsake another competitor if no contractual relationship exists between the latter two. A person is likewise free to carry on his business, including reduction of prices, advertising, and solicitation in the usual lawful manner although some third party may be induced thereby to breach his contract with a competitor in favor of dealing with the advertiser. Again, if two parties have separate contracts with a third, each may resort to any legitimate means at his disposal to secure performance of his contract even though the necessary result will be to cause a breach of the other contract. A party may not, however, under the guise of competition actively and affirmatively induce the breach of a competitor's contract in order to secure an economic advantage over that competitor. The act of inducing the breach must be an intentional one. If the actor had no knowledge of the existence of the contract or his actions were not intended to induce a breach, he cannot be held liable though an actual breach results from his lawful and proper acts.

. . . The case *of Katz v. Kapper, supra,* relied upon by defendants, held only that a person by the use of lawful means could interfere with advantageous business relationships of a competitor by inducing customers to trade with him instead. The case did not involve a breach of contract, and the court specifically stated: "In deciding whether the conduct of defendants, alleged in the complaint, is actionable, it is necessary to apply certain well-settled rules relating to competition in business. These may be generally stated as follows: 'Competition in business, though carried to the extent of ruining a rival, is not ordinarily actionable, but every trader is left to conduct his business in his own way, so long as the methods he employs do not involve wrongful conduct such as fraud, misrepresentation, intimidation, coercion, obstruction, or molestation of the rival or his servants or workmen, *or the procurement of the violation of contractual relations . . .'.*" (Italics added.) In California, therefore, an action will lie for unjustifiably inducing a breach of contract.

The complaint in the present case alleges that defendants actively induced Coker to violate his contract with plaintiffs so that they might sell ice to him. The contract gave to plaintiff the right to sell ice in the stated territory free from the competition of Coker. The defendants, by virtue of their interest in the sale of ice in that territory, were in effect competing with plaintiff. By inducing Coker to violate his contract, as alleged in the complaint, they sought to further their own economic advantage at plaintiff's expense. Such conduct is not justified. Had defendants merely sold ice to Coker without actively inducing him to violate his contract, his distribution of the ice in the forbidden territory in violation of his contract would not then [have] rendered defendants liable. They may carry on their business of selling ice as usual without incurring liability for breaches of contract by their customers. It is necessary to prove that they intentionally and actively induced the breach. Since the complaint alleges that they did so and asks for an injunction on the grounds that damages would be inadequate, it states a cause of action, and the demurrer should therefore have been overruled.

The judgment is reversed.

––––––––––

1.   Note the aggressive and injurious business practices that are condoned by the court. They can lead to bankrupting a corporation. How is the line drawn between permitted practices and those that will support an action in tortious interference with contract?

2.   Define "justification." What does the court say of "malice"?

SMITH v. FORD MOTOR COMPANY
Supreme Court of North Carolina, 1976
221 S.E.2d 282

Prior to 20 January 1971, Hull Dobbs Company operated a Ford dealership in Winston-Salem, the defendants Keesee and Dobbs being stockholders and directors of that company. Due to the poor performance of that dealership, Ford Motor Company (hereinafter called Ford) recommended a change of its name and the bringing in of a new general manager under an agreement allowing him to purchase 100 per cent of the stock of Hull Dobbs Company over a five-year period. The plaintiff [Smith] then had a profitable position with a Ford dealership in Atlanta. He gave up that position, moved to Winston-Salem and took over the management of the said dealership in Winston-Salem, the name of which was changed to Cloverdale Ford. Due to the plaintiff's efforts and skill the dealership was immediately changed from a losing to a profitable operation and continued to be such throughout the plaintiff's management of it.

. . . .

LAKE, JUSTICE.

. . . [T]he contract of employment upon which the plaintiff relies . . . contains no provision whatever as to the duration of such employment. "Where a contract of employment does not fix a definite term, it is terminable at the will of either party, with or without cause". . . . Consequently, Cloverdale committed no breach of its contract when it terminated the plaintiff's employment even if, as the plaintiff alleges, there was no "just cause" for such termination. The complaint, therefore, does not state a claim against Cloverdale upon which relief can be granted and there was no error in dismissing the action as to Cloverdale.

. . . .

Under the caption "Unsatisfactory Management," the contract of 18 May 1971, which the plaintiff made part of the complaint, provides:

"The parties hereto agree that if [the plaintiff], in his position as President and General Manager of the Corporation [i.e., Cloverdale], shall prove to be unsatisfactory in the opinion of [Keesee, Dobbs and Goodwin] *and* James W. Davis, *or the* Ford Motor Company *from the standpoint of profits earned or the manner of operation of the Corporation*, the employment of [the plaintiff] as President and Manager may be terminated by the Corporation. *Upon such termination* [the plaintiff] agrees to sell to James W. Davis the capital stock owned by him at book value of such stock at the end of the month preceding such termination and for cash." (Emphasis added.)

. . . .

As to Ford the substance of the complaint is: (1) Ford knew the plaintiff had a contract with Cloverdale, a Ford dealer, for employment by it, terminable at the will of Cloverdale; (2) the plaintiff was performing well his duties under that contract and, as a result, Cloverdale was prospering and was a successful dealer in Ford products; (3) but for the "wrongful, malicious and unlawful interference" by Ford therewith, this employment would have been continued by Cloverdale; (4) Ford "wrongfully, maliciously, and unlawfully exerted pressure" upon Cloverdale to terminate the plaintiff's employment; (5) the sole reason for Ford's interference with the employment relation between the plaintiff and Cloverdale was the plaintiff's refusal to discontinue his personal participation in the Ford Dealer Alliance, "a group of Ford dealers who had gathered together for the purpose of protecting their own interest in transactions with the defendant Ford Motor Company"; (6) due to pressure so exerted upon it by Ford, Cloverdale terminated the plaintiff's employment; and (7) thereby, the plaintiff was damaged.

. . . .

The question presented to us by this appeal is: If A, knowing B is employed by C under a contract terminable at will by C, maliciously causes C to discharge B, which C would not otherwise have done, by threatening, otherwise, to terminate A's own contract with C, which contract is terminable at will by A, the sole motive for A's action being A's resentment of B's personal affiliation with an organization disapproved by A, which affiliation does not impair C's performance of its contract with A, can B maintain in the courts of this State an action against A for damages? Our conclusion is that he can.

In *Childress v. Abeles*, 240 N.C. 667, 84 S.E. 2d 176 (1954), Justice Parker, later Chief Justice, speaking for this Court, said:

"[T]he overwhelming weight of authority in this nation is that an action in tort lies against an outsider who knowingly, intentionally and unjustifiably induces one party to a contract to breach it to the damage of the other party.

"To subject the outsider to liability for compensatory damages on account of this tort, the plaintiff must allege and prove these essential elements of the wrong: *First*, that a valid contract existed between the plaintiff and a third person, conferring upon the plaintiff some contractual right against the third person. *Second*, that the outsider had knowledge of the plaintiff's contract with the third person. *Third*, that the outsider intentionally induced the third person not to perform his contract with the plaintiff. *Fourth*, that in so doing the outsider acted without justification. *Fifth*, that the outsider's act caused the plaintiff actual damages." (Citations omitted.)

As we have noted above, there was no breach by Cloverdale of its contract with the plaintiff, but an exercise by Cloverdale of its legal right to terminate that contract. This circumstance does not, however, defeat the plaintiff's right of action against Ford. *Childress v. Abeles, supra,* expressly so states. The wrong for which the courts may give redress includes also the procurement of the termination of a contract which otherwise would have continued in effect. Hughes, later Chief Justice, said in *Truax v. Raich, supra,* "The fact that the employment is at the will of the parties, respectively, does not make it one at the will of others."

The fact that the plaintiff's contract with Cloverdale contained an express provision that Cloverdale might terminate the plaintiff's employment if the plaintiff "shall prove to be unsatisfactory in the opinion of . . . the Ford Motor Company from the standpoint of profits earned or the manner of operation of the corporation," is not the basis of a defense to Ford in the present action. On the contrary, it clearly indicates that dissatisfaction for the stated reasons was intended by the parties to be the *only* justification for Ford's expressing to Cloverdale its displeasure over the continuation of the plaintiff's employment. . . . While Ford was not a party to the contract of 18 May 1971, wherein this provision appears, it is obvious that Ford knew of the contract and of this provision in it. Nowhere in the record is it suggested that Ford was, or had any basis whatever for being, dissatisfied with the plaintiff's performance as president and general manager of Cloverdale "from the standpoint of profits earned or the manner of operation of Cloverdale." The complaint clearly alleges that Ford brought about the plaintiff's discharge because, and solely because, the plaintiff, in his personal capacity, belonged to the Ford Dealer Alliance and refused to withdraw therefrom.

. . . .

Ford contends that it did nothing to cause the termination of the plaintiff's contract with Cloverdale, except to threaten to terminate its own franchise agreement with Cloverdale if the plaintiff were not discharged, and that its contract with Cloverdale was expressly terminable at will by Ford upon the giving of proper notice. Consequently, Ford says, the complaint charges Ford with doing nothing except that which Ford had a right to do and its exercise of its own lawful right to terminate its contract with Cloverdale cannot be a tort against the plaintiff.

. . . .

Section 766 of the Restatement of Torts (1939) states:

"Except as stated in Section 698 [not applicable here], one who, without a privilege to do so, induces or otherwise purposely causes a third person not to

(a)   perform a contract with another, or

(b)   enter into or continue a business relation with another is liable to the other for the harm caused thereby."

Professor Carpenter, writing in 41 Harv. L. Rev. 728, 746 (1928), under the title *Interference With Contract Relations,* says:

"The privilege [to interfere] is conditional or qualified; that is, it is lost if exercised for a wrong purpose. In general, a wrong purpose exists where the act is done other than as a reasonable and *bona fide* attempt to protect the interest of the defendant which is involved."

. . . .

We hold: To exert economic pressure upon an employer for the purpose of procuring the termination by him of his employment of another is a qualified privilege even though, as between the actor and the employer, the actor has an absolute right to do that which produces such pressure upon the employer. The actor is liable in damages to the employee for so procuring such termination of the employment if the actor so acted with malice and for a reason not reasonably related to the protection of a legitimate business interest of the actor. . . .

The complaint of the plaintiff in this action alleges the malicious interference by the defendant with the plaintiff's employment relation without such justification. . . . [T]he dismissal of the action as against the Ford Motor Company was error. The matter is, therefore, remanded to the Court of Appeals for the entry by it of a judgment further remanding it to the Superior Court for trial of the plaintiff's alleged cause of action against Ford.

. . . .

As to the defendant Ford Motor company, reversed and remanded.

---

1. What definition does the court give to qualified privilege? To malice?

2. What did Ford do? Why is Ford's act wrongful? Could Ford argue self-defense? Why not?

3. Did Ford commit a separate tort apart from interfering with Smith's contract?

4. In *Nix v. Temple University*, 596 A.2d 1132 (Pa. Super. Ct. 1991), the court held that defendants were parties to the contract (at will) and therefore tortious interference did not lie.

ADLER, BARISH, DANIELS, LEVIN AND CRESKOFF v. EPSTEIN
Supreme Court of Pennsylvania, 1978
393 A.2d 1175

ROBERTS, JUSTICE.

OPINION:

Appellant, the law firm of Adler, Barish, Daniels, Levin and Creskoff . . . sought to enjoin appellees, former associates of Adler Barish, from interfering with existing contractual relationships between Adler Barish and its clients. The court of common pleas entered a final decree granting the requested relief, but a divided

Superior Court dissolved the injunction and dismissed Adler Barish's complaint. We granted allowance of appeal. We now reverse and direct reinstatement of the decree of the court of common pleas.

From the formation of Adler Barish in February, 1976, through March of the next year, appellees were salaried associates of Adler Barish. Appellees were under the supervision of Adler Barish partners, who directed appellees' work on cases which clients brought to the firm.

While still working for Adler Barish, appellees decided to form their own law firm and took several steps toward achieving their goal. They retained counsel to advise them concerning their business venture, sought and found office space, and early in March, 1977, signed a lease.

Shortly before leaving Adler Barish, appellees procured a line of $150,000 from First Pennsylvania Bank. As security, appellees furnished bank officials with a list of eighty-eight cases and their anticipated legal fees, several of which were higher than $25,000, and together exceeded $500,000. No case on the list, however, was appellees'. Rather, each case was an Adler Barish case on which appellees were working.

Appellee Alan Epstein's employment relationship with Adler Barish terminated on March 10, 1977.[5] At his request, Epstein continued to use offices of Adler Barish until March 19. During this time, and through April 4, when Adler Barish filed its complaint, Epstein was engaged in an active campaign to procure business for his new law firm. He initiated contacts, by phone and in person, with clients of Adler Barish with open cases on which he had worked while a salaried employee. Epstein advised the Adler Barish clients that he was leaving the firm and that they could choose to be represented by him, Adler Barish, or any other firm or attorney.

Epstein's attempt to procure business on behalf of the firm did not stop with these contacts. He mailed to the clients form letters which could be used to discharge Adler Barish as counsel, name Epstein the client's new counsel and create a contingent fee agreement. Epstein also provided clients with a stamped envelope addressed to Epstein. . . .

On April 4, the court of common pleas granted Adler Barish preliminary relief, enjoining appellees' campaign to obtain the business of Adler Barish clients.

. . . .

Appellees appealed to the Superior Court, which reversed. In addition to granting Adler Barish's petition for allowance of appeal, we granted a stay and expedited argument. . . .

The facts found by the court of common pleas . . . demonstrate that, while

---

[5] The firm received documents relating to cases for which it apparently had no file. Contrary to the firm's procedure, Epstein personally maintained files for some cases. Likewise, Epstein did not adhere to Adler Barish policy concerning certain fees. Adler Barish obtained a case which was assigned to Epstein. He sent the file to an out-of-state attorney for further handling. Instead of turning over the forwarding fee to the firm, Epstein kept it for himself. It appears that these events led to termination of Epstein's employment.

leaving Adler Barish, appellees made numerous contacts with Adler Barish clients on whose active cases appellees were working before leaving Adler Barish. Adler Barish argues that appellees' conduct constitutes an intentional interference with existing contractual relationships between Adler Barish and its clients. According to Adler Barish, appellees' conduct is "deserving of censure, not encouragement." Appellees, on the other hand, contend that their conduct was "privileged," and that therefore no right of action for intentional interference lies. Moreover, they argue that their conduct is protected under the first and fourteenth amendments to the Constitution of the United States.

"[S]peech which does 'no more than propose a commercial transaction' " is no longer outside the protection of the first and fourteenth amendments to the Constitution of the United States. *Virginia Pharmacy Board v. Virginia Consumer Council*, 425 U.S. 748, 762, 96 S. Ct. 1817, 1825, 48 L. Ed. 2d 346 (1976) (striking down state statute deeming licensed pharmacists' advertising of prescription drugs "unprofessional conduct"). Accordingly, states are barred from imposing blanket prohibitions against truthful advertising of "routine" legal services. *Bates v. State Bar of Arizona*, 433 U.S. 350, 97 S. Ct. 2691 53 L. Ed. 2d 810 (1977). Such a blanket prohibition "serves to inhibit the free flow of commercial information and to keep the public in ignorance."

Nothing in the challenged decree prohibited appellees from engaging in the truthful advertising protected under *Bates*. Appellees could inform the general public, including clients of Adler Barish, of the availability of their legal services, and thus the "free flow of commercial information" to the public is unimpaired. Moreover, the injunction expressly permitted appellees to announce "formation of their new professional relationship in accordance with the requirements of DR 2-102 of the Code of Professional Responsibility." Appellees therefore were permitted to mail announcements to "lawyers, clients, former clients, personal friends, and relatives." Code of Professional Responsibility, DR 2-102(A)(2). This would include the very clients of Adler Barish whose business appellees sought. See Committee on Professional Ethics of the American Bar Association, Informal Decision No. 681 (August 1, 1963) (permitting departing attorney to send announcements "to those clients of the old firm for whom he had worked").

What the injunction did proscribe was appellees' "contacting and/or communicating with those persons who up to and including April 1, 1977, had active legal matters pending with and were represented by the law firm of ADLER, BARISH, DANIELS, LEVIN and CRESKOFF." Our task is to decide whether the conduct of appellees is constitutionally subject to sanction.

. . . .

Ohralik v. Ohio State Bar Association, 436 U.S. 447, 98 S. Ct. 1912, 56 L. Ed. 2d 444 (1978), makes plain that, after *Bates*, states may constitutionally impose sanctions upon attorneys engaging in conduct which violates these disciplinary rules, even though the conduct involves "commercial speech." In *Ohralik*, the state bar association suspended an attorney who "solicited" persons injured in an automobile accident by making visits to the hospital room where the persons were recovering. Mr. Justice Powell, speaking for the Court, emphasized that commercial speech does not enjoy the same constitutional protections traditionally afforded other forms of speech. . . .

. . . .

[Here] appellees were actively attempting to induce the clients to change law firms in the middle of their active cases. Appellees' concern for their line of credit and the success of their new law firm gave them an immediate, personally created financial interest in the clients' decisions. In this atmosphere, appellees' contacts posed too great a risk that clients would not have the opportunity to make a careful, informed decision. Compare Code of Professional Responsibility, EC 2-10 (directing that standards for attorney advertising "facilitate informed selection of lawyers by potential consumers of legal services"). "[T]o reduce the likelihood of overreaching and the exertion of undue influence on lay persons; to protect the privacy of individuals; and to avoid situations where the lawyer's exercise of judgment on behalf of the client will be clouded by his own pecuniary self-interest," *Ohralik v. Ohio State Bar Association*, 436 U.S. at 461, 98 S. Ct. at 1921, we must reject appellees' argument and conclude that, just as in *Ohralik*, the Constitution permits regulation of their conduct. . . .

Thus, we turn to whether the court of common pleas properly concluded that Adler Barish is entitled to relief. In *Birl v. Philadelphia Electric Co.*, 402 Pa. 297, 167 A.2d 472 (1961), this Court adopted Section 766 of Restatement of Torts and its definition of the right of action for intentional interference with existing contractual relations. There we stated:

> At least since *Lumley v. Gye*, 2 Ell. & Bl. 216, 1 Eng. Rul. Cas. 706 (1853), the common law has recognized an action in tort for an intentional, unprivileged interference with contractual relations. It is generally recognized that one has the right to pursue his business relations or employment free from interference on the part of other persons except where such interference is justified or constitutes an exercise of an absolute right: Restatement, Torts, § 766. The Special Note to comment m. in § 766 points out: There are frequent expressions in judicial opinions that "malice" is requisite for liability in the cases treated in this Section. But the context and course of decision make it clear that what is meant is not malice in the sense of ill will but merely purposeful interference without justification.
>
> . . .

. . . The American Law Institute has reviewed each section of the Restatement of Torts, including Section 766. Section 766 of the Restatement (Second) of Torts (Tent. Draft No. 23, 1977), states the Institute's present view of what constitutes the elements of the cause of action before us:

Intentional Interference with Performance of Contract by Third Person

> One who intentionally and improperly interferes with the performance of a contract (except a contract to marry) between another and a third person by inducing or otherwise causing the third person not to perform the contract, is subject to liability to the other for the pecuniary loss

resulting to the other from the third person's failure to perform the contract.

. . . .

An examination of this case in light of Restatement (Second) of Torts, § 766, reveals that the sole dispute is whether appellees' conduct is "improper." There is no doubt that appellees intentionally sought to interfere with performance of the contractual relations between Adler Barish and its clients. While still at Adler Barish, appellees' behavior, particularly their use of expected fees from Adler Barish clients' cases, indicates appellees' desire to gain a segment of the firm's business. This pattern of conduct continued until the court of common pleas enjoined it. Indeed, appellees' intentional efforts to obtain a share of Adler Barish's business were successful. The record reveals that several clients signed the forms Epstein prepared on behalf of appellees notifying Adler Barish that the clients no longer wished the services of Adler Barish. Likewise, the record reveals that Adler Barish and its clients were parties to valid, existing contracts. . . .

In assessing whether appellees' conduct is "improper," . . . [w]e are guided . . . by Section 767 of Restatement (Second) of Torts, which focuses on what factors should be considered in determining whether conduct is "improper:"

In determining whether an actor's conduct in intentionally interfering with an existing contract or a prospective contractual relation of another is improper or not, consideration is given to the following factors:

(a) The nature of the actor's conduct,

(b) The actor's motive,

(c) The interests of the other with which the actor's conduct interferes,

(d) The interests sought to be advanced by the actor,

(e) The proximity or remoteness of the actor's conduct to the interference and

(f) The relations between the parties.[17]

. . . [T]he rules which apply to those who enjoy the privilege of practicing law in this Commonwealth expressly disapprove appellees' method of obtaining clients. Supra Part IIA, discussing Code of Professional Responsibility, DR 2-103(A). We find such a departure from "[r]ecognized ethical codes" "significant in evaluating the nature of [appellees'] conduct." . . .

Appellees' conduct . . . also had an immediate impact upon Adler Barish. Adler Barish was prepared to continue to perform services for its clients and therefore could anticipate receiving compensation for the value of its efforts. . . . Adler Barish's fee agreements with clients were a source of anticipated revenue protected from outside interference.

---

[17] Thus, new Restatement (Second) of Torts focuses upon whether conduct is "proper," rather than "privileged." . . . "The issue in each case is whether the interference is improper or not under the circumstances; whether, upon a consideration of the relative significance of the factors involved, the conduct should be permitted without liability, despite its effect of harm to another." [Comment b § 767].

It is true that, upon termination of their employment relationship with Adler Barish, appellees were free to engage in their own business venture. See Restatement (Second) of Agency, § 396(a) (1958) ("[u]nless otherwise agreed, after termination of the agency, the agent . . . has no duty not to compete with the principal"). . . .[21]

. . . .

Order of the Superior Court reversed and court of common pleas directed to reinstate its final decree. Each party pay own costs.

WALNUT STREET ASSOCIATES, INC. v. BROKERAGE CONCEPTS, INC.
Supreme Court of Pennsylvania, 2011
20 A.3d 468

Mr. Chief Justice Castille.

We consider whether Restatement (Second) of Torts § 772(a) applies in Pennsylvania to preclude an action for tortious interference with contractual relations where it is undisputed that the defendant's interfering statements were truthful.[1] We hold that Section 772(a) is applicable, and we affirm the decision of the Superior Court.

Appellant, Walnut Street Associates ("WSA"), provides insurance brokerage services and assists employers in obtaining health insurance for their employees. Since the 1980s, WSA was the broker of record for health insurance provided to employees of Procacci Brothers Sales Corporation ("Procacci"). Appellee, Brokerage Concepts, Inc. ("BCI"), is a third party administrator of employee benefit plans. In 1994, at the recommendation of WSA, Procacci retained BCI as administrator of its insurance plans, and BCI paid commissions to WSA based on premiums paid by Procacci.

In 2005, Procacci requested that BCI lower costs, but BCI would not meet Procacci's proposal. Procacci then notified BCI that it would be moving its business to another third-party administrator. Shortly thereafter, BCI's employee Kimberly Macrone wrote a letter to Procacci asking it to reconsider its decision, and in the process advising Procacci of the amount of compensation WSA had been receiving as broker of record. The amount was apparently higher than Procacci believed WSA

---

[21] Appellees suggest that injunctive relief was inappropriate. "It is well settled that equity will act to prevent unjustified interference with contractual relations." . . . [We] believe the court of common pleas could properly conclude that equitable relief was necessary to protect all the interests at stake in this case.

[1] Section 772 provides:

One who intentionally causes a third person not to perform a contract or not to enter into a prospective contractual relation with another does not interfere improperly with the other's contractual relation, by giving the third person:

(a) truthful information, or

(b) honest advice within the scope of a request for the advice.

had been earning, but there is no dispute that Macrone's statements about WSA's compensation were true. As a result of Macrone's letter, Procacci terminated its longstanding contractual relationship with WSA.

WSA then filed this action against BCI and Macrone. . . . WSA alleged that BCI had tortiously interfered with the WSA/Procacci contractual relationship by disclosing the amount of WSA's compensation. In its answer and new matter, BCI alleged, *inter alia*, that it could not be held liable for tortious interference because the information it provided to Procacci was truthful, or otherwise justified and privileged, and not confidential. The parties went to trial on the tortious interference claim. At the charging conference, BCI requested a jury instruction on truthfulness as a defense pursuant to Section 772(a), but the court denied it. . . . . The jury . . . specifically found that BCI had intentionally and improperly interfered with the WSA/Procacci contract, caused Procacci to terminate that contract, and awarded WSA $330,000 in damages. After its post-trial motion was denied, BCI filed an appeal to Superior Court.

The Superior Court reversed, holding that Macrone's truthful statements to Procacci regarding WSA's compensation could not support a claim for tortious interference with contractual relations. The court relied on Restatement Section 772(a), which, as noted above, provides that one who intentionally causes a third person not to perform a contract with another does not interfere improperly with the other's contractual relation by giving the third person truthful information. Because Macrone's statements to Procacci about WSA's compensation were true, the court held as a matter of law that BCI's interference with the WSA/Procacci contract was not actionable as tortious interference, and remanded for entry of judgment notwithstanding the verdict in favor of BCI. In doing so, the Superior Court predicted that this Court would adopt and apply Section 772(a) under these circumstances, and noted that "the courts of sister jurisdictions have nearly universally adopted" it. . . . We granted allocatur in part, rephrasing the issue as follows:

> Did the Superior Court err in adopting and applying Restatement (Second) of Torts § 772(a), and holding that truthful statements could not form the basis of a claim for tortious interference with contractual relations?

Appellant WSA argues that the Superior Court's decision adopting and applying Section 772(a) was erroneous. WSA insists that the trial court properly held that truth is not a defense to a claim for tortious interference with contractual relations. According to WSA, the court properly instructed the jury to consider the following factors in evaluating Macrone/BCI's conduct: a) the nature of the actor's conduct; b) the actor's motive; c) the interest of the other with which the actor's conduct interferes; d) the interests sought to be advanced by the actor; e) the social interest in protecting the freedom of action of the actor and the contractual interests of the other; and f) the relations between the parties. See RESTATEMENT (SECOND) OF TORTS § 767 (listing factors relevant to determining whether interference is improper). Applying these factors alone, WSA argues, the jury correctly determined that BCI's conduct was improper and unjustified, and caused the termination of the Procacci account, to WSA's financial detriment. . . .

Ours is a free society where citizens may freely interact and exchange information. Tortious interference, as a basis for civil liability, does not operate to burden such interactions, but rather, to attach a reasonable consequence when the defendant's intentional interference was "improper". . . .

Together with Sections 766 and 767, Section 772 is now part of a larger scheme of Second Restatement provisions regarding tortious interference with contractual relations, and further defines the core concept of "improper" interference.[11] Indeed, commentary appended to Section 767 provides that "Sections 769–773 deal with other special situations in which application of the factors enumerated in this Section [767] have produced more clearly identifiable decisional patterns. The specific applications in these Sections [769–773] therefore supplant the generalization expressed in this Section." RESTATEMENT (SECOND) OF TORTS § 767, cmt. a (emphasis added). This is not an extraordinary proposition; this is the manner in which the law often progresses. As general principles are tested in practice, more specific and accurate paradigms arise. Indeed, the commentary indicates that in situations where a Section 772(a) truthfulness defense is raised against claims of tortious interference, analysis of the general factors enumerated in Section 767 is not necessary. The commentary further supports this conclusion by recognizing that there are some situations where "the process of weighing the conflicting factors set forth in this Section has already been performed by the courts. . . . When this has been accomplished and the scope of the more or less crystallized rule or privilege has been indicated by the decisions, the responsibility in the particular case is simply to apply it to the facts involved; and there is no need to go through the balancing process afresh. Some of the situations in which this development has occurred are stated in §§ 769–773." *See* RESTATEMENT (SECOND) OF TORTS § 767, cmt. j (determination of whether actor's conduct is improper or not).

We do not view Section 772(a) as intending to alter the traditional understanding of the tort; as the Second Restatement makes clear, the elaborations are a product of experience and refinement. . . .

There is no dispute that BCI's employee Macrone intentionally imparted information about WSA's compensation to Procacci, when Procacci was seeking lower employee health insurance costs, and that the information was truthful. As a result of its learning that truth, Procacci fired WSA as insurance broker of record. The question is whether BCI's intentional interference with the Procacci/WSA contract was improper, and thus actionable. The jury found that the interference was improper, but only after being instructed on the Section 767 factors. The parties do not dispute that, if the trial court had deemed Section 772(a) applicable as BCI advocated, BCI would have been entitled to judgment as a matter of law. In our

---

[11] The Second Restatement provides a detailed framework for analyzing claims of tortious interference with contractual relations, including provisions describing "improper" conduct. See generally RESTATEMENT (SECOND) OF TORTS §§ 766 (intentional interference with performance of contract by third person); 766A (intentional interference with another's performance of his own contract); 766B (prospective contractual relations); 766C (negligent interference); 767 (factors in determining whether interference is improper); 768 (competition); 769 (actor having financial interest in business of person induced); 770 (actor responsible for welfare of another); 771 (inducement to influence another's business policy); 772 (advice as proper or improper interference); 773 (asserting a bona fide claim); 774 (agreement illegal or contrary to public policy); 774A (damages).

view, the Superior Court properly determined that Section 772(a) — the more specific Restatement provision regarding truthful disclosures — was available to BCI, rather than the more general Section 767 factors, exclusively.

As we have noted, Section 772 addresses a particular, recurring subclass of cases involving the construction of what may be deemed to be "improper" (and hence actionable) interference with contractual relations. Section 772 provides that it is not improper interference if the defendant is merely giving the third person: "(a) truthful information, or (b) honest advice within the scope of a request for the advice." The comments to Section 772 amplify the meaning of subsection (a):

> *a.* This Section is a special application of the general test for determining whether an interference with an existing or prospective contractual relation is improper or not, as stated in §§ 766–766B and 767. Comments to those Sections may be relevant here.

> *b. Truthful information.* There is of course no liability for interference with a contract or with a prospective contractual relation on the part of one who merely gives truthful information to another. The interference in this instance is clearly not improper. This is true even though the facts are marshaled in such a way that they speak for themselves and the person to whom the information is given immediately recognizes them as a reason for breaking his contract or refusing to deal with another. It is also true whether or not the information is requested. Compare § 581A, on the effect of truth in an action for defamation.

RESTATEMENT (SECOND) OF TORTS § 772, cmts. a-b (emphasis added [by the Court]).

Of course, the fact that the Second Restatement contains this refinement, and explicitly provides that the conveyance of truthful information is not "improper" interference, is not reason alone for this Court to "adopt" the provision, or to deem it a proper statement of Pennsylvania law. We adopt the provision, instead, because we believe the formulation is consistent with the very nature of the tort, and with Pennsylvania law. And, in this instance, we need not belabor the reasons why we believe that the elaboration is a proper understanding of what comprises improper conduct. The Restatement commentary we have set forth above amply explains why the conveyance of truthful information cannot reasonably be deemed to be "improper" interference. It would be strange, indeed, to deem disclosures of mere truth to be actionable. Those who would shield their contracting partners from non-privileged information that might affect those partners' business decisions properly run a risk that speech in the form of a truth, when disclosed, might imperil the relationship. Application of these precepts to the facts in this case leads us to hold as a matter of law that BCI's truthful statement to Procacci about WSA was not an improper interference, and cannot, on its own, support a claim for tortious interference with contractual relations. . . .

Order affirmed.

B.   TORTIOUS INTERFERENCE WITH PROSPECTIVE ECONOMIC RELATIONS

DELLA PENNA v. TOYOTA MOTOR SALES, U.S.A., INC.
Supreme Court of California, 1995
45 Cal. Rptr. 2d 436

ARABIAN, JUSTICE.

We granted review to reexamine, in light of divergent rulings from the Court of Appeal and a doctrinal evolution among other state high courts, the elements of the tort variously known as interference with "prospective economic advantage," "prospective contractual relations," or "prospective economic relations," and the allocation of the burdens of proof between the parties to such an action. We conclude that those Court of Appeal opinions requiring proof of a so-called "wrongful act" as a component of the cause of action, and allocating the burden of proving it to the plaintiff, are the better reasoned decisions; we accordingly adopt that analysis as our own, disapproving language in prior opinions of this court to the contrary. Such a requirement . . . sensibly redresses the balance between providing a remedy for predatory economic behavior and keeping legitimate business competition outside litigative bounds. We do not in this case, however, go beyond approving the requirement of a showing of wrongfulness as part of the plaintiff's case; the case, if any, to be made for adopting refinements to that element of the tort — requiring the plaintiff to prove, for example, that the defendant's conduct amounted to an independently tortious act, or was a species of anticompetitive behavior proscribed by positive law, or was motivated by unalloyed malice — can be considered on another day, and in another case.

In this case, after the trial court modified the standard jury instruction to require the plaintiff automobile dealer to show that defendant Toyota's interference with his business relationships was "wrongful," the jury returned a verdict for Toyota. The Court of Appeal reversed the ensuing judgment and ordered a new trial on the ground that plaintiff's burden of proof did not encompass proof of a "wrongful" act and that the modified jury instruction was therefore erroneous. Given our conclusion that the plaintiff's burden *does* include proof that the defendant's conduct was wrongful by some measure other than an interference with the plaintiff's interest itself, we now reverse the Court of Appeal and direct that the judgment of the trial court be affirmed.

I

John Della Penna, an automobile wholesaler doing business as Pacific Motors, brought this action for damages against defendant Toyota Motor Sales, U.S.A., Inc., and its Lexus division, alleging that certain business conduct of defendants both violated provisions of the Cartwright Act, California's state antitrust statute (*Bus. & Prof. Code, § 16700* et seq.), and constituted an intentional interference with his economic relations. The impetus for Della Penna's suit arose out of the 1989 introduction into the American luxury car market of Toyota's Lexus automobile.

Prior to introducing the Lexus, the evidence at trial showed, both the manufacturer, Toyota Motor Corporation, and defendant, the American distributor, had been concerned about the possibility that a resale market might develop for the Lexus in Japan. Even though the car was manufactured in Japan, Toyota's marketing strategy was to bar the vehicle's sale on the Japanese domestic market until after the American rollout; even then, sales in Japan would only be under a different brand name, the "Celsior." Fearing that auto wholesalers in the United States might reexport Lexus models back to Japan for resale, and concerned that, with production and the availability of Lexus models in the American market limited, reexports would jeopardize its fledgling network of American Lexus dealers, Toyota inserted in its dealership agreements a "no export" clause, providing that the dealer was "authorized to sell [Lexus automobiles] only to customers located in the United States. [Dealer] agrees that it will not sell [Lexus automobiles] for resale or use outside the United States. [Dealer] agrees to abide by any export policy established by [distributor]."

Following introduction into the American market, it soon became apparent that some domestic Lexus units were being diverted for foreign sales, principally to Japan. To counter this effect, Toyota managers wrote to their retail dealers, reminding them of the "no-export" policy and explaining that exports for foreign resale could jeopardize the supply of Lexus automobiles available for the United States market. In addition, Toyota compiled a list of "offenders" — dealers and others believed by Toyota to be involved heavily in the developing Lexus foreign resale market — which it distributed to Lexus dealers in the United States. American Lexus dealers were also warned that doing business with those whose names appeared on the "offenders" list might lead to a series of graduated sanctions, from reducing a dealer's allocation to possible reevaluation of the dealer's franchise agreement.

During the years 1989 and 1990, plaintiff Della Penna did a profitable business as an auto wholesaler purchasing Lexus automobiles, chiefly from the Lexus of Stevens Creek retail outlet, at near retail price and exporting them to Japan for resale. By late 1990, however, plaintiff's sources began to dry up, primarily as a result of the "offenders list." Stevens Creek ceased selling models to plaintiff; gradually other sources declined to sell to him as well.

In February 1991, plaintiff filed this lawsuit against Toyota Motor Sales, U.S.A., Inc., alleging both state antitrust claims under the Cartwright Act and interference with his economic relationship with Lexus retail dealers. At the close of plaintiff's case-in-chief, . . . [t]he tort cause of action went to the jury, however, under the standard BAJI instructions applicable to such claims with one significant exception. At the request of defendant and over plaintiff's objection, the trial judge modified BAJI No. 7.82 — the basic instruction identifying the elements of the tort and indicating the burden of proof — to require plaintiff to prove that defendant's alleged interfering conduct was "wrongful."

The jury returned a divided verdict, nine to three, in favor of Toyota. After Delia Penna's motion for a new trial was denied, he appealed. In an unpublished disposition, the Court of Appeal unanimously reversed the trial court's judgment, ruling that a plaintiff alleging intentional interference with economic relations is not required to establish "wrongfulness" as an element of its prima facie case, and that it was prejudicial error for the trial court to have read the jury an amended instruction to that effect. The Court of Appeal remanded the case to the trial court for a new trial; we then granted Toyota's petition for review and now reverse.

II

A

. . . The opinion of the Queen's Bench in *Lumley v. Gye* (1853) 2 EL & BL 216 [118 Eng. Rep. 749], a case that has become a standard in torts casebooks, is widely cited as the origin of the two torts — interference with contract and its sibling, interference with prospective economic relations[2] — in the form in which they have come down to us. . . .

. . . .

As a number of courts and commentators have observed, the keystone of the liability imposed in *Lumley v. Gye, supra, 2 EL & Bl. 216*, and *Temperton* [*v. Russell* (1893)], 1 Q.B. 715, to judge from the opinions of the justices, appears to have been the "malicious" intent of a defendant in enticing an employee to breach her contract with the plaintiff, and in damaging the business of one who refused to cooperate with the union in achieving its bargaining aims. . . . Dean Keeton, assessing the state of the tort as late as 1984, remarked that "[w]ith intent to interfere as the usual basis of the action, the cases have turned almost entirely upon the defendant's motive or purpose and the means by which he has sought to accomplish it. As in the cases of interference with contract, any manner of intentional invasion of the plaintiff's interests may be sufficient if the purpose is not a proper one."

. . . .

Because the plaintiff's initial burden of proof was such a slender one, amounting to no more than showing the defendant's conscious act and plaintiff's economic injury, critics argued that legitimate business competition could lead to time consuming and expensive lawsuits (not to speak of potential liability) by a rival, based on conduct that was regarded by the commercial world as both commonplace and appropriate. The "black letter" rules of the Restatement of Torts surrounding the elements and proof of the tort, some complained, might even suggest to "foreign lawyers reading the Restatement as an original matter [that] the whole competitive order of American industry is prima facie illegal."

. . . Acknowledging criticism, the American Law Institute discarded the prima facie tort requirement of the first Restatement. A new provision, section 766B, required that the defendant's conduct be "improper," and adopted a multifactor

---

[2] Throughout this opinion, in an effort to avoid both cumbersome locutions and clumsy acronyms ("IIPEA"), we use the phrase "interference with economic relations" to refer to the tort generally known as "intentional interference with prospective contractual or economic relations" and to distinguish it from the cognate form, "intentional interference with contract".

"balancing" approach, identifying seven factors for the trier of fact to weigh in determining a defendant's liability. . . .

B

. . . .

[A] claim of interference with economic relations "is made out when interference resulting in injury to another is *wrongful by some measure beyond the fact of the interference itself.* Defendant's liability may arise from improper motives or from the use of improper means. They may be wrongful by reason of a statute or other regulation, or a recognized rule of common law, or perhaps an established standard of a trade or profession. No question of privilege arises unless the interference would be wrongful but for the privilege; it becomes an issue *only if the acts charged would be tortious on the part of an unprivileged defendant.*" [Top Serv. Body Shop, Inc. v. Allstate Ins. Co. (1978) 283 Or. 201, [582 P.2d 1365, 1371].]

. . . "The problem with the prima facie tort approach is that basing liability on a mere showing that defendant intentionally interfered with plaintiff's prospective economic relations makes actionable all sorts of contemporary examples of otherwise legitimate persuasion, such as efforts to persuade others not to . . . engage in certain activities, or deal with certain entities. The major issue in the controversy — justification for the defendant's conduct — is left to be resolved on the affirmative defense of privilege. In short, the prima facie approach to the tort of interference with prospective economic relations requires too little of the plaintiff." [Leigh Furniture and Carpet Co. v. Isam (Utah 1982) 657 P.2d 293, 303.]

. . . .

Over the past decade or so, close to a majority of the high courts of American jurisdictions have imported into the economic relations tort variations on the *Top Service* line of reasoning, explicitly approving a rule that requires the plaintiff in such a suit to plead and prove the alleged interference was either "wrongful," "improper," "illegal," "independently tortious" or some variant on these formulations.

III

In California, the development of the economic relations tort has paralleled its evolution in other jurisdictions. . . . In *Imperial Ice Co. v. Rossier*, (1941) 18 Cal. 2d 33 [112 P.2d 631], however, a unanimous court, speaking through Justice Traynor, pronounced these statements in *Boyson* "not necessary to the decision" and directed that they be "disregarded." *(Id.* at p. 38.) California thus joined the majority of jurisdictions in adopting the view of the first Restatement of Torts by stating that "an action will lie for *unjustifiably* inducing a breach of contract."

In the aftermath of *Imperial Ice Co. v. Rossier, supra*, 18 Cal. 2d 33, our early economic relations cases were principally of two types, either the classic master and servant pattern of the pre-*Lumley v. Gye* cases or those involving circumscribed kinds of business relations in which the plaintiff, typically a real estate broker or attorney on a contingency, sued to recover fees after defendant had refused to share property sales proceeds or a personal injury recovery.

. . . .

"In California," . . . "privilege or justification is an affirmative defense, and the lack thereof need not be shown by the original pleader." ([*Buckaloo v. Johnson* (1975)]14 Cal. 3d at pp. 827-828.) A note of caution, however, crept into our formulation of principles at this point. "Perhaps the most significant privilege or justification for interference with a prospective business advantage is free competition," we wrote, "Ours is a competitive economy in which business entities vie for economic advantage." . . .

Second, in 1990, BAJI, the Book of Approved Jury Instructions widely used by trial judges in civil cases, relying on the Restatement Second of Torts and Mr. Witkin's account of the tort, included an instruction providing that a defendant in an economic relations tort case could defeat liability by showing that its conduct was not independently "wrongful."

. . . .

IV

. . . .

The courts provide a damage remedy against third party conduct intended to disrupt an existing contract precisely because the exchange of promises resulting in such a formally cemented economic relationship is deemed worthy of protection from interference by a stranger to the agreement. Economic relationships short of contractual, however, should stand on a different legal footing as far as the potential for tort liability is reckoned. Because ours is a culture firmly wedded to the social rewards of commercial contests, the law usually takes care to draw lines of legal liability in a way that maximizes areas of competition free of legal penalties.

. . . Beyond that, we need not tread today. It is sufficient to dispose of the issue before us in this case by holding that a plaintiff seeking to recover for alleged interference with prospective economic relations has the burden of pleading and proving that the defendant's interference was wrongful "by some measure beyond the fact of the interference itself." . . .

Conclusion

We hold that a plaintiff seeking to recover for an alleged interference with prospective contractual or economic relations must plead and prove as part of its case-in-chief that the defendant not only knowingly interfered with the plaintiff's expectancy, but engaged in conduct that was wrongful by some legal measure other than the fact of interference itself. The judgment of the Court of Appeal is reversed and the cause is remanded with directions to affirm the judgment of the trial court.

MOSK, JUSTICE, concurring.

. . . [L]iability under the tort may threaten values of greater breadth and higher dignity than those of the tort itself.

One is the common law's policy of freedom of competition. "The policy of the common law has always been in favor of free competition, which proverbially is the life of trade. . . . In short, it is no tort to beat a business rival to prospective customers. . . ."

Another of these values expresses itself in the guaranty of freedom of speech in the First Amendment to the United States Constitution. . . .

A third reason for the common law's near incoherence on the tort of intentional interference with prospective economic advantage may be discovered in its focus on the interfering party's motive, that is, *why* he seeks whatever it is that he seeks through his interference, and on his moral character as revealed thereby.

. . . .

It follows that the tort may be satisfied by intentional interference with prospective economic advantage *by independently tortious means.*

The interfering party is properly liable to the interfered-with party in such a situation. That is most plainly true when the independently tortious means the interfering party uses are tortious *as to the interfered-with party himself.* By the tort's very nature, the interfered-with party is an intended (or at least known) victim of the interfering party. (See *Ramona Manor Convalescent Hospital v. Care Enterprises*, (1986) 177 Cal. App. 3d 1120, 1132-1134 [225 Cal. Rptr. 120].) But it is true as well when the independently tortious means the interfering party uses are independently tortious *only as to a third party.*

. . . .

So reformulated, the tort can be distinctly stated and consistently applied.

. . . .

Moreover, the tort's internally inconsistent "protectionist" premise is now removed. The interfered-with party is not favored over the interfering party by virtue of their respective status: the former is merely protected against the latter's use of independently tortious means and restraints of trade.

Furthermore, the tort itself does not now impair the common law's policy of freedom of competition. By its very terms, the freedom in question does *not* extend to the use of independently tortious means or restraints of trade.

Neither does the tort now undermine the First Amendment's guaranty of freedom of speech, freedom of association, or right of petition. That is because, to the extent that speech or association or petitioning is involved, the federal constitutional provision itself limits liability.

Finally, in any action based on the tort, it is the interfered-with party as plaintiff who should bear the burden of pleading and the burden of proof as to whether there has been intentional interference with prospective economic advantage either by independently tortious means or through restraint of trade by the interfering party as defendant. . . .

. . . .

Under the tort as reformulated, it is plain that the Court of Appeal erred. To be sure, the instructions appear erroneous. They did not expressly require objective, and unlawful, conduct or consequences. . . .

. . . .

On two major points, however, I am compelled to state my disagreement.

First, I would not adopt the "standard" of "wrongfulness." As I have noted, the term and its cognates are inherently ambiguous. They should probably be avoided. They should surely not be embraced. . . .

Second, if I were to adopt such a "standard," I would not allow it to remain undefined. . . . Formerly, the interfering party as defendant was left "knowing he was entitled to some defense, but not knowing what defenses would be accounted sufficient." (Dobbs, *Tortious Interference With Contractual Relationships, supra,* 34 Ark. L. Rev. at p. 345.) Now, it appears, the interfered-with party as plaintiff will find himself in a similar position, knowing he may assert a claim, but not knowing the substance of a crucial element. This is hardly an improvement. Any definition of the "standard," of course, should avoid suggesting that the interfering party's motive might be material for present purposes. As I have explained, the focus on this issue is inappropriate. (See, *ante,* at pp. 402-406.) A position of this sort, one must acknowledge, would result in the imposition of no liability on a person who is purely, *but merely,* "malicious" — who acts, to quote Justice Holmes, with "disinterested malevolence." . . .

---

1.   What elements of tortious interference with contract have created problems?

2.   What are the various tests that the courts have adopted for tortious interference with contract or interference with prospective economic relations?

3.   What problems does each test present?

4.   What is the difference between the tort of interference with contract and interference with prospective economic relations?

5.   What test does *Della Penna* adopt? Does it solve the problems or is it merely another step in the progression?

6.   What is Justice Mosk's concern with the majority in *Della Penna*? Is his proposal precisely the same as the majority's decision? If not, how does it differ?

7.   There is a tort known as "slander of title" for interfering with the plaintiff's ownership of land by means of a statement. In *Horning v. Hardy,* 36 Md. App. 419, 373 A.2d 1273 (1977), the court renamed the tort "injurious falsehood," and held it had not been shown. The plaintiff, a developer, brought the action against the Hardys because they had ruined his property development deal. The Hardys had asserted that they owned the land. The court held that the Hardys could exercise

self-defense by claiming ownership. Applying *New York Times v. Sullivan*, 376 U.S. 254 (1964), the court held that a survey was not a prerequisite to the claim of ownership, as long as the Hardys did not know the claim was false or act in reckless disregard of the truth. The verdict on appeal was for the Hardys.

8. Can one beneficiary under a will sue another for obtaining the property before the death of the testator? In *Cyr v. Cote*, 396 A.2d 1013 (Me. 1979), the Supreme Court of Maine recognized an action for wrongful interference with an expected legacy under a will..

9. Interfering with the marital contract is a popular activity. Some courts hold that there is an action by the former spouse against the intervening party, *Nash v. Baker*, 522 P.2d 1335 (Okla. Ct. App. 1974), but many do not. *See Speer v. Dealy*, 242 Neb. 542, 495 N.W.2d 911 (1993).

In regard to an action on behalf of a child based on interference with his parent's marriage, *Nash v. Baker, supra*, stated:

> The sole remaining question is whether a minor child has a common law right to sue a third person whose luring away of the father breaks up the parents' marriage and deprives the child of the father's society and guidance. The common law recognizes no such right in the child. That the . . . spouse has an action for alienation of affections . . . does not require that a cause of action be given to the child. [T]he majority of those jurisdictions which have passed on the question have denied the child an action.

What policies are involved in denial of the above suit?

C. A BRIEF NOTE ON TORTIOUS BREACH OF CONTRACT

Tortious interference with contract cases involve strangers to the contract. In other words, an entity that is not a party to the contract interferes with a party, and the performance of the contract, in some way. Unlike tortious interference cases, tortious breach of contract cases require that a party to the contract breach it in some way that itself involves an intentional wrong, abuse, or gross negligence.

Not all jurisdictions recognize tortious breach of contact as a separate cause of action. Those jurisdictions that do not recognize a separate cause of action for tortious breach of contract treat the facts that would constitute the tort as part of a breach of contract case.

Chapter 22

VICARIOUS LIABILITY

Vicarious liability, respondeat superior, agency, and imputed negligence deal with the liability of an entity, usually an employer, for the tort of someone else, usually an employee. The party whose liability is at issue in these cases is not the party who committed the act upon which the lawsuit is based. Rather, the plaintiff must first establish that the actor committed a tort, and then that the party upon whom the plaintiff seeks to impose liability should be held answerable in damages for that tort. The classic vicarious liability scenario involves an employer being held liable for the negligent tort of an employee committed while the employee was acting within the scope of his or her employment. Standard issues include: whether the employee was really an employee at all; whether the employment relationship was the kind of relationship in which it would be appropriate to impose liability on the employer; and whether the employee was acting within the scope of his or her employment at the time the tort was committed.

Because the tort must have been committed while the employee was acting within the scope of employment, employers are rarely liable for the intentional torts of their employees. Exceptions to this include security guards charged with false imprisonment and bouncers charged with battery. These are intentional torts, but may be committed within the scope of employment, which includes stopping suspected shoplifters and evicting unwanted patrons.

Vicarious liability is a form of strict liability. Once the underlying act of negligence has been established, and once the court has decided to impose liability based on the theory of imputed negligence, the liable entity has no defenses. Liability will be imposed no matter what standard of care the liable entity met; indeed, its standard of care will be irrelevant. This form of liability is in sharp contrast to negligence-based liability against the employer. Of course, if the employer was itself negligent, it may be sued directly for its failure to meet the applicable standard of care. Such a case is based on primary negligence: the employer is responsible for its own negligence. In imputed negligence cases, the employer is liable for someone else's negligence and the employer's conduct becomes irrelevant.

O'TOOLE v. CARR

Superior Court of New Jersey, Appellate Division, 2001
786 A.2d 121

Conley, J.A.D.

This appeal is generated by an automobile accident caused by defendant Paul J. Carr while driving from his home to his municipal court judgeship employment. The accident victims sued not only Carr but the Murray and Carr law firm in which, at the time of the accident, Carr was a partner. The law firm's alleged liability was premised upon principles of agency and respondeat superior vicarious liability. On leave granted by the Supreme Court, the firm appeals a March 16, 2001, order granting plaintiffs' and Carr's motion for summary judgment. In granting the motion, the judge concluded as a matter of law that the law firm was vicariously liable for Carr's negligence.

Although recognizing that more modern approaches in other jurisdictions to respondeat superior liability might provide a basis for vicarious liability under the particular circumstances here, we are constrained to abide by what we believe to be the current law in New Jersey and reverse. Under our existing law, Carr's automobile negligence while driving to the location of his municipal court judgeship cannot be imputed to the private law practice of Murray and Carr.

Most of the particular circumstances are not in dispute. On January 8, 1998, the O'Tooles' vehicle was struck by Carr's vehicle on Route 9 in the Township of Eagleswood. At the time of the accident, Carr was driving to the Tuckerton Municipal Court, where he presided as a part-time municipal judge. His car was leased. Lease payments, in addition to gas, tolls and other car expenses, were paid from Carr's corporate account. Income in this corporate account was derived from law firm disbursements after partnership overhead expenses were paid. No income, however, from Carr's judgeships, or Murray's (who also was a part-time municipal judge) judgeships, went into the partnership business account or their separate corporate accounts. Carr's vehicle was not leased in either the partnership or corporate name, but rather was leased by Carr in his personal capacity. The vehicle was insured by First Trenton Indemnity with bodily injury limits of $100,000 for each person and $300,000 for each accident. In contrast, the law firm had a million dollar automobile policy with CNA. The judge noted that plaintiffs had no underinsured motorists' coverage, thus enabling them to recover from either policy.

There are a few disputed facts. Carr had a portable cellular phone at the time of the accident which he had with him in the vehicle. Sometime before the accident, he claims to have made several law firm-related calls, one to his secretary to check his diary for the day and one or two to law firm clients. It was his deposition testimony that were it not for the accident, these clients would have been billed for the phone calls. Some question is raised as to the existence of the calls as phone bills purporting to be those of Carr's cell phone do not reflect the calls. The authenticity and accuracy of these records is disputed. Were there some basis for concluding that the accident occurred while Carr was engaged in one of the firm-related phone calls he claims to have made, the dispute of fact as to their existence might be critical. Carr, however, admitted in deposition testimony that he had finished the phone calls and was not on the cell phone at the time of the accident. There is no basis for concluding, therefore, that at the time of the accident, Carr was directly engaged in law firm business.

. . . .

The focus here is upon the "going and coming" or commuting anomalies that have been engrafted upon respondeat superior liability principles. A number of different tests have been employed by jurisdictions throughout the country to determine whether respondeat superior principles apply to commuting accidents so as to make the employer liable for the commuting employee's negligence. By far, the most liberal is that utilized in California. Employing what has been referred to as an enterprise theory of liability, California has concluded that "if the employee's trip to or from work 'involves an incidental benefit to the employer, not common to commute trips made by ordinary members of the work force,' the 'going and coming' rule will not apply." *Henderson v. Adia Servs. Inc.*, 182 Cal. App. 3d 1069, 227 Cal. Rptr. 745, 747-48 (Cal. App. Ct. 1986) (quoting *Hinman v. Westinghouse Elec. Co.*, 2 Cal. 3d 956, 88 Cal. Rptr. 188, 471 P.2d 988 (Cal. 1970)). "Categorization of an employee's action as within or outside the scope of employment thus begins with a question of foreseeability, i.e., whether the accident is part of the inevitable toll of a lawful enterprise." *Id.* 227 Cal. Rptr. at 748. The enterprise theory inquires whether "in the context of the particular enterprise the employee's conduct was so unusual or startling that it would seem unfair to include the loss resulting from it among other costs of the employer's business." *Id.* 227 Cal. Rptr. at 749-50 (citation omitted). See also *Alma W. v. Oakland Unified Sch. Dist*, 123 Cal. App. 3d 133, 176 Cal. Rptr. 287, 289 (Cal. Ct. App. 1981). It is not some element of control by the employer that is seen as the basis for imposing vicarious liability "but [rather] because the employer's enterprise creates inevitable risks as a part of doing business." *Bailey v. Filco, Inc.*, 48 Cal. App. 4th 1552, 56 Cal. Rptr. 2d 333, 335 (Cal. Ct. App. 1996).[3] See also *Potter v. Shaw*, 2001 Mass. Super. LEXIS 271, 2001 WL 914203, at *3 (Mass. May 29, 2001) (applying California law).

In *Potter v. Shaw, supra*, for example, the employer was found liable for the negligence of its employees who were involved in a car accident while sightseeing on a "day off" during a business trip. Under California law, the court found that the sightseeing was not "so unusual or startling that it would seem unfair to include the

---

[3] The enterprise theory has been described in the following fashion:

> what has emerged as the modern justification for vicarious liability is a rule of policy, a deliberate allocation of a risk. The losses caused by the torts of employees, which as a practical matter are sure to occur in the conduct of the employer's enterprise, are placed upon that enterprise itself, as a required cost of doing business. They are placed upon the employer because, having engaged in an enterprise, which will on the basis of all past experience involve harm to others through the torts of employees, and sought to profit by it, it is just that he, rather than the innocent injured plaintiff, should bear them; and because he is better able to absorb them, and to distribute them, through prices, rates or liability insurance, to the public, and so to shift them to society, to the community at large.

[W. Page Keeton, et al., Prosser and Keeton on the Law of Torts, 499, 500-01 (5th ed. 1984) (footnotes omitted).]

[accident] among the other costs of [the employer's] business," *id.* at 4, and concluded that the employer would have anticipated or foreseen that its employees would utilize the "day off by sightseeing or by doing other recreational activities." *Ibid.*

Applying this rationale here, it might be said that the law firm could have anticipated or foreseen that Carr would be engaged in commuting to the municipal court as both Murray and Carr were each part-time municipal judges. Indeed, the partnership was formed to provide a mechanism, primarily for accounting purposes, by which each could continue with their part-time municipal judgeships but also engage in their respective private practices. It was also understood that while commuting, each attorney might conduct some firm business with their cell phones. Carr's automobile negligence under these circumstances might not be "so unusual or startling that it would seem unfair to" impose liability upon the partnership as a risk of its enterprise.

We do not believe New Jersey's application of respondeat superior liability principles to "going and coming" commuting circumstances has yet gone so far as the California approach. Fundamentally, the California enterprise liability eschews the scope of employment test set forth in the Restatement (Second) of Agency §§ 218, 228, 229 (1957). As described by one commentator: "Under [the enterprise liability theory], the reason for imposing vicarious liability on employers is because their businesses should bear the losses incidental to those enterprises. [On the other hand] the [Restatement's] "scope of employment" test attempts to limit the reach of respondeat superior." Rhett B. Franklin, *supra*, 39 S.D.L. Rev. at 593 (footnotes omitted). Thus far, New Jersey follows the principles of the Restatement. *Di Cosala v. Kay*, 91 N.J. 159, 169, 450 A.2d 508 (1982); *Mannes v. Healey*, 306 N.J. Super. 351, 353, 703 A.2d 944 (App. Div. 1997). See also *Gilborges v. Wallace*, 78 N.J. 342, 351, 396 A.2d 338 (1978).

Under the Restatement principles, an employer is vicariously liable for the torts of an employee if the employee was acting within the scope of his or her employment at the time the tort was committed. *Di Cosala v. Kay, supra*, 91 N.J. at 169. An employee is acting within the scope of employment if the action is " 'of the kind [the employee] is employed to perform; it occurs substantially within the authorized time and space limits; [and] it is actuated, at least in part, by a purpose to serve the master.' " 91 N.J. at 169 (quoting Restatement (Second) of Agency, § 228 (1957)).[4]

---

[4] The Restatement defines scope of employment in § 228 and describes the type of conduct which falls within that scope in § 229.

§ 228 states:

   (a) it is of the kind he is employed to perform;

   (b) it occurs substantially within the authorized time and space limits;

   (c) it is actuated, at least in part, by a purpose to serve the master; and

   (d) if force is intentionally used by the servant against another, the use of force is not unexpectable by the master.

(2) Conduct of a servant is not within the scope of employment if it is different in kind from that authorized, far beyond the authorized time or space limits, or too little actuated by a purpose to serve the master

Generally, the Restatement scope of employment principles do not recognize ordinary travel commute as within the scope of employment. "An employee driving his or her own vehicle to and from the employee's workplace is not within the scope of employment for the purpose of imposing vicarious liability upon the employer for the negligence of the employee-driver. " *Mannes v. Healey, supra*, 306 N.J. Super., at 353-54. Some courts ascribe this rule to the theory that "employment is suspended from the time the employee leaves the work-place until he or she returns, or that in traveling to and from work, the employee is not rendering service to the employer." *Id.* at 354.

We recognize a number of exceptions to the general rule that ordinary travel commute is not within the scope of employment. Where, at the time of the negligent conduct, the employee is serving an interest of the employer as well as his or her own private interest, a "dual purpose" is established and the employer is vicariously liable. *Gilborges v. Wallace, supra*, 78 N.J. at 351. Such liability will also be imposed when the employee can be considered to have been on a special errand or mission on behalf of the employer. Another exception exists where the employee is required to drive his or her vehicle to work so that the vehicle is available for work-related duties. Finally, where an employee is "on call" and becomes involved in an accident while, at the request of the employer, [the employee] is traveling to a work site, respondeat superior liability will attach. *Mannes v. Healey, supra*, 306 N.J. Super., at 354-55.

Several recent cases are illustrative. *Pfender v. Torres*, 336 N.J. Super. 379, 392-94, 765 A.2d 208 (App. Div.), *certif. denied*, 167 N.J. 637 (2001), is an example of the employer required vehicle availability. There, defendant was a salesman for a car dealership which had provided its salesmen with vehicles for business as well as personal use, albeit retaining ownership. During working hours, the assigned vehicles were used for customer "demonstrators" and to run work-related errands. The vehicles so provided displayed the dealership's identification and were consid-

---

§ 229 states:

(1) to be within the scope of the employment, conduct must be of the same general nature as that authorized, or incidental to the conduct authorized.

(2) In determining whether or not the conduct, although not authorized, is nevertheless so similar to or incidental to the conduct authorized as to be within the scope of employment, the following matters of fact are to be considered:

(a) whether or not the act is one commonly done by such servants;

(b) the time, place and purpose of the act;

(c) the previous relations between the master and the servant;

(d) the extent to which the business of the master is apportioned between different servants;

(e) whether or not the act is outside the enterprise of the master or, if within the enterprise, has not been entrusted to any servant;

(f) whether or not the master has reason to expect that such an act will be done;

(g) the similarity in quality of the act done to the act authorized;

(h) whether or not the instrumentality by which the harm done has been furnished by the master to the servant;

(i) the extent of departure from the normal method of accomplishing an authorized result; and

(j) whether or not the act is seriously criminal.

ered to serve promotional and advertising benefits when used by the salesmen. At the time of the accident, defendant was driving to work and was not serving any particular purpose of the dealership. In, nonetheless, imposing vicarious liability upon the dealership, we said: "[The dealership's] liability under [the] well-recognized exception is clear since [defendant employee] was driving to work when the accident happened and he was required to use the car in the performance of his employment as a demonstrator to encourage sales and to run work-related errands." *Id.* at 394.

In *Carter v. Reynolds*, 345 N.J. Super. 67, 783 A.2d 724 (App. Div. 2001), we concluded vicarious liability should be imputed to the employer for an auto accident that occurred when the employee was commuting home from work because the employee's employment responsibilities required her to have a vehicle at work for off-site client visits. We pointed out that at least a third of her work time was off-site.

In contrast, we declined in *Mannes v. Healey, supra,* 306 N.J. Super, at 355, to impose vicarious liability under the special mission or special errand exception. There, defendant was driving her own vehicle from her home to her place of employment when she struck a pedestrian at 8:30 p.m. She had an undefined and flexible nature of employment which allowed her to go to the office after regular business hours. But we viewed this employment flexibility as an employee benefit, not a requirement of the job. Moreover, we noted that the varying hours and unrestricted access to the employer's office underscored the absence of control by the employer, often considered a necessary element of respondeat superior liability. 306 N.J. Super. at 355. We also pointed out that defendant was using her own car and that the employer did not control the manner in which defendant operated her car, the route of travel or when she chose to commute to the office for business purposes. All of these Restatement factors convinced us that the employee in *Mannes* was not acting within the scope of employment at the time of the accident and that none of the exceptions thereto applied.

We believe a similar result must be reached here under our existing respondeat superior law. To begin with, it would be violative of Canon 2 of the Code of Judicial Conduct[5] to say that Carr was serving any purpose of the law firm while commuting to his municipal judgeship position and thus the dual purpose exception does not apply. And, certainly he was not on a law firm special errand or mission. Neither does the record support a finding that the firm's practice required him to have a vehicle for off-site firm business. Finally, he was not in an "on-call" capacity.

We can, therefore, find no authority in New Jersey for imposing vicarious liability upon the law firm for Carr's auto negligence under the particular circumstances as they are reflected by the present record. We add the following brief comments. As we have said, were this jurisdiction to have adopted the enterprise liability approach that exists in California, the result might be different. We note, in this respect, that in *Carter v. Reynolds, supra,* we cited California precedent as "persuasive." We also rejected the concept of employer control as a relevant factor. As we have previously

[5] Canon 2 instructs, in part, that a "judge should not lend the prestige of office to advance the private interests of others. . . ."

said, the result in *Carter* is primarily guided by the employee-required vehicle exception that exists in our present law. The enterprise and control comments in *Carter* are, therefore, dicta. Moreover, to the extent *Carter* can be read to depart from the respondeat superior principles thus far applied in New Jersey and as depicted in *Mannes*, we decline to do so. We are an appellate court bound to follow the law as we believe it to be in this jurisdiction.

Until and unless our Supreme Court rejects the Restatement (Second) of Agency, §§ 218, 228, 229, as the appropriate governing principles for resolving respondeat superior liability issues in the "going and coming"/commuting context or concludes that enterprise liability is consistent with the Restatement principles, we cannot expand those principles to encompass such liability. We, thus, conclude that the motion judge erred in imposing vicarious liability upon the law firm for Carr's negligence.

Reversed.

This decision was affirmed by the New Jersey Supreme Court "substantially for the reasons expressed in Judge Conley's decision," with a further note that "[t]he Court declines to adopt the broader enterprise liability theory that is the standard for *respondeat superior* in California. . . ." *O'Toole v. Carr*, 815 A.2d 471 (N.J. 2003) (per curiam).

KAVANAUGH v. NUSSBAUM
Court of Appeals of New York, 1988
523 N.E.2d 284

KAYE, J., CHIEF JUDGE WACHTLER and JUDGES SIMONS, ALEXANDER, HANCOCK, JR., BELLACOSA and DILLON[*] concur.

KAYE, JUDGE

A physician who designates another doctor to "cover" for him, in the circumstances presented, is not liable for the covering doctor's own negligence in treating the regular physician's patient.

Plaintiff Justin Kavanaugh was born, in obvious distress, at 4:46 a.m., December 16, 1974, after only 31 weeks' gestation, weighing about three pounds. His mother, plaintiff Irene Gonzales, had engaged defendant Erol Caypinar, an obstetrician, on December 3, 1974, after Dr. William Nussbaum had for several months failed to diagnose that she was pregnant.[1] Mrs. Gonzales was then 44 years old; the youngest of her three children was more than 20 years old. On her two visits to Dr. Caypinar's office — December 3 and December 10, 1974 — Mrs. Gonzales complained of staining, and had elevated blood pressure.

---

[*] Designated pursuant to N.Y. Constitution, article VI, § 2.

[1] A verdict was directed in Dr. Nussbaum's favor at the close of the evidence; he is not a party to this appeal.

At about 9:30 p.m., December 15, Mrs. Gonzales began bleeding to such an extent that her husband took her to the emergency room of defendant Brookhaven Hospital. There she was treated by the emergency room physician, defendant Nareys Suteethorn, a hospital employee. Dr. Suteethorn examined Mrs. Gonzales, but testified that he saw no active bleeding. Whether Dr. Suteethorn inserted his finger into Mrs. Gonzales' cervix, and whether such an examination precipitated hemorrhaging because of an abnormally low placenta (placenta previa), were sharply disputed issues. Dr. Caypinar was at the time attending a meeting at another hospital, and had arranged for Dr. Albin W. Swenson, Jr. (not a defendant) to cover for him. Dr. Suteethorn reported his findings by telephone to Dr. Swenson who told him to send Mrs. Gonzales home and have her contact Dr. Caypinar in the morning.

After returning home, Mrs. Gonzales' bleeding increased, and at about 2:00 a.m., December 16, she was returned by ambulance to the Brookhaven emergency room, where she was again seen by Dr. Suteethorn, and this time admitted to the hospital. Dr. Caypinar, who was in the delivery room assisting another doctor, ordered a "double set up" to permit either an internal examination of Mrs. Gonzales or a Caesarian section, because he anticipated a potential emergency (possible placenta previa or placenta separation). For an hour or more Dr. Caypinar received reports from the labor room nurses who were monitoring Mrs. Gonzales, and thereafter himself attended her. A loss of the fetal heartbeat was reported beginning about 4:15 a.m., some 31 minutes before Justin's delivery by Caesarian section. In the delivery room, the infant required resuscitation; his APGAR (a score of zero to 10 assigned to newborns, based on observation) was one at one minute after birth, five at five minutes, and four at 10 minutes. He was transferred to North Shore Hospital, where a tracheotomy was performed to help him breathe. He was tube fed for about six months, after which he spent some 14 months at Down-state Medical Center. The evidence indicated that Justin suffered permanent debilitating injury, including a reduced ability to become educated, or to care for himself, or to sustain himself economically; he is retarded, has epilepsy (experiencing periodic grand mal seizures) and requires special education and therapy.

A special verdict form, consisting of several questions, was submitted to the jury. The jury found that Dr. Caypinar was culpably negligent in four respects: he failed to ascertain the nature and position of placenta implantation; he failed to use the available diagnostic procedure of sonography; he failed to advise the covering physician as to potential risks; and he failed to render proper care and treatment on December 16, 1974. A single question was submitted embodying three possible theories of liability of Dr. Suteethorn: that he negligently performed a prenatal internal examination of Mrs. Gonzales; that he failed to describe all pertinent findings of that examination, including a finding of vaginal bleeding, to Dr. Swenson; and that he failed to admit Mrs. Gonzales to the hospital on her first visit. The jury answered that question affirmatively.

The jury was further asked whether Dr. Swenson — the covering doctor — himself had failed to care for and treat Mrs. Gonzales in accordance with accepted standards and whether such departure was a proximate cause of Justin's injuries. It answered yes to both that question and the next: "Under the facts and circumstances of this case, and in accordance with the rules of law as I have charged,[2] do you find that the arrangement between Dr. Caypinar and Dr. Swenson was such as to impute to Dr. Caypinar any causally related acts of negligence on the part of Dr. Swenson?" Having answered both questions affirmatively, the jury was then asked whether any part of the finding of Dr. Caypinar's liability was a result of the imputation of negligence on the part of Dr. Swenson and, if so, how much. The jury answered, "Yes. 25%."

Total damages were fixed at $4,340,000: $2,500,000 for Justin's pain and suffering; $600,000 as the present value of future expenses for institutional custodial care; $740,000 as the present value of his diminished earning capacity, and $500,000 for Mrs. Gonzales' lost services. The jury apportioned fault 70% to Dr. Caypinar, 30% to Brookhaven (as Suteethorn's employer). The court denied defendants' motions challenging the jury's findings as to negligence and apportionment, but it reduced the award for pain and suffering to $1,500,000 and it set aside the awards for custodial care, diminished earning capacity and lost services, concluding that there was inadequate evidentiary support for these items of damage. On cross appeals, the Appellate Division sustained the judgment as to liability and the award for pain and suffering, but it restored both the $740,000 award for lost earning capacity and $35,000 of the award for lost services (129 A.D.2d 559). This court granted defendants' motions for leave to appeal.

Except as to the imputation to Dr. Caypinar of liability for the negligence of Dr. Swenson, we affirm the Appellate Division order in every respect. In that the parties have devoted a major portion of their argument to the question whether the liability of Drs. Caypinar and Suteethorn was established, we state at the outset that, as to both doctors, the affirmed findings of their own negligence and causation had support in the record, which is the limit of the scope of our review (*Humphrey v. State of New York*, 60 N.Y.2d 742).

Vicarious Liability

Dr. Caypinar, a sole practitioner, and Dr. Swenson both specialized in obstetrics and gynecology on Long Island, but were not partners in the practice of medicine, and did not share office space. Both participated with two colleagues who similarly enjoyed privileges at Brookhaven Hospital in an arrangement whereby each doctor took a turn covering for the other three, so there would be 24-hour-a-day, seven-day-a-week coverage of their patients. Each of the four retained the entire fee from his own patient, whatever service the others might have rendered that patient. The undisputed testimony was that it was common practice in the community for sole practitioners to cover for each other, and that such arrangements were standard practice at the hospital, which required doctors with privileges to be continuously available for emergencies. Pursuant to the covering arrangement, when Mrs. Gonzales arrived at Brookhaven Hospital the night of

---

[2] The court charged that liability for Dr. Swenson's negligence could be imputed to Dr. Caypinar if it found a "sufficient legal relationship or arrangement," considering the following factors: any fee arrangement; any mutual benefit; whether the hospital required the arrangement; whether Mrs. Gonzales had the opportunity to select who would treat her in Dr. Caypinar's absence; whether Dr. Caypinar advised her she would be treated by someone else if he was unavailable; and whether Dr. Caypinar advised her of the names and qualifications of the covering doctors.

December 15 and said she was Dr. Caypinar's patient, the emergency room physician consulted the roster and called Dr. Swenson, who was covering for him.

Both in sending the issue to the jury and in later refusing to set aside the verdict, the trial court concluded — essentially for three reasons — that the relationship or association between Drs. Caypinar and Swenson supported the imposition of vicarious liability. First, even if Drs. Caypinar and Swenson were not partners, employees or employers of each other and shared no fees, the covering arrangement was for their mutual benefit; their arrangement afforded continuous treatment for their patients and enabled them to satisfy what appeared to be the hospital's requirement for privileges. Second, Mrs. Gonzales had an ongoing relationship with Dr. Caypinar, and had the right to expect satisfactory treatment from him, which included persons to whom he directed her. Third, Mrs. Gonzales had no knowledge of the arrangement and no opportunity to participate in the selection of the covering doctor in any given instance, from which the court concluded that "it would not seem reasonable that she should bear the total responsibility for the no option situation presented to her."

Liability in negligence generally rests on a defendant's own fault. Underlying the doctrine of vicarious liability — the imputation of liability to defendant for another person's fault, based on defendant's relationship with the wrongdoer — is the notion of control. The person in a position to exercise some general authority or control over the wrongdoer must do so or bear the consequences (Prosser and Keeton, Torts § 69, at 500 [5th ed. 1984]). A classic example is liability of an employer for the acts of its employees within the course of employment, evidencing the public policy foundations of vicarious liability. The risk is allocated to the employer because it is better able than the innocent plaintiff to bear the consequences of employees' torts, and by the imputation of liability is also encouraged to act carefully in the selection and supervision of its employees. Vicarious liability applies to hospitals and physicians (*Bing v. Thunig*, 2 N.Y.2d 656).[4] Brookhaven Hospital thus unquestionably stands liable for the negligence of its employee Dr. Suteethorn. But Dr. Swenson was not an employee of Dr. Caypinar — indeed, plaintiffs make no such contention — and the imputation of Dr. Swenson's negligence to him therefore raises different concerns.

The central decision with respect to the vicarious liability of physicians is *Graddy v. New York Med. Coll.* (19 A.D.2d 426 [Bergan, J.], *mot. to dismiss appeal denied*, 13 N.Y.2d 1175). In *Graddy* the court refused to impute the negligence of the treating physician to the regular physician, although they shared office space, services, equipment and supplies, and even certain fees. As pertinent as the logic and result of the decision is the collection of authorities supporting the conclusion — still valid after 25 years — that "[in] the absence of some recognized traditional legal relationship such as a partnership, master and servant, or agency, between physicians in the treatment of patients, the imposition of liability on one for the negligence of the other has been largely limited to situations of joint action in

---

[4] *See, e.g.*, Business Corporation Law § 1505(a), providing that each "shareholder, employee or agent of a professional service corporation shall be personally and fully liable and accountable for any negligent or wrongful act or misconduct committed by him or by any person under his direct supervision and control while rendering professional services on behalf of such corporation."

diagnosis or treatment or some control of the course of treatment of one by the other." (*Id.*, at 429.) The court concluded that vicarious liability "ought not be extended to rest on a situation where there is neither a legal nor an actual control of the treating physician by the other physician and the relationship between them upon which responsibility is sought to be imputed turns upon a shared office and an agreement to service each other's patients for a shared fee." (*Id.*, at 430.) (*See also, Connell v. Hayden*, 83 A.D.2d 30, 57-58; *Feigelson v. Ryan*, 108 Misc. 2d 192.)

The years since *Graddy* have seen the development of medical clinics and group practices engendering new questions about imputed liability, but the guiding principle remains unchanged: vicarious liability for medical malpractice generally turns on agency or control in fact, or apparent or ostensible agency (not in issue here) (*Hill v. St. Clare's Hosp.*, 67 N.Y.2d 72, 79; *see also, Lanza v. Parkeast Hosp.*, 102 A.D.2d 741). The requisite showing was not made.

The issue of agency or control in fact necessarily focuses on the relationship between the two doctors, not their relationship with plaintiffs. The trial court, in its charge and its comprehensive posttrial discussion of the issue, sought to determine whether the Caypinar-Swenson relationship was "sufficiently substantial," whether there was a "sufficient legal relationship or arrangement so as to impose liability on Caypinar", whether it was "reasonable to consider them to be associated." That is not the test. No claim is even made that Dr. Caypinar retained Dr. Swenson to act as his agent, in his behalf. Instead, plaintiffs characterize the two doctors as partners or joint venturers. Neither term fits the relationship. By taking turns covering for each other, the doctors did not become partners or even joint venturers, both relationships typified by a sharing of the property and risks of the venture (*see, e.g., Matter of Steinbeck v. Gerosa*, 4 N.Y.2d 302, 317). Nor is this a case of concerted treatment, where the original physician participated in or exercised some degree of control over the acts of the treating physician (*Graddy v. New York Med. Coll*, 19 A.D.2d 426, *supra; Connell v. Hayden*, 83 A.D.2d 30, 53, *supra*). As the court observed in *Graddy*, what is presented here "is something less, and quite different from, a relationship of master and servant or agency upon which vicarious liability has thus far rested." (19 A.D.2d, at 430, *supra*.)

The trial court found persuasive, and a point of distinction, that the Caypinar-Swenson relationship was regular and mutually beneficial. But similar elements also existed in *Graddy;* indeed it is hard to imagine that any physicians would maintain a covering arrangement that did not offer mutual benefit. Still what is missing is some sort of legal or actual authority or control of the treating physician by the regular physician.

The pivotal consideration in extending vicarious liability is one of policy. We recognize that *Graddy* is distinguishable on its facts, but the policy concerns articulated there are perhaps even more compelling today. There the court wrote that the "implications of such an enlarged liability would tend to discourage a physician from arranging to have another care for his patients on his illness or absence and thus curtail the availability of medical service." (19 A.D.2d, at 430, *supra*.) Covering arrangements were common for sole practitioners in Dr. Caypinar's community, as they must be generally today; while it is in the nature of the medical profession that a patient's emergency can arise at any moment, surely no person expects that his or her regular physician will *always* be there to respond. If liability were now to be imposed vicariously on physicians for the independent negligence of their covering doctors, some would doubtless be discouraged from making arrangements for the continuous care of their patients, but those who chose to or had to — if they are now to be made insurers of their colleagues' independent acts — would be compelled to insure themselves accordingly. In either event, the public interest would ultimately be disserved.

Nor is the patient — or the public — left at risk by denying vicarious liability in such circumstances. Doctors remain answerable for their own fault in their covering arrangements, as in their treatment of patients (*see, Datiz v. Shoob*, 71 N.Y.2d 867; *Ravo v. Rogatnick*, 70 N.Y.2d 305, 310). They may, for example, be liable to their patients for negligence in their designation of covering doctors, or for their own joint participation with them in diagnosis or treatment or — as in this very case — for failing to advise the covering doctor of potential risks involved. By the same token, covering doctors are independently responsible, as treating physicians, for their negligence.[5] Thus, we decline to enlarge the doctrine of vicarious liability to reach the situation here, and conclude that it was error to do so.

. . . .

Disposition

Having concluded that the only error committed by the Appellate Division was in upholding the imposition of vicarious liability on Dr. Caypinar, we next consider what relief is necessary to remedy that error.

The jury's finding of negligence on the part of Dr. Swenson, for which it imposed liability on Dr. Caypinar, was only one of five grounds found against Dr. Caypinar. Our rejection of vicarious liability does not undermine the validity of the remaining incidents of negligence, which independently support his liability to plaintiffs. Thus, despite error in imposing vicarious liability, Dr. Caypinar remains jointly and severally liable with Brookhaven for the full amount of the verdict as modified by the Appellate Division, and plaintiffs may recover the whole of their damages from either defendant. As we have several times noted, plaintiffs are not obliged to include all joint tort-feasors as defendants, and they may recover their entire damages from any of the particular tort-feasors sued, regardless of the concurrent negligence of others (*see, Ravo v. Ragotnick*, 70 N.Y.2d 305, 313, *supra*; *Graphic Arts Mut. Ins. Co. v. Bakers Mut. Ins. Co.*, 45 N.Y.2d 551, 557; *Kelly v. Long Is. Light Co.*, 31 N.Y.2d 25, 30).

While our decision to reject vicarious liability in the circumstances is without practical significance to plaintiffs, it may well affect defendants' obligations as between each other. By overturning the finding against Dr. Caypinar for Dr. Swenson's negligence, we also of necessity set aside the apportionment of damages

---

[5] It bears note that, in deciding the legal issue, we do not condone a practice where a physician does not tell the patient what, if any, covering arrangements have been made. The regrettable fact that Dr. Caypinar did not mention the covering arrangements to Mrs. Gonzales cannot, however, make him vicariously liable for the independent negligence of the other physicians participating in the arrangements.

between the two defendants, because the jury may well have predicated the apportionment on its belief that Dr. Caypinar's share included responsibility for Dr. Swenson's negligence. How the jury would have apportioned fault between the two codefendants without the element of vicarious liability is a question we cannot answer. Therefore, while not disturbing the award to plaintiffs, we must remit the case to Supreme Court, Suffolk County, for a new apportionment of damages between defendants, without the imposition on Dr. Caypinar of vicarious liability for the negligence of Dr. Swenson.

Defendants' remaining points are without merit or unpreserved. . . .

The *Kavanaugh* court cites the following as its second possible source of vicarious liability against Dr. Caypinar: "Mrs. Gonzales had an ongoing relationship with Dr. Caypinar, and had the right to expect satisfactory treatment from him, which included persons to whom he directed her." Is this really vicarious liability? Doctors have a primary obligation to their patients to use reasonable care in referring them to other doctors. Dr. Caypinar had a duty directly to Mrs. Gonzales, and any negligence in referral would be a breach of that duty. Liability for such negligence would be primary and not vicarious, although such liability would require a negligent act on the part of the doctor to whom the patient had been referred as part of the case for negligence in referral. What kinds of evidence would a plaintiff need to present to prevail in a negligent referral case?

SCHLOTFELDT v. CHARTER HOSPITAL OF LAS VEGAS
Supreme Court of Nevada, 1996
910 P.2d 271

YOUNG, J. I concur: STEFFEN, C.J. ROSE, J., concurring in part and dissenting in part. SHEARING, J., with whom SPRINGER, J., joins, dissenting.

YOUNG, J.

FACTS

On Saturday, March 4, 1989, appellant/cross-respondent Debra Schlotfeldt ("Schlotfeldt") presented herself to respondent/cross-appellant Charter Hospital of Las Vegas, a Nevada corporation ("Charter") that specializes in the treatment of alcoholism and drug addiction. Charter personnel observed that Schlotfeldt was extremely depressed and displayed rapid changes in her emotions. Schlotfeldt admitted at trial that she had abused alcohol and ingested methamphetamine prior to her admission to Charter. Schlotfeldt stated during a psychiatric examination that she gambled out of control when under the influence of drugs, was depressed for over a year and a half, and had thoughts of suicide. In a statement revealing the depth of Schlotfeldt's emotional difficulties, Schlotfeldt told Charter staff that "I don't trust myself," "I feel like I'm going crazy," and "I feel like I am at the end of my rope." After this conversation, Schlotfeldt went home to retrieve personal belongings. Escorted by her husband, Schlotfeldt returned to Charter and signed documents requesting voluntary admission and authorizing such care and treatment as ordered by her attending physician.

A Charter psychiatrist prepared an admitting diagnosis of Schlotfeldt that concluded she suffered from major depression and suicidal ideation. Anil Batra, M.D., also examined Schlotfeldt and diagnosed a major depressive disorder. On Sunday morning, March 5, 1989, Gilles M.K. Desmarais, M.D. ("Desmarais") examined Schlotfeldt. According to Charter, Desmarais was an independent doctor who was not assigned by Charter to Schlotfeldt. Instead, Desmarais attended to Schlotfeldt at the request of a Charter psychiatrist who was busy with other patients. Desmarais' examination revealed that Schlotfeldt had marital problems that led to alcohol abuse, drug use and compulsive gambling. Desmarais concluded that Schlotfeldt was a suicide risk because her severe depression of one and a half years was nearing a pinnacle.

Schlotfeldt argues that she made repeated requests to return home after the morning of March 5, 1989. Charter admits that Schlotfeldt requested to return home, but claims that because she was a suicide risk and her husband was out of town, releasing her at the time was imprudent. Desmarais urged her to stay voluntarily until her husband returned. Eventually, Desmarais allowed Schlotfeldt to leave because the effects of the drugs had worn off, she was no longer a suicide risk, and her husband had returned. Schlotfeldt spent a total of sixty-six hours at Charter.

Eighteen months later, Schlotfeldt filed suit against Charter and Desmarais. Schlotfeldt's initial complaint contained numerous claims for relief. However, all claims except the false imprisonment claim were withdrawn prior to trial. Schlotfeldt claimed she was admitted to Charter against her will and that she requested to leave Charter, but Charter and Desmarais continued to hold her against her will. Charter claimed that Schlotfeldt admitted herself voluntarily and it was obligated to urge her to remain until she was no longer a danger to herself or others. The district court excluded evidence showing Schlotfeldt was hospitalized for her psychiatric condition on multiple occasions after her stay at the Charter facility. Also, the district court found, as a matter of law, that Charter was vicariously liable for the acts of Desmarais. At the conclusion of trial, a jury found Charter and Desmarais liable for false imprisonment and awarded Schlotfeldt $50,000.00 in compensatory damages. After the district court entered a second amended judgment on the jury's verdict, Schlotfeldt and Charter appealed.

DISCUSSION

. . . .

Agency relationship

The district court instructed the jury that Charter was vicariously liable, as a matter of law, for the acts of Desmarais.[2] Based on the ostensible agency theory,

_____

[2] The district court instructed the jury as follows:

the district court found that Charter should be held liable for the acts of Desmarais because he was chosen by Charter to examine Schlotfeldt. Charter opposed the instruction because it claimed an issue of fact existed as to whether an agency relationship existed between Charter and Desmarais. The district court's instruction, according to Charter, was improper and materially prejudiced its position by binding its liability to the improper acts of Desmarais.

The existence of an agency relationship is generally a question of fact for the jury if the facts showing the existence of agency are disputed, or if conflicting inferences can be drawn from the facts. *Latin American Shipping Co., Inc. v. Pan American Trading Corp.*, 363 So. 2d 578, 579-80 (Fla. Dist. Ct. App. 1978). A question of law exists as to whether sufficient competent evidence is present to require that the agency question be forwarded to a jury. *In re Cliquot's Champagne*, 70 U.S. 114, 140, 18 L. Ed. 116 (1865); 3 Am. Jur. 2d *Agency* § 362 (1986).

Determining whether an issue of fact exists for a jury to decide is similar to determining whether a genuine issue of fact is present to preclude summary judgment. In *Oehler v. Humana, Inc.*, 105 Nev. 348, 351-52, 775 P.2d 1271, 1273 (1989), this court affirmed a summary judgment order that found, as a matter of law, that agency *did not* exist between a hospital and a doctor. The *Oehler* court stated that "[a] hospital is not vicariously liable for acts of physicians who are neither employees nor agents of the hospital." *Id.* at 351, 775 P.2d at 1273. According to the court, evidence that a doctor rented office space in a building that was controlled by a hospital, and that the hospital may have subsidized rents in the building, was not sufficient to raise a question of fact that the doctor was an agent. *Id.*

Medical malpractice cases also serve as a guide for establishing the presence of agency between a doctor and hospital and evoking vicarious liability. Those cases have found that absent an employment relationship, a doctor's mere affiliation with a hospital is not sufficient to hold a hospital vicariously liable for the doctor's negligent conduct. *Hill v. St. Clare's Hosp.*, 67 N.Y.2d 72, 499 N.Y.S.2d 904, 490 N.E.2d 823, 827 (1986); *Ruane v. Niagara Falls Memorial Medical Center*, 60 N.Y.2d 908, 470 N.Y.S.2d 576, 458 N.E.2d 1253 (1983). A physician or surgeon who is on a hospital's staff is not necessarily an employee of the hospital, and the hospital is not necessarily liable for his tortious acts. *Evans v. Bernhard*, 23 Ariz. App. 413, 417, 533 P.2d 721, 725 (1975). A hospital does not generally expose itself to vicarious liability for a doctor's actions by merely extending staff privileges to that doctor. *Moon v. Mercy Hospital*, 150 Colo. 430, 373 P.2d 944, 946 (Colo. 1962); *Hundt v. Proctor Community Hospital*, 5 Ill. App. 3d 987, 284 N.E.2d 676, 678 (1972).

Further, evidence that a doctor maintains a private practice may tend to dispel any claim of an agency relationship between a doctor and a hospital. *Hundt*, 284 N.E.2d at 678.

The evidence admitted in this case on the issue of agency was limited. Desmarais testified that he was not an employee of Charter but had staff privileges. Desmarais

---

The law holds an employer responsible for the acts of his employees while acting in the course of their employment. The law also holds a principal liable for the acts of its agent. Therefore, defendant Charter Hospital is legally responsible for the acts and omissions of all its employees and the acts or omissions of defendant Dr. Desmarais.

also testified that he was covering for another doctor the night Schlotfeldt was admitted to Charter. Charter's administrator stated that Desmarais only had staff privileges at Charter and was covering for another Charter doctor during the period in question. Also, evidence indicated that Desmarais may have maintained an independent practice because he billed Schlotfeldt separately for the services he rendered at Charter. Other than the fact that Desmarais went to Schlotfeldt's room to conduct a medical examination, no evidence was presented to show an employment or agency relationship existed between Charter and Desmarais.

The district court based its determination that Charter and Desmarais were in an agency relationship on the ostensible agency theory. This theory is recognized in medical malpractice cases. *See Stewart v. Midani*, 525 F. Supp. 843 (N.D. Ga. 1981). The ostensible agency theory applies when a patient comes to a hospital and the hospital selects a doctor to serve the patient. The doctor has apparent authority to bind the hospital because a patient may reasonably assume that a doctor selected by the hospital is an agent of the hospital. 869 F.2d at 847-53. However, even in cases involving ostensible agency, questions of fact exist for the jury. In *Stewart*, the court used the ostensible agency theory to justify the denial of summary judgment because issues of fact remained for the jury. *Id.* Typical questions of fact for the jury include (1) whether a patient entrusted herself to the hospital, (2) whether the hospital selected the doctor to serve the patient, (3) whether a patient reasonably believed the doctor was an employee or agent of the hospital, and (4) whether the patient was put on notice that a doctor was an independent contractor. All these questions existed in the present case. Accordingly, the jury should have considered the factual determinations necessary in concluding whether Charter and Desmarais had an agency relationship.

Charter presented evidence suggesting that no employment relationship existed with Desmarais, that Desmarais merely had staff privileges, and that Desmarais operated a private practice. This evidence was sufficiently competent to raise a question of fact for the jury regarding the existence of agency. Further, the district court's use of the ostensible agency theory to find agency as a matter of law was improper because application of the theory required a determination of numerous issues of fact. Accordingly, the jury should have decided the agency issue. Because Charter was materially prejudiced by having its liability linked to the acts of Desmarais, the district court committed reversible error.

CONCLUSION

In considering this case, it is not necessary to resolve the issues raised by Schlotfeldt on appeal. The district court erred by excluding essential evidence and concluding as a matter of law that an agency relationship was present. Accordingly, the district court's judgment against Charter is reversed and this matter is remanded for a new trial.

MILLER v. KEATING

Supreme Court of Louisiana, 1977
349 So. 2d 265

CALOGERO, JUSTICE. SUMMERS, J., dissents.

CALOGERO, J.

The issue in this case is whether the defendant-employer, Kustom Homes, Inc., and its insurer, Hartford Accident and Insurance Indemnity Company, are liable in damages for the tortious acts of Kustom's employees who planned and committed a battery on plaintiff Thomas J. Miller, a former officer and employee of the corporation.

Miller and Dutriel Michael Keating had been organizers, principal stockholders and executive officers in a small Louisiana corporation engaged in the construction of steel frame homes, Kustom Homes, Inc. Johnny Lee Howren and James Guillet were carpenters employed by the corporation. Hartford Accident and Indemnity Insurance Company was the liability insurer of Kustom Homes, Inc., having issued a comprehensive general liability insurance policy, which included general liability and automobile liability provisions.

After a disagreement between Miller and Keating, Miller left the employ of Kustom Homes, Inc., resigning his position as vice president and construction superintendent. About three months later, on Monday April 13, 1973 at about ten o'clock in the evening, he was brutally beaten with a pipe as he returned to his trailer home in Lafayette, Louisiana.

Miller sued the corporation, its insurer, and the three corporation employees, Keating, Howren and Guillet, alleging that the employees in the course and scope of their employment for Kustom Homes, Inc. had conspired and together perpetrated the battery upon him in an effort to kill him and thereby generate certain insurance proceeds for the benefit of the corporation. The case was tried before a civil jury which awarded plaintiff damages in the sum of $25,500.00 jointly and solidarily against Keating, Howren, Guillet and Kustom Homes. The jury absolved the insurer Hartford. Judgment was rendered and signed by the trial judge in accordance with that verdict.

Keating and Howren did not appeal; plaintiff Miller appealed contending that his claim against Hartford should not have been dismissed and contending that the damage award was inadequate. Guillet and Kustom Homes, Inc. appealed complaining that judgments should not have been entered against them.

The Court of Appeal rejected Miller's contentions, affirming both the quantum award and dismissal of the claim against Hartford. That Court rejected Guillet's contention and allowed him to remain cast in judgment. Additionally, the Court of Appeal reversed the judgment as to Kustom Homes, finding no liability on the part of the corporation.

Only plaintiff Miller applied to us for review of that judgment. He argues that the assault and battery was committed by Keating, Howren and Guillet within the course and scope of their employment with Kustom Homes; that Kustom Homes was liable for the actions of all three named individual defendants; and that the corporation's insurer should be jointly and solidarily liable, on the basis of its automobile or general liability policy, with the corporation. We granted writs. 341 So. 2d 901 (La. 1977).

. . . .

In order to analyze whether the conduct of the individual defendants fell within the course and scope of their employment with Kustom Homes we find it necessary to relate certain of the pertinent facts. Of the five stockholders in Kustom Homes, Inc. two of them, Keating and Miller, owned a majority of the stock; Keating was president of the corporation and Miller vice-president. At the time of the incident Kustom Homes had loans outstanding in an amount somewhere between $125,000.00 and $130,000.00. President Keating was the corporate executive charged with raising and borrowing money.

Before Miller's resignation from the company there was an outstanding life insurance policy in the sum of $25,000.00 on which the joint beneficiaries were Miller's father and Kustom Homes. Shortly after Miller left the company and just a month or two before the attack upon him, Kustom Homes took out $75,000.00 worth of additional insurance on Miller's life with the corporation as beneficiary; thus the corporation stood to receive $87,500.00 in insurance proceeds in the event of Miller's death. Keating told Howren in the presence of Guillet (he says jokingly) that he wanted to have Miller done away with because of Keating's belief that Miller had stolen money from the company and also because of the existence of certain insurance on the life of Miller. Keating also acknowledged that he was upset at Miller's decision to leave the corporation.

It was established that Howren and Guillet were salaried employees of Kustom Homes and that Keating was their boss. Howren testified that throughout the incident he was following his boss's orders. On the night in question Howren and Guillet were at the company office working, preparing furniture to be moved from the office, just before they left for a pre-arranged meeting with Keating and perpetration of the attack upon Miller; the battery took place at about 10 p.m. A week earlier under similar circumstances they had failed to accomplish their objective because Miller had returned home before Howren and Guillet had arrived. Even prior to that unsuccessful attempt, Howren and Guillet had traveled to Houma, Louisiana and around the Lafayette area to find out, if they could, where Miller was then residing. On the night in question Guillet and Howren were traveling in a company vehicle and Keating in a second company vehicle; the vehicles were equipped with communication radios and the radios were used to coordinate activities of the three, particularly to allow Keating to advise Howren and Guillet when Miller left for home from the residence of his new employer.

The Court of Appeal found that the acts committed by Keating, Howren and Guillet were not committed during the course and scope of their employment or in the exercise of the functions in which they were employed. The Court of Appeal relied upon its interpretation of *LeBrane v. Lewis*, 292 So. 2d 216 (La. 1974), a case wherein a supervisor kitchen steward for the Capitol House Hotel in Baton Rouge,

Louisiana stabbed a subordinate employee in an altercation following the steward's firing the employee and while escorting him off the premises. The Court of Appeal noted that in *LeBrane* we considered four factors, "(1) whether the tortious act was primarily employment-rooted; (2) whether the violence was reasonably incidental to the performance of the employee's duties; (3) whether the act occurred on the employer's premises; and (4) whether it occurred during the hours of employment." 339 So. 2d at 44.

Then they applied those tests to the facts in the instant suit, and concluded that the acts committed by Keating, Howren and Guillet were not committed during the course and scope of their employment or in the exercise of the functions in which they were employed for Kustom Homes. This conclusion, we believe, was erroneous.

We did not mean to suggest in *LeBrane* that in all cases of an employer's vicarious liability for the intentional torts of his employee that these four inclusive factors must be met before liability may be found. In that case which involved the conduct of a kitchen steward, a relatively lower echelon employee of the employer hotel, we stated our reasons for finding liability in this way:

> "The dispute which erupted into violence was primarily employment-rooted. The fight was reasonably incidental to the performance of the supervisor's duties in connection with firing the recalcitrant employee and causing him to leave the place of employment. It occurred on the employment premises and during the hours of employment.

> In short, the tortious conduct of the supervisor was so closely connected in time, place, and causation to his employment-duties as to be regarded a risk of harm fairly attributable to the employer's business, as compared with conduct motivated by purely personal considerations entirely extraneous to the employer's interests. It can thus be regarded as within the scope of the supervisor's employment, so that his employer is liable in tort to third persons injured thereby." 292 So. 2d at 218.

It was our general evaluation of the circumstances of the tort in *LeBrane* as being one which evolved out of a dispute relating to the employment, one which was reasonably incident to the steward's duties as a hotel employee, and one which was closely connected to those duties, (rather than a purely personal matter) which prompted us to regard the incident as one where the risk of harm was fairly attributable to the employer's business.

Each question of an employer's response in damages for the intentional torts of his employee must be looked at on its own merits to determine whether the conduct is to be regarded as within the scope of the employee's employment. While considerations such as whether the tort occurred on employer premises and during working hours are relevant when assessing the conduct of a relatively subordinate employee such as the kitchen steward in *LeBrane*, they are largely irrelevant in assessing conduct of a corporation's chief executive officer, the president of the corporation such as defendant Keating. In the latter case the conduct must be shown to be employment rooted but not necessarily exclusively so. And it should be reasonably incidental to the performance of his official duties. Beyond these considerations there are no magical requirements. The mission and authority which a legal entity such as a corporation must be presumed to have given its chief executive officer and top human functionary is certainly much broader than that which an employer generally is likely to give or have given lower echelon employees.

In the case at hand, Keating's conspiracy to kill Miller was related to Miller's former employment with the corporation and Miller's presumed non-loyal departure, and it was in large part, although perhaps not exclusively, actuated by Keating's desire to improve the corporation's financial picture, an area of the corporation's concern which had almost exclusively been assigned to Keating, its president, from the inception of the company. Certainly the risk of harm faced by plaintiff Miller was fairly attributable to Keating's employment by Kustom Homes.

Keating's conduct, we conclude, was within the scope of his employment. His employer Kustom Homes, Inc. is thus answerable in damages for the injuries sustained by Miller. La. C.C. art. 2320; *LeBrane v. Lewis, supra; Blanchard v. Ogima*, 253 La. 34, 215 So. 2d 902 (1968).

Because we have found Kustom Homes, Inc. vicariously liable for the tort of its president Keating, we find it unnecessary to consider the question of whether the torts of Howren and Guillet were likewise committed in the course and scope of their employment with Kustom Homes, Inc.

We turn now to the matter of the liability of Hartford Accident and Indemnity Insurance Company. Hartford had issued to Kustom Homes, Inc. a comprehensive general liability insurance policy which included comprehensive general liability and comprehensive automobile liability insurance coverage. The provisions with respect to comprehensive general liability provide that the company will pay on behalf of the insured "all sums which the insured shall become legally obligated to pay as damages" because of bodily injury caused by an occurrence. Inasmuch as we have found that Kustom Homes, Inc. is legally obligated to pay damages to the plaintiff, the insurer Hartford is thus liable in damages under the general liability insurance provisions of that policy. The contrary determination by the jury is unsupported by law.

Because of our finding Hartford Accident and Indemnity Insurance Company liable under the general liability provisions of the insurance policy, we find it unnecessary to consider plaintiff's contention that operation of the company's pick-up trucks by Guillet and Howren and/or Keating on the night of the battery caused the insurance company to be responsible for plaintiff's damage under the automobile liability provisions of that policy.

For the foregoing reasons the judgment of the district court is reinstated except that plaintiff shall have judgment jointly and solidarily against Hartford Accident and Indemnity Insurance Company as well as the other defendants cast in the district court judgment. Costs are to be borne by the defendants.

AMENDED AND AFFIRMED.

SUMMERS, J., dissents for reasons assigned by court of appeal, La. App., 339 So. 2d 40.

Chapter 23

CIVIL RIGHTS TORTS

This chapter deals with the sensitive area of governmental liability for employee actions that are both torts and also violations of civil rights. Individual government employees can often claim qualified immunity, and respondeat superior does not apply in suits alleging civil rights violations. Thus, in order to obtain compensation from government entities, the plaintiff must show that the conduct at issue reached beyond the particular employee/tortfeasor to the governmental entity itself, a showing that is difficult to make as courts are wary of holding governmental bodies liable. Few cases are successful. Those that do succeed typically are characterized by horrendous facts recited by the courts in great detail in order to demonstrate the reprehensibility of the government's conduct and the concomitant clear justice of a ruling in the plaintiff's favor.

BACKGROUND

Originally enacted as part of the Civil Rights Act of 1871 and one of the major pieces of Reconstruction legislation enacted after the Civil War, 42 U.S.C. § 1983 provides:

> Every person who, under color of any statute, ordinance, regulation, custom, or usage, of any State or Territory or the District of Columbia, subjects, or causes to be subjected, any citizen of the United States or other person within the jurisdiction thereof to the deprivation of any rights, privileges, or immunities secured by the Constitution and laws, shall be liable to the party injured in an action at law, suit in equity, or other proper proceeding for redress. . . .

Together with other federal Reconstruction statutes (notably 42 U.S.C. §§ 1981, 1985) this provision enables individuals to bring suits in federal (as well as state) courts seeking damages for violation of constitutional and other federal civil rights. Although formally statutory in character, such lawsuits are often referred to as seeking redress for "constitutional torts." Section 1983 and its counterparts were largely dormant in the law from the late 1870s through the 1950s. But in the landmark case of *Monroe v. Pape*, 365 U.S. 167 (1961), which involved a suit against Chicago police officers and the City of Chicago for grotesque violations of innocent individuals' Fourth Amendment rights, the U.S. Supreme Court revived Section 1983, in part by ruling that government officials may be sued in federal court for violating constitutional rights "under color of law" independently of whether they might also be sued for state-law torts. *Monroe*, however, also held that local government entities were immune from suit, ruling that they could not be held vicariously liable under § 1983 for constitutional violations committed by individual government officials.

In *Monell v. Department of Social Services*, 436 U.S. 658 (1978), the Court overruled *Monroe's* holding that local governments are wholly immune from § 1983 liability. The *Monell* Court agreed that vicarious government liability was forbidden, but it held that municipal government entities[1] may be directly liable to injured victims where government policies or customs cause the deprivation of individuals' federal rights. The Court's decision in *Monell* has been a prolific source of federal litigation over such questions as what constitutes a government policy or custom, what constitutes a deprivation of federal rights, whether and when punitive damages may be awarded, what standards of care apply, what proof of causation is required, and so forth. There has also been substantial litigation over the circumstances in which individual government officers sued under § 1983 may claim personal immunity. For more information, see Mark Brown & Kit Kinports, Constitutional Litigation Under § 1983 (2d ed. 2008); Harold Lewis, Jr. & Elizabeth J. Norman, Civil Rights Law and Practice (2d ed. 2004).

One important issue in the wake of *Monroe* and *Monell* has been the level of culpability, or state of mind, required to make out a violation of § 1983. Often, in cases involving alleged constitutional violations, the required state of mind is a matter of constitutional interpretation. Many decisions require a high level of official culpability. In *Daniels v. Williams*, 474 U.S. 327 (1986), for example, the Court held that negligence of prison officials that led to a prison inmate's serious injury was not sufficient to establish a violation of Due Process. *County of Sacramento v. Lewis*, 523 U.S. 833 (1998), held that governmental liability for injuries resulting from a high-speed police chase requires a showing of "a purpose to cause harm unrelated to the legitimate object of arrest" that amounts to "arbitrary conduct shocking to the conscience." *DeShaney v. Winnebago County Dept. of Social Services*, 489 U.S. 189 (1989), held that a government social services department had no duty to protect a child in its care from his abusive father. And *Town of Castle Rock v. Gonzales*, 545 U.S. 748 (2005), held that there is no liability for government failure to enforce a court restraining order against an abusive husband. With respect to municipal liability, the Court held in *City of Canton v. Harris*, 489 U.S. 378 (1989), that municipal liability based on an official policy or custom at a minimum requires a showing of "deliberate indifference" to the rights of the victim. Deliberate indifference is a unique federal standard of care that has been applied in a variety of federal constitutional and statutory settings. Its precise contours are uncertain and can vary from setting to setting, but in general it lies somewhere between negligence and intent. *See Farmer v. Brennan*, 511 U.S. 825 (1994) (attempting to define deliberate indifference for purposes of Eighth Amendment cases involving claims of inadequate prison conditions).

---

[1] Damage suits against state government entities may not be brought under § 1983, in part because of federal constitutional principles of state sovereign immunity related to the Eleventh Amendment. *See Edelman v. Jordan*, 415 U.S. 651 (1974).

GRIFFIN v. CITY OF OPA-LOCKA
United States Court of Appeals for the Eleventh Circuit, 2001
261 F.3d 1295, *cert. denied*, 535 U.S. 1034 (2002)

FAY, CIRCUIT JUDGE:

I. Introduction

This is an appeal from a $2 million jury verdict and award in favor of Plaintiff A. Griffin ("Griffin") against the City of Opa-Locka ("the City") and its former City Manager, Earnie Neal ("Neal"), stemming from Neal's sexual harassment and assault against Griffin. Both the City and Neal appeal. Neal argues that the district court erred in denying his motion to bifurcate the trial against him and the City; that the district court committed reversible error in permitting expert testimony to bolster Griffin's allegations that she was raped; and that the district court abused its discretion in denying Neal's motion for a new trial due to emotional outbursts by Griffin and another witness in the presence of the jury. The City argues that the district court erred in denying the City's Renewed Motion for Judgment as a Matter of Law, Motion for New Trial, and its Motion for Remittitur.

We review the district court's rulings on the admissibility of evidence, mistrial, bifurcation, and requests for new trial for abuse of discretion. *Alexander v. Fulton County, Georgia*, 207 F.3d 1303, 1324-25 (11th Cir. 2000); *Hicks v. Talbott Recovery System, Inc.*, 196 F.3d 1226, 1242 (11th Cir. 1999); *Messer v. Kemp*, 760 F.2d 1080, 1087 (11th Cir. 1985), *cert. denied*, 474 U.S. 1088, 106 S. Ct. 864, 88 L. Ed. 2d 902 (1986). A trial court's denial of a motion to remit is reviewed for clear abuse of discretion. *Farley v. Nationwide Mutual Ins. Co.*, 197 F.3d 1322, 1335 (11th Cir. 1999). We review the district court's denial of the motion for judgment as a matter of law *de novo*, considering the evidence in the light most favorable to Griffin. If a reasonable jury could have found in favor of Griffin, we will affirm the trial court's decision. *Hicks*, 196 F.3d at 1236. For the reasons set forth more fully below, we affirm the district court's final judgment in favor of Griffin as against Defendant Neal on all claims. We reverse the district court's judgment against the City only as to the City's liability for the sexual assault against Griffin under § 1983. We affirm in all other respects.

II. Factual and Procedural History

Griffin is a 32-year old single mother who, prior to the birth of her son, attempted to pursue a musical career. In 1992, she commenced employment with the City as a temporary employee and eventually became a permanent billing clerk in the City's water department in 1993. The City, located in northwest Miami-Dade County is a small municipality with fewer than 200 employees. In June 1995, the City hired Earnie Neal as City Manager. As City Manager, Neal was the Chief Executive Officer for the City, in charge of its day-to-day operations and personnel decisions.

Almost immediately after Neal started his job with the City, he began harassing Griffin. He summoned her to work with him on the first day by demanding that the "big tit" or "big breasted" girl be sent to his office. Immediately, he began asking her a series of personal questions regarding where she lived, who she lived with, who cared for her child, whether she was married, whether she had a boyfriend, and where was her child's father. The next day, Neal telephoned Griffin and asked her to guess what the "P" in his name stood for. Griffin testified that Neal was referring to his penis and that he would not get off of the phone until she guessed. Neal told her that he was looking for a girlfriend and wondered whether she could help him with that. He also told her that he did not like where she was sitting and wanted her to sit in front of him so that he could see her.

According to Griffin, despite her rejecting all of his advances, Neal continually demanded hugs and questioned her whether she had a man, reiterating that he was still looking for a girlfriend. He also told her that she needed a "man like Neal with money." Griffin stated that on one occasion, Neal asked her in front of the Vice Mayor whether she was going to a specific function that night. When she replied that she was, Neal stated, "Good, so we can dance close together," at which point Neal and the Vice Mayor started laughing, and Neal sent Griffin back to her desk. Neal also repeatedly asked her to go out with him. Griffin recalled an occasion when Neal commented that he and Winston Mottley, one of her supervisors, were going to come over and wanted her to cook dinner for them. Both Mottley and Neal laughed at this comment.

On multiple occasions, Neal called Griffin into his office and told her he would have to replace her if she did not cook for him, tell him how good he looked, and take care of him. In addition, he commented on how she should wear her hair and that she was gaining too much weight. Griffin started dieting for fear she would lose her job. Neal also began regularly hugging her tightly to feel her breasts and look down her shirt. In addition to the daily hugs, Griffin testified that while she was sitting with a couple of officials at a City function, Neal sat behind her and rubbed his knee against her buttocks and whispered in her ear that "I'm still looking for a girlfriend." At another function, Neal put his hand on her hip and told her that she had hurt his feelings again because she would not sing at an event congratulating him for being City Manager.

Griffin also recalled Neal calling her at home on a day that the City offices were officially closed. He asked her whether she was sleeping next to her boyfriend and summoned her to the office for no apparent reason. Although Griffin was eventually supposed to go back and work for the water department, Neal would summon her every day to his office even though he gave her no work. When she asked Neal to return to her old job, he told her that he was hurt and that he could not believe she wanted to leave him. Griffin testified that she asked various other City officials to help her get her old job back because she was unhappy working for the City Manager. Several employees testified that she looked miserable during the time she worked in Neal's office in stark contrast to the cheerful and friendly demeanor she had before she started working for Neal.

In October 1995, after City employees were given a cost of living increase, Neal told Griffin that he personally had seen to it that she got a larger increase than other employees. He said, "You got a bigger raise than anybody, now will you go to dinner with me?" Griffin testified that she felt like he was trying to buy her to make her go out with him and that she had no choice but to start looking for another job. Shortly thereafter, Griffin tendered her resignation to be effective two weeks later because she could no longer tolerate Neal's sexual advances or her working environment. Griffin testified that Neal was shocked by her resignation and tried to talk her out of it. He also told her he would have to figure a way to take her out before she left. Griffin testified that she did not report Neal's conduct or complain to anyone because he was her boss, she did not have the courage to do so, and she did not want to create conflict.

After she tendered her resignation but before her job with the City ended, Griffin attended a Rotary Club function where she was scheduled to sing. The Rotary Club was very important in the workplace culture of the City and was attended by the Mayor, Commissioners, Neal, and several City department heads. Although Griffin arranged for a ride home with the City's police chief following the event, Neal told her and the police chief that he would take her home instead. Upon arriving at her apartment, Neal grabbed Griffin's music equipment and began carrying it upstairs, despite her telling him that she could take care of it herself. He followed her into her apartment uninvited and asked her to get him a drink. While she was getting him water or juice, Neal came up behind her in the kitchen and raped her.

Griffin testified that after the rape, she feared for her life and that she felt that calling the police might make it worse since Neal had previously served as a police chief in the nearby town of Florida City, Florida. She did not believe that anyone would take her side, and she tried to go on as if the rape had not occurred. She went to work the next day and every day until the end of her employment a few days later. Several months later, Griffin decided to come forward about the rape. She contacted an attorney and this lawsuit ensued.

Griffin sought damages against the City for sexual harassment and sexual assault under Title VII (Count I); the Florida Civil Rights Act (Count II); 42 U.S.C. § 1983 (Counts III and IX); and state tort law (Count VIII). She also alleged assault and battery claims against Neal (Count IV); violations of the Violence Against Women Act, 42 U.S.C. § 13981 (Count V); Intentional Infliction of Emotional Distress (Count VI); and Invasion of Privacy (Count VII). After a two-week trial, the jury concluded by special interrogatory that Neal sexually harassed Griffin, that the harassment was a custom or policy of the City, and that Neal raped her under color of law. The jury also concluded that the City was deliberately indifferent in hiring Neal and found against Neal on the tort claims. The jury awarded Griffin $500,000 for the harassment and $1.5 million for the rape.

III. Discussion

A. Neal's Appeal

. . . .

B. The City's Appeal

In its judgment against the City, the jury found that Neal sexually harassed Griffin, that the harassment was a custom or policy of the City, that Neal raped her under color of law, and that the City was deliberately indifferent in hiring Neal. The City claims several errors on appeal. First, the City argues that the judgment in favor of Griffin must be reversed because as a matter of law the City cannot be liable for any sexual assault committed by Neal; the City cannot be liable for sexual harassment; and the City was not deliberately indifferent in hiring Neal. Second, the City argues that it is entitled to a new trial because the district court abused its discretion in allowing testimony by certain witnesses and permitting evidence of prior bad acts for the purpose of showing bad character or propensity. Finally, in the alternative, the City argues that it is entitled to a remittitur in the amount of damages or a new trial on damages. We address each argument in turn.

1. City's Argument it is Entitled to Judgment as Matter of Law

a. Liability for Sexual Assault

i. Color of State Law

In order to prevail on a civil rights action under § 1983, a plaintiff must show that he or she was deprived of a federal right by a person acting under color of state law. *Almand v. DeKalb County, Georgia*, 103 F.3d 1510, 1513 (11th Cir.), *cert. denied*, 522 U.S. 966, 118 S. Ct. 411, 139 L. Ed. 2d 314 (1997). A person acts under color of state law when he acts with authority possessed by virtue of his employment with the state. *Id.* "The dispositive issue is whether the official was acting pursuant to the power he/she possessed by state authority or acting only as a private individual." *Edwards v. Wallace Community College*, 49 F.3d 1517, 1523 (11th Cir. 1995). It is firmly established that a defendant in a § 1983 suit acts under color of law when he abuses the position given to him by the State. *United States v. Classic*, 313 U.S. 299, 326, 61 S. Ct. 1031, 1043, 85 L. Ed. 1368 (1941).

The City maintains that as a matter of law, it cannot be liable for any sexual assault committed by Neal against Griffin because Neal was not acting under color of state law at the time of the assault. This Court has previously recognized that under certain circumstances, a rape of a person by a state actor or official could violate the Constitution and serve as the basis for a suit under § 1983. Whether a government employee is acting under color of law is not always an easy call, and the color of law analysis inevitably requires that we engage in line drawing.

Based on the totality of facts and circumstances of this case and construing all of the evidence in a light most favorable to Griffin, we believe that there is evidence from which a reasonable jury could conclude that Neal's actions in harassing and ultimately raping Griffin occurred while he was acting under color of law. The rape occurred following a Rotary Club meeting attended by Neal, Griffin, the Mayor, City Commissioners, and the City Department heads. That the Rotary Club meeting was not technically an official City function does not trouble us insofar as the color of law analysis goes. There was testimony by Griffin and others that City employees were expected to attend Rotary Club meetings. In fact, Neal testified that after he failed to attend one Rotary Club meeting, the Mayor made him "sternly aware" of the Club's significance, and he never again missed a meeting. Moreover, there was testimony that Griffin was at the event as a City employee. Neal himself testified that he attended the function as City Manager, that he was there "preserving his job" and "taking care of business," and that he stayed close to the Mayor or Commissioners in case they needed anything. Neal specifically asked Griffin and other City employees to attend the meetings, the Mayor of the City was the founder of the Rotary Club chapter, and the City paid for employees, including Griffin, to join. In short, participation in the Rotary Club was a command performance for City employees.

After learning that Griffin had arranged for the City's police chief to take her home following the Rotary event due to car troubles, the evidence supports the conclusion that Neal intervened and invoked his authority as City Manager to create the opportunity to be alone with Griffin, to take her home, and then to rape her. In front of various City officials, including the Mayor, several Commissioners, and the Assistant City Manager, Neal told Griffin that he would take her home and that she should advise the police chief that he, the City Manager, would take her.[5] In addition, Neal himself also instructed the police chief that he would take her home and that the situation was all taken care of.[6]

On the way to Griffin's home, Neal used his authority to permit Griffin to park her car inside the City's police department and told her that he would have the City fix it. During the ride from the police station to her apartment, Neal and Griffin discussed her work for the City, and Neal tried to dissuade her from leaving her job. Upon their arrival at her apartment and after insisting on helping her with her equipment, Neal came up behind Griffin while she was in the kitchen and said, "Angie, you know that I have been waiting a long time for this." When she refused his sexual advances, Neal, as he had done numerous times throughout the course of his harassment of her, reminded her of his authority by saying "I can't believe you are telling me no after everything that I have done for you." Neal then proceeded to rape her.

It appears that Neal continued to invoke his authority over Griffin to harass her and humiliate her even after the sexual assault. When Griffin reported to work the day after Neal assaulted her, Neal summoned her to his office, where he asked her for a hug and told other workers about the great time he had the previous night and that "I want to do it again like I did last night, I want to do it all over again." Neal also used his authority to have the City repair Griffin's car. After the rape, he instructed a City employee to repair the car and told him not to ask any questions

---

[5] Griffin testified that she did not protest or refuse because Neal was still her boss and she did not want to make a scene or be negative in front of all of the City officials because she needed to get good references from them.

[6] Neal also told another Rotary Club member who offered Griffin help that he should not be concerned and that everything was "taken care of and "arrangements had been made." The Rotarian testified that Griffin looked upset.

or answer any questions about the car repair.[7]

Although we are persuaded that the foregoing facts demonstrate that Neal utilized his authority as City Manager to facilitate the assault on Griffin and that he was therefore acting under color of law at the time of the assault, we do not believe that under the facts of this case that we are required to view the sexual assault in isolation or ignore Neal's persistent abuse of authority leading up to the assault in making our color of law determination. Rather, we believe that the entire pattern of abuse and harassment against Griffin that eventually culminated in her rape is relevant to our color of law analysis. In other words, Neal's official interactions with Griffin as her boss during and after work hours, his continual sexual harassment of her during those interactions, and the ultimate sexual assault constitute an indivisible, ongoing series of events.

The pattern of Neal's abuse of his authority began the first day of his employment with the City and did not end until after he sexually assaulted Griffin and she left her job at the City for good. From day one, he utilized his authority as City Manager to harass and intimidate her by repeatedly insisting she owed him something for "all of the things" that he did for her, including giving her a pay raise for which she was apparently not entitled, threatening her with her job if she did not do certain things for him like cook, lose weight, and tell him how good he looked, demanding that she work in his office (although he apparently gave her no work), touching her inappropriately, continually requesting hugs, dates, and favors despite her refusal to go out with him, and asking her intimate questions. It is within this context of Neal's continual exploitation of and leverage of his authority over Griffin that we find a sufficient nexus between his duties and obligations as City Manager and Griffin's boss and the abuse of that authority to facilitate his harassment and ultimate sexual assault of her.

Although we are unaware of any cases directly on point, we believe our conclusion that Neal was acting under color of law is supported by several cases where state employees were held to be acting under color of law when they utilized their authority to create the opportunity for or to facilitate a sexual assault. . . .

ii. Policy or Custom

The City next argues that even if Neal's assault upon Griffin was taken under color of state law, it cannot be liable because Neal's actions were not taken pursuant to a municipal custom or policy. The law is clear that a municipality cannot be held liable for the actions of its employees under § 1983 based on a theory of respondeat superior. *Monell v. Dept. of Social Services of the City of New York*, 436 U.S. 658, 663, 98 S. Ct. 2018, 2022, 56 L. Ed. 2d 611 (1978). Rather, only deprivations undertaken pursuant to governmental "custom" or "policy" may lead to the imposition of governmental liability. *Floyd v. Waiters*, 133 F.3d 786, 793 (11th Cir. 1998).

Clearly, the City did not have a formal policy condoning or endorsing sexual

---

[7] Upon learning that the car was Griffin's, the water department supervisor allegedly told another City employee that "Neal must have gotten to her. We have Angie's car in the back."

harassment or sexual assault by City employees. Nevertheless, § 1983 liability may be imposed on a municipality based on "governmental 'custom' even though such a custom has not received formal approval through the body's official decisionmaking channels." *Id.* at 795. This Court set out the standard for imposing such liability in *Brown*, stating that:

> to prove § 1983 liability against a municipality based on custom, a plaintiff must establish a widespread practice that, "although not authorized by written law or express municipal policy, is so permanent and well settled as to constitute a 'custom or usage' with the force of law."

Brown v. City of Ft. Lauderdale, 923 F.2d 1474, 1481 (citations omitted). In addition, we have also held that a municipality's failure to correct the constitutionally offensive actions of its employees can rise to the level of a custom or policy "if the municipality tacitly authorizes these actions or displays deliberate indifference" towards the misconduct. *Brooks v. Scheib*, 813 F.2d 1191, 1193 (11th Cir. 1987).

After reviewing the record in full and taking all inferences in favor of Griffin, the evidence establishes without any question that sexual harassment was the on-going, accepted practice at the City and that the City Commission, Mayor, and other high ranking City officials knew of, ignored, and tolerated the harassment. As such, we are persuaded that the jury's conclusion that sexual harassment was so persistent and widespread as to amount to a unconstitutional policy or custom is amply supported by the evidence.

The workplace was permeated with vulgar, demeaning, and sexually suggestive conversations about women, improper demands for sexual favors and dates, unwelcome sexual advances, as well as unfair treatment for those women unwilling to reciprocate such conduct and who were not considered "team players." *Bohen v. City of East Chicago, Indiana*, 799 F.2d 1180, 1187-89 (7th Cir. 1986) (finding policy or custom of sexual harassment at municipal fire department where female employees subjected to unwelcome touching, conversations at the workplace were filled with "lurid sexual descriptions," the department had no sexual harassment policy, management personnel "knew the general picture if not the details" of the pattern of sexual harassment, and complaints were addressed superficially or not at all). We detail much of the testimony presented to the jury to make clear the egregious and commonplace nature of the harassment at the City, as well as to demonstrate that the final policymakers, including the City Commissioners and the Mayor were aware of the problem and were completely indifferent to it.

At trial, several witnesses testified about repeated instances during which Neal and other male employees engaged in vulgar, sexually suggestive, and demeaning conversations describing their sexual escapades and desires. Neal was often overheard discussing his sex life in front of various department heads and other City employees, including women, detailing how great he was in bed and how many times he had sex the night before. In addition, Neal and other male employees would frequently compare female staff members' breasts, legs, and bodies and describe what they would do to the women sexually if they had them.[13] For example, Neal would say "If I had [Jane Doe], I could really rock her world." On one

---

[13] According to Mayor Ingram, this is just how men talk among themselves.

occasion, Neal told the City Attorney that he wanted to see a female employee from the finance department naked. On another occasion during a business meeting at a local hotel with several City employees and representatives from a firm looking to do business with the City, Neal told everyone how he had sex in all of the rooms with mirrors at the hotel. Following a City Commission meeting, Neal talked about going out "poking all night," and high-fived the male assistant city manager who was present. On another occasion, Neal described to a female employee an incident in which he had sex in the back of a patrol car.

The City Attorney, Griffin, and numerous other female employees also testified that Neal frequently asked them for dates or dinner despite their rejections. In addition, he asked them to cook for him, told them that they owed him something, and questioned them about their sex lives. On at least two occasions, a group of female City employees complained to the City Attorney that they were having problems with Neal making inappropriate sexual comments to them, touching them, asking for sexual favors and punishing those who refused, giving people raises when they did not deserve them, and showing favoritism. The City Attorney also received complaints from a City Clerk to the effect that Neal was asking her out, questioning her about who her lover was, and that he was giving her a hard time because she was not reciprocating his advances.

Several employees, including a Commissioner, testified that in reference to Griffin, they knew that Neal had requested that the "big breasted" or "big tit girl" work in his office. Neal asked the City Attorney to go to a nude bar with him and told her that he would like to see her drunk. Natacha Yacinthe, an administrative assistant, testified that Neal asked her details about her sex life, inquired whether she had slept with another City employee, and indicated to her that he wanted her to dress more provocatively. Ana Otero, the acting director of human resources, testified that on one occasion, Neal came up so close behind her while she was standing at a copy machine that she could feel his breath on her neck. Neal told Otero that he liked short, Puerto Rican women like herself, and according to Otero, came up and kissed her once in the elevator though she had done nothing to encourage it. Otero also described an incident where Neal summoned her to his office and asked her for an "intimate kiss."

Griffin, Irby, Ellis, and others testified that Neal made threats regarding their job or salary when they did not reciprocate his advances. Irby testified that Neal told her she'd be removed from her job because she was not "committed to him" and did not ask him out for dinner. Those who did not at least tolerate his advances were not considered team players. One woman who interviewed with Neal for a job at the City testified that Neal commented how nice her legs were, called her at home, asked for dates, talked about kinky sex, gave her a City credit card number and told her to get them a hotel room. She refused his advances and did not get the job.

Moreover, there is no question that the Mayor and City Commissioners knew about Neal's sexual harassment and misconduct. Commissioner Barrett testified that it was commonly known throughout the City that Neal had problems with sexual harassment and dealing with women both before he became City Manager and afterwards. First, at or around the time Neal was being considered for the permanent City Manager position, various faxes, articles, and cartoons addressed to the Mayor and City Commission were circulated throughout the City government warning that Neal had a problem with sexual harassment. Some of the articles apparently pertained to an incident involving sexual harassment at Neal's previous job. Another fax contained a list of sexual harassment charges against Neal. Other faxes included cartoons depicting a man harassing or assaulting a woman with a warning that "You are going to get this if you hire this guy." A City resident also tried to present these articles and faxes raising concerns about Neal's sexual harassment problems at a City Commission meeting where Neal's hiring was discussed. The resident was ignored.

There was also testimony that Neal was known as a womanizer.[14] Commissioner Barrett testified about a tape recording of a City Commission meeting with Mayor Ingram, the City Commissioners, and the City Attorney where the group erupted in laughter as Neal was repeatedly introduced as Earnie P. Neal. Commissioner Barrett explained that everyone laughed at the emphasis placed on Neal's middle initial because he was known as Earnie "Penis" Neal. At least two employees, including the City Attorney, complained to Commissioner Barrett about Neal's sexual harassment. In addition to the complaints to Commissioner Barrett, another female employee testified that she complained about Neal's behavior to two other Commissioners, the City Attorney, and the Mayor. Although Commissioner Barrett testified that he believed the City had a sexual harassment problem, no remedial action was ever taken. Barrett maintained that he never pursued removing Neal because he believed that the other Commissioners and the Mayor endorsed everything Neal did and would not vote to remove him no matter what.

The most egregious example, however, of the City's notice of sexual harassment and its complete indifference to the problem is evidenced by the testimony regarding the Mayor's response to complaints that Neal was sexually harassing several female employees. Patricia Ellis, the City Attorney, testified that she went to see Mayor Ingram specifically to advise him of the various sexual harassment and misconduct complaints she had received from female employees in regard to Neal. After advising the Mayor of the complaints, Ellis testified that the Mayor responded as follows:

> Heck, if I believe the rumors that I hear about Earnie Neal and Timothy Holmes, then they have a heck of a libido, and I want some of what they are taking.[16]

Other than his statement regarding his desire to take some of what Neal and Holmes were taking, the Mayor had no other response to the harassment

---

[14] There was testimony that it was known around the City that Neal had a sexual interest in Griffin. Griffin testified that on a least two occasions, Neal made reference to taking her out in the presence of other City officials. She described one incident where Neal summoned her, and in the presence of the Vice-Mayor, told her that he was glad she was going to a City function that night so that they could dance "close together." She testified that both Neal and the Vice-Mayor laughed at the comment and sent her back to her desk. In addition, when Neal told Griffin that he, not the police chief, would take her home following the Rotary Club function, Neal commented in the presence of several Commissioners and the Mayor that he "could take her out now." The City officials laughed at Neal's remark according to Griffin even though there was testimony that Griffin looked upset.

[16] Timothy Holmes was the City's Vice-Mayor and a member of the City Commission.

complaints and no remedial action was taken. The Mayor's statement is important to our decision today for several reasons. First and foremost, it constitutes the most egregious statement of gross indifference to sexual harassment of which this Court can conceive. For the mayor of a city to express an interest in getting in on the action when confronted with complaints of sexual misconduct by the city's chief executive officer is nothing short of reprehensible.

Second, the Mayor's statement suggests that he was aware of and had prior notice of sexual harassment and/or sexual misconduct involving not only Neal, but the Vice-Mayor as well. The jury was certainly entitled to infer from the Mayor's response that he had prior notice. This inference coupled with the fact that he took absolutely no remedial action and expressed an interest in "taking some of what [Neal and the other Commissioner] are taking" reasonably supports the conclusion that sexual harassment was tolerated and condoned at the City, if not encouraged.

In contending that it had no notice of the harassment, the City makes much of the fact that no prior lawsuits were filed against Neal for sexual harassment. Nevertheless, we do not believe that the absence of prior lawsuits or EEOC complaints is determinative on the issue whether the City is on notice of blatantly unconstitutional conduct by its high-ranking officials. Nor are we overly concerned with the lack of formal complaints within the City government either. The City did not have a sexual harassment policy, nor was there any specific person or entity designated to receive sexual harassment complaints. The lack of a sexual harassment policy or formal mechanism for complaints was particularly problematic in the instant case because Neal, the primary harasser, was the person in charge of personnel and the day-to-day functioning of the City. Neither the Mayor or [sic] Commissioners were at the City full-time, and apparently there was no one at the City on a daily basis superior to Neal. Under these circumstances, it is not surprising that the City received no formal complaints against Neal.

In sum, we believe that the Mayor and City Commissioners were on notice of Neal's unconstitutional behavior and failed to take the first remedial measure or preventative step to correct the known or suspected sexual harassment problem. The City never investigated the allegations of sexual harassment, no records were kept of complaints, and no one in charge ever questioned, disciplined, or even discussed sexual harassment with Neal. There was no sexual harassment training or evidence that the Mayor or Commission ever even considered formulating a sexual harassment policy until after Griffin left her job with the City. We believe it fair to say that the City's tolerance of gross sexual harassment, its failure to take remedial action despite actual and constructive knowledge of the problem and its complete lack of any sexual harassment policy or complaint procedure taken together clearly constitute a "moving force" behind the rampant sexual harassment at the City. As such, we uphold the jury's conclusion that the City had a policy or custom of ignoring or tolerating gross sexual harassment.

The more difficult question is whether when a City has such a policy it can be liable for a rape following this type of harassment. Under the facts of this case, however, we do not believe that we are required to answer this question. Upon review of the district court's instructions to the jury and the jury verdict form itself, it appears that the jury did not make the requisite findings to support § 1983 liability for the rape against the City. Specifically, in response to Question 6 of the verdict form, the jury concluded that the City had a policy or custom of allowing a sexually hostile or abusive work environment. The jury, however, rendered no express finding as to whether the City had a similar custom or policy of ignoring or tolerating rape or sexual assault. Nor did the jury verdict refer to the rape incident as part of the policy or custom of sexual harassment such that § 1983 liability for the rape could be sustained based on the custom of harassment. Because the record does not establish that the jury found that the City had a custom or policy of allowing rape or that the rape incident was part of the custom or pattern of sexual harassment, we cannot reasonably say that the jury found all essential aspects of the § 1983 case against the City.[21] As such, the verdict and judgment against the City for the rape cannot stand.

b. Liability for Sexual Harassment

Next, the City contends that it cannot be liable for sexual harassment because the evidence affirmatively established that the atmosphere in which Griffin worked did not constitute a hostile working environment under Title VII or § 1983. To prevail on a hostile environment claim, a plaintiff must demonstrate that the sexual harassment was sufficiently severe or pervasive to alter the terms and conditions of employment and create a discriminatory abusive working environment. *Gupta v. Florida Board of Regents*, 212 F.3d 571, 582 (11th Cir. 2000), *cert. denied*, 531 U.S. 1076, 121 S. Ct. 772, 148 L. Ed. 2d 671 (2001).

Our discussion in previous sections of the opinion leaves little doubt as to our belief whether Neal's sexual harassment of Griffin was sufficiently severe or pervasive to constitute a hostile working environment. We clearly believe that it was, and the issue merits little discussion.

Construing the evidence in a light most favorable to Griffin, a reasonable jury could conclude that the harassment was severe and pervasive where there was testimony that it was known around the workplace that Neal had a sexual interest in Griffin; Griffin went to work with Neal in the first place because he demanded that the "big tit girl" work in his office; he repeatedly asked her to go on dates with him, cook for him, and to be his girlfriend; he made comments of a sexual nature and insulting remarks about her body, weight, and appearance; constantly requested hugs so that he could feel her breasts and look down her shirt; rubbed his knee against her buttocks and whispered that he was still looking for a girlfriend; and finally, after her repeated rejections of his advances, he raped her.

---

[21] Griffin argues that the City is properly liable for the rape because the rape was the culmination of, and therefore part of, the pattern of gross sexual harassment that existed at the City. By our decision today, we do not preclude the possibility that under some facts, a rape or sexual assault could be part of a pattern or custom of sexual harassment. Rather, we simply cannot say based on the record before us in this case that the jury, in fact, made this finding. It appears to us that the jury was never asked to do so.

c. Deliberate Indifference

Next, we consider whether a reasonable jury could conclude that the City's alleged deliberate indifference in hiring Neal by failing to investigate his background can support liability for sexual harassment under § 1983. In cases where a plaintiff presents a § 1983 claim based on a hiring decision and inadequate screening, the Supreme Court has stated that:

> Only where adequate scrutiny of an applicant's background would lead a reasonable policymaker to conclude that the plainly obvious consequence of the decision to hire the applicant would be the deprivation of a third party's federally protected right can the official's failure to adequately scrutinize the applicant's background constitute "deliberate indifference."

Board of the County Commissioners of Bryan County, Oklahoma v. Brown, 520 U.S. 397, 411, 117 S. Ct. 1382, 1392, 137 L. Ed. 2d 626 (1997).

To impose § 1983 liability based on a hiring decision, a plaintiff must demonstrate that the municipal actor disregarded a known or obvious consequence of hiring the applicant. It is not sufficient under this standard that a municipal actor's inadequate screening of an applicant's record reflects an "indifference" to the applicant's background. *Id.* at 411, 117 S. Ct. at 1392. Rather, a plaintiff must demonstrate that the municipal hiring decision reflects deliberate indifference to the risk that a violation of a particular constitutional or statutory right will follow the decision. *Id.*

Construing all inferences in favor of Griffin, we believe the evidence was sufficient for a finding that the City's inadequate screening of Neal's background was so likely to result in sexual harassment that the City could reasonably be said to have been deliberately indifferent to Griffin's constitutional rights. Neal was hired as City Manager according to some testimony without a resume, interview, background check, or any discussion of his qualifications.[22] As detailed in previous sections of the opinion, at the time when the City was considering hiring Neal, it was inundated with articles, faxes, and mail, warning of Neal's problems with sexual harassment and dealings with women. There was testimony that some of the faxes included a list of prior sexual harassment charges against Neal. Other faxes included explicit warnings that the City was going to have a sexual harassment and/or sexual assault problem if it hired Neal. Both a citizen who attempted to raise these complaints at a City Commission meeting and a City Commissioner who, concerned about the sexual harassment red flags, requested more information on Neal's background, were disregarded. Moreover, there was testimony that Neal was a known womanizer, commonly known to the Mayor and Commissioners as Earnie "Penis" Neal. Most importantly, however, there was testimony suggesting that the City officials were aware that Neal was sexually harassing City employees during the period of time between his appointment as acting City Manager and the time of his final confirmation as permanent City Manager. Despite these red flags indicating that Neal would have problems with sexual harassment, the City hired Neal for a permanent position.

---

[22] Mayor Ingram said that no particular experience was necessary for the job and the only qualifications needed were three votes by the Commission.

Moreover, it appears that a cursory check into Neal's prior employment history would have further alerted the City to prior complaints about Neal with regard to sexual harassment. The City apparently ignored its own policy of telephoning prior employers to conduct a background search and did not obtain Neal's employment files prior to hiring him as permanent City Manager. Neal's file indicated that during his employment with Florida City, there were complaints of sexual harassment against him. Further, the Mayor of Florida City testified that if he had been contacted by anyone at the City, he would have informed them of the sexual harassment complaints against Neal. Because we believe that the evidence supports the conclusion that the City ignored a known or obvious risk that Neal was highly likely to engage in sexual harassment if hired as the City's permanent City Manager, we uphold the jury's conclusion that the City acted with deliberate indifference in hiring Neal. The City is therefore properly liable for sexual harassment committed by Neal.

. . . .

IV. Conclusion

We hope that this is a unique case. It is difficult to believe that mature responsible adults would conduct themselves in this manner. It is even more troubling when the perpetrators of such intolerable activity are municipal officials. Our decision today should serve as a clear message to all that this type of behavior is contrary to our laws and will not be tolerated. For all of the foregoing reasons we affirm the verdict and judgment against Defendant Neal in all respects. We reverse the $1.5 million verdict against the City for Neal's sexual assault of Griffin under § 1983, but affirm the judgment against the City in all other respects.

AFFIRMED in part and REVERSED in part.

ANDERSON, CHIEF JUDGE, concurring specially:

I concur in all of Judge Fay's opinion in this very disturbing case, except to the extent that the opinion addresses the issue of whether Neal was acting under color of state law when he assaulted and raped Griffin. This issue was raised only by the City.[1] Because we hold that the jury did not find the City liable for the rape, there is no need to address the City's challenge relating to whether or not Neal was acting under color of law at that time. The jury found the City liable under § 1983 only for $500,000, and only for acts other than the rape (i.e., the sexual harassment excluding the rape). With respect to that issue, Judge Fay's opinion clearly establishes both that Neal acted under color of law and that he acted pursuant to a policy or custom of the City.

---

[1] The probable explanation for Neal's failure to raise the issue is because Neal was liable for the rape under several theories, including the state law claim of assault and battery.

HERRERA v. VALENTINE
United States Court of Appeals, Eighth Circuit, 1981
653 F.2d 1220

HEANEY, J.

This matter comes before the Court for a second time. We originally remanded the case to the district court to determine the amount that Jo Ann Yellow Bird is entitled to for attorney's fees and expenses. The district court has made its determination. We now reach the merits of the appeal and affirm the judgment of the court below except insofar as it relates to the award of attorneys' fees and expenses.

I

On September 15, 1976, Jo Ann Yellow Bird, an Indian woman visibly in the later months of pregnancy, was kicked in the stomach by Clifford Valentine, a police officer employed by the City of Gordon, Nebraska. Valentine was attempting to arrest Yellow Bird's husband at the time of the incident. As Yellow Bird went to the aid of her husband, Valentine kicked her in the abdomen, throwing her to the ground. After he had kicked her, Valentine handcuffed her and forced her into the back of his patrol car. Yellow Bird's pleas for medical attention were ignored. Instead of driving her a few blocks to the nearest hospital, Valentine drove her nearly twenty miles to the county jail. On the way to the jail, Valentine stopped the car and threatened to take Yellow Bird out into the country and shoot her. She was arrested and jailed; her requests for counsel were also ignored. As a result of the beating and inattention to her medical needs, she suffered physical and emotional injuries; her unborn child died in her womb and was delivered dead two weeks later.

Thereafter, Yellow Bird filed a lawsuit in federal district court alleging violations of her federal civil rights, as well as various state law claims. She named fourteen parties as defendants in the case, including Valentine and the City of Gordon. After a lengthy trial, the jury returned a verdict that found the City of Gordon and Valentine liable for violating Yellow Bird's federal civil rights. The jury awarded the plaintiff $300,000 in compensatory damages. The defendants' post-trial motions challenging the verdict were denied and this appeal followed.

On appeal, the appellants contend that the trial court erred by: (1) improperly submitting to the jury Yellow Bird's state law claims against the appellants; (2) permitting Yellow Bird to amend her complaint to conform to the evidence establishing a claim against the City under 42 U.S.C. § 1983; (3) denying their post-trial motions, which asserted that the verdict imposes liability vicariously upon the City and, alternatively, that there is insufficient evidence to sustain the verdict against the City and Officer Valentine; (4) instructing the jury that it could compensate Yellow Bird for the loss of her constitutional rights independent of any compensation due her for physical and emotional injury; (5) sustaining an excessive verdict; and (6) awarding excessive attorneys' fees and expenses.

. . . .

IV

The City asserts that Yellow Bird's claim against it is based solely upon the doctrine of *respondeat superior.* It is clear that a municipality cannot be held vicariously liable under section 1983 for the acts of its employees. *Monell v. Department of Soc. Serv.*, 436 U.S. 658, 691, 98 S. Ct. 2018, 2036, 56 L. Ed. 2d 611 (1978); *cf Parratt v. Taylor*, 451 U.S. 527, 101 S. Ct. 1908, 68 L. Ed. 2d 420 (1981); *Cotton v. Hutto*, 577 F.2d 453, 455 (8th Cir. 1978); *Sebastian v. United States*, 531 F.2d 900, 904 (8th Cir.), cert. denied, 429 U.S. 856, 97 S. Ct. 153, 50 L. Ed. 2d 133 (1976). Yellow Bird does not, however, assert that the City is liable under the doctrine of *respondeat superior.* Her claim is that the City's failure to properly hire, train, retain, supervise, discipline and control Valentine and the other police officers *directly* caused her tortious injury. See *Owen v. City of Independence*, 445 U.S. 622, 655 n.39, 100 S. Ct. 1398, 1418 n.39, 63 L. Ed. 2d 673 (1980). Under that theory, Yellow Bird was obligated to prove, by a preponderance of the evidence, that the City breached a duty owed to her and that that breach proximately caused the deprivation of her constitutional rights. *See Turpin v. Mailet*, 619 F.2d 196, 201-202 (2d Cir.), *cert. denied*, 449 U.S. 1016, 101 S. Ct. 577, 66 L. Ed. 2d 475 (1980); *McClelland v. Facteau*, 610 F.2d 693, 695-697 (10th Cir. 1979).

In order to prove her case, Yellow Bird had to establish that the City had notice of prior misbehavior and that its failure to act upon such knowledge caused her injury. "[W]here senior personnel have knowledge of a pattern of constitutionally offensive acts by their subordinates but fail to take remedial steps, the municipality may be held liable for a subsequent violation if the superior's inaction amounts to deliberate indifference or to tacit authorization of the offensive acts." *Turpin v. Mailet, supra*, 619 F.2d at 201.[1]

If a municipality fails to train its police force, or if it does so in a grossly negligent manner so that it inevitably results in police misconduct, "the municipality exhibits a 'deliberate indifference' to the resulting violations of a citizen's constitutional rights." *Leite v. City of Providence*, 463 F. Supp. 585, 590 (D.R.I. 1978); *cf. Goodman u. Parwatikar*, 570 F.2d 801, 803 (8th Cir. 1978); *Freeman v. Lockhart*, 503 F.2d 1016, 1017 (8th Cir. 1974). Moreover, a municipality's continuing failure to remedy known unconstitutional conduct of its police officers is the type of informal policy or custom that is amenable to suit under section 1983. *See Monell v. Department of Soc. Serv., supra*, 436 U.S. at 690-691 & n.56, 98 S. Ct. at 2035-2036 & n.56.

A

We are satisfied that Yellow Bird proved her case against the City of Gordon.[2] It is undisputed that racial tension was at a peak before, during and after the

---

[1] The Second Circuit Court of Appeals has noted that "an even stronger case for imposing liability for inaction occurs when the municipality fails to remedy a specific situation, the continuation of which causes a deprivation of constitutional rights." Turpin v. Mailet, 619 F.2d 196, 201 n.5 (2d Cir.), *cert. denied,* 449 U.S. 1016, 101 S. Ct. 577, 66 L. Ed. 2d 475 (1980).

[2] The trial of the case lasted for nearly a month. Almost every factual issue was disputed. At the close of the evidence, and after the jury had been properly instructed, the case was submitted to the jury for its deliberation. The jury returned a plaintiffs verdict. Now the appellants assert, inter alia, that the

incident giving rise to this lawsuit. Well before she was injured by the Gordon police, Yellow Bird, her husband and many other Indians and Caucasians as well, complained to the authorities of continuing police misconduct. Use of excessive force, sexual misconduct, racist conduct and selective enforcement of the laws were among the many infractions cited. The Yellow Birds were essentially spokespersons for the dissident group. Their complaints were a subject of community-wide knowledge.

Dissatisfied with the City's failure to remedy their complaints, Yellow Bird wrote to the Acting Director of the Nebraska Indian Commission, Stephen F. Janis. Because of numerous other complaints regarding the misconduct of the Gordon police, the Commission went to Gordon and convened a hearing in early 1976. At that hearing, attended by both Indians and Caucasians, the Commission received nearly forty separate complaints of police misconduct. These complaints were taken under advisement and later submitted to the Mayor of Gordon.

A few months later, the Commission reconvened in Gordon and heard more complaints. After this meeting, Janis appeared at a City Council meeting and personally handed the Mayor the citizens' complaints. The entire City Council was given a summary of the complaints that had been prepared by an attorney with Panhandle Legal Services. The Yellow Birds also appeared before the City Council and once again made known their various complaints. The meeting, and more particularly the Yellow Birds' participation, was well publicized in the local newspapers. The Commission asked the City to remedy the problem and report back to it. The City neither remedied the problem nor reported back. The matter was apparently turned over to the Sheridan County Attorney's Office, which later reported to the Mayor of Gordon that it was obvious that the City's police force considered themselves "overlords," whose orders were to be obeyed without question. A similar conclusion was reached by Security Services of Lincoln, Nebraska, an outside agency investigating the Gordon Police Department.

The foregoing demonstrates that the City was adequately notified that its five-member police force needed close and continuing supervision. It, however, permitted its over-zealous police force to continue its overlording. The inevitable result was the kind of misconduct that caused Yellow Bird's physical beating, the loss of her unborn child and her medical and emotional problems. The jury was properly and adequately instructed on the City's potential section 1983 liability. There was sufficient evidence to warrant those instructions and to sustain the jury's ultimate decision.

---

evidence is insufficient to sustain the jury's ultimate finding. We have long held, however, that an appellate court is not free to substitute its view of the facts for that of the jury. We consider the evidence in the light most favorable to the plaintiff, Jo Ann Yellow Bird. We assume that all conflicts in the evidence were resolved by the jury in the plaintiffs favor. We assume as proved all facts that Yellow Bird's evidence tends to prove. We give the plaintiff the benefit of all favorable inferences that reasonably may be drawn from the facts proved. Finally, if we determine that reasonable minds could differ as to the conclusions to be drawn, we must affirm the judgment of the district court. Northrup v. Archbishop Bergan Mercy Hospital, 575 F.2d 605, 607 (8th Cir. 1978).

B

Officer Valentine argues that the evidence against him is not sufficient to sustain the jury's verdict. We disagree. Reviewing the evidence in the light most favorable to Yellow Bird, we are convinced that the verdict is correct. Valentine kicked the visibly pregnant plaintiff in the stomach. He denied her necessary medical assistance even though she persisted in asking for it. Though a hospital was seven blocks away, she was driven to the county jail nearly twenty miles in the opposite direction. On the way to the jail, Valentine, who had been injured in the brawl and was visibly upset, pulled off to the side of the road, turned to Yellow Bird and said, "I don't know whether to take you people out in the country and shoot you or to take you to jail." Yellow Bird's medical expert testified that the kick and resulting lack of medical care caused the death of Yellow Bird's unborn child. Valentine's threat, in conjunction with the whole ordeal, caused her great emotional distress. The court's instructions were proper and more than adequate. The plaintiff's section 1983 verdict stands as rendered.

V

The court instructed the jury on damages under the plaintiff's state and federal claims separately. Three damage instructions were given with regard to Yellow Bird's federal claims. The jury was instructed that if it determined the issue of liability favorably to Yellow Bird, it would then assess damages based upon:

(1)   The physical harm that she suffered, including ill health and physical pain and discomfort;

(2)   The emotional and mental harm that she suffered, including fear, humiliation and mental anguish;

(3)   The extent and duration of her injuries, including their continuation into the future; and

(4)   The violation of her substantive constitutional right to liberty and to due process of law.

The court also properly instructed on the issue of punitive damages. The defendants' objections to the trial court's instructions were directed to the fourth element. Accordingly, we address the issue whether, independent of any recovery for actual physical and emotional injury, a plaintiff can be compensated for the deprivation of certain substantive constitutional rights.[6]

The trial court specifically instructed the jury as follows:

If you find that the plaintiff has been deprived of a constitutional right, you may award damages to compensate her for the deprivation. Damages

---

[6]   We are not faced here with a case that involves a violation of a constitutional right without injury. In this case, Yellow Bird proved, by a preponderance of the evidence, that she suffered severe and lasting physical injury and emotional anguish as a result of the constitutional deprivations. However, since the jury was instructed that it should compensate Yellow Bird for the loss of her constitutional rights independent of the physical and emotional injury she suffered, we inquire whether this is a proper element of damages.

for this type of injury are more difficult to measure than damages for a physical injury or injury to one's property. There are no medical bills or other expenses by which you can judge how much compensation is appropriate. In one sense, no monetary value we place upon constitutional rights can measure their importance in our society or compensate a citizen adequately for their deprivation. However, just because these rights are not capable of precise evaluation does not mean that an appropriate monetary amount should not be awarded.

The precise value you place upon any constitutional right which you find was denied to plaintiff is within your discretion. You may wish to consider the importance of the right in our system of government, the role which this right has played in the history of our republic, the significance of the right in the context of the activities which the plaintiff was engaged in at the time of the violation of the right.

A

Section 1983 serves basically two functions: it deters future governmental action that violates persons' civil rights, *Owen v. City of Independence, supra*, 445 U.S. at 651-652, 100 S. Ct. at 1415-1416; *Imbler v. Pachtman*, 424 U.S. 409, 442, 96 S. Ct. 984, 1000, 47 L. Ed. 2d 128 (1976) (White, J., concurring), and it compensates the injured party. *Carey v. Piphus*, 435 U.S. 247, 254, 98 S. Ct. 1042, 1047, 55 L. Ed. 2d 252 (1978). When these two purposes are achieved, the substantive constitutional guarantee at stake is vindicated and the harmed party is made whole.

The Supreme Court has long viewed money damages as an appropriate remedy for redressing the loss of a person's civil rights. *See Bivens v. Six Unknown Named Agents of Fed. Bureau of Narcotics*, 403 U.S. 388, 395-396, 91 S. Ct. 1999, 2004-2005, 29 L. Ed. 2d 619 (1971); *Giles v. Harris*, 189 U.S. 475, 485, 23 S. Ct. 639, 641, 47 L. Ed. 909 (1903) (Holmes, J.). In order to fully vindicate the challenged guarantees and deter future conduct that threaten their practical significance, full compensation is necessary.[7] To secure complete satisfaction, damage awards must take account of the intrinsic dimension that envelopes each substantive constitutional right. This concept is not a novel one. For example, the federal courts have traditionally compensated the intangible constitutional loss that results when a party's voting rights are infringed. *See generally Lane v. Wilson*, 307 U.S. 268, 59 S. Ct. 872, 83 L. Ed. 1281 (1939); *Nixon v. Condon*, 286 U.S. 73, 52 S. Ct. 484, 76 L. Ed. 984 (1932); *Nixon v. Herndon*, 273 U.S. 536, 47 S. Ct. 446, 71 L. Ed. 759 (1927); *Wayne v. Venable*, 260 F. 64 (8th Cir. 1919). Even if a plaintiff in a voting rights case cannot establish that the loss of his vote resulted in any consequential or actual injury, substantial nonpunitive damages are presumed to flow from the wrong itself. As Judge Walter Sanborn reasoned over sixty years ago,

---

[7] Many substantive constitutional guarantees may be violated without accompanying consequential or "actual" injury. If consequential injury were the touchstone for substantial compensatory awards, many blatant constitutional violations would remain unredressed. See Note, *Damage Awards for Constitutional Torts: A Reconsideration After Carey v. Piphus*, 93 Harv. L. Rev. 966, 976-977 & nn. 68-69 (1980).

In the eyes of the law [the right to vote] is so valuable that damages are presumed from the wrongful deprivation of it without evidence of actual loss of money, property, or any other valuable thing, and the amount of the damages is a question peculiarly appropriate for the determination of the jury, because each member of the jury has personal knowledge of the value of the right.

Wayne v. Venable, supra, 260 F. at 66.

A number of federal courts have recently ruled that substantial compensatory damages are recoverable when substantive constitutional rights have been violated. *See Dellums v. Powell,* 566 F.2d 167, 194-196, 184 U.S. App. D.C. 275 (D.C.Cir. 1977), *cert. denied,* 438 U.S. 916, 98 S. Ct. 3146, 98 S. Ct. 3147, 57 L. Ed. 2d 1161 (1978) (damages available to persons arrested for peaceful demonstration); *Tatum v. Morton,* 562 F.2d 1279, 1281-1285, 183 U.S. App. D.C. 331 (D.C.Cir. 1977) (damages available to plaintiffs unlawfully arrested for demonstrating peacefully); *Bryant v. McGinnis,* 463 F. Supp. 373, 388 (W.D.N.Y.1978) (damages available when inmates' rights to practice their religion were denied); *Mickens v. Winston,* 462 F. Supp. 910, 913 (E.D.Va.1978), *aff'd,* 609 F.2d 508 (4th Cir. 1979) (damages are presumed when inmate was racially segregated); *Manfredonia v. Barry,* 401 F. Supp. 762, 770-772 (E.D.N.Y.1975) (damages given for unlawful arrest while plaintiff was delivering a lecture on the use of contraceptives). We believe this to be the proper rule.

B

The appellants assert that *Carey v. Piphus, supra,* 435 U.S. 247, 98 S. Ct. 1042, 55 L. Ed. 2d 252, controls this case and prohibits an award for the violation of Yellow Bird's substantive constitutional rights, other than some nominal sum. We disagree. The holding in *Carey* was specifically limited to its facts. That case involved two students who were suspended from public schools for disciplinary reasons without any type of hearing in violation of the "procedural" requirements of the Due Process Clause. The Court, although noting that their procedural due process rights were infringed, nevertheless ruled that absent a showing by the two plaintiffs that some actual injury resulted from the violation, it would not presume damages. The Court distinguished the plaintiffs' procedural due process case from defamation and related tort law cases in which it has applied the doctrine of presumed damages, based in part upon the "ambiguous" causal link that usually accompanies cases in the former class.

The Court cautioned, however, that its analysis in *Carey* may not dictate a similar result when a different constitutional violation is involved. The Court stated:

[T]he elements and prerequisites for recovery of damages appropriate to compensate injuries caused by the deprivation of one constitutional right are not necessarily appropriate to compensate injuries caused by the deprivation of another.

Carey v. Piphus, supra, 435 U.S. at 264-265, 98 S. Ct. at 1052-1053.

The Court stated that we must consider the nature of the interest that is sought to be protected by the particular constitutional guarantee that is infringed. *Id.* at

265, 98 S. Ct. at 1053. It also directed us to consider the common law of torts, which has as one of its guiding principles that persons must be fairly compensated for the injuries and losses they suffer as a result of violations of their legal rights. *Id.* at 267, 98 S. Ct. at 1054.

C

We turn now to the specific constitutional guarantees involved in the instant case, mindful that "[a] damages remedy against the defending party is a vital component of any scheme for vindicating cherished constitutional guarantees, and the importance of assuring its efficacy is only accentuated when [among the wrongdoers] is the institution that has been established to protect the very rights . . . transgressed." *Owen v. City of Independence, supra*, 445 U.S. at 651, 100 S. Ct. at 1415.

The jury was instructed that it could find that the defendants: (1) used excessive force against the plaintiff; (2) knowingly failed to provide her with necessary medical assistance; (3) falsely arrested her; and (4) denied her counsel after her arrest and incarceration, all in violation of her federal constitutional rights.

Under our Constitution, persons are guaranteed to be free from the use of excessive force against them by their police officers. The Due Process Clause protects the security of one's life and limbs as well as property. There is clearly a liberty interest in freedom from punishment through bodily injury. *See Putman v. Gerloff*, 639 F.2d 415, 420-421 & n.6 (8th Cir. 1981). *See generally* Newman, *Suing the Lawbreakers: Proposals to Strengthen the Section 1983 Damage Remedy for Law Enforcers' Misconduct*, 87 Yale L.J. 447, 453 (1978).

Similarly, the Due Process Clause mandates that the right to needed medical assistance cannot be denied someone taken into custody. *See Fitzke v. Shappell*, 468 F.2d 1072 (6th Cir. 1972). It is clear that once someone is arrested and taken into custody, that person "becomes both vulnerable and dependent upon the state to provide certain simple and basic needs." *Id.* at 1076. The Due Process Clause guarantees that among these basic needs is the substantive right to medical assistance. *Id.; Scharfenberger v. Wingo*, 542 F.2d 328, 331 (6th Cir. 1976).

The Fourth Amendment creates an expectation of privacy and guarantees that citizens shall not be arrested without probable cause and reasonable grounds supporting the belief that they are committing a crime. *See, e.g., Butler v. Goldblatt Bros., Inc.*, 589 F.2d 323, 325 (7th Cir. 1978), *cert. denied*, 444 U.S. 841, 100 S. Ct. 82, 62 L. Ed. 2d 53 (1979); *Dellums v. Powell, supra*, 566 F.2d at 175-176; *cf. Wyland v. James*, 426 F. Supp. 304, 306 (N.D.Tex. 1977). The Fourth Amendment secures the citizens' substantive right to security from the government's unreasonable intrusions into privacy. *See generally* Comment, *Presumed Damages for Fourth Amendment Violations*, 129 U. Pa. L. Rev. 192, 212-216 (1980).

Finally, a person taken into custody has a Fifth Amendment right to counsel. *Edwards v. Arizona*, 451 U.S. 477, 101 S. Ct. 1880, 1883-1884, 68 L. Ed. 2d 378 (1981); *Miranda v. Arizona*, 384 U.S. 436, 467-473, 86 S. Ct. 1602, 1624-1627, 16 L. Ed. 2d 694 (1966). In *Miranda*, the Supreme Court reasoned that because a person can involuntarily make inculpatory statements during custodial interrogation, the right to counsel at that point in time provides the safeguard necessary to protect the criminal defendant's substantive right to remain silent and to assure a continuous opportunity to exercise that right. *Id.* at 460, 472, 86 S. Ct. at 1620, 1626.

Our recitation of the nature of the constitutional rights involved in this case is intentionally brief. Our aim here is simply to distinguish the substantive rights involved in this case from the right that was involved in *Carey.* The Court in *Carey* determined that the *procedural* right at issue there was nothing more than a mechanical process designed to avoid the mistaken or wrongful infringements of other *substantive* constitutional guarantees. In this case, by contrast, substantive constitutional rights, highly prized in our federal system of government, are clearly at stake.

D

As noted, *Carey* also directs us to inquire whether the specific constitutional guarantee at stake has a common law analogue. The Court reasoned there that "in some cases, the interests protected by a particular branch of the common law of torts may parallel closely the interests protected by a particular constitutional right. In such cases, it may be appropriate to apply the tort rules of damages directly to the § 1983 action." *Carey v. Piphus, supra,* 435 U.S. at 258, 98 S. Ct. at 1049. In the instant case, the interests protected by the particular constitutional rights at issue are analogous to the interests protected by the common law dignitary torts.[9] In cases involving invasions of dignitary rights, it is predictably difficult to place a value on the resulting injury. The injury that results from the invasion of dignitary expectations is often not an economic loss. Nevertheless, the common law has always redressed their breach with substantial damages. These damages are usually characterized as general damages the type that generally flow from the wrongful act. *See* D. Dobbs, Remedies § 3.2 at 138-139 (1973).

The general damages that may be recovered in the dignitary tort class of cases "do not require specific proof of emotional harm to the plaintiff. . . . Thus general damages for assault or false imprisonment and like torts are not dependent upon actual proof of such harm." *Id.* § 7.3 at 529. The value that is placed upon the dignitary loss is a question for the jury, subject, of course, to review by the courts. *See Wayne v. Venable, supra,* 260 F. at 66; Comment, *Presumed Damages for Fourth Amendment Violations,* 129 U. Pa. L. Rev. 192, 204-207 (1980). *But see* Love, *Damages: A Remedy for the Violation of Constitutional Rights,* 67 Cal. L. Rev. 1242, 1282-1285 (1979) (legislation needed to set specific presumed damage awards for violations of civil rights); Newman, *Suing the Lawbreakers: Proposals to Strengthen the Section 1983 Damage Remedy for Law Enforcers' Misconduct,* 87

---

[9] Professor Dobbs has stated that:

The list of dignitary actions is a fairly long one, though obscured in many instances by the fact that the plaintiff also has some economic claim as well. Many of these actions are recognized torts that involve some confrontation with the plaintiff in person or some indirect affront to his personality-assault, battery, false imprisonment, malicious prosecution, intentional infliction of mental anguish, libel and slander, invasion of privacy, alienation of affections are all in this category. These torts have their statutory and constitutional analogues, so that essentially the same sort of interests may be protected under federal or state civil rights statutes or under the federal Constitution.

D. Dobbs, Remedies § 7.1 at 509 (1973) (footnote omitted).

Yale L.J. 447, 465 (1978) (a liquidated damage sum should be awarded for violations of civil rights in addition to any actual damages).

The Court in *Carey* implicitly authorized the doctrine of presumed damages as it is applied to the dignitary torts of libel and defamation. The Court reasoned that in such cases injury is almost certain to result from the wrongful act, and that the specific injury is difficult to prove. Moreover, since the resulting injury is so likely, no purpose is served by requiring proof of this kind. *Carey v. Piphus, supra*, 435 U.S. at 262, 98 S. Ct. at 1051.

In this case, Yellow Bird was deprived of certain substantive constitutional rights that have been recognized as implicit in the Constitution, and highly prized in our federal system. It is reasonable to assume that violations of Yellow Bird's Fourth Amendment, Fifth Amendment and Fourteenth Amendment Substantive Due Process rights resulted in injury, just as injury is presumed to flow from an invasion of a person's dignitary rights in a voting rights case or a defamation action. The causal link between the wrongful deprivation of the substantive right and the resulting harm is anything but "ambiguous." *See Carey v. Piphus, supra*, 435 U.S. at 263, 98 S. Ct. at 1052.

Accordingly, the court's instruction to the jury permitting it to award damages to compensate Yellow Bird for violations of her constitutional rights independent of her other injuries is a proper instruction. As we stated earlier, Yellow Bird has proved actual physical and emotional injury. To the extent, however, that the overall verdict reflects, in part, an independent award for the violations of her civil rights, it stands as rendered.

. . . .

We affirm the judgment of the district court as modified.

While it is clear that the court had no need to award presumed damages in *Herrera v. Valentine*, it nonetheless left the door open to the possibility in an appropriate case. In the following case, the Supreme Court largely closed that door.

MEMPHIS COMMUNITY SCHOOL DISTRICT v. STACHURA
Supreme Court of the United States, 1986
477 U.S. 299

Justice Powell delivered the opinion of the Court.

This case requires us to decide whether 42 U.S.C. § 1983 authorizes an award of compensatory damages based on the factfinder's assessment of the value or importance of a substantive constitutional right.

I

Respondent Edward Stachura is a tenured teacher in the Memphis, Michigan, public schools. When the events that led to this case occurred, respondent taught seventh-grade life science, using a textbook that had been approved by the School Board. The textbook included a chapter on human reproduction. During the 1978-1979 school year, respondent spent six weeks on this chapter. As part of their instruction, students were shown pictures of respondent's wife during her pregnancy. Respondent also showed the students two films concerning human growth and sexuality. These films were provided by the County Health Department, and the Principal of respondent's school had approved their use. Both films had been shown in past school years without incident.

After the showing of the pictures and the films, a number of parents complained to school officials about respondent's teaching methods. These complaints, which appear to have been based largely on inaccurate rumors about the allegedly sexually explicit nature of the pictures and films, were discussed at an open School Board meeting held on April 23, 1979. Following the advice of the School Superintendent, respondent did not attend the meeting, during which a number of parents expressed the view that respondent should not be allowed to teach in the Memphis school system. The day after the meeting, respondent was suspended with pay. The School Board later confirmed the suspension, and notified respondent that an "administration evaluation" of his teaching methods was underway. No such evaluation was ever made. Respondent was reinstated the next fall, after filing this lawsuit.

Respondent sued the School District, the Board of Education, various Board members and school administrators, and two parents who had participated in the April 23 School Board meeting. The complaint alleged that respondent's suspension deprived him of both liberty and property without due process of law and violated his First Amendment right to academic freedom. Respondent sought compensatory and punitive damages under 42 U. S. C. § 1983 for these constitutional violations.

At the close of trial on these claims, the District Court instructed the jury as to the law governing the asserted bases for liability. Turning to damages, the court instructed the jury that on finding liability it should award a sufficient amount to compensate respondent for the injury caused by petitioners' unlawful actions:

> "You should consider in this regard any lost earnings; loss of earning capacity; out-of-pocket expenses; and any mental anguish or emotional distress that you find the Plaintiff to have suffered as a result of conduct by the Defendants depriving him of his civil rights." . . .

In addition to this instruction on the standard elements of compensatory damages, the court explained that punitive damages could be awarded, and described the standards governing punitive awards. Finally, at respondent's request and over petitioners' objection, the court charged that damages also could be awarded based on the value or importance of the constitutional rights that were violated:

> "If you find that the Plaintiff has been deprived of a Constitutional right, you may award damages to compensate him for the deprivation. Damages for this type of injury are more difficult to measure than damages for a

physical injury or injury to one's property. There are no medical bills or other expenses by which you can judge how much compensation is appropriate. In one sense, no monetary value we place upon Constitutional rights can measure their importance in our society or compensate a citizen adequately for their deprivation. However, just because these rights are not capable of precise evaluation does not mean that an appropriate monetary amount should not be awarded.

"The precise value you place upon any Constitutional right which you find was denied to Plaintiff is within your discretion. You may wish to consider the importance of the right in our system of government, the role which this right has played in the history of our republic, [and] the significance of the right in the context of the activities which the Plaintiff was engaged in at the time of the violation of the right." . . .

The jury found petitioners liable[3] and awarded a total of $275,000 in compensatory damages and $46,000 in punitive damages. The District Court entered judgment notwithstanding the verdict as to one of the defendants, reducing the total award to $266,750 in compensatory damages and $36,000 in punitive damages.

In an opinion devoted primarily to liability issues, the Court of Appeals for the Sixth Circuit affirmed, holding that respondent's suspension had violated both procedural due process and the First Amendment. *Stachura v. Truszkowski*, 763 F.2d 211 (1985). Responding to petitioners' contention that the District Court improperly authorized damages based solely on the value of constitutional rights, the court noted only that "there was ample proof of actual injury to plaintiff Stachura both in his effective discharge . . . and by the damage to his reputation and to his professional career as a teacher. Contrary to the situation in *Carey v. Piphus*, 435 U.S. 247 (1978) . . . , there was proof from which the jury could have found, as it did, actual and important damages." *Id.*, at 214.

We granted certiorari limited to the question whether the Court of Appeals erred in affirming the damages award in the light of the District Court's instructions that authorized not only compensatory and punitive damages, but also damages for the deprivation of "any constitutional right."[5] 474 U.S. 918 (1985). We reverse, and remand for a new trial limited to the issue of compensatory damages.

II

Petitioners challenge the jury instructions authorizing damages for violation of constitutional rights on the ground that those instructions permitted the jury to award damages based on its own unguided estimation of the value of such rights. Respondent disagrees with this characterization of the jury instructions, contending that the compensatory damages instructions taken as a whole focused solely on

---

[3] The jury found petitioners liable based both on the alleged deprivation of procedural due process and on the alleged violation of respondent's First Amendment rights.

[5] Since our decision in *Carey v. Piphus*, 435 U.S. 247 (1978), several of the Courts of Appeals have concluded that damages awards based on the abstract value of constitutional rights are proper, at least as long as the right in question is substantive. Other courts have determined that our reasoning in *Carey* forecloses such awards.

respondent's injury and not on the abstract value of the rights he asserted.

We believe petitioners more accurately characterize the instructions. The damages instructions were divided into three distinct segments: (i) compensatory damages for harm to respondent, (ii) punitive damages, and (iii) additional "compensatory" damages for violations of constitutional rights. No sensible juror could read the third of these segments to modify the first. On the contrary, the damages instructions plainly authorized — in addition to punitive damages — two distinct types of "compensatory" damages: one based on respondent's actual injury according to ordinary tort law standards, and another based on the "value" of certain rights. We therefore consider whether the latter category of damages was properly before the jury.

III

A

We have repeatedly noted that 42 U. S. C. § 1983 creates " 'a species of tort liability' in favor of persons who are deprived of 'rights, privileges, or immunities secured' to them by the Constitution' " *Carey v. Piphus*, 435 U.S. 247, 253 (1978), quoting *Imbler v. Pachtman*, 424 U.S. 409, 417 (1976). See also *Smith v. Wade*, 461 U.S. 30, 34 (1983); *Newport v. Fact Concerts, Inc.*, 453 U.S. 247, 258-259 (1981). Accordingly, when § 1983 plaintiffs seek damages for violations of constitutional rights, the level of damages is ordinarily determined according to principles derived from the common law of torts. See *Smith v. Wade, supra*, at 34; *Carey v. Piphus, supra*, at 257-258; *cf. Monroe v. Pape*, 365 U.S. 167, 196, and n. 5 (1961) (Harlan, J., concurring).

Punitive damages aside, damages in tort cases are designed to provide *"compensation* for the injury caused to plaintiff by defendant's breach of duty." 2 F. Harper, F. James, & O. Gray, Law of Torts § 25.1, p. 490 (2d ed. 1986) (emphasis in original), quoted in *Carey v. Piphus, supra*, at 255. See also *Bivens v. Six Unknown Federal Narcotics Agents*, 403 U.S. 388, 395, 397 (1971); *id.*, at 408-409 (Harlan J., concurring in judgment). To that end, compensatory damages may include not only out-of-pocket loss and other monetary harms, but also such injuries as "impairment of reputation . . . , personal humiliation, and mental anguish and suffering." *Gertz v. Robert Welch, Inc.*, 418 U.S. 323, 350 (1974). See also *Carey v. Piphus, supra*, at 264 (mental and emotional distress constitute compensable injury in § 1983 cases). Deterrence is also an important purpose of this system, but it operates through the mechanism of damages that are *compensatory* — damages grounded in determinations of plaintiffs' actual losses. *E. g.*, 4 Harper, James, & Gray, *supra*, § 25.3 (discussing need for certainty in damages determinations); D. Dobbs, Law of Remedies § 3.1, pp. 135-136 (1973). Congress adopted this common-law system of recovery when it established liability for "constitutional torts." Consequently, "the basic purpose" of § 1983 damages is "to *compensate persons for injuries* that are caused by the deprivation of constitutional rights." *Carey v. Piphus*, 435 U.S., at 254 (emphasis added). See also *id.*, at 257 ("damages awards under § 1983 should be governed by the principle of compensation").

Carey v. *Piphus* represents a straightforward application of these principles. *Carey* involved a suit by a high school student suspended for smoking marijuana; the student claimed that he was denied procedural due process because he was suspended without an opportunity to respond to the charges against him. The Court of Appeals for the Seventh Circuit held that even if the suspension was justified, the student could recover substantial compensatory damages simply because of the insufficient procedures used to suspend him from school. We reversed, and held that the student could recover compensatory damages only if he proved actual injury caused by the denial of his constitutional rights. *Id.*, at 264. We noted: "Rights, constitutional and otherwise, do not exist in a vacuum. Their purpose is to protect persons from injuries to particular interests. . . . " *Id.*, at 254. Where no injury was present, no "compensatory" damages could be awarded.

The instructions at issue here cannot be squared with *Carey*, or with the principles of tort damages on which *Carey* and § 1983 are grounded. The jurors in this case were told that, in determining how much was necessary to "compensate [respondent] for the deprivation" of his constitutional rights, they should place a money value on the "rights" themselves by considering such factors as the particular right's "importance . . . in our system of government," its role in American history, and its "significance . . . in the context of the activities" in which respondent was engaged. . . . These factors focus, not on compensation for provable injury, but on the jury's subjective perception of the importance of constitutional rights as an abstract matter. *Carey* establishes that such an approach is impermissible. The constitutional right transgressed in *Carey* — the right to due process of law — is central to our system of ordered liberty. See *In re Gault*, 387 U.S. 1, 20-21 (1967). We nevertheless held that *no* compensatory damages could be awarded for violation of that right absent proof of actual injury. *Carey*, 435 U.S., at 264. *Carey* thus makes clear that the abstract value of a constitutional right may not form the basis for § 1983 damages.[11]

Respondent nevertheless argues that *Carey* does not control here, because in this case a substantive constitutional right — respondent's First Amendment right to academic freedom — was infringed. The argument misperceives our analysis in *Carey*. That case does not establish a two-tiered system of constitutional rights, with substantive rights afforded greater protection than "mere" procedural safeguards. We did acknowledge in *Carey* that "the elements and prerequisites for recovery of damages" might vary depending on the interests protected by the constitutional right at issue. *Id.*, at 264-265. But we emphasized that, whatever the constitutional basis for § 1983 liability, such damages must always be designed "to

---

[11] We did approve an award of nominal damages for the deprivation of due process in Carey, 435 U.S., at 266. Our discussion of that issue makes clear that nominal damages, and not damages based on some undefinable "value" of infringed rights, are the appropriate means of "vindicating" rights whose deprivation has not caused actual, provable injury:

"Common-law courts traditionally have vindicated deprivations of certain 'absolute' rights that are not shown to have caused actual injury through the award of a nominal sum of money. By making the deprivation of such rights actionable for nominal damages without proof of actual injury, the law recognizes the importance to organized society that those rights be scrupulously observed; but at the same time, it remains true to the principle that substantial damages should be awarded only to compensate actual injury or, in the case of exemplary or punitive damages, to deter or punish malicious deprivations of rights." Ibid. (footnote omitted).

compensate injuries caused by the [constitutional] deprivation." *Id.*, at 265 (emphasis added).[13] See also *Hobson v. Wilson*, 237 U. S. App. D. C. 219, 277-279, 737 F.2d 1, 59-61 (1984), cert. denied, 470 U.S. 1084 (1985); *cf. Smith v. Wade*, 461 U.S. 30 (1983). That conclusion simply leaves no room for noncompensatory damages measured by the jury's perception of the abstract "importance" of a constitutional right.

Nor do we find such damages necessary to vindicate the constitutional rights that § 1983 protects. Section 1983 presupposes that damages that compensate for actual harm ordinarily suffice to deter constitutional violations. *Carey, supra*, at 256-257 ("To the extent that Congress intended that awards under § 1983 should deter the deprivation of constitutional rights, there is no evidence that it meant to establish a deterrent more formidable than that inherent in the award of compensatory damages"). Moreover, damages based on the "value" of constitutional rights are an unwieldy tool for ensuring compliance with the Constitution. History and tradition do not afford any sound guidance concerning the precise value that juries should place on constitutional protections. Accordingly, were such damages available, juries would be free to award arbitrary amounts without any evidentiary basis, or to use their unbounded discretion to punish unpopular defendants. Cf. *Gertz*, 418 U.S., at 350. Such damages would be too uncertain to be of any great value to plaintiffs, and would inject caprice into determinations of damages in § 1983 cases. We therefore hold that damages based on the abstract "value" or "importance" of constitutional rights are not a permissible element of compensatory damages in such cases.

B

Respondent further argues that the challenged instructions authorized a form of "presumed" damages — a remedy that is both compensatory in nature and traditionally part of the range of tort law remedies. Alternatively, respondent argues that the erroneous instructions were at worst harmless error.

Neither argument has merit. Presumed damages are a *substitute* for ordinary compensatory damages, not a *supplement* for an award that fully compensates the alleged injury. When a plaintiff seeks compensation for an injury that is likely to have occurred but difficult to establish, some form of presumed damages may possibly be appropriate. See *Carey*, 435 U.S., at 262; cf. *Dun & Bradstreet, Inc.* v. *Greenmoss Builders*, 472 U.S. 749, 760-761 (1985) (opinion of POWELL, J.); *Gertz v. Robert Welch, Inc., supra*, at 349. In those circumstances, presumed damages may

---

[13] Carey recognized that "the task . . . of adapting common-law rules of damages to provide fair compensation for injuries caused by the deprivation of a constitutional right" is one "of some delicacy." *Id.*, at 258. We also noted that "the elements and prerequisites for recovery of damages appropriate to compensate injuries caused by the deprivation of one constitutional right are notnecessarily appropriate to compensate injuries caused by the deprivation of another." *Id.*, at 264-265. *See also* Hobson v. Wilson, 237 U. S. App. D. C, at 279-281, 737 F.2d, at 61-63. This "delicate" task need not be undertaken here. None of the parties challenges the portion of the jury instructions that permitted recovery for actual harm to respondent, and the instructions that are challenged simply do not authorize compensation for injury. We therefore hold only that damages based on the "value" or "importance" of constitutional rights are not authorized by § 1983, because they are not truly compensatory.

roughly approximate the harm that the plaintiff suffered and thereby compensate for harms that may be impossible to measure. As we earlier explained, the instructions at issue in this case did not serve this purpose, but instead called on the jury to measure damages based on a subjective evaluation of the importance of particular constitutional values. Since such damages are wholly divorced from any compensatory purpose, they cannot be justified as presumed damages.[14] Moreover, no rough substitute for compensatory damages was required in this case, since the jury was fully authorized to compensate respondent for both monetary and nonmonetary harms caused by petitioners' conduct.

Nor can we find that the erroneous instructions were harmless. See 28 U. S. C. § 2111; *McDonough Power Equipment, Inc. v. Greenwood*, 464 U.S. 548 (1984). When damages instructions are faulty and the verdict does not reveal the means by which the jury calculated damages, "[the] error in the charge is difficult, if not impossible, to correct without retrial, in light of the jury's general verdict." *Newport v. Fact Concerts, Inc.*, 453 U.S., at 256, n. 12. The jury was authorized to award three categories of damages: (i) compensatory damages for injury to respondent, (ii) punitive damages, and (iii) damages based on the jury's perception of the "importance" of two provisions of the Constitution. The submission of the third of these categories was error. Although the verdict specified an amount for punitive damages, it did not specify how much of the remaining damages was designed to compensate respondent for his injury and how much reflected the jury's estimation of the value of the constitutional rights that were infringed. The effect of the erroneous instruction is therefore unknowable, although probably significant: the jury awarded respondent a very substantial amount of damages, none of which could have derived from any monetary loss. It is likely, although not certain, that a major part of these damages was intended to "compensate" respondent for the

---

[14] For the same reason, Nixon v. Herndon, 273 U.S. 536 (1927), and similar cases do not support the challenged instructions. In *Nixon*, the Court held that a plaintiff who was illegally prevented from voting in a state primary election suffered compensable injury. Accord, Lane v. Wilson, 307 U.S. 268 (1939). This holding did not rest on the "value" of the right to vote as an abstract matter; rather, the Court recognized that the plaintiff had suffered a particular injury-his inability to vote in a particular election-that might be compensated through substantial money damages. See 273 U.S., at 540 ("the petition . . . seeks to recover for private damage"). Nixon followed a long line of cases, going back to Lord Holt's decision in Ashby v. White, 2 Ld. Raym. 938, 92 Eng. Rep. 126 (1703), authorizing substantial money damages as compensation for persons deprived of their right to vote in particular elections. *E.g.*, Wiley v. Sinkler, 179 U.S. 58, 65 (1900); Wayne v. Venable, 260 F. 64, 66 (C.A. 8 1919). Although these decisions sometimes speak of damages for the value of the right to vote, their analysis shows that they involve nothing more than an award of presumed damages for a nonmonetary harm that cannot easily be quantified: "In the eyes of the law [the] right [to vote] is so valuable that damages are presumed from the wrongful deprivation of it without evidence of actual loss of money, property, or any other valuable thing, and the amount of the damages is a question peculiarly appropriate for the determination of the jury, because each member of the jury has personal knowledge of the value of the right." *Ibid*. See also Ashby v. White, supra, at 955, 92 Eng. Rep., at 137 (Holt, C. J.) ("As in an action for slanderous words, though a man does not lose a penny by reason of the speaking [of] them, yet he shall have an action"). The "value of the right" in the context of these decisions is the money value of the particular loss that the plaintiff suffered-a loss of which "each member of the jury has personal knowledge." It is not the value of the right to vote as a general, abstract matter, based on its role in our history or system of government. Thus, whatever the wisdom of these decisions in the context of the changing scope of compensatory damages over the course of this century, they do not support awards of noncompensatory damages such as those authorized in this case.

abstract "value" of his due process and First Amendment rights. For these reasons, the case must be remanded for a new trial on compensatory damages.

IV

The judgment of the Court of Appeals is reversed, and the case is remanded for further proceedings consistent with this opinion.

It is so ordered.

JUSTICE BRENNAN and JUSTICE STEVENS join the opinion of the Court and also join JUSTICE MARSHALL'S opinion concurring in the judgment.

JUSTICE MARSHALL, with whom JUSTICE BRENNAN, JUSTICE BLACKMUN, and JUSTICE STEVENS join, concurring in the judgment.

I agree with the Court that this case must be remanded for a new trial on damages. Certain portions of the Court's opinion, however, can be read to suggest that damages in § 1983 cases are necessarily limited to "out-of-pocket loss," "other monetary harms," and "such injuries as 'impairment of reputation . . . , personal humiliation, and mental anguish and suffering.'" See *ante*, at 307. I do not understand the Court so to hold, and I write separately to emphasize that the violation of a constitutional right, in proper cases, may itself constitute a compensable injury.

. . . .

Suits under Section 1983 require some governmental action. Under other civil rights statutes, such as 28 U.S.C. § 1981, civil rights violations may be actionable in the absence of direct governmental participation. Section 1981 claims, however, are limited to circumstances that involve denials of rights on the basis of race.

PHILLIP v. UNIVERSITY OF ROCHESTER
United States Court of Appeals for the Second Circuit, 2003
316 F.3d 291

POOLER, CIRCUIT JUDGE:

We are asked to decide whether the equal benefit clause of 42 U.S.C. § 1981 requires a showing of state action. Based primarily on the clear language of the statute, we hold that plaintiffs may sustain a claim for breach of the equal benefit clause without making a traditional state action showing. We caution, however, that this same statutory language constrains the breadth of the equal benefit clause. That is, plaintiffs must demonstrate that defendants, motivated by racial animosity, deprived or attempted to deprive plaintiffs of "the full and equal benefit" of a law or proceeding "for the security of persons and property." 42 U.S.C. § 1981(a). [Because defendants moved to dismiss the complaint as facially inadequate, we accept the factual allegations of the complaint as true.]

BACKGROUND

Nigel S. Phillip, Bernard Schmidt, St. Patrick Reid, and Grant Gittens are African-Americans and were, at the time of the pertinent events, students at the University of Rochester, a private university. In the early morning of April 30, 1999, the plaintiffs and other students, most of whom were minorities, gathered to socialize in the lobby of the university library. Within minutes, James Clukey, a university security officer, came up to the students and told them to "break it up" and "take it outside." Although the students attempted to comply with Clukey's order, he demanded that Gittens show his university identification and asked the other individuals whether they were students at the university. One of the students, Elizabeth Pena, reached into Gittens' pocket, pulled out his university identification and said, "there, you see he's a student here. We are all students here." Clukey snatched Gittens' identification card and radioed the Rochester Police Department ("RPD") for assistance. The officer also followed the students outside. Soon afterwards Raymond Pipitone, a university security supervisor, came to the scene along with other security officers.

Phillip tried to end the confrontation by bringing Gittens to a friend's car. Just as the car was about to leave the parking lot, Clukey placed himself in front of the car, would not allow it to leave, and began to copy its license plate.

Several police units then arrived. Police officers arrested the four plaintiffs, apparently based on conduct that the officers had observed. The plaintiffs stayed in jail overnight but received adjournments in contemplation of dismissal the following morning. Charges against all plaintiffs have been dismissed.

On May 11, 1999, University of Rochester President Thomas H. Jackson sent a memorandum to the entire university community. In his letter, Jackson acknowledged that the plaintiffs believed they had been "dealt with in a racist manner." He also admitted that "the performance of two of the University's Security personnel varied somewhat from normal policies and procedures, and their judgment did not meet expectations in this case." Finally, Jackson promised to request that the charges against the plaintiffs be dismissed.

Plaintiffs sued the university, Pipitone, and Clukey, claiming false arrest and imprisonment, battery and excessive use of force, assault, malicious prosecution, intentional and negligent infliction of emotional distress, and violation of the equal benefit clause of Section 1981. Defendants moved pursuant to Fed. R. Civ. P. 12(b)(6) to dismiss several of these claims including the Section 1981 claim. The district court dismissed plaintiffs' Section 1981 claim along with several of their other claims. With respect to the Section 1981 equal benefit clause claim, the court found plaintiffs could not prevail because they failed to allege state action. The parties subsequently stipulated to the dismissal of all remaining claims, and plaintiffs pursued this appeal, which is limited to the Section 1981 claim.

On appeal, plaintiffs contend that the district court's state action ruling was error. In addition to defending the district court's ruling, defendants contend that plaintiffs insufficiently pleaded racial motivation.

DISCUSSION

. . . .

II. Section 1981 and state action

To assess the need for state action in a Section 1981 equal benefit claim, we begin with the language of the statute both in its original form and as amended in 1991.

Before November 1991, Section 1981 provided only that

> All persons within the jurisdiction of the United States shall have the same right in every State and Territory to make and enforce contracts, to sue, be parties, give evidence, and to the full and equal benefit of all laws and proceedings for the security of persons and property as is enjoyed by white citizens, and shall be subject to like punishment, pains, penalties, taxes, licenses, and exactions of every kind, and to no other.

42 U.S.C. § 1981.

In 1991, Congress enacted amendments to Section 1981. The text just quoted now is denominated as subsection (a). A new subsection (b) repudiates *Patterson v. McLean Credit Union*, 491 U.S. 164, 109 S. Ct. 2363, 105 L. Ed. 2d 132 (1989), in which the Supreme Court held that breaches of contract are outside the scope of the "make and enforce contracts" clause of Section 1981. And, pertinent to this appeal, a new subsection (c) provides: "The rights protected by this section are protected against impairment by nongovernmental discrimination and impairment under color of State law." 42 U.S.C. § 1981(c).

On the face of the amended statute, it would seem that the answer to the question this appeal presents is clear: No state action is required for a Section 1981 claim.

Despite the apparent clarity of the statutory language, the courts of appeals [that] have considered whether the amended statute requires state action for an equal benefit clause claim have answered yes. *Youngblood v. Hy-Vee Food Stores, Inc.*, 266 F.3d 851, 855 (8th Cir. 2001), *cert. denied*, 535 U.S. 1017, 122 S. Ct. 1606, 152 L. Ed. 2d 621 (2002); *Brown v. Philip Morris Inc.*, 250 F.3d 789, 799 (3d Cir. 2001). The *Youngblood* holding rests on *Chapman v. Higbee Co.*, 256 F.3d 416 (6th Cir. 2001), *an opinion that since has been vacated and scheduled for rehearing en banc*, 270 F.3d 297 (6th Cir. 2001), and on dicta in *Mahone v. Waddle*, 564 F.2d 1018, 1029 (3d Cir. 1977), a pre-amendment case. *Brown* relies on *Mahone* and various district court cases. As we explain, we do not find *Youngblood*, *Brown*, or their sources sufficiently persuasive to displace the clear words of the statute.

Mahone, the primary and largely unexamined source for the holdings in *Youngblood* and *Brown*, merits close examination. In *Mahone*, the Third Circuit held that police officers who physically and verbally abused African-Americans, falsely arrested them, and gave false testimony against them could be sued under Section 1981's equal benefit clause. *Mahone*, 564 F.2d at 1028-29. In response to defendants' argument that construing Section 1981 to encompass their actions would federalize tort law, the court said in dicta that there was no such danger because the equal benefit clause requires state action. *Id.* at 1029. Although the court acknowledged that the "make and enforce contracts" clause of Section 1981 does not require state action, *id.* at 1029 (citing *Johnson v. Ry. Express Agency*, 421 U.S. 454, 95 S. Ct. 1716, 44 L. Ed. 2d 295 (1975), and *Runyon v. McCrary*, 427 U.S. 160, 96 S. Ct. 2586, 49 L. Ed. 2d 415 (1976)), it said that the rights to "make and enforce contracts" and to enjoy the "full and equal benefit of all laws and proceedings for the security of persons and property as is enjoyed by white citizens" were so different that the *Johnson* and *Runyon* holdings have no application to an equal benefit clause claim. *Id.* Because it is individuals who ordinarily make contracts, the court reasoned that individuals should be held liable for the racially motivated infringement of the contracts they make. *Id.* In contrast, the court said that the equal benefit clause "suggests a concern with relations between the individual and the state, not between two individuals" because states, not individuals, make laws and only the state can take away the protection of the laws it created. *Id.*

Because we do not agree with the premise of *Mahone*, we do not find its logic persuasive. Although the phrasing of the equal benefit clause does suggest that there must be some nexus between a claim and the state or its activities, the state is not the only actor that can deprive an individual of the benefit of laws or proceedings for the security of persons or property.

Having determined that individuals can deprive others of the equal benefit of laws and proceedings designed to protect the personal freedoms and property rights of the citizenry, we see no principled basis for holding that state action is required for equal benefit clause claims but not for contract clause claims. We therefore reject the analysis in *Mahone*. Nor does *Runyon* suggest a principled basis for limiting to the contract clause its conclusion that no state action is required under Section 1981. Although *Runyon* involved a contract clause claim, the Court held simply that " 42 U.S.C. § 1981 . . . reaches purely private acts of racial discrimination." *Runyon*, 427 U.S. at 170.

Finally, *Mahone* does not take into account the legislative history of the original version of Section 1981. This history suggests legislators' concern over private acts motivated by racial discrimination. Early on in its consideration of the bill that eventually became Section 1981, Congress considered a letter whose writer reported that "the hatred toward the negro as a freeman is intense among the low and brutal, who are the vast majority. Murders, shooting, whippings, robbing, and brutal treatment of every kind are daily inflicted upon them." Cong. Globe, 39th Cong., 1st Sess. 94 (1865). Another writer reported that an average of one black man was killed every day. *Id.* at 95. On January 22, 1866, Senator Creswell reported claims from two of his constituents that returning rebel soldiers persecuted, beat, and sometimes killed Negro soldiers who had fought for the Union. Cong. Globe, 39th Cong., 1st Sess. 339 (1866).

On January 29, 1866, Senator Trumbull, who sponsored the legislation, identified the rights protected by the Act as "fundamental rights." *Id.* at 476. Quoting *Corfield v. Coryell*, 6 F. Cas. 546, 4 Washington's Circuit Court Reports 380, Senator Trumbull identified these fundamental rights as

"protection by the Government; the enjoyment of life and liberty, with the right to acquire and possess property of every kind; and to pursue and obtain happiness and safety, subject, nevertheless to such restraints as the Government may justly prescribe for the general good of the whole [;] the right . . . to pass through, or to reside in any other State; . . . to claim the benefit of the writ of habeas corpus; to institute and maintain actions of any kind in the courts of the State; to take, hold, and dispose of property, either real or personal, and an exemption from higher taxes or impositions than are paid by the other citizens of the State."

Id. at 475. "As to these basic civil rights, . . . Senator [Trumbull] said, the bill would " 'break down all discrimination between black men and white men.' " *Jones v. Alfred H. Mayer Co.*, 392 U.S. 409, 432, 88 S. Ct. 2186, 20 L. Ed. 2d 1189 (1968) (quoting Cong. Globe, 39th Cong., 1st Sess.).

Throughout the legislative history, reports of abuses like those quoted above often are followed by statements suggesting that the writer was concerned about the freedmen's inability to obtain redress in southern courts. *See, e.g.*, Cong. Globe, 39th Cong., 1st Sess. at 94. However, the extensive description of racial abuses that individuals perpetrated, coupled with the Senate sponsor's broad view of the legislation's aims, persuades us that we should read Section 1981 as broadly as is consistent with the actual language of each clause. *Cf. Jones*, 392 U.S. at 426-37 (construing Section 1981's sibling statute, 42 U.S.C. § 1982).

Based on the general language of *Runyon*, the original legislative history, and *Mahone's* key analytical flaw — finding that individuals could not deny one another the equal benefit of a law or proceeding — we suspect that the Third Circuit erred by finding state action necessary to support a Section 1981 equal benefit clause claim.

Even assuming that the Third Circuit correctly decided *Mahone*, we believe that the 1991 amendment removes any doubt that the conduct of private actors is actionable under the equal benefit clause of Section 1981. Thus, we respectfully differ with the contrary conclusion reached by the Eighth and Third Circuits. As we discussed previously, these circuits primarily relied on *Mahone* and *Chapman*. *Youngblood*, 266 F.3d at 855; *Brown*, 250 F.3d at 799. We already have explained why we find *Mahone* unpersuasive. And, Section 1981(c) places *Mahone's* continuing viability in even greater doubt. Because the *Chapman* majority's arguments coincide with defendants' arguments and were adopted by reference in *Youngblood*, we consider their validity even though *Chapman* itself no longer has precedential force in the Sixth Circuit.

Unlike *Mahone, Brown*, and *Youngblood, Chapman* contains a lengthy analysis of the state action issue. The *Chapman* majority first accepted *Mahone's* conclusion that only the state can take away the benefits of laws and proceedings because only the state creates these laws and proceedings. *Chapman*, 256 F.3d at 420-21. It then parsed subsection (c), finding that it was

properly understood as clarifying the nature of the various "rights" enumerated in subsection (a). That is, the "rights . . . protected against impairment by nongovernmental discrimination" applies to the "make and enforce contracts" clause, while the "rights . . . protected against . . .

impairment under color of State law" refers to such clauses as the "full and equal benefit" clause of subsection (a).

Id. at 421. The court also held that a contrary interpretation would have "the absurd result of federalizing state tort law." *Id.* Finally, the court relied on the legislative history for subsection (c). This history states in its entirety:

> This subsection is intended to codify *Runyon v. McCrary.* In *Runyon,* the Court held that Section 1981 prohibited intentional racial discrimination in private, as well as public, contracting. The Committee intends to prohibit racial discrimination in all contracts, both public and private.

H. Rep. No. 40, 102d Cong., 1st Sess., Pt. II at 37 (1991), reprinted in U.S. Code Cong. & Admin. News at 549, 731.

In our view, each of *Chapman's* supporting arguments lacks merit. As we discussed in our consideration of *Mahone,* we reject the proposition that only the state can deprive an individual of the full and equal benefit of laws for the security of persons or property. We also do not believe that the *Chapman* panel's construction of subsection (c) is sustainable given the language of that subsection, which is, "the rights protected by this section are protected against impairment by nongovernmental discrimination and impairment under color of State law." 42 U.S.C. § 1981(c). In effect, the *Chapman* majority substituted for those clear words, the statement that "some of the rights protected by this section are protected against impairment by nongovernmental discrimination and others are protected against impairment under color of state law." The *Chapman* majority then decided that the rights protected against private interference were those within the contract clause while other rights — including those contained in the equal benefit clause — were protected only against state interference. If Congress had intended this result, it would have used language specifying which rights were protected against private interference, which against state interference, and which against both. The current language of subsection (c), however, can only be read to protect all of subsection (a)'s rights against both governmental and private interference.

Not only does *Chapman's* interpretation distort the language of the clause but it also fails on its own terms. It was clearly established prior to the 1991 amendment that Section 1981's contracts clause protects against violations by both state and private actors. *Patterson,* 491 U.S. at 171. Thus, the artificial dichotomy that the *Chapman* panel perceived does not exist, and its interpretation makes subsection (c) superfluous.

In view of the clarity of Section 1981(c), *Chapman's* resort to legislative history was ill advised. If a statute is clear on its face, a court is not permitted to use other interpretive tools, including legislative history, to discern the statute's meaning. *See, e.g., Brodie v. Schmutz (In re Venture Mort. Fund, L.P.),* 282 F.3d 185, 188 (2d Cir. 2002). In any event, the legislative history's reference to *Runyon v. McCrary* is consistent with our view of subsection (c) because, as noted previously, the language in that opinion does not limit its holding to the contracts clause. *Runyon,* 427 U.S. at 170.

For several reasons, we also decline defendants' invitation to modify the clear language of subsection (c) to avert a hypothesized federalization of tort law. First, we question our authority to do so. Second, neither the language of the statute nor the legislative history of the pre-amendment statute evinces a congressional purpose to preclude a wide federal role in protecting civil rights. Subsection (c), on its face, protects against both governmental and private interference with subsection (a) rights. The legislative history also suggests a broad goal of eliminating discrimination, whether private or public, between blacks and whites in areas affecting basic rights. Third, it is inconsistent to condemn the federalization of tort law when both Congress and the Supreme Court have made clear that Section 1981 reaches all contracts. *See Patterson*, 491 U.S. at 175; 42 U.S.C. § 1981(c). Because both contracts and torts are areas of particular state concern, there is no persuasive reason why racially motivated torts that deprive a plaintiff of the equal benefit of laws or proceedings for the security of persons and property should be outside the ambit of federal authority while racially motivated breaches of contract are not. Finally, we believe that any necessary safeguard against overuse of the equal benefit clause's protections is found in the words of the statute. Prospective plaintiffs first must prove a racial animus, not an easy task in itself; second must identify a relevant law or proceeding for the "security of persons and property;" and finally must persuade a fact-finder or the court that defendants have deprived them of "the full and equal benefit" of this law or proceeding. 42 U.S.C. § 1981(a).

We do not here attempt to define the universe of laws and proceedings for the security of persons and property, believing this task best resolved case by case. However, we do hold that plaintiffs here adequately alleged a deprivation of a law or proceeding for the security of persons and property. Accepting the truth of plaintiffs' allegations and according those allegations the most generous interpretation they support, defendants refused to allow Gittens and his friends to leave an area where they were peacefully assembled, confiscated Gittens' identification, and then called the police. We also accept the plausible inference that the police were called either to criminally investigate plaintiffs' behavior or to restore peace. We have no difficulty categorizing either a criminal investigation or the restoration of peace as a "proceeding for the security of persons and property" at the Rule 12(b)(6) stage. A full record and an adequately supported summary judgment motion may establish that the defendants' actions cannot be characterized as depriving plaintiffs of the equal benefit of proceedings for the security of persons and property. But at this stage, we address only the propriety of the district court's Rule 12(b)(6) decision. We hold that, assuming that Section 1981 requires a nexus to state proceedings or laws but not state action, plaintiffs' allegations are sufficient because plaintiffs claim that defendants attempted to trigger a legal proceeding against plaintiffs but would not have taken the same action had white students engaged in the same conduct.

III. Racial animus

Defendants argue in the alternative that we should affirm the district court's judgment based on plaintiffs' failure to adequately plead racial animus. It is true that plaintiffs plead few facts relevant to discriminatory intent. Nevertheless, we believe that their allegations are sufficient under the liberal standards applicable to Rule 12(b)(6) motions. Plaintiffs allege that they are African-Americans, describe defendants' actions in detail, and allege that defendants selected them for maltreatment "solely because of their color." A recent Supreme Court case, *Swierkiewicz v. Sorema*, 534 U.S. 506, 122 S. Ct. 992, 152 L. Ed. 2d 1 (2002), compels us to conclude that these allegations are sufficient. In *Swierkiewicz*, the Court held that a Title VII plaintiff need not set forth circumstances supporting an inference of discrimination in order to survive a Rule 12(b)(6) motion. *Id.* at 512-13. The Court found sufficient plaintiff's detailed account of the events leading up to his termination, which included the ages and nationalities of some of the decision makers, and his claim that his termination was motivated by age and national origin. *Id.* at 514. The Court said that these allegations "gave respondent fair notice of what petitioner's claims are and the grounds upon which they rest." *Id.* Like the *Swierkiewicz* complaint, the complaint here describes in great detail what the defendants actually did — actions that included confiscating without cause one plaintiff's identification, refusing to allow the plaintiffs to leave an area where they were peaceably assembled, and calling law enforcement officers without any misconduct on the students' part. In addition, although the complaint, like the complaint in *Swierkiewicz*, does not contain many evidentiary allegations relevant to intent, it does allege that the plaintiffs were singled out of a group that apparently also contained non-minority students. Based on *Swierkiewicz*, we find the allegations in plaintiffs' complaint sufficient to survive a Rule 12(b)(6) motion. This determination, of course, does not preclude a contrary determination on an appropriately supported summary judgment motion.

CONCLUSION

We hold that the equal benefit clause of Section 1981(a) does not require state action. We also find that plaintiffs' allegations state a claim that defendants, who were motivated by racial discrimination, attempted to deprive them of the "full and equal benefit" of a state proceeding "for the security of persons and property." Therefore, we vacate and remand. We emphasize that our holding is limited to the facts before us, and we intimate no view of the appropriate outcome for factual allegations less directly linked to "laws [or] proceedings for the security of persons and property."

Chapman v. Higbee, 319 F.3d 825 (6th Cir. 2003), *cert. denied*, 542 U.S. 945 (2004), agreed with *Phillip*'s conclusion that government action is not required for a Section 1981 "equal benefits" claim, but *Bilello v. Kum & Go, LLC*, 374 F.3d 656 (8th Cir. 2004), adhered to the position that "some sort of state action" is required. Although the Supreme Court has addressed the "make and enforce contracts" provision of Section 1981, *see Domino's Pizza, Inc. v. McDonald*, 546 U.S. 470 (2006), it has yet to address the issue whether, after the 1991 amendments, an "equal benefits" claim requires state action.

TABLE OF CASES

[References are to pages]

[References are to pages]

[References are to pages]

C

[References are to pages]

[References are to pages]

E

F

[References are to pages]

J

K

[References are to pages]

[References are to pages]

[References are to pages]

[References are to pages]

T

[References are to pages]

[References are to pages]

INDEX

[References are to pages.]

I-1

[References are to pages.]

[References are to pages.]